∞ tripadvisor®

The Best of Central America, by travellers like you

Visit TripAdvisor for millions of candid reviews by real travellers. Find the best places to eat, stay, and play... wherever you go.

Top-Rated Hotels

1 Hamanasi Adventure and Dive Resort ⊙⊙⊙⊙⊙
Hopkins, Belize
"Like being welcomed by your family"

2 The Phoenix Resort ⊙⊙⊙⊙⊙
Ambergris Caye, Belize
"Gorgeous, modern, and immaculate"

3 Villas Hermosas ⊙⊙⊙⊙⊙
Santa Teresa, Costa Rica
"Wow, what a great family vacation spot"

Popular Restaurants

1 Adventure Dining ⊙⊙⊙⊙⊙
Jacó, Costa Rica
"The views are absolutely breathtaking"

2 El Colibrí ⊙⊙⊙⊙⊙
San Juan del Sur, Nicaragua
"Simply but fantastically executed food"

3 Restaurante Sabor Español ⊙⊙⊙⊙⊙
Santa Elena, Costa Rica
"Delicious Spanish home cooking"

NOV - - 2014

Amazing Things to Do

1 Sante Wellness Center Day Spa ⊙⊙⊙⊙⊙
Roatan, Honduras
"The most relaxing few hours of my life"

2 Rancho Chilamate Adventures ⊙
San Juan del Sur, Nicaragua
"The ride to the beach was wonde

3 Safari Surf School ⊙⊙⊙⊙⊙
Nosara, Costa Rica
"Awesome surf school, super laid

D1058300

Central America Handbook

Richard Arghiris
Peter Hutchison

The tapering isthmus of Central America is fast emerging from its tempestuous past as a place of breezy self-confidence and stylish self-determination. Throughout the 20th century, the often-squabbling family of nations running from Southern Mexico to Panama were plagued by civil strife, Cold War intrigue and a succession of terminally cruel, dictatorial generals. Today, these former 'banana republics' are enjoying lasting democracy and robust economic growth, encouraging foreign investors and foreign visitors alike. From mushrooming city skylines to burgeoning new mega-projects, the isthmus is changing – and fast.

Fortunately, the nations of Central America are far too self-assured to lose themselves any time soon. Spanish-speaking Latino culture – with its devout Catholic festivals, its love of a raucous fiesta and its eternally gregarious disposition – permeates the isthmus in a multitude of forms, each with its own idiosyncratic customs, colourful jokes and slang. Head to the Caribbean coast, however, and you'll find the lilting roots and thumping reggaeton of a people very much descended from Africa and the West Indies. Central America's famous indigenous peoples – a tapestry of multi-culturalism in themselves – occupy the region's most remote and stunning locales. Hidden in vast jungles and mountains ranges, they practice ways of life that have changed little since their ancestors, the ancient Maya foremost among them.

Central America is, if anything, culturally diverse. But as a natural land bridge between the North and South American continents, it is one of the world's most biologically diverse places too. Exuberant swathes of rainforest host a staggering array of flora and fauna, all protected by one of the finest national park systems on the planet. Hiking, diving, climbing, birding, caving, kayaking, surfing, snorkelling and whitewater rafting are all well developed and popular options. No wonder Central America is looking so bright.

This page The Dance of the Conquest, often performed by indigenous dancers, is a satirical re-enactment of the Spanish Conquest

Previous page America's rambling shoreline conceals scores of secluded beaches, great for swimming, surfing or simply swinging in a hammock.

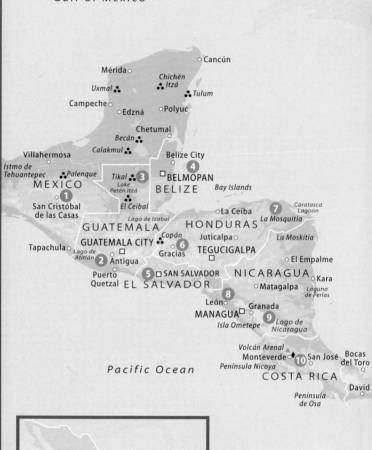

Gulf of Mexico

Cancún

Mérida

Chichén Itzá

Uxmal

Campeche

Edzná

Polyuc

Tulum

Chetumal

Becán

Calakmul

Villahermosa

Belize City

Istmo de Tehuantepec

Palenque

① MEXICO

Tikal

③ ④ **BELMOPAN**

Lake Petén Itzá

BELIZE

Bay Islands

San Cristóbal de las Casas

El Ceibal

Caratasca Lagoon

Lago de Izabal

La Ceiba

⑦ La Mosquitia

GUATEMALA

HONDURAS

La Moskitia

Tapachula

Copán

⑥ Juticalpa

Lago de Atitlán

GUATEMALA CITY

Gracias

TEGUCIGALPA

El Empalme

② Antigua

⑤ **SAN SALVADOR**

NICARAGUA

Kara

Puerto Quetzal

EL SALVADOR

Matagalpa

Laguna de Perlas

⑧ León

Granada

MANAGUA

⑨ Lago de Nicaragua

Isla Ometepe

Volcán Arenal

Monteverde

Bocas del Toro

Península Nicoya

⑩ San José

COSTA RICA

David

Península de Osa

Pacific Ocean

MEXICO

N

300 km

300 miles

Highlights See colour maps at the end of book

1 San Cristóbal de las Casas Kick back in bohemian San Cristóbal, the colonial jewel of the Chiapas highlands. ▸▸ page 71

2 Lake Atitlán Chill out on the tranquil shores of Lake Atitlán, home to thriving Mayan villages and colourful traveller hang-outs. ▸▸ page 239

3 Tikal Grab your machete and compass and explore the jungle-shrouded ruins of Tikal, the Mayan world's most enigmatic metropolis. ▸▸ page 325

4 Blue Hole Submerge yourself in the dazzling underwater world of Belize's Blue Hole, a premier dive site. ▸▸ page 368

5 Ruta de las Flores Soak up the warmth, colour and disarming rural charm of El Salvador's Route of Flowers. ▸▸ page 444

6 Gracias Don your hiking boots for the mountains around Gracias, including Las Minas, the highest peak in Honduras. ▸▸ page 521

7 La Mosquitia Enter another universe in the hard-to-reach Miskito coast, one of Central America's most isolated destinations. ▸▸ page 589

8 León Propose a toast to revolution in Nicaragua's hip and buzzing party town, a mere stone's throw from the Maribios volcano range. ▸▸ page 642

9 Isla Ometepe Sling a hammock on the magical island of Ometepe, home to twin volcanoes and mysterious pre-Columbian idols. ▸▸ page 679

10 Monteverde Spot birds and wildlife in the ethereal cloud forests of Monteverde, a setting straight out of a fantasy novel. ▸▸ page 771

11 Panama Canal Marvel at one of the world's greatest engineering feats, as impressive today as it ever was. ▸▸ page 899

12 Kuna Yala Go native in the indigenous Comarca Kuna Yala (San Blas archipelago), a string of some 400 pristine islets. ▸▸ page 913

CUBA

Caribbean Sea

Kuna Yala (San Blas Islands)

PANAMA CITY

Panama Canal

Lago Bayano

Campana

PANAMA

Pearl Islands

Yaviza

Península Azuero

The vast temples of Tikal, Guatemala, break through the jungle canopy, a testament to Mayan civilization at its height.

Nicaragua's tempestuous geological foundations have generated a host of smouldering and eternally photogenic volcanoes

Contents

SOUTHERN MEXICO

BELIZE

GUATEMALA

HONDURAS

EL SALVADOR

NICARAGUA

COSTA RICA

PANAMA

Contents

Essentials

Planning your trip

Where to go

The sheer variety of options in Central America means that for once the cliché is true – there is something for everyone. The diversity of landscapes, cultures and opportunities excites, entices and, to start with, just bewilders. The scope for adventurous holidays is vast, whether it be climbing a volcano, scuba-diving and snorkelling, whitewater rafting or seeking out the elusive quetzal bird from the forests of Guatemala right down to Panama. Equally enticing is the cultural variety; the pyramids and sculptures of the Maya; the Spanish colonial heritage, from the grandest cathedral to the smallest village church; the flora and fauna; indigenous markets; the modern and dynamic museums and art of the region; learning the language or local cooking techniques; or the mere prospect of lazing at some palm-shaded hideaway fringed with golden sands. One especially rewarding aspect of travel in Central America is the relatively compact size of many of the countries making it easy to move from one place to the next.

Southern Mexico

Southern Mexico is a land of scintillating cultural diversity. Ornate colonial towns, far-flung indigenous villages, brash young cities and gleaming pleasure resorts all punctuate the region, one of the most visited in Latin America. For otherworldly beauty, don't miss the grand Mayan ruins that pepper the landscape from jungle to shore – some of them are over a thousand years old. For living mysteries, head to the highlands of Chiapas, where shamans sacrifice live chickens and Christian crucifixes are really symbols for the Mayan world tree. Adventurists will find plenty of adrenalin-charged thrills to keep them occupied too. Trekking, reef diving and whitewater rafting are all popular, but the truly daring explore the eerie underwater world of the Yucatán's submerged cave system. If all that excitement sounds too much, rest assured, there are plenty of quiet palm-backed beaches to kick back on – and plenty of loud ones too. Viva variety! Viva colour! Viva southern Mexico!

Guatemala

Surely nobody could fail to be impressed by Guatemala. The expansive ruins of Tikal symbolize this rich and complex country, with majestic temples looking out across the endless rainforest canopy. To the south, the Maya, who once ruled these massive cities of stone, live on in hundreds of towns and villages, nestled among the intensely farmed foothills of scenic mountains and volcanoes. Each Guatemalan community has its own unique textile and its own fiesta; colourful markets welcome visitors, while packed buses ignore your pleas for a ride. But serenity and calm await. Not in the chaos of Guatemala City but amid the colonial charm of Antigua, the former capital, and in the hypnotic beauty of Lake Atitlán, which draws in even the most seasoned traveller. To the east, the lowland sierras offer trekking and hiking, while the Caribbean coast promises laid-back beach life and Garífuna culture. And, to the west, a fledgling ecotourism interest supports nesting turtles on the shores of the Pacific.

The #1 Essential Travel Download*

Get TripAdvisor Mobile - **FREE**

- Browse millions of traveller reviews, photos & maps
- Find hotels, restaurants & things to do
- See what's nearby
- Apps available for iPhone, Android, Nokia, Palm Pre, & Windows Mobile

Packing for Central America

Take as little as possible. Clothes that are quick and easy to wash and dry are a good idea. Loose-fitting clothes are more comfortable in hot climates and can be layered if it gets cooler. Sarongs are versatile: they can be used as a towel, beach mat, skirt, sheet, or scarf, to name but a few. But don't pack too many clothes; you can easily, and cheaply, buy things en route. Four musts are good walking shoes, a sun hat, sunglasses and flip-flops or sandals.

Don't load yourself down with toiletries either. They're heavy and can usually be found cheaply and easily everywhere. Items like contact lens solutions and tampons may be harder to find, but stock up in major cities as you go along and there shouldn't be a problem. Dental floss can be useful for backpack repairs as well.

Probably the most useful single item is a Swiss Army knife (with corkscrew), followed by a money belt, a headtorch/flashlight (not everywhere has 24-hour electricity), the smallest alarm clock you can find and a basic medical kit.

Pack photocopies of essential documents like passport, visas and traveller's cheque receipts, in case you lose the originals. For security, a small padlock is useful for locking your bag, and the doors of some of the more basic hotels. Finally, a climbing karabiner can be handy for clipping your bag on to something and foiling the grab thief.

Photographers using film will want to take all that they will require for the trip, ideally in a bag that is both water and dust proof. Digital photographers will need to take recharging gear and related adaptors.

Belize

Compact and accessible, but more expensive than its immediate neighbours, tiny Belize is frequently overlooked. Yet this Caribbean country is home to the Mesoamerican Barrier Reef – the longest in the Western Hemisphere – and offers some of the best diving in the world, not to mention a boatload of other watersports worth getting wet for. What's more, over 35% of the country is protected in national parks and reserves, including the world's only jaguar sanctuary at Cockscomb Basin. To the east, an intricate system of caves drains the rivers of Mountain Pine Ridge, many of which can be explored on foot, by boat or even inflated tube. And in the pine-clad hills to the south, Caracol, the largest of many ruins in Belize, remains mostly unexplored, revelling in the little-known fact that it once ruled over nearby Tikal.

El Salvador

Like Belize, El Salvador gets short shrift due to the popularity of its neighbours. The volcanic highlands and contrasting coastal plains are stunningly beautiful but a massive double earthquake in early 2001 ruined architectural treasures and human lives. El Salvador is challenging for independent travellers but ultimately enjoyable thanks to its genuinely friendly people. San Salvador, the country's capital, is close to unmissable volcanoes, lakes and national parks. Northern towns are moving out from the shadows of civil war and enjoying a cultural revival, while, to the south, long sandy beaches, prized by surfers for decades, stretch along the Costa del Sol to the Gulf of Fonseca. To the west are coffee plantations and the beautiful Ruta de las Flores. And who could resist a national park called 'El Imposible'.

Honduras

One of Central America's dark horses, Honduras has been pushing for a place in the limelight for years. The Bay Islands, off the Caribbean coast, are still the cheapest place to learn to scuba dive and, onshore, the adventure continues with whitewater rafting, hiking and birdwatching. Along the Atlantic, you can relax in the coastal communities of Omoa, Tela, La Ceiba and Trujillo and visit the isolated rainforest of La Mosquitia – Central America's 'Little Amazon'. In the west of the country, the villages are quieter and the hillside paths less travelled but there are colonial treasures and indigenous communities to discover. Close to the border with Guatemala, the stunning Copán ruins mark the southernmost reach of the Maya Empire.

Nicaragua

Although memories of the 1979 Sandinista Revolution still evoke images of work crews, comandantes and communist sympathies, 30 years on the Nicaragua of today is a very different and rapidly changing place. The country is embracing a deluge of tourist dollars that is set to increase as word gets around: Nicaragua is cool. There is a freshness about a country where the smiles are still warm, the questions still honest and the eyes undimmed by the attitudes of thoughtless travellers. Beautiful sites like the Island of Ometepe, Volcán Masaya, the Corn Islands, the Río San Juan and Pacific beaches are matched by some of Central America's oldest towns, including conservative Granada and liberal León. It's the contrasts that make Nicaragua so appealing.

Costa Rica

Peaceful, calm and 100% democratic … ah, that'll be Costa Rica. The wealth of national parks and biospheres, private reserves and national monuments in this country could make you believe that Ticos have a monopoly on nature. What makes the difference in Costa Rica is the sheer variety of wildlife on offer – something you only truly appreciate after pawing over large maps for ages: quetzales here, nesting turtles there, big cats at all points of the compass. World-class whitewater rafting from Turrialba, surfing on both coasts, experiencing the eruption of Arenal volcano and the steaming mudpools nearby, walking and hiking in the cloudforests of Monteverde or the rainforest of the Osa Peninsula; other countries may offer these things, but they don't pack them into such a compact, attractive bundle as Costa Rica. And they don't do it in quite the same laid-back way as the Ticos, who espouse *La Pura Vida*.

Panama

Panama is the crossroads of the world. The Panama Canal may not be natural but it is spectacular and pure Panamanian since the country successfully took control of the world's greatest shortcut at the end of 1999. Beyond modern Panama City, national and international visitors are opening their eyes to new discoveries on the Azuero Peninsula and in the Chiriquí Highlands, while Bocas del Toro on the Atlantic is developing into a hip coastal destination, with glassy waters and islands full of tiny multicoloured frogs. The 400 or so off-shore islands of the autonomous Kuna Yala province provide a precious haven of calm and tranquillity and, for the true adventurer, the wilderness of the Darién still offers one of the great challenges this side of space travel.

Three to four weeks

Not long enough to cover the region, but in three or four weeks you could explore a chunk of the Ruta Maya. In Guatemala, take a week or 10 days to take in the essentials of Antigua, Tikal and Lake Atitlán then head for Belize's Cayo district, and Caye Caulker for a bit of diving, before heading north to Mexico's Yucatán and west to the indigenous homelands of Chiapas, completing the loop. Any version of the Ruta Maya, taking in the main Maya sites of Guatemala, Belize and southern Mexico is possible in four weeks but doesn't really allow time for deviation. Another three- to four-week trip could focus on Costa Rica, with a great variety of national parks on offer: the most popular include Manuel Antonio National Park, Monteverde Cloud Forest Reserve, Tortuguero National Park to the east and Corcovado National Park to the south. The explosive Volcán Arenal never disappoints (unless it is shrouded in cloud). For the active there is whitewater rafting, surfing, horse riding and trekking. You could easily pop in to Nicaragua to the north, or Panama to the south. You could just about manage an overland trip from Guatemala through to Costa Rica in three to four weeks. If you're feeling particularly manic, you could even manage a mad dash down the Pan- American Highway from Mexico City all the way to Panama City.

Six to eight weeks

Six to eight weeks is long enough to travel across a few countries without feeling you've rushed too much. Start in Chiapas and the Maya ruins of Palenque. From here, continue south to Guatemala or west out to the Yucatán Peninsula for the beautiful beaches and more Maya ruins. Dropping south, Belize is worth some time. Diving, though more expensive than Honduras, is some of the best in the world and includes the famed Blue Hole. Head west for Guatemala and the eerie cave and river trips of the Cayo District or, to the south, the serenity around Placencia, the jaguar sanctuary at Cockscomb Basin and Maya villages close to Punta Gorda.

With six weeks you could squeeze in a short Spanish language course in Antigua, Quetzaltenango or even Todos Santos – world famous for its annual festival in November. After Guatemala, Honduras draws many to the affordable diving of the Bay Islands, which need at least a week. Other attractions include whitewater rafting on the Río Cangrejo close to La Ceiba. Inland, treks and hikes in the quiet hills around Gracias go through beautiful scenery and small indigenous communities, the very heart of Honduras. An alternative six-week trip might arrive in Guatemala City and head south overland flying out of San José, Costa Rica. While experiencing Guatemala and Costa Rica, you can travel at leisure through Honduras, dip into the lakes and volcanic beauty of El Salvador and visit Nicaragua where revolutionary history merges with colonial legacy to create one of Central America's most endearing nations. Honduras and Nicaragua are, for many travellers, the most challenging destinations, but for many the most memorable.

Three months

Three months is enough time for a thorough exploration of Central America. Use the Pan-American Highway as your guide and travel from southern Mexico to the Darién Gap, taking moments to pause, reflect and deviate at will. A month exploring the Ruta Maya is time well spent (see above), but a memorable trip through Honduras, El Salvador and Nicaragua could involve more daring expeditions to remote locales like the Mosquitia or the Río San Juan. In Costa Rica, it's relatively easy to switch between Pacific and Caribbean shores before finally crossing the border into Panama, where, from the city of David, you can blend adventure and beauty with a visit to the Chiriquí Highlands. Alternatively, cross over the mountains and head for the dive sites of Bocas del Toro, then head back inland towards the capital. A voyage through the Panama Canal would be the ideal way to end a trip of trans-continental travel before returning home, but don't miss the Kuna Yala archipelago before you do.

When to go

The best time to go is between November and April, although there are slight regional variations and a handful of microclimates that do not obey the rule. The rainy season works its way up from the south in May and runs through until October. At the start of the season, rain falls for a just couple of hours a day, usually in the afternoon. Towards the end, it is more torrential and disruptive. This is also hurricane season in the Caribbean. Despite the high-profile storm of Hurricane Wilma and a few lesser known local hurricanes and tropical storms, landfall is relatively rare. If a hurricane does arrive while you're in the area you can get details at www.nhc.noaa.gov.

If the time and mood is right, there is little to beat a Latin American festival. Fine costumes, loud music, the sounds of firecrackers tipped off with the gentle wafting of specially prepared foods all (normally) with a drink or two. Whether you're seeking the carnival or happen to stumble across a celebration, the events – big or small – are memorable.If you want to hit the carnivals there are a few broad dates generally significant throughout the region. Carnival is normally the week before the start of Lent. It's more important in Mexico but you'll probably find regional celebrations in most places. Semana Santa (Easter Week) is an understandably more spiritual affair. On 2 November is Día de los Muertos (Day of the Dead), again most popular in Mexico but significant throughout the region when families visit cemeteries to honour the dead. Christmas and New Year result in celebrations of some kind, but not always public.

Public holidays throughout the region lead to a complete shut-down in services. No banks, government offices, usually no shops and often far fewer restaurants and bars. It is worth keeping an eye on the calendar to avoid changing money or trying to make travel arrangements on public holidays.

What to do

Canyoning and caving

Options for caving and canyoning are developing in **Mexico** and Guatemala but the best caving in the region and the western hemisphere is found in Belize (see page 345) with some of the longest cave systems in the world.

Climbing

Across Central America, there are several volcanic peaks, active and dormant, that give excellent views and a challenging climb all the way through the isthmus down to

Panama. In **Guatemala** the active volcanic peak of Pacaya is a popular and safe excursion, while the Cuchumatanes Mountains in the mid-west of the country have the country's highest non-volcanic peaks. In **Belize** the highest climb is at Victoria Peak, best reached from the Cockscomb Basin Jaguar Sanctuary. Moving further south, climbing tends towards trekking. The peaks in **Honduras** include the hills around Gracias (the highest at 2849 m), such as Celaque, Puca and Opulaca. Close to La Ceiba is the rarely climbed Pico de Bonito. In **Nicaragua**,

Protect the reef

Belize, Mexico, Honduras and Panama offer some of the finest marine environments in the Caribbean Basin; the major challenge is to keep it that way. It's important that if you dive or snorkel you take responsibility for your own actions, and that your trip contributes to the preservation, rather than the destruction, of the reef. Here are a few ways to help:

- Don't touch the reef. Even a gentle brush can remove the protective covering of mucus from a coral colony and cause the death of an animal community that has taken hundreds of years to develop.
- Don't remove anything from the reef.
- Be aware of your fins and where they go. It's easy to lose track of that deadly (for the coral) 50 cm on the end of your foot.

- If you want to snorkel but haven't tried it before, practise your technique before you get close to a coral reef. A shallow bottom of a sandy beach or a swimming pool is perfect.
- When diving, stop your initial descent before you whack straight into the reef below.
- Lend a hand! Collect any plastic or rubbish you find on the reef or the cayes and make sure it's correctly disposed of. Lost fishing nets can be a huge problem for marine life, killing fish, turtles, even dolphins for years afterwards.
- Support an organization working to protect coral reefs, locally or worldwide. There are many excellent small-scale grassroots organizations that deserve your support.

Volcán Concepción and Madera on Isla de Omotepe are highlights of any trip through the region, but more volcanoes can be hiked in the highland belt northwest of León. In **Costa Rica** the highest peak is Cerro Chirripó and in **Panama** Volcán Barú is accessible from the nearby town of Boquete.

Diving

Opportunities for diving and snorkelling can be found throughout the region. Overall the best diving for safety and opportunity is probably in **Belize**, especially in the offshore Cayes, but prices tend to be higher than elsewhere. 2 diving hotspots in the region are the Blue Hole in Belize (page 368) and the Isla de Coco off Costa Rica (page 830). The cheapest place to learn to dive is off the Bay Island of Utila, **Honduras**: just US$200, even less in low season. If arriving in **Mexico**, learning to dive in the Cancún area is surprisingly affordable and you can dive off Isla Mujeres on your way south. Good diving

in **Costa Rica** is limited to the area around Puerto Viejo and Manzanillo on the Caribbean south coast, with the same good conditions continuing south to Bocas del Toro in **Panama**. The Corn Islands off **Nicaragua** (page 699) are another bastion of cheap diving instruction. For further details, see full-colour diving section in the middle of this book.

Cenote diving

There are more than 50 *cenotes* in the Mexico's Yucatán Peninsula. For details, see page 168.

Fishing

Sea and freshwater fishing are world class, with marlin and sailfish in the deep waters off **Costa Rica**, **Panama** and **Mexico**, bonefish a little closer to shore on the flats in **Belize**, and the freshwater dreams of snook and tarpon lurking in tropical streams along the Caribbean. Costs, however, are generally prohibitive, running to several hundred dollars for the day.

Hiking

A network of paths and tracks covers much of Central America. In Guatemala, which has a large indigenous population, you can walk just about anywhere, but in other countries, particularly Costa Rica, you can be limited to the many excellent national parks with hiking trails. Trekking should not be approached casually. Even if you only plan to be out a couple of hours you should have comfortable, safe footwear (which can cope with the wet) and a daypack to carry your sweater and waterproof. At high altitudes the difference in temperature between sun and shade is remarkable.

The longer trips mentioned in this book require basic backpacking equipment. Essential items are: a good backpack, sleeping bag, foam mat, stove, tent or tarpaulin, dried food (not tins), water bottle, compass, trowel for burying human waste. Hikers have little to fear from the animal kingdom apart from insects; robbery and assault are rare. You are much more of a threat to the environment than vice versa. Leave no evidence of your passing; don't litter and don't give gratuitous presents of sweets or money to rural villagers. Respect their system of reciprocity; if they give you hospitality or food, then is the time to reciprocate with presents.

Most Central American countries have an Instituto Geográfico, which sells topographical maps, scale 1:100,000 or 1:50,000. The physical features shown on these are usually accurate; the trails and place names less so. National Parks offices also sell maps.

Surfing

It's an endless summer of surfing all the way down the Pacific coast. In **El Salvador** there are good breaks close to La Libertad, with several all down the Pacific coast of Nicaragua. **Costa Rica** has well-documented breaks with the main centres at Tamarindo, Malpaís, Jaco and Dominical. Particular breaks are mentioned in the text. If looking to learn, your best chance is probably in Mexico or Costa Rica.

Wildlife and birdwatching

Central America offers spectacular wildlife-watching opportunities. You have the chance to dive with whale sharks between Mar and May in southern Belize and the Bay Islands, whilst another popular animal to see is the manatee, often found in the coastal lagoons of Central America's rambling Caribbean coastline. On land it is other mammals, particularly monkeys and the elusive wild cats, that quicken the heartbeat. In the air, or at least close to the ground, the sheer number of bird species – over 900 in Panama alone – mean ornithologists get positively overexcited by the prospect of Central America. The resplendent quetzal, with its beautifully flamboyant tail feather, is an essential sighting to start any twitcher's career. Although very rare, they populate the cloud forests around Cerro Punta, Panama, in great numbers. They can be spotted there without too much trouble.

For an introduction to the region's wildlife, see Background, page 1008.

Whitewater rafting

Being a potentially dangerous sport, whitewater rafting is not as widespread as it could be, but there are many world-class opportunities in the region. In Guatemala there are operators using the Cahabón, Motagua and Esclavos. In Honduras try the Cangrejal near La Ceiba in North Honduras. In Costa Rica the Reventazón and Pacuare are popular rivers, as is the Río Chiriquí and Chiriquí Viejo in Boquete, Panama.

Getting there

All countries in Latin America (in fact across the world) officially require travellers entering their territory to have an onward or return ticket and may at times ask to see that ticket. Although rarely enforced at airports, this regulation can create problems at border crossings. In lieu of an onward ticket out of the country you are entering, any ticket out of another Latin American country may suffice, or proof that you have sufficient funds to buy a ticket (a credit card will do). International air tickets are expensive if purchased in Latin America.

Air

Certain Central American countries impose local tax on flights originating there. Among these are Guatemala, Costa Rica, Panama and Mexico. Details of all the main airlines flying to each country are given in the relevant country Essentials sections.

Fares from Europe and North America to Latin American destinations vary. Peak periods and higher prices correspond to holiday season in the northern hemisphere. The very busy seasons are as follows: 7 December to 15 January and July to mid-September. If you intend travelling during those times, book as far ahead as possible. Check with an agency for the best deal for when you wish to travel. There is a wide range of offers to choose from in a highly competitive environment. Check the lists of discount flight agents for UK and Ireland, North America, and Australia and New Zealand. Also check the list of airline websites here and the list of tour operators in the UK and North America, on page 45. Many airlines share passengers across different routes to increase the areas that they can claim to cover. So you many fly the transatlantic leg with one airline before changing to a different airline for the final leg.

Most airlines offer discounted (cheaper than official) fares of one sort or another on scheduled flights. These are not offered by the airlines direct to the public, but through agencies that specialize in this type of fare. An indication of cost is difficult to give due to the large number of variables, not least the current fluctuations in currency and the wide variations in oil prices in recent years. The main factors are frequency of flights and popularity of destination at a particular time of year and there is a great price fluctuation. As a rough guide a three-month London–Mexico return in August is around US$1200. In November the same flight falls to US$1000. A three-month London–Costa Rica return is US$1250 in August, falling to US$1100 in November. Flying into one place and out of another can be very useful, but usually costs extra. Flying into Mexico City and out of Costa Rica in August is around US$1200, while in November look to pay around US$1050. While these are prices from London, the European prices are usually similar or cheaper as flights often involve European airlines such as **Martinair** or **Iberia**.

Travellers from Australia and New Zealand are getting an increasingly better deal compared with recent years, with special offers occasionally down to AUS$1900 flying direct to Mexico City. The more regular price is close to AUS$3200.

Other fares fall into three groups, and are all on scheduled services: **Excursion** (return) fares: these have restricted validity either seven to 90 days, or seven to 180 days, depending on the airline. They are fixed-date tickets where the dates of travel cannot be changed after issue without incurring a penalty. **Yearly fares**: these may be bought on a one-way or return basis, and usually the returns can be issued with the return date left

Border cooperation

In June 2006, Guatemala, El Salvador, Honduras, and Nicaragua entered into a 'Central America-4 (CA-4) Border Control Agreement'. Under the terms of the agreement, citizens of the four countries may travel freely across land borders from one of the countries to any of the others without completing entry and exit formalities at Immigration checkpoints. US citizens and other eligible foreign nationals, who legally enter any of the four countries, may similarly travel among the four without obtaining additional visas or tourist entry permits for the other three countries. Immigration officials at the first port of entry determine the length of stay, up to a maximum period of 90 days.

open. You must, however, fix the route. **Student** (or Under-26) fares: one way and returns available, or 'open jaws' (see below). There is also a wider range of cheap one-way student fares originating in Latin America than can be bought outside the continent. There is less availability in the busy seasons. The range of student fares is wider to Mexico than elsewhere. Some airlines are flexible on the age limit, others are strict.

Open-jaw fares For people intending to travel a linear route and return from a different point from that which they entered, there are 'open-jaw' or multi-stop flights, which are available on student, yearly, or excursion fares.

Flights from Europe
Airfares from Europe to Mexico City between February and June can be very low (see above), although the same does not apply to Cancún. Most European airlines have a regular weekly service to the capital throughout the year so it is worth considering Mexico City as an entry/exit point for a Mexican trip for the widest range of options and prices. If you do not stop over in Mexico City, low-cost add-ons are available to Mexican domestic destinations through links with the main airlines.

With the promotion of Cancún as a gateway from Europe, there has been an increase in the number of scheduled flights to Mexico (for example **Iberia** flies daily from Madrid and Barcelona to Cancún via Miami; **Air France/American Airlines** daily from Paris to Cancún; **Condor Flugdienst** from Frankfurt once a week to Cancún, **British Airways** operates a daily flight from London Gatwick to Cancún via Dallas Fort Worth).

Moving beyond Mexico there are few direct flights and asking a local discount supplier for the cheap options is the best way of finding out about flights. Seasonal charter flights can work out to be very affordable. **Martinair**, a subsidiary of **KLM**, flies Costa Rica–Netherlands, for around US$500 return. There are several cheap French charters to Mexico and Guatemala and a number of 'packages' that include flights from Mexico to Cuba can be bought locally in Mexico, Guatemala, Costa Rica or in advance. Travellers starting their journey in continental Europe should make local enquiries about charters and agencies offering the best deals.

Flights from the US and Canada
Flying to Mexico from the US and Canada offers a very wide range of options. The main US carriers – **American Airlines**, **Continental** and **United** – offer flights to many cities in Mexico. Direct international flights also serve many other cities in the country; the main

through points are Miami, Dallas/Fort Worth, Los Angeles and San Francisco. From Canada the options are less varied, but regular flights serve the main cities with direct flights from Montreal and Toronto. Keep an eye out for special offers, which can produce extremely cheap flights (often at very short notice). Fewer flights operate to Central America from the US and Canada.

Flights from Central and Latin America
Links throughout the isthmus are provided by **Taca**, a regional association linking five Central American national carriers. Main connections within the region and to other countries in Latin America and the Caribbean are provided through Mexico, San Salvador and Panama City. Prices for regional services are beginning to fall and are worth considering.

Flights from Australia and New Zealand
Flights to Central America and Mexico from Australia and New Zealand are with **United Airlines** and generally connect through Los Angeles.

General hints
Given complete free choice many people do not know where they will end up after several months travelling and would like to leave arranging the return leg of a ticket open in terms of date and departing airport or better still purchase a return leg when the time is right. In reality this is not a good idea. Two one-way tickets are always more expensive than a return and purchasing a ticket to the US or Europe from Central America is often more expensive than it would be from your home country; no frills Spirit airlines, however, is an exception. Meanwhile, if you have a return ticket you can normally change the return leg date of travel at the airport (normally at a charge) or at local travel agents.

If you buy discounted air tickets always check the reservation with the airline concerned to make sure the flight still exists. Also remember that airlines' schedules change in March and October each year, so if you're going to be away a long time it's best to leave return flight coupons open. If you know that you will be returning at the very busy seasons you should make a reservation. In addition, it is vital to check in advance whether you are entitled to any refund or re-issued ticket if you lose, or have stolen, a discounted air ticket.

E-tickets are increasingly common. If you are unsure about the use of an e-ticket, telephone the company concerned. If you can't locate a telephone number to call, it's probably best not to book with the company. At the booking stage, you should be reassured that you are buying a real ticket. If you find yourself stuck somewhere, you'll want to talk to a person – not a machine.

Weight allowances if going direct from Europe are generally 22 kg for economy and business class or 30 kg for first class. If you have special baggage requirements, check with an agency about anomalies that exist on different weight allowances one way, for example. Certain carriers (for example **Iberia** and **Air France**) offer a two-piece allowance out of the UK only, each piece up to 32 kg. Many people travel to Mexico and Central America via the US, and all carriers via the USA offer this allowance in both directions. Weight limits for internal flights are often lower, so it's best to enquire beforehand. For all the discussion of allowances, you're likely to have to carry your bag at times. So perhaps your personal carrying capacity is a more useful weight consideration.

Airport information

As a general rule, try to avoid arriving at night. If that's not possible, book a hotel for the first night at least and take a taxi or shuttle bus direct to your hotel. It may not be the cheapest way out of the airport, but it is the simplest and safest. Each country in the region charges an airport departure tax – information is given in each chapter for the relevant country.

Ticket agents and airlines

Most international and several domestic airlines have websites that are useful for gaining information about flights. However, you may not always get the best price online, so use the websites in an advisory capacity and discuss your options with an agent.

Airlines

For a full list of airline websites visit www.evasions.com/airlines1.htm.
AeroMéxico www.aeromexico.com
Air France www.airfrance.com
Alaska Airlines www.alaskaairlines.com
Alitalia www.alitalia.com
American Airlines www.aa.com
Avianca www.avianca.com
British Airways www.britishairways.com
Condor www.condor.de
Continental www.continental.com
Copa www.copaair.com
Cubana www.cubana.cu
Delta www.delta.com
Iberia www.iberia.com
Japan Airlines www.jal.com
KLM www.klm.com
LanChile www.lanchile.com
Lufthansa www.lufthansa.com
Martinair www.martinair.com
Mexicana www.mexicana.com
Northwest www.nwa.com
Qantas www.qantas.com.au
Spirit www.spirit.com
Taca www.taca.com
United www.united.com
Varig www.varig.com

Mexican low-cost airlines

Interjet www.interjet.com.mx
VivaAerobus www.vivaaerobus.com
Volaris www.volaris.com.mx

Web resources

www.expedia.com
www.lastminute.com
www.opodo.com
www.orbitz.com
www.priceline.com
www.travelocity.com

Discount flight agents
In the UK

Journey Latin America, 12-13 Heathfield Terrace, London, W4 4JE, T020-8747 8315; www.journeylatinamerica.co.uk.
South American Experience, Welby House, 96 Wilton Rd, London, SW1V 1DW, T0845-277 3366, www.southamerican experience.co.uk.
STA Travel, 45 branches in the UK (450 worldwide). Find your closest at T0871-230 0040, www.statravel.co.uk. Specialists in low-cost student/youth flights and tours, also good for student ID cards.
Trailfinders, 194 Kensington High St, London, W8 7RG, T020-7938 3939, www.trailfinders.com.

Rest of Europe

Die Reisegalerie, Grüneburgweg 84, 60323 Frankfurt, Germany, T069-9720-6000, www.reisegalerie.com.
Images du Monde, 14 rue Lahire, 75013 Paris, France, T1-4424-8788, www.imagenes-tropicales.com. Also with an office in Costa Rica.
Thika Travel, Kerkplein 6, 3628 AE, Kockengen (gem. Breukelen), Holland, T0346-242526, www.thika.nl.

North America

Air Brokers International, 685 Market St, Suite 400, San Francisco, CA94102, T01-800-883-3273, www.airbrokers.com.

Discount Airfares Databases Online,
www.etn.nl/discount.htm. Discount
agent links.
Exito Latin American Travel Specialists,
108 Rutgers Av, Fort Collins, CO 80525,
T1-800-655-4053, www.exitotravel.com.
STA Travel, T1-800-781-4040,
www.statravel.com. Branches
throughout the US and Canada.
Travel CUTS, 187 College St, Toronto, ON,
M5T 1P7, T1-888-359-2887, www.travel
cuts.com. Student discount fares.

Australia and New Zealand
Flight Centres, 82 Elizabeth St, Sydney 2000,
T133-133, www.flightcentre.com.au;
Unit 3, 239 Queen St, Auckland,
T0800-243544, www.flightcentre.co.nz.
With branches in other towns and cities.
STA Travel, 841 George St, Sydney, T134-782
(general enquires), www.statravel.com.au.
In NZ: 267 Queen St, Auckland,
www.statravel.co.nz, T0800-474-400. Also in
major towns and university campuses.
Travel.com.au, 76-80 Clarence St, Sydney,
T1300-130483, www.travel.com.au.
Trailfinders, 8 Spring St, Sydney, NSW 2000,
www.trailfinders.com.au, T1300-780-212.

Boat

Sailing your own vessel

Following the coastal route doesn't have to be done from the land side, as thousands of sailors who follow the good-weather sailing around the coast of Mexico and Central America can confirm. Indeed there seem to be increasing numbers of people travelling this way. Between California, the Panama Canal and Florida dozens of marinas await the sailor looking to explore the region from the sea. A guide to the marinas and sailing ports of the region is *Cruising Ports: the Central American Route*, and Mexico Boating Guide by Capt Pat Rains, published by Point Loma Publishing in San Diego. Captain Rain is an experienced navigator of Mexican and Central American waters with over 30 Panama transits under her cap (www.centralamericanboating.com).

Travelling by boat to the region is really only worth considering if you are shipping a vehicle from Europe or the US. Enquiries regarding passages should be made through agencies in your own country. In the UK, **Strand Voyages** have information on occasional one-way services to the Gulf of Mexico from Europe. Details on shipping cars are given in the relevant country sections.

In Europe

The Cruise People, 88 York St, London,
W1H 1QT, T020-7723-2450, www.cruise
people.co.uk; 1252 Lawrence Av East,
Suite 210, Toronto, Canada, M3A 1C3,
T416-444-2410.
Globoship, Neuengasse 30, CH – 3001 Bern,
Switzerland, T31-313 0004,
www.globoship.com.
Strand Voyages, 46 Gillingham St,
London SW1V 1HU, T020-7802-2199,
www.strandtravel.co.uk.

In the USA

Freighter World Cruises, 180 South
Lake Av, Suite 340, Pasadena,
CA 91101-2655, T1-800-531-7774,
www.freighterworld.com.
**Travltips Cruise and Freighter Travel
Association**, PO Box 580188, Flushing,
New York 11358, T1-800-872-8584,
www.travltips.com.

Road

Travel from the USA
There are a multitude of entry points from the US, the main ones being Tijuana, Nogales, Ciudad Juárez, Piedras Negras, Nuevo Laredo and Matamoros. Details of these and others are provided in the Footprint Mexico Handbook. Crossing the border is simple and hassle-free for foot passengers and reasonably straightforward for people travelling with their own vehicle. All border towns have bus terminals that provide long-distance bus services.

Getting around

Bus travel is the most popular style of transport for 'independent' travellers. An excellent network criss-crosses the region varying in quality from luxurious intercity cruisers with air conditioning, videos and fully reclining seats, to beaten-up US-style school buses or 'chicken buses' with busted suspension and holes in the floor.

Travelling under your own steam is also very popular. Driving your own vehicle – car, camper van, motorbike and bicycle – offers wonderful freedom and may not be as expensive or as bureaucratic as you think. From the letters we receive, the ever-greater cooperation between the nations of Central America is producing dramatic benefits at border crossings for those who decide to go it alone. Indeed, since 2006, when Guatemala, El Salvador, Honduras and Nicaragua signed the **Central America-4**, it's been even easier (see box, page 21). With the comprehensive road network it's easy to miss out on other sensible choices. Don't shun the opportunity to take a short flight. While you'll need to enquire about precise costs, the view from above provides a different perspective and the difference in cost may not be as great as you think. Getting around in Central America is rarely a problem whether travelling by bus, car, bike, in fact almost any mode of transport.

There is just one caveat that stands good across all situations: be patient when asking directions. Often Latin Americans will give you the wrong answer rather than admit they do not know. Distances are notoriously inaccurate so ask a few people.

Air

With the exception of El Salvador, all countries have a domestic flight service. Prices vary but it is definitely worth considering an aerial 'hop' if it covers a lot of difficult terrain and you get the bonus of a good view. If you know the outline of your itinerary, it may be worth booking internal flights before you arrive in the country. They are often cheaper.

Air passes
An option worth exploring is the airpass, usually offered by an airline or group of airlines. The standard scheme works on system of vouchers. A voucher covers a set distance between any two destinations. **All-America Airpass**, www.airallpass.com, operates one such scheme with 27 participating airlines from the US, Mexico, the Caribbean, Central and South America. These passes must be purchased in conjunction with an international air ticket. Low-frills airlines have arrived in the region, with five operating in Mexico. Keep an eye on websites for special offers; see page 23.

Boat

Keeping all options open, water transport has to be a consideration – although not a very realistic one in terms of reaching a distant destination. Most water transport consists of small boats with outboard motors. They travel relatively short distances in localized areas, usually along tropical rivers or between off-shore islands, where road transport is otherwise lacking. You'll find just a few regular ferry schedules that avoid circuitous land routes. The main journeys are between the Cayes of Belize and skipping down the coastline; from the Bay Islands of Honduras to the mainland; across Lake Nicaragua; and in Costa Rica, where there are connections between the mainland and the Osa and Nicoya peninsulas on the Pacific Coast. If heading from Panama to South America, if determined, you can work your way along the Caribbean coastline to Colombia using a number of small sporadically available vessels.

Beyond this functional travel one journey stands out: travelling the Panama Canal (as opposed to just seeing it!) and crewing a private yacht. Both of these require flexible schedules and good timing, but you might get lucky. Conditions of 'employment' vary greatly – you may get paid, you may get board and lodgings, you may even have to pay.

Road

Since 2007, the rising price of oil has had a noticeable impact on the cost of road travel. International currency fluctuations are complicating it. Whether travelling by bus or car, the price has changed. Fortunately, the price will always be cheap relative to your home country, where transport is likely to be affected in the same way.

Crossing borders

Travellers who are eligible for tourist cards or their equivalent (including most European, Australian and North American visitors) find that crossing borders in Central America a relatively straightforward process. Those travellers who require visas, however, may not always find them available; approach the relevant consulate (offices in the capital or big cities) before setting out for the border. Some crossings levy exit and entrance taxes, along with occasional *alcaldía* fees; the amounts vary. 'Unofficial' taxes are not uncommon and sometimes it can be easier to pay a few extra dollars than enter into drawn-out dispute. Asking for a *'factura'* (receipt) can help. Many immigration officers will ask for evidence of onward travel – either a return flight or a bus ticket – along with funds. If you use international buses, expect long queues and tedious custom searches. Sometimes the bus driver will collect everyone's passports; watch your fellow passengers and follow suit. If you're light on luggage, it is often quicker to use local buses and cross the border on your own. Some drivers may be subjected to bureaucratic delays. Preparation is the best guarantee of a speedy crossing – check in advance which documents you will require and make several copies before setting out (see Car documents, page 27 for more on procedures). The busiest borders are often frequented by unpleasant characters. Changing money is OK, but check the rate and carefully count what you're given – rip-offs can occur.

Bus

There is an extensive road system with frequent bus services throughout Mexico and Central America. Some of these services are excellent. In mountainous country, however, and after long journeys, do not expect buses to get to their destination anywhere near on time. Avoid turning up for a bus at the last minute; if it is full it may depart early. In general travellers tend to sit near the front – going round bends and over bumps has less impact on your body near the front axle, making the journey more comfortable and reducing the likelihood of motion sickness (on some long journeys it also means you are further from the progressively smelly toilets at the back of the bus). Tall travellers are advised to take aisle seats on long journeys as this allows more leg room. When the journey takes more than three or four hours, meal stops at country inns or bars, good and bad, are the rule. Often no announcement is made on the duration of the stop; ask the driver and follow him, if he eats, eat. See what the locals are eating – and buy likewise, or make sure you're stocked up on food and drink at the start. For drinks, stick to bottled water, soft drinks or coffee (black). The food sold by vendors at bus stops may be all right; watch if locals are buying. See page 43 for security in buses. Make sure you have a sweater or blanket to hand for long bus journeys, especially at night; even if it's warm outside, the air conditioning is often fierce.

International buses link the capital cities providing an effective way of quickly covering a lot of ground. There are several companies but the main operator is **Ticabus** with headquarters in Costa Rica, www.ticabus.com. However, bear in mind that Panama–Guatemala with **Ticabus** takes almost three days and costs over US$100, plus accommodation in Managua and San Salvador. You may want to consider flying if you need to get through more than one country quickly.

Car

If driving, an international driving licence is useful, although not always essential. Membership of motoring organizations can also be useful for discounts such as hotel charges, car rentals, maps and towing charges.

The kind of motoring you do will depend on your car. A 4WD is not necessary, although it does give you greater flexibility in mountain and jungle territory. Wherever you travel you should expect from time to time to find roads that are badly maintained, damaged or closed during the wet season, and delays because of floods, landslides and huge potholes.

Be prepared for all manner of mechanical challenges. The electronic ignition and fuel metering systems on modern emission-controlled cars are allergic to humidity, heat and dust, and cannot be repaired by mechanics outside the main centres. Standard European and Japanese cars run on fuel with a higher octane rating than is commonly available in North, Central or South America. Note that in some areas gas stations are few and far between. Fill up when you see one: the next one may be out of fuel.

Documents Land entry procedures for all countries are simple though time-consuming, as the car has to be checked by customs, police and agriculture officials (see Mexico, Getting around by car, page 57). All you need is the registration document in the name of the driver, or, in the case of a car registered in someone else's name, a notarized letter of authorization. Note that Costa Rica does not recognize the International Driving Licence, which is otherwise useful. In Guatemala, Honduras and Costa Rica, the car's entry is stamped into the passport so you may not leave the country even temporarily without it.

A written undertaking that the vehicle will be re-exported after temporary importation is useful and may be requested in Nicaragua, Costa Rica and Panama.

Most countries give a limited period of stay, but allow an extension if requested in advance. Of course, do be very careful to keep **all** the papers you are given when you enter, to produce when you leave. An army of 'helpers' loiters at each border crossing, waiting to guide motorists to each official in the correct order, for a tip. They can be very useful, but don't give them your papers. Bringing a car in by sea or air is much more complicated and expensive; generally you will have to hire an agent to clear it through.

Insurance for the vehicle against accident, damage or theft is best arranged in the country of origin. In Latin American countries it is very expensive to insure against accident and theft, especially as you should take into account the value of the car increased by duties calculated in real (that is non-devaluing) terms. If the car is stolen or written off, you will be required to pay very high duty on its value. A few countries (for example Costa Rica) insist on compulsory third-party insurance, to be bought at the border; in other countries it's technically required, but not checked up on (again, see page 57 for details on **Sanborn's** and other insurers, who will insure vehicles for driving in Mexico and Central America). Get the legally required minimum cover – not expensive – as soon as you can, because if you should be involved in an accident and are uninsured, your car could be confiscated. If anyone is hurt, do not pick them up (you become liable). Seek assistance from the nearest police station or hospital if you are able to do so. You may find yourself facing a hostile crowd, even if you are not to blame. Expect frequent road checks by police, military (especially Honduras, where there is a check point on entering and leaving every town), agricultural and forestry produce inspectors, and any other curious official who wants to know what a foreigner is doing driving around in his domain. Smiling simple-minded patience is the best tactic to avoid harassment.

For a good, first-hand overview of the challenges of travelling overland in your own vehicle, get hold of a copy of *Panama or Bust*, by Jim Jaillet, www.panamaorbust.com, which covers the challenges of preparing for and completing a year-long trip from the US to Panama and back.

Security Spare no ingenuity in making your car secure. Avoid leaving the car unattended except in a locked garage or guarded parking space. Remove all belongings and leave the empty glove compartment open when the car is unattended. Also lock the clutch or accelerator to the steering wheel with a heavy, obvious chain or lock. Street children will generally protect your car in exchange for a tip. Note down key numbers and carry spares of the most important ones, but don't keep all spares inside the vehicle.

Shipping a vehicle to Central America Two recommended shipping lines are **Wallenius Wilhelmsen** ① *head office in Norway at Box 33, N-1324 Lysaker, T+47-6758-4100, for other offices visit www.2wglobal.com*, and, in the US, **American Cargo Service Inc** ① *2305 Northwest 107 Av, Box 122, Miami, FL 331720, T305-592-8065*. Motorcyclists will find good online recommendations at www.horizonsunlimited.com.

Shipping from Panama to mainland South America is expensive; shop around to find the cheapest way. The shipping lines and agents, and the prices for the services from Panama and elsewhere change frequently. Current details and recommendations can be found in the Panama chapter under Shipping a vehicle, page 865.

Car hire

While not everyone has the time or inclination to travel with their own car, the freedom that goes with renting for a few days is well worth considering, especially if you can get a group of three or four together to share the cost. The main international car-hire companies operate in all countries, but tend to be expensive. Hotels and tourist agencies will tell you where to find cheaper rates, but you will need to check that you have such basics as a spare wheel, toolkit, functioning lights, etc. If you plan to do a lot of driving and will have time at the end to dispose of it, investigate the possibility of buying a second-hand car locally; since hiring is so expensive it may work out cheaper and will probably do you just as well.

Car hire insurance Check exactly what the hirer's insurance policy covers. In many cases it will only protect you against minor bumps and scrapes, not major accidents, or 'natural' damage (for example flooding). Ask if extra cover is available. Also find out, if using a credit card, whether the card automatically includes insurance. Beware of being billed for scratches that were on the vehicle before you hired it. When you return the vehicle make sure you check it with someone at the office and get signed evidence that it is returned in good condition and that you will not be charged.

Cycles and motorbikes

Cycling Unless you are planning a journey almost exclusively on paved roads – when a high-quality touring bike would probably suffice – a mountain bike is recommended. The good-quality ones are incredibly tough and rugged. Although touring bike and to a lesser extent mountain bike spares are available in the larger Latin American cities, you'll find that locally manufactured goods are often shoddy and rarely last. In some countries, such as Mexico, imported components can be found but they tend to be very expensive. Buy everything you can before you leave home. **Note** From Guatemala to Panama, border officials are likely to ask for a document of ownership and a frame number for your bicycle.

Recommended reading: *Richard's New Bicycle Book* (Pan) makes useful reading for even the most mechanically minded. Also recommended is *Latin America by Bike – A Complete Touring Guide,* Walter Sienko (The Mountaineers, 1993). For a first-hand account of travelling through the entire region by bike, look at *The Road That Has No End,* by Tim Travis (www.downtheroad.org). Tim and Cindie set out on a round the world trip in 2002 and are still going. This book covers the stretch from Mexico to Panama.

The **Expedition Advisory Centre** ⓘ *at the Royal Geographical Society, 1 Kensington Gore, London, SW7 2AR, T+44-(0)20-7591-3030, www.rgs.org,* has published a booklet on planning a long-distance bike trip titled *Bicycle Expeditions,* by Paul Vickers. Published in March 1990, it is available as a PDF from the website or £5 for a photocopy. In the UK the **Cyclists' Touring Club** ⓘ *CTC, Parklands, Railton Rd, Guildford, Surrey, GU2 9JX, T0844-736-8450, www.ctc.org.uk,* has information on touring, technical information and discusses the relative merits of different types of bikes.

Motorbikes People are generally very friendly to motorcyclists and you can make many friends by returning friendship to those who show an interest in you. Buying a bike in the States and driving down works out cheaper than buying one in Europe. In making your choice go for a comfortable bike. The motorcycle should be off-road capable, without necessarily being an off-road bike. A passport, International Driving Licence and bike registration document are required.

Security This is not a problem in most countries. Try not to leave a fully laden bike on its own. A D-lock or chain will keep the bike secure. An alarm gives you peace of mind if you leave the bike outside a hotel at night. Look for hotels that have a courtyard or more secure parking and never leave luggage on the bike overnight or whilst unattended. Also take a cover for the bike.

Shipping Bikes may be sent from Panama to Colombia by cargo flight. You must drain the fuel and oil and remove the battery, but it is easier to disconnect and seal the overflow tube. Tape cardboard over fragile bits and load the bike yourself. For details on Panama, see page 865.

Border crossings All borders in Central America seem to work out at about US$20 per vehicle. The exceptions to this are Mexico (see Getting around by car in Mexico) and Panama (approximately US$4.50). All borders are free on exit, or should be on most occasions. Crossing borders on a Sunday or a holiday normally incurs double the standard charges in Central American countries. It is sometimes very difficult to find out exactly what is being paid for. If in doubt, ask to see the boss and/or the rule book.

Hitchhiking

Hitchhiking in Latin America is reasonably safe and straightforward for males and couples, provided you speak some Spanish. It is a most enjoyable mode of transport – a good way to meet the local people, to improve one's languages and to learn about the country. If trying to hitchhike away from main roads and in sparsely populated areas, however, allow plenty of time, and ask first about the volume of traffic on the road. On long journeys, set out at the crack of dawn, which is when trucks usually leave. They tend to go longer distances than cars. However, it should be said that hitchhiking involves inherent risks and should be approached sensibly and with caution.

Train

Trains are like nature – they are treasured when threatened with extinction. Now that the privatization and subsequent closure of train lines in Mexico and Central America is almost complete there is a renaissance of interest in railway travel with a fledgling tourist service in **Costa Rica** and the **Trans-Isthmus** railroad in Panama. None of these are particularly epic routes, but you might also find unscheduled long-distance freight trains that take passengers. Be warned, however, they are very slow and sometimes attacked by bandits.

Maps

Maps from the **Institutos Geográficos Militares** in capital cities are often the only good maps available in Latin America. It is therefore wise to get as many as possible in your home country before leaving, especially if travelling overland. An excellent series of maps covering the whole region and each country is published by **International Travel Maps (ITM)** ① *12300 Bridgeport Rd, Richmond, BC, Canada, T604-273-1400, www.itmb.com,* most with historical notes by the late Kevin Healey.

An excellent source of maps is **Stanfords** ① *12-14 Long Acre, Covent Garden, London, WC2E 9LP, T+44-020-7836-1321, www.stanfords.co.uk, also in Bristol and Manchester.* Internet ordering and international delivery service available.

Sleeping

Hotels

At the top end of the market, mid- and upper-range hotel chains can be found throughout the region. A cheap but not bad hotel might be US$15 a night upwards in Mexico, less in some but not all of the Central American countries. In many of the popular destinations there is often an established preferred choice budget option. The quality of these fluctuates. The good ones stay on top of the game, the mediocre ones fade and bloom with the fashions. For those on a really tight budget, it is a good idea to ask for a boarding house – *casa de huéspedes, hospedaje, pensión, casa familial* or *residencial*, according to the country; they are normally to be found in abundance near bus and railway stations and markets. The very cheapest hotels may not have 24-hour water supplies so ask when the water is available. There are often great seasonal variations in hotel prices in resorts. In Mexico, couples should ask for a room with *cama matrimonial* (double bed), which is normally cheaper than a room with two beds. Note that in the text the term 'with bath' usually means 'with shower and toilet', not 'with bath tub'.

Motels, particularly in northern Mexico, are extremely popular and tend to provide accessible, economic accommodation close to the main roads. Further south, the term 'motel' picks up an altogether seedier interpretation.

Making reservations is a good idea, particularly at times you know are going to be busy or if you are travelling a long distance and won't have the energy to look around for a room. At the lower end of the market, having reservations honoured can be difficult. Ask the hotel if there is anything you can do to secure the room. If arriving late, make sure the hotel knows what time you plan to arrive.

Youth hostels

The **International Youth Hostel Association** ⓘ *www.hihostels.com*, has a growing presence in the region with several places in Mexico and Costa Rica. With other affiliated hostels joining it is worth considering getting membership if you are staying in Mexico for a while. While there is no shortage of cheap accommodation, youth hostels do still offer a fairly reliable standard of cleanliness. Members with an ID card normally get a discount.

The web has spawned some great communities and independent travellers should take a look at **www.couchsurfing.com**. It's a way of making friends by kipping on their couch. It's grown rapidly in the last couple of years– and appears to be a great concept that works.

Camping

Organized campsites are referred to in the text immediately below hotel lists, under each town. If there is no organized site in town, a football pitch or gravel pit might serve. Obey the following rules for 'wild' camping: (**1**) arrive in daylight and pitch your tent as it gets dark; (**2**) ask permission to camp from a person in authority; (**3**) never ask a group of people – especially young people; (**4**) avoid camping on a beach (because of sandflies and thieves). If you can't get information, camp in a spot where you can't be seen from the nearest inhabited place and make sure no one saw you go there.

If taking a cooker, the most frequent recommendation is a multifuel stove (for example MSR International Coleman Peak 1), which will burn unleaded petrol or, if that is not available, kerosene, *benzina blanca*, etc. Alcohol-burning stoves are simple, reliable, but slow and you have to carry a lot of fuel: for a methylated spirit-burning stove buy *alcohol*

Sleeping price codes

LL over US$200	**L** US$151-200	**AL** US$101-150
A US$66-100	**B** US$46-65	**C** US$31-45
D US$21-30	**E** US$12-20	**F** US$7-11
G under US$7		

LL-B Hotels in these categories can be found in most of the large cities but especially where there is a strong concentration of tourists or business travellers. They should offer pool, sauna, gym, jacuzzi, business facilities including email, restaurants and bars. A safe box is usually provided in each room. Credit cards are usually accepted and dollars cash changed occasionally at below market rates.

C Hotels in this category should provide more than the standard facilities and a fair degree of comfort. Many include a good breakfast and offer extras such as a colour TV, minibar and air conditioning. They may also provide tourist information and their own transport for airport pickups. Service is generally good and most accept credit cards although a lower rate is often offered for cash.

D and **E** Hotels in these categories range from very comfortable to bare and functional. There are some real bargains to be had. You should expect your own bathroom, constant hot water, a towel, soap and toilet paper. Some-times there'll be a restaurant and a communal sitting area. Wi-Fi is increasingly common in the better **D**-class hotels. In tropical regions, rooms are usually equipped with air conditioning although this may be rather old. Hotels used to catering for foreign tourists and backpackers often have luggage storage, money exchange and kitchen facilities.

F and **G** Hotels in these categories can be extremely simple with bedside or ceiling fans, shared bathrooms and little in the way of furniture. Standards of cleanliness may not be high, but it's not all gloomy; there are some spectacular places in this price range. In towns, a room with a window can often make the difference between OK and intolerable. Balance that with possible noise and security issues.

desnaturalizado, alcohol metílico, alcohol puro (de caña) or *alcohol para quemar* (avoid this in Honduras as it does not burn). Ask for 95%. In Mexico fuel is sold in supermarkets; in all countries it can be found in pharmacies. Gas cylinders and bottles are usually exchangeable, but if not can be recharged; specify whether you use butane or propane. Gas canisters are not always available. Camping supplies are usually only available in the larger cities, so stock up on them when possible.

Hammocks

A hammock can be an invaluable piece of equipment, especially if travelling on the cheap. It will be of more use than a tent because many places have hammock-hooks, or you can sling a hammock between trees or posts. A good tip is to carry a length of rope and some plastic sheeting. The rope gives a good choice of tree distances and the excess provides a hanging frame for the plastic sheeting to keep the rain off. Metal S-hooks or a couple of climbing karabiners can also be very useful, as can strong cord for tying out the sheeting. Don't forget a mosquito net if travelling in insect-infected areas.

Eating price codes

🍴🍴🍴 over US$15   🍴🍴 US$8-15   🍴 under US$8

Prices refer to the cost of a meal with a drink for one person.

Toilets

Almost without exception, used toilet paper should be placed in the receptacle provided and not flushed down the pan. This applies even in quite expensive hotels. Failing to observe this custom blocks the pan or drain.

Eating

There is a section on each nation's food at the start of each chapter and the listings give a cross section of the type of places available, and hopefully include the best of what is on offer. Naturally the dining experience varies greatly. An excellent general rule when looking for somewhere to eat is to ask locally.

Most restaurants serve a daily special meal, usually at lunchtime called a *comida corrida* or *comida corriente*, which works out much cheaper and is usually filling and nutritious. Vegetarians should be able to list all the foods they cannot eat; saying '*Soy vegetariano/a*' (I'm a vegetarian) or '*No como carne*' (I don't eat meat) is often not enough. Universally the cheapest place to eat is the local market.

Safety The golden rule is boil it, cook it, peel it or forget it, but if you did that every day, every meal, you'd never eat anywhere ... A more practicable rule is that if large numbers of people are eating in a regularly popular place, it's more than likely going to be OK.

Shopping

The range of gifts available is daunting, from the fine jade jewellery of Chiapas to the tacky T-shirts of the more popular spots, and from the textiles and clothing of Guatemala to the leather goods from Nicaragua and the finely crafted *molas* of Panama. If buying more expensive items, research before you leave home so you know if you're getting a good deal. Best buys and regional items are highlighted in each chapter. Generally, choice is better in the capital, but the price is often steeper. Always make sure you know the price before purchasing an item. Bargaining seems to be the general rule in most countries' street markets.

Festivals and events

If the time and mood is right, there is little to beat a Latin festival. Fine costumes, loud music, the sounds of firecrackers tipped off with the gentle wafting of specially prepared foods all (normally) with a drink or two. Whether you seek out the carnival or happen to stumble across a celebration, the events – big or small – are likely to be memorable.

If you want to hit the carnivals there are a few broad dates generally significant throughout the region. Carnival is normally the week before the start of Lent. It's more important in Mexico but you'll probably find regional celebrations in most places. *Semana Santa* (Easter Week) is an understandably more spiritual affair. On 2 November is *Día de los Muertos* (Day of the Dead), again most popular in Mexico but significant throughout the region when families visit cemeteries to honour the dead. Christmas and New Year result in celebrations of some kind, but not always public.

Public holidays throughout the region lead to a complete shut-down in services. No banks, government offices, usually no shops and often far fewer restaurants and bars. It is worth keeping an eye on the calendar to avoid changing money or trying to make travel arrangements on public holidays.

Mexico
Feb/Mar Carnival/Mardi Gras. Traditionally throughout Latin America, this week is a time for celebration before the hardships of Lent; in Mexico it is particularly popular in Mérida.
15 Sep Cry for Independence. Celebrations that are particularly impressive in Mexico City.
16 Sep Independence Day. Regional festivities and parades.
2 Nov Day of the Dead. The souls of the deceased return to earth and family and friends turn out in costume and to meet them.
12 Dec Pilgrimage of thousands to the Basílica de Guadalupe, in northeast Mexico City, the most venerated shrine in Mexico. Well worth a visit.

Guatemala
Mar/Apr Semana Santa, particularly colourful in Antigua with floats carrying Christ over wonderfully coloured and carefully placed carpets of flowers; also spectacular in Santiago Atitlán.
Nov Todos Santos Cuchumatán. All Saints' Day in the small town of Todos Santos, a colourful and drunken horse race with lots of dancing and antics. See page 272.

Belize
10 Sep St George's Cay Day, with celebrations in Belize City that start with river races in San Ignacio.
19 Nov Settlement Day, celebrating the liberation (or arrival) of the Garífuna from distant shores. Also celebrated in Guatemala and Honduras.

El Salvador
29 Nov Nuestra Señora de la Paz. Big celebrations in San Miguel.

Honduras
15 May San Isidro, La Ceiba's patron saint, followed by a fortnight of celebrations. The highlight is a huge carnival on the 3rd Sat in May.
1-4 Feb Supaya, southeast of Tegucigalpa, the most important shrine in Honduras with a tiny wooden image of the Virgen de Supaya.

Nicaragua
Keep an eye out for patron saints of villages and towns.
Dec La Purísima in honour of the patron saint of the Immaculate Virgin, celebrated with fireworks with 7 Dec being the high point.

Costa Rica
Late Jan/early Feb Fiesta de los Diablitos in the small towns of Boruca and Rey Curre, south Costa Rica, symbolic of the fight between cultures, religion and colonization.
2 Aug Virgin of Los Angeles, celebrated with pilgrimages to the basilica in Cártago.
15 Sep Independence Day with celebrations and parades in the capital San José and throughout the country.
12 Oct Día de la Raza (Columbus Day) celebrated with particular gusto in the Caribbean city of Puerto Limón.

Panama
3 Nov Independence Day.

Responsible travel

The travel industry is growing rapidly, and the impact is becoming increasingly apparent. These impacts can seem remote and unrelated to an individual trip or holiday, but air travel is clearly implicated in global warming and damage to the ozone layer, and resort location and construction can destroy natural habitats and restrict traditional rights and activities. With this in mind, individual choice and awareness can make a difference in many instances (see box, page 36); collectively, travellers can have a significant effect in shaping a more responsible and sustainable industry. In an attempt to promote awareness of and credibility for responsible tourism, organizations such as **EC3** ⓘ *Suite 8, Southern Cross House, 9 McKay Street, Turner, ACT, 2612, Australia, T+61-2-6257-9102, www.greenglobe.com*, offer advice on selecting destinations and sites that aim to achieve certain commitments to conservation and sustainable development. Generally, these are large mainstream destinations and resorts but they are still a useful guide and increasingly aim to provide information on smaller operations. Of course travel can have beneficial impacts and this is something to which every traveller can contribute – many national parks are part funded by receipts from visitors. Similarly, travellers can support small-scale enterprises by staying in locally run hotels and hostels, eating in local restaurants and by buying local goods, supplies and crafts. There has been a phenomenal growth in tourism that promotes and supports the conservation of natural environments and is also fair and equitable to local communities. This 'ecotourism' segment provides a vast and growing range of destinations and activities in Central America. For example, in Mexico, cultural heritage and ecotourism is being promoted by **Bioplanet@** ⓘ *T+52-55-5661-6156, www.bioplaneta.com, and in Belize through the Belize Ecotourism Association, T+501-722-2119, www.bzecotourism.org, and* PACT (the Protected Areas Conservation Trust) ⓘ *T+501-822-3637, www.pactbelize.org.*

How big is your footprint?

The point of a holiday is, of course, to have a good time, but if it's relatively guilt-free as well, that's even better. Perfect ecotourism would ensure a good living for local inhabitants, while not detracting from their traditional lifestyles, encroaching on their customs or spoiling their environment. Perfect ecotourism probably doesn't exist, but everyone can play their part. Here are a few points worth bearing in mind:

- Where possible choose a destination, tour operator or hotel with a proven ethical and environmental commitment.
- Spend money on locally produced (rather than imported) goods and services and use common sense when bargaining: your few dollars saved may be a week's salary to others.
- Use water and electricity carefully: travellers may receive preferential supply while the needs of local communities are overlooked.
- Consider staying in local accommodation rather than foreign-owned hotels: the economic benefits for host communities are far greater, and there are greater opportunities to learn about local culture.
- Protect wildlife and other natural resources; don't buy souvenirs or goods unless they are made from materials that are clearly sustainably produced and are not protected under CITES legislation (CITES controls trade in endangered species).
- Learn about local etiquette and culture; consider local norms and behaviour and dress appropriately for local cultures and situations.
- Always ask before taking photographs or videos of people.
- Make a voluntary contribution to counter the pollution caused by international air travel. Climate Concern calculates the amount of carbon dioxide you generate, and then offsets it by funding projects that reduce it; visit www.co2.org. Alternatively, you can offset CO2 emissions from air travel through Climate Care's CO2 reduction projects, www.climatecare.org.

Essentials A-Z

Children

Travel with children can bring you into closer contact with Latin American families and generally presents no special problems – in fact, the path is often smoother for family groups. Officials tend to be more amenable where children are concerned. Always carry a copy of your child's birth certificate and passport photos. For an overview of travelling with children, visit www.babygoes2.com.

Public transport

Overland travel in Latin America can involve a lot of time spent waiting for public transport. It is easier to take biscuits, drinks, bread, etc with you on longer trips than to rely on meal stops where the food may not be to taste. All airlines charge a reduced price for children under 12 and less for children under 2. Double check the child's baggage allowance – some are as low as 7 kg. On long-distance buses children generally pay half or reduced fares. For shorter trips it is cheaper, if less comfortable, to seat small children on your knee. Often there are spare seats that children can occupy after tickets have been collected. In city and local excursion buses, small children do not generally pay a fare, but are not entitled to a seat when paying customers are standing. On sightseeing tours you should always bargain for a family rate; often children can go free. Note that a child travelling free on a long excursion is not always covered by the operator's travel insurance.

Hotels

Try to negotiate family rates. If charges are per person, always insist that 2 children will occupy 1 bed only, therefore counting as 1 tariff. If rates are per bed, the same applies. It is quite common for children under 10 or 12 to be allowed to stay for no extra charge as long as they are sharing your room.

Customs and duty free

Duty free allowances and export restrictions for each country are listed in the beginning sections of each chapter. It goes without saying that drugs, firearms and banned products should not be traded or taken across international boundaries.

Disabled travellers

In most Latin American countries, facilities for disabled travellers are severely lacking. Most airports and hotels and restaurants in major resorts have wheelchair ramps and adapted toilets. While some cities such as San José in Costa Rica are all ramped, in general pavements are often in such a poor state of repair that walking is precarious.

Some travel companies specialize in exciting holidays, tailor-made for individuals depending on their level of disability. The Global Access-Disabled Travel Network Site, www.globalaccessnews.com, provides travel information for disabled adventurers and includes a number of reviews and tips from members of the public. You might also want to read *Nothing Ventured*, edited by Alison Walsh (Harper Collins), which gives personal accounts of worldwide journeys by disabled travellers, plus advice and listings.

Drugs

Users of drugs without medical prescription should be particularly careful, as some countries impose heavy penalties – up to 10 years' imprisonment – for even the simple possession of such substances. The planting of drugs on travellers, by traffickers or the police, is not unknown. If offered drugs on the street, make no response at all and keep walking. Note that people who roll their own cigarettes are often suspected of carrying drugs and are subjected to close searches.

If you are taking illegal drugs – even ones that are widely and publically used – be aware that authorities do set traps from time to time. Should you get into trouble, your embassy is unlikely to be very sympathetic.

Gay and lesbian travellers

Most of Latin America is not particularly liberal in its attitudes to gays and lesbians. Even in the cities people are fairly conservative, and more so in provincial towns and rural areas. Having said that, things are changing and you'll find there is a gay scene with bars and clubs at least in most of the bigger cities and resorts. Helpful websites include www.gay scape.com, www.gaypedia.com and www.iglta.org (International Gay and Lesbian Travel Association).

Health

See your GP or travel clinic at least 6 weeks before departure for general advice on travel risks and vaccinations. Try a specialist travel clinic if your own GP is unfamiliar with health conditions in Central America. Make sure you have sufficient medical travel insurance, get a dental check, know your own blood group and if you suffer a long-term condition such as diabetes or epilepsy, obtain a Medic Alert bracelet/ necklace (www.medicalert.co.uk). If you wear glasses, take a copy of your prescription.

Vaccinations

Vaccinations for tetanus, hepatitis A and typhoid are commonly recommended for all countries covered in this book. In addition, yellow fever vaccination is recommended for some areas of Panama; in most of the countries a yellow fever certificate is required if entering from an infected area. In all 8 countries vaccinations may also be advised advised against tuberculosis, hepatitis B, rabies and diptheria and, in the case of Guatemala, cholera. The final decision, however, should be based on a consultation with your GP or travel clinic. In all cases you should confirm your primary courses and boosters are up to date.

Health risks

The most common cause of travellers' **diarrhoea** is from eating contaminated food. In Central America, drinking water is rarely the culprit, although it's best to be cautious (see below). Swimming in sea or river water that has been contaminated by sewage can also be a cause; ask locally if it is safe. Diarrhoea may be also caused by viruses, bacteria (such as E-coli), protozoal (such as giardia), salmonella and cholera. It may be accompanied by vomiting or by severe abdominal pain. Any kind of diarrhoea responds well to the replacement of water and salts. Sachets of rehydration salts can be bought in most chemists and can be dissolved in boiled water. If symptoms persist, consult a doctor. Tap water in the major cities is safe to drink but it may be advisable to err on the side of caution and drink only bottled or boiled water. Avoid ice in drinks unless you trust that it is from a reliable source.

Travelling in high altitudes can bring on **altitude sickness**. On reaching heights above 3000 m, the heart may start pounding and the traveller may experience shortness of breath. Smokers and those with underlying heart or lung disease are often hardest hit. Take it easy for the first few days, rest and drink plenty of water, you will feel better soon. It is essential to get acclimatized before undertaking long treks or arduous activities.

Malaria precautions are essential for some parts of Mexico and Central America, particularly some rural areas. Once again, check with your GP or travel clinic well in advance of departure. Avoid being bitten by mosquitoes as much as possible. Sleep off the ground and use a mosquito net and some kind of insecticide. Mosquito coils release insecticide as they burn and are available in many shops, as are tablets of insecticide, which are placed on a heated mat plugged into a wall socket.

If you get sick

Contact your embassy or consulate for a list of doctors and dentists who speak your language, or at least some English. Doctors and health facilities in major cities are also listed in the Directory sections of this book. Good-quality healthcare is available in the larger centres but it can be expensive, especially hospitalization. Make sure you have adequate insurance (see below).

Useful websites

www.btha.org British Travel Health Association.
www.cdc.gov US government site that gives excellent advice on travel health and details of disease outbreaks.
www.fco.gov.uk British Foreign and Commonwealth Office travel site has useful information on each country, people, climate and a list of UK embassies/consulates.
www.fitfortravel.scot.nhs.uk A-Z of vaccine/health advice for each country.
www.numberonehealth.co.uk Travel screening services, vaccine and travel health advice, email/SMS text vaccine reminders and screens returned travellers for tropical diseases.

Insurance

Insurance is strongly recommended and policies are very reasonable. If you have financial restraints, the most important aspect of any insurance policy is medical care and repatriation. Ideally you want to make sure you are covered for personal items too. Read the small print **before** heading off so you are aware of what is covered and what is not, what is required to submit a claim and what to do in the event of an emergency.

Internet

Email is very common and public access to the internet is becoming endemic with cybercafés opening in both large and small towns. Hotels and even cafes in popular places are installing Wi-Fi that you can log on to if you have your own laptop or notebook. We list cybercafés in the text, but obviously these change.

Language

→ *See Footnotes, page 1016, for a list of useful words and phrases.*

Spanish is spoken throughout most of Mexico and Central America and, while you will be able to get by without knowledge of Spanish, you will probably become frustrated and feel helpless in many situations. English, or any other language, is useless off the beaten track (except in Belize). A pocket dictionary and phrase book together with some initial study or a beginner's Spanish course before you leave are strongly recommended. If you have the time, book 1-2 weeks of classes at the beginning of your travels.

Some areas have developed a reputation for language classes, Antigua and Quetzaltenango in Guatemala and San José and Heredia in Costa Rica. Many other locations also provide tuition. The better-known centres normally include a wide range of cultural activities and supporting options for homestay. A less well-known centre is likely to have fewer English speakers around. For details, see Language schools in the Directory sections of individual towns and cities.

Not all the locals speak Spanish, of course; you will find that some indigenous people in the more remote areas – the highlands of Guatemala for example – speak only their indigenous languages, although there will usually be at least one person in a village who can speak Spanish.

Language tuition

Arranging language tuition internationally is increasingly popular.

AmeriSpan, 1334 Walnut St (PO Box 58129), 6th floor, Philadelphia, PA 19107, T1-215-751-1100, T1-800-879-6640, www.amerispan.com (also with offices in Antigua, Guatemala). One of the most comprehensive options, offering Spanish immersion programmes, educational tours, volunteer and internship positions throughout Latin America.

Cactus Language, 4 Clarence House, 30-31 North St, Brighton, East Sussex, BN1 1EB, T0845-130-4775, www.cactuslanguage training.com. Spanish language courses from 1 week in duration in Mexico and Central America, with pre-trip classes in the UK. Also has additional options for volunteer work, diving and staying with host families.

Institute for Spanish Language Studies, in the US on T1-866-391-0394, www.isls.com. Has schools in Mexico, Costa Rica and Panama, offering innovative and flexible programmes.

Spanish Abroad, 5112 N 40th St, Suite 101, Phoenix, AZ 85018, USA, T1-888-722-7623 (USA and Canada), T1-602-778-6791 (worldwide), www.spanishabroad.com. Intensive Spanish immersion programmes throughout Latin America for those wishing to study abroad.

Media

World Band Radio Latin America has more local and community radio stations than practically anywhere else in the world; a shortwave (world band) radio offers a practical means to brush up on the language, sample popular culture and absorb some of the richly varied regional music. International broadcasters also transmit across Central America in both English and Spanish, these include the **BBC World Service**, www.bbc.co.uk/worldservice/index.shtml for schedules and frequencies, the **Voice** of America, www.voa.gov, and Boston (Mass)-based **Monitor Radio International**, operated by Christian Science Monitor, www.csmonitor.com. **Putumayo World Music**, www.putumayo.com specialize in the exotic sounds of Mexican music.

Details of the national newspapers, television and radio are given in the Essentials section at the beginning of each chapter.

Money

While most – but not all – countries in Mexico and Central America have their own currencies, the most useful foreign currency in the region is the US dollar. Consequently, that proportion of your money you take in cash and traveller's cheques (TCs) should be in US dollars. Banks and *casas de cambio* are increasingly able to change euros but the dollar is still the most readily accepted and changed.

The 3 main ways of keeping in funds while travelling are still with US dollars cash, US dollar TCs, or plastic (credit cards). It is recommended that you take all 3.

Cost of travelling

As a rough calculation budget travellers can get by on US$25-35 a day, but that means that you won't be able to afford to take many excursions. A more realistic and sustainable budget is US$35-50. Plenty of travellers manage on smaller budgets but it's probably better to spend a little longer at home saving up, and then have a good time while you're away, rather than find yourself adding up the small change on a Sat night to see if you can afford a weekly beer.

Cash

The chief benefit of taking US dollars is that they are accepted almost everywhere. They are used as national currency in El Salvador and Panama, and rates and

Exchange rates (June 2011)

	Unit of currency	US$1	€1	£1
Belize	Belize dollar	2.00	2.86	3.19
Costa Rica	Colón	502	737	823
El Salvador*	Colón	8.75	12.83	14.33
Guatemala	Quetzal	7.84	11.49	12.85
Honduras	Lempira	18.89	27.68	30.94
Mexico	Peso	11.79	17.28	19.31
Nicaragua	Córdoba	22.35	32.74	36.60
Panama*	Balboa	1.00	1.46	1.63

* US notes and coins are legal tender.

commissions are more competitive than for other currencies.

In many countries, US dollar notes are only accepted if they are in excellent condition – no small tears, rips, nicks, holes or scribbles. When ordering money at home bear this in mind. Take a selection of bills including several low-value US dollar bills (US$5 or US$10) which can be carried for changing into local currency if arriving in a country when banks or *casas de cambio* are closed, and for use in out of the way places when you may run out of local currency. They are also very useful for shopping: shopkeepers and *casas de cambio* tend to give better exchange rates than hotels or banks (but see below).

If your budget is tight it is essential to avoid situations where you are forced to change money regardless of the rate; watch weekends and public holidays carefully and never run out of local currency. Take plenty of local currency, in small denominations, when making trips away from the major towns and resorts.

Traveller's cheques

Traveller's cheques (TCs) provide reasonably accessible cash with peace of mind against theft. Denominations of US$50 and US$100 are preferable, with a few of US$20 to increase your options. Some banks will change the cheques for US dollars cash if you need to top up your supply. American Express or Visa US dollar TCs are recommended, but less commission is often charged on Citibank or Bank of America TCs if they are cashed at Latin American branches of those banks. American Express now has a plastic Traveller's Cheque Card, used in a similar way to paper TCs. While this should work in theory, experience shows that new financial ideas are not quickly adopted in Central America and you may have trouble using it.

Several banks charge a high fixed commission for changing TCs because they don't really want the bother. *Casas de cambio* are usually a much better choice for this service. Some establishments may ask to see a passport and the customer's record of purchase before accepting. Keep the original purchase slip in a separate place to the TCs and make a photocopy for security. The better hotels will normally change TCs for their guests (often at a poor rate).

Credit cards

Credit cards are ideal for travelling, providing ready access to funds without carrying large amounts of cash on your person. In an ideal world taking a couple of cards (one Visa and one MasterCard) will make sure you are covered in most options. It is straightforward to obtain a cash advance against a credit card and even easier to withdraw cash from ATMs. (Remove your credit card from the machine immediately after the transaction to avoid it being retained – getting it back can be difficult.) There are 2 acceptance systems, **Plus** and **Cirrus**. You may have to experiment to see what combination of options your require. Fortunately, most ATMs give you a 'language' option after you enter your card. The rates of exchange on ATM withdrawals are the best available for currency exchange but your bank or credit card company imposes a handling charge. If you lose a card, immediately contact the 24-hr helpline of the issuer in your home country (find out the numbers to call before travelling and keep them in a safe place). Most card issuers provide a telephone number where you can call collect from anywhere in the world in case of card loss or theft; be sure to request it before travelling.

For purchases, credit cards of the Visa and MasterCard groups, American Express (Amex), Carte Blanche and Diners Club can be used. Make sure you know the correct procedure if they are lost or stolen. Credit card transactions are normally at an officially recognized rate of exchange; they are often subject to sales tax. In addition, many establishments in Latin America charge a fee of about 5% on credit card transactions; although forbidden by credit card company rules there is not a lot you can do about this, except get the charge itemized on the receipt and complain to the card company. For credit card security, insist that imprints are made in your presence. Any imprints incorrectly completed should be torn into tiny pieces. Also destroy the carbon papers after the form is completed (signatures can be copied from them).

Changing money

Whenever possible change your money at a bank or a *casa de cambio*. Black markets and street changers have largely disappeared; avoid them if you can as you are unlikely to get a significantly better rate and you place yourself a greater risk of being ripped off. If you need to change money on the street, do not do so alone. If you are unsure about rates of exchange when you enter a country, check at the border with more than one changer, or ask locals or any traveller who may be leaving that country. Whenever you leave a country, sell any local currency before leaving – the further you get away from a country, the less the value of a country's money; in some cases you may not be able to change it at all.

Police

Probably the best advice with regards the police in Mexico and Central America is to have as little to do with them as possible. An exception to this rule are the Tourist Police, who operate in some of the big cities and resorts, and provide assistance. In general, law enforcement in Latin America is achieved by periodic campaigns, not systematically.

You may be asked for identification at any time and should therefore always have ID on you. If you cannot produce it, you may be jailed. If a visitor is jailed his or her friends should provide food every day. This is especially important for people on a special diet, such as diabetics. If you are jailed, you should contact your embassy or consulate and take advice. In the event of a vehicle accident in which anyone is injured, all drivers involved are automatically detained until blame has been established, and this does not usually take less than 2 weeks.

The giving and receiving of bribes is not recommended. However, the following advice may prove useful. Never offer a bribe unless you are fully conversant with the customs of the country. Wait until the official makes the suggestion, or offer money in some form that is apparently not bribery, for example 'In our country we have a system of on-the-spot fines (*multas de inmediato*). Is there a similar system here?'

Do not assume that officials who accept a bribe are prepared to do anything else that is illegal. You bribe them to do their job, or not do it, or to do it more quickly, or more slowly. You do not bribe them to do something which is against the law. The mere suggestion would make them very upset. If an official suggests that a bribe must be paid before you can proceed on your way, be patient (assuming you have the time) and he may relent. Bear in mind that by bribing you are participating in a system that may cause you immense frustration.

Post

Postal services vary in efficiency from country to country and prices are quite high; pilfering is frequent. All mail, especially packages, should be registered. Check before leaving home if your embassy will hold mail and if so for how long, in preference to the Poste Restante/General Delivery (*Lista de Correos*) department of a country's Post Office. Cardholders can use Amex agencies. If you're expecting mail and there seems to be no mail at the *Lista* under the initial letter of your surname, ask them to look under the initial of your forename or your middle name. If your name begins with 'W', look for letters under 'V' as well, or ask. For the smallest risk of misunderstanding, use title, initial and surname only.

Punctuality

Punctuality is more of a concept than a reality in Latin countries. The *mañana* culture reigns supreme and any arrangement to meet at, say 1900, will normally rendezvous somewhere between 2000 and 2100. However, the one time you are late to catch a bus, boat or plane, it will leave on time – the rule is hurry up and wait.

Safety

Generally speaking, most places in Latin America are no more dangerous than any major city in Europe or North America and the people, if anything, are friendlier and more open. In provincial towns, main places of interest, on daytime buses and in ordinary restaurants the visitor should be quite safe. Nevertheless, in large cities (particularly in crowded places such as markets and bus stations) crime exists, mostly of the opportunistic kind. If you are aware of the dangers, act confidently and use your common sense, you will lessen many of the risks. The following tips, endorsed by travellers, are meant to forewarn, not alarm.

Keep all documents secure; hide your main cash supply in different places or under your clothes. Extra pockets sewn inside shirts and trousers, pockets closed with a zip or safety pin, moneybelts, neck or leg pouches, and elasticated support bandages for keeping money and cheques above the elbow or below the knee have been repeatedly recommended. Pouches worn outside the clothes are not safe. Keep cameras in bags (preferably with a chain or wire in the strap to defeat the slasher) and don't wear fancy wristwatches or jewellery. Carry your small day pack in front of you.

Safety on public transport
When you have all your luggage with you at a bus station, be especially careful: don't get into arguments with any locals if you can help it and clip, tie or lock all the items together with a chain or cable if you are waiting for some time, or simply sit on top of your backpack. Take a taxi between airport/bus station/railway station and hotel, if you can afford it. Keep your bags with you in the taxi and pay only when you and your luggage are safely out of the vehicle (but keep an eye on it your luggage!). Avoid night buses unless essential or until you are comfortable travelling in the area; avoid

arriving at night whenever possible; and watch your belongings whether they are stowed inside or outside the cabin (rooftop luggage racks create extra problems, which are sometimes unavoidable – many bus drivers cover rooftop luggage with plastic sheeting, but a waterproof bag or outer sack can be invaluable for protecting your luggage and for stopping someone rummaging through the top of your bag). Major bus lines often issue a luggage ticket when bags are stored in the hold; this is generally a safe system. When getting on a bus, keep your ticket handy as you will probably have to show it at some point. Finally, be wary of accepting food, drink, sweets or cigarettes from unknown fellow travellers on buses or trains; although extremely rare, they may be drugged, and you could wake up hours later without your belongings. In this connection, never accept a bar drink from an opened bottle (unless you can see that the bottle is in general use); always have it uncapped in front of you. Do not take shared taxis with strangers you have met on the bus, no matter how polite or well-dressed; in Nicaragua, there have been a spree of armed robberies that begin that way.

Scams

A number of distraction techniques such as mustard smearers and paint or shampoo sprayers and strangers' remarks like 'what's that on your shoulder?' or 'have you seen that dirt on your shoe?' are designed to distract you for a few critical moments in which time your bag may be grabbed. Furthermore, supposedly friendly assistance asking if you have dropped money or other items in the street work on the same premise. If someone follows you when you're in the street, let him catch up with you and give him the 'eye'. While you should take local advice about being out at night, do not assume that daytime is any safer. If walking after dark on quiet streets, walk in the road, not on the pavement.

Be wary of 'plain-clothes policemen'; insist on seeing identification and on going to the police station by main roads. Do not hand over your identification (or money – which he should not need to see anyway) until you are at the station. On no account take them directly back to your lodgings. Be even more suspicious if he seeks confirmation of his status from a passer-by. If someone implies they are asking for a bribe, insist on a receipt. If attacked, remember your assailants may well be armed, and try not to resist.

It is best, if you can trust your hotel, to leave any valuables you don't need in a safe-deposit. Always keep an inventory of what you have deposited. If you don't trust the hotel, lock everything in your pack and secure that in your room. If you do lose valuables, you will need to report the incident to the police for insurance purposes.

Sexual assault

This is extremely rare, but if you are the victim of a sexual assault, you are advised in the first instance to contact a doctor (this can be your home doctor if you prefer). You will need tests to determine whether you have contracted any sexually transmitted diseases; you may also need advice on post-coital contraception. You should also contact your embassy, where consular staff are very willing to help in cases of assault.

Student and teacher travellers

If you are in full-time education you will be entitled to an **International Student Identity Card** (ISIC), which is distributed by student travel offices and travel agencies in over 100 countries. ISIC gives you special prices on all forms of transport (air, sea, rail, etc), and a variety of other concessions and services. Contact **International Student Travel Confederation** (ISTC), Herengracht 479, 1017 BS Amsterdam, The Netherlands,

T+31-20-421 2800, www.isic.org. Student cards must carry a photograph if they are to be of any use for discounts in Latin America. The ISIC website provides a list of card-issuing offices around the world. Teachers may want to take an **International Teacher Identity Card (ITIC)** distributed by ISTC (above), as discounts are often extended to teachers.

Tax

When departing, don't forget you'll have to pay departure tax if it isn't already included in your ticket. Check individual chapters for further details.

Telephone

Many of the telecommunications networks have been privatized and prices have fallen considerably. In some areas, services have even improved. Consequently keeping in touch by phone is no longer prohibitive. International telecom charge cards are useful and available from most countries; obtain details before leaving home. For the US AT&T's 'USA Direct', **Sprint** and **MCI** are all available for calls to the USA. It is much cheaper than operator-assisted calls. Internet calls (eg via Skype) may be possible.

Using a mobile in most of Mexico and Central America is very expensive. In addition to the hassle of having to charge your phone, research whether it is worth your while. Mobile phone calls will be cheaper if you buy a SIM card for the local network; in-country calls are likely to be considerably cheaper than using your home-based account. The initial cost of the SIM is getting more affordable (as little as US$3 in Honduras), but check the cost of calls. Also bear in mind, the number you use at home will not work.

Tour operators

In the UK
Condor Journeys and Adventures, 2 Ferry Bank, Colintraive, Argyll, PA22 3AR, T01700-841-318, www.condorjourneys-dventures.com, also offices in France.
Explore Worldwide, 55 Victoria Rd, Farnborough, Hants, GU14 7PA, T0845 013 1537, www.explore.co.uk.
Galapagos Classic Cruises, 6 Keyes Rd, London, NW2 3XA, T020-8933-0613, www.galapagoscruises.co.uk.
Journey Latin America, 12-13 Heathfield Terrace, London, W4 4JE, T020-8747-8315, www.journeylatinamerica.co.uk.
Last Frontiers, The Mill, Quainton Rd, Waddesdon, Buckinghamshire, HP18 0LP, T01296-653-000, www.lastfrontiers.com.
Select Latin America, 3.51 Canterbury Court, 1-3 Brixton Rd, London, SW9 6DE, T020-7407-1478, www.selectlatinamerica.com.

South America Adventure Tours,
336 Kennington Lane, Suite 25,
London, SE11 5HY, T0845-463-3389,
www.southamericaadventuretours.com.
Trips Worldwide, 14 Frederick Place,
Clifton, Bristol, BS8 1AS, T0800-840-0850,
www.tripsworldwide.co.uk.
Tucan Travel, 316 Uxbridge Rd, London, W3
9QP, T020-8896-1600, www.tucantravel.com.
Veloso Tours, 34 Warple Way, London,
W3 0RG, T020-8762-0616, www.veloso.com.
Western & Oriental Travel, 305 Upper St,
London, N1 2TU, T0845-277-3366,
www.WandOtravel.com.

In North America
Exito Travel, 6740 E. Hampden Av, Denver,
Colorado, T800-655-4053, www.exitotravel.com.
GAP Adventures, 19 Charlotte St, Toronto,
Ontario, M5V 2H5, T1-416-260-0999,
www.gapadventures.com.
Mila Tours, 100 S Greenleaf Av, Gurnee,
Il 60031, T1-800-367-7378, www.milatours.com.

S and S Tours, 4250 S Hohokam Dr,
Sierra Vista, AZ 85650, T866-780-2813,
www.ss-tours.com.

International
The following have operations in the US,
Canada, Europe, Australia and New Zealand.
Dragoman, T01728-861-133,
www.dragoman.co.uk.
Exodus Travels, T020-8675-5550,
www.exodus.co.uk.
LADATCO tours, 2200 S Dixie Highway,
Suite 704, Coconut Grove, FL 33133,
T1-800-327-6162, www.ladatco.com.

Tourist information

All countries in the region have a tourist
board but not all have an international
presence. Fortunately the internet makes
it possible to get the latest information
on developments in a country.

South American Explorers, Head Office in the USA at 126 Indian Creek Rd, Ithaca, NY 14850, USA, T607-277-0488, www.saexplorers.org, is a very useful resource. Despite the name, the whole of Latin America is covered and members receive help with travel planning as well as informed access on books and maps covering the region.

Useful websites

www.centralamerica.com Covers mainly Costa Rica but also touches on Guatemala, Belize, Honduras, Nicaragua and Panama.
www.latinnews.com Up-to-date site with political comment.
www.planeta.com A phenomenal resource, which is staggering for its detail on everything from ecotourism and language schools to cybercafés.
www.revuemag.com Growing regional guide in print and online, focusing on Guatemala with coverage of El Salvador, Honduras and Belize.
Google has country search engines for Mexico (.com.mx), El Salvador (.com.sv), Honduras (.com.hn), Nicaragua (.com.ni), Costa Rica (.com.cr) and Panama (.com.pa).

A couple of general travel websites that are worth a look are www.bootsnall.com and www.tripadvisor.com.

Visas and immigration

For information on visas and immigration, see the individual country chapters.
If you are thinking of travelling from your own country via the USA, or of visiting the USA after Latin America, you are strongly advised to get your visa and find out about any other requirements from a US Consulate in your own country before travelling. If you are eligible for a visa waiver, you are now required to register in advance with the **Electronic System for Travel Authorization** (ESTA), www.esta.cbp.dhs.gov/esta/. You will need to do this before setting out.

For US nationals, the implications of the **Western Hemisphere Travel Initiative**, which came into force on 1 Jan 2008 should be considered if entering Mexico. You will need a passport to reenter the US once you have left and visited Mexico.

All international travel requires that you have at least 6 months remaining on a valid passport. Beyond a passport, very little is required of international travellers to Mexico and Central America. However, there are a few little tricks that can make your life a lot easier. Latin Americans, especially officials, are very document-minded. If staying in a country for several weeks, it is worthwhile registering at your embassy or consulate.

Then, if your passport is stolen, the process of replacing it is faster and easier. It can also be handy to keep some additional passport-sized photographs together with photocopies of essential documents – including your flight ticket – separately from the originals.

It is your responsibility to ensure that your passport is stamped in and out when you cross borders. The absence of entry and exit stamps can cause serious difficulties; seek out the proper immigration offices if the stamping process is not carried out as you cross. Also, do not lose your entry card; replacing it can cause you a lot of trouble and possibly expense. If planning to study in Latin America for a long period, make every effort to get a student visa in advance.

Women travellers

Some women experience problems, whether accompanied or not; others encounter no difficulties at all. Unaccompanied Western women will at times be subject to close scrutiny and exceptional curiosity. Don't be unduly scared. Simply be prepared and try not to over-react. When you set out, err on the side of caution until your instincts have adjusted to the new culture. Women travelling alone could consider taking a wedding ring to prevent being hassled. To help minimize unwanted attention, consider your clothing choices. Do not feel bad about showing offence. When accepting an invitation, make sure that someone else knows the address you are going to and the time you left. Ask if you can bring a friend (even if you do not intend to do so). A good rule is always to act with confidence, as though you know where you are going, even if you do not. Someone who looks lost is more likely to attract unwanted attention. Do not disclose to strangers where you are staying.

Working

Two main areas provide opportunities for unskilled volunteers: childcare – often at orphanages or schools – and nature projects. Be warned, spontaneous volunteering is becoming more difficult. Organizations that use volunteers have progressed and plan their personnel needs so you may be required to make contact before you visit. Many organizations now charge volunteers for board and lodging and projects are often for a minimum of 4 weeks. Guatemala and Costa Rica in particular have fairly well-developed and organized volunteer programmes.

Many developed countries have nationally organized volunteer programmes. The **US Peace Corps**, Paul D Coverdell Peace Corps Headquarters, 1111 20th St NW, Washington, DC 20526, T1-800-424-8580, www.peacecorps.gov, is the most prominent in the region, working with countries on development projects with 2-year assignments for US citizens in countries throughout Mexico and Central America.

Variations on the volunteering programme are to enrol on increasingly popular gap-year programmes. These normally incorporate a period of volunteer work with a few months of free time at the end of the programme for travel.

Experiment in International Living, T+44-1684-562577, www.eiluk.org, is the UK element of a US international homestay programme that arranges stays with families in Mexico and Central America with social projects based on the ethos that if you want to live together, you need to work together. It's an excellent way to meet people and learn the language.

Contents

Footprint features

At a glance

⊖ **Getting around** Buses between cities and minibus shuttles for shorter distances. River boats cross into Guatemala on the Río Usumacinta.

◉ **Time required** 2-3 weeks to take in all the highlights.

☼ **Weather** Wet season runs May-Oct; dry season Nov-Apr. Temperatures generally mid-20°Cs, but chilly in the Chiapas highlands.

✕ **When not to go** Avoid the jungle lowlands of Chiapas during the wet season, unless you enjoy rain. Resorts are packed in the summer.

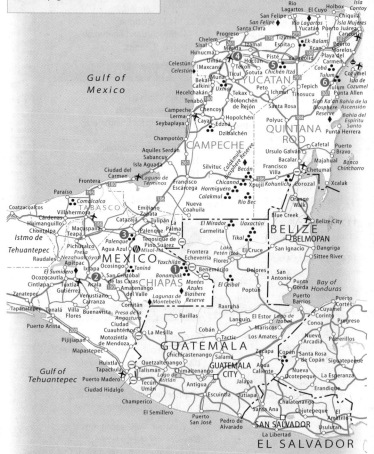

*Gulf of
Mexico*

*Gulf of
Tehuantepec*

Pacific Ocean

N

50 km

50 miles

Central America begins, geographically speaking, at the point where Mexico curls south and east, tapers into the slender isthmus of Tehuantepec, then opens out into the states of Tabasco, Chiapas and the vast limestone shelf of the Yucatán Peninsula. The shifting landscapes of these southernmost Mexican regions are wild and varied: fog-drenched mountain peaks, teeming lowland rainforests, jungle-shrouded wetlands, searing white-sand beaches, multi-coloured coral reefs and a vast network of underground caves and sinkholes – all invite intrepid exploration. Culturally, southern Mexico is as colourful and evocative as a bustling indigenous marketplace. Once the heartland of ancient Olmec and Mayan civilizations, scores of ruined cityscapes, pyramids and otherworldly monuments punctuate the region, all adorned with mysterious glyphs and artwork. Don't miss the jungle-shrouded temples of Palenque, the giant heads of La Venta, the magician's pyramid of Uxmal, or the immense, astronomically aligned architecture of Chichén Itzá, a site recently dubbed the Eighth Wonder of the World. The descendents of these ancient city-states today dwell in a network of intriguing Mayan villages. In some cases, life has changed little since pre-Columbian times – the rhythms of daily existence are still governed by a dazzling ritual cycle that invokes the old gods of rain and maize, planting and harvest, birth, marriage and death. But southern Mexico boasts plenty of urban culture too. For sheer colonial grandeur, try the highland city of San Cristóbal de las Casas, steeped in mist and endlessly photogenic mountain light, or, in the Yucatán Peninsula, the handsome pastel-coloured streets of Campeche, the urbane metropolis of Mérida and the laid-back town of Valladolid. Finally, for those seeking the convenience of well developed beach resorts, you can't do much better than the scintillating Caribbean shores of Quintana Roo, home to the famous party desinations of Cancún, Playa del Carmen and Tulum. Southern Mexico has something for everyone.

Essentials

Where to go

Tabasco's steamy coastal highway offers rapid overland access to the Yucatán Peninsula via the state capital, Villahermosa. Most travellers, however, prefer a more meandering route through the mountains, stopping off in the bohemian city of San Cristóbal de las Casas – an old colonial trade centre surrounded by lost-in-time Mayan villages. No trip to Chiapas would be complete without visiting the ancient ruins of Palenque, cloaked in mystery and exotic rainforest foliage, but hardcore Mayanists will want to head further afield to Yaxchilán and Bonampak, both perched on the Guatemalan border. Composed of three neighbouring states – Campeche, Yucatán and Quintana Roo – the Yucatán Peninsula boasts yet more ruins from Mayan history. The Puuc civilization reached its zenith at the regal city of Uxmal, whilst sprawling Chichén Itzá is famous for its shadow serpents which appear twice a year at the passing of the equinoxes. The Yucatán's beaches are as legendary as its archaeological sites and, if you like to party, you'll love Cancún, an American-style resort perched on Caribbean shores. If you're looking for something a little quieter, a short journey will take you to the beaches of Isla Mujeres or Tulum, where you can snorkel and dive, or simply relax in soothing waters. Equally, if you're seeking urban refinement, Mérida – the capital of Yucatán state and the so-called 'White City' – is steeped in history and grand colonial architecture.

Suggested itinerary

Begin your Central American journey in San Cristóbal de las Casas and take time to explore highland villages like San Juan Chamula. If you wish to skip the rest of Mexico, you can easily strike into Guatemala via the colonial city of Comitán, but it is recommended that you instead descend into the steamy Chiapas lowlands and spend a few days in Palenque. This is the starting point of the legendary Ruta Maya – an elliptical route that takes in the major Maya ruins of Mexico, Belize, Guatemala and Honduras – but you can adapt it to suit your needs. Heading in a clockwise arc around the Yucatán Peninsula, stop off in the colonial town of Campeche before making base at Mérida. Nearby, Chichén Itzá is an obligatory stop, also accessible from the nearby colonial town of Valladolid, but if you keep heading east you'll eventually land in Cancún. From here it's easy to jump between beaches and ruins en route south to the Belize border – Tulum and Coba are particularly recommended. After following the Ruta Maya through Belize, Honduras and Guatemala, you can loop back into Mexico at Frontera Echeverría, easily accessible from Tikal.

When to go

The best time to visit southern Mexico is from October to April when there is virtually no rain, although the mountains can be quite chilly, especially December to February. Rainy seasons lasts May to October, which is also hurricane season in the Caribbean. Don't be put off by the term 'rainy season' – most years, the rains only affect travellers for an hour or two a day. August is holiday time for Mexicans and this can make accommodation scarce in the smaller resorts. Semana Santa (Easter week), the Christmas holidays, Day of the Dead celebrations (at the beginning of November) and other important local fiestas are also busy times; book ahead.▸▸ *For festival dates, see page 62.*

Southern Mexico's coastline of reefs and lagoons, and its expanse of mountains cut by long rivers and protected areas make it extremely well suited to many types of outdoor adventure. The **Asociación Mexicana de Turismo de Aventura y Ecoturismo (AMTAVE)** ⓘ *Félix Cuevas 224-b, Col del Valle, CP 03100, México DF, T/F55-5575 7887, www.amtave.org,* is making steady progress in promoting and protecting ecotourism nationwide alongside adventure-related pursuits. The need for standards is important in some activities and **AMTAVE** is doing plenty to develop awareness in this field.

Caving

Caving, or speleology, in Mexico is more than just going down into deep dark holes. Sometimes it is a sport more closely related to canyoning as there are some excellent underground river scrambles. The biggest cave systems in the country are in Chiapas, especially around Tuxtla Gutiérrez, but you also have the option of diving in water-filled caves known as *cenotes*, a common and popular sport in the Yucatán, particularly around **Tulum**.

Diving

Quintana Roo offers warm-water reefs close to the shore and visibility of over 30 m. **Cozumel** has some of the best diving in the world. There are marine parks at Chankanaab and at Palancar Reef with numerous caves and gullies and a horseshoe-shaped diving arena. Also excellent on the west side of the island are Santa Rosa and sites off San Francisco beach. To the southwest are good sites off Laguna Colombia, while off Punta Sur there is excellent deep diving. There is concern, however, over the damage to the reef inflicted by the cruise ship pier, and more of these piers are planned. At **Isla Mujeres**, also in Quintana Roo, the most-dived sites include Los Manchones, La Bandera, a shallow dive south of the island, and El Frío, a deep wreck 1½ hrs to the north.

Rafting

The variety of Mexico's rivers opens the activity up to all levels of experience. The attraction is not just the run but the trek or rappel to the start and the moments between rapids, drifting in deep canyons beneath hanging tropical forests, some of which contain lesser-known and inaccessible ruins. Rafting in **Chiapas** covers the spectrum from sedate floats on rivers such as the Lacan-Há through the Lacandón jungle to Grade IV/V rapids on the Río Jataté, which gathers force where the Lacan Tum enters it and gradually diminishes in strength as it nears the Río Usumacinta. Jan and Feb are the preferred months because the climate is cooler.

Trekking

In Chiapas, there are good opportunities for trekking in the Triunfo Biosphere Reserve and the Lacandón jungle, but you should always seek advice before embarking on any expedition in the region – rebel Zapatistas and drug traffickers hide out in some areas of the countryside and there is a large military presence to deal with them. It's also possible to trek between ruins and *cenotes* (sink holes) in the tropical forests of the Yucatán Peninsula, but during the dry season they offer little shade and can be extremely hot. For more on trekking, see National parks, below.

National parks

Mexico has an immense range of habitats and wildlife – the far south is in the Neotropical kingdom, home to a wealth of tropical forest species. National parks in Mexico were set up a long time ago primarily to provide green recreation areas for city dwellers; they are generally small and have often been planted with imported species such as eucalyptus, and are thus of no biological value. However, the country does also have a good number of biosphere reserves, which are both of great biological value and suitable for tourism.

In Chiapas, **El Triunfo Biosphere Reserve** protects Mexico's only cloud forest, on the mountains (up to 2750 m) above the Pacific Coast; the main hiking route runs from Jaltenango (reached by bus from Tuxtla) to Mapastepec on the coastal highway. Groups need to book in advance through the **Instituto de Historia Natural** ① *Calzada de Hombres de la Revolución, by the botanical garden and Regional Museum (Apdo 391, Tuxtla 29000; T961-612-3663).*

Also in Chiapas is the immense **Selva Lacandona**, supposedly protected by the Azules Biosphere Reserve but in reality still being eaten away by colonization and logging. New plant species are still being discovered in this rainforest, best visited either from the Bonampak and Yaxchilán ruins, or by the road/boat route via Pico de Oro and Flor de Café to Montebello.

In the Yucatán the **Sian Ka'an Biosphere Reserve**, south of Cancún, is a mixture of forest, savannah and mangrove swamp, best visited on a day-trip run by **Amigos de Sian Ka'an** ① *Calle Fuego 2 SM, Cancún, T998-892 2958, www.amigosdesiankaan.org.* Also useful is the **Sian Ka'an Information Centre** ① *Av Tulum between Satelite and Geminis, Tulum, T/F984-871 2363, siankaan_tours@hotmail.com.* It is also well worth visiting the **Río Lagartos** and **Río Celestún** reserves on the north and west coasts of Yucatán, well known for their flamingos. The **Calakmul Biosphere Reserve** is important mainly for its Mayan ruins, seeming to the layman more like scrub than forest.

Information on national parks and biosphere reserves can be obtained from the **Instituto Nacional de Ecología** ① *Periférico 5000, Col Insurgentes Cuicuilco, CP 04530, Delegación Coyoacán, México DF, T55-5424 6400, www.ine.gob.mx,* a decentralized body of the Secretaría de Medio Ambiente y Recursos Naturales.

Non-governmental conservation organizations include **Naturalia** ① *Horquillas 43, Col Santa Fe, Hermosillo, 83249, Sonora, T55-5559 5696, www.naturalia.org.mx,* and **Pronatura, Asociación Mexicano por la Conservación de la Naturaleza** ① *Aspérgulas 22, Col San Clemente, CP 01740, México DF, T/F55-5635 5054, www.pronatura.org.mx.*

Getting there

Air

Airport information There are several international airports in Mexico, the two busiest are **Mexico City** and **Cancún**. If you are likely to be returning home at a busy time (eg between Christmas and New Year, or August) a booking is advisable on open-return tickets. When arriving in Mexico by air, make sure you fill in the immigration document before joining the queue to have your passport checked.

Departure tax Currently US$40 on international flights (dollars or pesos accepted); always check when purchasing if departure tax is included in ticket price. A sales tax of 15% is payable on domestic plane tickets bought in Mexico.

Student/youth and discount fares Some airlines are flexible on the age limit, others strict. One way and returns available, or 'Open Jaws' (flying into one point and returning from another). Do not assume student tickets are the cheapest, though they are often very flexible.

From Europe **To Mexico City**: there are several airlines that have regular direct flights. From Amsterdam with **KLM**; from Frankfurt with **Lufthansa** and **AeroMéxico** (**LTU** and **Condor** charter flights to Mexico City or Cancún); from London and Manchester with **British Airways**; from Barcelona with **Iberia**; from Madrid with **Iberia** and **AeroMéxico**; from Paris with **Air France** and **AeroMéxico**. Most connecting flights in Europe are through Madrid or Gatwick. Fares vary from airline to airline and according to time of year. Check with an agency for the best deal for when you wish to travel. **To Cancún**: From Amsterdam with **Martinair**, Dusseldorf with **LTU**, Frankfurt with **LTU** and **Condor**, Munich with **LTU** and **Condor**; Madrid with **AeroMéxico** and **Avianca**, Milan with **Lauda Air** and Paris with **American Airlines**.

From USA **To Mexico City**: A large number of airlines fly this route, including **American Airlines**, **AeroMéxico**, **Delta**, **Continental**, **United**, **Northwest**, **Taesa** and **Americawest**. Flights are available from most major cities, with the cheapest generally going through Miami, Dallas, Houston and sometimes Los Angeles. **To Cancún**: Flights leave from many cities across the USA.

From Canada **To Mexico City**: The options are less varied, but there are direct flights from Montreal and Toronto, as well as regular flights from other main cities. From Toronto with **United;** and from Vancouver with **Japan Airlines**. Keep an eye out for special offers, which can be extremely good value (often at very short notice).

From Australia and New Zealand From Sydney with **United** and from Auckland with **Air New Zealand**, all flying through Los Angeles.

From Latin America and the Caribbean Flights from Latin America have increased in recent years. Central America is covered by the **TACA** network, connecting the capitals of each country to Mexico City and some of the smaller regional cities. In South America, connections are to capitals and major cities. If planning a trip to Cuba there are flights from Cancún, Mérida and Mexico City with **Cubana**.

Road
From USA There are many border crossings with the US; the main ones are Tijuana, Mexicali, Nogales, Ciudad Juárez, Piedras Negras, Nuevo Laredo and Matamoros.

From Guatemala The main border town is Tapachula, with a crossing over the Talismán Bridge or at Ciudad Hidalgo. A more interesting route is via Ciudad Cuauhtémoc or heading northwest from Santa Elena/Flores towards Tenosique. There are also options for road and river travel.

From Belize The border crossing at Santa Elena is near Chetumal, where public transport can be arranged. A very quiet, and more challenging, crossing is at Blue Creek.

Air

Most medium-sized towns in Mexico have an airport. If you're looking to cover a great distance in a short time, several airlines fly internal routes (a few with international flights as well) including **Aeromar**, **Aeroméxico Connect**, **Taesa**, and **Aviacsa**. Low-cost airlines include: **Interjet** (www.interjet.com.mx), **Volaris** (www.volaris.com.mx) and **VivaAerobus** (www.vivaaerobus.com). General costs are comparable with the older airlines – you get the bargain if you can book ahead, travel at inconvenient times or if there is a special offer.

Bus → *Buses are often called camiones, hence 'Central Camionero' for bus station.*

The Mexican bus system is very extensive and efficient. In some cities there is a central bus terminal (in Mexico City there are four – one at each point of the compass), in others there are a couple – one for first-class services, one for second. A third variation is division by companies. The entire network is privatized and highly competitive, although in practise there is often little difference between carriers. Most inter-city routes are served by comfortable and very adequate first-class buses with reclining seats, air-conditioning, Spanish-language movies and on-board toilet. For those seeking extra luxury, several companies offer superior class services, so-called Primera Plus or Ejecutiva, which include a soft-drink, snack and almost horizontally aligned seats. It is highly advisable to book your tickets several days in advance when travelling at Christmas, Semana Santa or other national holidays. If your journey is longer than six hours, it is sensible to book 24 hours ahead. If travelling overnight, pack a sweater or blanket in your hand-luggage – the air-conditioning gets icy. Also avoid sitting near the toilet (it invariably smells) and bring snacks and water.

Fares Bus travel can use up a lot of your budget because the distances covered are great. As a very rough calculation, bus travel works out at around US$5 per hour spent travelling.

First-class fares are usually 10% dearer than second-class ones and the superior classes 30-40% more than first-class. On a long journey you can save the price of a hotel room by travelling overnight, but in some areas this is dangerous and not recommended.

Useful bus links
Some bus tickets can be purchased at **www.ticketbus.com.mx**, information on T01-800-702-8000.
ADO GL, www.adogl.com.mx, T01-800-702-8000. The Yucatán, southeast, Gulf and northeast Mexico.
Cristóbal Colón, T01-800-702-8000. South of Mexico City. Details on the Ticketbus system.

ETN, www.etn.com.mx, T01-800-8000-386.
Grupo Estrella, www.estrellablanca.com.mx, T01-800-507-5500. Most of Mexico through several companies.
Primera Plus, www.primeraplus.com.mx, T01- 800-375-7587. Mid-central to southern Mexico.

Bicycle

Southern Mexico offers plenty of enjoyable places for cycling. The main problems facing cyclists are heavy traffic, poor road conditions and a lack of specialized spare parts, particularly for mountain bikes, which can only be found in big cities. The easiest region for cycling is the Gulf of Mexico coast, but many of the roads are flat and boring. The mountains may appear intimidating, but gradients are as not difficult as they seem, and consequently offer some of the best cycling. The toll roads are generally preferable to the ordinary highways for cyclists; there is less traffic, more lanes and a wide paved shoulder, but take lots of water as there are few facilities. **Tip**: if you walk your bicycle on the pavement through the toll station you don't have to pay. Cycling on some main roads can be very dangerous; fit a rear-view mirror.

Car

Permits Vehicles may be brought into Mexico on a **Tourist Permit** for 180 days each year. You can enter and leave as often as you like during that time, but you must have a new tourist card or visa on each occasion you enter. The necessary documents are: passport, birth certificate or naturalization papers; tourist card; vehicle registration (if you do not own the car, a notarized letter from the vehicle's owner or the hire company is necessary); and a valid international or national driving licence. Two photocopies are required for each. US$16.50 is charged for the permit, payable only by credit card, not a debit card, in the name of the car owner. If you do not have a credit card, you have to buy a bond in cash to the value of the vehicle according to its age (a set scale exists). The payment is divided into two parts, the bond itself and administration costs; the latter is retained by the authorities and only the bond is refunded. On entry, go to *Migración* for your tourist card, then go to the **Banjército** desk and sign an *Importación Temporal de Vehículos/Promesa de retornar vehículo*, which bears all vehicle and credit card details so that if you sell your car illegally you can be debited for the import duty. Next you purchase the *Solicitud de importación temporal*, which costs US$12 and must be displayed on the windscreen. Then go to *Copias* to photocopy all necessary documents. There are heavy fines for overstaying or failing to surrender your entry documents at the end of your visit. It takes 10 days to extend a permit, so ask for more time than you need. The Sanborn's website (www.sanbornsinsurance.com) is an excellent source of information.

Insurance Foreign insurance will not be honoured; be sure that the company you insure with will settle accident claims inside Mexico. Entering Mexico from Guatemala presents few local insurance problems now. **Tepeyac** ⓘ *www.mapfretepeyac.com, or through English-speaking agents www.mexadventure.com, T800-485 4075*, has an office in Tapachula; and **Seguros La Provincial** ⓘ *Av General Utrillo 10A, upstairs, San Cristóbal de las Casas, also has an office in Cuauhtémoc: Av Cuauhtémoc 1217 ground floor, Sr García Figueroa, T5-604-0500*. Otherwise, try **Segumex** in Tuxtla Gutiérrez. In Mexico City, try **Grupo Nacional Provincial** ⓘ *Río de la Plata 48, T528-67732, www.gnp.com.mx*, which has offices in many towns; or **Sanborn's Mexican Insurance Service** ⓘ *2009 S 10th St, McAllen, TX 78505-0310, T956-686-0711, www.sanbornsinsurance.com*. Policy prices vary greatly between companies.

Petrol/diesel All *gasolina* is now unleaded and all petrol stations are franchised by Petróleos Mexicanos (PEMEX). Fuel costs the same throughout the country (approximately US$0.65 a litre). Diesel is also available. Petrol stations are not self-service; it is normal to give the attendant a small tip.

Assistance **Angeles Verdes** (Green Angels) patrol many of Mexico's main roads. Call them toll-free on T01-800-903-9200; every state also has an Angeles Verdes hotline. The drivers speak English, are trained to give first aid, make minor auto repairs and deal with flat tyres. Assistance is provided free of charge, you pay for the gas.

Border essentials

Mexico–Belize
Chetumal–Santa Elena

A popular crossing and often busy. Procedures can be slow, particularly at peak holiday times. No fresh fruit may be imported to Belize.

Currency exchange Plenty of money-changers. If entering Belize, it's not strictly necessary to change dollars – these are accepted everywhere at a fixed rate of 1:2. It's easier to change pesos here than inside Belize.

Mexican immigration Open 24 hours. Formalities are relaxed.

Belizean immigration Open 24 hours.

Onwards to Belize Corozal is 12 km south. On-going connections to Belize City, three or four hours.

Onwards to Mexico Chetumal, 11 km from the border, offers connections to the Yucatán Peninsula and the beaches of Quintana Roo.

La Unión A crossing for non-vehicular travellers, see pages 347 and 379.

Mexico–Guatemala
Ciudad Cuauhtémoc–La Mesilla

The fastest route between the mountain towns of Chiapas and western Guatemala.

Currency exchange Rates are not usually favourable at the border. Banrural in La Mesilla with ATM, or haggle in the street.

Mexican immigration Open 0600-2100. No town, just a few buildings, about 4 km from border.

Guatemalan immigration Open 0600-2100. Reports of 'unofficial' fees. Demand a receipt.

Onwards to Guatemala Services to Huehuetenango, two hours, with onward connections to the western highlands or Lago Atitlán. Transportes Velásquez offers express services to Guatemala City, seven hours.

Onwards to Mexico Access to Comitán and, beyond, to San Cristóbal de las Casas.

Talismán–El Carmen

Located at the international bridge over the Río Suchiate. Rarely sees much heavy traffic.

Currency exchange Better to change money in Tapachula, Mexico, than with the men at the border. Check rates before transacting.

Mexican immigration Open 24 hours. 200 m from Guatemalan immigration. The town of Talismán is 8 km from Tapachula.

Guatemalan immigration Open 24 hours. Drivers should expect lots of red tape.

Onwards to Mexico Highway access to coastal Chiapas and the Pan-American Highway.

Ciudad Hidalgo – Tecún Umán

Pacific coast crossing; 1-km-long bridge over the Río Suchiate; small cost for usage, boys can help carry luggage for a tip. Accommodation if you get stuck.

Currency exchange Numerous money-changers but nowhere to change TCs.

Mexican immigration Open 24 hours. A few blocks from the plaza at foot of bridge.

Guatemalan immigration Open 24 hours.
Onwards to Guatemala Connections to Coatepeque, Mazatenango and Retalhuleu. Four express buses daily to Guatemala City, five hours.
Onwards to Mexico Tapachula lies 8 km north, 30 minutes, with connections to coastal Chiapas and the Pan-American Highway.

La Palma – El Naranjo

Interesting and less travelled route along the Río San Pedro. Start early or you may not make transport connections (see page 88 for more details on Tenosique and the Río San Pedro route).
Currency exchange In Guatemala, you can change money at the grocery store opposite immigration. In Mexico, try the restaurants.
Guatemalan immigration A short way up the hill on the right. Beware unofficial charges.
Onwards to Guatemala Bus tickets to Flores/Santa Elena are available near immigration.
Onwards to Mexico Irregular services from La Palma to Tenosique. More reliably, catch a pickup to El Ceibo, where hourly buses depart for Tenosique behind the market.

Frontera Echeverría (Corozal) – Bethel/La Técnica

A relatively easy crossing on the Río Usumacinta (see page 87 for more). Note there have been reported robberies on the road to La Técnica; check locally on the security situation.
Currency exchange Try to bring the currency you need. Local shops or restaurants may exchange.
Mexican immigration Open 24 hours. You advised to get your tourist card/visa in advance if you need one.
Guatemalan immigration Open 24 hours.
Onwards to Guatemala Three daily buses to Flores/Santa Elena; arrive early and check schedules locally.
Onwards to Mexico At Corozal, a paved road leads 18 km to the frontier highway and 35 km to the San Javier junction. It's about four hours by bus to Palenque; set out early to make it.

Benemérito–Pipiles

The classic Río Usumacinta route is somewhat time-consuming; there are alternatives (see page 87 for more).
Currency exchange Bring currency before setting out. Shops and restaurants may exchange.
Mexican immigration Office is 3 km from Benemérito; bus will wait.
Guatemalan immigration Processing at the military post. You are advised to get a tourist card in advance to avoid paying bribes.
Onwards to Guatemala From Pipiles, the boat continues to Sayaxché. Connections to Flores from there.
Onwards to Mexico Seven to 12 hours to Palenque, reports of road improvements which would substantially diminish this. Set out early.

Road tolls A toll is called a *cuota*, as opposed to a non-toll road, which is a *vía libre*. There are many toll charges and the cost works out at around one peso per kilometre. Check out your route, and toll prices, on the **Traza Tu Ruta** section of www.sct.gob.mx.

In case of accident Do not abandon your vehicle. Call your insurance company immediately to inform it. Do not leave Mexico without first filing a claim. Do not sign any contract or agreement without a representative of the insurance company being present. Always carry with you, in the insured vehicle, your policy identification card and the names of the company's adjusters. A helpline for road accidents is available by phoning T02 and asking the operator to connect you to T55-5684 9715 or T55-5684 9761.

Warnings On all roads, if the driver flashes his lights he is claiming right of way and the oncoming traffic must give way. At *Alto* (Halt) signs, all traffic must come to a complete stop. Always avoid driving at night – night-time robberies are on the increase. 'Sleeping policemen' or road bumps can be hazardous as there are often no warning signs; they are sometimes marked *zona de topes*, or incorrectly marked as *vibradores*.

Car hire Car rental is very expensive in Mexico, from US$35-45 a day for a basic model (plus15% sales tax). Age limit is normally at least 25 and you'll need to place a deposit, normally against a credit card, for damage. It can be cheaper to arrange hire in the US or Europe. At some tourist resorts, however, such as Cancún, you can pick up a VW Beetle convertible for US$25 per day. Renting a vehicle is nearly impossible without a credit card. It is twice as expensive to leave a car at a different point from the starting point than it is to make a round trip. Rates will vary from city to city. Make sure you have unlimited mileage.

Hitchhiking

Hitchhiking in Mexico is not recommended as it is not universally safe (seek local advice). Do not, for example, try to hitch in parts of Chiapas state where even driving alone is not recommended. It is very easy to hitch short distances, such as the last few kilometres to an archaeological site off the main road; offer to pay something, like US$0.50.

Motorcycle

Motorcycling is good in southern Mexico as most main roads are in fairly good condition and hotels are usually willing to allow the bike to be parked in a courtyard or patio. In the major tourist centres, such as Playa del Carmen or Cancún, motorbike parts can be found as there are Honda dealers for bike and jet-ski rentals.

Taxi

To avoid overcharging, the government has taken control of taxi services from airports to cities. Only those with government licences are allowed to carry passengers from the airport and you can usually buy a ticket with a set price to your destination from a booth at the terminal. Tipping is not required unless the driver helps with heavy luggage or provides some extra service.

Maps

Guía Roji publish a wide range of regional maps, city plans and gazettes, available at most bookshops and news-stands. Guia Roji is online at http://guiaroji.com.mx with full street, town, city and state search facilities for the country.

Sleeping

Hotels and hospedajes

The cheapest places to stay are *casas de huéspedes*, but these are often very basic and dirty. Budget hotels are a gamble that sometimes pays off; always check amenities and room before accepting. The middle categories are still reasonable value by US and European standards, but high-end hotels have become increasingly expensive as tourism has flourished. Motels and auto-hotels are usually hourly rental, but can make clean and acceptable overnight lodgings for weary drivers.

There is a hotel tax, ranging between 1% and 4%, according to the state. Check-out time is commonly 1100 but bag storage is commonplace. Rooms are normally charged at a flat rate, or if there are single rooms they are around 80% the price of a double, so sharing works out cheaper. A room with a double bed is usually cheaper than one with two singles. A room with three or more sharing is often very economical, even in the mid-price range. Beware of 'helpers' who try to find you a hotel, as prices quoted at the hotel desk rise to give them commission. During peak season (November to April) it may be hard to find a room. The week after Easter is normally a holiday, so prices remain high. Discounts on hotel prices can often be arranged in the low season (May to October), but this is more difficult in the Yucatán.

Youth hostels

Hostels are very much on the increase and many of them are excellent. They are not always great value for couples, however – a shared hotel room is often more comfortable and economical. Both private and International Youth Hostel endorsed accommodation are widely available; the latter offers discounts for members. For more information contact **Hostelling International Mexico** ⓘ *Guatemala 4, Col Centro, Mexico City, T55-5518 1726, www.hostellingmexico.com.* Additionally, many towns have a **Villa Deportiva Juvenil**, the Mexican equivalent of a youth hostel, sometimes basic and normally very cheap.

Camping

Most sites are called 'trailer parks', but tents are usually allowed. However, due to their primary role as trailer parks they're often in locations more suited for people with their own transport than people on public transport. **Playas Públicas**, with a blue and white sign of a palm tree, are beaches where camping is allowed. They are usually cheap, sometimes free and some have shelters and basic amenities. You can often camp in or near national parks, although you must speak first with the guards, and usually pay a small fee.

Eating and drinking

Food

Food for most Mexicans represents an integral part of their national identity and much has been written since the 1960s about the evolution of Mexican cooking. Experts suggest that there have been three important developmental stages: first, the combination of the indigenous and the Spanish traditions; later, the influence of other European cuisines, notably the French in the 19th century; and finally the adoption of exotic oriental dishes and fast food from the USA in the 20th century. In 2010, the importance of Mexican food was recognized by its inclusion on the UNESCO Intangible Cultural Heritage List.

Mexican cooking is usually perceived as spicy or hot due to the prolific use of chilli peppers, but equally, maize is a very typical ingredient and has been a staple crop since ancient times. It is mainly consumed in *antojitos* (snacks) and some of the most common are tacos, *quesadillas*, *flautas*, *sopes*, *tostadas*, *tlacoyos* and *gorditas*, which consist of various shapes and sizes of *tortillas*, with a variety of fillings and usually garnished with a hot sauce.

Meals in Mexico consist of breakfast, a heavy lunch between 1400 and 1500 and a light supper between 1800 and 2000. Costs in modest establishments are US$2-3 for breakfast, US$2.50-3.50 for set lunch (US$4-6 for a special *comida corrida*) and US$5-10 for dinner (generally no set menu). A la carte meals at modest establishments cost about US$8-12. A very good meal can be had for US$15 at a middle-level establishment. Street stalls are by far the cheapest – although not always the safest – option. The best value is undoubtedly in small, family-run places. If self-catering, markets are cheaper than supermarkets.

Drink

There are always plenty of non-alcoholic *refrescos* (soft drinks) and mineral water. *Agua fresca* – fresh fruit juices mixed with water or mineral water – and *licuados* (milk shakes) are good and usually safe. Herbal teas, for example chamomile (*manzanilla*) and mint (*hierba buena*), are readily available.

The native alcoholic drinks are **pulque**, made from the fermented juice of the agave plant, **tequila** and **mezcal**, both made from distilled agave. Mezcal usually has a *gusano de maguey* (worm) in the bottle, considered to be a particular delicacy but, contrary to popular myth, is not hallucinogenic. *Puro de caña* (called *chingre* in Chinanteca and *posh* in Chamula) is distilled from sugar cane; it is stronger than *mezcal* but with less taste; it is found in Chiapas. National **beer** is also good with a wide range of light and dark varieties.

Festivals and events

If any of these holidays falls on a Thursday or a Tuesday, they are usually an excuse for a *puente*, a long weekend (which can have implications for travel, hotel accommodation and services).

National holidays
I Jan New Year
5 Feb Constitution Day
21 Mar Birthday of Benito Juárez
Mar/Apr Maundy Thu, Good Fri, Easter Sat
1 May Labour Day
5 May Battle of Puebla
1 Sep El Informe (Presidential Message)
16 Sep Independence Day
12 Oct Día de la Raza (Discovery of America)

20 Nov Día de la Revolución (Revolution Day)
25 Dec Christmas Day

Religious fiestas
There are more than 5000 religious festivals each year. The most widely celebrated are:
6 Jan Santos Reyes (Three Kings)
10 May Día de las Madres (Mothers' Day)
1-2 Nov Día de los Muertos (All Souls' Day)
12 Dec La Virgen de Guadalupe

Shopping

The colourful markets and craft shops are a highlight of any visit to southern Mexico. The *artesanía* is an amalgam of ancient and modern designS influenced mainly by the traditional popular art forms of local indigenous communities. Colonial towns such as Mérida and San Cristóbal de las Casas are convenient market centres for seeing the superb range of products from functional pots to scary masks hanging over delicately embroidered robes and gleaming lacquered chests.

Weaving and textile design go back a long way and the variety on offer is huge. They can be spun in cotton or wool on the traditional *telar de cintura*, a 'waist loom', or *telar de pie*, a pedal-operated loom introduced by the Spanish. Many woven items are on sale in the markets, from *sarapes* and *morrales* (shoulder bags) to wall-hangings, rugs and bedspreads. Synthetic fibres are often used, so make sure you know what you're getting. The Mayan villages around San Cristóbal are particularly well-known centres of weaving.

Essentials A-Z

Customs and duty free

The list of permitted items is extensive and generally allows for anything that could reasonably be considered for personal use. Adults entering Mexico are allowed to bring in up to 6 litres of wine, beer or spirits; 20 packs of cigarettes, or 25 cigars, or 200 g of tobacco and medicines for personal use. Goods imported into Mexico with a value of more than US$1000 (with the exception of computer equipment, where the limit is US$4000) have to be handled by an officially appointed agent. If you are carrying more than US$10,000 in cash you should declare it. There is no penalty but registration is required. Full details and latest updates are available at www.aduanas.sat.gob.mx.

Dress

Casual clothing is adequate for most occasions although men may need a jacket and tie in some restaurants. Dress conservatively in indigenous communities and small churches. Topless bathing is generally unacceptable.

Electricity

127 volts/60 Hz, US-style 2-pin plug.

Embassies and consulates

For details of Mexican embassies in the rest of the world, go to www.sre.gob.mx.
Australia, 14 Perth Av, Yarralumia, 2600 ACT, Canberra, T6273-3963, www.mexico.org.au.
Belize, 3 North Ring Rd, Belmopan, T822-0406.
Canada, 45 O'Connor St, Suite 1000, Ottawa, Ont, K1P 1A4, T613-233-8988, www.sre.gob.mx/canada.

Denmark, Bredgade 65, 1st floor 1260, Copenhagen, T3961-0500, www.sre.gob.mx/dinamarca.
France, 9 rue de Longchamp, 75116 Paris, T5370-2770, www.sre.gob.mx/francia.
Germany, Klingelhöferstrasse 3, 10785 Berlin, T30-269-3230, www.sre.gob.mx/alemania.
Holland, Nassauplein 28, 2585 EC, The Hague, T360-2900, www.embamex-nl.com.
Israel, 25 Hamared St, Trade Tower 5th floor, Tel Aviv 68125, T516-3938, www.sre.gob.mx/israel.
New Zealand, 185-187 Featherston St, level 2 (AMP Chambers), Wellington, T472-5555, www.sre.gob.mx/nuevazelandia.
Switzerland, Welpoststrasse 20, 5th floor, CH-3015, Berne, T357-4747, www.sre.gob.mx/suiza.
UK, 16 St George St, London, W1S 1FD, T020-7499-8586, www.sre.gob.mx/reinounido.
USA, 1911 Pennsylvania Av, NW, 20006 Washington DC, T202-728-1600, www.sre.gob.mx/eua.

Health

Social security hospitals are restricted to members, but will take visitors in emergencies; they are more up to date than the *Centros de Salud* and *Hospitales Civiles* found in most town centres, which are very cheap and open to everyone. A consultation in a private doctor's surgery may cost US$20-40.

Identification

ID is increasingly required when visiting offices or tourist sites within government buildings. It's handy to have some form of identification (*identificación* or *credencial*), a photocopied passport will usually do.

Internet

A list of useful websites is given on page 65. Every major town and these days most small villages now has at least one internet café, with more springing up daily. The better ones often cater for a wide range of internet services, including Skype. Prices vary from place to place but are normally around US$1.

Language

The official language of Mexico is Spanish. Outside of the main tourist centres, travelling without some knowledge of Spanish is a major hindrance. Adding to the challenges of communication, there are also numerous Mayan languages spoken in southern Mexico.

Media

The influential daily newspapers are: *Excelsior, Novedades, El Día, Uno Más Uno, El Universal, El Heraldo, La Jornada* (www.jornada.unam.mx, more to the left, with *Tiempo Libre*, listing cultural activities in Mexico City), *La Prensa* (a popular tabloid, with the largest circulation) and *El Nacional* (mouthpiece of the government). There are influential weekly magazines *Proceso, Siempre, Epoca* and *Quehacer Político*. The political satirical weekly is *Los Agachados*. *The Miami Herald* is stocked by most news-stands.

Money → *US$1=$11.79 pesos (June 2011).* The monetary unit is the Mexican peso, represented by '$' – the dollar sign – providing great potential for confusion, especially in popular tourist places where prices are higher and often quoted in US dollars (US$).

Exchange

US dollars cash can be easily changed at banks in all cities and towns and less economically at *casas de cambio*. Try to carry a mixture of large and small denominations; it can be hard to change notes of US$20 or higher in small villages. While it is possible to change the euro, sterling and other currencies, not all banks or *casas de cambio* will take them.

Traveller's cheques (TCs) from any well-known bank can be cashed in most towns if drawn in US dollars; TCs from other currencies are harder to cash. If you are stuck, branches of HSBC have been known to change other currencies. *Casas de cambio* are generally quicker than banks for exchange transactions and stay open later; fees are not charged but their rates may not be as good. You may be asked to show some ID. Amex and Visa US dollar TCs are the easiest to change.

Transfer

If you need to make a transfer ask your bank if they can transfer direct to a Mexican bank without using an intermediary, which usually results in greater delays. Beware of short-changing at all times. **Western Union**, www.westernunion.com, have outlets throughout Mexico but the service is more expensive than a traditional bank wire.

Credit cards

ATMs are now found even in small towns, allowing you to travel without carrying large amounts of cash or TCs. **MasterCard**, **Visa** and **American Express** are widely accepted in Mexico either when paying for goods, withdrawing cash from ATMs (*cajero automático*) or obtaining cash over the counter from banks. There is often a 6% tax on the use of credit cards. For lost or stolen cards call: **MasterCard** T001-800-307-7309; **Visa** T001-800-847-2911.

Cost of living and travelling

Couples and groups will make good savings. A basic room is likely to set you back about US$15 on average, with occasionally cheaper prices available. Comfortable rooms start at around US$20. Meals start from US$8 a day for those on tight budgets and activities cost US$20 per day and upwards. Travel is expensive compared to the rest of Central America and you should definitely calculate costs into your budget (see Getting around, page 56). An impoverished couple might just survive on US$15 per person per day, but US$25 is a more realistic. Prices are considerably higher in resorts – seek out those places preferred by the locals.

Student cards
Although an international student (ISIC) card offers student discounts, only national Mexican student cards permit free entry to museums, archaeological sites, etc.

Opening hours
Banks Mon-Fri 0900-1330 (some stay open later), Sat 0900-1230.
Business 0900/1000-1300/1400, then 1400/1500-1900 or later. Business hours vary considerably according to the climate and local custom.

Photography
There is a charge of US$3-5 for the use of video cameras at historical sites. For professional camera equipment, including a tripod, the fee is much higher. Never take photos of indigenous people without prior permission.

Post
International service has improved and bright red mailboxes, found in many parts of the city, are reliable for letters. Poste Restante (*lista de correos* in Mexico) functions quite reliably, but you may have to ask under each of your names; mail is sent back after 10 days.

Safety
Mexico is generally a safe country to visit, although the usual precautions over personal safety should be taken. Cars are a prime target for theft; never leave possessions visible inside the car and park in hotel car parks after dark. Avoid travelling at night; if at all possible make journeys in daylight. Avoid lonely beaches, especially if you are a single woman. Other than the tourist police who are helpful, speak some English and who you'll only come across in more touristy areas, it is best to avoid the police if at all possible; they are rarely helpful and tend to make complicated situations even worse. Speaking Spanish is a great asset for avoiding rip-offs targeting gringos, especially short changing and overcharging (both rife).

Telephone → *Country code T+52.*
IDD T00; **operator** T020; **international operator** T090; **directory enquiries** T040. Most destinations have a 7-digit number and 3-digit regional code (Mexico City is an exception). The format of a number, depending on the type of call, should be as follows: **local** 7- or 8-digit phone number; **regional** long-distance access code (01) + regional code (2- or 3-digit code) + 7- or 8-digit number; **international** international direct-dialling code + country code + regional code + 7- or 8-digit number. Most public phones take phone cards only (**Ladatel**) costing 30 or 50 pesos from shops and news kiosks everywhere. Reverse-charge (collect) calls can be made from any blue public phone; say you want to *llamar por cobrar*. Pre-paid phone cards are expensive for international calls. Of other pre-paid cards, the best value are **Ekofon**, www.ekofon.com.

Time
Southern Mexico is in Central Standard Time (CST), 6 hrs behind GMT. Daylight Saving Time runs from the first Sun in Apr to the last Sun in Oct (when it is 5 hrs behind GMT).

Tipping
Normally 10-15%; the equivalent of US$0.25 per bag for porters, the equivalent of US$0.20 for bell boys, and nothing for a taxi driver unless some kind of exceptional service.

Tourist information
Tourist offices are listed throughout the text. In Europe, information is available in several different languages by calling T00-800-1111-2266. In North America call T1-800-446-3942.

Useful websites
Mexico's web presence is phenomenal, some of the reliable, informative and

useful websites that have been round for a while include:

www.mexconnect.com General information.

www.mexperience.com Well-constructed site updated daily, with current affairs, feature articles and advice on travel in Mexico. Look out for the forum where comments from fellow travellers are exchanged.

www.sectur.gob.mx Tourism Secretariat's site, with less glossy links but equally comprehensive information.

www.visitmexico.com Mexico Tourist Board site, a comprehensive multilingual site with information on the entire country.

Visas and immigration

Virtually all international travellers require a passport to enter Mexico. Upon entry you will be issued a Mexican Tourist Card (FM-T), valid for up to 180 days. This must surrendered when leaving the country. If your stamp bears less than 180 days, you can extend it up to the limit at any **National Institute of Migration** office; you can find details at www.inm.gob.mx. To renew a tourist card by leaving the country, you must stay outside Mexico for at least 72 hrs. Take TCs or a credit card as proof of finance. At the border crossings with Belize and Guatemala, you may be refused entry into Mexico if you have less than US$200 (or US$350 for each month of intended stay, up to a maximum of 180 days). Likewise, if you are carrying more than US$10,000 in cash or TCs, you must declare it.

If a person **under 18** is travelling alone or with one parent, both parents' consent is required, certified by a notary or authorized by a consulate. A divorced parent must be able to show custody of a child. (These requirements are not always checked by immigration authorities and do not apply to all nationalities). Further details are available from any Mexican consulate (see page 63).

Weights and measures

The metric system is used.

www.mexperience.com Well-constructed site updated daily, with current affairs, feature articles and advice on travel in Mexico. Look out for the forum where comments from fellow travellers are exchanged.

www.sectur.gob.mx Tourism Secretariat's site, with less glossy links but equally comprehensive information.

www.visitmexico.com Mexico Tourist Board site, a comprehensive multilingual site with information on the entire country.

Weights and measures

The metric system is used.

Tabasco and Chiapas

The states of Tabasco and Chiapas merge to form a geographical block that separates Mexico from Guatemala and the Yucatán Peninsula. Until recently, low-lying, jungly Tabasco was considered an oil state with little appeal for tourists, but oil wealth has brought Villahermosa, the state capital, a certain self-assurance and vibrancy, and the parks, nature reserves and huge meandering rivers in the eastern and southern regions of the state are beginning to attract visitors. Its lands once gave rise to the first great civilization of Mesoamerica, the Olmec, whose influence was felt through vast zones of Mexico and further afield.

In Chiapas, the land of the Classic Maya (whose descendants still inhabit the highland villages today), the attractions are better known: San Cristóbal de las Casas is the end of the line for many travellers who base themselves in this delightful colonial and indigenous town while they soak up the atmosphere and explore the jungle waterfalls; the dramatic Sumidero Canyon; the multi-coloured lakes, and – highlight of any trip to Mexico – the ruins at Palenque, with a jungle setting that is arguably the most atmospheric and beautiful of all the Maya sites. Chiapas is also a good entry point for Guatemala. You can head straight for northern Guatemala and the ruins of Tikal or take a more genteel entry through the western highlands and idyllic Lake Atitlán.

Although in some ways Chiapas has fallen victim to the progress bug, it nevertheless seems impervious to the intrusion of outsiders. The Lost World feeling is created by indigenous inhabitants and their villages which make everything seem timeless. The appalling treatment the inhabitants have suffered over centuries was the fundamental cause of the rebellion on 1 January 1994, which led to the occupation of San Cristóbal by the revolutionaries of the EZLN (Zapatista Army of National Liberation) and their continuing struggle in and beyond the boundaries of Chiapas. ▸▸ *For routes to Guatemala, see page 87; for listings, see pages 90-111.*

Villahermosa → *For listings, see pages 90-111. Colour map 1, B1. Phone code: 993.*

Capital of Tabasco state, hot and humid Villahermosa is a busy, prosperous and attractive city on the Río Grijalva, which is navigable to the sea. Prices here tend to be high, although it is possible to find cheaper alternatives.

The **cathedral**, ruined in 1973, has been rebuilt, its twin steeples beautifully lit at night; it is not in the centre. There is a warren of modern colonial-style pedestrian malls throughout the central area. The **Centro de Investigaciones de las Culturas Olmecas** (CICOM) is set in a modern complex with a large public library, expensive restaurant, airline offices and souvenir shops, a few minutes' walk south, out of town along the river bank. The **Museo Regional de Antropología Carlos Pellicer** ① *Tue-Sun 0900-1700, US$2.50*, on three floors, has well laid-out displays of Maya and Olmec artefacts. Two other museums worth visiting are the **Museo de Cultura Popular** ① *Zaragoza 810, Tue-Sun 0900-2000, free*, and the **Museo de Historia de Tabasco** ① *Av 27 de Febrero corner of Juárez, Tue-Sun 0900-1900, US$1.50*. **Mercado Pino Suárez** ① *Pino Suárez corner of Bastar Zozaya*, offers a sensory overload as every nook and cranny is taken up with a variety of goods; everything from barbecued *pejelagarto* to cowboy hats, colourful handmade fabrics, spices and dangling naked chickens en route to the kettle. The local drink, *pozol*, is believed to cure a hangover. You can watch it being made here as the *pozoleros* grind the hominy into a thick dough to then mix it with cacao and water; its grainy starchiness is somewhat of an acquired taste. Nonetheless it is popular, and the *pozoleros* will serve you the drink *al gusto*, that is, with as much or as little sugar as you want. The **Institute of Tourism** ① *Av de los Ríos y Calle 13, T993-316 3633, www.vistetabasco.com, daily 0800-1800, English spoken*, is good for maps and advice on Tabasco state. Be sure to take insect repellent.

Parque Nacional La Venta
① *Blv Adolfo Ruiz Cortines, T993-314 1652, Tue-Sun 0800-1600, US$4; it takes up to 2 hrs to do the park justice; excellent guides speak Spanish and English, recommended.*

In 1925 an expedition of archaeologists discovered huge sculptured human and animal figures, urns and altars in almost impenetrable forest at **La Venta**, 120 km west of Villahermosa, and once the centre of the ancient Olmec culture. In the 1950s the monuments were threatened with destruction by the discovery of oil nearby. The poet Carlos Pellicer got them hauled all the way to a woodland area near Villahermosa, now the Parque Nacional de La Venta, also called the Museo Nacional de la Venta. The park, with scattered lakes, next to a children's playground, is almost opposite the old airport entrance (west of downtown). There, the 33 exhibits are dispersed in various small clearings. The huge heads, one of them weighing 20 tonne, are Olmec, a culture that flourished about 1150-150 BC. The figures have suffered a certain amount of damage through being exposed to the elements (those in the Xalapa Anthropological Museum are in far better condition) but to see them here, in natural surroundings, is an experience not to be missed. There is also a zoo with creatures from the Tabasco jungle, including monkeys, alligators, deer, wild pigs and birds. There is nothing to see at the original site of La Venta. Outside the park, on the lakeside, is an observation tower, **Mirador de las Aguilas** ① *free*, with excellent views, but only for the fit as there are lots of stairs. Taxis charge US$2 to the Parque. Bus Circuito No 1 from outside second-class bus terminal goes past Parque La Venta. From Parque Juárez in the city, take a 'Fraccionamiento Carrizal' bus and ask to be let off at Parque Tomás Garrido, of which La Venta is a part.

Parque Yumká
① *T993-356 0107, daily 0900-1600, US$5, most tour agencies offer round trips for about US$14*, a safari park containing 108 ha of Tabasco's three major habitats – jungle, savannah and lagoon, is a 'zoo without cages' offering walking, trolley and boat tours of each habitat. While the ecological park partly promotes the diversity of the region's flora and fauna, there are also animals from Asia and Africa. It's an easy day trip; take the *colectivo* to the airport and the park is next door.

South of Villahermosa
→ *For listings, see pages 90-111. Colour map 1, B1. Phone codes: Teapa 932; Bochil 932.*

South of Villahermosa on Route 195 the nice, clean little town of **Teapa** has several hotels and beautiful surroundings. Also in Teapa are the **Grutas de Cocona** ① *Tue-Sun 0900-1700, US$2.50*, which house a stunning array of stalagmites and beautiful displays of colour. The caves are approximately 500 m deep and a fresh and inviting river runs through them. There is a restaurant and campsite in the area.

Southwest of Teapa on Route 195 is **Pichucalco**, an affluent town with a lively and safe atmosphere. The zócalo throngs in the evening with people on after-dinner *paseos*. Buses run hourly to Villahermosa, US$4. There are hotels, restaurants and bars here. South of Pichucalco on Highway 195 on the way to Tuxtla Gutiérrez, is **Bochil**, an idyllic stopover.

The street system here is as follows: Avenidas run from east to west, calles from north to south. The avenidas are named according to whether they are north (Norte) or south (Sur) of the Avenida Central and change their names if they are east (Oriente) or west (Poniente) of the Calle Central. The number before avenidaavenida or callealle means the distance from the Centre measured in blocks. You know whether it's an avenidaavenida or a callealle by the order of the address: Avenidas have their number, then Sur or Norte followed by east or west; calles have the east or west position first. For example, 1 Norte Oriente is the eastern part of the first avenue north of Avenida Central; 2 Oriente Norte is the north part of the second street west of Calle Central. It sounds complicated, but as long as you check map and road signs very carefully, it is not difficult to navigate your way around. ↠ *See Transport, page 103.*

The capital of Chiapas, Tuxtla Gutiérrez is a busy, shabby city with a couple of points of interest to the tourist. The main sights are a long way from the centre and too far to walk:

Tuxtla Gutiérrez

N

200 metres
200 yards

Sleeping ⊖
Estrella 3
Hostal San Miguel 1
La Hacienda 4
María Eugenia 2
Palace Inn 5
Plaza Chiapas 8

Posada del Sol 6
Regional San Marcos 10

Eating ⊕
Antigua Fonda 1
Bonampak 11
Café Avenida 3
El Borrego Líder 2
El Huipil 5
El Mesón de Quijote 7
La Chata 6
Los Molcajetes 12
Mi Café 8

the gem is the zoo. The feast of the Virgen de Guadalupe is celebrated on 12 December. To get to the state **tourist office** ⓘ *Belisario Domínguez 950, Plaza Instituciones, T961-602 5127, www.turismo chiapas.gob.mx, daily 0800-1900*, take a *colectivo* from the junction of Avenida Central and Calle 2 Oriente. There is also a more convenient **municipal tourist office** ⓘ *4th floor of the Edificio Balencio, Av Central, between Calle 4a and 5a Pte Norte, Mon-Fri 0800-2000, Sat 0800-1400*.

Sights

In the Parque Madero at the east end of town (Calzada de los Hombres Ilustres) is the **Museo Regional de Chiapas** ⓘ *Tue-Sun 0900-1700, US$3.30*, with a fine collection of Maya artefacts, an auditorium and a library. Nearby is the **Jardín Botánico** (**botanical garden**) ⓘ *Mon-Fri 0900-1500, Sat 0900-1300, free*.

Tuxtla is best known for its superb **zoo** ⓘ *Tue-Sun 0900-1700, US$2; in Spanish only*, some 3 km south of town up a long hill. It was founded by Dr Miguel Alvarez del Toro, who died in 1996. His philosophy was to provide a free zoo for the children and indigenous people of the area. The zoo is very large and many of the animals are in open areas, with plenty of room to run about. Monkeys are not in cages, but in areas of trees pruned back so they cannot jump out of the enclosure. Some birds wander along the paths among the visitors. The zoo makes for a very pleasant and educational afternoon. Recommended. Take mosquito repellent. *Colectivos* to 'Zoológico' and 'Cerro Hueco' from Mercado (Calle 1a Oriente Sur y 7 Sur Oriente), pass the entrance every 20 minutes; taxis charge around US$3 from centre or town buses charge US$0.20. When returning, catch the bus from the same side you were dropped off as it continues up the hill to the end of the line where it fills up for the return journey.

Sumidero Canyon → *For listings, see pages 90-111. Colour map 1, B1.*

ⓘ *Daily 0600-1800, T961-600-6708, www.sumidero.com.*

The Sumidero Canyon, 1000-m deep, is a truly impressive spectacle. Native warriors, unable to endure the Spanish conquest, hurled themselves into this hungry chasm rather than submit to foreign domination. Fortunately, you don't have to do the same to experience the awesome energy of this place. There are two ways do it: from below, as a passenger on a high-speed boat; or from above, by visiting a series of miradors. The former method is highly recommended.

Boats depart from the river in **Chiapa de Corzo** (see below) when full, but you shouldn't have too wait long for other passengers. Tickets are available at the **Turística de Grijalva office** ⓘ *west side of the plaza, 0800-1700, US$10.* There is a second departure point beneath Cahuaré bridge, but it is hard to get to without your own vehicle. It takes two to three hours to traverse the canyon, where you'll see prolific wildlife including crocodiles, monkeys and vultures. The trip concludes near a hydroelectric dam – the engineering structure responsible for majority of the water in the canyon. Pack a sweater for the ride, as it gets chilly when you're speeding along.

Alternatively, you can view the canyon from a sublime series of miradors. **Autobús Panorámico** visits the main ones, Tuesday to Sunday 0900-1300, check with Tuxtla tourist office for more details. Otherwise you'll need your own vehicle or an expensive taxi. The best views are at La Coyota, especially at sunset, and there is a restaurant at the final Mirador. A trip to the Sumidero Canyon is a highlight of any visit to Chiapas. Organized tours including all transport costs are widely available in San Cristóbal and Tuxtla.

Chiapa de Corzo → *Colour map 1, B1. Phone code: 961. Altitude: 456 m.*

Fifteen kilometres beyond the canyon, Chiapa de Corzo, a colonial town on a bluff overlooking the Grijalva River, is more interesting than Tuxtla. In the centre is a fine 16th-century crown-shaped **fountain**; the 16th-century church of **Santo Domingo** with an engraved altar of solid silver; and craftsmen who work with gold, jewellery and lacquerwork. Chiapa de Corzo was a pre-Classic and proto-Classic Maya site and shares features with early Maya sites in Guatemala; the ruins are behind the Nestlé plant, and some unrestored mounds are on private property in a field near modern houses.

The waterfall at the **Cueva de El Chorreadero** is well worth a detour of 1 km. The road to the cave is 10 km past Chiapa de Corzo, a few kilometres after you start the climb into the mountains to get to San Cristóbal. Camping is possible but there are no facilities; take a torch.

San Cristóbal de las Casas

➔ For listings, see pages 90-111. Colour map 1, B1. Phone code: 967. Altitude: 2110 m.

One of Mexico's most beautiful towns, San Cristóbal de las Casas is stunningly located in the fertile Jovel valley, with the mountains of Huitepec to the west and Tzontehuitz to the east. The city is a charming blend of colonial architecture and indigenous culture, laid out in the colonial period with 21 indigenous barrios on the city's perimeter, which were later integrated into the totally *mestizo* city that existed by the 18th century. The indigenous population is today an important part of San Cristóbal's atmosphere, many of them earning a living by selling handicrafts in the town's two markets. The centre is rich in architectural variety, with excellent examples of baroque, neoclassical and plateresque, a Mexican style characterized by the intricate moulding of façades, resembling the work of silversmiths, hence the name, which means 'like a silversmith's'.

Ins and outs

Getting there The first class **OCC** and **ADO** bus terminal is at the junction of Insurgentes and Blv Sabines Gutiérrez, several blocks south of the centre. Other second-class lines and shuttle operators, including **AEXA** and **Rodolfo Figueroa**, also have nearby terminals on Gutiérrez, which soon becomes the Pan-American Highway. The airport serving San Cristóbal is now closed to commercial traffic; Tuxtla is the nearest point of entry. Those travelling to Palenque by car will have fine views but should avoid night-time journeys because of armed robberies. ▸▸ See Transport, page 104.

Getting around Most places are within walking distance of each other although taxis are available in town and to the nearby villages; the cheaper *colectivos* run on fixed routes only.

Best time to visit Due to its altitude, San Cristóbal has a pleasantly mild climate compared to the hotter Chiapas towns such as Palenque and Tuxtla. During June, July and August, it is warm and sunny in the morning, while in the afternoon it tends to rain, with a sharp drop in temperature. Warm, waterproof clothes are needed, although the heavy rains conveniently stop in the evening, when you can enjoy San Cristóbal's many cheap restaurants and friendly bars and cafés.

Tourist information The **tourist office** ① *Hidalgo 1, at the government offices, T967-678 6570, Mon-Sat 0800-2000, Sun 0900-1400*, is very helpful with all types of information and provides good maps; usually someone there speaks English. The **Municipal Office** ① *on the main plaza, in the Palacio Municipal, T967-678 0665*, has a good free map of the area.

Sights

The main square, **Plaza 31 de Marzo**, has a gazebo built during the era of Porfirio Díaz. In front of the plaza is the neoclassical **Palacio Municipal**, built in 1885. A few steps away is the **Catedral de San Cristóbal**, built in the 16th century, painted in ochre, brown and white, with a baroque pulpit added in the 17th century. Adjacent to the cathedral is the church of **San Nicolás**, which houses the historical archives of the diocese. The building dates from 1613, and is believed to be the only church in Mexico to preserve its original design in the architectural style of indigenous people's churches. Just off the plaza, at the beginning of Insurgentes, is the former **Casa de la Sirena**, now the **Hotel Santa Clara**. Built at the end of the 16th century, this is a rare example of colonial residential architecture in the plateresque

San Cristóbal de las Casas

Sleeping
Barón de las Casas **26** *C2*
Capri **1** *E2*
Casa Babylon **2** *D3*
Casa de Huéspedes
  Santa Lucía **4** *E1*
Casa Mexicana **6** *B2*
El Cerrillo **9** *B3*
Los Camellos **3** *C4*
Na Bolom **5** *A4*
Palacio de
  Moctezuma **10** *D3*
Posada 5 **30** *A2*
Posada Diego de
  Mazariegos **12** *B2*
Posada Doña Rosita **25** *B3*

Posada El Paraíso **13** *B1*
Posada Los Morales **15** *D1*
Posada Lucella **16** *E2*
Posada Lupita **17** *E2*
Posada Margarita **18** *C3*
Posada Media Luna **27** *D2*
Posada Real Jovel **14** *B3*
Posada San Agustín **28** *B2*
Posada Vallarta **19** *E2*
Posadita **20** *B3*
Rancho San Nicolás **7** *D4*
Real del Valle **21** *C2*
Suites Encanto **32** *B1*

Eating
Adelita **1** B4

Agapandos **7** *E2*
Café Museo Café **5** *B3*
Cocodrilo Café & Bar **8** *C2*
Craft Market **9** *A2*
El Fogón de Jovel **10** *B2*
El Gato Gordo **6** *C2*
El Mirador II **11** *C2*
Emiliano's Moustache **12** *C1*
Joveleño **4** *C3*
Juguería Ana Banana **14** *D2*
La Casa del Pan **33**
  B3, C2 & C3
La Fonda Argentina **15** *B3*
La Margarita **24** *C2*
La Paloma **2** *C2*
La Selva Café **16** *C1*

Madre Tierra **18** *D2*
María Cartones **19** *C2*
Namandí **20** *C1*
Naturalísimo **21** *B2*
París-México **22** *C2*
Tierra y Cielo **23** *C2*
Tuluc **25** *C2*

Bars & clubs
Barfly **26** *C1*
Blue Bar **28** *C1*
El Zirco **30** *B2*
Makia **27** *C2*
Revolución **32** *B2*

style. The interior has the four classic corridors of renaissance constructions. Heading off the plaza in the opposite direction, going north up 20 de Noviembre, you reach the **Church and Ex-Convento de Santo Domingo**. By far the most dramatic building in the city, it features an elaborate baroque façade in moulded mortar, especially beautiful when viewed in the late afternoon sun, which picks out the ornate mouldings with salmon pink hues. The church's altarpieces are covered in gold leaf, and the pulpit is intricately carved in a style known as churrigueresque, even more elaborate than the baroque style of Europe. Outside the market is the main handicraft market, with dozens of stalls selling traditional textiles, handmade dolls, wooden toys and jewellery. To the west of the centre, and up a strenuous flight of steps, is the **Templo del Cerrito**, a small church with fine views of the city and the surrounding mountains. The church is called *cerrito* (small hill) because it is set on an isolated, tree-covered hill. At the other end of the city, to the east, is another little church on a hill, the **Templo de Guadalupe**. This church is used by the indigenous people of the Barrio de Guadalupe, the nearest to the centre of the 21 such indigenous neighbourhoods. Each neighbourhood is characterized by the dress of the local people, depending on which indigenous group they belong to, and by the handicrafts produced by them. Guadalupe is the barrio of candle makers, saddle makers, and wooden toy makers. The other barrios, such as Mexicanos, the oldest in the city, are further afield and not recommended for unguided visits.

Na Bolom Museum and Cultural Centre ① *Vicente Guerrero 33, T967-678 1418, www.nabolom.org, guided tours daily, 1130 in Spanish, 1630 in English, US$4.50, US$3.50 without tour; library Mon-Fri 0930-1330, 1630-1900,* is situated in a neoclassical mansion dating from 1891. Na Bolom was founded in 1951 by the Danish archaeologist Frans Blom and his wife, the Swiss photographer Gertrudis Duby. After the death of Frans Blom in 1963, Na Bolom became a study centre for the universities of Harvard and Stanford, while Gertrudis Duby continued campaigning for the conservation of the Lacandón area. She died in 1993, aged 92, after which the centre has continued to function as a non-profit-making organization dedicated to conserving the Chiapan environment and helping the Lacandón people. The photographic archives in the museum are fascinating and contain a detailed visual history of 50 years of daily life of the Maya people with beautifully displayed artefacts, pictures of Lacondones, and information about their present way of life. There are five galleries with collections of pre-Columbian Maya art and colonial religious paintings. There is also a good library. A shop sells products made by the indigenous people helped by the centre.

Na Bolom runs various projects, staffed by volunteers. Prospective volunteers spend a minimum of three months, maximum six, at the centre. They must have skills that can be useful to the projects, such as anthropology, organic gardening, or be multi-linguists. Volunteers are given help with accommodation and a daily food allowance. Na Bolom also has 12 rooms to rent (see Sleeping, page 91). They run tours (Tuesday to Sunday) to San Juan Chamula and San Lorenzo Zinacantán; US$15 per person, good guides, thorough explanations, respectful to indigenous locals.

The **Museo de Los Altos** ① *Calzada Lázaro Cárdenas, next to Santo Domingo church, Tue-Sun 1000-1700, US$4, free on Sun and bank holidays,* is an anthropological museum that contains a history of San Cristóbal, with an emphasis on the plight of the indigenous people, as well as a good selection of locally produced textiles.

The **Templo del Carmen** ① *Crescencio Rosas y Alvaro Obregón,* with a unique archery tower in the Moorish style, is the home of **El Carmen Cultural Centre** ① *Tue-Sun 0900-1700, free.*

The **Centro de Desarrollo de la Medicina Maya** ① *Salomón González Blanco, Mon-Fri 0900-1800, Sat and Sun 1000-1600, US$2*, has a herb garden with detailed displays on the use of medicinal plants by the Maya for various purposes, including child delivery.

Villages near San Cristóbal

Travellers are strongly warned not to wander around in the hills surrounding San Cristóbal, as they could risk assault. Warnings can be seen in some places frequented by tourists. Remember that locals are particularly sensitive to proper dress (that is neither men nor women should wear shorts or revealing clothes) and manners; persistent begging should be countered with courteous, firm replies.

You are recommended to call at Na Bolom (see above) before visiting the villages, to get information on their cultures and seek advice on the reception you are likely to get. **Photography** is resisted by some of the indigenous people because they believe the camera steals their souls, and photographing their church is stealing the soul of God; it is also seen as invasive and sometimes profiteering. Either leave your camera behind or ask your guide to let you know when you can and cannot take pictures. Cameras have been taken by villagers when photography has been inappropriate. Much of the population does not speak Spanish. You can visit the villages of San Juan Chamula, Zinacantán and Tenejapa. While this is a popular excursion, especially when led by a guide, several visitors have felt ashamed at going to look at the villagers as if they were in a zoo; there were many children begging and offering to look after private vehicles.

Zinacantán

Zinacantán is reached by VW bus from the market, US$0.75, 30 minutes' journey, sometimes with frequent stops while the conductor lights rockets at roadside shrines; taxi US$4. The Zinacantán men wear pink/red jackets with embroidery and tassels, the women vivid pale blue shawls and navy skirts. Annual festival days here are 6 January, 19-22 January, 8-10 August; visitors are welcome. At midday every day the women prepare a communal meal, which the men eat in shifts. The main gathering place is

Around San Cristóbal de las Casas

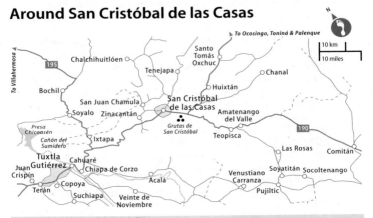

around the **church** ⓘ *US$1.50 for entering, official ticket from tourist office next door; photography inside is strictly prohibited*; the roof was destroyed by fire. There are two museums, but both have closed. Check before planning a visit. **Ik'al Ojov** ⓘ *off Calle 5 de Febrero, 5 blocks down Av Cristóbal Colón from San Lorenzo church, and 1 block to the left; donation requested*, includes two traditional *palapas* (huts) that people used to live in and there is a small collection of regional costumes. It occasionally holds shows and there is an annual festival on 17 February. There is also a tiny gift shop. The second museum is the **Museo Comunitario Autzetik ta jteklum** ⓘ *1 block from San Lorenzo church*, which is run by women from Zinacantán and also has exhibits on local culture.

Above the municipal building on the right, creative, resourceful Antonia has opened **Antonia's House** ⓘ *Isabel la Católica 7*. There is a small crafts shop and she and her family will demonstrate back-strap weaving, the making of tortillas and many other aspects of life in the village. She usually has some *posh* on the go – it's strong stuff, and the red variant will set your throat on fire... Be ready with a couple of litres of water! Antonia is very easy going and she may not charge for a sample of *posh*, however bear in mind that she makes her living from the shop, so buy something or leave a contribution. Tours from San Cristóbal cost US$15.

San Juan Chamula → *Colour map 1, B1.*

Signs in Chamula warn that it is dangerous to walk in the area on your own; robberies have occurred between Chamula and both San Cristóbal and Zinacantán. It's generally best to seek full advice on any travel outside San Cristóbal de las Casas.

In this Tzotzil village 10 km northwest of San Cristóbal the men wear grey, black or light pink tunics, while the women wear bright blouses with colourful braid and navy or bright blue shawls. One popular excursion is to visit the brightly painted **church** ⓘ *a permit (US$1) is needed from the village tourist office and photographing inside the church is absolutely forbidden*. There are no pews but family groups sit or kneel on the floor, chanting, with rows of candles lit in front of them, each representing a member of the family and certain significance attached to the colours of the candles. The religion is centred on the 'talking stones' and three idols as well as certain Christian saints. Pagan rituals are held in small huts at the end of August. The pre-Lent festival ends with celebrants running through blazing harvest chaff. This happens just after Easter prayers are held, before the sowing season starts. Festivals in Chamula should *not* be photographed; if you wish to take other shots ask permission, people are not unpleasant, even if they refuse (although children may pester you to take their picture for a small fee). For reasons of cultural understanding and safety it is recommended that you visit Chamula on a tour.

There are many handicraft stalls on the way up the small hill southwest of the village. This has a good viewpoint of the village and valley. Take the road from the southwest corner of the square, turn left towards the ruined church then up a flight of steps on the left.

To get to Chamula, you can catch a VW bus from the market in San Cristóbal every 20 minutes, last at 1700, last one back at 1900, US$1 per person (or taxi, US$4). It is an interesting walk from San Cristóbal to Chamula along the main road to a point 1 km past the crossroads with the Periférico ring road (about 2.5 km from town centre); turn right on to an old dirt road, not signposted but it is the first fork you come to between some farmhouses. Then head back via the road through the village of Milpoleta, some 8 km downhill; allow five hours for the round trip (one hour for Chamula). Best not done in hot weather. Also, you can hike from Chamula to Zinacantán in 1½ hours: when leaving Chamula, take the track straight ahead instead of turning left onto the San Cristóbal road;

Hardship for the Chiapanecos

For the visitor to Chiapas, the state's wonders are many: lush tropical jungle, quaint colonial villages, or the modern, prosperous capital, Tuxtla Gutiérrez. However, the peacefulness masks the troubles of the state's indigenous peoples. Their plight was splashed across the world's press with the Zapatista uprising of January 1994 and has remained a photogenic story ever since.

Chiapas, the southernmost state and one of Mexico's poorest, appears much like its neighbour, Guatemala, and shares many of the same problems. Subsistence has been a way of life for centuries, illiteracy and infant mortality are high, particularly among those who have retained their languages and traditions, shunning the Spanish culture. The Chiapas government estimates that nearly one million indigenous people live in the state, descendants of the great Maya civilization of AD 250-900. The indigenous Chiapanecos of today are spread out across the state, they do not speak the same language, nor dress alike, have the same customs nor the same types of tribal government.

The Tzotziles and Tzeltales total about 626,000 and live mainly on the plateau and the slopes of the high altitude zones. The Choles number 110,000 and live in the towns of Tila, Tumbalá, Salto de Agua, Sabanilla and Yajalón. The 87,000 Zoques live near the volatile Chichonal volcano.

The 66,000 Tojolabales live in Margaritas, Comitán, La Independencia, La Trinitaria and part of Altamirano. On the high mountains and slopes of the Sierra Madre are the 23,000 Mames and the 12,000 Mochós and Kakchikeles. The Lacandones, named after the rainforest they occupy, number only 500 today. Along the border with Guatemala are 21,500 Chujes, Kanjobales and Jacaltecos, although that number includes some refugees still there from the Guatemalan conflict, which ended in late 1996.

A minority of the indigenous population speaks Spanish, particularly in the Sierra Madre region and among the Zoques. Many have dropped their traditional clothing. Customary positions of authority along with stewardships and standard bearers have been dropped from tribal governance, but medicine men continue to practise. They still celebrate their festivals and they think about their ancestors as they have for centuries. Many now live in the large cities, but those who remain in *el campo* are, for the most part, poor. They get by, eating tortillas, some vegetables and occasionally beans. Many who leave for the city end up as domestic servants, labourers or street pedlars. The scarcity of land for indigenous people has been a political issue for many decades and limited land reform merely postponed the crisis that eventually erupted in the 1990s, and continues to cause the government difficulties.

turn left on a small hill where the school is (after 30 minutes) and follow a smaller trail through light forest. After about an hour you reach the main road 200 m before Zinacantán (but see warning, above).

Tenejapa → Phone code: 967.
Few tourists visit Tenejapa. The village is very friendly and many men wear local costume. Ask permission to take pictures and expect to pay. The Thursday market is traditionally for fruit and vegetables, but there are a growing number of other stalls.

The market thins out by noon. Excellent woven items can be purchased from the weavers' cooperative near the church. They also have a fine collection of old textiles in their regional ethnographic **museum** adjoining the handicraft shop. The cooperative can also arrange weaving classes.

Other excursions from San Cristóbal

Two other excursions can be made, by car or local bus, from San Cristóbal. The first goes south on the Pan-American Highway (30 minutes by car) to **Amatenango del Valle**, a Tzeltal village where the women make and fire pottery in their yards, and then southeast (15 minutes by car) to **Aguacatenango**, a picturesque village at the foot of a mountain. Continue one hour along this road past **Villa Las Rosas** (hotel) to **Venustiano Carranza**, where the women wear fine costumes, and there is an extremely good view of the entire valley. There is a good road from Las Rosas to Comitán as an alternative to the Pan-American Highway. There are frequent buses.

Las Grutas de San Cristóbal ① *daily 0900-1700, US$1*, are caves 10 km southeast of the town, which contain huge stalagmites and are 2445 m deep but only lit for 750 m. Refreshments are available. Horses can be hired at Las Grutas for US$15 for a five-hour ride (guide extra) on lovely trails in the surrounding forest. Some of these are best followed on foot. Yellow diamonds on trees and stones mark the way to beautiful meadows. Stay on the trail to minimize erosion. The land next to the caves is taken up by an army football pitch, but once past this, it is possible to walk most of the way back to San Cristóbal through woods and fields. Las Grutas are reached by **Autotransportes de Pasaje** '31 de Marzo' *colectivos* every 15 minutes (0600-1900, US$1) from Avenida Benito Juárez 37B, across the Pan-American Highway just south of the **Cristóbal Colón** bus terminal (or take a *camioneta* from Pan-American opposite San Diego church 500 m east of Cristóbal Colón). *Colectivos* are marked 'San Cristóbal, Teopisca, Ciudad Militar, Villa Las Rosas', or ask for minibus to 'Rancho Nuevo'. To the bus stop take 'San Diego' *colectivo* 1 block east of zócalo to the end of Benito Juárez. When you get to Las Grutas, ask the driver to drop you at Km 94; the caves are poorly signed.

Tours from San Cristóbal to the Sumidero Canyon (see page 70) including boat trip cost around US$20 with numerous travel agencies, 0900-1600. San Cristóbal can also serve as a base for exploring the Maya ruins at Palenque (210 km away, see page 80), Bonampak and Yaxchilán, near the Guatemalan border (see page 84).

Route to Palenque → *For listings, see pages 90-111.*

Ocosingo → *Colour map 1, B1. Phone code: 919.*
Palenque can be reached by paved road from San Cristóbal de las Casas, a beautiful ride via Ocosingo, which has a local airport, a colourful market and several hotels. It was one of the centres of fighting in the Ejército Zapatista de Liberación Nacional (EZLN) uprising in January 1994.

Toniná → *Colour map 1, B1.*
① *Daily 0900-1700, US$3.30, drinks are available at the site; also toilets and parking.*
The Maya ruins at Toniná are 12 km from Ocosingo, with bus links to San Cristóbal de las Casas. A tour from San Cristóbal to Toniná costs US$15; it is possible to drive in an ordinary car, or take a taxi (US$6). There are also *colectivos* (15 minutes, US$1) running from the market, or you can walk from Ocosingo.

Toniná is one of the last Classic Maya sites, with the palace high on a hill to your left. It is well worth visiting the ruins, which were excavated by a French government team. The temples are in the Palenque style with internal sanctuaries in the back room, but influences from many different Maya styles of various periods have been found. The huge pyramid complex, seven stone platforms making a man-made hill, is 10 m higher than the Temple of the Sun at Teotihuacán and is the tallest pyramidal structure in the Maya world. Stelae are in very diverse forms, as are wall panels, and some are in styles and of subjects unknown at any other Maya site. Ask the guardian to show you the second unrestored ball court and the sculpture kept at his house. He will show you round the whole site; there is also a small **museum**.

Agua Azul

① *Entry US$1.50, US$4 for cars. Entry price is not always included in day trips from Palenque, which allow you to spend up to 3 hrs at Agua Azul. Violent robberies have been reported so don't go alone; groups of at least 4 are best.*

The series of jungle waterfalls and rapids at Agua Azul run for 7 km and are breathtakingly beautiful. They are easily visited on a day trip from Palenque. All the travel agencies, and many hotels, offer a tour there for about US$10, including a visit to the waterfall at Misol-Há and Agua Clara (see below). Agua Azul's main swimming area has many restaurants and indigenous children selling fruit. Swimming is good, in clear blue water during good weather, in muddy brown water during bad (but still refreshing if very hot, which it usually is). Swimmers should stick to the roped areas where everyone else can see them; the various graves on the steep path up the hill alongside the rapids are testament to the dangers of swimming in those areas. One of the falls is called 'The Liquidizer', an area of white water in which bathing is extremely dangerous. On no account should you enter this stretch of water; many drownings have occurred. Even in the designated areas, the currents can be ferocious. Beware of hidden tree trunks in the water if it is murky. The path on the left of the rapids can be followed for 7 km, with superb views and secluded areas for picnics. There are also several *palapas* for hammocks, plenty of space for free camping and some rooms to rent.

Agua Clara and Misol-Há

Eight kilometres from Agua Azul along the river is **Agua Clara** ① *entry US$1*, a nature reserve. At Misol-Há there is a stunning waterfall usually visited first on day trips from Palenque. A narrow path winds around behind the falls, allowing you to stand behind the immense curtain of water. Swimming is possible in the large pool at the bottom of the tumbling cascade of water, but it is usually better to wait until you get to Agua Azul for a good swim. However, during the rainy season swimming is reported to be better at **Misol-Há** ① *entry US$1*, so go by bus or check with your tour operator, as some only allow a brief stop at Misol-Há.

Palenque town → *Colour map 1, B2. Phone code: 916.*

A friendly and, at times, hot, humid and airless little town whose sole reason to exist is to accommodate the tourists heading for the famous archaeological site nearby. There is plenty of accommodation for every budget, with dozens of cheap *posadas* around the centre, and a tourist barrio, **La Cañada**, with more expensive hotels, restaurants and bars. Souvenirs are available at lower prices than elsewhere on the Ruta Maya, making Palenque a convenient place to stop off en route to the southerly Chiapan towns of San

Cristóbal and Tuxtla Gutiérrez. Travellers coming to Palenque from Mérida, Campeche and other cities in the Yucatán Peninsula will find it much hotter here, particularly in June, July and August. The **Fiesta de Santo Domingo** is held on the first week of August.

The **tourist office** ⓘ *daily 0900-2100*, is on Juárez, a block below the plaza and next to the craft market. They are fairly useless but provide a good free map of Palenque and the ruins.

Five kilometres from Palenque town, but 3 km before the ruins, **El Panchán** ⓘ *www.palenquemx.com/elpanchan*, is host to a fascinating mix of philosophies, foods and intellectual interests. Don Moisés, founder of El Panchán, first came to Palenque as an archaeologist and was one of the first guides to the ruins. He bought a plot of land, named it El Panchán – Maya for 'heaven on earth' – and started to raise a family. Now he has divided lots among his children who run various businesses. It is about 10°C cooler at El Panchán than Palenque town due to the dense foliage cover. Although vastly different, all businesses at Panchan have intertwined themselves into the natural jungle that surrounds them, creating an almost Robinson Crusoe setting – if you don't want to stay in town and like the idea of being based in the forest, get a bus or taxi here soon after arriving in Palenque town. ▸▸ *See listings, pages 90-111.*

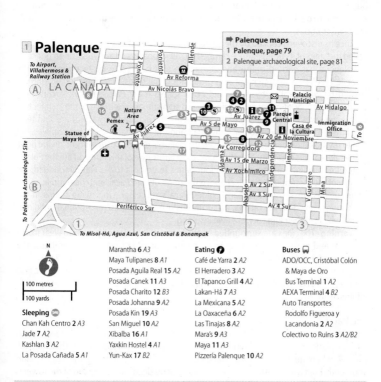

Palenque maps
1 Palenque, page 79
2 Palenque archaeological site, page 81

N
100 metres
100 yards

Sleeping 🛏
Chan Kah Centro **2** *A3*
Jade **7** *A2*
Kashlan **3** *A2*
La Posada Cañada **5** *A1*
Marantha **6** *A3*
Maya Tulipanes **8** *A1*
Posada Aguila Real **15** *A2*
Posada Canek **11** *A3*
Posada Charito **12** *B3*
Posada Johanna **9** *A2*
Posada Kin **19** *A3*
San Miguel **10** *A2*
Xibalba **16** *A1*
Yaxkin Hostel **4** *A1*
Yun-Kax **17** *B2*

Eating 🍴
Café de Yarra **2** *A2*
El Herradero **3** *A2*
El Tapanco Grill **4** *A2*
Lakan-Há **7** *A3*
La Mexicana **5** *A2*
La Oaxaceña **6** *A2*
Las Tinajas **8** *A2*
Mara's **9** *A3*
Maya **11** *A3*
Pizzería Palenque **10** *A2*

Buses 🚌
ADO/OCC, Cristóbal Colón
 & Maya de Oro
 Bus Terminal **1** *A2*
AEXA Terminal **4** *B2*
Auto Transportes
 Rodolfo Figueroa y
 Lacandonia **2** *A2*
Colectivo to Ruins **3** *A2/B2*

Palenque → *Colour map 1, B1.*

ⓘ *Daily 0800-1700, US$4.50, entrance to national park US$1; guided tours possible. There are lots of souvenir stalls at the main entrance. Water at the site is expensive, so bring your own. The cheapest food is the tacos from the stalls. Colectivos back to the town leave from outside the main entrance, US$1, every 6-18 mins. From Palenque town, take a colectivo from the main road near the 1st-class bus station.*

Built at the height of the Classic period on a series of artificial terraces surrounded by jungle, Palenque is one of the most beautiful of all the Maya ruins in Mexico. It was built for strategic purposes, with evidence of defensive apertures in some of the retaining walls. In the centre of the site is the Palace, a massive warren of buildings with an asymmetrical tower rising above them, and fine views to the north. The tower was probably used as an astronomical observatory and a watchtower. The outer buildings of the palace have an unusual series of galleries, offering shade from the jungle heat of the site.

From about the fourth century AD, Palenque grew from a small agricultural village to one of the most important cities in the prehispanic world, although it really achieved greatness between AD 600 and 800. During the long and illustrious reign of Lord Pacal, the city rapidly rose to the first rank of Maya states. The duration of Pacal's reign is still a bone of contention among Mayanists because the remains found in his sarcophagus do not appear to be those of an 81-year-old man, the age implied by the texts in the Temple of the Inscriptions.

Since its discovery, choked by the encroaching jungle that pushed against its walls and scaled the stairs of its temples once climbed by rulers, priests and acolytes, the architecture of Palenque has elicited praise and admiration and begged to be reconstructed. The corbelled vaults, the arrangement of its groupings of buildings, the impression of lightness created by walls broken by pillars and open spaces make Palenque-style architecture unique. It was only later that archaeologists and art historians realized that the architecture of Palenque was created mainly to accommodate the extraordinary sculptures and texts that referred not only to historical individuals and the important events in their lives, but also to mythological beings who endorsed the claims of dynastic continuity or 'divine right' of the rulers of this great city. The structures most illustrative of this function are the Palace, a group of buildings arranged around four patios to which a tower was later added, the Temple of the Inscriptions that rises above the tomb of Lord Pacal, and the temples of the Group of the Cross, used by Chan Bahlum, Pacal's successor, who made claims in the inscriptions carved on the tablets, pillars and balustrades of these exceptional buildings, claims which, in their audacity, are awe inspiring.

Warning The ruins are surrounded by thick, mosquito-infested jungle so wear insect repellent and make sure you're up to date with your tablets (May to November is the worst time for mosquitoes). It is extremely hot and humid at the ruins, especially in the afternoon, so it is best to visit early. Unfortunately, as well as mosquitoes, there have also been reports of criminals hiding in the jungle. As ever, try and leave valuables at home to minimize any loss.

The Palace

The Palace and Temple XI are located in the centre of the site. The Palace stands on an artificial platform over 100 m long and 9 m high. Chan Bahlum's younger brother, Kan Xul, was 57 when he became king. He devoted himself to enlarging the palace, and apparently built the four-storey tower in honour of his dead father. The top of the tower is almost at the level of Pacal's mortuary temple, and on the winter solstice the sun, viewed from here, sets directly above his crypt. Large windows where Maya astronomers could observe and chart the movement of the planets, ancestors of the royal lineage of Palenque, pierce the walls of the tower. Kan-Xul reigned for 18 years before being captured and probably sacrificed by the rulers of Toniná. During his reign Palenque reached its greatest degree of expansion, although recent excavations at the site may prove differently.

2 Palenque archaeological site

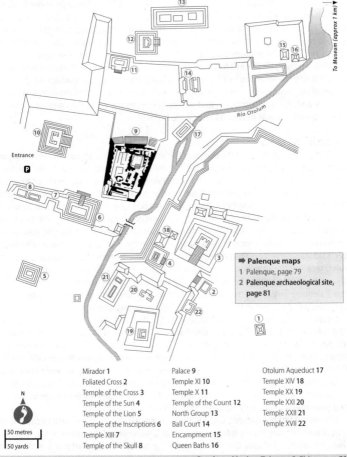

⇒ **Palenque maps**
1 Palenque, page 79
2 Palenque archaeological site, page 81

Mirador **1**	Palace **9**	Otolum Aqueduct **17**
Foliated Cross **2**	Temple XI **10**	Temple XIV **18**
Temple of the Cross **3**	Temple X **11**	Temple XX **19**
Temple of the Sun **4**	Temple of the Count **12**	Temple XXI **20**
Temple of the Lion **5**	North Group **13**	Temple XXII **21**
Temple of the Inscriptions **6**	Ball Court **14**	Temple XVII **22**
Temple XIII **7**	Encampment **15**	
Temple of the Skull **8**	Queen Baths **16**	

N
50 metres
50 yards

Temple of the Inscriptions

The Temple of the Inscriptions, along with Temple XII and Temple XIII, lies to the south of the Palace group of buildings and is one of the rare Maya pyramids to have a burial chamber incorporated at the time of its construction. This building was erected to cover the crypt in which Lord Pacal, the founder of the first ruling dynasty of Palenque, was buried. Discovered in 1952 by Alberto Ruz-Lhuillier, the burial chamber measured 7 m long, 7 m high and 3.75 m across, an incredible achievement considering the weight of the huge pyramid pressing down upon it. According to the inscriptions, Lord Pacal was born in AD 603 and died in AD 684. Inside, Ruz-Lhuillier discovered his bones adorned with jade jewellery. Around the burial chamber were various figures carved in stucco, depicting the Bolontikú, the Nine Lords of the Night of Maya mythology. There was a narrow tube alongside the stairs, presumably to give Pacal spiritual access to the outside world. Pacal also left a record of his forebears in the inscriptions. These three great tablets contain one of the longest texts of any Maya monument. There are 620 glyph blocks; they tell of Pacal's ancestors, astronomical events and an astonishing projection into the distant future (AD 4772). One of the last inscriptions reveals that, 132 days after Pacal's death, his son, Chan Bahlum, ascended to power as the new ruler of Palenque.

While finishing his father's funerary monument, Chan Bahlum had himself depicted as a child being presented as heir by his father. The portraits of Chan Bahlum, on the outer pillars of the Temple of the Inscriptions, display features that are both human and divine. He took and assumed attributes that rightly belong to the gods, thus ensuring that the heir to the throne was perceived as a divine human.

Group of the Cross

To the extreme southeast of the centre of the site lie Temple XIV and the buildings known as the *Grupo de la Cruz*. These include the Temple of the Sun, with beautiful relief carvings, which would probably have been painted in their day. The three temples in this group all have dramatic roof-combs, originally believed to have a religious significance, although traces of roof-combs have been found on buildings now known to have been purely residential. In all of the temples there was discovered a huge stone tablet with bas-relief, now removed to the museum, from whose images the name of each temple was taken.

Human and mythological time come together in the inscriptions of these temples. In each tableau carved on the tablets at the back of the temples, Chan Bahlum, the new ruler, receives the regalia of office from his father, Pacal, now in the underworld and shown much smaller than his living son. The shrines in the three temples are dedicated to the Palenque Triad, a sacred trinity linked to the ruling dynasty of the city, whose genealogy is explained in the inscriptions. They were certainly long lived: the parents of the triad were born in 3122 or 3121 BC and the children arrived on 19 October, 23 October and 6 November, 2360 BC. It has been shown that these were dates of extraordinary astronomical phenomena: the gods were intimately related to heavenly bodies and events. They also provided a mythological origin for the dynasty which is detailed on the three main tablets from the Group of the Cross. Rulers died and gods were born in an impressive merging of historical and mythological events. At their completion, the three temples of the Group of the Cross housed the divine sanction for the dynasty as a whole and gave the rationale for its descent through females and males.

On each set of balustrades, Chan Bahlum began his text with the birth of the patron god of each temple. On the left side of the stairs, he recorded the time elapsed between the birth of the god and the dedication of the temple. Thus, mythological time and

Sarcophagus

Pacal's sarcophagus, or coffin, is carved out of a solid piece of rock, with a carved slab covering it. Every element in the imagery of the sarcophagus lid is consistent with Maya iconography. It is exquisitely beautiful. The central image is that of Lord Pacal falling back into the fleshless jaws of the earth monster who will transport him to Xibalba, the realm of the dead. A cruciform world-tree rises above the underworld maw. The same world-tree appears on the tablets in the sanctuaries at the backs of the buildings known as the Group of the Cross. A long inscription runs around the edge of the lid, which includes a number of dates and personal names that records a dynastic sequence covering almost the whole of the seventh and eight centuries.

Four plugs in the corners of the lid filled the holes used with ropes to lower the lid into place; the plug in the southeast corner had a notch cut in it so that the channel, built into the stairway leading to the upper world, would allow spiritual communion between the dead king and his descendants above. Although the imagery of the sarcophagus lid refers to Pacal's fall into Xibalba, the location of the tower of the palace ensures that he will not remain there. The sun, setting over the crypt on the winter solstice, will have to do battle with the Nine Lords of the Night before re-emerging triumphantly in the east; the nine tiers of the pyramid represent the nine battles to be fought during his downward journey. Pacal, who awaits the sun at the point where the final battle had been fought, will accompany the sun as he re-emerges from Xibalba in the east. Palenque, the westernmost city of the Classic Maya, was in the 'dead zone', which placed it in the perfect position to accommodate the descent of the sun and Lord Pacal into the underworld.

contemporary time were fused. Each temple was named for the central image on its inner tablet. When Chan Bahlum died in 702 after ruling for 18 years, his younger brother and heir erected a fourth shrine to record the apotheosis of the departed king (Temple XIV). On these reliefs, Chan Bahlum emerges triumphantly from the underworld and dances towards his mother, Lady Ahpo-Hel.

The lengths to which the rulers of Palenque went to establish legitimacy for their claims of divine right could not guarantee the survival of Palenque after the collapse felt throughout the Classic Maya region, when the building of elite religious structures stopped and stelae were no longer engraved with the details of dynastic events. Toniná, the city that captured and probably sacrificed the Palenque ruler Kan-Xul, outlived the great centre made glorious by Pacal and Chan Bahlum. The last-known dated monument from the Maya region registers AD 909 at the lesser site; it is to be supposed that soon afterwards, Toniná went the way of the other centres of the Classic Maya world.

The **museum** ⓘ *Tue-Sun 0900-1630, free with ruins ticket*, is on the way back to the town, with an expensive restaurant and gift shop. Many of the stucco carvings retrieved from the site are here, as well as jade pieces of jewellery, funerary urns and ceramics. Readers wishing to learn more about the iconography and writing system of the Classic Maya could refer to: *A Forest of Kings*, L Schele and D Freidel, William Morrow and Company, NY 1990.

Yaxchilán, Bonampak and Lacanjá → *For listings, see pages 90-111. Colour map 1, B2.*

ⓘ *Yaxchilán 0800-1600, US$4.50; Bonampak 0800-1645, US$3.70 (free for under 13s, students and over 60s) plus US$11.50 for optional transport with the Jach Winik coop to the site; this includes toilet and locker and entry to the small museum. It's a 1-hr journey from Frontera Corozal to Bonampak.*

Yaxchilán

Yaxchilán is a major Classic Maya centre built along a terrace and hills above the Río Usumacinta, where there are more howler monkeys than people. The temples are ornately decorated with stucco and stone and the stone lintels are carved with scenes of ceremonies and conquests. Bonampak, originally under the political domination of Yaxchilán, was built in the late-Classic period on the Río Lacanjá, a tributary of the Usumacinta. It is famous for its murals, dated at AD 800, which relate the story of a battle and the bloody aftermath with the sacrificial torture and execution of prisoners.

From around AD 200 to the early 10th century, the era known as the Classic Maya witnessed the growth of many small settlements into great centres noted for wonderful architecture, sculpture, painted ceramics, impressive advances in mathematics and hieroglyphic writings, and the growth of an elite who often created alliances with other polities through marriage. Wide causeways, *sacbés*, were built between centres enabling the inhabitants to maintain contact with those of other towns. All these great advances came to an end around AD 909, when the Classic Maya civilization collapsed. For many years Mayanists have postulated about the cause of the collapse: some have suggested land exhaustion, others have suggested invasion from the Central Highlands, while still others believe in a peasant revolt against the conspicuous consumption of an expanding elite. The painted walls of Structure 1 at Bonampak illustrate well the extravagance indulged in by the elite of this centre on the margins of the Lacandón rainforest.

Bonampak

The murals at Bonampak are very realistic with an excellent use of colour and available space. Painted on the walls, vault rises and benches of three adjoining but not interconnecting rooms, they describe the rituals surrounding the presentation at court of the future ruler. Some of the rituals were separated by considerable intervals, which adds to the solemnity of the ceremony. It is very possible that the rituals illustrated were only a small selection of a far greater series of events. The people participating were mainly elite, including the royal family, and a strict hierarchy was observed in which eminent lords were attended by minor nobility.

In Room 1, the celebration opens with the presentation of the young prince, in which a porter introduces the child to an assembly of lords, dressed for the occasion in white robes. The king watches from his throne. Also present are two representatives from Yaxchilán, one male and one female. It is probable that the female is the wife or consort of Chaan-Muan, the ruler of Bonampak. After this simple opening, the spectacle begins. Lords are represented dressed in sumptuous clothing and jewellery, musicians appear playing drums, turtle carapaces, rattles and trumpets and they all line up for a procession, which will bemuse the peasantry, labourers and artisans waiting outside. We never see the lower orders but, open-mouthed, we can stand with them to observe the spectacle. The headdresses alone are enough to bedazzle us and the great diversity in the attire of the participants illustrates the wide spectrum of social functions fulfilled by those attending the ceremony.

The imagery and text of the sculptured lintels and stelae at nearby Yaxchilán proclaim the right of the heir to accede to the throne while emphasizing the need to take captives to be sacrificed in honour of the king-to-be. This need is echoed in the paintings of Room 2, Structure 1, at Bonampak. A ferocious battle is in progress in which the ruler, Chaan-Muan, proves his right to the throne. In the midst of battle, he shines out heroically. The local warriors pull the hair of those of the opposite side, whose identity is not known. Many captives were taken. In the ensuing scene, the full horror of the fate of those captured by the Maya is illustrated.

On a stepped structure, the ruler Chaan-Muan oversees the torture and mutilation of the captives taken in the recent battle. This event is clearly in the open air and surely witnessed by the inhabitants of Bonampak, whose loyalty is rewarded by admission to the bloody circus. The torture of the captives consisted of mutilation of the hands; some disconsolate individuals hold up their hands dripping blood, while one has clearly been decapitated, his head resting on a bed of leaves. It is to be supposed that the torture of the captives would be followed by death, probably by decapitation. The gods demanded sacrifice, which was provided by the rulers in an extravaganza of bloodletting. It must be understood that what appears to be outright bloodthirstiness was a necessary part of Maya ritual and probably accepted by all the polities throughout the Classic Maya region. It is very probable that the heir would not have been acceptable without this gory ritual.

The murals of the third room at Bonampak express the events that were meant to close the series of rituals designed to consolidate the claim to the throne by the son of the ruler. At first sight, the paintings that cover the walls of room three of Structure 1 appear to celebrate the sacrifices of the previous depictions in an exuberant public display of music, dance and perhaps song. The background is a pyramid, and ten elegantly dressed lords dance on different levels, colourful 'dance-wings' sprouting from their hips. The dominant dancer on the uppermost level is believed to be the ruler, Chaan-Muan. However, it has been noted that a very strong element of sacrifice accompanies the extrovert display. In a more private corner, the royal family is portrayed preparing to engage in blood sacrifice; a servant proffers them a container that the sacred bloodletting instruments. There are also indications that the male dancers had already drawn blood by means of penis perforation. As at Yaxchilán, blood endorsed the dynastic claims of the royal family.

The rituals portrayed on the walls of Structure 1 at Bonampak are thought to have been performed between 790 and 792, a time when the collapse of the Classic Maya was beginning to be felt. The extravagant use of enormous amounts of fine cloth, expensive jaguar pelts, jade beads and pectorals, elegant costumes, headdresses made from rare feathers, and spondylus shells was not enough to reverse the decadence of the civilization that had produced magnificent works in art, architecture, jewellery, mathematics, astronomy and glyphic writing: within a hundred years, the jungle was to claim it for its own.

Lacanjá

At Lacanjá (9 km from Bonampak) there is a community of Lacandones. For more details ask at **Na-Bolom** in San Cristóbal de las Casas. Local guides can be hired for hikes in the jungle and to the ruins of Bonampak. Lucas Chambor at the **Casa de Cultura** is a good source of advice. Lacanjá to Bonampak with locals costs US$6.50-9. The walk through the jungle is beautiful and crosses several streams. Another walk in the area is to the **Cascadas de Moctuniha** (one hour each way, US$6.50 with guide).

Comitán and around → *Phone code : 963.*

Comitán de Domínguez is a small but handsome colonial city located close to the border. It's a tranquil and elevated place, offering cool respite from the stifling lowlands and a good place to relax before or after visiting Guatemala. A large, shady zócalo marks the centre of town, where you'll find a **tourist office** ① *Juárez 6, just inside Pasaje Morales on the east side, Mon-Fri 0800-1800, Sat 0800-1600.* Visit the **Guatemalan Consulate** ① *1a Calle Sur Pte 26, T963-632 2979, Mon-Fri 0900-1700,* if you need a visa. There's a handful of small museums in town including the **Museo de Arte Hermila Domínguez de Castellanos** ① *Av Central Sur and 3a Sur Pte, Tue-Sat, 1000-1800, Sun 0900-1245, US$0.50,* with a collection of modern art; and **Casa Museo Belisario Domínguez** ① *Av Central Sur and 2a Sur Pte, Mon-Sat 1000-1800, Sun 0900-1245, US$0.50,* filled with memorabilia and dedicated to a local doctor who was assassinated after speaking out against President Huerta.

Lagunas de Montebello and Chinkultic

Six kilometres south of Comitán take a right turn for the Maya ruins of **Tenán Puente** ① *5 km situated in a forest, 0900-1600, US$2.50,* there is a shortcut on foot. In 1996 the tomb of a Maya nobleman (AD 1000) was discovered here. The buildings at Tenán are more restored than those at Chinkultic (see below). A road branches off the Pan-American Highway, 16 km further on, to a very beautiful region of vari-coloured lakes and caves, the **Lagunas de Montebello** (a national park). Off the road to Montebello, 30 km from the Pan-American Highway, lie the ruins of **Chinkultic** ① *0900-1700, US$3,* with temples, ball court, carved stone stelae and a *cenote* (deep round lake, good swimming) in beautiful surroundings; from the signpost the ruins are about 3 km along a dirt road. Watch and ask for the very small sign and gate where the road to the ruins starts (about 1 km back along the main road, towards Comitán from **Doña María's**, don't attempt any short cuts); worth visiting when passing. *Colectivo* from Comitán US$2.50.

Combi vans or buses marked 'Tziscao' or 'Lagos' to the Lagunas de Montebello National Park (60 km from Comitán, US$1.30 about one hour), via the **Lagunas de Siete Colores** (so called because the oxides in the water give varieties of colours), leave frequently from Avenida 2 Poniente Sur y Calle 3 Sur Poniente, four blocks from the plaza in Comitán; buses go as far as Laguna Bosque Azul, a one-hour journey. For those with their own transport there are several dirt roads from Comitán to the Lagunas; a recommended route is the one via La Independencia, Buena Vista, La Patria and El Triunfo (beautiful views), eventually joining the road west of the Chinkultic ruins.

Tziscao

Tziscao is 9 km along the road leading right from the park entrance, which is 3 km before Bosque Azul; hourly buses Comitán–Tziscao; the last bus and *colectivo* back connecting with the 1900 bus to San Cristóbal is at 1600. The last *combi* to Comitán is at 1700. A trip to the Lagunas de Siete Colores from Comitán can be done in a day (note that the less-accessible lakes are hard to get to even if staying in the vicinity). It is also possible to hire a *combi*, which takes 12 people, to go to the Lakes and Chinkultic for US$15 per hour. A day trip to Chinkultic and the lakes from San Cristóbal de las Casas is also possible, if exhausting (take passport and tourist card). The **Bosque Azul** area is now a reserve. The area is noted for its orchids and birdlife, including the famous *quetzal*, but it gets very busy at weekends and holidays. There are small caves nearby.

There are two main border crossings into Guatemala: one at Ciudad Cuauhtémoc (La Mesilla in Guatemala), reached via Route 190 from San Cristóbal de las Casas, and the other at Tapachula along the coastal Route 200 from the neighbouring state of Oaxaca. A third option is to cross the border by boat, east of Palenque, along the rivers Usumacinta or San Pedro. Note: if planning on returning to Mexico after an excursion to Guatemala, ensure you get an exit stamp, at the immigration office. Pick up your tourist card and a slip of paper, take this to any bank, pay US$23 and the slip is stamped. Not doing this can lead to problems when you try to leave Mexico again.

Ciudad Cuauhtémoc

South of San Cristóbal and heading for Guatemala, follow the 170-km paved road via **Teopisca** to **Comitán de Domínguez**. From Comitán the road winds down to the Guatemalan border at Ciudad Cuauhtémoc via La Trinitaria (near the turn-off to Lagunas de Montebello, restaurant but no hotel).

Ciudad Cuauhtémoc, despite its name, is not a city, but just a few buildings; the **Cristóbal Colón** bus station is opposite Immigration, with an overpriced restaurant and an excellent hotel. Be sure to surrender your tourist card and get your exit stamp at Mexican Immigration in Ciudad Cuauhtémoc before boarding a pickup for Guatemalan immigration; you will only have to go back if you don't. A pickup to the Guatemalan border, 4 km, costs US$0.65 per person. Walk 100 m to Immigration and Customs (open until 2100). Beyond the Guatemalan post at La Mesilla, see box, page 58, a beautiful stretch of road leads 85 km to Huehuetenango. This route is far more interesting than the one through Tapachula; the border crossing at Ciudad Cuauhtémoc is also reported as easier than that at Talismán.

Tapachula crossings: Talismán and Ciudad Hidalgo

The Talismán bridge lies 8 km from Tapachula and provides good onward connections to the western highlands and Quetzaltenango. It's a fairly grubby crossing with plenty of aggressive moneychangers who you should avoid doing business with. Further south, 37 km from Tapachula, Ciudad Hidalgo is a busy border town that connects with Guatemala's Pacific Highway.

Río Usumacinta route

The Río Usumacinta route takes you by road to Benemérito (southeast of Yaxchilán and Bonampak), boat to Sayaxché, Guatemala and then road to Flores. **Autotransportes Comitán Lagos de Montebello** buses (Avenida Manuel Velasco Suárez, Palenque, three blocks from food market) run eight a day starting at 0400 until 1530 to **Benemérito**, about six hours, on the Mexican side of the Usumacinta. You must visit immigration, about 3 km from Benemérito, to sign out of Mexico (the bus will wait).

Once in Benemérito where there is a 2100 curfew (two basic *pensiones*), hope for a boat to Guatemala; this may take a couple of days. The boat goes to Sayaxché and should stop at Pipiles for immigration. A trading boat takes two days, US$4-5; a motorized canoe eight hours, US$5-10. You can also charter a fast boat for about US$200. From Sayaxché, buses run to Flores.

For an alternative (and much easier) route, take the bus from Palenque to Frontera Corozal with Transportes Chamoan, Hidalgo 141, roughly hourly from 0500-1700, US$6. About an hour down this route at Km 61 is an excellent breakfast stop, Valle Escondido. Keep an eye out for hummingbirds. In Corozal there is an immigration post, two hotels and restaurants. It's a 30-minute *lancha* ride to Bethel, US$30 for one to two people, US$40 for three to four people; or a cheap five-minute ride to La Técnica, see box, page 58.

Tenosique and Río San Pedro route

The Río San Pedro route starts at Tenosique, a friendly place east of Palenque (money exchange at clothing shop, Ortiz y Alvarez at Calle 28 No 404, good rates for dollars to quetzales, poor for dollars to pesos). From here, the classic route takes you by road to La Palma, boat to El Naranjo, in Guatemala, and then road to Flores. A newer, more convenient route begins at El Ceibo, 60 km southeast of Tenosique.

From Tenosique to **La Palma** on the Río San Pedro, *colectivos* starting at 0600 from in front of the market, one hour, US$1, two hours by bus (from Tenosique bus station, which is outside town, take taxi, US$1.70 or *colectivo* to 'Centro', or walk 20 minutes). Taxi to La Palma US$7, shared by all passengers. From La Palma boats leave to El Naranjo when they have enough passengers, but timings are very irregular (they wait for a minimum of five passengers), at least 4½ hours, US$22. Be at the boat one hour early, it sometimes leaves ahead of schedule; if this happens ask around for someone to chase it, US$3-4 per person for three people. If there are fewer than five passengers, the boat may be cancelled, in which case you must either wait for the next one, or hire a *rápido* (US$125, maximum four people). You may be able to arrange a slower boat for up to six people for US$100. In La Palma, one restaurant will change money at weekends at a reasonable rate.

It is a beautiful boat trip, through mangroves with flocks of white herons and the occasional alligator, dropping people off at homesteads. There is a stop at the border post two hours into the journey to sign out of Mexico, a lovely spot with a lake and lilies. In the rain, your backpack will get wet; take waterproofs and a torch/flashlight. There are no officials on arrival at the jetty in El Naranjo; Immigration is a short way uphill on the right (entry will cost US$5 in quetzales or dollars, beware extra unofficial charges at customs); bus tickets to Flores are sold here.

For the newer, more reliable route, take an hourly bus from Tenosique to El Ceibo. They depart from calle 45 and 16, behind the market, 0600-1700, one hour. Once at the border, catch a pickup to Río San Pedro. There are frequent *lanchas* to El Naranjo until 1700, US$3.50, 30 minutes.

Route to Tapachula → *For listings, see pages 90-111.*

Travelling from the neighbouring state of Oaxaca, Routes 190 and 200 merge to cross the Isthmus of Tehuantepec. Accommodation is available at **Zanatepec**, and **Tapanatepec**, which is where Highway 190 heads northeast to Tuxtla Gutiérrez and Highway 200 continues southeast along the coast of Chiapas to the Guatemalan border.

Arriaga → *Colour map 1, B1. Phone code: 966.*

Arriaga is a good stopping place just across the state border that separates Oaxaca from Chiapas; many banks around zócalo for exchange. The road from Arriaga to Tapachula is a four-lane divided freeway.

From Arriaga, Route 200 continues to Tonalá, formerly a very quiet town but now noisy and dirty. Bus Tonalá–Tapachula, three hours, US$6.75; also buses to Tuxtla. This is by far the most direct road for travellers seeking the quickest way from Mexico City to Guatemala.

Puerto Arista → *Colour map 1, B1. Phone code: 961.*
Along the coast from Tonalá to Tapachula there are several fine-looking and undeveloped beaches, although waves and currents are dangerous. Puerto Arista (17 km south of Tonalá) is now being built up, but it is still a relatively peaceful area with 32 km of clean beach to relax on with no salespeople; bus/*colectivo* from Tonalá every hour, 45 minutes, US$0.60, taxi US$2; plenty of buses to Arriaga, US$0.75. Many hotels, motels and restaurants on the beach, which is hot and, in the wet season, has sandflies.

Buses also from Tonalá to **Boca del Cielo** further down the coast, which is good for bathing and has *cabañas* with hammocks, and similarly **Cabeza del Toro**. **Paredón**, on the huge Laguna del Mar Muerto, 14 km west of Tonalá, has excellent seafood and one very basic guesthouse. You can take a local fishing boat out into the lagoon to swim; the shore stinks because fishermen clean fish on the beach among dogs and pigs. There are frequent buses.

On the way to Tapachula you pass through **Pijijiapan** where there is the **Hotel Pijijilton** next to the **Cristóbal Colón** bus station. From **Huixtla**, a good, scenic road winds off into the mountains parallel to the border, towards Ciudad Cuauhtémoc and Comitán.

Tapachula and around → *For listings, see pages 90-111. Colour map 1, C1. Phone code: 962.*

Once little more than an obscure border town in a lesser visited corner of Chiapas, more than US$70 million has recently been invested in Tapachula, with a view to exploiting its strategic location on the Pacific coast. The result? Puerto Chiapas: a major new port large enough to receive the latest generation cruise, container and cargo ships. It's hoped that this ambitious new development will bring unprecedented visitors to Tapachula and Chiapas, and the tourist board's slick new brochures are an exercise in shameless self-promotion. Yet beyond the manicured lawns of the port, Tapachula is still the same shambling old border town it's always been, more characteristic of Central America than Mexico. For now, at least, this city has yet to blossom.

For orientation, **avenidas** run north–south, calles east–west (Oriente–Poniente). Odd-numbered **calles** are north of Calle Central, odd **avenidas** are east of Avenida Central. For information, contact the **municipal tourist office** ① *8a Av Norte and 3a Pte, T962-625 0441, www.turismotapachula.gob.mx*; or the **state tourist office** ① *Plaza Kamico, Central Ote, T962-625 5409*, away from the centre. Tapachula has an airport and is a major crossing junction for Guatemala.

There's little to see in town itself, save a small but captivating archaeological museum, **Museo Regional del Soconusco**, west side of the plaza. But beyond the city, a flurry of attractions have opened in anticipation of the big tourist influx.

Around Tapachula
La Ruta Café is an agro-tourism development that includes 13 coffee *fincas*, many of German origin. Some of them are stunningly positioned, with luxury, mountain-top accommodation and spas; others have facilities for adventure sports like biking and zip-lining. Speak to the tourist office for more details.

Caicrochis ① *F962-642 6692, Tue-Sun, 1000-1700, US$3,* is the oldest crocodile reserve in Mexico and home to around a thousand of the beasts. Don't dangle the kids too close! A couple of 'eco-parks' have opened that are really just touristy playgrounds with opportunities for activities like swimming, rock climbing and quad-biking. They include **Club Catay Maya** ① *Carretera a Carillopuerto San Agustín Jitotol, www.cataymaya.com;* and **Parque Ecoturístico La Changa** ① *Carretera a la Presa José Cecilio del Valle s/n, T626-5592, www.lachanga.com.mx.*

There are several beaches near Tapachula, including Playa Linda, San Benito, Las Escolleras and Barra Cahoacán. 5 km from Playa Linda you'll find **Laguna de Pozuelos**, a lagoon with rich mangroves and wildlife including snakes, lizards and aquatic birds. Similarly, **La Encrucijada Biosphere Reserve** is home to various species of local fauna.

The ruins of **Izapa** (proto-Classic stelae, small museum) lie just off the road to Talismán; the part of the site on the north is easily visible but a larger portion is on the south side of the highway, about 1 km away, ask caretaker for guidance. To reach Izapa take a combi from Unión Progreso bus station.

Forty-five kilometres northeast of Tapachula, beyond the turning to Talismán, is **Unión Juárez**, where you can have your papers stamped and proceed on foot via Talquián to the Guatemalan border at Sibinal.

A worthwhile hike can be made up the **Tacaná volcano** (4150 m), which takes two to three days from Unión Juárez. Ask for the road to Chiquihuete; no cars. The Tapachula tourist office can help; in Unión Juárez ask for Sr Umberto Ríos at **Restaurante Montaña**, he will put you in touch with guide Moisés Hernández, who charges US$15 a day. It is possible to stay overnight in Don Emilio Velásquez's barn halfway up, US$2; he offers coffee and *tortillas.* At the top are some *cabañas* in which you sleep for free; sleeping bag essential.

◉ Tabasco and Chiapas listings

For Sleeping and Eating price codes and other relevant information, see Essentials pages 31-33.

◉ Sleeping

Villahermosa *p67*

The price difference between a reasonable and a basic hotel can be negligible, so you might as well go for the former. Try to book in advance, especially during the holiday season (May onwards). Hotels tend to be full Mon-Thu; arrive before nightfall if you can. For cheaper options there are a number of hotels and guesthouses of varying standards and cleanliness along Av Constitución, in the centre, 1 block from the river.

AL-A Olmeca Plaza, Madero 418, T993-358 0102, www.hotelolmecaplaza. Large, central, professionally managed hotel with good services including restaurant, gym and pool. Some rooms have good views.

B-C Chocos, Lino Merino 100 and Constitución, T993-312 9444. Signposted from far away, not too hard to find. Clean, good-value rooms with a/c and telephone. Restaurant attached.

B-C Provincia Express, Lerdo 303, T993-314 5376, provincial _express@hotmail.com. Good, comfortable rooms with a/c and cable TV. American breakfast is included in the price.

C Hotel San Francisco, Av Madero 604, T993-312 3198. Reasonable central hotel, with adequate rooms, hot water, and fan.

C Oriente, Madero 425, T993-312 0121, hotel-oriente@hotmail.com. The rooms smell clean and fresh at this tidy hotel. They have hot showers and fan, pricier with a/c.

D-E Hotel Lino, Lino Merino 823, very close to **ADO** terminal. T993-148 1924. Basic rooms with good showers, quiet despite its location, more expensive with a/c.

Tuxtla Gutiérrez *p69, map p69*
There is plenty of budget accommodation near the former **ADO** terminal, Av 2 Norte Ote Pte 323, beyond the plaza. (Some of them also have left-luggage for a small fee even if you're not a hotel guest. Look for signs outside.)

A Hotel María Eugenia, Av Central Oriente 507, T961-613 3767, www.mariaeugenia. com.mx. Pleasant rooms in the heart of town. Internet, a/c, cable TV, parking, pool and restaurant.

B Palace Inn, Blv Belisario Domínguez 1081, 4 km from centre, T961-615 0574, palaceinn@ hotmail.com. Generally recommended, lovely garden, pool, noisy video bar.

C-D Plaza Chiapas, Av 2 Norte Ote y 2 Ote Norte, T961-613 8365. Small, clean rooms with hot showers, cable TV and a/c. Cheaper with fan. Enclosed car park. Recommended.

C-D Regional San Marcos, 1 Sur y 2 Ote Sur 176, T961-613 1940, hotelsanmarcos@prodigy. net.mx. Simple, but comfortable rooms with bath, fan or a/c, cheaper without TV.

D Hostal San Miguel, 3a Av Sur Poniente No 510, T961-611 4459, www.hostalsan miguel.com.mx. Nice, modern hostel with internet access, TV room, kitchen and lockers.

D Posada del Sol, 3a Pte Norte and 2a Pte Nte, T961-614 6220, 1 block from **Cristóbal Colón** buses. Rooms with hot shower and fan. Good service, good value, basic.

D-E Estrella, 2 Ote Norte 322, T961-612 3827. Friendly, clean hotel, slightly run-down, but good value. Rooms with bath and free drinking water, recommended.

Camping

E La Hacienda, Belisario Domínguez 1197 (west end of town on Route 190), T961-602 6946, www.lahaciendahotel.com. 4 spaces with hook-up, hot showers, restaurant, mini-pool, a bit noisy and not easily accessible for RVs over 6 m; owner speaks English.

San Cristóbal de las Casas *p71, map p72*
Look on the bulletin board outside the tourist office for guesthouses advertising cheap B&B.

AL-A Casa Mexicana, 28 de Agosto 1, T967-678 0698, www.hotelcasamexicana.com. This hotel is filled with art work and Mexican crafts. Services include sauna, Wi-Fi, parking and babysitters. The master suite has a jacuzzi, and the attractive courtyard is lush and filled with plants. There is a newer wing on the opposite side of the road with a good craft shop attached. Restaurant **Los Magueyes** and **Bar Cucaracha** attached to old wing, open 0700-2200. Highly recommended.

A Na Bolom Hotel Museo, Vicente Guerrero 33, T967-678 1418, www.nabolom.org. Beautiful, 17-room guesthouse in a cultural centre (see page 73). Rooms have bath and fireplace. Insightful tours available. Traditional Mexican meal every night at 1900 in the courtyard restaurant. Recommended.

A Posada Diego de Mazariegos, 5 de Febrero 1, 1 block north of plaza, T967-678 0833, www.diegodemazariegos.com.mx. Comfortable and quiet, almost convent-like atmosphere. Comfy common room. There's a travel agency and restaurant inside, as well as a bar, **Tequila Zoo**. Sun buffet at 1400. Recommended.

A-B Posada El Paraíso, Av 5 de Febrero 19, T967-678 0085, www.hotelposadaparaiso. Mexican/Swiss-owned. Impeccable rooms, many open onto pretty patio. Excellent, atmospheric restaurant, parking nearby beneath cathedral. Highly recommended.

A-B Posada Los Morales, Ignacio Allende 17, T967-678 1472, www.haciendalosmorales.com. An elegant hotel with beautiful views over the city. The cottages here have open fires, kitchen and hot showers. The owner is a collector and exporter of rustic-style Mexican furniture and the interior richly reflects this. Recommended.

B El Cerrillo, Belisario Domínguez 27, T967-678 1283, www.hotelesjardines.com. Nice carpeted rooms and a lovely rooftop patio. Wi-Fi and cable TV. Recommended.

B-C Posada Margarita, Real de Guadalupe 34, T967-678 0957, www.laposada margarita.com. This popular professionally managed hotel is spotless. Comfortable rooms have safes, cable TV and 24-hr hot water. There's a terrace, travel agency, free internet and an expensive restaurant serving wholefood.

C Barón de Las Casas, Belisario Domínguez 2, T967-678 0881, www.chiapas.turista.com.mx. Clean, comfortable, good value. Recommended.

C Capri, Insurgentes 54, T967-678 3018, hotel_capri81@hotmail.com, near first-class bus terminal. Large, reliable hotel with plenty of rooms and differing tariffs. Quieter rooms at the back. Clean and helpful. Recommended.

C Palacio de Moctezuma, Juárez 16, T967-678 0352, www.palaciodemoctezuma.com. Colonial-style hotel founded in 1727. Rooms have hot water and cable TV, good Mexican food is served in the restaurant. Rooms downstairs sometimes damp – 1st floor much better. Highly recommended.

C Posada Real Jovel, Flavio Paniagua 28, T967-678 1734, www.mundochiapas.com/hotelposadajovel. Villa-style hotel with clean, comfortable rooms. The beautiful garden is laden with fruit trees, and the roof terrace has fine views. There's a restaurant, and rooms over the road are half the price. Recommended.

C Suites Encanto, 10 de Marzo 42, T967-672 2679, suitesencanto5@gmail.com. This hotel has comfortable suites with fireplaces, cookers, fridges and sofas. There are cheap dorm beds too (**F**), and the manager can organize other accommodation if full. Excellent value. Highly recommended.

C-D Real del Valle, Av Real de Guadalupe 14, next to plaza, T967-678 0680, hrvalle@mundomaya.com.mx. Very clean and friendly. Avoid noisy room next to the kitchen. Rooms have hot water. Well maintained and good value.

C-E Los Camellos, Real de Guadalupe 110, T967-116 0097, loscamellos@hotmail.com. Popular backpackers' hostel with dorms and private rooms. There are 24-hr hot showers, free coffee and drinking water, book exchange, shisha café and hammocks. French/Mexican-run, friendly and hospitable staff.

D Posada San Agustín, Ejército Nacional 7, T967-678 1816. Large, clean, comfortable rooms, some with shared bath. Family-run and friendly. Recommended.

D Posada Vallarta, Hermanos Pineda, near 1st-class bus terminal, T967-678 0465. Quiet, clean, tidy, nice plants. Hot water and parking.

D-E Posada Lucella, Av Insurgentes 55, T967-678 0956, opposite Iglesia Santa Lucía (the bells can be noisy). Clean, economical rooms set around a patio, with bath, fan and hot water. Cheaper with shared bath.

D-F Casa Babylon, on Josefa Ortiz and Ramón Corona, T967-678 0590, www.casababylon.wordpress.com. Funky youth hostel with bargain dorm beds and private rooms (cheaper without bath). Somewhat messy, with communal kitchen, patio space, lockers, book exchange and laundry. Hot showers and free drinking water.

E Posada Lupita, near bus terminal on Insurgentes. Nice plant-filled courtyard, popular, often full.

E Posadita, Flavio Paniagua 30. With bath, clean, laundry facilities. Recommended.

E-F Posada 5, Comitán 13, T967-674 7660, www.posada5.com. Dorms and private rooms, with or without shared bath, nice garden, tours organized, book exchange, free internet, free coffee and tea, communal kitchen, friendly and laid-back.

E-F Posada Doña Rosita, Ejército Nacional 13, T967-678 8676, posadadn_rosita@hotmail.com. 3 blocks from main plaza. This *posada* is more like a friendly family home, presided over by Doña Rosita, an experienced healer who knows about herbs and local affairs. She heals sick guests, offers healthy organic breakfasts, and runs courses in cooking and natural medicine. Her dorms and rooms are basic, but there's hot water 24 hrs, just ask Rosita to switch it on as she has a good water-saving scheme. Highly recommended.

F Casa de Huéspedes Santa Lucía, Clemente Robles 21, 1 block from the Transportes Lacondia bus terminal, T967-678 0315. Basic rooms, some with bath, some without. There's hot water 24 hrs.

Camping

Rancho San Nicolás, T967-678 0057, at end of Francisco León, 1.5 km east of centre. Trailer park in a beautiful, quiet location, take warm blankets or clothing as the temperature really drops at night, hot showers, US$7 for room in *cabaña*, US$5 to camp, US$12 for camper van with 2 people (electric hook-up), children free, laundry facilities. Recommended.

Trailer park Bonampak, Route 190 at west end of town, T967-678 1621. Full hook-up, hot shower, heated pool in season, restaurant, US$10 per vehicle, US$5 per person.

Agua Azul *p78*

There are 2 places with *cabañas* for hammocks (hammock rental US$1.50 and up, US$3.50 per person in beds in dormitory); if staying, be very careful of your belongings; thefts have been reported.

Camping

Camping Casa Blanca is popular and reliable, opposite the parking lot; camping costs US$3.50, for a tent or hammock, and US$0.15 for use of toilets (all Agua Azul toilets charge up to US$0.50). You can also camp at the **Estación Climatológica** at Paso del Cayuco (**F**); it's about 15-20 mins' walk up the falls to the wire fence station.

RVs can stay overnight at Agua Azul, using the facilities, without paying extra (as long as you do not leave the park). Follow the path up the falls to a 2nd campsite, cheaper, less crowded. There are more *cabañas* and pleasant places to sling a hammock further upstream, all cheaper and less touristy than lower down.

Palenque town *p78, map p79*

Palenque town has a plethora of cheap lodgings, but it's generally a hot, dirty and unappealing place to stay. The exception is **La Cañada** district in the northwest, a burgeoning (and more expensive) tourist zone buffeted by lush jungle foliage and trees. With a number of new places opening up, though, the jungle setting is getting a bit thinner. Remember that humidity and bugs can be a real scourge in Palenque -- always check the room for dampness, odours and creepy-crawlies.

B Chan Kah Centro, corner of Juárez and Independencia, T916-345 0318. Restaurant and terrace bar overlooking the main plaza, www.chan-kah.com.mx. Sister hotel and convention centre (**AL**) with a pleasant pool and verdant setting, on the road to the ruins.

B-C Jade, Hidalgo 61, T916-345 0463. Family-run hotel with clean, comfortable rooms. Hot water, a/c and cable TV. Recommended. Peaceful. Will store luggage.

C Kashlan, 5 de Mayo 116, T916-345 0297, www.palenque.com.mx/kashlan. Long-standing Palenque favourite. Clean, mostly quiet rooms (except those facing the street) have bath, fan or a/c (**B**). The owners are helpful and friendly and offer a generous discount to holders of this book. Recommended.

C Posada Aguila Real, 20 de Noviembre s/n, T916-345 0004, www.posadaaguilareal.com. Very comfortable, attractive lodgings. Rooms are clean with hot water, cable TV and a/c. Helpful staff.

C Posada Kin, Abasolo s/n, 20 de Noviembre y 5 de Mayo, near zócalo, T916-345 1714, posada_kin@hotmail.com. Clean and large doubles with bathroom, fan, safe and luggage store. Recommended. Organizes tours in the area.

C-D San Miguel, Hidalgo and Aldama, above **Union Pharmacy**, T916-345 0152. Big clean rooms with balcony, hot water and fan. Pricier with TV and a/c. There are cheap dorms too. Good value.

D Marantha, 20 de Noviembre 19, T916-345 2348. Rooms have cable TV, hot water 24 hrs and fan, some with a/c (**C**). Family-run, friendly service.

D Yun-Kax, Av Corregidora 87 (behind Santo Domingo). Quiet, clean, large rooms with, hot water and fan (**C** with a/c). Recommended.

D-E Posada Canek, 20 de Noviembre 43. Nice rooms and dorm beds (**F**). More

expensive rooms have bath. English spoken, recently refurbished rooms have TV and a/c. Friendly, chatty and helpful owner.
E Posada Johanna, 20 de Noviembre and Allende, T916-345 0687. Tidy, family-run joint with basic, good value rooms.

La Cañada

A Maya Tulipanes, Cañada 6, T916-345 0201, www.mayatulipanes.com.mx. The slightly impersonal rooms have a/c and cable TV, and vary in price, size and quality. There's a garage, pool, bar and restaurant. The restaurant does karaoke in the evenings, but luckily also has soundproof walls.
B La Posada Cañada, Nicolás Bravo, T916-345 0437, nochepat@ hotmail.com. Cheapish, basic rooms, with hot water and fan. Kitchen facilities available to guests.
B-C Xibalba, Merle Green 9, T916-345 0411, www.hotelxibalba.com. A pleasant, hospitable hotel with 2 wings (1 older, 1 newer). Clean, comfortable, bug-free rooms, with safes and a/c. There's an impressive reproduction lid of Pacal's tomb, somewhat larger than the original. The owner is friendly and knowledgeable. Recommended.
D Yaxkin Hostel, Av Hidalgo corner with 5a Pte, T916-345 0102, www.hostalyaxkin.com. This is an economical alternative to the more upmarket hotels in La Cañada. Dorms and bungalows include a nice breakfast, popular with backpackers, free internet, movie lounge, *palapa*-style bar and restaurant area, kitchen, parking, laundry and luggage storage. Recommended.

Road to the ruins

Exuberant rainforest flanks the road to the ruins, making the accommodations interesting and attractive; **El Panchán**, a collection of budget *cabañas* is the most famous and popular. This area is plagued with bugs, ants and creepy-crawlies, in addition to raging humidity. Ensure your room or *cabaña* has secure screens and a net. Bring repellent, especially in the wet season.

AL Maya Tucán, Carretera Palenque, Km 0.5, T916-345 0290, www.tucan sihoplaya.com/palenque. Clean, pleasant hotel with swimming pool, bar and restaurant. Rooms have a/c and lovely views.
C-D Margarita and Ed's, El Panchán, edcabanas@yahoo.com (although the internet connection here is erratic). The plushest *cabañas* at El Panchán, all with private bath. If you don't fancy getting too close to nature, there are also modern rooms (**A**). A friendly, restful place oozing good vibes. The mattresses are amazing.
D Chato's, El Panchán, panchan@yahoo. com.mx, inside **Don Mucho's** restaurant. Cabins with private or shared bath.
D-E Jungle Palace, part of Chato's Cabañas. Economical rooms with private or share bath.
D-F Elementos Naturales, past El Panchán, www.elementosnaturales.org. Youth hostel where you can sling a hammock or camp. Includes breakfast. Pleasant outdoor feel.
D-F La Palapa, 1.5 km from the ruins inside the national park. *Cabañas*, camping with or without roof cover, space for hammocks. A bit basic, but the owners are restoring this pretty site right by a lake. They grow organic fruit and veg and run a Mexican restaurant where the food is prepared in front of you on a grill. There's an all-night bar with dancing, which can make it a bit noisy. All toilets are separate from the *cabañas* in order to keep the nearby lake clean. Group discounts.
E Jaguar, on the quieter side, across over the road from El Panchán, but the philosophy is still the same. Shared bath only.
E-F Rakshita, El Panchán. Delightful Rakshita has seen better days – the meditation area has been dismantled, the hippies have fled and the vegetarian restaurant has closed. Still, the cabins are intact and it remains a friendly, economical place to stay. Dorm beds (**G**) and very cheap hammock spaces (**F**) are also available.
Camping Trailer Park Mayabell, 2 km before entrance to ruins, T916-341 6977, www.mayabell.com.mx. Space for tents, hammocks and caravans. There are also

comfortable *cabañas* with a/c and private bath. Pool and live music in the evenings. Recommended.

Yaxchilán, Bonampak and Lacanjá *p84*

There is basic accommodation at Bonampak; take hammock and mosquito net. Thieving has been reported. **Camping** is restricted to the INAH site on the Usumacinta.

At Lacanjá there are 4 campsites where you can sling a hammock: **Kin Bor, Vicente K'in, Carlos Chan Bor** and **Manuel Chan Bor**.

Comitán and around *p86*

Accommodation is inferior in quality and almost twice the price of San Cristóbal.

B Internacional, Av Central Sur Belisario Domínguez 22, near plaza, T963-632 0110. Comfortable, attractive rooms with cable TV. There's a decent restaurant attached. Rooms are cheaper in older part of hotel.

B Los Lagos de Montebello, Belisario Domínguez 144, corner of 3 Av, T963-632 0657, www.hotellagosdemontebello.com. Noisy but good.

C Pensión Delfín, Av Domínguez 21, on plaza, T963-632 0013, www.hotel-delfin-comitan.com. Pleasant colonial-style building with comfortable rooms, garden and court-yard. There's parking and cable TV. Recommended, but don't leave valuables near windows even if they appear closed.

D Hospedaje Montebello, 1a Calle Norte Pte 10, T963-632 3572, 1 block from **Delfín**. Clean, sunny courtyard, laundry, TV, internet and parking, friendly. Recommended.

E San Francisco, 1a Av Ote Norte 13A, T963-110 6244. The rooms are clean and economical, but still slightly pokey. There's cable TV and hot water 24 hrs.

Río Usumacinta route *p87*

D Centro Turístico and Grutas Tsolk'in, Benemérito, www.ecoturlacandona.com. Clean, well-kept rooms with communal bathrooms. Much more friendly and helpful than the nearby **Escudo Jaguar** (which is overpriced and unfriendly). Less than 5 mins'

walk from the dock. Take a right turning opposite immigration office.

Tenosique and Río San Pedro route *p88*

D Rome, Calle 28, 400, T934-342 2151. Clean, will change dollars for residents, bath, not bad.

E Azulejos, Calle 26, 416. With bath, fan, clean, hot water, friendly, helpful owner speaks some English, opposite church.

E Casa de Huéspedes La Valle, Calle 19. With bath, good, but a little grubby.

Route to Tapachula *p88*

AL Argovia Finca Resort, Carretera Nueva Alemania Km 39 + 2, Tapachula, T962-692 3051, www.argovia.com.mx. Nice new eco-friendly spot with 12 cabins that sleep 2 each; outside of town.

C Galilea, Av Hidalgo 111 and Callejón Ote, Tonalá, T966-663 0239. With bath, a/c, good, basic cheap rooms on 1st floor, balconies, on main square, with good restaurants.

C Hotel El Estraneo, Av Central, Pijijiapan, T918-645 0264. Very nice, parking in courtyard.

C Posada San Rafael, Zanatepec. Motel. Very comfortable, safe parking.

C-D Ik-Lumaal, 1a Av Norte 6, near zócalo, Arriaga, T966-662 1164. A/c, clean, quiet, good restaurant.

D Motel La Misión, Tapanatepec, on Hwy 190 on northern outskirts, T971-717 0140. Fan, hot water, clean, TV, hammock outside each room, affiliated restaurant, very good.

D-E Colonial, Callejón Ferrocarril 2, Arriaga, next to bus station, T966-662 0856. Clean, friendly, quiet, limited free parking.

E Sabrina, Pijijiapan. Nice, clean and quiet, safe parking.

F Hotel Iris, Callejón Ferrocarril, Arriaga, near bus station. Bath, fan, basic.

Camping

José's Camping Cabañas (ask *colectivo* from Tonalá to take you there, US$0.60 extra), at east edge of Puerto Arista, follow signs. Canadian-run, well organized, clean, laundry, restaurant (including vegetarian), library.

Tapachula and around *p89*

AL Loma Real, Carretera Costera 200, Km 244, 1 km north of city, T962-626 1440, www.hotel lomareal.com.mx. Large, upmarket hotel with comfortable rooms, suites and bungalows. With pool, gym and parking.

A-B San Francisco, Av Central Sur 94, 15 mins from centre, T962- 620 1000, www. sucasaentapachula.com. This large, professional hotel has clean, modern rooms with a/c and hot water. With pool, gym, bar and restaurant.

C Santa Julia, next to OCC terminal, T962-626 2486. Bath, phone, TV, a/c, clean, good. Some discounts in high season. Its location next to main road and bus station can make it very noisy, particularly early mornings.

C-D Galerias Hotel & Arts, 4a Av Norte 21, T962-642 7596, www.galeriasartshotel.com. Modern hotel with an arty focus, 5% discount if paying by cash, a/c, cable TV, hot and cold water, Wi-Fi and parking in the town centre.

C-D Hotel Plaza Guizar, 4a Av Norte 27, T962-626 1400. Clean, tidy and basic, with fan. Plenty of rooms and sitting space. Good views over the city from balcony.

D San Román, Calle 9 Pte between Av 10 y 12 Norte. Very cheap motel-style place. Parking for cars and bikes. Friendly.

🍴 Eating

Villahermosa *p67*

In high season a number of eateries, bars and discos open up along the riverfront. Good for sunset drinks and dining, but take mosquito repellent.

♥♥♥-♥♥ Los Manglares, Madero 418, inside Hotel Olmeca Plaza. Attractive restaurant serving seafood, meat, chicken and breakfast. Excellent 4-course lunch buffet.

♥♥♥-♥♥ Los Tulipanes, Malecón, south of Paseo Tabasco, 2 blocks from Puente Grijalva 2. Thu-Sun 0800-1800, Mon-Wed 1300-1800, not open for dinner. Nice location, friendly staff, good fish and seafood. Recommended.

♥♥♥-♥♥ Villa Rica, Corredor Turístico Malecón. Open 1200-2000, sometimes closed in low season. A pleasant, modern restaurant with an enticing waterfront location. Tasty seafood including fish fillets and shellfish.

♥♥ Capitán Beuló II, Malecón Carlos A Madrazo, kiosko I, T993-314 4644, Ventas3@hotelolmecaplaza.com. A novel dining experience, with gastronomic cruises along Villahermosa's waterways, accompanied by the sounds of live marimba. Gastro tour Sun, 1430, sightseeing tour Wed-Fri 1700 and Sat-Sun 1200, 1430, 1730 and 1930. Children under 10 pay half price.

♥♥ El Matador, Av César Sandino No 101a, www.elmatador.com.mx. Open daily 24 hrs. Local meat dishes, *tacos al pastor*, good value.

♥♥ Rodizio do Brasil, Parque la Choca, Stand Grandero, T993-316 2895, informacion@ restauranterodizio.com. Speciality *espadas*, good Brazilian food.

♥ For good tacos head to Calle Aldama, Nos 611, 613 and 615, where there are 3 decent places. These are cheap and cheerful, but very good value, with great selections.

Cafés

Café La Cabaña, Juárez 303-A, across the way from the Museo de Historia de Tabasco. Has outdoor tables where town elders congregate to debate the day's issues over piping cups of cappuccino. Very entertaining to watch. No meals.

El Café de la Calle Juárez, Juárez 513, indoor/outdoor café. Great for breakfast, good coffee, a new menu every month. Outdoor tables are great for people-watching.

South of Villahermosa *p68*

♥♥ Restaurante Familiar El Timón, Carretera Villahermosa–Teapa Km 52.5 s/n, Teapa.

Tuxtla Gutiérrez *p69, map p69*

♥♥ Bonampak, Blv Belisario Domínguez 180, T961-602 5916. Formerly an upmarket hotel, now only the restaurant remains. Decent Mexican and North American dishes, quite pricey.

♯-♯ **El Borrego Líder**, 2 Ote Norte 262. Breakfasts and meat dishes, popular with locals.
♯-♯ **El Mesón de Quijote**, Central Ote 337. Clean, cheap place on the central avenue, serves Mexican fare, tacos for less than US$1.
♯-♯ **Las Pichanchas**, Av Central Ote 857, T961-612 5351, www.laspichanchas.com.mx. Daily 1200-2400. Pretty courtyard, typical food, live marimba music 1430-1730 and 2030-2330 and folkloric ballet 2100-2200, daily. Sister restaurant at **Mirador Copoya**, overlooking the Sumidero Canyon.
♯ **Antigua Fonda**, 2 Ote Sur 182, opposite La Chata. *Tortas*, *licuados*, breakfasts and general Mexican fare.
♯ **El Huipil**, 2 Ote Norte 250a. Clean locals' place serving *comida corrida* and *menú del día*. Also has a good breakfast selection.
♯ **La Chata**, opposite Hotel San Marcos. One of the few touristy places, grilled meat and *menú del día*, OK.
♯ **Los Molcajetes**, in the arches behind the cathedral. Cheap all-day meal deals including tacos, *enchiladas suizas*, *chilaquiles* and other staples. Several other restaurants lining the arches offer similar good value.

Cafés and ice cream parlours
Café Avenida, Central Pte 230. Good coffee shop, does cappuccino and espresso.
Mi Café, 1a Pte Norte 121. Interesting locals' place serving organic coffee by the bag or cup.

Chiapa de Corzo *p70*
There are good seafood restaurants by the river.
♯ **Parachic's**, near the main plaza, opposite the church. Excellent breakfasts and lunches.

San Cristóbal de las Casas *p71, map p72*
There are several cheap, local places on Madero east of Plaza 31 de Marzo.
♯♯♯ **Agapandos**, Calzada Roberta 16, inside Parador San Juan de Dios. This elegant restaurant is very secluded and quiet, overlooking a fragrant garden at the foot of the mountains. They serve sumptuous

crêpes, eggs, chicken and meat dishes with a local flavour and Mediterranean twist.
♯♯♯-♯♯ **La Fonda Argentina**, Adelina Flores 12, Good selection of steaks, fillets and other carnivorous, Argentine cuisine.
♯♯♯ **El Fogón de Jovel**, Av 16 Septiembre 11, opposite the Jade Museum. One of the best restaurants in town and a great place to experiment and try out a variety of local dishes. Try the local liquor, *posh*. Colourful vibe with 2 themed rooms – **Revolution** and **Mask**. Live music at night.
♯♯♯ **La Paloma**, Hidalgo 3, a few doors from zócalo. Inventive regional dishes at reasonable prices; international cuisine. Classy place, popular with tourists, best coffee, good breakfast, good pasta, art gallery next door, live music at weekends.
♯♯♯ **Madre Tierra**, Insurgentes 19 (opposite Franciscan church), T967-678 4297. Anglo-Mexican owned, European dishes, vegetarian specialities, good breakfasts, wholemeal breads from bakery (also takeaway), pies, brownies, chocolate cheesecake, Cuban and reggae music in the evenings, popular with travellers.
♯♯♯ **Tierra y Cielo**, Juárez 1, www.tierraycielo. com.mx. International food, with a menu that changes every Sun. Modern and clean. Good breakfast buffets Thu, Sat and Sun.
♯♯♯ **Tuluc**, Insurgentes 5. Good value especially breakfasts, fresh *tamales* every morning, near plaza, popular, classical music, art for sale and toys on display.
♯♯♯-♯ **Cocodrilo Café & Bar**, Plaza 31 de Marzo. Smart café/bar on the south side of the plaza serving snacks, cocktails and cappuccinos. They host live music, salsa and merengue.
♯♯♯-♯ **Emiliano's Moustache**, Av Crescencio Rosas 7. *Taquería*, popular with Mexicans, tacos from US$0.40. Excellent-value lunch menu. Recommended.
♯♯♯-♯ **Joveleño**, Real de Guadalupe 66, T674-6278. Pretty setting, fountain inside restaurant. Breakfast, lunch and dinner. Excellent selection of Thai, Arab and Indian dishes. Great service. A nice change from the usual beans, good value. Great atmosphere. Highly recommended.

La Margarita, inside Posada Margarita (see Sleeping) at Real de Guadalupe 34. Open from 0700. Live music in the evenings, flamenco, rumba and salsa, good tacos.

María Cartones, Plaza 31 de Marzo, T967-631 6002. Old-time favourite, with tables overlooking the plaza. Breakfasts, *comida típica*, coffee and sandwiches.

París-México, Madero 20. Smart, French cuisine vegetarian dishes, excellent breakfasts, reasonably priced *comida corrida*, classical music. Tequilas for US$1 in the evenings. Highly recommended.

Adelita, María Adelina Flores No 49. Great selection of tacos in a traditional, *charro*-themed restaurant. 2 for 1 tacos on Tue and tacos from US$0.30 any day.

Craft market, Insurgentes. The stalls here are the cheapest places for lunch in San Cristóbal. They do set meals for US$1.20, usually beef or chicken. Numerous stalls nearby sell punch, often made with *posh*.

El Gato Gordo, Real de Guadalupe 20, T962-678 8313. Funky place, popular with backpackers. Cheap set breakfast, crêpes, *tortas*, vegetarian options.

El Mirador II, Madero. Good local and international food, excellent *comida corrida* US$3 and pizzas US$2.50. Recommended.

Juguería Ana Banana, Av Miguel Hidalgo 9B. Good typical Mexican food and fresh juices.

Tierradentro, Real de Guadalupe 24. Small cultural centre serving economical breakfasts, lunch menus, baguettes, snacks and coffee.

Cafés, juice stalls and bakeries

Café Museo Café, Flores 10. Big, breezy café selling fine coffee by the bag or cup. There's an interesting museum inside charting the history of coffee in Chiapas – both café and museum are open daily.

La Casa del Pan, Dr Navarro 10 and B Domínguez. Excellent wholemeal bread, breakfasts, lunchtime buffet, live music, closed Mon. Has another branch at El Puente and in Real de Guadalupe 55. Highly recommended but not cheap. Good food and a great atmosphere.

La Selva Café, Crescencio Rosas and Cuauhtémoc. 30 types of really delicious organic coffees, owned by growers' collective, art gallery, lively in evenings. Good healthy breakfast and cakes. Recommended.

Namandí, Diego de Mazariegos 16. Crêpes, baguettes, juices, coffee and cake. They have Mexican staples too, if you fancy something more substantial. Has several branches in town including one in Insurgentes opposite El Templo del Carmen.

Naturalísimo, 20 de Noviembre 4. Healthy, low-fat vegetarian food, fresh (delicious) yoghurt, fruit sherbet and juices, wholewheat bread and home-baked goodies, pleasant courtyard inside. Recommended.

Palenque town *p78, map p79*

The classier restaurants are in Barrio La Cañada, behind the Maya head as you enter town.

El Tapanco Grill, Av Hidalgo 65, 2 blocks below plaza above **Bing** ice cream shop. Good steak, balcony dining.

Pizzería Palenque, Juárez 168 and Allende, T916-345 0332. Good pizzas and prices.

Lakan-Há, Juárez 20. Good tacos, fast and efficient. Also serves breakfast, Mexican staples and *menú del día*.

La Mexicana, Juárez and 5 de Mayo. Typical Mexican fare and breakfasts.

Mara's, Juárez 1, by the zócalo, cheap set menus.

Restaurante Maya, Hidalgo and Independencia. Popular, set menu lunches and à la carte dinner. Good meat dishes, efficient service and free Wi-Fi.

Café de Yarra, Hidalgo 68. Clean, stylish café serving good value, tasty breakfasts. Occasional live music.

El Herradero, Av Juárez 120. Breakfast and reasonably priced meals, fast service, open 24 hrs. Recommended.

La Oaxaceña, Juárez 122, opposite the **ADO** bus station. Economical Mexcian staples and *menú del día*.

Las Tinajas, 20 de Noviembre 41 and Abasolo. Family-run, excellent food, huge portions, recommended.

Road to the ruins

La Selva, Km 0.5 on Hidalgo. Open 1300-2300. Excellent, smart dress preferred, live music at weekends, recommended.

Don Mucho, El Panchán. Outdoor restaurant serving excellent Italian-Mexican food and fantastic breakfast. There's good evening entertainment, including fire dancing; quite exotic given the forest backdrop. They also host 'passing through' travelling musicians.

El Mono Blanco, El Panchán. Cheaper than Don Mucho's and much lower key. They serve Mexican food, breakfasts and à la carte menus.

Comitán p86

Café Gloria II, 1a Calle Sur Pte 47. The place for a wholesome evening meal.

Doña Chelo, Calle Central Pte 67. Traditional Mexican fare and seafood.

Restaurant Acuario, Belisario Domínguez 9, on the plaza opposite the church. In league with Vick's/Vicky restaurant (the sign has 2 different names) next door. Good Mexican standard grub, *tortas* and *comida corrida*, but do double check your bill before paying.

Café

Café Quiptic, part of Centro Cultural Rosario Castellanos, on the plaza. Good Chiapanecan coffee and snacks.

Tapachula and around p89

There are a couple of decent and reasonably priced eateries along the south side of the main plaza, for breakfasts lunch and dinner.

Vainilla Cous Cous, 4a Av Sur No 6, T962-118 0083. Tue-Sat 0930-2330 and Sun 0930-1700, with live music Fri and Sat 2100-2200. Run by a chef and a photographer this is a stylish place with some of the nicest dining in town. International cuisine with a North African twist, fine wines and a gallery next door. Also does yoga classes Mon and Thu.

El 7 Mares, Díaz Ordáz 11. Decent seafood, sometimes pricey.

Restaurant Prontos, 1a Calle Poniente 11, T962-626 5680. Open 0600-2200. Meat and more meat dishes.

Entertainment

San Cristóbal de las Casas *p71, map p72*

Bars and clubs

Barfly, Crecencio Rosas 4. Open 2000-2400. DJs play reggae, house and funk. Free drink on entry.

Bar Makia, Hidalgo, just off plaza, above a shop. Fri and Sat from 2200 until very late.

Blue Bar, Av Crescencio Rosas 2. Live music after 2300, salsa, rock, reggae, pool table, good atmosphere.

Cocodrilo, Insurgentes 1, T967-678 0871. Cappuccinos, cocktails, beer and live music every night: reggae, *trova*, flamenco and rumba.

El Zirko, 20 de Noviembre 7, a couple of blocks north of the zócalo. Live music.

Emiliano's Moustache (see page 97) has a bar open until 0100.

Revolución, 20 de Noviembre and 1 de Marzo. Café, bar with internet upstairs, happy hour 1200-1900, live soul, blues and rock music at 2000, good atmosphere.

Cinema and theatre

Centro Bilingüe at the Centro Cultural El Puente (see Cultural centres, page 110), Real de Guadalupe 55. Films Mon-Sat 1800, US$2, with later showings Fri and Sat, 2000. Film schedules are posted around town.

La Ventana, Real de Guadalupe 46. Cinema club showing a good range of films.

Teatro Municipal Daniel Zebadúa, 20 de Noviembre and 1 de Marzo, film festivals each month, films at 1800 and 2100 US$2 (US$1.50 students).

Palenque town *p78, map p79*

Road to the ruins

La Palapa (see Sleeping), has an all-night bar with dancing. Also numerous new bars and restaurants are springing up in the La Cañada district.

⊗ Festivals and events

Villahermosa *p67*
Feb Ash Wednesday is celebrated from 1500 to dusk by the throwing of water bombs and buckets of water at anyone who happens to be on the street!

Chiapa de Corzo *p70*
The fiestas here are outstanding.
Jan Daylight fiestas, **Los Parachicos**, on 15, 17 and 20 Jan to commemorate the miraculous healing of a young boy some 300 years ago, and the **Chunta Fiestas**, at night, 8-23 Jan. There **are parades** with men dressed up as women in the evenings of the 8, 12, 17 and 19 Jan. All lead to the climax, 20-23 Jan, in honour of **San Sebastián**, with a pageant on the river.
25 Feb El Santo Niño de Atocha.
25 Apr Festival de San Marcos, with various *espectáculos*.

San Cristóbal de las Casas *p71, map p72*
Jan/Feb Carnival is held during the 4 days before Lent, dates vary.
Mar/Apr There is a popular spring festival on Easter Sun and the week after.
Early Nov Festival Maya-Zoque, which lasts 4 days, promoting the 12 different Maya and Zoque cultures in the Chiapas region, with dancing and celebrations in the main plaza.
12 Dec La Fiesta de Guadalupe.

○ Shopping

Villahermosa *p67*
A small number of shops along Madero sell Tabasqueña handicrafts and souvenirs of varying quality and there are also some stalls set up daily along the same street. Bargain.

San Cristóbal de las Casas *p71, map p72*
Bookshops
La Pared, Av Miguel Hidalgo 2, T967-678 6367, lapared9@yahoo.com, opposite the government tourist office. Open daily,

1000-1400 and 1600-2000. Books in English and a few in other European languages, many travel books including **Footprint** handbooks, book exchange, American owner Dana Gay very helpful.
Soluna, Real de Guadalupe 13B, has a few English guidebooks, a wide range of Spanish titles and postcards.

Crafts
Amber Museum, Diego de Mazariegos, next to La Merced. There are also many shops on Av Real de Guadalupe selling amber and jade plus other *artesanías*. The market north of Santo Domingo is worth seeing as well.
Casa de Artesanías, Niños Héroes and Hidalgo. Top-quality handicrafts. Shop and museum.
Ex-Convento de Santo Domingo has been partly converted into a cooperative, **Sna Jolobil**, selling handicrafts from many local villages especially textiles (best quality and expensive); also concerts by local groups. Well worth a visit.
La Casa del Jade, Av 16 de Septiembre 16. The shop, which sells top-quality jade, also has a museum with replicas of jade relics and the Tomb of Pakal (Maya King of Palenque).
Taller Leñateros, Flavio A Paniagua 54, T967-678 5174, www.tallerlenateros.com. A paper-making workshop run primarily by a Maya group. Their paper and prints are made from natural materials and their profits help support around 30 Maya families. Souvenir markets on Utrilla between Real de Guadalupe and Comitán.

The **craft market** at Parque Fray Bartolomé de las Casas has an assortment of local sweets such as *cocada* (caramelized shredded coconut), as well as small animal figurines made, strangely enough, of sweetened hard-boiled egg yolks. Different, yet tasty.

Palenque town *p78, map p79*
Av Juárez is lined with souvenir shops selling hammocks, blankets, Maya figurines and hats. Sales staff are less pushy than in towns in the Yucatán Peninsula; bargain for the best prices.

▲ Activities and tours

Villahermosa *p67*
Tour operators
Creatur Transportadora Turística,
Paseo Tabasco 715, T993-317 7717,
www.creaturviajes.com. Tour operator
organizing tours along the 7 touristic routes
of the state, including a gastronomic tour,
the cacao route, whitewater rafting. Tours
only run at weekends in low season.
Recommended.

Tuxtla Gutiérrez *p69, map p69*
Tour operators
Carolina Tours, Sr José Narváez Valencia
(manager), Av Central Pte 1138, T961-612
4281; reliable, recommended; also coffee
shop at Av Central Pte 230.
Lacandona Tours, 6a Sur Pte 1276,
T961-612 9872, www.lacantours.com.
Tours to all the attractions in Chiapas
including the Lacandón rainforest,
Bonampak and the Sumidero canyon.
Viajes Miramar, Av Central Pte 1468, T961-
613 3983, www.viajesmiramar.com.mx. Good,
efficient service for national flight bookings.

San Cristóbal de las Casas *p71, map p72*
Horse riding
Horse-riding tours are widely available in
San Cristóbal, most going to Chamula and
costing US$8-12 for 4-5 hrs. Hotels, tourist
offices and travel agencies can easily
organize them, or look for advertising flyers
in touristy cafés and restaurants. Also Señor
Ismael rents out horses and organizes treks.
T961-678 1511.

Rafting
There are several rivers in the San Cristóbal
area that offer great rafting opportunities.
Explora-Ecoturismo y Aventura, 1 de Marzo
30, T967-674 6660, www.ecochiapas.com.
Eco-sensitive company with good
recommendations offer rafting, caving,
sea kayaking, river trips and multi-day
camping expeditions on a variety of rivers.

Tour operators and guides
There are many agencies to choose from.
As a rough guide to prices: to San Juan
Chamula and Zinacantán, US$12. Horse
riding to San Juan Chamula, US$12.
Sumidero Canyon, US$15. Montebello Lakes
and Amatenango del Valle, US$18. Palenque
ruins, Agua Azul and Misol-Há, US$22. Toniná
ruins, US$26. There's also a 3-day jungle trip
option taking in Agua Azul, Misol-Há, the
ruins at Bonampak, Cedro River Falls,
Yaxchilán and Palenque ruins, camping in
the jungle, US$250. Day trips to Bonampak
and Yaxchilán are also possible, but they are
much cheaper if booked in Palenque; take
care to check what is included in packages.
Na Bolom Museum and Cultural Centre,
Vicente Guerrero 33, T967-678 1418,
www.nabolom.org. This internationally
renowned and widely respected cultural
centre has close, long-standing ties with
Mayan communities. They run superlative
tours to the villages and expeditions to the
Lacandón rainforest (see page 73).
Otisa Travel, Real de Guadalupe 3,
T967-678 1933, otisa@otisatravel.com.
Daily tours to Sumidero Canyon, San Juan
Chamula and Zinacantán, Lagunas de
Montebello, Yaxchilán and Bonampak,
among other places.
Pronatura, Pedro Moreno 1. Organizes
guided bird walks with Javier Gómez, 2½ hrs
starting at 0700, from US$7 and plant walks,
leaving at any time of day depending on
demand. These last 1½ hrs, from US$5.
Raúl and Alejandro, T967-678 3741,
alexyraultours@yahoo.com.mx. Tours to San
Juan Chamula, Zinacantán and other villages.
They depart from in front of the cathedral at
0930 and return at 1400, in blue VW minibus,
US$15, in English, Spanish and Italian.
Friendly, very good, highly recommended.
Roberto Molina, T967-672 2679. Roberto
has good knowledge of medicinal plants and
the ancient art of pulse-reading. He offers a
spiritual interpretation of the land around
San Cristóbal and can organize tours to the
outlying villages, horse riding or hiking trips

in the surrounding mountain areas. Find him at **Posada Doña Rosita** (see page 92).
Travesía Maya, 20 de Noviembre 3, T967-674 0824, www.travesiamaya.com.mx. This friendly agency offers informative, economical tours to attractions in Chiapas, as well as private planes and direct buses to Guatemala.
Viajes Pakal, Cuauhtémoc 6-A, T967-678 2818, www.pakal.com.mx. A reliable agency with culturally friendly tours, several branches in other cities. Good for flight bookings, though some require 4 days' notice. Recommended.

Misol-Há *p78*
Tour operators
All the travel agencies in Palenque do a cheap tour to both Misol-Há and Agua Azul, about US$10 per person. Most tours allow about 30 mins at Misol-Há and 3-4 hrs at Agua Azul. Bring a swimsuit and plenty of drinking water. *Colectivos* from Hidalgo y Allende, Palenque, for Agua Azul and Misol-Há, 2 a day, US$8; *colectivos* can also be organized between Misol-Há and Agua Azul, in either direction. Taxi US$45 with 2 hrs at Agua Azul, or to both falls US$55.

Palenque town *p78, map p79*
Horse riding
Tours can be booked at the **Clínica Dental Zepeda**, Juárez s/n – the dentist owns the horses. Also through **Cabañas de Safari** in Palenque archaeological zone Km 1, T916-345 0026. **Gaspar Alvaro** also hires horses. He can be located at his house on the road to the ruins, directly in front of Mayabel. Gaspar will take you on a 3-hr ride through rainforested trails in the surrounding area of the ruins. Good chance of seeing monkeys and toucans. US$15 for 3 hrs. Tell him specifically that you want to go through the rainforest and not on the road.

Tour operators and guides
Alonso Méndez is a well-versed guide with extensive knowledge of flora, fauna, medicinal uses of plants and an intimate knowledge of the Palenque ruins. A respected authority on Chiapanecan ethnobotany, Alonso has a gift of academic and spiritual understanding of the rainforest. He speaks English, Spanish and Tzeltzal and can be found at his home in **El Panchán** camping site. Full-day hiking trips US$50 for a group of 6-8 people. Highly recommended.
Fernando Mérida, T044 916-103 3649 (mob). Fernando is a Lacandón guide with some interesting and unconventional views of the Maya and Mayan prophecies. He runs a range of unusual tours not offered by other companies, across Chiapas, including birdwatching expeditions on Sun lagoon. He speaks English and Italian. Look for his desk set up near **Chan Kan Centro**, Av Juárez, T961-600 1516.
José Luis Zúñiga Mendoza, T916-341 4736, tentzun@hotmail.com. Very easy going, José has excellent knowledge of the Palenque area and in addition to guided trips around the ruins offers jungle walks and stays with local communities.
Na Chan Kan, corner of Hidalgo and Jiménez, across from Santo Domingo church, T916-345 0263, www. nachankan.com/ viajesnachan. Offers a wide selection of packages ranging from tours to Agua Azul to excursions to the Yaxchilán and Bonampak ruins as well as transport to Guatemala.
Shivalva (Marco A Morales), Merle Green 9, La Cañada, T916-345 0411, www.hotelxibalba.com. Tours of Palenque, Yaxchilán, Bonampak and waterfalls. Friendly and well established.
Turística Maya Chiapas, Av Juárez 123, T916-345 0798, www.mayachiapas.com.mx. Tours to the waterfalls, Lacandón jungle. Tikal and other parts of Guatemala, as well as Belize. English spoken. Recommended.

Yaxchilán, Bonampak and Lacanjá *p84*
Tour operators
Operators from Palenque offer 1- and 2-day trips to Bonampak and Yaxchilán, all transport and food included. To see both sites independently, it's recommended you take

at least 2 days and stay overnight in Lacanjá. Otherwise, be prepared for a long, tough day of at least 14 hrs.

Local Spanish-speaking guides can be found by asking around in Lacanjá or enquiring at the entrance to Bonampak. The entire area is beautiful and worth exploring.

Tenosique and Río San Pedro route *p88*
Several agencies in Palenque offer tours to Flores by minibus and/or taxi, boat and public bus, via Tenosique, La Palma and El Naranjo. You probably won't meet any other travellers, so be prepared to fund the whole trip yourself, especially in low season.

Tapachula and around *p89*
Tour operators
Agencia de Viajes Chávez Tours, a few doors down from the OCC terminal, past Hotel Santa Julia, does tours of the area.

⊖ Transport

Villahermosa *p67*
Air
Airport Carlos R Pérez (VSA), 18 km from town, receives international flights from **Havana** and **Houston**, and has good national connections. VW bus to town US$5 each, taxi US$11.
   Airline offices AeroMéxico, Blv Ruiz Cortines 102 local 8, T993-352 4129. Aviacsa, Vía 3 No 120, T993-316 5731.

Bus
Reserve your seat as soon as you can; buses to Mexico City can sometimes be booked up well in advance. 1st-class ADO bus terminal is on Javier Mina and Lino Merino, 12 blocks north of centre, computerized booking system. Beware of long queues at the 1st-class ticket counters. The Central Camionera 2nd-class bus station is on Av Ruiz Cortines, near roundabout with fisherman statue, 1 block east of Javier Mina, opposite Castillo, 4 blocks north of ADO.

To **Mexico City** (TAPO, Norte or Tasqueña), regular departures, 10-12 hrs, US$52-84. To **Cancún**, many daily, 12 hrs, US$52.50. To **Chetumal**, 7 daily, 8½ hrs, US$27. To **Campeche**, many daily, 6 hrs, US$18. To **Mérida**, many daily, 8 hrs, US$25-36. To **Palenque**, OCC 2 daily, ADO 6 daily, 2½ hrs, US$8. To **Puebla**, 4 ADO services daily, US$40; and 4 luxury services, US$49. To **San Andrés Tuxtla**, ADO services, 0255, 0930, 1100, 1925, 6 hrs, US$16. To **San Cristóbal de las Casas**, 2 OCC services at 0930 and 1230, 7 hrs, US$16. Tto **Tapachula**, 1 OCC at 1915, 10 hrs, US$41; and 1 ADO luxury at 0335, US$50. To **Veracruz**, many daily including luxury services, 8 hrs, US$26. To **Xalapa**, with ADO at 1055, 1800, 1925, 2230, 8 hrs, US$31; and 2 luxury services at 2100 and 2120, US$37 and US$48. To **Emiliano Zapata**, many daily, 2½ hrs, US$8. To **Tenosique** (for Río San Pedro crossing into Guatemala, see page 108), many daily 3½ hrs, US$10.

Car
Car hire Hertz car rental is available from the airport. **Agrisa**, Paseo Tabasco corner of El Malecón, T993-312 9184, good prices, eg US$40 per day including taxes and insurance, but it is expensive to return the car to another city. Under no circumstances should you travel to Belize or Guatemala with a rental car unless you have all the paperwork at hand.

Taxi
City taxis charge US$1 for journeys in the centre.

South of Villahermosa *p68*
Bus There are buses between Teapa and **Villahermosa**, 50 km, 1 hr, US$2.20. Also to **Chiapa de Corzo** at 0730, through lovely, mountainous landscape.

Tuxtla Gutiérrez *p69, map p69*
Air
Aeropuerto Angel Albino Corzo is Tuxtla's international airport, 27 km south of the city. A taxi into town costs around US$15 and

from town to airport US$8 **ADO** buses to the airport from the OCC terminal, US$3.50.

Airline offices Aviacsa, Av Central Pte 1144, T961-612 8081. All lines also have ticket offices at the airport.

Bus

There is a 1st-class **ADO** and **OCC** bus terminal at 5a Norte Poniente, corner of Angel Albino Corzo, next to the large Plaza del Sol mall. There's a 2nd-class terminal at 3a Av Sur Ote and 7a Oriente Sur, about 1 km southeast of the centre.

To **Cancún**, OCC, 1055 and 1310, US$53; and **ADO GL**, 1430 and 1800, US$66. To **Córdoba**, 1st class (OCC and ADO), 1720, 1950, 7½ hrs, US$38. To **Chetumal**, OCC, 1310, 13 hrs, US$37; and **ADO GL**, 1430, US$44. To **Cd Cuauhtémoc**, Guatemalan border, **OCC**, 0630, 1015, 1615, 4½ hrs, US$13. To **Comitán**, OCC, many daily, 3 hrs, US$6. To **Mexico City**, 1st class, many daily, 12 hrs, US$57. To **Villahermosa**, 1st class, many daily, 4-7 hrs, US$17. To **Mérida**, OCC, 1500, 14 hrs, US$40; and **ADO GL**, 1800, US$48; otherwise change at Villahermosa. The scenery between Tuxtla and Mérida is very fine, and the road provides the best route between Chiapas and the Yucatán. To **Oaxaca**, OCC, 1130, 1920, 2355, 10 hrs, US$25; and **ADO GL**, 2130, US$30. To **Palenque**, 7 with OCC, 6 hrs, US$12; and **ADO GL**, 1430, US$15. To **Pochutla**, OCC, 2025 and 2310, 10 hrs, US$23. To **Puebla**, 1st class, many daily, same times as Mexico City, 10 hrs, US$50. To **Salina Cruz**, 1st class and luxury services, 1410, 1645, 2025, 2245, US$14.50. Take travel sickness tablets for Tuxtla–Oaxaca road if you suffer from queasiness. To **San Cristóbal de las Casas**, OCC, frequent services, 1 hr, US$3. To **Tapachula**, 1st class, many daily, 7½ hrs, US$183. To **Tonalá**, 1st and 2nd class, many daily, US$7-9. To **Tulum**, OCC, 1055, 1310, 17 hrs, US$48; and an **ADO GL**, 1430, US$57. To **Veracruz**, OCC, 2255, 2335, US$47; and an **ADO GL**, 2245, US$46.

Shuttles To **Chiapa de Corzo**, from 1 Sur Ote and 5a Ote Norte; and from the Transportes Chiapa–Tuxtla station, 2a Oriente Sur and 1a Av Sur Ote, 20 mins, US$0.70. To **San Cristóbal de las Casas**, from 2a Sur Ote 1203, between 11 and 12 Oriente Sur, 1 hr, US$2.50.

Taxis

Easy to flag down anywhere. US$3 within the centre, US$4 to the zoo, US$6 to Chiapa de Corzo (for Sumidero Canyon).

Chiapa de Corzo *p70*
Bus

Frequent buses to Tuxtla depart from Avenida 21 de Octubre on the plaza. Buses to San Cristóbal now bypass Chiapa de Corzo, meaning you'll have to pick one up on the highway or go via Tuxtla.

San Cristóbal de las Casas *p71, map p72*
Air

San Cristóbal has a small airport about 15 km from town, but at present does not serve passenger planes. Tuxtla Gutiérrez is now the principal airport.

Bicycle

Bike hire Los Pingüinos, Av Ecuador 4B, T967-678 0202, www.bikemexico.com/pinguinos, 0915-1430, 1600-1900, rents mountain bikes for US$10 for 4 hrs or US$14 per day. Guided biking tours half or full days, as well as longer guided tours. English, German spoken, beautiful countryside and knowledgeable guides, highly recommended.

Bus

For reasons of cultural sensitivity, it is recommended that you visit Mayan villages as part of a tour. A good guide will explain the workings of a Mayan community and introduce you to villagers personally, making your visit welcome and enlightening. If you go independently, be prepared for culture shock and some suspicious treatment. Crowded microbuses to Chamula,

Zinacantán, San Andrés Larráinzar, Tenejapa and other villages depart from around the market, north of the centre on Utrilla. Don't get stranded, as there isn't any tourist infrastructure.

There is a **Ticketbus** office in the pedestrianized part of Real de Guadalupe in the centre of San Cristóbal that stays open until 2200, daily. Very convenient for booking tickets without venturing as far as the OCC terminal.

Long distance The 1st-class OCC and ADO bus terminal is at the junction of Insurgentes and Blvd Sabines Gutiérrez, several blocks south of the centre. Other 2nd-class lines and shuttle operators, including AEXA and Rodolfo Figueroa, also have nearby terminals on Gutiérrez, which soon becomes the Pan-American Highway. There's also a variety of smaller bus companies and shuttles services that leave from the main road near the OCC bus station, with departures as far afield as Tijuana and other parts of northern Mexico, as well as Ocosingo, Palenque and nearby villages.

From the 1st-class terminal to **Campeche**, OCC, 1820, 10 hrs, US$25. To **Cancún**, OCC, 1215, 1430, 17 hrs, US$46; and ADO GL, 1545, US$58. To **Chetumal**, 1st class (OCC and ADO), 1215, 1430, 1605, 12 hrs, US$33, ADO GL, 1545, US$40. To **Cd Cuauhtémoc**, OCC, 0745, 1130, 1730, 3 hrs, US$6. To **Comitán**, OCC, frequent services, 1½ hrs, US$3. To **Mérida**, OCC, 1820, 13 hrs, US$36. To **Mexico City**, OCC, 1610, 1740, 1810, 2230, 14 hrs, US$60 and ADO GL 1700, 13 hrs, US$72. To **Oaxaca**, OCC, 1805, 2000, 10 hrs, US$34; and ADO GL, 2000, US$33. To **Palenque**, 8 daily with OCC and ADO GL, 5 hrs, US$9-11. To **Playa del Carmen**, OCC, 1215, 1430, US$56; and ADO GL, 1545, US$68. To **Pochutla**, OCC, 1915, 2200, 12 hrs, US$27. To **Puebla**, 4 daily with OCC and 2 with ADO GL daily, 11 hrs, US$64-53. To **Puerto Escondido**, OCC, 1915, 2200, 13 hrs, US$30. To **Tapachula**, 7 OCC daily, 8 hrs, US$16. To **Tuxtla**

Gutiérrez, OCC, many daily, 1 hr, US$2. To **Tulum**, OCC, 1215, 1430, 1605, 14½ hrs, US$44; and ADO GL, 1545, 16 hrs, US$52. To **Veracruz**, OCC, 2045, 8½ hrs US$40; and ADO GL, 2115, 9 hrs, US$47. To **Villahermosa**, OCC, 1120, 2300, 7 hrs, US$16. AEXA buses to **Palenque**, 0630, 1150, US$6. To **Agua Azul**, 0630, 1150, US$4. To **Tuxtla Gutiérrez**, *combis* every 10 mins from outside AEXA terminal from 0500, US$2. 50. 1st-class OCC buses depart for **Ciudad Cuautémoc** and the border daily. Alternatively, there are frequent departures to **Comitán**, from where you can catch a pickup or *colectivo*, hourly from 0700, around US$1. For details on crossing the border at **La Mesilla**, see page 58.

Shuttles Shuttles to **Tuxtla** regularly depart from the terminals on Gutiérrez, near the 1st-class bus terminal, 1 hr, US$3. You'll find shuttles to **Ocosingo** in the same area. Several operators run direct shuttles to the Guatemalan border and beyond, including **Travesia Maya**. Destinations include **La Mesilla**, **Quetzaltenango**, **Antigua**, **Flores** and **Panajachel**, US$30-60. It's a convenient and comfortable option if you can afford it. There are also regular departures to **Guatemala** from the OCC terminal itself, all departing at 0745 daily. To **Huehuetenango**, US$14. To **Los Encuentros**, US$19. To **Cuatro Caminos**, US$17 and to **Guatemala City**, US$24.

Car
Car hire Optima, Diego de Mazariegos 39, T967-674 5409; and Hertz, Villas Mercedes, Panagua 32, T967-678 1886. Rental is for within Chiapas only; do not attempt to go beyond.

Scooters
Croozy Scooters, Belisario Domínguez 7, www.prodigyweb.net.mx/croozyscooters. Swiss-British run, Open Tue-Sun 0900, closing times vary. Rents out bikes and small scooters, a good way of moving around. Minimum payment US$14, 2 hrs, US$25 per

day. They provide maps and suggested routes. Deposit and ID required. Bikes US$2 per day. Friendly. Recommended.

Taxi
US$1.75 anywhere in town, *colectivo* US$0.70.

Ocosingo *p77*
Many buses and *colectivos* to **Palenque**, 2½ hrs, US$3.30 and **San Cristóbal de Las Casas**.

Misol-Há *p78*
Several buses from Palenque daily (direction San Cristóbal de las Casas or Ocosingo), to crossroads leading to the waterfall, such as **Transportes Chambalu** to both Misol-Há and **Agua Azul**, leaving at 0900, 1000 and 1200, US$8.50, 2nd class, 1½ hrs. You can also purchase bus tickets from **Transportes Figueroa**, about 100 m from the **ADO** bus station (in direction of the town centre) in Palenque. Bus time is approximately 1½ hrs from Palenque to the turn-off to the Agua Azul road. From the crossroads walk the 4 km downhill to the falls on a beautiful jungle-lined road (or hitch a ride on a minibus for US$1). If, after a long day at the falls, you have no desire to walk the 4 km back to the main road (steep) you can always catch a ride back to Palenque on tour buses that have extra space, US$4. They leave from the Agua Azul parking lot 1500-1800. Back from the junction 1400-1600 with **Transportes Maya** buses. There are buses between San Cristóbal de las Casas and Palenque (to 2nd-class bus station, **Transportes Maya**), which will stop there, but on a number of others you must change at Temo, over 20 km away, north of Ocosingo. Tour companies can also arrange bus tickets with **AEXA** from the crossroads to San Cristóbal and other places if you don't wish to return all the way to Palenque to catch an onward bus.

Palenque town *p78, map p79*
Air
Commercial traffic through Palenque's small airport has dwindled, and it's now mainly used for specially chartered planes. Speak to a tour agent if you would like to organize flights within Chiapas (including Yaxchilán and Bonampak), Yucatán or Guatemala.

Bus
Local Micro buses run back and forth along the main street, passing the bus station area, to and from the ruins, every 10 mins, US$0.70 (taxi US$6). Catch one of these for **El Panchán** and other nearby accommodation.

Long distance There are 3 bus terminals. The 1st class **ADO/OCC** terminal is at the western end of Juárez. The Rodolfo Figueroa y Lacandonia terminal is on the opposite side of the road, with a few 2nd-class departures to San Cristóbal. An **AEXA** terminal is almost next door to the 1st-class terminal, serving a handful of destinations in Chiapas. Also on Juárez is **Autotransportes Tuxtla**, with 2nd-class departures to **Quintana Roo**.

To **Cancún**, 1st class (ADO and OCC), 1720, 1935, 2100, 13 hrs, US$40; and ADO GL, 2100, US$48. To **Campeche**, 1st class, 0800, 2100, 2200, 2325, 5 hrs, US$17.50. To **Escárcega**, 1st class, 6 daily, 3 hrs, US$10. To **Mérida**, 1st class, 0800, 2100, 2200, 2325, 8 hrs, US$26. To **Mexico City**, ADO, 1830 (TAPO), 2100 (Norte), 14 hrs, US$55. To **Oaxaca**, ADO, 1730, 15 hrs, US$39. To **San Cristóbal**, 1st class, 8 daily, 5 hrs, US$9.50; and an ADO GL. Also some 2nd-class departures. To **Tulum**, 1st class, 1720, 1935, 2000, 2110, 11 hrs, US$34; and ADO GL, 2100, US$40. To **Tuxtla Gutiérrez**, OCC, 8 daily, 6 hrs, US$12; and an ADO GL, US$14.50. To **Villahermosa**, 1st class, 11 daily, 2 hrs, US$7.50.

Shuttles To **Agua Azul** and **Misol-ha**, Transportes Chambalú, Allende and Juárez, 0900, 1000, 1200, US$8.50. They stop for 30 mins at Misol-Há and 3 hrs at Agua Azul. To **Frontera Corozal** (for **San Javier**, **Bonampak**, **Lacanjá** and **Yaxchilán**), Transportes Chamoan, Hidalgo 141, roughly hourly from 0500-1700, US$5. To **Tenosique**, Transportes Palenque, Allende and 20 de Noviembre, hourly, US$5. **Playas de Catazajá** (for Escárcega and Campeche) Transportes Pakal, Allende between 20 de Noviembre and Corregidora, every 15 mins, US$1.50.

Taxi
Taxis charge a flat rate of US$1.50 within the town, US$4 to **El Panchán** and nearby **Maya Bell** camping areas.

Yaxchilán, Bonampak and Lacanjá p84
Air
Flights from **Palenque** to Bonampak and Yaxchilán, in light plane for 5, about US$600 per plane, to both places, whole trip 6 hrs. Prices set, list available. **Viajes Misol-Há**, Juárez 48 at Aldama, T916-345 1614, run charter flights to Bonampak and Yaxchilán for US$150 per person return, minimum 4 passengers.

Boat
From **Bethel**, Guatemala, *lanchas* charge US$93 per boat return to visit Yaxchilán. From Palenque to Bethel US$20 and there are also connection direct to Flores US$25. From **La Técnica**, Guatemala, US$53 return. From **Frontera Corozal** to Yaxchilán it costs between US$50-60 per boat, although you may find other tourists to share the cost. Bargain the boatmen down (be warned, they're stubborn), or hitch a ride with a tour group. If you are travelling from Frontera Corozal to **Guatemala**, register with the immigration office before crossing the border and have your documents stamped. River crossings at Río Usumacinta US$3.50.

Bus
A few different companies run hourly *colectivo* services between **Palenque** and **Frontera Corozal**, including Transportes Chamoan (see Palenque shuttles, above). For Lacanjá or Bonampak, catch one of these and exit at the junction and military checkpoint at San Javier. From there, you will need to hike or take a taxi, if you can find one.

Bear in mind this is a remote destination, so pack water, travel light and plan your time accordingly. For Yaxchilán, take a boat from **Frontera Corozal**.

Car
Bonampak is over 30 km from Frontera Corozal and can be reached from the San Javier crossroads on the road to Corozal.

Comitán p86
Bus
Buses to **San Cristóbal de las Casas**, OCC, many daily, 2 hrs, US$3, also 2 luxury services US$4. To **Mexico City** (TAPO and Norte), OCC, 1410, 1550, 1640, 2040, 15½ hrs, US$64. To **Puebla**, same timings as for Mexico City, 13 hrs, US$57.To **Palenque**, OCC, 1345, 2115, 6½ hrs, US$14.50. **Tapachula**, OCC, 6 daily, 5½ hrs, US$12. To **Tuxtla Gutiérrez**, OCC, many daily, 3 hrs, US$5. To Cancún, OCC, 1345, 20½ hrs, US$56.

Frequent *combis*, shuttles and taxis for nearby **Ciudad Cuauhtémoc**, US$2, every 15 mins. To **San Cristóbal**, US$2.50 *combi*, US$3 taxi, 1 hr 10 mins, **Tuxtla** and other nearby places, transport leaves from the main boulevard, Belisario Domínguez, a few block north from the OCC terminal. Since these are only marginally cheaper than the much more comfortable buses, this is only worth it if you're strapped for cash or time.

Ciudad Cuauhtémoc p87
Bus
Long distance OCC 1st-class buses to **Comitán**, 1215, 1240, 1855, 200, 1½ hrs, US$3. There are also frequent de paso 2nd-class buses and *combis*. To **Mexico City**, OCC, 1240, 17 hrs, US$68. To **San Cristóbal de las Casas**, OCC, 1215, 1240, 1855, 2200, 3 hrs, US$6. To **Tuxtla Gutiérrez**, OCC, 1240, 1855, 2200, 4½ hrs, US12. To **Tapachula** (via Arriaga), OCC, 1100, 1445, 1755, 2045, 4½ hrs, US$8. If crossing the border, there are hourly buses to **Huehuetenango** or **Quetzaltenango** departing from the Guatemalan side.

Shuttles To **Comitán**, various operators, frequently from the border, 1½ hrs, US$3. More national connections in Comitán, including services to **San Cristóbal** and **Tuxtla**.

Río Usumacinta route *p87*
Shuttles
From Frontera Corozal to **Palenque**, hourly, 0400-1600, 2½ hrs US$5. Operators include **Transportes Chamoan**. Crossing the Río Usumacinta at Frontera Corozal by *lancha*, US$3.50.

Boat
Lanchas to **Yaxchilán**, 30 mins, US$50-60. To **Bethel**, 30 mins, US$30 for 2 people, US$40 for 4. To **Técnica**, US$5 per person. To **Piedras Negras**, 2-3 days, prices negotiable (around US$100-150 per person), and best organized as a group. Ensure your papers are in order before crossing the border. Visit immigration offices on both sides for exit and entry stamps, and keep a photocopy of your passport handy for possible military inspection.

Tapachula crossings: Talismán *p87*
Bus
There are few buses between the Talismán bridge and **Oaxaca** or **Mexico City**; it is advisable therefore to travel to **Tapachula** for connection; delays can occur at peak times.

Taxi
Combi vans run from near the Unión y Progreso bus station, about US$1; *colectivo* from outside **Posada de Calú** to Talismán, US$0.60, also from Calle 5 Pte between Av 12 y Av 14 Norte. Taxi **Tapachula–Talismán**, negotiate fare to about US$2. A taxi from Guatemala to Mexican Immigration will cost US$2, but it may be worth it if you are in a hurry to catch an onward bus.
    Hitchhikers should note that there is little through international traffic at the Talismán bridge. As a rule, hitchhiking is not advisable in Chiapas.

Tapachula crossings: Ciudad Hidalgo *p87*
Bus
From Calle 7 Pte between Av 2 Norte and Av Central Norte, Tapachula, buses go to 'Hidalgo', US$1.

Tenosique and Río San Pedro route *p88*
Bus
To **Emiliano Zapata**, ADO, many daily, 1 hr, US$3. To **Mexico City**, ADO, 1700, 15 hrs, US$57. To **Villahermosa**, ADO, frequent services, 3½ hrs, US$10.
    Shuttles To **Palenque**, hourly with Transportes Palenque, US$3.50. Or, catch a Villahermosa bus to **El Crucero de la Playa** and pick up a frequent *colectivo* from there.

Arriaga *p88*
Bus
To many destinations, mostly 1st class. To **Mexico City**, 1600, 1705, 1930, 2150, 12-13 hrs, US$50. To **Tuxtla**, with Fletes y Pasajes at 1400 and 1600, 4 hrs, US$7. To **Oaxaca**, 6 hrs, US$7.

Tapachula *p89*
Air
Tapachula airport is 25 mins from town centre and has flights to **Mérida** and **Mexico City**, daily, for other destinations connect via Mexico City. *Combis* to airport from Calle 2 Sur No 40, T962-625 1287, US$1, taxis US$7. From airport to border, minibuses charge US$26 for whole vehicle, so share with others, otherwise take *colectivo* to 2nd-class bus terminal and then a bus to Cd Hidalgo.
    Airline offices Aviacsa, Central Norte and 1a Pte, T962-625 4030. AeroMéxico, Central Ote, T962-626 7757.

Bus
OCC bus **Mexico City–Guatemala City** takes 23 hrs, with a change at the border to **Rutas Lima**. There is a variety of direct buses to many parts of Central America from

Tapachula all leaving from the OCC Terminal. Ticabus has some of the best connections. To **Guatemala City**, US$12. To **San Salvador**, US$24. To **Managua**, US$43. To **San José**, US$59. To **Panama City**, US$79. Also Línea Dorada, www.tikalmayanworld.com, operates buses between Tapachula and **Flores**, **Guatemala City** and **Río Dulce**. Guatemala and Galgos go to **Guatemala City** and **San Salvador**. To **Mexico City**, OCC, 9 daily, 17 hrs, including 3 luxury services from US$64. To **Oaxaca**, OCC, 1915, 12 hrs, US$25. To **Puebla**, OCC, 5 daily, 14½ hrs, US$55; and 3 luxury services, US$65-82. To **San Cristóbal de las Casas**, OCC, 0730, 0915, 1430, 1730, 2120, 7½ hrs, US$16. To **Tuxtla Gutiérrez**, OCC, 12 daily, 7 hrs, US$18; many 2nd-class and 2 luxury services, 1545 and 2359, US$33. To **Salina Cruz**, OCC, 2245, 7 hrs, US$20. To **Tehuantepec**, OCC, 1915, 7½ hrs, US$19.

⊙ Directory

Villahermosa *p67*
Banks American Express, Turismo Nieves, Sarlat 202, T01800-504 0400. **Banamex**, Madero and Reforma, Mon-Fri 0900-1700. HSBC, Juárez and Lerdo, changes TCs at good rates. There is also a good branch on Constitución and Merino, 0900-1700, Mon-Fri. **Cultural centres** Centro Cultural, Corner of Madero and Zaragoza, T993-312 5473. Presentations of local artists and photographers. Live music, workshops in literature, local handicrafts and musical interpretation, among others. El Jaguar Despertado, Sáenz 117, T993-314 1244, forum for artists and local Villahermosino intellectuals. Hosts concerts, art exhibitions and book presentations. Friendly. **Internet** Many along the pedestrianized section of Benito Juárez, all charging about US$1.50 per hr. Others scattered around town.
Post On Sáenz and Lerdo in the centre. DHL, parcel courier service, Paseo Tabasco and Malecón Carlos A Madrazo.

Tuxtla Gutiérrez *p69, map p69*
Banks Most banks open 0900-1600, HSBC has longer opening hours. Bancomer, Av Central Pte y 2 Pte Norte, for Visa and TCs, 0900-1500. HSBC, Mon-Fri 0900-1900, Sat 0900-1500, good rates and service. For cheques and cash: 1 Sur Pte 350, near zócalo. There are ATMs in various branches of Farmacia del Ahorro, all over the city.
Immigration, 1 Ote Norte. **Internet** Free at library of Universidad Autónoma de Chiapas, Route 190, 6 km from centre. Various other internet cafés all over town, especially on Av Central, costing about US$1 per hr. **Post** On main square.
Telephone International phone calls can be made from 1 Norte, 2 Ote, directly behind post office, 0800-1500, 1700-2100 (Sun1700-2000).

San Cristóbal de las Casas *p71, map p72*
Banks Banamex, Insurgentes 5, changes cheques without commission, 0900-1300. Banca Serfín on the zócalo, changes euro, Amex, MasterCard, TCs. **Bancomer**, Plaza 31 de Marzo 10, charges commission, cash advance on Visa, Amex or Citicorp TCs, good rates and service. **Casa Margarita** will change dollars and TCs. Banks usually open for exchange 0900-1600. HSBC, Diego de Mazariegos 6, good rates for cash and TCs (US$ only), fast, efficient, cash advance on MasterCard, open Sat afternoons. **Casa de Cambio Lacantún**, Real de Guadalupe 12, Mon-Fri 0900-1400, 1600-1900, Sat and Sun 0900-1300 (may close early), no commission, at least US$50 must be changed and much lower exchange than at the banks. 24-hr ATM at **Banorte**, 5 de Febrero, adjacent to cathedral. Quetzales can be obtained for pesos or dollars in the *cambio* but better rates are paid at the border. **Cultural centres** The Casa de Cultura, opposite El Carmen church on junction of Hermanos Domínguez and Hidalgo, has a range of activities on offer: concerts, films, lectures, art exhibitions and conferences. They also do marimba music and *danzón* on the

plaza outside the centre some evenings. **Casa/Museo de Sergio Castro**, Guadalupe Victoria 47 (6 blocks from plaza), T967-678 4289, 1800-2000 (but best to make appointment), entry free but donations welcome. Excellent collection of indigenous garments, talks (in English, French or Spanish) and slide shows about customs and problems of the indigenous population. **El Puente**, Real de Guadalupe 55, 1 block from the plaza, T967-678 3723, www.elpuenteweb.com, Spanish lessons with a restaurant, internet centre and a small cinema. Check their notice board for forthcoming events. A good place to meet other travellers. **Na Bolom Museum and Cultural Centre**, see page 73 and Sleeping, above. **Immigration** On Carretera Panamericana and Diagonal Centenario, opposite Hotel Bonampak. From zócalo take Diego de Mazariegos west, after crossing bridge take Diagonal on the left towards Hwy, 30-min walk. **Internet** There are many internet cafés all over town with rates around US$0.80 per hr. Service is generally good. **Language schools** Centro Cultural El Puente, Real de Guadalupe 55, T967-678 3723, www.elpuenteweb.com (Spanish programme), rates around US$10 per hr, US$145/week, 1-to-1 lessons, homestay programmes available from US$230 per week, registration fee US$35. Mixed reports. **Instituto Jovel**, Francisco Madero 27, T967-678 4069, www.institutojovel.com. Group or 1-to-1 classes, homestays arranged, said to be the best school in San Cristóbal as their teachers undergo an obligatory 6-week training course; very good reports from students, all teachers bilingual to some extent. **Universidad Autónoma de Chiapas**, Av Hidalgo 1, Dpto de Lenguas, offers classes in English, French and Tzotzil. **Laundry Superklin**, Crescencio Rosas 48, T967-678 3275, US$1.30 per kg, for collection after 5 hrs. **La Rapidita**, Insurgentes 9, coin-operated machines for self-service or they will launder clothes for you 1-3 kg

US$3.50. **Medical services** Doctors: Servicio Médico Bilingüe, Av Juárez 60, T967-678 0793, Dr Renato Zarate Castañeda speaks English, is highly recommended and if necessary can be reached at home, T967-678 2998. **Hospitals and clinics:** Red Cross, Prolongación Ignacio Allende, T967-678 0772. Recommended. **Pharmacies:** Widely available around town. **Post** Allende and Mazariegos, Mon-Fri 0800-1600, Sat 0900-1200. **Telephone** Casetas Telefónicas can be found all over the city. There are also **Ladatel** phones on the plaza, but these are generally more expensive than *casetas*.

Palenque town *p78, map p79*
Banks Exchange rate only comes through at 1000. Bancomer, changes TCs, good rates, Mon-Fri 0830-1600, Sat 0900-1500. Banamex, Juárez 28, Mon-Fri 0830-1600, Sat 0900-1500, slow. ATMs at **Bancomer** and **Banamex**, but often with long queues. Many travel agencies also have *casas de cambio*, but don't usually change TCs. **Internet** Several internet cafés along Juárez with good service and prices ranging from US$1-1.50 per hr. **Laundry** Opposite Hotel Kashlan, US$2 per 3 kg, 0800-1930. At the end of Juárez is a laundry, US$3 per 3 kg. **Post** Independencia, next to Palacio Municipal, helpful, Mon-Fri 0900-1300. **Telephone** Long-distance telephones at *casetas* along Juárez and at the bus terminals.

Comitán *p86*
Banks Bancomer, on plaza will exchange Amex TCs, bring ID; 2 others on plaza, none change dollars after 1200; also a *casa de cambio*. **Embassies and consulates** Guatemala, 1a Calle Sur Pte 35, 3rd floor (hard to spot, look for Guatemalan flag on top of building), T963-672 0491. Mon-Fri 0800-1300, 1400-1700, visas US$25 (not needed by most nationalities); tourist card US$10 (even for those for whom it should be free), valid 1 year, multiple entry. **Internet** Several internet cafés in the streets near the

main plaza, US$0.50 per hr. **Post** Av Central Sur Belisario Domínguez, 2 blocks south of main plaza.

Ciudad Cuauhtémoc *p87*

Banks Don't change money with the Guatemalan customs officials: the rates they offer are worse than those given by bus drivers or in banks (and these are below the rates inside the country). There is nowhere to change TCs at the border and bus companies will not accept cheques in payment for fares. However, 300 m after the border you can get good rates for TCs at the **Banco de Café**. The briefcase-and-dark-glasses brigade changes cash on the Guatemalan side only, but you must know in advance what the rates are.

Tapachula *p89*

Banks Avoid the crowds of streetwise little boys at the border; exchange is better in the town, bus station gives a good rate (cash only). **Banamex**, Blv Díaz Ordaz, 0830-1230, 1400-1600, disagreement over whether TCs are changed. **HSBC** is the only bank open Sat, changes TCs. **Casa de Cambio Tapachula**, Av 4 Norte y Calle 3 Pte, changes dollars, TCs, pesos, quetzales and lempiras (open late Mon-Sat), but not recommended, poor rates. Very difficult to change money or find anywhere open at weekends. Try the supermarket. **Embassies and consulates** El Salvador, Calle 2 Ote 31 and Av 7 Sur, T962-626 1252, Mon-Fri 0900-1700. Guatemala, Av 5a Norte, No 5, 3rd floor, Mon-Fri 1000-1500 and 1600-1800; tourist card US$10, friendly and quick, take photocopy of passport, photocopier 2 blocks away. **Immigration** Av 14 Norte 57, T962-626 1263. **Laundry** There is a laundry, at Av Central Norte 99 between Calle 13 y 15 Ote, US$3 wash and dry, 1 hr service, about 2 blocks from OCC bus station, open Sun. Also on Av Central Norte between Central Ote y Calle 1, opens 0800, closed Sun. **Telephone** Several long-distance phone offices, eg **Esther**, Av 5 Norte 46; **La Central**, Av Central Sur 95; **Monaco**, Calle 1 Pte 18.

Yucatán Peninsula

The Yucatán Peninsula, which includes the states of Campeche, Yucatán and Quintana Roo, is sold to tourists as the land of Maya archaeology and Caribbean beach resorts. And there's no denying it, the warm turquoise sea, fringed with fine white-sand beaches and palm groves of the 'Mayan Riviera' are second to none. And it would be a crime not to tread the beaten path to the sensational ruins at Chichén Itzá, Uxmal and Tulum. But it more than pays to explore beyond the main itineraries to visit some of the lesser-known Maya sites such as Cobá, Edzná or Dzibilchaltún, or the imposing Franciscan monastery and huge pyramid at Izamal. There are flamingo feeding grounds at Celestún and Río Lagartos and over 500 other species of bird, many of which are protected in Sian Ka'an Biosphere Reserve, which covers 4500 sq km of tropical forest, savannah, and coastline. Ever since Jacques Cousteau filmed the Palancar Reef in the 1960s, divers have swarmed to the clear waters of Cozumel, the 'Island of the Swallows', to wonder at the many species of coral and other underwater plants and creatures, at what has become one of the most popular diving centres in the world. Also popular and specialized is diving in the many cenotes (sink holes), including the famous Nohooch Nah Chich, part of the world's largest underground cave system.

Background

After the Maya arrived in Yucatán about 1200 BC, they built monumental stone structures during the centuries leading up to the end of the pre-Classic period (AD 250). Later they rebuilt their cities, but along different lines, probably because of the arrival of Toltecs in the ninth and 10th centuries. Each city was autonomous, and in rivalry with other cities. Before the Spaniards arrived the Maya had developed a writing system in which the hieroglyphic was somewhere between the pictograph and the letter. Fray Diego de Landa collected their books, wrote a very poor summary, the *Relación de las Cosas de Yucatán*, and with Christian but unscholarly zeal burnt most of the codices, which he never really understood.

The Spaniards found little to please them when they first arrived in the Yucatán: no gold, no concentration of natives; nevertheless Mérida was founded in 1542 and the few natives were handed over to the conquerors in *encomiendas*. The Spaniards found them difficult to exploit: even as late as 1847 there was a major revolt, fuelled by the inhumane conditions in the *henequén* (sisal) plantations, and the discrimination against the Maya in the towns, but it was the expropriation of Maya communal lands that was the main source of discontent. In July 1847 a conspiracy against the *Blancos*, or ruling classes from Mexico, was uncovered in Valladolid and one of its leaders, Manuel Antonio Ay, was shot. This precipitated a bloody war, known as the *Guerra de Castas* (Caste War) between the Maya and the *Blancos*. The first act was the massacre of all the non-Maya inhabitants of Tepich, south of Valladolid. The Maya took control of much of the Yucatán, laying siege to Mérida, only to abandon it to sow their crops in 1849. This allowed the governor of Yucatán to counter-attack, driving the Maya by ruthless means into southern Quintana Roo. In Chan Santa Cruz, now called Felipe Carrillo Puerto, one of the Maya leaders, José María Barrera, accompanied by Manuel Nahuat, a ventriloquist, invented the 'talking cross', a cult that attracted thousands of followers. The sect, called Cruzob, established itself and renewed the resistance against the government from Mexico City. It was not until 1901 that the Mexican army retook the Cruzob's domain.

People

The people are divided into two groups: the Maya, the minority, and the *mestizos*. The Maya women wear *huípiles*, or white cotton tunics (silk for fiestas), which may reach the ankles and are embroidered round the square neck and bottom hem. Their ornaments are mostly gold. A few of the men still wear straight white cotton (occasionally silk) jackets and pants, often with gold or silver buttons, and when working protect this dress with aprons. Carnival is the year's most joyous occasion, with concerts, dances and processions. Yucatán's folk dance is the *jarana*, the man dancing with his hands behind his back, the woman raising her skirts a little, and with interludes when they pretend to be bullfighting. During pauses in the music the man, in a high falsetto voice, sings *bambas* (compliments) to the woman. The Maya are a courteous gentle people. They drink little, except on feast days, speak Mayan languages, and profess Christianity laced with a more ancient nature worship.

Access to sites and resorts

Many tourists come to the Yucatán, mostly to see the ancient **Maya sites** and to stay at the new coastal resorts. A good paved road runs from Coatzacoalcos through Villahermosa, Campeche and Mérida (Route 180). An inland road from Villahermosa to Campeche gives easy access to Palenque (see page 80). If time is limited, take a bus from Villahermosa to Chetumal via Escárcega, which can be done overnight as the journey is not very interesting (unless you want to see the Maya ruins off this road). From Chetumal travel up the coast to Cancún, then across to Mérida. Route 307, from Chetumal to Cancún and Puerto Juárez is all paved and in very good condition. Air services from the US and Mexico City are given under Mérida, Cancún and Cozumel.

Quintana Roo (and especially Cozumel) is the main area for **diving** and **watersports** in the Yucatán Peninsula. However, water sports in Quintana Roo are expensive and touristy, although operators are generally helpful; snorkelling is often in large groups. On the more accessible reefs the coral is dying and there are no small coral fish, as a necessary part of the coral life cycle. Further from the shore, though, there is still much reef life to enjoy.

A useful website on places and activities in the Yucatán is www.yucatantoday.com, the web version of the monthly *Yucatán Today* magazine.

State of Campeche

Take time out to explore the State of Campeche. Colonial architecture is plentiful, there are several fortified convents and Campeche city itself was fortified to protect its citizens from pirate attacks. There are many archaeological sites, most demonstrating influences of Chenes-style architecture. Relax at the resorts of Sihoplaya and Seybaplaya while watching pelicans dive and iguanas scurry. You can try the beaches at Ciudad del Carmen, eat delicious red snapper and buy a cheap, but sturdy, Panama hat. The exhibits at several museums reflect the seafaring nature of the area and the pre-Conquest civilization that occupied these lands. The official government website is at www.campeche.gob.mx. ▸▸ For listings, see pages 122-126.

Tabasco to Campeche → For listings, see pages 122-126.

There are two routes to Campeche from the neighbouring state of Tabasco: the inland Highway 186, via Escárcega, with two toll bridges (cost US$5), and the slightly longer coastal route through Ciudad del Carmen, Highway 180; both converge at Champotón, 66 km south of Campeche. Highway 186 passes Villahermosa's modern international airport and runs fast and smooth in a sweeping curve 115 km east to the Palenque turn-off at Playas del Catazajá; beyond, off the highway, is **Emiliano Zapata** (fiesta 26 October), a busy cattle centre, with a Pemex station.

Francisco Escárcega → Colour map 1, B2. Phone code: 982.

Escárcega is a major hub for travellers on their way south to the states of Tabasco and Chiapas, north to Mérida in the state of Yucatán, east to Maya sites in Campeche and Quintana Roo states, and further east to the city of Chetumal. The town itself is not particularly enticing, set on a busy highway with a dusty wild west atmosphere. If stuck here overnight, there are a couple of hotels, a bank and several cheap restaurants.

Coast road to Campeche → For listings, see pages 122-126.

Although Highway 180 via Ciudad del Carmen is narrow, crumbling into the sea in places and usually ignored by tourists intent on visiting Palenque, this journey is beautiful and more interesting than the fast toll road inland to Campeche. The road threads its way from Villahermosa 78 km north through marshland and rich cacao, banana and coconut plantations, passing turnings to tiny coastal villages with palm-lined but otherwise mediocre beaches. It finally leads to the river port of **Frontera**, where Graham Greene began the research journey in 1938 that led to the publication of *The Lawless Roads* and later to *The Power and the Glory*. The **Feria Guadalupana** is held from 3-13 December, with an agricultural show, bullfights, *charreadas* and regional dances.

The road touches the coast at the Tabasco/Campeche state border. It then runs east beside a series of lakes (superb birdwatching) to the fishing village of **Zacatal** (93 km), at the entrance to the **Laguna de Términos** (named for the first Spanish expedition, which thought it had reached the end of the 'island' of Yucatán). Just before Zacatal is the lighthouse of **Xicalango**, an important pre-Columbian trading centre. Cortés landed near here in 1519 on his way to Veracruz and was given 20 female slaves, including 'La Malinche', the indigenous princess baptized as Doña Marina who, as the Spaniards' interpreter, played an important role in the Conquest. A bridge crosses the lake's mouth to Ciudad del Carmen.

Ciudad del Carmen → *Colour map 1, B1. Phone code: 938.*
This is the hot, bursting-at-the-seams principal oil port of the region. The site was established in 1588 by a pirate named McGregor as a lair from which to raid Spanish shipping; it was infamous until the pirates were wiped out by Alfonso Felipe de Andrade in 1717, who named the town after its patroness, the Virgen del Carmen.

Most streets in the centre are numbered; even numbers generally run west-east, and odd south-north. Calle 20 is the seafront *malecón* and the road to the airport and university is Calle 31. There's a **tourist office** ⓘ *at the main plaza, near the seafront Malecón, 0800-1500.*

The attractive, cream-coloured **cathedral** (Parroquia de la Virgen del Carmen), begun 1856, is notable for its stained glass. **La Iglesia de Jesús** (1820) opposite Parque Juárez is surrounded by elegant older houses. Nearby is the Barrio del Guanal, the oldest residential quarter, with the church of the **Virgen de la Asunción** (1815) and houses with spacious balconies and tiles brought from Marseilles.

There are several good beaches with restaurants and watersports, the most scenic being Playa Caracol (southeast of the centre) and Playa Norte, which has extensive white sand and safe bathing. Fishing excursions can be arranged through the **Club de Pesca** ⓘ *Nelo Manjárrez, T938-382 0073, at Calle 40 and Calle 61.* Coastal lagoons are rich in tarpon (*sábalo*) and bonefish. The town's patroness is honoured with a cheerful fiesta each year between 15 and 30 June.

Maya sites in south Campeche → *For listings, see pages 122-126.*

Calakmul → *Colour map 1, B2.*
ⓘ *Daily 0800-1700, US$3.70, cars US$4, entrance to biosphere reserve US$4.*
Three hundred kilometres southeast from Campeche town, and a further 60 km off the main Escárcega–Chetumal road, the ruins of Calakmul are only accessible by car. The site has been the subject of much attention in recent years, due to the previously concealed scale of the place. It is now believed to be one of the largest archaeological sites in Mesoamerica, and certainly the biggest of all the Maya cities, with somewhere in the region of 10,000 buildings in total, many of them as yet unexplored. There is evidence that Calakmul was begun in 300 BC, and continually added to until AD 800. At the centre of the site is the Gran Plaza, overlooked by a pyramid whose base covers 2 ha of ground. One of the buildings grouped around the **Gran Plaza** is believed, due to its curious shape and location, to have been designed for astronomical observation. The **Gran Acrópolis**, the largest of all the structures, is divided into two sections: **Plaza Norte**, with the ball court, was used for ceremonies; **Plaza Sur** was used for public activities. The scale of the site is vast, and many of the buildings are still under excavation, which means that information on Calakmul's history is continually being updated. To reach Calakmul, take Route 186 until Km 95, then turn off at Conhuás, where a paved road leads to the site, 60 km.

Xpujil → *Colour map 1, B3. Phone code: 983.*
ⓘ *Tue-Sun 0800-1700, US$3.40, US$3 to use a camcorder.*
The name means a type of plant similar to a cattail. The architectural style is known as Río Bec, characterized by heavy masonry towers simulating pyramids and temples, usually found rising in pairs at the ends of elongated buildings. The main building at Xpujil features an unusual set of three towers, with rounded corners and steps that are so steep they are unscalable, suggesting they may have been purely decorative. The façade

features the open jaws of an enormous reptile in profile on either side of the main entrance, possibly representing Itzamná, the Maya god of creation. Xpujil's main period of activity was AD 500-750; it began to go into decline around 1100. Major excavation on the third structure was done as recently as 1993, and there are still many unexcavated buildings dotted about the site. It can be very peaceful and quiet in the early mornings, compared with the throng of tourist activity at the more accessible sites such as Chichén Itzá and Uxmal. To get there, see Transport, page 125.

The tiny village of Xpujil, on the Chetumal–Escárcega highway, is conveniently located for the three sets of ruins in this area, Xpujil, Becán and Chicanná. There are two hotels and a couple of shops. Guided tours to the more remote sites, such as Calakmul and Río Bec, can be organized through either of the two hotels, costing about US$20-30 per person for the whole day.

Becán → Colour map 1, B3. Phone code: 996.
① Daily 0800-1700, US$3.70.
Seven kilometres west of Xpujil, Becán is another important site in the Río Bec style. Its most outstanding feature is a moat, now dry, which surrounds the entire city and is believed to be one of the oldest defence systems in Mesoamerica. Seven entrance gates cross the moat to the city. The large variety of buildings on the site are a strange combination of decorative towers and fake temples, as well as structures used as shrines and palaces. The twin towers, typical of the Río Bec style, feature on the main structure, set on a pyramid-shaped base supporting a cluster of buildings that seem to have been used for many different functions.

Chicanná → Colour map 1, B2. Phone code: 981.
① Daily 0800-1700. US$3.40.
Located 12 km from Xpujil, Chicanná was named upon its discovery in 1966 in reference to Structure II: *chi* (mouth), *can* (serpent) and *ná* (house), 'House of the Serpent's Mouth'. Due to its dimensions and location, Chicanná is considered to have been a small residential centre for the rulers of the ancient regional capital of Becán. It was occupied during the late pre-Classic period (300 BC-AD 250); the final stages of activity at the site have been dated to the post-Classic era (AD 1100). Typical of the Río Bec style are numerous representations of the Maya god Itzamná, or Earth Mother. One of the temples has a dramatic entrance in the shape of a monster's mouth, with fangs jutting out over the lintel and more fangs lining the access stairway. A taxi will take you from Xpujil bus stop to Becán and Chicanná for US$10, including waiting time.

Hormiguero → Colour map 1, B2.
① Daily 0800-1700, US$2.50.
Twenty kilometres southwest of Xpujil, Hormiguero is the site of one of the most important buildings in the Río Bec region, whose elaborate carvings on the façade show a fine example of the serpent's-mouth entrance, with huge fangs and a gigantic eye.

Río Bec
Río Bec is south off the main highway, some 10 km further along the road to Chetumal. Although the site gave its name to the architectural style seen in this area, there are better examples of it at the ruins listed above. Río Bec is a cluster of several smaller sites, all of which are very difficult to reach without a guide.

Champotón → *Colour map 1, A2.*

Back near the west coast of Campeche state, Route 261 runs 86 km due north from Escárcega through dense forest to the Gulf of Mexico, where it joins the coastal route at Champotón, a relaxed but run-down fishing and shrimping port spread along the banks of Río Champotón. In pre-Hispanic times it was an important trading link between Guatemala and Central Mexico; Toltec and Maya mingled here, followed by the Spaniards; in fact blood was shed here when Francisco Hernández de Córboba was fatally wounded in a skirmish with the inhabitants in 1517. The remnants of a 1719 fort built as a defence against the pirates who frequently raided this coast can be seen the south side of town. The Feast of the Immaculate Conception (8 December) is celebrated with a joyous **festival** lasting several days.

Sihoplaya and Seybaplaya → *Colour map 1, A2. Phone code: 982.*

Continuing north, Highways 180 and 261 are combined for 17 km until the latter darts off east on its way to Edzná and Hopelchen (bypassing Campeche, should this be desired). A 66-km toll *autopista*, paralleling Highway 180, just inland from the southern outskirts of Champotón to Campeche, is much quicker than the old highway. Champotón and Seybaplaya are bypassed. But from the old Highway 180, narrow and slow with speed bumps, you can reach the resort of **Sihoplaya** (regular buses from Campeche US$1). A short distance further north is the larger resort of **Seybaplaya**. This is an attractive place where fishermen mend nets and pelicans dry their wings along the beach. On the highway is the open-air **Restaurant Veracruz**, serving delicious red snapper (fresh fish at the seafront public market is also good value), but in general there is little to explore. Only the **Balneario Payucán** at the north end of the bay makes a special trip worthwhile; this is probably the closest decent beach to Campeche (33 km), although a little isolated, as the water and sand get filthier as one nears the state capital. Nevertheless, there is still much reef life to enjoy.

Campeche → *For listings, see pages 122-126. Colour map 1, A2. Phone code: 981.*

Campeche's charm is neatly hidden behind traffic-blocked streets, but once inside the city walls it reveals itself as a good place to break your journey out to the Yucatán. At the end of the 20th century, the town of Campeche was declared a World Heritage Site by UNESCO. The clean streets of brightly painted houses give the town a relaxed Caribbean feel. The Malecón is a beautiful promenade where people stroll, cycle, walk and relax in the evening in the light of the setting sun.

Ins and outs

Like many Yucatán towns, Campeche's streets in the Old Town are numbered rather than named. Even numbers run north/south beginning at Calle 8 (no one knows why) near the Malecón, east to Calle 18 inside the walls; odd numbers run east (inland) from Calle 51 in the north to Calle 65 in the south. Most of the points of interest are within this compact area. A full circuit of the walls is a long walk; buses marked 'Circuito Baluartes' provide a regular service around the perimeter.

The **state tourist office** ① *T981-811 9229, www.campechetravel.com, 0800-2100 daily*, is on the Malecón in front of the Palacio de Gobierno (walk down Calle 61 towards the sea). There is another smaller **tourist office** ① *on the northeastern corner of the zócalo, next to the cathedral, daily 0900-2100*. For a good orientation take the Centro Histórico tour, a regular **tourist tram** ① *daily on the hour from 0900-1200 and 1700-2000, 45 mins, US$7.50, English and Spanish spoken*, running from the main plaza.

Background

Highway 180 enters the city as the Avenida Resurgimiento, passing either side of the huge **Monumento al Resurgimiento**, a stone torso holding aloft the Torch of Democracy. Originally the trading village of Ah Kim Pech, it was here that the Spaniards, under Francisco Hernández de Córdoba, first disembarked on Mexican soil (22 March 1517) to replenish their water supply. For fear of being attacked by the native population, they quickly left, only to be attacked later by the locals further south in Champotón, where they were forced to land by appalling weather conditions at sea. It was not until 1540 that Francisco de Montejo managed to conquer Ah Kim Pech, founding the city of Campeche on 4 October 1541, after failed attempts in 1527 and again in 1537. The export of local dyewoods, *chicle*, timber and other valuable cargoes soon attracted the attention of most of the famous buccaneers, who constantly raided the port from their bases on Isla del Carmen, then known as the Isla de Tris. Combining their fleets for one momentous swoop, they fell upon Campeche on 9 February 1663, wiped out the city and slaughtered its inhabitants. Five years later the Crown began fortifying the site, the first Spanish colonial settlement to be completely walled. Formidable bulwarks, 3 m thick and 'a ship's height', and eight bastions (*baluartes*) were built in the next 36 years. All these fortifications soon put a stop to pirate attacks and Campeche prospered as one of only two Mexican ports (the other was Veracruz) to have had the privilege of conducting international trade. After Mexican Independence from Spain, the city declined into an obscure fishing and logging town. Only with the arrival of a road from the 'mainland' in the 1950s and the oil boom of the 1970s has Campeche begun to see visitors in any numbers, attracted by its historical monuments and relaxed atmosphere (*campechano* has come to mean an easy-going, pleasant person).

Sights

Of the original walls, seven of the *baluartes* and an ancient fort (now rather dwarfed by two big white hotels on the seafront) remain. Some house museums (see below).

The heart of the city is the zócalo, where the austere Franciscan **cathedral** (1540-1705) has an elaborately carved façade; inside is the Santo Entierro (Holy Burial), a sculpture of Christ on a mahogany sarcophagus with a silver trim. There is plenty of shade under the trees in the zócalo, and a small pagoda with a snack bar.

Right in front of the zócalo is the **Baluarte de Nuestra Señora de la Soledad**, the central bulwark of the city walls, from where you can do a walking tour of the **Circuito Baluartes**, the remains of the city walls. Heading east, you will come to the **Puerta del Mar**, formerly the entrance for those permitted to enter the city from the sea, which used to come up to this point. Next along the *Circuito* is a pair of modern buildings, the **Palacio de Gobierno** and the **Congreso.** The latter looks like a flying saucer, and makes for a bizarre sight when viewed with the 17th-century **Baluarte de San Carlos** in the background. Baluarte de San Carlos now houses a museum. Heading west on the continuation of the *Circuito*, you will come to **Templo de San José**, on Calle 10, an impressive baroque church with a beautifully tiled façade. It has been de-consecrated, and is now an educational centre. Back on to the *Circuito*, you will next reach the **Baluarte de Santa Rosa**, now the home of the tourist information office. Next is **Baluarte de San Juan**, from which a large chunk of the old city wall still extends, protecting you from the noisy traffic on the busy road beyond it. The wall connects with **Puerta de la Tierra** ① *Tue, Fri and Sat 2000 (for information, contact the tourist office)*, where a *Luz y Sonido* (Light and Sound) show takes place, US$4. The continuation of the *Circuito* will take you past the **Baluarte de San Francisco**, and then past the market, just outside the line of the city walls. **Baluarte de San Pedro** flanks the northeast corner of the city centre, and now houses a museum. The *circuito* runs down to the northwest tip of the old city, where the **Baluarte de Santiago** houses the Botanical Gardens.

Further from the city walls is the **Batería de San Luis**, 4 km south from the centre along the coast road. This was once a lookout post to catch pirates as they approached the city from a distance. The **Fuerte de San Miguel**, 600 m inland, is now a museum. A 20-minute walk along Avenida Miguel Alemán from Baluarte de Santiago is the **San Francisco** church, 16th century with wooden altars painted in vermilion and white. Nearby are the **Portales de San Francisco**, a beautifully restored old entrance to the city, with several good restaurants in its shadow.

The **Museo de la Escultura Maya** ⓘ *Baluarte de Nuestra Señora de la Soledad, Tue-Sun, 0800-1930, US$2.50*, has three well-laid-out rooms of Maya stelae and sculpture. **Jardín Botánico Xmuch'Haltun** ⓘ *Baluarte de Santiago, Tue-Sun 0900-1600*, is a small, but

Campeche

Sleeping	La Posada del Angel **4**	Iguana Azul **5**
América **7**	Monkey Hostal Campeche **3**	Lafitte's **6**
Colonial **9**	Reforma **12**	La Parroquia **7**
Best Western Hotel	Regis **5**	La Pigua **4**
del Mar **2**		Tulum **3**
Francis Drake **10**	Eating	Turix Café **8**
Hostal San Carlos **11**	Campeche **1**	Marganzo **2**
La Parroquia **8**	Casa Vieja Los Arcos **9**	

perfectly formed collection of tropical plants and flowers in a peaceful setting. The **Fuerte de San Miguel** ① *Tue-Sun 0900-1930, US$2.50*, on the Malecón 4 km southwest, is the most atmospheric of the forts (complete with drawbridge and a moat said to have once contained either crocodiles or skin-burning lime, take your pick!); it houses the **Museo Arqueológico**, with a well-documented display of pre-Columbian exhibits including jade masks and black funeral pottery from Calakmul and recent finds from Jaina.

> The word 'cocktail' is said to have originated in Campeche, where 17th-century English pirates enjoyed drinks adorned with palm fronds resembling cocks' tails.

Around Campeche

Lerma is virtually a small industrial suburb of Campeche, with large shipyards and fish-processing plants; the afternoon return of the shrimping fleet is a colourful sight. The **Fiesta de Polk Kekén** is held on 6 January, with traditional dances. The nearest decent beaches are at Seybaplaya (see page 117), 20 km south of Campeche. There, the beaches are clean and deserted; take your own food and drink as there are no facilities. Crowded, rickety buses marked 'Lerma' or 'Playa Bonita' run from Campeche, US$1, 8 km.

Maya sites east of Campeche → *For listings, see pages 122-126.*

A number of city remains (mostly in the Chenes architectural style) are scattered throughout the rainforest and scrub to the east of Campeche; little excavation work has been done and most receive few visitors. Getting to them by the occasional bus service is possible in many cases, but return trips can be tricky. The alternatives are one of the tours run by some luxury hotels and travel agencies in Campeche (see Tour operators, page 124) or renting a vehicle (preferably with high clearance) in Campeche or Mérida. Whichever way you travel, carrying plenty of drinking water is strongly advised.

Edzná → *Colour map 1, A2.*
① *Tue-Sun 0800-1700, US$3; local guides available.*
The closest site to the state capital is Edzná ('House of Grimaces'), reached by the highway east to Cayal, then a right turn onto Highway 261, a distance of 61 km. A paved shortcut southeast through China and Poyaxum (good road) cuts off 11 km; follow Avenida Nacozari out along the railway track. Gracefully situated in a lovely, tranquil valley with thick vegetation on either side, Edzná was a huge ceremonial centre, occupied from about 600 BC to AD 200, built in the simple Chenes style mixed with Puuc, Classic and other influences. The centrepiece is the magnificent, 30-m-tall, 60-sq-m **Temple of the Five Storeys**, a stepped pyramid with four levels of living quarters for the priests and a shrine and altar at the top; 65 steep steps lead up from the Central Plaza. Opposite is the **Paal U'na**, Temple of the Moon. Excavations are being carried out on the scores of lesser temples by Guatemalan refugees under the direction of Mexican archaeologists, but most of Edzná's original sprawl remains hidden away under thick vegetation. Imagination is still needed to picture the network of irrigation canals and holding basins built by the Maya along the valley below sea level. Some of the stelae remain in position (two large stone faces with grotesquely squinting eyes are covered by a thatched shelter); others can be seen in various Campeche museums. There is also a good example of a *sacbé* (sacred road). There is a small *comedor* at the entrance. Edzná is well worth a visit especially in July, when a Maya ceremony to honour Chac is held, to encourage or to celebrate the arrival of the rains (exact date varies). To get there see Transport, page 125.

Hochob

① Daily 0800-1700, US$2.70.

Of the more remote and less-visited sites beyond Edzná, Hochob and Dzibilnocac are the best choices for the non-specialist. Hochob is reached by turning right at Hopelchén on Highway 261, 85 km east of Campeche. This quiet town has an impressive fortified 16th-century church but only one hotel. From here a narrow paved road leads 41 km south to the village of **Dzibalchén**. Don Willem Chan will guide tourists to Hochob (he also rents bikes for US$3.50 per day), helpful, speaks English. Directions can be obtained from the church here (run by Americans); you need to travel 18 km southwest on a good dirt road (no public transport, hopeless quagmire in the rainy season) to the village of Chenko, where locals will show the way (4 km through the jungle). Bear left when the road forks; it ends at a small *palapa* and, from here, the ruins are 1 km uphill with a magnificent view over the surrounding forest. Hochob once covered a large area but, as at Edzná, only the hilltop ceremonial centre (the usual Plaza surrounded by elaborately decorated temple buildings) has been properly excavated; although many of these are mounds of rubble, the site is perfect for contemplating deserted, yet accessible Maya ruins in solitude and silence. The one-room temple to the right (north) of the plaza is the most famous structure: deep-relief patterns of stylized snakes moulded in stucco across its façade were designed to resemble a mask of the ferocious rain god Chac. A door serves as the mouth. A fine reconstruction of the building is on display at the Museo de Antropología in Mexico City. Early morning second-class buses serve Dzibalchén, but, returning to Campeche later in the day is often a matter of luck.

Dzibilnocac

① Daily 0800-1700, free.

Twenty kilometres northeast of Dzibalchén at Iturbide, this site is one of the largest in Chenes territory. Only three temples have been excavated here (many pyramidal mounds in the forest and roadside *milpas*); the first two are in a bad state of preservation, but the third is worth the visit: a unique narrow edifice with rounded corners and remains of a stucco façade, primitive reliefs and another grim mask of Chac on the top level. Much of the stonework from the extensive site is used by local farmers for huts and fences. A bus leaves Campeche at 0800, three hours, return 1245, 1345 and 1600, US$3.35. If driving your own vehicle, well-marked 'km' signs parallel the rocky road to Iturbide (no accommodation); bear right around the tiny zócalo and its attendant yellow church and continue (better to walk in the wet season) for 50 m, where the right branch of a fork leads to the ruins. Other sites in the region require 4WD transport and appeal mostly to archaeologists.

Becal

Becal is the centre for weaving Panama hats, here called *jipis* (pronounced 'hippies') and ubiquitous throughout the Yucatán. Many of the town's families have workshops in cool, moist backyard underground caves, which are necessary for keeping moist and pliable the shredded leaves of the *jipijapa* palm from which the hats are made. Most vendors give the visitor a tour of their workshop, but are quite zealous in their sales pitches. Prices are better for *jipis* and other locally woven items (cigarette cases, shoes, belts, etc) in the **Centro Artesanal, Artesanías de Becaleña** *① Calle 30 No 210*, than in the shops near the plaza, where the hat is honoured by a hefty sculpture of three concrete *sombreros*! More celebrations take place on 20 May during the **Feria del Jipi**.

For Sleeping and Eating price codes and other relevant information, see Essentials pages 31-33.

◉ Sleeping

Francisco Escárcega *p114*
C Escárcega, Justo Sierra 86, T982-824 0187, around the corner from the bus terminal (turn left twice). Clean, bath, parking, hot water, good restaurant, small garden.
C María Isabel, Justo Sierra 127, T982-824 0045. A/c, restaurant, comfortable, back rooms noisy from highway.
C Motel Akim Pech, T982-824 0240, on Villahermosa highway. A/c or fans and bath, reasonable rooms, restaurant in motel, another across the street, and a Pemex station opposite.

Coast road to Campeche *p114*
C San Agustín, Pino Suárez, Frontera, T913-332 0037. Very basic, fan, no mosquito net.
D Chichén Itzá, Aldama 671, Frontera, T913-332 0097. Not very clean, fan, shower, hot water.

Ciudad del Carmen *p115*
Hotel accommodation is generally poor value and can be difficult to come by Mon-Thu; book in advance and arrive early. You'll find a handful of 'economical' hotels opposite the ADO bus station.
A EuroHotel, Calle 22 No 208, T938-382 3044, reganem@prodigy.net.mx. Large and modern, 2 restaurants, pool, a/c, disco, built to accommodate the flow of Pemex traffic.
B Lino's, Calle 31 No 132, T938-382 0788 A/c, pool, restaurant, also has 10 RV spaces with electricity hook-ups.
D Zacarías, Calle 24 No 58B, T938-382 3506. Modern, some cheaper rooms with fans, brighter a/c rooms are better value. Recommended.

Campeche *p117, map p119*
In general, prices are high. Beware of over-charging and, if driving, find a secure car park.

AL Best Western Hotel Del Mar, Av Ruiz Cortines 51, T981-811 9191, www.delmar hotel.com.mx. 5-star hotel on the waterfront, has pleasant rooms with seaview and balconies, all mod cons and free Wi-Fi in the rooms. Pool, gym, good bar and restaurant.
A Hotel Francis Drake, Calle 12 No 207, between Calle 63 and Calle 65, T981-811 5626, www.hotelfrancisdrake.com. Classy colonial hotel with well-equipped rooms, restaurant, bar and a good business centre.
B América, Calle 10 252, T981-816 4588, www.hotelamericacampeche.com. This centrally located hotel is clean, tidy and well staffed. The rooms here have Wi-Fi and breakfast is included in the price. An attractive mid-range option.
C El Regis, Calle 12 No 148, between 55 and 57, T981-816 3175. Housed in a lovely old colonial building, the reception is a bit dark and dingy, but the hotel sports clean, spacious rooms and a stylish chequered floor.
C La Posada Del Angel, Calle 10 No 307, T981-816 7718 (on the side entrance of the cathedral). Clean, carpeted, comfortable rooms, some without windows, some with a/c (**B**). Friendly and recommended.
D Hotel Reforma, Calle 8 No 257, between Calle 57 and 59, T981-816 4464. Has a/c, hot water, TV and internet. A bit grotty, but right in the centre just a minute from the main plaza.
D-E Hostal San Carlos, Calle 10, No 255, Barrio de Guadalupe, a few blocks out of town, T981-816 5158, info@hostelcampeche. com.mx. Private rooms and dorms, continental breakfast included. Well-kept hostel with hot water, internet, currency exchange, laundry service and bike rental.
D-F La Parroquia, Calle 55, between 10 y 12, T981-816 2530, www.hostalparroquia.com. 3 dorms and rooms in one of Campeche's historic buildings. Services include free breakfast, kitchen, internet, bike rental book exchange, TV room with DVDs, and a tranquil terrace complete with sun loungers.

E Hotel Colonial, Calle 14 No 122, between Calle 55 and 57, T981-816 2630. Rooms have fans or a/c (more expensive) and hot water. A nice old colonial building, this quaint old hotel open since 1946, is living up to its name. Slightly scruffy, but very friendly.

E-F Monkey Hostel Campeche, Calle 57 No 10 overlooking the zócalo, T981-811 6605, www.hostalcampeche.com. Dorms and private rooms. There are lockers, laundry, internet, bike hire, kitchen and book exchange. Price includes breakfast and can arrange local tours. Luggage storage US$2.

Camping
Club Náutica, 15 km south of town, on the highway out of Campeche, Km 180, T981-816 7545. Big campsite with good facilities. Good spot for a few days.

🍴 Eating

Francisco Escárcega *p114*
There are few places used to serving tourists, but there is a good and cheap *lonchería* opposite the bus terminal.

🍽 **Titanic**, corner of the main highway and the road to the train station (first turning on the right after turning right out of the bus terminal). For a more expensive meal with a/c.

Ciudad del Carmen *p115*
🍽 **El Kiosco** Calle 33 s/n, between Calle 20 and 22, in **Hotel del Parque** with view of zócalo. Modest prices, eggs, chicken, seafood and Mexican dishes.

🍽-🍽 **El Pavo**, tucked away down Calle 36A, in Col Guadalupe. This superb, family-run restaurant serves excellent seafood dishes at cheap prices. Very popular with the locals.

🍽-🍽 **La Fuente**, Calle 20. 24-hr snack bar with view of the Laguna.

🍽 **La Mesita**, outdoor stand across from the old ferry landing. Well-prepared shrimp, seafood cocktails, extremely popular all day.

Cafés
There are several tiny cafés along the pedestrian walkway (Calle 33) near the zócalo.
Café Vadillo, Calle 33. The 'best coffee in town'.

Casa Blanca, Calle 20, between Calle 29 and 27. This popular and modern café-bar overlooks the seafront *malecón*. It serves filter coffee, cappuccinos and espressos.

Mercado Central, Calle 20 and 37, not far northwest of zócalo. Inexpensive snacks are available in the thriving market.

Campeche *p117, map p119*
Campeche is known for its seafood, especially *camarones* (large shrimps), *esmedregal* (black snapper) and *pan de cazón* (baby hammerhead shark sandwiched between corn tortillas with black beans). Food stands in the market serve *tortas*, tortillas, *panuchos* and *tamales* but hygiene standards vary widely; barbecued venison is also a marketplace speciality.

🍽-🍽 **Casa Vieja Los Arcos**, Calle 10, No 319A, on the zócalo, T981-100 5522. Beautiful balcony dining on top of the portales overlooking the main plaza. Specializes in local dishes, including *camarones*. Romantic setting.

🍽-🍽 **Lafitte's Restaurant**, inside **Hotel del Mar**. Pirate-themed restaurant with excellent Mexican dishes and good bar. There's a terrace overlooking the sea for outdoor dining. Recommended.

🍽 **La Pigua**, Av Miguel Alemán 179A, www.lapigua.com.mx. A locally renowned, clean, modern restaurant that specializes in seafood. It's open for lunch and dinner, and there's a pleasant garden setting.

🍽 **RestauranteTulum**, Calle 59 No 9, between Calle 10 and 12. This friendly, modern restaurant employs emerging talent from Campeche's gastronomic college. The menu is varied and international, offering white and red meats, baguettes, crêpes and salads. Open from lunchtime.

🍽-🍽 **Iguana Azul**, Calle 55, between C10 and C12. Bar with live music and dancing, snacks and good selection of drinks.

ⁱ†-ⁱ La Parroquia, Calle 55 No 8, part of the hotel with the same name. This busy locals' joint – staffed by smartly attired and friendly waiters – is open 24 hrs. It serves meat, fish and Mexican staples. Good breakfasts and a decent and economical *menú del día*. Free Wi-Fi. Recommended.

ⁱ†-ⁱ Marganzo, Calle 8. An elegant and widely respected fine-dining establishment. It boasts a very interesting menu of seafood and *comida típica*, and regularly lays on music with a trio of musicians and regional dancing.

ⁱ†-ⁱ Restaurant Campeche, right on the zócalo, opposite the cathedral, has an extensive menu, big portions and is very good value.

ⁱ Turix, Calle 57 between Calle 10 and 12. Arts and crafts centre combined with gourmet. This little cute café and art space a short hop from the zócalo does a variety of salads, sandwiches and good desserts. Art and crafts for sale.

⊛ Festivals and events

Campeche *p117, map p119*
Feb/Mar Good Carnival.
7 Aug State holiday.
Sep Feria de San Román, 2nd fortnight.
4-13 Oct Fiesta de San Francisco.

Maya sites east of Campeche *p120*
13-17 Apr A traditional Honey and Corn Festival is held in Holpechén.
3 May Día de la Santa Cruz.

◯ Shopping

Campeche *p117, map p119*
Excellent cheap **Panama hats** *(jipis)*, finely and tightly woven so that they retain their shape even when crushed into your luggage (within reason); cheaper at the source in Becal. Handicrafts are generally cheaper than in Mérida. There are souvenir shops along Calle 8, such as **Artesanía Típica Naval**,

Calle 8 No 259, with exotic bottled fruit like *nance* and *marañón*. Many high-quality craft items are available from the **Exposición** in the Baluarte San Pedro, **and Casa de Artesanías Tukulná**, Calle 10 No 333, between C59 and C31, open daily 0900-2000.

The **market**, from which most local buses depart, is beside Alameda Park at the south end of Calle 57. Plenty of bargains here. Try the ice cream, although preferably from a shop rather than a barrow. **Super 10** supermarket behind the post office has an excellent cheap bakery inside.

▲ Activities and tours

Campeche *p117, map p119*
Tour operators
Intermar Campeche, Av 16 de Septiembre 128, T981-816 9006, www.travel2mexico.com. Tours, ground transport, flights and car rental.
Viajes Chicanná, Av Augustín Melgar, Centro Comercial Triángulo del Sol, Local 12, T981-811 3503. Flight bookings to Cuba, Miami and Central America.
Viajes del Golfo, Calle 10 No 250 D, T981-816 1745, viajesdelgolfo@hotmail.com. Domestic and international flights; tours to archaeological sites.
Viajes Xtampak Tours, Calle 57 No 14, T981-816 6473, www.xtampak.com. Daily transport to ruins including Edzná, Calakmul, Uxmal and Palenque – they'll collect you from your hotel with 24 hrs' notice. There's a discount for groups and guide services at an extra cost. Recommended.

⊖ Transport

Tabasco to Campeche *p114*
Bus Buses from Emiliano Zapata, all **ADO**. To **Tenosique**, almost hourly, 1½ hrs US$3. To **Villahermosa**, frequent services, 2½ hrs,

US$7. To **Mérida**, 0900, 1120, 1500, 2215, 7 hrs, US$23.50. To **Escárcega**, 0900, 1500, 2 hrs, US$7.50. To **Chetumal**, 2100, 6 hrs, US$20.

Francisco Escárcega p114
Bus Most buses from Chetumal or Campeche drop you off at the 2nd-class terminal on the main highway. To buy tickets, you have to wait until the outgoing bus has arrived; sit near the ticket office and wait for them to call out your destination, then join the scrum at the ticket office. There is an ADO terminal west of the 2nd-class terminal, a 20-min walk. From there, 1st-class buses go to **Palenque**, 0410, 0630, 1250, 2335, 3 hrs, US$10. To **Chetumal**, frequent services, 4 hrs, US$13. To **Campeche**, frequent services, 2 hrs, US$7.50. From the 2nd-class terminal, there are buses to **Campeche**, 16 a day, 2½ hrs, US$5.60. To **Chetumal**, 3 a day, 4 hrs, US$11. To **Playas de Catazajá**, connecting with *colectivos* to **Palenque**, frequent, US$5. To **Villahermosa**, 12 a day, 4 hrs, US$12.50. *Colectivos* to **Palenque** leave from outside the 2nd-class terminal, US$5.50. From 1st class terminal to **Mérida**, frequent, 4½ hrs, US$16.50.

Ciudad del Carmen p115
Air
Carmen's airport (CME, 5 km east of the plaza) currently only has direct flights to **Mexico City**, from where there are connections to the rest of the country.

Bus
The ADO bus terminal is some distance from the centre. Take bus or *colectivo* marked 'Renovación' or 'ADO'; they leave from around the zócalo. There are frequent ADO and ATS services to **Campeche**, 2½-3 hrs, US$11. To **Mérida**, 6 hrs, US$21. To **Villahermosa** via the coast, 3 hrs, US$9, where connections can be made to **Palenque**. Buses also travel via **Escárcega**, where you can connect to **Chetumal** and **Belize**.

Car
Car hire Budget, Calle 31 No 117, T938-382 0908. Auto-Rentas del Carmen, Calle 33 No 121, T938-382 2376.

Xpujil p115
Bus 2nd-class buses from **Chetumal** and **Escárcega** stop on the highway in the centre of Xpujil, some 800 m east of the 2 hotels. There are 4 buses a day to **Escárcega**, between 1030 and 1500, 3 hrs, US$6. 8 buses a day to **Chetumal**, 2 hrs, US$5. Change at Escárcega for buses to **Palenque** or **Campeche**. 1st-class buses will not stop at Xpujil.

Campeche p117, map p119
Air
Modern, efficient airport (CPE) on Porfirio, 10 km northeast. AeroMéxico direct daily to **Mexico City**, T981-816 3109. If on a budget, walk 100 m down service road (Av Aviación) to Av Nacozari, turn right (west) and wait for 'China–Campeche' bus to zócalo.

Bus
The easiest way to reach **Edzna** is on a tourist minibus. They depart hourly and operators include Xtampak, Calle 57 No 14, between Calle 10 and 12, T981-812 8655, xtampac_7@ hotmail.com, US$21.50 (prices drop depending on no of passengers); and Transportadora Turística Jade, Av Díaz Ordaz No 67, T981-827 4885, Jade_tour@ hotmail.com, US$14. To get there on public transport, catch a morning bus to Pich and ask to be let out at Edzna – it's a 15-min walk from the highway. Ask the driver about return schedules, as services are quite infrequent and subject to change. There's no accommodation at Edzná and hitchhiking isn't recommended. Buses to **Seybaplaya** leave from the tiny Cristo Rey terminal opposite the market, 9 a day from 0615, 45 mins, US$1.

Long distance The bus station is about 3 km south of the centre. Buses from outside the terminal travel the *circuito* road. A taxi costs US$2.20. The 2nd-class bus terminal is about 1 km east of the centre along Av Gobernadores, but services are steadily moving to the main terminal. To **Cancún**, 7 daily with **ADO** and **ADO GL**, 7 hrs, US$32-24.50. To **Chetumal**, 1200, 6 hrs, US$42. To **Ciudad del Carmen**, frequent **ADO** services, 3 hrs, US$11. To **Escárcega**, frequent, 2 hrs, US$7.50. To **Mérida**, frequent **ADO** services, 2½ hrs, US$9.50. To **Mexico City**, **ADO** at 1230, 2225, 2345, 18 hrs, US$68, and 2 **ADO GL** services at 1430 and 1635, 16 hrs, US$82. To **San Cristóbal de las Casas**, **OCC** at 2145, 11 hrs, US$25. To **Veracruz**, luxury only, **ADO GL** at 2215, 11½ hrs, US$52.50. To **Villahermosa**, frequent **ADO** services, 6-7 hrs, US$21.

Car
Car hire Maya nature, Av Ruiz Cortines 51, inside Hotel del Mar, T981-811 9191. **Hertz** and **Autorent** car rentals at airport.

---

❶ Directory

Ciudad del Carmen *p115*
Banks Banamex, Calle 24 No 63 or Banorte, Calle 30 and 33. **Post** Calle 22 No 136.

Campeche *p117, map p119*
Banks Banorte, Calle 8 No 237, between C57 and C59; Mon-Fri 0900-1700; HSBC, Calle

10 No 311, Mon-Fri 0900-1700, Sat 0900-1500; Santander Serfín, Calle 57 No 8; American Express, T981-811 1010, Calle 59, Edificio Belmar, oficina 5, helpful for lost cheques, etc. Plenty of ATMs and places to get cash on credit cards. **Cultural centres** Casa del Teniente de Rey, Calle 59 No 38 between 14 and 16, houses the Instituto Nacional de Antropología e Historia (INAH), dedicated to the restoration of Maya ruins in the state of Campeche, as well as supporting local museums. INAH can be visited for information regarding any of the sites in the state, T981-811 1314, www.inah.gob.mx. The Centro Cultural Casa 6, Calle 57, between Calle 8 and 10, 0900-2100 daily, US$0.35, is housed in a handsome building on the main plaza. It conjures the opulence and splendour of Campeche's golden days. **Immigration** The Oficina de Migración is inside the Palacio Federal. **Internet** Many internet places around town, including Cybercafé Campeche, Calle 61 between Calle 10 and 12, 0900-1300, US$1.50 per hr. **Laundry** Antigua, Calle 57 between Calle 12 and 14, US$1 per kg. **Medical services** Red Cross, T981- 815 2411. **Post** Av 16 de Septiembre (Malecón) and Calle 53 in Edificio Federal); Mon-Fri 0800-2000, Sat 0900-1300 for *Lista de Correos*, registered mail, money orders and stamps. **Telephone** Telmex, Calle 8 between Calle 51 y 53, free; Calle 51 No 45, between Calle 12 and 14.

State of Yucatán

The archaeological sites of Chichén Itzá, Oxkintoc, Uxmal, Kabah and Labná are just a few of the many strewn throughout the State of Yucatán. Try not to miss Dzibilchaltún; the intrusion of European architecture is nowhere more startling than here. The region's many cenotes (deep pools created by the disintegration of the dry land above an underground river) were sacred to the Maya, who threw precious jewels, silverware and even humans into their depths; many are perfect for swimming. On the coast, boat trips are organized to observe pelicans, egrets and flamingos in their natural habitat. It is possible to visit some of the impressive henequén *(sisal) haciendas in the more rural areas and admire the showy mansions that line the Paseo de Montejo in Mérida.* ▸▸ *For listings, see pages 140-152.*

North to Mérida

At **Maxcanú**, the road to Muná and Ticul branches east; a short way down it is the recently restored Maya site of **Oxkintoc** ① *US$3*. The Pyramid of the Labyrinth can be entered (take a torch) and there are other ruins, some with figures. Ask for a guide at the village of Calcehtoc, which is 4 km from the ruins and from the Grutas de Oxkintoc (no bus service). These, however, cannot compare with the caves at Loltún or Balankanché (see pages 133 and 137). Highway 180 continues north towards Mérida through a region of numerous *cenotes*, soon passing a turn-off to the turn-of-the-20th-century Moorish-style *henequén* (sisal) hacienda at **San Bernardo**, one of a number in the state that can be visited; an interesting museum chronicling the old Yucatán Peninsula tramway system is located in its spacious grounds. Running beside the railway, the highway continues 47 km to its junction with the inland route at **Umán**, a *henequén* processing town with another large 17th-century **church** and convent dedicated to St Francis of Assisi; there are many *cenotes* in the flat surrounding limestone plain. If driving, Highway 180/261 is a divided four-lane motorway for the final 18-km stretch into Mérida. There is a ring road around the city.

Mérida → *For listings, see pages 140-152. Colour map 1, A2. Phone code: 999.*

The capital of Yucatán state and its colonial heart, Mérida is a bustling, tightly packed city full of colonial buildings in varying states of repair. There is continual activity in the centre, with a huge influx of tourists during the high season mingling with busy Meridanos going about their daily business. Although the city has been developed over many years for tourism, there is plenty of local flavour for the traveller to seek out off the beaten track. Attempts to create a sophisticated Champs Elysées-style boulevard in the north of the city at Paseo Montejo have not been quite successful; the plan almost seems to go against the grain of Mérida's status as an ancient city, which has gradually evolved into a place with its own distinct identity.

Ins and outs

Getting there All buses from outside Yucatán State arrive at the CAME terminal on Calle 70 between Calle 69 y 71, a few blocks from the centre. There is another bus terminal around the corner on Calle 69, where buses from local destinations such as Uxmal arrive. The airport is 8 km from the city, bus 79 takes you to the centre. Taxis to the centre from the airport charge US$9.

Getting around You can see most of Mérida on foot. Although the city is big, there is not much to concern the tourist outside a few blocks radiating from the main plaza. The VW Beetle taxis are expensive, due to their scarcity; fares start at US$3 for a short journey. *Colectivo* buses are difficult to locate; they appear suddenly on the bigger roads in the city, you can flag them down anywhere. They terminate at the market; flat fare US$0.25.

Tourist information The main **tourist office** ⓘ *Calle 60 y Calle 57 (just off Parque Hidalgo), daily 0800-2000*, is very helpful. There are other tourist offices on the main plaza by the Palacio Municipio and at the airport. You'll find good information online at www.mayayucatan.com.mx and www.yucatantoday.com.

Safety Mérida is a safe city, with its own **tourist police** ⓘ *T999-930 3200*, recognizable by their brown and white uniforms.

Best time to visit During July and August, although very hot, Mérida is subject to heavy rains during the afternoon.

Background
Mérida was originally a large Maya city called Tihoo. It was conquered on 6 January 1542, by Francisco de Montejo. He dismantled the pyramids of the Maya and used the stone as the foundations for the cathedral of San Ildefonso, built 1556-1559. For the next 300 years, Mérida remained under Spanish control, unlike the rest of Mexico, which was governed from the capital. During the Caste Wars of 1847-1855, Mérida held out against the marauding forces of indigenous armies, who had defeated the Mexican army in every other city in the Yucatán Peninsula except Campeche. Reinforcements from the centre allowed the Mexicans to regain control of their city, but the price was to relinquish control of the region to Mexico City.

Sights
The city revolves around the large, shady zócalo, site of the **cathedral**, completed in 1559, the oldest cathedral in Latin America, which has an impressive baroque façade. It contains the Cristo de las Ampollas (Christ of the Blisters), a statue carved from a tree that burned for a whole night after being hit by lightning, without showing any damage at all. Placed in the church at Ichmul, it then suffered only a slight charring (hence the name) when the church was burned to the ground. To the left of the cathedral on the adjacent side of the plaza is the **Palacio de Gobierno**, built 1892. It houses a collection of enormous murals by Fernando Castro Pacheco, depicting the struggle of the Maya to integrate with the Spanish. The murals can be viewed until 2000 every day. **Casa de Montejo** is on the south side of the plaza, a 16th-century palace built by the city's founder, now a branch of Banamex. Away from the main Plaza along Calle 60 is Parque Hidalgo, a charming tree-filled square, which borders the 17th-century **Iglesia de Jesús.** A little further along Calle 60 is the **Teatro Peón Contreras**, built at the beginning of the 20th century by an Italian architect, with a neoclassical façade, marble staircase and Italian frescoes.

There are several 16th- and 17th-century churches dotted about the city: **La Mejorada**, behind the Museum of Peninsular Culture (Calle 59 between 48 and 50), **Tercera Orden**, **San Francisco** and **San Cristóbal** (beautiful, in the centre). The **Ermita**, an 18th-century chapel with beautiful grounds, is a lonely, deserted place 10 to 15 minutes from the centre.

Mérida

To **3 8** & Progreso

Felipe Carrillo
Puerta Monument

Museo de
Antropología
e Historia

Parque
Santa Ana

Paseo de Montejo

Museo de
la Canción
Yucateca

Plaza
Santa
Lucía

Mercado
Municipal 2

Casa
Catherwood

Teatro Peón
Contreras

Jesús

Museo
de Arte
Popular

La Mejorada

Museum of
Peninsular
Culture

Parque
Hidalgo

Palacio
Municipal

Palacio de
Gobierno

Zócalo

Cathedral

Museo Macay

Las
Monjas

Casa de
Montejo

Colectivos to
Plaza de Los
Americas

Combis to
Izamal

LOCK buses to
Celestún,
Izamal etc.

Municipal

San
Cristóbal

To Chichén-Itzá & Cancún

To Campeche & Mexico City

Parque
San Juan

CAME

Terminal de
Autobuses

Parque
San
Sebastián

La Ermita

N

300 metres
300 yards

Sleeping

Casa Becil **1** *D2*
Casa Bowen **2** *D2*
Casa MExilio **10** *B1*
Casa San Angel **18** *A3*
Casa San Juan **16** *D2*
Dolores Alba **4** *C4*
Gobernador **5** *B2*
Gran **6** *C3*
Hacienda Xcanatún **8** *A3*
Hostal Zócalo **17** *C2*
La Misión de
  Fray Diego **7** *C2*
Las Monjas **9** *C2*

Margarita **11** *C2*
Medio Mundo **19** *B2*
Mucuy **12** *B3*
Nómadas Youth
  Hostal **13** *B2*
Posada Toledo **14** *B3*
San José **15** *C2*
Trailer Park Rainbow **3** *A3*
Trinidad **22** *B2*

Eating

Alberto's Continental **5** *B2*
Amaro **1** *B2*
Café Alameda **16** *B3*

Café Chocolate **23** *B3*
Café El Hoyo **15** *B2*
Café La Habana **8** *B2*
Café Petropolis **2** *D2*
Colonial **12** *B2*
El Colón Sorbetes y
  Dulces Finos **10** *C3*
El Nuevo Tucho **4** *B3*
El Trapiche **3** *C2*
Flor de Santiago **14** *B1*
Italian Coffee
  Company **9** *C2*
Jugos California **6** *C2*
La Casa de Frida **24** *C2*

La Vía Olympo **11** *C2*
Los Almendros **7** *B4*
Marlín Azul **18** *B2*
Marys **21** *C3*
Mérida **20** *C2*
Pórtico del Peregrino **17** *B2*
Villa Maria **13** *B1*
Vito Corleone's Pizza **19** *B2*

Bars & clubs

La Parranda **22** *C3*
Panchos **12** *B2*

Museo de Antropología e Historia ⓘ *Paseo de Montejo 485, Tue-Sat 0800-2000, Sun 0800-1400, US$3.70*, housed in the beautiful neoclassical Palacio Cantón, has an excellent collection of original Maya artefacts from various sites in the Yucatán state. The displays are very well laid out, and the explanations are all in Spanish. There are many examples of jade jewellery dredged from *cenotes*, and some examples of cosmetically deformed skulls with sharpened teeth. This is a good overview of the history of the Maya.

Museo Macay ⓘ *Calle 60, on the main plaza, www.macay.org, daily 1000-1730, free*, has a permanent exhibition of Yucatecan artists, with temporary exhibits by contemporary local artists. **Museo de Arte Popular** ⓘ *Calle 59 esq 50, Barrio de la Mejorada, Tue-Sat 0900-2000, Sun 0800-1400, free*, has a permanent exhibition of Maya art, handicrafts and clothing, with a good souvenir shop attached. **Museo de la Canción Yucateca** ⓘ *Calle 57 between 50 and 48, www.merida.gob.mx/historia/lugaresmuseocancion.html, Tue-Sun 0900-1700, US$1.50*, in the Casa de la Cultura, has an exhibition of objects and instruments relating to the history of music in the region. **Pinacoteca Juan Gamboa Guzmán** ⓘ *Calle 59 between Calle 58 and 60, Tue-Sat 0800-2000, Sun 0800-1400, free*, is a gallery showing old and contemporary painting and sculpture. Fans of John Lloyd Steven's seminal travelogue *Incidents of Travel in Central America, Chiapas and Yucatán* should check out **Casa Catherwood** ⓘ *Calle 59 between 72 and 74, daily 0900-1400 and 1700-2100, US$5*. Dedicated to Steven's companion and illustrator, Mr Catherwood, this museum contains stunning colour lithographs of Mayan ruins, as they were found in the 19th century.

Around Mérida → *For listings, see pages 140-152. Colour map 1, A2.*

Celestún → *Phone code: 988.*

A small, dusty fishing resort west of Mérida much frequented in summer by Mexicans, Celestún stands on the spit of land separating the Río Esperanza estuary from the ocean. The long beach is relatively clean except near the town proper, with clear water ideal for swimming, although rising afternoon winds usually churn up silt and there is little shade; along the beach are many fishing boats bristling with *jimbas* (cane poles), used for catching local octopus. There are beach restaurants with showers. A plain zócalo watched over by a simple stucco church is the centre for what little happens in town. Cafés (some with hammock space for rent) spill onto the sand, from which parents watch offspring splash in the surf. Even the unmarked **post office** ⓘ *Mon-Fri 0900-1300*, is a private residence the rest of the week.

The immediate region is a biosphere reserve, created to protect the thousands of migratory waterfowl who inhabit the lagoons; fish, crabs and shrimp also spawn here, and kingfishers, black hawks, wood storks and crocodiles may sometimes be glimpsed in the quieter waterways. In the winter months Celestún plays host to the largest flamingo colony in North America, perhaps more than 20,000 birds – in the summer most of the flamingos leave Celestún for their nesting grounds in the Río Lagartos area. Boat trips to view the wildlife can be arranged at the **visitor centre** ⓘ *below the river bridge 1 km back along the Mérida road* (US$60 for one six people, plus US$4 per person for the reserve entrance fees, 1½ hours). Make sure your boatman takes you through the mangrove channel and to the Baldiosera freshwater spring in addition to visiting the flamingos. It is often possible to see flamingos from the bridge early in the morning and the road to it may be alive with egrets, herons and pelicans. January to March is the best time to see them. It's important to wear a hat and use sunscreen. Hourly buses to Mérida's terminal at Calle 50 and 67, 0530-2000, two hours, US$4.

Know your hammock

Different materials are available for hammocks. Some you might find include **sisal**, which is very strong, light, hard-wearing but rather scratchy and uncomfortable, and is identified by its distinctive smell; **cotton**, which is soft, flexible, comfortable, not as hard-wearing but, with care, is good for four or five years of everyday use. It is not possible to weave cotton and sisal together, although you may be told otherwise, so mixtures are unavailable. **Cotton/silk** mixtures are offered, but will probably be an artificial silk. **Nylon** is very strong and light but it's hot in hot weather and cold in cold weather.

Never buy your first hammock from a street vendor and never accept a packaged hammock without checking the size and quality. The surest way to judge a good hammock is by weight: 1.5 kg (3.3 lb) is a fine item, under 1 kg (2.2 lb) is junk (advises Alan Handleman, a US expert). Also, the finer and thinner the strands of material, the more strands there will be, and the more comfortable the hammock. The best hammocks are the so-called 3-ply, but they are difficult to find. There are three sizes: single (sometimes called *doble*), *matrimonial* and family (buy a *matrimonial* at least for comfort). If judging by end-strings, 50 would be sufficient for a child, 150 would suit a medium-sized adult, 250 a couple. Prices vary considerably so shop around and bargain hard.

Progreso and around → *Phone code: 969.*

Thirty-six kilometres north of Mérida, Progreso has the nearest beach to the city. It is a slow-growing resort town, with the facilities improving to service the increasing number of US cruise ships that arrive every Wednesday. Progreso is famous for its industrial pier, which at 6 km is the longest in the world. It has been closed to the public since someone fell off the end on a moped. The beach is long and clean and the water is shallow and good for swimming.

A short bus journey (4 km) west from Progreso are **Puerto Yucalpetén** and **Chelem**. Balneario Yucalpetén has a beach with lovely shells, but also a large naval base with further construction in progress.

Five kilometres east of Progreso is another resort, **Chicxulub**; it has a narrow beach, quiet and peaceful, on which are many boats and much seaweed. Small restaurants sell fried fish by the *ración*, or kilogram, served with tortillas, mild chilli and *cebolla curtida* (pickled onion). Chicxulub is reputed to be the site of the crater made by a meteorite crash 65 million years ago, which caused the extinction of the dinosaurs. (The site is actually offshore on the ocean floor.) The beaches on this coast are often deserted and, between December and February, 'El Norte' wind blows in every 10 days or so, making the water turbid and bringing in cold, rainy weather.

Dzibilchaltún

ⓘ *0800-1700, US$5.80.*

Halfway between Mérida and Progreso turn right for the Maya ruins of Dzibilchaltún. This unique city, according to carbon dating, was founded as early as 1000 BC. The site is in two halves, connected by a *sacbé* (sacred road). The most important building is the **Templo de Las Siete Muñecas** (Temple of the Seven Dolls), at the east end, which is partly restored. At the west end is the ceremonial centre with temples, houses and a large plaza in which the open chapel, simple and austere, sticks out like a sore thumb. The evangelizing friars had clearly hijacked a pre-Conquest sacred area in which to erect a symbol of the invading religion. At its edge is the **Cenote Xlaca** containing very clear water that is 44 m deep (you can swim in it, take mask and snorkel as it is full of fascinating fish); there's a very interesting nature trail starting halfway between the temple and the *cenote*; the trail rejoins the *sacbé* halfway along. The **museum** is at the entrance by the ticket office (site map available). *Combis* stop here en route to **Chablekal**, a village along the same road.

The Convent Route → *For listings, see pages 140-152.*

The route takes in Maya villages and ruins, colonial churches, cathedrals, convents and *cenotes*. It is best to be on the road by 0800 with a full gas tank. Get on the Periférico to Ruta 18 (signs say Kanasín, not Ruta 18). At **Kanasín**, La Susana is known especially for local delicacies like *sopa de lima, salbutes* and *panuchos*. Clean, excellent service and abundant helpings at reasonable prices. Follow the signs to **Acanceh**. Here you will see the unusual combination of the Grand Pyramid, a colonial church and a modern church, all on the same small plaza (similar to the Plaza de las Tres Culturas in Tlatelolco, Mexico City). About four blocks away is the Temple of the Stuccoes, with hieroglyphs. Eight kilometres further south is **Tecoh**, with an ornate church and convent dedicated to the Virgin of the Assumption. There are some impressive carved stones around the altar. The church and convent both stand at the base of a large Maya pyramid. Nearby are the caverns of **Dzab-Náh**; you must take a guide as there are treacherous drops into *cenotes*. Next on the route is **Telchaquillo**, a small village with an austere chapel and a beautiful *cenote* in the plaza, with carved steps for easy access.

Mayapán and around
ⓘ *US$2.40.*

A few kilometres off the main road to the right you will find the Maya ruins of Mayapán, a walled city with 4000 mounds, six of which are in varying stages of restoration. Mayapán, along with Uxmal and Chichén Itzá, once formed a triple alliance, and the site is as big as Chichén Itzá, with some buildings being replicas of those at the latter site. The restoration process is ongoing; the archaeologists can be watched as they unearth more and more buildings of this large, peaceful, late-Maya site. Mayapán is easily visited by bus from Mérida (every 30 minutes from terminal at Calle 50 y 67 behind the municipal market, one hour, US$1 to Telchaquillo). It can also be reached from Oxcutzcab.

Thirty kilometres along the main road is **Tekit**, a large village containing the church of San Antonio de Padua, with many ornate statues of saints. The next village, 7 km further on, is called **Mama**, with the oldest church on the route, famous for its ornate altar and bell-domed roof. Another 9 km is **Chumayel**, where the legendary Maya document *Chilam Balam* was found. Four kilometres ahead is **Teabo**, with an impressive 17th-century church. Next comes **Tipikal**, a small village with an austere church.

Maní
Twelve kilometres further on is Maní, the most important stop on this route. Here you will find a large church, convent and museum with explanations in English, Spanish and one of the Maya languages. It was here that Fray Diego de Landa ordered important Maya documents and artefacts to be burned, during an intense period of Franciscan conversion

of the Maya people to Christianity. When Diego realized his great error, he set about trying to write down all he could remember of the 27 scrolls and hieroglyphs he had destroyed, along with 5000 idols, 13 altars and 127 vases. The text, entitled *Relation of Things in Yucatán*, is still available today, unlike the artefacts. To return to Mérida, head for Ticul, to the west, then follow the main road via Muná.

Ticul and Oxkutzcab → *Colour map 1, A2. Phone code: 997.*

Eighty kilometres south of Mérida, Ticul is a small, pleasant little village known for its *huípiles,* the embroidered white dresses worn by the older Maya women. You can buy them in the tourist shops in Mérida, but the prices and quality of the ones in Ticul will be much better. It is also a good base for visiting smaller sites in the south of Yucatán state, such as Sayil, Kabah, Xlapak and Labná (see below).

Sixteen kilometres southeast of Ticul is Oxkutzcab, a good centre for catching buses to Chetumal, Muná, Mayapán and Mérida (US$2.20). It's a friendly place with a market by the plaza and a church with a 'two-dimensional' façade on the other side of the square.

Grutas de Loltún and around

ⓘ *Tue-Sun 0930, 1100, 1230 and 1400. US$3 with obligatory guide, 1 hr 20 mins. Recommended. Caretaker may admit tours on Mon, but there is no lighting.*

Nearby, to the south, are the caverns and pre-Columbian vestiges at Loltún (supposedly extending for 8 km). Take pickup (US$0.30) or truck from the market going to Cooperativa (an agricultural town). For return, flag down a passing truck. Alternatively, take a taxi, US$10 (can be visited from Labná on a tour from Mérida). The area around Ticul and Oxkutzcab is intensively farmed with citrus fruits, papayas and mangoes. After Oxkutzcab on Route 184 is **Tekax** with restaurant **La Ermita** serving excellent Yucatecan dishes at reasonable prices. From Tekax a paved road leads to the ruins of **Chacmultún**. From the top you have a beautiful view. There is a caretaker. All the towns between Muná and Peto, 14 km northeast of Oxkutzcab off Route 184, have large old churches. Beyond the Peto turn-off the scenery is scrub and swamp as far as the Belizean border.

The Puuc Route

Taking in the four sites of Kabah, Sayil, Xlapak and Labná, as well as Uxmal, this journey explores the hilly (or *puuc* in Maya) region to the south of Mérida. All five sites can be visited in a day on the 'Ruta Puuc' bus, which departs from the first-class bus station in Mérida every day at 0800, US$11, entry to sites not included. This is a good whistle-stop tour, but does not give you much time at each of the ruins, but five sites in one day is normally enough for most enthusiasts; if you want to spend longer seeing these sites, stay overnight in Ticul.

Kabah

ⓘ *0800-1700, US$3.*

On either side of the main road, 37 km south of Uxmal and often included in tours of the latter, are the ruins of Kabah. On one side there is a fascinating **Palace of Masks** (*Codz-Poop*), whose façade bears the image of Chac, mesmerically repeated 260 times, the number of days in the Almanac Year. Each mask is made up of 30 units of mosaic stone. Even the central chamber is entered via a huge Chac mask whose curling snout forms the doorstep. On the other side of this wall, beneath the figure of the ruler, Kabal, are impressive carvings on the door arches, which depict a man about to be killed, pleading for mercy, and two men duelling. This side of the road is mostly reconstructed; across the road the outstanding feature is a reconstructed arch marking the start of the *sacbé* (sacred road), which leads all the way to Uxmal, and several stabilized, but impossible to climb mounds of collapsed buildings being renovated. The style is Classic Puuc.

Sayil, Xlapak and Labná
ⓘ *Entrance US$3 at each site.*

Sayil means 'The Place of the Ants'. Dating from AD 800-1000, this site has an interesting palace, which in its day included 90 bathrooms for some 350 people. The simple, elegant colonnade is reminiscent of the architecture of ancient Greece. The central motif on the upper part of the façade is a broad mask with huge fangs, flanked by two serpents surrounding the grotesque figure of a descending deity. From the upper level of the palace you can see a tiny ruin on the side of a mountain called the Nine Masks.

Thirteen kilometres from Sayil, the ruins of **Xlapak** have not been as extensively restored as the others in this region. There are 14 mounds and three partially restored pyramids.

Labná has a feature that ranks it among the most outstanding sites of the Puuc region: a monumental arch connecting two groups of buildings (now in ruins), which displays an architectural concept unique to this region. Most Maya arches are purely structural, but the one at Labná has been constructed for aesthetic purposes, running right through the façade and clearly meant to be seen from afar. The two façades on either side of the arch differ greatly; the one at the entrance is beautifully decorated with delicate latticework and stone carving imitating the wood or palm-frond roofs of Maya huts.

Uxmal → *For listings, see pages 140-152. Colour map 1, A2. Phone code: 997.*

ⓘ *Daily 0800-1700, US$9.50 including light and sound show; rental of translation equipment US$2.50. Shows are at 2000 in summer and 1900 in winter. Mixed reports. Guides available with 1½-hr tours. Tours in Spanish US$40, in English, French, German and Italian US$45. For transport to Uxmal, see page 150.*

Built during the Classic period, Uxmal is the most famous of the ruins in the Puuc region. The characteristic features of Maya cities in this region are the quadrangular layout of the buildings, set on raised platforms, and an artificially created underground water-storage system. The **Pyramid of the Sorcerer** is an unusual oval-shaped pyramid set on a large rectangular base; there is evidence that five stages of building were used in its construction. The pyramid is 30 m tall, with two temples at the top. The **Nunnery** is set around a large courtyard, with some fine masks of Chac, the rain god, on the corners of the buildings. The east building of the Nunnery is decorated with double-headed serpents on its cornices. There are some plumed serpents in relief, in excellent condition, on the façade of the west building. The **House of the Governor** is 100 m long, and is considered one of the most outstanding buildings in all of Mesoamerica. Two arched passages divide the building into three distinct sections that would probably have been covered over. Above the central entrance is an elaborate trapezoidal motif, with a string of Chaac masks interwoven into a flowing, undulating serpent-like shape extending to the façade's two corners. The stately two-headed jaguar throne in front of the structure suggests a royal or administrative function. The **House of the Turtles** is sober by comparison, its simple walls adorned with carved turtles on the upper cornice, above a short row of tightly packed columns, which resemble the Maya *palapas*, made of sticks with a thatched roof, still used today. The **House**

of the Doves is the oldest and most damaged of the buildings at Uxmal. It is still impressive: a long, low platform of wide columns topped by clusters of roof combs, whose similarity to dovecotes gave the building its name.

Izamal and around → *For listings, see pages 140-152. Colour map 1, A3. Phone code: 988.*

Sixty-eight kilometres east of Mérida is the friendly little town of Izamal. Once a major Classic Maya religious site founded by the priest Itzamná, Izamal became one of the centres of the Spanish attempt to Christianize the Maya.

Fray Diego de Landa, the historian of the Spanish conquest of Mérida (of whom there is a statue in the town), founded the huge **convent** and **church**, which now face the main **Plaza de la Constitución**. This building, constructed on top of a Maya pyramid, was begun in 1549 and has the second largest atrium in the world. If you carefully examine the walls that surround the magnificent atrium, you will notice that some of the faced stones are embellished with carvings of Maya origin, confirming that, when they had toppled the pre-Columbian structures, the Spaniards re-used the material to create the imported architecture. There is also a throne built for the Pope's visit in 1993. The image of the Inmaculada Virgen de la Concepción in the magnificent church was made the Reina de Yucatán in 1949, and the patron saint of the state in 1970. Just 2½ blocks away, visible from the convent across a second square and signposted, are the ruins of a great mausoleum known as the **Kinich-Kakmo pyramid** ① *0800-1700, free, entrance next to the tortilla factory.* You climb the first set of stairs to a broad, tree-covered platform, at the end of which is a further pyramid (still under reconstruction). From the top there is an excellent view of the town and surrounding *henequén* and citrus plantations. Kinich-Kakmo is 195 m long, 173 m wide and 36 m high, the fifth highest in Mexico. In all, 20 Maya structures have been identified in Izamal, several on Calle 27. Another startling feature about the town is that the entire colonial centre, including the convent, the arcaded government offices on Plaza de la Constitución and the arcaded second square, is painted a rich yellow ochre, giving it the nickname of the 'golden city'.

From Izamal you can go by bus to **Cenotillo**, where there are several fine *cenotes* within easy walking distance from the town (avoid the one *in* town), especially **Ucil**, excellent for swimming, and **La Unión**. Take the same bus as for Izamal from Mérida. Past Cenotillo is Espita and then a road forks left to Tizimín (see page 139).

The cemetery of **Hoctún**, on the Mérida-Chichén road, is also worth visiting; indeed it is impossible to miss, there is an 'Empire State Building' on the site. Take a bus from Mérida (last bus back 1700) to see extensive ruins at **Aké**, an unusual structure. Public transport in Mérida is difficult: from an unsigned stop on the corner of Calle 53 y 50, some buses to Tixkokob and Ekmul continue to Aké; ask the driver.

Chichén Itzá → *For listings, see pages 140-152. Colour map 1, A3.*

① *Daily 0800-1730, US$9.50 including light and sound show, free bag storage, free for Mexicans on Sun and holidays, when it is incredibly crowded; you may leave and re-enter as often as you like on day of issue. Guided tours US$40 per group of any size; it is best to try and join one, many languages available. Best to arrive before 1030 to beat the crowds. The tourist centre at the entrance to the ruins has a restaurant and small museum, bookshop and souvenir shop with exchange facilities. Drinks, snacks and toilets are available at the entrance and at the cenote. Take a hat, suncream, sunglasses, shoes with good grip and drinking water.*

Chichén Itzá

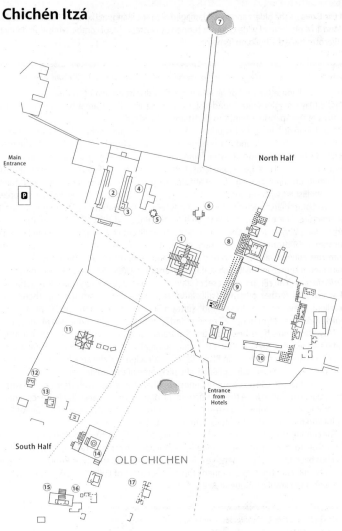

Main
Entrance

North Half

P

Entrance
from
Hotels

South Half

OLD CHICHEN

N

100 metres
100 yards

El Castillo **1**
Ball Court **2**
Temple of the Jaguar **3**
Platform of the Skulls
  (Tzompantli) **4**
Platform of Eagles **5**
Platform of Venus **6**

Cenote Sagrado (Well of
  Sacrifice) **7**
Temple of the Warriors
  & Chacmool Statue **8**
Group of a Thousand
  Columns **9**
Market **10**
Tomb of the High Priest **11**

House of the Deer **12**
Red House **13**
El Caracol (Observatory) **14**
Casa de las Monjas
  (Nunnery) **15**
'Church' **16**
Akabdzilo **17**

Chichén Itzá means 'mouth of the well of the water-sorcerer' and is one of the most spectacular of Maya sites. The Castillo, a giant stepped pyramid dominates the site, watched over by Chacmool, a Maya fertility god who reclines on a nearby structure. The city was built by the Maya in late Classic times (AD 600-900). By the end of the 10th century, the city was more or less abandoned. It was re-established in the 11th to 12th centuries, but much debate surrounds by whom. Whoever the people were, a comparison of some of the architecture with that of Tula, north of Mexico City, indicates they were heavily influenced by the Toltecs of Central Mexico.

The major buildings in the north half display a Toltec influence. Dominating them is **El Castillo** ① *1100-1500, 1600-1700, closed if raining*, its top decorated by the symbol of Quetzalcoatl/Kukulcán, the plumed serpent god. The balustrade of the 91 stairs up each of the four sides is also decorated at its base by the head of a plumed, open-mouthed serpent. The interior ascent of 61 steep and narrow steps leading to a chamber is currently closed; the red-painted jaguar that probably served as the throne of the high priest once burned bright, its eyes of jade, its fangs of flint.

There is a **ball court** with grandstand and towering walls, each set with a projecting ring of stone high up; at eye-level is a relief showing the decapitation of the winning captain (sacrifice was an honour; some theories, however, maintain that it was the losing captain who was killed). El Castillo stands at the centre of the northern half of the site, and almost at a right angle to its northern face runs the *sacbé* (sacred road), to the **Cenote Sagrado** (Well of Sacrifice). Into the Cenote Sagrado were thrown valuable propitiatory objects of all kinds, animals and human sacrifices. The well was first dredged by Edward H Thompson, the US Consul in Mérida, between 1904 and 1907; he accumulated a vast quantity of objects in pottery, jade, copper and gold. In 1962 the well was explored again by an expedition sponsored by the National Geographic Society and some 4000 further artefacts were recovered, including beads, polished jade, lumps of *copal* resin, small bells, a statuette of rubber latex, another of wood, and a quantity of animal and human bones. Another *cenote*, the Cenote Xtoloc, was probably used as a water supply. To the east of El Castillo is the **Templo de los Guerreros** (Temple of the Warriors) with its famous reclining **Chacmool** statue. This pyramidal platform is closed off to avoid erosion.

Chichén Viejo (Old Chichén), where the Maya buildings of the earlier city are found, lies about 500 m by path from the main clearing. The famous **El Caracol**, or Observatory, is included in this group, as is the **Casa de las Monjas** (Nunnery). A footpath to the right of the Casa de las Monjas leads to the **Templo de los Tres Dinteles** (Temple of the Three Lintels) after 30 minutes' walking. It requires at least one day to see the many pyramids, temples, ball courts and palaces, all of them adorned with astonishing sculptures. Excavation and renovation is still going on. Interesting birdlife and iguanas can also be seen around the ruins.

● *On the morning and afternoon of the spring and autumn equinoxes, the alignment of the sun's shadow casts a serpentine image on the side of the steps of El Castillo.*

Grutas de Balankanché

① *0900-1700, US$5 (allow about 45 mins for the 300-m descent), closed Sat afternoons. The caretaker turns lights on and off, answers questions in Spanish, every hour on the hour, minimum 6, maximum 20 persons.*
Tours run daily to the Grutas de Balankanché caves, 3 km east of Chichén Itzá just off the highway. There are archaeological objects, including offerings of pots and *metates* in an extraordinary setting, except for the unavoidable, awful *son et lumière* show (five a day in

Spanish; 1100, 1300 and 1500 in English; 1000 in French; it is very damp and hot, so dress accordingly). To get there, take the Chichén Itzá or Pisté-Balankanché bus hourly at a quarter past, US$0.50, taxi US$15.

Valladolid and around → *For listings, see pages 140-152. Colour map 1, A3. Phone code: 985.*

Situated roughly halfway between Mérida and Cancún, Valladolid is a pleasant little town, until now untouched by tourism. Its proximity to the famous ruins of Chichén Itzá, however, means that Valladolid has been earmarked for extensive development by the Mexican government.

Valladolid is set around a large plaza, flanked by the imposing Franciscan cathedral. Most of the hotels are clustered around the centre, as well as numerous restaurants catering for all budgets, favouring the lower end. There is a slightly medieval feel to the city, with some of the streets tapering off into mud tracks. The Vallisoletanos, as they are known, are friendlier than their Meridano neighbours, and Valladolid's location makes it an ideal place to settle for a few days, while exploring the ruins of Chichén Itzá, the fishing village of Río Lagartos on the north coast, and the three beautiful *cenotes* in the area, one of which is right in the town itself, on Calle 36 y 39.

The **tourist office** ① *southeast corner of the plaza*, is not very helpful but they give a useful map. Much more helpful information can be obtained from **Antonio 'Negro' Aguilar** ① *Calle 44 No 195*. Something of a local celebrity, he was a baseball champion in the 1950s and 60s, playing for Mexican squad, the Leones de Yucatán as well as the US team, the Washington Senators. Now he runs a shop selling sports equipment, rents bicycles and rents very cheap accommodation (see Sleeping, page 143). He is glad to offer information on any of the tourist attractions in the area; if cycling around, he will personally draw you a map of the best route you should take. Antonio can also help organize tours in a minivan to the ruins at Ek-Balam, minimum four people, US$3 per person.

Valladolid

100 metres
100 yards

Sleeping		Eating
Albergue La Candelaria 1	María Guadalupe 4	Bazar 1
Antonio 'Negro' Aguilar 2	Mesón del Marqués 5	La Sirenita 3
Hostal del Fraile 7	San Clemente 6	Las Campanas 2
María de la Luz 3		

Cenote Zací ⓘ *Calle 36 between Calle 37 and 39, daily 0800-1800, US$2, half price for children*, right in town, is an artificially lit *cenote* where you can swim, except when it is occasionally prohibited due to algae in the water. There is a thatched-roof restaurant and lighted promenades. A small town **museum** ⓘ *Calle 41, free*, housed in Santa Ana church, shows the history of rural Yucatán and has some exhibits from recent excavations at the ruins of Ek-Balam.

Seven kilometres from Valladolid is the beautiful **Cenote X-Kekén** ⓘ *daily 0800-1800, US$2.50*, at **Dzitnup**, the name by which it is more commonly known. It is stunningly lit with electric lights, the only natural light source being a tiny hole in the cavernous ceiling dripping with stalactites. Swimming is excellent, the water is cool and refreshing, although reported to be a little dirty, and harmless bats zip around overhead. Exploratory walks can also be made through the many tunnels leading off the *cenote*, for which you will need a torch. *Colectivos* leave when full from in front of **Hotel María Guadalupe**, US$1, they return until 1800, after which you will have to get a taxi back to Valladolid, US$4. Alternatively, hire a bicycle from Antonio Aguilar (see above) and cycle there, 25 minutes. Antonio will explain the best route before you set off. There is also the easily reached *cenote* close by, called **Samulá** ⓘ *US$2.25*, only recently opened to the public.

Ek-Balam
ⓘ *Daily 0800-1700, US$2.50.*

Twenty-five kilometres north of Valladolid are the Maya ruins of Ek-Balam, meaning 'Black Jaguar'. The ruins contain an impressive series of temples, sacrificial altars and residential buildings grouped around a large central plaza. The main temple, known as 'The Tower', is an immaculate seven-tiered staircase leading up to a flattened area with the remains of a temple. The views are stunning, and because they are not on the tourist trail, these ruins can be viewed at leisure, without the presence of hordes of tour groups from Cancún. To get there by car, take Route 295 north out of Valladolid. Just after the village of Temozón, take the turning on the right for Santa Rita. The ruins are some 5 km further on. A recommended way for those without a car is to hire a bike, take it on the roof of a *colectivo* leaving for Temozón from outside the **Hotel María Guadalupe**, and ask to be dropped off at the turning for Ek-Balam. From there, cycle the remaining 12 km to the ruins. There are also minivans to Ek-Balam run by Antonio Aguilar (see above).

Río Lagartos and around → *Colour map 1, A3.*

Tizimín is a dirty, scruffy little town en route to Río Lagartos, where you will have to change buses. If stuck, there are several cheap *posadas* and restaurants, but with frequent buses to Río Lagartos, there should be no need to stay the night here.

Río Lagartos is an attractive little fishing village on the north coast of Yucatán state, whose main attraction is the massive biosphere reserve containing thousands of pink flamingos, as well as 250 other species of bird. The people of Río Lagartos are extremely friendly and very welcoming to tourists. The only route is on the paved road from Valladolid; access from Cancún is by boat only, a journey mainly made by tradesmen ferrying fish to the resort. Development in Río Lagartos, however, is on the horizon.

Boat trips to see the flamingo reserve can be easily arranged by walking down to the harbour and taking your pick from the many offers you'll receive from boatmen. You will get a longer trip with fewer people, due to the decreased weight in the boat. As well as flamingos, there are 250 other species of bird, some very rare, in the 47-sq-km reserve. Make sure your boatman takes you to the larger colony of flamingos near **Las Coloradas**

(15 km), recognizable by a large salt mound on the horizon, rather than the smaller groups of birds along the river. Early morning boat trips can be arranged in Río Lagartos to see the flamingos (US$35, in eight to nine seater, 2½ to four hours, cheaper in a five-seater, fix the price before embarking; in mid-week few people go so there is no chance of negotiating, but boat owners are more flexible on where they go; at weekends it is very busy, so it may be easier to get a party together and reduce costs). Check before going whether the flamingos are there; they usually nest here during May and June and stay through July and August (although salt mining is disturbing their habitat).

◉ State of Yucatán listings

For Sleeping and Eating price codes and other relevant information, see Essentials pages 31-33.

● Sleeping

Mérida *p127, map p129*
The prices of hotels are not determined by their location with budget hotels close to the plaza and the better hotels often further away. If booking into a central hotel, always try to get a room away from the street side, as noise on the narrow streets begins as early as 0500.
LL Hacienda Xcanatún, Km 12 Carretera Mérida–Progreso, T999-941 0273, www.xcanatun.com. Carefully restored hacienda, 10 mins out of town, relaxed atmosphere, full breakfast included, restaurant, Casa de Piedra, possibly the best in Mérida, located in a converted machine room with ceilings high enough to give you vertigo, live music Thu, Fri and Sat. Highly recommended.
L-AL Casa San Angel, Paseo de Montejo 1 with Calle 49, T999-928 1800, www.hotel casasanangel.com. A colonial building with gorgeous, high-ceilinged rooms on the ground floor and more rooms upstairs. Quiet, tranquil relaxation pool, restaurant and craft shop. Pleasant.
AL-A Gobernador, Calle 59 No 535, corner of 66, T999-930 4141, www.gobernador merida.com.mx. Good clean hotel with 2 small pools. All rooms with a/c, cable TV and phone. 'Executive' rooms are better. Restaurant offers buffet breakfast. Promotional rates and free Wi-Fi. Recommended.

AL-A La Misión de Fray Diego, Calle 61 No 524 between Calle 64 and 66, T01-800-221-0599, www.lamisiondefraydiego.com. Very pleasant colonial-style hotel situated around 2 shady courtyards. Section nearest the road is original 17th century, formerly connected to the convent behind. Minibar and TV in all rooms, small pool and restaurant.
A Casa Mexilio, Calle 68, between Calle 59 and 57, T999-928 2505, casamexilio@ earthlink.net. This fabulous, old-fashioned colonial building has 3 floors complete with antique sitting room, lush courtyard and a pleasant pool. Part of a bygone world and a soothing place to stay. Breakfast included. Friendly hosts. Recommended.
A-B Gran Hotel, Parque Hidalgo, Calle 60 No 496, esq Calle 59, T999-923 6963, www.granhoteldemerida.com.mx. A great place to stay with a good atmosphere. Popular with the stars of film and stage, and politicians, including Fidel Castro. All rooms are clean and have a/c, TV, hot water and phone; not all have windows. Free parking.
A-B Medio Mundo, Calle 55 No 533 between Calle 64 and 66, T999-924 5472, www.hotelmediomundo.com. Renovated old home now a charming hotel with 12 tasteful, high-ceiling rooms, lush garden patio and swimming pool. Friendly, pleasant and quaint. Nice handicraft shop forms part of the hotel. Recommended.
B Dolores Alba Mérida, Calle 63 No 464 between Calle 52 and 54, T999-858 1555, www.dolores alba.com. This large, modern hotel has 2 sections and price bands. The more comfortable and expensive rooms

overlook the pool and courtyard. The cheaper rooms are slightly smaller and have no views. Cool, airy atmosphere and a nice pool. All rooms have a/c, and there's a sister establishment in Chichén Itzá.

B-C Casa San Juan, Calle 62 No 545A between Calle 69 and 71, T999-986 2937, www.casasanjuan.com. This restored 19th-century house, close to the bus station, has a pleasant, tranquil atmosphere. The multilingual owner is helpful and friendly, the rooms are large, and prices include American breakfast. Book ahead in high season.

B-C Posada Toledo, Calle 58 No 487 esq 57, T999-923 1690, hptoledo@prodigy.net.mx. This charming old hotel has a strong, if slightly tired, character. Elegant, high-ceiling rooms surround a plant-filled courtyard, all adorned with interesting woodwork and occasionally weathered, antique furniture. Cheap breakfast, parking (US$4) and colour TV.

C-D Trinidad, Calle 62 No 464 esq 55, T999-923 2033, www.hotelestrinidad.com. This old house, popular with budget travellers and backpackers, has a relaxed, friendly vibe. Pool table, DVDs, courtyard and rooftop jacuzzi – the perfect way to unwind after a hard day pounding the streets. Continental breakfast included in the price. Simply lovely and highly recommended.

D Casa Becil, Calle 67 No 550-C, between Calle 66 and 68, T999-924 6764, hotelcasa becil@yahoo.com.mx. The rooms are bright and clean, if simple. They all have fan, bath, hot water and cable TV. The owner is English-speaking and hospitable. There's also a communal kitchen. Conveniently located for the bus station. Recommended.

D Casa Bowen, restored colonial house, corner of Calle 66 No 521-B, esq 65, T999-928 6109. Open 24 hrs, if locked ring bell. The staff are friendly and English-speaking, and rooms have bath and hot water, cheaper with fan. Often full at weekends. Avoid rooms overlooking the main street – they're noisy. Nicely located between the CAME 1st-class bus terminal and the centre.

D Margarita, Calle 66 No 506 and 63, T999-923 7236. With shower, clean, good, rooms a bit dark and noisy downstairs, cheaper rooms for 5 (3 beds), parking, friendly, excellent value. Some rooms have TV and a/c (pricier).

D Mucuy, Calle 57 No 481, between Calle 56 and 58, T999-928 5193, www.mucuy.com. Good, but 1st-floor rooms are very hot. There's a pool and garden, hot water and optional TV. Run by a lovely English-speaking, elderly woman and her daughter. Highly recommended.

D-E Hostal Zócalo, on the south of the plaza, T999-930 9562, hostel_zocalo@yahoo.com. Popular hostel with economical rooms and big, clean dormitories. There's TV, DVD, kitchen, laundry and internet. Full breakfast included with the private rooms. Friendly management and good location.

D-E Las Monjas, Calle 66A No 509 between Calle 61 and 63, T999-928 6632. Simple, family-run lodgings. Clean, quiet, friendly and good value. Can organize tours. Recommended.

D-E San José, west of plaza on Calle 63 No 503 between Calle 64 and 66, T999-928 6657, san_jose92@latinmail.com. Bath, hot water, basic, clean, friendly, rooms on top floor are baked by the sun, one of the cheapest, popular with locals, will store luggage, good cheap meals available, local speciality *poc chuc*.

D-F Nómadas Youth Hostal, Calle 62 No 433, end of Calle 51, 5 blocks north of the plaza, T999-924 5223, www.nomadas travel.com. A clean and friendly hostel with private rooms and dorms. General services include hot water, full kitchen, drinking water, hammocks, swimming pool and internet. Owner Raúl speaks English and is very helpful. Good value and a great place to meet other travellers. Free salsa classes every night. Live 'trova' music Mon, Wed. Fri. Recommended.

Camping

Trailer Park Rainbow, Km 8, on the road to Progreso, T999-926 1026 US$18 for 1 or 2, hot showers, all facilities and good bus connection into town. Reports of excessive charging for use of amenities.

Celestún *p130*

Most lodgings are along Calle 12.

LL Hotel Eco Paraíso Xixim, Km 10 off the old Sisal Hwy, T988-916 2100, www.ecoparaiso.com. In coconut grove on edge of reserve, pool, tours to surrounding area including flamingos, turtle nesting, etc.

C Gutiérrez, Calle 12 (the Malecón) No 127, T988-916 2609. Large beds, fans, views, clean.

D San Julio, Calle 12 No 92, T988-916 2062. Large bright rooms and clean bathrooms, owner knowledgeable about the area.

Progreso and around *p131*

B-D Tropical Suites, Calle 19 No 143, T969-935 1263. Suites and rooms with cable TV, a/c, sea views.

D Progreso, Calle 29 No 142, T969-935 0039. Simple rooms in the centre.

Ticul and Oxkutzcab *p133*

C Trujeque, Calle 48 No 102-A, Oxkutzcab, T997-975 0568. A/c, TV, clean, good value, discount for stays over a week.

D Casa de Huéspedes, near bus terminal, Oxkutzcab. Large rooms with bath, TV, fan, friendly. Recommended.

D Hotel Rosalía, Calle 54 No 101 Oxkutzcab, T997-975 0167, turn right out of bus station, right again. Double room, shower, cable TV.

D-E Motel Bugambilias, Calle 23 No 291, Ticul, T997-972 1368. Clean, basic rooms.

E Sierra Sosa, Calle 26, near zócalo, Ticul, T997-972 0008. Cheap rooms that are dungeon-like, but friendly, clean and helpful.

Uxmal *p134*

There is no village at Uxmal, just the following hotels. For cheap accommodation, go to Ticul, 28 km away (see above).

AL The Lodge at Uxmal, entrance to ruins, T997-976 2102, www.mayaland.com/Lodge Uxmal. Same owners as **Hacienda Uxmal**. Comfortable, a/c, bath, TV, fair restaurant.

AL-A Hacienda Uxmal, T997-976 2012, www.mayaland.com/HaciendaUxmal, 300-400 m from ruins. Good, efficient and relaxing, good Yucatecan restaurant, a/c, gardens, pool.

A Misión Uxmal, 1-2 km from ruins on Mérida road, Km 78, T997-976 2022, www.hoteles mision.com.mx. Rooms a bit dark, with a pool.

A Villas Arqueológicas de Uxmal, Carretera Mérida–Uxmal, Km 78, about 12 km north of ruins, T997-976 2040, www.villasarqueo logicas.com.mx. Boutique-style new hotel, with birdwatching and jungle tour packages.

B Rancho Uxmal, Carretera Mérida–Uxmal, Km 70, about 4 km north of ruins, T997-977 6254. Comfortable rooms, hot and cold water, camping for US$5, pool, reasonable food but not cheap (no taxis to get there).

C-D Sacbé Hostel, at Km 127 on Hwy 261, T997-858 1281. A mix of private rooms (private bath), dorms and campsite, with space for hammocks, and solar-powered showers, with breakfast and dinner for a little more.

Camping

No camping allowed at the site, but there is a campsite at **Sacbé Hostel**, see above. 2nd-class buses from Mérida to Campeche pass by, ask to be let out at the **Campo de Baseball**. French and Mexican owners, beautiful park, fastidiously clean and impeccably managed. 9 electric hook-ups (US$7-10 for motor home according to size), big area for tents (US$2.75 per person with tent), *palapas* for hammocks (US$2.65 per person), for cars pay US$1, showers, toilets, clothes-washing facilities, also 3 bungalows with ceiling fan (**E**), breakfast, vegetarian lunch and dinner available (US$2.65 each). Highly recommended.

Izamal and around *p135*

B Macan-Che, Calle 22 No 305 between Calle 33 and 35, T988-954 0287, www.macanche. com. 4 blocks north of plaza, pleasant bungalows, breakfast. Recommended.

Chichén Itzá *p135*

LL-L Hacienda Chichén, T999-924 8407, www.haciendachichen.com. Luxury resort and spa, close to the ruins, with tasteful rooms, suites and bungalows. There's a garden, library and restaurant, all contained by historic colonial grounds.

AL-A Villas Arqueológicas, T997-974 6020, Apdo Postal 495, Mérida, www.villasarqueo logicas.com.mx. Close to the ruins. Pool, tennis, restaurant (expensive and poor). Both are on the other side of the fenced-off ruins from the bus stop; either walk all the way round, or take taxi (US$1-1.50).

A-B Hotel Chichén Itzá, Pisté, T999-851 0022, www.mayaland.com. 3 types of rooms and tariffs. The best are clean, tasteful, overlook the garden and have a/c, internet, phone and fridge. Cheaper rooms (**A**) overlook the street.

B Dolores Alba Chichén, Km 122, T985-858 1555, www.doloresalba.com. Small, Spanish-owned hotel, 2.5 km on the road to Puerto Juárez (bus passes it), 40 clean bungalows with shower, a/c and cable TV. Pool, restaurant, English is spoken. Sister hotel in Mérida.

B-C Pirámide Inn Resort, 1.5 km from ruins, at the Chichén end of Pisté, Km 117, T999-851 0115, www.chichen.com. This long-standing Pisté favourite has been remodelled. It has many clean, comfortable rooms, a pool, hammocks and *palapas*. Temazcal available, book 24 hrs in advance. Camping costs US$5, or US$15 with a car. Friendly owner, speaks English.

B-C Posada Olalde, 100 m from the main road at the end of Calle 6, between Calle 15 and 17. This lovely, family-run hotel has a handful of economical rooms and basic Yucatecan *cabañas* built the old-fashioned way. There's a lush, tranquil garden and the Mayan owners are kind and friendly.

C Posada Maya, Calle 8 No 70, just off the main road. Small, simple rooms, desperately in need of a deep clean. However, there's space to sling a hammock if you're terribly impoverished (**F**).

C Stardust Posada Annex, Pisté, about 2 km before the ruins if coming from Mérida (taxi to ruins US$2.50). Simple, basic rooms and a range of tariffs to suit your budget. Slightly run-down, but acceptable. There's also a pool and an average restaurant.

Valladolid *p138, map p138*

AL-A Mesón del Marqués, Calle 39 with Calle 40 and 42, north side of Plaza Principal, T985-856 2073, www.mesondelmarques.com. Housed in a handsome colonial edifice, this hotel has 90 tasteful rooms, all with a/c and cable TV. There's a swimming pool, Wi-Fi, garden and laundry service. Recommended.

A-B María de la Luz, Calle 42 No 193-C, Plaza Principal, T985-856 1181, www.mariadelaluz hotel.com. Good clean rooms, tours to Chichén Itzá and Río Lagartos, excellent restaurant.

B-C María Guadalupe, Calle 44 No 198, T985-856 2068. Simple, clean rooms with fan. Good value, hot water, washing facilities. Recommended.

C San Clemente, Calle 42 No 206, T985-856 2208, www.hotelsanclemente.com.mx. Many clean, comfortable rooms with a/c (cheaper with fan) and cable TV. There's a pool, restaurant, garden and free parking. Recommended.

C Antonio 'Negro' Aguilar rents rooms for 2, 3 or 4 people. The best budget deal in the town for 2 or more, clean, spacious rooms on a quiet street, garden, volleyball/basketball court. The rooms are on Calle 41 No 225, before the **Maya Hotel**, but you need to book them at Aguilar's shop (Calle 44 No 195, T985-856 2125). If the shop's closed, knock on the door of the house on the right of the shop.

D Albergue La Candelaria, Calle 35 No 201-F, T985-856 2267, candelaria_hostel@hot mail.com. Good cheap option, especially for solo travellers. Single-sex dorms with fan, clean, hot water, kitchen, washing facilities, hammocks out the back in the garden, TV room. Recommended.

E-F Hostal del Fraile, Calle de los Frailes 212-C, T985-856 5852. Youth hostal with 20 beds, free breakfast, clean, quiet, friendly. Best budget lodgings in town.

Río Lagartos and around *p139*

B Villa de Pescadores, Calles 14 x 93 y 9-A, T986-862 0020. 9 rooms, best hotel in town, friendly and helpful.

D Tere and Miguel, near the harbour (ask at the bus terminal). 3 rooms for rent, very nicely furnished, double and triple rooms, 1 with an extra hammock, sea views.

Ⓕ Eating

Mérida p127, map p129

There are a number of taco stands, pizzerias and sandwich places in Pasaje Picheta, a small plaza off the Palacio de Gobierno.

Alberto's Continental, Calle 64 No 482 corner Calle 57. Yucatecan, Lebanese and international food, mouth-watering steaks and seafood, all inside a colonial mansion. Highly recommended.

Casa de Piedra 'Xcanatún', in Hacienda Xcanatún (see Sleeping). Km 12 Carretera Mérida–Progreso, T999-941 0213. Fine dining, best restaurant in the area (although a bit out of town). Popular with locals. Reserve if possible. Highly recommended.

Villa María, Calle 59 No 553 and Calle 68, T999-923 3357, www.villamariamerida.com. Classical music spills over the white table-cloths at this sophisticated, fine-dining establishment. The interior is beautiful and they serve French, Mediterranean and Mexican cuisine.

Café La Habana, Calle 59 y Calle 62. Neither the coffee nor the food is fantastic, but it's OK for a snack. A fine spot for people-watching, open 24 hrs. Free Wi-Fi.

El Nuevo Tucho, Calle 60 near University. Good local dishes, mostly meat and fish, and occasional live music. Healthy and extensive drinks menu. Evening entertainment also.

La Casa de Frida, Calle 61, between Calle 66 and 66A, www.lacasadefrida.com.mx. Open Mon-Sat 1800-2200. Frida Kahlo-themed restaurant in a colourful courtyard setting, traditional Mexican cuisine, including mole and chiles en nogada.

Los Almendros, Calle 50A No 493 esq 59. Housed in a high-vaulted, white-washed thatched barn, this award-winning restaurant specializes in 1st-rate traditional

Yucatecan cuisine, serving tasty dishes like pollo pibil and poc chuc. Confusingly, the entrance is through the car park.

Pórtico del Peregrino, Calle 57 between Calle 60 and 62. Dining indoors or in an attractive leafy courtyard, excellent food.

Amaro, Calle 59 No 507 between Calle 60 and 62, near the plaza. Open late daily. With open courtyard and covered patio, good food, especially vegetarian, try chaya drink from the leaf of the chaya tree; their curry, avocado pizza and home-made bread are also very good.

Café Chocolate, Calle 60 No 442 y Calle 49, T999-928 5113, www.cafe-chocolate.com.mx. This café and art space does good mole, as well as an excellent breakfast buffet, a lunchtime menu and evening meals. They also have home-made fresh bread and pasta, and an excellent selection of fruit drinks and teas. Cosy and classy at the same time, with antique furniture, free Wi-Fi and art and photography exhibitions in beautiful surroundings, with sofas indoors or outdoor courtyard seating. Highly recommended.

Flor de Santiago, Calle 70 No 478, between Calle 57 and 59. Reputedly the oldest restaurant in Mérida. There's a cafeteria and bakery in one section, serving cheap snacks and à la carte meals. The patio out back is sophisticated and serves Yucatecan specialities. Breakfast buffet is good value.

La Vía Olympo (formerly La Valentina) on main plaza opposite cathedral. Good-value Mexican and Yucatecan dishes, brisk service and outdoor seating. Good for breakfasts, free Wi-Fi.

Restaurant Colonial, Calle 62 and 57. Average coffee, but this place lays on an 'all you can eat' breakfast buffet for US$6, with fruit, coffee, good juice, eggs, cereal and other offerings. Fill up on several courses and then come back for the lunch buffet ¬ this time there are steaks, but drinks aren't included.

Café Alameda, Calle 58 No 474 between Calle 57 and 55. Arabic and Mexican cuisine, breakfast and lunch only, 0730-1700.

El Trapiche, near on Calle 62 half a block north of the plaza. Good local dishes, excellent pizzas, sandwiches, omelettes, *tortas*, tacos, burgers and freshly made juices.

Marlín Azul, Calle 62, between Calle 57 and 59. The place for cheap seafood fare, mostly frequented by locals. Get a shrimp cocktail breakfast for a couple of dollars.

Marys, Calle 63 No 486, between Calle 63 and 58. Mainly Mexican customers. Possibly the cheapest joint in town. *Comida corrida* for US$2.50. Recommended.

Mérida, Calle 62 between Calle 59 and 61. Full 3 course for US$2.50 – a bargain, and it's tasty Yucatecan fare as well.

Vito Corleone's Pizza, Calle 59 No 508, between Calle 62 and 60. Open from 1800. Serves pop and pizza, by the slice or whole, eat in or take away. Popular with students and young Mexicans.

Cafés, juices and ice cream parlours

Café El Hoyo, Calle 62, between Calle 57 and 59. A chilled out spot with a patio, popular with students, serving coffee, beer and snacks.

Café Petropolis, Calle 70 opposite CAME terminal. Existed long before the terminal was built, family-run, turkey a speciality, excellent quality, good *horchata* and herb teas.

El Colón Sorbetes y Dulces Finos, Calle 61 and 60. Serving ice cream since 1907, great sorbets, *meringue*, good menu with explanation of fruits in English. Highly recommended. About 30 different flavours of good ice cream.

Italian Coffee Company, Calle 62 between Calle 59 and 61. A bit like a Mexican Starbucks, but nevertheless serves excellent coffee, decent toasted baguettes, and tasty cakes for those feeling a trifle decadent.

Jugos California, Calle 62 and 63 good fruit salads and juices. Next door **Jugos Janitzio** also good.

There's a good *panadería* at Calle 62 y 61. Parque Santa Ana, is good for cheap street fare. Closed middle of the day.

Celestún *p130*

Many beachside restaurants along Calle 12, but be careful of food in the cheaper ones; recommended is **La Playita**, for fried fish, seafood cocktails. Food stalls along Calle 11 beside the bus station should be approached with caution.

Chivirico, across the road from **Playita**, offers descent fish, shrimp and other seafood.

El Lobo, Calle 10 and 13, on the corner of the main square. Best spot for breakfast, with fruit salads, yoghurt, pancakes, etc. Celestún's best pizza in the evenings.

Progreso and around *p131*

The Malecón at Progreso is lined with seafood restaurants, some with tables on the beach. For cheaper restaurants, head for the centre of town, near the bus terminal.

Las Palmas and **El Cocalito** are 2 of several reasonable fish restaurants in Chelem.

Casablanca, **Capitan Marisco** and **Le Saint Bonnet**, Malecón, Progreso, all recommended.

Ticul and Oxkutzcab *p133*

Los Almendros, Calle 23 207, Ticul. Nice colonial building with patio, good Yucatecan cuisine, reasonable prices.

Pizzería La Góndola, Calle 23, Ticul. Good, moderately priced pizzas.

El Colorín, near Hotel Sierra Sosa on Calle 26, Ticul. Cheap local food.

Uxmal *p134*

Restaurant at ruins, good but expensive.

Izamal and around *p135*

There are several restaurants on Plaza de la Constitución.

Kinich-Kakmó, Calle 27 No 299 between Calle 28 and 30. Near ruins of same name, local food.

Tumben-Lol, Calle 22 No 302 between Calle 31 and 33. Yucatecan cuisine.

El Norteño at bus station. Good and cheap.

Wayane, near statue of Diego de Landa. Friendly, clean.

Chichén Itzá *p135*

Mostly poor and overpriced in Chichén itself (cafés inside the ruins are cheaper than the restaurant at the entrance, but still expensive). Restaurants in Pisté close 2100-2200.

¶¶ Fiesta Maya, Calle 15 No 59, Pisté. Reportedly the best restaurant in town. Serves Yucatecan food, tacos, meat and sandwiches. Lunch buffet every day at 1200, US$10.

¶ Pollo Mexicano on the main road in Pisté. One of several simple places that serves mouth-watering, barbequed chicken.

¶ Sayil in Pisté. Serves Yucatecan dishes like *pollo pibil*, as well as breakfast *huevos al gusto*.

Valladolid *p138, map p138*

There is a well-stocked supermarket on the road between the centre and bus station.

¶¶ El Mesón del Marqués, Calle 39, between Calle 40 and 42. Award-winning restaurant serving seafood and Yucatecan cuisine in a tranquil setting. Intimate and romantic.

¶¶ La Sirenita, Calle 34N, between Calle 29 and 31, T985-856 1655, few blocks east of main square. Closes 1800, closed Sun. Highly recommended for seafood, popular and friendly.

¶¶ Plaza Maya, Calle 41 No 235, a few blocks east of main square. Great regional food and good *comida corrida*, step up from the rest.

¶ Bazar, northeast corner of Plaza Principal, next to **Mesón del Marqués**. Wholesome grub.

Cafés

Las Campanas, Calle 41 and 42, opposite the plaza, serves various types of coffee.

Río Lagartos and around *p139*

For a fishing village, the seafood is not spectacular, as most of the good fish is sold to restaurants in Mérida and Cancún.

¶¶ Isla Contoy, Calle 19 No 134. Average seafood, not cheap for the quality.

¶¶ Los Negritos, off the plaza. Moderately priced seafood.

☺ Entertainment

Mérida *p127, map p129*
See the free listings magazine *Yucatán Today*.

Bars and clubs

There are several good bars on the north side of the plaza, beer is moderately priced at US$1, although food can be expensive. There are a number of live-music venues around Parque Santa Lucía, a couple of blocks from the main plaza.

El Cielo, Paseo de Montejo and Calle 25, T999-944 5127, www.elcielobar.com. Sexy, white leather lounge-bar that plays house, techno and pop. Don your dancing shoes and say 'buenas noches' to the beautiful people.

El Tucho, also known as **El Nuevo Tucho**, Calle 55 between 60 and 58. A restaurant open till 2100 only, with live music, often guest performers from Cuba play. Good food as well.

La Parranda, Calle 60, between 59 and 61, T999-938 0435, laparrandamerida.com. This touristy cantina is always buzzing with atmosphere in the evenings. Live music Thu-Sat and always a steady flow of beer.

Mambo Café, Plaza Las Americanas Shopping Mall, T999-987 7533, www.mambo cafe.com.mx. Big club in Mérida, mainly salsa but all kinds of music. Wed-Sat from 2100.

Panchos, Calle 59 between Calle 60 and 62. Very touristy, staff in traditional gear, but lively and busy, live music, patio.

Cinema

There is a cinema showing subtitled films in English on Parque Hidalgo.

Teatro Mérida, Calle 62 between 59 and 61, shows European, Mexican and independent movies as well as live theatre productions. The 14-screen multiplex **Cinepolis** is in the huge Plaza de las Américas, north of the city; *colectivo* and buses take 20 mins and leave from Calle 65 between 58 and 60. Hollywood Cinema, near Parque Santiago, has 4 screens.

Theatre

Teatro Peón Contreras, Calle 60 with 57. Shows start at 2100, US$4, ballet, etc.

⊛ Festivals and events

Mérida *p127, map p129*

Every **Thu** there is a cultural music and dance show in Plaza Santa Lucía. **Sat** brings En El Corazón de Mérida, with music and dance in bars, restaurants and in the street. Every **Sun** the central streets are closed off to traffic, live music and parades abound. **6 Jan** Mérida celebrates its birthday. **Feb/Mar** Carnival takes place the week before Ash Wed (best on Sat). Floats, dancers in regional costume, music and dancing around the plaza and children dressed in animal suits.

Chichén Itzá *p135*

21 Mar and 21 Sep On the morning and afternoon of the spring and autumn equinoxes, the alignment of the sun's shadow casts a serpentine image on the side of the steps of El Castillo. This occasion is popular and you'll be lucky to get close enough to see the action. Note that this phenomenon can also be seen on the days before and after the equinox, 19th-23rd of the month.

Río Lagartos *p139*

17 Jul A big local fiesta, with music, food and dancing in the plaza. **12 Dec** Virgen de Guadalupe. The whole village converges on the chapel built in 1976 on the site of a vision of the Virgin Mary by a local non-believer, who suddenly died, along with his dog, shortly after receiving the vision.

○ Shopping

Mérida *p127, map p129*

Bookshops

Amate, Calle 60 453A, between 49 and 51, T999-924 2222, www.amatebooks.com. You'll find a superb stock of literature here, covering everything from architecture to Yucatecan cuisine, but anthropology, archaeology, history and art are the mainstay. Another branch in Oaxaca.
Librerías Dante, Calle 59, No 498 between 58 and 60. Calle 61 between 62 and 64 (near Lavandería La Fe), used books.

Crafts and souvenirs

You'll find an abundance of craft shops in the streets around the plaza. They sell hammocks (see box, page 131), silver jewellery, Panama hats, *guayabera* shirts, *huaraches*, baskets and Maya figurines. The salesmen are ruthless, but they expect to receive about half their original asking price. Bargain hard, but maintain good humour, patience and face. And watch out for the many touts around the plaza, using all sorts of ingenious ploys to get you to their shops.

There are 2 main craft markets in the city: the **Mercado Municipal**, Calle 56a and 67 and the **García Rejón Bazaar**, also known as Casa de la Artesanía, Calle 65 and 60. The former sprawls, smells and takes over several blocks, but it's undeniably alive and undeniably Mexican. It sells everything under the sun and is also good for a cheap, tasty meal, but check the stalls for cleanliness. The latter is excellent for handicrafts and renowned for clothing, particularly leather *huaraches* and good-value cowboy boots – good, cheap Yucatecan fare.

If you're looking for a hammock, several places are recommended, but shop around for the best deal. **El Mayab**, Calle 58 No 553 and 71, are friendly, have a limited choice but good deals available; **La Poblana**, Calle 65 between Calle 58 and 60, will bargain, especially for sales of more than 1 – they have a huge stock. **El Aguacate**, Calle 58

No 604, corner of Calle 73, good hammocks and no hard sell. Recommended. **Casa de Artesanías Ki-Huic**, Calle 63, between Calle 62 and 64, is a friendly store with all sorts of handicrafts from silver and wooden masks, to hammocks and batik. Shop owner Julio Chay is very knowledgeable and friendly, sometimes organizes trips for visitors to his village, Tixkokob, which specializes in hammocks. Open daily, 0900-2100. Julio can also organize trips to other nearby villages and the shop has tequilas for sampling.

For silver, there are a handful of stores on Calle 60, just north of the plaza.

Mexican folk art, including *calaveras* (Day of the Dead skeletons), is available from **Minaturas**, Calle 59 No 507A; and **Yalat**, Calle 39 and 40.

If you're in the market for a *guayabera* shirt, you'll find stores all over the city, particularly on Calle 62, between 57 and 61.

Supermarkets
Supermaz, Calle 56, between 65 and 63.

Progreso and around *p131*
Mundo Marino, Calle 80 s/n, 1 block from the beach, T969-915 1380. Shark-related souvenirs.

Izamal and around *p135*
Market, Calle 31, on Plaza de la Constitución, opposite convent, closes soon after lunch.
Hecho a mano, Calle 31 No 332 between 36 and 38. Folk art; postcards, textiles, jewellery, papier-mâché masks.

▲ Activities and tours

Mérida *p127, map p129*
Tour operators
Most tour operators can arrange trips to popular local destinations including Chichén Itzá, Uxmal, Celestún and nearby *cenotes*.
Amigo Yucatán, Av Colón No 508-C and offices in 3 hotels, T999-920 0104, www.amigoyucatan.com. Interesting

gastronomy and tasting tours of Yucatán, as well as excursions to Maya ruins, Izamal, Puuc Route and Celestún. It's possible to book all tours online, 24 hrs in advance recommended, but also possible before 0830 on the same day (best to do this in person or on the phone). Friendly. Recommended.
Carmen Travel Services, Calle 27 No 151, between 32 and 34, T999-927 2027, www.carmentravel.com, 3 other branches. This well-established agency can organize flights, hotels and all the usual trips to the sights. Recommended.
Ecoturismo Yucatán, Calle 3 No 235, between Calle 32A and 34, T999-920 2772, www.ecoyuc.com.mx. Specializes in educational and ecotourism tours including jungle trips, birding expeditions and turtle-hatching tours. Also offers adventure and archaeological packages.
Yucatan Connection, Calle 33 No 506, T999-163 8224, www.yucatan-connection. com. Tours to lesser visited Mayan sites like Mayapán, Tecoh and Ochil. Staff are fluent in English, Czech and Slovak.
Yucatán Trails, Calle 62, No 482, Av 57-59, T999-928 2582, www.yucatantrails.com. Canadian owner Denis Lafoy is friendly, English-speaking and helpful. He runs tours to all the popular local destinations, stores luggage cheaply, has a book exchange and throws famous parties on the first Fri of every month.

⊖ Transport

Mérida *p127, map p129*
Air
Aeropuerto Rejón (MID), 8 km from town. From Calle 67, 69 and 60, bus 79 goes to the airport, marked 'Aviación', US$0.35, roughly every 20 mins. Taxi set price voucher system US$8; *colectivo* US$2.50. Good domestic flight connections. International flight connections with **Belize City**, **Houston**, **Miami** and **Havana**. Package tours Mérida–Havana–

Mérida available (be sure to have a confirmed return flight). For return to Mexico ask for details at Secretaría de Migración Av Colón and Calle 8.

Airline offices Aerolínenas Aztecas, T01-800-229-8322. **AeroMéxico**, Av Colón 451 and Montejo, T999-920 1260, www.aeromexico.com. **Aviacsa**, T999-925 6890, www.aviasca.com.mx. **Aviateca**, T999-926 9087. **Continental**, T999-926 3100, www.continental.com. **Delta**, T01-800-123-410, www.delta.com.

Bus
There are several bus terminals in Mérida.

The **CAME terminal** Buses to destinations outside Yucatán State, Chichén Itzá and Valladolid operating **ADO** and **UNO** buses leave from the 1st-class CAME terminal at Calle 70, No 555, between Calle 69 and 71. The station has lockers and is open 24 hrs, left luggage charges from US$0.30 per bag, depending on size. About 20 mins' walk to centre, taxi US$2.50. Schedules change frequently.

The **ADO terminal** Around the corner, has left luggage open 24 hrs, and is for Yucatán destinations except Chichén Itzá with fleets run by **Mayab**, **ATS**, **Sur** and **Oriente**.

There are also 1st-class departures from the **Hotel Fiesta Americana**, Calle 60 and Colón, which are mostly luxury services to Cancún.

Buses to **Progreso** depart every 15 mins, US$1.50, from their own terminal at Calle 62 No 524, between 65 and 67.

There is another 2nd-class terminal near the market at Calle 50 and 65. It deals with obscure local destinations, including **Timzimín**, **Cenotillo**, **Izamal** and many Maya villages specializing in different crafts, including **Tixkokob**.

To **Cancún**, hourly 1st-class **ADO** services, 4 hrs, US$18, and frequent 2nd-class services, US$15. To **Campeche**, frequent ADO and 2nd-class services, 2 hrs, US$7-10. To **Chichén Itzá** (ruins and Pisté), **ADO**

services at 0630, 0915, 1240, 2 hrs, US$7, and cheaper, frequent 2nd-class buses stop on their way to Cancún. To **Celestún**, frequent 2nd-class **Oriente** services, 2 hrs, US$3.50. To **Coatzacoalcos**, ADO services at 1210, 1830, 1930 and 2130; 12 hrs, US$38. To **Palenque**, ADO services at 0830, 1915, 2200, 8 hrs, US$26. To **Ruta Puuc**, 2nd-class **ATS** service, 0800, US$10. To **Tulum**, ADO services at 0630, 1040, 1240, 1745, 1945 6 hrs, US$9-14. To **Uxmal**, 2nd-class **SUR** services at 0600, 0905, 1040, 1205, 1705, 1½ hrs, US$3. To **Valladolid**, hourly ADO services, 1½ hrs, US$9, and 5 2nd-class buses, all in the afternoon and evening, US$5.50. To **Villahermosa**, frequent ADO services, 9 hrs, US$30.50 and several ADO GL services, US$36. To **Tuxtla Guitérrez**, an OCC service at 1915, 15 hrs, US$40, and ADO GL services at 1900 and 2315, US$55. To **San Cristóbal de las Casas**, an OCC service at 1915, 13 hrs, US$36. To **Tenosique**, an ADO service at 2100, US$29.

To Guatemala Take a bus from Mérida to San Cristóbal and change there for Comitán, or to Tenosique for the route to Flores. Another alternative would be to take the bus from Mérida direct to Tuxtla Gutiérrez (times given above), then connect to Cd Cuauhtémoc or to Tapachula.

To Belize Take a bus to **Chetumal**, ADO services at 0730 (except Wed and Sat), 1300, 1800, 2300, 6 hrs, US$21 and cross the border. **Premier** operate services from Chetumal to **Belize City** at 1145, 1445 and 1745, 5 hrs, US$10, schedules are subject to change.

Car
Car hire Car reservations should be booked well in advance if possible. Hire firms charge around US$45-50 a day although bargains can be found in low season. All agencies allow vehicles to be returned to Cancún for an extra charge, and most have an office at the airport where they share the same counter and negotiating usually takes place. Agencies include: **Budget**, at the airport,

T999-946 1323; **Executive,** Calle 56A No 451, corner of Av Colón, at the Hotel Fiesta Americana, T999-925 8171, www.executive. com.mx; **Easy Way Car Rental,** Calle 60, between 55 and 57, T999-930 9500, www.easywayrentacar-yucatan.com; **Mexico Rent a Car,** Calle 57A Depto 12, between 58 and 60, T999-923 3637, mexicorentacar@hotmail.com.

Car service Servicios de Mérida Goodyear, Calle 59, near Av 68. Very helpful, competent, owner speaks English, good coffee while you wait for your vehicle. Honest car servicing or quick oil change.

Taxi
There are 2 types: the Volkswagens, which you can flag down, prices range from US$3.50-7; cheaper are the 24-hr radio taxis, T999-928 5328, or catch 1 from their kiosk on Parque Hidalgo. In both types of taxi, establish fare before journey; there are set prices depending on the distance, the minimum is an expensive US$2.50 even for a few blocks.

Celestún *p130*
Bus Buses leave every 1-2 hrs from the local bus station on Calle 65 between 50 and 52, in Mérida, 2-hr journey, 1st class US$3.50, 2nd class US$3.

Progreso and around *p131*
Boat Boats can be hired to visit the reef of **Los Alacranes** where many ancient wrecks are visible in clear water.

Bus Buses from **Mérida** leave from the terminal on Calle 62 between 67 and 65, next to Hotel La Paz, every 10 mins. US$0.80 1-way/ US$2 return. Returns every 10 mins until 2200.

Dzibilchaltún *p131*
Bus 5 direct buses a day on weekdays, from Parque San Juan, marked 'Tour/Ruta Polígono'; returns from the site entrance on the hour, passing the junction 15 mins later,

taking 45 mins from the junction to **Mérida** (US$0.60).
Shuttles Leave from Parque San Juan in Mérida, corner of Calle 62 y 67A, every 1 or 2 hrs between 0500 and 1900.

Ticul and Oxkutzcab *p133*
Colectivo There are frequent VW *colectivos* to Ticul from Parque San Juan, **Mérida,** US$2.50.

Uxmal *p134*
Bus 5 buses a day from **Mérida,** from the terminal on Calle 69 between Calle 68 and 70, US$4. Return buses run every 2 hrs, or go to the entrance to the site on the main road and wait for a *colectivo*, which will take you to Muná for US$0.50. From there, many buses (US$1.70) and *colectivos* (US$1.40) go to Mérida.

Car Parking at the site costs US$1 for the whole day. Uxmal is 74 km from **Mérida,** 177 km from **Campeche,** by a good paved road. If going by car from Mérida, there is a circular road round the city: follow the signs to Campeche, then 'Campeche via ruinas', then to 'Muná via Yaxcopoil' (long stretch of road with no signposting). Muná–Yaxcopoil is about 34 km. Parking US$1.

Izamal and around *p135*
Bus Bus station is on Calle 32 behind government offices, can leave bags. 2nd class to **Mérida,** every 45 mins, 1½ hrs, US$1.50, lovely countryside. Bus station in Mérida, Calle 67 between 50 and 52. 6 a day to/from **Valladolid** (96 km), about 2 hrs, US$2.30-3.

Chichén Itzá *p135*
ADO bus office in Pisté is between **Stardust** and **Pirámide Inn.** Budget travellers going on from Mérida to Isla Mujeres or Cozumel should visit Chichén from Valladolid (see below), although if you plan to go through in a day you can store luggage at the visitor centre.
Bus Frequent 2nd-class buses depart from Mérida to Cancún, passing Chichén Itzá and Pisté. Likewise, there are frequent departures to/from Valladolid. The bus

station in Pisté is between Stardust and Pirámide Inn. To **Mérida**, 2nd class, hourly, US$5; and 1st class, 1420 and 1720, US$7. To **Cancún**, 2nd class, hourly, US$9. To **Valladolid**, 2nd class, hourly, US$2.50. To **Tulum**, 2nd class, 0810, 1420, 1615, US$11. The ruins are a 5-min ride from Pisté – the buses drop off and pick up passengers until 1700 at the top of the coach station opposite the entrance.

Valladolid *p138, map p138*
Bus The main bus terminal is on Calle 37 and Calle 54. To **Cancún**, ADO, frequent, 2½ hrs, US$9; and many 2nd class, 3-4 hrs, US$5.50. To **Chichén Itzá**, ADO, many daily, 30 mins; US$3; and many 2nd class, US$1.50. To **Mérida**, ADO, 16 daily, 2½ hrs, US$9. To **Playa del Carmen**, 1st and 2nd class, 11 daily, 3½ hrs, US$8.50. To **Tizimín** (for Río Lagartos), frequent1 hr, US$1.30. To **Tulum**, frequent ADO and ATS services, 3 hrs, US$5.

Río Lagartos and around *p139*
Bus There are 2 terminals side by side in Tizimín. If coming from Valladolid en route to Río Lagartos, you will need to walk to the other terminal. Tizimín–Río Lagartos, 7 per day, 1½ hrs, US$2. To **Valladolid**, frequent, 1 hr, US$1.30. To **Mérida**, several daily, 4 hrs, US$4. There are also buses to **Cancún, Felipe Carrillo Puerto** and **Chetumal**.

It is possible to get to Río Lagartos and back in a day from **Valladolid**, if you leave on the 0630 or 0730 bus (taxi Tizimín–Río Lagartos US$25, driver may negotiate). Last bus back from Río Lagartos at 1730.

---

❶ Directory

Mérida *p127, map p129*
Banks Banamex, at Calle 56 and 59 (Mon-Fri 0900-1300, 1600-1700), ATM cash machine. Many banks on Calle 65, off the plaza. Most have ATM cash machines, open 24 hrs. The beautiful Casa de Montejo, on the main plaza is also a Banamex branch. Open

0900-1600, Mon-Fri. HSBC usually changes TCs and stays open later than other banks, 0900-1900, Mon-Fri and 0900-1500 Sat. **Cultural centres** Alliance Française, Calle 56 No 476 between 55 and 57, T999-927 2403. Has a busy programme of events, films (Thu 1900), a library and a *cafetería* open all day. **Embassies and consulates** Austria, Av Colón No 59, T999-925 6386. Belize, Calle 53 No 498, corner of 58, T999-928 6152. Cuba, Calle 42 No 200, T999-944 4216. France, Calle 60 No 385, between 41 and 43, T999-930 1542. Germany, Calle 49 No 212, between 30 and 32, T999-944 3252. Honduras, Instituto Monte Líbano, Calle 54 No 486, between 57 and 59, T999-926 1922. Netherlands, Calle 64 No 418 between 47 and 49, T999-924 3122. USA, Calle 60 No 338, T999-942 5700. **Internet** Multitude of internet cafés, most charging US$1-1.50. **Language schools** Centro de Idiomas del Sureste, Calle 52 No 455, between 49 and 51, T999-923 0083, www.cisyucatan.com.mx, is a well-established Spanish school offering tried and tested language and cultural programmes. Modern Spanish Institute, Calle 15 No 500B, between 16A and 18, T999-911 0790, www.modernspanish.com, courses in Spanish, Maya culture, homestays. **Laundry** Lavandería, Calle 69 No 541, 2 blocks from bus station, about US$4.50 a load, 3-hr service. La Fe, Calle 61, No 518, between 62 and 64. US$4.50 for 3 kg. Highly recommended (shoe repair next door). Self-service hard to find. **Libraries** Mérida English Library, Calle 53 No 524 between 66 and 68, T999-924 8401, www.meridaenglish library.com. Many books on Mexico, used book for sale, bulletin board, magazines, reading patio. Mon-Fri 0900-1300; Mon 1830-2100; Thu 1600-1900; Sat 1000-1300. **Medical services** Hospitals: Centro Médico de las Américas (CEMA), Calle 54 No 365 between 33A and Av Pérez Ponce, T999-926 2111, emergencies T999-927 3199, www.cmasureste.com, affiliated with Mercy Hospital, Miami, Florida, US. Red Cross,

T999-924 9813. **Dentists: Dr Javier Cámara Patrón**, Calle 17 No 170, between 8 and 10, T999-925 3399, www.dentistyucatan.com. **Post** Calle 53, between 52 and 54. Will accept parcels for surface mail to US only, but don't seal parcels destined overseas; they have to be inspected. For surface mail to Europe try Belize, or mail package to US, Poste Restante, for collection later if you are heading that way. **Telephone** International calls are possible from caseta telefónicas. You'll find them all over town, but especially on Calle 62 and 60, north of the plaza. Calls to Europe cost around 4 pesos a minute, 2-3 pesos to the USA.

Izamal and around *p135*
Banks Bank on square with statue to Fray Diego de Landa, south side of convent. **Post** On opposite side of square to convent.

Chichén Itzá *p135*
Banks ATMs on the main street. **Internet** Available in Pisté. **Telephone** International calls may be placed from **Teléfonos de México**, opposite Hotel Xaybe.

Valladolid *p138, map p138*
Banks Santander Serfin, Calle 39 No 229; Bancomer, Calle 40 No 196; HSBC, Calle 41 No 201; Banamex, Calle 42, No 206. **Internet** Phonet, west side of the plaza, daily 1000-2100, internet costs US$1 per hr and there are long-distance call facilities. There are many other internet cafés. **Laundry** Teresita, Calle 33 between 40 and 42, US$6 for 5.5 kg. **Post** On east side of plaza, 0800-1500 (does not accept parcels for abroad). **Telephone** Telmex phone office on Calle 42, just north of square; expensive **Computel** offices at bus station and next to Hotel San Clemente; **Ladatel** phonecards can be bought from *farmacias* for use in phone booths.

State of Quintana Roo

The burgeoning international destinations of Cancún, Playa del Carmen, Isla Mujeres and Cozumel overshadow the eastern coast of the Yucatán and the State of Quintana Roo. Resorts: you either love them, hate them or simply enjoy the beautiful beaches, package tours and reliable restaurants. If Cancún is your port of entry for a trip through Mexico and Central America, it will certainly make for a good contrast to other regions. Diving in the area is popular, either off the coast of Isla Mujeres or Cozumel, or in the underwater caves or cenotes found in the region. The Maya ruins of Tulum are gloriously located, and the quieter spot of Cobá is worth a trip, as is the wilderness reserve of Sian Ka'an. To the far south, Chetumal seems a world away from the tourist hot spots, but it is the stepping-off point for travel to Belize and Guatemala. ▸▸ *For listings, see pages 170-190.*

Isla Holbox → *Colour map 1, A3. Phone code: 984.*

Also north of Valladolid, but in the neighbouring state of Quintana Roo, turn off the road to Puerto Juárez after Nuevo Xcan to Isla Holbox. Buses to **Chiquilá** for boats, three times a day; also direct from Tizimín at 1130, connecting with the ferry, US$2.20. The ferry leaves for Holbox 0600 and 1430, one hour, US$1, returning to Chiquilá at 0500 and 1300. A bus to Mérida connects with the 0500 return ferry. If you miss the ferry a fisherman will probably take you (for about US$14). You can leave your car in the care of the harbour master for a small charge; his house is east of the dock. Take water with you if possible. During 'El Norte' season, the water is turbid and the beach is littered with seaweed.

There are five more uninhabited islands beyond Holbox. Beware of sharks and barracuda, although very few nasty occurrences have been reported. Off the rough and mostly unpopulated bulge of the Yucatán coastline are several islands, once notorious for contraband. Beware of mosquitoes in the area.

Cancún → *For listings, see pages 170-190. Colour map 1, A3. Phone code: 998.*

In 1970, when Cancún was 'discovered' by the Mexican tourist board, it was an inaccessible strip of barren land with beautiful beaches; the only road went straight past Cancún to Puerto Juárez for the ferry to Isla Mujeres, which had been a national tourist destination since the 1950s. Massive international investment and government sponsorship saw the luxury resort of Cancún completed within 25 years. The 25-km hotel zone, set on a narrow strip of land in the shape of a number seven alongside the coast, is an ultra-modern American-style boulevard, with five-star hotels, high-tech nightclubs, high-class shopping malls and branches of McDonald's, Burger King and Planet Hollywood.

Love or hate Cancún, its presence on the international tourism market is indisputable. From all-in-one package tours to international government conferences, Cancún has an enviable record. It's worth a trip just to see what it's like. Jump on a Ruta 1 or Ruta 2 bus and you'll quickly see the international hotel chains with hundreds of rooms, packed along the sinuous sand bar. Spotted along the way Hotel Zone international shopping brands, restaurants and entertainment centres provide the complete holiday experience. All this is the more impressive given that the area has had to cope with some of the worst hurricanes of the century as well as incidents of drug violence. Fortunately for the region's economy, the violence is never directed at (or usually even on the radar screens of) tourists, but take their toll instead on the local population, generally in the most isolated areas.

Ins and outs

Getting there Cancún airport, www.cancun-airport.com, is 16 km south of the city. A fixed price *colectivo* taxi to the **Hotel Zone** or the centre costs US$9; pay at the kiosk outside airport. Drivers go via the Hotel Zone, but must take you to whichever part of the city centre you want. If going to the centre, make sure you know the name and address of your hotel before you get in the taxi, or the driver may offer to take you to a budget hotel of his own choice. **ADO** shuttle buses go to the centre via Avenida Tulum every 30 minutes from the airport. There is a tourist information kiosk in the airport, and a *casa de cambio*.

Getting around Ruta 1 and Ruta 2 buses go from the centre to the Hotel Zone, US$0.60; Ruta 1 runs 24 hours and goes via Avenida Tulum; Ruta 2 runs 0500-0330 and goes via

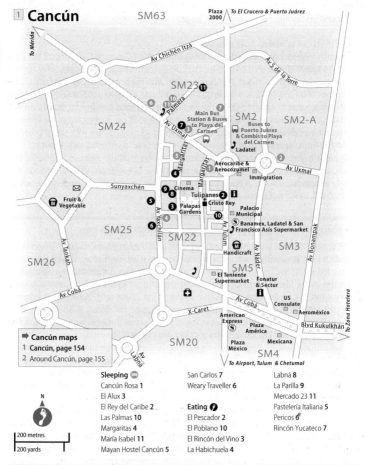

Cancún

Cancún maps
1 Cancún, page 154
2 Around Cancún, page 155

200 metres
200 yards

N

Sleeping
Cancún Rosa **1**
El Alux **3**
El Rey del Caribe **2**
Las Palmas **10**
Margaritas **4**
María Isabel **11**
Mayan Hostel Cancún **5**

San Carlos **7**
Weary Traveller **6**

Eating
El Pescador **2**
El Poblano **10**
El Rincón del Vino **3**
La Habichuela **4**

Labná **8**
La Parilla **9**
Mercado 23 **11**
Pastelería Italiana **5**
Pericos **6**
Rincón Yucateco **7**

Avenida Cobá to the bus terminal. Buses to the Hotel Zone can be caught from many stops along Avenida Tulum. Buses to **Puerto Juárez** for the boat to Isla Mujeres leave from outside **Cinema Royal**, across Avenida Tulum from the bus terminal, US$0.55. To get around in the centre, board a bus at Plaza 2000 and ask the driver if he's going to Mercado 28; those buses go along Avenida Yaxchilán; all others go to the Hotel Zone. Taxis are cheap and abundant in Cancún. Flat rate for anywhere within the centre is US$1.50; Hotel Zone from centre US$10-20. Many taxis stop at **El Crucero**, the junction of Avenida Tulum and Avenida López Portillo outside Plaza 2000, but there are often queues.

Downtown Cancún is a world apart from the Hotel Zone. It evolved from temporary shacks housing the thousands of builders working on the Hotel Zone, and is now a massive city with very little character. The main avenue is Tulum, formerly the highway running through the city when it was first conceived. It is now the location of the handicraft market, the main shops, banks and the municipal tourist office. There are also restaurants, but the better ones are along Avenida Yaxchilán, which is also the main centre for nightlife.

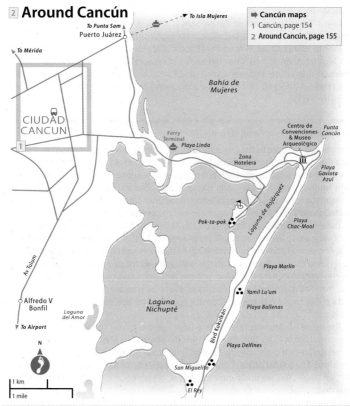

2 **Around Cancún**

⇨ **Cancún maps**
1 Cancún, page 154
2 **Around Cancún, page 155**

The cheaper end of the city, and a good area for budget travellers to base themselves, is around **El Crucero** (see above). The rest of the city is fairly expensive, but not as much as the Hotel Zone. The city is laid out in *supermanzanas* (SM), the blocks of streets between avenues, with smaller *manzanas* (M), or blocks, within them. Often the address you are given is, for example, SM24, M6, L3. L stands for *lote*, and is the precise number of the building within its *manzana*. This can lead to confusion when walking about, as the streets also have names, often not mentioned in the addresses. Look closely at street signs and you will see the SM and the M numbers. Taxi drivers generally respond better to addresses based on the *manzana* system.

Tourist information The **tourist office** ⓘ *Av Tulum 26, www.qroo.gob.mx, in a building that also houses local government offices,* is not very helpful; you'll get a glossy pocket guide to Cancún full of adverts for expensive restaurants and even more expensive hotels. There is a newer and well-equipped office at the **Conventions and Visitor Bureau** ⓘ *corner of Av Cobá and Av Bonampak, T884-6531.* Here the staff are helpful and friendly with information on new attractions, hotels and excursions.

Cancún to Isla Mujeres

A strip of coastline north of **Punta Sam** is officially part of Isla Mujeres. It is being developed as a luxury resort, but without the high-rise buildings of Cancún's Hotel Zone.

Puerto Juárez, about 3 km north of Cancún, is the dock for the cheaper ferry services to Isla Mujeres; there is also a bus terminal, but services are more frequent from Cancún. There are many buses between Cancún and Puerto Juárez, for example No 8 opposite the bus terminal (US$0.70). A taxi from Puerto Juárez to Downtown Cancún should be no more than US$2.

Isla Mujeres → *For listings, see pages 170-190. Colour map 1, A3. Phone code: 998.*

A refreshing antidote to the urban sprawl of Cancún, Isla Mujeres is a good place to relax for a few days away from the hurly-burly of package tourism. The island is especially nice in the evening, when all the Cancún day trippers have gone. The town is strictly low-rise, with brightly coloured buildings giving it a Caribbean island feel. The island's laws prohibit the construction of any building higher than three floors, and US franchises such as **McDonald's** and **Walmart** are not allowed to open branches here.

There are several good beaches on Isla Mujeres, the best being **Playa Cocos** on the northwest coast, five minutes' walk from the town. Further south, there are several places to swim, snorkel and observe marine life. Restaurants and nightspots are plentiful, good quality and cheaper than those on the mainland, and the people are friendlier. There are several ways to explore the island: you can rent a golf cart, many of which chug around the streets all day, good for families; mopeds and bicycles are cheap and plentiful to rent, and a public bus runs all the way from the town to El Paraíso, almost at the southern tip of the island.

The name Isla Mujeres refers to the large number of clay female idols found by the Spaniards here in 1518. The island contains the only known Maya shrine to a female deity: Ixchel, goddess of the moon and fertility. The ruins of the shrine are at the southern tip of the island. The **tourist office** ⓘ *Rueda Medina, opposite the ferry dock, Mon-Fri 0900-1600, Sat-Sun 0900-1400, www.isla-mujeres.com.mx,* is very helpful. The immigration office is next door.

In October there is a festival of music, with groups from Mexico and the US performing in the main square, and from 1-12 December, during the fiesta for the Virgin of Guadalupe, there are fireworks and dances until 0400 in the plaza.

Sights

Most of the sights south of the town can be seen in a day. The first of these, 5 km from the town, is the **Turtle Farm** ⓘ *daily 0900-1700, US$2*, with hundreds of sea turtles weighing from 170 g to 270 kg in a humane setting. To get there, take the bus to the final stop, Playa Paraíso, double back and walk five minutes along the main road.

At the centre of the island are the curious remains of a pirate's domain, called **Hacienda Mundaca** ⓘ *daily 0900-1700, US$2*. A big, arch gate marks its entrance. Paths have been laid out among the large trees, but all that remains of the estate (called Vista Alegre) are one small building and a circular garden with raised beds, a well and a gateway. Fermín Mundaca, more of a slave-trader than a buccaneer, built Vista Alegre for the teenage girl he loved. She rejected him and he died, broken-hearted, in Mérida. His epitaph there reads *Como eres, yo fui; como soy, tu serás* ('As you are I was; as I am you shall be'). See the poignant little carving on the garden side of the gate, *La entrada de La Trigueña* (the girl's nickname). To get there, get off the bus at the final stop, and turn the opposite way to the beach; the house is a short walk away.

El Garrafón ⓘ *T998-877 1100, www.garrafon.com*, is a snorkelling centre 7 km from the town, being developed into a luxury resort in the style of Xcaret on the mainland. Snorkelling is still possible, with a 12-m bronze cross submerged offshore for your exploration; by tour only. There is an expensive restaurant and bar at El Garrafón, and a small beach. The snorkelling is good past the pier, along a reef with some dead coral. Large numbers of different coloured fish can be seen at very close range. If you want to walk to El Garrafón from the bus stop at Playa Paraíso, take the second path on the right to the beach from the main road. The first path leads through **Restaurant Playa Paraíso**, which charges US$1 for the privilege of walking through their premises to the beach. Once on the beach, you can walk all the way to El Garrafón along the coast, although it gets very rocky for the final part. It is easier to go as far as the cluster of beach villas, then cut through one of them (ask for permission) to the main road. The whole walk takes about half an hour. When you arrive at El Garrafón, turn right at the building site, go down the hill to **Hotel Garrafón** del Castillo, which is the entrance to the snorkelling centre.

A further 15 minutes' walk from El Garrafón, at the tip of the island, are the ruins of the Maya shrine **Santuario Maya a la Diosa Ixchel**, US$2, dedicated to Ixchel the goddess of fertility. These were once free to visit, but unfortunately they have been bought and developed as part of the **El Garrafón 'National Park'** ⓘ *US$5.50*. A cultural centre has also been built here with large sculptures by several international artists.

South of Cancún → *For listings, see pages 170-190. Colour map 1, A3.*

Puerto Morelos → *Phone code: 998.*

A quiet little village 34 km south of Cancún, Puerto Morelos is one of the few places that still retains some of the charm of an unspoilt fishing village (but not for much longer), making it a good place to stop over en route to larger towns further south, such as Playa del Carmen. The village is really just a large plaza right on the seafront with a couple of streets going off it. If on arrival at Cancún airport you don't wish to spend the night in the city, you could get a taxi directly to Puerto Morelos. This is also the place to catch the car ferry to the island of Cozumel (see below). The **Sinaltur** office on the plaza offers a range of good snorkelling, kayak and fishing trips. **Goyos**, just north of the plaza, offers jungle adventures and rooms for rent, although erratic hours are maintained.

Playa del Carmen → *Phone code: 984.*

What used to be a pleasant little town on the beach has lost the charms of its former existence as a fishing village. Recent development for tourism has been rapid, but Playa, as it is known locally, has not had the high-rise treatment of Cancún. The beach is dazzling white, with crystal-clear shallow water, ideal for swimming, and further out there is good

Playa del Carmen

100 metres
100 yards

N

Sleeping
Alhambra **1** *B4*
Casa Tucán **5** *B3*
Cielo & El Carboncito
  Restaurant **7** *B3*
Happy Gecko **4** *A3*
Hostel Playa **8** *A2*
Las Molcas **6** *D3*

Mom's **11** *B2*
Posada Marinelly **13** *C2*
Tides Riviera Maya **2** *A1*
Urban Hostel **14** *B3*

Eating
Billy the Kid **1** *B2*
Buenos Aires **6** *B3*
El Fogón **8** *A2*
Glass Bar **12** *A4*
Habita Bookshop &
  Café **18** *A4*

Java Joe's **2** *A4*
Karen's **9** *C3*
La Parrilla **11** *A4*
Los Comales **10** *B3*
Maktub **22** *A4*
Pez Vela **5** *C3*
Rolandi **4** *D3*
Sushi-Tlan **23** *A4*
Tortas del Carmen **3** *B2*
Yaxche **7** *A3*

Bars & clubs
Beer Bucket **13** *A3*
Blue Parrot Inn **21** *A4*
Carlos 'n' Charlies **19** *D3*
Coco Maya **16** *A4*
El Cielo **17** *A4*
Habibi & Los
  Aguachiles **24** *A4*
OM **15** *A4*
Señor Frog's **20** *D3*
Tequila Barrel **14** *A4*

scuba-diving. There is lodging for every budget, and plenty of good restaurants and bars of every type. Many travellers choose Playa as their base for trips to the ruins of Tulum in the south, and archaeological sites such as Cobá in the interior.

The town is laid out in a grid system, with the main centre of tourist activity based on Avenida 5 (pedestrianized in the central section at night between 1800 and 0200), one block from and parallel with the beach. This is where the more expensive hotels and restaurants are, as well as being the centre for nightlife. Cheaper accommodation can be found up Avenida Juárez and further north of the beach.

Tourist information is scant, although there is a **tourism office** ① *corner of Av Juárez and Av 15, T984-873 2804*, which has useful information and maps, and the kiosk on the main plaza will provide a copy of *Destination Playa del Carmen,* a useful guide with maps produced by US residents.

Cozumel → *For listings, see pages 170-190. Colour map 1, A3. Phone code: 987.*

The town, properly San Miguel de Cozumel, but always shortened to Cozumel, is a seedy, overpriced version of Playa del Carmen. Daily tour groups arrive on cruises from Miami and Cancún, and the town's services seem geared towards this type of tourist. But Cozumel is a mecca for scuba divers, with many beautiful offshore reefs to explore, as well as much interesting wildlife and birdlife. Travellers looking for a beach holiday with some nightlife will find the island disappointing compared to Playa del Carmen. There is only one nice beach on the west side, and the eastern, Atlantic coast is far too rugged and choppy for swimming.

Ins and outs
The airport is just north of Cozumel with a minibus shuttle service to the hotels. There are 10-minute flights to and from the airstrip near Playa del Carmen, as well as flights linking to Mexico City, Cancún, Chichén Itzá and Houston (Texas). The passenger ferry from Playa del Carmen runs every two hours (see above), and the car ferry leaves twice daily from Puerto Morelos (see page 157). There are no local buses, but Cozumel town is small enough to visit on foot. To get around the island, there are organized tours or taxis; otherwise, hire a jeep, moped or bicycle.

San Miguel de Cozumel
The island's only town has very little character, mainly due to the construction of a US air base during the Second World War, whose airfield has now been converted for civilian use. There is a variety of accommodation, with a few budget hotels, but mainly focusing on the luxury end of the market.

On the waterfront between Calle 4 and 6, the **Museo de la Isla** ① *US$3.30,* provides a well-laid-out history of the island. There is a bookshop, art gallery and rooftop restaurant, which has excellent food and views of sunset, good for breakfast, from 0700 (**The Quick** is excellent value). Recommended.

Beaches
In the north of the island the beaches are sandy and wide, although those at the Zona Hotelera Norte were damaged in 1989 and again in 2005 and are smaller than they used to be. At the end of the paved road, walk up the unmade road until it becomes 'dual carriageway'; turn left for the narrow beach, which is a bit dirty. Cleaner beaches are

accessible only through the hotels. South of San Miguel, **San Francisco** is good if narrow (clean, very popular, lockers at **Pancho's**, expensive restaurants), but others are generally narrower still and rockier.

All the main hotels are on the sheltered west coast. The east, Caribbean coast is rockier, but very picturesque; swimming and diving on the unprotected side is very dangerous owing to ocean underflows. The only safe place is at a sheltered bay at **Chen Río**. Another bay with possibilities is **Punta Morena**, which is a good surf beach, there is good accommodation (contact Matt at **Deep Blue**, on Salas 200, for more information and transport) and seafood (try the *ceviche*). Three good (and free) places for snorkelling are: the beach in front of **Hotel Las Glorias**, 15 minutes' walk south from ferry (you can walk through the hotel's reception); **Playa Corona**, further south, is too far to walk, so hitch or

① Cozumel

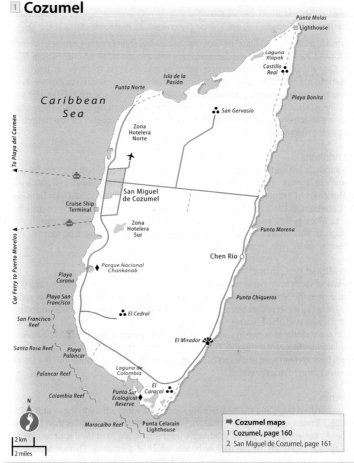

Punta Molas
Lighthouse

Laguna
Xlapak
Castillo
Real

Isla de la
Pasión

Punta Norte

Playa Bonita

Caribbean
Sea

San Gervasio

Zona
Hotelera
Norte

To Playa del Carmen

San Miguel
de Cozumel

Cruise Ship
Terminal

Zona
Hotelera
Sur

Punta Morena

Car Ferry to Puerto Morelos

Chen Río

Parque Nacional
Chankanab

Playa
Corona

Playa San
Francisco

Punta Chiqueros

San Francisco
Reef

El Cedral

Santa Rosa Reef   Playa
Palancar

El Mirador

Palancar Reef

Laguna de
Colombia

Colombia Reef

El
Caracol

Punta Sur
Ecological
Reserve

N

Maracaibo Reef   Punta Celarain
Lighthouse

2 km
2 miles

➡ **Cozumel maps**
1 Cozumel, page 160
2 San Miguel de Cozumel, page 161

take a taxi (there is a small restaurant and pier); and **Xul-Ha**, further south still, which has a bar and comfortable beach chairs.

Archaeological sites

There are some 32 archaeological sites on Cozumel; those on the east coast are mostly single buildings (thought to have been lookouts, navigational aids). The easiest to see are the restored ruins of the Maya-Toltec period at **San Gervasio** ① *0900-1800, US$6, guides are on hand, or you can buy a self-guiding booklet at the bookshop on the square in San Miguel, or at the flea market, for US$1*. It is in the north of the island (7 km from Cozumel town, then 6 km to the left up a paved road, toll US$1), an interesting site, quite spread out, with *sacbés* (sacred roads) between the groups of buildings. There are no large structures, but a nice plaza, an arch, and pigment can be seen in places. It is also a pleasant place to listen to birdsong, see butterflies, animals (if lucky), lizards, land crabs and insects. **Castillo Real** is one of many sites on the northeastern coast, but the road to this part of the island is in very bad condition and the ruins themselves are very small. **El Cedral** in the southwest (3 km from the main island road) is a two-room temple, overgrown with trees, in the centre of the village of the same name. Behind the temple is a ruin, and next to it a modern church with a green and white façade (an incongruous

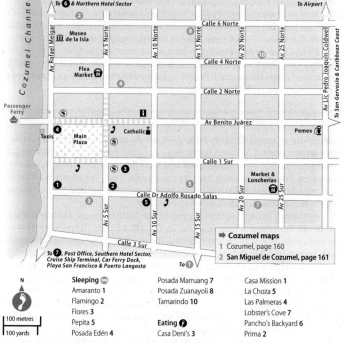

② San Miguel de Cozumel

Cozumel maps
1 Cozumel, page 160
2 San Miguel de Cozumel, page 161

N
100 metres
100 yards

Sleeping
Amaranto 1
Flamingo 2
Flores 3
Pepita 5
Posada Edén 4
Posada Marruang 7
Posada Zuanayoli 8
Tamarindo 10

Eating
Casa Dení's 3
Casa Mission 1
La Choza 5
Las Palmeras 4
Lobster's Cove 7
Pancho's Backyard 6
Prima 2

pairing). In the village are large, permanent shelters for agricultural shows, rug sellers and locals who pose with *iguanas doradas* (golden iguanas). **El Caracol**, where the sun, in the form of a shell, was worshipped, is 1 km from the southernmost Punta Celarain. At Punta Celarain is an old lighthouse.

Around the island

A circuit of the island on paved roads can easily be done in a day. Head due east out of San Miguel (take the continuation of Avenida Juárez). Make the detour to San Gervasio before continuing to the Caribbean coast at **Mescalito's** restaurant. Here, turn left for the northern tip (road unsuitable for ordinary vehicles), or right for the south, passing Punta Morena, Chen Río, Punta Chiqueros (restaurant, bathing), El Mirador (a low viewpoint with sea-worn rocks, look out for holes) and Paradise Cove. At this point, the paved road heads west while an unpaved road continues south to Punta Celarain. Here there is the **Punta Sur Ecological Reserve** ① *T987-872 0914, www.cozumelparks.com.mx, 1000-1700, US$10*, an ecotourism development, with a variety of natural landscapes with lagoons and mangrove jungles. A snorkelling centre has opened here as well as a viewing platform. On the road west, opposite the turn-off to El Cedral, is a sign to **Restaurante Mac y Cía**, an excellent fish restaurant on a lovely beach, popular with dive groups for lunch. Next is Playa San Francisco (see above). A few more kilometres leads to the former **Holiday Inn**, the last big hotel south of San Miguel.

Just after this is **Parque Chankanab** ① *0800-1800, US$16, snorkelling mask and fins US$5, use of underwater camera US$25*, which used to be an idyllic lagoon behind the beach (9 km from San Miguel). After it became totally spoilt, it was restored as a National Park, with the lagoon, crystal clear again, a botanical garden with local and imported plants, a 'Maya Area' (rather artificial), swimming (ideal for families with young children), snorkelling, dive shops, souvenirs, expensive but good restaurants and lockers (US$2). Soon the road enters the southern Hotel Zone at the **Stouffer Presidente**, coming to the cruise ship dock and car ferry port on the outskirts of town.

South of Playa del Carmen → *For listings, see pages 170-190. Colour map 1, A3/B3.*

The Maya site of **Xcaret** ① *T01-800-292-2738, www.xcaret.com, US$59 adults, under 5s free*, an ancient port called Polé, was the departure point for voyages to Cozumel. It has now been turned into an overpriced and very tacky theme park catering exclusively for day-trippers. There is a 1-km walk from the entrance to Xcaret. The alternative is to take a taxi, or a tour from Playa del Carmen or Cancún (in a multicoloured bus). You can also walk along the beach from Playa del Carmen (three hours).

A luxury resort, 102 km south of Cancún, 20 km north of Tulum, **Akumal** is reached easily by bus from there or from Playa del Carmen (30 minutes). There is a small lagoon 3 km north of Akumal, with good snorkelling. The coastline from Playa del Carmen down to just short of Tulum to the south is known as the 'Riviera Maya' – a strip of upmarket, generally all-inclusive hotels. Two ferries run daily to Cozumel. Also just south of Akumal are **Chemuyil** (*palapas* for hammocks, US$4, free shower, expensive restaurant, laundry facilities) and **Xcacel** (campground has water, bathrooms, cold showers and restaurant, very clean, US$2 per person, vehicles free, snorkel hire US$5 a day, beautiful swimming in the bay). Ask guards if you can go on turtle protection patrol at night (May to July).

Thirteen kilometres north of Tulum, 122 km from Cancún (bus from Playa del Carmen, 45 minutes), the beautiful clear lagoon of **Laguna Xel-Há** ① *daily 0800-1630, US$10*, is full of fish, but fishing is not allowed as it is a national park. Snorkelling gear can be rented at US$7 for a day, but it is often in poor repair; better to rent from your hotel. Lockers cost US$1.50. Arrive as early as possible to see fish as the lagoon is full of tourists throughout most of the day. Snorkelling areas are limited by fencing. Bungalows, first-class hotels and fast-food restaurants are being built. The food and drink is very expensive. There is a marvellous jungle path to one of the lagoon bays. Xel-Há ruins, known also as **Los Basadres** ① *US$3.35*, are located across the road from the beach of the same name. Few tourists but not much to see. You may have to jump the fence to visit; there is a beautiful *cenote* at the end of the ruins where you can have a lovely swim.

Tulum → *Colour map 1, A3. Phone code: 984.*
① *Daily 0800-1800, entry US$4.50, parking US$1.50, students with Mexican ID free.*

The Maya-Toltec ruins of Tulum are perched on coastal cliffs in a beautiful setting above the azure sea. The ruins are 12th century, with city walls of white stone. The temples were dedicated to the worship of the Falling God, or the Setting Sun, represented as a falling character over nearly all the west-facing doors (Cozumel was the home of the Rising Sun). The same idea is reflected in the buildings, which are wider at the top than at the bottom.

The main structure is the **Castillo**, which commands a view of both the sea and the forested Quintana Roo lowlands stretching westwards. All the Castillo's openings face west, as do most, but not all, of the doorways at Tulum. Look for the alignment of the **Falling God** on the temple of that name (to the left of the Castillo) with the pillar and the back door in the **House of the Chultún** (the nearest building in the centre group to the entrance). The majority of the main structures are roped off so that you cannot climb the Castillo, nor get close to the surviving frescoes, especially on the **Temple of the Frescoes**.

Tulum is crowded with tourists (best time to visit is between 0800 and 0900). Take towel and swimsuit if you wish to scramble down from the ruins to one of the two beaches for a swim (the larger of the two is less easy to get to). The reef is from 600 m to 1000 m from the shore, so if you wish to snorkel you must either be a strong swimmer, or take a boat trip.

There is a tourist complex at the entrance to the ruins. Guide books can be bought in the shops, local guides can also be hired. About two hours are needed to view at leisure. The parking area is near Highway 307, and there's a handicraft market. A small train takes you from the parking area to the ruins for US$2, or it is an easy 500 m walk. The paved road continues down the coast to **Boca Paila** and beyond, access by car to this road from the car park is closed. To reach the road south of the ruins, access is possible 1 km from Tulum village. Public buses drop passengers at El Crucero, a crossroads 500 m north of the car park for Tulum Ruinas (an easy walk) where there is an ADO bus terminal that is open for a few hours from 0800; at the crossroads are some hotels, a shop (will exchange traveller's cheques), on the opposite side of the road a naval base and airstrip, and a little way down Highway 307 a Pemex station.

If staying in the area, the beach running south of the ruins is dotted with quiet, isolated *palapas*, *cabañas* and hotels to fit most budgets. Alternatively the village of **Tulum** (as opposed to the ruins) is 4 km south of El Crucero. A taxi from the village to the ruins costs US$3. It is not very large but is growing rapidly and has a bus station, post office, bank (HSBC), several grocery shops, two bakeries, hotels and restaurants. There is a **tourist information office** in the village, next to the police station, two blocks north of the bus terminal. The information centre set up by the *Weary Traveller* backpacker centre has taken over as the primary source of information for this area. Located at the southern end

Sweating it out

The *temazcal* is a ritual ceremony that has been practised by the indigenous peoples of Mexico for hundreds of years. The Mexican version of the sweat lodge, it is a thanksgiving to the four elements, and a healing for the spirit as well as the body. You enter the womb of mother earth when you enter the *temazcal*, and when you exit you are born a new being. Traditionally, it was done in a square or dome-shaped building constructed from branches and then covered with blankets, and was preceded by a day of fasting. There are *temazcal* sessions open to newcomers all over Mexico. Done properly, the experience can be very intense.

Red-hot rocks are placed in the centre of the construction, and a group sits around them. The door is closed, and a medicine man leads the group in prayer and songs, all designed to connect the insiders to each of the four elements. During the ceremony, the door is opened four times, to allow people who want to leave (there is no returning), and to bring in more hot rocks. Different emotions and thoughts come up for different people, and everyone is encouraged to contribute something from their own traditions if they feel the need. After each contribution, herbal water is poured over the rocks to create more healing steam. This continues till everyone is in agreement to open the fourth and final door. Everyone then leaves, rinses off (hopefully in the sea or lagoon if you're near the coast), then shares soup and tea to break their fast.

of town a block away from the ADO bus terminal. Friendly and knowledgeable staff give fairly impartial information on hotels, excursions and restaurants. Another source of information is the **Sian Ka'an Information Centre** ① *Av Tulum between Satélite and Géminis, Tulum, T984-871 2363, siankaan_tours@hotmail.com*, which has information about visiting the reserve (see below) and several other areas of interest.

Cobá → *Colour map 1, A3. Phone code: 985.*
① *Daily 0800-1700, US$4.50.*

An important Maya city in the eighth and ninth centuries AD, whose population is estimated to have been between 40,000 and 50,000, Cobá was abandoned for unknown reasons. The present-day village of Cobá lies on either side of Lago Cobá, surrounded by dense jungle, 47 km inland from Tulum. It is a quiet, friendly village, with few tourists staying overnight.

The entrance to the ruins of this large but little-excavated city is at the end of the lake between the two parts of the village. A second lake, **Lago Macanxoc**, is within the site. There are turtles and many fish in the lakes. It is a good birdwatching area. Both lakes and their surrounding forest can be seen from the summit of the **Iglesia**, the tallest structure in the **Cobá Group**. There are three other groups of buildings to visit: the **Macanxoc Group**, mainly stelae, about 1.5 km from the Cobá Group; **Las Pinturas**, 1 km northeast of Macanxoc, with a temple and the remains of other buildings that had columns in their construction; the **Nohoch Mul Group**, at least another kilometre from Las Pinturas. Nohoch Mul has the tallest pyramid in the northern Yucatán, a magnificent structure, from which the views of the jungle on all sides are superb. You will not find at Cobá the great array of buildings that can be seen at Chichén Itzá or Uxmal, or the compactness of

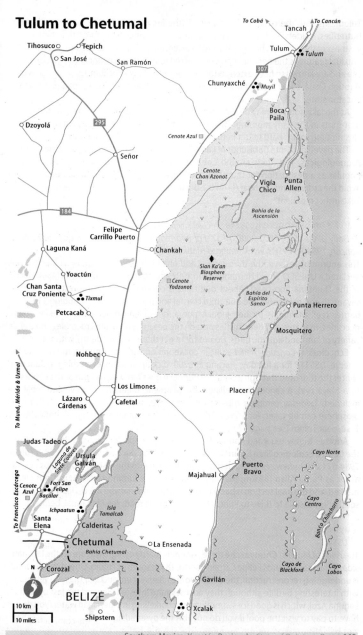

Tulum to Chetumal

To Cobá
Tancah
To Cancún

Tihosuco
Tepich
San José
San Ramón
Tulum
Tulum

Chunyaxché
Muyil

Boca Paila

Dzoyolá
295
Cenote Azul

Señor
Cenote Chan Azonot
Vigía Chico
Punta Allen

184
Bahía de la Ascensión

Felipe Carrillo Puerto
Chankah

Laguna Kaná
Sian Ka'an Biosphere Reserve

Yoactún
Cenote Yodzonot

Chan Santa Cruz Poniente
Tixmul
Bahía del Espíritu Santo

Petcacab
Punta Herrero

Mosquitero

Nohbec

Los Limones
Placer

Lázaro Cárdenas
Cafetal

Judas Tadeo
Cayo Norte

Laguna de Siete Colores
Ursula Galván

To Mund, Merida & Uxmal
Majahual
Puerto Bravo

Cenote Azul
Fort San Felipe
Bacalar

Cayo Centro

Ichpaatun
Isla Tamalcab

Banco Chinchorro

Santa Elena
Calderitas

To Francisco Escárcega

Chetumal
Bahía Chetumal
La Ensenada

N

Corozal
Cayo de Blackford
Cayo Lobos

BELIZE
Gavilán

10 km
10 miles

Xcalak

Shipstern

Tulum. Instead, the delight of the place is the architecture in the jungle, with birds, butterflies, spiders and lizards, and the many uncovered structures that hint at the vastness of the city in its heyday (the urban extension of Cobá is put at some 70 sq km). An unusual feature is the network of *sacbés* (sacred roads), which connect the groups in the site and are known to have extended across the entire Maya Yucatán. Over 40 *sacbés* pass through Cobá, some local, some of great length, such as the 100-km road to Yaxuná in Yucatán state.

At the lake, toucans may be seen very early; also look out for greenish-blue and brown mot-mots in the early morning. The guards at the site are very strict about opening and closing time so it is hard to get in to see the dawn or sunset from a temple.

The paved road into Cobá ends at **Lago Cobá**; to the left are the ruins, to the right **Villas Arqueológicas**. The roads around Cobá are badly potholed. Cobá is becoming more popular as a destination for tourist buses, which come in at 1030; arrive before that to avoid the crowds and the heat (ie on the 0430 bus from Valladolid, if not staying in Cobá). Take insect repellent.

Sian Ka'an Biosphere Reserve → *Colour map 1, A3.*
ⓘ *Daily 0900-1500, 1800-2000, US$2. For information, visit Los Amigos de Sian Ka'an in Cancún, T984-884 9583, www.amigosdesiankaan.org; very helpful.*

This enormous reserve, the third-largest and one of the most diverse in all Mexico, was declared a UNESCO World Heritage Site in 1987 and now covers 652,000 ha (4500 sq km) of the Quintana Roo coast. About one-third is covered in tropical forest, one-third is savannah and mangrove and one-third coastal and marine habitats, including 110 km of barrier reef. Mammals include jaguar, puma, ocelot and other cats, monkeys, tapir, peccaries, manatee and deer; turtles nest on the beaches; there are crocodiles and a wide variety of land and aquatic birds. Do not try to get there independently without a car.

Ecocolors ⓘ *Cancún, T/F884-9580*, in collaboration with **Los Amigos**, run tours to the reserve, US$115 for a full day, starting at 0700, pick up at hotel, everything included; in winter the tour goes through a canal, in summer it goes birdwatching, in both cases a visit to a Maya ruin, a *cenote*, snorkelling, all equipment, breakfast and evening meal are included. Two-day camping trips can be arranged. Two-hour boat trips through the biosphere can be taken for US$75. Trips can also be arranged through **Cabañas Ana y José**, near Tulum (see page 174).

Another highly regarded non-profit outfit that perhaps does a better job than any is the **Centro Ecológico Sian Ka'an** ⓘ *Carretera Nacional Cancún–Tulum at Km 68 in Tulum, T984-871 2499, www.cesiak.org*. It is possible to drive into the reserve from Tulum village as far as Punta Allen (58 km; the road is opposite the turning to Cobá; it is not clearly marked, and the final section is badly potholed); beyond that you need a launch. From the south it is possible to drive to Punta Herrero (unmade road, see Mahahual, below).

Muyil
ⓘ *US$4.*

The ruins of Muyil at **Chunyaxché** three pyramids (partly overgrown) are on the left-hand side of the road towards Felipe Carrillo Puerto, 18 km south of Tulum. One of the pyramids is undergoing reconstruction; the other two are relatively untouched. They are very quiet, with interesting birdlife although they are mosquito infested. Beyond the last pyramid is Laguna Azul, which is good for swimming and snorkelling in blue, clean water (you do not have to pay to visit the pool if you do not visit the pyramids).

Felipe Carrillo Puerto → *Colour map 1, A3.*

The cult of the 'talking cross' was founded here. The **Santuario de la Cruz Parlante** is five blocks west of the Pemex station on Highway 307. The beautiful main square, which has playground equipment for children, is dominated by the Catholic church, built by the Cruzob in the 19th century (see page 112). Legend has it that the unfinished bell tower will only be completed when the descendants of those who heard the talking cross reassert control of the region.

Mahahual and around → *Colour map 1, A3.*

Further south on Route 307, at Cafetal, a good road heads east to Mahahual (Majahual) on the coast (56 km from Cafetal), a peaceful, unspoilt place with clear water and beautiful beaches. The cruise ship dock gives a clue to the occasional interruption to the peace and calm with Mahahual welcoming cruise ships travelling up and down the Mexican and Central American coast. ADO buses leave from the main terminal in Chetumal at 0530 and 1930, returning at 0630 and 1830. An offshore excursion is possible to **Banco Chinchorro**, where there is a coral bank and a white-sand beach.

About 2 km before Mahahual a paved road to the left goes to **Puerto Bravo** and on to Placer and **Punta Herrero** (in the Sian Ka'an Biosphere Reserve, see above).

Just over 3 km along this road a right turn goes to the **Sol y Mar** restaurant, with rooms to rent, coconut palms and beach. Another 10.5 km along the Punta Herrero road, again on the right, is **Camidas Trailer Park**, see Sleeping, page 176.

Xcalak → *Colour map 1, B3.*

Across the bay from Chetumal, at the very tip of Quintana Roo, is Xcalak, which may be reached from Chetumal by private launch (two hours), or by the unpaved road from Cafetal to Mahahual, then turning south for 55 km (186 km by road from Chetumal, suitable for passenger cars but needs skilled driver). *Colectivos* from Chetumal leave daily between 0700 and 1900 (16 de Septiembre 183 and Mahatma Ghandi); check return times. Buses run Friday 1600 and Sunday 0600, returning Saturday morning and Sunday afternoon (details from the Chetumal tourist office). Xcalak is a fishing village with a few shops selling beer and basic supplies and one small restaurant serving Mexican food. A few kilometres north of Xcalak are two hotels, **Costa de Cocos** and **Villa Caracol**, both American-run; the latter is good, with comfortable *cabañas*, although expensive (it has sport fishing and diving facilities). From here trips can be arranged to the unspoiled islands of **Banco Chinchorro** or to San Pedro, Belize. In the village you may be able to rent a boat to explore Chetumal Bay and Banco Chinchorro. Do not try to walk from Xcalak along the coast to San Pedro, Belize; the route is virtually impassable.

Chetumal → *For listings, see pages 170-190. Colour map 1, B3. Phone code: 983.*

The state capital of Quintana Roo, Chetumal, is a necessary stopover for travellers en route to Maya sites in the south of the peninsula, and across the frontier to Belize and Guatemala. Although attractions are thin on the ground, Chetumal does have the advantage of being a small Mexican city not devoted to tourism, and thus has a more authentic feel than other towns on the Riviera Maya. It is also the logical spot for obtaining exit and entry visas. It is 240 km south of Tulum. The Chetumal bay has been designated a natural protected area for manatees, and includes a manatee sanctuary.

Cenote diving

There are more than 50 *cenotes* in this area – accessible from Ruta 307 and often well signposted – and cave diving has become very popular. However, it is a specialized sport and, unless you have a cave diving qualification, you must be accompanied by a qualified dive master.

A cave diving course involves over 12 hours of lectures and a minimum of 14 cave dives using double tanks, costing around US$600. Accompanied dives start at around US$60. Specialist dive centres offering courses are: Mike Madden's **CEDAM Dive Centres**, PO Box 1, Puerto Aventuras, T/F984-873 5129; **Aquatech**, Villas de Rosa, PO Box 25, T984-875 9020, www.cenotes.com. **Aventuras Akumal No 35**, Tulum, T984-875 9030; **Aktun Dive Centre**, PO Box 119, Tulum,

T984-871 2311, and **Cenote Dive Center**, Tulum, T984-871 2232, www.cenotedive. com, Norwegian owned.

Two of the best *cenotes* are 'Carwash', on the Cobá road, good even for beginners, with excellent visibility; and 'Dos Ojos', just off Ruta 307 south of Aventuras, the second largest underground cave system in the world. It has a possible link to the Nohoch Nah Chich, the most famous cenote and part of a subterranean system recorded as the world's largest, with over 50 km of surveyed passageways connected to the sea.

A word of warning: *cenote* diving has a higher level of risk than open-water diving – do not take risks and only dive with recognized operators.

The avenues are broad, busy and in the centre lined with huge shops selling cheap imported goods. The main local activity is window-shopping, and the atmosphere is more like a North American city, with an impression of affluence that can be a culture shock to the visitor arriving from the much poorer country of Guatemala. The **tourist office** ① *on the main plaza, opposite the Museo de Cultura Maya, Mon-Fri 0900-1900, Sat 0900-1300*, is mainly for trade enquiries. There is very little tourist information in Chetumal; it is usually best to go to a travel agent such as **Tu-Maya** (see page 184).

The *paseo* near the waterfront on Sunday night is worth seeing. The State Congress building has a mural showing the history of Quintana Roo. The **Museo de la Cultura Maya** ① *Av Héroes de Chapultepec by the market, Tue-Sun 0900-1900, US$5*, is highly recommended. It has good models of sites and touch screen computers explaining the Maya calendar and glyphs. Although there are few original Maya pieces, it gives an excellent overview; some explanations are in English, guided tours are available, and there's a good bookshop with English magazines.

Around Chetumal → *For listings, see pages 170-190.*

Towards Bacalar

Six kilometres north of Chetumal are the stony beaches of **Calderitas**, bus every 30 minutes from Colón, between Belice and Héroes, US$1.80, or taxi US$5, many fish restaurants. There is camping at Calderitas, signposted, OK, US$2.75. Beyond are the unexcavated archaeological sites of **Ichpaatun** (13 km), **Oxtancah** (14 km) and **Nohochmul** (20 km). Sixteen kilometres north on Route 307 to Tulum is the **Laguna de los Milagros**, a beautiful lagoon for swimming. Further on, 34 km north of Chetumal, is **Cenote Azul**, over 70 m deep, with a waterside restaurant serving inexpensive and good seafood and regional food (but awful coffee) until 1800. Both the *laguna* and the *cenote* are deserted in the week.

About 3 km north of Cenote Azul is the village of **Bacalar** (nice, but not special) on the **Laguna de Siete Colores**, which has swimming and skin-diving; *colectivos* from terminal (Suchaa) in Chetumal, corner of Miguel Hidalgo and Primo de Verdad, 0700-1900 every 30 minutes, US$1.60, return from plaza when full; also buses from Chetumal bus station every two hours or so, US$1.60. There is a Spanish fort there overlooking a beautiful shallow, clear, freshwater lagoon, and abundant birdlife on the lake shore. This is the fort of **San Felipe**, said to have been built around 1729 by the Spanish to defend the area from the English pirates and smugglers of logwood. There is a plaque praying for protection from the British and a small **museum** ⓘ *US$0.70*. The British ships roamed the islands and reefs, looting Spanish galleons laden with gold, on their way from Peru to Cuba. There are many old shipwrecks on the reef and around the Banco Chinchorro, 50 km out in the Caribbean (information kindly provided by Coral Pitkin of the **Rancho Encantado**, see page 176). There is a dock for swimming from north of the plaza, with a restaurant and disco next to it. North of Bacalar a direct road (Route 293) runs to Muná, on the road between Mérida and Uxmal. Gasoline is sold in a side-street.

Chetumal

María Dolores **7**
Real Azteca **8**
Ucúm **10**

Eating 🍴
El Emporio **2**
El Fenicio **3**
Los Milagros **4**
Pantoja **5**
Sergio Pizza **1**

Sleeping 🛏
Caribe Princess **2**
Cristal **3**
El Dorado **4**
Los Cocos **6**

Towards Francisco Villa

From Chetumal you can visit the fascinating Maya ruins that lie west on the way (Route 186) to Francisco Villa and Escárcega, if you have a car. There are few tourists in this area and few facilities. Take plenty of drinking water. About 25 km from Chetumal at **Ucum** (where fuel is available), you can turn off 5 km south to visit **Palmara**, located along the Río Hondo, which borders Belize; there are swimming holes and restaurant.

Just before Francisco Villa (61 km from Chetumal), the ruins of **Kohunlich** ⓘ *0800-1700, US$3*, lie 8.5 km south of the main road, 1½ hours' walk along a sweltering, unshaded road; take plenty of water. Descriptions in Spanish and English. Every hour or so the van passes for staff working at **Explorer Kohunlich**, a luxury resort hotel halfway to the ruins, which may give you a lift, but you'll still have 4 km to walk. There are fabulous masks (early Classic, AD 250-500) set on the side of the main pyramid, still bearing red colouring; they are unique of their kind (allow an hour for the site). About 200 m west of the turning for Kohunlich is an immigration office and a stall selling beer; wait here for buses to Chetumal or Xpujil, which have to stop, but first-class buses will not pick up passengers. *Colectivos* 'Nicolás Bravo' from Chetumal, or bus marked 'Zoh Laguna' from bus station pass the turning.

Other ruins in this area are **Dzibanché** and **Knichná** ① *0900-1700, US$3*. Both are recent excavations and both are accessible down a dirt road off the Chetumal–Morocoy road. In the 1990s the remains of a Maya king were disinterred at Dzibanché, which is thought to have been the largest Maya city in southern Quintana Roo, peaking between AD 300 and 1200. Its discoverer, Thomas Gann, named it in 1927 after the Maya glyphs he found engraved on the sapodilla wood lintels in Temple VI – *Dzibanché* means 'writing on the wood' in Maya. Later excavations revealed a tomb in Temple I, believed to have belonged to a king because of the number of offerings it contained. This temple is also known as the **Temple of the Owl** because one of the artefacts unearthed was a vase and lid carved with an owl figure. Other important structures are the **Temple of the Cormorants** and **Structure XIII**, known as 'The Captives', due to its friezes depicting prisoners. Knichná means 'House of the Sun' in Maya, christened by Thomas Gann in reference to a glyph he found there. The **Acropolis** is the largest structure. To reach these sights follow the Chetumal-Escárcega road, turn off at Km 58 towards Morocoy, 9 km further on. The road to Dzibanché is 2 km down this road, crossing the turning for Knichná.

◉ State of Quintana Roo listings

Hotel and guesthouse prices

LL over US$200	L US$151-200	AL US$101-150
A US$66-100	B US$46-65	C US$31-45
D US$21-30	E US$12-20	F US$7-11
G under US$7		

Restaurant prices

¶¶¶ over US$15	¶¶ US$8-15	¶ under US$8

See pages 31-33 for further information.

● Sleeping

Isla Holbox *p153*

Holbox has almost exclusively high-end accommodation; what else remains is not recommended.

AL Faro Viejo, Av Juárez, on the beach, T984-875 2217, www.faroviejoholbox. com.mx. Large, breezy rooms looking over the beach. Some rooms with kitchens.
AL Mawimbi, T984-875 2003, www.mawimbi.com.mx. Stylishly decorated *cabañas* with kitchenette, stepping out onto the beach.
AL Villa Los Mapaches, Av Pedro Joaquín Coldwell s/n, on beach, T984-875 2090,

www.losmapaches.com. Secluded, romantic cabins away from it all and fully furnished. Kitchenettes.
AL-A La Palapa, Av Morelos 231, T984-875 2121, www.hotellapalapa.com. Very clean cabins, leading onto the beach.
AL-A Villa Delfines, on the beach, T984-875 2196, www.villasdelfines.com. 20 romantic palm-roofed bungalows, leading onto the beach, pool, garden and bar, expensive but nice.

Camping

Best camping on beach east of village (north side of island).

Cancún *p153, maps p154 and p155*

Almost all accommodation – decent or otherwise – in the Hotel Zone now starts at around US$100, rises quickly and is best arranged as part of a package holiday. The increased costs – already the highest in Mexico – are also the result of a government-mandated rebuilding drive after

2 devastating hurricanes required all existing hotels to upgrade structures for safety. The beaches are supposedly public so you don't have to stay in a hotel to hang out on the beach, although this is not advertised and meandering along the strand is not encouraged by the larger hotels. The centre or downtown area has many cheaper options, but prices are still higher than other parts of the Yucatán Peninsula.

Hotel Zone

Some of these hotels have special offers during Jul and Aug, listed in *Riviera Maya Hotels Guide*, available free at the airport. Discounts can be considerable here as with anywhere on the coast during low season. 2 good high-end options are:

LL Le Meridien, Retorno del Rey Km 14, T998- 881 2200, www.starwoodhotels.com/lemeridien.

L Presidente Inter-Continental, Av Kukulcán Km 7.5, T998-848 8700, www.presidentecancun.com.

Town centre

Many hotels, especially the budget ones, tend to be full during Semana Santa and in Jul, and increasingly so over the Dec-Jan holidays. It is best to get to them as early as possible in the morning, or try to make a reservation if planning to return to Cancún after a trip to the interior or Isla Mujeres. Prices drop considerably in the low season. El Crucero, location of some of the budget hotels, is said by locals to be safe during the day, but unsafe at night.

AL-A El Rey del Caribe, Av Uxmal 24 and Náder, T998-884 2028, www.reycaribe.com. This hotel has clean, comfortable a/c rooms, some with cooker and fridge. There's a lush garden slung with hammocks and the spa has interesting treatments, such as chocolate or honey and milk massage.

AL-A Margaritas, Yaxchilán 41 and Jasmines, T998-884 7870, www.margaritas cancun.com. A clean and modern hotel with a range of efficient services including restaurant, bar, car rental, laundry and pool. There are over 100 rooms, all with a/c, balcony and cable TV.

B-C Cancún Rosa, Margaritas 2, local 10, T998-884 0623. Located close to the bus terminal, this hotel has tidy rooms of various sizes (including family size), all with cable TV and a/c. Management is friendly.

B-D Mayan Hostel Cancún, Margaritas 17 SM22, T998-892 0103, www.mayan hostel.com. Price per person. *Palapa*-style dorms, private rooms, fan or a/c, Breakfast, dinner and internet included in the price. Laundry and kitchen. Good service.

C El Alux, Av Uxmal 21, T998-884 0556, www.hotelalux.com. Turn left and first right from bus station. Clean rooms with a/c and bath. Some are cheaper and good value. Beware of the persistent tout outside, trying to take you to a cheap hovel. Recommended.

C-D María Isabel, Palmera 59, T998-884 9015, hotelmariaisabelcancun@yahoo. com.mx, near bus station and Av Tulum. A small hotel with clean and relatively economical rooms, all with a/c and TV. Friendly and recommended, but can be noisy.

C-D San Carlos, Cedro 40 (5th turning onto Cedro from bus terminal), opposite Mercado 23, T998-884 0602, www.hotelsancarlo scancun.com, handy for the bus terminal. Mixed bag of rooms, with mixed tariffs. Some rooms are a bit noisy and smelly, the upper floor is OK and a bit cheaper, but beware of very rickety stairs.

C-E Las Palmas, Palmeras 43, T998-884 2513, www.hotel-laspalmascancun.com. This friendly family-run hotel has very clean, good- value rooms with cable TV and a/c, and they'll store luggage. Breakfast is included and there's a cheap dormitory too. Recommended.

E Weary Traveller, Palmera 30, entrance in Av Uxmal, T998-887 0191, reservations@ wearytravelerhostel.com. Funky budget hostel with dormitories and private rooms (**C**). There's free internet, breakfast included in the price, TV, lockers and chillout space.

Camping

A big trailer park has been built opposite Punta Sam, 150 spaces, camping (**E** per person), shop selling basic commodities. Irregular bus service there, or hitchhike from Puerto Juárez. Check to see if restaurant is open evenings. Take mosquito repellent.

Isla Mujeres p156

LL-L Condominio Nautibeach, Playa Los Cocos, T998-877 0606, www.nautibeach.com. This hotel feels a bit like a giant warren, but has comfortable, a/c apartments and condos, right on the beach, facing the sunset. Sunset Grill, attached, is perfect for sundowners and there's a nice pool too.

L-A María del Mar, Av Carlos Larzo 1, on the road down to the north beach, T998-877 0179, www.cabanasdelmar.com. Good clean rooms and *cabañas*, close to the best beach. There's a restaurant, pool, beach bar, hammocks and a cool, tranquil garden for chilling out. Organizes fishing excursions and cultural tours.

AL-A Rocamar, Nicolás Bravo and Zona Marítima, T998-877 0101, www.rocamar-hotel.com. A large, well-established hotel, located on the quieter, eastern side of the island, where the sea is wilder and swimming not recommended. There's a range of rooms; the more expensive overlook the sea and the Caribbean sunrise and also have a jacuzzi.

B Hotel Bucaneros, Hidalgo 11, T998-877 1222, www.bucaneros.com. A pleasant, professionally managed hotel, right in the heart of town. It has 18 modern rooms, all with calm, neutral interiors. There's a good restaurant attached.

C-D Hotel Carmelina, Guerrero 4, T998-877 0006. Motel-style place with parking. The rooms are good and clean, with fridge, bath and fan. Good value.

C-D Posada Edelmar, Hidalgo, next to Bucanero hotel and restaurant. Economical alternative slap-bang in the middle of the pedestrianized section of town, seconds from the main restaurants and bars. Spacious rooms with good showers.

Ask for a room at the back if you want some peace and quiet.

C-D Vistalmar, Av Rueda Medina on promenade close to the ferry dock and Pemex station, T998-877 0209 (**D** for longer stays). Clean, comfortable rooms with fan, bath, balcony and TV. Some have a/c (**C**). Ask for a room on the top floor.

D-E Hostel Posada del Mar, Av Juárez s/n, T998-100 0759. This hostel features dorms and a couple of private rooms, all with fan, hot water and safety boxes. Continental breakfast included.

D-F Pocna Hostel (price per person), top end of Matamoros on the northeast coast, T998-877 0090, www.pocna.com. This is an island institution. Large, busy and warren-like Pocna has a plethora of dorms and rooms. There's internet access, lounge and beach bar, space to sling a hammock (**F**), yoga lessons and live music in the evenings. Book in advance – this is one of few hostels on the island, and as such is popular.

Puerto Morelos p157

AL Rancho Sak-Ol Libertad, next door to Caribbean Reef Club, T009-871 0181, www.rancholibertad.com. Thatched *cabañas*; the price includes breakfast, scuba-diving and snorkelling gear for rent.

B Posada Amor, Av Javier Rojo Gómez, opposite the beach, T998-871 0033. Very pleasant, well-built *cabañas* with good mosquito nets, the cheaper ones have outdoor communal showers, there is also a good restaurant and prices are reduced considerably out of season.

Playa del Carmen p158, map p158

Accommodation in Playa del Carmen is generally expensive and poor value, particularly around the beach and Av 5. The prices given below are for the high season, and can drop by as much as 50% at other times of the year.

LL Tides Riviera Maya, Rivera Maya Playa, Xcalacoco, Fracc 7, T984-877 3000, www.tidesrivieramaya.com. This boutique hotel boasts 30 well-designed villas in a jungle garden, and unpretentious service. The beach here is rocky, but they have built decking out to the sea so you can swim away from the rocks. See Activities and tours, page 183.

LL-AL Alhambra, Calle 8 Norte, corner with the beach, T984-873 0735, www.alhambra-hotel.net. Nice, airy palatial feel at this hotel with spiritual inclinations. All rooms have balcony or sea view, and general services include yoga instruction, jacuzzi, massage and there is a spa. Quiet and peaceful, despite its setting near beach bars. Family-run, French and English spoken. Recommended.

A Hotel Cielo, Calle 4, between 5 and 10, T984-873 1227, www.hotelcielo.com. Right in the centre of town, rooms have a/c, cable TV, safe and also throw in beach towels and breakfast. The corridors are a bit dark and narrow, but the views from the roof terrace superb. Great tacos at Restaurant **Carboncito**, attached.

A-B Casa Tucán, Calle 4 Norte, between Av 10 and 15, T984-873 0283, www.casatucan.de. German-owned hotel with simple, rustic *cabañas* and rooms. Rambling and labyrinthine, but there's a lovely lush garden, beautifully painted murals, and a deep pool where diving instruction takes place. There's also a restaurant, internet café and other handy outlets attached.

A-B Hotel Las Molcas, T984-873 0070, www.molcas.com.mx, near ferry pier. Strange but interesting architecture at this hotel, where some of the Moorish-style corridors seem to recede into infinity. There's a pool and staff are friendly.

B-C Mom's Hotel, Calle 4 and Av 30, T984-873 0315, www.momshotel.com, about 5 blocks from bus station or beach. Excellent value, friendly, family-run hotel with a pool. There are studios and apartments and good rates for long-term stays. Recommended.

C Posada Marinelly, Av Juárez between Calle 10 and 15, T984-873 0140. Centrally located with light, bright, comfortable rooms. More expensive with a/c (**A**). Handy for the ADO terminal. Friendly, bit basic.

C-D Happy Gecko, Av 10 between 6 and 8, T984-147 0692, happygeckohotel@yahoo.com. Canadian-owned, this hotel has good rooms with kitchen, fan and bath, some with a/c. Laundry service and movies available.

C-E Urban Hostel, Av 10 between 4 and 6, T984-803 3378, urbanhostel@gmail.com Funky backpackers' place with private rooms and dorms. Price includes breakfast. There's DVD, Xbox, internet and Wi-Fi, 2 terraces and kitchen.

D-E Hostel Playa, Av 25 with Calle 8, T984-803 3277, www.hostelplaya.com. A clean, professionally run hostel with various dorms, private rooms, kitchen and lounge space. There's a comfortable, friendly atmosphere. Prices per person, not per room.

Camping

Punta Bete, 10 km north, the right-hand one of 3 campsites at the end of a 5-km road, on beach. US$3 for tent, also 2 restaurants and *cabañas*.

Cozumel *p159, map p160 and p161*
Hotels are generally expensive and poor value. Expect prices to drop by up to 50% during low season.

AL-A Flamingo, Calle 6 Norte 81, T954-315 9236, www.hotelflamingo.com. Tasteful, comfortable rooms with a/c, Wi-Fi, balcony and fridge. There's a penthouse on the roof, good for families. Friendly staff.

A Amaranto, Calle 5 Sur, Av 15-20, T987-564 4262, www.cozumel.net/bb/amaranto. Lovely thatched-roof Mayan-style bungalows and suites, complete with hammocks. Spanish, English and French are spoken by the owners, Elaine and Jorge. There's a pool, and childcare is available on request.

A Tamarindo, Calle 4 Norte 421, between Av 20 and 25, T987-872 3614, www.cozumel.net/bb/tamarind. Intimate bed and breakfast, also owned by Elaine and Jorge. There's a shared kitchen, hammocks, dive-gear storage and rinse tank, purified drinking water, laundry, and safe-deposit box.

B Posada Marruang, A R Salas 440, between Av 20 Sur and 25 Sur, T987-872 1678. Very spick and span, large spartan rooms set back from road; barking dog ensures occasional noise and total security.

B-C Pepita, Av 15 Sur 120 y Calle 1 Sur, T987-872 0098, www.hotelpepitacozumel. com. Very pleasant rooms around a plant-filled courtyard. Modern fittings, a/c, cable TV, fridge in all rooms. Free coffee in the morning. Recommended.

B-C Posada Zuanayoli, Calle 6 Norte 272 between Av 10 and Av 15 Norte, T987-872 0690. Tall, old and slightly knackered building in a quiet street. Clean rooms have TV, fridge, fan, some with a/c (**B**). Free coffee and drinking water for guests.

C Posada Edén, Calle 2 Norte 124, T987-872 1166, gustarimo@hotmail.com. Clean, economical rooms with the usual bare necessities, including fan or a/c (**B**). There are apartments for long-term rental, 1 month minimum.

C-D Flores, A R Salas 72, off plaza, T987-872 1429. A range of basic, acceptable rooms with cable TV, fan or a/c (**B**). Only 50 m from the sea and very cheap for the location.

Tulum *p163*
Tulum village

Tulum village is a blossoming, but still relatively uninspiring destination. Scores of new budget hotels and restaurants are opening apace, making it a good base for backpackers and cost-conscious travellers. However, expect to offset those lower hotel rates with additional transport costs. There are no buses to the beach, only taxis and infrequent *colectivos*. For places to stay in Sian Ka'an Biosphere Reserve, see page 179.

C Hotel Maya, T984-871 1234, Av Tulum near the bus station (do not let taxis take you to Hotel Maya Tulum, an altogether much more expensive hotel). Large hotel with plenty of economical rooms, all with fan and bath. There's a restaurant next door serving home-cooked Mexican fare.

C-E Rancho Tranquilo, T984-871 2784, www.ranchotranquilo.com.mx, far south end of town. Friendly backpackers' place with dorms, *cabañas* and large rooms with private bath. There's also a lounge, library, shared kitchen and verdant garden. Friendly and highly recommended.

D-E Mayan Hostel Tulum, Carretera Coba– Boca Paila SN, 400 m from El Crucero, T998-112 1282, www.mayanhostel.com. Private rooms in *palapas*, dorms with a/c, breakfast and internet included in price. Bike rentals, book exchange, free short-term luggage storage.

D-E Weary Traveller Hostel, T984-871 2390, www.wearytravelerhostel.com, 1 block south of **ADO** bus terminal. Tulum's premier backpackers' hostel has bunk dorms, a book exchange and internet. They run transport to the beach, regular salsa classes and you can even cook your own food on the BBQ. A good place to meet fellow travellers. Breakfast included.

Tulum beach

A plethora of lodgings run the length of the coast from Tulum ruins to the Sian Ka'an Biosphere reserve. Development has been mercifully low-key, with ramshackle *cabañas* existing alongside luxury ecolodges. There is little infrastructure beyond these hotels, and it's best to reach them by taxi; official rates are posted on a sign at the rank in the village. Expect room costs to vary with views and proximity to the sea. Bear in mind this is a long stretch of beach and it's not always plausible to walk from hotel to hotel.

LL Ana y José, T984-880 5629, www.anayjose.com, 7 km south of ruins. Once only a collection of humble *cabañas*, Ana y José now offer elegant suites and luxurious spa accommodation. First-rate service and attention.

LL-AL Nueva Vida de Ramiro, Carretera Tulum–Boca Paila Km 8.5, No 17, T984-877 8512, www.tulumnv.com. If you must stay in high-end style in Tulum, these ecobungalows will do the trick. Straight on the beach.

L-AL Posada Margherita, T984-801 8493, www.posadamargherita.com. A decent, hospitable hotel with complete wheelchair access. There's 24-hr electricity and an excellent Italian restaurant attached. Recommended.

AL-A Cabañas Diamante K, T984-876 2115, www.diamantek.com, on the beach quite near the ruins. Rustic and friendly, with an array of interesting statues and hints of The Crystal Maze. *Cabaña* prices vary according to location and amenities, much cheaper with shared bath. There's a good bar and restaurant.

AL-B Dos Ceibas, T984-877 6024, www.dosceibas.com, 9 km from the ruins. This verdant ecolodge on the edge of the Sian Ka'an Biosphere reserve has a handful of comfortable *cabañas*. Massage and yoga instruction available. Friendly and tranquil ambience.

AL-B Los Arrecifes, T984-155 2957, www.losarrecifestulum.com, 7 km from ruins. *Cabañas,* trampoline, live music and shows, restaurant.

A Hotel Zazil-Kin, T984-124-0082, www.zazilkintulum.com, near the ruins. A popular, well-established Tulum favourite. A bit basic for the price, it offers a wide range of lodgings from rooms to *cabañas*, as well as restaurant, bar and gift shop.

B Playa Condesa, next door to Diamante K. Simple, airy wooden *cabañas*, not particularly good value for the price. Electricity a few hours each evening. There's a basic, but pricey grocery shop attached.

B-F Mar Caribe, near the ruins. Smaller complex than its neighbour, Zazil-Kin, but a friendly atmosphere, and much more peaceful. Very cheap if you bring your own hammock or tent. Organizes tours.

Cobá *p164*
A-B Villas Arqueológicas (Club Méditerranée), about 2 km from site on lake shore, T985-858 1527, www.villasarqueologicas.com.mx. Open to non-members, excellent, clean and quiet,

a/c, swimming pool, good restaurant with moderate prices, but expensive beer. Don't arrive without a reservation, especially at weekends; and yet making a reservation by phone seems to be practically impossible.

E-F Hotel Restaurant El Bocadito, in the village, on the street leading to the main road, T984-876 3738, www.cancunsouth.com/bocadito/. Run-down, spartan rooms with fan, intermittent water supply, poor security, good but expensive restaurant (which is popular with tour groups), books and handicrafts for sale. Recommended.

Sian Ka'an Biosphere Reserve *p166*
LL-AL Rancho Sol Caribe, Punta Allen, T984-139 3839, www.solcaribe-mexico.com. 4 comfortable *cabañas*, with bath, restaurant. Very expensive but recommended.

A Centro Ecológico Sian Ka'an, T984-871 2499, www.cesiak.org. Environmentally considerate and sensitive accommodation in the heart of the Reserve. Tours, kayaking and fly fishing arranged.

Felipe Carrillo Puerto *p167*
C El Faisán y El Venado, Av Benito Juárez, Lote 781, 2 blocks northeast of main square. Mixed reports on cleanliness, but hot water and good-value restaurant, popular with locals.

C María Isabel, near the plaza. Clean, friendly, laundry service, quiet, safe parking.

C San Ignacio, Av Benito Juárez 761, near Pemex. Good value, a/c, bath, towels, TV, secure car park.

C-D Chan Santa Cruz, Calle 68, 782, just off the plaza, T983-834 0021, www.hotelchansantacruz.com. Good, clean and friendly. A/c, cable TV, handicap accessible, fridge (Restaurante 24 Horas is open, as you'd imagine, 24 hrs).

Mahahual and around *p167*
There are plenty of options for sleeping with hammocks, camping and *cabañas*.
B-E Kabah-na, T983-838 8861, www.kabahna. com. *Cabañas* for 2 or space to hang a hammock, right on the beach.

C Sol y Mar restaurant, en route to Puerto Bravo, near Mahahual, with rooms to rent, bathrooms and spaces for RVs, also coconut palms and beach.

D-E Kok Hal, Mahahual, on the beach close to the old wharf. Shared bath and hot showers.

Camping
Camidas Trailer Park, Punta Herrero road, with palm trees, *palapas*, restaurant and space for 4 RVs, US$5 per person, car free.

Chetumal *p167, map p169*
AL-A Los Cocos, Av Héroes de Chapultepec 134, T983-835 0430, www.hotelloscocos. com.mx. Large, professionally managed hotel with clean, comfortable rooms and suites. There's a pool, bar and restaurant. Recommended.

A-B Caribe Princess, Av Obregón 168, T983-832 0520, www.caribeprincess chetumal.com. Good, clean rooms with a/c and TV. Recommended.

B Ucúm, Gandhi 167 corner of 16 de Septiembre, T983-832 6186, www.hotel ucumchetumal.com. Rooms with a/c, fan and bath. Pool and enclosed car park. Good-value restaurant next door.

B-C Palma Real, Obregón 103, T983-833 0963. Friendly and helpful place with big, clean rooms. Bath, cable TV and a/c.

C El Dorado, Av 5 de Mayo 42, T983-832 0315. Comfortable rooms with hot water and a/c. Friendly and quiet. Recommended.

C-D Hotel Cristal, Cristóbal Colón 207, T983-832 3878. Simple rooms with fan and bath. Parking available.

C-D Real Azteca, Av Belice 186, T983-832 0720. Cheerful, friendly, but no hot shower. 2nd-floor rooms best, but still not too good.

D María Dolores, Av Alvaro Obregón 206, T983-832 0508. Bath, hot water, fan, clean, windows don't open, noisy, restaurant **Solsimar** downstairs good and popular. Recommended.

Towards Bacalar *p168*
LL Akal Ki, Carretera Federal 307, Km 12.5, Bacalar Lagoon, T983-106 1751, www.akalki.com. A marvellously peaceful retreat with *palapas* built right over the water. Though surrounded by jungle, this strip of the lagoon has few rocks and little vegetation, making it crystal clear and ideal for swimming. Minimum stay 3 days. See Activities and tours, page 184.

AL-A Rancho Encantado, 3 km north of Bacalar, on the west shore of the lagoon. Resort hotel, half-board available, Apdo 233, Chetumal, T983-101 3358, www.encantado.com. With private dock, tour boat, canoes and windsurf boards for rent, private cabins with fridge and hammock, very good. See Activities and tours, page 184.

A-B Hotel Las Lagunas, Bvl Costero 479, about 2 km south of Bacalar (on left-hand side of the road going towards the village), T983-834 2206. It is very good, wonderful views, helpful, clean, comfortable, hot water, swimming pool and opposite a freshwater lake; restaurant is poor and overpriced.

C Hotel América, Av 5 258, Bacalar, 700 m north of the bus stop on the plaza (walk in the opposite direction to Chetumal). Recommended.

Camping
Camping is possible at the end of the road 100 m from the lagoon, toilets and shower, US$0.10, but lagoon perfect for washing and swimming.

❼ Eating

Cancún *p153, maps p154 and p155*
The **Hotel Zone** is lined with expensive restaurants, with every type of international cuisine imaginable, but with a predominance of Tex-Mex and Italian. Restaurants in the centre are cheaper, and the emphasis is on local food.

The cheapest area for dinner is SM64, opposite **Plaza 2000**. Popular with locals, especially on Sun when it is hard to get a table; there are 4 or 5 small, family-run restaurants serving local specialities. *Comida corrida* for as little as US$2. **Mercado 28** is the best budget option for breakfast or lunch, with many cheap outdoor and indoor *loncherías* serving *comida corrida*, very popular with locals, quick service. Another good option is **Mercado 23**, 5 blocks north of the **ADO** terminal, along Calle Cedro.

₸₸₸ El Pescador, Tulipanes 28. Good seafood, well established with excellent reputation. Expensive.

₸₸₸ La Habichuela, Margaritas 25. Award-winning restaurant serving delicious Caribbean seafood in a tropical garden setting. Great ambience and jazz music.

₸₸₸ La Parilla, Yaxchilán 51. Mouth-watering grill platters, ribs and steaks. A buzzing, lively joint, always busy and popular. Try the enormous margaritas in exotic flavours – hibiscus flower and tamarind.

₸₸₸ Pericos, Av Yaxchilán 71, T998-884 3152, www.pericos.com.mx. Chicken, meat, fish fillets and seafood platters at this themed Mexican restaurant where the staff wear fancy dress. It's touristy, it's cheesy, but the atmosphere is great.

₸₸₸-₸₸ El Rincón del Vino, Alcatraces 29. Tapas with a seafood emphasis. As the name suggests, there's a healthy stock of wine. A tranquil and pleasant place, with a range of international food.

₸₸₸-₸₸ Labná, Margaritas 29. The best in Yucatecan cooking, serving dishes like *poc chuc* and *pollo pibil*. Try the platter and sample a wide range of this fascinating regional cuisine. Good lunchtime buffet.

₸₸ El Poblano, Tulum and Tulipanes. Tacos, kebabs, grilled meats and steaks – carnivores call it dinner. A friendly, unpretentious restaurant, popular with Mexicans.

₸₸ Rincón Yucateco, Av Uxmal 24. Good grills and traditional Mexican grub from lunchtime.

Cafés

Pastelería Italiana, Yaxchilán, just before Sunyaxchén turning. Excellent coffee and pastries, friendly. There are a few other cheap eateries along Yaxchilán, tucked away between the pricey themed restaurants, some open during the day only.

Isla Mujeres *p156*

Hidalgo is the most popular for restaurants.

₸₸₸ Mesón del Bucanero, Hidalgo, opposite Rolandis. Steaks, seafood, pasta and crêpes at this classy restaurant. There's a rich offering of cocktails too. Nice al fresco seating.

₸₸ Bamboo, Hidalgo. A sleek and trendy restaurant-bar serving sushi, Thai curries, seafood and fresh fruit juices. Live music at the weekends.

₸₸ Comono, Hidalgo. Open 1400-2230, Mon-Fri. Israeli-run kitchen and bar that serves Mediterranean food, beer and shakes. There are nightly movies, live music on Fri, and hookah pipes if you fancy smoking some molasses. Popular with backpackers.

₸₸ Los Amigos Restaurant, Hidalgo. Small, with 2 tables outside, excellent pizzas and pasta.

₸₸ Mamma Rosa, Hidalgo and Matamoros. Formerly La Malquerida. Italian-run restaurant serving pasta and seafood with a good selection of Italian wines.

₸₸ Miguel's Moon Lite, Hidalgo 9. Good hospitality at this lively restaurant-bar. When the booze isn't flowing, there's tacos, steaks and seafood. Ask for a free shot of pomegranate tequila.

₸₸ Rolandis, Hidalgo, T998-877 0700. Terrace overlooking the street. Excellent Italian food, including a good range of tasty pizzas and pastas, seafood and meat dishes. Has many branches across Mexico.

₸ La Susanita, Juárez 5. Excellent home cooking, at this cute little locals' place; when closed it is the family's living room.

₸ Lonchería La Lomita, Juárez 25B. Nice and clean and at US$3, quite possibly the best value, tasty food in town.

Loncherías, northwest end of Guerrero, around the municipal market. Open till 1800. Busy and bustling, good for breakfast, snacks and lunch. All serve the same local fare at similar prices.

Poc-Chuc, Juárez y Madero. Somewhat rough and ready locals' joint, serving up big portions and good *tortas*.

Cafés

Aluxes Café, Av Matamoros, next to Aquí Estoy Pizza. A cheery place serving cappuccinos, filter coffee and home-made snacks.

Cafecito, Matamoros 42. Cool and tranquil. A nice breakfast place, serving waffles, juice, sandwiches.

Puerto Morelos p157
Johnny Cairo. Good typical food.
Pelícano. Very good seafood.

Playa del Carmen p158, map p158
The majority of the town's restaurants line Av 5, where most tourists limit themselves and a meal costs no less (and usually a bit more) than US$10. Popular, big name restaurants dominate the southern end of the street. Quieter, subtler settings lie north, beyond Calle 20. For budget eating, head west, away from the main drag.

Buenos Aires, Calle 6 Norte between Av 5 and 10, on Plaza Playa. Speciality Argentine meats, run by Argentines, nice for a change from Mexican food.

The Glass Bar, Calle 10, between Av 1 and 5, www.theglassbar.com.mx. A sophisticated Italian restaurant serving fine wine, Mediterranean cuisine and seafood. The place for an intimate, romantic dinner.

Karen's, Av 5, between Calle 2 and 4. Always a lively, family atmosphere here. The menu includes Mexican staples, good pizzas, grilled meats and tacos. There's live music most nights. Popular.

La Parrilla, Av 5 y Calle 8. Large portions, good service, live mariachi band every night, popular.

Yaxche, Calle 8 between Av 5 and 10. Traditional Maya cuisine. Cheaper lunchtime menu (🍴🍴).

Los Comales, Av 5 and Calle 4. Popular seafood restaurant. Dishes include Veracruz fish fillet, seafood platters, surf n turf, *fajitas* and other Mexican fare. There's a good-value breakfast buffet for US$5.50.

Maktub, Av 5, between Calle 28 and 30. Arab and Lebanese cuisine, clean and pleasant, with outdoor seating.

Sushi-Tlan, Av 5, between Calle 28 and 30. Something different; a clean, fresh, brightly lit sushi bar.

Pez Vela, Av 5 y Calle 2. Good atmosphere, food, drinks and music.

Rolandi, Av 5, close to the ferry dock. Superb pasta and pizza at this popular Italian place. Branches across Mexico.

Billy the Kid, Av 15 and Calle 4. This very cheap, rough-and-ready locals' haunt does tacos and *tortas*.

El Fogón, Av 30 and Calle 6. Locals' taco joint that serves grilled meat, wholesome *tortas* and *quesadillas*.

Tortas del Carmen, Av 15, between Calle 4 and 2. Tasty *tortas* and *licuados*, open from 0830.

Cafés and bakeries
Java Joe's, Calle 10, between Av 5 and 10. Italian and gourmet coffees, sandwiches, pastries. Next door's café/bookshop **Habita** is worth a peek for its art, books and alternative cultural space.

Cozumel p159, map p160 and p161
There are few eating options for budget travellers. The cheapest places for breakfast, lunch or an early dinner are the *loncherías* next to the market on A R Salas, between Av 20 and 25. They serve fairly good local *comida corrida*, 0800-1930.

Lobster's Cove, Av Rafael Melgar 790, 987-24022. Quality seafood, live music, happy hour 1200-1400.

Pancho's Backyard, Rafael Melgar 27, in **Los Cinco Soles** shopping complex in big courtyard out the back. Mexican food and wine elegantly served, good food.

ΨΨΨ **Prima**, Salas 109. Open 1600-2400. Northern Italian seafood, handmade pasta, brick-oven pizzas, non-smoking area.

ΨΨΨ-ΨΨ **Casa Mission**, Av 55, between Juárez and Calle 1 Sur, www.missioncoz.com. Open daily 1700-2300. Established in 1973, this restaurant survived hurricanes Wilma and Gilbert and is now a Cozumel institution. Fine Mexican, international and seafood in an elegant hacienda setting.

ΨΨΨ-ΨΨ **La Choza**, Salas 198 and Av 10, www.lachozarestaurant.com. Decent Mexican and regional cuisine. Popular.

ΨΨ **Las Palmeras**, at the pier (good people-watching spot), Av Melgar. Open 0700-1400. Very popular for breakfast, always busy. Recommended.

ΨΨ-Ψ **Casa Deni's**, Calle 1 Sur 164, close to plaza. Open-air restaurant, very good, cheapish prices.

Tulum *p163*

Tulum village

Testament to Tulum's growing popularity, a plethora of new restaurants have opened in town, mostly along Av Tulum. Wander along in the evening and take your pick of everything from Argentine *parrillas* to seafood and pizzas.

ΨΨΨ-ΨΨ **El Pequeño Buenos Aires**, Av Tulum, Argentine steak and grill house, one great meat feast, open air setting on the main drag.

ΨΨ **Don Cafeto**, Av Tulum 64. Popular place serving Mexican fare. Usually buzzing in the evenings. Beach branch currently shut, but set to re-open in late 2009.

ΨΨ **La Nave**, Av Tulum. Italian restaurant and pizzeria, set on 2 floors, nice rustic wooden decor. Cosy in the evenings.

Ψ **Doña Tinas**, good basic and cheap, in a grass hut at southern end of town. El Mariachito next door also does good, cheap and cheerful grub.

Ψ **El Mariachi**, cheap taco bar with good *fajitas*.

Tulum beach

Restaurants on the beach tend to be owned by hotels. For dinner, book in advance where possible. Strolling between establishments after dark isn't advisable.

ΨΨΨ-ΨΨ **La Zebra**, Carretera Tulum–Boca Paila Km 7.5, www.lazebratulum.com. Fresh, tasty barbequed fish, shrimps, *ceviche* and Mexican fare. Lashings of Margarita at the Tequila Bar.

ΨΨΨ-ΨΨ **Mezzanine**, Carretera Tulum–Boca Paila Km 1.5. Excellent authentic Thai cuisine and Martini bar attached.

ΨΨΨ-ΨΨ **Restaurant Margherita**, Carretera Tulum–Boca Paila Km 4.5, in Posada Margeherita. Closed Sun. Excellent, freshly prepared Italian food in an intimate setting. Hospitable, attentive service. Book in advance. Recommended.

Cobá *p164*

There are plenty of restaurants in the village, on the road to Villas Arqueológicas and on the road to the ruins, all quite pricey. There's also a grocery store by El Bocadito and souvenir shops.

ΨΨ **Pirámides**, on corner of track leading to Villas Arqueológicas. Highly recommended.

Ψ **Nicte-Ha**, good and friendly.

Sian Ka'an Biosphere Reserve *p166*

ΨΨ-Ψ **La Cantina**, Punta Allen, a good, non-touristy restaurant (US$3-4 for fish).

Felipe Carrillo Puerto *p167*

ΨΨ **Danburger Maya**, next door to hotel San Ignacio. Good food, reasonable prices, helpful.

Ψ **Restaurant Addy**, on main road, south of town. Good, simple.

Chetumal *p167, map p169*

ΨΨΨ-ΨΨ **El Emporio**, Merino 106. Delicious Uruguayan steaks served in a historic old house near the bay.

ΨΨ **Barracuda**, about 4 blocks north of market, then 3 blocks west (another area with many restaurants). Good seafood.

Sergio Pizza, Av Obregón 182. Pizzas, fish, and expensive steak meals, a/c, good drinks, excellent service.

El Fenicio, Héroes and Zaragoza, open 24 hrs, with mini-market at the back. Chicken, steaks, burgers and Mexican grub.

Los Milagros, Zaragoza and 5 de Mayo. This locals' café serves economical Mexican fare, *comida corrida* and breakfasts.

Mercado. Cheap meals in the market at the top of Av Héroes, but the service is not too good and tourists are likely to be stared at.

Pantoja, Ghandi 87. Busy locals' joint serving the usual economical fare.

Towards Bacalar *p168*

La Esperanza, 1 block north from plaza. Thatched barn, good seafood.

Punta y Coma, Orizaba, 3 blocks from zócalo. Inexpensive, large menu including vegetarian. Recommended.

⦿ Entertainment

Cancún *p153, maps p154 and p155*
Bars and clubs

The action happens in the Zona Hotelera, around 9 km from downtown on Kukulcan Blv, where big clubs play to big crowds. Girls will often drink for free, and there's a distinctly North American flavour. Downtown has a thriving scene too, mostly focused on Yaxchilán and the surrounding streets.

If you get the chance to see local dance band **Balancê** (www.balancelabanda.com), don't miss it.

Bulldog, Blv Kukulcán Km 9, www.bulldog cafe.com/cancun.html. Rock, hip-hop, pop and salsa. A popular, well-organized mega club with sophisticated light and sound rigs.

Coco Bongo, Forum by the sea mall, www.cocobongo.com.mx. Open Wed-Sat. Cancún's most famous nightclub. Expect wild theatrical displays, including dance, acrobatics, laser shows and gallons of dry ice. Loud, pumping dance music is played.

Dady Rock, Blv Kukulcán Km 9.5, www.dady rock.com.mx. 2 floors, 4 bars, DJs, MCs and live bands. **Dady Rock** lays on the entertainment with boundless paternal generosity. There's frequent bikini, 'sexy legs' and 'wet body' contests too, if that's your sort of thing.

Señor Frog's, Blv Kukulcán km 9.5, www.senorfrogs.com. You'll get a yard glass on entry, fill it with the booze of your choice, open wide and drink. A notorious 'Spring Break' dive, Señor Frogs is a long-standing Cancún favourite; it's spawned branches in most Mexican resorts and across the Caribbean with an array of dubious, themed merchandise to match. Cover US$5.

Cinemas

Cinepolis, Tulum 260, SM7. Large complex showing English-language, subtitled films.

Isla Mujeres *p156*
Bar and clubs

Most of the bars have a permanent happy hour, with 2 drinks for the price of 1. Happy Hour here also tends to favour women, who sometimes get to drink for free. There are many bars along Hidalgo and the beach – take your pick.

Chile Locos, along the beach, with live marimba music.

La Adelita, Hidalgo 12. Adelita stocks over 200 types of tequila, the bar staff really know their stuff and are happy to make recommendations. Pull up a stool, roll up your sleeves – it's going to be a long night.

La Palapa, on Playa Los Cocos. Serves cocktails and snacks and is busy during the day until everyone leaves the beach, then fills up again after midnight for drinking and dancing.

Om Bar, Matamoros 15. Open Wed-Sat, from 1900. Chilled-out hippy lounge. Drink beer and cocktails under the *palapa*, relax to reggae or Latin jazz. Free shots.

Playa del Carmen *p158, map p158*
Bars and clubs
Nightlife in Playa del Carmen is famously hedonistic. The best clubs are situated on Calle 12 and 14. There are also some bars in the 'gringo zone' by the ferry dock – Señor Frog's and Carlos 'n' Charlies, most notably.
Beer Bucket, Calle 10, between Av 5 and 10. Want a simple, unpretentious beer? Try this place, popular with expats, where the grog and conversation flow cheaply.
Blue Parrot Inn, Calle 12 y Av 1, next to beach. Dance, trance and house at this famous, sexy nightclub on the beach. Ladies night on Mon and Thu, with free drinks.
Coco Maya, Calle 12 and the beach. Beach club playing R and B, hip-hop, house and dance. Lots of TV screens, all under a *palapa*.
El Cielo, Calle 12, between Av 5 and the beach. Swanky disco playing dance and pumping tunes. Popular and well-known. Cover for men US$5, women free.
Habibi and Los Aguachiles, next door to OM (below) are upmarket and trendy watering holes for the hip and happening. Worth a peek, if a bit pricey.
OM, Calle 12, between Av 5 and the beach. Suave lounge-bar with sofas, sheeshas and ethereal white drapes. Electronic music.
Tequila Barrel, Av 5 between Calle 10 and 12. Tex-Mex Bar and grill, friendly owner (Greco) and staff. Girls who dance on the bar get a free shot of tequila.

Cozumel *p159, map p160 and p161*
Bars and clubs
1.5 Tequila Lounge, Melgar and Calle 11 Sur. Boozy, sociable lunch bar, popular with visitors straight off the cruise ships.
Carlos 'n Charlies, Plaza Punta Langosta. Big-name chain bar, always busy with tourists.
Neptuno, Melgar and Calle 11 Sur. Long-standing Cozumel disco, playing salsa, dance and reggae.
Señor Frog's, Plaza Punta Langosta, www.senorfrogs.com. Chain bar popular with North Americans and other tourists.

○ Shopping

Cancún *p153, maps p154 and p155*
There are several US-style shopping malls in the Hotel Zone. The main one, **Plaza Kukulcán**, known as Luxury Avenue, www.luxuryavenue.com, has over 200 shops, restaurants, a bowling alley and video games. It is open from 1000-2200 daily, and the prices are high for most things, including souvenirs. The main **craft market** is on Av Tulum near Plaza Las Américas; it is a huge network of stalls, all selling exactly the same merchandise: silver jewellery from Taxco, ceramic Maya figurines, hammocks, jade chess sets. Prices are hiked up to the limit, so bargain hard: most vendors expect to get half what they originally ask for. The market called **Mercado 23** (at the end of Calle Cedro, off Av Tulum) has cheaper souvenirs and less aggressive salesmen it's a bit tatty and tacky, although good for cheap food; *guayabera* shirts are available on one of the stalls. Several smoking shops have appeared, cashing in on the craze for Cuban cigars; (inspect your purchase thoroughly – if the price seems too good to be true, rest assured that it is); these are all located on or just off Av Tulum. Note that genuine Cuban cigars will be seized by US Customs if entering the States. Cheaper clothes shops than the Hotel Zone can be found at the north end of Av Tulum, near Plaza 2000. Pricey leather goods, clothes and jewellery can be bought in the **Plaza 2000** shopping mall.

Isla Mujeres *p156*
Cigars
Tobacco & Co, Hidalgo 14. Cuban cigars and smoking paraphernalia. There are several other shops in the centre selling Cuban cigars.

Souvenirs
Av Hidalgo is lined with souvenir shops, most of them selling the same things: ceramic Maya figurines and masks; hammocks; blankets; and silver jewellery

from Taxco. Bargaining is obligatory – try and get the desired item for half the original asking price, which is what the vendors expect to receive. There are more souvenir shops along the harbour front, where the salesmen are more pushy, and more shops along **Av Morelos**.

Playa del Carmen *p158, map p158*

Lots of expensive souvenir shops clustered around the plaza; cheaper shops, for day-to-day items, are on Av Juárez. There's a cheap *panadería* at the beginning of Av Juárez. For developing photos and buying film, there are several places along Av 5.

Chetumal *p167, map p169*

Shops are open 0800-1300, 1800-2000. Av Héroes is the main shopping street. Good for foreign foodstuffs – cheaper at the covered market in the outskirts than in the centre.

▲▲ Activities and tours

Cancún *p153, maps p154 and p155*
Boat trips and cruises
Aquaworld, Blv Kukulcán 15.2, T998-848 8327, www.aquaworld.com.mx. A range of boat trips and cruises including day-trips to Isla Mujeres and Cozumel; dinner cruises on the 'Cancun Queen'; and underwater explorations on their 'Sub See Explorer' submarine. They also organize parasailing, jungle tours and swimming with dolphins.

Bullfighting
Plaza de Toros, Av Bonompak south, has a folkloric show and bullfight every Wed at 1530, 2½ hrs. Admission US$38, tickets available at travel agents and the ring.

Dolphin encounters
Dolphin Discovery, Kukulcán Km 5, T998-849 4748, www.dolphindiscovery.com. Splash around with dolphins, manatees and seals, and get in touch with your inner sea mammal. A real winner for families.

Golf
Club de Golf Cancun, Kukulcán Km 7.5, T998-883 1230, www.cancungolfclub.com, 18-hole championship course, driving range and putting greens.
Hilton Cancun Beach and Golf Resort, Kukulcán Blvd Km 17, T998-881 8000, www.hiltoncancun.com/golf.htm. An attractive 18-hole course on the banks of a lagoon.

Scuba-diving and snorkelling
See also Aquaworld, above.
Scuba Cancun, Kukulcán Km 5, T998-849 5226, www.scubacancun.com.mx. A medium-sized dive centre run by Captain Luis Hurtado who has 54 years' diving experience. It offers a range of dives, snorkelling tours and accelerated PADI courses.

Tour operators
American Express, Av Tulum 208, esq Agua, SM 4, T998-884 5441.
Mayan Destinations, Cobá 31, Edificio Monaco, SM22, T998-884 4308, www.mayan destinations.com. All the usual destinations, such as Chichén Itzá, Xcaret, Tulum, as well as flights to Cuba. Many others in the centre and at larger hotels. Most hotels on the hotel zone have their own travel agency.

Water sports
A variety of watersports can be organized on the beaches along the hotel zone, including parasailing, waterskiing, windsurfing and jet-skiing.

Isla Mujeres *p156*
Birdwatching
Amigos de Isla Contoy, T998-884 7483, www.amigosdeislacontoy.org and www.islacontoy.org. This environmental organization keeps lists of authorized tour boats to Isla Contoy – a protected bird sanctuary, 30 km north of Isla Mujeres. More than 10,000 birds spend the winter on this island, including cormorants, frigates, herons, boobies and pelicans.

Scuba-diving and snorkelling
Carey, Av Matamoros 13-A, T998-877 0763. Small groups, bilingual staff and good range of dives, including reef dives, night dives, cenote dives and whale shark swimming. **El Garrafón**, T998-193 3360, www.garrafon. com, southern tip of the island. This water-sports centre offers a range of diving and snorkelling programmes, with a sunken cross off-shore for divers to explore. They also do dolphin encounters, kayaking and cycling. **Sea Hawk**, Zazil-Ha (behind **Hotel Na-Balam**) T998-877 1233, seahawkdivers@ hotmail.com. Certified PADI instructors, 2-tank dive US$50, introductory course including shallow dive US$85. Also snorkelling trips and fishing trips.

Tour operators
Mundaca Travel, Av Rueda Medina, T998-877 0845, inside the ferry terminal. Tours to Chichén Itzá, Tulum, Xel-Ha and Xcaret. Bus tickets and flights to Cuba. Friendly and helpful.

Playa del Carmen p158, map p158
Massage
Tides Riviera Maya, see Sleeping, page 172. Offers yoga, *temazcal*, massage, a range of other therapies, jacuzzis and steam rooms.

Scuba-diving and snorkelling
Abyss, Av 1a, between Calle 10 and 12, T984-873 2164, www.abyssdiveshop.com, inside **Hotel Tropical Casablanca**. Said to be the best. Run by fully certified Canadian Instructor David Tomlinson. Services include PADI courses; reef, night and cenote dives. Good value dive packages.
Tank-Ha, Calle 10, between Av 5 and 10, T984-873 0302, www.tankha.com. Experienced and well-established dive centre offering a range of packages.
Yucatek Divers, Av 15 Norte, between Calle 2 and 4, T984-803 2836, www.yucatek-divers.com. Open 0730-1730. General diving and snorkelling, including programmes for

disabled people. Also a snorkelling with whale sharks option.

Tour operators
Alltournative, Av 5, between Calle 12 and 14 and another office between Calle 2 and 4 (opposite the **ADO** terminal), T984-803 9999, www.alltournative.com. Open daily 0900-1900. Culturally and ecologically sensitive tours have won this company several awards. Services include tours to archaeological sites, Mayan villages, forests, lagoons and *cenotes*.
Viajes Felgueres, Calle 6 between Av 5 and Av 10, T984-873 0142. Long-standing and reliable agency with a branch in Cancún, tours to Chichén Itzá, including transport from hotel, guide, entry, food, also bookings for national and international flights, helpful staff.

Cozumel p159, map p160 and p161
Scuba-diving
See box, Cenote diving, page 168. The island is famous for the beauty of its underwater environment. The best reef for scuba-diving is **Palancar**, reached only by boat. Also highly recommended are **Santa Rosa** and **Colombia**. For more experienced divers the reefs at **Punta Sur**, **Maracaibo** and **Baracuda** should not to be missed. There are at least 20 major dive sites. Almost all Cozumel diving is drift diving, so if you are not used to a current, choose an operator you feel comfortable with.

Dive centres There are 2 different types of dive centre: the larger ones, where the divers are taken out to sea in big boats with many passengers; the smaller, more personalized dive shops, with a maximum of 8 people per small boat.

The best of the smaller centres is said to be **Deep Blue**, A R Salas 200, corner of Av 10 Sur, T987-872 5653, www.deepblue cozumel.com. Matt and Deborah, an English/Colombian couple, run the centre. All PADI and NAUI certifications, eg 3-5-day dive packages US$207-325; cavern and *cenote* diving, including 2 dives, transport and lunch.

Other small dive centres are: **Black Shark**, Av 5 between A R Salas and Calle 3 Sur, T987-872 5657, www.blackshark.com.mx; **Blue Bubble Divers**, Carretera Costera Sur Km 3.5, T987-872 4240, www.blue bubble.com; **Diving Adventures**, Calle 15 Sur, between Av 19 and 21, T987-872 3009, www.divingadventures.net.

Decompression centres Buceo Médico Mexicano, Calle 5 Sur No 21B, T987-872 1430, immediate localization (24-hr) VHF 16 and 21. It is supported by US$1 per day donations from divers with affiliated operators. **Cozumel Hyperbarics** in Clínica San Miguel, Calle 6 Norte No 135 between Av 5 and Av 10, T987-872 3070, VHF channel 65.

Tulum *p163*
Diving
Several dive shops all along the Tulum corridor. See box, page 168, for cave diving operators and specialist courses – highly recommended if you like diving. There are many untrained snorkelling and diving outfits, so take care.

Massage
Eco Tulum, www.ecotulum.com. Offers affordable local Maya treatments including clay massage. Yoga, *temazcal* and holistic massage also available.

Chetumal *p167, map p169*
Tour operators
Bacalar Tours, Alvaro Obregón 167A, T987-832 3875, Tours to Mayan ruins and car rental.
Tu-Maya, Alvaro Obregón 312, T983-832 0555, www.casablancachetumal.com/tumaya. 1-day tours to Guatemala, Belize and Calakmul.

Towards Bacalar *p168*
Massage
Akal Ki (see page 176), www.akalki.com. A retreat offering yoga, meditation, *temazcal* and *jenzu*, a seawater massage.

Rancho Encantado (see Sleeping, page 176), www.encantado.com. A holistic resort offering *lomi lomi*, a form of massage, *temazcal*, *qigong* and meditation.

⊜ Transport

Cancún *p153, maps p154 and p155*
Air
Cancún airport (CUN) has expensive shops and restaurant, exchange facilities, double check your money, especially at busy times, poor rates too, 2 hotel reservation agencies (no rooms under US$45). 2 terminals: **Main** and **South** (or 'FBO' building), white shuttle minibuses between them. From Cancún there are domestic flights and connections throughout the country. For international connections, see Getting there on pages 20 and 54. For airline websites, see page 23.

Airline offices Aviacsa, Aerocosta, Tulum 29, T998-884 0383; **Aeromar**, airport, T998-886 1100; **AeroMéxico**, Cobá 80, T998-287 1868; **Aviasca**, Cobá 39, T01-800-284-2272; **Continental Airlines**, airport, T998-886 0006; **Delta airlines**, airport, T998-886 0668.

Bus
For ferries to Isla Mujeres, several buses to the terminals at Gran Puerto and Puerto Juárez run from Av Tulum – try R-13, or R-1 marked Pto Juárez, US$0.80. Taxi to Puerto Juárez, US$2.50.

Long distance Cancún bus terminal, at the junction of Av Tulum and Uxmal, is small, well organized and handy for the cheaper hostels. The bus station is the hub for routes west to Mérida and south to Tulum and Chetumal, open 24 hrs, left luggage from US$0.30 per small bag, per hr, prices rising depending on size of bag, open 0600-2200. To **Cancun Airport**, every 30 mins, 30 mins, US$3.50. To **Chetumal**, ADO, frequent departures, 6 hrs, US$17.50. To **Chichén Itzá**; all 2nd-class buses to Mérida stop here, fewer 1st-class buses, 4 hrs,

US$7.50-11.50. To **Mérida**, ADO, frequent departures, 4½ hrs, US$15. To **Palenque**, 1st class (**ADO** and **OCC**), 1415, 1545, 1930, 2030, 12½ hrs, US$40; and an **ADO GL**, 1745, 13 hrs, US$48. To **Playa del Carmen** ADO shuttle, every 10 mins, 1 hr, US$3. To **Puerto Morelos**, ADO, frequent departures, 30 mins, US$1. To **San Cristóbal**, OCC, 1415, 1545, 2030 18 hrs, US$49, **ADO GL**, 1745, US$58. To **Tulum**, ADO, frequent departures, 2½ hrs, US$5, and many cheaper 2nd-class buses. To **Valladolid**, frequent departures, 2½ hrs, US$9. To **Villahermosa**, 1st class, many departures, 13 hrs, US$52.50-73.50. To **Xcaret**, frequent departures, 1¾ hrs, US$3. To **Xel-Há**, frequent departures, 2 hrs, US$4. **Expreso de Oriente** also has services to the more obscure destinations of **Tizimín** (3 hrs, US$8), **Izamal**, **Cenotillo** and **Chiquilá**.

Car
Car hire There are many car hire agencies, with offices on Av Tulum, in the Hotel Zone and at the airport; look out for special deals, but check vehicles carefully. They include: **Budget**, Av Tulum 231, T998-884 6955; **Alamo**, Cancún Airport, T998-886 0179; **Payless**, Blvd Luid Colosio Km 12, T998-886 2812; **Master Car**, Av Uxmal 20, T01-800-711-3344; **Top Rent a Car**, Blv Kukulcán Km 14.5.

Car parking Do not leave cars parked in side streets; there is a high risk of theft. Use the parking lot on Av Uxmal.

Ferry
Ferries to **Isla Mujeres** depart from terminals at Gran Puerto and nearby Puerto Juárez, north of Av Tulum, every 30 mins between 0600-2300, 20 mins by fast ferry, US$2.50, US$5 return (doesn't need to be on the same day). The car ferry departs from Punta Sam, US$18.50 for a driver and vehicle, US$1.50 for each additional passenger.

Isla Mujeres *p156*
Air
The small airstrip in the middle of the island is mainly used for private planes, best arranged with a tourist office in Cancún.

Bicycle and moped
Many touts along Hidalgo offer moped rentals at similar rates: US$7 per hr, US$25 full day. **Sport Bike**, Av Juárez y Morelos, has good bikes. **Cárdenas**, Av Guerrero 105, T/F998-877-0079, for mopeds and golf carts. Bicycles are usually offered by the same places as mopeds for about US$11 per day.

Bus
A public bus runs from the ferry dock to Playa Paraíso every 30 mins, US$0. 30. Timings can be erratic, especially on Sun.

Ferry
For information on ferries to and from the island, see Cancún, above.

Taxi
A taxi from town to **El Garrafón** and vice versa is US$4.30. For the return journey, sharing a taxi will work out marginally more expensive than the bus for 4 people. A taxi from El Garrafón to the bus stop at Playa Paraíso is US$1. Taxis charge an additional US$1 at night. Beware that the prices are fixed, but inflated on this stretch and a taxi ride to the southernmost tip of the island, a short walk from El Garrafón, is cheaper at US$2.80. There are several places renting **golf carts**, eg Ciros, on Matamoros near Playa Cocos. Rates are generally US$32-39 per day. A credit card is usually required as a deposit.

Puerto Morelos *p157*
Bus
There are buses to **Cancún** and **Playa del Carmen** every 30 mins. Buses depart from the main road, taxi to bus stop US$3.

Ferry

Car ferries to **Cozumel** depart at 0500, 1030, 1600, the dock is 500 m south of the plaza. They return at 0800, 1330, 1900, but always check schedules in advance. Taxi from Cancún airport to Puerto Morelos costs US$25-35.

Playa del Carmen *p158, map p158*

Air

There are flights to **Cozumel** from the nearby airstrip, speak to a tourist office in Playa del Carmen about chartering a plane.

Bus

The **ADO** bus terminal is on Av Juárez between Av 5 and 10. All buses depart from here. The following prices and times are for ADO buses (1st class, a/c, usually showing a video on longer journeys); Premier, also 1st class; Maya de Oro, supposed to be 1st class but quality of buses can be poor; OCC, good 1st-class service. To **Cancún**, frequent departures, 1½ hrs, US$3; 2nd-class services with Mayab, less frequent, US$2. To **Cancún airport**, Riviera, frequent between 0700 and 1915, 1 hr, US$6.50. To **Chetumal**, ADO, frequent departures, 4½ hrs, US$14.50; and many 2nd-class buses. To **Chichén Itzá**, 4 departures, 0610, 0730, 0800, 1150, 4 hrs, US$8.50-15.50. To **Mérida**, frequent departures, 5 hrs, US$20.50. To **Mexico City**, ADO, 1230, 1930, 2130, 24½ hrs, US$87. To **San Cristóbal de las Casas**, OCC, 1545, 1715, 2200, 16 hrs, US$46.50; an ADO GL, 1900, US$55.50; and 3 **TRF** departures, US$30. To **Tulum**, frequent departures, 1 hr, US$3.50. To **Valladolid**, frequent, 3 hrs, US$8.50 (most buses going to Mérida stop at Valladolid. 2nd-class buses to Valladolid go via Tulum). To **Xcaret**, frequent departures, 15 mins, US$0.80. To **Xel Há**, frequent departures, 1 hr, US$3.50.

Car

Car hire Avis, T984-873 1964; Budget, 3s and 5a, T984-873 2772; Executive, 5a and 12N, T984-873 2354, Happy Rent a Car, 10a and Constituyentes, T984-873 1739; Hertz

Rent-a-Car, Plaza Marina, T984-873 0703; Rodar, 5a between 2 and 4, T984-873 0088.

Ferry

Ferries to **Cozumel** depart from the main dock, just off the plaza. There are 2 competing companies, right next to each other, journeys take 30 mins with both, hourly departures on the hour from 0500 until 2200, US$20 return, more to bring a car across. Buy ticket 1 hr before journey.

Taxi

Cancún airport US$35. Beware of those who charge only US$5 as they are likely to charge an extra US$20 for luggage. Tours to **Tulum** and **Xel-Há** from kiosk by boat dock US$30; tours to Tulum, Xel-Há and **Xcaret**, 5-6 hrs, US$60; taxi to Xcaret US$6.65. Taxis congregate on the Av Juárez side of the square (Sindicato Lázaro Cárdenas del Río, T998-873 0032).

Cozumel *p159, map p160 and p161*

Airline offices

Most are based at the airport, 2 km north of the town. **Continental**, T987-872 0847. **Mexicana**, P Joaquín between Salas and Calle 3 Sur, next to Pemex, T987-872 0157.

Bicycle and moped

There is no bus service, but taxis are plentiful. The best way to get around the island is by hired moped or bicycle. Mopeds cost US$25-35 per day, credit card needed as deposit; bicycles are around US$15 per day, US$20 cash or TC deposit. El Aguila, Av Melgar, between 3 and 5 Sur, T987-872 0729; and El Dorado, Av Juárez, between 5 and 10, T987-872 2383.

Car

Car rental There are many agencies, including Avis, airport, T987-872 0219; Budget, Av 5 between 2 and 4 Norte, T987-872 0219; Hertz, Av Melgar, T987-872 3955; Ejecutivo, 1 Sur No 19, T987-872 1308.

Tulum *p163*
Bicycle
Bikes can be hired in the village from **Iguana Bike Shop**, Calle Satélite Sur and **Andrómeda**, T984-119-0836 (mob) or T984-871 2357; a good way to visit local centres (**Cristal** and **Escondido** which are recommended as much cheaper, US$2, and less commercialized than **Xcaret**).

Bus
Regular buses go up and down the coastal road travelling from Cancún to Tulum en route to Chetumal, stopping at most places in between. Some buses may be full when they reach Tulum; very few buses begin their journeys here. To **Chetumal**, frequent departures, 4 hrs, 2nd class, US$10, 1st class US$12. To **Cobá**, 8 departures daily, 45 mins, US$3. To **Escárcega**, ADO, 1645, 1715, 7 hrs, US$24.50. To **Felipe Carrillo Puerto**, frequent departures, 1½ hrs, US$5. To **Mérida**, ADO, 2400, 0140, 0500, 1240, 1430, 4 hrs, US$14; and several 2nd-class departures. To **Mexico City**, ADO, 1340, 23½ hrs, US$85. To **Palenque**, OCC, 1655, 1825, 10-11 hrs, US$34; and ADO GL, 2015, US$40.50. To **San Cristóbal**, OCC, 1655, 1825, 15 hrs, US$43.50; and an ADO GL, 2015, US$52. To **Villahermosa**, ADO, 1340, 2324, 11 hrs, US$38.

Taxi
Tulum town to Tulum ruins US$3.50. To the *cabañas* US$3.50. To **Cobá** about US$25 1 way – bargain hard. **Tucan Kin** run shuttles to Cancún airport, T01-800-702-4111 for reservations, about US$20-25 for 2 people, 1 hr 45 mins.

Cobá *p164*
Bus
Buses into the village turn round at the road end. To **Cancún**, ADO, 1330, 1530, 3 hrs, US$8. To **Playa del Carmen**, ADO, 1330, 1530, 2 hrs, US$5. To **Tulum**, ADO, 1330, 1530, 1 hr, US$2.50.

Taxi
A taxi to **Tulum** should cost you around US$25. If you miss the bus there is a taxi to be found at **El Bocadito**.

Felipe Carrillo Puerto *p167*
Bus
Bus station opposite Pemex. To **Cancun**, frequent 1st and 2nd-class departures, 4 hrs, US$13. To **Chetumal**, frequent departures, 2½ hrs, US$8. To **Playa del Carmen**, frequent departures, 2½ hrs, US$9. To **Tulum**, frequent departures, 1½ hrs, US$5.

Chetumal *p167, map p169*
Air
Airport (CTM) 2.5 km from town. Flights to **Cancún**, **Mérida**, **Belize City**, **Mexico City**, **Monterrey** and **Tijuana**.
  Airline offices Aviacsa, T983-832 7765.

Bus
Bus information T983-832 5110. The main bus terminal is 3 km out of town at the intersection of Insurgentes y Belice. Taxi into town US$1.50. There is a bus into the centre from Av Belice. **Left-luggage** lockers cost US$0.20 per hr. If buying tickets in advance, go to the **ADO** office on Av Belice esq Ghandi, 0800-1600. There are often more buses than those marked on the display in the bus station. Always ask at the information desk. Many buses going to the border, US$0.30; taxi from Chetumal to border, 20 mins, US$6 for 2. Long-distance buses are often all booked a day ahead, so avoid unbooked connections. Expect passport checks on buses leaving for Mexican destinations.
  To **Bacalar**, very frequent 1st- and 2nd-class departures, 1 hr, US$2. To **Campeche**, ADO, 1200, 6 hrs, US$20. To **Cancún**, many 1st-class departures, 6 hrs, US$17.50. To **Córdoba**, ADO, 1130, 16 hrs, US$57. To **Emiliano Zapata**, 1st class (OCC and ADO), 2150, 2345, 6½ hrs,

US$20.50. To **Escárcega**, ADO, 11 daily, 4 hrs, US$13. To **Felipe Carrillo Puerto**, many 1st- and 2nd-class departures, 2½ hrs, US$8. To **Mérida**, ADO, 0730, 1330, 1700, 2330, 5½ hrs, US$21. To **Mexico City**, ADO, 1130, 1630, 20½ hrs, US$73.50. To **Minatitlán**, ADO, 2000, 12 hrs, US$36. To **Palenque**, OCC, 0220, 2020, 2150, 7 hrs, US$23; and ADO GL, 2350, US$27. To **Playa del Carmen**, frequent 1st- and 2nd-class departures, 5 hrs, US$14.50. To **Puebla**, ADO, 2300, 17 hrs, US$66.50. To **San Cristóbal**, OCC, 0220, 2020, 2150, 12 hrs, US$33; and ADO GL 2350, US$39.50. To **Tulum**, frequent 1st- and 2nd-class departures, 4 hrs, US$12. To **Tuxtla Gutiérrez** OCC, 2030, 2150, 13 hrs, US$36.50; and ADO GL 2350, US$43.50. To **Veracruz**, 1830, 17 hrs, US$50. To **Villahermosa**, ADO, 6 daily, 8½ hrs, US$27. To **Xpujil**, 13 ADO, Sur and OCC, 2 hrs, US$6.

To Belize Premier run buses between Chetumal and **Belize City**, 1145, 1445, 1745, 5 hrs, US$10. En route, they stop at **Orange Walk**, 2½ hrs, US$5. Money-changers in the bus terminal offer marginally poorer rates than those at the border. If intending to stay in Belize City, do not take a bus that arrives at night as you are advised not to look for a hotel in the dark.

To Guatemala Línea Dorada operate daily buses to **Flores** in Guatemala at 0600, US$29. Schedules are very subject to change, and sometimes-lengthy searches are always a possibility, so always check times in advance, and be prepared to spend a night in Chetumal if necessary.

Car

There's a petrol/gas station just outside Chetumal on the road north at the beginning of the road to Escárcega, and another at Xpujil.

Garage Talleres Barrera, helpful, on Primo de Verdad; turn east off Héroes, then past the electrical plant.

Taxi

There are no city buses; taxis run on fixed-price routes, US$1.50 on average. Cars with light-green licence plates are a form of taxi.

Colectivos To **Bacalar** and **Francisco Villa** (for Kohunlich and Xpujil) depart from the junction of Av Miguel Hidalgo and Francisco Primo de Verdad.

① Directory

Cancún *p153, maps p154 and p155*
Banks There are 11 Mexican banks along Av Tulum, all in SM4 and SM5. **American Express**, for changing their own TCs at better rates than anywhere else, is on Av Tulum, just south of Av Cobá. Many *casas de cambio* in the centre, mainly around the bus terminal and along Av Tulum. *Casas de cambio* in the Hotel Zone give slightly lower rates for TCs than those in the centre. **Cultural centres** Casa Tabasco, Av Tulum 230, displays and handicrafts for sale from the state of Tabasco, a good place to go if bored of the same old souvenirs in Cancún. **Embassies and consulates** Austria, Cantera 4, SM15, Centro, T998-884 7505. Canada, Plaza Caracol, 3rd floor, Hotel Zone, T998-883 3360. France,Fonatur St, T998-267 9722. Germany, Punta Conoco 36, SM24, Centro, T998-884 1598; Italy, Alcatraces 39, SM22, Centro, T998-884 1261. Netherlands, Hotel Presidente, Hotel Zone, T998-883 0200. Spain, Oasis Corporativo, Hotel Zone, T998-848 9900. Sweden, Switzerland, Av Cobá 12, T998-884 8446. UK, Hotel Royal Sands, Hotel Zone, T998-881 0100. US, Plaza Caracol, 3rd floor, Hotel Zone, T998-883 0272. **Immigration office** On the corner of Av Náder and Av Uxmal. There is also an office in the airport, T998-886 0492, where the staff are better trained and speak English. **Internet** Numerous cafés charging US$1-1.50 per hr. Generally good servers, open until around 2300. **Language schools** El Bosque del Caribe, Av Náder 52 and Uxmal, T998-884 1065, www.cancun-

language.com.mx. **Laundry** Alborada, Nader 5, behind tourist information building on Av Tulum. **Cox-boh**, Av Tankah 26, SM24. **Medical services** American Hospital (24-hr), Viento 15, Centro, T998-884 6133. Total Assist (24-hr) Claveles 5, Centro, T998-884 1058. **American Medical Centre**, Plaza Quetzal, Hotel Zone Km 8, T998-883 0113. **Post** At the end of Av Sunyaxchén, near Mercado 28, Mon-Fri 0800-1900, Sat 0900-1300. **Telephone** Many public phones and call shops everywhere, phone cards available from general stores and pharmacies. Collect calls can be made without a card. Also many public phones designed for international calls, which take coins and credit cards. Fax at post office, Mon-Sat, and at San Francisco de Asís shopping mall, Mon-Sat until 2200.

Isla Mujeres *p156*

Banks HSBC, Av Reuda Medina, opposite the ferry dock. Good rates, varying daily, are offered by several *casas de cambio* on Av Hidalgo. The one opposite **Rolandis** is open daily 0900-2100. **Internet** Several internet cafés operate on the island US$1.50 per hr, but speeds can be a little slow. Many cafés and restaurants have free Wi-Fi. **Laundry** Tim Pho, Juárez y Abasolo. **Medical services** Doctors: Dr Antonio Salas, Hidalgo, next to **Farmacia**, T998-877 0477. 24 hrs, house calls, English spoken, air ambulance. **Post** At the end of Guerrero towards the beach. **Telephone** Phone cards can be bought at some of the souvenir shops along Hidalgo.

Puerto Morelos *p157*

Internet There is an internet café on the corner of the plaza opposite **Posada Amor**, US$2.50 per hr, Mon-Sat 1000-1400, 1600-2100.

Playa del Carmen *p158, map p158*

Banks Bancomer, Av Juárez between Calle 25 and 30. Banamex, Av Juárez between Calle 20 and 25. A few doors down is Santander. Banorte, Av 5 between Av Juárez and the beach. **Inverlat**, Av 5 between Av Juárez and Calle 2. HSBC, Av Juárez between Calle 10 and 15, also at Av 30 between Calle 4 and 6. There are several *casas de cambio* along Av 5, which change TCs with no commission. Count your money carefully as short changing is not uncommon and rates can be hit and miss. **Immigration office** Centro Comercial, Plaza Antigua, Av 10 Sur, T984-873 1884. **Internet** All the cybercafés in town charge between US$1.50-2 per hr. **Language schools** Playalingua,Calle 20 between Av 5 and 10, T984-873 3876, www.playa lingua.com, weekend excursions, a/c, library, family stays, US$85 enrolment fee, US$220 per wk (20 hrs). **Solexico Language and Cultural Center**, Av 35 between 6 and 6 bis, T984-873 0755, www.solexico.com. Variable programme with workshops, also have schools in Oaxaca and Puerto Vallarta. **Laundry** Av Juárez, 2 blocks from bus station; another on Av 5. **Maya Laundry**, Av 5 between Calle 2 and Calle 4, Mon-Sat 0800-2100. Laundry in by 1000, ready in the afternoon, many others around town. **Medical services** Dentist: Perla de Rocha Torres, Av 20 Norte between 4 and 6, T984-873 0021, speaks English. Recommended. International Medical Services: Dr Victor Macías Orosco, Av 35 between Calle 2 and 4, T984-873 0493. 24-hr emergency service, land and air ambulance, ultrasound, most major insurance accepted. **Tourist Divers Medical Centre**, Dr Mario Abarca, Av 10 between Av Juárez and Calle 2, T984-873 0512. Air and land ambulance service, hyperbaric and diving medicine, affiliated with South Miami Hospital, all insurance accepted. **Police** Av Juárez, T984-873 0291. **Post** Calle 2 and Av 20, Mon-Fri 0800-1700, Sat 0900-1300.

Cozumel *p159, map p160 and p161*

Banks 4 banks on the main square (all with ATMs), all exchange money in morning only, but not at same hours: **HSBC**, on Juárez, **Bancomer, Banamex, Banorte**. *Casas de cambio* on Av 5 Norte and around square.

Internet Several internet cafés charging around US$1.50 per hr. **Laundry** Express, Salas between Av 5 and Av 10, T987-872 3655. Coin-op, service washes, US$9 medium load, collection service and dry cleaning.

Medical services Dentist: Dr Hernández, T987-872 0656. **Hospitals and clinics: Red Cross**, A R Salas between Calle 20 and 25 Sur, T987-872 1058. **Centro Médico de Cozumel**, Calle 1 Sur No 101, esq Av 50, T987-872 3545. English spoken, international air ambulance, 24-hr emergency service. **Pharmacy:** Salas between Av 12 and Av 20, 0700-2400.

Post Av Rafael Melgar y Calle 7 Sur, Mon-Fri 0900-1800, Sat 0900-1200. **Telephone** Ladatel phones (if working) on main square at corner of Av Juárez and Av 5, or on Salas, just up from Av 5 Sur, opposite **Roberto's Black Coral Studio**. For calls to the US, go to **The Stadium**. Telmex phone offices on the main square next to Restaurant Plaza Leza, 0800-2300, and on Salas between Av 10 and 15. There are also expensive **Computel** offices in town, eg at the cruise ship dock. **Telephone centre** for long distance on corner of Rafael Melgar and Calle 3 Sur. Also public telephone *caseta* at Av 5 esq Calle 2, 0800-1300, 1600-2100.

Tulum *p163*

Banks HSBC, Av Tulum open 0900-1900, has an ATM, but doesn't change TCs. **Scotiabank** further along the same road is open Mon-Fri, 0900-1600, changes TCs and cash. Several *casas de cambio* in Av Tulum closer to the **ADO** terminal. **Telephone and internet** Long-distance phones on Av

Tulum near and opposite the **ADO** terminal in town. Internet cafés on the same road.

Chetumal *p167, map p169*

Banks The banks all close at 1430. There are several ATMs. For exchange, **Banamex**, Obregón y Juárez, changes TCs. **Banco Mexicano**, Juárez and Cárdenas, TCs or US$ cash, quick and courteous service. Several on, or near, Av Héroes with ATMs. Banks do not change quetzales into pesos.

Embassies and consulates Guatemala, Av Héroes de Chapultepec 354, T983-832 6565. Open for visas, Mon-Fri 0900-1700. It is best to organize your visa, if required, in your home country before travel. **Belize**, Hon Consul, Lic Francisco Lechón Rosas, Rotondo Carranza 562 (behind Super San Francisco), T983-878 7728; visas can take up to 3 weeks to get, and many are only issued in Mexico City. **Internet** Eclipse, 5 de Mayo 83 between PE Calles and Zaragoza. 0930-1500, 1800-2100, not very friendly but cheap at US$3 per hr. **Los Cebollones**, Calzada Veracruz 452, T983-832 9145, also restaurant and cocktail bar. **Laundry** Lavandería Automática 'Lava facil', corner of Héroes and Confederación Nacional Campesina.

Medical services Malaria prophylaxis available from **Centro de Salud**, opposite hospital (request tablets for paludismo).

Post 16 de Septiembre y PE Calles. Mon-Fri 0800-1730, Sat 0900-1300. Packets to be sent abroad must be taken unwrapped to the bus terminal to have them checked by customs before taking them to the post office. Better to wait until another town. Parcel service not available Sat. **Western Union** office attached to post office, same hours.

Contents

Footprint features

Guatemala

At a glance

🚌 **Getting around** Bus and the odd flight for long distances, minibus shuttles for shorter distances. Boats to Belize on the Caribbean coast.

🕐 **Time required** 3-4 weeks; any less and you'll have to rush around.

🌤 **Weather** Mid-20°Cs, but chilly at higher altitudes. Wet season is May-Oct.

✖ **When not to go** Lowlands in the wet season, if you don't like rain.

Laguna del Tigre & Biotopo
El Mirador
Río Azul
Uaxactún
BELIZE

Carmelita
El Perú
Paso Caballos
El Zotz
Tikal
6

El Naranjo
La Joyanca
Reserva de la Biosfera Maya
El Remate
Nakum
Xunantunich
Melchor de Mencos

Piedras Negras
Yaxhá & Topoxte

MEXICO
Bethel
Frontera Echeverría
Flores
Santa Elena
Ixcún

La Libertad
Sayaxché
Dolores
Naj Tunich Cave

Pipiles
El Ceibal
Poptún
Punta Gorda

Dos Pilas
Aguateca
Modesto Méndez
Punta de Manabique

Gracias a Dios
San Mateo Ixtatán
Playa Grande
Chisec
Raxruhá
Fray Bartolomé de Las Casas
Río Dulce
Livingston
5
Puerto Barrios

Todos Santos Cuchumatán
3
Barillas
Laguna Lachuá
Sebol
Cahabón
El Estor
Morales

La Mesilla
Chajul
Lanquín
Senahú
Lago de Izabal
Quiriguá

Chiantla
Nebaj
Cotzal
Cobán
Semuc Champey
Santa Cruz Verapaz
Los Amates

Huehuetenango
Sacapulas
Tactic
Río Hondo
HONDURAS

Momostenango
Santa Cruz del Quiché
Biotopo del Quetzal
Salamá
Estanzuela

San Francisco El Alto
Utatlán
Rabinal
Zacapa
El Florido
Chiquimula

El Carmen
4
Chichicastenango
Sanrate
El Rancho
Esquipulas

Quetzaltenango
Panajachel
El Progreso
Agua Caliente

Volcán Sta María
Solalá
2
Antigua
GUATEMALA CITY
Ipala

Tecún Umán
Lake Atitlán
1
Volcán Fuego
Anguiatú

Retalhuleu
Santiago Atitlán
Volcán Acatenango
Volcán Agua
Volcán Pacaya
Jutiapa

Champerico
Santa Lucía Cotzumalguapa
Escuintla
Valle Nuevo
San Cristóbal Frontera

El Tulate
Taxisco
EL SALVADOR

El Semillero
Sipacate
Puerto San José
Monterrico
Pedro de Alvarado

Pacific Ocean

★ **Don't miss ...**
1 Antigua, page 222.
2 Lake Atitlán, page 239.
3 Todos Santos Cuchumatán, page 271.
4 Around Quetzaltenango, page 277.
5 Lívingston and Río Dulce, pages 299 and 300.
6 Tikal, page 325.

N

50 km
50 miles

Guatemala has a monopoly on colour – from the red lava tongues of the volcanoes in the Western Highlands to the creamy shades of the caves in the southern Petén, and from the white sand of the Caribbean coast near Lívingston to the black sand and fabulous orange sunsets over the Pacific. And that's just nature's palette. Completing this work of art are traditional Maya fiestas, arcane religious rituals where idol worship and Roman Catholicism merge, and jungle temples where ancient ruins tell of long-lost civilizations. Deep in Guatemala's northern jungle, the majestic cities of the Maya are buried. Temples, stelae and plazas have been discovered here, along with evidence of human sacrifice and astronomical genius, to reveal their dynastic history and traditions.

Antigua is the colonial centre of the New World. Gracefully ruined after an 18th-century earthquake, its cobbled streets are lined with columned courtyards, toppled church arches, preserved pastel-coloured houses, flowers and fountains galore.

Formed by an explosion that blew the lid off the top of a volcanic mountain, Lake Atitlán and its three volcanoes are truly breathtaking. Further west, the bustling city of Quetzaltenango makes an excellent base from which to explore the volcanoes, markets and villages of the Western Highlands, such as the mountain community of Todos Santos, where the colourful clothes of the Maya and the All Saints' Day horse race are major attractions. In the Verapaces, rivers run through caves stuffed with stalagmites and stalactites. On the humid lower slopes of the Pacific, Olmec-influenced ruins are buried among coffee bushes and turtles nest on the shore, while on the Caribbean coast, the Garífuna rock to the sound of the punta and dolphins frolic in the sea.

Essentials

Guatemala City is a modern, polluted capital. It is the main entry point for travellers by air and long-distance bus. While there are some sites of interest, a couple of excellent museums in the city centre and some great nightlife, few stay long, preferring to head west to the clean air and relaxed atmosphere of **Antigua**. Once the capital, Antigua was built by the Spanish conquistadors. Later destroyed by several huge earthquakes, the grand ruins of colonial architecture remain, the dramatic location at the foot of three volcanoes and its prominence as a centre for Spanish studies, make Antigua a justifiably popular destination.

Heading northeast from Guatemala City, lie the highlands of the Verapaz region. **Cobán** is the main focus, with access to nearby traditional villages, the caves at Lanquín, the natural bridge of Semuc Champey and, at Purulhá, the Mario Dary Rivera Reserve which protects the habitat of the quetzal, Guatemala's national bird. Skirting the northern shores of Lago de Izabal is the Bocas del Polochic Wildlife Reserve, which is full of monkeys, avifauna and other wildlife.

South of the lake, the highway runs close to **Quiriguá**, which once competed with Tikal and nearby Copán, in Honduras, for dominance of the Maya heartlands. On Guatemala's short Caribbean shore is **Lívingston**, popular with young travellers and, near **El Golfete Biotopo Chocón-Machacas**, a manatee and wildlife reserve and the fabulous Río Dulce gorge. From Lívingston boats go inland to Río Dulce, north to Punta Gorda in Belize, or head for Puerto Barrios for Placencia in Belize, or south overland to Honduras.

The forested northern lowlands of **El Petén** hide most of Guatemala's archaeological sites. The majestic **Tikal** is the most developed for tourism, but many others can be reached including Uaxactún, Yaxhá and El Ceibal. **Flores**, sitting on an island in Lago Petén Itzá, is the centre for exploring El Petén with routes from here to Belize and Mexico.

West of Guatemala City, beyond La Antigua, the mountainous highlands overflow with Maya communities. Market days filled with colour, fiestas crammed with celebrations, and each community characterized by unique clothes and crafts. Several villages are dotted around the shores of **Lago de Atitlán**, a spectacular and sacred lake protected on all sides by silent volcanic peaks. From **Panajachel**, ferries and trails link the small communities. **San Pedro La Laguna** is the chief chill-out and hang-loose spot on the lake's shores, with **San Marcos** the favourite for true relaxation; but there are other less touristy and more interesting options to explore.

An hour north of Lake Atitlán is the famous market of **Chichicastenango**, a town where Maya and visitors converge in a twice-weekly frenzy of buying general goods and produce, alongside textiles and tapestry. The market is alive with colour and is a must for any visitor.

Towards the Mexican border, the towns of **Quetzaltenango**, **Retalhuleu** and **Huehuetenango** provide good opportunities for discovering the charms of western Guatemala, including volcanoes and Maya towns. To the north, in the heart of the Cuchumatanes mountains, **Todos Santos Cuchumatán** stands firm as a town that has restricted western influences and is increasingly popular as a place to learn about the Mam way of life, including language and weaving classes. Along the Pacific coastline, the turtle-nesting sites of **Monterrico** are attracting visitors to this little-explored district of Guatemala.

Suggested itinerary

The most natural trip in Guatemala, if you're travelling through the region, is to enter the country from the north from Mexico or Belize, visit Tikal and then head south. After some time in La Antigua and around Lake Atitlán, explore the towns of the Guatemalan highlands. Continuing south, there are many options for crossing the border. Head for El Florido, for best access to Copán, or out to the Caribbean and the crossing at Entre Ríos–Corinto near Puerto Barrios for the Bay Islands. Three to four weeks is a good stay in Guatemala; any less and you'll have to rush around.

When to go

Climate is dependent upon altitude and varies greatly. Most of the population lives at between 900 m and 2500 m, where the climate is healthy – with warm days and cool nights, so you'll need warm clothes at night. The majority of visitors spend most of their time in the highlands, where the dry season lasts from November to April. The central region around Cobán has an occasional drizzle-like rain called *chipi chipi* in February and March. Some places enjoy a respite from the rains (the *canícula*) in July and August. On the Pacific and Caribbean coasts you can expect rain all year round, heaviest on the Pacific in June and September with a dry spell in between, but with no dry season on the Caribbean. In the lowlands of El Petén, the wet season is roughly May to October, when the mosquitoes are most active. December to February are cooler months, while March and April are hot and dry. All of this is increasingly settled, according to Guatemalans, who say that the clear divisions of the seasons are blurring. In terms of festivals, the key events are **Semana Santa** at Easter in Antigua, see page 228, and **All Saints' Day** in Todos Santos, see page 272.

What to do

Archaeology

Archaeology is the big attraction. Consequently there are numerous organizations offering tours. Some companies operate out of Flores and Santa Elena in the Petén using local villagers to help with expeditions.
Maya Expeditions, 15 Calle "A", 14-07, Zona 10, Guatemala City, T2363-4955, www.mayaexpeditions.com, offers trips to **Piedras Negras** (with archaeologists who worked on the 1990s excavation of the site), **Río Azul**, the **Petexbatún** area, **El Mirador**, led by Dr Richard Hansen (the chief archaeologist of the site) and a trip to the more recently discovered **Cancuén** site, led by its chief archaeologist, Dr Arthur Demarest.
Explorations, in the USA, T1-239-992-9660, www.explorationsinc.com, has tours led by archaeologist and Maya specialist Travis Doering.

Mountain biking

Mountain biking is an increasingly popular activity in Guatemala. There are numerous tracks and paths that weave their way across the country, passing hamlets as you go.
Old Town Outfitters, 5 Av Sur 12 "C", Antigua, T7832-4171, www.adventure guatemala.com, is a recommended operator, offering mountain-bike tours starting at US$25 for a half day. They also deals in the gear.

Mountain and volcano climbing

Guatemala represents a wealth of opportunity for climbers, with more than 30 volcanoes on offer. There are also the heights of the Cuchumatanes Mountains in the highlands, which claims the highest non-volcanic peak in the country at 3837 m, and those of the relatively unexplored Sierra de Las Minas in eastern Guatemala close to the Río Motagua Valley.

Fundación Defensores de la Naturaleza, 2a Av 14-08, Zona 14, Guatemala City, T2310-2929, are the people to contact for a *permiso* to climb in the Sierra de las Minas Biosphere Reserve.

Turismo Ek Chuah, 3 Calle 6-24, Zona 2, www.ekchuah.com, offer volcano-specific tours, see page 217. For other operators offering volcano climbing around Guatemala City and Antigua, see page 235.

Nature tourism

The majority of tour operators listed in this guide will offer nature-oriented tours. There are several national parks, *biotopos* and protected areas in Guatemala, each with their highlights. **CECON** (Centro de Estudios Conservacionistas) and **INGUAT** have set up conservation areas for the protection of Guatemalan wildlife (the quetzal, manatee, jaguar, etc) and their habitats. Several other national parks (some including Maya archaeological sites) and forest reserves have been set up or are planned.

CONAP (Consejo Nacional de Areas Protegidas) Av, 6-06, Zona 1, Guatemala City, T2238-0000, http://conap.online.fr, is the national parks and protected areas authority.

Proyecto Ecológico Quetzal, 2 Calle, 14-36, Zona 1, Cobán, T7952-1047, www.eco quetzal.org, a non-profit-making project, is another useful organization.

Spiritual interest

There is a spiritual centre on the shores of Lake Atitlán that offers courses in accordance with the cycle of the moon: **Las Pirámides del Ka**, in San Marcos La Laguna, offers yoga and meditation as well as spiritual instruction year round (see also page 257). At the **Takilibén Maya Misión** in Momostenango, day keeper Rigoberto Itzep (leave a message for him on T7736-5537), 3 Av "A", 6-85, Zona 3, offers courses in Maya culture.

Textiles and weaving

It is possible to get weaving lessons in many places across the highlands. Weaving lessons can also be organized through Spanish schools.

Watersports
Diving

La Iguana Perdida, Santa Cruz La Laguna, T5706-4117, www.laiguanaperdida.com, for diving in Lake Atitlán with ATI Divers.

Kayaking

Old Town Outfitters, Antigua, www.adventure guatemala.com, run kayaking tours.

Waterskiing

La Iguana Perdida, Santa Cruz La Laguna, see above for contact info, also organize waterskiing.

Whitewater rafting

Rafting is possible on a number of rivers in Guatemala across a range of grades. However, none of the trips are turn-up-and-go – they have to be arranged in advance. In general, the larger the group, the cheaper the cost.

Maya Expeditions, see address under Archaeology, above, is the country's best outfitter. It rafts the **Río Cahabón** in Alta Verapaz (Grade III-V), the **Río Naranjo** close to Coatepeque (Grade III), the **Río Motagua** close to Guatemala City (Grade III-IV), the **Río Esclavos**, near Barbarena (Grade III-IV), the **Río Coyolate** close to Santa Lucía Cotzumalguapa (Grade II-III) and the **Río Chiquibul** in the Petén (Grade II-III). It also runs a rafting and caving tour in the Petén and a combined archaeology and rafting tour where you would raft through a canyon on the **Río Usumacinta** (Grade II). For a little extra excitement, Maya Expeditions also arrange bungee jumping in Guatemala City.

Getting there

Air

From the USA **American** (Atlanta; Chicago; Dallas Fort Worth; Miami), **Continental** (Houston), **Delta** (Atlanta), **United** (Los Angeles), **Grupo Taca** (Miami).

From Canada Connections are made through San Salvador, Los Angeles or Miami.

From Europe **Iberia** flies directly from Madrid and via Miami, with connecting flights from other European cities. Long-haul operators from Europe will share between airlines, taking passengers across the Atlantic normally to Miami, and using **Taca**, for example, to link to Guatemala City.

From Central America Connections available throughout Central America, in most cases travelling through the capital city. There are exceptions with connections to Belize from Flores. See page 25 for regional airpasses. **Taca** from the Caribbean and **Cubana** from Havana.

From South America **Lacsa** from Bogotá via San José, **Copa** via Panama.

Road

There are good road crossings with all of Guatemala's neighbouring countries. There are several crossing points to southern **Mexico** from western Guatemala with additional routes through the jungle from Palenque. From **Belize** it is possible to cross from Benque Viejo del Carmen. Links with **Honduras** are possible on the Caribbean near Corinto, and for the ruins at Copán the best crossing is El Florido. There are four road routes into **El Salvador**.

An unofficial tourist tax (10-30 quetzales) is sometimes charged on leaving or entering overland at some borders (borders may not be open 24 hours). Bribery is now less common at border crossings. Ask for a receipt and, if you have time and the language ability, do not give in to corrupt officials. Report any problems to INGUAT.

Sea

Connections by sea with daily boats between **Punta Gorda** in Guatemala and **Lívingston**.

Getting around

Air

Grupo Taca, www.taca.com, links Guatemala City with Flores/Santa Elena. **TAG**, www.tag.com.gt, also flies this route daily, US$135 one way. See page 325 for (overland) services to Tikal. Private charters are on the increase.

Road

Bus There is an extensive network of bus routes throughout the country. The chicken buses (former US school buses) are mostly in a poor state of repair and overloaded. Faster and more reliable Pullman services operate on some routes. Correct fares should be posted. We receive regular complaints that bus drivers charge tourists more than locals, a practice that is becoming more widespread. One way to avoid being overcharged is to

Border essentials

Guatemala–Mexico
For crossings between Guatemala and Mexico (Ciudad Cuauhtémoc–La Mesilla, Talismán–El Carmen, Ciudad Hidalgo–Tecún Umán, La Palma–El Naranjo, Frontera Echeverría (Corozal)–Bethel/La Técnica, Benemérito–Pipiles), see page 58.

Guatemala–Belize
For crossing between Guatemala and Belize (Benque-Viejo–Menchor de Mencos, Punta Gorda–Puerto Barrios/Lívingston), see page 348.

Guatemala–Honduras
El Florido
Popular and busy crossing, but straightforward for pedestrians. If entering Honduras just to visit Copán Ruinas, you can get a temporary 72-hour exit pass, but you must return on time. The consulate at Hotel Payaquí, Esquipulas, can help arrange a visa if you need one.
Currency exchange Numerous money-changers; better rates in Copán.
Guatemalan immigration Open 0700-1900.
Honduran immigration Open 0700-1900. Get a receipt for 'extra' charges.
Onwards to Honduras Minibuses run all day until 1700 to Copán Ruinas.
Onwards to Guatemala There are numerous minibus services to Guatemala City/Antigua.

Entre Ríos–Corinto
Caribbean coast crossing. A road now connects Puerto Barrios (Guatemala) and Puerto Cortés (Honduras) with a bridge over the Motagua river.
Guatemalan immigration Get your exit stamp in Puerto Barrios or Lívingston if you are leaving by boat to Honduras. If you arrive by boat, go straight to either of these offices.
Honduran immigration At Corinto if crossing from Puerto Barrios in Guatemala. Also facilities at Puerto Cortés, to be used if arriving by boat.
Onwards to Honduras Connections to the northern coast. Buses leave Corinto for Omoa and Puerto Cortés every hour or so.
Onwards to Guatemala Highway access to Guatemala City and Santa Elena/Flores.

Agua Caliente
A busy crossing, but quicker, cheaper and more efficient than the one at El Florido. There are three banks, a tourist office, *comedor* and *hospedaje* on the Honduran side. The consulate at Hotel Payaquí, Esquipulas, can help arrange a visa.
Currency exchange Money-changers outside Honduran immigration. If leaving Honduras, keep some lempiras for the ride from Agua Caliente to Esquipulas.
Guatemalan immigration Open 0600-1900.
Honduran immigration Open 0700-1800.
Onwards to Honduras Several buses daily from Agua Caliente to San Pedro Sula, six or seven hours. Also frequent services to Nueva Ocotepeque.
Onwards to Guatemala Minibuses go to Esquipulas with connections to Guatemala City, Chiquimula and the highway to Flores.

Guatemala–El Salvador
Frontera–San Cristóbal
The main Pan-American Highway crossing, used by international buses and heavy traffic.
Currency exchange Money-changers.
Guatemalan immigration Open 0600-2200, but usually possible to cross outside these hours with extra charges.
Salvadorean immigration Open 0600-2200.
Onwards to El Salvador Regular buses to Santa Ana, bus 201, with connections to San Salvador, 1½ hours.
Onwards to Guatemala Connections to Guatemala City, two or three hours.

Valle Nuevo–Las Chinamas
The fastest road link from San Salvador to Guatemala City. Busy.
Currency exchange Change with the women in front of the ex-ITSU office. Good quetzal-dollar rate.
Guatemalan immigration Open 0800-1800.
Salvadorean immigration Open 0800-1800. A straightforward crossing; quick service if your papers are ready.
Onwards to El Salvador Frequent buses to Ahuachapán, No 265, 25 minutes, with connecting services to San Salvador, No 202. Alternatively, try to negotiate a seat with an international Pullman bus, most pass between 0800 and 1400.
Onwards to Guatemala Connections to Guatemala City, two hours.

Ciudad Pedro Alvarado–La Hachadura
This border is at the bridge over the Río Paz, with a filling station and a few shops nearby. Increasingly popular thanks to improved roads. Private vehicles require a lot of paperwork and can take two hours to process.
Currency exchange Money-changers.
Salvadorean immigration Facilities on either side of the bridge; a relaxed crossing.
Onwards to El Salvador Access to El Salvador's Pacific coast. Services to San Salvador's Terminal Occidente, No 498, three hours. Also services to Ahuachapán, No 503, one hour. Last bus to Sonsonate at 1800.
Onwards to Guatemala Access to the Pacific coast and Guatemala City.

Anguiatú
Normally a quiet border crossing, except when there are special events at Esquipulas in Guatemala.
Guatemalan immigration Open 0600-1900.
Salvadorean immigration Open 0600-1900. The usual requirements, a relaxed process.
Onwards to El Salvador Buses to Santa Ana, No 235A, 1¾ hours. Also services to Metapán, 40 minutes, from where a rough but very scenic road runs to El Poy.
Onwards to Guatemala Best highway access if you're heading north to Tikal. Head for the Padre Miguel junction 19 km from the border; there you can make connections to Chiquimula and Esquipulas.

watch for what the locals pay or ask a local, then tender the exact fare on the bus. Many long-distance buses leave very early in the morning. Make sure you can get out of your hotel/*pensión*. For international bus journeys make sure you have small denomination local currency or US dollar bills for border taxes. At Easter there are few buses on Good Friday or the Saturday and buses are packed with long queues for tickets for the few days before Good Friday. Many names on bus destination boards are abbreviated: (Guate – Guatemala City; Chichi – Chichicastenango; Xela/Xelajú – Quetzaltenango, and so on). On many tourist routes there are **minibus shuttles**; quick, comfortable, and convenient, they charge a little more than the regular buses, but can be useful. They can be booked through hotels and travel agencies and will pick you up from your hotel.

Car and motorcycle Think carefully before driving a vehicle in Guatemala as it can be hazardous. Of the 14,000 km of roads, the 30% that are paved have improved greatly in recent years and are now of a high standard, making road travel faster and safer. Even cycle tracks (*ciclovías*) are beginning to appear on new roads. However, a new driving hazard in the highlands is the deep gully (for rainwater or falling stones) alongside the road. High clearance is essential on many roads in remoter areas and a 4WD vehicle is useful.

Bringing a vehicle into Guatemala requires the following procedure: presentation of a valid International Driving Licence; a check by **Cuarantena Agropecuaria** (Ministry of Agriculture quarantine) to check you are not importing fruit or veg; at **Aduana** (Customs) you must pay US$4.50 for all forms and a tourist vehicle permit for your vehicle. A motorcycle entry permit costs the same as one for a car. The description of your vehicle on the registration document must match your vehicle's appearance exactly. You must own the car/motorcycle and your name must be on the title papers. When entering the country, ask the officials to add any important accessories you have to the paper. Car insurance can be bought at the borders.

On leaving the country by car or motorcycle, two stamps on a strip of paper are required: surrender of the vehicle permit at customs and the **Cuarantena Agropecuaria** (quarantine) inspection, which is not always carried out. It is better not to import and sell foreign cars in Guatemala, as import taxes are very high.

Gasoline 'Normal' costs US$3.80, 'premium' US$3.90, and diesel is US$3.50 for the US gallon, though prices are rising constantly (prices correct as of January 2011). Unleaded (*sin plomo*) is available in major cities, at Melchor de Mencos and along the Pan-American Highway, but not in the countryside, although it is gradually being introduced across the country.

Security Spare no ingenuity in making your car or motorbike secure. Try never to leave the car unattended except in a locked garage or guarded parking space. Lock the clutch or accelerator to the steering wheel with a heavy, obvious chain or lock. Street children will generally protect your car fiercely in exchange for a tip. Don't wash your car: smart cars attract thieves. Be sure to note down key numbers and carry spares of the most important ones. Try not to leave your fully laden motorbike on its own. An Abus D or chain will keep a bike secure. A cheap alarm gives you peace of mind if you leave the bike outside a hotel at night. Most hotels will allow you to bring the bike inside. Look for hotels that have a courtyard or more secure parking and never leave luggage on the bike overnight or whilst unattended. Also take a cover for the bike. Just about all parts and accessories are available at decent prices in Guatemala City at FPK, 5 Calle 6-75, Zona 9.

Border crossings From Mexico to Western Guatemala: **Ciudad Tecún Umán/Ciudad Hidalgo** is the main truckers' crossing. It is very busy and should be avoided at all costs by car. **Talismán**, the next border crossing north, is more geared to private cars. **La Mesilla** is the simplest for private cars and you can do your own paperwork with ease. All necessary documents can be obtained here.

Car hire Average rates are US$35-100 per day. Credit cards or cash are accepted for rental. Local cars are usually cheaper than those at international companies; if you book ahead from abroad with the latter, take care that they do not offer you a different vehicle claiming your original request is not available. Cars may not always be taken into neighbouring countries (none are allowed into Mexico or Belize); rental companies that do allow their vehicles to cross borders charge for permits and paperwork. If you wish to drive to Copán, you must check this is permissible and you need a letter authorizing you to take the vehicle in to Honduras. **Tabarini** and **Hertz** allow their cars to cross the border.

Cycling The scenery is gorgeous, the people friendly and colourful, but the hills are steep and sometimes long. The Pan-American Highway is OK from Guatemala City west; it has a shoulder and traffic is not very heavy. Buses are frequent and it is easy to load a bicycle on the roof; many buses do so, charging about two-thirds of the passenger fare. On the road, buses are a hazard for cyclists; Guatemala City is particularly dangerous. Look out for the cycle tracks (*ciclovías*) on a few main roads.

Hitchhiking Hitching is comparatively easy, but risky, especially for single women. Also beware of theft of luggage, especially in trucks. The best place to try for a lift is at a bridge or on a road out of town; be there no later than 0600, but 0500 is better as that is when truck drivers start their journey. Trucks usually charge US$1-1.50 upwards for a lift/day. Travellers have suggested it can be cheaper by bus. In remote areas, lifts in the back of a pickup are usually available; very crowded, but convenient when bus services are few and far between, or stop early in the day.

Sea

You can get around Lake Atitlán and from Puerto Barrios to Lívingston by public boat services. Private boat services are possible from Puerto Barrios to Belize and Honduras and around El Estor and Río Dulce and around Lake Petén Itzá.

Sleeping

The tourist institute INGUAT publishes a list of maximum prices for single, double and triple occupancy of hundreds of hotels throughout the country in all price ranges, though the list is thin at the budget end. They will deal with complaints about overcharging if you can produce bills or other proof. Room rates should be posted in all registered hotels. Ask if taxes (*impuestos*) are included when you are given the room rate. INGUAT tax is 10% and service charge is usually an additional 12%. Busiest seasons are Easter, December and July to August. Most budget hotels do not supply toilet paper, soap or towels. There are no official campsites in Guatemala.

Eating and drinking

Traditional Central American/Mexican food such as tortillas, tamales, tostadas, etc, are found everywhere. Tacos are less spicy than in Mexico. *Chiles rellenos* (chillies stuffed with meat and vegetables) are a speciality in Guatemala and may be *picante* (spicy) or *no picante*. *Churrasco*, charcoal-grilled steak, is often accompanied by *chirmol*, a sauce of tomato, onion and mint. Guacamole is also excellent. Local dishes include *pepián* (thick meat stew with vegetables) in Antigua, *patín* (small fish from Lake Atitlán wrapped in leaves and served in a tomato-based sauce) from Lake Atitlán, *cecina* (beef marinated in lemon and bitter orange) from the same region. *Fiambre* is widely prepared for families and friends who gather on All Souls' Day (1 November). It consists of all kinds of meat, fish, chicken, vegetables, eggs or cheese served as a salad with rice, beans and other side dishes. Desserts include *mole* (plantain and chocolate), *torrejas* (sweet bread soaked in egg and *panela* or honey) and *buñuelos* (similar to profiteroles) served with hot cinnamon syrup. For breakfast try *mosh* (oats cooked with milk and cinnamon), fried plantain with cream, black beans in various forms. *Pan dulce* (sweet bread), in fact bread in general, and local cheese are recommended. Try *borracho* (cake soaked in rum).

Drink

Local beers are good (Monte Carlo, Cabra, Gallo and Moza, a dark beer); bottled, carbonated soft drinks (*gaseosas*) are safest. Milk should be pasteurized. Freshly made *refrescos* and ice creams are delicious made of many varieties of local fruits; *licuados* are fruit juices with milk or water, but hygiene varies, so take care. Water should be filtered or bottled. By law alcohol cannot be consumed after 2000 on Sundays.

Festivals and events

Although specific dates are given for fiestas, there's often a week of jollification beforehand.
1 Jan New Year.
Mar/Apr Holy Week (4 days). Easter celebrations are exceptional in Antigua and Santiago Atitlán. Bus fares may be doubled.
1 May Labour Day.
15 Aug Public holiday Guatemala City only.
15 Sep Independence Day.
12 Oct Discovery of America. Not a business holiday.

20 Oct Revolution Day.
1 Nov All Souls' Day. Celebrated with abandonment and drunkeness in Todos Santos. In Santiago Sacatepéquez, the *Día de los Muertos* is characterized by colourful kite-flying (*barriletes*).
24 Dec Christmas Eve. From noon, although not a business holiday.
25 Dec Christmas Day.
31 Dec Public holiday from noon.

Shopping

Visiting a **market** in Guatemala can be one of the most enjoyable and memorable experiences of any trip. Bartering in the markets is the norm and is almost expected and unbelievable discounts can be obtained. You won't do better anywhere else in Central America, but getting the discount is less important than paying a fair price. Woven goods are normally cheapest bought in the town of origin. Try to avoid middlemen and buy direct from the weaver. Guatemalan coffee is highly recommended, although the best is exported; coffee sold locally is not vacuum-packed.

Essentials A-Z

Customs and duty free

You are allowed to take in, free of duty, personal effects and articles for your own use, 2 bottles of spirits and 80 cigarettes or 100 g of tobacco. Temporary visitors can take in any amount in quetzales or foreign currencies. The local equivalent of US$100 per person may be reconverted into US dollars on departure at the airport, provided a ticket for immediate departure is shown.

Drugs

If caught with drugs you'll wind up in prison where the minimum penalty is 5 years. A number of police have been installed in the traditional laid-back travellers' drug haven of San Pedro on Lake Atitlán.

Electricity

Generally 110 volts AC, 60 cycles, US-style plug. Electricity is usually reliable in the towns but can be a problem in more remote areas like Petén.

Embassies and consulates

Belgium, Av Winston Churchill 185, 1180, Brussels, T(+322) 345-9058 (also covers Luxembourg).
Belize, 8 A St, Belize City, T223-3150.
Canada, 130 Albert St, Suite 1010, Ottawa, Ontario, K1P 5G4, T613 233-7188.
Costa Rica, del Gimnasio Fitsimons 100 m sur, 50 m oeste Sabana Sur, San José, T2291-6208.
El Salvador, 15 Av Norte No 135, between C Arce and 1 C Pte, San Salvador, T2271-2225.
France, 66 Rue Grignan, 13001, Marseille, T8866-3012 (also covers Portugal and Switzerland).
Germany, Joachim-Karnatz-Allee 45-47 D-10557, Berlin, T30 206-4363.
Honduras, Calle Arturo López Rodezno No 2421, Col Las Minitas, Tegucigalpa, T2232-1580.
Israel, Medinat Hayeydim 103, Ackerstein building, entry B, floor 2, Herzliya Pituah, T957-7335.

Italy, Vía dei Colli della Farnesina 128, 1-00194, Rome, T3638-1143.
Japan, 38 Kowa Bldg, 9th floor, room 905, Nishi-Azabu, Tokyo 106-0031, T3 3400-1830.
Mexico, Av Explanada No 1025, Col Lomas de Chapultepec, 11000 México DF, T5540-7520.
Nicaragua, Km 11.5 on road to Masaya, Managua, T2799-609.
Panama, Edificio Altamira, 9th floor, office 925, Vía Argentina, El Cangrejo, Corregimiento de Bella Vista, Panama City, T2369-3475.
Spain, Calle Rafael Salgado No 3, 10a derecha, 28036, Madrid, T1-344-1417 (also covers Morocco).
UK, 13 Fawcett St, London, SW10 9HN, T020-7351-3042, embaguategtm@ btconnect.com.
USA, 2220 R St NW, Washington DC, 20008, T202 745-4952, www.guatemala-embassy.org.

Health

Guatemala is healthy enough if precautions are taken about drinking water, milk, uncooked vegetables and peeled fruits; carelessness on this point is likely to lead to amoebic dysentery, which is endemic. In Guatemala City 2 good hospitals are **Bella Aurora**, 10 Calle, 2-31, Zona 14, T2368-1951 and **Herrera Llerandi**, 6 Avenida, 8-71, Zona 10, T2334-5959, but you must have full medical insurance or sufficient funds to pay for treatment. English and other languages are spoken. Most small towns have clinics. At the public hospitals, which are seriously underfunded and where care for major problems is not good, you may have an examination for a nominal fee, but drugs are expensive.

Internet

Internet cafés are found in all tourist destinations, ask around in the cities for the best rates. Rates are US$0.50-1.50 per hr.

Language

The official language is Spanish and Guatemala is one of the biggest centres for learning Spanish in Latin America. Outside the main tourist spots few people speak English. There are over 20 Mayan languages.

Regarding pronunciation in Guatemala, 'X' is pronounced 'sh', as in Xela (shay-la).

Media

The main newspaper is *Prensa Libre* (www.prensalibre.com). The *Guatemala Post*, www.guatemala post.com, is published in English online. *Siglo Veintiuno*, www.sigloxxi.com, is a good newspaper. Mega popular is *Nuestro Diario*, a tabloid with more gory pics than copy. The *Revue*, www.revuemag.com, produced monthly in Antigua, carries articles, maps, advertisements, lodgings, tours and excursions, covering Antigua, Panajachel, Quetzaltenango, Río Dulce, Monterrico, Cobán, Flores and Guatemala City.

Money → *US$1=7.84 quetzales (June 2011)*
The unit is the quetzal, divided into 100 centavos. There are coins of 1 quetzal, 50 centavos, 25 centavos, 10 centavos, 5 centavos and 1 centavo. Paper currency is in denominations of 5, 10, 20, 50, 100 and 200 quetzales.

There is often a shortage of small change; ask for small notes when you first change money to pay hotel bills, transport, etc.

ATMs and exchange

There are numerous banks in Guatemala and in cities and towns most have ATMs (*cajeros automáticos*). All will change US dollars cash into quetzales, the majority will accept Visa and MasterCard to obtain cash, and some will change TCs, up to US$5000, although they are becoming less commonly accepted. **Banco Industrial** in Guatemala City and at the international airport will change sterling, Canadian dollars and yen. **Banco Uno** will change euros and Mexican pesos.

Banks usually charge up to 2% per transaction to advance quetzales on a credit card. Citicorp and Visa TCs are easier to change outside the main cities than Amex. Your passport is required and in some cases the purchase receipt as well, especially in the capital.

Credit cards

Visa and MasterCard are the most widely recognized and accepted bank cards. Some establishments may make a charge for use of credit cards – usually about US$3. Check before you sign. In the main it is only higher-class hotels and restaurants that accept cards. **Visa assistance**, T1-800-999-0115/ T2331-8720; **MasterCard**, T1-800-999-1480/T2334-0578. **American Express**, T1-800-999-0245/ T2470-4848. Amex cards are not very widely accepted.

Cost of living and travelling

Guatemala is one of the cheapest Central America countries, and those travelling on a tight budget should be able to get by on US$25 a day or less. With shorter distances, especially compared with Mexico to the north, travel becomes much less of a demand on your budget with the exception of the trip north to Tikal.

Opening hours

Banks Mon-Fri 0900-1500, Sat 0900-1300. Some city banks are introducing later hours, up to 2000; in the main tourist towns and shopping malls, some banks are open 7 days a week. **Shops** 0900-1300 and 1500-1900, often mornings only on Sat.

Post

Airmail to **Europe** takes 10-14 days. Letters cost US$1.10 for the first 20 g, US$3.40 for up to 100 g and US$37 for up to 2 kg. Airmail letters to the **US and Canada** cost US$0.1.10 for the first 20 g. Airmail parcel service to US is reliable (4 to 14 days) and costs US$2.70 for up 100 g and US$30 for up to 2 kg. Parcels over 2 kg can be sent from Guatemala City, Correos y Telégrafos, 7 Av y 12 Calle, Zona 1, and Antigua US$55 for up to 4.5 kg.

See under Panajachel and Chichicastenango (pages 266 and 267) for alternative services.

Prohibition
Take care with gambling in public places and do not take photos of military installations. See also Drugs, above.

Safety
In some parts of the country you may be subject to military or police checks. Local people can be reluctant to discuss politics with strangers. Do not necessarily be alarmed by 'gunfire', which is much more likely to be fireworks and bangers, a national pastime, especially early in the morning.

Robberies and serious assaults on tourists are becoming more common. While you can do nothing to counter the bad luck of being in the wrong place at the wrong time, sensible precautions can minimize risks. Single women should be especially careful. Tourist groups are not immune and some excursion companies take precautions. Do not travel at night if at all possible and take care on roads that are more prone to vehicle hijacks – the road between Flores and the Belizean border, the highway between Antigua and Panajachel and the principal highway between the capital and El Salvadorean border. Assaults and robberies on the public (former US) buses have increased. There have been a high number of attacks on private vehicles leaving the airport.

Consult www.fco.gov.uk, http://guatemala.usembassy.gov/recent_incidents.html and http://travel.state.gov.

Asistur, T1500/2421-2810 is a 24-hr, year-round tourist assistance programme for any problem or question. There is also a national tourist police force, **POLITUR**, T5561-2073, or for emergencies: T120/122/123. Other useful numbers include: **National police** T110; and **tourist police** in Antigua T832-7290.

Tax
There is a 17% ticket tax on all international tickets sold in Guatemala. There is also a US$30 or quetzal equivalent international departure tax.

The tourist institute **INGUAT** tax is 10%. Service charge is usually an extra 12%.

Telephone → *Country code T+502, Directory enquiries T+154.*
All phone numbers in the country are on an 8-figure basis. There are 2 main service providers – **Telgua** and **Telefónica**. Telefónica sells cards with access codes, which can be used from any private or public Telefónica phone. Telgua phone booths are ubiquitous and use cards sold in values of 20 and 50 quetzales. From a Telgua phone, dial 147 before making an international call.

Most businesses offering a phone-call service charge a minimum of US$0.13 for a local call, making a phone card a cheaper option.

International calls can be made from phone booths, however, unlike the local calls, it is cheaper to find an internet café or shop, which tend to offer better rates.

Mobile phone sim cards are affordable, with good deals costing around US$10-20 for the card, which includes free calls. Comcel and PCS offer mobile phone services. Rates are around US$0.03 a minute for a national call, US$1.20 for international.

Operator calls are more expensive. For international calls via the operator, dial T147-110. For calling card and credit-card call options, you need a fixed line in a hotel or private house. First you dial 9999 plus the following digits: For **Sprint USA**, dial 136; **AT&T Direct**: 190; **Germany**: 049; **Canada**: 198; **UK (BT)**: 044; **Switzerland**: 041; **Spain**: 034, **Italy**: 039.

Collect calls may be made from public Telgua phones by dialling T147-120.

Time
- 6 hrs GMT.

Tipping
Tip hotel and restaurant staff 10% in the better places (often added to the bill). Tip airport porters US$0.25 per bag.

Tourist information
Instituto Guatemalteco de Turismo (INGUAT), 7 Av, 1-17, Zona 4, Centro Cívico, Guatemala City, T2421-2800, www.visit guatemala.com. INGUAT provides bus times, hotel lists and road maps. Staff are helpful. Open Mon-Fri 0800-1600. Also office at the airport, open for all arrivals. The INGUAT airport office is open daily 0600-2400.

The Guatemalan Maya Centre, 94b Wandsworth Bridge Rd, London SW6 2TF, T020-7371-5291, www.maya.org.uk, has information on Guatemala, the Maya, a library, video archive and a textile collection; visits by prior appointment.

INGUAT offices outside Guatemala
See also Embassies and consulates, page 203.
Germany, Joachim Karntaz-Alle 45-47, 10557, Berline Tiergarten.
Italy, Viale Prassilla 152, 00124, Rome, T390-6-5091-6626.
Mexico, T00-52-5202-1457, turismoembagua@prodigy.net.mx.
Spain, Calle Rafael Salgado 9, 4th Izquierda, 28036 Madrid, T/F34-91-457-3424.
USA, T001-202-518-5514.

Useful websites
Regional websites covering some of the more popular areas include **www.atitlan.com**, **www.mayaparadise.com** (Río Dulce/ Lívingston), **www.cobanav.net** (Cobán) and **www.xelapages.com** (Quetzaltenango). Posada Belén in Guatemala City run a very informative site packed with information, www.guatemalaweb.com.

Of the several publications with websites, the *Revue*, **www.revuemag.com**, is probably the most useful to the visitor.

Visas and immigration
Only a valid passport is required for citizens of all Western European countries; USA, Canada, Mexico, all Central American countries, Australia, Israel, Japan and New Zealand. The majority of visitors get 90 days on arrival.

Visa renewal must be done in Guatemala City after 90 days, or on expiry. Passport stamp renewal on expiry for those citizens only requiring a valid passport to enter Guatemala must also be done at the immigration office at **Dirección General de Migración**, 6 Avenida, 3-11, Zona 4, Guatemala City, T2411-2411, Mon-Fri 0800-1600 (0800-1230 for payments). This office extends visas and passport stamps only once for a further period of time, depending on the original time awarded (maximum 90 days). Since 2006, when Guatemala signed a Central America-4 (CA-4) Border Control Agreement with El Salvador, Honduras, and Nicaragua you will have to visit a country outside of these 3 to re-enter and gain 90 days. These rules have been introduced to stop people leaving the country for 72 hrs (which is the legal requirement) every 6 months and returning, effectively making them permanent residents.

Working and volunteering
If you would like to volunteer, it is best to try and make contact before arriving, if only by a few days. Such is the demand for positions that unskilled volunteers very often have to pay for board and lodgings. Work needs to be planned and, although there is always work to do, your time will be used most efficiently if your arrival is expected and planned for.
Asociación de Rescate y Conservación de Vida Silvestre (ARCAS), T2478-4096,

www.arcasguatemala.com. Runs projects involving working with nature and wildlife, returning wild animals to their natural habitat.

Casa Alianza, 13 Av, 0-37, Zona 2 de Mixco, Col la Escuadrilla Mixco, Guatemala City, T2250-4964, www.casa-alianza.org. A project that helps street kids.

Casa Guatemala, 14 Calle, 10-63, Zona 1, Guatemala City, T2331-9408, www.casa-guatemala.org. Runs a project for abandoned and malnourished children at Río Dulce.

Comité Campesino del Altiplano, on Lake Atitlán, 10 mins from San Lucas, T5804-9451, www.ccda.galeon.com. This Campesino Cooperative now produces Fair Trade organic coffee buying from small farmers in the region; long-term volunteers are welcome but Spanish is required.

Fundación Mario Dary, Diagonal 6, 17-19, Zona 10, Guatemala City, T2333-4957, fundary@intelnet.net.gt. Operates conservation, health and education projects on the Punta de Manabique and welcomes volunteers.

Proyecto Ak' Tenamit, 11 Av 'A', 9-39, Zona 2, Guatemala City, T2254-1560, www.aktenamit.org, based at Clínica Lámpara, 15 mins upriver from Lívingston. This project was set up to help 7000 civil-war-displaced Q'eqchi' Maya who now live in the region in 30 communities.

Proyecto Mosaico Guatemala, 3 Av Norte 3, Antigua. T7832-0955, www.promosaico.org. An information centre and clearing house for volunteers, with access to opportunities all over the country.

Quetzaltrekkers, Casa Argentina, 12 Diagonal, 8-37, Zona 1, Quetzaltenango, T7765-5895, www.quetzaltrekkers.com. Volunteer opportunities for hiking guides and office workers, minimum 3-month commitment.

UPAVIM, Calle Principal, Sector D-1, Col La Esperanza, Zona 12, Guatemala City, T2479-9061, www.upavim.org. This project helps poor families, providing social services and education for the workers using fair-trade principles.

There are also opportunites to work in children's homes in Quetzaltenango (Xela). 2 organizations are **Casa Hogar de Niños** and the **Asociación Hogar Nuevos Horizontes**. See page 288. Also check out Xela-based volunteering information organization www.entremundos.org. Several language schools in Xela fund community development projects and seek volunteers. Make enquiries in town or via www.xelapages.com.

The London-based **Guatemala Solidarity Network**, www.guatemalasolidarity.org.uk, can assist with finding projects that look at human rights issues.

Guatemala City

→ *Colour map 2, C2. Altitude: 1500 m.*
Smog-bound and crowded, Guatemala City is the commercial and administrative centre of the country. It is a sprawl of industrial activity lightly sprinkled with architectural treasures and out-of-place tributes to urban sculpture. Rarely rated by visitors, this is the beating heart of Guatemala and is worth a couple of days if you have time and can bear the noise and pollution in Zona 1. Guatemala City is surrounded by active and dormant volcanoes easily visited on day trips. → *See listings, pages 213-222.*

Ins and outs

Getting there
The airport is in the south part of the city at La Aurora, 4 km from the Plaza Central, T2331-8392. It has banks, ATMs, internet, bars and restaurants. A taxi to Zona 10 is US$8, Zona 1, US$10 and from Antigua, US$25-30. Shuttles from outside airport to Antigua meet all arriving flights, US$10. The Zona 4 chicken bus terminal between 1-4 Avenida and 7-9 Calle serves the Occidente (west), the Costa Sur (Pacific coastal plain) and El Salvador. The area of southern Zona 1 contains many bus offices and is the departure point for the Oriente (east), the Caribbean zone, Pacific coast area towards the Mexican border and the north, to Flores and Tikal. First-class buses often depart from company offices in Zona 1 (see map, page 210). Note that some companies have been moved from Zona 1 and Zona 4 out to Zona 7 and 12. → *See Transport, page 217.*

Getting around
Any address not in Zona 1 – and it is absolutely essential to quote zone numbers in addresses – is probably some way from the centre. Addresses themselves, being purely numerical, are usually easy to find. For example, 19 Calle, 4-83 is on 19 Calle between 4 Avenida and 5 Avenida at No 83.

If driving, *Avenidas* have priority over *calles* (except in Zona 10, where this rule varies).

Tourist information
INGUAT ① *7 Av, 1-17, Zona 4 (Centro Cívico), 24 hrs T1801-464-8281, T2421-2800, www.visitguatemala.com, Mon-Fri 0800-1600, English is sometimes spoken.* They are very friendly and provide a hotel list, a map of the city, and general information on buses, market days, museums, etc. They also have an office in the **airport arrivals hall** ① *T2331-4256, 0600-2100*, where staff are exceptionally helpful and on the ball.

Background

Guatemala City was founded by decree of Carlos III of Spain in 1776 to serve as capital after earthquake damage to the earlier capital, Antigua, in 1773. Almost completely destroyed by earthquakes in 1917-1918, it was rebuilt in modern fashion, or in copied colonial, only to be further damaged by earthquake in 1976. Most of the affected buildings have been restored.

Sights

The old centre of the city is Zona 1. It is still a busy shopping and commercial area, with some good hotels and restaurants, and many of the cheaper places to stay. However, the main activity of the city has been moving south, first to Zona 4, now to Zonas 9, 10 and 14. With the move have gone commerce, banks, embassies, museums and the best hotels and restaurants. The best residential areas are in the hills to the east, southeast and west.

Around Zona 1

At the city's heart lies the **Parque Central**. It is intersected by the north-to-south-running 6 Avenida, the main shopping street. The eastern half has a floodlit fountain; on the west side is **Parque Centenario**, with an acoustic shell in cement used for open-air concerts and public meetings. The Parque Central is popular on Sunday with many *indígenas* selling textiles.

① **Guatemala City orientation**

➡ **Guatemala City maps**
1 Orientation, page 209
2 Zona 1, page 210
3 Zona 9, 10 & 13, page 212

To the east of the plaza is the **cathedral** (www.catedral.org.gt). It was begun in 1782 and finished in 1815 in classical style with notable blue cupolas and dome. Inside are paintings and statues from ruined Antigua. Solid silver and sacramental reliquary are in the east side chapel of the Sagrario. Next to the cathedral is the colonial mansion of the Archbishop. Aside from the cathedral, the most notable public buildings constructed between 1920 and 1944, after the 1917 earthquake, are the **Palacio Nacional** ① *visits every 15 mins Mon-Fri 0900-1645; every 30 mins Sat and Sun 0900-1630*, built of light green stone, the Police Headquarters, the Chamber of Deputies and the Post Office. To the west of the cathedral are the Biblioteca Nacional and the Banco del Ejército. Behind the Palacio Nacional is the Presidential Mansion.

Museums in Zona 1 include the **Museo Nacional de Historia** ① *9 Calle, 9-70, T2253-6149, Mon-Fri 0900-1600, Sat-Sun 0900-1200 and 13001600, US$6*, which has historical documents and objects from Independence onward. **Museo de la Universidad de San Carlos de Guatemala (MUSAC)** ① *9 Av, 9-79, T2232-0721, www.musacenlinea.org, Mon, Wed-Fri 0930- 1730, Sat 0930-1700, closed Tue and Sun, US$1; guided tours at 1000 and 1400*, charts the history of the university. The Salón Mayor is where Guatemala signed its Independence from Mexico in 1823, and in 1826, the Central American Federation, with Guatemala as the

N

300 metres

300 yards

Sleeping 🛌
Chalet Suizo **4** C2
Continental **6** B2
Pan American **7** A2
Pensión Meza **8** B3
Posada Belén **1** C3

Spring **9** C2

Eating 🍴
Altuna **1** C2
Arrin Cuan **2** A2
Café de Imeri **3** A1
Helados Marylena **5** A1
Los Canalones **6** B2
Vegetariano
  Rey Sol **7** A2

Bars & clubs 🍸
El Portal **12** A2

Europa **4** B2
La Bodeguita del
  Centro **10** B1
Las Cien Puertas **14** A2

Transport 🚍
ADN to Santa
  Elena **5** C2
Escobar y Monja
  Blanca to Cobán **1** C2
Fuente del Norte to
  Río Dulce & Santa
  Elena/Flores **2** D2

Línea Dorada to Río
  Dulce & Flores **3** D3
Marquensita to
  Quetzaltenango **6** E1
Rutas Orientales to
  Chiquimula &
  Esquipulas **7** D3
Transportes Galgos
  to Mexico **12** D2
Transportes Litegua
  to Puerto Barrios &
  Río Dulce **13** C3

seat of power, abolished slavery in the union. Also, Doctor Mariano Gálvez, the country's president from 1831-1838, is buried behind part of the salon wall and a marble bust of him sits outside the door. The Universidad de San Carlos was the first university in Guatemala City. **Casa MIMA** ⓘ *8 Av, 14-12, T2253-6657, casamima@hotmail.com, Mon-Sat 0900-1230, 1400-1500, US$1, no photography,* is the only authentic turn-of-the-19th-century family home open to the public, once owned by the family Ricardo Escobar Vega and Mercedes Fernández Padilla y Abella. It is furnished in European-influenced style with 15th- to mid-20th-century furniture and ornaments.

Most of the churches worth visiting are in Zona 1. **Cerro del Carmen** ⓘ *11 Av y 1 Calle A,* was built as a copy of a hermitage destroyed in 1917-1918, containing a famous image of the Virgen del Carmen. Situated on a hill with good views of the city, it was severely damaged in the earthquake of 1976 and remains in poor shape. **La Merced** ⓘ *11 Av y 5 Calle,* dedicated in 1813, has beautiful altars, organ and pulpit from Antigua as well as jewellery, art treasures and fine statues. **Santo Domingo** ⓘ *12 Av y 10 Calle,* built between 1782 and 1807, is a striking yellow colour, reconstructed after 1917, with an image of Nuestra Señora del Rosario and sculptures. **Sagrado Corazón de Jesús,** or **Santuario Expiatorio** ⓘ *26 Calle y 2 Av,* holds 3000 people; the colourful, exciting modern architecture was by a young Salvadorean architect who had not qualified when he built it. Part of the complex, built in 1963 (church, school and auditorium) is in the shape of a fish. The entrance is a giant arch of multicoloured stained glass, wonderfully illuminated at night. The walls are lined with glass confessionals. **Las Capuchinas** ⓘ *10 Av y 10 Calle,* has a very fine St Anthony altarpiece, and other pieces from Antigua. **Santa Rosa** ⓘ *10 Av y 8 Calle,* was used for 26 years as the cathedral until the present building was ready. The altarpieces are from Antigua (except above the main altar). **San Francisco** ⓘ *6 Av y 13 Calle,* a large yellow and white church that shows earthquake damage outside (1976), has a sculpture of the Sacred Head, originally from Extremadura, in Spain. **Carmen El Bajo** ⓘ *8 Av y 10 Calle,* was built in the late 18th century; again the façade was severely damaged in 1976.

North of the centre
Parque Minerva ⓘ *Av Simeón Cañas, Zona 2, 0900-1700, US$1.50,* has a huge relief map of the country made in 1905 to a horizontal scale of 1:10,000 and a vertical scale of 1:2,000. The park has basketball and baseball courts, bar and restaurant and a children's playground (unsafe at night). To get there, take bus V21 from 7 Avenida, Zona 4. Just beyond is a popular park, the **Hipódromo** which is packed on Sundays with bumper cars and mechanical games, and a great little train for kids.

South of the centre: Avenida La Reforma
The modern **Centro Cívico**, which links Zona 1 with Zona 4, includes the Municipalidad, the Palacio de Justicia, the Ministerio de Finanzas Públicas, the Banco de Guatemala, the mortgage bank, the social-security commission and the tourist board. The curious **Teatro Nacional** ⓘ *Mon-Fri 0800-1630 for tours, US$4,* with its blue and white mosaic, dominates the hilltop of the west side of the Centro Cívico. There is an excellent view of the city and surrounding mountains from the roof. An old Spanish fortress provides a backdrop to the open-air theatre adjoining the Teatro Nacional.

Cuatro Grados Norte, located on Vía 5 between Ruta 1 and Ruta 2, is a pedestrianized area that has grown up around the IGA theatre and bookshop (a cultural centre, which sometimes has interesting concerts and exhibitions). Cafés and bars have tables on the street and it's safe and fun to wander around at night. The **Centro Cultural de España** is located here with live music, films, exhibitions and conferences, there is also a branch of **Sophos**, an excellent bookshop. On Saturdays there is a street market with craft and jewellery stalls, often cultural events in the street. On Sundays there are clowns and events for children. It's a strange mix of wealthy Guatemalans strolling with their poodles and alternative street-market types; sit back and enjoy watching the people.

To see the finest residential district go south down 7 Avenida to Ruta 6, which runs diagonally in front of Edificio El Triángulo, past the orange **Capilla de Yurrita** (Ruta 6 y Vía 8). Built as a private chapel in 1928 on the lines of a Russian Orthodox church, it has been described as an example of "opulent 19th-century bizarreness and over-ripe extravagance". There are many woodcarvings, slender white pillars, brown/gold ornamentation and an unusual blue sky window over the altar. Ruta 6 runs into the wide tree-lined Avenida La Reforma.

③ Zona 9, 10 & 13

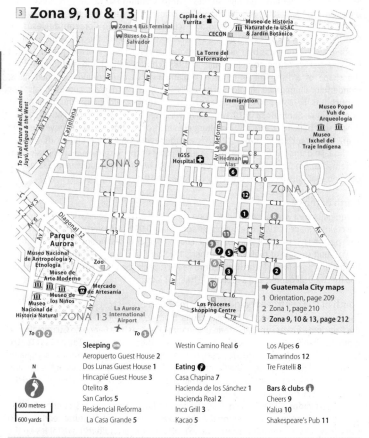

Sleeping 🛏	Westin Camino Real 6	Los Alpes 6
Aeropuerto Guest House 2		Tamarindos 12
Dos Lunas Guest House 1	**Eating** 🍴	Tre Fratelli 8
Hincapié Guest House 3	Casa Chapina 7	
Otelito 8	Hacienda de los Sánchez 1	**Bars & clubs** 🍸
San Carlos 5	Hacienda Real 2	Cheers 9
Residencial Reforma	Inca Grill 3	Kalua 10
La Casa Grande 5	Kacao 5	Shakespeare's Pub 11

N

600 metres
600 yards

To the east, in Zona 10, are some excellent museums. **Museo Ixchel del Traje Indígena** ⓘ *Campus of Universidad Francisco Marroquín, 6 Calle Final, T2331-3623, www.museoixchel.org, Mon-Fri 0900-1700, Sat 0900-1300, US$4*, has a collection of indigenous dress. In addition to the clothes there are photos from the early 20th century, paintings and very interesting videos. A shop sells beautiful textiles that aren't available on the tourist market, prices are fixed, and quality costs. **Museo Popol Vuh de Arqueología** ⓘ *6 Calle Final, T2338-7896, www.popolvuh.ufm.edu.gt, Mon-Fri 0900-1700, Sat 0900-1300, US$5.50, US$3 charge to take photographs*, has an extensive collection of pre-Columbian and colonial artefacts, as well as a replica of the Dresden Codex, one of the only Maya parchment manuscripts in existence. **Museo de Historia Natural de la USAC y Jardín Botánico** ⓘ *Calle Mcal Cruz 1-56, T2334-6065, Mon-Fri 0800-1600, Sat 0830-1230, US$1.30*, has gardens, stuffed animals and live snakes.

In **Parque Aurora**, Zona 13, in the southern part of the city, are La Aurora International Airport, the Observatory, racetrack and **Parque Zoológico La Aurora** ⓘ *T2472-0507, Tue-Sun 0900-1700, US$1.10*. The newer areas show greater concern for the animals' well-being. There are also several museums: **Museo Nacional de Antropología y Etnología** ⓘ *Salón 5, Parque Aurora, Zona 13, T2475-4406, Tue-Fri 0900-1600, Sat-Sun 0900-1200, 1330-1600, US$5, no photos*. Outstanding Maya pieces including stelae from Piedras Negras and typical Guatemalan dress, as well as good models of Tikal, Quiriguá and Zaculeu. There are sculptures, murals, ceramics, textiles, a collection of masks and an excellent jade collection. Around the corner is the **Museo Nacional de Historia Natural** ⓘ *6 Calle, 7-30, Zona 13, T2472-0468, Mon-Fri 0900-1600, Sat-Sun 0900-1200, 1400-1600, US$5*, which houses a collection of national fauna, including stuffed birds, animals, butterflies, geological specimens, etc. Opposite the archaeology museum, the **Museo de Arte Moderno** ⓘ *Salón 6, Parque Aurora, Zona 13, T2472-0467, US$5, Tue-Fri 0900-1600*, has a modest but enjoyable collection. Next door is the **Museo de los Niños** ⓘ *T2475-5076, Tue-Fri 0830-1200, 1300-1630, US$4*, an interactive museum with a gallery of Maya history and the Gallery of Peace which houses the world's largest single standing artificial tree – a *ceiba*.

◉ Guatemala City listings

◉ Sleeping

You can get better prices in the more expensive hotels by booking corporate rates through a travel agent or simply asking at the desk if any lower prices are available. Hotels are often full at holiday times, eg Easter and Christmas. At the cheaper hotels, single rooms are not always available. There are many cheap *pensiones* near bus and railway stations and markets; those between Calle 14 and Calle 18 are not very salubrious.

Hoteles Villas de Guatemala, reservations 8 Calle 1-75 Zona 10, T2223-5000, www.villasdeguatemala.com, rents luxury villas throughout Guatemala.

Zona 1 *p209, map p210*

AL-A Pan American, 9 Calle, 5-63, T2232-6807, www.hotelpanamerican.com.gt. Quiet and comfortable rooms with TV, but try to avoid rooms on the main-road side. Parking, and breakfast included. Restaurant with good food in the mid-range price bracket.

B Posada Belén, 13 Calle "A", 10-30, T2232-9226, www.posadabelen.com. A colonial-style house run by the friendly Francesca and René Sanchinelli, who speak English. Quiet, comfy rooms with good hot showers. Laundry, email service, luggage store and good meals. Parking. Tours available. A lovely place to stay, highly recommended.

B Spring, 8 Av, 12-65, T2230-2858. Bright rooms with TV in this quiet haven of tranquillity and flowers amid the pollution of Zona 1. Rooms without private shower are cheaper. Patio garden, good breakfasts, and parking near by. Free coffee, email service, phone calls, luggage store. Probably the best choice in Zona 1 at this price.

C Continental, 12 Calle, 6-10, T2251-8237. 2 floors up with a very secure street entrance. It has vast, comfortable rooms, but they're spartan; some quadruples available. All are very clean with private bath. Credit cards accepted.

C-D Chalet Suizo, 7a Calle, 14-34, T2251-3786, chaletsuizo@gmail.com. In a good central position with constant hot-water showers (cheaper with shared bathroom). It is popular, so often crowded. There is a locked luggage store, safety box, and the rooms are secure. Those rooms facing the main street are noisy. Avoid rooms 9-12 as a noisy pump will disturb sleep and 19-21 have very thin walls. Free parking.

D-E Pensión Meza, 10 Calle, 10-17, T2232-3177. A large ramshackle place with beds in dorms. It's popular with helpful staff and English is spoken. It's sometimes noisy and some rooms are damp. Other rooms are darker than a prison cell, but cheered by graffiti, poetry and paintings. There is a ping-pong table, book exchange, internet at US$80 per hr, or free Wi-Fi.

South of the centre: Avenida La Reforma *p211, map p212*

L Westin Camino Real, Av La Reforma y 14 Calle, Zona 10, T2333-3000, www.starwoodhotels.com. Excellent value, good restaurants open 0600-2330,

gym, pool, spa, airport shuttle, piano bar and live Cuban music Fri and Sat at 2100.

AL Otelito, 12 Calle, 4-51, T2339-1811, Zona 10, www.otelito.com. 12 lovely rooms in this small boutique hotel. Includes breakfast, shuttle to hotel and internet. Restaurant open Mon-Wed 0630-2100, Thu-Sat 0630-2230, Sun 0630-2030.

A Residencial Reforma La Casa Grande, Av La Reforma, 7-67, Zona 10, T2332-0914, www.casagrande-gua.com. Near US Embassy, with nicer rooms than the next door **San Carlos**. Colonial style, all rooms come with TV. Good, small restaurant, open 0630-2100, a bar and internet service. Good value.

A San Carlos, Av La Reforma, 7-89, Zona 10, T2362-9076, www.hsancarlos.com. A small, charming hotel, with pool and plant-filled patio. Includes breakfast and free airport transfer.

B Hincapié Guest House, Av Hincapié, 18-77, Zona 13, T2332-7771, ruedapinillos@ yahoo.com. On the far side of the airport runway. Continental breakfast included and free airport transport. Cable TV in the rooms.

B Hotel Aeropuerto Guest House, 5 mins' walk from the airport at 15 Calle "A", 7-32, Col Aurora 1, Zona 13, T2332-3086, www.aeropuertoguesthouse.com. Free transport to and from the airport. With or without bath, and is clean and safe, breakfast included. Free internet.

D Dos Lunas Guest House, 21 Calle, 10-92, Zona 13, T2261-4248, www.hoteldos lunas.com. Private rooms and dorms in a comfy B&B. Very close to the airport with free transport to or from the airport. Storage service, free breakfast and water and tourist information. Lorena, the landlady, also organizes shuttles and taxis and tours. English spoken. Reservations advisable as often full.

🍴 Eating

Zona 1 *p209, map p210*
There are all kinds of food available in the capital, from the simple national cuisine to

French, Chinese and Italian food. There is a plethora of fast-food restaurants and traditional *comedores* where you will get good value for money; a reasonable set meal will cost no more than US$3. The cheapest places to eat are at street stalls and the various markets – take the normal precautions.

¶¶¶ **Altuna**, 5 Av, 12-31. Serves tasty Spanish food in huge portions. Lobster available but expensive. Delicious coffee. This hotel has a beautiful traditional Spanish bar interior. There is a branch in Zona 10 at 10 Calle, 0-45.

¶¶¶ **Hotel Pan American**, 9 Calle, 5-63 (see Sleeping). Best lunchtime menu.

¶¶ **Arrin Cuan**, 5 Av, 3-27. A famous local institution specializing in traditional food from Cobán (*subanik*, *gallo en chicha*, and *kak ik*). The restaurant is centred around a small courtyard with a little fountain and live lunchtime marimba music. Breakfast available. Also on 16 Calle, 4-32, Zona 10.

¶¶ **Los Canalones – Parrillada Argentina**, 6 Av A, 10-39. Mon-Sat 1200-1630. Barbecue on the street outside, for serious meat eaters. Alejandro *El Argentino* does tasty chunks of meat and chorizo served with excellent salad, get there early. Meals include soup, endless tortillas and *refresco*.

¶¶-¶ **Café de Imeri**, 6 Calle, 3-34. Closed Sun. Sandwiches, salads, soups and pastries in a patio garden. Set lunch and excellent cakes. It's popular with young professional Guatemalans. Try the *pay de queso de elote* (maize cheesecake). Its bakery next door has a rare selection of granary breads, birthday cakes, etc.

¶ **Restaurante Vegetariano Rey Sol**, 8 Calle, 5-36. Closed Sun. A prize vegetarian find – wholesome food and ambience oasis amid the fumes of Zona 1, and popular with the locals. Delicious veggie concoctions at excellent prices served canteen-style by friendly staff. Breakfasts and *licuados* also available. Newer, larger and brighter branch at 11 Calle, 5-51.

Ice cream parlours

¶ **Helados Marylena**, 6 Calle, 2-49. Open daily 1000-2200. Not quite a meal but almost.

This establishment has been serving up the weirdest concoctions for 90 years. From the probably vile – fish, chilli, yucca and cauliflower ice cream – to the heavenly – beer and sputnik (coconut, raisins and pineapple). The *elote* (maize) is good too. This city institution is credited with making children eat their vegetables! Anyone travelling with fussy eaters should stop by here.

South of the centre: Avenida La Reforma *p211, map p212*

Most of the best restaurants are in the 'Zona Viva', within 10 blocks of the Av La Reforma on the east side, between 6 Calle and 16 Calle in Zona 10. **Zona 9** is just across the other side of Av La Reforma.

There are several options in the area around **Cuatro Grados Norte** providing tapas, sushi, *churros* and chocolate. Lively, especially on Fri and Sat nights.

¶¶¶ **Café Rouge**, Cuatro Grados Norte, Vía 5 between Ruta 1 and Ruta 2. Good cappuccinos, chocolate things and apple pie.

¶¶¶ **Hacienda de los Sánchez**, 12 Calle, 2-25, Zona 10. Good steaks and local dishes, but seriously crowded at weekends, and so not the most pleasant of settings compared with other steakhouses in the vicinity.

¶¶¶ **Hacienda Real**, 15 Calle, 15, Zona 10. An excellent steak selection. Candles and palms create a garden-like atmosphere. Nice little bar with Mexican leather chairs on one side.

¶¶¶ **Inca Grill**, 2 Av 14-32, Zona 10. Tasty Peruvian food, live Andean music.

¶¶¶ **Kacao**, 2 Av, 13-44, Zona 10. A large variety of delicious local and national dishes, which are attractively prepared and served in ample portions. The setting is fantastic – a giant thatched room, *huípiles* for tablecloths, beautiful candle decorations; some options are expensive.

¶¶¶ **L'Osteria**, Cuatro Grados Norte, Vía 5 between Ruta 1 and Ruta 2. Popular Italian on the corner with leafy terrace; brick pizza oven.

¶¶¶ **Tamarindos**, 11 Calle, 2-19A, Zona 10, T2360-2815. Mixed Asian, sushi, Vietnamese rolls, mushrooms stuffed with almonds and crab are some of the tantalizing options at this very smart Asian restaurant with spiral shades and soothing bamboo greens.

†††† **Tre Fratelli**, 2 Av 13-25, Zona 10. Good Italian food; tasty bread and parmesan cheese; very lively and popular, some outside tables.

††† **Arguileh**, Cuatro Grados Norte, Vía 5 between Ruta 1 and Ruta 2. Eastern-style kebabs and *pan árabe*, wooden decor, looks good.

††† **Café Vienés**, in the Westin Camino Real (see Sleeping). One of the best places for German- style coffee and cakes, your chance to try a chocolate fondu.

††† **Casa Chapina**, 1a Av, 13-42, Zona 10, T4212-2746. Near the quality hotels, friendly service, reasonable prices and a wide range of traditional and international dishes to choose from.

††† **Los Alpes**, 10 Calle, 1-09, Zona 10. Closed Mon. A Swiss/Austrian place with light meals, which also offers a smorgasbord of excellent cakes and chocolates. Popular with Guatemalan families.

††† **Tarboosh**, Cuatro Grados Norte, Vía 5 between Ruta 1 and Ruta 2, not far from L'Ostería. Mediterranean cuisine in a funky upstairs setting with loud live music acts.

†††-† **Cafesa**, 6 Av, 11-64, Zona 9. 24-hr diner serving Western and Guatemalan food with some seriously cheap options.

ⓔ Entertainment

Guatemala City *p208, maps p209, p210 and p212*
Bars and clubs
Cheers, 13 Calle, 0-40, Zona 10. A basement sports bar with pool tables, darts, and large cable TV. Mon-Sat 0900-0100, Sun 1300-2400ish. Happy hour until 1800.

El Portal, Portal del Comercio, 8 Calle, 6-30, Zona 1. Mon-Sat 1000-2200. This was a favourite spot of Che Guevara and you can imagine him sitting here holding court

at the long wooden bar. A stuffed bull's head now keeps watch over drinkers. To get there, enter the labyrinths of passageways facing the main plaza at No 6-30 where there is a Coke stand. At the first junction bear round to the left and up on the left you will see its sign. *Comida típica* and marimba music, beer from the barrel.

Europa, 11 Calle, 5-16, Zona 1. Mon-Sat 0800-0100. Popular peace-corps/travellers' hang-out, sports bar, shows videos, books for sale.

Kalua, 1 Av, 15-06. Huge club, 3 floors with different tunes, stylish.

La Bodeguita del Centro, 12 Calle, 3-55, Zona 1, T2239-2976. The walls of this hip place in an old stockhouse are adorned with posters of Che Guevara, Bob Marley and murdered Salvadorean Archbishop Romero. There's live music Thu-Sat at 2100, talks, plays, films, exhibitions upstairs. Wooden tables are spread over 2 floors; seriously cheap nachos and soup on the menu. It's an atmospheric place to spend an evening. Call in to get their **Calendario Cultural** leaflet.

Las Cien Puertas, Pasaje Aycinea, 7 Av, 8-44, just south of Plaza Mayor, Zona 1. Daily 1600-2400. Has a wonderful atmosphere with political, satirical and love missives covering its walls. There's excellent food and outdoor seating and it's friendly.

Sabor Latino, 1 Av, 13 Calle, Zona 10. A club that's under **Rock and Salambo** on the same block as **Mi Guajira**. The night begins with salsa and graduates to a more hip-hop beat.

Shakespeare's Pub, 13 Calle, 1-51, Zona 10. Mon-Fri 1100-0100, Sat and Sun 1400-0100. English-style basement bar with a good atmosphere, American owner, a favourite with ex-pats and locals, safe for women to go and drink.

Cinema and theatre
There are numerous cinemas and they often show films in English with Spanish subtitles.
Teatro Nacional, Centro Cívico.
Most programmes are Thu-Sun.

○ Shopping

Guatemala City *p208, maps p209, p210 and p212*

Bookshops
Museo Ixchel, page 213, has a bookshop.
Museo Popol Vuh bookshop, page 213, has a good selection of books on pre-Columbian art, crafts and natural history.

Maps
Maps can be bought from the **Instituto Geográfico Nacional** (IGN), Av Las Américas, 5-76, Zona 13, T2332-2611. Mon-Fri 0900-1730. The whole country is covered by about 200 1:50,000 maps available in colour or photocopies of out of print sections. None is very up to date. There is, however, an excellent 1996, 1:15,000 map of Guatemala City in 4 sheets. A general *Mapa Turístico* of the country is available here, also at INGUAT.

Markets and supermarkets
The Central Market operates underground behind the cathedral, from 7 to 9 Av, 8 Calle, Zona 1. One floor is dedicated to textiles and crafts, and there is a large, cheap basketware section on the lower floor. Silverware is cheaper at the market than elsewhere in Guatemala City. Other markets include the **Mercado Terminal** in Zona 4, and the **Mercado de Artesanía** in the Parque Aurora, near the airport, which is for tourists. Large shopping centres are good for a wide selection of local crafts, artworks, funky shoes, and clothes. Don't miss the *dulces*, candied fruits and confectionery.

The best shopping centres are **Centro Comercial Los Próceres**, 18 Calle and 3 Av, Zona 10, the **Centro Comercial La Pradera**, Carretera Roosevelt and Av 26, Zona 10. There is a large **Paiz** supermarket on 18 Calle and 8 Av and a vast shopping mall **Tikal Futura** at Calzada Roosevelt and 22 Av, Zona 11. *Artesanías* for those who shop with a conscience at the fair-trade outlet **UPAVIM**, Calle Principal, Col La Esperanza, Mesquital Zona 12, T2479-9061, www.upavim.org, Mon-Fri 0800-1800, Sat 0800-1200.

▲ Activities and tours

Guatemala City *p208, maps p209, p210 and p212*
Aire, Mar y Tierra, Plaza Marítima, 6 Av, 20-25, Zona 10, T2337-0149. Recommended.
Clark Tours, Plaza Clark, 7 Av 14-76, Zona 9, T2412-4700, www.clarktours.com.gt, and several other locations. Long-established, very helpful, tours to Copán, Quiriguá, etc.
Four Directions, 1 Calle, 30-65, Zona 7, T2439-7715, www.fourdirections.com.gt. Recommended for Maya archaeology tours. English spoken.
Maya Expeditions, 15 Calle "A", 14-07, Zona 10, T2363-4955, www.mayaexpeditions.com. Very experienced and helpful, with varied selection of short and longer river/hiking tours, whitewater rafting, bungee jumping, cultural tours, tours to Piedras Negras.
Setsa Travel, 8 Av, 14-11, Zona 1, T2230-4726, karlasetsa@intelnet.net.gt, very helpful, tours arranged to Tikal, Copán, car hire.
Tourama, Av La Reforma, 15-25, Zona 10, T2368-1820, turama@intelnet.net.gt. English spoken. Recommended.
Trolley Tour, T5907-0913, Tue-Sat 1000-1300, Sun 1000. Pickups from Zona 10 hotels for 3-hr city tours, US$20, children, US$10.
Turismo Ek Chuah, 3 Calle 6-24, Zona 2, T2220-1491, www.ekchuah.com. Nationwide tours as well as some specialist and tailor-made tours on bicycle and horseback.

⊖ Transport

Guatemala City *p208, maps p209, p210 and p212*
Air
Flights to **Flores** with **Grupo Taca** 0820, 1605 and 1850, and **TAG** at 1630 daily.

Charter airlines Aero Ruta Maya, Av Hincapié and 18 Calle, Zona 13, T2339-0502.

Domestic airlines Aerocharter, 18 Calle and Av Hincapié, Zona 13,

T5401-5893, to **Puerto Barrios**. Phone for schedule. **Aeródromo**, Av Hincapié and 18 Calle, Zona 13, T5539-9364, to **Huehuetenango**. Phone for schedule. **Aerolucía**, 18 Calle and Av Hincapié, T5959-7008 to **Quetzaltenango**. Phone for schedule. **Grupo Taca** at the airport and Av Hincapié, 12-22, Zona 13, T2470-8222, www.taca.com. **Tag**, Av Hincapié y 18 Calle, Zona 13, T2361-1180, www.tag.com.gt.

International airlines **American Airlines**, Hotel Marriot, 7 Av, 15-45, Zona 9, T2422-0000. **Continental Airlines**, 18 Calle, 5-56, Zona 10, Edif Unicentro, T2385-9610. **Copa**, 1 Av, 10-17, Zona 10, T2385-5555. **Cubana de Aviación**, Edificio Atlántis, 13 Calle, 3-40, Zona 10, T2361-0857. **Delta Airlines**, 15 Calle, 3-20, Zona 10, Edif Centro Ejecutivo, T2263-0600. **Iberia**, Av La Reforma, 8-60, Zona 9, Edif Galerías Reforma, T2332-7471/ 2332-0911, www.iberia.com. **Inter Jet**, T1-800-835-0271, www.interjet.com.mx. **Mexicana**,13 Calle, 8-44, Zona 10, Edif Plaza Edyma, T2333-6001. **Spirit Air**, www.spiritair.com. **Taca** (includes Aviateca, Lacsa, Nica and Inter), see above. **United**, Av La Reforma, 1-50, Zona 9, Edif La Reformador, 2nd floor, T1-800-835-0100.

Bus
Local
Buses operate between 0600-2000, after which you will have to rely on taxis.
In town, US$0.13 per journey on regular buses and on the larger red buses known as *gusanos* (worms) except on Sun and public holidays when they charge US$0.16.) One of the most useful bus services is the **101**, which travels down 10 Av, Zona 1, and then cuts across to the 6 Av, Zona 4, and then across Vía 8 and all the way down the Av La Reforma, Zona 10. The **82** also travels from Zona 1 to 10 and can be picked up on the 10 Av, Zona 1 and the 6 Av, Zona 4. Bus **85**, with the same pickup points, goes to the cluster of museums in Zona 13. Buses **37**, **35**, **32** all head for the INGUAT building,

which is the large blue and white building in the Centro Cívico complex. **R40** goes from the 6 Av, Zona 4, to the Tikal Futura shopping complex – a good spot to catch the Antigua bus, which pulls up by the bridge to the complex. Buses leaving the 7 Av, Zona 4, just 4 blocks from the Zona 4 bus terminal, for the Plaza Mayor, Zona 1, are *gusano* **V21**, **35**, **36**, **82**, and **101**.

Long distance
Watch your bags everywhere, but like a hawk in the Zona 4 terminal.
There are numerous bus terminals in Guatemala City. The majority of 1st-class buses have their own offices and departure points around Zona 1. Hundreds of chicken buses for the south and west of Guatemala leave from the Zona 4 terminal, as well as local city buses. However, there was a plan, at the time of writing, to redirect all buses for the southern region to leave from Central sur, Col Villalobos. International buses (see below) have their offices scattered about the city. (The cheaper Salvador buses leave from near the Zona 4 terminal.) The Zona 4 bus terminal has to be the dirtiest and grimmest public area in the whole of the city.
The main destinations with companies operating from Guatemala City are:
Antigua, every 15 mins, 1 hr, US$1, until 2000 from Av 23 and 3 Calle, Zona 3. To **Chimaltenango** and **Los Encuentros**, from 1 Av between 3 y 4. Calle, Zona 7. **Chichicastenango** hourly from 0500-1800, 3 hrs, US$2.20 with **Veloz Quichelense**. **Huehuetenango**, with Los Halcones, Calzada Roosevelt, 37-47, Zona 11, T2439-2780, 0700, 1400, 1700, US$7, 5 hrs, and **Transportes Velásquez**, Calzada Roosevelt 9-56, Zona 7, T2440-3316, 0800-1630, every 30 mins, 5 hrs, US$7. For La Mesilla, see below.
Panajachel, with Transportes Rebulí, 41 Calle, between 6 y 7 Av, Zona 8, T2230-2748, hourly from 0530-1530, 3 hrs, US$2.20; also to **San Lucas Tolimán**

0530-1530, 3 hrs US$2.10 **San Pedro La Laguna** with Transportes Méndez, 41 C, between 6 y and Av, Zona 8, 1300, 4 hrs. **Santiago Atitlán**, with various companies, from 4 C, between 3 y 4 Av, Zona 12, 0400-1700, every 30 mins, 4 hrs, US$4.

Quetzaltenango (Xela) and **San Marcos**. 1st-class bus to Xela with Transportes Alamo, 12 Av "A", 0-65, Zona 7, T2471-8626, from 0800-1730, 6 daily 4 hrs, US$7. Líneas Américas, 2 Av, 18-47, Zona 1, T2232-1432, 0500-1930, 7 daily, US$7. Galgos, 7 Av, 19-44, Zona 1, T2232-3661, between 0530-1700, 5 daily, 4 hrs, US$7 to **Tapachula** in Mexico through the El Carmen border. Marquensita, 1 Av, 21-31, Zona 1, T2230-0067. From 0600-1700, 8 a day, US$6.10, to Xela and on to San Marcos. To **Tecpán**, with Transportes Poaquileña, 1 Av corner of 3 and 4 Calle, Zona 7, 0530-1900, every 15 mins, 2 hrs, US$1.20.

To **Santa Cruz del Quiché**, Sololá and Totonicapán, buses depart from 41 Calle between 6 and 7 Av, Zona 8.

To **Biotopo del Quetzal** and **Cobán**, 3½ hrs and 4½ hrs respectively, hourly from 0400-1700, US$6 and US$7.50, with Escobar y Monja Blanca, 8 Av, 15-16, Zona 1, T2238-1409. **Zacapa**, **Chiquimula** (for **El Florido**, Honduran border) and **Esquipulas** with Rutas Orientales, 19 Calle, 8-18, Zona 1, T2253-7282, every 30 mins 0430-1800. To **Zacapa**, 3¼ hrs, to **Chiquimula**, 3½ hrs, to **Esquipulas**, 4½ hrs, US$6.

Puerto Barrios, with Transportes Litegua, 15 Calle, 10-40, Zona 1, T2220-8840, www.litegua.com, 0430-1900, 31 a day, 5 hrs, US$6.80, 1st class US$12 and **Río Dulce**, 0600, 0900, 1130, 5 hrs, US$6.20.

El Petén with Fuente del Norte (same company as Líneas Máxima de Petén), 17 Calle, 8-46, Zona 1, T2251-3817, going to **Río Dulce** and **Santa Elena/Flores**. There are numerous departures 24 hrs; 5 hrs to Río Dulce, US$6.50; to Santa Elena, 9-10 hrs, US$12; buses vary in quality and price, breakdowns not unknown. The 1000 and 2130 departures are a luxury bus Maya

del Oro with snacks, US$18, the advantage being it doesn't stop at every tree to pick up passengers. Línea Dorada, 16 Calle, 10-03, Zona 1, T2220-7990, www.tikalmayan world.com, at 1000, US$16 to **Flores**, 8 hrs and on to **Melchor de Mencos**, 10 hrs. To **Santa Elena** ADN, 8 Av, 16-41, Zona 1, T2251-0050, www.adnautobuses delnorte.com, luxury service, 2100 and 2200, returns at 2100 and 2300, US$19, toilets, TV and snacks.

To **Jalapa** with Unidos Jalapanecos, 22 Calle 1-20, Zona 1, T2251-4760, 0430-1830, every 30 mins, 3 hrs, US$2.50 and with Transportes Melva Nacional, T2332-6081, 0415-1715, every 30 mins, 3 hrs 30 mins, US$2.50. Buses also from the Zona 4 terminal. To **San Pedro Pinula** between 0500-1800.

To **Chatia Gomerana**, 4 Calle y 8 Av, Zona 12, to **La Democracia**, every 30 mins from 0600-1630 via Escuintla and Siquinala, 2 hrs. Transportes Cubanita to **Reserva Natural de Monterrico** (La Avellana), 4 Calle y 8 Av, Zona 12, at 1030, 1230, 1420, 3 hrs, US$2.50. To **Puerto San José** and **Iztapa**, from the same address, 0430-1645 every 15 mins, 1 hr. To **Retalhuleu** (Reu on bus signs) with Transportes Fortaleza del Sur, Calzada Aguilar Batres, 4-15, Zona 12, T22230-3390, between 0010-1910 every 30 mins via Escuintla, Cocales and Mazatenango, 3 hrs, US$6.80. Numerous buses to **Santa Lucía Cotzumalguapa** go from the Zona 4 bus terminal.

International buses
Reserve the day before if you can. Taking a bus from Guatemala City as far as, say, San José, is tiring and tiresome (the bus company's bureaucracy and the hassle from border officials all take their toll).

To **Honduras** avoiding El Salvador, take a bus to **Esquipulas**, then a minibus to the border. Hedman Alas, 2 Av, 8-73, Zona 10, T2362-5072, www.hedmanalas.com, to **Copán** via El Florido, at 0500 and 0900, 5 hrs, US$30. Also goes on to **San Pedro**

Sulas, US$45, and **La Ceiba**, US$52. Pullmantur to **Tegucigalpa** daily at 0700 via San Salvador, US$66 and US$94. **Ticabus** to **San Pedro Sula**, US$34 and **Tegucigalpa**, US$34 via San Salvador. **Rutas Orientales**, 19 C, 8-18, T2253-7282 goes to **Honduras** at 0530 via Agua Caliente, 8 hrs, US$28.

To **Mexico** with **Trans Galgos Inter**, 7 Av, 19-44, Zona 1, T2223-3661, www.transgalgos inter.com.gt to **Tapachula** via **El Carmen**, 0730, 1330, and 1500, 7 hrs. **Línea Dorada**, address above, to **Tapachula** at 0800, US$24. **Transportes Velásquez**, 20 Calle, 1-37, Zona 1, T2221-1084, 0800-1100, hourly to **La Mesilla**, 7 hrs, US$5. **Transportes Fortaleza del Sur**, Calzada Aguilar Batres, 4-15, Zona 12, T2230-3390 to **Ciudad Tecún Umán**, 0130, 0300, 0330, 0530 via **Retalhuleu**, 5 hrs.

To **Chetumal** via **Belize City**, with **Línea Dorada** change to a minibus in Flores. Leaves 1000, 2100, 2200 and 2230, 2 days, US$42. Journey often takes longer than advertised due to Guatemala–Belize and Belize–Mexico border crossings.

To **El Salvador** via **Valle Nuevo**, border crossing, with **Ticabus**, 0600 and 1300 daily to San Salvador, US$17 1st class, 5 hrs. From **Ticabus** terminal, Calzada Aguilar Batres 22-25, T2473-0633, www.ticabus.com, clean, safe, with waiting area, café, toilets, no luggage deposit.

Shuttles
Shuttles are possible between Guatemala City and all other destinations, but it's a case of reserving them first. Contact shuttle operators in Antigua (see Antigua Transport, page 236). Guatemala City to **Antigua**, US$15, **Panajachel** US$30, Chichicastenango US$30, **Copán Ruinas**, US$40, **Cobán** US$30 and **Quetzaltenango**, US$25.

Car
Car hire companies Hertz, at the airport, T2470-3800, www.hertz.com. **Budget**, at the airport; also at 6 Av, 11-24, Zona 9, www.budget.co.uk. **Tabarini**, 2 Calle "A", 7-30,

Zona 10, T2331-2643, airport T2331-4755, www.tabarini.com. **Tally**, 7 Av, 14-60, Zona 1, T2232-0421, very competitive, have pickups. Recommended.

Car and motorcyle repairs Mike and Andy Young, 27 Calle, 13-73, Zona 5, T2331-9263, Mon-Fri 0700-1600. Excellent mechanics for all vehicles, extremely helpful. Honda motorcycle parts from **FA Honda**, Av Bolívar, 31-00, Zona 3, T2471-5232. Some staff speak English. Car and motorcycle parts from **FPK**, 5 Calle, 6-75, Zona 9, T2331-9777. **David González**, 32 Calle, 6-31, Zona 11, T5797-2486, for car, bike and bicycle repairs. Recommended.

Taxi
If possible call a taxi from your hotel or get someone to recommend a reliable driver; there are hundreds of illegal taxis in the city that should be avoided.

There are 3 types of taxis – **Rotativos**, **Estacionarios** and the ones that are metered, called **Taxis Amarillos**. *Rotativos* are everywhere in the city cruising the length and breadth of all zones. You will not wait more than a few mins for one to come along. They are numbered on their sides and on their back windscreen will be written TR (*Taxi Rotativo*) followed by 4 numbers. Most of them have a company logo stamped on the side as well. *Estacionarios* also have numbers on the sides but are without logo. On their back windscreen they have the letters TE (*Taxi Estacionario*) followed by 4 numbers. They are to be found at bus terminals and outside hotels or in other important places. They will always return to these same waiting points (good to know if you leave something in a taxi). Do not get in a taxi that does not have either of these labels on its back windscreen. *Rotativos* and *Estacionarios* are unmetered, but *Estacionarios* will always charge less than *Rotativos*. The fact that both are unmetered will nearly always work to your advantage because of traffic delays.

You will be quoted an inflated price by *Rotativos* by virtue of being a foreigner. *Estacionarios* are fairer. It is about US$8 from the airport to Zona 1. From Zona 1 to 4 is about US$4. The metered *Taxi Amarillo* also moves around but less so than the *Rotativos*, as they are more on call by phone. They only take a couple of minutes to come. **Amarillo Express**, T2332-1515, are 24 hr.

Directory

Guatemala City *p208, maps p209, p210 and p212*

Banks

The legal street exchange for cash may be found on 7 Av, between 12 and 14 Calle, near the post office (Zona 1), but be careful; don't go alone. Banks change US dollars into quetzales at the free rate, but actual rates and commission charges vary; if you have time, shop around. **Banco Industrial**, Av 7, opposite the central post office, Visa cards only, Mon-Fri 0900-1530. **Bancared**, near Parque Centanario on 6 Calle and 4 Av has 24-hr ATM for Visa/Cirrus. **Lloyds Bank plc**, 6 Av, 9-51, Zona 9, Edif Gran Vía, also at 14 Calle and 4 Av, Zona 10, with ATM. Mon-Fri 0900-1500. **Banco Uno**, 10 Calle, 5-40, Visa and ATM. Mon-Fri 0930-1730, Sat 1000-1300. Quetzales may be bought with MasterCard at **Credomatic**, beneath the Bar Europa, at 11 Calle, 5-6 Av, Zona 1. Mon-Sat 0800-1900. MasterCard ATM also at **Banco Internacional**, Av La Reforma and 16 Calle, Zona 10. **Western Union**, T2360-1737, collect T1-800-360-1737.

Embassies and consulates

Australia, Australians should report loss or theft of passports at the Canadian Embassy. Nearest Australian embassy is in Mexico. **Austria**, in Mexico (T+52) 55 52 510806, www.embajadadeaustria.com.mx. **Belgium**, in Costa Rica, T(+506) 225 6633. **Belize**, 5 Av 5-55, Zona 14, Europlaza Torre II, office 1502, T2367-3883. Mon-Fri 0900-1200, 1400-1600.

Canada, 13 Calle, 8-44, Zona 10, T2363-4348. Mon-Thu, 0800-1700, Fri 0800-1330. **Costa Rica**, 15 C 7-59, Zona 10, T2366-9918. Mon-Fri 0900-1400. **El Salvador**, Av de las Américas 16-46, Zona 13, T2360-7670. Mon-Fri 0800-1500. **France**, 5 Av, 8-59, Zona 14, Edif Cogefar, T2421-7370. Mon-Fri 0900-1200. **Germany**, 20 Calle, 6-20, Zona 10, T2364-6700. Mon-Fri 0900-1200. **Honduras**, 19 Av "A", 20-19, Zona 10, T2363-5495. Mon-Fri 0900-1700. **Israel**, 13 Av, 14-07, Zona 10, T2333-6951. Mon-Fri 0800-1600. **Japan**, Av La Reforma, 16-85, Zona 10, Edif Torre Internacional, T2367-2244. Mon-Fri 0930-1230, 1400-1630. **Mexico**, 2 Av, 7-57, Zona 10, T2420-3430. Mon-Fri 0900-1300, 1400-1700. **Netherlands** 16 Calle, 0-55, Zona 10, T2381-4300. Mon-Fri 0800-1700. **Nicaragua**, 10 Av, 14-72, Zona 10, T2368-0785. Mon-Fri 0900-1300. **Panama**, 12 Av, 2-65, Zona 14, T2366-3331. Mon-Fri 0900-1400. **Spain**, 6 Calle, 6-48, Zona 9, T2379-3530. Mon-Fri 0800-1400. **Switzerland**, 16 Calle, 0-55, Zona 10, Edif Torre Internacional, 14th floor, T2367-5520. Mon-Fri 0900-1130. **UK**, 16 Calle, 0-55, Zona 10, T2367-5425-29. Embassy open Mon-Thu 0800-1230, 1330-1700, Fri 0800-1200. Consulate Mon-Thu 0830-1200, Fri 0830-1100. **USA**, Av La Reforma, 7-01, Zona 10, T2326-4000, http://guatemala.usembassy.gov, Mon-Fri 0800-1700.

Emergency

T128 for ambulance, T122 for the fire brigade (*bomberos*) who also get called to accidents.

Immigration

Immigration office Dirección General de Migración, 6 Av, 3-11, Zona 4, T2411-2411. For extensions of visas. If you need new entry stamps in a replacement passport (ie if one was stolen), a police report is required, plus a photocopy and a photocopy of your passport. They also need to know your date and point of entry to check their records.

Internet
There's an internet café in **Edificio Geminis** in Zona 10.

Medical services
Doctors Dr Boris Castillo Camino, 6 Av, 7-55, Zona 10, Of 17, T2334-5932. 0900-1230, 1430-1800. Recommended.
Dentists Centro Médico, 6 Av, 3-47, Zona 10, T2332-3555, English spoken by some staff.
Hospitals Hospital de las Américas, 10a. Calle 2-31, Zona 14, T2384-3535,

info@hospitalesdeguatemala.com.
Private hospital, must be able to demonstrate you have funds for treatment. **Roosevelt Hospital**, Calzada Roosevelt, Zona 11, T2471-1441. Public hospital affiliated with University San Carlos School of Medicine.
Opticians Optico Popular, 11 Av, 13-75, Zona 1, T2238-3143, excellent for repairs.

Post
The main post office is at 7 Av and 12 Calle, Zona 1. Mon-Fri 0830-1700.

Antigua and around

→ *Colour map 2, C2.*
Antigua is rightly one of Guatemala's most popular destinations. It overflows with colonial architecture and fine churches on streets that are linked by squat houses, painted in ochre shades and topped with terracotta tiles, basking in the fractured light of the setting sun. Antigua is a very attractive city and is the cultural centre of Guatemala; arts flourish here. Maya women sit in their colourful clothes amid the ruins and in the Parque Central. In the late-afternoon light, buildings such as Las Capuchinas are beautiful, and in the evening the cathedral is wonderfully illuminated as if by candlelight. Around Antigua are a cluster of archaeological sites, highland villages and volcanoes to explore. ►► *See listings, pages 230-238.*

Ins and outs

Getting around *Avenidas* run north to south and *calles* run from east to west. House numbers do not give any clue about how far from the Parque Central a particular place is. ►► *See Transport, page 236.*

Tourist information **INGUAT office** ① *2a C Ote,11 (between Av 2 and Av 3 Norte), Mon-Fri 0800-1700, Sat and Sun 0900-1700, T7832-3782, info-antigua@inguat.gob.gt, www.visitguatemala.com*, is very helpful, with maps and information; occasional exhibitions in rooms around courtyard behind office. Information available about volunteer work. English, Italian and a little German spoken. The monthly magazine *The Revue* is a useful source of tourist information in English with articles, maps, events and advertisements; it's free and widely available in hotels and restaurants.

Safety Unfortunately, despite its air of tranquillity, Antigua is not without unpleasant incidents. Take care and advice from the tourist office on where to go or not to go. There are numerous tourist police (green uniforms) who are helpful and conspicuous; their office is at 4 Avenida Norte at the side of the Municipal Palace. If you wish to go to Cerro de la Cruz (see page 226), or the cemetery, they will escort you, leaving 1000 and 1500 daily. Antigua is generally safe at night, but it's best to keep to the well-lit area near the centre. Report incidents to police and the tourist office. Tourist assistance 24 hours, T2421-2810. ►► *See also page 205.*

Background

Until it was heavily damaged by an earthquake in 1773, Antigua was the capital city. Founded in 1543, after the destruction of an even earlier capital, Ciudad Vieja, it grew to be the finest city in Central America, with numerous great churches, a university (1676), a printing press (founded 1660), and a population of around 50,000, including many famous sculptors, painters, writers and craftsmen.

Antigua has consistently been damaged by earthquakes. Even when it was the capital, buildings were frequently destroyed and rebuilt, usually in a grander style, until the final cataclysm in 1773. For many years it was abandoned, and most of the accumulated treasures were moved to Guatemala City. Although it slowly repopulated in the 19th century, little was done to prevent further collapse of the main buildings until late in the 20th century when the value of the remaining monuments was finally appreciated. Since 1972, efforts to preserve what was left have gained momentum, and it is now a UNESCO World Heritage Site. The major earthquake of 1976 was a further setback, but you will see many sites that are busy with restoration, preservation or simple clearing. If the city was not treasure enough, the setting is truly memorable. Volcán Agua (3766 m) is due south and the market is to the west, behind which hang the imposing peaks of Volcán Acatenango (3976 m) and Volcán Fuego (3763 m), which still emits the occasional column of ash as a warning of the latent power within.

Sights

In the centre of the city is the **Parque Central**, the old Plaza Real, where bullfights and markets were held in the early days. The present park was constructed in the 20th century though the fountain dates back to the 18th century. The **cathedral** ① *US$0.40*, to the east, dates from 1680 (the first cathedral was demolished in 1669). Much has been destroyed since then and only two of the many original chapels are now in use. The remainder can be visited. The **Palacio de los Capitanes Generales** is to the south. The original building dates from 1558, was virtually destroyed in 1773, was partly restored in the 20th century, and now houses police and government offices. The **Cabildo**, or **Municipal Palace**, is to the north and an arcade of shops to the west. You can climb to the second floor for a great view of the volcanoes (Monday to Friday 0800-1600). The **Museo de Santiago** ① *Tue-Fri 0900-1600, Sat-Sun 0900-1200, 1400-1600, US$4*, is in the municipal offices to the north of the plaza, as is the **Museo del Libro Antiguo** ① *same hours and price*, which contains a replica of a 1660 printing press (the original is in Guatemala City), old documents and a collection of 16th- to 18th-century books (1500 volumes in the library). The **Museo de Arte Colonial** ① *Tue-Fri 0900-1600, Sat-Sun 0900-1200, 1400-1600, US$4*, is half a block from Parque Central at Calle 5 Oriente, in the building where the San Carlos University was first housed. It now has mostly 17th- to 18th-century religious art, well laid out in large airy rooms around a colonial patio.

Hotel Casa Santo Domingo is one of Antigua's most beautiful sights – a converted old Dominican church and also monastery property. Archaeological excavations have turned up some unexpected finds at the site. During the cleaning out of a burial vault in September 1996, one of the greatest finds in Antigua's history was unearthed. The vault had been filled with rubble, but care had been taken in placing stones a few feet away from the painted walls. The scene is in the pristine colours of natural red and blue, and depicts Christ, the Virgin Mary, Mary Magdalene and John the Apostle. It was painted in

Antigua

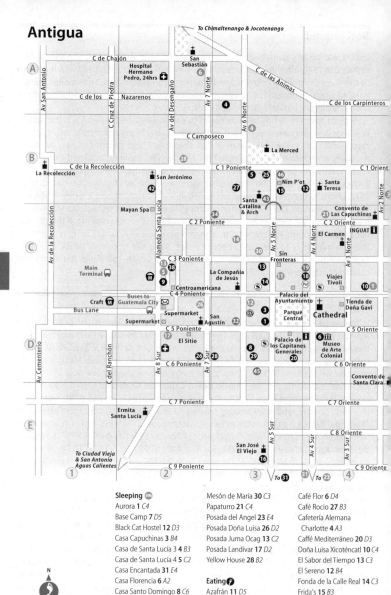

Sleeping 🛏
Aurora **1** C4
Base Camp **7** D5
Black Cat Hostel **12** D3
Casa Capuchinas **3** B4
Casa de Santa Lucía 3 **4** B3
Casa de Santa Lucía 4 **5** C2
Casa Encantada **31** E4
Casa Florencia **6** A2
Casa Santo Domingo **8** C6
El Descanso **11** C3
Jungle Party Hostal **14** C3
Las Camelias Inn **2** C5

Mesón de María **30** C3
Papaturro **21** C4
Posada del Angel **23** E4
Posada Doña Luisa **26** D2
Posada Juma Ocag **13** C2
Posada Landivar **17** D2
Yellow House **28** B2

Eating 🍴
Azafrán **11** D5
Bagel Barn **1** D3
Café Barroco **2** C5
Café Condesa **3** D3

Café Flor **6** D4
Café Rocio **27** B3
Cafetería Alemana
  Charlotte **4** A3
Caffé Mediterráneo **20** D3
Doña Luisa Xicoténcatl **10** C4
El Sabor del Tiempo **13** C3
El Sereno **12** B4
Fonda de la Calle Real **14** C3
Frida's **15** B3
Hector's **5** B3
Helas Taberna Griega **18** C4
La Antigua Viñería **16** E3

To Cerro de la Cruz   To Guatemala City

C de la Candelaria

♦ La Candelaria

♦ Santa Rosa

Plazuela
Santa Rosa

C de la Beatas Indias

C de los Duelos

♦ Santo Domingo

Av 1 Norte

C 3 Oriente

C 4 Oriente

♦ La Concepción

C del Hermano Pedro

Av 1 Sur

C de los Pasos

♦ San
Francisco

C del Hermano Pedro

♦ Santa Cruz

To Escuela
de Cristo &
El Calvario

To Santa Isabel, San Juan
del Obispo & Santa María
de Jesús

La Casa de los Mixtas **38** *C2*
La Casserole **41** *C5*
Peroleto **42** *B2*
Quesos y Vinos **25** *B3*
Rainbow Café &
  Travel Center **26** *D2*
Sabe Rico **8** *D3*
Típico Antigüeño **9** *C2*
Tostaduría Antigua **28** *D3*
Travel Menu **29** *D3*
Vivero y Café de
  la Escalonia **31** *E3*

Bars & clubs 🍸
Café 2000 **32** *D3*
Casbah **43** *B3*
La Chiminea **34** *C3*
La Sala **45** *D3*
Reilly's Irish Pub **46** *B3*
Riki's **19** *C4*

1683, and was only discovered with the help of ultraviolet light. Within the monastery grounds are the **Colonial Art Museum**, with displays of Guatemalan baroque imagery and silverware and the **Pre-Columbian Art Museum, Glass Museum, Museum of Guatemalan Apothecary** and the **Popular Art and Handicrafts of Sacatepequez Museum** ⓘ *3 Calle Ote 28, 0900-1700, US$5 for each museum.*

There are many fine colonial religious buildings: 22 churches, 14 convents and 11 monasteries, most ruined by earthquakes and in various stages of restoration. Top of the list are the cloisters of the convent of **Las Capuchinas** ⓘ *2 Av Norte y 2 Calle Ote, 0900-1700, US$3.90,* with immensely thick round pillars (1736) adorned with bougainvillea. The church and convent of **San Francisco** ⓘ *1 Av Sur y 7 Calle Ote, 0800-1200, 1400-1700, US$0.40,* with the tomb of Hermano Pedro, is much revered by all the local communities. He was canonized in 2002. The church has been restored and now includes the **Museo de Hermano Pedro** ⓘ *Tue-Sun 0900-1200, 1300-1630, US$0.40.* The convent of **Santa Clara** ⓘ *6 Calle Ote y 2 Av Sur, 0900-1700, US$3.90,* was founded in about 1700 and became one of the biggest in Antigua, until the nuns were forced to move to Guatemala City. The adjoining garden is an oasis of peace. **El Carmen** ⓘ *3 Calle Ote y 3 Av Norte*, has a beautiful façade with strikingly ornate columns, tastefully illuminated at night, but the rest of the complex is in ruins. Likewise **San Agustín** ⓘ *5 Calle Pte y 7 Av Norte*, was once a fine building, but only survived intact from 1761 to 1773; earthquake destruction continued until the final portion of the vault collapsed in 1976, leaving an impressive ruin. **La Compañía de Jesús** ⓘ *3 Calle Pte y 6 Av Norte, 0930-1700,* at one time covered the whole block. The church is closed for restoration but you can access the rest of the ruins from 6 Avenida Norte.

The church and cloisters of **Escuela de Cristo** ① *Calle de los Pasos y de la Cruz,* a small independent monastery (1720-1730), have survived and were restored between 1940 and 1960. The church is simple and has some interesting original artwork. **La Recolección** ① *Calle de la Recolección, 0900-1700, US$3.90,* despite being a late starter (1700), became one of the biggest and finest of Antigua's religious institutions. It is now the most awe-inspiring ruin in the city. **San Jerónimo** ① *Calle de la Recolección, 0900-1700, US$3.90,* was a school (early 1600s) for La Merced, three blocks away, but later became the local customs house. There is an impressive fountain in the courtyard. **La Merced** ① *1 Calle Pte y 6 Av Norte, 0800-1700,* with its white and yellow façade dominates the surrounding plaza. The church (1767) and cloisters were built with earthquakes in mind and survived better than most. The church remains in use and the **cloisters** ① *US$0.80,* are being further restored. Antigua's finest fountain is in the courtyard. **Santa Teresa** ① *4 Av Norte,* was a modest convent, but the church walls and the lovely west front have survived. It is now the city's men's prison.

Other ruins including **Santa Isabel**, **Santa Cruz**, **La Candelaria**, **San José El Viejo** and **San Sebastián** are to be found round the edges of the city, and there is an interesting set of the Stations of the Cross, each a small chapel, from San Francisco to **El Calvario** church, which was where Pedro de Betancourt (Hermano Pedro) worked as a gardener and planted an esquisuchil tree. He was also the founder of the **Belén Hospital** in 1661, which was destroyed in 1773. However, some years later, his name was given to the **San Pedro Hospital**, which is one block south of the Parque Central.

There is a fabulous panorama from the **Cerro de la Cruz**, which is 15 minutes' walk from the northern end of town along 1 Avenida Norte.

Around Antigua → *For listings, see pages 230-238.*

Ciudad Vieja – the former capital – is 5.5 km southwest of Antigua at the foot of Volcán Agua. In 1527, Pedro de Alvarado moved his capital, known then as Santiago de Los Caballeros, from Iximché to San Miguel Escobar, now a suburb of Ciudad Vieja. On 11 September 1541, after days of torrential rain, an immense mudslide came down the mountain and swallowed up the city. Alvarado's widow, Doña Beatriz de la Cueva, newly elected governor after his death, was among those drowned. Today Ciudad Vieja is itself a suburb of Antigua, but with a handsome church, founded in 1534, and one of the oldest in Central America. There's a fiesta on December 8. Between Ciudad Vieja and San Miguel de las Dueñas is the **Valhalla macadamia nut farm** ① *T7831-5799, www.exvalhalla.net, free visits and nut tasting, 0800-1700.*

About 3 km northwest of Ciudad Vieja is **San Antonio Aguas Calientes**. The hot springs unfortunately disappeared with recent earthquakes, but the village has many small shops selling locally made textiles. **Carolina's Textiles** is recommended for a fine selection, while on the exit road **Alida** has a shop. You can watch the weavers in their homes by the roadside. Local fiestas are 16-21 January, Corpus Christi (a moveable feast celebtrated around June) and 1 November.

Beyond San Juan del Obispo, beside Volcán Agua, is the charming village of **Santa María de Jesús**, with its beautiful view of Antigua. In the early morning there are good views of all three volcanoes from 2 km back down the road towards Antigua. Colourful *huípiles* are worn, made and sold from a couple of stalls, or ask at the shops on the plaza. The local fiesta is on 10 January.

Just north of Antigua is **Jocotenango**. The music museum, **Casa K'ojom** ⓘ *Mon-Fri 0830-1630, Sat 0830-1600, US$4*, is in the **Central Cultural La Azotea**, with displays of traditional Maya and colonial-era instruments. The village also has public saunas at the **Fraternidad Naturista Antigua**.

Five kilometres beyond San Lucas Sacatepéquez, at Km 29.5, Carretera Roosevelt (the Pan-American Highway), is **Santiago Sacatepéquez**, whose fiesta on 1 November, *Día de los Muertos* (All Souls' Day), is characterized by colourful kite-flying (*barriletes*). They also celebrate 25 July. Market days are Wednesday and Friday.

Visiting a **coffee farm** is an interesting short excursion. **Tour Finca Los Nietos** ⓘ *on the outskirts of Antigua, near the Iglesia San Felipe de Jesús, T7728-0812, www.filadelfiaresort.com,* runs two-hour tours (US$18) three times a day. They are very informative and interesting with expert multilingual guides, in beautiful manicured grounds and restored colonial buildings; also with restaurant and shop.

North of Guatemala City is **Mixco Viejo**, the excavated site of a post-Classic Maya fortress, which spans 14 hilltops, including 12 groups of pyramids. Despite earthquake damage it is worth a visit and is recommended. It was the 16th-century capital of the Pokomam Maya.

Volcanoes → *For listings, see pages 230-238.*

Each of the four volcanoes that are immediately accessible from Antigua provides a unique set of challenges and rewards. Agua, Fuego and Acatenango volcanoes directly overlook Antigua whilst Volcan Pacaya is about an hour's drive away. All of these volcanoes can be experienced either as part of a day trip (a cheaper and faster option that requires only lightweight packs) or with an overnight excursion (heavier packs making climbing times longer, but with better light conditions for lava viewing and enhancing already spectacular views with beautiful sunset and sunrises). Whatever option you choose, it is important to prepare properly for the unique features of each volcano (Pacaya is a relatively quick climb in a secure national park, while the three volcanoes on Antigua's perimeter are longer climbs with much greater risk of robberies and attacks). At a minimum, ensure that you have appropriate clothing and footwear (as summits are cold and volcanic ash is sharp bring fleeces and ideally use climbing boots), enough water (very important) and snacks for the trip and make informed decisions about safety (although you can climb each of these volcanoes independently, you will significantly decrease your risks of getting lost, attacked or not finding shelter by using a professional guiding service – **Outdoor Excursions (OX)**, which runs trips with expert guides and armed security, is particularly recommended). Remember that altitude takes its toll and for the longer hikes it is important to start early in the morning to allow enough time to ascend and descend in daylight. As a general rule, descents take from a third to a half of the ascent time.

Volcán Pacaya

ⓘ *Tours are available for US$6 upwards and are sold in most tour companies in Antigua. The popular and best time for organized trips is to leave Antigua at 1300 and return at 2100. Departures also 0600 returning 1300. There is also a US$3.50 fee to be paid at the entrance to the Volcán Pacaya National Park in San Francisco de Sales (toilets available).*

At 2552 m, the still-active Volcán Pacaya can't be missed and is the most exciting volcano to climb. Pacaya has erupted about 20 times since 1565, but since the mid-1960s it has been continuously active, meaning it can reward climbers with some spectacular lava

Semana Santa

This week-long event is a spectacular display of religious ritual and floral design. Through billowing clouds of incense, accompanied by music, processions of floats carried by purple-robed men make their way through the town. The cobbled stones are covered in *alfombras* (carpets) of coloured sawdust and flowers.

The day before the processions leave from each church, Holy Vigils (*velaciones*) are held, and the sculpture to be carried is placed before the altar (*retablo*), with a backdrop covering the altar. Floats (*andas*) are topped by colonial sculptures of the cross-carrying Christ. He wears velvet robes of deep blue or green, embroidered with gold and silver threads, and the float is carried on the shoulders by a team of 80 men (*cucuruchos*), who heave and sway their way through the streets for as long as 12 hours. The processions, arranged by a religious brotherhood (*cofradía*), are accompanied by banner and incense carriers, centurions, and a loud brass band.

The largest processions with some of the finest carpets are on **Palm Sunday** and **Good Friday**. Not to be missed are: the procession leaving from **La Merced** on **Palm Sunday** at 1200-1300; the procession leaving the church of **San Francisco** on **Maundy Thursday**; the 0200 sentencing of Jesus and 0600 processions from **La Merced** on **Good Friday**; the crucifixion of Christ in front of the **cathedral** at noon on **Good Friday**; and the beautiful, candlelit procession of the crucified Christ which passes the **Parque Central** between 2300 and midnight on **Good Friday**.

This is the biggest Easter attraction in Latin America so accommodation is booked far ahead. If you plan to be here and haven't reserved a room, arrive a few days before Palm Sunday. If unsuccessful, commuting from Guatemala City is an option. Don't rush; each procession lasts up to 12 hours. The whole week is a fantastic opportunity for photographs – and if you want a decent picture remember the Christ figure always faces right. Arm yourself with a map (available in kiosks in the Parque Central) and follow the processional route before the procession to see all the carpets while they are still intact. (There are also processions into Antigua from surrounding towns every Sunday in Lent.)

flows. The cone – now split in two since the most recent eruption, in 2010 – is covered in black basaltic rock, shed from the crater. The rocks get warm and are lethally sharp. One of the results of the eruption is that shallow tunnels have formed, creating natural open-air saunas. They offer quite a spectacular experience, though for obvious safety reasons you should only enter these at the advice of an experience guide. Take torch/flashlight refreshments and water and – it may sound obvious – wear boots or trainers, not sandals. Walking sticks are also offered at the park entrance – don't be too proud, on the steeper slopes, the crumbly lava screes can be very tricky to climb up or down. If you bring marshmallows to toast on the lava, make sure you have a long stick – lava is (rather unsurprisingly) very hot! Security officers go with the trips and police escorts ensure everyone leaves the area after dark. Check the situation in advance for **camping** (well below the crater lip). Sunrise comes with awesome views over the desolate black lava field to the distant Pacific (airborne dust permitting) and the peaks of Fuego, Acatenango and Agua. And as the sun sets on the horizon, Agua is silhouetted in the distance, a weak orange line streaked behind it.

Volcán Agua

ⓘ *Most organized tours with Antigua tour operators are during the day – you should enure that costs include both a guide and security. Trips normally leave Antigua about 0500.*

At 3760 m, Agua is the easiest but least scenic of the three volcanoes overlooking Antiqua. The trail, which can be quite littered, begins at **Santa María de Jesús**. Speak to Aurelio Cuy Chávez at the **Posada El Oasis**, who offers a guide service or take a tour with a reputable agency. You have to register first at the Municipalidad; guides are also available in the main square, about US$50 a day per guide. For Agua's history, see Ciudad Vieja. The crater has a small shelter (none too clean), which was a shrine, and about 10 antennae. There are great views of Volcán Fuego. It's a three- to five-hour climb if you are fit, and at least two hours down. To get the best views before the clouds cover the summit, it is best to stay at the radio station at the top. Agua can also be climbed from **Alotenango**, a village between Agua and Fuego, south of Ciudad Vieja. It's 9 km from Antigua and its name means 'place surrounded by corn'. Alotenango has a fiesta from 18-20 January.

Volcán Acatenango

ⓘ *If you do this climb independently of a tour agency, ask for a guide in La Soledad. However, it is strongly recommended that you use a professional guiding service, ideally with security.*

Acatenango is classified as a dormant volcano and is the third tallest in the country (3975 m) with two peaks to its name. Its first recorded eruption was in 1924. Two other eruptions were reported in 1924-1927 and 1972. The best trail heads south at **La Soledad**, 2300 m (15 km west of Ciudad Vieja), which is 300 m before the road (Route 5) turns right to Acatenango (see Sleeping). A small plateau, La Meseta on maps, known locally as **El Conejón**, provides a good camping site half way up (three or four hours). From here it is a further three or four hours' harder going to the top. The views of the nearby (lower) active crater of Fuego are excellent.

Volcán Fuego

ⓘ *This is an active volcano with trails that are easy to lose – it is recommended that you use a guiding service and do not venture up to the crater.*

This volcano (3763 m) can be climbed via Volcán Acatenango, sleeping between the two volcanoes, then climbing for a further two to three hours before stopping a safe distance from the crater. This one is for experienced hikers only. Do not underestimate the amount of water needed for the climb. It is a seven-hour ascent with a significant elevation gain – it's a very hard walk, both up and down. There are steep, loose cinder slopes, which are very tedious, in many places. It is possible to camp about three-quarters of the way up in a clearing. Fuego has regular eruptions that shoot massive boulders from its crater – often without warning. Check in Antigua before attempting to climb. If driving down towards the south coast you can see the red volcanic rock it has thrown up.

Hotel and guesthouse prices

LL over US$200	**L** US$151-200	**AL** US$101-150
A US$66-100	**B** US$46-65	**C** US$31-45
D US$21-30	**E** US$12-20	**F** US$7-11
G under US$7		

Restaurant prices

₮₮₮ over US$15	₮₮ US$8-15	₮ under US$8

See pages 31-33 for further information.

● Sleeping

Antigua *p222, map p224*

In the better hotels, advance reservations are advised for weekends and Dec-Apr. During Holy Week, hotel prices are significantly higher, sometimes double for the more expensive hotels. In the Jul-Aug period, find your accommodation early in the day.

LL Posada del Angel, 4 Av Sur 24-A, T7832-5303, www.posadadelangel.com. Breakfast included, dining room, exercise pool, fireplaces, 5 suites individually decorated, roof terrace, romantic, exclusive and private. Bill Clinton once stayed here.

LL-AL Casa Santo Domingo, 3 Calle Ote 28, T7820-1220, www.casasanto domingo.com.gt. This is a beautifully designed hotel with 126 rooms in the ruins of a 17th-century convent with prehispanic archaeological finds, with good service, beautiful gardens, a magical pool, good restaurant with breakfast included. Worth seeing just to dream. See Sights, page 223.

LL-AL Hotel Mesón de María, 3 Calle Pte 8, T7832-6068, www.hotelmesondemaria.com. Great little place with a wonderful roof terrace. 20 stylish rooms are decorated with local textiles. Free internet and breakfast included at a local restaurant. Friendly and attentive service. Showers have large skylights.

LL-A Casa Encantada, 9 Calle Pte1, esq Av 4 Sur, T7832-7903, www.casaencantada-antigua.com. This sweet colonial boutique hotel with 10 rooms is a perfect retreat from the centre of Antigua. It has a small rooftop terrace where breakfast is served and a

comfortable sitting room with open fire, books, lilies and textile-lined walls. 2 rooms are accessed by stepping stones in a pond. The suite, with jacuzzi, enjoys views of the 3 volcanoes.

L-A Casa Capuchinas, 2 Av Norte 7, T7832-0121, www.casacapuchinas.com. 5 large, colonially furnished rooms, with fireplaces and massive beds, adjoining beautiful tiled bathrooms and special touches. A continental breakfast is included.

L-A Casa Florencia, 7 Av Norte 100, T7832-0261, www.cflorencia.net. A sweet little hotel enjoying views towards Volcán Agua. 11 rooms with all the usuals including safety box and kitchen for guests. The balcony has *cola de quetzal* plants lining it. Staff are very welcoming. Recommended.

L-A Las Camelias Inn, 3 Calle Ote 19, T/F7832-5780, www.cameliasinn.com. 16 rooms, some with bath. There's a small patio and balconies to hang out on. There are also 3 apartments for rent. Parking.

AL Aurora, 4 Calle Ote 16, T7832-0217, www.hotelauroraantigua.com. The oldest hotel in the city with old plumbing (but it works) and 1970s features. Quieter rooms face a patio overflowing with beautiful flowers. Continental breakfast included, English spoken.

B Papaturro, 2 Calle Ote 14, T7832-0445. Family atmosphere, rooms around attractive restaurant/bar area, run by a Salvadorean couple, 5 rooms, 1 with bath and mini kitchen, breakfast included, full board available, good deals for longer stays.

B Posada Landivar, 5 Calle Pte 23, close to the bus station, T7832-2962. Rooms with private bathroom and a/c. It's safe and in a good position. Discounts for longer stays. Parking. Recommended.

C El Descanso, 5 Av Norte 9, T7832-0142. Rents 4 clean rooms on the 2nd floor, with private bath. There's a family atmosphere here and the place is extremely friendly and welcoming.

C Posada Doña Luisa, 7 Av Norte 4, T7832-3414, posadadoluisa@hotmail.com. Near San Agustín church, good view of romantically lit ruins at night, a clean and very friendly place with a family atmosphere. It has 8 rooms with private bath and a small cafeteria. Parking.

D Casa de Santa Lucía No 3, 6 Av Norte, T7832-3302. There are 20 standard clean rooms here all with private bathrooms, towels, soap, hot water and free drinking water. Beautiful views of La Merced and Volcán de Fuego. Parking.

D Casa de Santa Lucía No 4, Alameda Sta Lucía Norte 5, T7832-3302. Way more attractive than Nos 2 and 3, with 30 rooms for the same price. Only 14 years old, it has been built in a colonial style, with dark wood columns and is decorated with large clay bowls in the patio. Parking.

D Posada Juma Ocag, 8 Av Norte 13 (Alameda Santa Lucía), T7832-3109. A small, but clean and nicely decorated hotel, using local textiles as bedspreads. It has an enclosed roof terrace, is quiet and friendly, shared bathrooms.

D Yellow House, 1 Calle Pte 24, T7832-6646. 8 clean rooms in this hostel run by the welcoming Ceci. Breakfast included. Colonial style, laundry service, free internet. 3 rooms with bath, kitchen, patio, parking. Recommended.

D-E Base Camp, 1 Av 4b, T7832-0074, www.basecamphostel.com. 6 dorm beds and 2 double rooms with lots of shared space. Runs adventure tours through **Outdoor Excursions**.

E Black Cat Hostel, 6 Av Norte 1, T7832-1229. A hostel with dorm rooms. Services include a bar, free breakfasts and DVD screenings. There's also an upmarket option at 9 Calle Ote 5, T7832-2187 with private rooms, free breakfast and a terrace bar.

E Jungle Party Hostal and Café, 6 Av Norte 20, T7832-0463, www.junglepartyhostal.com. Price per person. 33 beds spread across 6 rooms and 3 shared showers. Friendly management. Hot water, lockers, small patio, TV, free breakfast and movies. BBQ on Sat.

Apartments
Look on the notice boards in town. Rooms and apartments are available from about US$25 a week up to US$500 per month. One recommended family is **Estella López**, 1 Calle Pte 41A, T7832-1324, who offer board and lodging on a weekly basis. The house is clean, and the family friendly.

Around Antigua *p226*
F Pensión, Volcán Acatenango. Basic, with good cheap meals.

🍴 Eating

Antigua *p222, map p224*
For the cheapest of the cheap go to the stalls on the corner of 4 Calle Pte and 7 Av Norte, and those at the corner of 5 Calle Pte and 4 Av Sur. During the Easter period, the plaza in front of La Merced is transformed into a food market. At all these places you can pick up *elote, tortillas, tostadas* and *enchiladas*.

♥♥♥ Azafrán, La Casa de los Sueños, 1 Av Norte 1, T7832-5215. Tue-Sun 1200-1500, 1900- 2200. Serves international cuisine with tables on the patio. Recommended.

♥♥♥ El Sereno, 4 Av Norte 16, T7832-0501. Open 1200-1500, 1800-2300. International/ Italian cuisine. Grand entrance with massive heliconia plants in the courtyard. It has a lovely terrace bar up some stone steps and a cave for romantic dining; it's popular at weekends.

♥♥♥ La Casserole, Callejón de Concepción 7, T7832-0219 close to **Casa Santo Domingo**. Tue-Sat 1200-1500, 1900-2200, Sun 1200-1500, closed Mon. Sophisticated French cooking with fresh fish daily served at tables set in a beautiful courtyard, exclusive. Rigoberta Menchú dined with Jacques Chirac here.

♥♥♥-♥♥ Caffé Mediterráneo, 6 Calle Pte 6A, T7832-7180. Wed-Mon 1200-1500, 1830-2200. 1 block south of the plaza. Mouth-watering Italian cuisine with great candlelit ambience. Recommended.

♥♥♥-♥♥ Fonda de la Calle Real, 5 Av Norte 5 and No 12, T7832 0507, also at 3 Calle Pte 7 (which wins over the others for the setting). Its speciality is *queso fundido*. It also serves local dishes including *pepián* (and a vegetarian version) and *Kak-ik*, a Verapaz speciality.

¶¶ El Sabor del Tiempo, Calle del Arco and 3 Calle Poniente, T7832 0516. Good steaks, burgers, seafood and pasta in tastefully converted former warehouse, with polished wood and glass cabinets. A bit pricey but full of antiquey character.

¶¶ Frida's, 5 Av Norte 29, Calle del Arco, T7832-0504. Daily 1200-0100. Ochre and French navy colours decorate this restaurant's tribute to Mexico's famous female artist. It is quite dark inside but Frida memorabilia and colander-like lampshades lighten the interior. Efficient service. 2nd-floor pool table, Wed and Thu ladies' night.

¶¶ Hector's, 1 Calle Poniente No 9, 7832-9867. Small, busy and welcoming restaurant that serves wonderful food at good prices. Highly recommended.

¶¶ La Antigua Viñería, 5 Av Sur 34A, T7832-7370. Mon-Thu 1800-0100, Fri-Sun 1300-0100. Owned by Beppe Dángella, next door to San José ruins. Amazing photographic collection of clients in various stages of inebriation, excellent selection of wines and grappa, you name it. Very romantic, feel free to write your comments on the walls, very good food, pop in for a reasonably priced *queso fundido* and glass of wine if you can't afford the whole hog.

¶¶ Quesos y Vinos, Calle Poniente 1, T7832-7785. Wed-Mon 1200-1600, 1800-2200. Authentic Italian food and owners, good selection of wines, wood-fired pizza oven, sandwiches, popular.

¶¶ Sabe Rico, 6 Av Sur No 7, 7832-0648. Herb garden restaurant and fine-food deli that serves healthy, organic food in tranquil surroundings.

¶¶-¶ Café Flor, 4 Av Sur 1, T7832-5274. Full-on delicious Thai/Guatemalan-style and Tandoori food, delivered up between 1100-2300. The stir-fries are delicious, but a little overpriced. Discounts sometimes available. Friendly staff.

¶¶-¶ Café Rocio, 6 Av Norte 34. This is a palace of Asian food delight. Virtually everything on the menu is mouth-wateringly delicious. Don't leave without indulging in the *mora crisp*: hot blackberry sauce sandwiched between slices of vanilla ice cream! Highly recommended.

¶¶-¶ Helas Taberna Griega, 4 Av Norte 4, inside **La Escudilla**. Open 1800-0100, from 1300 weekends, closed Wed. Delicious food including pitta bread stuffed with goodies, Greek olives, tzatsiki, all surrounded by a Greek ruin and sea mural, fishing net and shells.

¶¶-¶ Rainbow Café, 7 Av Sur, on the corner of 6 Calle Pte. Consistently delicious vegetarian food served in a pleasant courtyard surrounded by hanging plants, good filling breakfasts, indulgent crêpes, popular, live music evenings, good book exchange. Bar at night with happy hour and ladies' nights. Recommended.

¶ In front of La Merced, in the back of the shop opposite La Merced, open until about 1900. Where local people eat it's ridiculously cheap, large proportions. Arrive respectfully and enjoy a real Guatemalan experience.

¶ La Casa de los Mixtas, 3 Calle Pte 3 Callejón 2A. Mon-Sat 0900-1900. Cheap Guatemalan fodder with a few tables on the pavement next to **Casa de Don Ismael**, good breakfasts, set lunch way above average, friendly family. Recommended.

¶ Típico Antigüeño, Alameda Sta Lucía 4, near the PO, T7832-5995. This locally run place offers an absolute bargain of a *menú del día* (fish, chicken), which includes soup and sometimes a drink. It is extremely popular and can get ridiculously busy, so best to turn up before 1300 for lunch. Recommended.

¶ Travel Menu, 6 Calle Pte 14. Big fat juicy sandwiches and tofu stir-fry, in candlelit place, friendly.

Cafés and delis

Bagel Barn, 5 Calle Pte 2. Open 0600-2200. Popular, breakfast, snack deals with bagels and smoothies, videos shown nightly, free.

Café Barroco, Callejón de la Concepción 2, T7832-0781. Peaceful garden, stylish, delicious cakes, coffees, huge selection of English teas for the deprived.

Café Condesa, 5 Av Norte 4. Open 0700-2100.West side of the main plaza in a pretty courtyard, popular, a little pricey for the portions, breakfast with free coffee fill-ups, desserts, popular Sun brunches.

Cafetería Alemana Charlotte, Callejón de los Nazarenos 9, between 6 and 7 Av Norte. Good breakfasts, cakes, good coffee, German books, newspapers, and films.

Doña Luisa Xicoténcatl, 4 Calle Ote 12, 1½ blocks east of the plaza, 0700-2130 daily. Popular meeting place with an excellent bulletin board, serving breakfasts, tasty ice cream, good coffee, burgers, large menu, big portions. Good views of Volcán Agua upstairs. Shop sells good selection of wholemeal, banana bread, yogurts, etc; don't miss the chocolate and orange loaf if you can get it.

Peroleto, Alameda Sta Lucía 36. Run by a Nicaraguan, next to San Jerónimo church, stop by here for the wickedest *licuados* in town and you probably won't be able to bypass the cake cabinet either. It has a *ceviche* restaurant next door open until 1800.

Tostaduría Antigua, 6 Calle Pte/Av Sur Esquina. 0900-1300,1430-1800. Roasts and brews good Antiguan coffee, many say the best in town. You can smell the coffee half a block away in each direction.

Vivero y Café de La Escalonia, 5 Av Sur Final 36 Calle, T7832-7074. This delightful place is well worth the walk – a café amid a garden centre with luscious flowers everywhere, pergola, classical music, *postres*, herb breads, salads andcold drinks. Bird of paradise flowers and tumbergia. Daily 0900-1800.

Tue-Sat 1930-2300. Kicking most nights with indie music, and hard, cool lines in decor, but the free films or sports events shown on a giant screen can alter the balance in the bar between those on a bender and those glued to the screen. Good salads.

Casbah, 5 Av Norte 30. Mon-Sat 1800-0100. Cover charge includes a drink. Gay night Thu. Has a medium-sized dance floor with a podium and plays a mix of good dance and Latin music, the closest place to a nightclub atmosphere in Antigua.

La Chimenea, 7 Av Norte 18. Mon-Sat 1700-2430. Happy hour every day, seriously cheap, relaxed atmosphere, mixed young crowd, dance floor, salsa, rock.

La Sala, 6 Calle Pte, T5671-3008. One of the most popular salsa dancing and watering holes in town.

Reilly's Irish Pub, 5 Av Norte 32. Daily 1400-0100, happy hour 1600-2000. Guinness and other other imported beers available, very popular with sports fans for its international games shown on big TV screens; reasonably priced food.

Riki's Bar, 4 Av Norte 4, inside **La Escudilla**. Usually packed with gringos, but attracts a young Guatemalan crowd as well, and popular with the gay fraternity. Good place to meet people. A good mix of music, including jazz.

Cinemas

Antigua must be the home of the lounge cinema. All show films or videos in English, or with subtitles.

Café 2000, 6 Av Sur. Free films daily and the most popular spot in town to watch movies.

Cine Sin Ventura, 5 Av Sur 8. The only real screen in town, auditorium can get cold, and they need to hit the brightness button.

🌑 Entertainment

Antigua *p222, map p224*
Bars and clubs
Café 2000, 6 Av Norte 8, between 4 and 5 Calle Pte. Daily 0800-0100. Happy hour

🌑 Festivals and events

Antigua *p222, map p224*
Feb International Culture Festival: dance, music and other top-quality performers from around the globe come to Antigua.

Mar/Apr Semana Santa: see box, page 228.
21-26 Jul The feast of San Santiago.
31 Oct-2 Nov All Saints and All Souls, in and around Antigua.
7 Dec Quema del Diablo (burning of the Devil) by lighting fires in front of their houses and burning an effigy of the Devil in the Plazuela de La Concepción at night, thereby starting the Christmas festivities.
8 Dec Fiesta in Ciudad Vieja
15 Dec The start of what's known as the Posadas, where a group of people leave from each church, dressed as Mary and Joseph, and seek refuge in hotels. They are symbolically refused lodging several times, but are eventually allowed in.

○ Shopping

Antigua *p222, map p224*
Antigua is a shopper's paradise, with textiles, furniture, candles, fabrics, clothes, sculpture, candies, glass, jade and ceramics on sale. The **main municipal market** is on Alameda Santa Lucía next to the bus station, where you can buy fruit, clothes and shoes. The *artesanía* market is opposite, next to the bus lane.

Art
Galería de Arte Antigua, 4 Calle Ote 27 y 1 Av. Tue-Sat. Large art gallery.

Bookshops
Numerous bookshops sell books in English and Spanish, postcards, posters, maps and guides including **Footprint Handbooks**.
Un Poco de Todo, near Casa del Conde on the plaza. **Casa del Conde**, 5 Av Norte 4; has a full range of books from beautifully illustrated coffee-table books to guides and history books. **Rainbow Cafe**, 7 Av Sur 18, second-hand books. **Hamlin and White**, 4 Calle Ote 12A. Books on Guatemala are cheaper here than at **Casa del Conde**.

Crafts, textiles, clothes and jewellery
Many other stores sell textiles, handicrafts, antiques, silver and jade on 5 Av Norte between 1 and 4 Calle Pte and 4 Calle Ote.
Casa Chicob, Callejón de la Concepción 2, www.casachicob.com. Beautiful textiles, candles and ceramics for sale.
Casa de Artes, 4 Av Sur 11, www.casade artes.com.gt, for traditional textiles and handicrafts, jewellery, etc. Very expensive.
Casa de los Gigantes, 7 Calle Ote 18, for textiles and handicrafts.
Diva, at 5 Av Norte 16. For Western-style clothes and jewellery.
El Telar, Loom Tree, 5 Av Sur 7, all sorts of coloured tablecloths, napkins, cushion covers and bedspreads are sold here.
Huipil market, held in the courtyard of La Fuente every Sat 0900-1400. The display is very colourful and if the sun is out this is an excellent place for photos.
Mercado de Artesanías, next to the main market at the end of 4 Calle Pte.
Nativo's, 5 Av Norte, 25 "B", T7832-6556. Sells some beautiful textiles from such places as Aguacatán.
Nim P'ot, 5 Av Norte 29, T7832-2681, www.nimpot.com, a mega-warehouse of traditional textiles and crafts brought from around the country. Excellent prices.
Textura, 5 Av Norte 33, T7832-5067 for lots of bedroom accessories.

Food
Doña María Gordillo, 4 Calle Ote 11. Famous throughout the country. It is impossible to get in the door most days but, if you can, take a peek, to see the *dulces*, as well as the row upon row of yellow wooden owls keeping their beady eyes on the customers.
La Bodegona, 5 Calle Pte 32, opposite Posada La Quinta, on 5 Calle Pte and with another entrance on 4 Calle Pte, large supermarket.
Tienda de Doña Gavi, 3 Av Norte 2, behind the cathedral, sells all sorts of lovely potions and herbs, candles and home-made biscuits. Doña Gaviota also sells Guatemala City's most

famous ice creams in all sorts of weird and wonderful flavours (see **Helados Marylena**, page 215).

▲ Activities and tours

Antigua *p222, map p224*
Spas
Antigua Spa Resort, San Pedro El Panorama, lote 9 and 10 G, T7832-3960. Daily 0900-2100. Swimming pool, steam baths, sauna, gym, jacuzzi, beauty salon. Reservations advised.
Mayan Spa, Alameda Sta Lucía Norte 20, T7832-3537. Mon-Sat 0900-1800. Massages and pampering packages, including sauna, steam baths and jacuzzi, are available.

Riding
Ravenscroft Riding Stables, 2 Av Sur 3, San Juan del Obispo, T7830-6669. You can also hire horses in Santa María de Jesús.

Swimming
Porta Hotel Antigua, non-residents may use the pool for a charge.
Villas de Antigua (Ciudad Vieja exit), T7832-0011-15, for buffet lunch, swimming and marimba band.

Tour operators
Adrenalina Tours, 3a Calle Poniente, T7882 4147, www.adrenalinatours.com. Xela's respected tour operator has opened up in Antigua too. As well as shuttles all around Guatemala, there are minibuses to San Cristóbal de las Casas, Mexico, US$55. Also customized packages, weekend trips to Xela and discounted Tikal trips. Recommended.
Adventure Travel Center Viareal, 5 Av Norte 25B, T7832-0162, daily trips to Guatemalan destinations (including Río Dulce sailing, river and volcano trips), Monterrico, Quiriguá, El Salvador and Honduras.
Antigua Tours, Casa Santo Domingo, 3 Calle Ote 22, T7832-5821, www.antiguatours.net. Run by Elizabeth Bell, author of 4 books on Antigua. She offers walking tours of the city

(US$20 per person), book in advance, Mon, Thu 1400-1700, Tue, Wed, Fri, Sat 0930-1230. During Lent and Holy Week there are extra tours, giving insight into the processions and carpet making. Highly recommended.
Aventuras Naturales, Col El Naranjo No 53, Antigua, T5381-6615, http://aventuras naturales.tripod.com. Specialized trips including guided birding tours.
Aventuras Vacacionales, T5306-3584, www.sailing-diving-guatemala.com. Highly recommended sailing trips on *Las Sirenas* owned byCaptain John Clark and sailed by Captain Raúl Hernández (see also under Río Dulce, page 307).
CATours, 6 Calle Oriente Casa 14, T7832-9638, www.catours.co.uk. British-run motorcycle tour operators, with trips all around Guatemala and to El Salvador, from 1- to 14-day tours. Recommended.
CA Tours, 6 Calle Oriente Casa 14, T7832-9638, www.catours.co.uk. British-run motorbike tour company. Recommended.
Eco-Tour Chejo's, 3 Calle Pte 24, T832-5464, ecotourchejos@hotmail.com. Well-guarded walks up volcanoes. Interesting tours also available to coffee *fincas*, flower plantations, etc, shuttle service, horse riding, very helpful.
Gran Jaguar, 4 Calle Pte 30, T7832-2712, www.guacalling.com/jaguar/. Well- organized fun volcano tours with official security. Also shuttles and trips to Tikal and Río Dulce. Very highly recommended for the Pacaya trip.
Old Town Outfitters, 5 Av Sur 12 "C", T7832-4171, www.adventureguatemala.com. Action adventure specialists, with mountain-bike tours (½-day tour, US$39), kayak tours hiking and climbing, outdoor equipment on sale, maps, very helpful.
Outdoor Excursions, 1 Av Sur 4b, T7832-0074, www.guatemalavolcano.com. Professional, knowledgeable and fun Volcano tour company with private security. Overnight tours to Fuego (US$79), Acatenango (US$79) and Pacaya (US$59).
Rainbow Travel Center, 7 Av Sur 8, T7931-7878, www.rainbowtravelcenter.com. Full local travel service, specialists in student

flights and bargain international flights, they will attempt to match any quote. It also sells ISIC, Go25 and teachers' cards. English, French, German and Japanese spoken.

Sin Fronteras, 5a Av Norte 15 "A", T7720-4400, www.sinfront.com. Local tours, shuttles, horse riding, bicycle tours, canopy tours, national and international air tickets including discounts with ISIC and Go25 cards. Also sells travel insurance. Agents for rafting experts **Maya Expeditions**. Reliable and highly recommended.

Tivoli Travel, 4 Calle Ote 10, T7832-4274, antigua@tivoli.com.gt. Closed Sun. Helpful with any travel problem, English, French, Spanish, German, Italian spoken, reconfirm tickets, shuttles, hotel bookings, good-value tours. Useful for organizing independent travel as well as tours.

ViaVenture, 2 Calle Ote 2, T7832-2509, www.viaventure.com. Professional tour operator offering special interest and tailor-made tours.

Guatemala Reservations.com, 3 Av Norte 3, T7832-3293, www.guatemalareservations.com. Closed Sun. A wide range of tours and transport services. Frequently recommended. Also has guidebooks for reference or to buy, along with a water bottle-filling service to encourage recycling. Cheap phone call service. Shuttles and tours.

⊖ Transport

Antigua p222, map p224
Bus
To **Guatemala City**. Buses leave when full between 0530 and 1830, US$1, 1-1½ hrs, depending on the time of day, from the Alameda Santa Lucía near the market, from an exit next to **Pollo Campero** (not from behind the market). All other buses leave from behind the market. To **Chimaltenango**, on the Pan-American Hwy, from 0600-1600, every 15 mins, US$0.65, for connections to **Los Encuentros** (for **Lake Atitlán** and **Chichicastenango**), **Cuatro Caminos**

(for **Quetzaltenango**) and **Huehuetenango** (for the Mexican border). It is possible to get to Chichicastenango and back by bus in a day, especially on Thu and Sun, for the market. Get the bus to Chimaltenango and then change. It's best to leave early. See Chimaltenango for connections. The only direct bus to **Panajachel** is Rebuli, leaving at 0700, from 4 Calle Pte, in front of La Bodegona supermarket, US$5, 2½ hrs, returning 1100. Other buses to **Pana** via Chimaltenango with **Rebuli** and **Carrillo y Gonzalez**, 0600-1645, US$2.50. To **Escuintla** 0530-1600, 1 hr, US$1.25.

International To **Copán** and other cities in Honduras, including **Tegucigalpa**, with **Hedman Alas**, www.hedmanalas.com, from Posada de Don Rodrigo to its terminal in Guatemala City for a connection to Copán. Leaves at 0330 and 0630 from Antigua, US$41, US$77 return and 0500 and 0900 from Guatemala City, US$35, US$65 return. Return times are 1330 and 1800 to Guatemala City; the earlier bus continues to Antigua.

Shuttles Hotels and travel agents run frequent shuttle services to and from **Guatemala City** and the **airport** (1 hr) from 0400 to about 2000 daily, US$10-15 depending on the time of day: details from any agency in town. There are also shuttles to **Chichicastenango**, US$5-18, **Panajachel**, US$5-12, **Quetzaltenango**, US$16, **Monterrico**, US$15, **Flores**, US$20-40, **Copán**, US$8-25 and other destinations, but check for prices and days of travel. **Plus Travel** (www.plustravelguate.com) has some of the best prices and range of destinations, with offices in Antigua (6a Calle Pte No 19, T7832-3147) and Copán Ruinas. Recommended.

Around Antigua p226
Bus To **Ciudad Vieja**, US$0.30, every 30 mins, 20 mins. **San Miguel de las Dueñas**. Take a bus marked 'Dueñas', every 30 mins, 20 mins, US$0.30. To **San Antonio Aguas Calientes**, every 30 mins, 30 mins, US$0.30.

To **Santa María de Jesús** every 30 mins, 45 mins, US$0.50. There are a few buses a day between **Mixco Viejo** and the Zona 4 terminal, Guatemala City. The bus goes to Pachalum; ask to be dropped at ruins entrance.

Volcán Agua *p229*
Bus From Antigua to **Alotenango** from 0700-1800, 40 mins.

Volcán Acatenango *p229*
Bus To reach **La Soledad**, take a bus heading for Yepocapa or Acatenango village and get off at La Soledad.

Car Tabarini, 6 Av Sur 22, T7832-8107, also at the **Hotel Radisson Villa Antigua**, T7832-7460, www.tabarini.com.

Motorcycle hire La Ceiba, 6 Calle Pte 15, T7832-0077.

Taxi Servicio de Taxi 'Antigua', Manuel Enrique Gómez, T5417-2180, has been recommended.

Horse-drawn carriage Available at weekends and during fiestas around the plaza.

Tuk-tuk Motorbike taxis with a seat for 2 will whizz you around town for US$1.50.

ⓘ Directory

Antigua *p222, map p224*
Banks Banks are closed Wed-Sun of Holy Week and none change money between Christmas and New Year. Most banks are open Mon-Fri 0900-1800, some until 1900 and Sat 0900-1300. **Banco de América Central**, on the plaza, Visa and MasterCard ATM (Cirrus and Plus), but bank hours only. **Banco Industrial**, 5 Av Sur 4, near plaza, gives cash on Visa ATM (24 hr) and Visa credit card at normal rates, no commission. Extremely quick service. **Banco Industrial** on plaza, good rates, no commission, MasterCard (Cirrus) ATM.

Internet Some internet cafés offer discount cards, which are worth buying if you are in town for any length of time. The following are recommended: **Enlaces**, 6 Av Norte 1. **Funky Monkey**, Paseo de los Corregidores, 5 Av Sur 6.

Language schools Footprint has received favourable reports from students for the following language schools: **Academia Antigüeña de Español**, 1 Pte 10, T7832-7241, www.spanishacademy antiguena.com. **Alianza Lingüística 'Cano'**, Av El Desengaño 21A, T7832-0370. Private classes are also available. **Amerispan**, 6 Av Norte 40 and 7 Calle Ote, T7832-0164, www.amerispan.com. In the US, 1334 Walnut St, 6th floor, Philadelphia PA 19107. **Centro Lingüístico Maya**, 5 Calle Pte 20, T7832-1342, www.clmmaya.com. **CSA** (Christian Spanish Academy), 6 Av Norte 15, Aptdo Postal 320, T7832-3922, www.learncsa.com. **Don Pedro de Alvarado**, 6 Av Norte 39, T5872-2469, www.donpedro spanishschool.com. 25 years' experience. **Proyecto Bibliotecas Guatemala (PROBIGUA)**, 6 Av Norte 41B, T7832-2998, www.probigua.org. Gives a percentage of profits towards founding and maintaining public libraries in rural towns; frequently recommended. **Proyecto Lingüístico Francisco Marroquín**, 6 Av Norte, www.plfm-antigua.org. **Sevilla Academia de Español**, 1 Av Sur 8, T7832-5101, www.sevillantigua.com. **Tecún Umán**, 6 Calle Pte 34A, T7832-2792, www.tecunuman.centramerica.com. **Private lessons** Check ads in **Doña Luisa's** and others around town and the tourist office. Recommended: **Julia Solís**, 5 Calle Pte 36, T7832-5497, julisar@hotmail.com (she lives behind the tailor's shop). **Armalia Jarquín**, Av El Desengaño 11, T7832-2377. There are, unbelievably, numerous No 11s on this road. Armalia's has a sign up and is opposite No 75, which has a tiled plaque. **Laundry** All charge about US$1 per kg and most close Sun and half-day Sat. **Delilah** in La Unión on 1 Av Sur provides an excellent service. **Lavandería Gilda**, 5 Calle Pte between 6 and 7 Av, very good and can do a wash and dry in 2 hrs.

Learning the lingo

Antigua is overrun with language students and so some say it is not the most ideal environment in which to learn Spanish. There are about 70-plus schools, open year round. At any one time there may be 300-600 overseas students in Antigua. Not all schools are officially authorized by INGUAT and the Ministry of Education. INGUAT has a list of authorized schools in its office. Rates depend on the number of hours of tuition per week, and vary from school to school. As a rough guide, the average fee for four hours a day, five days a week is US$120-200, at a reputable school, with homestay, though many are less and some schools offer cheaper classes in the afternoon. You will benefit more from the classes if you have done a bit of study of the basics before you arrive. There are guides who take students around the schools and charge a high commission (make sure this is not added to your account). They may approach tourists arriving on the bus from the capital.

All schools offer one-to-one tuition; if you can meet the teachers in advance, so much the better, but don't let the director's waffle distract you from asking pertinent questions. Paying more does not mean you get better teaching and the standard of teacher varies within schools as well as between schools. Beware of 'hidden extras' and be clear on arrangements for study books. Some schools have an inscription fee. Several schools use a portion of their income to fund social projects and some offer a programme of activities for students such as dance classes, Latin American film, tours, weaving and football. Before making any commitment, find somewhere to stay for a couple of nights and shop around at your leisure. Schools also offer accommodation with local families, but check the place out if possible before you pay a week in advance. Average accommodation rates with a family with three meals a day are US$75-100 per week. In some cases the schools organize group accommodation; if you prefer single, ask for it.

Central, 5 Calle Pte 7B. **Medical services** Casa de Salud Santa Lucía, Alameda Sta Lucía Sur 7, T7832-3122. Open 24 hrs, good and efficient service. Consultation prices vary. **Hospital Privado Hermano Pedro**, Av El Desengaño 12A, T7832-6419. **Optica Santa Lucía**, 5 Calle Pte 28, T7832-0384. Opticians selling contact-lens solution and accessories. **Police** Tourism police, Rancho Nimejay, 6 Calle, between 8 Av and 4 Calle del Ranchón, T7832-7290. The office is open 24 hrs. Just knock on the door or ring their number. **National Police** are based in Antigua, in the Palacio de los Capitanes General, on the south side of the plaza. **Post** Post office at Alameda Sta Lucía and 4 Calle Pte, near the market. Mon-Fri 0800-1730, Sat 0900-1430. The only place

in town to buy stamps. Large parcels, up to 4.5 kg, cost approx US$60 to UK and rest of Europe; take about a week to arrive. If you get a cardboard box for your parcel from nearby supermarket, the post office will wrap it up in brown paper and tape it up for you. **Courier services** There are several in town, including DHL, 6 Calle Pte and 6 Av Sur. Quicker and maybe more reliable than regular post but nearly three times the cost. **Telephone** Telgua, 5 Av Sur, corner of the plaza for international and local calls. There are public phone boxes inside the **Telgua** building, which are quieter to use than the couple under the arches on the west side of the square. Mon-Fri 0800-1800, Sat 0800-1200. Try **Funky Monkey** for internet calls.

Lake Atitlán and around

→ Colour map 2, C1.

Beautiful scenery stretches west of the capital through the Central Highlands. Here, volcano landscapes are dotted with colourful markets and the Maya wearing traditional clothes in the towns and villages. Aldous Huxley called Lake Atitlán "the most beautiful lake in the world" and attractive villages flank its shores. Further north you can explore the streets of Chichicastenango as the town fills with hawkers and vendors at the weekly markets serving tourists and locals alike. North of Chichicastenango, the Quiché and Ixil Triangle regions have small, very traditional, hamlets set in beautiful countryside that are easily explored by bus.

▶ For listings, see pages 254-267.

Ins and outs

The easiest way to get to the Lake Atitlán area is by the numerous buses that ply the Pan-American Highway, changing at Los Encuentros or El Cuchillo junctions. Alternatively, shuttles go to Panajachel from most big tourist centres. Villages around the lake are connected to Panajachel by boat services. Some are served by buses. Some Hurricane Stan damage from October 2005 is still visible and some small roads remain unrepaired. Access is not affected, though. Panabaj, the village that was completely destroyed behind Santiago Atitlán, was declared a mass graveyard. Tropical Storm Agatha caused further destruction in 2010, with roads all around the lake badly affected and slowing down transport access. ▶ See Transport, page 263.

Towards Lake Atitlán

The Pan-American Highway heads west out of the capital passing through Chimaltenango and on to Los Encuentros where it turns north for Chichicastenango, Santa Cruz del Quiché, Nebaj and the Ixil Triangle, and south for Sololá and the Lake Atitlán region. It continues to the western highland region of Quetzaltenango (see page 277), Totonicapán, Huehuetenango and the Cuchumatanes Mountains (see pages 270 and 271).

Chimaltenango and around

Chimaltenango is busy with traffic. Here, another road runs south for 20 km to Antigua. This tree-lined road leads to Parramos where it turns sharp left. Straight on through the village, in 1.5 km, is a well known inn and restaurant (see Sleeping, page 254). This road continues through mountains to Pastores, Jocotenango and finally to Antigua. Some 6 km south of Chimaltenango, **San Andrés Itzapa** is well worth a visit; there is a very interesting **chapel to Maximón** ① *open till 1800 daily.* Shops by the chapel sell prayer pamphlets and pre-packaged offerings. Beyond Chimaltenango is **Zaragoza**, a former Spanish penal settlement, and beyond that a road leads 13 km north to the interesting village of **Comalapa**. This is the best place to see *naíf* painting and there are plenty of galleries. The **tourist information office** ① *Av 3-76, T5766-3874*, is in the house of Andrés Curuchich, a popular artist). There's a colourful market on Monday and Tuesday.

Routes west: Tecpán and Los Encuentros

Returning to the Pan-American Highway the road divides 6 km past Zaragoza. The southern branch, the old Pan-American Highway, goes through Patzicía and Patzún (see below) to Lake Atitlán, then north to Los Encuentros. The northern branch, the new

Pan-American Highway, which is used by all public transport, goes past Tecpán (see below) and then to Los Encuentros. From Los Encuentros there is only the one road west to San Cristóbal Totonicapán, where it swings northwest to La Mesilla/Ciudad Cuauhtémoc, at the Mexican border.

From Zaragoza the Pan-American Highway runs 19 km to near **Tecpán**, which is slightly off the road at 2287 m. It has a particularly fine church with silver altars, carved

Lake Atitlán

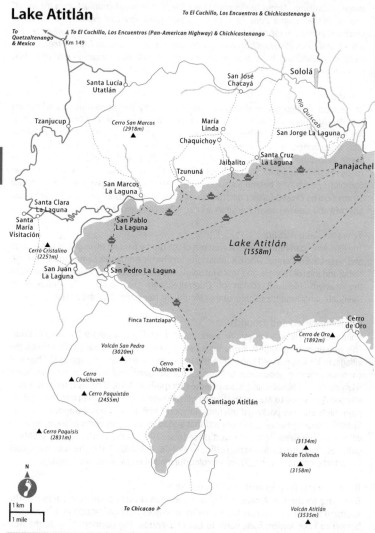

To El Cuchillo, Los Encuentros & Chichicastenango

To El Cuchillo, Los Encuentros (Pan-American Highway) & Chichicastenango

To Quetzaltenango & Mexico

Km 149

Sololá

Santa Lucía Utatlán

San José Chacayá

Río Quiscab

Tzanjucup

Cerro San Marcos (2918m)

María Linda

San Jorge La Laguna

Chaquichoy

Jaibalito

Santa Cruz La Laguna

Panajachel

Tzununá

San Marcos La Laguna

Santa Clara La Laguna

Santa María Visitación

Cerro Cristalino (2251m)

San Pablo La Laguna

Lake Atitlán (1558m)

San Juan La Laguna

San Pedro La Laguna

Finca Tzantziapa

Cerro de Oro

Volcán San Pedro (3020m)

Cerro Chuitinamit

Cerro de Oro (1892m)

Cerro Chuichumil

Cerro Paquixtán (2455m)

Santiago Atitlán

Cerro Paquisís (2831m)

N

1 km
1 mile

To Chicacao

(3134m)

Volcán Tolimán

(3158m)

Volcán Atitlán (3535m)

wooden pillars, odd images and a wonderful ceiling that was severely damaged by the 1976 earthquake. There is accommodation, restaurants and banks. Near Tecpán are the important Maya ruins of **Iximché** ⓘ *5 km of paved road south of Tecpán, 0800-1700, US$3.25*, once capital and court of the Cakchiqueles. The first capital of Guatemala after its conquest was founded near Iximché; followed in turn by Ciudad Vieja, Antigua and Guatemala City. The ruins are well presented with three plazas, a palace and two ball courts on a promontory surrounded on three sides by steep slopes.

The old and new Pan-American highways rejoin 11 km from Sololá at the **El Cuchillo** junction. About 2 km east is **Los Encuentros**, the junction of the Pan-American Highway and the paved road 18 km northeast to Chichicastenango, see page 249.

To Lake Atitlán along the old Pan-American Highway

With amazing views of Lake Atitlán and the surrounding volcanoes, travellers of the southern road from Zaragoza to Lake Atitlán encounter a much more difficult route than the northern option, with several steep hills and many hairpin bends. Nevertheless, if you have both the time and a sturdy vehicle, it is an extremely rewarding trip. Note that there is no police presence whatsoever along the old Pan-American Highway.

The route goes through **Patzicía**, a small Maya village founded in 1545 (no accommodation). Market days are Wednesday and Saturday and the local fiesta is 22-27 July. The famous church, which had a fine altar and beautiful silver, was destroyed by the 1976 earthquake. Beyond is the small town of **Patzún**; its church, dating from 1570, is severely damaged and is not open to the public. There is a Sunday market, which is famous for the silk (and wool) embroidered napkins and for woven *fajas* and striped red cotton cloth; other markets are on Tuesday and Friday and the town fiesta is 17-21 May. For accommodation, ask at the *tiendas*.

The road leaves Patzún and goes south to Xepatán and on to **Godínez**, the highest community overlooking the lake. From

Map labels:
To Las Trampas, Guatemala City & Zaragoza
Río Panajachel
San Andrés Semetabaj
Las Canoas
Santa Catarina Palopó
Godínez
To Patzún
San Antonio Palopó
Tzampetey
Agua Escondida
Pachitulúl
Panaranjo
San Lucas Tolimán
San Gabriel
To Cocales & Pacific Highway

Godínez, a good paved road turns off south to the village of San Lucas Tolimán and continues to Santiago Atitlán.

The main (steep, paved) road continues straight on for Panajachel. The high plateau, with vast wheat and maize fields, now breaks off suddenly as though pared by a knife. From a viewpoint here, there is an incomparable view of Lake Atitlán, 600 m below. The very picturesque village of **San Antonio Palopó** is right underneath you, on slopes leading to the water. It is about 12 km from the viewpoint to Panajachel. For the first 6 km you are close to the rim of the old crater and, at the point where the road plunges down to the lakeside, is **San Andrés Semetabaj** which has a beautiful ruined early 17th-century church. Market day is Tuesday. Buses go to Panajachel.

Sololá → *Colour map 2, C1. Altitude: 2113 m.*

On the road down to Panajachel is Sololá, which has superb views across Lake Atitlán. Outside the world of the tourist, this is the most important town in the area. A fine, modern, white church, with bright stained-glass windows and an attractive clocktower dominates the west side of the plaza. Sololá is even more special for the bustling market that brings the town to life every Tuesday and Friday, when the Maya gather from surrounding commuities to buy and sell local produce. Women and particularly men wear traditional dress. While it is primarily a produce market, there is also a good selection of used *huípiles*. Even if you're not in the market to buy, it is a colourful sight. Markets are mornings only; Friday market gets underway on Thursday. There's a fiesta 11-17 August.

From Sololá the old Pan-American Highway weaves and twists through a 550-m drop in 8 km to Panajachel. The views are impressive at all times of day, but particularly in the morning. Time allowing, it is quite easy to walk down direct by the road (two hours); you also miss the unnerving bus ride down (US$0.40).

Panajachel → *For listings, see pages 254-267. Colour map 2, C1.*

The old town of Panajachel is charming and quiet but the newer development, strung along a main road, is a tucker and trinket emporium. It's busy and stacked cheek by jowl with hundreds of stalls and shops along the main road. Some of the best bargains are here and textiles and crafts from across the country can be found. Panajachel is a gringo magnet, and if you want to fill up on international cuisine and drink then it's a good place to stay for a few days. There are also stunning views from the lakeshore.

Ins and outs

Getting there and around Good connections from most large town in the highlands, including Antigua, Chichicastenango and Quetzaltenango. The town centre is the junction of Calle Principal and Calle (or Avenida) Santander. The main bus stop is here, stretching south back down Calle Real, and it marks the junction between the old and the modern towns. It takes about 10 minutes to walk from the junction to the lake shore. Calle Rancho Grande is sometimes called Calle del Balneario and other streets have variants.
▸ *See Transport, page 264.*

Tourist information **INGUAT** ⓘ *Calle Real Principal and Av Los Arboles, T7762-1106, daily 0900-1300 and 1400-1700.* Helpful with information about buses, boats and good local knowledge. Also see www.atitlan.com.

Safety There have been reports from travellers who have suffered **robbery** walking around the lake between San Juan and San Pablo and between San Marcos and Tzununá. Seek local advice from **INGUAT**, other travellers and local hotels/hostels before planning a trip.

Panajachel

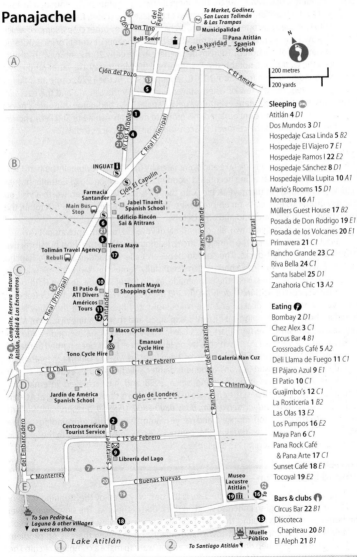

200 metres
200 yards

Sleeping

Atitlán **4** D1
Dos Mundos **3** D1
Hospedaje Casa Linda **5** B2
Hospedaje El Viajero **7** E1
Hospedaje Ramos I **22** E2
Hospedaje Sánchez **8** D1
Hospedaje Villa Lupita **10** A1
Mario's Rooms **15** D1
Montana **16** A1
Müllers Guest House **17** B2
Posada de Don Rodrigo **19** E1
Posada de los Volcanes **20** E1
Primavera **21** E1
Rancho Grande **23** C2
Riva Bella **24** C1
Santa Isabel **25** D1
Zanahoria Chic **13** A2

Eating

Bombay **2** D1
Chez Alex **3** C1
Circus Bar **4** B1
Crossroads Café **5** A2
Deli Llama de Fuego **11** C1
El Pájaro Azul **9** E1
El Patio **10** C1
Guajimbo's **12** C1
La Rosticería **1** B2
Las Olas **13** E2
Los Pumpos **16** E2
Maya Pan **6** C1
Pana Rock Café
  & Pana Arte **17** C1
Sunset Café **18** E1
Tocoyal **19** E2

Bars & clubs

Circus Bar **22** B1
Discoteca
  Chapiteau **20** B1
El Aleph **21** B1

Background

The original settlement of Panajachel was tucked up against the steep cliffs to the north of the present town, about 1 km from the lake. Virtually all traces of the original Kaqchikel village have disappeared, but the early Spanish impact is evident with the narrow streets, public buildings, plaza and church. The original Franciscan church was founded in 1567 and used as the base for the Christianization of the lake area. Later, the fertile area of the river delta was used for coffee production, orchards and many other crops, some of which are still grown today and can be seen round the back of the tourist streets or incorporated into the gardens of the hotels. Tourism began here in the early 20th century with several hotels on the waterfront, notably the **Tzanjuyú** and the **Monterrey**, the latter originally a wooden building dating from about 1910, rebuilt in 1975. In the 1970s came an influx of young travellers, quite a few of whom stayed on to enjoy the climate and the easy life. Drugs and the hippy element eventually gave Panajachel a bad name, but rising prices and other pressures have encouraged this group to move on – some to San Pedro across the lake. Others joined the commercial scene and still run services today.

Sights

The old town is 1 km from the lake and dominated by the **church**, originally built in 1567, but now restored. It has a fine decorated wooden roof and a mixture of Catholic statues and Maya paintings in the nave. A block up the hill is the daily market, worth a visit on Sunday mornings especially for embroideries. The local fiesta runs from 1-7 October, the main days are at the weekend and on 4 October.

In contrast, the modern town, almost entirely devoted to tourism, spreads out towards the lake. Calle Santander is the principal street, leading directly to the short but attractive **promenade** and boat docks. The section between Calle Santander and Calle Rancho Grande has been turned into a park, which delightfully frames the traditional view across the lake to the volcanoes. Near the promenade, at the **Hotel Posada de Don Rodrigo**, is the **Museo Lacustre Atitlán** ① *daily 0900-1200, 1400-1800, US$4.40*, created by Roberto Samayoa, a prominent local diver and archaeologist, to house some of the many items found in the lake. The geological history is explained and there is a fine display of Maya classical pottery and ceremonial artefacts classified by period. A submerged village has been found at a depth of 20 m, which is being investigated. It has been named **Samabaj** in honour of Don Roberto. For those interested in local art, visit **La Galería** (near **Rancho Grande Hotel**), where Nan Cuz, an indigenous painter, sells her pictures evoking the spirit of village life. She has been painting since 1958 and has achieved international recognition. On the road past the entrance to **Hotel Atitlán** is the **Reserva Natural Atitlán** ① *T7762-2565, www.atitlanreserva.com, daily 0800-1800, US$5.50*, a reserve with a bird refuge, butterfly collection, monkeys and native mammals in natural surroundings, with a picnic area, herb garden, waterfall, visitor centre, café, zip-lines and access to the lakeside beach. Camping and lodging are available.

Around Lake Atitlán → *For listings, see pages 254-267.*

Getting around Travelling round the lake is the best way to enjoy the stunning scenery and the effect of changing light and wind on the mood of the area. The slower you travel the better, and walking round the lake gives some fantastic views (but take advice on safety). With accommodation at towns and villages on the way, there is no problem finding somewhere to bed down for the night if you want to make a complete circuit. The lake is 50 km in circumference and you can walk on or near the shore for most of it. Here and there the cliffs are too steep to allow for easy walking and private properties elsewhere force you to move up 'inland'. For boat information see Transport, Panajachel. At almost any time of year, but especially between January and March, strong winds (*El Xocomil*) occasionally blow up quickly across the lake. This can be dangerous for small boats. ▸▸ *See Transport, page 263.*

Santa Catarina Palopó

The town, within easy walking distance (4 km) of Panajachel, has an attractive adobe church. Reed mats are made here, and you can buy *huípiles* (beautiful, green, blue and yellow) and men's shirts. Watch weaving at **Artesanías Carolina** on the way out towards San Antonio. Bargaining is normal. There are hot springs close to the town and an art gallery. Houses can be rented and there is at least one superb hotel, see Sleeping. The town fiesta is 25 November.

San Antonio Palopó

Six kilometres beyond Santa Catarina, San Antonio Palopó has another fine 16th-century church. Climbing the hill from the dock, it lies in an amphitheatre created by the mountains behind. Up above there are hot springs and a cave in the rocks used for local ceremonies. The village is noted for the clothes and head dresses of the men, and *huípiles* and shirts are cheaper than in Santa Catarina. A good hike is to take the bus from Panajachel to Godínez, take the path toward the lake 500 m south along the road to Cocales, walk on down from there to San Antonio Palopó (one hour) and then along the road back to Panajachel via Santa Catarina Palopó (three hours). You can walk on round the lake from San Antonio, but you must eventually climb steeply up to the road at Agua Escondida. The local fiesta is 12-14 June.

San Lucas Tolimán

San Lucas is at the southeastern tip of the lake and is not so attractive as other towns. It is known for its fiestas and markets especially Holy Week with processions, arches and carpets on the Thursday and Friday, and 15-20 October. Market days are Tuesday, Friday and Sunday (the best). There are two banks and an internet centre. **Comité Campesino del Altiplano** ⓘ *T5804-9451, www.ccda.galeon.com,* is based in the small village of Quixaya, 10 minutes from San Lucas. This Campesino Cooperative now produces fair trade organic coffee buying from small farmers. You can visit its organic processing plant on a small coffee *finca* and learn about its *café justicia,* and political work. Long-term volunteers welcome, Spanish required.

Volcán Atitlán and Volcán Tolimán

ⓘ *Ask Father Gregorio at the Parroquia church, 2 blocks from the Central Plaza, or at the Municipalidad for information and for available guides in San Lucas. Father Greg has worked in the area for more than 40 years so has a vested interest in recommending safe and good guides. One such is Carlos Huberto Alinan Chicoj, leaving at 2400 with torches to arrive at the summit by 0630 to avoid early cloud cover.*

From San Lucas the cones of **Atitlán**, 3535 m, and **Tolimán**, 3158 m, can be climbed. The route leaves from the south end of town and makes for the saddle (known as Los Planes, or Chanán) between the two volcanoes. From there it is south to Atitlán and north to the double cone (they are 1 km apart) and crater of Tolimán. Though straightforward, each climb is complicated by many working paths and thick cover above 2600 m. If you are fit, either can be climbed in seven hours, five hours down. Cloud on the volcano is common, but least likely from November to March. There have been reports of robbery so consider taking a guide, and ask local advice before setting out.

Santiago Atitlán

Santiago is a fascinating town, as much for the stunningly beautiful embroidered clothing of the locals, as for the history and character of the place with its mix of Roman Catholic, evangelical and Maximón worship. There are 35 evangelical temples in town as well as the house of the revered idol Maximón. The Easter celebrations here rival Antigua's for interest and colour. These are some of the most curious and reverential ceremonies in the world. If you only visit Guatemala once in your lifetime and it's at Easter and you can't bear to leave Antigua, come to Santiago at least for Good Friday. Commemorative events last all week and include Maximón as well as Christ.

You will be taken to the house of Maximón for a small fee. The fine church, with a wide nave decorated with colourful statues, was founded in 1547. The original roof was lost to earthquakes. There is a plaque dedicated to priest Father Francis Aplas Rother who was assassinated by the government in the church on 28 August 1981. At certain times of the year, the square is decked with streamers gently flapping in the breeze. The Tz'utujil women wear fine clothes and the men wear striped, half-length embroidered trousers (the most beautiful in Guatemala). There is a daily market, best on Friday and all sorts of art work and crafts can be bought. **Asociación Cojol ya weaving centre** ① *T5499-5717, Mon-Fri 0900-1600, Sat 0900-1300, free, weaving tours also.* As well as Holy Week, the local fiesta takes place 23-27 July.

Near town is the hill, **Cerro de Oro**, with a small village of that name on the lake. The summit (1892 m) can be reached from the village in 45 minutes.

For more information on the **Lake Atitlán Medical project** and volunteer opportunities, see www.puebloapueblo.org.

San Pedro La Laguna

San Pedro is a small town set on a tiny promontory with coffee bushes threaded around tracks lined with hostels and restaurants on the lakeside fringes. The tourists and long-term gringos have colonized the lakeside while the **Tz'utujil Maya** dominate the main part of the town up a very steep hill behind. San Pedro is now the favourite spot to hang out in for a couple of days or longer. It's a place to relax, to soak in hot baths, learn a bit of Spanish, horse ride and trek up Nariz de Maya. Some of the semi-permanent gringo inhabitants now run bars and cafés or sell home-made jewellery and the like. The cobbled road from the dock facing Panajachel (known as the *muelle)* climbs up to the centre and another goes down, more or less at right angles, to the other dock (known as the *playa* – beach) facing Santiago with the town arranged around. There's a mazy network of *callejones* and paths that fringe the shoreline between the two ferries. Market days are Thursday and Sunday (better) and there's a fiesta 27-30 June with traditional dances.

The town lies at the foot of the **Volcán San Pedro** (3020 m), which can be climbed in four to five hours, three hours down. It is now in the Parque Ecológico Volcán San Pedro, and the US$15 entrances includes a guide. **Politur** also work in the park and there have been no incidents of robbery since the park's inauguration. Camping is possible. Go early (0530) for the view, because after 1000 the top is usually smothered in cloud; also you will be in the shade all the way up and part of the way down.

Descubre San Pedro has set up a museum of local culture and coffee, with natural medicine and Maya cosmovision tours.

Evangelical churches are well represented in San Pedro, and you can hardly miss the yellow and white **Templo Evangélico Bautista Getsemaní** in the centre. A visit to the

San Pedro La Laguna

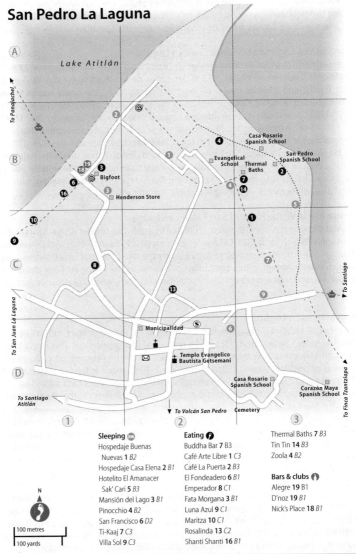

Sleeping 🛏
Hospedaje Buenas Nuevas **1** B2
Hospedaje Casa Elena **2** B1
Hotelito El Amanacer Sak' Cari **5** B3
Mansión del Lago **3** B1
Pinocchio **4** B2
San Francisco **6** D2
Ti-Kaaj **7** C3
Villa Sol **9** C3

Eating 🍴
Buddha Bar **7** B3
Café Arte Libre **1** C3
Café La Puerta **2** B3
El Fondeadero **6** B1
Emperador **8** C1
Fata Morgana **3** B1
Luna Azul **9** C1
Maritza **10** C1
Rosalinda **13** C2
Shanti Shanti **16** B1

Thermal Baths **7** B3
Tin Tin **14** B3
Zoola **4** B2

Bars & clubs 🍸
Alegre **19** B1
D'noz **19** B1
Nick's Place **18** B1

N

100 metres
100 yards

rug-making cooperative on the beach is of interest and backstrap weaving is taught at some places. A session at the **thermal baths** ⓘ *about US$10, Mon-Sat 0800-1900*, is a relaxing experience. Note that the water is solar heated, not chemical hot springs. Best to reserve in advance. Massage is also available, US$10.

For general local information ask at **Bigfoot**, page 262, who will advise you on horse riding to neighbouring villages, guides for climbing Volcán San Pedro and whatever else you have in mind. Canoes are made in San Pedro and hire is possible.

San Juan La Laguna and Santa Clara La Laguna

The road north from San Pedro passes around a headland to San Juan La Laguna (2 km), a traditional lakeside town. Look for **Los Artesanos de San Juan** ⓘ *8 Av, 6-20, Zona 2, T5963-9803*, and another image of Maximón displayed in the house opposite the Municipalidad. **Rupalaj Kistalin** ⓘ *close to the textile store, LEMA, T5964-0040, daily 0800-1700*, is a highly recommended organization run by local guides. **LEMA** ⓘ *T2425-9441, lema@sanjuanlalaguna.com*, the women weavers' association that uses natural dyes in their textiles, is also in town. Weaving classes are also possible (T7759-9126). On the road towards San Pablo there's a good viewpoint from the hilltop with the cross; a popular walk. A more substantial walk, about three hours, is up behind the village to Santa Clara La Laguna, 2100 m, passing the village of **Cerro Cristalino** with its attractive, white church with images of saints around the walls.

Santa María Visitación and San Pablo La Laguna

A short distance (500 m) to the west, separated by a gully, is a smaller village, Santa María Visitación. As with Santa Clara La Laguna, this is a typical highland village, and unspoilt by tourism. San Juan is connected to San Pablo by the lakeshore road, an attractive 4 km stretch mainly through coffee plantations. San Pablo, a busy village set 80 m above the lake, is known for rope making from *cantala* (maguey) fibres, which are also used for bags and fabric weaving.

San Marcos La Laguna

San Marcos' location is deceptive with the main part of the community 'hidden' up the hill. The quiet village centre is set at the upper end of a gentle slope that runs 300 m through coffee and fruit trees down to the lake, reached by two paved walkways. If arriving by boat and staying in San Marcos, ask to be dropped at the Schumann or the Pirámides dock. The village has grown rapidly in the last few years with a focus on the spiritual and energy – there is lots of massage, yoga, and all sorts of other therapies. It is the ideal place to be pampered. Beyond the centre, 300 m to the east is the main dock of the village down a cobbled road. Down the two main pathways are the hotels; some with waterfront sites have their own docks. There is a slanting trail leaving the village up through dramatic scenery over to Santa Lucía Utatlán, passing close to Cerro San Marcos, 2918 m, the highest point in the region apart from the volcanoes.

San Marcos to Santa Cruz

From the end of San Marcos where the stone track goes down to the dock, a rough track leads to **Tzununá**, passable for small trucks and 4WD vehicles, with views across the lake all the way. The village of Tzununá is along the tree-lined road through coffee plantations with a few houses up the valley behind. There is also a hotel with wonderful views (see Sleeping). There is a dock on the lakeside but no facilities. From here to Panajachel there are no roads or vehicular tracks and the villages can only be reached by boat, on horse or on foot. Also from here are some of the most spectacular views of the lake and the southern volcanoes. **Jaibalito** is smaller still than Tzununá, and hemmed in by the mountains with wonderful accommodation, see Sleeping. Arguably the best walk in the Atitlán area is from Jaibalito to Santa Cruz.

Santa Cruz La Laguna
Santa Cruz village is set in the most dramatic scenery of the lake. Three deep ravines come down to the bay separating two spurs. A stone roadway climbs up the left-hand spur, picks up the main walking route from Jaibalito and crosses over a deep ravine (unfortunately used as a garbage tip) to the plaza, on the only flat section of the right spur, about 120 m above the lake. The communal life of the village centres on the plaza. The hotels, one of them overflowing with flowers, are on the lake shore. Behind the village are steep, rocky forested peaks, many too steep even for the locals to cultivate. The fiesta takes place 7-11 May.

There is good walking here. Apart from the lake route, strenuous hikes inland eventually lead to the Santa Lucía Utatlán–Sololá road. From the left-hand (west) ravine reached from the path that runs behind the lake shore section, a trail goes through fields to an impossible looking gorge, eventually climbing up to Chaquijchoy, **Finca María Linda** and a trail to San José Chacayá (about four hours). In the reverse direction, the path southwest from San José leads to the Finca María Linda, which is close to the crater rim from where due south is a track to Jaibalito, to the left (east) round to the trail to Santa Cruz. Others follow the ridges towards San José and the road. These are for experienced hikers, and a compass (you are travelling due north) is essential if the cloud descends and there is no one to ask. From Santa Cruz to Panajachel along the coast is difficult, steep and unconsolidated, with few definitive paths. If you do get to the delta of the Río Quiscab, you may find private land is barred. The alternatives are either to go up to Sololá, about 6 km and 800 m up, or get a boat.

Chichicastenango → *For listings, see pages 254-267. Colour map 2, B1. Altitude: 2071 m.*

Chichicastenango is a curious blend of mysticism and commercialism. It is famous for its market where hundreds come for a bargain. On market mornings the steps of the church are blanketed in flowers as the women, in traditional dress, fluff up their skirts, amid baskets of lilies, roses and blackberries. But, with its mixture of Catholic and indigenous religion readily visible, it is more than just a shopping trolley stop. On a hilltop peppered with pine, villagers worship at a Maya shrine; in town, a time-honoured tradition of brotherhoods focuses on saint worship. Coupled with the mist that encircles the valley in the late afternoon, you can sense an air of intrigue. The **tourist office** ① *5 Av and Teatro Municipalidad, 1 block from church, daily 0800-2000, T7756-2022,* is helpful and provides a free leaflet with map, and local tour information.

Ins and outs
Getting there Chichicastenango is served by numerous chicken buses that head north from Los Encuentros or south from Santa Cruz del Quiché. There are direct buses from Xela and Guatemala City and shuttles from Antigua, the city and Pana. ▶▶ *See Transport, page 265.*

Background

Often called 'Chichi' but also known as Santo Tomás, Chichicastenango is the hub of the Maya-K'iche' highlands. The name derives from the *chichicaste*, a prickly purple plant-like a nettle, which grows profusely, and *tenango*, meaning 'place of'. Today the locals call the town 'Siguan Tinamit' meaning 'place surrounded by ravines'. The townsfolk are also known as *Masheños*, which comes from the word *Max*, also meaning Tomás. About 1000 *ladinos* live in the town, but 20,000 Maya live in the hills nearby and flood the town for the Thursday and Sunday markets. The town itself has winding streets of white houses roofed with bright red tiles, which wander over a little knoll in the centre of a cup-shaped valley surrounded by high mountains. The men's traditional outfit is a short-waisted embroidered jacket and knee breeches of black cloth, a woven sash and an embroidered kerchief around the head. The cost of this outfit, now over US$200, means that fewer and fewer men are wearing it. Women wear *huípiles* with red embroidery against black or brown and their *cortes* have dark blue stripes.

Chichicastenango

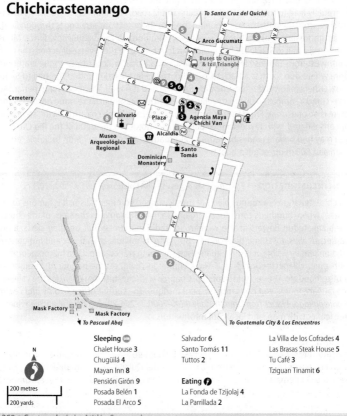

Sleeping 😊
Chalet House **3**
Chugüilá **4**
Mayan Inn **8**
Pensión Girón **9**
Posada Belén **1**
Posada El Arco **5**

Salvador **6**
Santo Tomás **11**
Tuttos **2**

Eating 🍴
La Fonda de Tzijolaj **4**
La Parrillada **2**

La Villa de los Cofrades **4**
Las Brasas Steak House **5**
Tu Café **3**
Tziguan Tinamit **6**

N

200 metres
200 yards

Sights

A large plaza is the focus of the town, with two white churches facing one another: **Santo Tomás** the parish church and **Calvario**. Santo Tomás, founded in 1540, is open to visitors, although photography is not allowed, and visitors are asked to be discreet and enter by a side door (through an arch to the right). Next to Santo Tomás are the cloisters of the Dominican monastery (1542). Here the famous *Popol Vuh* manuscript of the Maya creation story was found. A human skull wedged behind a carved stone face, found in Sacapulas, can be seen at the **Museo Arqueológico Regional** ① *main plaza, Tue, Wed, Fri, Sat 0800-1200, 1400-1600, Thu 0800-1600, Sun 0800-1400, closed Mon, US$0.70, photographs and video camera not permitted*. There's also a jade collection once owned by 1926-1944 parish priest Father Rossbach.

The Sunday and Thursday markets are both very touristy, and bargains are harder to come by once shuttle-loads of people arrive mid-morning. Articles from all over the Highlands are available: rugs, carpets and bedspreads; walk one or two streets away from the main congregation of stalls for more realistic prices, but prices are cheaper in Panajachel for the same items and you won't find anything here that you can't find in Panajachel.

The idol, **Pascual Abaj**, a god of fertility, is a large black stone with human features on a hill overlooking the town. Crosses in the ground surrounding the shrine are prayed in front of for the health of men, women and children, and for the dead. Fires burn and the wax of a thousand candles, flowers and sugar cover the shrine. One ceremony you may see is that of a girl from the town requesting a good and sober husband. If you wish to undergo a ceremony to plead for a partner, or to secure safety from robbery or misfortune, you may ask the *curandero* (US$7 including photographs). To reach the deity, walk along 5 Avenida, turn right on 9 Calle, down the hill, cross the stream and take the second track from the left going steepest uphill, which passes directly through a farmhouse and buildings. The farm now belongs to a mask-maker whom you can visit and buy masks from. Follow the path to the top of the pine-topped hill where you may well see a Maya ceremony in progress. It's about half an hour's walk. The site can be easily visited independently (in a small group), or an INGUAT-approved guide arranged through the local tourist committee can take you there and explain its history and significance (US$6.50, one or two hours, identified by a license in town).

Santa Cruz del Quiché and around → *Population: 7750. Altitude: 2000 m.*

Santa Cruz del Quiché, often simply called Quiché, is a quaint, friendly town, with a colourful daily market covering several blocks. There are few tourists here and prices are consequently reasonable. Its main attraction is **Utatlán**, the remains of the Maya K'iche' capital. The large Parque Central has a military garrison on the east side with a jail on the lower floor and a sinister military museum with reminders of recent conflicts above. The town's fiesta – about 14-20 August – varies around the Assumption.

Three kilometres away are the remains of temples and other structures of the former Quiché capital, **Gumarcaj**, sometimes spelt **K'umarkaaj**, and now generally called **Utatlán** ① *0800-1700, US$1.30, from the bus station, walk west along 10 Calle for 40 mins until you reach a small junction with a blue sign (SECP), take the right lane up through gates to the site*. The city was largely destroyed by the Spaniards, but the stonework of the original buildings can be seen in the ruins, which can be reached on foot; the setting is very attractive and well maintained. There are two subterranean burial chambers (take a torch, as there are unexpected drops) still used by the Maya for worship and chicken sacrifices. The seven plazas, many temples, ball court, gladiator's archway and other features are marked.

There is a paved road east from Quiché to (8 km) **Santo Tomás Chiché**, a picturesque village with a fine, rarely visited Saturday market (fiesta 25-28 December). There is also a road to this village from Chichicastenango. Although it is a short-cut, it is rough and virtually impassable in any vehicle. It makes a good, three- to four-hour walk, however. Further east (45 km) from Chiché is **Zacualpa**, where beautiful woollen bags are woven. The church has a remarkably fine façade and there is an unnamed *pensión* near the plaza. Market days are Sunday and Thursday.

At **Joyabaj** women weave fascinating *huípiles* and there is a colourful Sunday market, followed by a procession at about noon from the church led by the elders with drums and pipes. This was a stopping place on the old route from Mexico to Antigua. There is good walking in the wooded hills around, for example north to Chorraxaj (two hours), or across the Río Cocol south to Piedras Blancas to see blankets being woven. During fiesta week (9-15 August) Joyabaj has a *Palo Volador* and other traditional dances. There is a restaurant next to the Esso station on the Santa Cruz end of the plaza with a bank opposite (will change US dollars cash).

The road east to Cobán
The road east from **Sacapulas** is one of the most beautiful mountain roads in all Guatemala, with magnificent scenery in the narrow valleys. There is accommodation in **Uspantán** and this is the place to stay for the night enroute to Cobán. The road is not paved beyond Uspantán. ▶ *See Transport, page 266.*

It's a five-hour walk from Uspantán south to **Chimul**, the birthplace of **Rigoberta Menchú**, Nobel Peace Prize winner in 1992. The village was virtually wiped out during the 1980s, but the settlement is coming to life again. Only pickups go to the village.

The Ixil Triangle → *For listings, see pages 254-267.*

The Ixil Triangle is made of up of the highland communities of Nebaj, Chajul and Cotzal. The forested mountainous scenery provides great walking opportunities, although sadly, out of local necessity, many of the slopes have been badly deforested and the wood burnt for fires. The traditional dress of the Nebaj women – an explosion of primary colours – is spectacular. Much of this area was decimated during the Civil War and then repopulated with the introduction of 'model villages' established by the government. Evidence of wartime activities can still be seen and more remote Maya Ixil-speaking villages are gradually opening up to visitors with the introduction of hostel and trekking facilities.

Nebaj and around → *Colour map 2, B1.*

The town of Nebaj is high in the Cuchumatanes Mountains and its green slopes are often layered with mist. It is coloured by the beautiful dress worn by the local women, in an extravaganza of predominantly green, with red, yellow, orange, white and purple. The *corte* is mainly maroon with vertical stripes of black and yellow; some are bright red, and the *huípil* is of a geometric design. The women also wear a headdress with colourful bushy pom-poms on them. The men hardly ever wear the traditional costume; their jacket is red and embroidered in black designs. The main plaza is dominated by a large, simple white church. At the edge of the plaza there are weaving cooperatives selling *cortes, huípiles* and handicrafts from the town and the surrounding area – bargaining is possible. When you arrive, boys will meet you from incoming buses and will guide you to a *hospedaje* – they expect a tip. Nebaj has Sunday and Thursday markets and a fiesta on 12-15 August with traditional dancing. There is an excellent website for Nebaj, www.nebaj.com, run by **Solidaridad Internacional**, with useful phrases in Ixil and your daily Maya horoscope. There's a **tourist office** ① *6a Av and 8a Calle Cantón Vitzal, T7755-8337.*

La tumba de la Indígena Maya is a shrine just outside Nebaj (15 minutes) where some of those massacred during the war were buried. Take the same route as to Ak'Tzumbal, but at the bottom of the very steep hill, immediately after the bridge over the river, take a left, walk straight on over a paved road, then you come to a small junction – carry straight on until you see a minor crossroads on a path with an orange house gate to your left. Look up and you will see a small building. This is the shrine. Walk to your right where you will see a steep set of stairs leading to the shrine.

There is a walk to **Ak'Tzumbal**, through fields with rabbits, and through long, thin earth tunnels used by the military and guerrillas during the war. You need a guide to walk this cross-country route. Alternatively you can take the road to Ak'Tzumbal, where the new houses still display signs warning of the danger of land mines. Walk down 15 Avenida de Septiembre away from the church, and take a left just before **El Triangulo** gas station past **El Viajero Hospedaje**, then left and then right down a very steep hill and keep walking (1½ hours). When you reach a small yellow tower just before a fork – take the right (the left goes to Salquil Grande) to reach the 'model village'. Above the village of Ak'Tzumbal is **La Pista**, an airstrip used during the war. Next to it bomb craters scar the landscape. Only a few avocado trees, between the bomb holes, survive, and the *gasolinera* to refuel planes, is still there, although it is now covered in corrugated iron. Ask around for directions.

Chajul and Cotzal

Chajul, the second largest village in the Ixil Triangle, is known for its part in the Civil War, where Rigoberta Menchú's brother was killed in the plaza, as relayed in her book *I, Rigoberta Menchú*. According to the Nobel Peace Prize winner on 9 September 1979, her 16-year-old brother Petrocinio was kidnapped after being turned in for 15 quetzales. He was tortured in the plaza by the army along with numerous others. Villagers were forced to watch the torture under threat of being branded communists. People were set on fire, but the onlookers had weapons and looked ready to fight. This caused the army to withdraw. Chajul's main fiesta is the second Friday in Lent. There is also a pilgrimage to Christ of Golgotha on the second Friday in Lent, beginning the Wednesday before (the image is escorted by 'Romans' in blue police uniforms). Market day is Tuesday and Friday. It is possible to walk from Chajul to Cotzal. It is a six-hour walk from Nebaj to Chajul. A couple of very basic *hospedajes* are in town.

Cotzal is spread over a large area on a number of steep hills. The village's fiesta is 22-25 June, peaking on the day of St John the Baptist (24 June). Market days are Wednesday and Saturday. You can hire bikes from **Maya Tour** on the plaza next to the church. Nebaj to Cotzal is a pleasant four-hour walk. There's no accommodation or restaurants in other small villages and it is difficult to specify what transport is available in this area as trucks and the occasional pickup or commercial van are affected by road and weather conditions. For this reason, be prepared to have to spend the night in villages.

For Sleeping and Eating price codes and other relevant information, see Essentials pages 31-33.

⊜ Sleeping

Chimaltenango and around p239

B La Posada de Mi Abuelo, Carretera a Yepocapa, Parramos, T7849-5930, www.laposadademiabuelo.com. A delightful inn formerly a coffee farm, good restaurant. Packages with horse riding, biking and meals are available.

F Pixcayá, 0 Av, 1-82, Comalapa, T7849-8260. Hot water, parking.

Sololá p242

E Del Viajero, 7 Av, 10-45, on Parque Central (also annexe around the corner on Calle 11) T7762-3683. Rooms with bath, cheaper without, spacious, clean and friendly, good food in restaurant on plaza (El Cafetín).

F El Paisaje, 9 Calle, 5-41, 2 blocks from Parque Central, T7762-3820. Pleasant colonial courtyard, shared baths and toilets, clean, hot water, restaurant, good breakfast, family-run, laundry facilities.

Panajachel p242, map p243

AL Atitlán, 1 km west of centre on lake, 2nd turning off the road to Sololá, T7762-1441, www.hotelatitlan.com. Full board available, colonial style, excellent rooms and service, beautiful gardens with views across lake, pool, private beach, top-class restaurant.

A Posada de Don Rodrigo, final Calle Santander, overlooks the lake, T7762-2326, www.posadadedonrodrigo.com. Pool, sauna, terrace, gardens, good restaurant, excellent food and service, comfortable and luxurious bathrooms, fireplaces.

A Rancho Grande, Calle Rancho Grande, Centro, T7762-1554, www.ranchogrande inn.com. Cottages in charming setting, 4 blocks from beach, popular for long stay, good, including breakfast with pancakes. Pool with café in spacious gardens with good children's play equipment. Staff are helpful. Recommended.

B Dos Mundos, Calle Santander 4-72, Centro, T7762-2078, www.hoteldosmundos.com. Pool, cable TV, some rooms surround pool, good Italian restaurant (La Lanterna). Breakfast included.

B Posada de los Volcanes, Calle Santander, 5-51, Centro, T7762-0244, www.posadade losvolcanes.com. 12 rooms with bath, hot water, clean, comfortable, quiet, friendly owners, Julio and Jeanette Parajón.

C Müllers Guest House, Calle Rancho Grande 1-81, Centro, T7762-2442. Comfortable, quiet, good breakfast included. Recommended.

C Primavera, Calle Santander, Centro, T7762-2052, www.primaveratitlan.com. Clean, bright rooms, with TV, cypress wood furniture, gorgeous showers, washing machine available, friendly. Recommended. **Chez Alex** next door serves French food but lovely patio setting at the back. Don't get a room overlooking the street at weekends.

D Montana, Callejón Don Tino, near bell tower in the old town, T7762-2180, www.hotelmontanapanajachel.com. Comfortable, TV, hot water, parking, Wi-Fi, large patio filled with plants.

D Riva Bella, Calle Real, 2-21, Centro, T7762-1348. Bungalows with parking, with bath, good, clean, nice garden. Recommended.

E Hospedaje Casa Linda, Callejón El Capulín, Centro, T7762-0386. Hot shower in shared or private bathrooms, garden, friendly, clean and quiet. Good value. Recommended.

E Hospedaje El Viajero, final Calle Santander, Centro, T7762-0128, www.sleeprentbuy.com/ elviajero. With bath, comfortable large, clean rooms, hot water, friendly, laundry facilities, nice flower garden.

E Hospedaje Ramos I, close to public beach, T7762-0413. Run by Maya family, friendly, safe, with bath, hot water, clean, good value, some rooms have TV. View from 2nd floor.

E Mario's Rooms, Calle Santander esq Calle 14 Febrero, Centro, T7762-1313. Cheaper without bath, with garden, clean, bright rooms, hot showers, good breakfast, but not included, popular and friendly.

E Santa Isabel, Calle del Embarcadero 8-86, Centro, T7762-1462. 2 rooms in large house, quiet, hot water, with bath, friendly, nice gardens, parking, also fully equipped bungalow for longer rent. Recommended.

E Zanahoria Chic, 3 Av 0-46, Av de los Arboles, old town, T7762-1249, www.zanahoriachic.com. Restaurant, rooms above, clean, TV, hot water in shared or private bathrooms, colonial style, friendly, coffee, luggage store.

F Hospedaje Sánchez, Calle El Chali 3-65, Centro, T7762-2224. Clean, friendly, hot shower, family-run, quiet, comfortable. Recommended.

F Hospedaje Villa Lupita, Callejón Don Tino, old town, T5054-2447. Pretty courtyard, hot showers, clean, friendly, parking, good value. Recommended.

Apartments

Ask around for houses to rent; available from US$125 a month for a basic place, to US$200, but almost impossible to find in Nov and Dec. Break-ins and robberies of tourist houses are not uncommon. Water supply is variable.

Apartamentos Bohemia, Callejón Chinimaya, rents furnished bungalows.

Camping

Possible in the grounds of **Hotel Visión Azul** and **Tzanjuyú** – see above for details.

Santa Catarina Palopó p245

You can stay in private houses (ask around) or rent rooms (take sleeping bag).

LL Casa Palopó, Carretera a San Antonio Palopó, Km 6.8, less than 1 km beyond Santa Catarina, on the left up a steep hill, T5773-7777, www.casapalopo.com. One of the finest hotels in the country, 9 beautiful rooms all richly furnished, flowers on arrival, excellent service, heated pool, spa, gym,

top-class restaurant overlooking the lake – reservations necessary.

L Tzam Poc Resort, Vía Rural Km 6.5, T7762-2680, www.atitlanresort.com. Resort on the slopes above Santa Catarina with an amazing infinity pool. Lovely villas and spa. There's also an archery range.

A Villa Santa Catarina, T7762-1291, www.villasdeguatemala.com. 36 comfortable rooms with balconies around the pool, most with view of the lake. Good restaurant.

B Hotel Terrazas del Lago, T7762-0157, www.hotelterrazasdellago.com. On the lake with view, bath, clean, restaurant, a unique hotel built up over the past 30 plus years.

San Lucas Tolimán p245

A Toliman, Av 6, 1 block from the lake, T7722-0033. 18 rooms and suites in colonial style washed in terracotta colours with some lovely dark wood furniture. Suite No 1 is very romantic with lit steps to a sunken bath, good but expensive restaurant (reservations), fine gardens, pool, partial lake views. Recommended.

D Casa Cruz Inn, Av 5 4-78, a couple of blocks from the park. Clean, comfortable beds, run by an elderly couple, garden, quiet, good value.

D Hotel y Restaurante Don Pedro, Av 6, on lakeside, T7722-0028. Unattractive building – a sort of clumsy rustic, 12 rooms, a little rough around the edges, restaurant, bar.

D La Cascada de María, Calle 6, 6-80, T7722-0136. With bath, TV, parking, garden, restaurant, good.

Santiago Atitlán p246

Book ahead for Holy Week.

A-C Posada de Santiago, 1.5 km south of town, T7721-7366, www.posadade santiago.com. Highly recommended relaxing lakeside lodge with comfortable stone cottages (some cheaper accommodation), restaurant with home-grown produce and delicious food, tours and pool. Massage and language classes arranged. Friendly and amusing management – David, Susie and his mum, Bonnie – quite a trio. Has its own dock or walk from town.

B Bambú, on the lakeside, 500 m by road towards San Lucas, T7721-7332, www.ecobambu.com. 10 rooms, 2 bungalows and 1 *casita* in an attractive setting with beautifully tended gardens, restaurant, a secluded pool, a few mins by *lancha* from the dock. Kayaks available.

D-E Chi-Nim-Ya, walk up from the dock, take the first left and walk 50 m and it's there on the left, T7721-7131. Good, clean, comfortable and friendly, cheaper without bath, good value, good café, cheap, large helpings.

E Tztuhil, on left up the road from the dock to centre, above **Ferretería La Esquina**, T7721-7174. With bath and TV, cheaper without, restaurant, great views, good.

Camping
Camping is possible near **Bambú**.

San Pedro La Laguna *p246, map p247*
Accommodation is mostly cheap and laid back; your own sleeping bag, etc, will be useful.

D Hotelito El Amanecer Sak' Cari, T7721-8096, www.hotelsakcari.com. With bath, hot water, lovely rooms with great garden – get those with fabulous lake views. Extremely good value. Recommended.

D Mansión del Lago, T7721-8041, www.hotelmansiondellago.com. Up a hill with good views, with bath, hot water, TV costs more, very good value.

E Hospedaje Casa Elena, along the path behind **Nick's Place**. With large bathrooms or shared bath (some are nicer than others), clean, excellent views of lake. Recommended.

E Hotel San Francisco. Rooms with lake view, garden, cooking facilities, cold water, helpful owner, washing facilities, cheaper without bath, good value. Tours offered.

E Pinocchio. Rooms with private bath, nice garden and use of kitchen. Hammocks available.

E Ti-Kaaj, uphill from Santiago dock, 1st right. Simple rooms, hammock space, popular with backpackers, lovely garden and small pool; basic, but worth it for pool.

E Villa Sol, T2334-0327. With bath, cheaper shared, but the rooms aren't as nice. The newer part is a lot nicer. There are 2 bungalows with kitchen facilities, friendly staff, nice rooms. Recommended.

F Hospedaje Buenas Nuevas. Small, friendly, with hot shower.

San Juan La Laguna *p248*
A-B Hotel Uxlabil, T5990-6016/2366-9555 (in Guatemala City), www.uxlabil.com. This is an eco-hotel set up on the hill with its own dock (flooded, like all the village shore, in 2010), a short walk from the town centre. It's run by very friendly people with a small restaurant, and beautiful views from its rooftop terrace. It is a perfect, relaxing getaway, with Maya sauna and tended gardens, in this most unassuming and interesting of towns. It has links with the ecotourism association in town. Recommended.

San Marcos La Laguna *p248*
A-B Aaculaax, Las Pirámides dock, on a path from the **Centro Holístico**, T5287-0521, www.aaculaax.com. A Hansel-and-Gretel affair on the lake shore. It is a blend of cave work with Gaudí-type influence from the stained-glass work down to the sculptures and lamp shades. A corner of artistic Nirvana on Lake Atitlán – this place is highly recommended. Each of the 7 rooms with private bathroom is different, with quirky decor. It is run on an eco-basis, compost toilets and all. It is run by a German, Niels. There is a restaurant, bar, bakery and massage room. Also glass and papier mâché workshops.

B-D Posada Schumann, 2nd dock, T5202-2216, www.posadaschumann.com. With waterfront and dock, bungalows in attractive gardens, some with kitchenettes, sauna, restaurant, restaurant.

D-E Hotel Jinava, 2nd dock, left at the top of first pathway, T5299-3311, www.hoteljinava.com. This is heaven on a hill. With fabulous views, it clings to a steep slope with lovely rooms, restaurants, terraces and a patio. Books and games and solitude if you want it. Close to the lakeshore with its own dock where launches will drop you. Only 5 rooms, breakfast included. German-owned. Recommended.

E La Paz, 2nd dock, first pathway, T5702-9168. Bungalows and 1 dorm (**F** per person), vegetarian restaurant, quiet with nice communal area, popular.

E Las Pirámides del Ka, Las Pirámides dock, www.laspiramidesdelka.com. A residential, meditation centre. See also page 196.

F Quetzal, Las Pirámides dock, 2nd pathway, T5306-5039. Price per person. 4 bunk rooms, shared bath, restaurant.

F Unicornio, Las Pirámides dock, 2nd pathway. With self-catering, bungalows, shared kitchen and bathrooms. Has a little post office.

San Marcos to Santa Cruz *p248*
A Lomas de Tzununá, Tzununá, T7820-4060, www.lomasdetzununa.com. This hotel enjoys a spectacular position high up above the lake. The views from the restaurant terrace are magnificent. The 10 spacious rooms, decorated with local textiles, have 2 beds each with lake views and a balcony. The hotel, run by a friendly Belgian family, offers walking, biking, kayaking and cultural tours. The restaurant (♔-♔) uses home-made ingredients, the hotel is run on solar energy and the pool does not use chlorine. Board games, internet, bar and giant chess available. The family are reforesting a hill. Breakfast and taxes included.

B La Casa del Mundo, Jaibalito, T5218-5332, www.lacasadelmundo.com. Enjoys one of the most spectacular positions on the entire lake. Room No 15 has the best view followed by room No 1. Cheaper rooms have shared bathrooms. Many facilities, standard family-style dinner, lakeside hot tub, a memorable place with fantastic views. Repeatedly recommended.

Santa Cruz La Laguna *p249*
AL-B Villa Sumaya, Paxanax, beyond the dock, about 15 mins' walk, T5810-7199, www.villasumaya.com. Including breakfast, with its own dock, sauna, massage and healing therapies, yoga, comfortable, peaceful.

B-D La Casa Rosa, to the right as you face the dock from the water, along a path, T5416-1251, www.atitlanlacasarosa.com. Bungalows and rooms, with bath, cheaper without, home-made meals, attractive garden, sauna. Candlelit dinners at weekends.

C-E Arca de Noé, to the left of the dock, T5515-3712. Bungalows, cheaper rooms with shared bathrooms, good restaurant, BBQ, lake activities arranged, nice atmosphere, veranda overlooking a really beautiful flower-filled gardens and the lake. Low-voltage solar power.

C-E La Iguana Perdida, opposite dock, T5706-4117, www.laiguanaperdida.com. Rooms with and without bathroom and dorm (**F** per person) with shared bath, lively, especially weekends, delicious vegetarian food, BBQ, popular, friendly, great atmosphere. ATI Divers centre (see page 262), waterskiing; kayaks and snorkelling. Bring a torch.

Chichicastenango *p249, map p250*
You won't find accommodation easily on Sat evening, when prices are increased. As soon as you get off the bus, boys will swamp you and insist on taking you to certain hotels.

AL Santo Tomás, 7 Av, 5-32, T7756-1061. A very attractive building with beautiful colonial furnishings and parrots in patios. It is often full at weekends, pool, sauna, good restaurant and bar. Buffet lunch (US$14) on market days in stylish dining room, with attendants in traditional dress.

A Mayan Inn, corner of 8 Calle, 1-91, T7756-1176, www.mayaninn.com.gt. A classic, colonial-style courtyard hotel, filled with plants, polished antique furniture, beautiful dining room and bar with fireplaces. Gas-heated showers and internet The staff are very friendly and wear traditional dress. Secure parking.

C Posada El Arco, 4 Calle, 4-36, T7756-1255. Clean, very pretty, small, friendly, garden, washing facilities, negotiate lower rates for stays longer than a night, some large rooms, good view, parking, English spoken.

C-D Chalet House, 3 Calle, 7-44, T7756-1360, www.chalethotelguatemala.com. A clean, guesthouse with family atmosphere, hot water. Don't be put off by the dingy street.

D Chugüilá, 5 Av, 5-24, T7756-1134, hotelchuguila@yahoo.com. Some rooms with fireplaces. Avoid the front rooms, which are noisy, restaurant.

E Tuttos, 12 Calle, near **Posada Belén**, T7756-7540. Reasonable rooms.

E Pensión Girón, Edif Girón on 6 Calle, 4-52, T7756-1156. Clean rooms with bath, cheaper without, hot water, parking, 17 rooms.

F Posada Belén, 12 Calle, 5-55, T7756-1244. With bath, cheaper without, hot water, clean, will do laundry, fine views from balconies and hummingbirds in attractive garden, good value. Recommended.

F Salvador, 10 Calle, 4-47. 55 large rooms with bath, a few with fireplace (wood for sale in market), good views over town, parking. Cheaper, smaller rooms without bath available.

Santa Cruz del Quiché and around *p251*

Several very basic options around the bus arrival/departure area.

D Rey K'iché, 8 Calle, 0-9, 2 blocks from bus terminal. Clean, comfortable, hot water, parking, restaurant, TV.

E Maya Quiché, 3 Av 4-19, T7755-1667. With bath, hot water, restaurant.

E San Pascual, 7 Calle, 0-43, good location 2 blocks south of the central plaza, T5555-1107. With bath, cheaper without, quiet, locked parking.

G La Cascada, 10 Av, 10 Calle. Friendly, clean.

The road east to Cobán *p252*

There are a couple of *hospedajes* in Uspantán.

E Galindo, 4 blocks east of the Parque Central. Clean, friendly, recommended.

The Ixil Triangle *p252*

F Solidaridad Internacional supports 6 hostels in the villages of **Xexocom**, **Chortiz**, **Xeo**, **Cocop**, **Cotzol** and **Párramos Grande** where there is room for 5 people. Contact them at the PRODONT-IXIL office, Av 15 de Septiembre, Nebaj.

Nebaj and around *p252*

C-E Hotel Turansa, 1 block from plaza down 5 Calle, T7755-8219. Tiny rooms, but very clean, soap, towels, 2nd-floor rooms are nicer, cable TV and parking, little shop in entrance, phone service.

D-E Hotel Mayan Ixil, on north side of main square, T7755-8168. Just 5 rooms with private bath and gas hot water. Small restaurant overlooking the plaza, internet service downstairs.

D-E Ilebal Tenam, Cantón Simecal, bottom of Av 15 de Septiembre, road to Chajul, T7755-8039. Hot water, shared and private bath, very clean, friendly, parking inside, attractive decor.

E Hospedaje Esperanza, 6 Av, 2-36. Very friendly, clean, hot showers in shared bathroom, noisy when evangelical churches nearby have activities, hotel is cleaner than it looks from the outside.

F Hostal Ixil Don Juan, 0 Av A, 1 Calle B, Canton Simocol. Take Av 15 de Septiembre and take a left at **Comedor Sarita**, opposite grey office of PRODONT-IXIL, then it's 100 m to the right, on the right, T7755-4014/1529. Part of **Programa Quiché**, run with the support of the EU, there are 6 beds in 2 rooms, each bed with a locked strongbox, and hot showers. The colonial building has a traditional sauna, *chuj*.

F Media Luna MediaSol, T5749-7450, www.nebaj.com/hostel.htm. A backpackers' hostel close to **El Descanso** restaurant with dorms and private rooms. The hostel's also got a little kitchenette, DVD player and Wi-Fi.

Cotzal p253

F Cafetería and Hospedaje Christian, alongside the church. Basic.

F Hostal Doña Teresa. Has a sauna, patio and honey products for sale.

🍴 Eating

Panajachel p242, map p243

🍴🍴🍴 Chez Alex, Calle Santander, centre, T7762-0172. Open 1200-1500 and 1800-2000. French menu, good quality, mainly tourists, credit cards accepted.

🍴🍴🍴 Tocoyal, annexe to Hotel del Lago. A/c, groups welcome, buffet on request but tourist prices.

🍴🍴 Circus Bar, Av Los Arboles 0-62, T7762-2056. Open 1200-2400. Italian dishes including delicious pasta and pizzas, good coffee, popular. Live music from 2030, excellent atmosphere. Recommended.

🍴🍴 Crossroads Café, Calle de Campanario 0-27. Tue-Sat 0900-1300,1500-1900. Global choice of quality coffee, but you can't go wrong with Guatemalan! Excellent cakes.

🍴🍴 El Patio, Calle Santander. Good food, very good large breakfasts, quiet atmosphere but perfect for people-watching from the garden. Try the amaretto coffee.

🍴🍴 Guajimbo's, Calle Santander. Good atmosphere, excellent steaks, fast service, popular, live music some evenings. Recommended.

🍴🍴 La Rosticería, Av Los Arboles 0-42, T7762-2063. Daily 0700-2300. Good food, try eggs 'McChisme' for breakfast, good fresh pasta, excellent banana cake, good atmosphere, popular, a bit pricey. Live piano music at weekends, friendly service.

🍴🍴 Los Pumpos, Calle del Lago. Varied menu, bar, good fish and seafood dishes.

🍴🍴 Pana Rock Café with Pana Arte upstairs, Calle Santander 3-72. Buzzing around happy hour (2 for 1), salsa music, very popular, international food, pizza.

🍴🍴 Sunset Café, superb location on the lake. Open 1100-2400. Excellent for drinks, light

meals and main dishes, live music evenings, but you pay for the view.

🍴-🍴 Bombay, Calle Santander near Calle 15 Febrero, T7762-0611. Open 1100-2130. Vegetarian recipes, including spicy curries, German beer, Mexican food, good food and wines, set lunch popular, good service. Very highly recommended.

🍴-🍴 El Pájaro Azul, Calle Santander 2-75, T7762-2596. Café, bar, crêperie with gorgeous stuffed sweet or savoury crêpes, cakes and pies. Vegetarian options available. Reasonable prices, good for late breakfasts. 1000-2200. Recommended.

🍴 Deli Llama de Fuego, Calle Santander, T7762-2586. Thu-Tue 0700-2200. Sweet little café with a giant cheese plant as its focus. Breakfasts, muffins, bagels, pizzas, pasta, Mexican food and vegetarian sandwiches.

🍴 Restaurante Las Olas, overlooking the lake at the end of Calle Santander, down by the dock. Serves the absolute best nachos, great for just before catching the boat.

Bakeries

Maya Pan, Calle Santander 1-61. Excellent wholemeal breads and pastries, banana bread comes out of the oven at 0930, wonderful, cinnamon rolls and internet too. Recommended.

San Lucas Tolimán p245

🍴 La Pizza de Sam, Av 7, 1 block down from the plaza towards the lake. Pizzas and spaghetti.

🍴 Restaurant Jardín, orange building on corner of plaza. *Comida típica* and *licuados*.

Santiago Atitlán p246

There are many cheap *comedores* near the centre. The best restaurants are at the hotels.

🍴🍴🍴 El Pescador, on corner 1 block before Tzutuhil. Full menu, good but expensive.

🍴🍴🍴 Posada de Santiago, 1.5 km south of town, T/F7721-7167. Delicious, wholesome food and excellent service in lovely surroundings. Highly recommended.

🍴 Restaurant Wach'alal, close to Gran Sol. Daily 0800-2000. A small yellow-painted café serving breakfasts, snacks and cakes. Airy and pleasant.

San Pedro La Laguna *p246, map p247*

Be careful of drinking water in San Pedro; both cholera and dysentery exist here.

††-† Café Arte Libre, up the hill from **Hotel San Pedro**. All meals, vegetarian dishes, good value.

††-† Luna Azul, along shore. Popular for breakfast and lunch, good omelettes.

††-† Restaurant Maritza, with commanding views over lake. Chilled place to hang out with reggae music. Service is slow though. 5 rooms also to rent with shared bath. (**F**).

††-† Tin Tin. Good value, Thai food, delightful garden. Recommended.

† Buddha Bar. Shows movies every night and has a rooftop and sports bar.

† Café La Puerta, on the north shore coastal path. Open daily 0800-1700. Cheap, tasty dishes, with tables in a quirky garden, or looking out over the lake. Beautiful.

† Comedor Sta Elena, near Nick's Italian. Seriously cheap and filling breakfasts.

† El Fondeadero. Good food, lovely terraced gardens, reasonable prices.

† Emperador, up the hill. *Comedor* serving good local dishes.

† Fata Morgana, near the Panajachel dock, great focaccia bread sandwiches, with pizza and fine coffee too.

† Rosalinda, near centre of village. Friendly, breakfasts (eg *mosh*), local fish and good for banana and chocolate cakes.

† Shanti Shanti. Run by Israelis, Italian dishes.

† Thermal Baths, along shore from *playa*. Good vegetarian food and coffee, expensive.

† Zoola. Open 0900-2100. Close to the north shore, a quiet, hideaway with pleasant garden. A great spot .

San Marcos La Laguna *p248*

All hotels and hostels offer food.

††-† Il Giardino, up the 2nd pathway. Attractive garden, Italian owners, good breakfasts.

Chichicastenango *p249, map p250*

The best food is in the top hotels, but is expensive. On market days there are plenty of good food stalls and *comedores* in the centre of the plaza that offer chicken in different guises or a set lunch for US$1.50. There are several good restaurants in the **Centro Comercial Santo Tomás**, on the north side of the plaza (market).

†† La Fonda de Tzijolaj, on the plaza. Great view of the market below, good meals, pizza, prompt service, reasonable prices.

†† Las Brasas Steak House, 6 Calle 4-52, T7756-2226. Nice atmosphere, good steak menu, accepts credit cards.

††-† La Villa de los Cofrades, on the plaza. Café downstairs, breakfasts, cappuccinos, espressos, good value. There is a 2nd restaurant 2 blocks up the street towards Arco Gucumatz, more expensive, great people-watching upstairs location and an escape during market days, popular for breakfast.

††-† Tziguan Tinamit, on the corner of 5 Av, esq 6 Calle. Some local dishes, steaks, tasty pizzas, breakfasts, good pies but a little more expensive than most places, good.

† Caffé Tuttos, See Sleeping. Daily 0700-2200. Good breakfast deals, pizzas, and *menú del día*, reasonable prices.

† La Parrillada, 6 C 5-37, Interior Comercial Turkaj. Escape the market bustle, courtyard, reasonable prices, breakfast available.

† Tu Café, 5 Av 6-44, on market place, Santo Tomás side. Open 0730-2000. Snacks, budget breakfast, sandwiches, set lunch, good value.

Santa Cruz del Quiché and around *p251*

Try *sincronizadas*, hot tortillas baked with cubed ham, spiced chicken and cheese.

† La Cabañita Café, 1 Av, 1-17. Charming, small café with pinewood furniture, home-made pies and cakes, excellent breakfasts (pancakes, cereals, etc), eggs any way you want 'em, great snacks, for example *sincronizadas*.

† La Toscan, 1 Av just north of the church, same road as **La Cabañita**. A little pizza and *pastelería* with checked cloth-covered tables. Lasagne lunch a bargain with garlic bread and pizza by the slice also.

Nebaj and around *p252*

Boxboles are squash leaves rolled tightly with *masa* and chopped meat or chicken, boiled and served with salsa and fresh orange juice.

† **El Descanso**. Popular volunteer hang-out, good food and useful information about their other community-based projects (see www.nebaj.com).

† **Maya Ixil**, on the parque Central. Substantial food, local and international dishes, pleasant family atmosphere.

† **Pizza del César**. Daily 0730-2100. Breakfasts, mouth-wateringly good strawberry cake, and hamburgers as well as pizzas.

Cotzal *p253*

† **Comedor and Hospedaje El Maguey**. Bland meal, but decent size, plus drink, are served up for for US$1.70. Don't stay here though, unless you're desperate.

⊕ Entertainment

Panajachel *p242, map p243*

Circus Bar, Av los Arboles. Open daily 1200-0200. Good live music from 2030.
Discoteca Chapiteau, Av los Arboles 0-69, nightclub Thu-Sat 1900-0100.
El Aleph, Av los Arboles. One of a number of bars, Thu-Sat 1900-0300.

San Pedro La Laguna *p246, map p247*

Nick's Place, overlooking the main dock, is popular, and well frequented in the evening. Nearby are **Bar Alegre**, a sports bar (www.thealegrepub.com) and **D'noz**.
Ti Kaaj is another popular spot.

⊛ Festivals and events

Chichicastenango *p249, map p250*

1 Jan Padre Eterno.
20 Jan San Sebastián.
19 Mar San José.
Feb/Apr Jesús Nazareno and María de Dolores (both Fri in Lent).
Mar/Apr Semana Santa (Holy Week).
29 Apr San Pedro Mártir.
3 May Santa Cruz.
29 Jun Corpus Christi.
18 Aug Virgen de la Coronación.
14 Sep Santa Cruz.
29 Sep San Miguel.
30 Sep San Jerónimo Doctor.
1st Sun of Oct Virgen del Rosario.
2nd Sun in Oct Virgen de Concepción.
1 Nov San Miguel.
13-22 Dec Santo Tomás, with 21 Dec being the main day. There are processions, traditional dances, the *Palo Volador* (19, 20, 21 Dec) marimba music, well worth a visit – very crowded.

○ Shopping

Panajachel *p242, map p243*

Bartering is the norm. There are better bargains here than in Chichicastenango. The main tourist shops are on Calle Santander.
Tinamit Maya Shopping Centre, Calle Santander. Bargain for good prices. Maya sell their wares cheaply on the lakeside; varied selection, bargaining is easy/expected.
Librería del Lago, Calle Santander Local A-8, T7762-2788. Daily 0900-1800. Great bookshop selling a good range of quality English-language and Spanish books.

Chichicastenango *p249, map p250*

Chichicastenango's markets are on Sun and Thu. See page 251.
Ut'z Bat'z, 5a Avenida and 5a Calle, T50085193, is a women's Fair Trade weaving workshop, with free demonstrations; high-quality clothes and bags for sale.

▲ Activities and tours

Panajachel p242, map p243

Diving

ATI Divers, round the back of El Patio, Calle Santander, T5706-4117, www.laiguana perdida.com. A range of options including PADI Open Water US$220, fun dive US$30, 2 for US$50. PADI Rescue and Dive Master also available. Altitude speciality, US$80. Dives are made off Santa Cruz La Laguna and are of special interest to those looking for altitude diving. Here there are spectacular walls that drop off, rock formations you can swim through, trees underwater, and because of its volcanic nature, hot spots, which leaves the lake bottom sediment boiling to touch. Take advice on visibility before you opt for a dive.

Fishing

Lake fishing can be arranged, black bass (*mojarra*) up to 4 kg can be caught. Boats for up to 5 people can be hired for about US$15. Check with INGUAT for latest information.

Hang-gliding

Rogelio, contactable through **Americo's Tours**, Calle Santander, and other agencies will make arrangements, at least 24 hrs' notice is required. Jumps are made from San Jorge La Laguna or from above Santa Catarina, depending on weather conditions.

Kayaking and canoing

Kayak hire is around US$2 per hr. Ask at the hotels, INGUAT and at lakeshore. **Diversiones Acuáticos Balán**, in a small red and white tower on the lakeshore, rent out kayaks. Watch out for strong winds that occasionally blow up quickly across the lake; potentially dangerous in small boats.

Tour operators

All offer shuttle services to Chichicastenango, Antigua, the Mexican borders, etc, and some to San Cristóbal de las Casas (see Transport)

and can arrange most activities on and around the lake. There are a number of tour operators on Calle Santander, including those listed below. **Americo's Tours**, T7762-2021. **Centroamericana Tourist Service**, T7832-5032. **Tierra Maya**, T7725-7320. Friendly and reliable tour operator, which runs shuttles to San Cristóbal de las Casas as well as within Guatemala. **Toliman Travel**, T7762-1275. Also **Atitrans** on Edif Rincón Sai, T7762-2336, www.atitrans.com.

Waterskiing

Arrangements can be made with **ATI Divers** at **Iguana Perdida** in Santa Cruz.

Santiago Atitlán p246

Aventura en Atitlán, Jim and Nancy Matison, Finca San Santiago, T7811-5516. 10 km outside Santiago. Riding and hiking tours. **Francisco Tizná** from the Asociación de Guías de Turismo, T7721-7558, is extremely informative. Ask for him at the dock or at any of the hotels. Payment is by way of donation.

San Pedro La Laguna p246, map p247

A growing list of activities from hiking up the Nariz de Maya (5 hrs, US$13) and other local trips, through to local crafts. Yoga for all levels is available down towards the shore (US$5 for 1½ hrs).
Bigfoot, 0800-1900. Run by the super-helpful Juan Baudilio Chipirs, T7721-8203. Also close to the small streets away from the docks.

San Juan La Laguna p248

Rupalaj Kistalin, T5964-0040, rupalajkistalin@ yahoo.es, offers interesting cultural tours of the town visiting painters, weavers, *cofradías* and traditional healers. As well as this cultural circuit there is an adventure circuit taking in Panan forest and a canopy tour at Park Chuiraxamolo' or a nature circuit taking in a climb up the Rostro de Maya and fishing and kayaking. Highly recommended. Some of the local guides speak English.

San Marcos La Laguna *p248*
Wellbeing
Casa Azul Eco Resort, T5070-7101,
www.casa-azul-ecoresort.com, is a gorgeous
little place offering yoga and reiki, among
other therapies and writers' workshops
hosted by Joyce Maynard. There's also a
sauna, campfire and café/restaurant serving
vegetarian food. You can reach it from the
first dock, or from the centre of the village.
Las Pirámides del Ka, www.laspiramides
delka.com. The month-long course costs
US$420, or US$15 by the day if you stay for
shorter periods, accommodation included.
Courses are also available for non-residents.
In the grounds are a sauna, a vegetarian
restaurant with freshly baked bread and a
library. This is a relaxing, peaceful place.
San Marcos Holistic Centre, up the 2nd
pathway, beyond **Unicornio**, www.sanm
holisticcentre.com. Mon-Sat 1000-1700.
Offers iridology, acupuncture, kinesiology,
Indian head massage, reflexology and
massage. Classes in various techniques
can also be taken.

Chichicastenango *p249, map p250*
Maya Chichi Van, 6 Av, 6-45, T7756-2187,
mayachichivan@yahoo.com. Shuttles
and tours ranging from US$10-650.

Nebaj and around *p252*
Guías Ixiles (El Descanso Restaurant),
www.nebaj.com ½- to 3-day hikes, bike
rental. There's also a 3-day hike to Todos
Santos.
Solidaridad Internacional, Av 15 de
Septiembre, www.nebaj.org. Inside the
PRODONT-IXIL (Proyecto de Promoción
de Infraestructuras y Ecoturismo) office,
in a grey building on the right 1 block after
the **Gasolinera El Triángulo** on the road to
Chajul. For further information call in to see
the director Pascual, who is very helpful.
2-, 3- and 4-day hikes, horses available.
Options to stay in community *posadas*, with
packages available, from 1-4 days, full board,
from about US$100-200 per person.

Chajul and Cotzal *p253*
Ask Teresa at **Hostal Doña Teresa** about
trips from the Cotzal or ask for Sebastián
Xel Rivera who leads 1-day camping trips.

Transport

Chimaltenango and around *p239*
Bus
Any bus heading west from Guatemala
City stops at Chimaltenango. To **Antigua**
leave from the corner of the main road and
the road south to Antigua where there is a
lime green and blue shop – **Auto Repuestos
y Frenos Nachma**, 45 mins, US$0.34. To
Chichicastenango, every 30 mins, 0600-
1700, 2 hrs, US$2. To **Cuatro Caminos**,
2½ hrs, US$2.50. To **Quetzaltenango**,
every 45 mins, 0700-1800, 2½ hrs, US$2.80.
To **Tecpán** every 30 mins, 0700-1800, 1 hr.

**Routes west: Tecpán and
Los Encuentros** *p239*
Bus
From Tecpán to **Guatemala City**, 2¼ hrs,
buses every hour, US$2.20; easy day trip
from Panajachel or Antigua.

**To Lake Atitlán along the old
Pan-American Highway** *p241*
Bus
To and from **Godínez** there are several
buses to Panajachel, US$0.45 and 1 bus
daily Patzún–Godínez. To **San Andrés
Semetabaj**, bus to Panajachel, US$0.40.

Sololá *p242*
Bus
To **Chichicastenango**, US$0.50, 1½ hrs; to
Panajachel, US$0.38, every 30 mins, 20 mins,
or 1½-2 hrs' walk. To **Chimaltenango**,
US$1.20. To **Quetzaltenango**, US$1.8.
Colectivo to **Los Encuentros**, US$0.20.
To **Guatemala City** direct US$2.50, 3 hrs.

Panajachel *p242, map p243*

Boat

There are 2 types of transport – the scheduled ferry service to Santiago Atitlán and the *lanchas* to all the other villages. The tourist office has the latest information on boats. The boat service to **Santiago Atitlán** runs from the dock at the end of Calle Rancho Grande (Muelle Público) from 0600-1630, 8 daily, 20 mins in launch, US$3.10, 1 hr in the large **Naviera Santiago** ferry, T7762-0309 or 20-35 mins in the fast *lanchas*. Some *lanchas* to all the other villages leave from here, but most from the dock at the end of Calle Embarcadero run by **Tzanjuyú** from 0630-1700 every 45 mins or when full (min 10 people). If you set off from the main dock the *lancha* will pull in at the Calle Embarcadero dock as well. These *lanchas* call in at **Santa Cruz**, **Jaibalito**, **Tzununá**, **San Marcos**, **San Pablo**, **San Juan** and **San Pedro**, US$1.20 to US$2.50 to **San Marcos** and beyond. To **San Pedro** US$3.10. The first boat of the day is at 0700. If there is a demand, there will almost always be a boatman willing to run a service but non-official boats can charge what they like. Virtually all the dozen or so communities round the lake have docks, and you can take a regular boat to any of those round the western side. Note that, officially, locals pay less. The only reliable services back to Panajachel are from **Santiago** or **San Pedro** up to about 1600. If you wait on the smaller docks round the western side up this time, you can get a ride back to Panajachel, flag them down in case they don't see you, but they usually pull in if it's the last service of the day. Only buy tickets on the boat – if you buy them from the numerous ticket touts on the dockside, you will be overcharged. There are no regular boats to Santa Catarina, San Antonio or San Lucas: pickups and buses serve these communities, or charter a *lancha*, US$30 return to Santa Catarina and San Antonio. Bad weather can, of course, affect the boat services. Crossings are generally rougher in the afternoons, worth bearing in mind if you suffer from sea-sickness.

Boat hire and tours *Lanchas* can be hired to go anywhere round the lake, about US$100 for 5 people for a full day. For round trips to **San Pedro** and **Santiago** and possibly **San Antonio Palopó**, with stopovers, go early to the lakefront and bargain. Trip takes a full day, eg 0830-1530, with stops of 1 hr or so at each, around US$6-7, if the boat is full. If on a tour, be careful not to miss the boat at each stage – if you do, you will have to pay again.

Bus

Rebuli buses leave from opposite Hotel Fonda del Sol on Calle Real, otherwise, the main stop is where Calle Santander meets Calle Real. **Rebuli** to **Guatemala City**, 3½ hrs, US$3.30, crowded, hourly between 0500 and 1500. To **Guatemala City** via **Escuintla** south coast, 8 a day plus 3 Pullman a day. Direct bus to **Quetzaltenango**, 7 a day between 0530 and 1415, US$2.70, 2½ hrs. There are direct buses to **Los Encuentros** on the Pan-American Hwy (US$0.75). To **Chichicastenango** direct, Thu and Sun, 0645, 0700, 0730 and then hourly to 1530. Other days between 0700-1500, US$2, 1½ hrs. There are 4 daily direct buses to **Cuatro Caminos**, US$1.60 from 0530, for connections to Totonicapán, Quetzaltenango, Huehuetenango, etc. To **Antigua** take a bus up to Los Encuentros through Sololá. Change for a bus to **Chimaltenango** US$3.10, and change there for Antigua. There is also a direct bus (**Rebuli**) to **Antigua** leaving 1030-1100, daily, US$4.40. To **Sololá**, US$0.40, 20 mins, every 30 mins. You can wait for through buses by the market on Calle Real. The fastest way to southern **Mexico** is probably by bus south to Cocales, 2½ hrs, 5 buses between 0600 and 1400, then many buses along the Pacific Hwy to **Tapachula** on the border. For **La Mesilla**, take a bus up to Los Encuentros, change west for Cuatro Caminos. Here catch a bus north to La Mesilla. Some travel agencies go direct to

San Cristóbal de las Casas via La Mesilla, daily at 0600. See Tour operators, above.

Shuttles Services are run jointly by travel agencies, to **Guatemala City**, **Antigua**, **Quetzaltenango**, **Chichi** and more. Around 4 a day. **Antigua**, US$14, **Chichicastenango**, on market days, US$15, **Quetzaltenango** US$20 and the Mexican border US$40. Atitrans, Calle Santander, next to Hotel Regis, T7762-0146, is recommended.

Bicycle
Several rental agencies on Calle Santander, eg **Maco Cycle Rental** and **Tono Cycle Rental**. Also **Alquiler de Bicicletas Emanuel**, on Calle 14 de Febrero. Prices start at US$2 per hr or about US$10 for a day.

Motorcycle
Motorcycle hire About US$6 per hr, plus fuel and US$100 deposit. Try **Maco Cycle** near the junction of Calle Santander and 14 de Febrero, T7762-0883.
Motorcycle parts David's Store, opposite **Hotel Maya Kanek**, has good prices and also does repairs.

Santa Catarina Palopó *p245*
There are frequent pickups from Panajachel and boat services.

San Antonio Palopó *p245*
Frequent pickups from Panajachel. Enquire about boats.

San Lucas Tolimán *p245*
Boat Enquire about boats. Private *lancha*, US$35.
Bus To **Santiago Atitlán**, hourly and to **Guatemala City** via **Panajachel**.

Santiago Atitlán *p246*
Bus To **Guatemala City**, US$2.60 (5 a day, first at 0300). 2 **Pullmans** a day, US$3.40. To **Panajachel**, 0600, 2 hrs, or take any bus and change on main road south of San Lucas.

Boat 4 sailings daily to Pana with *Naviera*, 1¼ hrs, US$1.80, or by *lancha* when full, 20-35 mins, US$1.30-2. To **San Pedro** by *lancha* several a day, enquire at the dock for times, 45 mins, US$1.80.

San Pedro La Laguna *p246, map p247*
Boat
Up to 10 *lanchas* to **Panajachel**. To **Santiago**, leave when full (45 mins, US$2.50). To **San Marcos**, every 2 hrs. Private *lanchas* (10 people at US$2 each).

Bus
There are daily buses to **Guatemala City**, several leave in the early morning and early afternoon, 4 hrs, US$4.50, to **Antigua** and to **Quetzaltenango**, in the morning, 3½ hrs, US$3.

San Marcos La Laguna *p248*
Boat Service roughly every ½ hr to **Panajachel** and to **San Pedro**. Wait on any dock. Fare US$1.80 to either.
Bus San Pedro to Pan-American Hwy can be boarded at San Pablo. **Pickup** Frequent pickups from the village centre and anywhere along the main road. To **San Pedro**, US$0.50, less to villages en route.

Chichicastenango *p249, map p250*
Bus
Buses passing through Chichi all stop at 5 Av/5 Calle by the **Hotel Chugüilá**, where there are always police and bus personnel to give information. To **Guatemala City**, every 15 mins 0200-1730, 3 hrs, US$3.70. To **Santa Cruz del Quiché**, every ½ hr 0600-2000, US$0.70, 30 mins or 20 mins, if the bus driver is aiming for honours in the graduation from the School of Kamikaze Bus Tactics. To **Panajachel**, ½ hr, US$2, several until early afternoon or take any bus heading south and change at Los Encuentros. Same goes for **Antigua**, where you need to change at Chimaltenango. To **Quetzaltenango**, 5 between 0430-0830, 2½ hrs, US$3.80. To **Mexico**, and all points west, take any bus

to Los Encuentros and change. To **Escuintla** via Santa Lucía Cotzumalguapa, between 0300 and 1700, 3 hrs, US$2.80. There are additional buses to local villages especially on market days.

Shuttles operate to the capital, **Xela, Panajachel, Huehuetenango** and Mexican border. Maya Chichi Van, see Tour operators, above.

Santa Cruz del Quiché and around *p251*
Bus

Terminal at 10 Calle y 1 Av, Zona 5. To **Guatemala City**, passing through Chichicastenango, at 0300 until 1700, 3 hrs, US$4.50. To **Nebaj** and **Cotzal**, 8 a day, US$3.20, 2 hrs. Buses leave, passing through Sacapulas (1 hr, US$2.50), roughly every hour from 0800-2100. To **Uspantán**, via **Sacapulas**, for **Cobán** and **San Pedro Carchá** every hour, 2 hrs, US$3.90. To **Joyabaj**, several daily, via Chiché and Zacualpa, US$1.80, 1½ hrs. First at 0800 with buses going on to the capital. Last bus back to Quiché at 1600. It is possible to get to **Huehuetenango** in a day via Sacapulas, then pickup from bridge to **Aguacatán** and bus from there to Huehuetenango. Last bus to Huehue from Aguacatán, 1600. Daily buses also to **Quetzaltenango**, **San Marcos**, and to **Panajachel**. To **Joyabaj**, Joyita bus from **Guatemala City**, 10 a day between 0200 and 1600, 5 hrs, US$1.80. There are buses from **Quiché** to **San Andrés Sajcabajá**.

The road east to Cobán *p252*
Bus and truck

Several trucks to Cobán, daily in the morning from **Sacapulas**; 7 hrs if you're lucky, usually much longer. Start very early if you wish to make it to Cobán the same day. **Transportes Mejía** from Aguacatán to **Cobán** stops in Sacapulas on Tue and Sat mornings. Also possible to take Quiché–Uspantán buses (0930, 1300, 1500), passing Sacapulas at about 1030, 1400, 1600. Then take the early morning buses at 0300 and 0500 from

Uspantán to Cobán or the **Transportes Mejía** buses. After that, pickups leave when full. Hitchhiking to Cobán is also possible. Buses to Quiché 0300, 2200, other early-morning departures.

Nebaj and around *p252*
Bus

The bus ride to Quiché is full of fabulous views and hair-raising bends but the road is now fully paved. Buses to **Quiché** (US$3.20, 2½ hrs) passing through **Sacapulas** (1¾ hr from Nebaj, US$1.30) leave hourly from 0500-1530. Bus to **Cobán** leaves Gazolinera Quetzal at 0500, 4-5 hrs, US$6.50. Cobán to Nebaj at 1300. Alternatively get to Sacapulas on the main road, and wait for a bus.

Chajul and Cotzal *p253*
Bus

Buses to Chajul and Cotzal do not run on a set schedule. It is best to ask the day before you want to travel, at the bus station. There are buses and numerous pickups on Sun when villagers come to Nebaj for its market, which would be a good day to visit the villages. Alternatively, bargain with a local pickup driver to take you on a trip.

❶ Directory

Panajachel *p242, map p243*
Banks Banco Industrial, Calle Santander (TCs and Visa ATM), Calle Real, US$, TCs and cash, Visa ATM opposite. There is a *cambio* on the street near **Mayan Palace** for US$ cash and TCs. **Internet** Many in centre, shop around for best prices; standard is US$1 per hr. Cheaper in the old town. **Medical services** Centro de Salud Calle Real, just downhill from the road to San Antonio Palopó. **Farmacia Santander**, top end of Calle Santander, very good and helpful. **Post** Calle Santander. Difficult but not impossible to send parcels of up to 1 kg abroad as long as packing requirements are met. **Get Guated Out**, Centro Comercial,

Av Los Arboles, T/F7762-0595, good but more expensive service, they use the postal system but pack and deal with formalities for you. DHL, Edif Rincón Sai, Calle Santander. **Telephone** Telgua, Calle Santander and internet cafés. **Language schools** Jardín de América, Calle 14 de Febrero, T7762-2637, www.jardindeamerica.com. US$80 for 20 hrs per week tuition, lodging with family costs an additional US$60 per week. Jabel Tinamit, behind Edif Rincón Sai, T7762-0238, www.jabeltinamit.com. Similar tariff.

San Lucas Tolimán *p245*
Banks Banrural and Corpobanco.
Internet Available in the plaza.

Santiago Atitlán *p246*
Banks G&T Continental, opposite the church. **Internet** Next to Chim-ni-ya.

San Pedro La Laguna *p246, map p247*
Banks Banrural changes cash and TCs; Visa ATM. **Internet** There are several internet and phone offices. **Language schools** This is a popular place for learning Spanish. Students may make their own accommodation arrangements but homestays are possible. Casa Rosario, www.casarosario.com, offers classes from US$70 a week for 20 hrs a week. Corazón Maya, T7721-8160, www.corazonmaya.com, from US$49 a week. Tz'utujil classes also. Run by the welcoming Marta Navichoc. San Pedro, T5715-4604, www.sanpedrospanish school.org, from US$75 per week. School has a great location with gardens close to the lakeshore. **Medical services** Centro Médico opposite Educación Básica school has a good doctor who does not speak English.

San Juan La Laguna *p248*
Banks Banrural, diagonally opposite Nick's Place. Changes cash and TCs.
Internet There are a couple of places in town.

San Marcos La Laguna *p248*
Language schools Casa Rosario, T5613-6401. San Marcos Spanish School, T5852-0403, www.sanmarcos spanishschool.com. From US$76 per week.

Chichicastenango *p249, map p250*
Banks There are a number of banks in town taking Visa and MasterCard. Mayan Inn will exchange cash. **Internet** Aces, inside Hotel Girón, 6 Calle, 4-52. **Post** 7 Av, 8-47. Cropa Panalpina, 7 Av, 8-60, opposite post office, T7756-1028, www.cropa.com.gt. Will pack and ship your purchases back home by air cargo. **Telephone** Telgua, 6 Calle between 5 y 6.

Santa Cruz del Quiché and around *p251*
Banks Banco Industrial, 3 Calle y 2 Av, top corner of Parque Central, cash on Visa cards and TCs; G&T Continental, 6 Calle y 3 Av, Visa and MasterCard TCs. **Post** 3 Calle between 1 Av and 0 Av, Zona 5. **Telephone** Telgua, 1 Av/2 Calle, Zona 5.

Nebaj and around *p252*
Banks Banrural, TCs and Visa ATM. There are now a couple of ATMS. **Internet** There are a couple of internet services in town. **Language schools** The Nebaj Language School, www.nebajlanguageschool.com, US$145 a week including accommodation. **Post** Behind the bank.

Western highlands

Just before the volcanic highlands reach their highest peaks, this part of the western highlands takes the form of scores of small market towns and villages, each with its own character – the loud animal market at San Francisco El Alto, the extra-planetary landscape at Momostenango, and its Maya cosmovision centre, and the dancing extravaganzas at Totonicapán. The modern ladino town of Huehuetenango sits at the gateway to the Sierra de los Cuchumatanes, within which hides, in a cold gash in a sky-hugging valley, the indigenous town and weaving centre of Todos Santos Cuchumatán. ▸▸ *For listings, see pages 273-276.*

Ins and outs

This area is well connected by buses from the Cuatro Caminos junction, Quetzaltenango or Huehuetenango. The road from Cobán is another access option, although a much slower one. ▸▸ *See Transport, page 275.*

Nahualá and Cuatro Caminos

Before the major four-way junction of Cuatro Caminos, the Pan-American Highway runs past Nahualá, a Maya village at 2470 m. The traditional *traje* is distinctive and best seen on market days on Thursday and Sunday, when finely embroidered cuffs and collars are sold, as well as very popular *huípiles*. The **Fiesta de Santa Catalina** is on 23-26 November (25th is the main day). There is an unpaved all-weather road a little to the north and 16 km longer, from Los Encuentros (on the Pan-American Highway) through Totonicapán (40 km) to San Cristóbal Totonicapán. The route from Chichicastenango to Quiché, Xecajá and Totonicapán takes a day by car or motorcycle, but is well worth taking and recommended by cyclists. There are no buses. There is also a scenic road from Totonicapán to Santa Cruz del Quiché via San Antonio Ilotenango. It takes one hour by car or motorcycle and two hours by pickup truck. There are no buses on this route either.

Cuatro Caminos is a busy junction with roads, east to Totonicapán, west to Los Encuentros, north to Huehuetenango and south to Quetzaltenango. Buses stop here every few seconds so you will never have to wait long for a connection. There is a petrol station and lots of vendors to keep you fed and watered. Just north of Cuatro Caminos is **San Cristóbal Totonicapán**, noted for its *huípiles*.

Totonicapán → *Colour map 2, B1. Altitude: 2500 m.*

The route to San Miguel Totonicapán, the capital of its department, passes through pine-forested hillsides, pretty red-tiled roofs and *milpas* of maize on the road side. The 18th-century beige church stands on one of the main squares, unfortunately now a parking lot, at 6 y 7 Avenida between 3 and 4 Calle. The market is considered by Guatemalans to be one of the cheapest, and it is certainly very colourful. Saturday is the main market noted for ceramics and cloth, with a small gathering on Tuesdays. There is a traditional dance fiesta on 12-13 August, music concerts and a chance to see *cofradía* rituals. The annual **feria** is on 24-30 September in celebration of the Archangel San Miguel, with the main fiesta on 29 September. The **Casa de Cultura** ① *8 Av, 2-17, T56300554 www.larutamayaonline.com/aventura.html*, run by Carlos Humberto Molina, displays an excellent collection of fiesta masks, made on site at the mask factory, and for sale. It has a cultural programme with a number of tour options, cultural activities and bicycle adventures. You need to reserve in advance.

San Francisco El Alto

San Francisco stands high on a great big mound in the cold mountains at 2640 m above the great valley in which lie Totonicapán, San Cristóbal and Quetzaltenango. It is famous for its market, which is stuffed to capacity, and for the animal market held above town, where creatures from piglets to kittens to budgies are for sale. The town's fiesta is on 1-6 October, in honour of St Francis of Assisi.

The market is packed to bursting point on Fridays with locals buying all sorts, including woollen blankets for resale throughout the country. It's an excellent place for buying woven and embroidered textiles of good quality, but beware of pickpockets. Go early to see as much action as possible. Climb up through the town for 10 minutes to see the animal market (ask for directions all the time as it's hard to see 5 m ahead, the place is so packed).

The **church** on the main square is magnificent; notice the double-headed Hapsburg eagle. It is often full on market days with locals lighting candles, and their live purchases ignoring the 'Silencio' posters. The white west front of the church complements the bright colours of the rest of the plaza, especially the vivid green and pink of the Municipalidad.

Momostenango → *Colour map 2, B1.*

Momostenango is set in a valley with ribbons of houses climbing higgledy-piggledy out of the valley floor. Momostenango, at 2220 m, represents *Shol Mumus* in K'iche', meaning 'among the hills', and on its outlying hills are numerous altars and a hilltop image of a Maya god. Some 300 medicine men are said to practise in the town. Their insignia of office is a little bag containing beans and quartz crystals. Momostenango is the chief blanket-weaving centre in the country, and locals can be seen beating the blankets (*chamarras*) on stones, to shrink them. There are also weird stone peaks known as the *riscos* – eroded fluted columns and draperies formed of volcanic ash – on the outskirts of town.

The town is quiet except on Wednesday and Sunday market days, the latter being larger and good for weaving, especially the blankets. On non-market days try **Tienda Manuel de Jesús Agancel** ① *1 Av, 1-50, Zona 4, near bank*, for good bargains, especially blankets and carpets. There is also **Artesanía Paclom** ① *corner of 1 Calle and 3 Av, Zona 2*, just five minutes along the road to Xela. This family have the weaving looms in their back yard and will show you how it's all done if you ask.

The **Feast of Wajshakib Batz' Oj** (pronounced 'washakip'), is celebrated by hundreds of *Aj Kij* (Maya priests) who come for ceremonies. New priests are initiated on this first day of the ritual new year; the initiation lasting the year. The town's very popular fiesta is between 21 July and 4 August, with the town's patron saint of Santiago Apóstol celebrated on 25 July. The **Baile de Convites** is held in December with other dances on 8, 12 and 31 December and 1 January. At **Takilibén Maya Misión** ① *3 Av 'A', 6-85, Zona 3, T7736-5537; wajshakibbatz13@yahoo.es*, just after the Texaco garage on the right on the way in from Xela, Chuch Kajaw (day keeper/senior priest) Rigoberto Itzep welcomes all interested in learning more about Maya culture and cosmology. He offers courses in culture and does Maya horoscope readings. He also has a **Maya sauna** (*Tuj*).

Just outside town are three sets of *riscos* (eroded columns of sandstone with embedded quartz particles), creating a strange eerie landscape of pinnacles that look like rocket lollipop ice creams. To get there, take the 2 Calle, Zona 2, which is the one to the right of the church, for five minutes until you see a sign on a building pointing to the left. Follow the signs until you reach the earth structures (five to 10 minutes).

Huehuetenango and around

→ For listings, see pages 273-276. Colour map 2, B1. Altitude: 1905 m.

Huehuetenango – colloquially known as Huehue – is a pleasant, large town with little to detain the visitor. However, it is a busy transport hub serving the Cuchumatanes Mountains and the Mexican border. Its bus terminal, 2 km from town, is one of the busiest in the country. There are Maya ruins near the town, which were badly restored by the infamous **United Fruit Company**, and new adventure tourism opportunities opening up nearby. Trips, including horse rides, to more remote spots in the Huehuetenango region to see forests, haciendas and lakes are organized by **Unicornio Azul**. A useful website is www.interhuehue.com.

The neoclassical **cathedral** was built between 1867 and 1874, destroyed by earthquake in 1902, and took 10 years to repair. In 1956, the image of the patron saint, the Virgen de la Concepción was burnt in a fire. Then, during the 1976 earthquake, 80% of it was damaged, save the bells, façade and cupola. The skyline to the north of the city is dominated by the Sierrra de los Cuchumatanes, the largest area over 3000 m in Central America.

Huehuetenango

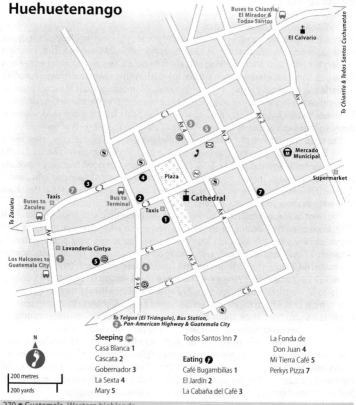

N
200 metres
200 yards

Sleeping 💤
Casa Blanca **1**
Cascata **2**
Gobernador **3**
La Sexta **4**
Mary **5**

Todos Santos Inn **7**

Eating 🍴
Café Bugambilias **1**
El Jardín **2**
La Cabaña del Café **3**

La Fonda de
Don Juan **4**
Mi Tierra Café **5**
Perkys Pizza **7**

The ruins of **Zaculeu** ① *0800-1800, US$6.40,* the old capital of the Mam Maya, are 5 km west of Huehuetenango on top of a rise with steep drops on three sides – a site chosen because of these natural defence measures. Its original name in Mam was *Xinabajul,* meaning 'between ravines'. In K'iche' it means 'white earth'. It was first settled in the Early Classic period (AD 250-600), but it flourished during the late post-Classic (AD 1200-1530). In July 1525, Gonzalo de Alvarado, the brother of Guatemala's conqueror, Pedro de Alvarado, set out for Zaculeu with 80 Spaniards, 40 horses and 2000 indigenous fighters, passing Mazatenango and Totonicapán on the way. The battle lasted four months, during which time the soldiers and residents of Zaculeu were dying of hunger, and eating their dead neighbours. The weakened Kaibil Balam, the Zaculeu *cacique* (chief), called for a meeting with Gonzalo. Gonzalo told the Mam chief that peace was not on the cards. Negotiations followed with the outcome being that Kaibil Balam be instructed in Christianity, obey the Spanish king and leave the city, whereupon Gonzalo de Alvarado would take possession of the Mam kingdom settlement in the name of the Spanish crown.

Aguacatán → *Colour map 2, B1. Altitude: 1670 m.*

The women of Aguacatán wear the most stunning headdresses in the country. On sale in *tiendas* in town, they are a long, slim belt of woven threads using many colours. The women also wear beautiful clothes – the *cortes* are dark with horizontal stripes of yellow, pink, blue and green. The town fiesta is 40 days after Holy Week, Virgen de la Encarnación.

Towards Todos Santos Cuchumatán

To get to Todos Santos, you have to climb the front range of the Cuchumatanes Mountains above Chiantla by a steep road from Huehuetenango. **Chiantla** has the **Luna Café** with art gallery and the nearby paleontological site of **El Mamutz**. Looking down on a clear day the cathedral at Huehuetenango resembles a blob of orange blancmange on the plain. At the summit, at about 3300 m, there is **El Mirador**. The paved road continues over bleak moorland to Paquix where the road divides. The unpaved road to the north continues to Soloma. The other to the west goes through Aldea Chiabel, noted for its outhouses, more obvious than the small dwellings they serve. Here, giant agave plants appear to have large pom-poms attached – reminiscent of the baubles on Gaudí's Sagrada Familia in Barcelona. On this journey you often pass through cloud layer, eventually surfacing above it. On cloudier days you will be completely submerged until descending again to Huehuetenango. The road crosses a pass at 3394 m before a difficult long descent to Todos Santos, about 50 km from Huehuetenango. The walk northwest from Chiantla to Todos Santos Cuchumatanes can be done in around 12-14 hours, or better, two days, staying overnight at **El Potrillo** in the barn owned by Rigoberto Alva. This route crosses one of the highest parts of the sierra at over 3500 m. Alternatively, cycle the 40-km part-gravel road, which is steep in places, but very rewarding.

Todos Santos Cuchumatán

→ *For listings, see pages 273-276. Colour map 2, B1. Altitude: 2470 m.*

High in the Cuchumatanes, the Mam-speaking Todos Santeros maintain a traditional way of life with their striking, bright, traditional dress and their adherence to the 260-day Tzolkin calendar. The town is hemmed in by 3800-m-high mountains either side that squeeze it into one long, 2-km street down the valley. The town is famous for its weaving, and even more famous for the horse race, see box, page 272.

Todos Santos festival

The horse racing festival of Todos Santos is one of the most celebrated and spectacular in Central America – it is also a frenzied day that usually degenerates into a drunken mess. Quite simply riders race between two points, having a drink at each turn until they fall off.

According to Professor Margarito Calmo Cruz, the origins of the fiesta lie in the 15th or 16th century with the arrival of the *conquistadores* to Todos Santos. They arrived on horses wearing large, colourful clothes with bright scarves flowing down their backs and feathers in their hats. The locals experimented, imitating them, enjoyed it and the tradition was born. When the day begins, the men are pretty tipsy, but sprightly and clean. The race is frantic and colourful with scarves flying out from the backs of the men. As the day wears on, they get completely smashed, riding with arms outstretched – whip in one hand and beer bottle in the other. They are mudspattered, dishevelled and are moaning and groaning from the enjoyment and the alcohol which must easily have reached near comatose level.

At times the riders fall, and look pretty lifeless. They are dragged by the scruff of the neck, regardless of serious injury or death, to the edge of the fence as quickly as possible, to avoid trampling.

The men guzzle gallons of beer and the aim is to continue racing all day. A fall means instant dismissal from the race. There are wardens on the side lines with batons, whose primary job is the welfare of the horses, changing them when they see necessary. But they also deal with protesting fallen riders, who try and clamber back onto their horses. By the end of the day the spectacle is pretty grotesque. The horses are drenched with sweat and wild-eyed with fear. The men look hideous and are paralytic from booze. The edge of the course and the town is littered with bodies.

The race takes place on the road that winds its way out of town, not the incoming road from Huehue. It starts at 0800. There are about 15 riders on the course at any one time. It continues until noon, stops for cerveza guzzling and begins again at 1400, ending at 1700.

Some of Guatemala's best weaving is done in Todo Santos. Fine *huípiles* may be bought in the cooperative on the main street and direct from the makers. The men wear the famous red-and-white striped trousers. Some wear a black wool over-trouser piece. Their jackets are white, pink, purple and red-striped with beautifully coloured, and intricately embroidered, collars and cuffs. Their straw hat is wrapped with a blue band. You can buy the embroidered cuffs and collars for men's shirts, the red trousers, and gorgeous colourful crocheted bags made by the men. The women wear navy blue *cortes* with thin, light blue, vertical stripes.

There is a colourful Saturday market and a smaller one on Wednesday. The **church** near the park was built in 1580.

Around Todos Santos

The closest walk is to **Las Letras**, where the words 'Todos Santos' are spelt out in white stone on a hillside above the town. The walk takes an hour. To get there take the path down the side of **Restaurant Cuchumatlán**. The highest point of the Cuchumatanes, and the highest non-volcanic peak in the country, **La Torre** at 3837 m, is to the northeast of Todos Santos and can be reached from the village of **Tzichem** on the road to Concepción

Huista. When clear, it's possible to see the top of Volcán Santa María, one of the highest volcanoes in Guatemala. The hike takes about five hours. The best way to do it is to start in the afternoon and spend the night near the top. It is convenient for camping, with wood but no water. A compass is essential in case of mist. From Todos Santos, you can also hike south to **San Juan Atitán**, four to five hours, where the locals wear an interesting *traje típico*. Market days are on Mondays and Thursdays. From there you can hike to the Pan-American Highway – it's a one day walk. The local fiesta is 22-26 June.

Jacaltenango to the Mexican border

The road from Todos Santos continues northwest through **Concepción Huista**. Here the women wear towels as shawls and Jacalteco is spoken. The fiesta, 29 January-3 February, has fireworks and dancing. The hatmaker in Canton Pilar supplies the hats for Todos Santos, he welcomes viewers and will make a hat to your specifications (but if you want a typical Todos Santos leather *cincho*, buy it there).

Beyond Jacaltenango is **Nentón**, and **Gracias a Dios** at the Mexican border. When the road north out of Huehue splits at Paquix, the right fork goes to **San Mateo Ixtatán**, with ruins nearby. The road from Paquix crosses the roof of the Cuchumatanes, before descending to **San Juan Ixcoy, Soloma** and **Santa Eulalia**, where the people speak O'anjob'al as they do in Soloma. East along a scenic route is **Barillas**. There are several *pensiones* in these places and regular buses from Huehue.

⊙ Western highlands listings

For Sleeping and Eating price codes and other relevant information, see Essentials pages 31-33.

⊜ Sleeping

Totonicapán *p268*
D-E Hospedaje San Miguel, 3 Calle, 7-49, Zona 1, T7766-1452. Rooms with or without bath, hot water, communal TV.
E Pensión Blanquita, 13 Av and 4 Calle. 20 rooms, hot showers, good. Opposite this *pensión* is a Shell station.

San Francisco El Alto *p269*
D-E Vista Hermosa, 2 Calle, 2-23, T7738-4010. 36 rooms, cheaper without bathroom, hot water, TV.
F Hotel Vásquez, 4 Av, 11-53, T7738-4003. Rooms all with private bathroom. Parking.

Momostenango *p269*
E Hospedaje y Comedor Paclom, close to central plaza, at 1 Calle, 1-71, Zona 4. Pretty inner courtyard with caged birds and plants, hot water in shared bathrooms.

E Estiver Ixcel, 1 Calle, 4-15, Zona 4, downhill away from plaza, T7736-5036. 12 rooms, hot water, cheaper without bath, clean.
E-F La Villa, 1 Av, 1-13, Zona 1, below bank, T7736-5108. 6 rooms, warm water only, clean and nicely presented.

Huehuetenango and around *p270, map p270*
B Casa Blanca, 7 Av, 3-41, T7769-0777. Comfortable, good restaurant in a pleasant garden, buffet breakfast, set lunch, very popular and good value, parking.
C Cascata, Lote 4, 42, Zona 5, Col Alvarado, Calzada Kaibil Balam, close to the bus station, T7769-0795, www.hotelcascata.ya.st. Newish hotel with 16 rooms with Wi-Fi and private bathrooms. It is owned by Dutch, French and English folk and the service is excellent.
D La Sexta, 6 Av, 4-29, T7764-6612. With bath, cheaper without, cable TV, restaurant, good for breakfast, clean, good value, phone call facility, stores backpacks without charge.
D Mary, 2 Calle, 3-52, T7764-1618. With bath, cheaper without, good beds,

hot water, cable TV, parking, clean, quiet, safe, well-maintained, good value. Recommended.

E Hotel Gobernador, 4 Av 1-45, T7764-1197. Garden, parking, with bath cheaper without, clean, good value.

E Todos Santos Inn, 2 Calle, 6-74, T7764-1241. Shared bath and private bath available, hot water, TV, helpful, clean, laundry, some rooms a bit damp, luggage stored. Recommended.

Todos Santos Cuchumatán p271

Reservations are necessary in the week before the Nov horse race, but even if you turn up and the town is full, locals offer their homes.

E Casa Familiar, up the hill, close to central park, T7783-0656. Run by the friendly family of Santiaga Mendoza Pablo. Hot shower, sauna, breakfast, dinner, delicious banana bread, spectacular view, popular. The Mendoza family make and sell *típicas* and give weaving lessons.

E Hotelito Todos Santos, above the central park. Hot water, clean, small café, but beware of boys taking you to the hotel quoting one price, and then on arrival, finding the price has mysteriously gone up.

E Hotel Mam, above the central park, next to **Hotelito Todos Santos**. Friendly, clean, hot water, but needs 1 hr to warm up, not too cold in the rooms as an open fire warms the building, good value.

E-F Hospedaje El Viajero, around the corner and then right from **Hotelito Todos Santos**, 5 rooms, 2 shared baths with hot water.

E-F Hotel La Paz. Friendly, great view of the main street from balconies, excellent spot for the 1 Nov fiesta, shared showers have seen better days, enclosed parking.

Around Todos Santos p273

F Hospedaje San Diego, San Juan Atitán. Only 3 beds, basic, friendly, clean, food available.

❶ Eating

Totonicapán p268
♆ **Comedor Brenda 2**, 9 Av, 3-31. Good, serving local food.
♆ **Comedor Letty**, 3 Calle, 8-18. Typical Guatemalan fare.

Momostenango p269
♆ **Comedor Santa Isabel**, next door to Hospedaje y Comedor Paclom. Friendly, cheap and good breakfasts.
♆ **Flipper**, 1 Calle y 2 Av A. Good *licuados* and a range of fruit juices.
♆ **Hospedaje y Comedor Paclom**, close to the central plaza and where buses arrive from Xela, 1 Calle, 1-71, Zona 4. Cheap meals, including snacks in a pretty inner courtyard.

Huehuetenango and around
p270, map p270
♆♆-♆ **Casa Blanca**, see Sleeping. Open 0600-2200. Try the breakfast pancake with strawberries and cream. The plate of the house is a meat extravaganza, fish and good salads served, set lunch good value.
♆♆-♆ **La Cabaña del Café**, 2 Calle, 6-50. Log cabin café with to-die-for cappuccino, snack food and good *chapín* breakfasts, good atmosphere. Recommended.
♆ **Café Bugambilias**, 5 Av 3-59, on the plaza. large, unusual 4-storey building, most of which is a popular, cheap, restaurant, very good breakfasts, *almuerzos*, sandwiches. Recommended.
♆ **El Jardín**, 6 Av 2-99, Zona 1. Meat dishes, breakfasts, good pancakes and local dishes. It's worth eating here just to check out the toilets, which are right out of the 3rd-and-a-half floor of the office in the movie *Being John Malkovich*!
♆ **La Fonda de Don Juan**, 2 Calle, 5-35. Italian restaurant and bar (try the *cavatini*), sandwiches, big choice of desserts, *licuados*, coffees, good pizzas, also *comida típica*, with reasonable prices all served in a bright environment with red and white checked tablecloths.

Mi Tierra Café, 4 Calle, 6-46, T7764-1473.
Good drinks and light meals, Mexican
offerings – try the *fajitas*, nice setting,
popular with locals and travellers.
Recommended.
Perkys Pizza, 3 Av esq, 4 Calle. Wide
variety of pizzas, eat in or takeaway,
modern, clean, good value.

Todos Santos Cuchumatán *p271*
There are *comedores* on the 2nd floor
of the market selling very cheap meals.
Comedor Katy. Will prepare vegetarian
meals on request, good-value *menú
del día*.
Cuchumatlán. Has sandwiches, pizza
and pancakes, and is popular at night.

⊛ Festivals and events

Todos Santos Cuchumatán *p271*
1 Nov Horse race. The festival begins
on 21 Oct. See box, page 272.
2 Nov Day of the Dead, when locals
visit the cemetery and leave flowers
and food.

◎ Shopping

Todos Santos Cuchumatán *p271*
The following shops all sell bags, trousers,
shirts, *huípiles*, jackets and clothes. Prices
have more or less stabilized at the expensive
end, but the best bargains can be had at the
Tienda Maribel, further up the hill from
Casa Familiar and the **Cooperativa Estrella
de Occidente**, on the main street. **Casa
Mendoza**, just beyond Tienda Maribel,
is where Telésforo Mendoza makes clothes
to measure. **Domingo Calmo** also makes
clothes to measure. His large, brown house
with tin roof is on the main road to the
Ruinas (5 mins) – follow the road up from
Casa Familiar. Ask for the **Casa de Domingo**.

▲ Activities and tours

Huehuetenango and around *p270,
map p270*
Unicornio Azul, based in Chancol,
T5205-9328, www.unicornioazul. com.
Horse-riding trips, trekking, mountain biking
and birdwatching in the Cuchumatanes.

⊖ Transport

Totonicapán *p268*
Bus Every 15 mins to **Quetzaltenango**,
US$0.40, 45 mins. To **Los Encuentros**,
US$2.20. To **Cuatro Caminos**, 30 mins, US$0.30.

San Francisco El Alto *p269*
Bus 2 km along the Pan-American Hwy
heading north from Cuatro Caminos is a
paved road, which runs to San Francisco El
Alto (3 km) and then to Momostenango
(19 km). Bus from **Quetzaltenango**, 50 mins
on Fri, US$0.75. The last bus back is at 1800.

Momostenango *p269*
Bus From **Cuatro Caminos** (US$0.50) and
Quetzaltenango, 1-1½ hrs. Buses to Xela
every 30 mins from 0430-1600.

Huehuetenango and around *p270,
map p270*
Bus and taxi
Local From the terminal to town, take 'Centro'
minibus, which pulls up at cathedral, 5 mins.
Taxis from behind the covered market. Walking
takes 20-25 mins. Bus leaves Salvador Osorio
School, final Calle 2, every 30 mins, 15 mins, to
Zaculeu, last return 1830. Taxi, US$8, including
waiting time. To walk takes about 1 hr – either
take 6 Av north, cross the river and follow the
road to the left, through Zaculeu modern village
to the ruins, or go past the school and turn right
beyond the river. The signs are barely visible.

Long distance To **Guatemala City**,
5 hrs, US$11, **Los Halcones**, 7 Av, 3-62,
Zona 1 (they do not leave from the terminal)

at 0430, 0700, 1400, reliable. From the bus terminal there are numerous services daily to the capital from 0215-1600 via **Chimaltenango**, 5 hrs, US$4. Via **Mazatenango** there are 5 daily.

North To **Todos Santos Cuchumatán**, 10 daily until 1630, 2-3 hrs, US$3.60. To **Barillas**, via **San Juan Ixcoy** (2½ hrs), **Soloma** (3 hrs), and **San Mateo Ixtatan** (7 hrs), 10 daily from 0200-2330, US$7. There are also buses to **San Rafael la Independencia** passing through Soloma and **Sta Eulalia**.

Northwest To **La Mesilla** for Mexico, frequent buses between 0530-1800, US$3.50, 2½ hrs, last bus returning to Huehue, 1800. To **Nentón**, via La Mesilla twice a day. To **Gracias a Dios**, several times a day.

South To **Quetzaltenango**, 13 a day from 0600-1600, US$3, 2-2¼ hrs. To **Cuatro Caminos**, US$2, 2 hrs. To **Los Encuentros**, for Lake Atitlán and Chichicastenango, 3 hrs.

East To **Aguacatán**, 12 daily, 0600-1900, 1 hr 10 mins, US$1.20. To **Nebaj** you have to get to Sacapulas via Aguacatán. To **Sacapulas**, 1130, 1245. To **Cobán**, take the earliest bus/pickup for Aguacatán and then Sacapulas and continue to Uspantán to change for Cobán.

Aguacatán *p271*
Bus From **Huehue**, 1 hr 10 mins. It is 26 km east of Huehuetenango on a semi-paved route (good views). Returning between 0445 and 1600. Buses and pickups for **Sacapulas** and for onward connections to Nebaj and Cobán leave from the main street going out of town. Wait anywhere along there to catch your ride. It is 1½ hrs from Aguacatán to Sacapulas. To **Guatemala City** at 0300, 1100.

Todos Santos Cuchumatán *p271*
Bus To **Huehuetenango**, 2-3 hrs, crowded Mon and Fri, 0400, 0500, 0600, 0615-0630, 1145, 1230, 1300. Possible changes on Sat so ask beforehand. For petrol, ask at **El Molino**.

Jacaltenango to the Mexican border *p273*
Bus From **Huehuetenango** at 0330, 0500, returning at 1130 and 1400; also pickups.

San Francisco El Alto *p269*
Banks G&T Continental, 2 Av, 1-95, takes MasterCard and changes TCs; Banco Industrial, 2 Calle, 2-64, cashes TCs, takes Visa.

Momostenango *p269*
Banks Banrural, on plaza, TCs only.
Language schools Patzite, 1 Calle, 4-33, Zona 2, T7736-5159, www.patzite.20m.com.

Huehuetenango and around *p270, map p270*
Banks Some banks open Sat morning. The bigger banks change TCs. Mexican pesos available from Camicard, 5 Av, 6-00. **Internet** Several places around town. **Language schools** Some operate in summer months only (see box, page 238). Huehuetenango is a good spot to learn Spanish, as there are fewer chances of meeting gringos and conversing in your own tongue. Señora de Mendoza, 1 Calle, 1-64, Zona 3, T7764-1987. Rodrigo Morales (at Sastrería La Elegancia), 9 Av, 6-55, Zona 1. Recommended. Spanish Academy Xinabajul, 4 Av, 14-14, Zona 5, T7764-6631, www.world wide.edu/guatemala/xinabaj/index.html. Abesaida Guevara de López, 10 Calle 'A', 10-20, Zona 1, T7764-2917. Recommended. Information on schools and other tourist info is posted in Mi Tierra Café. **Post** 2 Calle, 3-54. **Telephone** Telgua, Edif El Triángulo, 9 Av, 6-142, on main road out of town.

Todos Santos Cuchumatán *p271*
Bank Banrural TCs and dollars cash only.
Language schools All local coordinators are on friendly terms but are competing for your business. Take your time and visit all 3 schools. Hispano Maya, opposite Hotelito Todos Santos, www.hispanomaya.org. Nuevo Amanecer, escuela_linguistica@yahoo.com. Working There is also a volunteer project to teach English in a nearby village where food and board is provided. Weaving can be taught. **Post** Parque Central.

Quetzaltenango and around

→ *Colour map 2, C1. Altitude: 2335 m.*

Quetzaltenango (commonly known as Xela – pronounced 'shayla') is the most important city in western Guatemala. The country's second city is set among a group of high mountains and volcanoes, one of which, Santa María, caused much death and destruction after an eruption in 1902. The bulk of the city is modern, but its 19th-century downtown revamp and its narrow streets give the centre more of a historic feel. There are breathtaking views and a pleasant park with its beautifully restored façade of the colonial church. It is an excellent base from which to visit nearby hot springs, religious idols, volcanoes and market towns. ▶▶ *For listings see pages 283-288.*

Ins and outs

Getting there Most visitors arrive by bus, a 30-minute (14.5 km) journey southwest of Cuatro Caminos. Buses pull into the Zona 3 Minerva Terminal. To get a bus into the city centre, take a path through the market at its far left or its far right, which brings you out in front of the Minerva Temple. Watch out for very clever pickpockets walking through this market. Buses for the town centre face away (left) from the temple. All Santa Fe services go to Parque Centro América, US$0.15. Alternatively take a taxi. ▶▶ *See Transport, page 286.*

Getting around The town centre is compact and all sites and most services are within walking distance. The Santa Fe city bus goes between the terminal, the *rotonda* and the town centre. Out of town destination buses stop at the *rotonda* and it is quicker to get here from the town centre than to the Minerva Terminal. City buses for the terminal leave from 4 Calle and 13 Avenida, Zona 1, and those straight for the *rotonda* leave from 11 Avenida and 10 Calle, Zona 1, US$0.15. A taxi within Zona 1, or from Zona 1 to a closer part of Zona 3, is about US$3.20.

Tourist information INGUAT ① *7 Calle, 11-35, on the park, T7761-4931, Mon-Fri 0900-1600, Sat 0900-1300.* Not recommended. Try the recommended tour operators (page 285) for information instead. General information can be found at www.xelapages.com and www.xelawho.com, which has good listings.

Background

The most important battle of the Spanish conquest took place near Quetzaltenango when the great K'iche' warrior Tecún Umán was slain. In October 1902 the Volcán Santa María erupted, showering the city with half a metre of dust. An ash cloud soared 8.6 km into the air and some 1500 people were killed by volcanic fallout and gas. A further 3000 people died a short while later from malaria due to plagues of mosquitoes which had not been wiped out by the blast. Some 20 years on, a new volcano, born after the 1902 eruption, began to erupt. This smaller volcano, Santiaguito, spews clouds of dust and ash on a daily basis and is considered one of the most dangerous volcanoes in the world. The city's prosperity, as seen by the grand neoclassical architecture in the centre, was built on the back of the success of the coffee *fincas* on the nearby coastal plain. This led to the country's first bank being established here. The town's fiestas are 9-17 September, Holy Week and the October fiesta of La Virgen del Rosario.

Sights

The central park, **Parque Centro América**, is the focus of the city. It is surrounded by the cathedral, with its beautifully restored original colonial façade, and a number of elegant neoclassical buildings, constructed during the late 19th and early 20th century. The modern cathedral, **Catedral de la Diócesis de los Altos**, was constructed in 1899 and is set back behind the original. The surviving façade of the 1535 **Catedral del Espíritu Santo** is beautiful, intricately carved and with restored portions of murals on its right side. On the south side of the park is the **Casa de la Cultura**. Inside are the **Museo de la Marimba** with exhibits and documents relating to the 1871 Liberal Revolution. On the right-hand

Quetzaltenango

Quetzaltenango maps
1 Quetzaltenango, page 278
2 Quetzaltenango centre, page 279

200 metres
200 yards

Sleeping
Casa Argentina &
Quetzaltrekkers 1
Hotel del Campo 2

Eating
Bakeshop 1
Chocolate Doña Pancha 2

side of the building is the totally curious **Museo de Historia Natural** ⓘ *Mon-Fri 0800-1200, 1400-1800, US$0.90.* Deformed stuffed animals are cheek by jowl with pre-Columbian pottery, sports memorabilia, fizzy drink bottles, a lightning-damaged mirror and dinosaur remains. It satisfies the most morbid of curiosities with displays of a

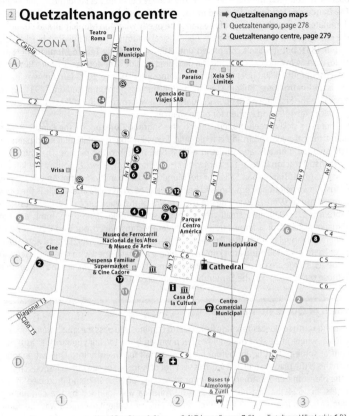

Quetzaltenango centre

➡ Quetzaltenango maps
1 Quetzaltenango, page 278
2 Quetzaltenango centre, page 279

Sleeping 😴
Altense **1** *D3*
Anexo Modelo **3** *B1*
Black Cat Hostel **10** *B2*
Casa Mañen **6** *C3*
Hostal Don Diego **9** *C1*
Kiktem-Ja **11** *C2*
Los Olivos **12** *B2*
Pensión Andina **2** *C3*
Pensión Bonifaz **4** *B2*
Villa de Don Andrés **7** *C2*
Villa Real Plaza **15** *B2*

Eating 🍴
Asados Puente **17** *C2*
Blue Angel Café **2** *C1*
Café Baviera **1** *C2*
Café Taberna Enanos **7** *C2*
Café y Chocolate
  La Luna **8** *C3*
Cardinali **3** *B2*
Casa Antigua **12** *B2*
El Apaste **4** *C2*
El Deli Crepe **5** *B2*
Las Calas **9** *B1*
Royal París & Guatemaya
  Intercultural Travel
  Agency **10** *B1*
Salón Tecún **16** *C2*

Tertulianos Villas Lesbia **6** *B2*
Ut'z Hua **11** *B2*

Bars & clubs 🍸
El Duende **14** *A1*
El Zaguán **13** *A1*
La Taberna de Don
  Rodrigo **15** *A2*
Ojalá **19** *B1*

two-headed calf, Siamese twin pigs, an eight-legged goat, and a strange sea creature that looks like an alien, known as *Diabillo del Mar* (little sea devil). On the park's southwest side is the **Museo de Arte**, with a collection of contemporary Guatemalan art, and the **Museo del Ferrocarril Nacional de los Altos** ⓘ *7 Calle and 12 Av, Mon-Fri 0800-1200, 1400-1800, US$0.90*, recounting the story of an electric railway between Xela and the Pacific slope. The **Banco de Occidente**, founded in 1881, and the first bank to opened in Guatemala, dominates the northern edge of the park. The overly wired-up **Municipalidad** straddles the eastern edge of the park with its neoclassical columns. Its first building blocks were laid in 1881, but it wasn't completed until 1897. The stately **Teatro Municipal** (1892-1896) is on 14 Avenida y 1 Calle and can be visited outside of performance hours. Restored at a cost of four million quetzales, it has an imposing presence. To its left, on Avenida 14 "A", is the Teatro Roma. Building began in 1898, but was not completed until 1931, when it became the first cinema to open in Guatemala. It was restored in 2000 as a theatre with a capacity for 1400 and is open for performances.

There is a sickly green modern church, the **Sagrado Corazón**, on the Parque Benito Juárez near the market. Inside is a gigantic, free-standing, Chagall-influenced painting with swooping angels, and Christ in a glass box, built into the picture. The church of **La Transfiguración** ⓘ *near the corner of 11 Calle and 5 Av, Zona 1*, houses the largest crucified Christ figure (San Salvador del Mundo) to be found in Central America – it is almost 3 m in height and now housed behind glass. At 20 Avenida and 4 Calle is the city's **Cementerio** ⓘ *0700-1900*. Inside are the remains of the Quetzalteco President, Estrada Cabrera (1898-1920) in a small cream neoclassical temple. Behind his tomb are the unmarked graves of a large number of cholera victims wiped out in a 19th-century epidemic. Manuel Lisandra Barillas (Guatemalan President 1885-1892) is also entombed here. There is a small patio area known as Colonia Alemana lined with graves of German residents; a large area where those that died as martyrs in the civil war lie; and a memorial to those that perished in the September Revolution of 1897.

North of Quetzaltenango → *For listings, see pages 283-288.*

Heading south to Quetzaltenango from Cuatro Caminos you pass the small *ladino* town of **Salcajá**, where *jaspé* skirt material has been woven since 1861. If you fancy a taste or a whiff of some potent liquor before bracing yourself for an entry into Quetzaltenango, then this is the place to halt. It is worth a visit not only for the booze but its famous church – the oldest in Central America – and for its textiles, often seen being produced in the streets. In 1524 the first church in Central America was founded by the conquering Spaniards. **San Jacinto** is a small church on 6 Avenida y 2 Calle; it may not always be open. *Caldo de frutas*, a highly alcoholic drink with quite a kick, is not openly sold but is made in the town and drunk on festive occasions. It is illegal to drink it in public places. It is a concoction of nances, cherries, peaches, apples and quinces and is left to ferment in rum. There is also *rompope*, a drink made with eggs. Salcajá is a town that also revolves around textiles, with shops on every street. Yarn is tied and dyed, untied, and wraps are then stretched around telephone poles along the road or on the riverside. One of these can be seen outside San Jacinto church. Market day is Tuesday.

San Andrés Xecul is a small village in stunning surroundings with an extraordinarily lurid coloured church, 8 km north of Xela. Painted a deep-mustard yellow in 1900, its figurines, including angels, have been given blue wings and pastel-pink skirts. Climb the hill a bit above the town and catch a glimpse of the fantastic dome – mulitcoloured like a beach ball. With your back to the church climb the cobbled street leading up the right-hand side of the plaza to a yellow and maroon chapel peering out across the valley. The view from here is spectacular. Market day is Thursday, opposite the church. The town's fiestas are on 21 November, 30 November and 1 December.

South of Quetzaltenango → For listings, see pages 283-288.

Souteast of Xela is **Cantel** which has the largest and oldest textile factory in the country. Sunday is market day and the town's fiesta is 12-18 August (main day 15 August). At Easter a passion play is performed. A little further on, on the outskirts of town, on the right-hand side (one minute on the bus), is the white **Copavic glass factory** ① *T7763-8038, www.copavic.com, Mon-Fri 0500-1300, Sat 0500-1200,* where you can watch and photograph the workers blow the recycled glass.

Zunil

Pinned in by a very steep-sided valley is the town of Zunil, 9 km from Quetzaltenango. It is visited for the nearby hot thermal baths that many come to wallow in, and for its worship of its well-dressed idol San Simón (Maximón). The market is held on Mondays. The town's fiesta is 22-26 November (main day 25) and there is a very colourful Holy Week. The **church** is striking both inside and out. It has a large decorated altarpiece and a small shrine to murdered Bishop Gerardi at the altar. The façade is white with serpentine columns wrapped in carved ivy.

San Simón (Maximón) is worshipped in the town and is often dressed in different clothes at different times. A small charge is made for the upkeep and to take photos; ask anyone in the town to escort you to his house. To the left of the church is the **Santa Ana Cooperative,** which sells beautiful *huípiles*, shirt and skirt materials, as well as bags and bookmarks.

The nearby extinct **Volcán Pico Zunil**, rises to 3542 m to the southeast of the town. On its slopes are the **thermal baths of Fuentes Georginas** ① *0700-1900, US$2.70,* which you'll know you're approaching by the wafts of sulphurous fumes that come your way. There are several different-sized pools set into the mountainside surrounded by thick, luscious vegetation and enveloped in the steam that continuously rises up in wafts from the hot pools. There are spectacular views on the way to the baths.

The thermal baths of **Aguas Amargas** ① *0800-1700, US$2, children, US$1.30,* are on Zunil Mountain below Fuentes Georginas. They are reached by following the road south and heading east (left) by Estancia de La Cruz. This road passes fields of flowers and would make a great trip on a bike.

El Viejo Palmar

This is Guatemala's Pompeii. The river that cuts through here flows directly down from the active Santiaguito volcanic cone following a series of serious lahars (mudflows of water and volcanic material) that took place in the 1990s. The small town of 10,000 was evacuated, leaving an extraordinary legacy. In August 1998, the whole south end of the ghost town was destroyed by a massive lahar that crushed the church. This also shifted the course of the Río Nimá I, which began to flow directly through the centre of the church remains. Very heavy erosion since has left the west front and the altar separated by a 30-m deep ravine – an unbelievable sight.

Volcán Santa María and Santiaguito

Santiaguito's mother, Santa María (3772 m), is a rough 5½-hour climb (1500 m). You can see Santiaguito (2488 m) below, erupting mostly with ash blasts and sometimes lava flows from a mirador. It is possible to camp at the summit of Santa María, or on the saddle west of the summit, but it is cold and windy, but worth it because dawn provides views of the entire country's volcanic chain and an almighty shadow is cast across the area by Santa Maria's form. Santiaguito is a fairly new volcano that formed after the eruption of Santa María out of its crater. Do not attempt to climb Santiaguito: it erupts continuously on a daily basis throwing up ash and is considered one of the most dangerous volcanoes in the world. To see it erupting you need to climb Santa María, where you can look down on this smaller volcano. ▸▸ *See Tour operators, page 285.*

Laguna Chicabal

San Martín rangers' station ⓘ *0700-1800, US$2,* is where the two-hour climb to Laguna Chicabal starts. This is a lime-green lake, at 2712 m, in the crater of the extinct volcano (2900 m) of the same name, with wild white lilies, known as *cartucho,* growing at the edges. The Maya believe the waters are sacred and it is thought that if you swim in the lake you will become ill. The highlight of a trip here is the sight of the clouds tumbling down over the circle of trees that surround the lake, and then appearing to bounce on the surface before dispersing. Ceremonies of Maya initiation are held at the lake in early May, known as *Jueves de la Ascensión.* The walk from San Martín takes about two hours.

West of Quetzaltenango → *For listings, see pages 283-288.*

To Mexico from Quetzaltenango

It takes half an hour to reach **San Juan Ostuncalco**, 15 km away. It's a pleasant, prosperous town with a big white church noted for its good weekly market on Sunday and beautiful sashes worn by men. Its fiesta, Virgen de la Candelaria, is held on 29 January to 2 February. The road, which is paved, switchbacks 37 km down valleys and over pine-clad mountains to a plateau looking over the valley in which are San Pedro and San Marcos. **San Marcos** has a few places to stay and eat. It is a transport hub with little to see. **San Pedro Sacatepéquez** has a huge market on Thursday. The Maya women wear golden and purple skirts.

The extinct **Volcán Tajumulco**, at 4220 m, is the highest in Central America. Start very early in the day if you plan to return to San Marcos by nightfall. It's about a five-hour climb and a three-hour descent. Once you have reached the ridge on Tajumulco, turn right along the top of it; there are two peaks, the higher is on the right. The peak on the left (4100 m) is used for shamanistic rituals.

Dormant **Volcán Tacaná** (4093 m) on the Mexican border may be climbed from the village of Sibinal. Its last eruption was 1949, but there was activity in 2001, so check before climbing. It is the second highest volcano in Guatemala with a 400-m wide crater and fumaroles on its flanks. Take a bus to Sibinal from San Marcos. It is a six-hour difficult climb to the summit and it's recommended that you ask for a guide in the village. About 15 km west of San Marcos the road begins its descent from 2500 m to the lowlands. In 53 km to **Malacatán** it drops to 366 m. It is a winding ride with continuous bends, but the scenery is attractive. There is accommodation.

The road to the coastal plain from San Juan Ostuncalco is the most attractive of all the routes down from the highlands, bypassing most of the small towns through quickly changing scenery as you lose height. After San Juan, go south for 1.5 km to **Concepción**

Chiquirichapa, with a bright blue and yellow church, which is one of the wealthiest villages in the country. It has a small market early every Thursday morning and a fiesta on 5-9 December. About 6 km beyond is **San Martín Sacatepéquez**, which used to be known as San Martín Chile Verde, and is famous for its hot chillies. This village appears in Miguel Angel Asturias' *Mulata de Tal*. It stands in a windy, cold gash in the mountains. The slopes are superbly steep and farmed, giving fantastic vistas on the climb up and down from Laguna Chicabal (see above). The men wear very striking long red and white striped tunics, beautifully embroidered around the hem. Market day is Sunday. The fiesta runs from 7-12 November (main day 11 November).

◉ Quetzaltenango and around listings

For Sleeping and Eating price codes and other relevant information, see Essentials pages 31-33.

● Sleeping

Quetzaltenango *p277, maps p278 and p279*
At Easter, 12-18 Sep and Christmas, rooms need to be booked well in advance.
B Casa Mañen, 9a Av, 4-11, Zona 1, T7765-0786. Reports are consistently good, serves great breakfasts and friendly staff offer a very warm welcome. Room 2 is a great option with a bed on a mezzanine. Some rooms have microwave, fridge and TV. All are comfortable, and furnished with attractive wooden accessories. There is a small, pretty courtyard area and secure parking.
B Pensión Bonifaz, 4 Calle, 10-50, Zona 1, T7765-1111. 75 clean, comfortable rooms with TV. Pool, which is occasionally heated. Good restaurant and bar. Parking.
C Hotel del Campo, Km 224, Carretera a la Costa Sur, T7931-9393, www.hoteldel campo.com.gt. Large 91602 red-brick hotel 4 km from town, popular with family weekenders, with indoor heated swimming pool, playground and meeting rooms. 92 spacious bedrooms with private bath, cable TV, and Wi-Fi, breakfast included. Recommended.
C Hotel Villa de Don Andrés 13 Av 6-16, Zona 1, T7761-2014. www.hotelvilladedon andres.com. Boutique B&B hotel in old city centre one block from Parque Central, 5 prettily decorated rooms with private bath, minibar, cable TV and Wi-Fi, breakfast extra. Laundry service and parking space. Recommended.

C Los Olivos, 13 Av, 3-22, T7761-0215, Zona 1. 26 pleasant rooms above parking area with private bathroom, TV and a restaurant with cheap breakfasts and meals.
C Villa Real Plaza, 4 Calle, 12-22, Zona 1, T7761-4045. Dignified colonial building, 58 rooms with TV. Restaurant has good vegetarian food, and is good value. Parking.
D Kiktem-Ja, 13 Av, 7-18, Zona 1, T7761-4304. A central location with 16 colonial-style rooms, nicely furnished, locally made blankets on the beds, wooden floors, all with bath, hot water, open fires, car parking inside gates.
E Altense, 9 Calle, 8-48, Zona 1, T7765-4648. 16 rooms with bath, hot water, parking, secure and friendly. However, if your room is on the 9 Av side, you'll be woken by rush-hour traffic. This is a good town centre deal for single travellers. Recommended.
E-G Black Cat Hostel, 13 Av, 3-33, Zona 1, T7761-2091, www.blackcathostels.net. A hostel in the old Casa Kaehler. Dorms (**F** per person) and private rooms all with shared bathrooms. Breakfast included.
F Hostal Don Diego, 6 Calle, 15-12, Zona 1, www.hostaldondiegoxela.com. Sweet hostel, set about an interior courtyard with rooms with shared bathroom. Hot water and breakfast included. Bright and clean. Weekly and monthly rents available; tours office (branch of **Adrenalina Tours**).
F Pensión Andina, 8 Av, 6-07, Zona 1, T7761-4012. Private bathrooms, hot water, friendly, clean, sunny patio, restaurant, good value, parking.

G Casa Argentina, Diagonal 12, 8-37, Zona 1, T7761-2470. 25 clean rooms, hot water, 10 shared bathrooms, cheaper in 18-bed dorm, rooms with private bath, cooking facilities with purified water, friendly, laundry service. Ask about cheap monthly room rates.

Zunil p281

A-B Las Cumbres Eco-Saunas y Gastrono-mía, T5399-0029, www.las cumbres.com.gt. Daily 0700-1800. Beyond Zunil on the left-hand side of the road heading to the coast (Km 210). This is the place for some R&R with saunas emitting natural steam from the geo-thermal activity nearby. There are 12 rooms with sauna, cheaper without, and separate saunas and jacuzzis for day visitors (US$2.50 per hr) and a restaurant serving good regional food and natural juices. Highly recommended. See Transport, page 287 for transfers.

D Turicentro Fuentes Georginas. 6 cold bungalows with 2 double beds and 2 bunga-lows with 3 single beds. They have cold showers, fireplaces with wood, electricity 1700-2200 and barbecue grills for guests' use near the baths. Guests can use the baths after public closing times. Reasonably priced restaurant with breakfasts, snacks and drinks, 0800-1800 (destroyed by Tropical Storm Agatha in 2010, but being rebuilt early 2011).

🍴 Eating

Quetzaltenango *p277, maps p278 and p279*

🍴🍴-🍴 **Cardinali**, 14 Av, 3-25, Zona 1. Owned by Benito, a NY Italian, great Italian food, including large pizzas with 31 varieties: 2 for 1 on Tue and Thu; tasty pastas of 20 varieties, extensive wine list. Recommended. Also does home delivery in 30 mins (T7761-0924).

🍴🍴-🍴 **Las Calas**, 14 Av "A", 3-21, Zona 1. Mon-Sat. Breakfasts, salads, soups, paella and pastas served around a courtyard with changing art hanging from walls. The food is tasty with delicious bread to accompany, but small portions are served. The breakfast service is far too slow. Adjoining bar.

🍴🍴-🍴 **Restaurante Royal París**, 14 Av "A", 3-06, Zona 1. Delicious food (try the fish in a creamy mushroom sauce), excellent choices, including vegetarian. Also cheap options. Run by Stéphane and Emmanuelle. Recommended. Live music from 2000 on Fri.

🍴🍴-🍴 **Restaurante Tertulianos Villa Lesbia**, 14 Av, 5-26, Zona 3, T7767-4666. Gourmet quality, specializing in meat, cheese and chocolate fondues, and scrumptious desserts. Recommended.

🍴🍴 **El Apaste**, 5 Calle, 14-48, Zona 3, T7776-6249. Local Xela cuisine, rich stews and meats, traditionally served in the eponymous *apaste* (terracotta dish).

🍴🍴 **Ut'z Hua**, Av 12, 3-02, Zona 1. This prettily decorated restaurant with purple tablecloths does typical food, which is always very good and filling. Don't miss the *pollo con mole* or fish. Recommended.

🍴🍴-🍴 **Asados Puente**, 7 Calle, 13-29. Lots of veggie dishes with tofu and tempeh. Also ceviche. Popular with expats. Run by Ken Cielatka and Eva Melgar. Some profits go towards helping ill children.

🍴🍴-🍴 **Salón Tecún**, Pasaje Enríquez, off the park at 12 Av y 4 Calle, Zona 1. Bar, local food, breakfasts also, TV. Always popular with gringos and locals.

🍴 **Café Taberna Enanos**, 5 Calle near Av 12 and Parque Central, Zona 1. Mon-Sat 0715- 2000. Good cheap breakfast, also has *menú del día*.

🍴 **El Deli Crepe**, 14 Av, 3-15, Zona 1. Good tacos, *almuerzo* with soup, great milkshakes, savoury and sweet crêpes, juicy *fajitas* that arrive steaming.

Cafés and bakeries

Bakeshop at 18 Av, 1-40, Zona 3. Mennonite bakery that is Xela's answer to *dulce* heaven. They bake a whole range of cookies, muffins, breads and cakes and sells fresh yoghurt and cheeses. Tue and Fri 0900-1800 so get there early as the goodies go really fast.

Blue Angel Café, 7 Calle, 15-79, Zona 1. Great salads, light meals, service a little slow though, movies shown on a monthly rotation, useful noticeboard.

Café Baviera, 5 Calle, 13-14, Zona 1. Open 0700-2000. Good cheap meals and excellent pies, huge cake portions (try the carrot cake) and coffee in large premises, with walls lined from ceiling to floor with old photos and posters. Good for breakfasts, but a little on the expensive side. Popular, but lacks warmth.

Chocolate Doña Pancha, 10a Calle 16-67 Zona 1, T7761-9700. High-quality chocolate factory, with great range of drinks, cakes and pastries, also chocolate products to take away.

Café y Chocolate La Luna, 8 Av, 4-11, Zona 1. Delicious hot chocolate with or without added luxuries, good cheap snacks, also top chocolates and *pasteles* (the strawberry and cream pie is recommended), pleasant atmosphere in a colonial house decorated with moon symbols, fairy lights, and old photos; a good meeting place.

⊕ Entertainment

Quetzaltenango *p277, maps p278 and p279*
Bars and clubs
El Duende, 14 Av "A", 1-42, Zona 1. Popular café-bar, 1800-2330. A favourite among Guatemalans and gringos.

El Zaguán, 14 Av "A", A-70, Zona 1. A disco-bar Wed, Thu 1900-2430, Fri, Sat 2100-2430, US$3.25, drink included; plays salsa music.

La Taberna de Don Rodrigo, 14 Av, Calle C-47, Zona 1. Cosy bar, reasonable food served in dark wood atmosphere, draught beer.

Ojalá, 15 Av "A", 3-33, an entertainment venue, popular with locals and gringos, which also shows films.

Cinemas
Cine Sofía, 7 Calle 15-18. Mon-Fri 1800. See Blue Angel and Ojala, above.
La Pradera, 5 screens in shopping mall in Zona 3, next to bus terminal. Latest releases.

Dance
Trópica Latina, 5 Calle 12-24, Zona 1, T5892-8861, tropicalatina@xelawho.com. Classes Mon-Sat.

Theatre
Teatro Municipal, 14 Av and 1 Calle, main season May-Nov, theatre, opera, etc.

⊙ Shopping

Quetzaltenango *p277, maps p278 and p279*
Bookshops
Vrisa, 15 Av, 3-64, T7761-3237, a good range of English-language second-hand books.

Markets
The **main market** is at Templo de Minerva on the western edge of town (take the local bus, US$0.10); at the southeast corner of Parque Centro América is the **Centro Comercial Municipal**, a shopping centre with craft and textile shops on the upper levels, food, clothes, etc below. There is another **market** at 2 Calle y 16 Av, Zona 3, south of Parque Benito Juárez, known as La Democracia. Every first Sun of the month there also is an art and handicrafts market, around Parque Centro América.

Supermarkets
Centro Comercial Mont Blanc, Paiz, 4 Calle between 18-19 Av, Zona 3.
Despensa Familiar, 13 Av, 6-94.
La Pradera, near the Minerva Terminal.

North of Quetzaltenango *p280*
The smallest bottle of bright yellow *rompope* is sold in various shops around Salcajá, including the **Fábrica de Pénjamo**, 2 Av, 4-03, Zona 1, US$1.55, and it slips down the throat very nicely!

▲ Activities and tours

Quetzaltenango *p277, maps p278 and p279*
When climbing the volcanoes make sure your guides stay with you all the time; it can get dangerous when the cloud rolls down.
Adrenalina Tours, inside Pasaje Enríquez, T7761-4509, www.adrenalinatours.com. Numerous tours are on offer including bike,

fishing, rafting, horse riding, rock climbing and volcano tours as well as packages to Belize, Honduras and the Petén and trips to Huehue and Todos Santos. Specializes in hikes and treks all over Guatemala. Highly recommended.

Agencia de Viajes SAB, 1 Calle, 12-35, T7761-6402. Good for cheap flights.

Guatemaya Intercultural Travel Agency, 14 Av "A", 3-06, T7765-0040. Very helpful.

Mayaexplor, T7761-5057, www.maya explor.com. Run by Thierry Roquet, who arranges a variety of trips around Xela and around the country. He can also arrange excursions into Mexico, Belize and Honduras and treks, eg Nebaj–Todos Santos. French-speaking. His website offers useful info for travellers. A proportion of funds goes towards local development projects. Recommended.

Quetzaltrekkers, based inside **Casa Argentina** at Diagonal 12, 8-37, T7765-5895, www.quetzaltrekkers.com. This recommended, established, non-profit agency is known for its 3-day hike (Sat am-Mon pm) from Xela across to Lake Atitlán. Proceeds go to the **Escuela de la Calle School** for kids at risk, and a dorm for homeless children. Also offers trek from Nebaj–Todos Santos, 6 days, full-moon hike up Santa María and others. Hiking volunteers are also needed for a 3-month minimum period: hiking experience and reasonable Spanish required.

Tranvia de los Altos, www.tranviadelos altos.com, provides daytime and nighttime walking tours in Xela as well as excursions. Guided city tour is only US$4. Recommended.

Zunil *p281*

See **Las Cumbres Eco-Saunas y Gastronomía**, T5399-0029, under Sleeping, above.

⊖ Transport

Quetzaltenango *p277, maps p278 and p279*
Bus
Local City buses run between 0600 and 1900. Between the town centre and Minerva

Terminal, bus No 6, Santa Fe, US$0.20, 15-30 mins, depending on traffic. Catch the bus at the corner of 4 Calle and 13 Av by Pasaje Enríquez. Buses to the Rotonda leave from the corner of 11 Av and 10 Calle, US$0.20, or catch bus No 6, 10 or 13, from Av 12 y 3 Calle as they come down to the park, 15 mins.

To catch buses to **San Francisco El Alto**, **Momostenango**, the **south coast** and **Zunil**, get off the local bus at the Rotonda, then walk a couple of steps away from the road to step into a feeder road where they all line up.

Long distance To **Guatemala City**, **Galgos**, Calle Rodolfo Robles, 17-43, Zona 1, T7761-2248, 1st-class buses, at 0400, 1230, 1500, US$5, 4 hrs, will carry bicycles; **Marquensita** several a day (office in the capital 21 Calle, 1-56, Zona 1), leaves from the Minerva Terminal, US$4.60, comfortable, 4 hrs. **Líneas América**, from 7 Av, 3-33, Zona 2, T7761-2063, US$5, 4 hrs, between 0515-2000, 6 daily. **Línea Dorada**, 12 Av and 5 C, Zona 3, T7767-5198, 0400 and 1530, US$9. **Transportes Alamo** from 14 Av, 5-15, Zona 3, T7763-5044, between 0430 and 1430, 7 a day, US$5, 4 hrs.

The following destinations are served by buses leaving from the Minerva Terminal, Zona 3 and the Rotonda. For **Antigua**, change at Chimaltenangoby either taking a chicken bus or Pullman. To **Almolonga**, via **Cantel**, every 30 mins, US$0.50, 10 mins. (Buses to Almolonga and Zunil not via Cantel, leave from the corner of 10 Av and 10 Calle, Zona 1.) To **Chichicastenango** with Transportes Veloz Quichelense de Hilda Esperanza, several from 0500 to 1530, US$3.80, 2½ hrs. To **Cuatro Caminos** US$0.50, 30 mins. To **Huehuetenango** with Transportes Velásquez, every 30 mins 0500-1730, US$2.50, 2½ hrs. To **La Mesilla** at 0500, 0600, 0700, 0800, 1300, 1400 with Transportes Unión Fronteriza, US$3.60, 4 hrs. To **Los Encuentros**, US$2.20. To **Malacatán**, US$3.60, 5 hrs. To **Momostenango**, US$1.20, 1½ hrs. To **Panajachel**, with Transportes Morales, at 0500, 0600, 1000, 1200, 1500,

US$3.20, 2½-3 hrs. To **Retalhuleu**, US$1.20, 1½ hrs. To **Salcajá**, every 30 mins, US$0.40, 15 mins. To **San Andrés Xecul** every 2 hrs, US$0.60, 30 mins. To **San Cristóbal Totonicapán**, every 30 mins, US$0.40, 20 mins. To **San Francisco El Alto**, US$0.70. **San Marcos**, every 30 mins, US$1, 1 hr. **San Martín Sacatepéquez/San Martín Chile Verde**, US$0.70, 1 hr. **Santiago Atitlán**, with **Ninfa de Atitlán** at 0800, 1100, 1230, 1630, 4½ hrs. To **Ciudad Tecún Umán** every 30 mins, 0500-1400, US$3.60, 4 hrs. To **Totonicapán**, every 20 mins, US$1.20, 1 hr. To **Zunil**, every 30 mins, US$0.70, 20-30 mins.

Shuttle Adrenalina Tours, see Tour operators, above, runs shuttles. To **Cobán**, US$45, Panajachel US$20 and Antigua, US$25. Adrenalina also runs a shuttle to and from **San Cristóbal de las Casas**, Mexico, US$35.

Car
Car hire Tabarini Renta Autos, 9 Calle, 9-21, Zona 1, T7763-0418.
Mechanic José Ramiro Muñoz R, 1 Calle, 19-11, Zona 1, T7761-8204. Also **Goodyear Taller** at the Rotonda and for motorbikes **Moto Servicio Rudy**, 2 Av, 3-48, Zona 1, T7765-5433.

Taxi
Found all over town, notably lined up along Parque Centro América.
Taxis Xelaju, T7761-4456.

North of Quetzaltenango *p280*
Bus All buses heading to Quetzaltenango from Cuatro Caminos pass through **Salcajá**, 10 mins. From Xela to **San Andrés Xecul**, US$0.60, 30 mins. Or take any bus heading to Cuatro Caminos and getting off at the Esso station on the left-hand side, and then almost doubling back on yourself to take the San Andrés road. There are pickups from here.

South of Quetzaltenango *p281*
Bus Cantel is 10-15 mins by bus (11 km), and US$0.24 from Xela on the way to Zunil, but you need to take the bus marked for Cantel Fábrica and Zunil, not Almolonga and

Zunil. From **Zunil** to Xela via Almolonga leaves from the bridge. Walk down the left-hand side of the church to the bottom of the hill, take a left and you'll see the buses the other side of the bridge, US$0.60. **Fuentes Georginas** is reached either by walking the 8 km uphill just to the south of Zunil, 2 hrs (300-m ascent; take the right fork after 4 km, but be careful as robbery has occurred here), by pickup truck in 15 mins (US$10 return with a 1 hr wait), or hitch. If you come by bus to Zunil and are walking to the Fuentes, don't go down into town with the bus, but get off on the main road at the Pepsi stand and walk to the entrance road, which is visible 100 m away on the left. See also Shuttles, left, for transfer to the thermal pools.

El Viejo Palmar *p281*
Bus Just before San Felipe, and just before the Puente Samalá III, if you're heading south, is the turn to the right for El Viejo Palmar. Take any bus heading to the south coast and asked to be dropped off at the entrance and walk. Or, take a pickup from San Felipe park. Ask for Beto or Brígido.
Taxi From Xela round trip is US$25, or take a tour from town.

Volcán Santa María and Santiaguito *p282*
Bus To reach the volcano take the bus to **Llano del Pinal**, 7 km away, from the Minerva Terminal (every 30 mins, last bus back 1800). Get off at the crossroads and follow the dirt road towards the right side of the volcano until it sweeps up the right (about 40 mins), take the footpath to the left (where it is marked for some distance); bear right at the saddle where another path comes in from the left, but look carefully as it is easily missed.

Laguna Chicabal *p282*
Bus/car The last bus to **Quetzaltenango** leaves at 1900, 1 hr. Parking at the entrance, US$2. It is a 40-min walk from the car park (and you'll need a sturdy vehicle if you attempt the steep first ascent in a car).

To Mexico from Quetzaltenango *p282*
Bus Volcán Tajumulco can be reached by getting to the village of **San Sebastián** from San Marcos, which takes about 2 hrs.

❶ Directory

Quetzaltenango *p277, maps p278 and p279*
Banks Many banks on Parque Centro América. Non-Amex TCs are difficult to change here. Maestro can't be used in ATMs. There is a **Bancard**, 24 hr Visa ATM on the park next to **Banrural** which has a MasterCard ATM **Banco Industrial**, corner of 5 Calle y 11 Av, 24 hr Visa ATM, Visa accepted. **G&T Continental**, 14 Av, 3-17. Advances on MasterCard. **Embassies and consulates** Mexican Consulate, 21 Av, 8-64, Zona 3, T7767-5542, Mon-Fri 0800-1100, take photocopies of your passport. **Emergencies** Police: T7761-5805; Fire: T7761-2002; Red Cross: T7761-2746. **Internet** Lots of places around town. **Language schools** See also box, page 238. Many of Xela's schools can be found at www.xelapages.com/schools.htm. There are many schools offering individual tuition, accommodation with families, extra-curricular activities and excursions. Some also offer Mayan languages. Several schools fund community-development projects, and students are invited to participate with voluntary work. Some schools are non-profit making; enquire carefully. Extra-curricular activities are generally better organized at the larger schools. Prices start from US$130 per week including accommodation, but rise in Jun-Aug to US$150 and up. The following have been recommended: Centro de Estudios de Español Pop Wuj, 1 Calle, 17-72, T7761-8286, www.pop-wuj.org. Guatemalensis, 19 Av, 2-14, Zona 1, T7765-1384, www.geocities.com/spanland/. Sol Latino, Diagonal 12, 6-58, Zona 1, T5613-7222, www.spanishschoollatino.com. Instituto Central América (ICA), 19 Av, 1-47 Calle, Zona 1, T/F7763-1871. INEPAS (Instituto de Estudios Español y Participación en Ayuda

Social), 15 Av, 4-59, T7765-1308, www.inepas.org. Keen on social projects and has already founded a primary school in a Maya village, extremely welcoming. Juan Sisay Spanish School, 15 Av, 8-38, Zona 1, T7761-1586, www.juansisay.com. Kie-Balam, Diagonal 12, 4-46, Zona 1, T7761-1636, kie_balam@hotmail.com. Offers conversation classes in the afternoon in addition to regular hours. La Paz, Diagonal 11, 7-36, T7761-2159, xela.escuelalapaz@gmail.com. Minerva Spanish School, 24 Av, 4-39, Zona 3, T7767-4427, www.minervaspanish school.com. Proyecto Lingüístico Quetzalteco de Español, 5 Calle, 2-40, Zona 1, T7765-2140, hermandad@plqe.org. Recommended. Proyecto Lingüístico 'Santa María', 14 Av "A", 1-26, T/F7765-1262. Volunteer opportunities and free internet access. Sakribal, 6 C, 7-42, Zona 1, T7763-0717, www.sakribal.com. Community projects are available. Ulew Tinimit, 4 C, 15-23, Zona 1, T7761-6242, www.spanish guatemala.org. Utatlán, 12 Av, 14-32, Pasaje Enríquez, Zona 1, T7763-0446, utatlan_xela@hotmail.com. Voluntary work opportunities, one of the cheaper schools. **Laundry** Minimax, 14 Av, C-47. Lavandería Pronto, 7 Calle, 13-25, good service. Lavandería El Centro, 15 Av, 3-51, Zona 1, very good service. **Medical services** San Rafael Hospital, 9 Calle, 10-41, T7761-2956. Hospital Rodolfo Robles, a private hospital on Diagonal 11, Zona 1, T7761-4229. Hospital Privado Quetzaltenango, Calle Rodolfo Robles, 23-51, Zona 1, T7761-4381. Medical tourism, www.turismosaludquetzaltenango.com, T5308-5106, a new service supported by many doctors, and Adrenalina Tours (see above). **Post** 15 Av y 4 Calle. **Telephone** Telgua, 15 Av "A" y 4 Calle. Kall Shop, 8 Av, 4-24, Zona 1. **Voluntary work** Asociación Hogar Nuevos Horizontes, www.ahnh.org, T7761-6140. EntreMundos, El Espacio, 6 Calle, 7-31, Zona 1, T7761-2179, www.entremundos.org, puts people in touch with opportunities. Hogar de Niños, Llanos de Urbina, Cantel, T7761-1526, hogardeninos@hotmail.com.

Southern Guatemala

The southern coastal plain of Guatemala supports many plantations of coffee, sugar and tropical fruit trees and its climate is unbearably hot and humid. Amid the fincas some of the most curious archaeological finds have been unearthed, a mixture of monument styles such as Maya and Olmec, including Abaj Takalik, the cane field stones at Santa Lucía Cotzumalguapa and the big 'Buddhas' of Monte Alto.

On the coast are the black-sand beaches and nature reserves of the popular and laid-back Monterrico and Sipacate resorts, where nesting turtles burrow in the sand and masses of birds take to the skies around. Casting a shadow over the coast, the Central Highland volcanoes of Lake Atitlán, and the Antigua trio of Fuego, Acatenango and Agua, look spectacular, looming on the horizon above the lowlands. ▸▸ *For listings, see pages 293-296.*

Ins and outs

Numerous buses travel from Guatemala City and along the CA2 Highway that runs through the transport hub of Escuintla and through towns either side to the Mexican and El Salvadorean borders. ▸▸ *See Transport, page 295.*

Guatemala City to the Pacific coast

The main road from the capital heads to Escuintla, which connects Guatemala City with all the Pacific ports. There is also a direct route to Escuintla from Antigua. South of Guatemala City is **Amatitlán** on the banks of the lake of the same name. The lake is seriously polluted. The main reason for coming here would be for the **Day of the Cross** on 3 May, when the Christ figure is removed from the church and floated out of a boat amid candles and decorations. A *teleférico* has opened on the lake. **Palín** has a Sunday market in a plaza under an enormous ceiba tree. The textiles are exceptional, but are increasingly difficult to find. There are great views of Pacaya to the east as you head down to the coast, Volcán Agua to the northwest, and the Pacific lowlands to the west. An unpaved road runs northwest from here to Antigua via **Santa María de Jesús**. The town's fiesta is on 24-30 July. **Escuintla** is a large, unattractive provincial centre in a rich tropical valley. It is essentially a transport hub for travellers in the area.

Puerto San José, Chulamar and Iztapa

South of Escuintla the fast tarmacked highway heads to Puerto San José. Puerto San José used to be the country's second largest port and first opened for business (especially the coffee trade) in 1853. The climate is hot, the streets and most of the beaches dirty, and at weekends the town fills up with people from the capital. Fishing is available (see under Iztapa, below), and there are swimming beaches near by, but beware of the strong undercurrent. Some 5 km to the west of Puerto San José is Chulamar, a popular beach at weekends with good bathing. Iztapa is world renowned for deep-sea fishing. Sail fish, bill fish, marlin, tuna, dorado, roosterfish, yellowfin and snapper are to be found in large numbers. The **Chiquimulilla Canal** runs either side of Puerto San José parallel to the coast, for close to 100 km. From here a trip can be taken through the canal by *lancha* to the old Spanish port of Iztapa, now a bathing resort, a short distance to the east.

Monterrico → *For listings, see pages 293-297. Colour map 2, C2.*

Monterrico is a small, black-sand resort where the sunsets are a rich orange and the waves crash spectacularly on to the shore. If you are in the area between September and January, you can sponsor a baby turtle's waddle to freedom.

Ins and outs
The landing stage is 10 minutes' walk from the ocean front, where you'll find the main restaurants and places to stay. When you step off the dock take the first left, and keep left, which heads directly to the main cluster of beach hotels. This road is known as Calle del Proyecto or Calle del Muelle. Walking straight on from the dock takes you to the main drag in town. When you get to the main drag and want to walk to the main group of hotels, take a left along the beach or take the sandy path to the left one block back from the beach where the sand is a tiny bit easier to walk on.

Sights
Monterrico's popularity is growing fast but mainly as a weekend and holiday resort with views that are undisturbed by high-rise blocks. All the hotels, mostly rustic and laid-back, are lined up along the beach, and there are a few shops and *comedores* not linked to hotels, in this village of just 1500 people. The village is surrounded by canals carpeted in aquatic plants and mangrove swamps with bird and turtle reserves in their midst. These areas make up the **Monterrico Nature Reserve**. Anteater, armadillo, racoon and weasel live in the area. It is worth taking a boat trip at sunrise or sunset, to see migratory North and South American birds, including flamingo. However, the real stars in this patch are the olive ridleys – *Parlama blanca* and *Parlama negra* turtles, which lay eggs between July and October, and the Baule turtle, which lays between between October and February. There is a **turtle hatchery** ① *daily 0800-1200, 1400-1700, US$1*. Just behind the hatchery there are 300 breeding crocodiles, 150 turtles and iguanas. The turtle liberation event takes place every Saturday night between October and February.

Santa Lucía Cotzumalguapa → *For listings, see pages 293-297. Colour map 2, C2.*

Amid the sugar-cane fields and *fincas* of this Pacific town lie an extraordinary range of carved stones and images with influences from pre-Maya civilizations, believed mostly to be ancient Mexican cultures, including the Izapa civilization from the Pacific coast area of Mexico near the Guatemalan border. The town is just north of the Pacific Highway, where some of the hotels and banks are.

Ins and outs
You can visit all the sites on foot. However, you are advised not to go wandering in and out of the cane fields at the Bilbao site as there have been numerous assaults in the past. You can walk along the tarmacked road north to the El Baúl sites (6 km and 8 km respectively from town), but there is no shade, so take lots of water. Ask for directions. There is an occasional 'Río Santiago' bus, which goes as far as Colonia Maya, close to the El Baúl hilltop. Only workers' buses go to **Finca El Baúl** in the morning, returning at night. To get to the museum, walk east along the Pacific Highway and take a left turn into the *finca* site. Alternatively, take a taxi from town (next to the plaza) and negotiate a trip to all four areas. They will charge around US$20. **Note** Do not believe any taxi driver who tells

you that Las Piedras (the stones) have been moved from the cane fields to the museum because of the increasing assaults.

Sights

There is considerable confusion about who carved the range of monuments and stelae scattered around the town. It is safe to say that the style of the monuments found in the last 150 years is a blend of a number of pre-Columbian styles. Some believe the prominent influence is Toltec, the ancestors of the Maya K'iche', Kaqchikel, Tz'utujil and Pipiles. It is thought the Tolteca-Pipil had been influenced in turn by the Classic culture from Teotihuacán, a massive urban state northeast of the present Mexico City, which had its zenith in the seventh century AD. However, some experts say that there is no concrete evidence to suggest that the Pipiles migrated as early as AD 400 or that they were influenced by Teotihuacán. All in all, the cultural make-up of this corner of Guatemala may never be known.

Four main points of interest entice visitors to the area. **Bilbao**, **El Baúl**, **Finca El Baúl** and the **Museo de Cultura Cotzumalguapa**. The remnants at **Bilbao**, first re-discovered in 1860, are mainly buried beneath the sugar cane but monuments found above ground show pre-Maya influences. It is thought that the city was inhabited 1200 BC-AD 800. There are four large boulders – known as *Las Piedras* – in sugar-cane fields, which can be reached on foot from the tracks leading from the end of 4 Avenida in town. **El Baúl** is a Late Classic ceremonial centre, 6 km north of Santa Lucía, with two carved stone pieces to see; most of its monuments were built between AD 600 and 900. **Finca El Baúl** has a collection of sculptures and stelae gathered from the large area of the *finca* grounds. The **Museo de Cultura Cotzumalguapa** ① *Finca Las Ilusiones, Mon-Fri 0800-1600, Sat 0800-1200, US$1.30, less than 1 km east of town, ask the person in charge for the key*, displays numerous artefacts collected from the *finca* and a copy of the famous Bilbao Monument 21 from the cane fields.

Santa Lucía Cotzumalguapa to the Mexican border

Beyond Santa Lucía Cotzumalguapa is **Cocales**, where a good road north leads to Patulul and after 30 km, to Lake Atitlán at San Lucas Tolimán. The Pacific Highway continues through San Antonio Suchitepéquez to **Mazatenango** (where just beyond are the crossroads for Retalhueleu and Champerico) and on to Coatepeque and Ciudad Tecún Umán for the Mexican border. Mazatenango is the chief town of the Costa Grande zone. While not especially attractive, the Parque Central is very pleasant with many fine trees providing shade. There is a huge fiesta in the last week of February, when hotels are full and double their prices. At that time, beware of children carrying (and throwing) flour.

Retalhuleu and around → *Colour map 2, C1.*

Retalhuleu, normally referred to as 'Reu' (pronounced 'Ray-oo') is the capital of the department. The entrance to the town is grand with a string of royal palms lining the route, known as Calzada Las Palmas. It serves a large number of coffee and sugar estates and much of its population is wealthy. The original colonial church of **San Antonio de Padua** is in the central plaza. Bordering the plaza to the east is the neoclassical **Palacio del Gobierno**, with a giant quetzal sculpture on top. The **Museo de Arqueología y Etnología** ① *Tue-Sat 0830-1300, 1400-1800, Sun 0900-1230, US$1.30, next to the palacio*, is small. Downstairs are exhibits of Maya ceramics.

If you fancy cooling off, near Reu are the **Parque Acuático Xocomil** ① *Km 180.5 on the road from Xela to Champerio, T7722-9400, www.irtra.org.gt, Thu-Sun 0900-1700, US$9.60.*

Nearby is the enormous theme park with giant pyramids of **Xetulul** ① *T7722-9450, www.irtra.org.gt, Thu-Sun 100-1800, US$26.*

Abaj Takalik
① *Daily 0700-1700, US$3.25, guides are volunteers so tips are welcomed.*
One of the best ancient sites to visit outside El Petén is Abaj Takalik, a ruined city that lies, sweltering, on the southern plain. Its name means 'standing stone' in K'iche'. The site was discovered in 1888 by botanist Doctor Gustav Brühl. It is believed to have flourished in the late pre-Classic period of 300 BC to AD 250 strategically placed to control commerce between the highlands and the Pacific coast. There are some 239 monuments, which include 68 stelae, 32 altars and some 71 buildings, all set in peaceful surroundings. The environment is loved by birds and butterflies, including blue morphos, and by orchids, which flower magnificently between January and March. The main temple buildings are mostly up to 12 m high, suggesting an early date before techniques were available to build Tikal-sized structures.

Towards the Mexican border
The main road runs 21 km east off the Pacific Highway to **Coatepeque**, one of the richest coffee zones in the country. There is a bright, modern church in the leafy Plaza Central. The local fiesta takes place from 11-19 March. There are several hotels, *hospedajes* and restaurants. **Colomba**, an attractive typical village east of Coatepeque in the lowlands, has a basic *hospedaje*.

Routes to El Salvador
Three routes pass through Southern Guatemala to El Salvador (see box, page 199, for border-crossing information). The main towns are busy but scruffy with little to attract the visitor. If travelling by international bus to El Salvador, see page 220.

Route 1 **The Pan-American Highway**: The first route heads directly south along the paved Pan-American Highway from Guatemala City (CA1) to the border at San Cristóbal Frontera. **Cuilapa**, the capital of Santa Rosa Department, is 65 km along the Highway. About 9 km beyond Los Esclavos is the El Molino junction. Beyond, just off the Pan-American Highway, is the village of **El Progreso**, dominated by the imposing Volcán Suchitán, at 2042 m, now part of the Parque Regional Volcán Suchitán run by La Fundación de la Naturaleza. There is accommodation. The town fiesta with horse racing is from 10-16 November. From El Progreso, a good paved road goes north 43 km via Jalapa through open, mostly dry country, with volcanoes always in view. There are several crater lakes including **Laguna del Hoyo** near Monjas that are worth visiting. The higher ground is forested. Beyond Jutiapa and El Progreso the Pan-American Highway heads east and then south to Asunción Mita. Here there is a turning left to Lago de Güija. Before reaching the border at **San Cristóbal Frontera** (see box, page 199), the Pan-American Highway dips and skirts the shores (right) of **Lago Atescatempa**, with several islands set in heavy forest.

Route 2 **Via Jalpatagua**: The second, quicker way of getting to San Salvador is to take a highway that cuts off right from the first route at El Molino junction, about 7 km beyond the Esclavos bridge. This cut-off goes through El Oratorio and Jalpatagua to the border at **Valle Nuevo** (see page 199), continuing then to Ahuachapán and San Salvador.

Route 3 El Salvador (La) via the border at Ciudad Pedro de Alvarado: This coastal route goes from Escuintla to the border bridge over the Río Paz at La Hachadura (El Salvador). It takes two hours from Escuintla to the border. You pass **Auto Safari Chapín** ① *Km 87.5, T2363-1105, Tue-Sun 0900-1700, US$5*, east of Escuintla, an improbable wildlife park, but busy at weekends and holidays. **Taxisco** is 18 km beyond and just off the road. It's a busy place, which has a white church with a curious hearts and holly design on the façade. To the east is Guazacapán, which merges into **Chiquimulilla**, 3 km to the north, the most important town of the area, with good-quality leather goods available. There is accommodation on offer. A side excursion can be made from Chiquimulilla up the winding CA 16 through coffee *fincas* and farmland. About 20 km along there is a turning to the left down a 2- to 3-km steep, narrow, dirt road that goes to **Laguna de Ixpaco**, an impressive, greenish-yellow lake that is 350 m in diameter. It is boiling in some places, emitting sulphurous fumes and set in dense forest. This trip can also be made by heading south off the Pan-American Highway after Cuilapa (just before Los Esclavos) towards Chiquimulilla on the CA 16, with old trees on either side, some with orchids in them, where you will reach the sign to Ixpaco, after 20 km. Thirty kilometres beyond on the Pacific Highway is **Ciudad Pedro de Alvarado** on the border. See box, page 199.

◉ Southern Guatemala listings

For Sleeping and Eating price codes and other relevant information, see Essentials pages 31-33.

⬤ Sleeping

Puerto San José, Chulamar and Iztapa *p289*

There are a number of *comedores* in town.
L Soleil Pacífico, Chulamar, T7879-3131, www.gruposoleil.com. Usual luxuries with day passes available.
A Hotel y Turicentro Eden Pacific, Barrio El Laberinto, Puerto San José, T7881-1605. 17 a/c rooms with TV, private beach and pools.
C-D Hotel Club Sol y Playa Tropical, 1 Calle, 5-48, on the canal, Iztapa, T7881-4365. With pool, friendly staff and standard rooms with fans. Good food at restaurant.

Monterrico *p290*

Most hotels are fully booked by Sat midday and prices rise at weekends – book beforehand if arriving at the weekend.
B Hotel Pez de Oro, at the end of main strip to the east, T2368-3684, www.pezdeoro.com. 18 spacious bungalows attractively set around a swimming pool. All rooms have private bathroom, mosquito lamps, pretty

bedside lights and fan. Some with a/c. Recommended.
B-C San Gregorio, Calle del Proyecto, behind El Kaimán, T2238-4690. 29 modern rooms with bath, fan and mosquito nets. There is a large part-shaded pool, a restaurant set around the pool. Non-guests can pay to use the pool.
B-D El Mangle, main strip, T5514-6517. Rooms with fans, bathrooms, and mosquito nets (some are a little dark), centred around a nice, clean pool, set a little back from the beach front. It's quieter than some of the others. Recommended.
C Hotel Restaurante Dulce y Salado, some way away from the main cluster of hotels and a 500-m hard walk east through sand if you are on foot, T5817-9046. The sea view and the uninterrupted view of the highland volcanoes behind is fantastic. Run by a friendly Italian couple, Fulvio and Graziella. Clean, nice rooms, with bath, fans and mosquito nets, set around a pool. Breakfast included, good Italian food.
C-D Café del Sol, 250 m west of the main drag next to Eco Beach Place, T5810-0821, www.cafe-del-sol.com. 13 rooms pleasant rooms. Rooms across the road in an annexe

are much more spartan. There is a pleasant bar area and a restaurant.

C-G Johnny's Place, main strip. Equipped bungalows, rooms with bath, cheaper without, and a dorm (**F** per person). All windows have mosquito netting. Internet, table tennis, swimming pools, fishing and a restaurant with free coffee fill-ups. Recommended.

E-F El Delfín, T5904-9167, eldelfin99@ yahoo.com. Bungalows, with mosquito nets, fans and private bathroom and rooms. Restaurant with vegetarian food. Organizes shuttles at any hour. Recommended.

F Hotel y Restaurant Kaiman, on the beach side, T5617-9880, big bar ('1000 'til you're done' at the weekends) and restaurant. The rooms are very clean, with bath, fan, and mosquito nets. There are 2 pools for adults and children, but they're not in top shape. Discounts for longer stays.

Santa Lucía Cotzumalguapa *p290*
B Santiaguito, Pacific Hwy at Km 90.4, T7882-5435. A/c, TV and hot and cold water, pool and restaurant. Non-guests can use the pool for US$2.60.

D-E Hotel El Camino, diagonally opposite Santiaguito across the highway at Km 90.5, T7882-5316. Rooms with bath, tepid water, fan, some rooms with a/c (more expensive). All have TV. Good restaurant.

F Hospedaje La Reforma, a stone's throw from the park on 4 Av, 4-71. Lots of dark box rooms and dark shared showers. Clean.

Retalhuleu and around *p291*
B La Colonia, 1.5 km to the north at Km 180.5, T7772-2048. Rooms with a/c and TV, pool, and good food.

B Posada de Don José, 5 Calle, 3-67, T7771-0180, posadadonjose@hotmail.com. Rooms with a/c and fan, TV. Also a very good restaurant serving such mouth-watering temptations as lobster sautéed in cognac. Restaurant and café are set beside the pool. Non-guests can use the pool for a small fee.

C Astor, 5 Calle, 4-60, T7771-2559, hotelastor@intelnett.com. A colonial-style place with with 27 rooms, a/c, hot water, TV, set around a pretty courtyard where there's a pool and jacuzzi. Parking and restauarant. **Bar La Carreta** is inside the hotel. Non-guests can use the pool and jacuzzi here (nicer than the one at **Posada de Don José**) for a fee.

C Siboney, 5 km northwest of Reu in San Sebastián, Km 179, T7772-2174, www.hotelsiboney.com. Rooms are with bath, a/c and TV, set around pool. Try the *caldo de mariscos* or *paella* in the excellent restaurant. Non-guests can pay to use the pool.

⊖ Eating

Monterrico *p290*
Be careful especially with *ceviche*. There are lots of local *comedores* along Calle Principal, which leads to the beach.

♔ **Restaurant Italiano**, at the end of the main strip to the east, at **Hotel Pez de Oro**. Popular and consistently good. Recommended.

Santa Lucía Cotzumalguapa *p290*
♔ **Pastelería Italiana**, Calzada 15 de Septiembre, 4-58. Open early for bakery.

Retalhuleu and around *p291*
♔ **Restaurante La Luna**, 5 Calle, 4-97, on the corner of the plaza. Good *típico* meals served.
♔ **El Patio**, corner of 5 Calle, 4 Av. *Menú del día* and cheap breakfasts. Limited.

⊕ Entertainment

Monterrico *p290*
El Animal Desconocido, on beach close to **Johnny's Place**. Open from 2000 in the week.

▲ Activities and tours

Monterrico *p290*
Tour operators
Those preferring to stay on land can rent horses for a jaunt on the beach. *Lancha* and turtle-searching tours are operated by a couple of agencies in town.

⊖ Transport

Guatemala City to the Pacific coast *p289*
Bus To and from Guatemala City to **Amatitlán** (every 30 mins, US$0.50) from 0700-2045 from 14 Av, between 3 y 4 Calle, Zona 1, Guatemala City. From **Escuintla** (1½ hrs) to the capital from 8 Calle y 2 Av, Zona 1, near the corner of the plaza in Escuintla. Buses that have come along the Pacific Hwy and are going on to the capital pull up at the main bus terminal on 4 Av. From the terminal there are buses direct to **Antigua** every 30 mins, 1-1½ hrs, US$1.20. To **Taxisco** from Escuintla, every 30 mins, 0700-1700, 40 mins, for connections onwards (hourly) to La Avellana, for boats to Monterrico. Frequent buses to **Iztapa** with the last bus departing at 2030.

If you are changing in Escuintla for **Santa Lucía Cotzumalguapa** to the west, you need to take a left out of the bus terminal along the 4 Av up a slight incline towards the police fortress and take a left here on its corner, 9 Calle, through the market. Head for 3 blocks straight, passing the **Cinammon Pastelería y Panadería** on the right at 9 Calle y 2 Av. At the end here are buses heading to Santa Lucía and further west along the Pacific Hwy. It is a 5- to 10-min walk. Buses leave here every 5 mins. To **Santa Lucía Cotzumalguapa** (the bus *ayudantes* shout 'Santa'), 35 mins, US$1.20. On the return, buses pull up at the corner of the 8 Calle y 2 Av, where Guatemala City buses also pass.

Puerto San José, Chulamar and Iztapa *p289*
Bus Regular buses from the capital passing through **Escuintla**, 2-3 hrs. If you are heading further east by road from Iztapa along the coast to **Monterrico** (past loofah plantations), see below.

Monterrico *p290*
Bus and boat
There are 3 ways of getting to Monterrico: 2 by public transport, the 3rd by shuttle. The **first route** to Monterrico involves heading direct to the Pacific coast by taking a bus from the capital to **Puerto San José**, 1 hr, and changing for a bus to **Iztapa**. Or take a direct bus from Escuintla to Iztapa. Then cross river by the toll bridge to **Pueblo Viejo** for US$1.60 per vehicle (buses excluded), or US$0.80 per foot passengers, 5 mins. The buses now continue to Monterrico, about 25 km east, 1 hr. Buses run to and from Iztapa between 0600-1500, from the corner of main street and the road to Pueblo Viejo to the left, 3 blocks north of the beach, just past the Catholic church on the right.

The **second route** involves getting to Taxisco first and then La Avellana. There are also direct buses to La Avellana from Guatemala City, see page 218. If you are coming from Antigua, take a bus to **Escuintla** 1-1½ hrs. From there, there are regular departures to **Taxisco**, 40 mins. From Taxisco to La Avellana, buses leave hourly until 1800, US$1, 20 mins. If you take an international bus from Escuintla (45 mins), it will drop you off just past the Taxisco town turn-off, just before a bridge with a slip road. Walk up the road (5 mins) and veer to the right where you'll see the bus stop for **La Avellana**. At La Avellana take the **motor boats** through mangrove swamps, 20-30 mins, US$0.60 for foot passengers, from 0630 and then hourly until 1800. The journey via this route from Antigua to Monterrico takes about 3¼ hrs if your connections are good. Return boats to La Avellana leave at 0330, 0530, 0700, 0800,

0900, 1030, 1200, 1300, 1430, 1600. Buses leave La Avellana for Taxisco hourly until 1800. Buses pull up near the **Banco Nor-Oriente** where numerous buses heading to Guatemala and Escuintla pass.

Shuttles Alternatively, numerous travel agencies in Antigua run shuttles, US$10-12 1 way. You can book a return shuttle journey in Monterrico by going to the language school on the road that leads to the dock. There are also mini buses operating from Monterrico to **Iztapa** and vice-versa.

Santa Lucía Cotzumalguapa *p290*
Bus Regular departures to the capital. Buses plying the Pacific Hwy also pass through, so if you are coming from Reu in the west or Escuintla in the east you can get off here. **Car** If you are driving, there are a glut of 24-hr **Esso** and **Texaco** gas stations here. See under Guatemala City to the Pacific coast for catching transport from **Escuintla**.

Santa Lucía Cotzumalguapa to the Mexican border *p291*
Bus 5 a day **Cocales-Panajachel**, between 0600 and 1400, 2½ hrs. Frequent buses to **Mazatenango** from Guatemala City, US$5. To the border at **Ciudad Tecún Umán**, US$2.10, an irregular service with Fortaleza del Sur.

Retalhuleu and around *p291*
Bus Services along the Pacific Hwy to Mexico leave from the main bus terminal, which is beyond the city limits at 5 Av 'A'. To **Coatepeque** (0600-1800), **Malacatán**, **Mazatenango** and **Champerico** (0500-1800). Buses also leave from here to **El Asintal**, for Abaj Takalik, 30 mins, every 30 mins from 0600-1830, last bus back to Reu 1800. Or catch them before that from the corner of 5 Av 'A' and the Esso gas station as they turn to head for the village. Leaving from a smaller terminal at 7 Av/10 Calle, there are regular buses to **Ciudad Tecún Umán**, **Talismán** and **Guatemala City** via the Pacific route, and to Xela (1¾ hrs, every hour 0500-1800).

Abaj Takalik *p292*
Bus Take a bus to El from **Retalhuleu** and walk the hot 4 km to the site entrance. Or, take any bus heading along the Pacific Hwy and get off at the **El Asintal** crossroads. Take a pickup from here to El Asintal; then a pickup from the town square to Abaj Takalik. As there are only *fincas* along this road, you will probably be on your own, in which case it is US$5 to the site or US$10 round trip, including waiting time. Bargain hard.

Taxi and tour A taxi from central plaza in Reu to the site and back including waiting time is US$13. Alternatively, take a tour from Xela.

Towards the Mexican border *p292*
Bus From Quetzaltenango to **Coatepeque**, catch any bus heading to Ciudad Tecún Umán from Reu.

⊕ Directory

Monterrico *p290*
Language school Proyecto Lingüístico Monterrico, http://monterrico-guatemala. com/spanish-school.htm. **Medical services** There is a clinic behind El Delfín open at weekends. **Post** Near Hotel Las Margaritas on the Calle Principal.

Santa Lucía Cotzumalguapa *p290*
Banks Banco G&T Continental, on the highway, accepts MasterCard. Banco Industrial, accepts Visa, 3 Av between 2 and 3 Calle. There's a Bancared Visa ATM on the plaza. **Telephone** Telgua, Cda 15 de Septiembre near the highway.

Retalhuleu and around *p291*
Banks There are plenty of banks in town taking Visa and MC. ATMs also. **Embassies and consulates** Mexico, inside the Posada de Don José. Mon-Fri 0700-1230, 1400-1800. **Medical services** Hospital Nacional de Retalhuleu, Blvd Centenario, 3 Av, Zona 2, 10 mins along the road to El Asintal, T7771-0116. **Post** On the plaza. **Telephone** 5 Calle, 4-18.

Guatemala City to the Caribbean

From the capital to the Caribbean, the main road passes through the Río Motagua Valley, punctuated by cacti and bordered by the Sierra de Las Minas mountains rising abruptly in the west. Dinosaur remains, the black Christ and the Maya ruins of Quiriguá can be found on or close to the highway. The banana port of Puerto Barrios is a large transport and commercial hub and jumping-off point for the Garífuna town of Livingston. Trips down the lush gorge of the Río Dulce are a highlight; nearby are some great places to see and stay on its banks, as well as accommodation around Lago de Izabal. ⏭ *For listings, see pages 302-310.*

Ins and outs

Getting there The Carretera al Atlántico, or Atlantic Highway, stretches from Guatemala City all the way to Puerto Barrios on the Caribbean coast in the department of Izabal. Most of the worthwhile places to visit are off this fast main road, along the Río Motagua valley, where cactus, bramble, willow and acacia grow. There are numerous buses plying the route. ⏭ *See Transport, page 308.*

Along the Atlantic Highway

Before Teculután is **El Rancho** at Km 85, the jumping-off point for a trip north to Cobán (see page 313). There are a few places to stay here. Geologists will be interested in the **Motagua fault** near Santa Cruz, between Teculután and Río Hondo. Just before Río Hondo (Km 138), a paved road runs south towards Estanzuela. Shortly before this town you pass a monument on the right commemorating the 1976 earthquake, which activated a fault line that cut across the road. It can still be seen in the fields on either side of the road. The epicentre of this massive earthquake, which measured 7.5 on the Richter scale, and killed 23,000 people, was at **Los Amates**, 65 km further down the valley towards Puerto Barrios.

Estanzuela

Estanzuela is a small town fronting the highway. Its **Museo de Palaeontología, Arqueología y Geología** ⓘ *daily 0800-1700, free,* displays the incredible reconstructed skeletal remains of a 4-m prehistoric giant sloth found in Zone 6, Guatemala City and a giant armadillo, among others. Take a minibus south from Río Hondo and ask to be dropped at the first entrance to the town on the right. Then walk right, into the town, and continue for 600 m to the museum, 10 minutes. When you reach the school, walk to the right and you will see the museum.

Chiquimula, Volcán de Ipala and the Honduran border

Chiquimula is a stop-off point for travellers who stay here on their way to or from Copán Ruinas, Honduras, if they can't make the connection in one day (see page 198 for border crossing). The fiesta, which includes bullfighting, is from 11-18 August. An alternative route to Chiquimula and Esquipulas is from the southeast corner of Guatemala City (Zona 10), where the Pan-American Highway heads towards the Salvadorean border. After a few kilometres there is a turning to **San José Pinula** (fiesta: 16-20 March). After San José, an unpaved branch road continues for 203 km through fine scenery to **Mataquescuintla**, **Jalapa** (several *hospedajes*, good bus connections; fiesta: 2-5 May), **San Pedro Pinula**, **San Luis Jilotepeque** and **Ipala** to Chiquimula. Southwest of Chiquimula, the extinct Volcán de Ipala (1650 m) can be visited. The crater lake is cool and good for swimming.

At **Vado Hondo**, 10 km south of Chiquimula on the road to Esquipulas, a smooth dirt road branches east to the Honduran border (48 km) and a further 11 km to the great Maya ruins of Copán. The border is 1 km after the village.

Esquipulas → *Colour map 2, C3.*

Esquipulas is dominated by a large, white basilica, which attracts millions of pilgrims from across Central America to view the image of a Black Christ. The town has pulled out the stops for visitors, who, as well as a religious fill, will lack nothing in the way of food, drink and some of the best kitsch souvenirs on the market. If it's possible, stop at the mirador, 1 km from the town, for a spectacular view on the way in of the basilica, which sits at the end of a 1.5-km main avenue. The history of the famous *Cristo Negro* records that in 1735 Father Pedro Pardo de Figueroa, suffering from an incurable chronic illness, stood in front of the image to pray, and was cured. A few years later, after becoming Archbishop of Guatemala he ordered a new church to be built to house the sculpture. The **basilica** ⓘ *open until 2000*, was completed in 1758 and the *Cristo Negro* was transferred from the parish church shortly after that. Inside the basilica, the Black Christ is on a gold cross, elaborately engraved with vines and grapes. It was carved by Quirio Cataño in dark balsam wood in 1595. The image attracts over 1,000,000 visitors per year, some crawling on their hands and knees to pay homage. The main pilgrimage periods are 1-15 January (with 15 January being the busiest day), during Lent, Holy Week and 21-27 July.

Quiriguá

ⓘ *Daily 0730-1630, US$4. Take insect repellent. There are toilets, a restaurant, a museum and a jade store and you can store your luggage with the guards. There is no accommodation at the site (yet), but you can camp (see Sleeping). The site is reached by a paved road from the Atlantic Highway. The village of Quiriguá is about halfway between Zacapa and Puerto Barrios on the highway, and about 3 km from the entrance road to the ruins.*

The remarkable Late Classic ruins of Quiriguá include the tallest stelae found in the Maya world. The UNESCO World Heritage Site is small, with an excavated acropolis to see, but the highlight of a visit is the sight of the ornately carved tall stelae and the zoomorphic altars. The Maya here were very industrious, producing monuments every five years between AD 751 and 806, coinciding with the height of their prosperity and confident rule. The earliest recorded monument dates from AD 480.

It is believed that Quiriguá was an important trading post between Tikal and Copán, inhabited since the second century, but principally it was a ceremonial centre. The Kings of Quiriguá were involved in the rivalries, wars and changing alliances between Tikal, Copán and Calakmul. It rose to prominence in the middle of the eighth century, around the time of Cauac Sky who ascended to the throne in AD 724. Cauac Sky was appointed to the position by 18 Rabbit, powerful ruler of Copán (now in Honduras), and its surrounding settlements. It seems that he was fed up with being a subordinate under the domination of Copán, and during his reign, Quiriguá attacked Copán and captured 18 Rabbit. One of the stelae tells of the beheading of the Copán King in the plaza at Quiriguá as a sacrifice after the AD 738 battle. After this event 18 Rabbit disappears from the official chronicle and a 20-year hiatus follows in the historical record of Copán. Following this victory, Quiriguá became an independent kingdom and gained control of the Motagua Valley, enriching itself in the process. And, from AD 751, a monument was carved and erected every five years for the next 55 years. The tallest stelae at Quiriguá is **Stelae E**, which is 10.66 m high with another 2.5 m or so buried beneath. It is 1.52 m wide and weighs

65 tonnes. One of its dates corresponds with the enthronement of Cauac Sky, in AD 724, but it's thought to date from AD 771. All of the stelae, in parkland surrounded by ceiba trees and palms, have shelters, which makes photography difficult. Some monuments have been carved in the shape of animals, some mythical, all of symbolic importance to the Maya.

Thirteen kilometres from Quiriguá is the turn-off for **Mariscos** and Lago de Izabal (see page 302). A further 28 km on are the very hot twin towns of Bananera/Morales. From Bananera there are buses to Río Dulce, Puerto Barrios and the Petén.

Puerto Barrios → *Colour map 2, B3.*

Puerto Barrios, on the Caribbean coast, is a hot and dusty port town, still a central banana point, but now largely superseded as a port by Santo Tomás. The launch to the Garífuna town of Lívingston leaves from the municipal dock here. While not an unpleasant town, it is not a destination in itself, but rather a launch pad to more beautiful and happening spots in Guatemala. It's also the departure point for the Honduran Caribbean. On the way into town, note the cemetery on the right-hand side, where you will pass a small Indian mausoleum with elephant carvings. During the 19th century, *culi* (coolies) of Hindu origin migrated from Jamaica to Guatemala to work on the plantations. The fiesta is 16-22 July.

Lívingston and around → *For listings, see pages 302-310. Colour map 2, B3.*

Lívingston, or La Buga, is populated mostly by Garífuna, who bring a colourful flavour to this corner of Guatemala. With its tropical sounds and smells, it is a good place to hang out for a few days, sitting on the dock of the bay, or larging it up with the locals, *punta*-style. *Coco pan* and *cocado* (a coconut, sugar and ginger *dulce*) and locally made jewellery are sold in the streets. The town is the centre of fishing and shrimping in the Bay of Amatique and only accessible by boat. It is nearly 23 km by sea from Puerto Barrios and there are regular daily boat runs that take 35 minutes in a fast *lancha*. The bulk of the town is up a small steep slope leading straight from the dock, which is at the mouth of the Río Dulce estuary. The other part of town is a linear spread along the river estuary, just north of the dock and then first left. The town is small and everything is within walking distance. The Caribbean beach is pretty dirty nearer the river estuary end, but a little further up the coast, it is cleaner, with palm trees and accommodation. Closer to the town are a couple of bars and weekend beach discos. The town's **Centro Cultural Garífuna-Q'eqchi'** is perched on a hillock, and has the best views in the whole of Lívingston. The town's fiestas are 24-31 December, in honour of the Virgen del Rosario, with dancing including the *punta*, and Garífuna Day, 26 November. The small but helpful **tourist office** ① *on the east side of the Parque Municipal, www.livingston.com.gt, daily 0600-1800*, with a café and exhibition space behind.

Around Lívingston

Northwest along the coastline towards the Río Sarstún, on the border with Belize (where manatee can be seen), is the **Río Blanco beach** (45 minutes by *lancha* from Lívingston), followed by **Playa Quehueche** (also spelt Keueche). Beyond Quehueche, about 6 km (1½ hours) from Lívingston, are **Los Siete Altares**, a set of small waterfalls and pools hidden in the greenery. They are at their best during the rainy season when the water cascades down to the sea. In the drier seasons much of the water is channelled down small, eroded grooves on large slabs of grey rock, where you can stretch out and enjoy the sun. Early *Tarzan* movies were filmed here. Don't stroll on the beach after dark and be careful of your belongings at the Siete Altares end. Police occasionally accompany tourists to the falls; check on arrival what the security situation is. Boats can be hired in Lívingston to visit beaches along the coast towards San Juan and the Río Sarstún.

For one of the best trips in Guatemala take a boat up the **Río Dulce** through the sheer-sided canyon towards El Golfete, where the river broadens. Trees and vegetation cling to the canyon walls, their roots plunging into the waters for a long drink below. The scenery here is gorgeous, especially in the mornings, when the waters are unshaken. Tours can be arranged from Lívingston for US$12. You can also paddle up the Río Dulce gorge on *cayucos*, which can be hired from some of the hotels in Lívingston.

The **Biotopo Chocón Machacas** ① *0700-1600, US$2.50 (private hire at US$125 is the only transport option)*, is one place where the elusive manatee (sea cow) hangs out, but you are unlikely to see him munching his way across the lake bottom, as he is very shy and retreats at the sound of a boat motor. (The manatee is an aquatic herbivore, which can be up to 4 m long when adult, and weigh more than 450 kg. It eats for six to eight hours daily

Lívingston

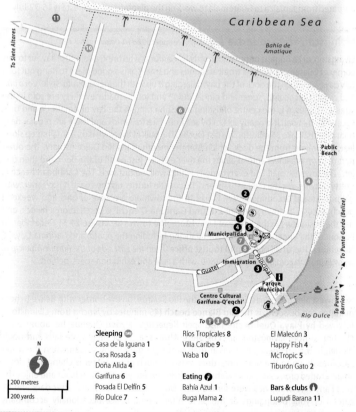

Sleeping 🛏
Casa de la Iguana **1**
Casa Rosada **3**
Doña Alida **4**
Garífuna **6**
Posada El Delfín **5**
Río Dulce **7**

Ríos Tropicales **8**
Villa Caribe **9**
Waba **10**

Eating 🍴
Bahía Azul **1**
Buga Mama **2**

El Malecón **3**
Happy Fish **4**
McTropic **5**
Tiburón Gato **2**

Bars & clubs 🍸
Lugudi Barana **11**

and can consume more than 10% of its body weight in a 24-hour period.) Administered by CECON, the reserve is a mangrove zone, halfway between Río Dulce town and Lívingston, on the northern shore of **El Golfete** – an area where the Río Dulce broadens into a lake 5 km across. Four Q'eqchi' communities of 400 people live on land within the 6245-ha reserve. Within the reserve are carpets of water lilies, dragonflies, blue morpho butterflies, pelicans and cormorants. On land, spot army ants, crabs, mahogany trees and the *labios rojos* ('hot lips') flower.

Proyecto Ak' Tenamit ⓘ *www.aktenamit.org*, meaning 'new village' in Q'eqchi', is 15 minutes upriver from Lívingston. It was set up to help 7000 Q'eqchi' Maya displaced by the civil war. Volunteers are needed for a minimum of a month's work (board and transport, and weekends off). A working knowledge of Spanish is required. There's also a shop and restaurant, with excursions, run by locally trained volunteer guides, and accommodation is available (see Sleeping). Near here is the **Río Tatín tributary** the wonderfully sited **Finca Tatín** and **Hotelito Perdido**, see Sleeping. **Reserva Ecológica Cerro San Gil**, with its natural pools, karstic caves and biostation, can be visited from here, or from Río Dulce. Contact **FUNDAECO** ⓘ *www.fundaeco.org.gt*.

Punta de Manabique

Punta de Manabique is a fine, finger-shaped peninsula northeast of Puerto Barrios and just visible across the bay from Lívingston, coated in a beach of white sand on its eastern side, and by mangrove on the other. Travelling north to the point of the peninsula, you pass the Bahía de Graciosa, where dolphins frolic and manatees silently graze under the surface. In its virgin tropical forest live howler monkeys, parrots, snakes, pizote, tapirs and peccary and, on its beaches, turtles. There is a visitor centre, scientific station and a hotel. For more information contact the **Fundación Mario Dary** ⓘ *www.guate.net/fundarymanabique/fundacion.htm*, which operates conservation, health, education and ecotourism projects.

Lago de Izabal → *For listings, see pages 302-310. Colour map 2, B3.*

The vast Lago de Izabal narrows to form a neck at the town of Fronteras. Better known as Río Dulce, it is famed for its riverside setting and there are some beautiful places around the lake and river in which to stay. Just south of Río Dulce on the lake is the Castillo de San Felipe. On the northern shore of the lake is the town of El Estor, and on its southern shore the smaller town of **Mariscos**. Further east, beyond Río Dulce, the river broadens out to El Golfete, where there is the Biotopo Chacón Machacas, see above. It then narrows into one of the finest gorges in the world, and opens out at its estuary, with Lívingston at its head. This area can be wet in the rainy season, but it experiences a lull in July, known as the *canícula*.

Fronteras/Río Dulce and around

Río Dulce is a good place to stop and kick back for a couple of days. Allow yourself to be tempted to laze on a boat for the afternoon, walk in the nearby jungle, or eat and drink at one of several dockside restaurants. Río Dulce, www.mayaparadise.com, is 23 km upstream from Lívingston at the entrance to Lago de Izabal, is easily accessible from Puerto Barrios by road, and is the last major stop before the Petén. It's also a good place to collect information about the area stretching from El Estor to Lívingston.

On the shore of Lago de Izabal is **Casa Guatemala** ⓘ *14 Calle, 10-63, Zona 1, Guatemala City, T2231-9408, www.casa-guatemala.org* (also known as **Hotel Backpacker's**), an orphanage where you can work in exchange for basic accommodation and food. At the entrance to Lago de Izabal, 2 km upstream, is the old Spanish fort of **Castillo de San Felipe** ① *0800-1700, US$3.30*. The fortification was first built in 1643 to defend the coast against attacks from pirates; it has been well preserved and in lovely grounds; great views from the battlements. Between Río Dulce and El Estor is **Finca El Paraíso**, a hot waterfall with waters that plunge into a cool-water pool below.

El Estor and around → *Colour map 2, B3.*

El Estor enjoys one of the most beautiful vistas in Guatemala. It is strung along the northwest shore of Lago de Izabal, backed by the Santa Cruz mountain range and facing the Sierra de las Minas. The lake is the largest in Guatemala at 717 sq km. It's a great place to relax, swim (down a nearby canyon), go fishing and spot manatee. Some businesses are expecting the new road to bring a surge of tourists visitors. For the next few years, you'll still have the place mostly to yourself. The town dates back to the days when the Europeans living in the Atlantic area got their provisions from a store situated at this spot, now the **Hotel Vista al Lago**. Briton Skinner and Dutchman Klee supplied the region from *el store* 1815-1850. Nickel-mining began just outside town in 1978, but was suspended at the **Exmibal plant** after the oil crisis of 1982, because the process depended on cheap sources of energy.

You can hire a boat from Río Dulce to El Estor, passing near the hot waterfall, inland at Finca El Paraíso, which can be reached by a good trail in about 40 minutes. The Río Sauce cuts through the impressive **Cañón El Boquerón**, where you can swim with the current all the way down the canyon, which is brilliant fun. It's a deep canyon with lots of old man's beard hanging down, strange rock formations and otters and troops of howler monkeys whooping about. One of the locals will paddle you upstream for about 800 m (US$1). Exploring the Río Zarco, closer to town, also makes for a good trip, with cold swimming. The **Refugio de Vida Silvestre Bocas del Polochic** (Bocas del Polochic Wildlife Reserve) is a 23,000-ha protected area on the western shores of the lake. Howler monkeys are commonly seen. In addition to over 350 bird species, there are iguanas, turtles and the chance of sighting crocodiles and manatees. The NGO **Defensores de la Naturaleza** ① *2 Calle and 5 Av, El Estor, T2440-8138 in the capital, www.defensores.org.gt*, has a research station at Selempim with bunk beds (F per person), food, showers and kitchen. Its a two- or three-hour boat ride from El Estor to Ensenada Los Lagartos. Tours available from town for US$30 for two people. Contact the office in El Estor or ask at a hotel about boat services.

Mariscos is on the southern shore of Lago de Izabal. The best reason to come here is the nearby **Denny's Beach**.

◎ Guatemala to the Caribbean listings

For Sleeping and Eating price codes and other relevant information, see Essentials pages 31-33.

● Sleeping

Chiquimula *p297*
C Posada Perla del Oriente, 2 Calle between 11 and 12 Av, T7942-0014. All rooms with TV, some with a/c, parking, pool, quiet. Restaurant. Recommended.

E Hernández, 3 Calle, 7-41, T7942-0708. Cheaper without bathroom, fans. TVs in rooms and a pool add to its attractions. Family-run, quiet and friendly.
E Hotel Posada Don Adán, 8 Av, 4-30, T7942-0549. All rooms with private bathroom, a/c, TV. Run by a friendly, older couple.
E Victoria, 2 Calle, 9-99, next to the bus station (so ask for rooms away from street), T7942-2732. All rooms have bath, cold water,

fan, cable TV, towels, soap, shampoo, some rooms have a/c, drinking water provided, good restaurant, good value, will store luggage. Recommended.

Esquipulas p298

There are plenty of hotels, *hospedajes* and *comedores* all over town, especially in and around 11 Calle, also known as Doble Vía Quirio Cataño. Prices tend to double before the Jan feast day. They also rise at Easter and at weekends. When quiet, midweek, bargain for lower room prices.

A Payaquí, 2 Av, 11-26, T7943-1143, www.hotelpayaqui.com. The 40 rooms are lovely, with *frigobars*, full of beers for the pilgrims to guzzle, hot-water showers and free drinking water, swimming pool, parking, restaurant, bar; credit cards, Honduran lempiras and US dollars accepted.

B Hotel Chortí, on the outskirts of town at Km 222, T7943-1148. All 20 rooms have a/c, TV, phone and *frigobar*. There are 2 pools, a restaurant and bar.

B-C Hotel El Peregrino, 2 Av, 11-94, T7943-1054. Clean rooms in the newer part.

C Hotel Villa Zonia, 10 Calle, 1-84, T7943-1133. Looks a little Alpine and very nice.

C Legendario, 3 Av and 9 Calle, T7943-1824, www.portahotels.com. Built around a garden with 2 pools, restaurant, parking.

C Los Angeles, 2 Av, 11-94, T7943-1254. Spotless rooms with bath, TV and fans, parking, friendly service. Recommended.

D Hotel Calle Real, 3 Av, 10-00, T7943-2405. Rooms all with private bathroom, with TV, hot water, clean.

F Pensión Casa Norman, 3 Av, 9-20, T7943-1503. Rooms with bath and hot water.

F San Carlos 2, used to be known as *París*, 2 Av, 10-48, T7943-1276. 28 very clean rooms. Cheaper without bath, hot water showers.

Quiriguá p298

C Hotel Restaurante Santa Mónica, in Los Amates, 2 km south of Quiriguá village on the highway, T7947-3838. 17 rooms all with private bath, TV and fan, pool, restaurant.

It is opposite a 24-hr Texaco gas station. Convenient if you don't want to walk the 10-15 mins into Quiriguá village for the 2 hotels there. There are a couple of shops, banks, and *comedores* here.

F Hotel y Cafetería Edén, T7947-3281. Helpful, cheaper with shared bath, basement rooms are very dark, clean. The bus comes as far as here, which is where the back route walk to the ruins starts.

F Hotel y Restaurante Royal, T7947-3639. With bath, cheaper without, clean, mosquito netting on all windows, good place to meet other travellers, restaurant.

Camping

You can camp in the car park of the ruins for free, but facilities are limited to toilets and very little running water. There is a restaurant and a project in the pipeline to open a hotel and waterpark opposite the entrance.

Puerto Barrios p299

B Hotel Valle Tropical, 59 rooms on 12 Calle between 5 and 6 Av, T7948-7084, vtropical@guate.net. All rooms with a/c and private bathroom, inviting pool and restaurant, parking. Non-guests can use pool (US$7).

B-C El Reformador, 16 Calle and 7 Av 159, T7948-5489. 51 rooms with bathroom, a/c and TV, some with a/c, restaurant, laundry service, clean, quiet, accepts credit cards. Recommended. The same management run the **Oguatour** travel agency across the road.

C-E Hotel del Norte, at the end of 7 Calle, T7948-2116. A rickety, old wooden structure with sloping landings on the seafront side. All rooms have bath, some with a/c. There's a pool and expensive restaurant, but worth it for the English colonial tearoom atmosphere, no credit cards, but will change dollars.

D Hotel Europa, 8 Av, between 8 and 9 Calle, T7948-1292. 23 clean rooms, with bath, fan, 2 more expensive rooms with a/c, good restaurant, parking, friendly Cuban management.

F Hotel Lee, 5 Av, between 9 and 10 Calle, T7948-0830. Convenient for the

bus station and dock, 24 rooms with fan and TV, with private bath, cheaper without. Noisy restaurant opposite. Friendly service.
F Hotel Xelajú, 9 Calle, between 6 and 7 Av, T7948-0482. Rooms, with bath, cheaper without, fans, quiet, and ultra-clean shared bathrooms.

Lívingston *p299, map p300*
A Hotel Villa Caribe, up Calle Principal from the dock on the right, T7947-0072, www.villasdeguatemala.com. All rooms have sea view and baths. There is a swimming pool (available to non-guests when the hotel is not busy for US$6.50), bar and a large restaurant overlooking the sea.
B Posada El Delfín, T7947-0694, www.posadaeldelfin.com. Good-quality hotel, with over 20 attractive rooms with a/c and hot water.
C Hotel Doña Alida, in a quiet location, T7947-0027, hotelalida@yahoo.es. Direct access to the beach, some rooms with great sea views and balconies, with restaurant.
D Hotel Ríos Tropicales, T7947-0158, www.mctropic.com. This place has some nice touches to distinguish it from the majority of other places in town, like terracotta-tiled floors. 11 rooms, with fans, 5 with private bath, book exchange and the **McTropic** restaurant up the road with internet and a tour operator.
E Casa de la Iguana, T7947-0064. Very cool hostel with jungle hut style accommodation and hot showers. 3 private rooms, each with bath as well as dorms and space for tents and hammocks.
E Casa Rosada, a pastel-pink house set on the waterfront, 600 m from the dock, T7947-0303, www.hotelcasarosada.com. 10 bungalows furnished with attractive hand-painted furniture. The room upstairs overlooks the bay. Meals are set for the day, ranging from pasta to delicious shrimps bathed in garlic. Reservations advisable.
F Garífuna (see map), T7947-0183. 8 comfortable, ultra-clean rooms with private bath, laundry and internet. Recommended.

F Hotel Río Dulce, main street, T7947-0764, An early 19th-century wooden building, with a seriously sloping landing on the 1st floor, a good place from which to watch life pass by. Try and get a room upstairs rather than behind the old building. Rooms with or without bathrooms. There is a restaurant on the ground floor with some tables directly on the street.
F Waba, Barrio Pueblo Nuevo, T7947-0193. Run by a friendly family offering upstairs rooms with a balcony and sea views. All rooms have private bath and are clean and cool, with fan. *Comida típica* is served at a little wooden restaurant (0700-2130) on site. Good value and recommended.

Around Lívingston *p299*
D Hotelito Perdido, hideaway on the River Lampara, can be dropped off on the Lívingston–Río Dulce boat service, T5725-1576, www.hotelitoperdido.com. Quiet hideaway, with rustic, basic and clean accommodation. Food extra at around US$15 a day (no local alternatives available).
E Centro Turístico Quehueche, 15 mins upriver from Lívingston, T254 1560, www.aktenamit.org; run by Ak'Tenamit Foundation, community-led project. Ecolodge wooden cabins with private bath, lovely jungle setting. Highly recommended.
E Finca Tatín, Río Tatín tributary, with great dock space to hang out on, T5902-0831, www.fincatatin.centro america.com. It's B&B, whether you opt for a room with private bath, or a dorm bed. Tours available. Take a *lancha* from Lívingston (US$4) to get there.
E Hotel Ecológico Salvador Gaviota, along the coast, towards Siete Altares, beyond **Hotel Ecológico Siete Altares**, T7947-0874, www.hotelecologicosalvador gaviota.com. Rooms are with shared bath, but the bungalows for 2 or 4 people have private bath. Rooms available for monthly rent. All set in lush surroundings. There is a bar and restaurant (0730-2200), and free *lancha* service – ring beforehand. Tours available. The beach here is lovely, hummingbirds flit about and the owner Lisette is friendly. Highly recommended.

Camping
Biotopo Chocón Machacas, 400 m from the entrance, next to a pond, with grills for cooking on, and toilets, but no food or drink for sale.

Punta de Manabique *p301*
E Eco-Hotel El Saraguate, www.guate.net/ fundarymanabique/saraguate.htm. Rooms and a restaurant run by Fundación Mario Dary.

Fronteras/Río Dulce and around *p301*
A Catamaran Island Hotel, T7930-5494, www.catamaranisland.com. Finely decorated *cabañas*, 40 rooms set around the lake edge, an inviting pool, large restaurant with good food, *lancha* from Río Dulce, 10 mins downstream, or call for a pickup. Recommended.

A Hotel La Ensenada, Km 275, in town 500 m to the right at the Shell station on road to Petén, T7930-5340. Riverside location, breakfast included, restaurant, pool, nice gardens, camping and campervan facilities.

B-C Hacienda Tijax, T7930-5505, www.tijax.com. 2 mins by *lancha* from the dock, jungle lodges and cabins (a/c costs extra); yacht moorings available. There is a beautiful jungle trail with canopy walkway, a rubber plantation, bird sanctuary, pool with whirlpool and jacuzzi, natural pools to swim in, horse riding, kayaking, sailing and rowboat hire and a medicine trail. Excellent food in the riverside bar and restaurant, tranquil and beautiful. Highly recommended.

C-D Tortugal Marina, T5306-6432, www.tortugal.com. 3 beautifully presented bungalows with gorgeous soft rugs on the floor and other types of accommodation. Plentiful hot water. There is a riverside restaurant and bar, pool table in a cool upstairs attic room with books, satellite TV, internet, phone and fax service. Very highly recommended.

C-F Bruno's, in town on the lake, a stone's throw from the where the buses stop,

T7930-5721, www.mayaparadise.com/ brunoe.htm. Best rooms overlook the lake, also dorms, camping, campervan parking, pool, restaurant. Non-guests can pay to use pool. The marina has 28 berths. Restaurant service is consistently not up to scratch.

E Café Sol, in town 500 m north of the bridge on the road to Tikal, T7930-5143. Friendly, clean, fans, good-value rooms, cheaper without bath, TV costs a bit extra. Useful if you have to catch an early bus.

E La Cabaña del Viajero, 500 m from the castle, T7930-5062. Small place with pool, traditional *cabañas* as well as larger family-style *cabañas* with private bathroom and some cute little attic rooms as well.

F Hotel Backpacker's, in town by the bridge on the south bank of the river, T7930-5169, www.hotelbackpackers.com. Restaurant and bar, dorms (**G** per person) with lockers, and private rooms with bathroom, internet and telephone service, profits go to **Casa Guatemala** (see page 301). Recommended.

El Estor and around *p302*
C Marisabela, 8 Av and 1 Calle on the waterfront, T7949-7215. Large rooms with tiled private bathrooms, some with TV, internet service.

D-F Denny's Beach, T5398-0908, www.dennysbeach.com. With its gorgeous lakeside location, accessible by *lancha* from Río Dulce (minimum fee US$41), or free from Mariscos if you call ahead. Tours, wake boarding and horse riding arranged. Internet service. A remote and complete get away.

E Hotel Vista al Lago, 6 Av, 1-13, T7949-7205. 21 clean rooms with private bath and fan. Ask for the lakeview rooms, where there is a pleasant wooden balcony on which to sit. Friendly owner Oscar Paz will take you fishing, and runs ecological and cultural tours.

E Villela, 6 Av, 2-06, T7949-7214. 9 big rooms with bath, clean, some quite dark though. Flower-filled garden with chairs to sit out in. Recommended.

ⓞ Eating

Chiquimula p297

Ⴈ Magic, corner of 8 Av and 3 Calle. A good place from which to watch the world go by, and most of what's on offer is seriously cheap. Sandwiches, *licuados* and burgers.

Ⴈ Pastelería Las Violetas, 7 Av, 4-80, and another near **Hotel Victoria**. An excellent cake shop with a fine spread, good-value sandwiches too, plus great cappuccino, and a/c. Next door is its bakery.

Esquipulas p298

There are plenty of restaurants, but prices are high for Guatemala.

ⴈⴈⴈ La Hacienda, 2 Av, 10-20. Delicious barbecued chicken and steaks. Kids' menu available, breakfasts available. One of the smartest restaurants in town.

ⴈⴈ Restaurante Payaquí, 2 Av, 11-26, inside the hotel of the same name. Specialities include turkey in *pipián*, also lunches and breakfasts. A poolside restaurant makes a pleasant change.

Ⴈ Café Pistachos, close to **Hotel Calle Real**. Clean, cheap snack bar with burgers, hotdogs, etc.

Puerto Barrios p299

ⴈⴈⴈ-ⴈⴈ Restaurante Safari, at the north end of 5 Av and 1 Calle, overlooking the bay with views all around. Basically serving up oceans of fish, including whole fish, *ceviche* and fishburgers.

ⴈⴈ La Fonda de Quique, an orange and white wooden building at 5 Av and corner of 12 Calle. Nicely a/c with handmade wooden furniture, serving lobster, fish and meats, plus snacks.

Lívingston p299, map p300

Fresh fish is available everywhere; ask for *tapado* in restaurants – a rich soup with various types of seafood, banana and coconut. Women sell *pan de coco* on the streets.

ⴈⴈ Bahía Azul, Calle Principal. Excellent breakfasts, but dreadful coffee. Tables on the street as well as a dining-room. Specializes in salsas, *camarones* and *langosta*. There is a tourist service and the **Exotic Travel Agency**.

ⴈⴈ Buga Mama, an excellent example of an innovative development project. Local Mayan young people staff this large restaurant located next to the water as part of their training with the Ak'Tenamit project (www.aktenamit.org). The food is OK, the service excellent, and a great spot too – well worth checking out.

ⴈⴈ El Malecón, 50 m from the dock on the left. Serves *chapín* and Western-style breakfasts, seafood and chicken *fajitas*, all in a large, airy wooden dining area.

ⴈⴈ Happy Fish, just along from the **Hotel Río Dulce**. A popular restaurant with internet café. Serves a truckload of fish (not quite so happy now) with good coffee. Occasional live music at weekends.

ⴈⴈ Hotel Río Dulce, see Sleeping. The restaurant serves delicious Italian food prepared with panache. Recommended.

Ⴈ McTropic, opposite the **Hotel Río Dulce**. Street tables, great breakfasts, and cocktails. Good service and popular.

Ⴈ Rasta Mesa Restaurant, in Barrio Nevago, just past the cemetery, www.site.rasta mesa.com. Garífuna cultural centre and restaurant. Music, history, classes in cooking and drumming. Great place to hang out.

Ⴈ Tiburón Gato, far end of Calle Principal. A simple open-fronted place, serving a good range of fish, seafood and pasta; open for breakfasts too.

Fronteras/Río Dulce and around p301

There are restaurants in the hotels – **Bruno's** is a relaxing location – and a couple along the main road.

ⴈⴈ-Ⴈ Ranchón Mary, El Relleno, T7930-5103. Thatch-roofed waterfront deck with tables, serving delicious fish and seafood and ice-cold beer.

♔♔ Rosita's Restaurant, San Felipe de Lara, T5054-3541. Lovely waterfront location with open deck, overlooking the bridge, 5 mins by *lancha* from Río Dulce. Great seafood, nachos and home-made banana pie.

El Estor and around *p302*

♔ **Dorita**. A *comedor* serving seafood, very good meals, excellent value and popular with the locals.

♔ **Marisabela**, 8 Av and 1 Calle. Good and cheap spaghetti, as well as fish and chicken, with lake views.

♔ **Restaurant del Lago**, west side of main square. Restaurant overlooking the main square. Popular with local dishes.

♔ **Restaurant Elsita**, 2 blocks north of the market on 8 Av. This is a great people-watching place. There's a large menu and the food's good.

☻ Entertainment

Puerto Barrios *p299*

The Container, just past the **Hotel del Norte** overlooking the sea, is an unusual bar constructed from the front half of an old ship equipped with portholes, and a number of banana containers from the massive banana businesses just up the road. Open 0700-2300.

Mariscos de Izabal, one of the most popular spots in Puerto Barrios. A thatched bar that is mostly a drinking den but with tacos, tortillas and burgers served amid beating Latin rhythms. You can hang out until here 0100.

Lívingston *p299, map p300*

Lugudi Barana, a disco that's also on the beach and popular with visitors and locals. Sun only, 1500-0100.

☻ Festivals and events

Lívingston *p299, map p300*

24-31 Dec In honour of the **Virgen del Rosario**, with traditional dancing.
26 Nov Garífuna Day.

▲ Activities and tours

Lívingston *p299, map p300*

Exotic Travel Agency, in the Bahía Azul restaurant, T7947-0133, www.blue caribbeanbay.com.

Happy Fish, on the main road, T7947-0661, www.happyfishresort.com.

Captain Eric, located at the Pitchi Mango snack bar on the main street, T4265-5278. Will arrange 1- to 2-day boat tours for groups of up to 5 people to the surrounding region.

You can also contract any of the *lancheros* at the dock to take you to Río Dulce, Playa Blanca and Siete Altares.

Fronteras/Río Dulce *p301*

Sailing

Captain John Clark's sailing trips on his 46-ft Polynesian catamaran, *Las Sirenas*, are highly recommended. Food, taxes, snorkelling and fishing gear, and windsurf boards included. Contact **Aventuras Vacacionales SA**, Antigua, www.sailing-diving-guatemala.com.

Coastguard For emergencies, call Guarda Costa on VHF channel 16, T4040-4971.

Tour operators

Atitrans Tours, on the little road heading to the dockside. To **Finca Paraíso** for US$20.

Otiturs, opposite Tijax Express, T5219-4520. Run by the friendly and helpful Otto Archila. Offers a minibus service as well as tours to local sites, internal flights and boat trips.

Tijax Express, opposite Atitrans, T7930-5505, info@tijax.com. Agent for Hacienda Tijax (over the river).

Lancheros offer trips on the river and on Lago de Izabal. They can be contacted at the muelle principal, under the bridge. Ask for Cesár Mendez, T5819-7436, or ask at **Atitrans** for collection.

⊘ Transport

Estanzuela p297

Bus From **Guatemala City** to Zacapa, with Rutas Orientales, 0430-1800, every 30 mins, 2¾-3 hrs. To **Esquipulas** with same service that continues from Zacapa, US$6, 1½ hrs.

Chiquimula, Volcán de Ipala and the Honduran border p297

Bus Take an early bus to **Ipala** from Chiquimula; stay on the bus and ask the driver to let you off at Aldea El Chaparroncito (10 mins after Ipala). From here it's a 1½-hr ascent, following red arrows every now and then. Another ascent goes via Municipio Agua Blanca. Take a minibus to **Agua Blanca** from Ipala and get out at the small village of El Sauce, where the trail starts. The last bus from Ipala to Chiquimula is 1700.

Chiquimula

Bus There are 3 terminals in Chiquimula, all within 50 m of each other. To **Guatemala City**, Transportes Guerra and Rutas Orientales, hourly, US$4, 3¼-3½ hrs, leave from 11 Av between 1 and 2 Calle, as do buses for **Puerto Barrios**, several companies, every 30 mins, between 0300-1500, 4 hrs, US$6.50. To **Quiriguá**, US$3.20, 1 hr 50 mins. Take any Puerto Barrios-bound bus. On to **Río Dulce** take the Barrios bus and get off at La Ruidosa junction and change, or change at Bananera/Morales. To **Flores** with Transportes María Elena, 8 hrs, 0400, 0800, 1300. Buses to **Ipala** and **Jalapa** also leave from here; 4 buses daily to Jalapa between 0500-1230, 4½ hrs, US$5.80; to Ipala, US$2.20. Supplemented by minibuses 0600-1715 to Ipala. To **Zacapa**, 25 mins, from the terminal inside the market at 10 Av between 1 and 2 Calle. Same for those to **Esquipulas**, every 10 mins, US$2.70, until 1900. To and from **Cobán** via El Rancho (where a change must be made). Buses to **El Florido** (Honduras border) leave with Transportes Vilma from inside the market at 1 Calle, between 10 and 11 Av, T7942-2253, between 0530-1630,

US$2.70, 1½ hrs. Buses return from the border at 0530, 0630 and then hourly 0700-1700. See box, page 198, for border-crossing information.

Esquipulas p298

Bus Rutas Orientales. Leaving Esquipulas, 1 Av "A" and 11 Calle, T7943-1366, for **Guatemala City** every 30 mins from 0200-1700, 4½ hrs, US$8.50. To **Chiquimula** by minibus, every 30 mins, 0430-1830, US$1.40.

Quiriguá p298

Bus Emphasize to the bus driver if you want Quiriguá *pueblo* and not the *ruinas*. Countless travellers have found themselves left at the ruins and having to make a return journey to the village for accommodation.

To get to the **ruins** directly, take any bus heading along the highway towards Puerto Barrios and ask to be let off at the *ruinas*. At this ruins crossroads, take a pickup (very regular), 10 mins, US$0.50, or bus (much slower and less regular) to the ruins 4 km away. Last bus back to highway, 1700. You can walk, but take lots of water, as it's hot and dusty with little shade.

To get to the **village** of Quiriguá, 3 km south from the ruins entrance road, it is only a 10-min walk to the **Hotel Royal**. Keep to the paved road, round a left-hand bend, and it's 100 m up on the left. Or take a local bus heading from the highway into the village. The **Hotel Edén** is a further 5 mins on down the hill. There is a frequent daily bus service that runs a circular route between Los Amates, Quiriguá village and then on to the entrance road to the ruins. You can also walk through the banana plantations from Quiriguá village to the ruins as well. From **Hotel Royal** walk past the church towards the old train station and the **Hotel Edén**, and follow the tracks branching to the right, through the plantation to the ruins.

Puerto Barrios p299
Boat

It's a 10-min walk to the municipal dock at the end of Calle 12, from the **Litegua** bus station. Ferries *(barca)* leave for Lívingston at 1030 and 0500 (1½ hrs, US$2.50). *Lanchas* also leave when a minimum of 12 people are ready to go, 30 mins, US$3.80. The only scheduled *lanchas* leave at 0630, 0730, 0900 and 1100, and the last will leave, if there are enough people, at 1800. **Transportes El Chato**, 1 Av, between 10 and 11 Calle, T7948-5525, pichilingo2000@yahoo.com, also does trips from here to Punta de Manabique, and other places near and far.

To Belize *Lanchas* leave for **Punta Gorda** at 1000 with **Transportes El Chato**, address above, returning at 1400, 1 hr 20 mins, US$22. Also services with Requena to Punta Gorda at 1400, returning at 0900.

Bus
To **Guatemala City**, with **Litegua**, 6 Av between 9 and 10 Calle, T7948-1002, www.litegua.com. 18 a day, 5 hrs, US$11-7.50. Bus to **El Rancho** (turn-off for Biotopo del Quetzal and Cobán), 4 hrs, take any bus to Guatemala City. To **Quiriguá**, 2 hrs, take any capital-bound bus. To **Chiquimula**, operated by **Carmencita**, 4 hrs. Alternatively, catch a bus to Guatemala City, getting off at Río Hondo, and catch a *colectivo* or any bus heading to Chiquimula. For **Río Dulce**, take any bus heading for Guatemala City and change at **La Ruidosa** (15 mins). For minibuses to **Entre Ríos**, for the El Cinchado border crossing to **Honduras** (**Corinto**), with connections to **Omoa**, **Puerto Cortés** and **La Ceiba**, see page 198.

Lívingston *p299, map p300*
Boat
Ferry to **Puerto Barrios** to (22.5 km), 1½ hrs, US$1.60 at 0500 and 1400 Mon-Sat. Private *lanchas* taking 16-25 people also sail this route, 30 mins, US$4. They leave at 0630 and 0730 each day and at 0900 and 1100 Mon-Sat to Puerto Barrios and then when full. Lívistingon to **Río Dulce**, with short stops at **Aguas Calientes** and the **Biotopo Chacón Machacas**, US$15.50 1 way. *Lanchas* definitely leave at 0900 and 1430 for

Río Dulce, but these make no stops. To **Honduras** (Omoa, Puerto Cortés, La Ceiba), *lanchas* can be organized at the dock or through tour operators, see above. To **Belize** (Punta Gorda, Placencia, Cayos Zapotillos), check with tour operators, see above, about boats to Belize. Anyone who takes you must have a manifest with passengers' names, stamped and signed at the immigration office. On Tue and Fri fast *lanchas* make the trip to Punta Gorda (US$22). Enquire at the dock and negotiate a fare with the *lanchero* association. Boats to Placencia and the Zapotilla cayes can also be arranged.

Fronteras/Río Dulce and around *p301*
Boat
Lanchas colectivas leave for **Lívingston** at 0930 and 1300, US$15.50. Private *lanchas* can be arranged at the dock to any of the river or lakeside hotels.

Bus
Local To get to **Castillo de San Felipe**, take a boat from Río Dulce, or *camioneta* from the corner of the main road to Tikal, and the first turning left after the bridge by **Pollandia**, 5 mins, or a 5-km walk. From Río Dulce to **Finca El Paraíso**, take the same road, 45 mins, US$1.70. Buses to Río Dulce pass the *finca* between 40 and 50 mins past the hour. To **El Estor**, from the same Pollandia turn-off, US$2.50, 1½ hrs on a paved road, 0500-1600, hourly, returning 0500-1600. To **Puerto Barrios**, take any bus to **La Ruidosa** and change, 35 mins to junction then a further 35 mins to Puerto Barrios.

Long-distance To **Guatemala City** and **Flores**: through buses stop at Río Dulce. To **Guatemala City** with **Litegua**, T7930-5251, www.litegua.com, 7 a day between 0300 and 1515, US$7.54, 6 hrs. **Fuente del Norte**, T5692-1988, 23 services daily, US$6.30. Luxury service 1300, 1700 and 2400, US$13. **Línea Dorada**, at 1300, luxury service, 5 hrs, US$13. To **Flores** from 0630-0300, 25 buses daily, 4½ hrs with Fuente del Norte, US$8. Luxury service,

1430, US$13. This bus also stops at **Finca Ixobel** and **Poptún**, US$3.90. Línea Dorada, to Flores, 1500, 3 hrs, luxury service with a/c, TV and snacks, US$13, and on to **Melchor de Mencos** for Belize. Fuente del Norte, also to **Melchor de Mencos**, at 1300, 2130 and 2330, 6 hrs, US$12.50. Also to, **Sayaxché** at 2200 and one to **Naranjo** at 2100.

Shuttles Atitrans, T7930-5111, www.atitrans.com, runs shuttles to **Antigua**, **Flores**, **Copán Ruinas** and **Guatemala City**.

El Estor and around *p302*
Bus The ferry from Mariscos no longer runs, but a private *lancha* can be contracted.

To **Río Dulce**, 0500-1600, hourly, 1 hr, US$2.20. Direct bus to **Cobán**, at 1300, 7 hrs, US$5.60. Also via either Panzós and Tactic, or Cahabón and Lanquín, see page 319. For the **Cañón El Boquerón**, take the Río Dulce bus and ask to be dropped at the entrance. Or hire a bike from town (8 km) or a taxi, US$6.50, including waiting time.

To **Cobán**, with **Transportes Valenciana**, 1200, 0200, 0400 and 0800, 8 long and dusty hrs, with no proper stop. To **Guatemala City**, 0100 direct, via Río Dulce, 7 hrs, US$6.30, or go to Río Dulce and catch one. At 2400 and 0300 via Río Polochic Valley. For **Santa Elena, Petén** take a bus to Río Dulce and pick on up from there.

⊙ Directory

Chiquimula *p297*
Banks There are several banks accepting MasterCard and Visa, and ATMs. **Post** Close to the bus terminal inside the market. **Telephone** Office on the plaza.

Esquipulas *p298*
Banks There are a number of banks and ATMs in town close to the park, Visa and MasterCard accepted. There are money changers in the centre if you need *lempiras*. Better rates than at the borders. **Post** End of 6 Av, 2-43.

Puerto Barrios *p299*
Banks Banco G&T Continental, 7 Calle and 6 Av, with ATMs. TCs. Banco Industrial, 7 Av, 7-30, 24-hr Visa ATM and cash on Visa cards. **Immigration** Corner of 12 Calle and 3 Av, open 24 hrs. **Internet** A couple of places in town. **Post** Corner of 6 Calle and 6 Av. **Telephone** Telgua, corner of 10 Calle and 8 Av.

Lívingston *p299, map p300*
Banks Banco Reformador, cash advance on Visa and MasterCard, TCs and cash changed. Has a 24-hr Visa-only ATM. There is also a Banrural. Some hotels will change cash, including Casa Rosada. **Immigration** Calle Principal, opposite Hotel Villa Caribe, T7947-0240. Just knock if the door is shut. **Internet** There are a couple of places in town, including Café Buga Net, opposite Buga Mama, daily 0730-2100, US$0.80 per hr. Gaby's in Barrio Marcos Sánchez Díaz is open 0900-2100 daily and charges US$1.25 an hour. **Laundry** Lavandería Doña Chila, opposite Casa Rosada. **Language schools** Livingston Spanish School, T5715-4604, www.livingstonspanishschool.org. 1-2-1 classes, 20 hrs a week, US$95 a week including food and lodging. **Post** Next to Telgua, behind the Municipalidad, take the small road to the right. **Telephone** Telgua, behind the Municipalidad, 0800-1800.

Fronteras/Río Dulce and around *p301*
Banks There are 2 banks: Visa, TCs and cash only. ATMS available. **Internet** Captain Nemo's Communications behind Bruno's, and phone call service and Tijax Express. **Post** Near the banks.

El Estor *p302*
Banks Banco Industrial and Banrural have ATMs. **Internet** Xbox 360 open 0800-2100, Mon-Sat. Good machines with a/c keeping machines and people cool. **Post** In the park.

The Verapaces

Propped up on a massive limestone table eroded over thousands of years, the plateau of the Verapaz region is riddled with caves, underground tunnels, stalagtites and stalagmites. Cavernous labyrinths used by the Maya for worship, in their belief that caves are the entrances to the underworld, are also now visited by travellers who marvel at the natural interior design of these subterranean spaces. Nature has performed its work above ground too. At Semuc Champey, pools of tranquil, turquoise-green water span a monumental limestone bridge; beneath the bridge a river thunders violently through. The quetzal reserve also provides the opportunity to witness a feather flash of red or green of the elusive bird, and dead insects provide curious interest in Rabinal, where their body parts end up on ornamental gourds. The centre of this region – the imperial city of Cobán – provides respite for the traveller with a clutch of museums honouring the Maya, coffee and orchid, and a fantastic entertainment spectacle at the end of July with a whirlwind of traditional dances and a Maya beauty contest. ▸▸ *For listings, see pages 316-320.*

Ins and outs

The principal road entrance to the Verapaces leaves the Atlantic Highway at El Rancho heading up to Cobán. This junction is one hour from Guatemala City. ▸▸ *See Transport, page 318.*

Background

Before the Spanish conquest of the region, Las Verapaces had a notorious reputation – it was known as Tezulutlán (land of war) for its aggressive warlike residents, who fought repeated battles with their neighbours and rivals, the K'iche' Maya. These warring locals were not going to be a pushover for the Spanish conquerors and they strongly resisted when their land was invaded. The Spanish eventually retreated and the weapon replaced with the cross. Thus, Carlos V of Spain gave the area the title of Verdadera Paz (true peace) in 1548. The region's modern history saw it converted into a massive coffee- and cardamom-growing region. German coffee *fincas* were established from the 1830s until the Second World War, when the Germans were invited over to plough the earth by the Guatemalan government. Many of the *fincas* were expropriated during the war, but some were saved from this fate by naming a Guatemalan as the owner of the property. The area still produces some of Guatemala's finest coffee – served up with some of the finest cakes! The Germans also introduced cardamom to the Verapaces, when a *finquero* requested some seeds for use in biscuits. Guatemala is now the world's largest producer of cardamom.

Baja Verapaz → *For listings, see pages 316-320.*

The small region of Baja Verapaz is made up of a couple of Achi'-Maya speaking towns, namely Salamá, Rabinal, San Jerónimo and Cubulco. The department is known for the quetzal reserve, the large Dominican *finca* and aqueduct, and the weird decorative technique of the crafts in Rabinal.

Sierra de las Minas Biosphere Reserve → *Colour map 2, B3.*

ⓘ *To visit, get a permit in San Augustín from the office of La Fundación de Defensores de la Naturaleza, Barrio San Sebastián, 1 block before the Municipalidad, T7936-0681, ctot@ defensores.org.gt, www.defensores.org.gt. The contact is César Tot. Alternatively, contact the Fundación offices in Santa Elena, Petén, at 5 Calle, 3 Av "A", Zona 2, T7926-3095, lacandon@ defensores.org.gt, or in the capital at 7 Av, 7-09, Zona 13, T2440-8138.*

Just north of El Rancho, in the Department of El Progreso, is **San Agustín Acasaguastlán**, an entrance for the Sierra de las Minas Biosphere Reserve, one of Guatemala's largest conservation areas with peaks topping 3000 m and home to the quetzal, harpy eagle and peregrine falcon, puma, jaguar, spider monkey, howler monkey, tapir and pizote.

Biotopo del Quetzal

ⓘ *Daily 0700-1600, US$2.60, parking, disabled entrance. Run by Centro de Estudios Conservacionistas (CECON), Av Reforma, 0-63, Zona 10, Guatemala City, T2331-0904, cecon@usac.edu.gt.*

The Biotopo del Quetzal, or **Biosphere Mario Dary Rivera**, is between Cobán and Guatemala City at Km 160.5, 4 km south of Purulhá and 53 km from Cobán. There are two trails. Increasing numbers of quetzals have been reported in the Biotopo, but they are still very elusive. Ask for advice from the rangers. The area around the Biotopo has been protected as a 'Corredor Biológico Bosque Nuboso, with numerous privately run reserves and restaurants by the roadside offering birdwatching trails, waterfalls, natural swimming holes and caves. For more information, see www.bosquenuboso.com.gt.

Salamá, Rabinal and Cubulco

Just before Salamá is **San Jerónimo**, where there is a Dominican church and convent, from where friars tended vineyards, exported wine and cultivated sugar. There is an old sugar mill (*trapiche*) on display at the *finca* and a huge aqueduct of 124 arches to transport water to the sugar cane fields and the town. Salamá sits in a valley with a colonial cathedral, containing carved gilt altarpieces as its centrepiece. The town also has one of a few remaining *Templos de Minerva* in the country, built in 1916. Behind the Calvario church is the hill Cerro de la Santa Cruz, from where a view of the valley can be seen. Market day is Monday and is worth a visit. The village of **Rabinal** was founded in 1537 by Fray Bartolomé de las Casas. It has a 16th-century church, and a busy Sunday market, where lacquered gourds, beautiful *huípiles* and embroidered napkins are sold. The glossy lacquer of the gourd is made from the body oil of a farmed scaly insect called the *niij*. The male *niij* is boiled in water to release its oil, which is then mixed with soot powder to create the lacquer. The **Museo Rabinal Achí** ⓘ *2 Calle y 4 Av, Zona 3, T5311-1536, museoachi@hotmail.com*, displays historical exhibits and has produced bilingual books about the Achí culture. West of Rabinal, set amid maize fields and peach trees, Cubulco is known for its tradition of performing the pole dance, *Palo Volador*, which takes place every 20-25 July. Men, attached by rope, have to leap from the top of the pole and spiral down, accompanied by marimba music. There are three basic *hospedajes* in town.

Alta Verapaz → *For listings, see pages 316-320.*

The region of Alta Verapaz is based on a gigantic mountain, Sierra de Chamá. Dinosaurs roamed the area more than 65 million years ago before it was engulfed by sea. It later emerged, covered with limestone rock, which over millions of years has left the area riddled with caves, and dotted with small hills. In the far northwest of the department are the mystical, emerald-green waters of **Laguna Lachuá**.

Santa Cruz Verapaz and around

Santa Cruz Verapaz has a fine white 16th-century church with a fiesta between 1-4 May when you can see the wonderful Danza de los Guacamayos (scarlet macaws). This **Poqomchi' Maya** village is 15 km northwest of Tactic, at the junction with the road to Uspantán. To get there, take the San Cristóbal Verapaz bus, 25 minutes, or take a bus heading to the capital, get off at the junction and walk 200 m into town. The local fiestas are 15, 20 January, 21-26 July with the *Palo Volador*. The devil-burning dance can be seen on 8 December. Six kilometres west towards Uspantán is **San Cristóbal Verapaz**, which has a large, white, colonial church. From the church, a 1-km long, straight, road (Calle del Calvario) slopes down and then curves upwards to a hilltop **Calvario Church**. At Easter, the whole road is carpeted in flowers that rival those on display in Antigua at this time of year. There is **Museo Katinamit** ① *T7950-4039, cecep@intelnet. net.gt, Mon-Fri 0900-1200, 1500-1700*, run by the *Centro Comunitario Educativo Poqomchi'*, dedicated to the preservation and learning of the Poqomchi' culture.

Cobán and around → *For listings, see pages 316-320. Colour map 2, B2. Altitude: 1320 m.*

The cathedral and centre of the Imperial City of Cobán (www.cobanav.net), is perched on a long, thin plateau with exceptionally steep roads climbing down from the plaza. To the south the roads are filled with the odd, well-preserved colonial building and a coffee *finca*. There is year-round soft rainfall, known as *chipi-chipi*, which is a godsend to the coffee and cardamom plants growing nearby. Most visitors use the city as a base for visiting sights in the surrounding area, trips to Semuc Champey, Languin and as a stepping off point for rafting trips on the Río Cahabón. English is spoken at the **city tourist office** ① *Parque Central*, where they have lots of information and can help organize tours. **INGUAT office** ① *7 Av 1-17, in Los Arcos shopping centre, T79510216, Mon-Fri 0800-1600, Sat 0900-1300*, is very helpful with leaflets and maps on the whole Verapaz region. For online information on northern Alta Verapaz and the southern Petén, check www.puertamundomaya.com.

Sights

The **cathedral** is on the east side of the Parque Central and dates from the middle of the 16th century. The chapel of **El Calvario**, in the northwest, has its original façade still intact. On the way up to the church are altars used by worshippers who freely blend Maya and Roman Catholic beliefs. Its worth climbing the 142 steps to get a bird's-eye view of Cobán. The **Museo El Príncipe Maya** ① *Mon-Sat 0900-1300, 1400-1800, US$1.30, 6 Av, 4-26, Zona 3*, is a private museum of pre-Columbian artefacts. The **Parque Nacional Las Victorias** ① *just west of El Calvario, daily 0700-1800, US$0.80*, has two little lagoons in its 84 ha. There are paths and you can picnic and camp, loos but no showers, but check with the tourist office about safety before going. The daily market is near the bus terminal. Starbucks coffee fans can check out where their mug of the old bean comes from – direct from **Finca Santa Margarita** ① *on the edge of town, 3 Calle, 4-12, Zona 2, T7951-3067, Mon-Fri 0800-1230, 1330-1700, Sat 0800-1200, 45-min tour with English/Spanish-speaking guides, US$2.50*. Don't miss a visit to the flower-filled world of **Vivero Verapaz** ① *0900-1200, 1400-1700 daily, US$1.30, 2.5 km southwest of town, 40-min walk, or taxi ride; US$1.30 for guided tour*, an orchid farm with more than 23,000 specimens, mostly flowering from December to February – the best time to go – with the majority flowering in January.

Around Cobán

Southeast of Cobán (8 km) is **San Juan Chamelco** with an old colonial church. A one-hour walk from here is **Aldea Chajaneb** (see Sleeping). Along this road are the caves of **Grutas Rey Marcos** ① *US$1.30*, and **Balneario Cecilinda** ① *0800-1700*. **San Pedro Carchá** is 5 km east of Cobán on the main road and used to be famous for its pottery, textiles, wooden masks and silver, but only the pottery and silver are available now. The local food speciality here is *kaq Ik*, a turkey broth.

Lanquín and Semuc Champey → *For listings, see pages 316-320. Colour map 2, B2.*

Lanquín is surrounded by mountainous scenery reminiscent of an Alpine landscape. It nestles in the bottom of a valley, where a river runs. With this mountain ambience, caves and the clear water pools at Semuc Champey, it is worth kicking back for a few days and inhaling the high altitude air. Lanquín is 56 km east of Cobán, 10 km from the Pajal

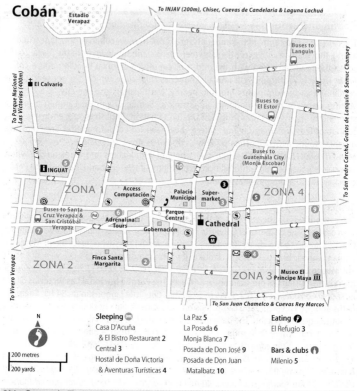

Cobán

Sleeping 🛏
Casa D'Acuña
  & El Bistro Restaurant 2
Central 3
Hostal de Doña Victoria
  & Aventuras Turísticas 4

La Paz 5
La Posada 6
Monja Blanca 7
Posada de Don José 9
Posada de Don Juan
  Matalbatz 10

Eating 🍴
El Refugio 3

Bars & clubs 🍸
Milenio 5

junction. Just before the town are the **Grutas de Lanquín** ⓘ *0800-1600, US$3, 30-min walk from town*. The caves are lit for 200 m and strange stalactite shapes are given names, but it's worth taking a torch. The cave, whose ceiling hangs with thousands of stalactites, is dangerously slippery from guano mud, although handrails will help you out. The sight of the bats flying out at dusk is impressive. Outside the cave you can swim in the river and camp for free.

From Lanquín you can visit the natural bridge of **Semuc Champey** ⓘ *0600-1800, US$6, parking available*, a liquid paradise stretching 60 m across the Cahabón Gorge. The limestone bridge is covered in stepped, glowing blue and green water pools, that span the length and breadth of it. Upstream you can see the water being channelled under the bridge. As it thunders through, it is spectacular. At its voluminous exit you can climb down from the bridge and see it cascading. You can swim in all the pools and little hot flows pour into some of them. Tours of Semuc Champey from Cobán cost around US$31.

Parque Nacional Laguna Lachuá
ⓘ *T5704 1509 to hire a guide for the day, US$4, main entrance, US$5.20, Mon-Sat 0900-1700.*
Near **Playa Grande**, northwest of Cobán, is Parque Nacional Laguna Lachuá. The deep velvet-green lake, formed by a meteor impact, is 5 sq km and 220 m deep in places. It is surrounded by virtually unspoilt dense jungle, and the chances of seeing wildlife at dawn and dusk are high. There is a guided nature trail and camping and a basic guesthouse. In this area is the **Río Ikbolay**, a green river that runs underground through caves. When it emerges the other side it is blue. The river has changed its course over time leaving some of its run-through caves empty, making it possible to walk through them. The **Proyecto Ecológico Quetzal**, see page 318, runs jungle hikes in this area.

North of Cobán and southern Petén crossroads → *For listings, see pages 316-320.*

About 100 km northeast of Cobán is **Sebol**, reached via **Chisec** (www.visitchisec.com with information on the Grutas de Candelaria and Laguna Lachuá, see above) and unappealing **Raxrujá**. From here roads go north to Sayaxché and east to Modesto Méndez via Fray Bartolomé de las Casas. West of Raxrujá are the **Grutas de Candelaria** ⓘ *US$5.35 including a guided tour*, an extensive cavern system with stalagmites. Tubing is available. Take the road to Raxrujá and look for the Candelaria Camposanto village at Km 310 between Chisec and Raxrujá or look for a sign saying 'Escuela de Autogestión Muqbilbe' and enter here to get to the caves and eco-hotel. Camping is possible. Both points of access offer activities for visitors. North of Raxrujá is the Maya site of **Cancuén** ⓘ *www.puertamundomaya.com, ask in Cobán about tours*, reached by *lancha* in 30 minutes (US$40 for one to 12 people), from the village of La Unión (camping and meals are available at the site). Ten kilometres east of Sebol, and 15 minutes by bus, is **Fray Bartolomé de las Casas**, a town that is just a stop-off for travellers on the long run between Poptún and Cobán or Sayaxché. A road (that is nearly all tarmacked) links Fray Bartolomé de las Casas, Sebol and Sayaxché via Raxrujá. The scenery is beautiful with luscious palms, solitary sheer-sided hills and thatched-roofed homes.

The Verapaces listings

For Sleeping and Eating price codes and other relevant information, see Essentials pages 31-33.

Sleeping

Sierra de las Minas p312

C La Cabaña de Los Albores, Chilascó. A 130-m-high waterfall, el salto de Chilascó, is near this ecotourism project with 2 cabins and 8 beds with shared hot water showers.

Biotopo del Quetzal p312

B Posada Montaña del Quetzal, at Km 156, www.hposadaquetzal.com. Bungalows or rooms with private bathrooms, hot water, café, bar, swimming pool and gardens.
C Ram Tzul, km 185.5, T5908-4066, http://m-y-c.com.ar/ramtzul. Lovely bedrooms in wooden *cabañas*. Dozens of excursions can be arranged.
F Hospedaje Ranchitos del Quetzal, Km 160.8, near the Biotopo entrance, T7823-5860. Clean rooms with shared or private bathrooms, hot water, *comedor*.

Salamá, Rabinal and Cubulco p312

E San Ignacio, 4 Calle "A", 7-09, Salamá, T7940-1797. Behind the Telgua building, with bath and TV, clean and friendly.
F Posada San Pablo, 3 Av, 1-50, T7938-8025, Rabinal. Clean and friendly, will do laundry, but hard beds.

Santa Cruz Verapaz and around p313

B Hotel Park, Km 196, on the main road south of the junction to the Poqomchi' Maya village, Santa Cruz, Verapaz, T7952-0807, www.parkhotelresort.com. Rooms of varying prices with TV, restaurant, bar, gym and excellent gardens.
E Eco Hotel Chi' Ixim, Km 182.5, just beyond Tactic, T7953-9198. Rooms with private bath, hot water and fireplaces, restaurant.
F Hotel El Portón Real, 4 Av, 1-44, Zona 1, Santa Cruz Verapaz, T7950-4604. Dreary from the outside, but inside this hotel is lovely with lots of wood furnishings. It's run by a very friendly *señora*. Rooms with bath, cheaper without, hot water and free drinking water. The hotel closes its doors at 2130.

Cobán p313, map p314

Accommodation is extremely hard to find on the Fri and Sat of Rabin Ajau (last week of Jul) and in Aug. For Rabin Ajau you need to be in town a few days beforehand to secure a room, or ring and reserve.
B Hotel Posada de Don Juan Matalbatz, 3 Calle, 1-46, Zona 1, T7952-1599, info@discoveryguate.com. A colonial-style hotel with rooms set around a courtyard. Despite the nearby bus terminal it is very quiet and safe. All rooms have TV and there's a restaurant, pool table and parking. Tours offered.
B La Posada, 1 Calle, 4-12, Zone 2, T7952-1495, www.laposadacoban.com. 16 attractively decorated rooms all with private tiled bathrooms and fireplaces, colonial hotel with well-kept flourishing gardens, credit cards accepted, stylish restaurant with terrace and fireplace, stop by for a drink if nothing else. Café too, see Eating.
D Hostal de Doña Victoria, 3 Calle, 2-38, Zona 3, T7951-4213. In a 400-year-old former Dominican convent with colonnaded gallery, attractive gardens and a good restaurant (see Eating). Excursions arranged, recommended.
E Central, 1 Calle, 1-79, T7952-1442. A stone's throw from the cathedral. 15 very clean large rooms, around a patio, with hot shower. Rooms with TV cost a little extra.
E Monja Blanca, 2 Calle, 6-30 Zona 2, T7952-1712. All rooms are set around a pretty courtyard, very peaceful, old-fashioned dining room, breakfast good value. The place is run by a slightly eccentric *señora* and looks shut from the outside. Recommended.

E Posada de Don José, 6 Av, 1-18, Zona 4, T7951-4760. 13 rooms with private bathroom, TV, cheaper without, clean general bathrooms, laundry, friendly, courtyard, good budget option.

E-G Casa D'Acuña, 4 Calle, 3-11, Zona 2, T7951-0482, casadeacuna@yahoo.com. 2 bunk beds to a room, ultra-clean bathrooms with hot water, laundry service, internet, excellent meals, tempting goodies and coffee in El Bistro restaurant in a pretty courtyard (see Eating). The owners run a tourist office, shop and tours. Recommended.

F La Paz, 6 Av, 2-19, T7952-1358. Hot water, safe parking, pleasant, 35 rooms, cheaper without bath, laundry, café, garden, popular.

Around Cobán p314

C Don Jerónimo's, Km 5.3 Carretera a Chamil, Aldea Chajaneb, T5301-3191, www.dearbrutus.com/donjeronimo. Bungalows to rent, with full board including 3 vegetarian meals a day and activities such as hiking, swimming and tubing included, massage available, a great place for relaxation. From Cobán in a taxi, 30 mins, about US$8. Or, take a bus from Cobán to Chamelco, then bus or pickup to Chamil and ask to be let off at Don Jerónimo's.

Lanquín and Semuc Champey p314

There is a backpackers' hostel at Semuc Champey, **E-F**. Otherwise try:

D El Recreo, Lanquín, at the village entrance, T7983-0056, hotel_el_recreo@hotmail.com. Big, spacious wooden lodge in riverside grounds, with clean rooms, good meals, friendly; parking space. Recommended

C-E El Retiro, 5 mins from Lanquín on the road to Cahabón, T4585-4684. Campsite, cabañas, dorms and restaurant, in a gorgeous riverside location. There's an open fire for cooking, hammocks to chill out in, and inner tubes for floating on the river. To get there don't get off in town, continue for 5 mins and ask to be dropped off. Highly recommended.

F Hospedaje El Centro, Lanquín, close to the church. Friendly, good simple dinner, basic.

Camping

It is possible to camp for as long as you want at Semuc Champey once you've paid the entrance fee. There are toilets and cooking areas. Take insect repellent, a mosquito net, and all food and water. See also **El Retiro**, above.

Parque Nacional Laguna Lachuá p315

E National park accommodation, T5704-1509. Price per person. Bunk beds with mosquito netting or camping (tents available). Bring your own food and rubbish bags. There are fireplaces, showers and toilets.

F Finca Chipantun, on the borders of the national park on the bank of the Río Chixoy, T7951-3423, www.geocities.com/chipantun/main.html. With rooms, hammocks or camping space. 3 meals a day are provided at extra cost but at excellent value – the most expensive is dinner at US$3.50. Horse riding, boating, kayaking and guided tours possible.

North of Cobán and the southern Petén crossroads p315

C-D Complejo Cultural y Ecoturístico Cuevas de Candelaria, T7861-2203, www.cuevasdecandelaria.com. Thatched cabañas in a country setting with one large room with 10 beds and private rooms. Restaurant and café on site. Full board available.

E Las Diamelas, Fray Bartolomé de las Casas, just off park, T5810-1785. Cleanest rooms in town. Restaurant food is OK and cheap.

F Rancho Ríos Escondidos, near Grutas de Candelaria, on the main road. Camping possible at this farmhouse. Ask for Doña América.

🍴 Eating

Cobán *p313, map p314*

†††-†† **El Bistro**, in Casa D'Acuña (see Sleeping), T7951-0482. Excellent menu and massive portions. Try the blueberry pancakes, great yogurt, don't walk through the restaurant without putting your nose into the cake cabinet! Recommended.
†† **El Refugio**, 2 Av, 2-28, Zona 4, T7952-1338, 1030-2300. Excellent waiter service and substantial portions at good-value prices – steaks, fish, chicken and snacks, set lunch. Also cocktails, big screen TV and bar.
†† **Hostal de Doña Victoria** (see Sleeping). Serves up breakfast, lunch and supper in a semi-open area with a pleasant, quiet ambience. Good Italian food, including vegetarian options, is the speciality of the house. Also mini cellar bar.

Cafés

Café Fantasia, 1 Calle, 3-13, western end of the main park. Handy spot open for breakfast.
Café La Posada, part of La Posada (see Sleeping). Divine brownies and ice cream, sofas with a view of the Parque Central. Open afternoons.

Lanquín and Semuc Champey *p314*
There are *tiendas* in Lanquín selling good fruit and veg, and there are a couple of bakeries, all open early, for stocking up for a trip to Semuc Champey.
† **Comedor Shalom**, Lanquín. Excellent value, if basic, including drink.

🎭 Entertainment

Cobán *p313, map p314*
Bars and clubs
Milenio, 3 Av 1-11, Zona 4, 5 rooms, dance floor, live music weekends, beer by the jug, pool table, big screen TV, week ends minimum consumption US$3, popular place with a mature crowd.

Cinema
At Plaza Magdalena, a few blocks west of town. Multi-screen cinema with latest releases usually showing.

🎉 Festivals and events

Cobán *p313, map p314*
Mar/Apr Holy Week.
Last week of Jul Rabin Ajau, the election of the Maya Beauty Queen. Around this time the **Paa banc** is also performed, when the chiefs of brotherhoods are elected for the year.
1-6 Aug Santo Domingo, the town's fiesta in honour of its patron.

⛰️ Activities and tours

Cobán *p313, map p314*
Adrenalina Tours, west of the main square. Reliable tour operator, with a national presence.
Aventuras Turísticas, 3 Calle, 2-38, Zona 3, T7952-2213, www.aventurasturisticas.com. Also offers tourist information.
Proyecto Ecológico Quetzal, 2 Calle, 14-36, Zona 1, Cobán, T7952-1047, www.ecoquetzal.org. Contact David Unger. Trips are organized to the multicoloured Río Ikbolay, northwest of Cobán, see page 315, and the mountain community of Chicacnab.

🚌 Transport

Biotopo del Quetzal *p312*
Bus
From **Guatemala City**, take a Cobán bus with Escobar-Monja Blanca and ask to be let out at the Biotopo, hourly from 0400-1700, 3½ hrs, US$3.50. From **Cobán**, 1 hr, US$0.80, take any capital-bound bus or a minibus from Campo 2 near football stadium every 20 mins, US$0.80. From **El Rancho**–Biotopo, 1¼ hrs. Cobán–Purulhá,

local buses ply this route between 0645-2000 returning until 1730, 1 hr 20 mins.

Salamá, Rabinal and Cubulco p312
Bus
Salamá-Rabinal, 1-1½ hrs. Rabinal is reached by travelling west from Salamá on a paved road. From **Guatemala City**, 5½ hrs, a beautiful, occasionally heart-stopping ride, or via El Progreso, and then Salamá by bus. Buses leave 0330-1600 to Guatemala City via Salamá from Cubulco. There is a bus between Rabinal and Cubulco, supplemented by pickup rides.

Santa Cruz Verapaz and around p313
Bus
From **Cobán** between 0600-1915 every 15 mins, US$0.700, 40 mins. All capital-bound buses from Cobán run through **Tactic**, or take a local bus between 0645-2000, returning between 0500-1730, 40 mins, US$0.80. Bus from Cobán to **Senahú**, 6 hrs, from opposite INJAV building, from 0600-1400, 4 daily, US$2.90. If you are coming from El Estor, get off at the Senahú turn-off, hitch or wait for the buses from Cobán. Trucks take this road, but there is little traffic, so you have to be at the junction very early to be in luck.

Cobán p313, map p314
Bus
The central bus terminal has attempted to group the multitude of bus stations into one place. While many now depart from this bus terminal, there are still a number of departure points scattered around town. Seek local advice for updates or changes.

To **Guatemala City** with **Transportes Escobar-Monja Blanca**, T7951-3571, every 30 mins from 0200-1600, 4-5 hrs, US$7, from its own offices near the terminal. **El Estor**, 4 daily from Av 5, Calle 4, first at 0830, and mostly morning departures, but check in the terminal beforehand, 7 hrs, US$5.60.

To **Fray Bartolomé de las Casas**, between 0600-1600 by bus, pickup and trucks, every 30 mins. Route **Raxrujá– Sayaxché–Flores** there are minibuses **Micro buses del Norte** that leave from the terminal del norte near INJAV 0530 and 0630, 5 hrs, US$7.20. In Sayaxché you take a passenger canoe across the river (there is also a car ferry) where minibuses will whisk you to Flores on a tarmacked road in 45 mins. To **Uspantán**, 1000 and 1200, 5 hrs, US$2 from 1 Calle and 7 Av, Zona 2. Cobán can be reached from **Santa Cruz del Quiché** via Sacapulas and Uspantán, and from **Huehuetenango** via Aguacatán, Sacapulas and Uspantán.

Around Cobán p314
Bus
Every 20 mins from Cobán to **San Juan Chamelco**, US$0.25, 20 mins from Wasen Bridge, Diagonal 15, Zona 7 To **San Pedro Carchá**, every 15 mins, US$0.25, 20 mins from 2 Calle and 4 Av, Zona 4.

Lanquín and Semuc Champey p314
Bus
From **Cobán** there are minibuses that leave from the 3 Av, 5-6 Calle, 9 a day 0730-1745, US$3.80. From Lanquín to Semuc Champey hire a pickup, see below. From Lanquín to **Flores**, take a Cobán-bound bus to **Pajal**, 1 hr, then any passing bus or vehicle to **Sebol**, 2-2½ hrs (there are Las Casas–Cobán buses passing hourly in the morning only) and then pickup, hitch or bus to Sayaxché and then Flores.

Semuc Champey is a 10-km walk to the south from Lanquín, 3 hrs' walking along the road, which is quite tough for the first hour as the road climbs very steeply out of Lanquín. If planning to return to Lanquín the same day, start very early to avoid the midday heat. To get there in a pickup start early (0630), US$0.85, or ask around for a private lift (US$13 return). Transport is very irregular so it's best to start walking and keep your fingers crossed. By 1200-1300 there are usually people returning to town to hitch a lift with. If you are on your own and out of season, it would be wise to arrange a lift back.

Car
There is a gas station in Lanquín near the church.
   Car hire Inque Renta Autos, T7952-1431, Tabarini, T79521-1504.

Parque Nacional Laguna Lachuá *p315*
Heading for **Playa Grande** from Cobán, also known as **Ixcan Grande**, ask the bus driver to let you off before Playa Grande at 'la entrada del parque', from where it's a 4.2-km (1-hr) walk to the park entrance. Minibuses leave Cobán every 30 mins via Chisec, 4 hrs, US$8 opposite INJAV.

North of Cobán and the southern Petén crossroads *p315*
Bus
Local transport in the form of minibuses and pickups connects most of these towns before nightfall.
   Bus to **Poptún** from Fray Bartolomé de las Casas leaves at 0300 from the central park, 5¾ hrs, US$5.10. This road is extremely rough and the journey is a bone-bashing, coccyx-crushing one. Buses to **Cobán** at 0400 until 1100 on the hour. However, do not be surprised if one does not turn up and you have to wait for the next one. To **Flores** via Sebol, Raxrujá and Sayaxché at 0700 (3½ hrs) a further 30 mins-1 hr to Flores. The road from **Raxrujá** via Chisec to Cobán is very steep and rocky. **Chisec** to Cobán, 1½ hrs. The Sayaxché–Cobán bus arrives at Fray Bartolomé de las Casas for breakfast and continues between 0800 and 0900. You can also go from here to Sebol to Modesto Méndez to join the highway to **Flores**, but it is a very slow, killer of a journey. Buses leave from Cobán for Chisec from Campo 2 at 0500, 0800, 0900.

❶ Directory

Cobán *p313, map p314*
Banks Most banks around the Parque Central will change money. MasterCard accepted at **G&T Continental**, corner of 1 Calle and 2 Av. **Internet** Access Computación, same building as Café Tirol. Fax and collect-call phone service only. Infocel, 3 Av, between 1-2 Calle, Zona 4. **Language schools** Active Spanish School, 3 Calle, 6-12, Zona 1, T7952-1432 (Nirma Macz). La Escuela de Español Muq'bil' B'e, 6 Av, 5-39, Zona 3, T7951-2459 (Oscar Macz), muqbilbe@ yahoo.com. Offers Spanish and Q'eqchi'. **Laundry** Lavandería Providencia, opposite Café Tirol. **Medical services** Policlínica y Hospital Galen, a private institution on 3 Av, 1-47, Zona 3, T7951-2913. **Post** Corner of 2 Av and 3 Calle. **Telephone** You can make international calls from **Telgua** and Access Computación (see above).

El Petén

Deep in the lush lowland jungles of the Petén lie the lost worlds of Maya cities, pyramids and ceremonial centres, where layers of ancient dust speak ancient tales. At Tikal, where battles and burials are recorded in intricately carved stone, temples push through the tree canopy, wrapped in a mystical shroud. Although all human life has vanished from these once-powerful centres, the forest is humming with the latter-day lords of the jungle: the howler monkeys that roar day and night. There are also toucans, hummingbirds, spider monkeys, wild pig and coatimundi. Jaguar, god of the underworld in Maya religion, stalks the jungle but remains elusive, as does the puma and tapir. Further into the undergrowth away from Tikal, the adventurous traveller can visit El Mirador, the largest Maya stronghold, as well as El Zotz, El Perú, El Ceibal and Uaxactún by river, on foot and on horseback. ▸▸ *For listings, see pages 334-340.*

Ins and outs
Best time to visit The dry season and wet season offer different advantages and disadvantages. In the months of November through to early May, access to all sites is possible as tracks are bone-dry. There are also less mosquitoes and if you are a bird lover, the mating season falls in this period. In the rainy winter months, from May to November, tracks become muddy quagmires making many of them impassable, also bringing greater humidity and mosquitoes. Take plenty of repellent, and reapply frequently. It's also fiercely hot and humid at all times in these parts so lots of sun screen and drinking water are essential.

Background
Predominantly covered in jungle, the Petén is the largest department of Guatemala although it has the smallest number of inhabitants. The northern area was so impenetrable that its Maya settlers, the Itzás, were not conquered by the Spaniards until 1697. In 1990, 21,487 sq km of the north of the Petén was declared a *Reserva de la Biósfera Maya* (Maya Biosphere Reserve), by **CONAP**, the National Council for Protected Areas. It became the largest protected tropical forest area in Central America. Inside the boundaries of the biosphere are the Parque Nacional Tikal, Parque Nacional Mirador–Río Azul and Parque Nacional Laguna del Tigre.

Poptún → *Colour map 2, B3.*
Poptún is best known for its association with **Finca Ixobel**, see Sleeping, page 334. Otherwise, it is just a staging-post between Río Dulce and Flores, or a stop-off to switch buses for the ride west to Cobán.

Flores and Santa Elena → *For listings, see pages 334-340. Colour map 2, A2.*

Flores is perched on a tiny island in Lake Petén Itzá. Red roofs and palm trees jostle for position as they spread up the small hill, which is topped by the white twin-towered cathedral. Some of the streets of the town are lined with houses and restaurants that have been given lashings of colourful paint, giving Flores a Caribbean flavour. A pleasant new lakeshore *malecón* has been built around the island, with benches, street lamps and jetties for swimming. *Lanchas*, drifting among the lilies and dragonflies, are pinned to the lake edges. Boat trips around the lake go from the Flores end of the causeway, about US$20 for 40 minutes, but it's worth bargaining.

Santa Elena is the dustier, less elegant and noisier twin town on the mainland where the cheapest hotels, banking services and bus terminal can be found.

Ins and outs

Getting there and around Flores is 2 km from the international airport on the outskirts of Santa Elena. The airport departures hall has an internet place. Tour operator and hotel representatives are based in the arrival halls. A causeway links Flores with Santa Elena. A taxi from the airport into Santa Elena or Flores costs US$1.30 and takes five minutes, but

Flores

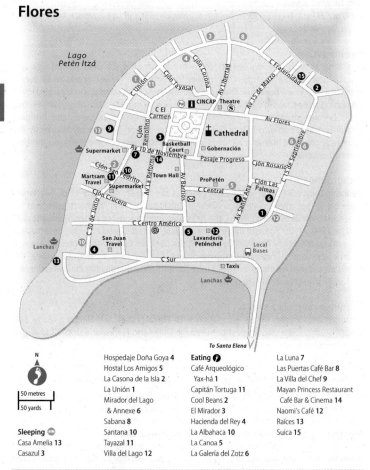

N

50 metres
50 yards

Sleeping
Casa Amelia **13**
Casazul **3**
Hospedaje Doña Goya **4**
Hostal Los Amigos **5**
La Casona de la Isla **2**
La Unión **1**
Mirador del Lago
  & Annexe **6**
Sabana **8**
Santana **10**
Tayazal **11**
Villa del Lago **12**

Eating
Café Arqueológico
  Yax-há **1**
Capitán Tortuga **11**
Cool Beans **2**
El Mirador **3**
Hacienda del Rey **4**
La Albahaca **10**
La Canoa **5**
La Galería del Zotz **6**

La Luna **7**
Las Puertas Café Bar **8**
La Villa del Chef **9**
Mayan Princess Restaurant
  Café Bar & Cinema **14**
Naomi's Café **12**
Raíces **13**
Suica **15**

To Santa Elena

bargain hard. If you arrive by long-distance bus from Guatemala City, Mexico or Belize, the terminal is 10 blocks south of the causeway. There are hotels in Santa Elena and Flores across the causeway (10 to 15 minutes from Santa Elena). Chicken buses run between the two, US$0.35. Tuc-tucs charge US$0.90 for journeys between the two.

Tourist information **INGUAT** ⓘ *in the airport, T7956-0533, daily 0700-1200, 1500-1800.* **ProPetén** ⓘ *Calle Central, T7867-5155, www.propeten.org,* associated with **Conservation International. CINCAP (Centro de Información sobre la Naturaleza, Cultura y Artesanía de Petén)** ⓘ *on the plaza, T7926-0718, www.alianzaverde.org,* has free maps of Tikal, and other local information. Housed in the same building is the **Alianza Verde** ⓘ *closed Mon,* an organization promoting sustainable ecotourism. If you wish to make trips independently to remote Maya sites, check with **ProPetén** to see if they have vehicles making the journey.

Safety Roadside robbery used to be a problem on the road to Tikal and to Yaxhá. Get independent, up-to-date advice before visiting these places and leave all valuables at your hotel. **Asistur,** see Safety, page 205, can assist and have a base at Tikal.

Santa Elena

To Flores

Lago Petén Itzá

Lanchas

To San Benito, Bancafé, San Andrés & San José

C 1
C 1A
C 2
C 3
C 4

Av 4
Av 5
Av 6
Av 7
Av 8

Taxis
Parque Central Fraternidad
San Juan Travel Agency
Catholic
Taxis
Taxis
Supermarket
Explore

To Airport, Tikal, Guatemala City, INGUAT & Tikal Connection

To Actún Kan Caves & Long-distance Bus Terminal (4 blocks)

N

100 metres
100 yards

Sleeping 🛏
Casa de Elena **1**
Casona del Lago **6**
Maya Internacional **2**

Patio Tikal **3**
Petén Espléndido **4**
San Juan **5**

Eating 🍴
El Petenchel **1**
El Rodeo **2**
Mijaro **3**

Background

This jungle region was settled by the Maya Itzá Kanek in about AD 600, with their seat then known as La Isla de Tah Itzá (Tayasal in Spanish), now modern-day Flores. The Itzás were untouched by Spanish inroads into Guatemala until the Mexican conquistador Hernán Cortés and Spanish chronicler Bernal Díaz del Castillo dropped by in 1525 on their way from Mexico to Honduras. In 1697 Martín Urzua y Arismendi, the governor of the Yucatán, fought the first battle of the Itzás, crossing the lake in a galley killing 100 indigenous people in the ensuing battle, and capturing King Canek. He and his men destroyed the temples and palaces of Tayasal and so finished off the last independent Maya state.

Sights

The **cathedral**, Nuestra Señora de los Remedios y San Pablo del Itzá, is plain inside, and houses a Cristo Negro, part of a chain of Black Christs that stretches across Central America, with the focus of worship at Esquipulas. **Paraíso Escondido** is home to the **zoo** ① *US$2.70*. A dugout to the island costs US$16 round trip. Near the zoo is **ARCAS** (**Asociación de Rescate y Conservación de Vida Silvestre**) ① *US$2, T5208-0968, www.arcasguatemala.com*, where they care for rescued animals and release them back into the wild. Volunteers are welcome. There is a centre and interactive trails at the site. Boat tours of the whole lake cost from about US$10 per boat, calling at the zoo and **El Mirador** on the Maya ruin of **Tayasal** ① *US$2.70*. **Actún Kan caves** ① *0800-1700, US$2.70*, are a fascinating labyrinth of tunnels where, legend has it, a large serpent lived. They are 3 km south of Santa Elena and a 30 to 45 minutes' walk. To get there take the 6 Avenida out of Santa Elena to its end, turn left at a small hill, then take the first road to the right where it is well marked. South of Santa Elena, at Km 468 is **Parque Natural Ixpanpajul** ① *T2336-0576, www.ixpanpajul.com*, where forest canopy Tarzan tours, zip-wire, night safari, birdwatching and horse riding and more are on offer. Local fiestas include 12-15 January, the Petén *feria*, and 11-12 December in honour of the Virgen de Guadalupe.

Around Lake Petén Itzá

San Andrés, 16 km by road from Santa Elena, enjoys sweeping views of Lake Petén Itzá, and its houses climb steeply down to the lake shore. There is a language school, see Directory. Adonis, a villager, takes good-value tours to El Zotz and El Mirador and has been recommended. Ask around for him; his house is close to the shoreline. You can also volunteer in the village with **Volunteer Petén** ① *Parque Nueva Juventud, T5711-0040, www.volunteerpeten.com*, a conservation and community project. The attractive village of **San José**, a traditional Maya Itzá village, where efforts are being made to preserve the Itzá language and revive old traditions, is 2 km further northeast on the lake from San Andrés. Its painted and thatched homes huddling steeply on the lake shore make it a much better day trip than San Andrés. Some 4 km beyond the village a signed track leads to the Classic period site of **Motul**, with 33 plazas, tall pyramids and some stelae depicting Maya kings. It takes 20 minutes to walk between the two villages. On 1 November San José hosts the **Holy Skull Procession**.

At the eastern side of Lake Petén Itzá is **El Remate**. The sunsets are superb and the lake is flecked with turquoise blue in the mornings. You can swim in the lake in certain places away from the local women washing their clothes and the horses taking a bath. There are many lovely places to stay, as it is also a handy stop-off point en route to Tikal. West of El

Remate is the 700-ha **Biotopo Cerro Cahuí** ① *daily 0800-1600, US$2.70, administered by CECON*. It is a lowland jungle area where three species of monkey, deer, jaguar, peccary, ocellated wild turkey and some 450 species of bird can be seen. If you do not wish to walk alone, you can hire a guide. Ask at your *posada*.

Parque Nacional Tikal → *For listings, see pages 334-340. Colour map 2, A2.*

① *Open daily 0600-1800, US$19 per day, payable at the national park entrance, 18 km from the ruins (park administration, T7920-0025). An overall impression of the ruins may be gained in 5 hrs, but you need at least 2 days to see them properly. If you enter after 1600 your ticket is valid for the following day. If you stay the night in the park hotels, you can enter at 0500 once the police have scoured the grounds. This gives you at least a 2-hr head start on visitors coming in from Flores. At the visitor centre there is a post office, which stores luggage, a tourist guide service (see below), exchange facilities, toilets, a restaurant and a few shops that sell relevant guidebooks. Take a hat, mosquito repellent, water and snacks with you as it's extremely hot, drinks at the site aren't cheap and there's a lot of legwork involved.*

With its Maya skyscrapers pushing up through the jungle canopy, Tikal will have you transfixed. Steep-sided temples for the mighty dead, stelae commemorating the powerful rulers, inscriptions recording the noble deeds and the passing of time, and burials that were stuffed with jade and bone funerary offerings, make up the greatest Maya city in this tropical pocket of Guatemala.

Ins and outs

Getting there From Flores, it's possible to visit Tikal in a day. **San Juan Travel Agency** minibuses leave hourly between 0500 and 1000, one at 1400 and return at 1230 and hourly between 1400 and 1700 (though on the way back from Tikal, buses are likely to leave 10-15 minutes before scheduled), one hour, US$7.50 return. Several other companies also run trips such as **Línea Dorada** at 0500, 0830, 1530, returning 1400 and 1700. If you have not bought a return ticket you can often get a discounted seat on a returning bus if it's not full. Minibuses also meet Guatemala City–Flores flights. A taxi to Tikal costs US$60 one way. You can also visit Tikal with a one-day or two-day package tour from Guatemala City or Antigua.

Best time to visit Try to visit the ruins after 1400, or before 0900, as there are fewer visitors. From April to December it rains every day for a while; it is busiest November to January, during the Easter and summer holidays and most weekends. The best time for bird tours is December to April, with November to February being the mating season. Mosquitoes can be a real problem even during the day if straying away from open spaces.

Tourist information A guide is highly recommended as outlying structures can otherwise be missed. The official **Tourist Guide Association** offers tours of varying natures and in different languages. A private guide can be hired for US$60 or you can join up with a group for US$15 per person. Tours are available in Spanish, English, Italian, German and French. The guidebook *Tikal*, by W R Coe, in several languages, has an excellent map; or you can buy a reasonable leaflet/map at the entrance, US$2.50. Free transport around the site is available for elderly and disabled visitors, in an adapted pickup truck, with wheelchair access.

Background

At its height, the total 'urban' area of Tikal was more than 100 sq km, with the population somewhere between 50,000 and 100,000. The low-lying hill site of Tikal was first occupied around 600 BC during the pre-Classic era, but its buildings date from 300 BC. It became an important Maya centre from AD 300 onwards, which coincided with the decline of the mega power to the north, El Mirador. It was governed by a powerful dynasty of 30-plus rulers between about the first century AD until about AD 869, with the last known named ruler being Hasaw Chan K'awill II.

Tikal

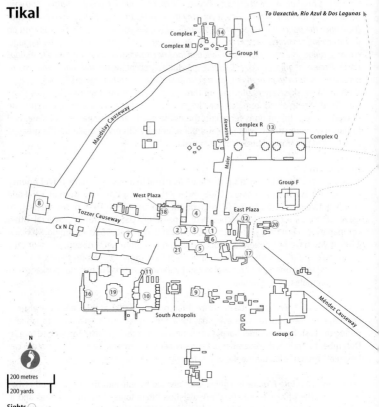

Sights ○

Temple I (Temple of the
  Great Jaguar) **1**
Temple II (Temple of the
  Masks) **2**
Great Plaza **3**
North Acropolis **4**
Central Acropolis **5**

Ball Court **6**
Temple III (Temple of the
  Jaguar Priest) **7**
Temple IV (Temple of the
  Double-Headed Serpent) **8**
Temple V **9**

Plaza of the Seven
  Temples **10**
Triple Ball Court **11**
Market **12**
Twin Pyramid Complexes
  Q & R **13**

North Group **14**
Temple VI (Temple of
  Inscriptions) **15**
El Mundo Perdido (Lost
  World) **16**

Tikal's main structures, which cover 2.5 sq km, were constructed from AD 550 to 900 during the Late-Classic period. These include the towering mega structures of temples – shrines to the glorious dead – whose roof combs were once decorated with coloured stucco figures of Tikal lords. Doorways on the temple rooms were intricately carved – using the termite-resistant wood of the sapodilla tree – with figures and symbols, known as lintels. Tikal's stelae tell of kings and accessions and war and death. Its oldest stela dates from AD 292. Many Central Mexican influences have been found on the stelae imagery, in burial sites at Tikal and in decorative architectural technique, which led archaeologists to conclude that the city was heavily influenced from the west by forces from the great enclave of Teotihuacán, now just outside Mexico City. This war-like state bred a cult of war and sacrifice and seemed intent on spreading its culture. After the collapse of Teotihuacán in AD 600, a renaissance at Tikal was achieved by the ruler Ah Cacao (Lord Cocoa, Ruler A, Moon Double Comb, Hasaw Chan K'awil I, Sky Rain) who succeeded to the throne in AD 682 and died sometime in the 720s. However, in the latter part of the eighth century the fortunes of Tikal declined. The last date recorded on a stela is AD 889. The site was finally abandoned in the 10th century. Most archaeologists now agree the collapse was due to warfare with neighbouring states, overpopulation, which resulted in environmental destruction, and drought. Tikal's existence was first reported by Spanish monk Andrés de Avendaño, but its official discovery is attributed to Modesto Méndez, Commissioner of the Petén, and Ambrosio Tut, Governor of the Petén, in 1848. They were both accompanied by the artist Eusebio Lara.

Wildlife

Tikal is a fantastic place for seeing animal and bird life of the jungle. Wildlife includes spider monkeys, howler monkeys, three species of toucan (most prominent being the keel-billed toucan), deer, foxes and many other birds and insects. Pumas have been seen on quieter paths and coatimundis (*pizotes*), in large family groups, are often seen rummaging through the bins. The ocellated turkeys with their sky-blue heads with orange baubles attached are seen in abundance at the entrance, and at **El Mundo Perdido**.

Museo Cerámico 1
Park Administration 2
Disused Airfield 3
Minibus Park
Entrance & Tickets
Museo Lítico
Visitor Centre
Comedores
Entrance
To Flores

Structure 5D 38 **17**
Structure 5D II **18**
Great Pyramid **19**
Sweat House **20**
Structure 5D 73 **21**

Sleeping
Jaguar Inn **1**
Jungle Lodge **2**
Tikal Inn **3**

The ruins

The **Great Plaza (3)** is a four-layered plaza with its earliest foundations laid around 150 BC and its latest around AD 700. It is dwarfed by its two principal temples – Temples I and II. On the north side of the plaza between these two temples are two rows of monuments. It includes Stela 29, erected in AD 292, which depicts Tikal's emblem glyph – the symbol of a Maya city – and the third century AD ruler Scroll Ahau Jaguar, who is bearing a two-headed ceremonial bar.

Temple I (Temple of the Great Jaguar) (1), on the east side of the Great Plaza, rises to 44 m in height with nine stepped terraces. It was ordered to be built by the ruler Ah Cacao, who ruled between AD 682 to around AD 720-724, who probably planned it for use as his shrine. His tomb, the magnificent Burial 116, was discovered beneath Temple I in 1962 with a wealth of burial goods on and around his skeleton. The display is reconstructed in the Museo Cerámico/Tikal.

Temple II (Temple of the Masks) (2) faces Temple I on the Great Plaza and rises to 38 m, although with its roof comb it would have been higher. It's thought Ah Cacao ordered its construction as well. The lintel on the doorway here depicted a woman wearing a cape, and experts have suggested that this could be his wife.

The **North Acropolis (4)** contains some 100 buildings piled on top of earlier structures in a 1-ha area and is the burial ground of all of Tikal's rulers until the break with royal practice made by Ah Cacao. In 1960, the prized Stelae 31, now in the Museo Cerámico/Tikal, see below, was found under the Acropolis. It was dedicated in AD 445. Its base was deliberately burnt by the Maya and buried under Acropolis buildings in the eighth century. This burning was thought to be like a 'killing', where the burning ritual would 'kill' the power of the ruler depicted on the monument, say, after death. It's thought to depict the ruler Siyah Chan K'awil (Stormy Sky), who died sometime around AD 457 having succeeded to the throne in AD 411. Yax Moch Xok (Great Scaffold Shark) is thought to be entombed in the first century AD grave, Burial 85. Surrounding the headless male body were burial objects and a mask bearing the royal head band. Under a building directly in the centre of this acropolis Burial 22 – that of ruler Great Jaguar Paw, who reigned in the fourth century, and died around AD 379 – was discovered. Also found here was Burial 10, thought to be the tomb of Nun Yax Ayin I (Curl Nose), who succeeded to the throne in AD 379 after Great Jaguar Paw. Inside were the remains of nine sacrificed servants as well as turtles and crocodile remains and a plethora of pottery pieces. The pottery laid out in this tomb had Teotihuacán artistic influences, demonstrating Tikal's links to the powers of Teotihuacán and Teotihuacán-influenced Kaminal Juyú. Burial 48 is thought to be the tomb of Curl Nose's son, Siyah Chan K'awil (Stormy Sky).

Central Acropolis (5) is made up of a complex of courts connected by passages and stairways, which have expanded over the centuries to cover 1.6 ha. Most of the building work carried out took place between AD 550-900 in the Late-Classic era. The **East Plaza** behind Temple I is the centre of the highway junctions of the Maler Causeway in the north, and the Méndez Causeway heading southeast.

On the western side of the **West Plaza** is structure 5D II under which Burial 77 was brought to light. The skeleton was adorned with a jade pendant, which was stolen from the site museum in the 1980s.

Temple III (Temple of the Jaguar Priest) (7) is so called because of the scene of a figure in a glamorous jaguar pelt on a lintel found on the temple. Some experts believe this figure is Ah Chitam (Nun Yax Ayin II, Ruler C), son of Yax Kin, and grandson of the great

Ah Cacao, and so propose that this is his shrine, although there has been no confirmation of this. Temple III was constructed around AD 810 and is 55 m tall.

Temple IV (Temple of the Double-Headed Serpent) (8) is the highest building in Tikal at 70 m. It was built in the Late-Classic period around AD 741, as proven by hieroglyphic inscriptions and carbon dating. It's thought it was built to honour Yax Kin, the son of Ah Cacao, who became ruler in AD 734. A date on the lintel is AD 741, the same year that Temple I was dedicated.

Temple V (9), constructed between AD 700-750 during the reign of Yax Kin, is 58 m high. It is the mortuary temple of an unknown ruler.

El Mundo Perdido (The Lost World) (16). The **Great Pyramid** is at the centre of this lost world. At 30 m high, it is the largest pyramid at Tikal. It is flat topped and its stairways are flanked by masks. From the top a great view over the canopy to the tops of other temples can be enjoyed. Together with other buildings to the west, it forms part of an astronomical complex. The Lost World pyramid is a pre-Classic structure, but was improved upon in the Early Classic. East of El Mundo Perdido is the **Plaza of the Seven Temples (10)**, constructed during the Late Classic period (AD 600-800). There is a triple ball court lying at its northern edge.

Temple VI (Temple of the Inscriptions) (15) was discovered in 1951. The 12 m-high roof comb is covered on both sides in hieroglyphic text and is the longest hieroglyphic recording to date. It was carved in AD 766, but the temple was built under the rule of Yax Kin some years before. Altar 9 is at the base of the temple as is Stela 21, said to depict the sculptured foot of the ruler Yax Kin to mark his accession as ruler in AD 734. Unfortunately because of the location of this temple away from the rest of the main structures it has become a hideout for robbers and worse. Some guides no longer take people there. Take advice before going, if at all.

The North Group has several twin pyramid complexes, including Complexes Q and R, marking the passing of the *katun* – a Maya 20-year period.

The **Museo Cerámico (Museo Tikal)** ① *near the Jungle Lodge, Mon-Fri 0900-1700, Sat and Sun, 0900-1600, US$1.30*, has a collection of Maya ceramics, but its prize exhibits are Stela 31 with its still clear carvings, and the reconstruction of the tomb of Tikal's great ruler, Ah Cacao. In the **Museo Lítico** ① *in side the visitor centre, Mon-Fri 0900-1700, Sat and Sun, 0900-1600*, there are stelae and great photographs of the temples as they were originally found, and of their reconstruction, including the 1968 rebuild of the Temple II steps. **Note** Photography is no longer permitted in either of these museums.

Other Maya ruins → *For listings, see pages 334-340.*

There are literally hundreds of Maya sites in the Petén. Below are a handful of sites, whose ruins have been explored, and of whose histories something is known.

Uaxactún → *Colour map 2, A3.*

In the village of Uaxactún (pronounced Waash-ak-tún) are ruins, famous for the oldest complete Maya astronomical complex found, and a stuccoed temple with serpent and jaguar head decoration. The village itself is little more than a row of houses either side of a disused airstrip. Uaxactún is one of the longest-occupied Maya sites. Its origins lie in the Middle pre-Classic (1000-300 BC) and its decline came by the early post-Classic (AD 925-1200) like many of its neighbouring powers. Its final stelae, dated AD 889, is one of the last to be found in the region. The site is named after a stela, which corresponds to

Baktun 8 (8 x 400 Maya years), carved in AD 889 – *uaxac* means 8, *tun* means stone. South of the remains of a ball court, in **Group B**, a turtle carving can be seen, and Stela 5, which marks the takeover of the city, launched from Tikal. Next door to this stela under Temple B-VIII were found the remains of two adults, including a pregnant woman, a girl of about 15 and a baby. It is believed this may have been the governor and his family who were sacrificed in AD 378. From Group B, take the causeway to **Group A**. In Group A, Structure A-V had 90 rooms and there were many tombs to be seen. The highest structure in the complex is Palace A-XVIII, where red paint can still be seen on the walls. In **Group E** the oldest observatory (E-VII-sub) ever found faces structures in which the equinoxes and solstices were observed. When the pyramid (E-VII) covering this sub-structure was removed, fairly well preserved stucco masks of jaguar and serpent heads were found flanking the stairways of the sub-structure. The ruins lie either side of the village, the main groups **(Group A** and **Group B)** are to the northwest (take a left just before **Hotel El Chiclero** and follow the road round on a continuous left to reach this group). A smaller group **(Group E)** with the observatory is to the southwest (take any track, right off the airstrip, and ask. This group is 400 m away. The site is 24 km north of Tikal on an unpaved road. It is in fairly good condition taking less than one hour in any vehicle.

El Zotz

El Zotz, meaning bat in Q'eqchi', is so called because of the nightly flight from a nearby cave of thousands of bats. There is an alternative hiking route as well (see below). Incredibly, from Temple IV, the highest in the complex at 75 m, it is possible to see in the distance, some 30 km away, Temple IV at Tikal. The wooden lintel from Temple I (dated AD 500-550) is to be found in the Museo Nacional de Arqueología y Etnología in the capital. Each evening at about 1850 the sky is darkened for 10 minutes by the fantastic spectacle of tens of thousands of bats flying out of a cave near the camp. The 200-m-high cave pock-marked with holes is a half-hour walk from the camp. If you are at the cave you'll see the flight above you and get doused in falling excrement. If you remain at the campsite you will see them streaking the dark blue sky with black in straight columns. It's also accessible via Uaxactún. There is some basic infrastructure for the guards, and you can camp.

One of the best trips you can do in the Petén is a three-day hike to El Zotz and on through the jungle to Tikal. The journey, although long, is not arduous, and is accompanied by birds, blue morpho butterflies and spider monkeys chucking branches at you all the way.

El Perú and the Estación Biológica Guacamayo

A visit to El Perú is included in the **Scarlet Macaw Trail**, a two- to five-day trip into the **Parque Nacional Laguna del Tigre**, through the main breeding area of the scarlet macaw. There is little to see at the Maya site, but the journey to it is worthwhile. In 2004 the 1200 year old tomb and skeleton of a Maya queen were found. A more direct trip involves getting to the Q'eqchi'-speaking isolated community of **Paso Caballos** (1¾ hours). Here, the **Comité de Turismo** can organize transport by *lancha* along the Río San Pedro. From Paso Caballos it is one hour by *lancha* to the El Perú campsite and path. It's possible to stop off at the **Estación Biológica Guacamayo** ① *US$1.30, volunteers may be needed, contact Propeten, www.propeten.org*, where there is an ongoing programme to study the wild scarlet macaws (*ara macao*). The chances of seeing endangered scarlet macaws during March, April and May in this area is high because that's when they are reproducing. A couple of minutes upriver is the landing stage, where it's a 30-minute walk to the campsite of El Perú: howler monkeys, hummingbirds, oropendola birds and fireflies abound. From there, it is a two-hour walk to the El Perú ruins. Small coral snakes slither about, howler monkeys roar, spider monkeys chuck branches down on the path. White-lipped peccaries, nesting white turtles, eagles, fox and kingfishers have also been seen. The trip may be impossible between June and August because of rising rivers during the rainy season and because the unpaved road to Paso Caballos may not be passable. Doing it on your own is possible, although you may have to wait for connections and you will need a guide, about US$20 per day.

El Mirador, El Tintal and Nakbé → *Colour map 2, A2.*

El Mirador is the largest Maya site in the country. It dates from the late pre-Classic period (300 BC-AD 250) and is thought to have sustained a population of tens of thousands. It takes five days to get to El Mirador. From Flores it is 2½ to three hours to the village of Carmelita by bus or truck, from where it is seven hours walking, or part horse riding to El Mirador. It can be done in four days – two days to get there and two days to return. The route is difficult and the mosquitoes and ticks and the relentless heat can make it a trying trip. Organized tours are arranged by travel agents in Flores – get reassurance that your agents have enough food and water. If you opt to go to El Mirador independently, ask in Carmelita for the **Comité de Turismo**, which will arrange mules and guides. Take water, food, tents and torches. It is about 25 km to El Tintal, a camp where you can sling a hammock, or another 10 km to El Arroyo, where there is a little river for a swim near a *chiclero* camp. It takes another day to El Mirador, or longer, if you detour via Nakbé. You will pass *chiclero* camps on the way, which are very hospitable, but very poor. In May, June and July there is no mud, but there is little chance of seeing wildlife or flora. In July to December, when the rains come, the chances of glimpsing wildlife is much greater and there are lots of flowers. It is a lot fresher, but there can be tonnes of mud, sometimes making the route impassable. The mosquitos are also in a frenzy during the rainy season. Think carefully about going on the trip (one reader called it "purgatory"). The site, which is part of the Parque Nacional Mirador-Río Azul, is divided into two parts with the **El Tigre Pyramid** and complex in the western part, and the **La Danta** complex, the largest in the Maya world, in the east, 2 km away. The larger of two huge pyramids – La Danta – is 70 m high; stucco masks of jaguars and birds flank the stairways of the temple complex. The other, El Tigre, is 55 m in height and is a wonderful place to be on top of at night, with a view of endless jungle and other sites, including Calakmul, in Mexico. In **Carmelita** ask around for space to sling your hammock or camp. There is a basic *comedor*. **El Tintal**, a day's hike from El Mirador, is said to be the second largest site in Petén, connected by a causeway to El Mirador, with great views from the top of the pyramids. **Nakbé**, 10 km southeast of El Mirador, is the earliest known lowland Maya site (1000-400 BC), with the earliest examples of carved monuments.

Río Azul and Kinal

From Uaxactún a dirt road leads north to the campamento of Dos Lagunas. It's a lovely place to camp, with few mosquitoes, but swimming will certainly attract crocodiles. The guards' camp at Ixcán Río, on the far bank of the Río Azul, can be reached in one long day's walk, crossing by canoe if the water is high. If low enough to cross by vehicle you can drive to the Río Azul site, a further 6 km on a wide, shady track. It is also possible to continue into Mexico if your paperwork is OK. A barely passable side track to the east from the camp leads to the ruins of Kinal. The big attraction at Río Azul are the famous black and red painted tombs, technically off limits to visitors without special permission, but visits have been known.

Yaxhá, Topoxte, Nakum and Melchor de Mencos
About 65 km from Flores, on the Belize road ending at Melchor de Mencos, is a turning left, a dry weather road, which brings you in 8.5 km to Laguna Yaxhá. On the northern shore is the site of Yaxhá (meaning Green Water), the third largest known Classic Maya site in the country, accessible by causeway. Open 0800-1700. This untouristy site is good for birdwatching and the views from the temples of the milky green lake are outstanding. The tallest structure, **Templo de las Manos Rojas**, is 30 m high In the lake is the unusual Late Post Classic site (AD120-1530) of Topoxte. (The island is accessible by boat from Yaxhá, 15 minutes.) About 20 km further north of Yaxhá lies Nakum, which it's thought was both a trading and ceremonial centre. You will need a guide and your own transport if you have not come on a tour. The group of sites has been designated as a national park, entry to each US$9 (www.conap.com.gt, T7861-0250). **Note** For the Belize border crossing, see box, page 348.

Northwest Petén and the Mexican border
An unpaved road runs 151 km west from Flores to **El Naranjo** on the Río San Pedro, near the Mexican border. Close by is **La Joyanca**, a site where the chance of wildlife spotting is high. You can camp at the *cruce* with the guards.

Parque Nacional Laguna del Tigre and Biotopo
The park and biotopo is a vast area of jungle and wetlands north of El Naranjo. The best place to stay is the CECON camp, across the river below the ferry. This is where the guards live and they will let you stay in the bunk house and use their kitchen. Getting into the reserve is not easy and you will need to be fully equipped, but a few people go up the Río Escondido. The lagoons abound in wildlife, including enormous crocodiles and spectacular bird life. Contact CECON.

Sayaxché → *Colour map 2, B2.*
Sayaxché, south of Flores on the road to Cobán, has a frontier town feel to it as its focus is on a bend on the Río de la Pasión. It is a good base for visiting the southern Petén including a number of archaeological sites, namely El Ceibal. You can change US dollar bills and traveller's cheques at **Banoro**.

El Ceibal
This major ceremonial site is reached by a 45-minute *lancha* ride up the Río de la Pasión from Sayaxché. It is about 1.5 km from the left bank of Río de la Pasión hidden in vegetation and extending for 1.5 sq km. The height of activity at the site was from 800 BC to the first century AD. Archaeologists agree that it appears to have been abandoned in between about AD 500 and AD 690 and then repopulated at a later stage when there was an era of stelae production between AD 771 and 889. It later declined during the early decades of the 10th century and was abandoned. You can sling a hammock at El Ceibal and use the guard's fire for making coffee if you ask politely – a mosquito net is advisable, and take repellent for walking in the jungle surroundings. Tours can be arranged in Flores for a day trip to Sayaxché and El Ceibal (around US$65) but there is limited time to see the

site. From Sayaxché the ruins of the **Altar de los Sacrificios** at the confluence of the Ríos de la Pasión and Usumacinta can also be reached. It was one of the earliest sites in the Péten, with a founding date earlier than that of Tikal. Most of its monuments are not in good condition. Also within reach of Sayaxché is **Itzán**, discovered in 1968.

Piedras Negras

Still further down the Río Usumacinta in the west of Petén is Piedras Negras, a huge Classic period site. In the 1930s Tatiana Proskouriakoff first recognized the periods of time inscribed on stelae here coincided with human life spans or reigns, and so began the task of deciphering the meaning of Maya glyphs. Advance arrangements are necessary with a rafting company to reach Piedras Negras. **Maya Expeditions** (address on page 195) run expeditions, taking in Piedras Negras, Bonampak, Yaxchilán and Palenque. This trip is a real adventure. The riverbanks are covered in the best remaining tropical forest in Guatemala, inhabited by elusive wildlife and hiding more ruins. Once you've rafted down to Piedras Negras, you have to raft out. Though most of the river is fairly placid, there are the 30-m **Busilhá Falls**, where a crystal-clear tributary cascades over limestone terraces and two deep canyons, with impressive rapids to negotiate, before reaching the take-out two days later.

Petexbatún

From Sayaxché, the Río de la Pasión is a good route to visit other Maya ruins. From **Laguna Petexbatún** (16 km), a fisherman's paradise can be reached by outboard canoe from Sayaxché. Excursions can be made from here to unexcavated ruins that are generally grouped together under the title Petexbatún. These include **Arroyo de la Piedra**, Dos Pilas and Aguateca. **Dos Pilas** has many well-preserved stelae, and an important tomb of a king was found here in 1991 – that of its Ruler 2, who died in AD 726. Dos Pilas flourished in the Classic period when as many as 10,000 lived in the city. There are many carved monuments and hieroglyphic stairways at the site, which record the important events of city life. **Aguateca**, where the ruins are so far little excavated, gives a feeling of authenticity. The city was abandoned in the early ninth century for unknown reasons. Again, a tour is advisable. It's a boat trip and a short walk away. The site was found with numerous walls (it's known the city was attacked in AD 790) and a chasm actually splits the site in two. The natural limestone bridge connects a large plaza with platforms and buildings in the west with an area of a series of smaller plazas in the east. These places are off the beaten track and an adventure to get to.

For Sleeping and Eating price codes and other relevant information, see Essentials pages 31-33.

◉ Sleeping

Poptún *p321*

C-G Finca Ixobel, T5410-4307, www.finca ixobel.com. A working farm owned by Carole Devine, widowed after the assassination of her husband in 1990. This highly acclaimed 'paradise' has become the victim of its own reputation and is frequently crowded especially at weekends. However, you can still camp peacefully and there are great treehouses, dorm beds, private rooms and bungalows. One of the highlights is the food. The *finca* offers a range of trips that could keep you there for days. Recommended.

Flores *p321, map p322*

B Hotel Casazul, Calle Fraternindad, T7867-5451, www.hotelesdepeten.com. 9 rooms, all blue and most with lakeside view. All with cable TV, a/c and fan.

B Hotel Santana, Calle 30 de Junio, T7867-5123, www.santanapeten.com. Lakeside restaurant, pool, clean rooms, all with their own terrace a/c, and TV.

B La Casona de la Isla, Callejón San Pedrito, on the lake, T7867-5163, www.hotelesde peten.com. Elegant rooms, fans, TV, clean, friendly, good restaurant, nice breakfasts, bar, garden, pool.

C Sabana, Calle La Unión, T7867-5100. Huge, airy rooms, good service, clean, pleasant, with funky green wavy paintwork in lobby; good view, caters for European package tours, lakeside pool and restaurant.

C Villa del Lago, 15 de Septiembre, T7926-0508. Very clean rooms with a/c and fan, cheaper with shared bath, some rooms with lake view and balcony. Breakfast is served on a terrace with lake view, but the service is excruciatingly slow. The breakfast menu is open to non-guests, but avoid it in high season unless you don't mind a long wait.

E Hospedaje Doña Goya, Calle Unión, T7926-3538. 6 basic but clean rooms, 3 with private bath, cheaper without, 3 with balcony, terrace with superb views, internet, book exchange, kitchen, hammocks on thatched roof terrace; friendly, family-run.

E-G Tayazal, Calle Unión, T7867-5333. Rooms of various sizes, a bit dingy but OK, with fan, showers downstairs, some with private bath as well as dorms, roof terrace, very accommodating, can arrange a Tikal trip. Travel agency in reception.

F La Unión, Calle La Unión, T7867-5531. Basic but clean rooms with tiny balcony and lake view, very friendly.

F Mirador del Lago, Calle 15 de Septiembre, T7926-3276. Beautiful view of the lake and a jetty to swim from. All with private bathrooms and (irregular) hot water. One of the better budget hotels and it has lake access. The annexe opposite is quiet. All with fan.

F-G Hostal Los Amigos, Calle Centro América and Av Barrios, T7867-5075, www.amigos hostel.com. Dorms with 20 beds, private rooms, luxury dorms and hammocks with a funky courtyard. Good, cheap restaurant; bar and internet available. Very helpful and friendly. Very popular with backpackers but can be crowded and noisy; highly recommended. It also rents out hammocks and mosquito nets for tours to Tikal.

Santa Elena *p321, map p323*

L Hotel Casona del Lago, overlooking the lake, T7952-8700, www.hotelesdepeten.com. 32 spacious rooms, some with balcony, in this lovely duck-egg blue and white hotel. Pool, restaurant, internet and travel agency.

AL Petén Espléndido, 1 Calle, T7926-0880, www.petenesplendido.com. Small but well-furnished rooms with a/c, TV and some with lake view. A great lakefront restaurant setting (0600-2200), with beautiful pool on the lake. Pool open to non-guests for a small fee. Range of business services available.

A Maya Internacional, lakefront, T7926-2083, www.villasdeguatemala.com. Bungalows and rooms beautifully situated and with all services. Room 52 is particularly delightful. Restaurant and pool open to non-guests, 0630-2100.

B Hotel del Patio Tikal, corner of Calle 2 and Av 8, T7926-0104, www.hoteldelpatio.com.gt. Clean, modern rooms with a/c, TV, expensive restaurant, beautiful pool and gym. It's best booked as part of a package for cheaper rates.

C Casa de Elena, Av 6, just before the causeway, T7926-2235. With a beautiful tiled staircase, rooms have cable TV, pool, restaurant 0630-2100.

E-G San Juan, Calle 2, close to the Catholic church, T7926-0562, sanjuanttravel@ hotmail.com.gt. Full of budget travellers in the older rooms, cheaper with shared bath, not always spotless. Some remodelled rooms with a/c and TV. Exchanges US dollars and Mexican pesos and buys Belizean dollars. It's not the nicest place to stay but it's safe, there's a public phone inside and parking. Note that the Tikal minibuses leave from 0500 so you will probably be woken early.

Around Lake Petén Itzá *p324*

To reach the lodgings along the north shore of the lake can be up to a 2-km walk from El Remate centre, depending on where you stay (turn left, west on the Flores–Tikal main road). There is street light up to the Biotopo entrance until 2200.

L Bahía Taitzá Hotel and Restaurant, Barrio El Porvenir, San José, T7928-8125, www.taitza.com. 8 lovely rooms decorated with local furnishings set behind a beautiful lawn that sweeps down to the lakeshore. Rates include breakfast and transfer. Restaurant on site.

L-AL La Lancha, T7928-8331, www.blanca neaux.com. Francis Ford Coppola's attractive, small hotel has 10 tastefully furnished rooms, 4 of which have lake views from balconies. There's a pool and terrace restaurant serving excellent local cuisine, and local arts and crafts have been used to decorate the rooms.

Quiet and friendly in a lovely setting, with horse riding and kayaking trips available.

AL Camino Real, 1.8 km from the western entrance of Biotopo Cerro Cahuí, El Remate, T7926-0204, www.caminorealtikal.com.gt. All rooms have views, good restaurant, a/c, cable TV, lovely pool in an attractive setting.

A Hotel Ni'tun, 2 km from San Andrés on the Santa Elena road, T5201-0759, www.nitun.com. Luxury *cabañas* on a wooded hillside above the lake, run by friendly couple Bernie and Lore, who cook fantastic vegetarian meals and organize expeditions to remote sites.

C Hotel Casa Amelia, Calle La Unión, T7867-5430, www.hotelcasamelia.com. Cheerful and friendly hotel with 15 comfortable, a/c rooms – 6 of which have lake views. Guests can enjoy a terrace and pool table.

D La Casa de Don David, 20 m from the main road, on the El Remate side, T7928-8469, www.lacasadedondavid.com. Clean and comfortable; all rooms with private bath and some with a/c. Great view from the terrace restaurant with cheap food, bike hire free. Transport to Tikal and other tours offered. There's a wealth of information here and helpful advice is offered.

D-F Hotel y Restaurante Mon Ami, on the El Remate side, T7928-8413, www.hotelmon ami.com. Guided tours to Yaxhá and Nakum organized with the owner who is a conservationist. Lovely bungalows, dorms (**F** per person) and hammocks for sleeping. English, French and Spanish spoken. Restaurant 0700-2130, with wines and seriously cheap chicken, pastas and other dishes served.

E La Unión, Calle Unión, T7867-5634, gulzam75@hotmail.com. Formerly a restaurant and now a hotel with 14 rooms, all with hot water and private bathroom. Internet café in lobby and also rents kayaks.

E-F Sun Breeze Hotel, exactly on the corner, on the El Remate side, T7928-8044. Run by the very friendly Humberto Castro. Little wooden rooms with views over the lake. Fans and *mosquiteros* in each room. 2 rooms with private bathroom. He runs a daily service to Tikal and can run other trips.

F La Casa Doña Tonita, on the El Remate side, T5701-7114. One of the most chilled out places along the shore and popular, with a friendly, warm family running the place. Shared bathroom, rooms and a dorm. Enormous portions of good food. Highly recommended.

F-G La Casa Roja, on the El Remate side, T5909-6999. A red house with a tranquil, oriental feel. Rooms are under thatched roofs, with separate bathrooms in attractive stone and wood design. The rooms don't have doors but there are locked trunks. Hammock space and camping possible. Kayaks for rent and trips arranged. Recommended.

G El Mirador del Duende, on the main Flores–Tikal road in El Remate Village, T7926-0269, miradordelduende@gmail.com. Overlooks lake, camping, cabins, veggy food, jungle trips, canoes, boat trips, mountain bikes, horses and guides are available.

G La Casa de Don Juan, on the main Flores–Tikal road in El Remate Village, T5309-7172, casadonjuan@hotmail.com. Rooms out the back behind the restaurant. Owner Don Juan offers tours.

Camping

Campsite with hammock facilities at El Sotz, just before El Remate.

Parque Nacional Tikal *p325*
You are advised to book when you arrive; in high season, book in advance. Take a torch: 24-hr electricity is not normally available.

A-B Tikal Inn, T7926-1917. Bungalows and rooms, hot water 1800-1900, electricity 0900-1600, 1800-2200, beautiful pool for guest use only. Natural history tours at 0930 for US$10, minimum 2 people, helpful.

A-C Jungle Lodge, T5361-4098, www.quik. guate.com/jltikal/index.html. Spacious, comfortable bungalows, with bath, 24-hr hot water and fan (electricity 0700-2100), pool; cheaper without bath. It will cash TCs, full board available (although we've had consistent reports of unsatisfactory food, slow service and small portions). Jungle Lodge's Tikal tours have been recommended.

B Jaguar Inn, T7926-0002, www.jaguar tikal.com. Full board, less without food. There is also a dorm with 6 beds. Hammocks with mosquito nets and lockers. Electricity 1800-2200, hot water in the morning or on request Mar-Oct and Nov-Feb, 0600-2100. It will provide a picnic lunch and stores luggage.

Camping

G Camping Tikal, run by the Restaurante del Parque, reservations T2370-8140, or at the Petén Espléndido, T7926-0880. If you have your own tent or hammock it is US$5. If you need to rent the gear it is US$8. There are also *cabañas* with mattresses and mosquito nets for US$7 per person. It also does deals that include breakfast, lunch and dinner ranging from US$15-30 for a double. Communal showers available. Take your own water as the supply is very variable.

Uaxactún *p329*
E-G El Chiclero, T7926-1095. Neat and clean, hammocks and rooms in a garden, also good food by arrangement.

G Aldana's Lodge, T5801-2588, edeniaa@ yahoo.com. Little white *casitas*, tent and hammock space behind El Chiclero. Just before El Chiclero take a left on the road to the ruins and then first right until you see a whitewashed *casita* on the right (2 mins). Clean and run by a friendly family.

Sayaxché *p332*
D-E Guayacán, close to ferry, T7928-6111. Owner Julio Godoy is a good source of information.

D-F Hotel Posada Segura, turn right from the dock area and then first left, T7928-6162. Some rooms with bath, TV, clean; one of the best options in town.

Petexbatún *p333*
A Chiminos Island Lodge, T2335-3506, www.chiminosisland.com. Remote, small ecolodge close to a Maya site on a peninsula on the river. Great for exploring local sites, fishing and wildlife spotting. Includes all food.

A Posada Caribe, T7928-6117, including 3 meals, comfortable *cabañas* with bathroom and shower, excursion to **Aguateca** by launch and a guide for excursions.

Camping

Camping is possible at Escobado, on the lakeside.

● Eating

Flores *p321, map p322*

¶¶¶-¶¶ Raíces, T5521-1843 raicesrestaurante@gmail.com. Excellent waterfront restaurant beside the *lanchas* near the far west end of Calle Sur. Specialities include *parillas* and kebabs. Great seafood.

¶¶-¶ Café Arqueológico Yax-há, Calle15 de Septiembre, T5830-2060, www.cafeyaxha.com. Cheap daily soups, Maya specialities, such as chicken in tamarind sauce, great smoothies, and home-made nachos. German owner Dieter offers tours to little-known Maya sites (speaks English too) and works with local communities to protect them.

¶¶-¶ Hacienda del Rey, Calle Sur. Expensive Argentine steaks are on the menu, but the breakfasts are seriously cheap.

¶¶-¶ La Albahaca, Calle 30 de Junio. 1st-class home-made pasta and chocolate cake.

¶¶-¶ La Luna, Av 10 de Noviembre. Closed Sun. Refreshing natural lemonade, range of fish, meat and vegetarian dishes. The restaurant has a beautiful courtyard with blue paintwork set under lush pink bougainvillea. Recommended.

¶¶ La Villa Del Chef, T4366-3822, lavilladelchef_guatemala@yahoo.com. Friendly German-owned restaurant at the South end of Calle Unión that specializes in *pescado blanco*. Has a happy hour and also rents canoes for lake tours. Recommended.

¶¶ Mayan Princess Restaurant Café Bar and Cinema, Reforma and 10 de Noviembre. Closed Sun. Has the most adventurous menu on the island including daily specials, many with an Asian flavour, relaxed atmosphere,

with bright coloured textile cloths on the tables. Internet and free films.

¶¶-¶ Capitán Tortuga, Calle 30 de junio. Pizzas, pasta and bar snacks, with dayglo painted walls and lakeside terrace.

¶¶-¶ La Galería del Zotz, 15 de Septiembre. A wide range of food, delicious pizzas, good service and presentation, popular with locals.

¶¶-¶ Las Puertas Café Bar, Av Santa Ana and Calle Central, T7867-5242. Closes at 2300 for food and 2400 completely. Closed Sun. Cheap breakfasts, huge menu, good large pasta portions. It's popular at night with locals and travellers and is in an airy building, chilled atmosphere, games available.

¶ Café Uka, Calle Centro América. Open from 0600. Filling breakfasts and meals.

¶ Cool Beans, Calle Fraternidad, T5571-9240, coolbeans@itelgua.com. Cheap food with home-made bread and pastries.

¶ El Mirador, overlooking the lake but view obscured by restaurant wall. Seriously cheap food and snacks but service slow.

¶ La Canoa, Calle Centro América. Good breakfasts (try the pancakes), dinners start at US$1.50, with good *comida típica*, very friendly owners.

¶ Suica, Calle Fraternidad. Small place serving an unusual mix of sushi, tempura and curries (open 1200-1900, closed Sun).

Santa Elena *p321, map p323*

¶¶ El Rodeo, 1 Calle. Excellent, reasonable prices, classical music and sometimes impromptu singing performances.

¶ El Petenchel, Calle 2. Vegetarian food served here as well as conventional meats and meals. Excellent breakfasts. Good-value *menú del día*. Music played, prompt service.

¶ Restaurante Mijaro, Calle 2 and Av 8. Great filling breakfasts and a bargain *menú del día* at US$1.70, all in a thatched-roofed roadside location.

Uaxactún *p329*

¶ Comedor Imperial, at village entrance. Bargain *comida típica* for US$1.30.

Sayaxché *p332*

♦♦♦ **El Botanero Café Restaurante and Bar**, straight up from the dock and 2nd left. A funky wooden bar with logs and seats carved from tree trunks.

♦ **Restaurant La Montaña**, near dock. Cheap food, local information given.

♦ **Yakín**, near dock. Cheap, good food; try the *licuados*.

▲ Activities and tours

Flores and Santa Elena *p321*, maps *p322 and 323*

Conservation Tours Tikal, Calle 15 de Septiembre, opposite Oficina Contable Tayasal, run by Lucía Prinz, T7926-0670, nermeild@yahoo.com.gt.php?id=3 (or ask at Las Puertas). This organization, funded by UNESCO, employs people from Petén communities to take visitors on tours to local sites. English and Spanish spoken. Also walking tours in the jungle, birdwatching, horse and kayak tours also. 5% of profits go to conservation.

Equinoxio, Calle Unión, T4250- 6384, sergioequinoxio@yahoo.es. Bus and airline tickets as well as Tikal tours.

Explore, 2a Calle 3-55, Sta Elena, T7926-2375, www.exploreguate.com. Very helpful, reliable and professional operator offering tours to Tikal, Aguateca, Dos Pilas, Ceibal and Yaxhá.

Martsam Travel, Calle 30 de Junio, T7867-5377, www.martsam.com. Guided tours to Tikal, El Zotz, El Mirador, El Perú, Yaxhá, Nakum, Aguateca, Ceibal and Uaxactún. Guides with wildlife and ornithological knowledge in addition to archaeological knowledge. Highly recommended.

San Juan Travel Agency, T7926-0042, www.corporacionsanjuandelnorte.com, offers transport (US$7.50 return) to Tikal and excursions to Ceibal, Uaxactún, and Yaxhá (US$80). Service to Belize, US$20, 0500 and 0700, 5 hrs, pickup from hotels Also to Chetumal, Mexico, at 0500 and 0730, US$20, 7 hrs. To Palenque at 0500, US$35, 7 hrs.

Tikal Connection, International Airport, T7926-1537, www.tikalcnx.com, runs tours to El Perú, El Mirador, Nakbé, El Zotz, Yaxhá, Dos Aguadas, Uaxactún. It also sells bus tickets.

Viajes de Tivoli, Calle Centroamerica, T5436-6673, www.tivoli.com.gt. Trips to local sites as well as general agency services.

Uaxactún *p329*

For guided walks around the ruins ask for one of the trained guides, US$10. For expeditions further afield, contact Elfido Aldana at **Posada Aldana**. Neria Baldizón at **El Chiclero** has high-clearance pickups and plenty of experience in organizing both vehicle and mule trips to any site. She charges US$200 per person to go to Río Azul.

Sayaxché *p332*

Viajes Don Pedro, on the river front near the dock, T7928-6109, runs launches to El Ceibal (US$35 for up to 3), Petexbatún and Aguateca (US$60 for up to 5), Dos Pilas (US$50 for small group). Trip possible by jeep in the dry season, Altar de los Sacrificios (US$100 minimum 2 people) and round trips to Yaxchilán for 3 days (US$400). Mon-Sat 0700-1800, Sun 0700-1200.

◉ Transport

Poptún *p321*
Bus

Take any **Fuente del Norte** bus or any bus heading to the capital from **Flores**, 2 hrs. To Flores catch any Flores-bound bus from the capital. To **Río Dulce**, 2 hrs. Buses will drop you at the driveway to **Finca Ixobel** if that's your destination, just ask. From there it's a 15-min walk. Or, get off at the main bus stop and arrange a taxi there or through **Finca Ixobel**. To **Guatemala City** there are plenty daily, 7-8 hrs, US$10-13. The only bus that continues to **Fray Bartolomé de las Casas** (Las Casas on the bus sign) leaves at 1030, 5¾ hrs, US$8.

Flores and Santa Elena *p321,*
maps p322 and p323

Air
Be early for flights, as overbooking is
common. The cost of a return flight is
between US$180-220, shop around. **Grupo
Taca**, T2470-8222, www.taca.com, leaves
Guatemala City daily at 0645, 0955, 1725,
1 hr, returns 0820, 1605 and 1850. **Tag**,
T2360-3038, www.tag.com.gt, flies at 0630
returning 1630. To **Cancún**, Grupo Taca.
To **Belize City**, Tropic Air, www.tropicair.com.

Boat
Lanchas moor along Calle Sur, Flores;
behind the **Hotel Santana**; from the dock
behind **Hotel Casona de Isla**; and beside
the arch on the causeway.

Bus
Local Local buses (chicken buses), US$0.26,
Flores to Santa Elena, leave from the end of
the causeway in Flores.

Long distance All long-distance buses
leave from the relocated bus terminal,
6 blocks south of the Calle Principal in Santa
Elena. It has a snack bar, toilets, seating and
ATM. Opposite are restaurants, *comedores*,
and a bakery. Banrural is down the side.
To **Guatemala City**, Línea Dorada, daily
office hours 0500-2200, www.tikalmayan
world.com, leaves 1000, 2100, 1st class,
US$30; 2200, US$16, 8 hrs. **Autobuses del
Norte (ADN)**, T7924-8131, www.adnauto
busesdel norte.com, luxury service, 1000,
2100, 2300, US$23. **Fuente del Norte**,
T7926-0666, office open 24 hrs, buses every
45 mins-1 hr, 0330-2230, US$12, 9 hrs.
At 1000, 1400, 2I00, 2200, US$20, 7-8 hrs.
2nd-class buses, **Rosita**, T7926-5178 and
Rápidos del Sur, T7924-8072, also go to
the capital, US$13. If you are going only to
Poptún, 2 hrs, or **Río Dulce**, 3½-4 hrs, make
sure you do not pay the full fare to Guatemala
City. To **Sayaxché** with Pinita, T9926-0726,
at 1100, returns next day at 0600, US$2.50.
With **Fuente del Norte** at 0600, US$1.70,

returning 0600. *Colectivos* also leave every
15 mins 0530-1700, US$2.40. Buses run
around the lake to **San Andrés**, with one
at 1200 with **Pinita** continuing to **Cruce dos
Aguadas,** US$2.90 and **Carmelita**, US$3.30
for access to El Mirador. Returning from
Carmelita at 0500 the next day. Minibuses
also run to San Andrés. To **Chiquimula**, take
Transportes María Elena, T5550-4190, at
0400, 0800, 1300, US$3. The **María Elena** bus
continues onto **Esquipulas**, 9 hrs, US$12.
Fuente del Norte to **Cobán**, 0530, 0630,
1230, 1330, 5 hrs, US$8. Or take a minibus
to Sayaxché and change. Shuttle transfers
may also be possible. To **Jutiapa**, 0500,
0530, 7 hrs, returning 0900, US$10-12.

International To **Belize City**, see page 348.
To **Melchor de Mencos** at the Belize border,
0500, 0600, 1630, 2300, 1½ hrs, US$3.30.
Returning 0200, 0500, 0600, 1630, 2300.
Also with **Línea Dorada** and on to **Chetumal**,
Mexico, see also box, page 58.
   To **Copán Ruinas**, **Honduras**, take
Transportes María Elena, T5550-4190,
to Chiquimula at 0400, 0800, 1300,
US$13 then from Chiquimula to El
Florido (see page 198) and finally on to
Copán Ruinas. Alternatively, take any bus
to the capital and change at Río Hondo.
To **Mexico**, see box, page 58. To **San
Salvador**, 0600, 8 hrs, US$26.70.

Car
There are plenty of agencies at the airport,
mostly Suzuki jeeps, which cost about
US$65-80 per day. **Hertz**, at the airport,
T7926-0332. **Garrido** at Sac-Nicte Hotel,
Calle 1, Santa Elena, T7926-1732.
   Petrol is sold in Santa Elena at the 24-hr
Texaco garage on the way to the airport.

Around Lake Petén Itzá *p324*
Boat
Public *lanchas* from San Benito have virtually
come to a stop. Visitors can still charter a
lancha from Flores for about US$10.

Bus

There's a bus ticket and internet office opposite the turning to El Remate. Any bus/shuttle heading for Tikal can stop at El Remate, US$2.50, last bus around 1600; taxi around US$10. Returning to **Flores**, pick up any shuttle heading south (this is a lot easier after 1300 when tourists are returning). There is a bus service heading to **Flores** from El Remate at 0600, 0700, 0830, 0930, 1300 and 1400. Shuttles leave every 30 mins for San Andrés, US$0.70, 30 mins and go on to San José.

Uaxactún *p329*

Bus To Uaxactún from Santa Elena at 1200 arriving between 1600-1700, US$2.60, returning 0500 with **Transportes Pinita**. Foreigners have to pay US$2 to pass through Parque Nacional Tikal on their way to Uaxactún, payable at the main entrance to Tikal.

El Mirador, El Tintal and Nakbé *p331*

Bus 1 bus daily with **Transportes Pinita** to **Carmelita**. See Flores for information.

Northwest Petén and the Mexican border *p332*

Boat and bus To **El Naranjo** at 0500 and 1000, returning at 0500, 1100 and 1300, US$4. Or hire a *lancha* from Paso Caballos.

Sayaxché *p332*

Bus There are buses to **Flores**, 0600, 0700, 1-2 hrs, and microbuses every 30 mins. To **Raxrujá** and on to **Cobán** via **Chisec** at 0400, US$.80, 6½ hrs direct to Cobán. There are pickups after that hourly and some further buses direct and not via Chisec. For **Lanquín** take the bus to Raxrujá, then a pickup to Sebol, and then a pickup to Lanquín, or the Lanquín *cruce* at Pajal, and wait for onward transport. If you are heading to **Guatemala City** from here it could be quicker to head north to Flores rather than take the long road down to Cobán. However, this road has now been entirely tarmacked.

Petaxbatún *p333*

Boat It is 30-40 mins in *lancha* from Sayaxché to the stop for **Dos Pilas** to hire horses. It's 50 mins-1 hr to **Chiminos** lodge and 1 hr 20 mins to the **Aguateca** site. To Dos Pilas and Aguateca from Chiminos, US$27 return to each site.

● Directory

Flores and Santa Elena *p321, maps p322 and 323*

Banks Banrural, Flores, next to the church. TCs only. **Banco del Café**, Santa Elena, best rates for Amex TCs. Do not use its ATM: it eats cards by the dozen. **Banco de los Trabajadores**, Santa Elena, MasterCard accepted. **Banco Agromercantil**, Santa Elena, open until 1800. **Banco Industrial**, MasterCard only. The major hotels and travel agents change cash and TCs. There's a bank opposite the bus terminal. **Immigration** at the airport, T7926-0984. **Internet** There are plenty of places. Hotel internet terminals tend to have fairer prices than the internet shops. **Laundry** Lavandería Petenchel, wash and dry. Open 0800-1900. **Medical services** Hospital Nacional, in San Benito, T7926-1333, open 24 hrs. **Centro Médico Maya**, 4 Av 335, Santa Elena, T7926-0810, speaks some English. Recommended. **Post** In Flores and in Santa Elena. **Telephone** Telgua in Santa Elena and some travel agencies. **Volunteering** See ARCAS, page 206. Also www.volunteer peten.com, and Women's Association for the Revival of Traditional Medicine, T5514-8889.

Around Lake Petén Itzá *p324*

Language schools Eco-Escuela Español, San Andrés, T5940-1235, www.ecoescuelaespanol.org. 20 hrs of classes, homestay and extra curricular activities for a week, US$150. The Escuela Bio-Itzá, San José, www.ecobioitza.org offers classes, homestay and camping for the same price.

Contents

Belize

At a glance

⊖ **Getting around** Bus and plane, with the odd boat trip out to the cayes. Boats to Guatemala and Honduras.

◉ **Time required** You'll get a feel for the country in a fortnight – but longer is better.

☀ **Weather** Warm throughout the year, wettest from Jun-Oct.

✕ **When not to go** Jun and Jul are the wettest months – a real dampener if you're on the beach.

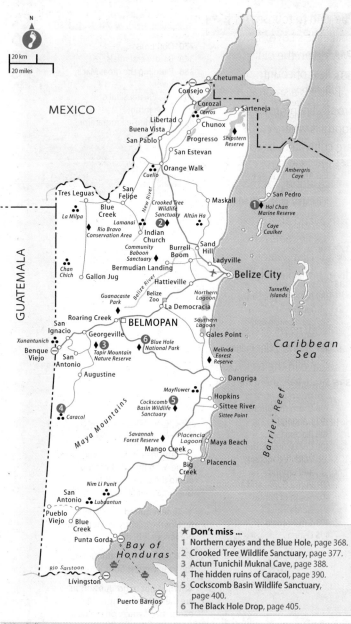

N

20 km
20 miles

MEXICO

Chetumal
Consejo
Corozal ○ Sarteneja
Cerros
Libertad
Buena Vista ○ Chunox
San Pablo ○ Progresso
San Estevan *Shipstern Reserve*
Cuello
Orange Walk

Tres Leguas *Ambergris Caye*

San Felipe ○ San Pedro **1** ◆ Hol Chan Marine Reserve

GUATEMALA

Blue Creek
La Milpa Lamanai ○ Crooked Tree Wildlife Sanctuary ○ Maskall
◆ Rio Bravo Conservation Area *Caye Caulker*
2 ◆ Altún Ha
Indian Church

Chan Chich Community Baboon Sanctuary ○ Burrell Boom ○ Sand Hill
Bermudian Landing ◆ Ladyville
Gallon Jug ○ Hattieville ✈ ○ **Belize City**

Guanacaste Park ◆ Belize River *Northern Lagoon* *Turneffe Islands*
Roaring Creek Belize Zoo ○ La Democracia
San Ignacio ○ **BELMOPAN** *Southern Lagoon*
Xunantunich ○ Georgeville ◆ Gales Point
Benque Viejo ○ **3** ◆ Tapir Mountain Nature Reserve **6** ◆ Blue Hole National Park *Caribbean Sea*
San Antonio ○ Melinda Forest Reserve

Augustine ○ *Mayflower* ◆ ○ Dangriga

4 ◆ Cockscomb Basin Wildlife Sanctuary **5** ◆ Hopkins
Caracol ○ Sittee River
Sittee Point

Maya Mountains Savannah Forest Reserve ◆ *Placencia Lagoon* *Barrier Reef*
Mango Creek ○ Maya Beach
Big Creek ○ Placencia

San Antonio ○ Nim Li Punit
Lubaantun
Pueblo Viejo ○ Blue Creek
Punta Gorda ○

Bay of Honduras

Rio Sarstoon

Lívingston ○

Puerto Barrios ○

★ Don't miss ...
1 Northern cayes and the Blue Hole, page 368.
2 Crooked Tree Wildlife Sanctuary, page 377.
3 Actun Tunichil Muknal Cave, page 388.
4 The hidden ruins of Caracol, page 390.
5 Cockscomb Basin Wildlife Sanctuary, page 400.
6 The Black Hole Drop, page 405.

"Be kind to tourists," says the big friendly voice in the advert on Belize's Love FM, as the beaten-up school bus works its way down the old Hummingbird Highway. Sometimes this smallest of countries appears innocent, naïve and relaxed.

Belize is a smorgasbord of landscapes, from mountainous, tropical rainforests with abundant wildlife to fertile subtropical foothills where cattle are reared, and sugar, rice and fruit trees are cultivated, or coastal wetlands filled with birds and small islands – known as cayes – with beautiful beaches.

Measuring 174 miles north to south and just 80 miles across, the country nestles on the coast between Mexico and Guatemala, with a land area of about 8860 sq miles, including hundreds of cayes. The reefs and cayes form a 184-mile barrier reef with crystal-clear water and are a major attraction for world-class diving, snorkelling and sport fishing. And hidden beneath the depths is the magnificent Blue Hole, one of the world's best dives.

Inland, rivers and rainforest invite you to head out, trekking, paddling and biking, to visit the ancient ruins of the Maya, or to cave in their spiritual underworld. For the beginner and the specialist birdwatching is an endless pleasure.

With a Caribbean history and a Central American geography, Belize is a subtle blend of cultures that encourages the laid-back attitude of the small (just 311,000) but ethnically diverse population, who paint an intriguing picture in this culturally different, English-speaking Central American nation.

Essentials

Where to go

The reputation of **Belize City** is not good but the authorities are working hard to clean it up and present a better face to tourists. Special tourist police have been introduced and crime is much less widespread than it was. That said, you may still be offered drugs on the streets. It is worth spending a day or two having a look around Belize City and getting a feel for the old town – it's not possible to really know Belize if you haven't spent some time in the city. Generally, the longer people stay the better they like it and resident Belizeans are friendly and welcoming. The short journey to visit **Belize Zoo** is definitely worthwhile. A little further on is the tiny capital of **Belmopan**, an hour from Belize City.

The **northern cayes**, a series of paradise islands with crystal-clear waters, palm-fringed beaches and mangroves, are the main hub of tourism. **Ambergris Caye**, more upmarket, and **Caye Caulker**, popular with budget travellers, are the two most developed cayes, from where you can take trips to the smaller cayes and marine parks. They attract a wide range of travellers wishing to sample the delights of a Caribbean island. The atmosphere is laid-back with plenty of watersports for the active, spectacular diving and snorkelling on the barrier reef and outlying cayes and the world-famous **Blue Hole**.

On the mainland, the Northern Highway leads from Belize City to the Mexican border through some of the most productive farmland in the country. There is still plenty of room for wildlife at the **Community Baboon Sanctuary**, for black howler monkeys; the **Crooked Tree Lagoons and Wildlife Sanctuary**, for birds. The archaeological remains of **Lamanai** with a 112-ft temple (the tallest known pre-Classic Maya structure) is easily visited from Orange Walk, and **Altún Ha**, once a major Maya ceremonial site, are essential visits for 'Maya-philes'. The largest town in the north, **Orange Walk**, is a multi-racial city of Mennonites, Creoles, Maya and other Central Americans making their living from agriculture.

The Western Highway leads from Belize City, skirting the capital Belmopan, to **San Ignacio** and the Guatemalan border. San Ignacio and its twin town Santa Elena have a pleasant climate and are in a beautiful setting of wooded hills straddling the Macal River. A side trip to the **Mountain Pine Ridge** area offers great hiking, amid spectacular broadleaf forests, rivers, rapids, waterfalls and caves, making a worthwhile excursion with much to be enjoyed along the entire route to Caracol. There are several Maya sites, notably **Cahal Pech**, on the edge of town; **El Pilar**, north through Bullet Tree Falls; **Xunantunich**, across the Mopan River by hand-cranked ferry at San José Succotz with plazas, temples, ball court and *castillo*; and **Caracol**, the country's largest site to date rivalling Tikal in size, where the Sky Palace pyramid reaches a height of 138 ft.

The Southern Highway runs along the eastern edge of the Maya Mountains, through sparsely populated countryside dotted with indigenous settlements, to Dangriga and Hopkins Village and then past the world-famous **Cockscomb Basin Wildlife (Jaguar) Sanctuary**. The coastal area around **Placencia** offers idyllic palm-fringed beaches, diving and sport fishing, with plenty of accommodation choices for all budgets. Offshore cayes are reached by boat from **Dangriga** or Mango Creek. In the far south is **Punta Gorda** with the ruins of **Lubaantun**, a late-Maya ceremonial site where the infamous Crystal Skull was discovered. You can stay at guesthouses in Maya villages nearby as part of a community tourism project.

Suggested itineraries

There are two simple options: coming from Mexico's Yucatán Peninsula, head south into Belize City, pop out to the cayes then make your way south through Placencia to Punta Gorda and on to Guatemala or Honduras; or go west through San Ignacio visiting the caves of the highlands, and then to Tikal in Guatemala. If coming from Guatemala, visit San Ignacio, Belize City and the cayes before heading south. You can get a good feel for Belize in a fortnight.

When to go

The high season runs from mid-December to March and pushes into May with clear skies and warm temperatures (25-30°C). Inland, in the west, day temperatures can reach 38°C, but the nights are cooler and usually pleasant. Between November and January there are cold spells during which the temperature at Belize City may fall as low as 13°C. Humidity is normally high, making it 'sticky' most of the time in the lowlands.

There are sharp annual variations in rainfall. From 1270 mm in the north and around 1650 mm in Belize City, there is a huge increase up to 4310 mm down in the south. The driest months are April and May; in June and July there are heavy showers followed by blue skies. Around August the *mauger* occurs, a mini dry season of about six weeks. September to November tend to be overcast and there are more insects during these months.

Hurricanes threaten the country from June to November along the coast. An efficient warning system was put in place after Hurricane Mitch and most towns and large villages have hurricane shelters. 'Hurricane Preparedness' instructions are issued annually. Do not ignore local instructions about what to do following a forecast.

What to do

Archaeology

The protection of Belize's Maya heritage and its development into tourism sites is high on the agenda. Further excavation and protection of sites, better access, construction of tourist facilities like visitor centres and small souvenir shops, the availability of brochures and knowledgeable guides are all part of the plan. For information contact the **Archaeology Department**, T822-2106, in Belmopan, where there are plans underway for a Museum of Archaeology.

Caving

Belize has some of the longest caving systems in the world. Main attractions in caves are crystal formations, but most of the caves in Belize were also used by the Maya, and in some Maya artefacts have been found. While government permission is required to enter unexplored systems, simple cave

exploration is easy. From San Ignacio, tours go to Chechem Ha, Barton Creek and Actun Tunichil Muknal Cave, known for their Maya artefacts. The best one-stop shop for all levels is the **Caves Branch Jungle Lodge** (see page 405) on the Hummingbird Highway close to the entrance to the Blue Hole National Park.

Diving

The shores are protected by the longest barrier reef in the Western Hemisphere. The beautiful coral formations are a great attraction for scuba-diving, with canyons, coves, overhangs, ledges, walls and endless possibilities for underwater photography.

Lighthouse Reef, the outermost of the 3 north-south reef systems, offers pristine dive sites in addition to the incredible Blue Hole. Massive stalagmites and stalactites are found along overhangs down the sheer vertical walls of the Blue Hole. This outer reef lies beyond the access of most land-based diving resorts and even beyond most fishermen, so the marine life is undisturbed. An ideal way to visit is on a live-aboard boat. An exciting marine phenomenon takes place during the full moon each Jan in the waters around Belize when thousands of the Nassau groupers gather to spawn at Glory Caye on Turneffe Reef.

Note There are decreasing numbers of small fish – an essential part of the coral lifecycle – in the more easily accessible reefs, including the underwater parks. The coral reefs around the northerly, most touristy cayes are dying, probably as a result of tourism pressures, so do your bit to avoid further damage.

Fishing

Belize is a very popular destination for sport fishing, normally quite pricey but definitely worth it if you want to splash out. The rivers offer fewer and fewer opportunities for good fishing, and tilapia, escaped from regional fish farms, now compete with the catfish, tarpon and snook for the food supply. The sea still provides game fish such as sailfish, marlin, wahoo, barracuda and tuna. On the flats, the most exciting fish for light tackle – the bonefish – is found in great abundance.

Note In addition to the restrictions on turtle and coral extraction, the following regulations apply: no person may take, buy or sell crawfish (lobster) between 15 Feb and 14 Jun, shrimp between 15 Mar and 14 Jul, or conch between 1 Jul and 30 Sep.

Nature tourism

Conservation is a high priority in Belize. Tourism vies for the top spot as foreign currency earner in the national economy, and is the fastest-growing industry. Nature reserves are supported by a combination of private and public organizations including the Belize Audubon Society, the government and international agencies.

The **Belize Audubon Society** ① *PO Box 1001, 12 Fort St, Belize City, T223-5004, www.belizeaudubon.org*, manages seven protected areas including Half Moon Caye Natural Monument (3929 ha), Cockscomb Basin Wildlife Sanctuary (41,800 ha – the world's only jaguar reserve), Crooked Tree Wildlife Sanctuary (6480 ha – swamp forests and lagoons with wildfowl), Blue Hole National Park (233 ha), Guanacaste National Park (20.25 ha), Tapir Mountain Nature Reserve (formerly known as Society Hall Nature Reserve; 2731 ha – a research area with Maya presence) and the Shipstern Nature Reserve (8910 ha – butterfly breeding, forest, lagoons, mammals and birds, contact BAS or the International Tropical Conservation Foundation, through www.shipstern.org).

The **Río Bravo Management and Conservation Area** (105,300 ha) bordering Guatemala to the northwest of the country, covers some 4% of the country and is managed by the **Programme for Belize** ① *PO Box 749, 1 Eyre St, Belize City, T227-5616, www.pfbelize.org*.

Other parks include the Community Baboon Sanctuary at Bermudian Landing, Bladen Nature Reserve (watershed and primary forest) and Hol Chan Marine Reserve (reef eco-system). More recently designated national parks and reserves include: Five Blue Lakes National Park, based on an unusually deep karst lagoon, and a maze of exotic caves and sinkholes near St Margaret Village on the Hummingbird Highway; Kaax Meen Elijio Panti National Park, at San Antonio Village near the Mountain Pine Ridge Reserve; Vaca Forest Reserve (21,060 ha); and Chiquibul National Park (107,687 ha – containing the Maya ruins of Caracol). There's also Laughing Bird Caye National Park (off Placencia), Glovers Reef Marine Reserve, and Caye Caulker, which now has a marine reserve at its north end.

Belize Enterprise for Sustained Technology (BEST) ⓘ *Mile 54 Hummingbird Highway, PO Box 35, Belmopan, T822-3043, www.best.org.bz*, is a non-profit organization committed to the sustainable development of Belize's disadvantaged communities and community-based ecotourism, for example Gales Point and Hopkins Village.

On 1 June 1996 a **National Protected Areas Trust Fund (PACT)** ⓘ *www.pactbelize.org*, was established to provide finance for the "protection, conservation and enhancement of the natural and cultural treasures of Belize". Funds for PACT come from a US$3.75 conservation fee paid by all foreign visitors on departure by air, land and sea, and from 20% of revenues derived from protected areas entrance fees, cruise ship passenger fees, etc. Visitors pay only one PACT tax every 30 days, so if you go to Tikal for a short trip from Belize, show your receipt in order not to pay twice.

Getting there

Air

From North America and Europe With the exception of neighbouring countries, international services to Belize go through the USA, with **American Airlines**, **Continental**, **Delta** and **United**. There are no direct flights from Europe. Most flights from Europe go through the US and require an overnight stop in Miami or Houston.

From Central America There are daily connections to San Salvador with **Grupo Taca** and Flores (Guatemala) with **Maya Island Air**, www.mayaislandair.com, and **Tropic Air**, www.tropicair.com.

Road

The most commonly used routes are with the Petén Department of Guatemala at Benque Viejo del Carmen (see page 348) and, to the north, at the border with Chetumal on Mexico's Yucután Peninsula (see page 58). Both immigration offices have been remodelled, reducing the waiting times. A less widely used crossing, for non-vehicular travellers, is at La Unión, where there are immigration facilities.

Sea

Boat services link the south of the country with Honduras and Guatemala. From Puerto Barrios, Guatemala, there is a boat service to Punta Gorda (see page 348); from Puerto Cortés, Honduras, a boat goes to Placencia, via Mango Creek. Obtain all necessary exit stamps and visas before sailing – see under each town for details.

Getting around

Air

Maya Island Air and **Tropic Air** (see page 362) both provide in-country flights to the cayes, Corozal, Dangriga, Placencia and Punta Gorda; both have good safety records and regular schedules. It costs less to fly from the Municipal Airport in Belize City than from the International Airport to the same destination. There is one exception: if making a connection for an international flight, it is cheaper to arrive at the International Airport, than to take a taxi the 10 miles from the Municipal Airport to the International Airport.

Border essentials

Belize–Mexico

For crossings between Belize and Mexico (Chetumal–Santa Elena), see page 58.

Belize–Guatemala

Benque Viejo–Menchor de Mencos

A popular crossing with travellers heading between Belize and Tikal. Taxi rip-offs are common; bargain hard.

Currency exchange Good rates for quetzales, Belizean dollars and Mexican pesos on the street; or try Banrural at the border (0700-2000).

Belizean immigration Open 0600-2000.

Guatemalan immigration Open 0500-2100.

Onwards to Guatemala There are several buses a day from Melchor de Mencos to Sana Elena, two or three hours; colectivos 1½ hours.

Onwards to Belize Regular buses to Belize City. If you leave Santa Elena, Guatemala, at 0500, you can be in Belize City by 1200. Also direct buses Flores–Chetumal (Mexico) with Línea Dorado.

Punta Gorda–Puerto Barrios/Lívingston

Various boat services go from Punta Gorda in Belize to Puerto Barrios and Lívingston in Guatemala. They include Requena Water Taxi (12 Front Street, T722-2070), departing from the dock opposite immigration. Schedules are changing and irregular; arrive as early as possible or better yet, arrange in advance. Bike and motorbike shipment difficult; no permits available in Lívingston.

Currency exchange Money-changers at both sides, but better to buy quetzales in Guatemala. Nowhere to change TCs.

Belizean immigration Obtain stamps from the customs house near the pier on Front Street. Allow up to two hours for processing.

Guatemalan immigration If you arrive in Guatemala by boat, check into immigration immediately. Offices are in Puerto Barrios and Lívingston, both open 24 hours. Exit fees to leave Guatemala by boat are US$10.

Onwards to Guatemala Highway connections from Puerto Barrios to Guatemala City and Flores.

Onwards to Belize Connections with southern Belize.

Airport information The main international airport and arrival point is the **Phillip SW Goldson International Airport** ① *IATA code BZE, Northern Highway, Ladyville, T225-2045, www.pgiabelize.com*, 10½ miles (17 km) from Belize City in. For airport details, see page 355. When leaving by air you'll pay US$20 (payable in US dollars only) including PACT conservation tax (see page 347) plus a US$1.50 security bag fee per person. Departing overland costs US$18.75; by boat, US$3.75.

Road

Bus Public transport between most towns is by bus and, with the short distances involved, there are few long journeys to encounter. Trucks carry passengers to many isolated destinations. Most buses are ex-US school buses with small seats and limited legroom. There are a few ex-**Greyhounds**, mostly used for 'express' services and charters. It is recommended to buy tickets for seats in advance at the depot before boarding the bus. To find out about bus companies schedules go to www.guidetobelize.info (then select travel and then bus). Most buses have no luggage compartments so bags that do not fit on the luggage rack are stacked at the back. Get a seat at the back to keep an eye on your gear, but rough handling is more of a threat than theft.

Belize Shuttles ① *Belize International Airport Ladyville, T631-1749, in the USA T757-383 8024 and Canada T647-724 2004, www.belizeshuttlesandtransfers.com*, offer transfers to and from Belize City, to many other parts of the country, and to Cancún in Mexico and Flores in Guatemala (for the ruins at Tikal). Transport is in US-style air-conditioned minivans and cars. Prices are very reasonable: for example, to Belize City, municipal airport and boat docks (11 daily coinciding with flight arrivals, US$15 per person and US$5 for each additional passenger), San Ignacio (US$25-35 per person and US$5 for each additional person), Placencia via Dangriga and Hopkins (US$35 per person and US$5 for each additional person).

Car Motorists should carry their own driving licence and certificate of vehicle ownership. Third-party insurance is mandatory and can be purchased at any border: US$12.50 a week, US$25 a month, cars and motorbikes are the same, cover up to US$10,000 from the **Insurance Corporation of Belize** ① *7 Daly St, Belize City, T224-5328, www.icbinsurance.com*. Border offices are open Monday-Friday 0500-1700, Saturday 0600-1600. There are also offices in every district. Valid International Driving Licences are accepted in place of Belize driving permits. Fuel costs about US$4.95. Unleaded gasoline is now available in Belize.

Car hire When choosing a car rental company (see page 363) check if it will release registration papers to enable cars to enter Guatemala or Mexico. Without obtaining them at the time of hire it is impossible to take hire cars across national borders. Car hire cost is high in Belize owing to the heavy wear and tear on the vehicles. You can expect to pay between US$65 for a Suzuki Samuri and US$125 for an Isuzu Trooper per day. Drive carefully as road conditions are constantly changing and totally unpredictable, with speed bumps, cyclists and pedestrians appearing around every bend. When driving in the Mountain Pine Ridge area it is prudent to check carefully on road conditions at the entry gate; good maps are essential. Emory King's annually updated *Drivers' Guide to Belize* is helpful when driving to the more remote areas.

Hitchhiking While practised freely by locals, hitchhiking is risky and not recommended for travellers. If, however, this is your preferred mode of travel, be prepared for long waits and break the journey down into smaller legs.

Sea
Boats Several boats ferry passengers to the most popular cayes of Caye Caulker and Ambergris Caye, with regular daily services from the Marine Terminal by the swing bridge in Belize City. Further south, boat transport is available at Dangriga to nearby cayes, with a service to Puerto Cortés, Honduras, also stopping at Placencia, as well as from Punta Gorda, with service to Puerto Barrios and Lívingston, Guatemala. In the north there is a daily service between Corozal and San Pedro, Ambergris Caye.

Sleeping

Accommodation throughout the country varies greatly. For the budget traveller there are options in most towns of interest, although prices are higher than in neighbouring countries. While standard hotel options exist, the area around San Ignacio offers several secluded hideaways of varying price and to the south there are options for staying in Maya communities which helps to maintain the cultural identity of the region. The Belize Tourist Board promotes good hotels under US$60 a night through the **Toucan Trail** ⓘ *www.toucantrail.com*. **Belize Travel Services** ⓘ *www.BelizeTravelServices.com*, have the best collection of small, up- and mid-market hotels and guesthouses in the coutry and can organize tours and trips. Because of their concession, rates can be better than booking direct. All hotels are subject to 9% government hotel tax (on room rate only) and 10% service charge is often added. Camping sites are gaining in popularity, and there are private camping facilities to be found in most tourist areas, with a variety of amenities offered. Camping on the beaches, in forest reserves or in any other public place is not allowed. Butane gas in trailer/Coleman stove-size storage bottles is available in Belize, and white gas for camp stoves is available at **Brodies** in Belmopan.

Eating and drinking

Dishes suffer a wonderful preponderance of rice'n'beans – a cheap staple to which you add chicken, fish, beef and so on. For the cheapest meals, order rice which will come with beans and (as often as not) banana or plantain, or chicken, vegetables or even a blending of beef with coconut milk. Belize has some of the best burritos in Central America but you have to seek them out, normally in hidden-away stalls in the markets. Along the coastal region and on the cayes seafood is abundant, fresh and reasonably cheap, but avoid buying lobster between 15 February and 14 June (out of season) as stocks are worryingly low. (Conch is out of season between 1 July and 30 September; Nassau grouper, between 1 December and 31 March.) Better restaurants offer a greater variety and a break from the standards, often including a selection of Mexican dishes; there are also many Chinese restaurants, which are not always good and are sometimes overpriced.

Belikin beer is the local brew, average cost US$3 a bottle. Many brands of local rum are available too. Several local wines and liqueurs are made from available fruit. One favourite, called *nanche*, is made from *crabou* fruit and is very sweet, as is the cashew wine, made from the cashew fruit rather than the nut. All imported food and drink is expensive. A 9% sales tax is added to meals and a 10% service charge may be added as well.

Festivals and events

1 Jan New Year's Day.
Feb Weekend before or after Valentine's Day, Annual Sidewalk Arts Festival, Placencia.
9 Mar Baron Bliss Day; see also page 386.
Early Mar San José Succotz Fiesta.
Mar/Apr Good Fri and Sat and Easter Mon.
Late Apr or May National Agricultural and Trade Show (Belmopan).
1 May Labour Day.
May (variable) Cashew Festival (Crooked Tree), Cayo Expo (San Ignacio), Coconut Festival (Caye Caulker).
24 May Commonwealth Day.
23-25 Jun Lobster Fest, Placencia.
Early to Mid-Jul Benq ue Viejo Fiesta.
Aug International Costa Maya Festival (San Pedro, Ambergris Caye).
10 Sep St George's Caye Day.

21 Sep Belize Independence Day.
11 Oct Pan-American Day.
19 Nov Garífuna Settlement Day, festival normally over the weekend.

25 Dec Christmas Day.
26 Dec Boxing Day.

Most services throughout the country close down Good Friday to Easter Monday; banks close at 1300 on the Thursday, buses run limited services Holy Saturday to Easter Monday, though local flights and boats to the cayes are available. Christmas and Boxing Day are also limited in terms of services. Many shops will open for a few hours on holiday mornings, but still may have limited choices for food. Independence Celebrations begin on St George's Caye Day, 10 September, and there are events occurring daily through to Independence Day, 21 September. The 'September Celebrations', as they are locally called, often start two or three days in advance and require a lot of energy. The most colourful of Belizean festivals is Garífuna Settlement Day in November with celebrations concentrated around Dangriga, Seine Bight and Placencia. The tone of the festival varies greatly with a more public celebration of music and dance in Dangriga, with a more spiritual and quieter ambience in Seine Bight.

Shopping

Indigenous arts and crafts are noticeable primarily for their absence. Carved hardwood objects are widely available. Jewellery made of black coral is occasionally offered but should not be bought. There are some fine Belikin/diving T-shirts. If you want to buy music, Andy Palacio is one of the best punta rock artists.

Essentials A-Z

Customs and duty free

Clothing and articles for personal use are allowed in without payment of duty, though laptop computers, video cameras, mobile phones and CD players and radios that you bring may be stamped on your passport to ensure they leave with you. Other import allowances are: 200 cigarettes or ½ lb of tobacco; 1 litre of alcohol; 1 bottle of perfume. Visitors can take in an unspecified amount of other currencies. No fruit or vegetables may be brought into Belize; searches are infrequent, but can be thorough. Pets must have proof of rabies inoculations and a vet's certificate of good health.

Electricity

110/220 volts single phase, 60 cycles. Some hotels use 12-volt generators.

Embassies and consulates

For the latest information, visit www.belize.gov.bz .

El Salvador, Calle El Bosque Norte and Calle Las Lomas, Candeleria No 1, Block P, Col Jardines de la Cima 1st Stage, San Salvador, T+503-248 1423.

European Communities, Blvd Brand Whitlock 136, 1200 Brussels, Belgium, T+32-2-732 6204, embelize@skynet.be.

Guatemala, 5 Av 5-55, Zona 14, Europlaza, Torre II, Oficina 1502, Guatemala City, T+502-2367 3883, F2367-3884.

Honduras, Hoteles de Honduras, R/do Hotel Honduras Maya, Tegucigalpa, Honduras CA, T+504-238 4616, F238-4617.

Mexico, 215 Calle Bernardo de Galvez, Col Lomas de Chapultepec, Mexico DF 11000, T+52-5520 1274.

Panama, Calle 22, Villa de Las Fuentes, No 1, F-32, Panama City, R de P, T/F+507-236 4132.

UK, 3rd floor, 45 Crawford Place, London, W1H 4LP, T/F+44-20-7723 3603.
USA, 2535 Massachusetts Av, NW Washington DC 20008, T1-202-332-9636.

Health

Those taking standard precautions will find the climate pleasant and healthy. There are no mandatory inoculations required to enter the country unless coming from a country where yellow fever is a problem. Malaria prophylaxis is necessary only if staying in rural areas with poor medical care. Dengue fever is also rare but possible for travellers, and using insect repellent for mosquitoes is the best prevention for both diseases. Insect bites should be carefully scrutinized if not healing or if odd symptoms occur, as the possibilities of Chagas, leishmaniasis, or botfly larvae are all present. **Medical services** have improved in recent years with the completion of the **Karl Heusner Memorial Hospital** in Belize City, though many Belizeans still seek medical care for serious ailments in Mérida or Guatemala City. The **British High Commission** in Belmopan (T822-2146) has a list of doctors and dentists. See page 38 for further information.

Internet

The relatively high cost of telephone calls makes internet surfing and cafés prohibitive. With the exception of San Ignacio, Ambergris Caye and Caye Caulker, internet cafés are less common than in neighbouring countries. When you do find one, the cost is upwards of US$2 per hr.

Language

English is the official language, but Spanish is very widely used, especially in border areas. Creole is spoken by some throughout the country. Mennonite settlers in the north speak a Low German dialect. Several Mayan languages and Garífuna are spoken by ethnic groups to the south.

Media

There are no daily newspapers in Belize. News is available in the weeklies, which generally come out on Friday morning, with the forthcoming Sunday's date: *The Belize Times* (PUP supported), *The Guardian* (UDP supported), *The Reporter* and *Amandala*. Good coverage of Ambergris Caye is provided by *The San Pedro Sun*; likewise, *Placencia Breeze* covers Placencia. Small district newspapers are published sporadically. Radio station *Love FM* (95.1FM) is the perfect summary of Belize on the airwaves. Try www.belizeweb.com for Belizean internet radio.

Money

→ *US$1=Bz$2 (stabilized).*
The monetary unit is the **Belize dollar**. Currency notes issued by the Central Bank are in denominations of 100, 50, 20, 10, 5 and 2 dollars, and coins of 2 dollars and 1 dollar; 50, 25, 10, 5 and 1 cent coins are in use. The American expressions quarter (25c), dime (10c) and nickel (5c) are used, although 25c is sometimes referred to as a shilling. US dollars are accepted everywhere. A common cause for complaint or misunderstanding is uncertainty about which currency you are paying in. The price tends to be given in US$ when the hundred Belizean dollar mark is breached; make sure it is clear from the start whether you are being charged in US or Belizean dollars.

Exchange

See Banks, Belize City, page 363. The government has restricted the exchange of foreign currency to government-licensed *casas de cambio*, but these only operate in major towns. You can still find some money changers at the borders, but the exchange rate is not as high as it has been, and there is a risk of both you and the money changer being arrested and fined.

Cost of living and travelling

The cost of living is high, compared to neighbouring countries, because of the heavy reliance on imports and extra duties. Budget travellers will still be able to get by on about US$45 per person per day if travelling in pairs. Budget travellers can find exploring the interior difficult because public transport is limited to main highways and car hire is beyond the means of many. VAT has been replaced by a 9% sales tax, which is charged on all services, but should not be charged on top of the 9% hotel tax charged on your room. A 1% 'Environmental Tax' is levied on all goods brought into the country.

Opening hours

Businesses 0800-1200, 1300-1600 and Fri 1900-2100, with half day on Wed. Small shops open additionally most late afternoons and evenings, and some on Sun 0800-1000. **Government and commercial offices** Mon-Fri 0800-1200, 1300-1600.

Post

Airmail to Europe takes 8 days and costs US$0.38 for a letter, US$0.20 for a postcard. A letter to USA costs US$0.30 and a postcard costs US$0.15. A letter to Australia costs US$0.50 and a postcard costs US$0.30, and takes 2-3 weeks. **Parcels:** US$3.50 per 0.5 kg to Europe, US$0.38 per 0.5 kg to USA. The service to Europe and USA has been praised, but surface mail is not reliable. Belize postage stamps are very attractive, much in demand, and a trip to the **Philatelic Bureau** in Belize City may provide you with your most treasured souvenir.

Safety

While attacks on foreigners are extremely rare, precautions are still advised, particularly if travelling alone or at night or in deserted areas. Crimes against travellers are harshly punished. Despite the apparent availability of illegal drugs, the authorities are keen to prevent their use. The penalties for possession of marijuana are 6 months in prison or a US$3000 fine, minimum.

Telephone → *Country code T+501*

Information T113. International operator T115.

If you have many calls to make, a card phone works out much cheaper. There is a direct-dialling system between the major towns and to Mexico and USA. Local calls cost US$0.25 for 3 mins, US$0.12 for each extra min within the city, US$0.15-0.55 depending on zone. **Belize Telemedia Ltd**, 1 Church St, Belize City, Mon-Sat 0800-1800, Sun and holidays 0800-1200, has an international telephone, telex and internet service. The entire country's telephone directory is online at www.belizetelemedia.net.

The much-maligned Belizean telephone system is steadily modernizing. Formed in 2007 out of the old BTL, Belize Telemedia is promising to provide the world down the phone line.

Most people now have a mobile phone and most parts of the country have coverage. All towns have a telephone office and in most villages visitors can use the community phone. Payphones and card phones are fairly commonplace in Belize City and elsewhere.

Time

- 6 hrs GMT.

Tipping

In restaurants, 10% of the bill. Taxi drivers are tipped depending on the length of the transfer, whether 'touring' took place or for extra stops, from US$1-10.

Tourist information

The quality and quantity of tourist information in Belize varies greatly. In the popular centres of the cayes, Placencia and the developed sections of Cayo there is a steady supply of information available. Moving away from these popular areas the information is less reliable.

There is an ID card system to validate official tourist guides, which works well in the popular areas. Off the main routes there is less government checking of guides so a more ad hoc system works.

Maps of the country are limited and topographical maps have not been readily available for several years. The best internationally available maps are from ITMB.

Belize Tourism Board, 64 Regent St, Belize City, T227-2420, www.travelbelize. org, also with an office in the Tourism Village, provides information on hotels and a variety of handouts on parks and reserves.

Useful websites

www.belizenet.com, **www.belize.net** and **www.belize.com** Good search engines with general information.
www.governmentofbelize.gov.bz The government site on the country, packed with information on the official angle.
www.belizeaudubon.org and **www.pfbelize.org** Cover many protected areas and have a strong conservation focus.
www.ambergriscaye.com, **www.gocaye caulker.com**, **www.placencia.com** and **www.southernbelize.com** Useful sites.
www.belizex.com Covers the Cayo area.

www.belizereport.com The online version of the *Belize Report*.
www.belizenews.com. Local news and links to the local newspapers (*Amandala*, *The Belize Times*, *The Reporter* and *The Guardian*).

Visas and immigration

All nationalities need passports, as well as sufficient funds and, officially, an onward ticket, although this is rarely requested for stays of 30 days or less. Visas are not usually required by nationals from countries within the EU, Australia and New Zealand, most Caribbean states, the USA and Canada. Citizens of India, Israel, Austria and Switzerland do need a visa. There is a Belizean Consulate in Chetumal, Mexico, at Armada de México 91, T+52-983-21803, US$25. If you need a visa it is best to obtain one in Mexico City or your home country before arriving at the border.

Weights and measures

Imperial and US standard weights and measures.

Belize City and Belmopan

Hardly large enough to warrant the title 'city', in any other country Belize City would be a dusty backwater, but in Belize it is the centre of the country, a blend of Latin American and Caribbean influences. Clapboard houses line dusty streets while people huddle in groups as the world drifts idly by. Born of the Belize River when the logs used to float downstream, it is still the main hub for maritime communications with boat services to the cayes. Nearby Belize Zoo is a model for zoos throughout the world. The capital, Belmopan, enjoys the cursed pleasure of being a planned city. Founded after a devastating hurricane struck Belize City, it has survived as the country's political centre, and has recently grown after several hurricanes have hit the country. ⇥ *For listings, see pages 359-364.*

Belize City → *For listings, see pages 359-364. Colour map 3, A1. Population: 66,700.*

Belize City is the old capital and the largest town in Belize. Many of the houses are wooden, with galvanized-iron roofs. Most stand on seven-foot-high piles – signs of a bygone age when the city used to experience regular flooding. The city has improved greatly in recent years with the cleaning of the canals. Reclaimed land and a spate of building around the Eyre Street area, the Museum of Belize, renovation of the Bliss Institute and the House of Culture suggest plans to improve the city are well underway. The introduction of tourist police has had a marked effect on crime levels, and the situation now requires sensible caution rather than paranoia. However, some areas of the city – particularly to the south and west – are neither particularly safe nor pleasant. Just under a quarter of the total population live here. Humidity is high, but the summer heat is offset by the northeast trades.

Hurricane Keith hit Ambergris Caye in 2000, Hurricane Iris in 2002 and Hurricane Richard in 2010, acting as reminders of the inherent risks of Belize City's lowland location.

Ins and outs

Getting there International flights arrive at **Phillip Goldson International Airport** ⓘ *IATA code BZE, Northern Highway, Ladyville, T225-2045, www.pgiabelize.com,* 10½ miles from Belize City from Belize City along the northern highway. Facilities in the check-in area include toilets, a restaurant, internet, bank (daily 0830-1200 and 1230-1800), viewing deck and duty-free shop. There are no facilities on the arrivals side but you can just walk round to the check-in area. Taxi fares to town are US$25, 30 minutes; taxi drivers strongly discourage sharing so team up, if need be, before getting outside. Make sure your taxi is legitimate by checking for the green licence plates. Taxis all operate on a fixed rate, so you should get the same price quoted by every driver. Ask to see a rate sheet if you have doubts about the price. Any bus going up the Northern Highway passes the airport junction (US$1), then it's a 1½-mile walk. If transferring direct to or from the islands or elsewhere in Belize with a domestic carrier be sure to stipulate that you would like a connection through the international airport. This will cost an extra US$20 or so, offset by avoiding an unnecessary transit through Belize City to the municipal airport or boat dock (and an associated US$25 taxi fare).

Most domestic flights, including the island hops operated by **Maya Island** and **Tropic Air** arrive at the pocket-sized **Belize City Municipal Airport** ⓘ *IATA code TZA,* which is 2 miles north of the city centre on the seafront. A taxi to the city centre will cost around US$10.

Belize City

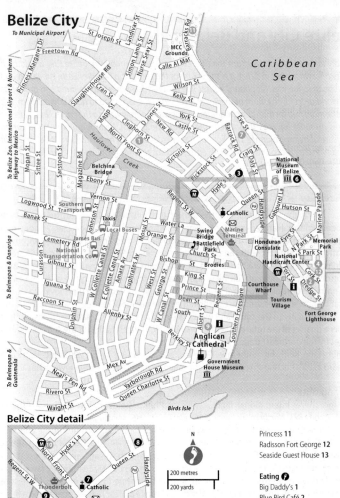

Belize City detail

N

200 metres
200 yards

Sleeping
Bakadeer Inn 1
Chateau Caribbean 4
Freddie's 7
Great House 2
Isabel Guest House 8
Ma Ma Chen 6
Mopan 9
North Front Street Guest House 10
Princess 11
Radisson Fort George 12
Seaside Guest House 13

Eating
Big Daddy's 1
Blue Bird Café 2
Celebrity 6
Dario's 3
Deep Sea Marlin 9
DIT's 4
El Centro 5
Judith's Pastries 7
Nerie's 8

The main **bus station** is on West Collette Canal Street to the west of town, an area that requires some caution. If taking an early morning bus, arrange for a taxi as walking through this part of town in darkness with luggage can be dangerous. Likewise, if arriving after dark take a taxi from outside the station; approximately US$3 to the centre. See Transport, page 362. For **boats** to the Cayes and Mexico, see also page 362.

Getting around Belize City is small enough to walk around when exploring. If going further afield, jump in a cab.

Tourist information **Belize Tourist Board** ① *64 Regent St, Belize City, T227-2420, www.travel belize.org, Mon-Thu 0800-1200, 1300-1700, Fri 0800-1200, 1300-1630,* provides a bus schedule with a map of Belize City, as well as hotel lists. There's also an office in the Tourism Village.

Safety **Tourist police** wearing dark green uniforms patrol the city centre in an attempt to control crime and give advice; their introduction has been encouraging and crime in the city is greatly reduced. Nevertheless, a common-sense approach is needed and a careful eye on your possessions recommended. Watch out for conmen. Guides have to be licensed and should carry a photo ID. Street money changers are not to be trusted. It is wise to avoid small, narrow sidestreets and stick to major thoroughfares, although even on main streets you can be the victim of unprovoked threats and racial abuse. Travel by taxi is advisable, particularly at night and in the rain.

Cars should only be left in guarded car parks. For a tip, the security officer at hotels with secure parking will look after cars for a few days while you go to the cayes.

Sights

Haulover Creek divides the city and is crossed by the antiquated **swing-bridge**, which opens to let large vessels pass, if required, usually between 1730 and 1800. Three narrow canals further divide the city. The main commercial area is either side of the swing-bridge, with most shops on the south side, many being located on Regent and Albert streets and with offices and embassies generally on the northern side. The area around **Battlefield Park** (formerly Central Park) is always busy, with the former colonial administration and court buildings bordering the overgrown park adding to the sense of mischief in the area. At the southern end of Regent Street, the **Anglican Cathedral** (St John's) and **Government House** nearby are interesting. Both were built in the early 19th century and draw on the romantic and grand memories of colonialism. In the days before the foundation of the Crown Colony, the kings of the Mosquito coast were crowned in the cathedral, which was built with bricks brought from England as ships' ballast. In the **cathedral** ① *Mon-Fri 0900-1500 and during Sun services, donation requested,* note the 19th-century memorial plaques that give a harrowing account of early deaths from 'country fever' (yellow fever) and other tropical diseases.

In Government House, the **museum** ① *Mon-Fri 0830-1630, US$5,* contains some interesting pictures of colonial times, displays of furniture and silver and glassware, as well as a one showing fishing techniques and model boats. There are pleasant gardens surrounding the museum if you are looking for somewhere quiet.

The **jail building** (1857) in front of the Central Bank on 8 Gabourel Lane has been beautifully renovated and is now the **National Museum of Belize** ① *T223-4524, www.nichbelize.org Mon-Thu 0830-1700, Fri 0830-1630, US$5,* with exhibits on the history of Belize City and a permanent exhibit on the Maya sites of Belize.

Continuing to the right, pop into the **Image Factory Art Foundation**ⓘ *91 North Front St, www.imagefactorybelize.com, Mon-Fri 0900-1700, free,* for a peek at exhibitions by local artists – more grassroots than the other galleries. Moving towards the end of the peninsula is the **Tourism Village** consisting of souvenir and gift shops and snack bars, along with several handicraft shops. This development caters to tourists arriving from cruise ships. A little further on, at the tip of the peninsula on Marine Parade, is **Memorial Park**, with a small obelisk, two cannon and concrete benches peppered with the holes of land crabs. The views across the bay can be spectacular in the early morning. The park by the **Fort George Lighthouse** has a children's play area and is a popular meeting place. Baron Bliss' tomb is also here. **Belize Zoo** (see page 386) is definitely worth a visit and not far from Belize City. The trip is very easy with buses from Belize City passing the entrance every half hour.

Belmopan and around → *For listings, see pages 359-364. Colour map 3, A1. Population: 20,000.*

As capital of Belize, Belmopan has been the seat of government since August 1970. It is 50 miles inland to the west of Belize City, near the junction of the Western Highway and the Hummingbird Highway to Dangriga (Stann Creek Town). Following the devastation caused in Belize City by Hurricane Hattie in 1961, plans were drawn up for a town that could be a centre for government, business and study away from the coast: Belmopan is the result.

The hurricanes of recent years have prompted a renewed interest in plans to develop the capital, and several government organizations are in the process of relocating to the city, injecting a desperately needed 'heart' to this most eerie of capitals. One possible site of interest would be the **Department of Archaeology**, in the government plaza, which has a vault containing specimens of the country's artefacts. Unfortunately, the vault is currently closed and there are no plans to open it in the near future, although there is a small display and plans to build a museum. Part of the collection is displayed in the **National Museum of Belize** (see above).

Belmopan has the National Assembly building, two blocks of government offices (with broadly Maya-style architecture), the national archives, police headquarters, a public works department, a hospital, over 700 houses for civil servants, a non-governmental residential district to encourage expansion and a market. The Western Highway from Belize City is now good (a one-hour drive), continuing to San Ignacio, and there is an airfield (for charter services only).

Guanacaste National Park
ⓘ *US$2.50.*

One very good reason for stopping nearby is Guanacaste National Park, just outside Belmopan, which is well worth a visit. As Belmopan's accommodation is so expensive it may be better to take an early bus to the park from Belize City or San Ignacio rather than go from the capital. See also page 386.

Belize City and Belmopan listings

Hotel and guesthouse prices

LL over US$200 L US$151-200 AL US$101-150
A US$66-100 B US$46-65 C US$31-45
D US$21-30 E US$12-20 F US$7-11
G under US$7

Restaurant prices

℡℡℡ over US$15 ℡℡ US$8-15 ℡ under US$8

See pages 31-33 for further information.

Sleeping

Belize City p355, map p356

On the north side of the swing-bridge, turn left up North Front St for some of the cheaper hotels.

LL Radisson Fort George, 2 Marine Parade, T223-3333, www.radisson.com/ belizecitybz. In 3 wings (**Club Wing**, where rooms have marble floors and panoramic views of the Caribbean; the **Colonial Section** with balconies overlooking the sea and **Villa**), rooms with partial sea view or pool view. Rooms are excellent with a/c, TV, and bathtubs. The staff are helpful and service is good. Good main restaurant (and **Stonegrill Restaurant** where food is cooked on hot, volcanic stones). 2 lovely pools, fitness room and small garden. Fri pm live music. Bar with large TV screen, open until 2400 at weekends. **Le Petit Café** is also on the premises.

LL-L The Great House, 13 Cork St, T223-3400, www.greathousebelize.com. A beautifully restored white colonial building with 16 rooms furnished in homey style. 2 rooms have ocean view. Ask to read about its interesting history from 1927.

LL-A Princess, King's Park, T223-2670, www.princessbelize.com. On seafront (but not central), marina facilities, casino and bowling, cinema, a/c, good food and service in restaurant and bar (a/c with sea views, expensive), good business facilities, informal calypso bar near the dock is lively at night, nice pool and children's play area.

AL Chateau Caribbean, 6 Marine Parade, by Fort George, T223-0800, www.chateaucaribbean.com. Main building is colonial. Rooms looking a little dated with a/c, good bar, restaurant (excellent Chinese and seafood), sea view, good service, parking.

A-B Mopan, 55 Regent St, T227-7351, www.hotelmopan.com. 14 rooms with bath, a/c, cheaper with fan, TV, in historic house, has restaurant and bar, management very keen to help.

A-D Bakadeer Inn, 74 Cleghorn St, T223-0659. Private bath, a/c, TV, fridge, friendly. Recommended.

B-C Isabel Guest House, 3 Albert St, above Matus Store, T207-3139. Just 3 double rooms, 1 huge triple room, fans and fridges, quiet except when nearby disco operating at weekends, private shower, clean, friendly, safe, Spanish spoken. Isabel is very friendly. Highly recommended.

B-D Seaside Guest House, 3 Prince St, T227-8339, www.seasideguesthouse.org. 6 rooms with private and shared baths, very clean, pleasant veranda with view out to the bay, a great place to stay and meet other travellers. Breakfast, drinks, book swap, credit cards accepted, internet access on site. Consistently recommended.

C Freddie's, 86 Eve St, T223-3851, freddies@btl.net. 3 double rooms with shower and toilet, fan, hot water, clean, very nice, secure, very small.

C Ma Ma Chen, 5 Eve St, T223-4568, ann_chou36@yahoo.com.tw. 4 clean rooms with a/c or fan and private and shared bath. Run by quiet Chinese family with restaurant next door.

D North Front Street Guest House, 124 North Front St, T227-7595. A block north of post office, 4 rooms, no hot water, some have fans, friendly, good information, keep windows closed at night and be sure to lock your door, on street and a bit noisy. Laundry and internet across street.

Belmopan and around *p358*

Belmopan has been described as a disaster for the budget traveller.

L-AL Belmopan Hotel, Constitution Drive, opposite bus stop and market, T822-2130. A/c, hot water, swimming pool, restaurant, bars.

A Bull Frog Inn, 25 Half Moon Av, a 15-min walk east of the market through the parliament complex or a short taxi ride from the bus station, T822-2111, www.bullfroginnbelize.com. A/c, good, reasonably priced, laundry, karaoke nights on Thu (popular with locals).

B-C El Rey Inn, 23 Moho St, T822-3438, www.belmopanhotels.com. Big rooms with fan, hot and cold water, basic, clean, friendly, laundry on request, central.

🍽 Eating

Belize City *p355, map p356*

It can be difficult to find places to eat between 1500-1800.

ⓎⓎⓎ Stone Grill at Radisson Fort George, see Sleeping. The best restaurant in Belize City (as is reflected by the bill), offering traditional Belizean cooking and seafood. Portions are modest.

ⓎⓎⓎ-ⓎⓎ Smoky Mermaid, 13 Cork St, at The Great House (see Sleeping) T223-4759, www.smokymermaid.com. Popular with locals and specializes in snapper and pasta dishes.

ⓎⓎ Celebrity, Marine Parade BLDV, T223-7272, www.celebritybelize.com. Recommended restaurant that serves a wide range of food, from burgers to seafood.

ⓎⓎ Deep Sea Marlin, 13 Regent St West, overlooking Belize River, T227-6995. Varied menu, good seafood.

ⓎⓎ El Centro, 4 Bishop St, T227-2413. Local dishes and burgers. A/c dining room and delivery available.

ⓎⓎ Nerie's, corner Queen and Daly St, T223-4028, www.neries.bz. Belizean food, also burgers, salads and fresh fruit juices. At the Douglas Jones St branch there is also a bar.

Ⓨ Big Daddy's, 2nd floor of market building, Church St, opposite BTL office. Good food, with pleasant view over the harbour. Closes when the food runs out.

Ⓨ Blue Bird Café, Albert St. Cheap fruit juices, specialities, basic, clean, reasonable. Inside tables are perfect for people-watching.

Ⓨ Dario's, 33 Hyde's Lane, T203-5197. Classic Belizean hot meat pies, try 1 and then buy in bulk if you like them.

Ⓨ DIT's, 50 King St. Good for pastries, rice'n'beans and desserts.

Ⓨ Judith's Pastries, 147 Queen St, T223-3789. Good cakes and pastries.

Belmopan and around *p358*

Eating options are limited in Belmopan. There are several cheap *comedores* at the back of the market and a couple of bakeries near Constitution Drive. Cafés are closed on Sun.

ⓎⓎ Caladium, at Market Square in front of bus terminal. Limited fare, moderately priced, small portions.

ⓎⓎ Pasquales Pizza, Forest Drive and Slim Lane, T822-4663. Also serves pasta and hot and cold sandwiches.

ⓎⓎ Perkup Café, Shopping Center, T822 0001, www.perkupcoffeeshop.com. Good coffee, snacks and ice cream.

🎭 Entertainment

Belize City *p355, map p356*

Bars and clubs

Lots of bars, some with jukeboxes, poolrooms and karaoke nights. Try the local drink, anise and peppermint, known as 'A and P'; also the powerful 'Old Belizeno' rum. The local beer, Belikin, is good, as is the 'stout', strong and free of gas.

Fri night is the most popular night for going out in Belize. Clubs often have a cover charge of US$5 and drinks are expensive once inside. Happy hour on Fri starts at 1600 at **Radisson Fort George** and continues at **Biltmore, Calypso** and elsewhere. The best and safest bars are found at major hotels, **Fort George**, **Biltmore Plaza**, **Bellevue** and **Princess**. **Club Calypso**, at the **Princess Hotel**, see Sleeping, has top bands at weekends. **The Wet Lizard**, near the Tourism Village, has good American/Creole fare, great view.

Cinema
Princess Hotel, see Sleeping, has a 2-theatre modern cinema, showing recent movies for US$7.50.

○ Shopping

Belize City *p355, map p356*
The whole city closes down on Sun except for a few shops open in the morning, eg **Brodies** in the centre of town. Banks and many shops and offices are also closed on Sat afternoons.

Books
Brodies, Albert St, has decent selection of books on Belize and some paperback novels. It is now the only bookshop in the city.

Markets and supermarkets
The **market** is by the junction of North Front St and Fort St.
Brodies has widest grocery selection, though prices are slightly higher. Closed Sun.

Souvenirs
Handicrafts, woodcarvings and straw items are all good buys.
Zericote (or Xericote) wood carvings can be bought at **Brodies**, Central Park end of Regent St (which also sells postcards), the **Fort George Hotel**, see Sleeping, above, or **Egbert Peyrefitte**, 11a Cemetery Rd. Such wood carvings are the best buy, but to find a carver rather than buy the tourist fare in shops, ask a taxi driver. The wood sculpture of **Charles Gabb**, who introduced carving into Belize, can be seen at the Art Centre, near Government House. Wood carvers sell their work in front of the main hotels.

National Handicraft Center, South Park St. The Belize Chamber of Commerce's showcase promotes craftspeople from all over Belize; come here first for an overview of Belizean art and crafts.

Belize Audubon Society, across from the Tourist Village near the lighthouse, has a small but good selection of posters, T-shirts, gifts, and jewellery, all locally made in villages, and all at very reasonable prices.

▲ Activities and tours

Belize City *p355, map p356*
Diving
Hugh Parkey's **Belize Dive Connection**, www.belizediving.com, is based at the **Radisson's** dock and is a professional outfit.

Tour operators
Discovery Expeditions, 5916 Manatee Dr, Buttonwood Bay, T223-0748, www.discovery belize.com. An efficient and professional outfit offering interesting cultural and adventure tours out of the city and across the country. Recommended.
The Green Dragon, based out near Belmopan, but covering most of the country, T822-2124, www.greendragonbelize.com, is very helpful and will arrange hotel bookings and tours all over Belize.
Island Expeditions Co, Canada-based, www.island expeditions.com. Adventure and multi-sport wilderness, rainforest and reef trips.
Maya Travel Services, 42 Cleghorn St, T223-1623, www.mayatravelservices.com/contact.php, gets positive reports.
S&L Guided Tours, 91 North Front St, T227-7593, www.sltravelbelize.com. Recommended group travel (groups of 4 people for most tours, 2 people for Tikal). If booking tours in Belize from abroad it is advisable to check prices and services offered with a reputable tour operator in Belize first.

⊖ Transport

Belize City *p355, map p356*

Air

The International Airport is 10 miles from Belize City. The municipal airstrip for local flights is 15 mins' drive from the centre on the northern side of town, taxi, US$5, no bus service. Domestic services with **Tropic Air** and **Maya Island Air**, flights every 30 mins, 0700-1630. Flights to and from the islands can be taken from the international airport and companies link their flights to international arrivals and departures; flights from the international airport cost about US$15 more each way. **Maya** and **Tropic** also have services to **Flores**, Guatemala.

Airline offices American Airlines, San Cas Plaza, T223-2522 (reservations), Mon-Fri 0800-1800, Sat 0800-1200. **Continental Airlines**, 32 Albert St, T227-8309. **Belize Global Travel Services**, 41 Albert St, T227-7363, www.belizeglobal.bz, provides services for **Grupo Taca** and **US Airways**. **Maya Island Air**, Municipal Airstrip, Belize City, T223-1140, www.mayaislandair.com. **Tropic Air**, Albert St, Belize City, T226-2012, www.tropicair.com.

Boat

Boats to **Caye Caulker** continuing to **San Pedro** (Ambergris Caye) and **Chetumal Pedro** leave from 3 principal boat terminals in Belize City, with sailings at regular times – between around 0700 and 1730 each day. As long as you check schedules beforehand you are never more than 30 mins from a boat during the day time. The **Water Jets Express** (T226-2194, www.sanpedrowatertaxi.com) dock lies on Bird's Isle at the far end of Albert St in the southside of Belize City, just beyond St. John's Cathedral. The company has services 4 times daily to Caye Caulker (US$12 one way, 30-45 mins), San Pedro (US$18 one way, about 60-80 mins) and once daily, on to Chetumal in Mexico (US$35 from San Pedro and US$40 from Caye Caulker, both one way). The company are also an official agent for

Mexican ADO buses, and can book tickets from Chetumal or all along the Riviera Maya to Cancún, and connections beyond. Taxis to the San Pedro marine terminal from the city centre cost around US$8. Belize's other 2 boat terminals both lie on North Front St, a few hundred metres southeast of the swing bridge in the city centre. Closest to the bridge is the **Caye Caulker Water Taxi Association** terminal (T226-0992, www.cayecaulkerwatertaxi.com) also with 4 times daily to Caye Caulker (US$10 one way, 45 mins), San Pedro (US$15 one way, about 90 mins). A little further on up the same road right next to the cruise ship tourist facility in the **Brown Sugar Terminal**, is the Belize Water Taxi (Brown Sugar Market Square, 111 North Front St, T223-2225, http://belizewatertaxi.com). They have the same number of sailings to the same destinations as the Caye Caulker Water Taxi Association, for the same price, and once daily, on to Chetumal in Mexico (US$35 from San Pedro and US$40 from Caye Caulker, both one way). Both terminals have areas where you can leave a bag and the Caye Caulker Water Taxi Association terminal has a few shops and cafés. Booths outside the latter sell onward bus tickets – to destinations throughout Belize and beyond to Mexico and Guatemala.

Bus

Within the city the fare is US$0.50 run by **Belize in Transit** services. They originate next to the taxi stand on Cemetery Rd.

There are bus services to all the main towns. The **National Transportation Co** operates Northern Transport from West Collette Canal St (can store luggage, US$0.50).

North to **Chetumal** (see Mexico, page 167), about 15 daily each way, roughly every 30 mins, starting at 0500 until 1800, 3 hrs, US$2.50, express buses from 0600 stopping at **Orange Walk** and **Corozal** only, US$6.50, 2½ hrs. If taking a bus from Chetumal which will arrive in Belize City after dark, decide on a hotel and go there by taxi.

West towards **Guatemala** by bus to **Belmopan** and **San Ignacio**, express bus 0900, US$3, with a/c and refreshments, ordinary bus every 30 mins, Mon-Sat frequent 0600-1900, Sun 0630-1700. The 0600, 0630 and 1015 buses connect at the border with services to **Flores**, Guatemala. To **San Ignacio**, **Benque Viejo** and the **Guatemalan border** via Belmopan, US$2.50 to Belmopan, US$4 to San Ignacio, US$4.50 to Benque, hourly Mon-Sat, 1100-1900. The last possible bus connection to **Flores** leaves the border at 1600, but it is better to get an earlier bus to arrive in daylight. Many buses leave for **Melchor de Mencos**, 0600-1030. To **Flores**, Guatemala, minibuses leave the Marine Terminal on Front St in Belize City; make reservations the previous day.

1st-class express buses from Belize City to **Flores/Tikal** with Mundo Maya/Línea Dorada, www.tikalmayanworld.com, leave from Belize City daily at 1000 and 1700, with buses connecting to Guatemala City and beyond. Also with services heading north to **Chetumal**. Check the Mundo Maya counter in the Marine Terminal on North Front St.

South to Dangriga, via Belmopan and the Hummingbird Hwy. **Southern Transport** (T227-3937), from the corner of Vernon and Johnson St near the Belchina Bridge, several daily on the hour 0800-1600, plus Mon 0600, US$5. **James** (T702-2049), to **Punta Gorda** via **Dangriga**, **Cockscomb Basin Wildlife Sanctuary** and **Independence**, every hour from 0515 to 1015 and 1215 to 1515 with the last bus at 1545, 6-8 hrs, US$14.

Car

Car hire Cars start at US$75 plus insurance of around US$15 a day. Most rental firms have offices in Belize City and opposite the international airport terminal building. Avis, T203-4619, avisbelize@btl.net. Budget, 2½ miles, Northern Hwy, T223-2435, www.budget-belize.com. **Crystal Auto Rental**, Mile 5 Northern Hwy, T223-1600, www.crystal-belize.com, cheapest deals in town, but not always most reliable, wide selection of vehicles, will release insurance papers for car entry to Guatemala and Mexico. **Hertz**, 11a Cork St, beside Radisson Fort George Hotel, T223-5395, www.hertz belize.com, and International Airport, T225-3300. **Pancho's**, 5747 Lizarraga Av, T224-5554, www.panchosrentalbelize.com, locally owned rental company.

Taxi

Official cabs have green licence plates (drivers have ID card); within Belize, US$4 for 1 or 2 people; slightly more for 3 or more. There is a taxi stand on Central Park, another on the corner of Collet Canal St and Cemetery Rd, and a number of taxis on Albert St, Queen St and around town. Outside Belize City, US$1.75 per mile, regardless of number of passengers. Belize City to the resorts in Cayo District approximately US$100-125, 1-4 people. No meters, so beware of over-charging and make sure fare is quoted in Bz$ not US$.

Belmopan and around *p358*
Bus

To **San Ignacio**, hourly on the hour 0500-2100, 1 hr, US$2.50. To **Belize City**, Mon-Sat, every 30 mins, 0600-1900, hourly on Sun, 1 hr, US$3.50. Heading south hourly buses Mon-Sat 0830-1630 (fewer on Sun) to **Dangriga**, 1 hr, US$3, **Mango Creek**, 3 hrs, US$8 and **Punta Gorda**, 4½ hrs, US$9. James Bus leaves for **Belize City** and **Punta Gorda** from opposite the **National Transportation Co** bus station. To **Orange Walk** and **Corozal** take an early bus to Belize City and change.

❶ Directory

Belize City *p355, map p356*
Banks

All banks have facilities to arrange cash advance on Visa. Guatemalan quetzales and Mexican pesos are best bought at the border. There are several ATMs in Belize City **Atlantic**

Bank, 6 Albert St, quick efficient service, small charge for Visa/MasterCard, smaller queues than Belize Bank Belize Bank, 60 Market Sq, is particularly efficient and modern, US$0.50 commission on Amex cheques but a big charge for cash against Visa and MasterCard. It is easy to have money wired to Belize City.

Cultural centres
Audubon Society, see page 346. Baron Bliss Institute, public library, temporary exhibitions; has 1 stela and 2 large discs from Caracol on display. The Image Factory, 91 Front St, has exhibitions of contemporary art, Mon-Fri 0900-1800. The Belize National Handicraft Center sales room on South Park St has a good supply of books about Belize culture. Programme for Belize, 1 Eyre St, T227-5616, www.pfbelize.org, is a conservation organization that manages land reserves including Río Bravo. Society for the Promotion of Education and Research (SPEAR), 5638 Gentle Av, T223-1668, www.spear.org.bz, with a great reference library for everything Belizean.

Embassies and consulates
Many embassies and consulates are now located in Belmopan. For more countries visit www.mfa.gov.bz (see also Belmopan Directory, below). Canada (consulate), represented through Guatemala. France, covered by San Salvador. Guatemala, 8A St, T223-3150, 0830-1230, will not issue visas or tourist cards here; will tell you to leave it till you reach your exit point. Honduras, 114 Bella Vista, T224-5889, 0900-1200, 1300-1600. Italy (consulate), 18 Albert St, T227-8449. Nicaragua, 124 Newtown Barracks, T223-3868. Panama, consular services at Central American Blv and Mahogany St, T222-4551.

Internet
Service at BTL and in some hotels; prices around US$4 per hr. Keep an eye out for cheaper options. Mailbox, on Front St.

Laundry
Northside Laundromat, North Front St, 0900-2000, US$4 for 6 kg wash and dry. Belize Dry Cleaners and Launderomat, 3 Dolphin St.

Post
The main post office is at Queen St and North Front St, 0800-1700 (1630 Fri). Letters held for a month. Beautiful stamps for collectors around the corner on Queen St.

Telephone
Belize Telemedia Ltd, 1 Church St, just off Central Park, Mon-Sat, 0800-1800, Sun 0800-1200. Also public fax and booths for credit card and charge calls.

Belmopan and around *p358*
Banks
Scotia Bank 1915 Constitution Dr and Belize Bank, Constitution Dr, also provide cash advances.

Embassies and consulates
Costa Rica, Mountain View Apartments, Apartment 2, University Blv, Belmopan, T822-1582. El Salvador, 49 Nanche St, T822-3404. Mexico, Embassy Sq, Belmopan, T822-0406. UK High Commission, North Ring Rd, next to the Governor's residence, T822-6, www.britishhighbze.com, Mon-Thu 0800-1200 and 1300-1600, Fri 0800-1400. Has a list of recommended doctors and dentists. USA, Floral Park Rd, Belmopan, T822-4011, http://belize. usembassy.gov/; consulate is round the corner on Hutson St, office hours, Mon-Fri, 0800-1200, 1300-1700.

Internet
Techno Hub at bus station, US$4.50 per hr.

Post
The post office is next to the market (opposite the immigration office).

Northern cayes

The cayes off the coast are attractive, relaxing, slow and very 'Caribbean' – an excellent place for diving, sea fishing or just lazing about. Palm trees fringe the coastline, providing day-long shade for resting in your hammock looking out at the stunning azure seas. They are popular destinations, especially in August and between December and May.

There are some 212 sq miles of cayes. The cayes and atolls were home to fishermen and resting points to clean the catch or grow coconuts. But they have always been valued. The Maya built the site of Marco Gonzalez on the southwestern tip of Ambergris Caye, the largest and most populated of the islands. Nearby Caye Caulker is a popular destination for the more budget-minded visitor, while serious divers head for the Turneffe Islands. Other, smaller cayes are home to exclusive resorts or remain uninhabited, many being little more than mangrove swamps. St George's Caye, nine miles northeast of Belize, was once the capital and the scene of the battle in 1798 that established British possession. ▸▸ *For listings, see pages 369-376.*

Ins and outs

Most boats to Caye Caulker and Ambergris Caye leave from the Marine Terminal or the Triple J terminal. Boats leave regularly from 0630 to 1730 if you're just turning up. Otherwise check at your hotel as timetables change frequently. For the southern cayes, see page 396.

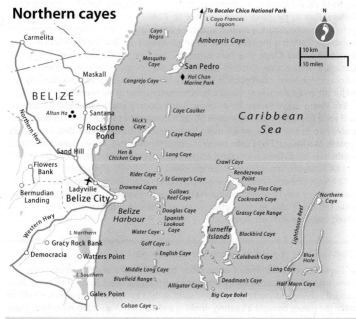

Northern cayes

To Bacalar Chico National Park
L Cayo Frances Lagoon
Cayo Negro
Ambergris Caye
Carmelita
Mosquito Caye
San Pedro
Maskall
Cangrejo Caye
Hol Chan Marine Park
BELIZE
Altun Ha
Santana
Hick's Caye
Caye Caulker
Caribbean Sea
Rockstone Pond
Caye Chapel
Sand Hill
Hen & Chicken Caye
Long Caye
Crawl Caye
Flowers Bank
Rider Caye
St George's Caye
Rendezvous Point
Drowned Cayes
Gallows Reef Caye
Dog Flea Caye
Northern Caye
Bermudian Landing
Ladyville
Belize City
Cockroach Caye
Grassy Caye Range
Belize Harbour
Douglas Caye
Spanish Lookout Caye
Turneffe Islands
Blackbird Caye
Lighthouse Reef
L Northern
Water Caye
Gracy Rock Bank
Goff Caye
Democracia
Watters Point
English Caye
Calabash Caye
Blue Hole
Middle Long Caye
Long Caye
Bluefield Range
Deadman's Caye
Half Moon Caye
Gales Point
Alligator Caye
Big Caye Bokel
Colson Caye
10 km
10 miles
N

This island (pronounced Am-*ber*-gris), along with the town of **San Pedro**, has grown rapidly over the last couple of years, with over 50 hotels and guesthouses on the island. Buildings are still restricted to no more than three storeys in height, and the many wooden structures retain an authentic village atmosphere. The very helpful **Ambergris tourist information office** ① *Mon-Sat 1000-1300, 1400-1900*, is next to the the town hall.

Although sand is in abundance, there are few beach areas around San Pedro town. You cannot, in practice, walk north along the beach from San Pedro to Xcalak, Mexico. The emphasis is on snorkelling on the nearby barrier reef and **Hol Chan Marine Park**, and the fine scuba-diving, sailing, fishing and board sailing. The main boat jetties are on the east (Caribbean Sea) side of San Pedro. It can be dangerous to swim near San Pedro as there have been serious accidents with boats. Boats are restricted to about 5 mph within the line of red buoys about 25 yards offshore, but this is not always adhered to. There is a 'safe' beach in front of the park, just to the south of the government dock. A short distance to the north and south of San Pedro lie miles of deserted beachfront, where picnic barbecues are popular for day-tripping snorkellers and birders who have visited the nearby small cayes hoping to glimpse rosets, spoonbills or white ibis. If you go north you have to cross a small inlet with hand-pulled ferry, US$0.50 for foreigners. **Note** Only very experienced snorkellers should attempt to swim in the cutting between the reef and the open sea.

Around Ambergris Caye

Just south of Ambergris Caye, and not far from Caye Caulker, is the **Hol Chan Marine Park** ① *US$12 entry fee; the park office (with reef displays and information on Bacalar Chico National Park to the north) is on Caribeña St, T226-2247, www.holchanbelize.org*. This underwater natural park is divided into three zones: Zone A is the reef, where fishing is prohibited; Zone B is the seagrass beds, where fishing can only be done with a special licence (the **Boca Ciega** blue hole is here); Zone C is mangroves where fishing also requires a licence. Only certified scuba-divers may dive in the reserve. Fish feeding, although prohibited, takes place at Shark Ray Alley, where about 15 sharks and rays are fed for the entertainment of tourists. Not the most natural of experiences.

San Pedro is well known for its diving. Long canyons containing plenty of soft and hard coral formations start at around 50-60 ft going down to 120 ft. Often these have grown into hollow tubes, which make for interesting diving. **Tackle Box**, **Esmeralda**, **Cypress, M & Ms** and **Tres Cocos** are only some of the dive sites. The visibility in this area is usually over 100 ft. There is a recompression chamber in San Pedro and a US$1 tax on each tank fill insures treatment throughout the island.

Although offshore, Ambergris Caye airport makes arranging tours to visit places on the mainland very easy (for example Altún Ha US$60 per person; Lamanai US$125 per person) while still being able to enjoy other water experiences (catamaran sailing, deep-sea fishing, manatee and Coco Solo).

Caye Caulker → *For listings, see pages 369-376. Colour map 3, A2.*

On Caye Caulker, a thin line of white sandy beach falls to a sea of turquoise blue and green, while the reef can be seen a mile and a half from the shore. By day on this laid-back island, it's diving and snorkelling, sea and sand; at dusk everyone heads up to the 'split' to watch the sunset; by night it's eating, drinking and dancing. A quiet lobster-fishing island

Caye Caulker

(closed season 15 February to 14 June) until fairly recently, its extremely relaxing atmosphere, gentle climate, postcard-perfect views and the myriad small restaurants and bars have drawn increasing numbers of tourists.

The caye is actually two islands separated by a small channel (the 'split'); swimming is possible here but beware of fishing and powerboats. All services are on the southern island and, in the north, is a **marine reserve** ⓘ *free for school parties, tourists are asked for a US$2 donation to help expansion and to increase the work in ecology education.* In the south, next to **Shirley's** is the **Caye Caulker Mini Reserve**.

Tour operators and hotels on the island have worked hard to improve services for visitors. The atmosphere is friendly and easy-going, but the usual common sense rules apply with regards to personal safety. Drugs are readily available, but they are illegal and you shouldn't expect any sympathy should you get into difficulties. Some think the atmosphere is more relaxed out of high season. Sandflies can be ferocious in season (December to February); take long trousers and a good

Sleeping 🛏
Anchorage Resort **2**
Barefoot Beach **3**
Belize Odyssey **4**
Caye Caulker Plaza **5**
China Town **6**
Edith's **8**
Ignacio Beach Cabins **9**
Iguana Reef Inn **10**
Lazy Iguana **11**
Marin's Guest House **13**
Pancho's Villa **16**
Rainbow **18**
Sandy lane **19**
Sea Dreams **20**
Seaside Cabañas **21**
Shirley's Guest House **22**
Tree Tops **25**
Tropical Paradise Resort **26**
Tropics **23**
Vega Inn **27**
Yumas House **24**

Eating 🍴
Amor y Cafe **1**
Cáfe Coco Loco **2**
Coco Plum Gardens **3**
Habanero's **4**
Happy Lobster **5**
Island Link Internet Café
 & Ice Cream Parlour **13**
Marin's **6**
Oceanside **7**
Popeye's **8**
Rainbow **9**
Rose's Bar & Grill **10**
Sandbox **11**
Syd's **12**

Bars & clubs 🍸
Herbal Tribes **13**
I & I **14**
Lazy Iguana **15**

repellent. Make sure you fix prices before going on trips or hiring equipment and, if you pay the night before, get a receipt.

A walk south along the shore takes you to the airstrip, the Caye Caulker Mini Reserve and to mangroves where the rare black catbird can be seen and its sweet song heard.

Around Caye Caulker

Reef trips are the same as those found on Ambergris Caye; for more details see under San Pedro (pages 366 and 373).

Generally all trips are offered at the same price by agreement between tour operators, eliminating the need to shop around for a good price. Tour operators share clients if numbers are not sufficient. This means that you can be certain there is always a trip, but make sure that the boat operator is reliable. Tour organizers must be licensed by the **Belize Tourist Board** and should have a licence to prove it. To encourage high standards, and for your own safety, insist on seeing proof that your guide is licensed.

Protect against sunburn on reef trips, even while snorkelling. Tours are slightly cheaper from Caye Caulker than Ambergris Caye. ▸▸ *See Activities and tours, page 373.*

Lighthouse Reef and Turneffe Islands → *For listings, see pages 369-376. Colour map 3, A2.*

ⓘ *On arrival you must register near the lighthouse with the warden who will provide maps and tell you where you can camp.*

Lighthouse Reef is the outermost of the three north-south reef systems off Belize and is some 45 miles to the east of Belize City. Trips out here are not cheap, but if you like diving and have the money, this is one of the most interesting and exciting dive sites in the world. There are two cayes of interest: Half Moon Caye (on which the lighthouse stands) and, **Long Caye**, where there is accommodation with Huracan Diving (see page 375). Between the two are some of the most pristine coral reefs in the Western hemisphere, including the diving shrine of the **Blue Hole** (see below) is found. **Half Moon Caye** is the site of the **Red-Footed Booby Sanctuary** ⓘ *US$20*, a national reserve. Besides the booby, magnificent frigate birds also nest on the island. The seabirds nest on the western side, which has denser vegetation (the eastern side is covered mainly in coconut palms). Of the 98 other bird species recorded on Half Moon Caye, 77 are migrants. The iguana, the wish willy (smaller than the iguana) and the Anolis allisoni lizard inhabit the caye, and hawksbill and loggerhead turtles lay their eggs on the beaches. The **Belize Audubon Society** in Belize City (see page 346) maintains the sanctuary, providing a lookout tower and a trail. The lighthouse on the caye gives fine views of the reef. It was first built in 1820: the present steel tower was added to the brick base in 1931 and nowadays the light is solar powered. Around sunset you can watch the boobies from the lookout as they return from fishing. They land beside their waiting mates at the rate of about 50 a minute, seemingly totally unperturbed by humans.

In Lighthouse Reef is the **Blue Hole** ⓘ *US$20, US$40 to snorkel or dive*, a National Monument that is a circular sinkhole, 1000 ft across and with depths exceeding 400 ft. The crater was probably formed by the collapsed roof of a subterranean cave, and was studied by Jacques Cousteau in 1984. Stalagmites and stalactites can be found and it is rated as one of the best dives in the world. Scuba-diving is outstanding at Lighthouse Reef, and includes two walls that descend almost vertically from 30-40 ft to a depth of almost 400 ft.

Caye Chapel was once a small, quiet caye dotted with palms and devoid of sandflies, close to its busier neighbour Caye Caulker, where you could escape to a bit of quiet and solitude. That has all changed, as it is now exclusive as well as secluded.

For Sleeping and Eating price codes and other relevant information, see Essentials pages 31-33.

◉ Sleeping

Ambergris Caye *p366*
San Pedro
LL-L Ramon's Village, T+1 601 649-1990, www.ramons.com. 61 rooms, a diving and beach resort, highly recommended even for non-divers (fishing, swimming, boating, snorkelling), comfortable rooms, pool with beach-club atmosphere.
LL-L Sun Breeze, T226-2191, www.sun breeze.net. Near airport, Mexican-style building, boxy a/c rooms, decent pool and

restaurant, and one of the best dive shops on the island – a branch of Hugh Parkey's (www.belizediving.com). Recommended.
L Mayan Princess, T+1 504 2445 5050, www.mayan princesshotel.com. Centre of town on seafront, clean, comfortable.
L-AL Changes in Latitude, T226-2986, T1-800-631-9834 (toll free), www.ambergris caye.com/latitudes. Sweet B&B with 6 rooms decorated in retro style. Guests have free use of bikes, a golf cart and the yacht club pool. Local artists occasionally hang out in the courtyard.
L-AL San Pedro Holiday Hotel, T+1 713 893-3825, www.sanpedroholiday.com. 16 rooms and a suite in good central

location, fun atmosphere with good facilities. Children 2-12 US$10.

L-A Spindrift, T226-2018, www.ambergris caye.com/spindrift. 24 rooms, 4 apartments, unattractive block but central location, good bar and restaurant; popular meeting place, a/c, comfortable.

AL-A Coral Beach, T226-2013, www.coralbeachhotel.com. Central location and good local feel.

AL-A Hotel San Pedrano, T226-2054, sanpedrano@btl.net. Another small hotel with a/c and fan rooms with private bathrooms. Children 6-12 years, US$5.

AL-A Tio Pil's Hotel, T206-2059, www.tiopilshotel.com (formerly Lilly's Caribbean Lodge), 6 rooms with sea view, 2 with partial view and 3 without view, all with a/c, clean and friendly.

B Tomas, 12 Barrier Reef Dr, T226-2061. 7 airy rooms with a/c, cheaper with fan, bath, drinking water, clean, friendly and family-run. Children under 6 stay free.

B-D Pedro's Inn, T226-3825, www.back packersbelize.com. The island's only real budget place with onsite bar, BBQ and pool. Rooms have shared bathroom.

B-D Ruby's, San Pedro Town on the beach, T226-2063, www.ambergriscaye.com/rubys. 26 a/c or fan rooms, with private or shared bath, good views, central. Recommended as best value in town.

Outside San Pedro

Several resort-style complexes outside the town offer seclusion and an ambience that borders on paradise.

LL Capricorn Resort, 3 miles north of town, T226-2809, www.ambergriscaye.com/ capricorn. Wooden cabins on beach with great restaurant.

LL Mata Chica Resort, 4 miles north of town, T226-5010, www.matachica.com. European owned and managed, beautiful and stylish stucco and thatched cabins on a lovely beach, fantastic **Mambo** restaurant.

LL Victoria House, 2 miles south of town, T226-2067, T1-800-247-5159 (US toll free)

www.victoria-house.com. This stunning resort, offers 4 different types of stylishly decorated rooms. There are also fully fitted villas in the grounds. Excellent facilities, lovely pool, good dive shop and watersports. Highly recommended.

LL-L El Pescador, on Punta Arena beach 3 miles north, Belize City, T226-2398, www.elpescador.com. Specialist fishing lodge with good reputation, a/c, good food and service. Access by boat.

LL-L Portofino, 6 miles north, PO Box 36, T888 240 1923 (toll free), T678-5096, www.portofino belize.com. A series of spacious, very comfortable thatched roof beach cabins gathered around a jewel-like pool and overlooking the sea. The Belgium owners organize excursions, diving and run one of the best kitchens on the island.

Caye Caulker *p366, map p367*

In all accommodation, take precautions against theft. The arrival pier is just about in the centre of town, with all the accommo-dation on or within a 15-min walk of the main street. The southern end of town is slightly quieter and has a smattering of mangrove and bird life, but it's quite a walk from the 'split' for swimming or snorkelling. Camping on the beach is forbidden.

LL-L Iguana Reef Inn, T226-0213, www.iguanareefinn.com. Probably the best place on the island, relaxing and quiet as it's on the back side. With 13 rooms, a bar and a pool.

LL-B Belize Odyssey, south end of island, T206-0244, http://belizeodyssey.com. Clean, old-fashioned but well-run resort hotel set on 4 acres of land. Owner Tony Vega has a wealth of knowledge about Caye Caulker, its history and local tours.

L-AL Lazy Iguana, southwest side of the island, a block from the cemetery. T226-0350, www.lazyiguana.net. Beauti-fully designed B&B with great views. Collects and uses rainwater. Offers onsite massages for guests.

L-AL Sea Dreams, at north end of the island, T226-0602, www.seadreamsbelize.com. Cosy rooms with good facilities in well-located hotel next to a dock. 10% of profits go to a community school established by co-owner Heidi Curry.

L-AL Seaside Cabañas, first place you reach off the boat, T226-0498, www.seasidecab anas.com. 16 comfortable rooms and cabins in Mexican style with Moroccan furnishings – some with their own roof terraces set around a pool. Excellent tours and very helpful.

L-A Barefoot Beach, Playa Asuncion, T2260205. Inviting, attractive establishment with nice rooms, all with private bath and some with kitchen.

L-B Vega Inn, T226-0142, www.vega belize.com. Suites, houses and budget rooms, camping (**E** per person) and credit cards accepted. All doubles, with ceiling fan, fresh linen and hot showers. Camping ground is guarded, hot water, clean toilets.

AL Anchorage Resort, to the south, near Ignacio's, T206-0304, www.anchorage resort.com. 3-storey building with 18 comfortable, tiled rooms with private bathrooms, pleasant atmosphere, friendly family, drinks served under shade on the beach.

AL Caye Caulker Plaza Hotel, Av Langosta, T226-0780, www.cayecaulkerplazahotel.com. 32 rooms, all with a/c. Good views from the rooftop.

AL Pancho's Villa, Pasero St, T226-0304, www.panchosvillasbelize.com. 6 attractive rooms with good facilities and Wi-Fi. Has sundeck with views of all the island.

AL-A Shirley's Guest House, south end of the village on the beach, T226-0145, www.shirleysguesthouse.com. Very relaxing with 5 green and white raised cabins, with private and shared bath. No kids.

AL-A Tree Tops, T226-0240, www.treetops belize.com. Spotless, spacious rooms and suites, most with private bath, comfortable beds with beach views, German spoken, powerful fan or ac, cable TV, friendly, good value. Children over 10 only. Recommended.

A-B China Town Hotel, Estrella St, T226-0228, www.chinatownhotelbelize.com. Efficient, matter-of-fact hotel with clean rooms and good facilities. Decent value.

A-B Rainbow Hotel, T226-0123, www.rain bowhotel-cayecaulker.com. Good street-front location facing the beach and the popular **Rainbow Grill**. 17 rooms and 2 apartments, with shower, hot water, good.

A-C Tropical Paradise Resort, T226-0124, www.tropicalparadisehotel.com. Cabins with hot showers, clean, restaurant, good excursions.

A-C Tropics Hotel, on the main street, T226-0374, www.thetropicshotel.com. Rooms with private bath and hot water. Cheaper for longer stays and discounts available on local tours. Good value.

A-D Ignacio Beach Cabins, T226-0175. 19 small purple huts raised very high on the beach just outside town to the south. Cheaper rooms are smaller with cold water bathrooms. Quiet and clean. Book exchange and kayak and bike rental. Recommended.

C Edith's, 2 blocks from the beach and close to the **I and I Bar**, T206-0069. Offering 11 rooms with bath, hot water, fan. Recommended.

C-D Sandy Lane, 1 block back from main street, T226-0117. Bungalow-type cabins, clean, private and cheaper shared bathrooms, hot showers, run by Rico and Elma Novelo. Also more expensive rooms with kitchen and TV for longer stays. Recommended.

D Marin's Guest House, Estrella St, 1½ blocks from the beach at the southern end, T226-0444. Good-sized rooms with private and shared facilities in wooden cabins on stilts in a small compound.

D-E Yumas House, formerly Tina's Backpackers, T206-0019, www.yumashouse belize.com. Cheapest on the caye, with dorms, 3 private rooms, or sling a hammock. Recently refurbished and still popular but no longer noisy.

Lighthouse Reef and the Turneffe Islands *p368*

Many cayes have package deals for a few days or a week.

LL Caye Chapel Island Resort, Caye Chapel, T226-8250, www.cayechapel.com. 22 villas with tennis courts, private airstrip and golf.

LL Turneffe Flats, Turneffe Islands (56 Eve St, Belize City), T220-4046, www.tflats.com. In a lovely location, offers week-long packages for fishing and scuba; takes 20 guests.

LL Turneffe Island Lodge, Big Caye Bokel, Turneffe Islands, T220-4142, www.turneffe lodge.com. Can accommodate 16 guests for week-long fishing and scuba packages.

LL-L Blackbird Caye Resort, Turneffe Islands (c/o Blackbird Caye Co, 8 Front St, Belize City), T223-2767, www.blackbirdresort.com. An ecological resort on this 4000-acre island is used by the **Oceanic Society** and is a potential site for a biosphere reserve underwater project. Weekly packages arranged. Diving or fishing packages available, no bar, take your own alcohol.

LL-L Huracan, PO Box 487, Belize City, T603 2930, www.huracandiving.com. Simple but elegant accommodation in a small chalet with polished wooden floors on a tiny island on the Lighthouse Reef. The sea views from the islands beaches and jetties are unforgettable, with a real sense of remoteness, the diving the best on the Reef (this is the only dive operator within 20 mins of the Blue Hole) and the cooking and hospitality from Ruth and her husband Karel warm and welcoming. Prices include transfers from Belize, full board and dives making this a very good-value option.

● Eating

Ambergris Caye *p366*
San Pedro

ᵗᵗᵗ Celi's, in San Pedro Holiday Hotel (see Sleeping). Good seafood overlooking the sea. Recommended. Closed Wed when there is a beach BBQ.

ᵗᵗᵗ Elvi's Kitchen, www.elviskitchen.com. Popular, upmarket, live music, roof built around flamboyant tree, can be very busy, has won international awards.

ᵗᵗᵗ Wild Mango's, south of main strip, T226-2859. Closed Mon. Run by Amy Knox, former chef at **Victoria House**. Rustic setting overlooking the sea. Try the rum-soaked bacon-wrapped shrimp. The delicious meals are tastefully presented. Recommended.

ᵗᵗᵗ-ᵗᵗ Ambergris Delight and Pizza, 35 Pescador Dr, T226-2464, Closed Tue. Pleasant place serving up Belizean cuisine and burgers.

ᵗᵗᵗ-ᵗᵗ Fido's Courtyard, towards north end of Front St. T226-2056, www.fidosbelize.com Lively bar-restaurant often with live music, good lunch and dinner. Sushi bar upstairs.

ᵗᵗ El Patio, south of town, beyond Belize Yacht Club. Good, Mexican-style food, live music in evenings.

ᵗᵗ Estel's Dine by the Sea on the beach close to water taxi terminal. Good food and 1940s-50s music.

ᵗ Dande's Frozen Custard, Middle St, www.dande.bz. Popular place for an ice cream cone, sorbet or frozen custard.

Caye Caulker *p366, map p367*

Beer is sold by the crate at the wholesaler on the dock by the generator; ice for sale at **Tropical Paradise**.

ᵗᵗᵗ Habanero's, very close to main dock, T226-0487. Closed Thu. Excellent and tasty food, the best in Belize according to some. Pricey.

ᵗᵗᵗ-ᵗᵗ Happy Lobster, Av Hicaco. Good food with majority fish dishes and pasta. Recommended. Closed Tue.

ᵗᵗᵗ-ᵗᵗ Rainbow Bar and Restaurant, on its own jetty. Delicious burritos good value, beautiful view.

ᵗᵗᵗ-ᵗᵗ Syd's Restaurant, Middle St. Closed Sun. Family-run and very popular with locals.

ᵗᵗᵗ-ᵗᵗ Tropical Paradise, on the beach (see Sleeping). Excellent seafood, varied menu, slightly more expensive than others.

Amor y Cafe, Av Hicaco. Open 0600-1130, closed Mon. Some say it is the best place on the island for breakfast.

Coco Plum Gardens, at the southern end of the island, with spa and art gallery. Open for breakfast and dinner, Mon-Sat and does a fabulous omelette.

Glenda's, Back St. Old-time island favourite. Good breakfast and lunches. Mornings only.

Marin's, 3 blocks south 1 west of the dock. Good seafood all day everyday, cable TV.

Oceanside, most popular bar on the island. Food OK, music and dancing until midnight.

Popeye's, on the beach. Live music some nights, opens at 0600 for breakfast.

Rose's Bar & Grill, Front St, a great grill with good seafood and burgers.

Sandbox, T226-0200. With a good atmosphere and sandy floors for that complete beach experience.

Café Coco Loco, Av Hicaco next door to the lighthouse. Delicious bagels, brownies and coffee. Try the fruit sorbet cooler made with ginger ale.

Island Link Internet Café & Ice Cream Parlour, Av Hicaco, T226-0592. Internet service and home-made ice cream; 8 different flavours.

● Entertainment

Ambergris Caye *p366*
Big Daddy's Disco, open evenings but cranks up at midnight. Try also 'Chicken Drop' in Pier Lounge at **Spindthrift Hotel** on a Wed night: you bet US$1 on which square the chicken will leave its droppings. **Jaguar's Temple** and **Barefoot Iguana** are current popular nightspots.

Caye Caulker *p366, map p367*
Many of the restaurants become bars in the evenings.
Herbal Tribes, near the north end of the island, is a bar and restaurant with a good atmosphere.

I and I Bar, which used to be the **Swing Bar** and still has the swings, should be tried later at night.
Lazy Lizard, right at the north tip of the island at 'the split', is an excellent place to watch the sunset.
Sunset cranks up big style after **Oceanside** closes at 2400 and is a lot of fun.

○ Shopping

Ambergris Caye *p366*
There are many gift shops in the centre of San Pedro town. It is better to shop around the smaller shops and groceries where prices are clearly marked. When paying check that the bill is correct.
Fidos has **Belizean Arts** (paintings and prints by local artists) and **Ambar Jewelry**.
Kasbah and **Orange** sell local crafts and jewellery.

Caye Caulker *p366, map p367*
There are at least 4 small 'markets' on the island where a variety of food can be bought; prices are 20-50% higher than the mainland. There are a couple of gift shops and a gallery in the same building as Coco Loco.
Chan's Mini Mart, Middle St, 1 street back from main street, open daily including Christmas and New Year's Day.

▲ Activities and tours

Ambergris Caye *p366*
Diving and snorkelling
Park fees are not included in prices quoted. US$10 for Hol Chan, US$30 for Blue Hole, US$10 Half Moon Caye and US$10 for Bacalar Chico. Be clear on what's included. You will likely be charged extra for equipment. Instruction to PADI Open Water level available, from US$350. Local 2-tank dive US$60, Turneffe US$140-160, Blue Hole US$185. Many operators practice chumming

to attract fish and sharks; divers should discourage operators from doing this. Accommodation and dive packages at some hotels are very good value. All dive operators offer snorkelling trips from US$25 for Shark Ray Alley to US$125 for the Blue Hole.

Note Check the diving shop's recent safety record before diving.

Ambergris Divers, T226-2634, www.amber grisdivers.com. Will collect divers from Caye Caulker for Blue Hole trip. Very good-value dive and accommodation packages with a number of hotels on the island.

Amigos del Mar, opposite Lily's, T226-2706, www.amigos dive.com. Gets a lot of return customers and has been recommended, but practices chumming at the Blue Hole.

Ramon's Village, www.ramons.com, T+1 (601) 649-1990. A bit more expensive than other operators. Check the diving shop's recent safety record before diving.

Fishing

Extreme Reef Adventures, office by the dock at Fido's, T226-3513. Parasailing, banana tubing and other sport tours.

Karibbean Water Sports, behind Spindrift Hotel, T226-3205, www.karibbean watersports.com. Rents out jet-skis for US$30 per 30 mins, or take a tour!

Sailsports, Holiday Hotel, T226-4488, www.sailsportsbelize.com. Windsurfing, sailing, kitesurfing lessons and rentals.

Therapies

Asian Garden Day Spa, T226-4072, www.asiangardendayspa.com.

The Art of Touch, T226-357, www.touchbelize.com.

Sol Spa, T226-2410, www.belizesolspa.com.

Spa Shangri-La, T226-3755.

Tour operators

Travel and Tour Belize in town, T226-2031. Helpful, all services and can arrange flights, with a request stop at Sarteneja (for the Shipstern Nature Reserve).

Tanishas Tour Daniel Núñez does trips to the Maya sites on the north of the caye in the Bacalar Chico National Park with his company.

Caye Caulker *p366, map p367*

Diving and snorkelling

Mask and snorkel hire from several dive and tour operators; normally US$2.50 per day.

Belize Diving Services, T226-0143, www.belizedivingservice.com. A dive shop on the island with similar prices to Frenchie's.

Big Fish Dive Center, T226-0450, bigfish dive@btl.net. Go to the Blue Hole, US$175, Lighthouse Reef and Turneffe. Also does PADI refresher courses and works with Frenchie's.

Frenchie's Diving, T226-0234, www.frenchiesdivingbelize.com. Charges US$310 for a 4-day PADI course, friendly and effective, 2-tank dive US$90, also advanced PADI instruction. Day excursion diving Blue Hole, etc, US$190, snorkellers welcome.

Fishing

Fishing can be arranged through tour operators or by ringing Eloy Badillo T226-0270.

Kayaking

Tour agencies on the main street rent kayaks.

Manatee watching

Available with most tour operators.

Sailing

See also Ras Creek and E-Z Boy Tours, below, for their sailing trips.

Raggamuffin Tours, T226-0348, www.raggamuffintours.com. Do a fun sunset cruise, US$25 per person, with booze and music on a sail boat as well as offering a 3-day all-inclusive sailing tour to Placencia leaving Tue and Fri, US$300 per person, minimum 8 people including all food and 2 nights' camping on Rendezvous Caye and Tobacco Caye. Beats travelling by bus and is an increasingly popular excursion.

Tour operators

Prices are consistent across all operators, so find someone you connect with and feel you can trust. The main excursion is snorkelling in Hol Chan Marine Park and visiting Shark Ray Alley and San Pedro, US$45, equipment included. Further afield there are other snorkelling trips, river and Maya site tours. Manatees and Goff Caye (a paradise-perfect circular island with good snorkelling around), US$60; fishing trips US$175. Snorkelling excursions to the Turneffe Islands, Half Moon Caye, Bird Sanctuary and Blue Hole on request. **Sunset Tours** are popular with snorkelling until dusk, US$30.

E-Z Boy Tours, on main street, T226-0349. As well as the usual snorkelling tours, E-Z offers a seahorse, a Maya archaeology and croc-spotting tour.

Javier Novelo at Anwar Tours, T226-0327, www.anwartours.com, is locally recommended for a range of snorkelling tours.

Raggamuffin Tours, see above, run trips to the Caye Caulker Marine Reserve and Hol Chan. They can also arrange fishing tours with local fishermen, full day, US$275.

Guides Recommended guides include **Ras Creek**, 'a big man with a big heart', in his boat, based at the water taxi dock, US$27.50 including lunch and entrance fee to the Caye Caulker Marine Reserve; seahorse trips, fishing trips, US$37.50; booze cruise, US$10 per person; canoe and snorkel rental. **Neno Rosado**, of Tsunami Adventures, T226-0462, www.tsunamiadventures.com, has been approved by the guide association and is reliable and knowledgeable.

Lighthouse Reef and the Turneffe Islands *p368*
Diving

The main dive in the Blue Hole is very deep, at least 130 ft; the hole itself is 480 ft deep. Check your own qualifications as the dive operator probably will not – you should be experienced and it is advisable to have at least the Advance Open Water PADI course, although an Open Water qualification is fine if you feel confident and don't have major problems equalizing.

Huracan Diving, PO Box 487, Belize City, T603-2930, www.huracandiving.com. The only hotel and dive operation on Lighthouse Reef itself. Excellent value (see Sleeping).

Dive operators on Ambergris and on Caye Caulker run trips to Half Moon Caye, the Blue Hole and Turneffe Islands, see above. It's also possible to go from Belize City with:

Hugh Parkey's Belize Dive Connection, based at the Radisson's dock, www.belize diving.com.

Sunrise Travel, Belize City, T227-2051 or T223-2670, helps arrange trips, advance book.

⊝ Transport

Ambergris Caye *p366*
Air

Tropic Air, T226-2012, and Maya Island Air, T226-2435, have flights to/from both **Belize City** airports, many hourly, to **Caye Caulker** and **Corozal**. Charter services are available.

Bicycle and golf cart

Bicycles US$2.50 per hr, negotiate for long-term rates. Golf carts from US$15 per hr and up to US$300 per week, battery or gas powered, driver's licence needed.

Boat

More interesting than going by air are the boats. All these call at **Caye Caulker** and San Pedro. **San Pedro Belize Express water taxi**, http://belizewatertaxi.com, to **Caye Caulker** and **Belize City** at 0700 (express to Belize City), 1130, 1430, 1630 and 1800. With **San Pedro Jet Express** at 0600, 1030, 1500 and 1730. Many regular boats to Caye Caulker.

The *Island Ferry*, T226-3231, from Fido's dock, services the north of the island every 2 hrs from 0700-1700 then hourly 1800- 2200. Also at 2400 and 0200 on Wed, Fri and Sat. Returns 0600-2200 every 2 hrs, US$10-25.

Caye Caulker *p366, map p367*

Air

Maya Island Air flies to/from **Belize City**, **Corozal** and **San Pedro**, several daily. Also flights with **Tropic Air**, T226-2439.

Bicycle and golf cart

Island Boy Rentals, T226-0229. Golf cart rental for US$10 per hr. Bike hire for US$7.50 per day.

Boat

Boats leave from the main dock in front of Seaside Cabañas to **Belize City** with the **Caye Caulker Water Taxi Association** at 0630, 0730, 0830, 1000, 1100, 1200, 1330, 1500, 1600, 1700, 45 mins 1 way (can be 'exciting' if it's rough). To **San Pedro** 0700, 0820, 0845, 0950, 1120, 1250, 1420, 1550 and 1720. **Triple J** leave from the **Rainbow Hotel** dock.

Caye Caulker *p366, map p367*

Banks Rates for cash and TCs are reasonable. **Atlantic Bank** Visa advances; US$5 commission and now with 24-hr ATM with Visa and MasterCard, Mon-Fri 0800-1400, Sat 0830-1200, and many other places for exchange. Gift shops will charge a commission. **Internet** Caye Caulker Cyber Café, 0700-2200, or Cayeboard Connection 0800(ish) to 2100(ish), both about US$7.50 per hr. **Laundry** There are 3 laundries with self-service options, the one next to Rose's Cafe being the most central. **Post** ½ block west of Big Fish Dive Center. **Telephone** International service from the telephone exchange (0900-1230, 1400-1630); card-phone outside the **BTL** office can be used for international calls. Collect calls possible at least to North America at no charge.

⊙ Directory

Ambergris Caye *p366*

Banks Atlantic Bank and Bank of Belize, Mon-Thu 0800-1500, Fri 0800-1630. ATMs. Small denominations of US$ in regular use. **Internet** Caribbean Connection, Barrier Reef Dr. **Medical services** San Pedro Polyclinic II, T226-2536. Emergencies, T226-2555. Hyperbaric chamber, T226-2851.

North Belize

North Belize is notable for the agricultural production of sugar, fruit and vegetables and for providing much of the country's food. But among the fields of produce are some well-hidden sights and wildlife magnets. The Maya ruins of Lamanai are just about visible in the spectacular setting of the dense jungle. Wildlife can easily be seen at the Community Baboon Sanctuary, the Crooked Tree Wildlife Sanctuary – home to thousands of beautiful birds – and the wildlife reserves of Shipstern near Sartaneja. The vast Río Bravo Conservation Area nudges up to the Guatemalan border and contains the truly isolated ruins and lodge of Chan Chich.

Heading north out of Belize City, the Northern Highway leads to the Mexican border. You can do the journey in just a few hours, passing through Orange Walk and Corozal, but you won't see a thing. It's definitely worth stopping off if you have time. ▶▶ *For listings, see pages 381-384.*

Bermudian Landing and the Community Baboon Sanctuary

About 15 miles out of Belize City a road heading west leads to the small Creole village of Bermudian Landing (12 miles on a rough road from the turn-off), which has been thrust into the global conservation spotlight. This was once a transfer point for the timber that floated down the Belize River, but now there's a local wildlife museum sponsored by the WWF, and the **Community Baboon Sanctuary** ⓘ *daily 0900-1700, www.howlermonkeys.org, 45- to 60-min guided tours from US$5,* including a visit to the small museum; guided wildlife walks are available when booked ahead and simple homestay accommodation is available, where visitors can see black howler monkeys, many of whom are so used to people that they come very close.

Crooked Tree Wildlife Sanctuary

ⓘ *US$4; you must register at the visitor centre, drinks are on sale, but take food. There is a helpful, friendly warden, Steve, who will let you sleep on the porch of the visitor centre. It is easy to get a lift to the sanctuary, and someone is usually willing to take visitors back to the main road for a small charge.*

The Northern Highway continues to **Sand Hill**, and a further 12 miles to the turn-off for the Crooked Tree Wildlife Sanctuary, which was set up in 1984 and is a rich area for birds. The network of lagoons and swamps is an internationally protected wetlands under the RAMSAR programme, and attracts many migrating birds. The dry season, October to May, is a good time to visit. You may see the huge jabiru stork, the largest flying bird in the Western Hemisphere at a height of 5 ft and a wingspan of 11-12 ft, which nests here, as well as herons, ducks, vultures, kites, ospreys, hawks, sand pipers, kingfishers, gulls, terns, egrets and swallows. In the forest you can also see and hear howler monkeys. Other animals include coatimundi, crocodiles, iguanas and turtles. Glenn Crawford is a good guide.

The turn-off to the sanctuary is signposted but keep an eye out for the intersection, which is 22 miles from Orange Walk and 33 miles from Belize City. There is another sign further south indicating the sanctuary but this just leads to the park boundary, not to the Wildlife Sanctuary. The mango and cashew trees in the village of Crooked Tree are said to be 100 years old. Birdwatching is best in the early morning but, as buses do not leave Belize City early, for a day trip take an early Corozal bus, get off at the main road (about 1¼ hours from Belize City) and hitch to the sanctuary. The village is tiny and quaint, occupied mostly by Creoles. Boats and guides can be hired for approximately US$80 per boat (maximum four people). It may be worth bargaining as competition is fierce. Trips include a visit to an unexcavated Maya site.

Altún Ha → *Colour map 3, A1.*
ⓘ *Daily 0900-1700, US$5, insect repellent necessary.*

The Maya remains of Altún Ha, 31 miles north of Belize City and 2 miles off the Old Northern Highway, are worth a visit. Altún Ha was a major ceremonial centre in the Classic period (AD 250-900) and also a trading station linking the Caribbean coast with Maya centres in the interior. There are two central plazas surrounded by 13 partially excavated pyramids and temples. What the visitor sees now is composite, not how the site would have been at any one time in the past. The largest piece of worked Maya jade ever found, a head of the Sun God Kinich Ahau weighing 9½ lb (4.3 kg), was found here in the main temple (B-4) in 1968. It is now in a bank vault in Belize City. Nearby is a large reservoir, now called **Rockstone Road**.

Orange Walk → *Colour map 3, A1. Population: 15,990.*

The Northern Highway runs to Orange Walk (66 miles), the centre of a district where Creoles, Mennonites and Maya earn their living from timber, sugar planting and general agriculture. Nearby, the impressive ruins of Lamanai make a good day trip – see below. This is also the departure point for Sartaneja and the Shipstern Peninsula and for the long overland trip to Río Bravo Conservation Area, Chan Chich and Gallon Jug.

There is little to draw the visitor for an extended stay in Orange Walk. An agricultural centre and the country's second city, it is busy with the comings and goings of a small town. Orange Walk is a truly multicultural centre with inhabitants from all over Central America, making Spanish the predominant language. Originally from Canada, Mennonites live in nearby colonies using the town as their marketing and supply centre. The only battle fought on Belizean soil took place here, during the Yucatecan Caste Wars (1840-1870s): the Maya leader, Marcus Canul, was shot in the fighting in 1872. The **House of Culture** on Main Street shows a history of the town's development.

Buses plying the route from Belize City to the Mexican border stop on Queen Victoria Avenue, the main street, close to the town hall. While a few pleasant wooden buildings remain on quiet side streets, most are worn out and badly in need of repair. Many have been pulled down and replaced by the standard concrete box affairs, which lack both inspiration and style.

A toll bridge now spans the New River a few miles south of the town at Tower Hill. There is a market overlooking New River, which is well organized with good food stalls and interesting architecture.

West and south of Orange Walk

From Orange Walk a road heads west, before turning south, running parallel to the Mexican and then Guatemalan border, where it becomes unpaved. Along this road are several archaeological sites. First is **Cuello**, 4 miles west on San Antonio road, behind Cuello Distillery (ask there for permission to visit); taxi about US$3.50. The site dates back to 1000 BC, but, although it has yielded important discoveries in the study of Maya and pre-Maya cultures, there is little for the layman to appreciate and no facilities for visitors. At **Yo Creek** the road divides, north to San Antonio, and south through miles of cane fields and tiny farming settlements as far as **San Felipe** (20 miles via San Lázaro, Trinidad and August Pine Ridge). At August Pine Ridge there is a daily bus to Orange Walk at 1000. You can camp at the house of Narciso Novelo or 'Chicho' (T323-3019), a little-known secret and a relaxing place to stay set amongst bananas, pine tres, bushes and flowers; no fixed cost, just pay what you think. Chicho will meet you off the bus if you call ahead. At San

Felipe, a branch leads southeast to Indian Church/Lamanai, 35 miles from Orange Walk (one hour driving, 4WD needed when wet). Another road heads west to Blue Creek Village on the Mexican border (see below).

Lamanai → *Colour map 3, A1.*
ⓘ *US$5.*

Near Indian Church, one of Belize's largest archaeological sites, Lamanai is on the west side of New River Lagoon, 22 miles by river south of Orange Walk. Difficult to get to and hidden in the jungle, it is a perfect setting to hide the mysteries of the Maya and definitely worth a visit. While the earliest buildings were erected about 700 BC, culminating in the completion of the 112-ft major temple, N10-43, about 100 BC (the tallest known pre-Classic Maya structure), there is evidence the site was occupied as long ago as 1500 BC. As a Maya site, it is believed to have the longest history of continuous occupation and, with the Spanish and British sites mentioned below and the present-day refugee village nearby, Lamanai's history is impressive. The Maya site has been partially cleared, but covers a large area so a guide is recommended. The views from temple N10-43, dedicated to Chac, are superb; look for the Yin-Yang-like symbol below the throne on one of the other main temples, which also has a 12-ft-tall mask overlooking its plaza. Visitors can wander freely along narrow trails and climb the stairways. There is a very informative museum housing the only known stela found at the site. There is also a fine jungle lodge, see Sleeping, page 382.

At nearby **Indian Church**, a Spanish mission was built over one of the Maya temples in 1580, and the British established a sugar mill here. The remains of both buildings can still be seen. The archaeological reserve is jungle and howler monkeys are visible in the trees. There are many birds and the best way to see them is to reach Lamanai by boat, easily arranged in Orange Walk or by taking a day trip from Belize City, see Tour operators, page 361. The earlier you go the better, but the trips from Orange Walk all leave at pretty standard times. The mosquitoes are vicious in the wet season (wear trousers, take repellent). The community phone for information on Indian Church, including buses, is T309-3015.

Blue Creek and around → *Colour map 3, A1.*
West of San Felipe is Blue Creek (10 miles), the largest of the Mennonite settlements. Many of the inhabitants of these close-knit villages arrived in 1959, members of a Canadian colony that had migrated to Chihuahua, Mexico, to escape encroaching modernity. They preserve their Low German dialect, are exempt from military service, and their industry now supplies the country with most of its poultry, eggs, vegetables and furniture. Some settlements, such as Neustadt in the west, have been abandoned because of threats by drug smugglers in the early 1990s. Belize and Mexico have signed an agreement to build an international bridge from Blue Creek across the river to La Unión, together with a river port close to the bridge. It is not known when work will start; at present there is a canoe-service for foot passengers across the Blue Creek.

A vast area to the south along the **Río Bravo** has been set aside as a conservation area (see page 346). Within this, there is a study and accommodation centre near the Maya site of **La Milpa**. The site is at present being excavated by a team from the University of Texas and Boston University, USA.

A good road can be followed 35 miles south to **Gallon Jug**, where a jungle tourism lodge has been built in the **Chan Chich** Maya ruin, see Sleeping. The journey to Chan Chich passes through the Río Bravo Conservation Area, is rarely travelled and offers some of the best chances to see wildlife. Chan Chich is believed to have the highest number of jaguar sightings in Belize, and is also a birdwatchers' paradise. Another road has been cut south through Tambos to the main road between Belmopan and San Ignacio, but travel in this region is strictly a dry-weather affair.

Sartaneja and northeast of Orange Walk

From Orange Walk a complex network of roads and tracks converge on **San Estevan** and Progresso to the north. The Maya ruins near San Estevan have reportedly been 'flattened' to a large extent and are not very impressive. Ten miles from San Estevan is a road junction; straight on is **Progresso**, a village picturesquely located on the lagoon of the same name. The right turn, signposted, runs off to the Mennonite village of **Little Belize** and continues (in poor condition) to **Chunox**, a village with many Maya houses of pole construction. In the dry season it is possible to drive from Chunox to the Maya site of Cerros (see below).

Three miles before Sarteneja is the visitor centre for Shipstern Nature Reserve, which covers 22,000 acres of this northeastern tip of Belize. Hardwood forests, saline lagoon systems and wide belts of savannah shelter a wide range of mammals (coatis and foxes, and all the fauna found elsewhere in Belize, except monkeys), reptiles and 200 species of bird. There are mounds of Maya houses and fields everywhere. The most remote forest, south of the lagoon, is not accessible to short-term visitors. There is a botanical trail leading into the forest with trees labelled with Latin and local Yucatec Maya names; a booklet is available. At the visitor centre is the **Butterfly Breeding Centre** ① *daily 0800-1700, US$5 including excellent guided tour*. Visit on a sunny day if possible; on dull days the butterflies hide themselves in the foliage. There is rather poor dormitory accommodation at the visitor centre, US$10 per person. A day-trip by private car is possible from Sarteneja or Orange Walk. Mosquito repellent is essential.

Leaving the Northern Highway, a road heads east to **Sarteneja**, a small fishing and former boat-building settlement founded by Yucatán refugees in the 19th century. The main catch is lobster and conch. On Easter Sunday there is a popular regatta, with all types of boat racing, dancing and music. There are the remains of an extensive Maya city scattered throughout the village, and recent discoveries have been made and are currently being explored to the south around the area of Shipstern Lagoon.

Corozal and around → *Colour map 3, A1. Population: 9110.*

The Northern Highway continues to Corozal (96 miles from Belize City), formerly the centre of the sugar industry, now with a special zone for the clothing industry and garment exports. Much of the old town was destroyed by Hurricane Janet in 1955 and it is now a mixture of modern concrete commercial buildings and Caribbean clapboard seafront houses on stilts. Like Orange Walk it is economically depressed but Corozal is much the safer place. It is open to the sea with a pleasant waterfront where the market is held. There is no beach but you can swim in the sea and lie on the grass. You can check out the local website at www.corozal.com.

Between Orange Walk and Corozal, in San José and San Pablo, is the archaeological site of **Nohmul**, a ceremonial centre whose main acropolis dominates the surrounding cane fields (the name means 'Great Mound'). Permission to visit the site must be obtained from Sr Estevan Itzab, whose house is opposite the water tower.

From Corozal, a road leads 7 miles northeast to **Consejo**, a quiet, seaside fishing village on Chetumal Bay. No public transport, taxi about US$10.

Six miles northeast of Corozal, to the right of the road to Chetumal, is **Four Mile Lagoon**, about a quarter of a mile off the road (buses will drop you there). Clean swimming, better than Corozal bay, some food and drinks available; it is often crowded at weekends.

Across the bay to the south of Corozal stand the mounds of **Cerros**, once an active Maya trading port whose central area was reached by canal. Some of the site is flooded but one pyramid, 69-ft-high with stucco masks on its walls, has been partially excavated. Take a boat from Corozal, walk around the bay (a boat is needed to cross the mouth of the New River) or do the dry-season vehicular trail from Progresso and Chunox (see above). Trips can be arranged with **Hotel Maya** and **Hok'Ol K'in Guest House**, from US$60 for a water taxi carrying up to six people.

◉ North Belize listings

For Sleeping and Eating price codes and other relevant information, see Essentials pages 31-33.

● Sleeping

Bermudian Landing and the Community Baboon Sanctuary *p377*
L-B Black Orchid Resort, T225 9158, www.blackorchidresort.com. Selection of rooms with shared bath through to luxury villas on the banks of the Belize River. Restaurant, fresh water swimming pool, and very good tours along the Belize River in search of history, howler monkeys and crocodiles, with friendly owner Doug Thompson. A great alternative choice to Belize City or Crooked Tree. Airport transfers easily arranged.
A-B Howler Monkey Lodge, 400 m from museum, T220-2158, www.howlermonkey lodge.com. Screened windows, fans, shared bath cheaper, student discount, TCs, Visa, MasterCard accepted, camping US$5 per person, bring tent, river tours US$25 per person, recommended. Transport from Belize City in pickup US$40, 1-4 people, on request. Breakfast, lunch and dinner, US$5-9. Many good tours including nighttime crocodile adventures US$40. Canoe rentals in Burrell Boom for trips on Belize River to see birds, howler monkeys, manatee and other wildlife.
C Community Baboon Sanctuary, *cabañas* are available alongside the visitor centre, bath, hot water. Basic lodging is also available with families in the village and can

be arranged through the Baboon Sanctuary office.

Crooked Tree Wildlife Sanctuary *p377*
AL-A Crooked Tree Lodge, T+1 (207) 404 9066, www.crookedtreelodgebelize.com. Relaxing birdwatching on the lagoon, and wildlife- and nature-related tours. Run by Mick and Angie Webb.
AL-B Bird's Eye View Lodge, T203-2040, www.birdseyeviewbelize.com. Owned by the Gillett family. Single and double rooms, shower, fan, meals available, boat trips, horse riding, canoe rental, nature tours with licensed guide. Ask for information at the **Belize Audubon Society** (see page 346).

Orange Walk *p378*
Parking for vehicles is very limited at hotels.
A-B Hotel de la Fuente, 14 Main St, T322-2290, www.hoteldelafuente.com. With recently renovated suites of rooms, with kitchenettes, simple wooden desks and wildlife paintings by a local artist. Tours to Lamanai available.
B D'Victoria, 40 Belize Rd (Main St), T322-2518, www.dvictoriabelize.com. A/c, shower, hot water, parking, pool, quite comfortable but somewhat run-down.
B-C St Christopher's, 12 Main St, T/F302-1064, www.stchristophershotelbze.com. Beautiful clean rooms and bathrooms, highly recommended and the best in town.
C-D Akihito Japanese Hotel, 22 Belize Corozal Rd, T302-0185, akihitolee@

hotmail.com. An affordable place in the centre of town.

D-E Lucia's Guest House, 68 San Antonio Rd, T322-2244, osiris-rod@yahoo.com. One of the budget places in town that gets recommendations, 5 mins west of town.

Lamanai *p379*

AL Lamanai Outpost Lodge, at Indian Church, T223-3578, www.lamanai.com. Run by the incredibly friendly Howells, this beautiful lodge is a short walk from Lamanai ruins, overlooking New River Lagoon, package deals available, day tours, thatched wooden cabins with bath and fan, hot water, 24-hr electricity, restaurant, excellent and well-informed guides. Juvenile crocodile study underway and guests are invited to participate.

Camping

Nazario Ku, the site caretaker, permits camping or hammocks at his house, opposite path to Lamanai ruins, good value for backpackers.

Blue Creek and around *p379*

LL Chan Chich, Chiun Chah, T223-4419, www.chanchich.com. A beautifully sited lodge in the midst of Maya ruins with an extensive trail system in the grounds, delicious food, fantastic birdwatching and wildlife-watching opportunties; very good guides; pool. Recommended. Phone before setting out for Chan Chich for information on the roads.

AL La Milpa Field Station, La Milpa, for information call T323-0011, or contact the Programme for Belize in Belize City (T227-5616, www.pfbelize.org). Makes a good base for exploring trails in the region and birdwatching. To reach La Milpa, go 6 miles west from Blue Creek to Tres Leguas, then follow the signs south towards the Río Bravo Escarpment. The reserve is privately owned and you will need proof of booking to pass the various checkpoints. 4 double *cabañas*, spacious, comfortable, with a

thatched roof overhanging a large wooden deck, or a dormitory sleeping up to 30.

C Hill Bank Field Station, on the banks of the New River Lagoon. Also a good base for exploring trails in the region and birdwatching, and with a dormitory sleeping up to 30. See **La Milpa Field Station**, above, for contact details.

Sartaneja and northeast of Orange Walk *p380*

B-C Fernando's Guest House, on seafront near centre of Sartaneja, T423-2085, sartenejabelize@hotmail.com.

E Backpacker's Paradise, http://backpackers. bluegreenbelize.com, 5 mins from the village. Cabins and camping, kitchen and restaurant and a range of activities. Attracts a young and boisterous crowd.

Corozal and around *p380*

AL-A Las Palmas Hotel, 123, 5th Av South, T422-0196, www.laspalmashotelbelize.com. With bath and fan, OK, *refrescos* available, good food, lively bar downstairs.

AL-B Tony's, South End, T422-2055, www.tonysinn.com. With a/c, clean, comfortable units in landscaped grounds. Recommended, but restaurant overpriced.

A Copa Banana, 409 Corozal Bay Rd, T422-0284, www.copabanana.bz. Newest place in town, with 5 suites all with private bathrooms. US-owned so complimentary coffee each morning. Ask the bus driver to drop you off.

A Hok'Ol K'in Guest House, 4th Av and 4th St South, T422-3329, www.corozal.net. Immaculate rooms. Runs tours to Cerros.

D Caribbean Village Resort, South End, T422 2725. Hot water, US$5 camping, US$12 trailer park, restaurant, recommended.

Camping

Caribbean Motel and Trailer Park, see **Caribbean Village Resort**, above. Camping possible but not very safe (US$4 per person), shaded sites, restaurant.

❶ Eating

Orange Walk *p378*
Most restaurants in town are Chinese.
We've received encouraging reports about
La Hacienda Steakhouse and **Marvias**.
ᵗᵗ Nahil Mayab, www.nahilmayab.com,
Orange Walk Town. Contemporary Mexican
cuisine, grilled meat and vegetarian dishes.
Best in town. Closed Sun.
Ψ Central Plaza Restaurant, behind the
main bus terminal. A popular choice in
a handy location.
Ψ Diner, Clarke St, behind the hospital.
Good meals, very friendly, taxi US$4 or walk.

Corozal and around *p380*
There are many Chinese restaurants in town.
ᵗᵗ Cactus Plaza, 5th Av South. A loud bar
with lots of fluorescent lighting and great
a/c. Worth trying if you're stuck in town
for the night.
ᵗᵗ Purple Toucan, No 52, 4th Av North.
Good restaurant and lively bar with pool
table and good music. Opposite is **Marcelo's**,
which serves good pizza.
Ψ Border, 6th Av South. Friendly Chinese,
good food.
Ψ Corozal Garden, 4th Av, 1 block south.
Good, quick local food.
Ψ Gongora's Pastry, southwest corner
of main square. Hot pizza pieces, cakes
and drinks.
Ψ Newtown Chinese, 7th Av, just north of
the gas station on the other side of the main
road. Large portions, good quality but
slow service.
Ψ RD's Diner, 7-4th Av, T422-3796. Burgers
and American-style food.

▲ Activities and tours

Orange Walk *p378*
Jungle River Tours, 20 Lovers Lane, T302-
2293, lamanaimayatour@btl.net. In Lovers'
Café on the southeastern corner of the park.
Organize and run trips to Lamanai (US$40

plus entrance of US$5, including lunch,
departing 0900 returning 1600), Altún Ha and
New River area, regular trips, *the* specialists on
the region and consistently recommended.
They also provide trips to any destination in
Belize with a minimum of 4 people.

❸ Transport

**Bermudian Landing and the
Community Baboon Sanctuary** *p377*
Bus
From **Belize City**, Mcfadzean Bus from corner
of Amara Av and Cemetery Rd at 1215 and
1715 Mon-Fri; 1200 and 1400 Sat. **Rancho
Bus (Pook's Bus)** from Mosul St, 1700
Mon-Fri, 1300 Sat, check details, US$1.50-2,
1 hr. Alternatively, any bus travelling the
Northern Hwy can drop you off at the
turn-off to Bermudian Landing where you
can wait for a bus, or hitch a ride. A day trip
giving any meaningful time in the sanctuary
is difficult by public transport, so it's best
to stay the night.

Crooked Tree Wildlife Sanctuary *p377*
Bus
Buses from **Belize City** with JEX (1035);
return from Crooked Tree at 0600-0700.

Altún Ha *p378*
Bus
With little transport on this road, hitching
is not recommended – best to go in a
private vehicle or a tour group. Vehicles
leave **Belize City** for the village of **Maskall**,
8 miles north of Altún Ha, several days a
week, but same-day return is not possible.

Orange Walk *p378*
Bus
Bus station is on street beside the fire station,
on the main road. All buses travelling from
Belize City to Corozal and beyond to
Chetumal stop in Orange Walk; from **Belize**,
US$3. From **Corozal**, US$1.50, 50 mins. For
Lamanai take bus to Indian Church (Mon,

Wed, Fri 1600). Buses to **Sarteneja** (which is 40 miles away) outside **Zeta's Store** on Main St, 5 between 1300 and 1900, US$2.50. Also to **Progresso** at 1100 and 1130.

Blue Creek and around *p379*
Air
Flights to Chan Chich from **Belize City** can be chartered.

Sartaneja and northeast of Orange Walk *p380*
Bus
Bus from **Belize City** at 1200, US$4.50, from the corner of Victoria and North Front St. Buses also leave from **Corozal** (1400), via Orange Walk (1530).

Corozal and around *p380*
Air
Maya Island Air, daily from Belize City via Caye Caulker and San Pedro (Ambergris Caye); **Tropic Air** daily from San Pedro. Airstrip 3 miles south, taxi US$1.50. Private charters to **Sartaneja** cost about US$75 for the 30-min journey (compared with 3 hrs by road).

Boat
To **Orange Walk**, leaving at 1400.

Bus
Heading south, buses leave every 30 mins, starting at 0400 running until 1830. Regular service 3 hrs, US$2.50, faster express service, 2½ hrs, US$3.50, leaves at 0600, 0700, 1200, 1500 and 1800. If heading north, buses from **Belize City** continue north to **Chetumal** terminal, with stopping time to allow for immigration procedures.

For those coming from Mexico who are interested in **Tikal** in Guatemala, it is possible to make the journey border to border in a day, with a change of bus in Belize City.

Taxi
Leslie's Taxi Service, T422-2377. Transfers from Corozol to the Mexican border, US$22 for a 4-person taxi. Ask for a quote for other services. Reliable and professional.

❶ Directory

Orange Walk *p378*
Banks Belize Bank on Main St (down Park St from Park, turn left). Scotia Bank on Park, US$0.50 commission. Shell Station will change TCs. **Internet** K&M, on Main St.

Corozal and around *p380*
Banks Atlantic Bank (charges US$2.50 for Visa cash advances), Bank of Nova Scotia, and Belize Bank. For exchange also ask at the bus station.
Internet Charlotte's Web, 5th Av between 5th and 6th St South, cybercafé and book exchange.

West Belize

Impressive sights – artificial and natural – line the route from Belize City to the Guatemalan border, starting with Belize Zoo – a pleasant break from the norm. Monkey Bay Wildlife Sanctuary and Guanacaste National Park are both worth a visit. From the bustling town of San Ignacio, there are canoe trips down the Macal River and dramatic cave systems, journeys into the impressive limestone scenery of Mountain Pine Ridge, and the spectacular Maya ruins of Caracol, Xunantunich and Cahal Pech to explore. Day trippers can also cross the border for a quick visit to Tikal in Guatemala. For listings, see pages 391-395.

Belize City to San Ignacio → For listings, see pages 391-395.

The Western Highway leaves Belize City past the cemetery, where burial vaults stand elevated above the boggy ground, running through palmetto scrub and savannah landscapes created by 19th-century timber cutting. At Mile 16 is **Hattieville**, originally a temporary settlement for the homeless after Hurricane Hattie in 1961. The highway roughly parallels the Sibun River, once a major trading artery where mahogany logs were floated down to the coast in the rainy season; the place name 'Boom' recalls spots where chains were stretched across rivers to catch logs being floated downstream.

San Ignacio

To 2 & Branch Mouth Rd
Burns Av
Savannah St
Hospital St
Tejidia St
West St
David's Adventure Tours
Collective Taxis to Benque de Viejo
Galvez
Far West St
Mayawalk Tours
Savannah Taxi Co-op
Pacz Tours
Maya St
To Bullet Tree Falls
Hudson St
Macal River
To Belize City, San Antonio & Mountain Pine Ridge
Church St
Far West St
Town Hall
Cayo Com
King St
Hawkesworth Bridge
To 9 11 Cahal Pech, Xunantunich, Che Chem Ha
Cave, Benque Viejo del Carmen & Guatemala

N
50 metres
50 yards

Sleeping
Casa Blanca Guesthouse **1**
Hi-Et **3**
Martha's Guest House **4**
Midas Resort **2**
San Ignacio Resort **11**
Venus **5**
Windy Hill Resort **9**

Eating
Flavia's **7**
Eva's Bar **2**
Mr Greedy's Pizzaria **4**
Maxim's **5**
Serendib **6**

Paddling the great Macal River

Time it right and you can paddle down the length of the Macal River taking part in La Ruta Maya canoe race. It's a gruelling three-day open canoe race, starting in San Ignacio covering 180 miles along the river before ending in Belize City on Baron Bliss Day (early March). All food and water is provided for the trip, but you'll need to be fit and healthy.

You'll struggle to compete at the racing end of the field unless you're a top athlete and have a canoe of modern design, but plenty of people enter the race for the challenge and with a bit of luck it's possible to turn up, talk with people around town and find yourself a place on a boat. For information, visit www.larutamayabelize.com.

The small but excellent **Belize Zoo** ① *daily 0900-1700, US$7.50, www.belizezoo.org, take any bus from Belize City along the Western Highway (1 hr)*, is at Mile 28½, watch out for the sign or tell the driver where you're going. It is a wonderful collection of local species (originally gathered for a wildlife film), lovingly cared for and displayed in wire-mesh enclosures amid native trees and shady vegetation, including jaguar and smaller cats, pacas (called gibnuts in Belize), snakes, monkeys, parrots, crocodile, tapir (mountain cow), peccary (wari) and much more. Highly recommended, even for those who hate zoos. Get there early to miss the coach party arrivals. Tours by enthusiastic guides, T-shirts and postcards sold for fundraising.

At Mile 31½, the **Monkey Bay Wildlife Sanctuary** protects 1070 acres of tropical forest and savannah between the highway and the Sibun River (great swimming and canoeing). Birds are abundant and there is a good chance of seeing mammals.

Forty-seven miles from Belize City, a minor road runs 2 miles north to **Banana Bank Lodge and Jungle Equestrian Adventure** (see Sleeping, page 391).

A mile beyond the **Banana Bank Lodge and Jungle Equestrian Adventure** turning is the highway junction for Belmopan and Dangriga. At the confluence of the Belize River and Roaring Creek is the 50-acre **Guanacaste National Park** ① *US$2.50*, protecting a parcel of 'neotropical rainforest' and a huge 100-year-old *guanacaste* (tubroos) tree, which shelters a wide collection of epiphytes including orchids. Many mammals (jaguarundi, kinkajou, agouti etc) and up to 100 species of bird may be seen from the 3 miles of nature trails cut along the river. This is a particularly attractive swimming and picnicking spot at which to stop or break the journey if travelling on to Guatemala. It has a visitor centre, where luggage can be left. To get there, take an early morning bus from Belize City, see the park in a couple of hours, then pick up a bus going to San Ignacio or Dangriga.

Soon after the junction to Belmopan is **Roaring Creek**, once a thriving town but now rather overshadowed by the barely illuminated capital nearby. At Camelote, a dirt road southwards takes you to **Roaring River**. At Teakettle, turn south along a dirt road for 5 miles to **Pook's Hill Reserve** (see Sleeping, page 391).

The important but unimpressive **Floral Park** archaeological site is just beyond the bridge over **Barton Creek** (Mile 64). Just 2 miles further is **Georgeville**, from where a gravel road runs south into the Mountain Pine Ridge Forest Reserve (see page 389). The highway passes the turn-off at Norland for **Spanish Lookout**, a Mennonite settlement area 6 miles north (**B & F Restaurant**, Centre Road, by Farmers' Trading Centre, clean, excellent value). The **Central Farm Agricultural College**, the village of **Esperanza** and other small settlements along the way keep the road interesting until it reaches **Santa**

Elena. Formerly only linked by the substantial Hawkesworth suspension bridge to its twin town of San Ignacio, it now has a small, one-lane 'temporary bridge' you must take to cross the river to San Ignacio.

San Ignacio and around → For listings, see pages 391-395. Colour map: 3, A1.

Some 68 miles from Belize City and 10 miles from the border, San Ignacio (locally called **Cayo**) is the capital of Cayo District and Western Belize's largest town, an agricultural centre serving the citrus, cattle and peanut farms of the area, and a good base for excursions into the Mountain Pine Ridge and west Belize. It stands amid attractive wooded hills at 200-500 ft, with a good climate, and is a nice town to rest in if coming from Guatemala. The town is on the eastern branch of the Old, or Belize River, known as the Macal. The 180-mile river journey down to Belize City is internationally famous as the route for the annual 'Ruta Maya Belize River Challenge', a gruelling three-day canoe race held the weekend of Baron Bliss Day, 9 March, see box, page 386.

A short walk from San Ignacio (800 m from **Hotel San Ignacio**) is **Cahal Pech** ① *daily 0600-1700, US$5*, an interesting Maya site and nature reserve on a wooded hill overlooking the town, with a visitor centre and small museum.

Four miles west of San Ignacio on a good road is **Bullet Tree Falls**, a pleasant cascade amid relaxing surroundings on the western branch of the Belize River, here in its upper course known as the Mopan River.

Twelve miles north of San Ignacio is **El Pilar**, an archaeological site that straddles the border with Guatemala. Although it is a large site (about 94 acres), much of it has been left intentionally uncleared so that selected architectural features are exposed within the rainforest. The preserved rainforest here is home to hundreds of species of birds and animals. There are five trails – three archaeological, two nature – the longest of which is 1½ miles. There are more than a dozen pyramids and 25 identified plazas. Unusually for Maya cities in this region, there is an abundance of water (streams and falls). Take the Bullet Tree Road north of San Ignacio, cross the Mopan River Bridge and follow the signs to El Pilar. The reserve is 7 miles from Bullet Tree on an all-weather limestone road. It can be reached by vehicle, horse or mountain bike (hiking is only recommended for the experienced; carry lots of water). The caretakers, who live at the south end of the site in a modern green-roofed house, are happy to show visitors around. The **Cayo Tour Guides Association** works in association with the **Belize River Archaeological Settlement Survey (BRASS)** and can take visitors. See also *Trails of El Pilar: A Guide to the El Pilar Archaeological Reserve for Maya Flora and Fauna*.

Dr Rosita Arvigo, a Maya healer, sells a selections of herbs (the jungle salve, US$5, has been found effective against mosquito bites) and a book on medicinal plants used by the Maya. The herbs and books are also sold in most local gift shops. She also runs the **Ix Chel Wellness Center** ① *25 Burns Av, T804-0264, by appointment only*, offering herbology and traditional Maya healing. For local medicines you could also talk to the García sisters (see San Antonio, page 389).

The **San Ignacio Resort Hotel** houses the **Green Iguana Exhibit and Medicinal Jungle Trail** ① *0700-1600, US$5.45 for a guided tour of the medicinal trail*, where you will learn about the life and habits of this vibrantly coloured reptile. Entrance fees are used to provide scholarships for local pupils. From March to May you're likely to see iguanas in the wild if you take the pleasant half hour walk from San Ignacio to where the Mopan and Macal rivers meet.

Local tour operators (see below) generally offer similar tours at similar prices. Canoe trips up the **Macal River** are worthwhile. They take about three hours upstream, 1½ hours on return. Hiring a canoe to go upstream without a guide is not recommended unless you are highly proficient as there are Grade II rapids one hour from San Ignacio. Another trip is to **Barton Creek Cave**, a 1½-hour drive followed by a 1½-hour canoe trip in the cave. The cave vault system is vast, the rock formations are beautiful, the silence is eerily comforting and all can be explored for a considerable distance by canoe (US$55 per person minimum two people). Tours can be arranged at almost every place in San Ignacio.

For a more adventurous caving tour, you shouldn't leave without going to **Actun Tunichil Muknal (ATM) Cave** (the Cave of the Stone Sepulchre), a one-hour drive from San Ignacio to the Tapir Mountain Nature reserve, a 45-minute jungle hike in the reserve and then 3½ hours of adventurous, exhilarating caving, US$75. Besides the beautiful rock formations, this cave is full of Maya artefacts and sacrificial remains. The guides from both **Emilio Awe's Pacz Tours** and **Mayawalk**, are recommended. Mayawalk also run an overnight ATM tour (US$180). Under 8s and pregnant women are discouraged from taking this tour. ▸▸ *See Activities and tours, page 394.*

Maya artefacts can be seen in **Che Chem Ha Cave** ① *T820-4063*, on the private property of the Moralez family on the Vaca Plateau, south of San Ignacio (Benque). In contrast to Barton Creek and Actun Tunichil Muknal this is a so-called dry cave. The family offers trips into the cave, a half-hour hike to the entrance, followed by a one- to 1½-hour walk in the cave. The view from the property is stunning and the family serves lunch. Tours start at 0900 and 1300. If you go by private transport be there in time for the tour and call the family in advance or, better still, book a tour with an agency in San Ignacio.

Trips to the nearby ruins of **Xunantunich** (see below) are very easy by bus, regular traffic going to the Guatemalan border. Tours of **Mountain Pine Ridge** are available (see below), but shop around carefully – if you decide to go with a taxi you probably won't get far in the wet season. Trips to **Caracol** are best arranged from San Ignacio, see page 394, and if you only want to visit Tikal in Guatemala, you can arrange a day trip that will maximize your time spent at the ruins. On a good road 9 miles west of San Ignacio is the tranquil town of **Benque Viejo del Carmen**, near the Guatemalan border. Many of the inhabitants are Maya Mopan. For information on the Benque Viejo–Melchor de Mencos border crossing, see page 348.

South of San Ignacio, halfway between Clarissa Falls turn-off and Nabitunich is Chial Road, gateway to adventure. A half-mile down the road is a sharp right turn that takes you through Negroman, the modern site of the ancient Maya city of **Tipu** which has the remains of a Spanish Mission from the 1500s. Across the river from here is **Guacamallo Camp**, rustic jungle camping and starting point for canoe trips on the Macal River. Two miles further up, also across the river, is **Ek Tun** (see Sleeping, page 392). **Belize Botanic Gardens** ① *T824-3101, www.belizebotanic.org, daily 0700-1700, US$2.50, guided walks 0730-1500, US$7.50*, on 50 acres of rolling hills, is next to the **Du Plooys'** lodge (see Sleeping, page 392) with hundreds of orchids, dozens of named tree species, ponds and lots of birds. Recommended.

Xunantunich → *Colour map 3, A1.*

① *Daily 0730-1600, US$5; a leaflet on the area is available from the site for US$4. Apart from a small refreshment stand, there are no facilities for visitors, but a museum has been built and a couple of stelae have been put on display in a covered area. It is an extremely hot walk up the hill, with little or no shade, so start early. Last ferry (free) back is at 1630.*

At Xunantunich ('Maiden of the Rock') there are Classic Maya remains in beautiful surroundings. The heart of the city was three plazas aligned on a north-south axis, lined with many temples, the remains of a ball court, and surmounted by the Castillo. At 130 ft, this was thought to be the highest artificial structure in Belize until the Sky Palace at Caracol was measured. The impressive view takes in the jungle, the lowlands of Petén and the blue flanks of the Maya Mountains. Maya graffiti can still be seen on the wall of Structure A-16 – friezes on the Castillo, some restored in modern plaster, represent astronomical symbols. Extensive excavations took place in 1959-1960 but only limited restoration work has been undertaken.

Just east of the ferry, **Magaña's Art Centre** and the **Xunantunich Women's Group** sell locally made crafts and clothing in a shop on a street off the highway. About 1½ miles further north are the ruins of **Actuncan**, probably a satellite of Xunantunich. Both sites show evidence of earthquake damage.

Mountain Pine Ridge → *For listings, see pages 391-395. Colour map 3, A1.*

Mountain Pine Ridge is a Forest Reserve (146,000 acres) that covers the northwest section of the Maya Mountains, an undulating landscape of largely undisturbed pine and gallery forest, and valleys of lush hardwood forests filled with orchids, bromeliads and butterflies. The devastation to large swathes of the pine forest first caused by an infestation of the southern pine bark beetle in 2001 continues to impact on the area. Note the frequent changes of colour of the soil and look out for the fascinating insect life. If lucky, you may see deer. There's river scenery to enjoy, high waterfalls, numerous limestone caves and shady picnic sites; it's a popular excursion despite the rough roads. The easiest way of visiting is on a trip from San Ignacio. Hitching is difficult but not impossible. Try contacting the **Forestry Conservation Officer** ⓘ *T824-3280*, who may be able to help.

Two roads lead into the reserve: from Georgeville to the north and up from Santa Elena via Cristo Rey. These meet near **San Antonio**, a Mopan Maya village with many thatched-roof houses and the nearby Pacbitun archaeological site (where stelae and musical instruments have been unearthed). At San Antonio, the García sisters have their workshop, museum and shop where they sell carvings in local slate. They also have a guesthouse (D). You can sample Maya food and learn about the use of medicinal plants. This is a regular stop on tours to the Mountain Pine Ridge. A donation of US$0.50 is requested; US$12.50 is charged to take photos of the sisters at work. Two buses a day from San Ignacio, 1000 and 1430, from market area; check times of return buses before leaving San Ignacio.

1000-ft falls

The main forest road meanders along rocky spurs, from which unexpected and often breathtaking views emerge of jungle far below and streams plunging hundreds of feet over red-rock canyons. A lookout point (with a small charge) has been provided to view the impressive falls, said to be 1000 ft high (often shrouded in fog October to January). On a clear day you can see Belmopan from this viewpoint. It is quite a long way from the main road and is probably not worth the detour if time is short, particularly in the dry season (February to May) when the flow is restricted. At this time of year, there is an ever-present danger of fire and open fires are strictly prohibited. Eighteen miles into the reserve the road crosses the **Río On**. Here, where the river tumbles into inviting pools over huge granite boulders; is one of Belize's most beautiful picnic and swimming spots. The rocks form little water slides and are fun for children.

Augustine

Five miles further on is the tiny village of Augustine (also called Douglas D'Silva or **Douglas Forest Station**), the main forest station where there is a shop, accommodation in two houses (bookable through the Forestry Dept in Belmopan, the area Forestry Office is in San Antonio) and a **camping ground** ⓘ *US$1, no mattresses (see rangers for all information on the area), keep your receipt, a guard checks it on the way out of Mountain Pine Ridge*. A mile beyond Augustine is a cluster of caves in rich rainforest. The entrance to the **Río Frío Cave** (in fact a tunnel) is over 65 ft high, and there are many spectacular rock formations and sandy beaches where the river flows out. Trees in the parking area and along the Cuevas Gemelas nature trail, which starts one hour from the Río Frío cave, are labelled. It's a beautiful excursion and highly recommended.

Forestry roads continue south further into the mountains, reaching **San Luis** (6 miles), the only other inhabited camp in the area, with post office, sawmill and forest station, and continuing on over the granite uplands of the Vaca Plateau into the **Chiquibul Forest Reserve** (460,000 acres).

The four forest reserves that cover the Maya Mountains are the responsibility of the Forestry Department, who have only about 20 rangers to patrol over a million acres of heavily forested land. A hunting ban prohibits the carrying of firearms. Legislation, however, allows for controlled logging; all attempts to have some areas declared national parks or biosphere reserves have so far been unsuccessful. You can stay in the area at **Las Cuevas Research Station and Explorers Lodge** (see Sleeping).

Caracol → *Colour map 3, A1.*

About 24 miles south-southwest of Augustine, Caracol (about one hour by 4WD) is a rediscovered Maya city. The area is now a National Monument Reservation. Caracol was established about 300 BC and continued well into the Late Classic period (glyphs record a victorious war against Tikal). Why Caracol was built in such a poorly watered region is not known, but Maya engineers showed great ingenuity in constructing reservoirs and terracing the fields. The **Sky Palace** (*Caana*) pyramid, which climbs 138 ft above the site, is being excavated by members of the University of Central Florida. Excavations take place between February and May, but there are year-round caretakers who will show you around. Very knowledgeable guides escort groups around the site twice daily, there's an information centre and an exhibition hall has been built. The road has been improved and is passable for much of the year with normal vehicles and year-round with 4WD. It is an interesting journey as you pass through the Mountain Pine Ridge, then cross the Macal River and immediately enter a broadleaf tropical forest. Take your own food as there is none at the site. Otherwise **Pine Ridge Lodge**, **Five Sister's Lodge** or **Blancaneaux Lodge** are open for lunch (see Sleeping).

For Sleeping and Eating price codes and other relevant information, see Essentials pages 31-33.

● Sleeping

Belize City to San Ignacio *p385*
L Jaguar Paw Jungle Resort, near Belize Zoo on curve of Caves Branch River on road south at Mile 31, T820-2023, www.jaguarpaw.com, with meals.
L-A Pook's Hill Lodge, Pook's Hill Reserve, T820-2017, www.pookshillbelize.com. A 300-acre nature reserve on Roaring Creek, 6 *cabañas*, horses and rafting.
AL Banana Bank Lodge and Jungle Equestrian Adventure, Guanacaste National Park, T820-2020, www.bananabank.com. Resort accommodation, with meals, horse riding on river side and jungle trails, birding and river trips.
C-E Tropical Education Centre, at Belize Zoo. Basic-style accommodation.
E Monkey Bay Wildlife Sanctuary, Mile 31 Western Hwy, Belmopan, T820-3032, www.watershedbelize.org. Dormitory accommodation or you can camp on a wooden platform with thatched roof, swim in the river, showers available, take meals with family.

San Ignacio and around *p387, map p385*
Some hotels in town and on Cahal Pech Hill may be noisy at weekends from loud music, and during the day from traffic and buses. In the area surrounding San Ignacio there are many jungle hideaways. Ranging from secluded and exclusive cottages to full activity resorts, and covering a wide range of budgets, these places are normally an adventure on their own. Before going, make sure you know what's included in the price; food is often extra.

San Ignacio
LL-L San Ignacio Resort Hotel, 18 Buena Vista Rd, T824-2125, www.sanignacio belize.com. Southern end of town, on the

road to Benque Viejo. Rooms with bath, a/c, hot water, some with balconies. Helpful staff, clean, swimming pool, tennis court, excellent restaurant. Live music every weekend at the Stork Club. **Green Iguana Exhibit** on site, see page 387, and tour agency.
L-A Midas Resort, Branch Mouth Rd, T824-3172, www.midasbelize.com. An attractive 7-acre family-run resort, located on the edge of town, yet with a more remote wilderness feel. *Cabaña* accommodation with Wi-Fi service and access to the river for swims.
AL Martha's Guest House, 10 West St, T804-3647, www.marthasbelize.com. 10 comfortable rooms, 2 with balcony, TV, a/c, cheaper without, lounge area, good restaurant, friendly, clean, kitchen facilities, the family also runs **August Laundromat**.
A-C Casa Blanca Guesthouse, 10 Burns Av, T824-2080, www.casablancaguesthouse. com. 8 clean rooms with 2 beds in each, private shower, fan or a/c, TV, use of kitchenette, free coffee, friendly.
C Venus Hotel, 29 Burns Av, T824-3203, www.venushotelbelize.com. Family-run hotel providing 32 rooms with private bathroom and TV.
C-D Hi-Et, 12 West St, T824-2828, thehiet@ yahoo.com. Lovely, red and cream old wooden building with 10 rooms and private shower, cheaper without. Reportedly noisy, nice balcony, friendly, helpful, family-run, stunning orchids in patio. Free coffee.

Around San Ignacio
LL Blancaneaux Lodge, Mountain Pine Ridge Rd, east of San Ignacio, Central Farm, Cayo District, T824-3878, www.blancaneaux lodge.com. Once the mountain retreat of Francis Ford Coppola and his family, now one villa and wonderful, huge *cabañas* decorated in Guatemalan textiles, horse riding, croquet, spa, hot pool, overlooking a stream, private air strip. Access to Big Rock Falls. Italian restaurant and bar. Recommended.

LL The Lodge at Chaa Creek, on the Macal River, south of San Ignacio off the Chial Rd, after the turn to Ix Chel Farm, T824-2037, www.chaacreek.com, or hotel office at 56 Burns Av, San Ignacio. Upscale accommodation, amenities and tours, with spa, conference centre, butterfly breeding centre, natural history movement and an adventure centre. Strong supporters of environmental groups and projects. Tours and excursions offered.

L Du Plooys', south of San Ignacio, past the Chaa Creek road, then follow (including one steep hill) to its end above the Macal River, T824-3101, www.duplooys.com. Choices of accommodation and packages are available, enjoy the **Hangover Bar** with cool drinks on the deck overlooking trees and river. The **Belize Botanic Gardens** (see page 388) is also run by the Du Plooy family.

L Ek Tun, south of San Ignacio, T820-3002, in USA T303-4426150, www.ektunbelize.com. A 500-acre private jungle retreat on the Macal River, boat access only, 2 very private deluxe thatched guest cottages, excellent food, spectacular garden setting. Great spot for romantic adventurers. Advance reservations only, no drop-ins, adults only and 3-night minimum.

L-AL Five Sisters Lodge, east of San Ignacio, 2½ miles beyond **Blancaneaux Lodge** (see above), T820-4005, www.fivesisterslodge.com. Rustic cottages lit by oil lamps, great views, good-value restaurant. Recommended.

AL Las Cuevas Research Station and Explorer's Lodge, in the Chiquibul Forest, T822-2149, www.lascuevas.org. Isolated research station open to non-researchers. Rivers, caves, archaeological sites nearby, a genuine wilderness experience.

AL Mountain Equestrian Trails, Mile 8, Mountain Pine Ridge Rd (from Georgeville), Central Farm PO, Cayo District, T699 1124, www.metbelize.com. Accommodation in 4 double *cabañas* with bath, no electricity, hot water, mosquito nets, good food in *cantina*, ½-day, full-day and 4-day adventure tours on horseback in Western Belize, packages,

birdwatching tours and other expeditions offered, excellent guides and staff.

AL Pine Ridge Lodge, east of San Ignacio, on the road to Augustine, just past turning to Hidden Valley Falls, T606-4557, www.pineridgelodge.com. *Cabañas* in the pinewoods, including breakfast.

AL Windy Hill Resort, 2 miles west of San Ignacio, on Graceland Ranch, T824-2017, www.windyhillresort.com. 14 cottage units, all with bath, dining room, small pool, nature trails, horseriding and river trips can be arranged, expensive.

AL-A Cohune Palms River Cabanas, Bullet Tree Falls, T824-0166, www.cohune palms.com. 4 *cabañas* separated by a fabulously beautiful garden walk.

AL-A Mopan River Resort, Benque Viejo, T823-2047, www.mopanriverresort.com. Belize's 1st all-inclusive, luxury resort on the Mopan River, opposite Benque Viejo, boat access only 12 thatched *cabañas* with verandas nestled in a lush coconut grove, pool, water garden, 7-night minimum.

AL-B Maya Mountain Lodge (Bart and Suzi Mickler), ¾ mile east of San Ignacio at 9 Cristo Rey Rd, Santa Elena, San Ignacio, T824-2164, www.mayamountain.com. Welcoming, special weekly, monthly and family rates. Restaurant, expensive excursions, self-guided nature trail, swimming, hiking, riding, canoeing, fishing can be arranged.

A-B Iguana Junction, Bullet Tree Falls, T824-2249, www.iguanajunction.com. British-run with good-quality *cabaña* accommodation in a tropical riverbank location. Hammocks available for kids.

B Cahal Pech Village, south of town, near Cahal Pech, T824-3740, www.cahalpech.com. Thatched cabins or a/c rooms, restaurant, bar, meeting facilities.

B Parrot Nest, near village of Bullet Tree Falls, 3 miles north of San Ignacio, T820-4058, www.parrot-nest.com. Family run with small, comfortable tree houses in beautiful grounds by the river. Breakfast and dinner are available, as well as free tubing. Can arrange local tours.

C **Aguada Hotel**, Santa Elena, across the river, T804-3609, www.aguadahotel.com. Full-service hotel, 12 rooms, private baths, a/c costs more, fresh water pond and heart-shaped swimming pool, quiet part of town, excellent restaurant and bar.

C **Cosmos Camping & Cabanas**, Branch Mouth Rd, T824-2116, cosmoscamping@btl.net. 4 very simple units, or camp on the site alongside the Macal River. Tents for rent, washing and cooking facilities, run by friendly Belizean family, good breakfasts, canoe and bikes for hire, good. Cabins available (**E**).

C-D **Clarissa's Falls**, on Mopan River, down a signed track on the Benque road, around Mile 70, T824-3916, www.clarissafalls.com. Owned by Chena Galvez, thatched cottages on riverbank by a set of rapids, also bunkhouse with hammocks or beds, camping space and hook-ups for RVs, rafting, kayaking and tubing available, wonderful food in the restaurants.

Camping

D-E **Barton Creek Outpost**, T662-4797, www.bartoncreekoutpost.com. Located in a gloriously beautiful jungle setting, this excellent campsite is worth the minor adventure of getting to it (the best bet is to contact the owners Jimmy and Jacqueline a few days prior to arrival). Camping is free if you have your own gear, and you can also rent mattresses and camp gear. Campers are offered discounts on a range of tours (most notably to Barton Creek itself). Hot meals are available for purchase.

D-E **Inglewood Camping Grounds**, west of San Ignacio at Mile 68¼, T824-3555, www.inglewoodcampingground.com. *Palapas*, camping, RV hook-ups, hot and cold showers, maintained grounds, some highway noise.

Eating

San Ignacio and around *p387, map p385*

ψψψ **Running W**, in the San Ignacio Resort Hotel (see Sleeping). One of the best restaurants in town. Also live music every 2nd Sat in the bar of the same hotel.

ψψ **Eva's Bar**, 22 Burns Av, T804-2267, Mon-Sat 0800-1500, 1800-late. Good diner-style restaurant, local dishes, helpful with good local information, bike rental, internet facilities, tours.

ψψ **Flavia's**, 4 Far West St, T824-2821. Vegetarian available, reasonable prices and proud of their pizza and seafood.

ψψ **Mr Greedy's Pizzaria**, 5 Burns Av. Daily 0600-2100. Popular with locals and foreigners. Italian style oven-cooked pizza, beach sand floor and bamboo bar.

ψψ **Sanny's Grill**, several blocks down the hill off the Western Hwy past the Texaco station. Serves the 'world's best conch ceviche', full dinner menu, charming setting.

ψψ **Serendib**, 27 Burns Av, T824-2302. Mon-Sat, 1030-1500, 1830-1100. Good food and good value, Sri Lankan owners, Indian-style food.

ψψ-ψ **Martha's Kitchen**, below Martha's Guest House (see Sleeping). Very good breakfasts and Belizean dishes, plus pizzas and burger. Garden patio.

ψ **Hode's Place**, Savannah Rd across park, just outside town. Open daily. Popular with locals and good value, Belizean food arriving in huge portions, pleasant yard to sit outside.

ψ **Long Luck Chinese restaurant**, George Price, up the hill on the left, just after the Hydro road, Benque Viejo. Best Chinese in town.

ψ **Maxim's**, Bullet Tree Rd and Far West St. Chinese, good service, cheap, very good food, popular with locals, noisy TV at the bar.

ψ **Old French Bakery**, JNC building. Good pastries for days out exploring.

ψ **Terry's**, north of San Ignacio, near the village of Bullet Tree Falls. Restaurant with limited menu but good food.

☻ Entertainment

San Ignacio and around *p387, map p385*
Cahal Pech, www.cahalpech.com, on a hill, with TV station, beside the road to Benque Viejo before the edge of town. Music and dancing at weekends, *the* place to be, live bands broadcast on TV and radio, good views. On a hill across the track from the club is Cahal Pech archaeological site.
Culture Club, same building as **Pitpan**, upstairs, live reggae Thu-Sat night, popular with foreigners and the local Rasta crowd.
Legends 200, Bullet Tree Rd. Disco, popular with locals.
Pitpan, right turn off King St to river. Open daily. The open-air bar is at the back of the building, popular spot.
Stork Club, San Ignacio Resort Hotel, see Sleeping, live music every 2nd Sat in the bar.

☉ Shopping

San Ignacio and around *p387, map p385*
Black Rock Gift Shop, near Flavias, linked to Black Rock Lodge, luggage can be left here if canoeing from Black Rock to San Ignacio, arts and crafts, workshop. **Celina's Supermarket**, Burns Av, next to the bus station. Not the cheapest but wide selection. Mon-Sat 0730-1200, 1300-1600, 1900-2100. **Maxim's**, West St, small, cheap supermarket. Fruit and veg market every Fri and Sat morning. Book exchange at **Snooty Fox**, Waights Av (opposite Martha's).

▲ Activities and tours

San Ignacio and around *p387, map p385*
Many of the resorts and lodges in this area organize a variety of tours and expeditions.

Therapies
See Dr Rosita Arvigo, page 387. Therapeutic Massage Studio, 38 West St, T604-0314. Mon-Fri 0800-1200, 1300-1630. Sat 0830-1200.

Tour operators
David's Adventure Tours, near bus terminal, T804-3674. Recommended for visits to Barton's Creek Cave, US$37, Mountain Pine ridge and Barton, US$67, Caracol, US$75, or guided canoe trips along the Macal River, including the medicinal trail and overnight camping, US$127. Always gets a good report.
Easy Rider, Bullet Tree Rd, T824-3734, horse riding. Full-day tours for US$40 with lunch.
Hun Chi'ik Tours, Burns Av, T670-0746, www.hunchiiktours.com. Cave and other tours, specializing in small groups but providing discounts for groups of more than 6 people.
Pacz Tours, 30 Burns Av, T824-0536, www.pacztours.net, offers great trips to Actun Tunichil Muknal Cave, US$75 including lunch and reserve fee of US$30. Excellent guides. Bob who runs the bar, is the best starting point for information on any of the trips and is very helpful. Your hotel will also have details and suggestions. Canoe trips on the Macal River, with bird and wildlife watching, medicinal plant trail, good value, US$65; Barton Creek Cave, US$55 for ½-day tour, Mountain Pine Ridge, US$65, Caracol and trip to pools, US$75, Tikal, US$135. Highly recommended.
Mayawalk Tours, 19 Burns Av, T824-3070, www.mayawalk.com, has received good recommendations. Similar rates to **Pacz**, also offer overnight rainforest and cave packages if you're looking for some true adventure.
Maya Mystic Tours, Savannah St, T804-0055. All trips organized including El Pilar, US$45 per person and river canoeing. Shuttles arranged.

☻ Transport

San Ignacio and around *p387, map p385*
Bus
National Transport Company Bus Station is on Burns Av. To **Belize City**, Mon-Sat 0430-1800 every hour, Sun hourly 0700-1800, 3½-4 hrs, US$2.50. To **Belmopan**, same

schedule as Belize City, 1 hr, US$1.70.
To **Benque Viejo**, every 2 hrs, Mon-Sat 0730-2300 (less on Sun), 30 mins, US$0.75. Change at Belmopan for Dangriga and the south. From the bus station at Benque, you need to get a taxi to the immigration post at **Melchor de Mencos**, US$1.25, 2 mins.

Minibuses also run to **Tikal**, making a day trip possible. Organized tours cost about US$70.

Taxi
Savannah Taxi Drivers' Co-op, T824-2155, T606-7239 (Manuel, 24 hrs). To **Guatemalan border**, US$15 (*colectivo* US$2.50, on the road, but US$12.50 if you pick them up from their base opposite David's). To **Xunantunich** US$30 return, to **Belize City** US$75, to **Tikal** US$175 return, to **Mountain Pine Ridge**, US$75, **Chaa Creek**, US$30, **Caracol**, US$175 return.

Xunantunich *p388*
Bus
Bus from San Ignacio towards the border as far as **San José Succotz** (7 miles), US$0.75, where a hand-operated ferry takes visitors and cars across the Mopan River (0800-1600, free); it is then a 20-min walk uphill on an all-weather road. Return buses to San Ignacio pass throughout the afternoon.

Mountain Pine Ridge *p389*
Taxi
There's no public transport. Apart from tours, the only alternatives are to take a taxi or hire a vehicle or mountain bike. Everything is well signposted. The private pickups that go into San Ignacio from Augustine are usually packed, so hitching is impossible. Taxis

charge around US$75-80 for 5 people. Roads are passable but rough Jan-May, but after Jun they are marginal and are impossible in the wet (Sep-Nov). It's essential to seek local advice at the time.

❶ Directory

San Ignacio and around *p387, map p385*
Banks Banks open Mon-Fri 0830-1500, Sat 0830-1300, all bunched together at the southern end of Burns Av, **Belize Bank** offers full service, TCs, Visa and MasterCard cash advance plus ATM. **Atlantic Bank**, also does cash advances and has an ATM. Both charge commission for cash advances. **Scotia Bank**, opposite Atlantic Bank, doesn't charge for cash advances. **Western Union**, has a branch in Celina's (supermarket), Burns Av, Mon-Thu 0800-1200 1300-1600, Fri and Sat also 1900-2100. **Eva's Bar** and **Martha's** both change TCs at good rates. Changers in the town square give better rates of exchange for US$ cash and TCs than you can get at the border with Guatemala. Change US$ into quetzales in Guatemala. **Internet** High charges from BTL mean internet services come and go. Cheapest places in town are **Cayo Community Computer Centre**, Hudson St, Mon-Sat 0800-2100, Sun 1000-1800 and Tradewinds **Eva's Bar**, US$3 for 30 mins. **Laundry** August Laundromat at Martha's and Mike's, and **Laundromat** at Burns Av. **Post** Hudson St, reliable parcel service, Mon-Thu 0800-1200 and 1300-1700, Fri 0800-1200 and 1300-1600. **Telephone** BTL office at further end of Burns Av, opposite **Venus Hotel**, long-distance calls and fax service.

South Belize and the southern cayes

Southern Belize is the most remote part of the country and has poor roads, but it is worth exploring. Dangriga is the largest of several Garífuna settlements that burst into life every year on Settlement Day. The paradise beaches of Hopkins and Placencia are perfect for watersports and relaxing. Cockscomb Basin Wildlife (Jaguar) Sanctuary offers one of the best chances of seeing a big cat in the wild, while the sparsely populated far south around Punta Gorda has many Maya settlements to visit in a region dotted with impressive Maya ruins.

▶ *For listings, see pages 405-414.*

South to Dangriga → *For listings, see pages 405-414. Colour map 3, A1.*

About 2 miles beyond the Belize Zoo on the Western Highway, the Coastal Highway (a good dirt road) runs southeast to **Gales Point**, a charming fishing village on a peninsula at the south end of Manatee Lagoon, 15 miles north of Dangriga. The villagers are keen to preserve natural resources and there are still significant numbers of the endangered manatee and hawksbill turtles. Boat tours of the lagoon are recommended.

Along the Hummingbird Highway

The narrow Hummingbird Highway branches off the Western Highway 48 miles west of Belize City, passes Belmopan and heads south. Skirting the eastern edge of Mountain Pine Ridge, the highway meanders through lush scenery of cohune palms, across vast flood

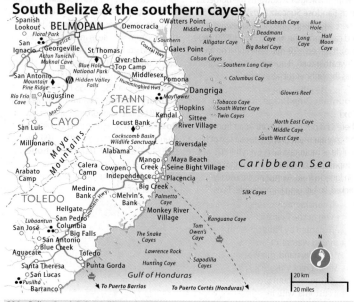

South Belize & the southern cayes

plains filled with citrus trees, which provide a spectacular backdrop for the 52-mile journey southeast to Dangriga.

The Hummingbird Highway climbs through rich tropical hardwood forest until reaching Mile 13, where a visitor centre marks a track leading off to **St Herman's Cave**. Two paths, with good birdwatching, lead through shady ferns before descending in steps to the cave entrance with its unique microclimate. You can walk for more than a mile underground but it can be slippery if wet; torch and spare batteries essential. There is a 3-mile trail to a campsite from the visitor centre.

Two miles further on is the **Blue Hole National Park** ① *daily 0800-1600, US$4, visitor centre at entrance,* an azure blue swimming hole fringed with vines and ferns, fed by a stream that comes from St Herman's Cave. This is typical karst limestone country with sinkholes, caves and underground streams. After its long journey underground, the water here is deliciously cool until it disappears again into the top of a large underwater cavern. Eventually this joins the Sibun River which enters the sea just south of Belize City. There is a rough 2½-mile trail (good hiking boots are required), through low secondary forest, between St Herman's Cave and the Blue Hole itself. A sign on the roadway warns visitors against thieves; lock your car and leave someone on guard if possible when swimming. An armed guard and more wardens have been hired to prevent further theft and assaults.

The peaks of the mountains dominate the south side of the highway until about Mile 30, when the valley of Stann Creek begins to widen out into Belize's most productive agricultural area, where large citrus groves stretch along the highway.

Canoeing or tubing trips can be organized down Indian Creek, visiting the imaginatively named Caves Five, Four and Three and then Daylight Cave and Darknight Cave, from **Over-the-Top Camp** on the Hummingbird Highway, or **Kingfisher/Belize Adventures** in Placencia. Vehicle support is brought round to meet you on the Coastal Highway near Democracia.

Turn east at Mile 32 for 4 miles along a gravel road to **Tamandua**, a wildlife sanctuary in **Five Blue Lakes National Park** ① *Friends of 5 Blues, PO Box 111, Belmopan, T809-2005, or the warden, Lee Wengrzyn, a local dairy farmer, or else Augustus Palacio (see Sleeping).* Follow the track opposite **Over-the-Top Camp**, turning right and crossing the stream for Tamandua, then for another 2 miles or so straight on following the signs for the national park, 1½ miles, where there is camping.

Dangriga → *For listings, see pages 405-414. Colour map 3, A1. Population: 11,600.*

The chief town of the Stann Creek District is on the seashore, which has the usual Belizean aspect of wooden clapboard houses elevated on piles, and is a cheerful and busily commercial place with a population largely of Black Caribs (Garífuna). North Stann Creek meets the sea at Dangriga, coming alive with flotillas of boats and fishermen. There are several gas stations, a good hospital and an airfield with regular flights. The beach has been considerably cleaned up and extended, being particularly pleasant at the far north of town at the **Pelican Beach Hotel**, where it is raked and cleaned daily. Palm trees have been planted by **Pal's Guest House** where the beach has been enlarged. Dangriga means 'standing waters' or 'sweet water' in Garífuna.

To understand more about the Garífuna culture, visit the **Gulisi Garífuna Museum** ① *Stann Creek Valley Rd, T502-0639, www.ngcbelize.org, Mon-Fri 1000-1700, Sat 0800-1200, US$5.* The museum includes information about the origins of the Garífuna people, history and customs, with music and a working garden of traditional plants and herbs.

Cayes near Dangriga

Tobacco Caye ⓘ *US$15, 35 mins by speedboat from Dangriga*, is a tiny and quite heavily populated island, but has lots of local flavour and charm and, though becoming a little commercialized, still has an authentic feel. It sits right on the reef and you can snorkel from the sandfly-free beach although there are no large schools of fish; snorkelling gear for rent. Boats go daily, ask at **Riverside Café** ⓘ *US$12-15 per person*.

South Water Caye, the focus of a marine reserve, is a lovely palm-fringed tropical island with beautiful beaches, particularly at the south end.

South of Dangriga → *Colour map 3, A1.*

The Southern Highway (now completely paved except for a stretch of a mile or so) connects Dangriga with Punta Gorda in the far south. Six miles inland from Dangriga the road branches off the Hummingbird Highway and heads south through mixed tropical forests, palmettos and pines along the fringes of the Maya Mountains. West of the road, about 5 miles from the junction with the Hummingbird Highway, a track leads to **Mayflower**, a Maya ruin. Some minimal work has begun on opening it up and some say it will eventually be the biggest archaeological site in southern Belize.

Fifteen miles from Dangriga, a minor road forks off 4 miles east to the Garífuna fishing village of Hopkins. Watch out for sandflies when the weather is calm. The villagers throw household slops into the sea and garbage on to the beach.

Turning east towards the Caribbean just before Kendal a road leads down the Sittee River to **Sittee River Village** and **Possum Point Biological Station**.

Glover's Reef

Glover's Reef, part of North East Cay and about 45 miles offshore, is an atoll with beautiful diving and has been a Marine Reserve since 1993, US$10. The reef here is pristine and the cayes are generally unspoilt, but yellow blight has hit the area killing most of the existing palm trees – especially on **Long Caye**. The combination of Hurricane Mitch and high water temperatures has damaged the coral, and the snorkelling is not as good as it once was.

Placencia → *For listings, see pages 405-414. Colour map 3, A1.*

Placencia, a former Creole fishing village 30 miles south of Dangriga, is a small seaside community on a thin sandy peninsula promoting the delights of the offshore cayes and marinelife and is a good base for inland tours too. Continuing down the Southern Highway a couple of hotel signs indicate a turning (nothing official, look carefully) to a road that heads east to Riversdale (after 9 miles) turning south to follow the peninsula to **Maya Beach**, **Seine Bight** and, eventually, **Placencia**. The peninsula road is very rough from Riversdale to Seine Bight, with sand mixed with mud; a 4WD is advisable.

Placencia is becoming more popular among people looking for an 'end of the road' adventure. It's a relaxing combination of chilling out on the beach, fishing, snorkelling and diving. If you time the trip right or get lucky, your visit may coincide with the migrations of the whale shark – the largest fish in the world at up to 55 ft – that passes through local waters from March to May. And, between January and March, hundreds of scarlet macaws gather at nearby Red Bank. Also worth hitting if you can time it right is the **Lobster Fest**, on the last full weekend in June, with two days of music, dancing and lobster and the **Sidewalk Arts Festival** held the weekend before or after Valentine's Day. Placencia is a natural base for one- and two-day trips to **Cockscomb Basin Wildlife**

Sanctuary – see page 400. **Big Creek**, on the mainland opposite Placencia, is 3 miles from Mango Creek.

There are no streets, just a network of concrete footpaths connecting the wooden houses that are set among the palms. The main sidewalk through the centre of the village is reported to be in the *Guiness Book of Records* as the world's narrowest street. The atmosphere has been described as laid back, with lots of Jamaican music, particularly after Easter and Christmas celebrations.

The local **Placencia Tourism Center** ⓘ *T523-4045, www.placencia.com, Mon-Fri 0900-1700, closed public holidays, and 1130-1300 during low season*, is in Placencia Village Square, with lots of useful information. It also produces the local monthly news-sheet, *Placencia Breeze* (www.placenciabreeze.com).

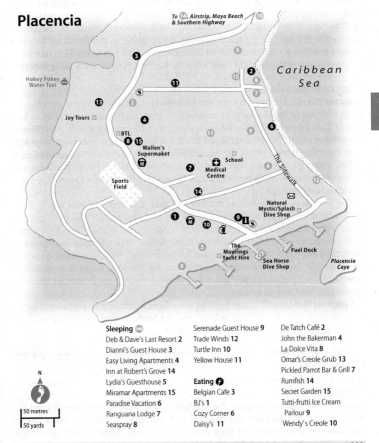

Placencia

Sleeping 😴
Deb & Dave's Last Resort **2**
Dianni's Guest House **3**
Easy Living Apartments **4**
Inn at Robert's Grove **14**
Lydia's Guesthouse **5**
Miramar Apartments **15**
Paradise Vacation **6**
Ranguana Lodge **7**
Seaspray **8**

Serenade Guest House **9**
Trade Winds **12**
Turtle Inn **10**
Yellow House **11**

Eating 🍴
Belgian Cafe **3**
BJ's **1**
Cozy Corner **6**
Daisy's **11**

De Tatch Café **2**
John the Bakerman **4**
La Dolce Vita **8**
Omar's Creole Grub **13**
Pickled Parrot Bar & Grill **7**
Rumfish **14**
Secret Garden **15**
Tutti-frutti Ice Cream Parlour **9**
Wendy's Creole **10**

Around Placencia

Trips can be made to local cayes and the **Barrier Reef**, approximately 18 miles offshore. Day trips include snorkelling, with a beach BBQ lunch of lobster and conch. Offshore cayes include **Laughing Bird Caye**. **Gladden Spit** and **Silk Cayes Marine Reserve** (reserve fee US$10), also protected by **Friends of Nature**. Whale sharks visit the spit in March, April, May and June for 10 days after the full moon to feed on the spawn of aggregating reef fish.

Several hotels and guide services have kayaks that can be rented to explore some of the nearer islands or the quieter waters of the **Placencia Lagoon**. Those who want to keep their feet dry can go mountain biking on the peninsula or use it as a base for trips to **Cockscomb Basin Wildlife Sanctuary** and Maya ruins.

Day tours by boat south along the coast from Placencia to **Monkey River** and **Monkey River Village** are available. Monkey River tours, US$20 per person, feature howler monkeys, toucans, manatees and iguanas. Monkey River Village can be reached by a rough road, which is not recommended in wet weather. The road ends on the north side of the river and the town is on the south side, so call over for transport. Trips upriver can also be arranged here with locals but kayaking is best organized in Placencia. Trips can be arranged to Red Bank for the scarlet macaws, which gather in their hundreds between January and March. For information on travelling to or from Puerto Cortés in Honduras, see pages 974 and 563. North of Placencia is the Garífuna community of **Seine Bight**.

Cayes near Placencia

Ranguana Caye is a private caye reached from Placencia (US$5). Getting there is free if it fits in with one of the regular trips, otherwise it costs US$150 each way for up to four people. Divers must bring their own scuba equipment. Day trips for diving, snorkelling or just relaxing cost US$45-50, and include lunch. For longer stays, see Sleeping, page 407.

At the southernmost end of the Mesoamerican Barrier Reef are the **Sapodilla Cayes**, US$10. Tours are arranged from Guatemala (for example see under Río Dulce and Lívingston) or can be made from Placencia. There are settlements on a few of the Cayes including **Hunting Caye**.

The **Silk Cayes**, also known as the **Queen Cayes**, is a small group of tiny, picture-perfect islands, which sits on the outer barrier reef and, together with Gladdens Spit, has become the core zone of the country's newest marine reserve. The Silk Cayes have superb diving, especially on the North Wall. Coral in the deeper areas is in good condition with many tube and barrel sponges and sharks, turtles and rays often seen cruising the reef wall. The Silk Cayes are a popular destination for Placencia-based dive operators, however, it's not possible to dive in this area during periods of rough weather. The rainy season lasts from June to January.

Laughing Bird Caye ⓘ *reserve fee US$4, www.friendsofnaturebelize.org*, used to be the home of the laughing gull (*Larus articilla*), now it's home to other sea birds and has an exciting array of underwater life around its shores.

Cockscomb Basin Wildlife Sanctuary and around

→ *For listings, see pages 405-414. Colour map 3, A1.*
ⓘ *US$5.*

Some 20 miles south of Dangriga, the Southern Highway crosses the Sittee River at the small village of **Kendal** (ruins nearby). One mile beyond is the village of **Maya Centre** from where a poor seven-mile track winds west through Cabbage Haul Gap to the

The Crystal Skull of Lubaantun

In 1927, a young woman by the name of Anna Mitchell-Hedges woke for her 17th birthday. For her it proved more eventful than most as she explored the recently excavated Maya site of Lubaantun to discover a finely crafted crystal skull made of pure quartz – setting off a tale of intrigue that remains to this day.

The size of a small watermelon, the translucent skull of reflected light weighs just over 5 kg. The skull is one of only two ever found in Central America. Its date of manufacture is unknown – but some put it at over 3600 years old – and its purpose is equally curious. Local Maya people gave the skull to Anna's father, the British explorer FA Mitchell-Hedges as a gift, saying it was used for healing and, more sinisterly, for willing death.

Dating the skull precisely is difficult because of the purity of the crystal, but the details of the finding are equally mysterious, with speculation that the skull was 'placed' to make that birthday so special.

Cockscomb Basin Wildlife Sanctuary (21,000 acres), the world's first jaguar sanctuary and definitely worth an extended visit if you have two or three days. The sanctuary was created out of the Cockscomb Basin Forest Reserve in 1986 to protect the country's highest recorded density of jaguars (*Panthera onca*), and their smaller cousins the puma (red tiger), the endangered ocelot, the diurnal jaguarundi and that feline cutey, the margay. Many other mammals share the heavily forested reserve, including coatis, collared peccaries, agoutis, anteaters, Baird's tapirs and tayras (a small weasel-like animal). There are red-eyed tree frogs, boas, iguanas and fer-de-lances, as well as over 290 species of bird, including king vultures and great curassows. The sanctuary is a good place for relaxing, showering under waterfalls, tubing down the river, or listening to birds – hundreds of bird species have been spotted and there are several types of toucan, hummingbirds and scarlet macaws to be seen by early risers. The reserve is sponsored by the Belizean government, the **Audubon Society**, the **Worldwide Fund For Nature** and various private firms. Donations are very welcome.

Park HQ is at the former settlement of Quam Bank (whose milpa-farming inhabitants founded the **Maya Centre** outside the reserve). Here there is an informative visitor centre. An 18-mile network of jungle trails spreads out from the centre, ranging in distance from a few hundred yards to 2½ miles. Walkers are unlikely to see any of the big cats as they are nocturnal, but if you fancy a walk in the dark you may be lucky. Note that the guards leave for the day at 1600. You will see birds, frogs, lizards, snakes and spiders. Longer hikes can be planned with the staff. Nearby is one of Belize's highest summits, **Victoria Peak** (3675 ft), which is an arduous four- or five-day return climb and should not be undertaken lightly. There is virtually no path, a guide is essential; February to May are the best months for the climb. ▸▸ *For guides, see Activities and tours, page 411.*

Punta Gorda and around → For listings, see pages 405-414. Colour map 3, B1. Population: 5255.

The turn-off from the Southern Highway for Mango Creek, Independence and Big Creek comes 15 miles after the Riversdale turn-off, and the road runs 4 miles east through the **Savannah Forest Reserve** to the mangrove coast opposite Placencia. About 35 miles beyond the junction, 10½ miles north of the T-junction for Punta Gorda, half a mile west of the road, is the **Nim Li Punit** archaeological site which has a visitor centre and clean spacious housing for the stelae. Nim Li Punit ('The Big Hat') was only discovered in 1974. A score of stelae, 15-20 ft tall, were unearthed, dated AD 700-800, as well as a ball court and several groups of buildings. The site is worth visiting – look for the sign on the highway. Day trips also offered from Placencia. A short distance beyond, the highway passes **Big Falls Village**, almost completely destroyed by Hurricane Iris. Take a short hike back to the hot springs for a swim, camp or sling a hammock, but first seek permission from the landowner, Mr Peter Aleman. Four miles from Big Falls, the Highway reaches a T-junction, know locally as the 'Dump', marked by a Shell station; the road to San Antonio branches right (west), the main road turns sharp left and runs down through a forest reserve for 13 miles to Punta Gorda. The road is paved from Big Falls to Punta Gorda.

Punta Gorda is the southernmost town of any size in Belize, a marketing centre and fishing port with a varied ethnic makeup of Creoles, Q'eqchi', Mopan, Chinese, East Indians and descendants of the many races brought here over the years as labourers in ill-fated settlement attempts. Three miles north of **Toledo** are the remains of the sugar cane settlement founded by Confederate refugees after the American Civil War. The coast, about 10 ft above sea level, is fringed with coconut palms. The seafront is clean and enjoyable – once you get away from Front Street, where the lively and colourful market on Wednesday, Friday and Saturday comes with the associated smells of fish and rotting vegetables. The *Voice of America* has an antenna complex to the south of town.

At **Toledo Visitors' Information Center**, also called **Dem Dats Doin** ① *in booth by pier, PO Box 73, T722-2470, demdatsdoin@btl.net, free, irregular opening hours*, Alfredo and Yvonne Villoria, provide information on travel, tours, guiding, accommodation with indigenous families (Homestay Programme), message service and book exchange, for the whole of Toledo district. **Tourist Information Centre** ① *Front St, T/F722-2531, Mon-Sat 0800-1200 and 1300-1700*, provides a wealth of information about the area, including bus schedules to local Maya villages, and can organize reservations for flights and for hotels, tours and boat trips to Honduras. The **Toledo Ecotourism Association** has an office in the same building. Information on the **Village Guesthouse** and **Ecotrail** programme, as well as booking and transport to the villages.

Around Punta Gorda

Rainfall in this region is particularly heavy, with more than 170 inches annually, and the vegetation is consequently luxuriant. There are many tours that can be enjoyed on the numerous rivers in the Toledo District. Countless species of birds make their homes along the rivers, as do troops of howler monkeys and other wildlife. Kayaking is a good way to view wildlife on the rivers. There are many white-sand beaches on the cayes off Punta Gorda for the beachcomber, or camper. Fly fishing is becoming a popular sport and sport fishing, snorkelling and scuba-diving are available. **Toledo** is off the beaten path and has some of the most spectacular views, waterfalls, rainforest, cayes and friendly people.

South of Punta Gorda → *For listings, see pages 405-414. Colour map 3, B1.*

San Pedro Columbia

Inland from Punta Gorda there are several interesting villages in the foothills of the Maya Mountains. Take the main road as far as the 'Dump', the road junction with the Southern Highway. Take the road west to San Antonio. After nearly 2 miles, there is a branch to San Pedro Columbia, a Q'eqchi' village where the Maya inhabitants speak the Q'eqchi' language and the women wear colourful costumes, including Guatemalan-style *huípiles*. There are many religious celebrations, at their most intense on **San Luis Rey Day** (5 August).

Lubaantun

ⓘ *0800-1600 daily, beyond San Pedro, continuing left around the church, then right and downhill to the concrete bridge, then left for a mile, a caretaker will point out things of interest. Take refreshments.*

Lubaantun ('Fallen Stones') was the major ceremonial site of southern Belize. The site has a visitor centre and has undergone extensive work to restore a large part of the ruins. It was found to date from AD 800-900, late in the Maya culture and therefore unique. A series of terraced plazas surrounded by temples and palaces ascend along a ridge from south to north. The buildings were constructed with unusual precision and some of the original lime-mortar facings can still be discerned. Excavation revealed whistle figurines, iron pyrite mirrors, obsidian knives, conch shells from Wild Cane Caye, etc. One of the great controversies of the site was the discovery in 1927 of the Crystal Skull by the daughter of the explorer FA Mitchell-Hedges (see box, page 401). This whole region is a network of hilltop sites, mostly unexcavated and unrecognizable to the untrained eye.

Blue Creek

Blue Creek is another attractive indigenous village which has a marked trail to **Blue Creek Caves** ⓘ *US$12.50 per person, the caretaker is the guide*, and their Maya drawings. The trail leads through forest and along rock-strewn creeks. Swimming nearby is good swimming but choose a spot away from the strong current. Turn off 3 miles before San Antonio at **Roy's Cool Spot** (good restaurant; daily truck and all buses pass here).

Pusilhá

Pusilhá is one of the most interesting Maya cities, only accessible by boat. Many stelae have been found here dating from AD 573-731, and carvings are similar to those at Quiriguá, Guatemala. Rare features are a walled-in ball court and the abutments remaining from a bridge that once spanned the Moho River. Swimming in the rivers is safe. There are plenty of logging trails and hunters' tracks penetrating the southern faces of the Maya Mountains but if hiking in the forest, do not go alone.

San Antonio → *For listings, see pages 405-414. Colour map 3, B1.*

San Antonio (21 miles from Punta Gorda) was founded by refugees from San Luis in Guatemala in the late 19th century. Nearby there are Maya ruins of mainly scientific interest. There's a community phone for checking buses and other information, T702-2144. **Dem Dats Doin** in Punta Gorda (see page 402) will also be able to give information. There's a medical centre in the village.

There are no roads to the southern border with Guatemala along the Sarstún River. The **Sarstoon-Temash National Park** is a wilderness of red mangroves and unspoilt rainforest. There are no visitor facilities at present. At **Barranco**, the only coastal hamlet south of Punta Gorda, there is a village guesthouse (part of TEA, see box, page 404). A dirt road goes to Barranco through the village of Santa Ana, or you can go by boat.

Guesthouse programme

An interesting alternative to Punta Gorda is to stay in indigenous villages as part of the Guesthouse Programme, run by villagers and the non-competitive cooperative the Toledo Ecotourism Association (TEA).

A number of villages have joined together and developed a visitor scheme. Each has built a well-appointed guesthouse, simple, but clean, with sheets, towels, mosquito nets, oil lamps, ablutions block, and a total of eight bunks in two four-bunk rooms. Visitors stay here, but eat in the villagers' houses on rotation, so each household gains equal income and only has to put up with intrusive foreigners for short periods. Villages taking part include San Miguel, San José (Hawaii), Laguna and Blue Creek. Santa Elena is an isolated village beyond the Dump towards San Ignacio. Medina Bank is more accessible as its location is just off the southern highway. Barranco is a Garífuna village south of Punta Gorda, accessible by boat or poor road.

Local attractions include: San Antonio waterfall; caves at San José (Hawaii); Uxbenka ruins and caves 2½-hour walk from San Antonio (turn right just before Santa Cruz), with commanding view from ruins; and Río Blanco waterfalls, 10 minutes beyond the village. For Uxbenka and Santa Cruz, take Chun's bus on Wednesday and Saturday at 1300 from San Antonio and arrange return time. Do not take Cho's bus, it does not return. Many village men and children speak English. The local indigenous people have been relearning old dances from elderly villagers and are trying to rescue the art of making and playing the harp, violin, marimba and guitar for evening entertainments. Home-made excursions are arranged; these vary from a four-hour trek looking at medicinal plants and explaining agriculture, to seeing very out-of-the- way sights like caves and creeks (take boots, even in dry season). The village tour could be skipped, although by doing this on your own you deprive the 'guide' of income.

One night for two people, with a forest tour and two meals, costs US$42.50 for a basic package or US$55 for a full package (including music and dancing); all profits go direct to the villages, with no outsiders as middlemen. Dorms are US$11 per person. Profits are ploughed back into the villages' infrastructure, schools and other community projects. A US$5 registration fee is payable at the TEA Office at the Tourist Information Center (BTB Building) in Punta Gorda, T722-2096, before visiting the village. The staff provide information about participating villages, key attractions, tours and courses, and take bookings and arrange transport. You may have to arrange your own transport, or a vehicle can be hired. Staff at TEA will be able to advise. Hitching is not recommended as some villages are remote. 'Market' buses leave Punta Gorda every Monday, Wednesday, Friday and Saturday at 1130 or 1200 depending on the village. They come from the villages on the morning of the same days departing early at 0400, 0500 or 0600, depending on the village.

Toucan Trail organize cultural exchange programmes with the Maya in San José, Na Luum Ca and Aguacate villages. Accommodation is no-frills and there is full immersion in tribal life. Guests sleep with the family in one- or two-room palm-thatch and adobe houses. There's little privacy and shared outhouse 'bathrooms' with no warm water. Meals of corn tortillas, beans and fish or meat are eaten communally. Men are expected to help work the *milpa* fields and women to grind corn and attend to other traditional duties. Prices start at US$30 per night and guests must make their own way to the village (details at www.southernbelize.com/tea.html).

For Sleeping and Eating price codes and other relevant information, see Essentials pages 31-33.

● Sleeping

South to Dangriga *p396*

LL Manatee Lodge, Gales Point, T220-8040, www.manateelodge.com. Resort on the shores of the Southern Lagoon, trips to local areas. Prices include transfers, meals and tours.

LL-E Caves Branch Jungle Lodge, ½ mile past St Herman's Cave, T/F673 3454, www.cavesbranch.com. Reached along ½-mile track, signed on the left, any bus between Belmopan and Dangriga will stop. A secluded spot on the banks of Caves Branch River, comfortable *cabañas* with private baths or **E** per person in the bunkhouse, camping US$5 per person, good, clean, shared bathrooms, great 'jungle showers', delicious meals served buffet style. More than just accommodation, this is very much an activity centre. Great trips through caves, 7-mile underground floats, guided jungle trips, overnight trips as well, tubing, kayaking, mountain biking and rappelling, including the adrenalin-busting **Black Hole Drop**. Excellent guides, pricey for some budgets starting at around US$60 but highly recommended. See also page 345.

E Gales Point Bed and Breakfast Association, contact Hortence Welch on arrival or call T220-9031 in advance. Basic accommodation, no indoor plumbing, meals available.

Dangriga *p397*

LL Bonefish, Mahogany St, on seafront near post office, T522-2243, www.blue marlinlodge.com. A/c, US cable TV, hot water, takes Visa. Restaurant, diving and fishing. Packages are all inclusive.

L-AL Pelican Beach, outside town, on the beach north of town, T522-2044, www.pelicanbeachbelize.com. Private bath, hot water, a/c, veranda, pier, hammocks, 20 rooms, restaurant, bar, games lounge, gift shop, tours arranged, helpful (taxi from town, or 15-min walk from North Stann Creek).

B-D Pal's Guest House, 868 A Magoon St, Dangriga, T522-2095, www.pals belize. com. 19 units on beach, all with balconies, sea views, bath, fan, cable TV, cheaper rooms in main building, shared bath downstairs, private upstairs. **Dangriga Dive Centre** runs from next door (see Activities and tours).

C-D Bluefield Lodge, 6 Bluefield Rd, T522-2742, bluefield@btl.net. Bright hotel, owner Louise Belisle very nice, spotless, comfortable beds, very helpful, secure. Highly recommended.

C-D Chaleanor, 35 Magoon St, T522-2587, chaleanor@btl.net. Fairly large rooms, some with TV and fan and a/c some with sea views, rooftop restaurant.

Cayes near Dangriga *p398*
Tobacco Caye

There is no electricity on the island, but it has a good family atmosphere and great fun.

AL-B Lana's on the reef, T522-2571, T909-9434556 (USA). Has its own fishing pier, snorkelling equipment hire, good Caribbean-style food, mosquito net, shared and private shower. Recommended.

AL-B Reef's End Lodge, T522-2419, www.reefsendlodge.com. Basic, small rooms, boat transfer on request from Dangriga.

C Tobacco Caye Lodge, T520-5033, www.tclodgebelize.com. A-frame huts, campground, meals available, reef excursions, friendly, good value. Recommended.

South Water Caye

LL Blue Marlin Lodge, T522-2243, www.bluemarlinlodge.com. Excellent dive lodge offering various packages, small sandy island with snorkelling off the beach, good accommodation and food, runs tours.

LL Pelican's Beach Resort, T522-2044, www.pelicanbeachbelize.com, rooms in a 2-storey colonial building, and 3 secluded cottages. **Pelican University** is ideal for groups housing up to 23 people at US$60 per person per day including 3 meals.

South of Dangriga *p398*
LL Hamanasi, Sittee Point, T520-7073, www.hamanasi.com. 17-acre resort, 18 rooms and suites with a/c. Swimming pool, full dive operation.

LL-L Jaguar Reef Lodge, south of Hopkins, just north of Sittee River, T520-7040, www.jaguarreef.com. 18 a/c rooms with fridges. Central lodge on sandy beach, pool, diving, snorkelling, kayaking, mountain bikes, birdwatching and wildlife excursions.

L-AL Beaches and Dreams, Sittee Point, T523-7259, www.beachesanddreams.com. 4 extremely well-furnished beachfront rooms. Price includes full breakfast, Dangriga transfer, use of bikes and kayaks.

AL-A Hopkins Inn, on beach south of centre, T523-7283, www.hopkinsinn.com. White cabins with private bathroom, very clean and friendly, German spoken. Price includes breakfast, knowledgeable owners.

AL-E Sir Thomas at Toucan Sittee, T523-7039, www.sir-thomas-at-toucan-sittee.com. 400 yds down river from **Glover's**. Run by Neville Collins, lovely setting, rooms with screens and fans, bunkhouse, hot water, or fully equipped riverside apartments, grow most of their own fruit and veg, also over 50 medicinal plants.

C-D Tipple Tree Beya Inn, just before Sandy Beach Lodge, T520-7006, www.tippletree.com. English/American run, 4 rooms in a wooden house and small cabin apartment, camping possible.

E-F Glover's Guest House, on river bank, T802-2505. 5 rooms, restaurant, camping, jungle river trips, family-run and starting point for the boat to **North East Caye** (see below). Price per person.

Glover's Reef *p398*
North East Caye
B-E Glover's Atoll Resort, T520-5016 www.glovers.com.bz. 8 cabins with wood-burning stoves, you can also choose dorm or camping. Weekly rates include round-trip transportation from Sittee River. Occasional rice and seafood meals, bring food, some groceries and drinking water (US$2.50 a gallon) available. Best to bring everything you will need. Facilities are very simple and basic. Guests are sometimes invited to help out.

Placencia *p398, map p399*
Rooms may be hard to find in the afternoon (after arrival of the bus from Dangriga). Usually several houses to rent, US$200-550 per week, see the ads at the tourist information centre.

LL The Inn at Robert's Grove, north of the air strip and Rum Point Inn, T523-3565, www.robertsgrove.com. Luxury resort with 2 pools, massage service, boats and jacuzzis set on a white-sand beach shaded by the odd palm. Rooms are spacious, comfortable and quiet and the restaurant serves good, filling food. Entertainment and tours, including PADI diving from its own marina, are organized. Friendly bar staff.

LL Turtle Inn, on beach close to airstrip, T523-3244, www.turtleinn.com. Completely destroyed by Hurricane Iris, owner Francis Ford Coppola rebuilt this impressive resort in local and Balinese style set around a circular pool with restaurant and spa.

LL-L Miramar Apartments, T523 3658. Immaculate, fully equipped apartments close to the beach that range from 1-bed studios to 3-bed apartments.

L-AL Easy Living Apartments, T523-3481, www.easyliving.bz. Well-appointed roomy apartments with space for up to 4, at which point they represent good value – TV, fully equipped kitchen, good location at the centre of town, on the sidewalk.

AL Ranguana Lodge, T523-3112, www.ranguanabelize.com. Wooden cabins on the ocean, very clean.

AL-A Serenade Guest House, T523-3380, www.serenadeguesthouse.com. Spacious, airy rooms, all with a/c and private bath. Upstairs rooms more expensive.

Welcoming owners. Restaurant next door. Parking available.

AL-B Trade Winds Hotel, South Point, T523-3122, trdewndpla@btl.net. 9 very colourful cabins in a spacious private plot on the south beach.

AL-C Seaspray, T523-3148, www.seaspray hotel.com. Very nice, comfortable and friendly. Good-value rooms across a range of prices from beachside *cabañas* to small doubles in original building. Popular **De Tatch Café** on the beach, see Eating.

A Dianni's Guest House, T523-3159, www.diannisplacencia.com. 6 spacious rooms and 3 *cabañas* with a/c, most with 1 double and single bed. Fridge, coffee and tea provided, nice balcony with hammocks, internet available.

B-D Paradise Vacation Hotel, down by the piers, T523-3179, www.paradisevacation belize.com. 12 rooms with private baths and 4 rooms with shared.

C Deb and Dave's Last Resort, T523-3207, www.toadaladventure.com. 4 very good budget rooms with shared bathroom, hot water, kayak and bike rental. Walk-ins only, no advance reservations. Also runs tours in local area.

C The Yellow House, T523-3481, www.ctbelize.com. A bright yellow building, directly behind **Serenade**, with 4 very comfortable rooms with communicating doors, so excellent for a family or group of friends. Front rooms have microwave, coffee machines and fridges. Excellent value. Also runs **B-C Garden Cabañas**, www.garden cabanas.com, and **A-C Mahogany Beach**.

C-D Lydia's Guesthouse, T523-3117, www.lydiasguesthouse.com. 8 double rooms with shared toilet and shower, situated across the sidewalk on a quiet part of the beach. Kitchen facilities. Simple, but very chilled and with free Wi-Fi or a PC for hire. Recommended.

Camping
Sea Kunga, www.seakunga.com. Organizes camping tours on the beach.

Around Placencia *p400*
Maya Beach
L Green Parrot Beach Houses, T523-2488, www.greenparrot-belize.com. Beach houses on stilts, all with sea view, sleep up to 5, kitchenettes, open-air restaurant and bar.
L Singing Sands Inn, T520-8022, www.singingsands.com. 6 thatched cabins with bathrooms, hot water, fans, ocean view, snorkelling in front of the resort at False Caye, restaurant and bar on the beach.
L-AL Maya Breeze Inn, T523-8012. 4 cottages on the beach, 2 with a/c, restaurant across the road.
AL-A Barnacle Bill's, T523-8010, www.barnaclebills-belize.com. 2 *cabañas* with queen-sized bed, sleeper/sofa in the living/dining area, full kitchen, private bath and fans.

Mango Creek/Independence
C-D Ursela's Guest House, T503-2062. 9 simple rooms with shared or private bath, TV.
F Hotel above People's Restaurant. Very basic, ask to borrow a fan and lamp, shower is a bucket of water in a cabin, basic restaurant.

Cayes near Placencia *p400*
L Frank's Caye, reservations through Serenade Guesthouse, T523-3481, www.belizecayes.com. 3 *cabañas* with private baths, restaurant and bar.
L-AL Ranguana Caye, reservations through Robert's Grove,T523-3565, www.roberts grove.com. 3 *cabañas*, each with a double and single bed, gas stove, private hot showers and toilet in separate building. BBQ pits so bring food, but meals also available.

Camping
Lime Caye (tent camping is crowded). Very good fishing at certain times of the year (contact local guides for information).

Cockscomb Basin Wildlife Sanctuary and around p400

To guarantee accommodation, contact the **Belize Audubon Society**, see page 346.

L Mama Noots Backabush Resort, T422-3666, www.mamanoots.com. Electricity from solar, wind and hydro system, most fruits and vegetables grown organically on the grounds of the resort. 6 double rooms and 1 duplex thatched *cabaña* that sleeps up to 6. Private baths.

B-E Park HQ. Purpose-built cabins and dorms (**D-E** per person) with a picnic area. Drinking water is available, also earth toilets, but you must bring all your own food, drinks, matches, torch, sleeping bag, eating utensils and insect repellent. Nearest shop is at Maya Centre.

Punta Gorda and around p401

LL Cotton Tree Lodge, T670-0557, www.cottontreelodge.com. 11 charming thatched cabanas at the woody bank of Moho River, built and run in an eco-friendly manner, guests can visit local Mayan farmers and have a taste of their culture. Restaurant serves 3 meals a day. Families are welcome.

AL Sea Front Inn, 4 Front St, T722-2300, www.seafrontinn.com. 14 rooms with private bath hot water, a/c, TV, restaurant with great views. **Maya Island Air** and **Tropic Air** agents.

AL-A Hickatee, T622-4475, www.hickatee. com. English breakfast, afternoon tea and wonderful, comfortable accommation in wooden chalets set in a bird-filled glade in the heart of the rainforest. Helpful and very knowledgable owners who can organize trips around Toledo.

AL-C Tate's Guest House, 34 José María Nuñez St, T722-0147, tatesguesthouse@ yahoo.com. A/c, cheaper without, clean, hot water, bathroom, TV, parking, friendly, breakfast before 0730, laundry.

B-D Pallavi, 19 Main St, T702-2414, gracemcp@hotmail.com. Tidy, clean, friendly.

C Mahung's Inn, corner North and Main St, T722-2044, mahungsinn@hotmail.com.

Reasonable, private bath, cable TV, also rents mountain bikes, US$5 per day.

C St Charles Inn, 23 King St, T722-2149, stcharlespg@btl.net. All with bath, spacious rooms, fan or a/c, cable TV, good.

C-D Nature's Way Guest House, 65 Front St, T702-2119. Clean, friendly, good breakfast, camping gear for rent. Recommended.

D-E Wahima, on waterfront, T722-2542. Clean and safe, with private bath, owner Max is friendly and informative. Also rents kitchenettes.

F Airport Inn, 24 Main Middle St. Price per person, quiet, OK, communal bathrooms, clean, spartan. You can flag down the 0500 bus to Belize in front of **Wahima** or **Pallavi**, buy a ticket the night before to get a reserved seat.

South of Punta Gorda p402

Accommodation is restricted to community-based ecotourism projects where you can stay in the indigenous villages. There are 2 main projects: **TEA – Toledo Ecotourism Association**, T722-2096, www.southern belize.com/tea.html, where you can stay in your private accommodation within the village, and the **Homestay Programme**, where you stay with the family in their house. The Homestay Programme can be arranged via Blue Creek Rainforest Lodge see below. See also box, page 404.

B Blue Creek Rainforest Lodge, www.ize2 belize.com. Simple wooden bungalows in the middle of the forest and just 15 mins' walk from Blue Creek Village. Pack full with adventures trekking around the jungle, exploring caves and learning about local culture.

C Maya Mountain Research Farm, www.mmrfbz.org. An organization that promotes forestry research and welcome intership researches and volunteers from 1 week to 1 semester. You pay for your accommodation. See webpage for details.

San Antonio p403

D Bol's Hilltop Hotel. Showers, toilets, meals extra, clean.

❶ Eating

Dangriga p397

❚ **Riverside Café**, south bank of river, just east of main road. Nicer inside than it looks, good breakfast, good service and food, best place to get information on boats to Tobacco Caye.

Placencia p398, map p399

❚❚❚ **La Dolce Vita**, near Wallen's grocery, T523-3115. Italian restaurant who claim to have the best wine selection in town.

❚❚❚ **The Secret Garden**, near Wallen's grocery, T523-3617. International cuisine served in a relaxed, chilled out atmosphere

❚❚❚-❚❚ **Rumfish**, T523-3293, rumfish@btl.net. Good quality restaurant, popular with locals.

❚❚ **Belgian Cafe**, above Michelo, 21 Harbour Place. Mon-Fri 0700-1430. Friendly European-owned café, with Wi-Fi, great for breakfasts.

❚❚ **Cozy Corner**, on the beach, T523-3280. Very nice beachside bar and restaurant. Good, mid-priced barbecue and grilled seafood.

❚❚ **De Tatch Café**, just before the north end of the sidewalk. Closed Wed. Said to be the the best coffee in town, certainly is hugely popular with excellent seafood specials at night and snappy service; a winner.

❚❚ **Pickled Parrot Bar and Grill**, close to Wallen's Hardware. Closed Sun. Good pizza, chicken and seafood.

❚❚-❚ **BJ's Restaurant**, see map, T523-3131. Good fried chicken and traditional Creole food. Owners Percy and Betty offer good Asian stir-fries and pizza – inexpensive and popular with locals.

❚ **Daisy's**, sidewalk, close to De Tatch. Cheap meals and good ice cream.

❚ **John the Bakerman**, follow the signs. Freshly baked bread and cinnamon buns each afternoon at 1800 (takeaway only).

❚ **Omar's Creole Grub**, Creole diner.

❚ **Tutti-frutti Ice Cream Parlour**, Placencia Village Square. Great Italian ice cream, made by real Italians!

❚ **Wendy's Creole Restaurant and Bar**, close to the gas station. Good food but service can be very slow so leave plenty of time if you're meeting transport.

Around Placencia p400

❚❚ **Goyo's Inn/Restaurant Independence**, Mango Creek. Family-owned, good food.

❚ **Lola's Café and Art Gallery**, sign at south end of Seine Bight. For an entertaining evening with dinner, run by local artist Lola Delgado.

❚ **White house with green shutters**, Mango Creek, behind **People's**. Better than at **People's**. Book 2 hrs in advance if possible.

Punta Gorda p401

Several cafés around the market area with good views over the bay.

❚❚ **Bobby's** Main St. Serves excellent fish dishes, Bobby is a local fishing guide and arranges trips.

❚❚ **Earth Runnings Café and Bukut Bar**, Main Middle St, T702-2007, bukutbar@hotmail.com. Closed Tue. Great, idiosyncratic bar and café with regular live music that also provides tourist information, internet and occasional yoga and therapeutic massage.

❚❚ **Emery Restaurant**, Main St, T702-2990. Local dishes and seafood, popular with locals, reasonable prices, friendly.

❚❚ **Gomier's**, behind the **Sea Front Inn**. For vegan meals and soya products.

❚❚ **Marian's Bayview Restaurant**, 76 Front St, T722-0129. Serves traditional Belizean and East Indian dishes.

❚ **El Cafe**, opposite Mahung's Inn. Inexpensive café fare.

❚ **Marenco's Ice Cream Parlour**, Main St. Serves good ice cream and food as well.

San Antonio p403

❚ **Theodora** or **Clara**, next to hotel. Both do meals with advance notice. Local specialities are *jippy jappa/kula*, from a local plant, and chicken *caldo*.

☺ Entertainment

Dangriga *p397*
Listen for local music 'Punta Rock', a Garífuna/African-based Carib sound, now popular throughout Belize. **Local Motion Disco**, next to **Cameleon**, open weekends, punta rock, reggae, live music. **Riviera Club**, between bridge and **Bank of Nova Scotia**, popular nightclub at weekends. Home-made instruments are a Garífuna speciality, particularly drums. Studios can be visited.

Placencia *p398, map p399*
Tipsy Tuna Sports Bar, popular sports and karaoke beachside bar, from 1900. **Barefoot Beach Bar** at Tipsy Tuna is a very popular joint on the beach with live music and a happy hour 1700-1800. Closed Mon.

☺ Festivals and events

Dangriga *p397*
18-19 Nov Garífuna, or Settlement Day, re-enacting the landing of the Black Caribs in 1823, having fled a failed rebellion in Honduras. Dancing all night and next day; very popular. Booking advisable for accommodation. Private homes rent rooms, though. Boats from Puerto Barrios to Punta Gorda (see Transport) tend to be full, but launches take passengers for US$10 per person.

▲ Activities and tours

South to Dangriga *p396*
There is a wide variety of day and overnight excursions, from US$30 per boat holding 6-8 people. Contact Kevin Andrewin of **Manatee** Tour Guides Association on arrival. Community phone, T02-12031, minimum 48 hrs' notice is advisable, ask for Alice or Josephine.

Dangriga *p397*
Dangriga Dive Centre, T522-3262. Derek Jones arranges fabulous trips to the cayes.

Pelican Beach Hotel runs tours to Cockscomb Basin, Gales Point and citrus factories. **Rosado's Tours**, 35 Lemon St, T522-2119. Government Services.
Treasured Travels, 64 Commerce St, T522-2578, is very helpful, run by Diane.

South of Dangriga *p398*
Second Nature Divers, T523-7038, divers@btl.net, or enquire at **Hamanasi**. English-owned, good guides and equipment, recommended spot to visit is Sharks' Cave.

Glover's Reef *p398*
Off The Wall Dive Center, Dangriga, T614-6348, www.offthewallbelize.com, offers dive courses. Friendly owners Jim and Kendra Schofield offer packages that include transport, accommodation, meals and diving.

Placencia *p398, map p399*
Scuba-diving and snorkelling
Full PADI scuba-diving courses are available at most local dive shops, around US$350. Some dive operators listed below base themselves out of high-end resorts. Of the in-town operators **Seahorse**, **Joy Tours** and **Splash** enjoy solid reputations. However, environmental standards and genuine concern for the reef is somewhat lacking – this could be improved with a little encouragement. Prices are from about US$70, plus 9% sales tax, for 2-tank dives, US$105 to outer reef (gear extra). **Seahorse Dive Shop**, T523-3166, www.belizescuba.com, ask for Brian Young. Good selection of gear. **Splash**, T523-3058, www.splashbelize.com. Owners helpful – specialize in dive training and courses. **Joy Tours**, T651-0464, www.njoybelize.com, is locally recommended. **Naudi Dive Shop**, T523-3595, www.nauticalinn belize.com, and **Robert's Grove Dive Shop**, T523-3565, www.robertsgrove.com. **Ocean Motion Guide Service**, T523-3363, www.oceanmotion placencia.com, is a reputable snorkelling tour operator. Snorkel trips generally cost US$60-70 for a full day and US$30-45 for a half day, including gear. There is a whale shark and

snorkelling fee of US$15 in operation from 1 Mar-3 Jul charged by **Friends of Nature**.

Fishing
Fishing, especially saltwater fly-fishing, is excellent, with recognized world-class permit fishing. Reputable licensed guides and tour operators include **Kurt Godfrey**, T523-3277, and **Earl Godfrey**, T523-3433, lgodfrey@btl.net. **Destinations Belize**, offers combination cayes camping and fishing/snorkelling trips, plus whale shark interaction tours, T523-4018, www.destinationsbelize.com. **Bruce Leslie**, from **Tutti-frutti**, T523-3370. Rates for a full day of light tackle and fly fishing, including lunch, average US$325, maximum 2 anglers per boat for fly-fishing.

Kayaking
Toadal Adventures, T523-3207, www.toadala dventure.com, is a reputable tour operator for multi-day kayaking trips to the cayes and Monkey River.

Cockscomb Basin Wildlife Sanctuary and around *p400*
The **Belize Audobon Society**, see page 346, runs the reserve. The most knowledgeable guides to the reserve live in Maya Centre; contact **Julio Saqui**, of **Julio's Cultural Tours**, T608-4992, www.cockscombmayatours.com, who runs the village shop and can look after any extra luggage. At **Greg's Bar**, on the main road in the middle of the village, you can contact **Greg Sho**, an experienced river and mountain guide who can arrange kayak trips.

Full-day Mopan Mayan cultural tours of Maya Centre Village are available including visits to workshops on traditional Mayan cooking, crafts, language and natural tropical medicines. Contact **Liberato** or **Araceli Saqui** at Maya Centre Village. Tour operators in Placencia run day trips for US$65.

Punta Gorda *p401*
Green Iguana Eco Adventures, T722-2475, provides a wide range of tours and services. **Tide Tours**, Main St, T722-2129,
www.tidetours.org, organizes eco-tours. Also try **Sun Creek Tours**, suncreek@hughes.net.

⊖ Transport

South to Dangriga *p396*
Boat
Gales Point can be reached by inland waterways from **Belize City**, but buses have largely superseded boat services.

Bus
At least 2 daily **Southern Transport** buses run between **Belize City** and Dangriga on the coastal road.

Dangriga *p397*
Air
Maya Island Air and **Tropic Air**, T522-2129, from **Belize City** several daily, also from **Punta Gorda** via Placencia. Tickets from the airstrip, or **Pelican Beach Hotel**.

Boat
A fast skiff leaves 0900 (be there at 0800) on Sat for **Puerto Cortés**, **Honduras**. Irregular service, departing from north bank of river by bridge, T522-3227, ask for Carlos. Check procedures for exit formalities in advance. Enquire locally about hiring a boat for around US$25 per person in a group to **Belize City**.

Bus
From **Belize City**, Southern Transport, Magazine St, several daily from 0800, returning daily from 0530, US$5, 3½-4 hrs (bus passes entrance to the Blue Hole National Park); also via Coastal Hwy, 2 hrs. Bus to **Placencia** daily at 1200 and 1700, 3 hrs, US$5, via Hopkins and Sittee River, US$4. To **Belmopan**, 2½ hrs, US$4.50. The Southern Transport bus terminal is at the junction at the south end of town.

South of Dangriga p398

Bus

From Dangriga or Placencia, **Southern Transport** around 0700, 1500, 1530 and 1800, which travel on to Placencia or Dangriga. **James Bus** from Dangriga to Placencia around 1130 and 1700, Placencia to Dangriga around 0600 and 1400.

To **North East Caye**, 4 daily Southern Transport buses (T522-2160) from **Dangriga** to Sittee River and **Glover's Guest House** at Sittee River Village (see Sleeping). Also 3 daily buses from **Placencia**. Or, take any bus going south to the Sittee junction and take a ride to the guesthouse. If you get lost, phone ahead for help. At 0800 on Sun a sailing boat leaves for the reef, 5 hrs, US$20 per person 1 way (price included in accommodation package), returns Sat. At other times, charter a boat (skiff or sailing boat, US$200 1 way, up to 8 people, diesel sloop US$350, up to 30 people).

Placencia p398, map p399

Air

Placencia has its own airstrip. **Maya Island Air** and **Tropic Air** (T523-3410) fly several times a day to **Belize City** (international and municipal), also to **Dangriga** and **Punta Gorda**.

Boat

The **Hokie Pokie Water Taxi**, T523-2376, www.aguallos.com/hokeypokey. In Placencia leaves from the water taxi gas station terminal behind the **M'n M** store.
In Mango Creek the terminal is across the lagoon to **Independence**. US$5, check website for schedule (regular departures). From here, buses depart for **Punta Gorda** and **Belize City**.

The **Belize–Honduras Boat**, T632-0083, www.belizeferry.com, provides a regular weekly service linking Placencia and **Puerto Cortés** in Honduras. The journey can be quite choppy. From Placencia the boat leaves the dock near the petrol station at 0930 every Fri, passing Big Creek at 1000 to complete immigration formalities. It arrives in Puerto Cortés from 1200, US$50. Buy tickets in the

Placencia Tourism Center, US$55. Return service leaves Puerto Cortés on Mon at 1100 arriving 1330.

Bus

Placencia Peninsula Shuttle, T607-2711, runs from the Placencia dock to the **Zeboz Hotel** 5 times daily each way, US$2.50-5. See the tourist office for schedule. Buses to **Dangriga** direct at 0600, 0630, 1400, 3 hrs, US$5. Express, US$6. Direct buses to **Punta Gorda**, from Placencia with Southern Transport or James Buses. Alternatively take the **Hokie Pokie Water Taxi**, see above, to catch the James Bus Line buses from Independence Village, at 0930, 1045, 1500, 1630, 1645, 1½-2½ hrs. For buses to **Dangriga**, 1 hr, **Belmopan**, 2½ hrs and **Belize City**, 3½ hrs, also catch the boat to Independence. Buses leave at 0715, 0815, 1015, 1415 and 1645. Check times and fares at the Placencia tourist centre at the dock next to the Shell gas station.

Cockscomb Basin Wildlife Sanctuary and around p400

Bus

Can be booked at time of reservation, or locals will drive you from Maya Centre, otherwise it is a 6-mile, uphill walk from Maya Centre to the reserve – allow 2 hrs for the walk to Maya Centre. If you leave early in the morning going either way you are likely to see quite a lot of wildlife. All buses going south from **Dangriga** go through Maya Centre, 40 mins, US$4; and north from Placencia, return buses from 0700 onwards to Dangriga. If walking, leave all unwanted gear in Dangriga in view of the uphill stretch from Maya Centre, or you can leave luggage at Julio's little store in Maya Centre for a daily fee.

Taxi

A taxi from **Dangriga** will cost about US$50, it is not difficult to hitch back.

Punta Gorda p401

Air

Airstrip 5 mins' walk east of town. Daily flights with **Maya Island Air** and **Tropic Air**, T722-2008, from Dangriga, Placencia, Belize City (both airports). Tickets at **Alistair King's** (at Texaco station), **Bob Pennell's** hardware store on Main St, the **Sea Front Inn** on Front St or the offices alongside the airstrip. Advance reservations recommended.

Requena's Charter Services, T722-2070, leaves Punta Gorda for **Puerto Barrios, Guatemala**, at 0900 every day, US$20, 1 hr, return journey leaves at 1400. Guatemalan operator **Pichilingo** provides a similar service, leaving Puerto Barrios for **Punta Gorda** at 1000, returning at 1400.

Bus

James bus line to Belize City (6½ hrs, longer in heavy rain), daily at 0400, 0500, 0600, 0800, 1000 and 1200. **James** bus returns from Belize City daily, leaving hourly between 0515 and 1015, then 1215, 1315, 1515 and 1545. To **San Antonio** from square, see below; buses to **San Pedro Columbia** and San José, Wed and Sat 1200, return Wed and Sat morning. Buses can be delayed in the wet season. For the latest information on schedules, contact the Tourist Information Centre or **Dem Dats Doin** at the pier by the Customs House.

San Antonio p403

Bus and car

From **Punta Gorda**, 1-1½ hrs, US$1.50, Mon, Wed, Fri, Sat 1230, from west side of Central Park, also 1200 on Wed and Sat, continuing to **Santa Cruz**, **Santa Elena** and **Pueblo Viejo** (1 hr from San Antonio). Or, hire a pickup van in **Dangriga**; or get a ride in a truck from the market or rice cooperative's mill in Punta Gorda (1 leaves early afternoon); or go to the road junction at Dump, where the northern branch goes to Independence/Mango Creek, the other to San Antonio; 6 miles, either hitch or walk. Bus from San Antonio to **Punta Gorda**, Mon, Wed, Fri and Sat 0530, also

0500 Wed and Sat (having left Pueblo Viejo at 0400). If going to **Dangriga**, take the 0500, get out at Dump to catch 0530 Southern Transport bus going north. This area is full of places to explore and it is worth hiring a vehicle.

🄳 Directory

Dangriga p397

Banks Bank of Nova Scotia, MasterCard and Visa, and ATM. Belize Bank (Visa cash advances). **Immigration office** South end of Commerce St. **Internet** Val's laundry and Pelican Beach Hotel. **Laundry** Val's, Mahogany Rd near Bonefish, also has internet access. **Medical services** New Southern Regional Hospital, T522-3832. **Post** Mahogany Rd. **Telephone** BTL office is on the main street.

Placencia p398, map p399

Banks Atlantic Bank south end of the village witn ATM. Also ATM opposite Wendy's. **Internet** On the main road is Purple Space Monkey Village, and Placencia Office Supplies, on the main road near the centre. Good machines, fast access. also at De Tatch. **Medical services** Basic medical care available at Placencia Medical Center, T223-3292, behind St John's Memorial School on the sidewalk. **Post** Mon-Fri 0800-1200, 1330-1600. **Telephone** BTL office in the centre where you can make international calls. Payphones here, at the gas station and the ballfield.

Around Placencia p400

Banks Belize Bank, Mango Creek/ Independence, is open Fri only 0900-1200.

Punta Gorda p401

Banks Belize Bank, at one end of the park, will change excess Bz$ for US$ on production of passport and ticket out of the country. They do not change quetzales and charge US$5 for advancing cash against Visa and

MasterCard, changes TCs. Mon-Thu 0800-1300, Fri 0800-1630. You can change Bz$ for quetzales at Customs in Punta Gorda (ask for Emilio from **Grace** restaurant) and Puerto Barrios. **Western Union**, is run by Mahung's, corner North and Main St, Mon-Sat 0800-1200, 1330-1700. **Internet** Several places in town. **Internet**, next door to Sea Front Inn. **Carisha's**, by clock tower. **Laundry** Sony's Laundry Service near airstrip. **Telephone** The BTL office on Main St and King St.

Contents

Footprint features

El Salvador

At a glance

◉ **Getting around** Buses are efficient and economical.

◉ **Time required** 2-3 weeks would be best if you have the time.

◐ **Weather** High 20°Cs throughout the year, with most rainfall from May-Oct.

✖ **When not to go** The wettest weather and highest temperatures are in May, when it's hot and humid.

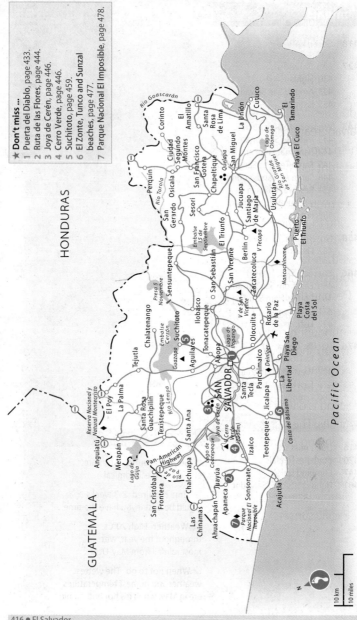

HONDURAS

GUATEMALA

Pacific Ocean

El Salvador is a lively country and the people are just as friendly – some say more so – than in the rest of Central America. Ornately painted and colourful buses bump from place to place, just as they do in Guatemala and Honduras, but El Salvador has better roads and the quality of the buses is superior to that of neighbouring countries. While the rest of Central America relies on tortillas, Salvadoreans fill them with beans, cheese or meat and call them *pupusas*. Pinning it down is difficult but there's a slightly different feel here from neighbouring countries.

Guidebooks tend to urge caution, but in reality El Salvador is no more dangerous than other Central American countries. During the civil war, Salvadoreans sought refuge abroad; now they're returning, bringing with them a gang culture and other less-than-favourable imports from the United States, although as a tourist you are rarely subjected to any of these social problems.

Despite the high rate of gang-related crime, frequent natural disasters and a tourist infrastructure less developed than its neighbouring countries, there are some compelling reasons why you should visit El Salvador: dramatic volcanic landscapes, blue-green lagoons, horizon-filling panoramas and golden beaches. In the northern hills around El Poy and Perquín the trekking is divine, with far-reaching views across staggered horizons. The stark cinder cone of Volcán Izalco offers a challenging but rewarding trek from the slopes of Cerro Verde, while El Imposible National Park provides the chance to visit a forest. Along the coast, choose from surfing, diving or simply lazing around and watching the endless display of Pacific sunsets.

Essentials

Life in El Salvador focuses strongly on San Salvador. All roads lead towards the capital with just a few exceptions. Planning your trip will involve either a visit to San Salvador or at least travelling through it. Fortunately the country is so small that the capital can make a convenient base, thus avoiding the hassle of dragging your bags across the country.

Where to go

San Salvador is a cosmopolitan city with a variety of architectural styles that have been created by the multitude of rebuilding projects in a history dogged by earthquakes. The city centre is always busy and widely thought of as unsafe at night, so newcomers are best advised to head for the western areas around Boulevard de los Héroes, with its shopping malls and restaurants, and the residential districts of Escalón and the Zona Rosa with its major shopping malls – Multiplaza, Hipermall and La Gran Vía – with fancy stores, branded boutiques and a variety of restaurants and nightclubs.

Throughout El Salvador volcanoes dominate the landscape, and the scenery is one of its main attractions. Close to the capital, **Parque Balboa** affords fine views through the dramatic Puerta del Diablo (Devil's Door) and from the Mirador in the centre of the mountain village of **Los Planes de Renderos**. Below Los Planes de Renderos is **Panchimalco**, an old village where cultural traditions are kept alive by a growing handicraft industry. The community hosts the yearly Procesión de Las Palmas, a spectacular floral procession in the beginning of May. **Parque Nacional Cerro Verde**, just west of San Salvador, is a popular excursion for its prospect over Izalco and Santa Ana volcanoes and the deep-blue waters of the beautiful **Lago de Coatepeque**. Closed for two years after earthquakes, Cerro Verde recuperated its unique flora and fauna, was declared a protected natural area and is now open to foreign visitors. Also a short distance west of the capital are the country's main archaeological sites of **San Andrés** and the **Joya de Cerén**, where a Maya settlement has been preserved under volcanic ash. There are no grand temples and sculptures, but the dwellings and everyday objects found here are the only ones of their type preserved from the Maya era in Central America. Just north of San Salvador is **Cihuatán**, El Salvador's largest archaeological park and the largest city in Mesoamerica at the time of the Toltecs. The main city of the west is **Santa Ana**, which is also a good base for visiting the sites of **Tazumal** and **Casa Blanca** to the west.

A little further south, **Sonsonate** is an interesting town leading to the **Ruta de las Flores** a handful of villages climbing the volcanic chains with good scenery and waterfalls, pleasant hiking and a smattering of crafts.

There are very few pockets of undisturbed land, mainly because El Salvador is farmed intensively. On the border with Guatemala and Honduras is **Montecristo**, a remnant of cloud forest administered jointly by the three countries, while another such survivor is **Parque Nacional El Imposible**, one of the largest national parks in Central America. Just south of El Imposible is the **Barra de Santiago** protected natural area, home to a wide variety of species in the best preserved mangrove in the country.

North of San Salvador, near the Honduran border, are the towns of **La Palma** and **San Ignacio**, where handicrafts of brightly painted wood and other styles are made. Also north, but heading more to the east, is **Suchitoto**, one of the best preserved colonial towns, currently enjoying a revival that takes advantage of the beautiful scenery around Cerrón Grande resevoir. In eastern El Salvador are the cities of **San Vicente** and **San Miguel**, the port of La Unión/Cutuco and many small traditional towns. Those interested in the recent civil war can visit **Perquín**.

The Pacific coast at **La Libertad** is only a short trip from the capital and is a good place to start exploring the Balsam coast to the west, the surfing beaches and to get a feel for the country as a whole. The beaches of the **Costa del Sol** are definitely worth a stop for their long stretches of sand and estuaries. The **Gulf of Fonseca** has islands with secluded beaches which you can explore. In some parts of the country the infrastructure for tourism is quite rudimentary, but in others (such as the capital and nearby places of interest and some of the beach resorts) it is well developed.

Suggested itinerary

With so many crossings and borders, the options for travel in and around El Salvador are very flexible. Points of interest are spread throughout the country so there is no natural route to travel. If you want to visit **Parque Nacional El Imposible**, go for the La Hachadura crossing, drift through **Apaneca** and on to **San Salvador** before heading north to **Suchitoto**. If you're going to Honduras, head to **El Poy** if you want to drop into Santa Rosa de Copán or Gracias, or **Perquín** if you want Gracias or Tegucigalpa. For Nicaragua head to El Amatillo. El Salvador is subtly different to the other Central American nations. You could shoot through the main highlights in 10 days or else hang out for two to three weeks and soak up the nuances; if you've got the time, you'll enjoy the difference.

When to go

The most pleasant months are from November to January. El Salvador is fortunate in that temperatures are rarely excessively high. The average for San Salvador is 28°C with a variation of only about 3°C. March to May are the hottest months; December to February the coolest. There is one rainy season, from May to October, with April and November being transitional periods; there are only light rains for the rest of the year: the average annual rainfall is about 1830 mm. Highest temperatures and humidity will be found on the coast and in the lowlands, with the heat at its greatest from March to May.

What to do

El Salvador has been a popular **surfing** destination for several decades, from La Libertad heading west. Beyond this there is some diving in the coastal area and volcano lagoons.

National parks provide opportunities for **trekking** and **nature walks** in particular at Parque Nacional Cerro Verde close to San Salvador and in the more remote parks of Montecristo and Parque Nacional El Imposible.

Getting there

Air

From Europe To Miami with any transatlantic carrier, then to San Salvador with **American Airlines** or **Taca. Iberia** flies from Barcelona and Madrid via Miami.

The international airport is at Comalapa, 62 km southeast of San Salvador off the Coastal Highway, reached by a four-lane toll highway. There is a tourist information desk at the

Border essentials

El Salvador–Guatemala

For crossings between El Salvador and Guatemala (Frontera–San Cristóbal, Valle Nuevo–Las Chinamas, Ciudad Pedro Alvarado–La Hachadura, Anguiatú), see page 199.

El Salvador–Honduras

El Poy

This crossing between northern El Salvador and southwestern Honduras is straightforward, but it's better to arrive early if you have a long journey ahead.
Currency Exchange Bargain with money-changers for the best deal.
Onwards to Honduras Shuttles carry passengers to Nueva Ocotopeque, 15-20 minutes, where you can catch highway connections north to Santa Rosa de Copán.
Onwards to El Salvador Buses to San Salvador depart hourly, three to four hours, passing La Palma en route, 30 minutes.

El Amatillo

The Río Goascarán forms the border at El Amatillo. If driving, you will be hounded by *tramitadores*, some of them are unethical, but their services aren't really required here anyway. Thorough car searches.
Currency exchange Money-changers.
Salvadorean immigration Open 0600-1700, closes for an hour or two at lunchtime.
Honduran immigration Open 0600-1700, closed at lunch.
Onwards to Honduras Hourly services to Tegucigalpa, four hours. To Choluteca, every 30 minutes, three hours.
Onwards to El Salvador Regular services to San Miguel, bus 330, 1½ hours.

Perquín–Sabanetas

The international boundary has been variously disputed throughout history. A treaty resolved the disagreement in 2006 and the border now lies 3 km north of Perquín. It may be impassable after heavy rains. Travel early morning for the best chance of transport connections. Rough road.
Currency exchange Money-changers.
Honduran immigration 5 km inside Honduras.
Salvadorean immigration There is apparently no immigration office at Perquín. Entering the country is possible, but illegal. Not recommended.
Onwards to Honduras Irregular daily services to Marcala.
Onwards to El Salvador Services to San Miguel.

airport, which is open sporadically. If closed, you can still pick up some useful leaflets. Taxis and buses provide regular links to the capital. ▸▸ *See Transport, page 439.*

There is a 13% tax on international air tickets bought in El Salvador and an airport departure tax of US$32 for anyone staying more than six hours. The airport departure tax is now included in the ticket. The phone number for the airport authorities (**CEPA**) is T2339-9455. The airport has offices for all the main car rental companies and there are two banks, a tourist office and **Grupo Taca** and **American Airline** offices. Border formalities tend to be relatively brief although searches may be carried out.

From USA and Canada The main connection is with Miami. Other cities with flights to San Salvador are Atlanta, Dallas/Fort Worth, Houston, Los Angeles, Montreal, New Orleans, New York, Orlando, Phoenix, San Diego, San Francisco, Washington and Toronto.

From Central America and Mexico There are flights from all capitals and many larger cities in Mexico.

From South America Good connections to Colombia with a few flights to Barranquilla and Bogotá. Also connections with Buenos Aires, Cali, Caracas, Cartagena, Cucutá, Guayaquil, Quito, Lima, Medellín, Santa Marta and Santiago. Some flights go via San José or Panama City.

Road

Several border crossings with neighbouring countries. To the west the Pan-American Highway arrives from Guatemala at San Cristóbal through Santa Ana, Las Chinamas and La Hachadura, which is handy for Parque Nacional El Imposible. To the northwest the crossing is at Anguiatú. Also to the northwest the crossing at El Poy leads to southern Honduras, as does the crossing to the northeast at Perquín and to the east at El Amatillo. *▶▶ For border crossings with Guatemala, see page 199; for crossings with Honduras, see page 420.*

Getting around

Road

Bus Bus services are good and cover most areas, although the buses are usually crowded. The best time to travel by bus is 0900-1500; avoid Friday and Sunday afternoons. All bus routes have a number, some also have a letter. Strange as it may seem, the system works and the route numbers don't change. Tickets are still unbelievably cheap, both within cities – usually around US$0.25 – and for long-distance journeys, which rarely cost more than US$1.50. Buses are brightly painted, particularly around San Miguel.

Transport is not difficult for the budget traveller as nearly all buses have luggage racks inside. For bigger bags there is sometimes space at the back where a couple of seats have been removed, so sit near there if you want to stay close to your bag. However, when problems on buses do occur they are usually at the back of the bus. The cheaper alternatives to the **Pullman buses**, which cross to Guatemala and Tegucigalpa from Puerto Bus Terminal in San Salvador, have luggage compartments beneath them and the luggage is tagged.

Taxi Apart from in the major cities taxis are rare, especially after dark. However, if you're eating out at night, you can usually arrange a lift at your hotel or restaurant for a small tip.

Car At the border, after producing a driving licence and proof of ownership, you are given a *comprobante de ingreso* (which has to be stamped by immigration, customs and quarantine), this is free of charge and you get the vehicle permit for 60 days. You need to have a passport from the same country as your driving licence or have an international licence and not have been in the country for more than 60 days. (If you are a foreigner residing in El Salvador you need to get a Salvadorean driver's licence.) You receive a receipt, vehicle permit and vehicle check document. Under no circumstances may the 60 days be extended, even though the driver may have been granted 90 days in the country. A few kilometres from the border the *comprobante* will be checked. When you leave the country a *comprobante de ingreso* must be stamped again and, if you don't intend to return, your permit must be surrendered. Do not overstay your permitted time unless you wish to be fined. Leaving the country for a few days in order to return for a new permit is not recommended as customs officials are wise to this and may fine you anyway. To bring a vehicle in permanently involves a complex procedure costing thousands of dollars.

Petrol costs per US gallon US$3.60 (super), US$3.20 (regular), US$2.80 (diesel), though as everywhere, prices are constantly rising. All fuel is unleaded. **Roads** are very good throughout the country, but look out for crops being dried at the roadside or in central reservations. Take care of buses, which travel very fast. Third-party, **insurance** is compulsory in El Salvador and can be arranged at the border (enquire first at consulates). Under the 1996 law, **seat belts** must be worn; the fine for not doing so is US$57. The fine for **drink-driving** is US$57. If your alcohol level is very high you go straight to jail and have to await the sentence. Do not attempt to bribe the officials. For more information, call **Ministerio de Transporte** ① *T2281-0678 0679*.

Sleeping

As the most industrialized of the Central American states El Salvador has an impressive selection of international-standard business hotels in San Salvador. The country also has a good selection of more expensive hotels for those taking weekend breaks from the capital. At the lower end there is no shortage of cheap accommodation, but there is a shortage of good, cheap accommodation. If you have the time, shop around, don't check into the first hotel you come to. If travelling at holiday times book accommodation in advance. **Ximena's Guest House** off Boulevard de Los Héroes is recognized as a hotel where backpackers meet up.

Eating

Pupusas, stuffed tortillas made of corn or ricemeal, are the quintessential Salvadorean dish. They come in several varieties including *chicharrón* (pork crackling), *queso* (cheese) and *revueltas* (mixed), and are typical, tasty and cheap. The ones sold at street stalls are better there than at restaurants, but beware stomach infection from the accompanying *curtido* (pickled cabbage). On Saturday and Sunday nights people congregate in *pupuserías*. *Pavo* (turkey) is common and good, as are *frijoles* (red beans). A *boca* is an appetizer, a small dish of yucca, avocado or chorizo, served with a drink before a meal. Apart from in San Salvador, restaurants tend to close early, around 2000.

Coffee makes an excellent souvenir and is good value and delicious.

Beer Light lagers are the norm, as elsewhere in Central America; Suprema is stronger than Pilsener, while Golden Light is a reduced-alcohol beer.

Chicha is a traditional alcoholic drink made from corn, sometimes with a trace of pineapple; El Salvador also has a stronger, distilled version called *chaparro*. Although illegal to sell, everyone has their source. When made well *chicha* can taste similar to white wine. It is a trademark of the Maya and is particularly well made in the western village of Izalco. Ask at the tourist office there for a *chicha* contact to purchase a sample. *Chaparro* *curado* contains fruit or honey. It is a favourite at election times when alcohol sales are banned. Water bottles are emptied and filled with the clear *chaparro* for illegal swigging on the streets.

Festivals and events

1 Jan New Year's Day.
Mar/Apr Holy Week (3 days, government 10 days).
1 May Labour Day.
10 May Mothers' Day.
First week of Aug Corpus Christi (half day).
15 Sep (half day).

2 and **5 Nov** (half day).
24 Dec (half day) and **Christmas Day**.
Government offices are also closed on religious holidays. Look in newspapers for details of regional fiestas and other fairs. There are many craft fairs, for example at San Sebastián and San Vicente.

Shopping

The best place to buy arts and crafts is in the village where the items are originally made; **Ilobasco** for ceramics, **San Sebastián** for hammocks and **La Palma** for painted wooden boxes, **Nahuizalco** for baskets and furniture of wicker and jute. If you cannot go there in person, the markets in **San Salvador** (Mercado Ex-Cuartel and Mercado de Artesanía) sell many of these items at a slightly higher prices. Branches of Nahanché have outlets in the major shopping malls with good quality handicrafts from all over the country.

Essentials A-Z

Accident and emergency
Police: 911; Fire service: T2527-7300; Red Cross: T2222-5155; **Hospitals**: T2225-4481; Public hospital: Rosales T2231-9200; Public maternity: Hospital de Maternidad T2529-8200; **Private Hospital Pro Familia**: T2244-8000; **Private Maternity**: T2271-2555; Hospital Ginecológico: T2247-1122.

Customs and duty free
All personal luggage is allowed in free. Also permitted: 50 cigars or 200 cigarettes, and 2 litres of liquor, 2 used cameras or a video recorder, 1 personal stereo, 1 portable computer and new goods up to US$1000 in value (best to have receipts). No restrictions on the import of foreign currency; up to the amount imported and declared may also be exported. Check with www.aduana.gob.sv for full information.

Phone numbers for Salvadorean border crossings: **Hachadura**: T2420-3767, Chinamas: T2401-3601; **San Cristóbal**: T2441-8109; **El Poy**: T2335-9401; **Angiatú**: T2401-0231; **Amatillo**: T2649-9388.

Electricity
110 volts, 60 cycles, AC (US-style flat-pin plugs). Supply is far from stable; important electrical equipment should have surge protectors.

Embassies and consulates
For more countries, visit www.rree.gob.sv.
Belgium, Av de Tervuren 171, 2nd floor, 1150 Brussels, T733-0485.
Canada, 209 Kent St K2P 1Z8, Ottawa, Ontario, T613-238-2939, also in Montreal and Vancouver.
Germany, Joachin-Karnatz-Allee 47, 10557, Berlín (Tiergarten), T30-206-4660, www.botschaft-elsalvador.de.

Israel, 4 Avigail, Apto 4, Abu-Tor, Jerusalem, Israel. 93551, T267-28411.

Italy, Via Gualtiero Castellini 13, Scala B int, 3, 00197 Roma, T06-807-6605.

Japan, Kowa 38, Building 803, Nishi Azabu 4 Ch, Tokyo, Japan 106, T33499-4461.

Spain, Calle Serrano 114, 2 Edif Izquierda, 28006 Madrid, T91-562-8002.

Mexico, Calle Temístocles 88 Col Polanco, México DF, T5281-5725.

UK, 2nd floor, 8 Dorset Sq, London, NW1 6PU, T020-7224-9800.

US: 1400 Sixteenth NW Washington, DC 20036, T202-387-6511; with consulates in several other large cities.

Health

Gastroenteritic diseases are most common. Visitors should take care over what they eat during the first few weeks, and should drink *agua cristal* (purified bottled water). The bags of water sold in the street are not always safe and taste somewhat of rubber. Cases of dengue are rare in adults. For diarrhoea, mild dysentery, amoebas and parasitic infections get *Nodik* tablets from any chemist or large supermarket, approx US$14 for a 3-day cure. El Salvador has one of the best health systems in Central America, so the capital is a good place to sort out problems. You can get a stool sample taken at the **Pro-Familia Hospital**, 25 Av Norte, near Metro Centro, which gives you the result in about 6-12 hrs. See also page 38.

Internet

Internet cafés are widespread in the capital and are now commonplace in smaller places outside San Salvador. Most hotels will offer both internet service and wireless connection.

Language

Spanish is the official language and English is widely understood in business and travel industry-related circles.

Media

Newspapers in San Salvador include *Diario de Hoy* (right wing), www.elsalvador.com, and *La Prensa Gráfica* (centre) every morning including Sun, www.laprensagrafica.com; both have the most complete listings of cultural events in San Salvador. *Co Latino* is a left-wing newspaper. *El Mundo* in the afternoons except Sun. US newspapers and magazines are available at leading hotels.

Of the 80 **radio stations**, 1 is government owned and several are owned by churches.

There are 4 commercial **television stations**, all with national coverage, and 1 government-run station with 2 channels. There are several cable channels, all with CNN news, etc. Most hotels and many guesthouses in San Salvador have cable.

Money → *US$1=8.75 colones (fixed)*.

El Salvador adopted the dollar on 1 Jan 2001 and the national currency – the colón – is now totally replaced. All US coinage and notes are widely used, although you may have problems with US$20 bills and above. There are some small shops and street merchants that still price their products in colones, but they are in the minority.

ATMs and exchange

Do not find yourself in the countryside without cash or credit cards; traveller's cheques (TCs) are of limited use outside the capital and major cities. You can use credit cards in pretty much any store (except small *tiendas*). See under San Salvador, Banks, page 441, regarding exchange of TCs. Be aware that some banks will want to see your original purchase receipt. Credit cards are widely accepted and are charged at the official rate. There are international Visa and MasterCard ATMs in El Salvador and larger cities throughout the country. For cash advances on Visa or MasterCard, go to **Aval-Visa** or **Banco de América Central de El Salvador**.

All ATMs and banks give US dollars in cash (so no need for exchange). Pretty much all gas stations have ATMs.

Cost of living and travelling

El Salvador is reasonably priced and 2 people should be able to travel for US$40 per person per day. However, the range of services open to the foreign tourist is still limited (although growing) so the quality of hotels is not as good as that offered in neighbouring countries for the same price.

Opening hours

Banks Mon-Fri 0900-1700, Sat 0900-1200, closed between 29-30 Jun and 30-31 Dec.
Businesses Mon-Fri 0800-1200, 1400-1730; Sat 0800-1200.
Government offices Mon-Fri 0730-1530.

Post

Airmail to and from Europe can take up to a month, but is normally about 15 days; from the USA, 1 week. Certified packets to Europe cost US$9.25 per kilo and regular service is US$8.50 per kilo, good service; swifter, but more expensive, is **EMS** (US$34 per kg to Europe). Courier services are much quicker, but cost more. The correct address for any letter to the capital is 'San Salvador, El Salvador, Central America'.

Safety

Traditionally El Salvador has a reputation for violence and crime. In part this is a legacy of many years of civil war although this has been improved through a more active role of the police in later years. The reality is that most people visiting El Salvador return with reports of friendly, open people; far from being targeted by criminals, you are much more likely to receive a warm welcome and genuine interest in your visit. Locals will talk incessantly about the country's problems and dangers but few actual examples materialize. Be cautious until you find your own level of comfort and always ask local advice. Statistically El Salvador has the unenviable distinction of having the worst levels of violent crime on the continent. This derives from Salvadorean gang culture (*maras*) and most visitors will see nothing of this activity.

If renting a car, buy a steering lock. Visitors to San Salvador should seek advice on where is not safe both inside and outside the city.

Telephone → *Country code T+503.*

The **international direct dialling** code (to call out of El Salvador) is T00; 144+00 for **Telefónica**. There are no local area codes within El Salvador. There is a network of public phones for telecommunications companies – all use prepaid phone cards that only work in the company's particular machines. Available at most street corners, supermarkets, gas stations to small stores they can be used for local and international calls, but make sure the card is from the same company as the public phone. The cards come in several denominations (US$1-3, US$5, US$10, US$25, etc). Mobile phones are very cheap. You can get a SIM card for US$3 and if you need a mobile phone you can get one from as little as US$12.

Some hotels will provide direct dialling – by far the easiest option. Dial T114 for **Information** (English spoken) and details of phone numbers in capital.

Time

- 6 hrs GMT.

Tipping

In upmarket restaurants: 10%, in others, give small change. Check your bill as most now add the 10% at the end (if they have, an additional tip is not needed). Nothing for taxi drivers except when hired for the day; airport porters, *boinas rojas* (red berets), US$2 per bag.

Tourist information

Corporación Salvadoreña de Turismo (**Corsatur**), at the Ministry of Tourism, Edificio Carbonel No1, Col Roma Alameda Dr Manuel Enrique Araujo Pasaje Carbonel San Salvador, T2243-7835; T2241-3200, www.elsalvador.travel. Provides information locally and on the web.

Revue, www.revuemag.com. English-language magazine published in Guatemala, with a section on El Salvador. Contains articles on places to visit and details of activities.

Useful websites

www.alfatravelguide.com Has a comprehensive listings of hotels throughout the country.

www.elsalvador.com Site of *El Diario de Hoy*– look in 'Otros Sitios' for tourist info.

www.diariocolatino.com Site of the leftist *Co Latino* newspaper.

www.laprensa.com.sv Site of *La Prensa Gráfica* newspaper.

www.mipatria.net and **www.theother elsalvador.com** Access to useful information.

www.turismo.com.sv Lists of hotels, restaurants and interesting places to visit.

www.utec.edu.sv Site of Centre for Investigation of El Salvadorean Public Opinion (CIOPS) with information in Spanish on El Salvadorean political and social issues.

Visas and immigration

Every visitor must have a valid passport. No visas are required for European, US, Canadian, Australian or New Zealand nationals. The government website www.rree.gob.sv has a full list of country requirements.

Overstaying the limit on a tourist card can result in fines. Immigration officials can authorize up to 90 days stay in the country; extensions may be permitted on application to Migración, Centro de Gobierno (see under San Salvador). As of 2006, when El Salvador signed a Central America-4 (CA-4) Border Control Agreement with Guatemala, Honduras, and Nicaragua, you have to visit a country outside of these 4 to re-enter and gain 90 days. Travel between these 4 countries now involves minimal customs control: no entry stamp in your passport, only an exit stamp from departing country. Nevertheless, always check at a Salvadorean consulate for any changes to the rules.

Weights and measures

The metric system is used alongside certain local units such as the *vara* (836 mm), *manzana* (7000 sq m) and the *quintal* (45 kg). Some US weights and measures are also used; US gallons are used for gasoline and quarts for oil.

San Salvador

→ *Colour map 3, C1. Altitude: 680-1000 m. Population: 2,297,282 including suburbs).*
Surrounded by a ring of mountains in a valley known as 'Valle de las Hamacas', San Salvador has suffered from both natural and man-made disasters. El Salvador's capital is a bustling cosmopolitan city with a rich blend of architectural styles; modern, yet retaining the charm of the Spanish era with the privilege of being one of the first European cities in the New World. Today, crumbling buildings await renovation and restoration, or the arrival of the next earthquake to deliver the final death knell. As always, some areas speed to recovery, and the shopping malls and wealthy suburbs to the west stand out in the pollution-filled valley. The further northwest you get from the city centre the higher you climb and the cleaner the air becomes.

San Salvador itself does not have many natural attractions, but there are several day trips to nearby volcanoes, crater lakes and beauty spots such as Los Planes de Renderos, the Puerto del Diablo and San Salvador's own volcano, Boquerón, which has a paved road all the way to the top. There are, surprisingly, many green areas and trees planted alongside the streets giving the city a refreshing atmosphere. If you spend a few days in the city and surrounding area you could be pleasantly surprised by how easy it is to get around and how much there is to do. ►► *For listings, see pages 435-442.*

Ins and outs

Getting there The **international airport** (SAL) is at Comalapa, 62 km southeast of San Salvador towards Costa del Sol beach, reached by a four-lane, toll highway. Some domestic flights use the old airport at Ilopango, 13 km east of the capital. Most **international buses** arrive at the Puerto Bus terminal, although luxury services and **Ticabus** have their own terminals. Domestic bus lines use terminals at the east, south and west ends of the city. ►► *See Transport, page 439.*

Getting around The main focal points of the city are the historical centre, the commercial district some 3 km to the west around Boulevard de los Héroes, and the residential and commercial districts of Escalón and Zona Rosa another 2 km further west. City buses and taxis are needed to get between the three (see page 439).

Four broad streets meet at the centre: Avenida Cuscatlán and its continuation Avenida España run south to north; Calle Delgado and its continuation Calle Arce, with a slight blip, from east to west. This principle is retained throughout: the *avenidas* run north to south and the *calles* east to west. The even-numbered *avenidas* are east of the central *avenidas*, odd numbers west; north of the central *calles*, they are dubbed Norte, south of the central *calles* Sur. The even-numbered *calles* are south of the two central *calles*, the odd numbers north. East of the central *avenidas* they are dubbed Oriente (Ote), west of the central *avenidas* Poniente (Pte). Sounding more complicated than it is, the system is straightforward and quickly grasped.

Tourist information **Corporación Salvadoreña de Turismo (Corsatur)** ① *Edificio Carbonel No 1, Col Roma Alameda Dr Manuel Enrique Araujo Pasaje Carbonel San Salvador, T2243-7835, www.elsalvador.travel, Mon-Fri 0800-1230, 1330-1730.* Good information on buses, archaeological sites, beaches and national parks. Texaco and Esso sell good maps at some of their service stations. The best maps of the city and country are available from the **Instituto**

Geográfico Nacional ⓘ *1 Calle Pte y 43 Av Norte 02310, Col Flor Blanca, T2260-8000.* The **Instituto Salvadoreño de Turismo (ISTU)** ⓘ *Calle Rubén Darío 619, San Salvador Centre, T2222-8000,* has useful information about the 13 government-run **Turicentros** recreation and water parks in the country and on Cerro Verde and Walter T Deininger national parks.

Best time to visit The climate is semi-tropical and healthy, and the water supply relatively pure. Days are often hot, especially in the dry season, but the temperature drops in the late afternoon and nights are usually pleasantly mild. Since it is in a hollow, the city has a very bad smog problem, caused mainly by traffic pollution. Efforts are being made to reduce vehicle emissions.

① San Salvador

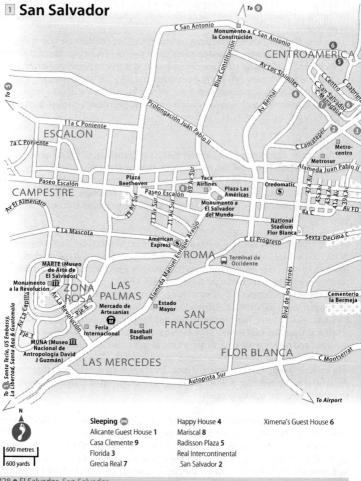

Sleeping 🛏
Alicante Guest House **1**
Casa Clemente **9**
Florida **3**
Grecia Real **7**

Happy House **4**
Mariscal **8**
Radisson Plaza **5**
Real Intercontinental
San Salvador **2**

Ximena's Guest House **6**

600 metres
600 yards

Safety The city centre is considered by many to be dangerous after dark, but the area north of Bulevar de los Héroes up to around San Antonio Abad is quite safe. As a general rule, stay out of poorly lit areas and keep to main roads where there are more people around. At night, taxis are a sensible alternative if you don't know where you're going exactly.

Armed security personnel are commonplace. There is a heightened atmosphere of tension in some areas. In downtown markets, don't carry cameras, don't wear watches or jewellery and don't flash money around.

San Salvador maps
1 San Salvador, page 428
2 San Salvador centre, page 430

Bars & clubs
Café La 7 **5**
El Arpa (Bar Irlandés) **6**
La Luna **3**

Sights

A number of important buildings are near the intersection of the main roads in the historic centre. On the east side of Avenida Cuscatlán is the **Plaza Barrios**, the heart of the city. A fine equestrian statue looks west towards the renaissance-style **Palacio Nacional** (1904-1911). To the north is the **New Cathedral**, which was left unfinished for several years after Archbishop Romero suspended its construction to use the money to reduce poverty. Work was resumed in 1990 and completed in 1999, the last consecration of a cathedral of the millennium. It now stands as a beacon of tranquillity amid the dirt and noise of the downtown capital. It commands a striking presence, gleaming white and modern, its façade flanked by two giant murals vividly splashed with the colourful work of the country's most famous artist, **Fernando Llort**. Inside it is quite bare, but for the fabulous circular stained-glass window of a dove surrounded by a hundred shards of brilliant yellow glass, which in turn is framed by yellow stars set in deep lapis lazuli-blue glass. Beneath the cathedral, a new chapel has been created to house the tomb of assassinated **Archbishop Oscar Romero**.

2 San Salvador centre

Sleeping
American Guest House **1**   El Palacio **3**
Centro Histórico **2**

East of Plaza Barrios, on Calle Delgado, is the **Teatro Nacional**, whose interior has been magnificently restored. If you walk along 2 Calle Oriente you pass, on the right, **Parque Libertad** with the rebuilt church of **El Rosario** on the eastern side where José Matías Delgado, father of the Independence movement, lies buried. The interior, decked out in modern sculpture, is fascinating; go early morning or late afternoon to see the stunning light effect of the modern stained-glass window. The **Palacio Arquiepiscopal** is next door. Not far away to the southeast, on 10 Avenida Sur, is another rebuilt church, **La Merced**, whose belltower rang out Father Delgado's tocsin call to Independence in 1811.

One block north, across Calle Delgado, is the **Teatro Nacional** ① *Plaza Morazán, T2222-5689*, with a monument to General Morazán. The theatre reopened in 2008, after a complete restoration following earthquake damage in 2001; it hosts a regular programme of performances, sometimes free, in a sumptuous auditorium with red velvet seats. Heading east along Delgado is the **Mercado Ex-Cuartel**, and the expected confusion of sounds and smells that besiege the senses. Nearby are some of the cheapest hotels in the city. Running west from the Teatro Nacional, Calle Arce leads to **Hospital Rosales** and its own gardens. On the way to the hospital is the great church of **El Sagrado Corazón de Jesús**, which is well worth a visit; don't miss the stained-glass windows. Turn left (south) here and after one block you come to the **Parque Bolívar**, with the national printing office to the south and the Department of Health to the north.

Four streets north of Calle Arce is the Alameda Juan Pablo II, an important road for bus transport, on which stands **Parque Infantil**, where you will find the Palacio de los Deportes. One block west is the **Centro de Gobierno**, with many official buildings.

The north side of Parque Bolívar is Calle Rubén Darío (2 Calle Poniente), which becomes Alameda Roosevelt, then Paseo General Escalón as it runs through the commercial and residential districts west of the centre. Heading west this boulevard first passes **Parque Cuscatlán**. A major junction is with 49 Avenida: to the south this avenue soon passes the national stadium, **Estadio Olímpico Flor Blanca**, before becoming the main highway to the international airport. To the north, 49 Avenida crosses Alameda Juan Pablo II beyond which it changes name to **Bulevar de los Héroes**, home to the fashionable shopping centres, **Metrocentro** and the newer **Metrosur**, the **Hotel Real Intercontinental**, some of the city's better restaurants and a glut of fast-food places, which is a busy area at all times, especially at night. At the Shell station by

➡ **San Salvador maps**
1 San Salvador, page 428
2 San Salvador centre, page 430

Parque Centenario

Alameda Juan Pablo II

5 C Ote

3 C Ote

4 Av Nte

6 Av Nte

8 Av Nte

10 Av Nte

12 Av Nte

1 C Ote

aza razán

Mercado Ex-Cuartel

C Delgado

Teatro acional

4 Av Sur

6 Av Sur

8 Av Sur

10 Av Sur

12 Av Sur

2 C Ote

Parque Libertad

El Rosario

4 C Ote

(Pol) Director General of Police

Metrocentro, mariachis and other musicians gather each evening, waiting to be hired; others wander around the restaurants, playing to diners.

Continuing west along Alameda Roosevelt, the next landmark at the Plaza Las Américas is the **Monumento al Salvador del Mundo**, a statue of Jesus standing on the Earth atop a column. From this junction the Pan-American Highway heads southwest to **Santa Tecla**. Straight ahead is Paseo General Escalón, Parque Beethoven and an area with many restaurants, shops and the Colonia Escalón residential district. Hidden behind the towering office blocks flanking the monument is the **Museo Forma** ① *Av Manuel Enrique Araujo, T2298-4269, www.fjuliadiaz.org, Mon-Fri 0900-1700, Sat 0900-1200, US$1.50*, a small modern art gallery housed in a neocolonial-style castle, with an interesting collection of paintings and sculpture by Salvadorean artists.

Another important residential and entertainment region is the **Zona Rosa** and **Colonia San Benito**, reached either from the Pan-American Highway or from Escalón. In this leafy suburb, some of the most elegant restaurants and the **Hotel Sheraton Presidente** and **Hotel Hilton Princess** (where former US president Clinton stayed while on his Central America tour) are found. **MUNA (Museo Nacional de Antropología David J Guzman)** ① *Feria Internacional, Av de la Revolución y Carretera a Santa Tecla, T2243-3750, Tue-Sun 0900-1700, US$3*, is a modern museum worth visiting, showcasing exhibits on the country's archaeological and historical past as well as numerous cultural events; descriptions in Spanish only, but free guided tours available in afternoons with English-speaking guides (check at desk as they only operate if enough visitors). Just north of the museum at the end of Avenida Revolución is **MARTE (Museo de Arte de El Salvador)** ① *T2243-6099, Tue-Sun 1000-1800, US$1.50 (free on Sun), café and shop (both closed Sun) in lobby*. This privately run modern arts museum has permanent exhibits depicting the history of Salvadorean painters with temporary exhibits of artists from Latin America and other parts of the world.

A little further north is **El Arbol de Dios** ① *La Mascota y Av Masferrer, T2224-6200, Mon-Sat 1000-2200*, an arts and crafts store, restaurant, museum and garden, operated by the famed Salvadorean artist Fernando Llort, who designed the façade of the Metropolitan Cathedral and is known for his naïf-style wood paintings. The display here also includes the work of other artists.

In Colonia San Benito is **Museo de Ciencias Físicas Stephen Hawking** ① *Av Reforma 179, T2223-3027, Mon-Sat 1000-1400, US$1.25*, with sections on astronomy, ecology, electronics and biochemistry. Interactive exhibits about the sciences with monthly lectures on scientific topics. This area also has many art galleries such as **Galería Espacio** ① *Av La Capilla*, **Galería 1-2-3** ① *Calle La Reforma*, **La Pinacoteca** ① *Blv Hipódromo*, to name a few. See local press for details.

Worth visiting is the **María Auxiliadora church**, locally known as 'don Rua', situated in Barrio San Miguelito. This multi-coloured marble temple – a copy of the cathedral in Turin (Italy) – is one of the city's landmarks, displaying a Venetian clock tower and with a spectacular view from the belltower.

Museo Militar de las Fuerzas Armadas ① *behind the presidential palace of San Jacinto at the former Cuartel El Zapote*, has a collection of exhibits of weapons, uniforms and decorations of the armed forces, and weapons captured from FMLN guerrillas. **Mercado de San Miguelito** is an indoor market located close to don Rua. Safer than many of the other city markets and famous for its *comedores* which offer typical Salvadorean dishes (difficult to find outside a traditional Salvadorean home) at economic prices. There are several food stalls throughout the place – look for the area dedicated just to *comedores* at the far end of the market. It's a great place to watch people go about their shopping and to enjoy the display of stalls.

A good sightseeing tour of the surrounding area heads south to a couple of local places of interest. Lasting most of the day by bus (No 12) or two to three hours by car it starts a few blocks southwest of the main square on the eastern side of the Mercado Central. It includes the **San Salvador Zoo** ① *T2270-0828, Wed-Sun 0900-1600, US$0.60*, which, although small, is quiet and attractive. Just three blocks away is the **Museo de Historia Natural** ① *Parque Saburo Hirao*, with interesting displays on prehistoric findings and a herbal medicine garden. To get there, take bus No 2 ' Zoo', and No 12 from the centre. You then pass the **Casa Presidencial** and go on up to the residential district in the mountain range of **Planes de Renderos**. This place is crowned by the beautiful **Parque Balboa** ① *daily 0800-1800*, and there's a good view of the city from El Mirador at the foot of the park. Parque Balboa is a **Turicentro**, with cycle paths, playground and gardens. From the park a scenic road runs to the summit of **Cerro Chulo**, from which the view, seen through the Puerta del Diablo (Devil's Door), is even better. There are local buses to Puerta del Diablo and Parque Balboa (No 12 from eastern side of Mercado Central and No 12-MC marked 'Mil Cumbres') almost hourly. Bus No 17 goes from the same location to Panchimalco through Los Planes de Renderos so you can get off at the junction there and take the No 12 to Parque Balboa and Puerta del Diablo.

The **Puerta del Diablo** consists of two enormous, nearly vertical rocks which frame a magnificent view of the Volcán San Vicente. The rocks are very steep but the sides can be climbed on reasonable paths for an even better view. A little beyond the car park and drinks stands at the Puerta del Diablo is a path climbing up a further summit, from which there are 360° views: to the coast, Lago Ilopango, the capital and volcanoes, including San Salvador, Izalco and Cerro Verde and San Vicente.

At the foot of Cerro Chulo is **Panchimalco** (see below). The route to Panchimalco (No 17 from Mercado Central) and the coast branches off the road to Parque Balboa at the village of **Los Planes**, a few kilometres before the park.

Around San Salvador

Many places can be visited in a day from San Salvador either on the frequent bus services or by car. To the south is the indigenous village of **Panchimalco**, heading east are the beautiful setting and views around **Lago de Ilopango**; and to the southwest the crater of **Volcán San Salvador** (see Santa Tecla, page 445).

Heading west towards Santa Ana, but still manageable in a day, are the archaeological sites of **Joyo de Cerén**, El Salvador's Pompeii, and **San Andrés** and the peaks of **Volcán Izalco** and **Cerro Verde** (see page 446) with the deep blue waters of **Lago de Coatepeque** in the crater below. The limits of a comfortable weekend trip will take you to the garden park of **Ichanmichen**, which is restful (see page 479), and the pyramid of **Tazumal** (west of Santa Ana) is also worth a visit (see page 449). At weekends the coast around La Libertad (see page 476) is very popular. Bus 495 from the Terminal del Occidente goes to the seaside resort of **Costa del Sol** (see page 479).

Panchimalco

This small town and the surrounding area is home to the Pancho, descendants of the Pipil tribes, one of the region's dominant indigenous groups prior to conquest. This is one of the few places in El Salvador where you can still see indigenous people in traditional dress. Streets of large cobbles, with low adobe houses, thread their way between huge boulders at the foot of Cerro Chulo. A very fine baroque colonial church, Santa Cruz, has a white façade with statues of eight saints. Inside are splendid woodcarvings and wooden columns, altars, ceilings and benches. There is a bell inscribed with the cipher and titles of the Holy Roman Emperor Charles V, and a colourful cemetery. The Casa de La Cultura in the main street has frequent cultural events and crafts stores. The **Fiesta de Santa Cruz de Roma** is held on 12-14 September, with music and traditional dances; on 3 May (or the second Sunday of the month) there is the procession of **Las Palmas**. Bus 17 from Mercado Central at 12 Calle Poniente, San Salvador, every 45 minutes (45 minutes), or minibus from near Mercado Central, very crowded but quicker (30 minutes), and cheaper (US$0.80).

Lago de Ilopango

Beyond the four-lane highway to Ilopango airport (14.5 km east) lie the deep waters of Lago de Ilopango. Surrounded by mountains, the views around El Salvador's largest and deepest crater lake are impressive. Before the conquest local people used to appease the harvest gods by drowning four virgins here every year. Private chalets make access to the lake difficult, except at clubs and the **Turicentro Apulo**, but it is well worth a visit. The eastern shore is less polluted and is reached from Cojutepeque. There are a number of lakeside cafés and bathing clubs, some of which hire dug-outs by the hour. The cafés are busy in the dry season (try **Teresa's** for fish dishes), but often closed in the middle of the year. **Hotel Vista del Lago** ① *3 km from Apulo turn-off on the highway*, is on a hill top. Bus 15, marked Apulo, runs from the bus stop on Parque Hula Hula to the lake (via the airport), 1¼ hours, US$1. Entrance to the Turicentro **camping site** costs US$0.60.

Volcán San Salvador

This large massif at 1839 m has an impressive crater, more than 1.5 km wide and 543 m deep, known as **El Boquerón**. About 2 km to the east is the equally dramatic peak of **El Picacho** (1960 m), which dominates the capital. Buses leave a block from Plaza Merliot. By car you turn right just after the Plaza Merliot Mall and continue to the end of the road where a paved road take you up the volcano. A walk clockwise round the crater takes about two hours; the first half is easy, the second half rough. The views are magnificent, if somewhat spoilt by TV and radio towers. The area by Boquerón is now a park administrated by the Ministry of Tourism. The area is closed off, with guards during opening hours (daily 0800-1500). **La Laguna** botanical garden is near the summit. The inner slopes of the crater are covered with trees, and at the bottom is a smaller cone from the eruption of 1917.

You can follow the road north and then turn right through extensive coffee plantations and forest to reach the summit of **El Picacho**. This also makes an excellent climb from the Escalón suburb of San Salvador, in the early morning preferably, which takes about three to four hours return trip (take a guide). The easy access, great views and fresh climate has made the Volcano of San Salvador a popular destination for people in the capital and, as a result, new restaurants have opened their doors in recent years. See Eating, page 436. Another access to the volcano from the city side is by **Ecoparque El Espino** ① *run by El Espino Cooperative T2289-0749/69 www.ecoparqueelespino.com, US$1.50*. The entrance is by the Polideportivo in Ciudad Merliot, take bus No 42 C especial and walk 100 m. They have several trails, bike rental and small cafeterias. The trails end at a mirador with a panoramic view of the city.

San Salvador listings

Hotel and guesthouse prices

LL over US$200	L US$151-200	AL US$101-150
A US$66-100	B US$46-65	C US$31-45
D US$21-30	E US$12-20	F US$7-11
G under US$7		

Restaurant prices

| ₸₸₸ over US$15 | ₸₸ US$8-15 | ₸ under US$8 |

See pages 31-33 for further information.

Sleeping

San Salvador *p427, maps p428 and p430*
In the downtown area, some hotels lock their doors very early. Many cheap *hospedajes* near **Terminal de Oriente** are of dubious safety and not recommended for single women. Foreigners are advised not to be out in the city centre after dark.

13% VAT (IVA) is added to bills at major hotels. Most of the cheaper hotels are around the Centro Histórico. Be careful in this area, particularly at night.

L Hotel Real Intercontinental San Salvador, Blv de los Héroes and Av Sisimiles, in front of the Metrocentro, T2211-3333, www.grupo real.com. A useful landmark, smart, formal atmosphere (popular with business visitors), Avis car hire, **Taca** desk, shop selling souvenirs, postcards, US papers and magazines.

A Radisson Plaza, 89 Av Norte and 11 Calle Pte, Col Escalón, T2257-0700, www.radisson.com. Elegant rooms with a/c and cable TV. Good value, with parking.

C Alicante Guest House, Calle las Rosas y Av Los Laureles 1, Col La Sultana, T2243-0889, www.alicante.com.sv. Telephone, cable TV, restaurant, internet access for guests, breakfast included. Discounts for extended stays.

C Grecia Real, Av Sisimiles 2922, Col Miramontes, 50 m west of **Hotel Real Intercontinental**, T2261-0555, www.greciareal.com. With good Greek restaurant. Recommended.

C Happy House, Av Sisimiles 2951, Col Miramonte, T/F2260-1568, www.hotel happy house-elsalvador.com. Good, friendly, parking, good breakfast.

C Mariscal, Paseo Escalón 3658, T2283-0220, www.hotelmariscal.com. Good apartments, a good deal for long-term stay.

D American Guest House, 17 Av Norte 119 between Calle Arce y 1 Calle Pte, 3 blocks from Puerto Bus, T2222-8789. With bath (cheaper without), hot water, fan, helpful, will store luggage, accepts credit cards, discounts for groups. Oldest guest house downtown, run by the young at heart Irma Estradain her 70s, weekly rates, **Cafetería La Amistad**, parking nearby, good.

D Centro Histórico, 1 Calle Pte 124 y 1 Av Norte, 2 blocks from cathedral, T2221-5086, www.hotelescentrohistorico.com.sv. A/c, TV, parking, good choice.

D Hotel Florida, Pasaje Los Almendros 15, Urbanización Florida and Blv de los Héroes, T2260-2540. All rooms with bath, fan, laundry service, some with a/c, thin walls but good value, secure. Recommended.

D-F Ximena's Guest House, Calle San Salvador 202, Col Centroamérica, T2260-2481, www.ximenasguesthouse.com. A variety of rooms with private bath and hot shower, cheaper in 6-bed dormitory. Wi-Fi. Friendly and knowledgeable staff (ask for Lena, speaks several languages). Variety of economic tours as well as transport to their beach house **Capricho** and **Lisa Guest House** at organic farm. Conveniently located, but not easy to find (behind the Esso station on Blv de los Héroes). Recommended.

E Casa Clementina, Av Morazán y Av Washington 34, Col Libertad, T2225-5962. Very friendly, clean, pleasant, garden.

E Centro, 9 Av Sur 410, T2271-5045, hotel_centro55@hotmail.com. A bit box-like, check out 1200, cable TV, internet, TV, phone, friendly, washing facilities, clean, safe. Recommended.

E Nuevo Panamericano, 8 Av Sur 113, T2222-2959. Cold shower, safe, open 24 hrs, parking. Recommended.

F Hospedaje España, 12 Av Norte 123, T2222-5248. Fan, clean, bright, good value.

🍴 Eating

San Salvador *p427, maps p428 and p430*
In the older downtown area few places are open to eat after 1830. Restaurants are open later in the western sections of the city. Along Blv Hipódromo, San Benito, restaurants are generally very good, but expensive. On Blv de los Héroes there are many restaurants, including US-style fast-food places. The strip along Calle San Antonio Abad has several local eateries.

🍴🍴🍴 **Al Pomodoro**, Paseo Escalón 3952, Col Escalón, T2257-2544, www.alpomodoro.com. Popular, good Italian, also does delivery.

🍴🍴🍴 **Dynasty**, Blv Hipódromo 738-B, T2263-9955. Known for serving the best Chinese food in the city.

🍴🍴🍴 **El Bodegón**, Paseo Escalón 3956 and 77 Av Norte, T2263-5283. The proprietor is Spanish, as is the food. Excellent.

🍴🍴🍴 **H'ola Beto's Escalón**, Pasaje Dordelly 4352 between 85 and 87 Av Norte (above Paseo Escalón). Best seafood in the city, also serves Italian. Great service, parking. Recommended.

🍴🍴🍴 **Kamakura**, 93 Av Norte 617, Col Escalón T2263-2401. Japanese food.

🍴🍴🍴 **La Hacienda Real**, just opposite of La Gran Vía Mall T, Km 8, Carretera Panamericana, next to Air Force offices, T2243-8567. Without a doubt the best steaks in El Salvador, excellent service and fingerlicking food.

🍴🍴🍴 **La Panetière**, Plaza Villaviciencio, local 5, Paseo Escalón. Delicious French pastry, crêpes, cappuccinos, popular with foreigners, a bit pricey but worth it.

🍴🍴 **Automariscos**, located next to roundabout by the Don Rua church, 5a Av Norte, Blv Tutunichapa, T2226-5363, also outlet in San Benito, Av Revolución No 179 (between Pizza Hut and Anthropological museum), T2243-3653. Out-of-the-ordinary seafood and huge portions. Recommended.

🍴🍴 **Café Café**, Calle El Tanque, 99 Av Norte y 7 y 9 Calle Pte bis 130, T2263-4034, www.cafe cafe.com.sv. Locally popular Peruvian restaurant. Recommended.

🍴🍴 **El Sopón Típico**, 71 Av Norte and 1 Calle Pte 3702, Col Escalón, T2298-3008 and Blv de Los Héroes, Pasaje Las Palmeras 130, Urb Florida T2260-2671, www.elsopontipico.com. Typical Salvadorean soups and other dishes, including *gallo en chicha* (chicken in maize wine) and *mariscada* (seafood chowder).

🍴🍴 **Kalpataru**, Calle La Mascota 928 and Calle Maquilishuat, just below **Arbol de Dios**. Open until 2230, full restaurant service and lunch buffet, nice atmosphere. Best vegetarian place in town.

🍴 **KREEF**, Plaza Kreef, 87 Av Sur and Av los Almendros Block G, Zona 11, Urb Maquilishuat T2264-7094, www.kreef.com. Restaurant and deli, specialities meat and juicy chicken filets, imported cheese, beer and wine. Live music weekends.

🍴 **Restaurante Sol y Luna**, Blv Universitario, in front of **Cines Reforma**, T2225-6637. Open Mon-Fri 0830-1730, Sat until 1600. Delicious vegetarian food.

🍴 **Zócalo Escalón**, 71 Av Norte, T2257-6851, next to Galerías mall. Excellent Mexican food in small, casual place, with outdoor tables; other branches around city, including Zona Rosa, San Benito and Santa Elena.

🍴-🍴 **Mercadito Merliot**, Antiguo Cuscatlán. Famous food market with fresh seafood dishes (among others).

🍴 **The Brother**, Calle San Antonio Abad. Meats grilled on outdoor BBQ, large dishes and low prices.

🍴 **Uncle Yang**, Paseo General Escalón, T2264-7118. Taiwanese rice and noodle dishes, huge portions (*grande* is big enough for 2); try the Taiwanese iced tea with little tapioca dumplings sucked up through a wide straw. Clean, tasty and great value.

Cafés, delis and juice stalls

There are numerous cafeterías serving cheap traditional meals such as *tamales*, *pupusas*, *frijoles*, rice with vegetables, etc. Often these places can be found around the major hotels. **Café de Don Pedro**, Roosevelt y Alameda, next to Esso filling station. Good range of food, mariachi groups, open all night, another branch in Chiltiuapan, near Plaza Merliot Mall, also 24 hrs.

Oh-la-la, 1 Calle Ote and 69 Av Norte 168, just around the corner of Galerías mall, T2223-0161. Fine pastries.

Shakes, 3 Calle Pte 5254, Lomas Verdes, Col Escalón, T2263-4533. Juice bar and delicious fresh cakes. Recommended.

Shaw's, Paseo Escalón, 1 block west of Plaza Beethoven, Zona Rosa and at Metrocentro. Pricey but good coffee and chocolates, also sell US magazines, a few English-language books and greetings cards.

Entertainment

San Salvador *p427, maps p428 and p430*
Bars and clubs
Check for gigs in *La Prensa Gráfica* and *El Diario de Hoy*. All leading hotels have their own nightclub. All discos have ladies' night on Wed and Thu when women enter free and get a discount on drinks; go in a group. Zona Rosa, Col San Benito, has many bars/discos/open-air cafés in a 5-block area, well-lit, crowded Fri-Sat night (disco cover charge is US$10), take bus No 30 B from near Esso/Texaco/Mundo Feliz on Blv de los Héroes before 2000, taxi thereafter. Just beyond Zona Rosa, the shopping malls of **Multiplaza** and **La Gran Vía** are the favourite places for going out; both have strips of night clubs, coffee shops and bars where young people gather at the weekends. Among the most popular discos in Multiplaza are **Envy** and **Stanza** and the bar **La Cueva**.

Café La T, run by German Anne, opposite Centro Comercial San Luis also has a fairtrade gift shop.

El Arpa Irlandés Av A 137 Col San José, run by Gerry from Ireland.

La Luna, Calle Berlín 228, off Blv de los Héroes, Urbanización Buenos Aires 3, T2260-2921, www.lalunacasayarte.com. Open Wed-Sun. Great food and atmosphere, live music some nights, decor and furniture

designed by local artists. Popular and fashionable place to hang out. Reasonably priced drinks and snacks; take taxi late at night.

Photo Café, Col El Roble, Pje 2 21, T2100-2469, near National University, is an artsy place run by photojournalists.

Cinema
A few older-style cinemas in the centre are being overshadowed by the multiplexes along the Blv de los Héroes; most screenings are in English with Spanish sub-titles. Look in local press for listings. Arthouse films are shown at **La Luna** and **Café La T** for free. See schedules for events. **Alliance Française** arranges film seasons, T2223-8084.

Music, dance and theatre
Ballet and theatre at the **Teatro Nacional de Bellas Artes**, and music or plays at the **Teatro Cámera**.

Spectator sports
Check *La Prensa Gráfica* and *El Diario de Hoy*.
Baseball On the field opposite Mercado Nacional de Artesanías, Tue-Fri 1700, Cuban and US coaches, local teams, entrance US$1.25.
Boat racing Club Náutico, at the Estero de Jaltepeque, is famous for its boat races across the mud flats at low tide.
Football Sun and Thu at the Cuscatlán and/or Flor Blanca stadiums.
Motor racing At the El Jabalí autodrome on lava fields near Quetzaltepeque.

Festivals and events

San Salvador *p427, maps p428 and p430*
Mar/Apr Holy Week.
Jul/Aug Celebrations of **El Salvador del Mundo** are held the fortnight preceding 6 Aug. As a climax, colourful floats wend their way up the Campo de Marte (the park encompasssing Parque Infantil and Palacio de Deportes; 9 Calle Pte and Av España). On 5 Aug, an ancient image of the Saviour is borne before the large procession, before

church services the next day, celebrating the **Feast of the Transfiguration**.

12 Dec Día del Indígena; there are colourful processions honouring the **Virgen de Guadalupe** (take bus No 101 to the Basílica de Guadalupe, on the Carretera a Santa Tecla).

○ Shopping

San Salvador *p427, maps p428 and p430*
Visa and MasterCard are accepted in most establishments.

Bookshops

Magazines and newspapers in English can be bought at leading hotels and many shops sell US magazines. **Cervantes**, 9 Av Sur 114 in the Centre and Edif El Paseo 3, Paseo Escalón; **Clásicos Roxsil**, 6 Av Sur 1-6, Santa Tecla, T2228-1212; **Editorial Piedra Santa**, Av Olímpica 3428, Av 65-67 Sur, T2223-5502; **Etc Ediciones** in Centro Comercial Basilea, San Benito. Some English books at Librería Cultural Salvadoreña in Metrosur.
Olivos, also café and restaurant, just below Hotel Princess, Zona Rosa, T2245-4221, www.olivoscafe.com. Has a wide selection of books, specializing in alternative medicine and health.

Crafts

You can buy fairtrade arts and crafts at **Café La T**, Calle San Antonio Abad, and **Nahanché**. Metrocentro, Centro Comercial Basilea and Multiplaza has a great selection of handicrafts from all over the country.
El Arbol de Dios, La Mascota y Av Masferrer, T2224-6200, see page 432.
Mercado Ex-Cuartel, 8 Av Norte, 1 Calle Ote. Crafts market, a few blocks east of the Teatro Nacional, rebuilt after a fire in 1995.
Mercado Nacional de Artesanías, opposite the Estado Mayor on the road to Santa Tecla (buses 101A, B or C, 42B, 79, 34, 30B), at prices similar to the Mercado Ex-Cuartel, open daily 0800-1800. A 1-stop craft shop with a good cross-section of items even

if not that well presented. Some of the cheapest prices.

Markets and malls

Metrocentro, large shopping mall on the Blv de los Héroes, northwest of the city centre. Together with **Metrosur** this is the largest shopping mall in Central America. Another shopping centre, **Villas Españolas**, is on the Paseo Escalón, 1 block south of the Redondel Masferrer; it is more exclusive, with expensive boutiques. **Galerías Escalón**, Col Escalón, has department stores and cybercafés. **El Paseo**, is the newish mall in Escalón, located just at the corner of 79 Av The area west of Zona Rosa has 3 newer malls named **Multiplaza**, **Hiper Mall Cascadas** and **La Gran Vía**.

▲ Activities and tours

San Salvador *p427, maps p428 and p430*
Tour operators
Inter Tours, Balam Quitze mall in Paseo Escalon, T2263-6188, www.viajero.com.sv. One of the most recognized travel agencies in the capital. They have excellent service and can track down that special rate you need.
OTEC Turismo Joven, Centro Comercial El Partenope, local 2, Paseo Escalón, T2264-0200, www.otec.com.sv. Official ISIC office in El Salvador and STA Travel representative, offering travel assistance, reissue of lost tickets, date changes and rerouting. Special prices for student, teacher and youth with ISIC card.
Pullmantur, Av La Revolución, T2243-1300. Luxury bus service to Guatemala and excellent package tours to Antigua.
Salva Natura, 33 Av Sur 640, Col Flor Blanca, T2279-1515, www.salvanatura.org. For information about Parque Nacional El Imposible in the southwest, near Tacuba and Ataco.
Tour In El Salvador, T2207-4155, www.tour inelsalvador.com. Minibus tours around the country and to Guatemala and Honduras;

experienced and very knowledgeable guide Jorge Martínez. Highly recommended.

Watersports
El Salvador Divers, Paseo Escalón 3 Calle Pte 5020, Col Escalón, T2264-0961, www.elsalvadordivers.com. Offer weekly excursions and classes. Located behind the Villavicencio Mall.
Ríos Aventuras, is part of **Tropic Tours**, Av Olímpica 3597, T2279-3235, www.riosaventuras. com.sv. Bilingual guides organize rafting trips to Río Paz on the Guatemalan border. Recommended.

⊖ Transport

San Salvador *p427, maps p428 and p430*
Air
The international airport (**SAL**), T2339-9455, at Comalapa is 62 km southeast from San Salvador towards Costa del Sol beach. **Acacya** minibus to airport, from 3 Calle Pte y 19 Av Norte, T2271-4937, airport T2339-9182, at 0600, 0700, 1000, 1400 (be there 15 mins before), US$3 one-way (leaves from airport when full, on right as you go out). **Acacya**, T2271-4937, also has a taxi service, US$25, the same as other radio taxi companies; ordinary taxis charge US$20. Taxi to **La Libertad** beach US$30. To **Costa del Sol** US$50. There is a post office, a tourist office, 2 exchange desks (including Citi Bank) and duty-free shopping for both departures and arrivals.
The old airport is at Ilopango, 13 km east of the city and is primarily used by the air force and for some domestic flights.
Airline offices American Airlines, Alameda Roosevelt, Edificio Centro-americana, 3107, T2298-0777. **Copa Airlines**, T2209-2600, www.copaair.com. **Delta**, 81 Av Norte y Calle El Mirador, Edif WTC, local 107, piso 4, Col Escalón T2275-9292, www.delta.com. **Grupo TACA**, Oficinas Centrales Santa Elena (behind American Embassy), T2267-8222, www.taca.com. **Mexicana**, Edificio Mejicana de Aviación,

2 nivel, Km 4.5, Carretera Sta Tecla, T2252-9999, www.mexicana.com. **United Airlines**, T2279-3900, www.united.com.

Bus
Local Most buses stop running at 2100. City buses charge US$0.20 and microbuses charges US$0.25 within the city – have the right change or a small bill to hand. Most run 0500-2000, after which use taxis.
Some useful routes: No 29 from Terminal de Oriente to Metrocentro via downtown; **No 30** Mercado Central to Metrocentro; **No 30B** from Mundo Feliz (100 m up from Esso station on Blv de los Héroes) to Escalón, 79 Av Norte, Zona Rosa (San Benito), Alameda Roosevelt and back to Metrocentro along 49 Av; **No 34** San Benito–Mercado de Artesanías–Terminal de Occidente–Mercado Central–Terminal Oriente; **No 52** 'Paseo' Parque Infantil–Metrocentro–Plaza Las Américas– Paseo Escalón–Plaza Masferrer; **No 52** 'Hotel' Parque Infantil–Metrocentro–Hotel Copa Airlines–Plaza Masferrer. Route **No 101** buses to/from Santa Tecla are blue and white for either class of service.

Long distance and international
Domestic services go from **Terminal de Occidente**, off Blv Venezuela, T2223-3784 (take city buses 4, 7C, 27, 44 or 34); **Terminal de Oriente**, end of Av Peralta in Centro Urbano Lourdes (take city buses No 29 from Metrocentro, 42 from Alameda, or No 4, from 7 Calle), T2281-3086, very crowded with buses and passengers, keep your eyes open for the bus you want; and **Terminal Sur**, San Marcos, Zona Franca, about 9 km from the city (take city bus No 26 from Universidad Nacional area or Av España downtown, take taxi to city after 1830). Terminal de Sonsonate, located just outside city centre, by main road to Acajutla T2450-4625, Terminal de Santa Ana T2440-0938. Routes and fares are given under destinations. For La Libertad and beaches west to Playa El Zonte, plenty of buses go from opposite Iglesia Ceiba

Guadalupe, short taxi ride from centre: Bus No 102 to La Libertad and Nos 107 or 192 to Playa El Zonte, approx 1 hr, US$1.

Heading south: Recognized international bus company **Ticabus** departs from Hotel San Carlos, Calle Concepción 121, T2222-4808, www.ticabus.com. Also with an office in Blv del Hipódromo, Zona Rosa, T2243-9764. To **Tapachula** 0600 and 1200 noon, 11 hrs, US$30. To **Guatemala**, 0600 and 1300, 5 hrs, US$15. To **Tegucigalpa**, 1200, 7 hrs, US$15. To **Managua**, 0500, 12 hrs, US$30. To **San José**, 33 hrs including overnight in Managua, US$50. To **Panama City**, depart 0500, arriving 1700 next day, US$75. They now have an executive coach service to **Nicaragua** for US$44, and **Costa Rica** US$58 (both depart 0300) and to **Panama** at 0500, US$93. **King Quality**, Puerto Bus Terminal, Alameda Juan Pablo II y 19 Av Norte, T2241-8704; in Zona Rosa T2271-1361, www.king-qualityca.com. You can walk there from city centre, but it's not advisable with luggage; take bus 101D from Metrocentro, or bus 29, 52 to 21 Av Norte, 2 blocks south of terminal (city buses don't permit heavy luggage). The terminal has a *casa de cambio* (good rates) and a restaurant. They have departures to Central America and Mexico. Departure times from Puerto Bus station (check office for times from Zona Rosa).

Service to Guatemala with domestic carriers include **Pezzarossi, Taca, Transesmer, Melva**, and **Vencedora**. All operate services to **Guatemala City** more or less hourly (5½ hrs, US$13). Departures between 0500 and 1600. **Confortlines** (sister company of **King Quality**) has departures to Guatemala at 0800 and 1400 for US$30 – higher-class bus than the regular service but no meals. **Pullmantur**, T2243-1300, runs a 0700 service Mon-Sat, 0830 Sun, and a daily luxury 1500 service from Hotel Marriott Presidente in Zona Rosa for US$35, with a/c, film, drinks and meals.

Service to Mexico also from Terminal de Occidente, **El Cóndor** goes to **Talismán**, Mexico via Sonsonate, La Hachadura and Escuintla, US$12, 0330, 9½ hrs, also 0700-0800 to Guatemala City. **Transgalgos** has direct departures to Mexico from Puerto Bus.

Car

Car hire Local insurance (about US$10-15 per day plus a deductible US$1000 deposit) is mandatory and 13% IVA applies. **Avis**, 43 Av Sur 137, Col. Flor Blanca www.avis.com.sv, T2500-2847; **Budget**, Hotel Sheraton Presidente, Col San Benito T2283-2908 and Calle Mirador and 85 Av Norte 648, Col Escalón, T2264-3888, www.budget.com; **Hertz**, corner of 91 Av Nte and 9 Calle Pte, T2264-2818, www.hertz.com; **Sandoval & Co**, T2235-4405, sub-compact late-model cars from US$10 per day, English spoken; **Euro Rent-Cars**, 29 Calle Pte and 7 Av Norte 1622, T2235-5232, chamba_r@hotmail.com, cheap daily rates from US$10.

Car repairs Modern service centres of **Record** and **Impressa**, are found throughout the capital. Good source of spare parts found at **Super Repuestos**, T2221-4440.

Insurance **Asesuiza** is widely used for car insurance T2209-5025 as is **La Centroamericana**, T2298-6666.

Car papers Ministerio de Hacienda, T2226-1900, 'Tres Torres', turn left on Blv de los Héroes, 300 m past Texaco station.

Taxi

Plenty (all yellow), don't have meters, ask fare before getting in. Trips within San Salvador will have a mininum cost of US$4 and most trips will be between US$4 and US$7. Airport is approximately US$25. Few drivers speak English. They will charge more in the rain. More expensive radio taxis may be hired through **Acacya**, T2271-4937.

○ Directory

San Salvador *p427, maps p428 and p430*
Banks
Most banks open Mon-Fri 0900-1600, Sat 0900-1200. The banks have branches in all the shopping malls and in large hotels such as Princess Hilton and Radisson. ATMs only give US dollars. Banco Agrícola Comercial de El Salvador, Paseo Escalón 3635, T2279-1033, English spoken. HSBC give good rates for TCs and Visa card advances. Most banks give cash advance on your credit card if you bring your passport. In emergency, for Visa International or MasterCard, T2224-5100; Visa TCs can only be changed by Visa cardholders. Visa ATMs can be found at Aval card 24-hr machines, the majority at Esso and Shell service stations (eg Esso, Blv de los Héroes), but also at Metrocentro, 8th floor food court, and Centro de Servicio, Av Olímpica. See also Yellow Pages. Western Union for money transfers, c/o HSCB branches, T2225-2503 (48 other branches throughout the country, look out for the black and yellow sign), head office Alameda Roosevelt 2419 between 45 y 47 Av Sur, T2298-1888, Mon-Fri 0800-1700, Sat 0800-1200, take passport and photographic ID (30 mins if from USA/Canada, 2-3 hrs from Europe). Banco de América Central (Ex-Credomatic), next to Siman in Metrocentro and CC San Luis gives cash advances on credit cards.

Cultural centres
Alianza Francesa, 5 Av Norte 152, Col Escalón, T2260-5807 and newer location in Col San Benito: Calle La Mascota 547, Pasaje 2, www.afelsalvador.com. Union Church, Calle 4 Final, Col La Mascota, T2263-8246, English-speaking interdominational international church, weekly church services and bible studies, volunteering opportunities. Centro de Intercambio y Solidaridad (CIS), Blv Universitario 4, next to Cine Reforma, T2226-2623, www.cis-elsalvador.org, for language classes, FMLN (Frente Farabundo Martí para la Liberación Nacional) programmes and schools. Instituto para el Rescate Ancestral Indígena Salvadoreño (RAIS), Av Santiago 20, Col San Mateo, has programmes for local aid to indigenous communities and the Nahual language and customs.

Embassies and consulates
Belize, Calle el Bosque Ote y Calle Lomas de Candelaria I, Block "P1", Col Jardines de la 1a Cima Etapa, T2248-1423. Costa Rica, Calle Cuscatlán 4415, between 81 and 83 Av Sur, Col Escalón, T2264-3863. Canada, Centro Financiero Gigante and Alameda Roosevelt y 63 Av Sur Lobby 2, local 6, T2279-4659. France, 1 Calle Pte 7380, Col Escalón, T2298-4260. Germany, 77 Av Norte y 7 Calle Pte 3972, T2263-2088. Guatemala, 15 Av Norte 135 between 1 Calle Pte and Calle Arce, T2271-2225. Holland, I Calle Pte 3796, T2298-2185. Honduras, 89 Av Norte 561, between 7 and 9 Calle Pte, Col Escalón, T2263-2808. Israel, Centro Financiero Gigante, Torre B, 11 piso, Alameda Roosevelt y 63 Av Sur, T2211-3434. Italy, La Reforma 158, Col San Benito, T2223-4806. Mexico, Pasaje 12 y Calle Circunvalación, San Benito, behind Hotel Presidente, T2248-9906. Nicaragua, Calle Mirador and 93 Av Norte 4814, Col Escalón, T2263-8849. Norway, Calle Cuscatlán 133 between 83 and 81 Av Sur, Col Escalón, T2263-8257. Panama, Av Buganvilia No21, Col San Francisco T2298-0773. Spain, Calles la Reforma 164, Col San Benito, T2257-5700. Sweden, Alameda Manuel E Araujo y 67 Av Sur 3515, T2281-7901. Switzerland, Pastelería Lucerna, 85 Av Sur y Paseo Escalón 4363, T2263-7485. USA, Blv Santa Elena, Antiguo Cuscatlán, T2278-4444, outside the city, reached by bus 101A.

Emergency
Fire service, T2555-7300. Red Cross, Av Henry Dunat y 17 Av Norte, T2224-5155, 24-hr. Police, T911, no coin needed from new coin phones. In San Salvador, metropolitan police deal with tourist complaints.

Immigration

Departamento de Inmigración, Centro de Gobierno, T2221-2111, Mon-Fri 0800-1600. Will consider extending tourist visas, but be prepared with photos and plenty of patience. **Migración y Extranjería**, Plaza Merliot and Hipermall Cascadas saves the trip to Centro de Gobierno and has quicker service.

Internet

Cafés (roughly US$1 per hr) are found through-out the city, especially at shopping malls.

Language schools

Centro de Intercambio y Solidaridad, Blv Universitario 4, T2226-2623, www.cisel salvador.org. Spanish school in the mornings 0800-1200, English school in the afternoons 1700-1900 (volunteer English teachers needed for 10-week sessions). **Cihuatan Spanish Language Institute** (Ximena's Guest House), Calle San Salvador 202, Col Centro América (near Hotel Real Intercontinental), T2260-2481, ximenas@navegante.com.sv; US$8 per hr.

Libraries

The **UCA** library (Universidad Centro-americana), José S Cañas, Autopista Sur, is said to be the most complete collection. US information library at **American Chamber of Commerce**, 87 Av Norte 720, Apto A, Col Escalón, Apdo Postal (05) 9, Sr Carlos Chacón, speaks English, helpful. **Centro Cultural Salvadoreño**, Av Los Sisimiles, Metrocentro Norte, T2226-9103, 0800-1100, 1400-1700, English library, excellent. **Intercambios Culturales de El Salvador**, 67 Av Sur 228, Col Roma, T2245-1488, extensive Spanish and English reference library, local artistic exhibitions, computer school.

Medical services

Hospitals and clinics Hospital de la Mujer, between 81 and 83 Av Sur y Calle Juan José Cañas, Col Escalón (south of Paseo, bus 52 Paseo), T2263-5181. **Hospital Pro-Familia**, 25 Av Norte 483, 11 blocks east of Metrocentro, T2244-8000, clinics and 24-hr emergency, reasonable prices. **Hospital Rosales**, 25 Av Norte y 3 Calle Pte, T2231-9200, long waits. **Clínicas Médicas**, 25 Av Norte 640 (bus 3, 9, 44 centro from Universidad Nacional), T2225-5233. If you contract a serious stomach problem, the doctor will send you for tests, which will cost US$5-6. **Doctors** Dr Cesar Armando Solano, at Av Bernal 568, Col Yurimuri T2261-1657, excellent dentist and low prices. English spoken. **Medicentro La Esperanza**, 27 Av Norte is a good place to find doctors in most specialist fields, afternoons mostly after 1500. **Dr Jorge Panameno**, T2225-9928, English-speaking, specialist in tropical diseases, makes house calls at night for about US$50.

Post

Central Post Office at the Centro de Gobierno with EMS, T2527-7600. Good service to Europe. Mon-Fri 0730-1700, Sat 0730-1200. **Lista de Correos**, Mon-Fri 0800-1200, 1430-1700, good service for mail collection. Branches throughout the city.

Telephone

Phone boxes throughout the city, card only, available at fast-food stores such as **Pollo Campero**; direct dialling to anywhere in the world, also collect calls. Telephone cards for sale in pharmacies and stores, denominations from US$1 upwards.

Work

UCA University Simeon Cañas, Blv Los Próceres San Salvador, T2210-6600, www.uca. edu.sv. An English-language programme always needing certified English teachers.

Western El Salvador

Compact and with good transport links, Western El Salvador combines the dramatic volcanic landscapes of Cerro Verde, Volcán Izalco and Lago de Coatepeque – essential for any visitor to the country – with the serene beauty and majesty of countless waterfalls and the colourful Ruta de las Flores around Sonsonate. Little indigenous villages and pre-Columbian ruins contrast with the vibrancy of Santa Ana, El Salvador's second largest city. Three routes lead to Guatemala, the northernmost passing close to the impressive cloud forests of Parque Nacional Montecristo on the border with Honduras. ▸▸ *For listings, see pages 452-457.*

Izalco to Sonsonate → *For listings, see pages 452-457.*

From the junction with the Pan-American Highway, just west of Colón, route CA 8 heads west, past Armenia, to the town of **Izalco** (population: 70,959) at the foot of Izalco volcano (8 km from Sonsonate, bus 53C). The town has evolved from the gradual merging of the *ladino* village of Dolores Izalco and the indigenous village of Asunción Izalco. In colonial times this was an important trading centre and experienced a communist rebellion in 1932. Today the town is experiencing a tourist revival with good colonial architecture, a prominent and active indigenous population, and rich heritage of religious imagery which blends indigenous and Roman Catholic beliefs, and produces regular processions and festivals. A week-long festival celebrating El Salvador del Mundo runs 8-15 August and there is also a local celebration from 24 November to 10 December. The Feast of John the Baptist runs from 17-24 June.

Note The town of Izalco and Izalco volcano are not directly connected by road. A paved road branches off the Pan-American Highway 14 km before the turning for Izalco town (about 22 km from Sonsonate) and goes up towards Cerro Verde, Volcán Izalco and Lago de Coatepeque (see page 446).

Sonsonate and around

→ *For listings, see pages 452-457. Colour map 3, C1. Altitude: 225 m. Population: 71,541.*

Sonsonate, 64 km from the capital, is the country's chief cattle-raising region. It also produces sugar, tobacco, rice, tropical fruits, hides and balsam. The city was founded in 1552 and is hot, dirty and crowded, but worth checking to see the colonial architecture in the city centre. The beautiful **El Pilar** church (1723) is strongly reminiscent of the church of El Pilar in San Vicente. The **cathedral** has many cupolas (the largest covered with white porcelain) and was badly damaged in the 2001 earthquake but is now fully restored. The old church of **San Antonio del Monte** (completed 1861), 1 km from the city, draws pilgrims from afar (fiesta 22-26 August). There is a small **railway museum**, look for the locomotive at the entrance to the city on the highway from San Salvador (Km 65). An important market is held each Sunday. The market outside the church is quite well organized. In the northern outskirts of the city there is a waterfall on the Río Sensunapán. Legend has it that an indigenous princess drowned there, and on the anniversary of her death a gold casket appears below the falls. The main annual event is **Feria de la Candelaria** in February. Easter Week processions are celebrated with particular fervour and are probably the most impressive in the whole country. On Easter Thursday and Holy Friday the streets are filled with thousands of members of the *cofradías* (brotherhoods).

Around Sonsonate

Route CA 8, northwest to Ahuachapán (see page 449), has spectacular scenery along the **Ruta de las Flores**, with frequent buses from Sonsonate (bus 249 and 285, two hours) covering the 40-km paved route. The road goes just outside the indigenous village of Nahuizalco (population: 49,081). Some of the older women here still wear the *refajo* (a doubled length of cloth made of tie-dyed threads worn over a wrap-round skirt), and various crafts are still made, including wood and rattan furniture. Although use of the indigenous language is dying out, you do still encounter people who speak Náhuatl. The night market, unique in El Salvador, opens at dusk and has traditional local food on sale. There's a religious festival 19-25 June, with music, **Danza de los Historiantes** and art exhibitions; also 24-25 December, with music and **Danza de los Pastores**. Take bus 53 D from Sonsonate.

Salcoatitán and Juayúa

A little further up the mountainside at Km 82 is **Salcoatitán** (population: 5484) at 1045 m above sea level, a colonial village with a beautiful park in front of the colonial church. This cosy village used to be only a drive-through on the way to Juayúa or Apaneca but has experienced a tourist revival lately with several new restaurants, art galleries and artisans shops. **Los Patios restaurant** (same owners Las Cabañas de Apaneca) just opened a restaurant and art gallery here.

Further along, the road branches off to Juayúa 2 km further north and the same bus from Sonsonate takes a detour into the village and back. **Juayúa** is the largest city on the Ruta de Las Flores – the name means 'River of Purple Orchids' in the local Náhuatl dialect – and sits nestled in a valley dominated by volcanoes. It's a peaceful spot where you can watch people at work and kids playing in the semi-cobbled street. The surrounding region is blanketed in coffee groves; the bean was introduced to the area in 1838 and today the town produces about 10% of the coffee exported from El Salvador. Its church houses an image of the **Cristo Negro** (Black Christ) carved by Quirio Cataño at the end of the 16th century. **Tourist information** is available from Jaime Salgado, at **Juayutur** ⓘ *T2469-2310, juayutur@navegante.com.sv*. He can provide good information about the activities available in the region, which include rappelling waterfalls, the hike of the seven waterfalls and the mountain lagoon with wild horses. Guides are trained local youngsters. Also check out the **Casa de la Cultura**, on the corner next to the park for information on Juayúa. Gaby and Julio Vega, the owners of **Akwaterra Tours** ⓘ *www.akwaterra.com*, run a mountain cabin at Finca Portezuelo named **La Escondida**; also a camping site with ready made-up tents on decks under covers. They're fluent in English and offer a wide range of activites at **Portezuelo Adventure Park** such as hiking, mountain biking, horseback riding, zip-wire circuit, ATVs and paragliding.

There are a number of excursions you can do in the area to see wildlife, including river otters, toucans, butterflies and many other animals. In the dry season **Laguna de las Ranas** (Laguna Seca) dries up, attracting numerous reptiles as it shrinks. There are also trips to the 30-m-high waterfall at **Salto el Talquezal**, the 50-m-high **Salto de la Lagunilla Azul** and several other waterfalls in the region (seven in one day if you take a tour), with swimming and picnics on the way (see below). Every weekend Juayúa celebrates the Feria Gastronómica, an opportunity to try a variety of traditional dishes, often accompanied by local events, music and shows.

The **Feria Gastrónomica Internacional** is in January and celebrates with dishes from all over the world; other festivals include **Día de los Canchules** (31 October), when people ask for candies and **Día de las Mercedes** (17 September), when the houses are decorated with branches and candles leading up to the procession of the Virgen de la Merced. Another local attraction is the **Museo del Café**, of the coffee cooperative La Majada ① *T2467-9008 ext 1451, www.cafemajadaoro.com.sv*, located in **San José La Majada**, just outside Juayua on the road to Los Naranjos. Tours include information on coffee processing and a trip to the processing plant. A coffee shop offers local brews and iced coffee.

Los Naranjos and around

Moving northeast of Juayúa, swirling up a scenic mountain road connecting Juayúa with Santa Ana you arrive at Los Naranjos, a small traditional coffee village located at the mountain pass between Santa Ana and the Pilón volcanoes. The lines of wind-breaking trees preventing damage to coffee trees are particularly beautiful, while the high altitude makes the climate cool with the scent of cypress forests. A series of restaurants and small cabins for lodging has popped up in recent years and is an excellent option for cool climate and countryside relaxation.

At Km 82 on the Carretera Salcoatitán to Juayúa is **Parque y Restaurante La Colina** ① *T2452-2916, www.lacolinajuayua.com*, with hammocks, arts and crafts, and horse riding available. **Apaneca** is a short distance uphill from Sonsonate, see page 443.

Several **waterfalls** and other sites of natural beauty can be found in the Sonsonate district. To the west, near the village of **Santo Domingo de Guzmán** (bus 246 from Sonsonate), are the falls of **El Escuco** (2 km north), **Tepechapa** (1.5 km further) and **La Quebrada** (further still up the Río Tepechapa), all within walking distance of both Santo Domingo and each other. Walk through the town, then follow the river, there are several spots to swim. Santo Domingo de Guzmán is also known for its *alfarería* (pottery) of *comales*, clay plates used to create tortillas and *pupusas* over the open fire, and its many Náhuatl-speaking habitants. There's a festival in Santo Domingo, 24-25 December. A short distance north is **San Pedro Puxtla** (bus 246), with a modern church built on the remains of an 18th-century edifice. From here you can visit the **Tequendama Falls** on the Río Sihuapán. Bus 219 goes east to **Cuisnahuat** (18th-century baroque church), where the Fiesta de San Judas takes place 23-29 November. From there it is 2 km south to the Río Apancoyo, or 4 km north to **Peñón El Escalón** (covered in balsam trees) and **El Istucal Cave**, at the foot of the Escalón hill, where indigenous rites are celebrated in November.

Santa Tecla to Santa Ana → *For listings, see pages 452-457.*

The new Pan-American Highway parallels the old one, continuing northwest to the border with Guatemala at San Cristóbal. Santa Ana, acting as a transport hub, has routes out to Ahuachapán to the west and the border at Las Chinamas, as well as north to Metapán and beyond to the border crossing of Anguiatú. ►► *See border essentials, page 199.*

Fifteen kilometres from Santa Tecla, 7 km beyond the junction with the Sonsonate road, there is a junction to the right. This road forks immediately, right to **Quezaltepeque**, left (at **Joya de Cerén** café) to **San Juan Opico**. After a few kilometres on the San Juan road, you cross the railway by the Kimberley-Clark factory.

Joya de Cerén

ⓘ *US$3, parking US$1, T2401-5782, www.fundar.org.sv/joyadeceren.*

After the girder bridge crossing the Río Sucio there is a grain store beside which is Joya de Cerén (32 km from the capital). This is a major archaeological site and on the World Heritage List of UNESCO (the only one in El Salvador), not for spectacular temples, but because this is the only known site where ordinary Maya houses have been preserved having been buried by the ash from the nearby Laguna Caldera volcano in about AD 600. Buildings and construction methods can be clearly seen; a painted book and household objects have been found. All the structures are covered with protective roofing. The site has a small but good museum, café, toilets and car park. Official tours are in Spanish but English-language tours are available upon request. ▸▸ *See Transport, page 456.*

San Andrés

ⓘ *Tue-Sun 0900-1600, US$3, popular for weekend picnics, otherwise it's quiet. Has a café. Take bus No 201 from Terminal de Occidente, US$1.50 (same bus from Santa Ana) T2319-3220, www.fundar.org.sv/sanandres.*

Back on the main road, heading west is the excavated archaeological site of San Andrés, halfway between Santa Tecla and Coatepeque on the estate of the same name (its full name is **La Campana de San Andrés**). It is located at Km 32.5 on the Pan-American Highway, just after the Hilasal towel factory. A **museum** at the site displays some of the ceramics found (others can be seen at the Museo Nacional de Antropología David J Guzmán – MUNA – in San Salvador, see page 432). The museum also features a special indigo section with information about this natural dye. El Salvador was the number one producer of indigo in the world during the colonial era. A large indigo *obraje* (processing basin) – probably the largest found in Latin America – was found at San Andrés during an archaeological excavation and has been preserved. There are good views of the nearby hills.

Lago de Coatepeque

At El Congo, 13 km before Santa Ana, a branch road leads south to the northern shore of the beautiful Lago de Coatepeque, a favourite weekend resort, with good sailing, watersports and fishing, near the foot of Santa Ana Volcano. Many weekend homes line the north and east shores, making access to the water difficult, but there are public *balnearios*. The lakeside hotels are a good option for having a meal and use their infrastructure for the day. You can also get boat rides on the lake through the hotels or by independent fishermen. There are *aguas termales* (hot springs) on the opposite side of the lake. A ride is between US$15 and US$45. There are two islands in the lake – **Anteojos** which is close to the hotels, and **Teopán** on the far side. The local Fiesta del Santo Niño de Atocha runs from 25-29 June.

Cerro Verde, Volcán Izalco and Volcán Santa Ana

ⓘ *Park entrance US$1, passport or photocopy required, car park US$0.70. Guided tour to the summit of Izalco or Santa Ana is included, leaving from the entrance daily 1100. The guided tour through the nature trail around the Cerro Verde Summit is US$0.25 per person and is led by local trained guides. The Turicentro Cerro Verde (the summit of Cerro Verde with its trails, the parking lot and departure point for the hikes to the volcano) is run by the Ministry of Tourism, for information T2222-8000, www.elsalvador.travel. The whole area covering the volcanoes Santa Ana, Cerro Verde and Izalco and surrounding area are part of the Parque Nacional de los Volcanes, which is administrated by Salvanatura, T2279-1515, www.salvanatura.org.*

Climbing Izalco

Izalco, as can be seen from the lack of vegetation, is a geologically young volcano. Historical records show that activity began in the 17th century as a sulphurous smoke vent but, in February 1770, violent eruptions formed a cone that was more or less in constant activity until 1957. There was a small eruption in 1966 through a blowhole on the southeast slope testified by two 1000-m lava flows. Since that time, it has been quiescent.

A path leads off the road (signposted) just below the car park on Cerro Verde. In 20-30 minutes, descend to the saddle between Cerro Verde and Izalco, then it's one to 1½ hours up (steep but manageable). The contrast between the green forest of Cerro Verde and the coal-black lava around Izalco is impressive.The climb is three hours from base. Beware of falling rocks when climbing. There's a spectacular view from the top so try to ensure that low cloud is not expected before planning to go. For a quick descent, find a rivulet of soft volcanic sand and half-slide, half-walk down in 15 minutes, then it's about one hour back up the saddle. This 'cinder running' requires care, strong shoes and consideration for those below.

If you wish to climb the volcano you need to take the first bus to Cerro Verde, as the park rangers wait for the passengers from this bus before they start the guided climb to the volcano at 1100.

In October 2005, Santa Ana volcano erupted for the first time in more than 100 years. The area was closed for a period, but it has now reopened.

From El Congo another road runs south, around the east shore of Lago Coatepeque. This road is locally known as Carretera Panorámica, due to the fantastic view of Coatepeque on one side and the mountains and valleys beyond the ridge. After reaching the summit, the paved road branches right, climbing above the south end of the lake to **Parque Nacional Cerro Verde** (2030 m) with its fine and surprising views of the Izalco volcano (1910 m), and Santa Ana volcano (2381 m), the highest volcano in the country. The road up to Cerro Verde is lined with beautiful flowers and halfway up there is a mirador with a great view of Lago Coatepeque. Cerro Verde is probably one of the most beautiful places in El Salvador due to the special flora and fauna, breathtaking views and fine volcano trekking.

A 30-minute walk along a nature trail leads you around the crater ridge, to a series of miradors with views of Lago Coatepeque and Santa Ana volcano. For the best view of Izalco, go in the morning, although the afternoon clouds around the cone can be enchanting. ▸▸ *For information on climbing Volcán Izalco, see box, above.*

The old hotel and its volcano-view terrace was destroyed in the 2001 earthquake but you can still go there for an amazing view over Izalco volcanic crater. There are now a couple of cabins available for US$35-55. For information call the **Turicentro** ① T7949-2751. To access Cerro Verde, take bus No 208 from Santa Ana at 0800, passing El Congo at 0815 am to catch the 1100 departure. If you come from Sonsonate side, take the No 209 bus from Sonsonate to Cerro Verde.

Santa Ana and around

→ For listings, see pages 452-457. Colour map 3, C1. Altitude: 776 m. Population: 245,421.

Santa Ana, 55 km from San Salvador and capital of its department, is the second largest city in the country. The basin of the Santa Ana volcano is exceptionally fertile, producing large amounts of coffee, with sugar cane coming a close second. The city, named Santa Ana La Grande by Fray Bernardino Villapando in 1567, is the business centre of western El Salvador. There are some fine buildings: the neo-Gothic **cathedral**, and several other churches, especially **El Calvario**, in neoclassical style. Of special interest is the classical **Teatro de Santa Ana** ① *on the north side of the plaza, a guide (small charge) will show you round on weekdays, refer to the local press for performances*, originally completed in 1910, now in the latter stages of interior restoration and one of the finest theatres in Central America. The Fiestas Julias take place from 1-26 July.

Chalchuapa → *Altitude: 640 m. Population: 96,727.*

About 16 km west of Santa Ana, on the road to Ahuachapán, lies Chalchuapa. President Barrios of Guatemala was killed in battle here in 1885, while trying to reunite Central America by force. There are some good colonial-style domestic buildings. The church of Santiago Apóstol is particularly striking; almost the only one in El Salvador which shows

Santa Ana

Sleeping 🛏
Casa Frolaz 5
El Faro 1
La Libertad 3
La Posada del Rey 2
Sahara 4

Eating 🍴
Expresión 1
Los Horcones 3
Lover's Steak House 2

strong indigenous influences (restored 1997-1998). Fiestas are on 18-21 July, Santiago Apóstol, and 12-16 August, San Roque. **Tazumal** ruins next to the cemetery in Chalchuapa, are the tallest and probably the most impressive in El Salvador. Built about AD 980 by the Pipil, with its 14-step pyramid. In 2004 the ruins suffered a partial collapse of the main pyramid due to the filtration of water which led to extensive excavations and application of new preservation techniques (getting rid of the old concrete) and many new discoveries were made. The excavations concluded in 2006. The site has been occupied since 5000 BC and in the **Museo Stanley H Boggs** ① *Tue-Sun 0900-1600, T2408-4295*, you find artefacts found in Tazumal since the first excavations in the 1950s.

Casa Blanca Archaeological Site ① *Km 78 Pan-American Hwy, T2408-4641, Tue-Sun 0900-1600, US$1*, just outside Chalchuapa, has several pyramids, ongoing excavations, and a museum that provides an insight into the archaeology of the area and information on indigo (*añil*) production. If you want to participate in the indigo workshop the cost is US$3. It's very interesting, educational and you can keep the products produced. Recommended.

Atiquizaya

The road continues 12 km west to Atiquizaya, a small, quiet town with one *hospedaje*, several good *pupuserías* (1600-2100) and **Restaurante Atiquizaya**, which can be found at the intersection with the main highway to Ahuachapán. At **Cataratas del Río Malacachupán** there is a beautiful 50-m-high waterfall cascading into a lagoon; it's a 1-km hike to get there. Nearby is **Volcán Chingo** on the Guatemalan border. Another attraction is **Aguas Calientes**, a hot spring that runs into the river and is excellent for a relaxing bath and for enjoying nature. It's a short ride from Atiquizaya, but bring a local guide.

Ahuachapán → *Colour map 3, C1. Altitude: 785 m. Population: 110,511.*

A quiet town with low and simple houses, 35 km from Santa Ana. Coffee is the main product. The main local attraction is the geothermal field of **Los Ausoles**, 3 km road from Ahuachapan and marked on the road out of town to Apaneca as 'Planta Geotérmica'. You can't go into the plant, but when you arrive take the road to the right where, just a little way up the hill on the left, you come to a little house, geysers of boiling mud with plumes of steam and strong whiffs of sulphur. The *ausoles* are used for generating 30% of the country's electricity. For a small tip the house owner will take you into his back garden to see the fumaroles and boiling pools. If you want a more professional tour, with an explanation on the thermal activity including a trip through the geothermal plant, contact **Tours Universales** in the city, see page 456.

Taking the northern road from Ahuachapán, 9 km west of town near the village of **Los Toles** are the **Tehuasilla Falls**, where the Río El Molino falls 60 m (bus No 293 from Ahuachapán to Los Toles, then walk 1 km). The road continues northwest through the treeless **Llano del Espino**, with its small lake, and across the Río Paz into Guatemala.

Tacuba → *Population: 29,585.*

Tacuba is an indigenous town, around 850 m above sea level, and 15 km west of Ahuachapán. Tacuba means 'the village of the football game', probably relating to the *juego de pelota* of the Maya, and the existence of many pre-Columbian mounds in the surrounding area suggest the region was heavily populated in the past. At the entrance to the town are the largest colonial church ruins in El Salvador, torn down by the earthquake of Santa Marta, the same tremors that ruined large parts of Antigua, Guatemala, in 1773. You can also visit the Casa de la Cultura office, **Concultura** ① *3 km on main st north, daily*

0900-1230, 1330-1600, to see an interesting display of photos. The town is near the northern entrance of Parque Nacional El Imposible (see page 478), which is accessed by hiking or 4WD in the dry season.

The surrounding area offers a wide range of opportunities including waterfalls, pristine rivers, mountain hikes and panoramic views. **Ceiba de los Pericos**, 15 minutes out of Tacuba by car, a 600-year-old ceiba tree where thousands of parrots flock together at dusk to sleep in its branches, ending the day with a deafening noise before resting for the night. In Tacuba centre the **Ceiba de las Garzas** is the rendezvous of hundreds of *garzas* (herons).

Local tour company **El Imposible Tours**, led by Tacuba native Manolo González, provide tours of the Tacuba area and to Parque Nacional El Imposible (see page 478). The dirt road leading from Tacuba to the cordillera, is steep and spectacular and provides impressive views; it is recommended although a 4WD is required.

Apaneca → *Altitude: 1450 m. Population: 8383.*

Between Ahuachapán and Sonsonate is Apaneca (91 km from San Salvador, 29 km from Las Chinamas on the border) an extremely peaceful town (and the highest town in the country), with small cobbled streets, marking the summit of the **Ruta de las Flores**. Founded by Pedro de Alvarado in 1543, Apaneca is known for its cool climate and winds – *apaneca* means 'rivers of wind' in Náhuatl. The town has a colonial centre, a traditional *parque* and a municipal market selling fruit, flowers and handicrafts. One of the oldest parochial churches in the country used to corner the central park but was demolished after damage caused by the 2001 earthquake. It has been partially reconstructed, with a modern twist. The artisans market is a great place to see the local arts and crafts. Other local industries include coffee, flowers for export and furniture. Have a look at the topiary creations outside the police station. Check out the **Casa de la Cultura** in the centre of town. There are two small lakes nearby to the north, **Laguna Verde** and **Laguna Las Ninfas**, whose crater-like walls are clothed in tropical forest and cypress trees. It is possible to swim in the former, but the latter is too shallow and reedy. According to local legend, a swim is meant to be very beneficial to your health and the lakes are very popular with tourists. This is the Cordillera de Apaneca, part of the narrow highland belt running southeast of Ahuachapán.

South of Apaneca is the **Cascada del Río Cauta**. To get there, take bus No 216 from Ahuachapán towards Jujutla, alight 3 km after the turn-off to Apaneca, then walk 300 m along the trail to the waterfall.

Santa Leticia archaeological site ① *US$2; 2-hr coffee tour US$20; both combined US$35, www.coffee.com.sv. Bus No 249 from Juayúa (10 mins),* is believed to be 2600 years old and was rediscovered in 1968 by the farm owner. Three huge monuments are buried among the coffee groves and you feel like a first-time discoverer as you travel the winding route to get there. There are three stone spheres with human characteristics weighing between 6000 and 11,000 kg.

Ataco

Concepción de Ataco, to give the town its full name, located just below Apaneca, is now a favourite on the Ruta de Las Flores. The village has undergone a complete renovation, and now boasts cobbled streets, old-fashioned benches and street lights, and a popular weekend festival with food, flowers, and arts and crafts. Some excellent coffee shops and restaurants, offering cuisine from Mexico to France, continue to open up, mainly for weekends only, making Ataco one of the most visited villages in the area, and well worth a weekend trip.

Look for the *marimba* and the traditional dances in the main square and drop by **Diconte & Axul**, an artsy café that offers anything from delicious home-made pies to original arts and crafts that are giving La Palma art a run for their money. The **House of Coffee** has an espresso machine and serves the excellent world-class coffee grown in Ataco at their own *finca* for five generations.

North of Santa Ana

Texistepeque, 17 km north of Santa Ana on the road to Metapán, has an 18th-century baroque church, with fiestas on 23-27 December and 15 January. The town was one of the main areas for indigo production, and colonial processing plants known as *obrajes* exist all around the area. Visit the indigo workshop and museum of **Licenciado Marroquín** just out of town.

Metapán is about 10 km northeast of Lago de Güija and 32 km north of Santa Ana. Its colonial baroque **Catedral de San Pedro**, completed by 1743, is one of the very few to have survived in El Salvador. The altarpieces have some very good silver work, and the façade is splendid. The Fiesta de San Pedro Apóstol runs from 25-29 June. There are lots of easy walks with good views towards **Lago de Metapán** and, further on, **Lago de Güija**. If planning to walk in the hills near Metapán, seek local advice and do not walk alone. **Parque Acuático Apuzunga** ① *20 mins' drive from Metapán towards Santa Ana, T2483-8952, www.apuzunga.com*, is an adventure park by the Río Guajoyo, with fun pools, slides, zip-wires and a range of activities, including whitewater rafting and kayaking. There's a restaurant overlooking the river offering great views of the rafts shooting the rapids and the zip-wire over the water.

Reserva Nacional y Natural Montecristo → *Colour map 3, C1.*

① *20 km from Metapán to the park. Park employees (guardabosques) escort visitors and a permit is obtained (via fax or email) through MARN (Ministry of Environment) in San Salvador, T2267-6259 (with Patrimonio Natural and ask for Solicitud de Ingreso a Parque Nacional Montecristo). You need to fill out a form and pay US$6 per person. A 4WD is necessary in the wet season (mid-May to mid-Oct). To hire a 4WD and driver, contact Sr Francisco Xavier Monterosa, Calle 15 de Septiembre Casa 40, T2402-2805/T7350-1111 (mob). The trails to the summit take 4 hrs. Camping is permitted, with 3 campsites inside the park, spacious and clean, under the pine trees, with toilets, barbecue grills and picnic benches and tables. An overnight stay is needed if you want to reach the summit – worthwhile to fully appreciate the dramatic changes in vegetation as you climb from 800-2400 m above sea level.*

A mountain track from Metapán gives access to El Salvador's last remaining cloud forest, where there is an abundance of protected wildlife. It now forms part of El Trifinio, or the International Biosphere 'La Fraternidad', administered jointly by Guatemala, Honduras and El Salvador. The summit of **Cerro Montecristo** (2418 m), is the point where the three borders meet, At the Casco Colonial, former finca, is a visitor centre, with small museum and wildlife exhibits. Nearby is an **orchid garden** with over 100 species (the best time to see them in flower is early spring), an orchard and a camping ground in the forest. The views are stunning, as is the change seen in flora and fauna with the altitude. This highest elevated part is closed for visitors during the mating and reproduction season of the animals (31 May to 31 October).

For Sleeping and Eating price codes and other relevant information, see Essentials pages 31-33.

⊖ Sleeping

Izalco *p443*

C La Casona de Los Vega, 2a Av Norte 24, in the center of Izalco. T2453-5951, www.lacasonadelosvega.com.sv. Colonial home converted into comfortable hotel and restaurant with good views.

D El Chele, Final Av Roberto Carillas, Calle La Violeta, Caserío Texcalito, T2453-6740. Ricardo Salazar, T7798-8079, www.izalcoel chelerestaurant.com, some 800 m north of Izalco at a *finca* surrounded by forest. Great view of Volcán Izalco. Escorted hikes and horse rides available to Cerro Verde and its surrounding slopes and Izalco with visits to 2 pre-Columbian ruins nearby. Free transport available, call to arrange. English spoken.

Sonsonate *p443*

C Agape, Km 63 on outskirts of town, take old road through Sonsonate, the hotel is on the exit street to San Salvador, just before the main roundabout on the right side, T2451-2667, www.hotelagape.com.sv. Converted convent, suites and rooms, a/c or fan, safe parking, fine restaurant, gardens, cable TV, pool and laundry service. Recommended.

Salcoatitán and Juayúa *p444*

B-D La Escondida, 6 km north of Juayúa at Finca El Portezuelo, T7888-4552, www.akwa terra.com. B&B in an exceptionally beautiful location, in a coffee plantation cradled between Laguna Verde and forest-clad mountains, with a view over to Ahuachapán to the north. Cosily furnished rooms, with fireplace, DVD, equipped kitchen. Contact Julio and Gaby (English spoken). They also offer coffee decks – a tent protected by a roofed wooden structure – and camping.

D Hotel Juayúa, Urb Esmeralda, Final 6a Av Norte, Juayúa, T2469-2109, www.hoteljuayua.com. Newest hotel in town, with great views.

D Doña Mercedes, 29 Av Sur, 6 Calle Oriente 3-6, Juayúa, 1 block south of **Farmacia Don Bosco**, T2452-2287. Discounts for longer stays. Recommended.

D-E Hostal Casa Mazeta, 4 blocks from main square opposite church, Juayúa, T2406-3403. Great backpackers' hostel in former family home, cosy rooms, dorm and covered hammock space, with garden, kitchen, Wi-Fi and lounge area with DVD library. French owner, also speaks English, German and Spanish. Tours, parking space and laundry. Recommended.

E El Mirador, a block from the park, Juayúa, T2452-2432, www.elmiradorjuayua.com. A 3-storey building with restaurant on top. Best option for low rates and central location.

E Anahuac, 1 Calle Pte and 5 Av Norte, Juayúa, T2469-2401, www.hotelanahuac.com. Dormitories and private rooms for back-packers and tours, with garden, hammocks, book exchange. Very friendly owner Cesar also runs nearby **Café Cadejo** (live music at weekends); extremely popular and highly recommended.

Los Naranjos and around *p445*

B Hotel and Restaurant Los Trozos, located on the road down to Sonsonate. T2415-9879, www.lostrozos.com.

North of Santa Ana *p451*

B Villa Limón, T2442-0149, www.canopy villalimon.com. 30 mins' drive up very rough road (4WD only) northwest of Metapán. Cosy, clean rooms in wooden *cabañas*, and a campsite in beautiful mountainside location, with huge zip-wires over the pine forests. Amazing views over Metapán, to lakes and volcanoes beyond. Full board, or bring your own food, advanced reservation essential; guided walks to nearby water-falls, and horse-riding trips available. Recommended.

Lago de Coatepeque p446

C Torremolinos, on pier out above the lagoon, T2441-6037, www.torremolinoslagocoatepeque.com. Pool, good rooms (all with hot showers), restaurant and bar, boating trips, popular at weekends with music, lively. Discounts for longer stays.

E-F Amacuilco, 300 m from Telecom, T7822-4061.Very helpful manager called Sandra. 6 rooms undergoing renovation at time of writing but still open, with basic but clean and airy rooms, some with lake view, and hammocks. Discounts for longer stays, *marimba* classes, Spanish and Náhuatl lessons, and an art gallery. All meals available, pool, great view with jetty over the lake, secure, boat excursions on lake, tours arranged from US$30-40 per day, kayaks and bikes for rent. Recommended.

Santa Ana p448, map p448

Many hotels close their doors from 2000, so arrive early if you can.

C Sahara, 3 Calle Pte y 10 Av Sur, T2447-8865, www.hotelsahara.com.sv. Good service, but a little overpriced.

D La Libertad, near cathedral, 4 Calle Ote 2, T2441-2358. With bath, good-value budget choice, friendly, clean, helpful. Safe car park across the street, US$2 for 24 hrs.

E Casa Frolaz, 29 Calle Pte 42-B between 8 and 10 Av Sur T2440-5302, www.casafrolaz.com. Beautiful and clean hostel with art, paintings, history books and a friendly reception, hot showers, tropical garden with hammocks and barbecue. Very popular with backpackers, constantly recommended.

E El Faro I, 14 Av Sur 9 entre 9 y 11 Calle Pte, T2447-7787, www.hoteleselfaro.com. Clean rooms, good price.

F La Posada del Rey, 10 Av Sur 71, between 13 and 15 Calle Pte, east side of Mercado Colón and 50 m from bus terminal, T2440-0787, hotellaposadadelrey@hotmail.com. Low prices and nice rooms, friendly and helpful owners. A good backpacker choice and recommended.

Ahuachapán p449

C Casa Blanca, 2 Av Norte y Calle Gerardo Barrios, T2443-1505. 2 good, clean rooms with a/c. Recommended. Owner's husband is a doctor.

C El Parador, Km 102.5 road to Guatemala, 1.5 km west of town, T/F2443- 0331. Hotel and restaurant, a/c, good service, motel-style, relaxing. Helpful owner, Sr Nasser. Buses to border stop outside. Recommended.

E San José, 6 Calle Pte, opposite the park, T2413-0033. Clean, friendly, with bath. Parking available.

Tacuba p449

B -C La Cabaña de Tacuba, 50 m west of Alcaldía, T2417-4332. Nice hotel with large park grounds, access to river and swimming pools, a/c, cable TV. Great food at restaurant.

D-F Hostal de Mama y Papa, Barrio El Calvario, 1 Calle 1, T2417-4268, www.imposibletours.com. Home of the delightful González family, dorm and private rooms with private bath available; roof terrace, DVDs, Wi-Fi access, crazy ducks guard the garden. Excellent, cheap food. The son, Manolo, runs El Imposible Tours, one of the most adventurous and expert outfits in the country.

Apaneca p450

A Santa Leticia, Carretera Sonsonate Km 86.5, south of Apaneca, T2433-0357, www.coffee.com.sv. Comfortable double rooms, decorated in locally carved wood. Solar-heated pool, gardens, live music on Sun, restaurant. Close to Santa Leticia archaeological site.

B Las Cabañas de Apaneca, T2433-0500, www.cabanasapaneca.com. 12 cabins in pleasant gardens, many with good views. More expensive with full board.

C Villas Suizas, at entrance to Apaneca, T2433-0193. Several log cabins with kitchen and living room. Lovely gardens.

C-E Las Orquídeas, Av Central Sur 4, T2433-0061. Clean rooms, accessible prices, centrally located. Also offer accommodation in a family home.

Laguna Verde

C Hotel Laguna Verde Guest House, T7859-2865, www.apanecasguesthouse. netfirms.com. A nice small domo house and a wood cabin located at the rim of a deep secondary crater with a spectacular view. Located 250 m from Laguna Verde and 3 km from Apaneca, a perfect departure point for hiking in the area. Micobuses serve the area several times a day; check current schedules.

Ataco *p450*

B Alicante Montaña, Km 93.5 Carr etera Apaneca/Ataco, T2433-0175, www.alicante apaneca.com. 26 very clean log-cabin rooms with hot water, cable TV. Huge, barnlike rest+aurant, good service and good value meals, pool, spa and jacuzzi; nice grounds with aviary. Very friendly and helpful, recommended.

C El Jardín de Celeste, Km 94, Carretera Apaneca/Ataco, T2433-0277, www.eljardinde celeste.com. 10 rustic cabins with local flair located in a coffee grove and surrounded by colourful plants. The restaurant has capacity for larger parties and conventions. Beautifully decorated throughout the place with antiques, orchids, plants and arts and crafts.

C La Posada de Don Oli, Ataco, a few kilometres west of Apaneca, T2450-5155, oogomezduarte@yahoo.com.mx. Hotel and restaurant in a colonial setting, owned by the local mayor, Oscar Gómez. Guides available for visits to the local sights.

C Las Flores de Eloisa, Km 92.5 Carr Apaneca/Ataco, T2433-0415. Seven small cabins located inside a plant nursery.

North of Santa Ana *p451*

C San José, Carretera Internacional Km 113, Metapán, near bus station, T2442- 0556, www.hoteleselsalvador.com. A/c, quiet, cable TV, safe parking, restaurant on ground floor.

F Hospedaje Central, 2 Av Norte y Calle 15 de Septiembre. Clean, friendly and popular, with bath.

🍴 Eating

Izalco *p443*

🍴 **Casa de Campo**, across from Turicentro Atecozol, T2453-6530. The old *casco* of the *finca* Cuyancúa has been restored with beautiful gardens, making it a good spot for a meal (only open at weekends). The fish raised in the artificial lake is served in the restaurant. Horses available for hire.

🍴 **Mariona**, in the centre, T2453-6580. One of several *comedores*. They serve a 55-year-old recipe for *sopa de gallina* (Creole chicken soup) which is famous all over Izalco.

🍴 **Restaurante El Cheles**, located in the centre of Izalco with another branch out of town at Final Av Roberto Carillas, Calle La Violeta, Caserío Texcalito, T2453-5392, www.izalcoelcheleres taurant.com. Owner Ricardo Salazar speaks English and can arrange escorted hikes and horse riding to Cerro Verde.

Sonsonate *p443*

🍴 **Doña Laura**, located inside Hotel Agape (see Sleeping, above). Open 0730-2100. Highly recommended.

🍴 **Burger House Plaza**, Pasaje Francisco Chacón. Open 0900-2000. Hamburgers, fried chicken with potato salad.

Salcoatitán and Juayúa *p444*

Each weekend the whole central plaza of Juayua is invaded by the Gastronomical Food Fair, grab a chair and a table if you can, the event attracts folks from far and near. During the week there are several other options. Check www.juayua. com. for a complete list of hotels and restaurants in this area.

🍴 **Baking Pizza**, 2a Calle Ote y 4a Av Sur, Juayua, T2469-2356 – home-made pizza.

🍴 **Comedor Laura's**, 1 block from the park on 1 Av Sur, Juayúa, T2452-2098. Open daily 0700-2000. 'The best in town' according to one reader, serving *comida a la vista*.

🍴 **La Terraza**, on corner of the park, Juayúa. A café and convenience store with a tourist kiosk nearby.

¶ **Parque Restaurante La Colina**, Km 82 on the turn-off between Juayúa and Salcoatitán, T2452-2916, old timer in the region, popular with families, also has hammocks for relaxation after the meal as well as cabins and horse rides for the kids.

¶ **Taquería La Guadalupana**, Av Daniel Cordón Sur and 2a Calle Ote, Juayúa T2452-2195. Good Mexican food.

Cafés

Pastelería y Cafetería Festival, 4 Calle Pte and 1 Av Sur, T2452-2269. Bakery and coffee shop – try the *pastelitos de ciruela* (plum pie) or the traditional *semita*. Good view overlooking the park.

Santa Ana *p448, map p448*
Restaurants close quite early, between 2000 and 2100. *Comedores* are usually cheap and good value or try the food stalls beside the plaza or in front of the cathedral. Look for excellent pineapples in season.

¶¶ **Los Horcones**, on main plaza next to the cathedral. Like a jungle lodge inside, with pleasant balcony dining, good cheap meals.

¶¶ **Lover's Steak House**, 4 Av Sur y 17 Calle Pte, T2440-5717. Great value, recommended.

¶¶ **Talitunal**, 5 Av Sur 6. Mon-Sat 0900-1900. Vegetarian, attractive, good lunch, owner is a doctor and expert on medicinal plants.

¶ **Expresión**, 11 Calle Pte 20, between Av 6 and 8, T/F2440-1410, www.expresion cultural.org. A great little coffee bar, restaurant, bookshop and internet café, with occasional art exhibitions. The owner, Angel, speaks English. An obligatory stop, recommended.

Chalchuapa *p448*
Several cheap and informal eateries with good-quality meals can be found around charming Parque Central.

¶¶ **Los Antojitos**, Calle Ramón Flores 6. Good meals.

Ahuachapán *p449*
There are now a handful of restaurants with lake views by Laguna del Espino just outside Ahuachapán.

¶¶ **Restaurant El Paseo**, **Restaurant Tanya** and **El Parador**, on the Las Chinamas road. All serve good meals.

Apaneca *p450*
Stalls in the municipal market offer cheap meals and typical dishes. Try the *budín* at the middle stall on the right side of market entrance (might be the best in El Salvador). A definite must for those on a budget or for experiencing local food.

¶¶¶-¶¶ **La Cocina de Mi Abuela**, in town, T2433-0100, open weekends; and **Cabañas de Apaneca**. The 2 largest restaurants, and the most popular spots. Attract people from far and wide.

¶¶ **El Rosario**, by the turn-off at Km 95 between Apaneca and Ataco, T2433-0205, www.negociosyturismoelrosario.com. Offers different grilled dishes, from regular *churrascos* to *pelibuey* (a mix between goat and sheep), *jaripeo* (Salvadorean version of rodeo), horse shows and musical entertainments weekends.

¶¶ **Entre Nubes**, Km 93.5, T2433-0345, exceptionally beautiful nursery plants surround this fine coffee shop (open weekends) great desserts and varieties of coffee.

¶¶ **Parque Ecoturístico Las Cascadas de Don Juan**, T2273-1380, lascascadasdedonjuan@ yahoo.com. Serving typical dishes and also offer hikes to the waterfalls, freshwater springs as well as a camping area.

¶ **Artesanías y Comedor Rosita**. Range of local dishes as well as arts and crafts.

¶ **Laguna Verde Restaurant**. Km 3.5 Carr El Caserío by La Laguna Verde, T2261-0167. A cosy and rustic spot serving typical dishes of the region. Only open weekends.

Ataco *p450*
A number of small restaurants and coffee shops have opened recently, most are only open at weekends.

¶-¶ The House of Coffee, T2450-5353, thoc@hotmail.com. Tue-Sun. A must visit, the café has the only professional espresso machine in town. Home-made cakes and steaming hot 'Cup of Excellence' award-winning coffee is available here.

¶-¶ Tayua, T7233-6508. A gem of a place 2 blocks uphill from the plaza, run by English-speaking and trained chef Veronica, and her husband. Wide range of dishes usually home-produced organic veg from the restaurant's own garden. Antique decor and background jazz. They also have a bakery, producing the best bread and pastries in town.

North of Santa Ana p451
Just before entering Metapán, 50 m off the highway, at the rim of the Lagunita Metapán, there are a couple of places with an international menu offering good fish from the lake, including **La Cocina de Metapán**, T2423-0014, which also has a pool and terrace. Both have a/c.

¶-¶ Balompie, Metapán, opposite church on main square, T2402-3567. Upstairs restaurant, nice balcony, serves good-value mix of meat, seafood, pasta and snacks. Also serves football stadium behind

▲ Activities and tours

Ahuachapán p449
Tour operators
Tours Universales, at Agencia de Viajes Morales, 2 Av Norte 2-4, T2413-2002. Speak to Beatriz Contreras.

Apaneca p450
Tour operators
Apaneca Aventura, Calle Los Platanares 2, T2433-0470, apanecaaventura@yahoo.com. Specialize in off-road buggy rides around the mountains and forests, including to Laguna Verde and Ausole de Santa Teresa geysers and thermal baths. English manager Becky, and with English-speaking guides, highly recommended.

Tacuba p449
El Imposible Tours, see Hostal de Mama y Papa, page 453. Range of activities including mountain biking, canyoning and hiking; overnight trips combining tour of Barra de Santiago and mangroves. Highly recommended.

⊖ Transport

Sonsonate p443
Bus No 248 to **Santa Ana**, US$1.50 along Carr 12 north, 39 km, a beautiful journey. To **Ahuachapán**, bus No 249, 2 hrs, slow, best to go early in the day. To Ataco, via Juayúa and Ahuachapán, No 23, US$1, 1½ hrs To **Barra de Santiago**, bus No 285. To **Los Cobanos** bus No 259. Take care at the bus terminal and on rural routes (eg in Nahuizalco area). From **San Salvador** to Sonsonate by bus No 530, US$0.80, 1½ hrs, very frequent.

Joya de Cerén p446
Bus No 108 from **San Salvador** Terminal de Occidente to San Juan; US$0.45, 1 hr. Bus No 201 from **Santa Ana**, US$0.60, 1 hr, ask the bus driver to drop you at Desvío Opico from where you can catch another bus to Joya de Cerén.

Lago de Coatepeque p446
Bus From **Santa Ana**, bus No 220 'El Lago' to the lake every 30 mins, US$0.35. From **San Salvador**; bus No 201 to El Congo (bridge at Km 50) on Pan-American Hwy, US$1, then pick up the No 220 bus to the lake, US$0.45. Other buses to **Guatemala** may also stop at El Congo, so it's worth checking.

Taxi From Santa Ana, US$10.

Cerro Verde and Volcán Izalco p446
Bus From **Santa Ana**, bus No 248 goes to Santa Ana and Cerro Verde via El Congo. If you come from San Salvador wait for the bus at the other side of the main road, near the turn-off to Lake Coatepeque. The departures from Santa Ana are 0800, 1000 1100 and 1300. The bus arrives approximately 30 mins

later at El Congo. The return bus leaves Cerro Verde at 1100, 1200, 1300, 1500, 1600 and 1730. The latest bus stops at El Congo and does not go all the way to Santa Ana. The journey between Cerro Verde at El Congo takes approximately 1 hr.

If you travel from **San Salvador** take the bus towards Santa Ana (No 205). Get off at the Shell gas station at El Congo, cross the bridge that goes over the highway and catch the No 248 at the junction from Santa Ana. If you come from the west take the bus from Esso gas station beween Izalco and Ateos that leads to Santa Ana and get off at junction 14 km below Cerro Verde summit and wait for No 248 that comes from El Congo.

Santa Ana *p448, map p448*
Bus No 201 from Terminal del Occidente, **San Salvador**, US$1-1.25, 1 hr, every 10-15 mins, 0400-1830. To **La Libertad**, take 'autopista' route bus to San Salvador and change buses in Nueva San Salvador. Buses (**Melva, Pezzarossi** and others) leave frequently from 25 Calle Pte y 8 Av Sur, T2440-3606, for **Guatemala City**, full fare as from San Salvador, 4-4½ hrs including border stops. Alternatively, there are local buses to the border for US$0.45; they leave from the market. Frequent buses to **Metapán** and border at **Anguiatú**. No 238 follows a beautiful route to **Juayúa**.

Atiquizaya *p449*
Bus There are frequent buses to the river from the central park in Atiquizaya; buses No 202 and 456 from Terminal Occidente in **San Salvador**, 2 hrs, US$0.90. From **Santa Ana**, 45 mins, US$0.40. All Ahuachapán buses stop in the Parque Central.

Ahuachapán *p449*
Bus Ahuachapán is 100 km from **San Salvador** by bus 202, US$0.90, every 20 mins, 0430-1830 to the capital, 2 hrs via **Santa Ana**. Microbuses to border from northwest corner of parque, US$0.45, 25 mins, slower buses same price. Bus No 210 to **Santa Ana** 1 hr, US$0.50. Bus No 235 El Express to

Metapán 1¼ hrs, US$0.90. Frequent buses and minivans to the border at Km 117.

Tacuba *p449*
Bus Buses leave the terminal in **Ahuachapán** every 30 mins, 0500-1530, return 1630-1700, via **Ataco**; US$0.60, 45 mins, rough road.

Apaneca *p450*
Bus Local buses stop by the plaza, others pass on the main road, a few blocks north, leaving you with a fairly long walk. **Laguna Verde** can be reached on foot from Apaneca to Cantón Palo Verde and Hoyo de Cuajuste, then a further 1 km from where the road ends.

North of Santa Ana *p451*
Bus and car From Santa Ana bus No 235, US$0.80, 1 hr. If driving **San Salvador–Metapán**, a bypass skirts Santa Ana. Bus No 211 to border at **Anguiatú**.

❶ Directory

Salcoatitán, Juayúa, Ahuachapán and Ataco *p444, p449 and p450*
Banks Scotia Bank (with ATM), Juayúa, opposite bus stop from Ahuachapan. Mon-Fri 0800-1600, Sat 0800-1200. There are several banks in Sonsonate and Ahuachapán. Ataco has Pro Credit and Western Union banks, 1 block from main square, both with ATMs. **Internet** Mini Librería, 4 Calle Ote, ½ block from main square, Juayúa. **Post** 1 block from main square, Ataco, towards market, 0900-1630.

Santa Ana *p448, map p448*
Banks Banks will change TCs, though becoming less widely accepted. HSBC and several other banks, Av Independencia Sur, between Calle 3 and 7. **Internet** Expresión, has a couple of computers on the go in a very comfortable setting. **Laundry** Lavandería Solución, 7 Calle Pte 29, wash and dry US$2.50 per load, ironing service, recommended. **Police** Emergency T911. **Post** 7 Calle Pte, between 2 Av and Av Independencia Sur.

Northern El Salvador

The route from San Salvador to western Honduras heads north, skirting the vast arm of the Cerrón Grande reservoir with volcanoes in the distance. Small villages are interspersed with brand new settlements tucked amongst the fields and hills as the road winds through mountainous landscape – a snapshot of the old way of life, and the emergence of the new. Currently enjoying a cultural revival, the charming colonial town of Suchitoto on the southern shore of the reservoir is definitely worth a visit. ▸▸ For listings, see pages 462-465.

North from San Salvador

The old highway, Troncal del Norte (CA 4) used to be the only acess to the north from the capital, but has been replaced with a modern highway. This can be accessed from Boulevard de la Constitución, in the northeastern part of San Salvador, and swirls west around the Volcán de San Salvador towards the Pan-American Highway and branches out to Nejapa, Quezaltepeque and Apopa to the north. Another advance in the northern road system is the road that connects Aguilares with Suchitoto. It is 2½ hours by car from San Salvador to La Palma, then 11 km to the border at El Poy.

Apopa and Tonacatepeque

ⓘ Bus 38 B from San Salvador to Apopa, US$0.35.

Apopa is a friendly town with a good market and a shopping centre. It is the junction with a road to Quezaltepeque (12 km). A paved road runs east from Apopa to Tonacatepeque, an attractive small town on a high plateau. It has a small textile industry and is in an agricultural setting – check out the charming park and the colonial church. There has been some archaeological exploration of the town's original site, 5 km away. A paved road from Tonacatepeque runs 13 km south to the Pan-American Highway, some 5 km from the capital. In the other direction, a dry-weather road runs north to Suchitoto. Three kilometres beyond Apopa, on CA 4 Km 17, is **Finca Orgánica Las Termópilas** where **Lisa's Guest House** is located (see page 462). There is also a Spanish-language school and they arrange volunteers for the 'Working Farm' project at Termópilas organic farm. Tours are available to the archaeological site Cihuatán (see below) as well as on horseback to Suchitoto and to Volcán Guazapa, which played a prominent part in the civil war. The panoramic views are amazing and you can visit the old guerrilla hide outs. Contact Lena and René Carmona at **Ximena's** (see page 435), T2260-2481. All buses from Terminal de Oriente to Aguilares pass the entrance (US$0.25).

Aguilares

From Apopa, it's 21 km to Aguilares, 4 km beyond which are the ruins of **Cihuatán**
ⓘ Tue-Sun 0900-1600, map of the site with the Sendero Interpretativo is available from Lisa's Guest House or Ximena's Guest House; alternatively, contact chief archaeologist Paul Amaroli at FUNDAR in San Salvador, T2235-9453, www.fundar.org.sv. The name means 'place of women' and was presided over by female royalty. This was the largest city in Mesoamerica during the Toltec period, when the city was surrounded by extended fortification measuring more than 10 sq km. The biggest archaeological site in the country has several tall pyramids, ball courts and temazcales (ritual saunas).

An improved road goes from Aguilares heading west to Suchitoto. If heading north, see page 460.

Suchitoto → *Population: 24,786.*

ⓘ *Good sites on Suchitoto are www.gaesuchitoto.com and www.suchitoto-el-salvador.com. For information in English, try to contact US citizen Roberto Broz who runs a Cyber Café Store and Restaurant El Gringo, just off the main plaza, see Eating, page 463.*

Suchitoto, meaning 'the place of birds and flowers' in Náhuatl, was founded by the Pipil more than 1000 years ago. In 1528 the capital was moved to Suchitoto for 15 years as the villa of San Salvador suffered attacks from local tribes. In 1853 an earthquake destroyed much of San Salvador and many affluent families moved to Suchitoto leaving a lasting impression on the town. Today it is a small, very attractive colonial town with cobbled streets, balconied houses and an interesting church. It is one of the favourite tourist spots in the country, with cultural traditions kept alive by the many artists living and working in the town. Several hotels and restaurants offer fantastic views towards Suchitlán and Volcán Guazapa. More than 200 species of bird have been identified in the area, and white-tailed deer inhabit the local woods.

The town was almost completely deserted in the early 1990s after 12 years of civil war which severely affected the region – 90% of the population left, leaving Suchitoto a virtual ghost town. However, a cultural revival has stimulated a range of activities and events, and the town is now considered the cultural capital of the country. Life centres on the main plaza which every evening becomes a bustle of people wandering the streets. Suchitoto's telegraph poles have been decorated by artist Paulo Rusconi, and Parque San Martín, to the west of town, is dotted with modern sculptures, some made using materials left over from the war. Arts and cultural festivals with internationally renowned artists take place every February. Another local festivity is the *Palo Encebado*, a competition involving attempts to clamber to the top of long greasy poles, and the *cerdo encebado* where a pig smeared with lard is chased through town and is kept by the first person who manages to grab it.

Sleeping
El Tejado 5
La Fonda El Mirador 2
Los Almendros de
   San Lorenzo 21
Posada Alta Vista 3
Posada de Suchitlán 4

Villa Balanza 6

Eating
Café Billard-Sánchez 2
Café El Obraje 1
Cyber Café Store &
   Restaurant El Gringo 7

El Dorado 6
Lupita del Portal 3
Pupusería La Bella
   Esquina 4
Pupusería Vista al Lago 5
Villa Balanza 8

The **Teatro de Las Ruinas** is almost fully restored and hosts concerts and events. Contact Sra Chavez, T2335-1086 for more information. **Iglesia de Santa Lucía** ⓘ *Mon-Sat 0800-1200, 1400-1600, all day Sun*, built in 1858 with wooden and hollow columns, has also been restored with a lot of stencil work inside. There is a splendid view from the church tower. **Casa Museo de Alejandro Cotto** ⓘ *daily 0900-1200 and 1400-1600, US$4, guided tour in Spanish (T2335-1140)*, home of movie director Alejandro Cotto, is an interesting museum with more than 132 paintings of El Salvador's most renowned artists, collections of books and music instruments.

The **tourist office** ⓘ *Calle Francisco Morazán 7, next to the telephone office, T2335-1782, daily 0800-1700, www.suchitoto-el-salvador.com*, offers daily tours of the city centre, to Los Tercios waterfall and to Lake Suchitlán. There is also a Ministry of Tourism **tourist office** ⓘ *Mon-Fri 0800-1700, Sat-Sun 0800-1600, T2335-1835*, in Suchitoto.

Around Suchitoto

A 30-minute walk north of town leads to the **Embalse Cerrón Grande** (also known as **Lago de Suchitlán**). **Proyecto Turístico Pesquero Puerto San Juan** is the a harbour with boat shuttle services and a complex of, restaurants, craft shops and cafés on the lake shore. This is the departure point for boat excursions across to remote areas in neighbouring Chalatenango, ask around and negotiate prices. Trips are available to five islands including **Isla de Los Pájaros**, which makes an interesting trip (one to 1½ hours).

Ferries cross the Embalse Cerrón Grande for San Luis del Carmen (25 minutes to San Luis, frequent departures all day), where there is Comedor Carmen, and buses to Chalatenango. The ferry also makes a stop at the small village of **San Francisco Lempa**.

Los Tercios, a waterfall with striking, gigantic, black, hexagonal-shaped basaltic columns, can be reached by car, foot and by *lancha*. It is at its most impressive in the wet season when the full force of nature is on show. Walk 10-15 minutes from town down the very steep road towards the lake known as Calle al Lago de Suchitlán. Lifts are available for about US$2-3 if you can't face the steep climb back to town afterwards, ask around. At the lake shore, where there are *comedores*, ask for a *lanchero*. A *lancha* to the base of the trail to Los Tercios is US$5-6 (negotiable) and takes 10 minutes (ask the *lanchero* to point out the trail).

La Ciudad Vieja, one-time site of the capital, is 10 km from Suchitoto. An original Pipil town, it was taken over by the Spanish who made it their central base for 17 years before electrical storms, lack of water, and cholera forced them to flee. It is a private site but can be visited. There are plans for a museum and a café.

Boat trips go to lakeside villages associated with the FMLN in the civil war. On the road to Aguilares, 12 km away, a **Bosque de la Reconciliación** is being developed at the foot of Cerro de Guazapa. Contact **CESTA** ⓘ *T2213-1400, www.cesta-foe.org*, in San Salvador, or contact the park directly on T2213-1403 and speak to Jesús Arriola. Also, 3 km along this road is **Aguacayo** and a large church, badly damaged during the war.

Chalatenango → *Colour map 3, C1. Altitude: 450 m. Population: 30,808.*

Highway 4 continues north from **Aguilares**, passing the western extremity of the **Cerrón Grande** reservoir. A branch to the east skirts the northern side of the reservoir to Chalatenango, capital of the department of the same name. Rural Chalatenango is mainly agricultural and has many remote villages, there are a number of non-governmental organizations working in the area. Chalatenango is a delightful little town with annual fairs and fiestas on 24 June and 1-2 November. It is the centre of an important region of

Handicrafts of El Salvador

The artists' village of **La Palma**, in a pine-covered valley under Miramundo mountain, is 84 km north of the capital 10 km south of the Honduran frontier. Here, in 1971, the artist **Fernando Llort** 'planted a seed' known as the *copinol* (a species of the locust tree) from which sprang the first artists' cooperative, now called **La Semilla de Dios** (Seed of God). The copinol seed is firm and round; on it the artisans base a spiritual motif that emanates from their land and soul.

The town and its craftspeople are now famous for their work in wood, including exotically carved *cofres* (adorned wooden chests), and traditional Christmas *muñecas de barro* (clay dolls) and ornamental angels. Wood carvings, other crafts and the designs of the original paintings by Llort, are all produced and exported from La Palma to the rest of El Salvador and thence worldwide.

In 1971 the area was almost exclusively agricultural. Today 75% of the population of La Palma and neighbouring San Ignacio are engaged directly or indirectly in producing handicrafts. The painter **Alfredo Linares** (born 1957 in Santa Ana, arrived in La Palma 1981 after studying in Guatemala and Florence) has a gallery in La Palma, employing and assisting local artists. His paintings and miniatures are marketed abroad, yet you will often find him working in the family pharmacy next to the gallery. Many of La Palma's images are displayed on the famous Hilasal towels. If you cannot get to La Palma,

visit the shop/gallery/workshop of Fernando Llort in San Salvador, **Arbol de Dios**.

Twenty kilometres from the capital is the indigenous town of **Panchimalco**, where weaving on the loom and other traditional crafts are being revived. Many Náhuatl traditions, customs, dances and the language survived here as the original indigenous people hid from the Spanish conquistadors in the valley beneath the Puerta del Diablo (now in Parque Balboa). In 1996 the painter Eddie Alberto Orantes and his family opened the **Centro de Arte y Cultura Tunatiuh**, named after a Náhuatl deity who is depicted as a human face rising as a sun over a pyramid. The project employs local youths (from broken homes, or former addicts) in the production of weavings, paintings and ceramics.

In the mountains of western El Salvador, villages in the coffee zone, such as **Nahuizalco**, specialize in weaving henequen, bamboo and reed into table mats and wicker furniture. There are also local artists like Maya sculptor **Ahtzic Selis**, who works with clay and jade. East of the capital, at **Ilobasco** (60 km), many ceramic workshops produce items including the famous *sorpresas*, miniature figures enclosed in an egg shell. In the capital there are craft markets, and throughout the country, outlets range from the elegant to the rustic. Everywhere, artists and artisans welcome visitors into their workshops.

traditional livestock farms. It has a good market and several craft shops, for example **Artesanías Chalateca**, for bags and hammocks. The weekly horse fairs, where horses, saddles and other equipment are for sale, are very popular.

La Palma and around → *Colour map 1, C1. Altitude: 1100 m. Population: 12,235.*

The main road continues north through Tejutla to La Palma, a charming village set in pine-clad mountains, and well worth a visit. It is famous for its local crafts, particularly brightly painted wood carvings and hand-embroidered tapestries. Also produced are handicrafts made from clay, metal, cane and seeds. There are a number of workshops in La Palma where the craftsmen can be seen at work and purchases made (see box, page 461). The **Fiesta del Dulce Nombre de María** takes place mid- or late February.

The picturesque village of **San Ignacio**, 6 km north of La Palma, has two or three small *talleres* producing handicrafts (20 minutes by bus, US$0.10 each way).

San Ignacio is the departure point for buses ascending a fairly new, safe but steep road leading up to the highest mountain of El Salvador, El Pital (2730 m). As you reach the pass below the mountain top, the road branches to **Las Pilas** to the left and **Miramundo** to the right. Both Miramundo and Las Pilas have small agricultural communities, specializing in organic crops. The extensive cabbage fields combined with the pine-clad mountains make for beautiful vistas.

If you take the road from the summit to the right, you end up in Miramundo which gives a view of pretty much all El Salvador. On clear days you can see almost all the volcanoes in the country, including Volcán Pacaya and Volcán Agua in Guatemala. No doubt the best view in the country.

Border with Western Honduras

The road continues north to the border at **El Poy**, for Western Honduras. From Citalá, there is a small town with a colonial church and a potent war history (you still see bullet holes in the walls of the houses on street corners). One kilometre west off the highway just before El Poy, an adventurous road leads to Metapán. Two buses daily take three hours to travel the 40 km, a rough but beautiful journey.

◉ Northern El Salvador listings

For Sleeping and Eating price codes and other relevant information, see Essentials pages 31-33.

● Sleeping

Apopa and Tonacatepeque *p458*
D-F Lisa's Guest House, Finca Orgánica Las Termópilas, 3 km beyond Apopa, on CA 4 Km 17.5, Troncal del Norte, www.ximenas guesthouse.com. Same owners as **Ximena's Guest House**, T2260-2481, in San Salvador, see page 435. Budget lodging in dorms with shared bath, and spacious family rooms with TV and private bath.

Suchitoto *p459, map p459*
L Los Almendros de San Lorenzo, 4 Calle Pte, next to police station, T2335-1200, www.hotelsalvador.com. In a restored colonial house with exclusive rooms, suites and delightful gardens. Delicious meals in the restaurant – people come from the capital

to lunch here at weekends. Art Gallery **Pascal**, across the street, has great exhibits, textiles and handicrafts (same French owner).
L-A Posada de Suchitlán, Final 4 Calle Pte, at the western end of town, T2335-1064, www.laposada.com.sv. Colonial-style, beautifully tiled and decorated, excellent hotel and restaurant, including local speciality, *gallo a chichi* (chicken cooked in maize wine); stunning lake views.
A-B El Tejado, 3 Av Norte 58, Barrio Concepción, T2335-1769, www.eltejado suchitoto.net. Beautifully restored colonial house with just nicely furnished and spotless rooms, some with balcony; pool and gorgeous view of Lake Suchitlán. Pretty terrace restaurant.
B Hacienda La Bermuda 1525, Km 34.8 Carretera a Suchitoto, T2226-1839, www.labermuda.com. Hotel and restaurant with frequent cultural activities, located just outside Suchitoto.

C Villa Balanza, north edge of Parque San Martín, T2335-1408, www.villabalanza restaurante.com. On the street behind the restaurant of the same name and 250 m to the right down the hill. Small rooms but nicely furnished, with lovely views of lake from the hotel balcony.

C-E Posada Alta Vista, on Av 15 de Septiembre 8, near the square, T2335-1645. Good rooms, although the cheaper ones can be hot. Helpful, friendly staff. Rooftop terrace with great view of the town.

D La Fonda El Mirador, Calle 15 de Septiembre, Barrio Concepción, on the road that leads to the lake, T2335-1126, quintanilladavid@yahoo.com. Next to restaurant of same name, with superb views of lake and good food too.

Chalatenango *p460*

D La Ceiba, 1a calle Pte, near 5a Av Norte, behind the military fort, Barrio Las Flores, T2301-1080. With shower and bath. Basic rooms but with a/c, in quiet corner of town.

La Palma and around *p461*

AL Entre Pinos, San Ignacio, T2335-9312, www.entrepinosresortandspa.com. 1st-class resort complex, a/c, pool, cable TV, sauna and shop.

B-C Hotel Maya, Km 77.5 Troncal del Norte, T2323-3758. Motel at the entrance of La Palma. Amazing panoramic view.

C Hotel La Palma, Troncal del Norte, 84 km Carretera, La Palma, T2335-9012, www.hotellapalma.com.sv. 32 large rooms, clean, with bath. Friendly, with good restaurant, beautiful gardens, nice pool, ceramics workshop, parking and gas station. Also runs guided walks around local trails, including El Tecomate, Río Nunuapa and Los Pozos. Recommended.

C La Posada de Reyes, San Ignacio, just behind the park, T2352-9223. Nice private rooms with bath, also has a restaurant.

D-E Las Praderas de San Ignacio, San Ignacio, a couple of kilometres before the border, T2350-9330, www.hotelpraderas

desanignacio.com. Cabins, beautiful gardens and an economic restaurant.

D-F Hostal Miramundo, Miramundo, T2219-6251, www.hotelmiramundo.com. Nice rooms with hot water. A restaurant, great food and great views. Recommended.

E-F Hotel Cayahuanca, San Ignacio, across the street at Km 93.5, T2335-9464. Friendly, with good but expensive restaurant.

F Casa de Huéspedes Las Orquídeas, Las Pilas. Run by a local farming family – ask for a guided trip to the mountain top nearby, for an unrivalled panoramic view and free peaches.

⦿ Eating

Apopa and Tonacatepeque *p458*

🍴 **La Posada de John Paul**, Finca Orgánica Las Termópilas. Serves food made with own-grown produce, as well as meat dishes and natural fruit juices. Excellent organic honey and coffee available, and fruit and vegetables when in season.

Suchitoto *p459, map p459*

Local specialities include *salporitas* (made of corn meal) and *chachamachas*. Try the *pupusas* in the market. Several eating options around the main plaza;many restaurants only open weekend evenings, especially during off season.

🍴🍴 **Los Almendros de San Lorenzo**, 4 Calle Pte, next to police station, Barrio El Centro (see Sleeping), T2335-1200, plebailly@hotel elsalvador.com. Best restaurant in Suchitoto. Has a French chef, serves succulent meals and visitors come from San Salvador on weekends to dine here.

🍴 **El Dorado**, by Lake Suchitlán, T2225-5103, www.gaesuchitoto.com. Bar and restaurant that hosts frequent concerts.

🍴 **Hacienda La Bermuda**, just out of Suchitoto, Km 34.8 Carretera a San Salvador (see Sleeping), T2389-9078, www.labermuda. com. B&B, colonial-style restaurant with pool and cultural events.

¶ **Lupita del Portal**, Parque Centenario, T2335-1679. The current hot spot, open until midnight. Serves gourmet *pupusas* with home-grown herbs, Salvadorean specialities and natural teas. Owner René Barbón also runs **Suchitoto Adventure Outfitters** (T2335-1429) from here, an excellent tour operator (see below).

¶ **Villa Balanza**, Parque San Martín, T2335-1408, www.villabalanzarestaurante.com. Rustic farm decor and antique bric-a-brac, serving excellent local cuisine, steaks and fish, and home-made fruit preserves.

¶ **Vista Conga Restaurant**, T2335-1679, Final Pasaje Cielito Lindo No 8 Barrio Concepción, vistacongasuchi@yahoo.com. Live music, only open at weekends.

¶ **Café Billard-Sánchez**, 4 Calle Pte, by El Cerrito, Barrio Santa Lucía, T2335-1464. Bar and disco.

¶ **Café El Obraje**, next to Santa Lucía church, T2335-1173. Clean and reasonably priced, with good breakfast variety. Closed Tue.

¶ **Cyber Café Store and Restaurant El Gringo**, T2335-1770, 8a Av Norte No 9, Barrio San José. Fri-Wed. Serves *pupusas* (normal and gourmet), Tex/Mex and typical Salvadorean foods. Famous for veggie burritos.

¶ **Pupusería La Bella Esquina**, on 15 de Septiembre and 4 Calle Ote. Very good, cheap food.

¶ **Pupusería Vista al Lago**, Av 15 de Septiembre 89, T2335-1134. Good food.

Chalatenango *p460*
Several restaurants to choose from including:
¶¶¶-¶ **Rinconcito El Nuevo**, next to the military fort. A la carte menu as well as *pupusas*, good. Check out bizarre collection of old sewing machines, irons, typewriters and other knick-knacks on display in the adjacent colonnade.

La Palma and around *p461*
In Ignacio, there are many local *comedores*, including **Comedor Elisabeth**, which offer delicious *comida a la vista* including fresh milk, cheese and cream.

¶ **El Poyeton**, Barrio San Antonio, 1 block from church, La Palma. Reliable, serves simple dishes.

¶ **La Estancia**, on Calle Principal, La Palma, T/F2335-9049. Open 0800-2000. Good menu, useful bulletin board.

▲ Activities and tours

Suchitoto *p459, map p459*
Suchitoto Adventure Outfitters, based in **Lupita del Portal** café on main square, T2335-1429, www.suchitotooutfitters.com. Excellent local tours, including 5-hr horse-riding trip up Volcán Guazapa to former guerrilla camp, fascinating insights on war history (US$35). Owner René Barbón speaks excellent English and is extremely knowledgeable and helpful.

◯ Shopping

La Palma and around *p461*
Handicrafts
There are more than 80 arts and crafts workshops in La Palma, www.lapalma elsalvador.com, provides a complete list of all the workshops and how to contact them. Many workshops have come together and formed a **Placita Artesanal** – an artisans market, which is located by the Catholic church on the central plaza.

Cooperativa La Semilla de Dios, Plaza San Antonio. The original cooperative founded by Fernando Llort in 1971, it has a huge selection of crafts and paintings, helpful.

Gallery Alfredo Linares, Sr Linares' house (if gallery is unattended, ask in the pharmacy), T2335-9049. Well-known artist whose paintings sell for US$18-75. Open daily 0900-1800, friendly, recommended.

Palma City, Calle Principal behind church. Sra Alicia Mata is very helpful and will help find objects, whether she stocks them or not (wood, ceramics, *telas*, etc).

⊖ Transport

Suchitoto *p459, map p459*
Bus To **Aguilares**, No 163 every
30 mins, 0500-1800, 30 mins. Regular
buses (No 129) from Terminal Oriente,
San Salvador, beginning at 0330. The bus
stops at the market and leaves town for
the capital from 3 Av Norte. To **Ilobasco**
by dirt road, 0800 and 1000, returning
1230 and 1430.

Ferry Cross the Embalse Cerrón Grande
(Lago de Suchitlán) for **San Luis del
Carmen** (25 mins to San Luis, frequent
departures throughout the day, will leave
whenever full, cars US$8, foot passengers
US$1) where there is **Comedor Carmen**,
and buses linking to **Chalatenango**. Small
lanchas also make the short crossing from
San Juan to San Francisco Lempa on the
north shore, with onward buses to
Chalatenango, US$5 for the whole boat
(up to approximately 10 passengers).

Chalatenango *p460*
Bus No 125 from Oriente terminal,
San Salvador, US$2, 2½ hrs.

La Palma and around *p461*
Bus From **San Salvador**, Terminal de
Oriente, No 119, US$2.25, 3 hrs, last bus at
1630. To La Palma from Amayo, crossroads
with Troncal del Norte (main highway to San
Salvador), and E-W road to Chalatenango,
bus No 119 every 30 mins, US$1.35.

❶ Directory

Suchitoto *p459, map p459*
Banks Western Union available. Mon-Fri
0800-1600, Sat 0830-1200. Will cash TCs.
No credit card facilities. **Internet** Cyber
Café El Gringo, daily 0800-2100, US$1per hr,
free Wi-Fi for laptops; Barrio San José;
2 places on the main square either side
of **Lupita del Portal**.

Chalatenango *p460*
Banks HSBC and Banco Pro Credit on
3 Av Sur, **Western Union** off plaza to right
of barracks, all with ATM.

La Palma and around *p461*
Banks Citibank, Calle Delgado and
Av Independencia, with 24-hr ATM.

Eastern El Salvador

A primarily agricultural zone, the central region is lined with dramatic volcanoes, impressive scenery and the small towns of the Lempa Valley. Along the coast, quiet beaches and islands can be found on the way to the stunning Gulf of Fonseca to the east. In the north towards the mountain range bordering Honduras was an area of fierce disputes between the army and guerrillas during the civil war (1980-1992). Small communities are now rebuilt and opening up to visitors providing several small quaint villages offer ecotourism and original crafts. There are two border crossings to Honduras: to the north at Perquín, and the east at El Amatillo. ▸▸ *For listings, see pages 472-475.*

East from San Salvador → *For listings, see pages 472-475.*

There are two roads to the port of La Unión (formerly known as Cutuco) on the Gulf of Fonseca: the Pan-American Highway, 185 km through Cojutepeque and San Miguel (see page 468); and the coastal highway, also paved, running through Santo Tomás, Olocuilta, Zacatecoluca and Usulután.

The Pan-American Highway is dual carriageway out of the city, but becomes single carriageway for several kilometres either side of Cojutepeque – sections that are twisty, rough and seem to induce some very bad driving.

At San Martín, 18 km from the capital, a paved road heads north to Suchitoto, 25 km on the southern shore of the Embalse Cerrón Grande, also known as Lago de Suchitlán. At Km 34.8 is **Hacienda La Bermuda**, see page 462.

Cojutepeque → *Colour map 3, C1. Population: 50,315.*

The capital of the Department of Cuscatlán, 34 km from San Salvador, is the first town on the Pan-American Highway encountered when heading east. There is a good weekly market. The town is famous for cigars, smoked sausages, *quesadillas* and tongue, and its annual feria on 29 August has fruits and sweets, saddlery, leather goods, pottery and headwear on sale from neighbouring villages, and sisal hammocks, ropes, bags and hats from the small factories of Cacaopera (Department of Morazán). There is also a **sugar cane festival** on 12-20 January. Lago de Ilopango is a short trip to the southwest.

Cerro de las Pavas, a conical hill near Cojutepeque, dominates Lago de Ilopango and offers splendid views of wide valleys and tall mountains. Its shrine of **Our Lady of Fátima** draws many pilgrims every year (religious ceremonies take place here on 13 May).

Ilobasco → *Population 61,510.*

From **San Rafael Cedros**, 6 km east of Cojutepeque, a 16-km paved road north to Ilobasco has a branch road east to Sensuntepeque at about Km 13. The surrounding area, devoted to cattle, coffee, sugar and indigo, is exceptionally beautiful. Many of Ilobasco's population are workers in clay; although some of its decorated pottery is now mass-produced and has lost much of its charm, this is definitely the best place to buy pottery in El Salvador. Check out miniature *sorpresas*, delicately shaped microscopic sceneries the size of an egg (don't miss the naughty ones). Try **Hermanos López** ① *entrance to town, or José y Víctor Antino Herrera i Av Carlos Bonilla 61, T2332-2324, look for the 'Kiko' sign*, where there are fine miniatures for sale. The annual fiesta is on 29 September.

San Sebastián → *Population 14,411.*

Four kilometres from the turning to Ilobasco, further south along the Pan-American Highway at **Santo Domingo** (Km 44 from San Salvador), a paved road leads for 5 km to San Sebastián, where colourfully patterned cloth hammocks and bedspreads are made. You can watch them being woven on complex looms of wood and string. Behind **Funeraria Durán** there is a weaving workshop. Sr Durán will take you past the caskets to see the weavers. The **Casa de Cultura**, about 50 m from the plaza, will direct you to weaving centres and give information on handicrafts. Before buying, check prices and beware of overcharging. Market day is on Monday.

San Vicente → *Colour map 3, C1. Population: 53,213.*

Founded in 1635, San Vicente is 61 km from the capital and lies a little southeast of the Highway on the Río Alcahuapa, at the foot of the double-peaked **Volcán San Vicente** (or **Chinchontepec**), with very fine views of the Jiboa valley to the west. The town enjoys a lovely setting and is a peaceful place to spend a night or two. Its pride and joy is **El Pilar** (1762-1769), the most original church in the country. It was here that the local chief, **Anastasio Aquino**, took the crown from the statue of San José and crowned himself King of the Nonualcos during the rebellion of 1832.

El Pilar stands on a small square 1½ blocks south of the Parque Central. On the latter is the **cathedral**, whose nave is draped with golden curtains. In the middle of the main plaza is a tall, open-work **clock tower**, quite a landmark when descending the hill into the city. Three blocks east of the main plaza is the *tempisque* tree under which the city's foundation

San Vicente

To Pan American Highway & San Salvador

Sleeping 🛌
Central Park **2**

Eating 🍴
Acapulco **1**
Comedor Rivolí **2**

200 metres
200 yards

charter was drawn up. The tree was decreed a national monument on 26 April 1984. There's an extensive market area a few blocks west of the centre and hammock sellers are on nearby streets. An army barracks takes up an entire block in the centre. There's a small **war museum**; ask the FMLN office here or in San Salvador. Carnival day is 1 November.

Around San Vicente

Three kilometres southeast of the town is the **Balneario Amapulapa** ⓘ *T2393-0412, US$0.80 entry and US$0.90 parking charges, a Turicentro*. There are three pools at different levels in a wooded setting. The tourist police patrols here and lately it's been considered a safe place for tourists, although women should not walk to the area alone. Reached by bus No 177 from Zacatecoluca bus station, and by pickup from the San Vicente Bus station. **Laguna de Apastepeque** ⓘ *T2389-7172*, near San Vicente off the Pan-American Highway, is small but picturesque. Take bus No 156 from San Vicente, or 499 from San Salvador. Ask in San Vicente for guides for climbing the San Vicente volcano.

San Miguel → Colour map 3, C2. Population: 218,410.

Set at the foot of the **Volcán San Miguel** (**Chaparrastique**), which last erupted in 1976 but has shown activity ever since, San Miguel is the third largest city in El Salvador, 136 km from San Salvador. The capital of its Department, the town was founded in 1530 as a military fortress by Don Luis de Moscoso. It now has one of the fastest growing economies in Central America, has two shady plazas: **Parque David J Guzmán**, containing the bare 18th-century cathedral, and the adjacent **Plaza Barrios**, flanked by overflowing market stalls. The city's **theatre** dates from 1909, but since the 1960s it has been used for various purposes other than the arts. After several years of restoration it reopened in 2003 in all its original glory. There is a Metrocentro shopping centre southeast of the centre, on Avenida Roosevelt Sur and the **Turicentro of Altos de la Cueva** ⓘ *T2669-0699*, is 1 km north (take bus No 94 in front of the cathedral in San Miguel, US$0.80). It offers swimming pools, gardens, restaurants, sports facilities and bungalows for rent (US$34), and is busy at weekends.

The arid climate all year round makes the region ideal for growing maize, beans, cotton and sisal, and some silver and gold are mined here. However, the biggest industry is the *remesas* (money received from family members who have emigrated to the US), as this part of the country experienced heavy migration both during and after the civil war.

The fiesta de la Virgen de la Paz is on the last Saturday in November, and one of the biggest carnivals in Central America, known as *El Carnaval de San Miguel*, also takes place here. The free festival features parades and marching bands filing down Avenida Roosevelt to the city centre, from 1900 until late. For more information contact the **Comite de Festejos** ⓘ *T2660-1326*. Apart from this event, San Miguel is not a place you're likely to want to linger; thee are traffic-clogged streets, stinking gutters, a hot, sticky climate and few conventional tourist attractions.

Routes from San Miguel → For listings, see pages 472-475.

Several routes radiate outwards from San Miguel. A paved road runs south to the Pacific Highway. Go south along it for 12 km, where a dirt road leads to Playa El Cuco (bus 320 from San Miguel, US$1.50). A mainly paved, reasonable road goes to west to San Jorge and Usulután: leave the Pan-American Highway 5 km west of San Miguel, where the road passes hills and coffee plantations with good views of the San Miguel volcano.

Another route heads northeast to the small town of Jocorro, where the road splits with options to Honduras. Heading north, San Francisco Gotera leads to the Perquín crossing; east of Jocorro the road leads to the border crossing at El Amatillo; and directly east from San Miguel lies La Unión, with connections north to El Amatillo.

San Francisco Gotera and around

The capital of Morazán Department can be reached directly from the Oriente terminal in San Salvador, or from San Miguel (bus No 328). There are places to stay (see Sleeping, page 472).

Beyond San Francisco, the road runs to **Jocaitique** (there is a bus) from where an unpaved road climbs into the mountains through pine forests to **Sabanetas**, near the Honduran border. Accommodation is available at Jocaitique and Sabanetas.

Northeast of San Francisco is **Corinto** ① *20 mins north of the village on foot, just east of the path to the Cantón Coretito, open daily*, which has two rock overhangs showing faint evidence of pre-Columbian wall paintings. Take an early bus, No 327, from San Miguel, US$1.

San Miguel

N
200 metres
200 yards

Sleeping	El Mandarín **6**	Plaza Floresta **1**
China House **2**	King Palace **3**	Trópico Inn **8**
Comfort Inn Real **4**	Motel Millián **5**	Victoria **10**

Ciudad Segundo Montes and around

Eight kilometres north of San Francisco Gotera is Ciudad Segundo Montes, a group of villages housing 8500 repatriated Salvadorean refugees (the community is named after one of the six Jesuit priests murdered at the Central American University in November 1989). Schafic Vive is a small museum with information on the community. If you wish to visit contact **PRODETUR** ⓘ *T2680-4086*, for information. No formal accommodation is available.

Fourteen kilometres north of San Francisco is **Delicias de la Concepción**, where fine decorated hammocks and ceramics are made. The prices are good and the people are helpful; worth a visit. Buses every 20 minutes from San Francisco.

Perquín and around → *Colour map 3, C2. Altitude: 1200 m. Population: 3158.*

Perquín – meaning 'Road of the Hot Coals'– is 205 km from San Salvador and was the guerrillas' 'capital', and the scene of much military activity. War damage used to be visible around the town, but all is now peaceful and the scenery is very beautiful, surrounded by pine-topped mountains. There is a small central square with a Casa de la Cultura, and post office. Opposite is the plain Iglesia Católica Universal Progresista, next to which is POLITUR, the very helpful and friendly police station. The police may give you a lift to the tourist office, below, now that it has rather inconveniently moved. It is now on the outskirts of town, past the turn-off to **La Posada de Don Manuel**, jointly run by **PRODETUR** and **Perkin Tours travel agency** ⓘ *T2680-4311, www.rutadepazelsalvador.com, Mon-Fri 0800-1700*.

The **Museo de la Revolución** ⓘ *T7942-3721, daily 0800-1700, US$1.20, no photos or filming allowed, guided tours in Spanish, camping permitted, US$1*, clearly signposted from the plaza, has temporary exhibits as well as one on Archbishop Romero and all the gory details of his murder – nothing is spared. The museum, run by ex-guerrillas, is badly lit, but fascinating with photographs, propaganda posters, explanations, objects, pictures of the missing, and military paraphernalia. In the garden is the wreckage of an American-made helicopter, shot down by guerrillas in 1984. Sprawled like a piece of modern art, it would look at home in a contemporary art gallery. There is also a room where a recreated cabin shows the place from where the clandestine radio *Venceremos* broadcast their programmes during the war.

Behind the town is the **Cerro de Perquín** ⓘ *US$0.25 to climb, it is advisable to bring a guide*. The views are fantastic with the town below nestling in the tropical scenery, green parrots flying through the pine trees, and the mountains stretching towards the border with Honduras. The **Festival de Invierno**, 1-6 August, is a mixture of music, exhibitions and film. Book accommodation in advance if planning to come for the festival. The **Festival de San Sebastián** is on 21-22 January, and the celebration of the **Virgen del Tránsito**, the patron saint of the church, takes place 14-15 August.

Nearby villages such as Arambala and El Mozote can be visited, or you can take a walking tour. At **El Mozote** is a memorial to a massacre that took place in 1981, during which more than 800 people, among them children and babies, were brutally murdered. Five kilometres west of Perquín is **Arambala**, which is slowly being rebuilt. Locals will give you a tour (free, but tips appreciated) of the town and church, which has been largely rebuilt since being destroyed by fire in the 1980s; a sad and deeply moving experience, well worth the effort. Opposite the church is a small crafts shop run by a local women's cooperative, some of whom are also guides. Near Perquín, turn-off 2 km south, are the park and trails of **Cerro Pelón**. Nearby is **El Llano del Muerto**, a tourist area of naturally heated pools and wells. North of Perquín, straddling the border with Honduras, is one of the few unpolluted rivers in the country. The people of Morazán are more reserved with strangers than in the rest of El Salvador. If travelling on your own, 4WD is advised.

Ruta de Paz run by **Perkin Tours** ① *T2680-4086, perkintours@yahoo.es, daily 0800-1700, 0800-2100 during the winter festival*, provides walks, culture and adventure tourism, and can organize accommodation. Tours last for between 25 minutes and two days, and are for one to 10 people. Ask for Serafín Gómez, who is in charge of the tours.

Santa Rosa de Lima → *Population: 27,693.*

The shortest route from San Miguel to the Honduran border takes the Ruta Militar northeast through Santa Rosa de Lima to the Goascarán bridge at El Amatillo, a total of 58 km on paved road.

Santa Rosa is a charming little place with a wonderful colonial church set in the hillside. There are gold and silver mines, a market on Wednesday, and a curiously large number of pharmacies and shoe shops. The FMLN office has details about the **Codelum Project**, a refugee camp in Monte Barrios. The fiesta is on 22-31 August.

La Unión → *For listings, see pages 472-475. Colour map 3, C2. Population: 34,045.*

It is another 42 km from San Miguel to the port of La Unión, on the Gulf of Fonseca. The spectacular setting on the west shore of the gulf does little to offset the heat and the faded glory of this port town which handles half the country's trade. Shortly before entering the town, the Pan-American Highway turns north for 33 km to the Goascarán bridge at **El Amatillo** on the border with Honduras (see box, page 420). A project to inaugurate the modern port of La Unión is scheduled to happen in the near future. This huge project includes foreign investments, such as a large Spanish tuna fish processing plant, with supporting infrastructure including new roads, hotels and a school running training in logistics and tourism.

Around la Unión

Conchagua is worth visiting to see one of the few old colonial churches in the country, and there is a good bus service from La Unión (No 382, US$0.10). The church was begun in 1693, after the original Conchagua had been moved to its present site following repeated attacks on the island settlements by the English. There are fiestas on 18-21 January and 24 July. There is also **Volcán Conchagua** (1243 m) which can be climbed but is a hard walk, particularly near the top where protective clothing is useful against the vegetation. It's about four hours up and two hours down, but you will be rewarded with superb views over Volcán San Miguel to the west and the Gulf of Fonseca, which is bordered by El Salvador, Honduras and Nicaragua (where the Cosigüina volcano is prominent) to the east.

In the Gulf of Fonseca are the Salvadorean islands of **Isla Zacatillo**, **Isla Conchagüita** and the largest, **Isla Meanguera** (about 4 km by 7 km). English and Spanish pirates occupied Isla Meanguera in the late 1600s, and international claims remained until the International Court of Justice in The Hague awarded the island to El Salvador in 1992, in preference to claims from Honduras and Nicaragua.

A *lancha* leaves La Unión for the town of **Meanguera del Golfo**, on Meanguera. The journey across the gulf is beautiful – tranquil waters, fishing boats and views to the surrounding mountains. The island has secluded beaches with good bathing, for example Majahual (a 45-minute walk), fringed with palm trees. About 2400 people live on this carefree island, where painted boats float in the cove surrounded by small *tiendas* and *comedores* that serve fish, shark and prawns. The highest point on the island is **Cerro de Evaristo** at 512 m. Launches leave La Unión daily at 1000, or private boats may leave earlier when full; the journey takes 45 minutes. It's possible to arrange transport with a local boatman to Coyolito (Honduras), Isla Amapala, or for day trips around the gulf (about US$80), but make sure the price is agreed beforehand. You can travel to Honduras or Nicaragua if you have visited immigration in La Unión first to get the necessary paperwork.

◉ Eastern El Salvador listings

For Sleeping and Eating price codes and other relevant information, see Essentials pages 31-33.

● Sleeping

San Vicente *p467, map p467*
D-E Central Park, on Parque Central, T2393-0383. Good, clean rooms, with bath, a/c and phone. Cheaper with fan, cheaper still without TV. Café and restaurant downstairs.
E Estancia Familiar, El Calvario (corner in front of Pollo Campero), budget option in town.

San Miguel *p468, map p469*
Most hotels are on the entrance roads, although there are plenty of cheap places near the bus station.
AL-A Hotel Comfort Inn Real, Av Roosevelt, in front of Metrocentro, T2600-0202, www.choicehotels.com. Comfortable, businesslike hotel, spick and span if spartan rooms, with a/c, cable TV; excellent buffet breakfast, tiny pool and adjacent bar/restaurant; laundromat. Convenient for Metrocentro mall, opposite.
B Hotel Plaza Floresta, Av Roosevelt Sur 704, T2640-1549, www.hotelplazafloresta.com. Pleasant, clean rooms facing central courtyard with tiny swimming pool; cable TV, Wi-Fi access. Handy location for nearby restaurants and nightlife.
B Trópico Inn, Av Roosevelt Sur 303, T2682-1082, tropicoinn@yahoo.com. Clean and comfortable, with reasonable restaurant, swimming pool, garden and safe parking for motorbikes. Recommended.

C El Mandarín, Av Roosevelt Norte, T2669-6969. A/c, pool, good Chinese restaurant.
C Motel Millián, Panamericana Km 136, in front of the Military Hospital, T2683-8100. Pool and a good restaurant. Recommended, value for money.
C Victoria, 8a Av Sur 101, El Calvario T2660-7208, hotelvictoriasanmiguel2008@hotmail.com. Private bath with a/c and cable TV.
D China House, 15 Av Norte, Pan-americana Km 137.5, T/F2669-5029. Clean, friendly.
E King Palace, opposite the bus station. Good breakfast.

San Francisco Gotera *p469*
C-E Hospedaje San Francisco, Av Morazán 29, T2654-0066. Nice garden and hammocks.

Perquín and around *p470*
B Hotel Perkin Lenca, Km 205.5 Carretera a Perquín, T/F2680-4080, www.perkinlenca.com. Cosy Swiss cabins with piping hot showers and thick blankets. Excellent meals in restaurant **La Cocina de Ma'Anita**, with panoramic terrace overlooking forested hills, open daily 0700-1900. US owner Ronald organizes tours to El Mozote with former guerrilla guides, a bit grim but very moving.
B Las Margaritas, T2613-1930, at the entrance to Perquín village.
C Arizona T2634-8990, at entrance to town on main street towards El Llano del Muerto.
D La Posada de Don Manuel, 5 mins from Perquín at the bottom of the hill, CTE Perquín T2680-4037. Previously called

El Gigante, countless partitioned rooms that would probably be noisy if full, but rarely are. Clean, with cold showers and meals. Have highly recommended restaurant and organize tours with guides. Friendly.
F Cocina Mama Toya y Mama Juana, at the entrance of Perquín village, T2680-4045. Small rooms with 3 beds, shared bath, parking.

Camping

It's possible to camp in the grounds of the **Museo de la Revolución**, near a crater formed by a 227-kg bomb dropped in Aug 1981. Ask in the nearby *tiendas*.

Near the Río Zapo, **PRODETUR**, T2680-4311, www.rutadepazelsalvador.com, has a great campground with facilities, and there are guides who can give you a tour of the area. Good for both trekking and hiking. There is also a simple cabin for rent here.

Santa Rosa de Lima *p471*

F Florida, Ruta Militar, T2641-2020. Helpful, fairly clean, basic, with 3 parking spaces (arrive early).
F Hospedaje Mundial, near the market. Basic rooms with fan. Friendly, lots of parking.
F Recreo, 2 blocks from town centre in front of police station and Telecom, 4 Av Norte, Barrio el Recreo, T2641-2126. Basic fan rooms, noisy but friendly. Recommended.

La Unión *p471*

E San Francisco, Calle General Menéndez 6-3, Barrio Concepción, T2604-4159. Clean and friendly, some rooms with hammocks and fan. Noisy and has some water supply problems, but OK. Safe parking.

Around La Unión *p471*

AL Hotel Joya del Golfo, Isla de Meanguera, T2648-0072. Wonderfully relaxing hotel in the next bay beyond the harbour (ask the *lancha* from La Unión to drop you off), run by extremely hospitable US-Salvadorean family. 4 lovely rooms, beautifully furnished, with 4-poster beds, a/c, cable TV and balcony. Excellent food in cosy family lounge, with

books, games and DVDs. Kayaks for guests and boat to nearby beaches (US$10), plus hikes around island. Reservations essential. Highly recommended.
D Hotel Paraíso, Meanguera del Golfo. Has rooms with TV, private bath and hot water. Recommended.

❷ Eating

Ilobasco *p466*

There are 2 pizzerias, several local *comedores*, a **Pollo Campero** and a **Taco Hut**.
❦ **Restaurante Ricky**, at 3 Av Sur. The town's only real restaurant with à la carte dining.

San Vicente *p467, map p467*

The San Vicente Gastronomical festival is held on the last Sat of the month at the central park. Close to Hotel Central Park are **Pops** and **La Nevería**, for good ice cream.
❦ **Acapulco**, by the central park. Good.
❦ **Casablanca**, next to the park, T2393-0549. Good shrimps, steaks, and you can swim in their pool for US$1.15.
❦ **Comedor Rivoli**, Av María de los Angeles Miranda. Good breakfast and lunches. Clean.
❦ **Evergreen**. Bar and restaurant. Wed-Sun.

San Miguel *p468, map p469*

Try *bocadillos de totopostes*, maize balls with either chilli or cheese; and *tustacos*, which are like small tortillas with sugar or honey. Both are delicious and traditional.
❦ **El Gran Tejano**, 4 Calle Pte, near the cathedral. Great steaks.
❦ **Restaurant Perkin Lenca**, Km 205.5 Carretera a Perquín, T/F2680-4080, www.perkinlenca.com. Daily 0700-2000. Part of the hotel of the same name, this restaurant serves traditional food.

Perquín and around *p470*

❦ **Antojitos Marisol**, T2680-4063, near the church on the south side of the plaza. Simple food and open late.

Comedor Blanquita, T2680-4223 near the church in the centre, *comida a la vista* and snacks.

La Cocina de Mi Abuela, at the entrance to town. T2502-2630, popular with locals with good, local dishes.

Santa Rosa de Lima *p471*

Martina, near the bridge. Good food including *sopa de apretadores* for US$7.

Chayito, Ruta Militar. Buffet, *comedor*.

La Unión *p471*

Bottled water is hard to find, but *agua helada* from clean sources is sold (US$0.25 a bag). There are several cheap *comedores* to choose from, try **Comedores Gallego** and **Rosita**, recommended. **Comedor Tere**, Av General Menéndez 2.2, is also fairly good.

Amanecer Marino, on the waterfront. Beautiful view of the bay and good for watching the world go by. Serves seafood.

Las Lunas, 3 blocks from the central park. Nice atmosphere. Very popular among locals.

Restaurante Puerto Viejo, located in front of El Dragón. Big portions, cheap. Best seafood in town – try *tazón de sopa de pescado*.

⊖ Transport

Cojutepeque *p466*

Bus No113 from Oriente terminal in **San Salvador** (US$0.80); buses leave from Cojutepeque on the corner of the plaza, 2 blocks from the main plaza.

San Sebastián *p467*

Bus No 110 from the Oriente terminal runs from San Salvador to San Sebastián (1½ hrs, US$1). There are also buses from Cojutepeque.

San Vicente *p467, map p467*

Bus No116 from Oriente terminal, **San Salvador**, every 10 mins or so (1½ hrs, US$0.90). Returning to the capital, catch bus from the bus station, Av Victoriano Rodríguez y Juan Crisóstomo Segovia; outside the cathedral; or on the road out of town. To **Zacatecoluca**, No 177 (US$0.50) from bus station. Buses to some local destinations leave from the street that runs west to east through the market. You have to take 2 buses to get to **San Miguel** (see below), the first to the Pan-American Hwy, where there is a bus and food stop, then another on to San Miguel (US$1.50 total).

San Miguel *p468, map p469*

Bus Nos 301, 306 and 346 from Oriente terminal, **San Salvador** US$2.50, every 30 mins from 0500 to 1630, 2½ hrs. There are also 3 comfortable express buses daily, 2 hrs, US$5.

There are frequent buses to the Honduran border at **El Amatillo**, US$1. 4 buses, No 332A, daily to **Perquín**, from 0600-1240, 2¾ hrs, US$1.60. Direct to Tegucigalpa, with King Quality Bus, T2271-0307, www.kingqualityca.com/, daily at 0830 and 1630, 6 hrs, US$35

Perquín and around *p470*

Bus From **San Miguel**, bus No 332A (2¾ hrs, US$1.50). The bus from Terminal Oriente in **San Salvador** (4½ hrs) is very crowded, luggage a hindrance. Bus or truck from **Cd Segundo Montes**. Transport back to Cd Segundo Montes or San Miguel may be difficult in the afternoons.

Car

If you're driving fill your tank before getting to Perquín because the last petrol station is 20 mins from the city and closes at 1700.

Santa Rosa de Lima *p471*

Bus To the Honduran border every 15 mins, US$0.50. Direct buses also to **San Salvador**, No 306, from 0400 until 1400, US$3.25, 3½ hrs.

La Unión *p471*

Bus The terminal is at 3 Calle Pte (block 3). To **San Salvador**, bus 304, US$2, 2-3 hrs, many daily, direct or via San Miguel, 1 passes the harbour at 0300. Bus 324 to **San Miguel,** US$1. Bus to Honduran border at **El Amatillo,** No 353, US$1.80.

❻ Directory

San Vicente *p467, map p467*
Banks Banco Hipotecario on main plaza, exchange counter at side. Also branches of HSBC, Citi Bank and Banco Agrícola Casa de Cambio León, Calle Dr Antonio J Cañas, off northeast corner of main plaza. **Post** In Gobernación, 2 Av Norte y Calle 1 de Julio 1823. **Telephone** Telecom, 2 Av Norte/Av Canónigo Raimundo Lazo, southeast of plaza.

San Miguel *p468, map p469*
Banks Daily 0900-1600. Citi Bank will change TCs, but you must produce receipt of purchase. Banco Agrícola is next to Trópico Inn. Casa de Cambio Lego, 2 Calle Pte, overlooking market. **Police** Emergency T911.

La Unión *p471*
Banks Open daily 0900-1600. Scotiabank, HSBC and Western Union between bus terminal and harbour, have 24-hr ATMs. **Customs** 3 Av Norte 3.9. **Immigration** Av General Cabañas and 1 Av Norte. **Internet** Infocentro, 1 Calle Pte, 2-4 Av Norte, Mon-Fri. **Police** Opposite Immigration office.

Pacific coast

Running the length of the country to the south, the Pacific coastline is a blend of stunning views, quiet beaches and private resorts. If basking in the sun isn't enough, the coast is a big hit with the surf crowd as some of the best surfing spots are located in the departments of La Libertad and Las Flores in San Miguel. For a little more activity, you can go west and visit the impressive Parque Nacional El Imposible. Heading east towards Nicaragua, the islands of the Gulf of Fonseca are equally cut off. ➤➤ *For listings, see pages 480-484.*

La Libertad → *For listings, see pages 480-484. Colour map 3, C1. Population: 35,997.*

Just before Santa Tecla, a branch road turns south for 24 km to the small fishing port of La Libertad, 34 km from San Salvador and just 25 minutes from the Comalapa International Airport. This is a popular, laid-back seaside resort in the dry season but is not very clean. However, the whole area has been remodelled and now boasts an amphitheatre, soccer and basketball courts and a **Complejo Turístico** where the old naval building once stood, with a *malecón* and several restaurants. **Tourist office** ① *T2346-1634, Mon-Fri 0800-1600, Sat, Sun 0900-1300.* The pier is worth seeing for the fish market awnings and, when the fleet is in, for the boats hauled up out of the water along its length. The cemetery by the beach has tombstones painted in the national colours, blue and white. On the seafront are several hotels and restaurants. At a small plaza, by the **Punta Roca** restaurant, the road curves left to the point, offering fine views of La Libertad bay and along the coast. The market street is two blocks inland across from the central church. The coast to the east and west has good fishing, surfing and bathing. The beaches are black volcanic sand (which can get very hot).

La Libertad gets very crowded at weekends and holidays and for overnight stays the beaches to the west of La Libertad are better. Service can be off-hand. Dedicated surfers may wish to stay for a while, as the breaks at Punta Roca in Puerto La Libertad are rated among the best 10 in the world. The season runs from November to April and the surf is excellent. Watch your belongings on the beach and don't stay out alone late at night.

The town holds an annual **Gastronomic Festival** in early December and has resurrected the tradition of *lunadas* (full-moon parties) in the dry season. Bonfires are lit on the beach, restaurants stay open late offering *comida típica*, and some places provide live music and themed nights. Find local information in Spanish at www.puertolalibertad.com.

Around La Libertad

The **Costa del Bálsamo** (Balsam coast), running west from La Libertad and Acajutla, gives its name to the pain-relieving balsam, once a major export of the region. On the steep slopes of the departments of Sonsonate and La Libertad, scattered balsam trees are still tapped for their aromatic juices. Buses travel along the coast to Sonsonate (at 0600 and 1300) and the journey offers stunning views of the rugged volcanic coast. The municipalities of San Julián, Cuisnahuat, Ixhuatan, Tepecoyo, Talnique, Jayaque, Chiltuipan, Comasagua and Teotepeque are all situated along the balsam coast. On the road from San Salvador to La Libertad is **Plaza Turística Zaragoza** ① *Tue-Sun 1000-1900, where you will find handicrafts, restaurants and amenities for children.*

At the very entrance of Puerto La Libertad is the **El Faro** shopping center, with **Selectos** supermarket, a shoe shop, **Nevería** ice cream shop and fried chicken **Pollo Campero**.

The eastern end of La Libertad is **Playa La Paz or Punta Roca**, 2 km beyond which is **Playa Obispo**. About 1 km east of La Curva, on the right towards San Diego is the **Fisherman's Club** ⓘ *T2262-4444, entry US$6*, with pool, tennis courts and a good restaurant. The beach is good too, but beware of the rip tide; it's only advisable for surfers.

West of La Libertad → *For listings, see pages 480-484.*

Continuing west from **Playa Conchalío** at Km 38 you reach **Playa El Majahual**, which does not have a safe reputation, nor is it very clean, but offers good waves for surfing. A little further on is **Playa El Cocal** and **Playa San Blas**. On both beaches there are several hotels catering primarily for surfers. One of the most popular beaches for foreigners is **Playa El Tunco**. To get here take bus No 80 from La Libertad and get off at the turn-off where all the surfer hotels signs are posted (**Roca Sunzal** is the most visible one). It is then a short walk (a couple of blocks) to the seafront. This is one of the best surfing beaches in this area with the two breaks, El Sunzal and La Bocana, both easily accessible. **Club Salvadoreño** ⓘ *www.clubsalvadoreno.com*, and **Club Tecleño** both have their beach premises here and El Tunco itself has several hotels and restaurants.

Further up the road at Km 43.5 is **El Sunzal**. Although the breaks are amazing at Sunzal, the small hotels are not as safe as at El Tunco and there have been reports of theft on the beach at dusk, so choose to stay at El Tunco. The exception in El Sunzal is the luxury hotel **Casa de Mar**, which is located just in front of the breaks, and is an option if you want a splurge or to dine in their gourmet seafood restaurant, **Café Sunzal**, which has great food and panoramic views of the beach.

At Km 49.5 is **Playa Palmarcito**. This tiny and inviting beach is great for escaping the crowds and is good for novice surfers, as the breaks are not as violent as on other beaches. Located just in front of the beach is **Restaurante Las Palmas**, offering great meals and low prices. An option for a few night's stay is **Hotel El Palmarcito**, which also has a restaurant, surf board rental and classes. Perched atop a cliff next to Palmarcito is the **Atami Beach Club** ⓘ *T2223-9000, access for US and other non-Central American passport-holders is US$10, including a cabaña for changing*, a beautiful place with a large pool, private beach, expensive restaurant, two bars and gardens. At the turn-off to the beach along the highway (next to police station) is the **Hotel Bosques del Río** (same owner as **Restaurante Las Palmeras**), where you can ask for discounts for longer stays.

Just a couple of kilometres out of La Libertad on the Carretera Litoral is **Parque Nacional Walter Deininger** ⓘ *run by the Ministry of Tourism, T2243-7835, www.el salvador.travel, for more information contact ISTU on T2222-8000, www.istu.gob.sv*, simply present your passport at the gate. There are rivers and caves, and the park is great for hiking. There is even a seed bank for endangered tree species, an array of medicinal plants and a nursery. The views are fantastic and it's a good way to learn more about the flora and fauna, guides are available upon request.

At Km 53.5 is **Playa El Zonte**, is another favourite among foreign tourists. It's a bit safer and quieter than El Tunco, being further away from La Libertad. The top-notch surf breaks has made El Zonte a place people stay longer than anticipated, and there are several well-established hotels with restaurant service. There are also several informal, cheap cafés and room rentals down at the beach.

The Carretera Litoral continues for a further 40 km or so to Acajutla past rocky bays, remote black-sand beaches and through tunnels. Take great care if you bathe along this coast, as it can be dangerous.

Acajutla and around → *Colour map 3, C1. Population: 52,359.*

At the junction of San Julián, a short journey south from Sonsonate, the coastal road heads south to the lowland city of Acajutla, El Salvador's main port serving the western and central areas, 85 km from San Salvador (the port is 8 km south of the Coastal Highway). It is a popular seaside resort during the summer for Salvadoreans, but lodging in the village is not considered safe for foreigners. There are some good seafood restaurants with panoramic views.

The rocky beach of **Los Cóbanos** (14 km south of Acajutla via San Julián, bus from Sonsonate) is very popular with weekending Salvadoreans and has one of only two coral reefs along the entire Central American Pacific coast, making it a popular dive spot. Fishermen arrange boat trips; negotiate a price. José Roberto Suárez at **Los Cobanos Village Lodge** ① *T2420-5248, sas_tun@hotmail.com,* speaks English and can be of assistance when renting boats and diving equipment.

The paved coastal road heads west running along the coast for 43 km before reaching the Guatemalan frontier at **La Hachadura**.

The black-sand beaches northwest of Acajutla at **Metalío** and Costa Azul (mostly full of private beach houses) and **Barra de Santiago** are recommended, although there are few public facilities. Barra de Santiago is a peninsula, 30 km west of Acajutla, the beach is reached along a 7 km compact dirt road or across a beautiful lagoon. The entire area is a protected natural area is in the process of being declared an ecological reserve to protect endangered species, including turtles, crocodiles and sea falcons. The *garza azul* (blue heron) is one of the amazing rare birds only found here. The mangrove is the third largest in El Salvador. This beach has an island named **El Cajete,** which has an archaeological site dating back to around AD 900. There are several pyramids but the area has not been excavated. **El Capricho Beach House** ① *T2260-2481, same owners as Ximena's in San Salvador, see page 435,* has a beautiful beach-front hotel here (see Sleeping, page 481).

Parque Nacional El Imposible

① *Park entrance is US$6, payable at the gate. For more information contact Salvanatura office, 33 Av Sur 640, Col Flor Blanca, San Salvador, T2279-1515, www.salvanatura.org. Voluntary donation of US$4-5 a day. To get to the park, take the San Salvador–Sonsonate bus, and then bus No 259 to Cara Sucia. Pickups leave for the park at 1100 and 1400. From Guatemala and the border, regular buses heading for San Salvador pass through Cara Sucia from where you catch the 1100 and 1400 pickups.*

So called because of the difficulty of transporting coffee through its ravines and down to the coast, today this 'impossibility' has helped preserve some of the last vestiges of El Salvador's flora and fauna on the rocky slopes and forests of the coastal **Cordillera de Apaneca**. Mule trains used to travel through the region, navigating the steep passes from which the park takes its name.

Among the mammals are puma, ocelot, agouti and ant bear; the birds include black-crested eagle, white hawk and other birds of prey, black and white owls, and woodpeckers. There is also a wide variety of reptiles, amphibians and insects, the greatest diversity in the country. There are eight different strata of forest, and over 300 species of tree have been identified. There is a small visitor centre, and rivers and natural pools to swim in. Trained naturalist guides from the nearby community of San Miguelito accompany visitors into the park, helping to identify season specific trails and routes, and pointing out interesting plants, animals and other attractions along the way.

The second route to La Unión runs east through the southern cotton lands. It begins on a four-lane motorway to the airport at Comalapa. The first place of any importance is at Km 13, **Santo Tomás** where there are pre-Hispanic ruins at **Cushululitán**, a short distance north. A road to the east, rising to 1000 m, runs south of Lago de Ilopango to join the Pan-American Highway beyond Cojutepeque. From Santo Tomás it's 10 km on to **Olocuilta**, an old town famed for its church and known worldwide for its rice dough *pupusas*. It hosts a colourful market on Sundays under a great tree. Both Santo Tomás and Olocuilta can be reached by bus 133 from San Salvador. The highway to the airport crosses the Carretera Litoral (CA 2) near the towns of San Luis Talpa and Comalapa. The coastal road goes east, through Rosario de la Paz, across Río Jiboa and on to Zacatecoluca.

Costa del Sol
Just after Rosario, a branch road to the south leads to **La Herradura** (bus 153 from Terminal del Sur to La Herradura, US$1.25, 1½ hours) and the Playa Costa del Sol on the Pacific, which is being developed as a tourist resort. The beach is on a narrow peninsula, the length of which are private houses which prevent access to the sand until you reach the **Turicentro** ① *0800-1800*. Here, *cabañas* can be rented for the day or for 24 hours, but they are not suitable for sleeping. Playa Costa del Sol is crowded at weekends and holidays, as there are extensive sandy beaches. However, the sea has a mild undertow; so go carefully until you are sure. Expensive hotels are continuously popping up but prices are a bit over the top; budget travellers might choose some of the smaller hotels by Playa Los Blancos. On the road to Costa del Sol, there is also a great water park, **Atlantis Water Park** ① *Km 51, carretera Costa del Sol, T2211-4103, www.atlantis.com.sv, US$8*. It's on bus routes No 495 and 143 (every 15 minutes). Options from San Salvador, include hotel pickup, small lunch and entrance from US$15-20.

Isla Tasajera
At the southeast end of the Costa del Sol road, near the **Pacific Paradise** hotel, a ferry (US$1.75) leaves for Isla Tasajera in the Estero de Jaltepeque (tidal lagoon). For boat excursions, take the Costa del Sol bus to the last stop at La Puntilla and negotiate with the local boatmen. Boat hire for the day costs US$75, including pilot. It's a great trip into the lagoon, with mangroves, dolphin watching and trips up to the river mouth of the Río Lempa (the longest river in the country).

Zacatecoluca → *Colour map 3, C1. Altitude: 201 m. Population: 65,826.*
The capital of La Paz Department is 56 km from San Salvador by road and 19 km south of San Vicente. This is a good place to buy hammocks (for example nylon 'doubles', US$13). José Simeón Cañas, who abolished slavery in Central America, was born here. There is a cathedral in the Moorish style and an excellent art gallery as well as a mall with a supermarket and several stores.

Ichanmichen
① *Admission and car parking US$0.75 per person, bungalow rental US$4.*
Near the town is the park and Turicentro of Ichanmichen ('the place of the little fish'). It is crossed by canals and decorated with natural spring pools where you can swim. It is very hot but there is plenty of shade.

Usulután, Playa El Espino and Laguna El Jocotal → *Colour map 3, C2.*

About 110 km from the capital is Usulután, capital of its department. It's a large, dirty and unsafe place, and only useful as a transit point (bus 302 from San Salvador, US$1.40). The coastal highway goes direct from Usulután to La Unión.

Playa El Espino can be reached from Usulután, by car (4WD), pickup or slow bus; it is very remote but lovely. Some small hotels and restaurants operate, but most only at weekends. To visit the reserve, enquire at the entrance; hire a boat to see more.

Beyond Usulután, the impressive silhouette of **Volcán Chaparrasque** rises out of the flat coastal plain. Two roads go northeast to San Miguel, the first from 10 km along at El Tránsito, the second a further 5 km east, which keeps to the low ground south and east of Volcán San Miguel. Two kilometres beyond this turning on the Carretera Litoral is a short road to the right leading to Laguna El Jocotal, a national nature reserve supported by the World Wildlife Fund, which has an abundance of birds and snakes.

Playa El Cuco and around
ⓘ *Bus No 320 to San Miguel, US$0.45, 1 hr, last bus 1600.*

About 12 km from the junction for San Miguel there is a turning to the right leading in 7 km to Playa El Cuco, a popular beach with several cheap places to stay near the bus station. The main beach is liable to get crowded and dirty at weekends and holidays, but is deserted mid-week. Single women should take care here; locals warn against walking along the beach after sunset. Cases of malaria have been reported. Another popular beach, **El Tamarindo**, is reached by following the coastal road a little further before taking a right turn.

◉ Pacific coast listings

For Sleeping and Eating price codes and other relevant information, see Essentials pages 31-33.

◉ Sleeping

La Libertad *p476*

B Pacific Sunrise, Calle Obispo, entrance of La Libertad, T2346-2000, www.hotelesel salvador.com. Hotel with pool, restaurant and rooms overlooking the Obispo beach, which can be accessed via an ingenious pedestrian overpass. Best hotel in La Libertad and good rates if more people share the rooms.
C Rick, behind **Punta Roca**. Clean rooms with bath. Friendly, good value. Has a restaurant.
D Hotel Surf Club, 2 Calle Pte 22-9. Big rooms, a/c, kitchen area. Supermarket downstairs.
F Comedor Margoth. Run-down but clean.

West of La Libertad *p477*
Playa El Conchalío
C El Malecón de Don Lito, T2355-3201. Good for children, plenty of space.
C Los Arcos del Mediterráneo, T2335-3490, www.hotelmedplaz.com.sv. 300 m from beach. A/c, TV, safe and quiet, with pool, garden and restaurant.

Playa El Majahual
B Hotel El Pacífico, T2310-6504. Pool, restaurant.
D Hotel y Restaurante Santa Fe, at the entrance to the Majahual beach, T2310-6508. Safe and nice, with pool. Recommended, relaxing and safe.

Playa El Cocal
C Punta Roca Surf Resort, T2300-0474, www.puntaroca.com.sv. Owned by National Champion Jimmy Rotherham, Punta Roca is an option for surfers (the beach has rocks!).

Playa El Sunzal

E El Hostal at the entrance of Playa El Sunzal run by a couple of guys from the US.

F Roots Camping, Km 42, Carretera Litoral, next to **Restaurante Roca Sunzal**, fruboza@ hotmail.com. Campsite with thatched-roof terrace for tents and hammocks.

Playa San Blas and Playa El Tunco

C Hotel Mopelia, T2389-6265, www.hotel mopelia-salvador.com. Owned by Frenchman Gilles, is a popular spot, also for its bar (open all week) and new pizzeria **Tunco Veloz**.

C Roca Sunzal, Km 42, T2389-6126, www.rocasunzal.com. Best hotel in El Tunco, beautifully located in front of the beach. Great views, pool, good food in restaurant. Value for money. They now have new suites with artsy and original decor. Good service. Recommended.

D La Guitarra, www.surfingeltunco.com, T2389-6390. 18 rooms with and without a/c, discounts for longer stays, Wi-Fi.

D Sol Bohemio, T7887-6241, www.sol bohemio.com. Reasonable rates, as do a couple of the smaller hostels, such as **Barriles**.

E La Sombra, info@lasombradelarte.com. Rooms with a/c and fan.

E Papayas Lodge, T2389-6231, www.papayalodge.com. Family-run surf hostel. Clean rooms with fans, use of kitchen and safe. Owned by Salvadorean surf legend, Papaya. Board sales and repair and surf classes. Recommended.

F Casa Tamanique, a couple of blocks up the road from El Tubo, fernandosgallegos@ yahoo.com. Newcomer with a tiny hostel.

Playa Palmarcito

C Atami Beach Club, Km 49.5, T2335-7301, www.atami.com.sv. Good rooms. Swimming pool and water slide. Seafood restaurant. In the grounds of the club is a private *rancho*.

D El Palmarcito, T7942-4879, www.elpal marcito.com, surf lessons, board rental, restaurant, beachfront.

Playa El Zonte

E Esencia Nativa, T7737-8879, www.esencianativa.com. Run by surfer Alex Novoa, with cheap rooms, dorm and pool. Popular restaurant serves range of options, including great veggie food and is busy at weekends. Surfing lessons and board rentals available. Popular with surfers.

E Horizonte Surf Camp, T2323-0099, saburosurfcamp@hotmail.com. Simple bungalows, some with a/c, nice garden, pool, restaurant, board rental, clean, good service. Good choice for surfers. Beach-front restaurant offers good food. Room for up to 6 people on the 3rd floor. Great view.

E La Casa de Frida Hotel, T2302-6068, www.lacasadefrida.com. Lodging in cabins behind restaurant with beachfront garden. Cosy place with hammocks.

Acajutla and around *p478*

L La Cocotera Resort & Ecolodge, Barra de Santiago, T2245-3691, www.lacocotera resort.com. Rates per person are fully inclusive – full-board and airport transfers. Small luxurious resort with thatched bungalows on the beach and with mangroves behind; swimming pool, kayaks, and tours available. Very peaceful, recommended.

B Los Cóbanos Village Lodge, Carretera Acajutla, turn right at **Restaurant Marsolie**, T2420-5248, www.loscobanos.com.sv. Beachfront cabins with pool and restaurant. Scuba-diving, surfing, fishing on offer. TV and internet available.

C-E Capricho Beach House, Barra de Santiago (same owners as **Ximena's**, see page 435), contact T2260-2481, www.ximenasguesthouse.com (under: Capricho). Private rooms with bath and a/c, cabin with dorms and ceiling fan, clean and safe. Beautiful beach and located in a wildlife reserve, close to mangroves and the tip of the peninsula. Tours of the mangroves, fishing, surf lessons and board rental all available. Transport from the capital and tours to **Parque Nacional El Imposible** available. Recommended. Take direct bus

No 285 to La Barra de Santiago, which departs twice daily from Sonsonate, or bus towards border and pickup from turn-off.

Parque Nacional El Imposible p478
C Hostal El Imposible, T2411-5484. With restaurant/bar area, swimming pool and small trail. 5 cabins sleeping 2-6 people have private bath, hot water and small terrace, also restaurant service. Information from **Salvanatura** in San Salvador, T2279-1515. www.salvanatura.org.

Costa del Sol p479
Cheaper accommodation can be found 1 km east at Playa Los Blancos and in La Herradura.
B Izalco Cabaña Club. 30 rooms and a pool. Good value, seafood is a speciality.
C Izalco Cabaña Club, T2338-2006 also has another hotel at Playa Torola.
E Miny Hotel y Restaurant Mila, Km 66, opposite police station. Very friendly, owner Marcos speaks English. Clean, simple, fan, pool, good food, beach access. Take bus No 495 from Terminal Sur, San Salvador; buses are very crowded at weekends, but the resort is quiet during the week.

Playa El Cuco and around p480
C Trópico Club, 2.5 km along the coast from Playa El Cuco, T2682-1073, tropicoinn@yahoo.com. Several cabins, pool and open-air dining. Leads directly to the beach. Run by the **Trópico Inn** in San Miguel (T2661-1800) see page 472.
E Cucolindo, 1 km along the coast, T2619-9012, hotelcucolindo@hotmail.com. Basic cabin for 4, with cold water. Mosquitos.
E Los Leones Marinos, El Cuco, T2619-9015. Clean and tidy with bath.

Playa Las Flores
LL-AL Las Flores Surf Resort, close to Playa El Cuco, T2619-9118, www.lasflores resort.com. Run by surf expert Rodrigo Barraza, boutique hotel, catering mostly for foreign tourists making an excellent choice for an upscale budget.

Playa Torola
C Torola Cabaña Club, Km 175, T2681-5528. Pool looking out to sea, great open-air bar/restaurant, friendly. Welcoming owner, recommended.

Playa El Tamarindo
C Tropi Tamarindo, T2682-1073, www.tropico inn.com.sv. Run by the **Trópico Inn** in San Miguel (T2661-1800), see page 472.

● Eating

La Libertad p476
There are cheap restaurants near the pier, in the market, and around Playa La Paz, Playa El Obispo and El Sunzal. An area with new buildings located where the old Marina used to be close to the pier now hosts a series of great seafood eateries.
♈ El Nuevo Altamar, 4 Calle Pte, Playa La Paz, T2335-3235. Good for seafood, steaks and bird.
♈ Mariscos Freddy and **La Marea**, on the beach at Playa Obispo. Good-value seafood restaurants.
♈-♈ Punta Roca, 5 Av Sur, T2335-3261. Mon-Fri 0800-2000, Sat and Sun 0800-2300. Try the shrimp soup. Owned by American ex-pat Robert Rotherham, father of the national surf champion Jimmy Rotherham.

Around La Libertad p476
East of the El Faro mall at the entrance there is a strip with very good restaurants. 2 of the best are:
♈ La Curva de Don Gere, T2335-34360. Legendary place run by Geremias Alvarado with several outlets in El Salvador (and the US). One of the trademarks is their seafood cream chowder in huge sizes including king crab legs and other goodies.
♈ La Dolce Vita, Playa Las Flores, 200 m east of the Shell gas station, T2335-3592. Excellent seafood and pasta restaurant.

West of La Libertad *p477*
El Sunzal
Around the Sunzal area are several very good restaurants, such Hola Beto's, Las Pamas Mirador and La Curva de Don Gere. All have beautiful vistas along the coast.

† **Café Sunzal**, Km 43.5 Carretera, T2389-6019, www.cafesunzal.com. Great seafood and steak house, exquisite international cuisine. Excellent views over El Sunzal beach.

Playa San Blas and Playa El Tunco
Tunco is on the rise and new places keep popping up.

† **Hotel and Restaurante Roca Sunzal**. Delicious seafood and a very good bar. All with an excellent beachfront location. Recommended.

† **Hotel Mopelia** (see Sleeping) has a pizzeria and their well-stocked bar is open all week.

†-† **La Bocana**, in front of the Tunco (pig). Owned and operated by Luis who's very friendly. Beachfront, offering great view from 2nd storey. Good seafood, great value.

† **Dale Dale Café**, behind Roca Sunzal. Coffee shop serving delicious brownies, muffins and coffee to go with it.

† **Erika**, T2389-6054. Run by owner Amelia Hernández. Very popular with the locals. 2nd-storey palm hatch with great atmosphere.

El Zonte
† **Esencia Nativa** (see Sleeping). Run by charismatic Alex Novoa, Esencia Nativa has an innovative menu, including good veggie options and pizzas, served at the poolside. Folks in the know come down from the capital just to get a bite.

† **Horizonte Surf Resort**. A nice restaurant at the beachfront run by Japanese Saburo. The view from 2nd floor is especially lovely. Good value.

† **La Casa de Frida**, El Zonte, T2253-2949, www.lacasadefrida.com. A great restaurant located in a large beachfront garden dotted with tables and hammocks.

Costa del Sol *p479*
† **Restaurante Kenny Mar**, Km 60, Carretera Costa del Sol, Playa San Marcelino, T2338-2578. Delicious seafood with beachfront view.

▲ Activities and tours

La Libertad *p476*
Watersports
Look for board rentals and surf lessons at hostels on the coast west of Puerto La Libertad. Also look at www.sunzal.com, which offers great surfing tours combined with photography by local photographer, El Vaquero.

Punta Roca, restaurant in La Libertad, T2335-3261 www.puntarocarockets.com. Owner Robert Rotherham (father of Surf Champion Jimmy Rotherham) runs surfboard rental, including boards for both pros and beginners (see website for details). He also arranges excursions including deep-sea fishing for up to 3 people, see www.punta roca.com.sv (which features webcam of area, surf and weather report) for more information. English spoken. Recommended.

⊖ Transport

La Libertad *p476*
Bus The station for the buses going down to Puerto La Libertad is now located at the 17th Av Sur at the intersection of Blv Venezuela by the general cemetery in San Salvador. The buses going to San Salvador from Puerto La Libertad leave from the terminal at the entrance of the city centre by the ball courts. Departures from Puerto La Libertad along the coast to Sonsonate at 0600.

For beaches around Acajutla and west, take the direct bus from Terminal de Occidente to Sonsonate and then on: No 285 to **Barra de Santiago**, No 28 to **Cara Sucia** and the border and No 252 to **Acajutla**.

For **Costa del Sol**, **Zacatecoluca** and connections toward eastern beaches go from Terminal del Sur by San Marcos in San Salvador.

Acajutla and around *p478*
Bus No 207 from Terminal Occidente, San Salvador (US$2.80), or No 252 from Sonsonate (US$0.30). 58 km from **Santa Ana**.

Zacatecoluca *p479*
Bus No133 from Terminal Sur, **San Salvador**. Direct bus to **La Libertad** 1540 (US$0.85), or take San Salvador bus, change at Comalapa, 2 hrs.

Playa El Cuco and around *p480*
Boat Boat from El Tamarindo across the bay leads to a short cut to **La Unión**.

Bus From **La Unión**, 20 mins.

❶ Directory

La Libertad *p476*
Banks There are no credit card facilities or international ATMs in La Libertad. Banco de Fomento Agropecuario, Mon-Fri 0800-1600, Sat 0800-1200. Also has **Western Union**. HSBC, takes TCs. **Internet** Infocentros, in main street close to Puerto Bello, cheap. **Language school** 5 Av Norte, close to Punta Roca restaurant, T2449-0331, salvaspanischool@mailcity.com. **Police** Calle Gerardo Barrios and 1 Av Sur. **Tourism police,** based here and patrol the town and beach areas at weekends. A tourist kiosk is in the new, gleaming white complex opposite the fish market pier, Mon-Fri 0800-1600, Sat and Sun 0900-1300, T2346-1634. **Post** Up the side of the Telecom office, 0800-1200, 1400- 1700. **Telephone** Telepunto, next to Hotel Puerto Bello, 2 Calle Pte (0630-0830). Cheap rates. **Telecom** on same road.

Contents

Footprint features

Honduras

At a glance

⊖ **Getting around** Buses, flights to cut out long journeys. Boats to the Bay Islands from La Ceiba, and to Belize from Puerto Cortés.

◎ **Time required** You could easily spend 3 weeks exploring.

☀ **Weather** Wettest Aug-Dec. From Jan-Mar it's chilly in the central highlands at night, hot on the coast.

✖ **When not to go** Rainy season if you don't like getting wet.

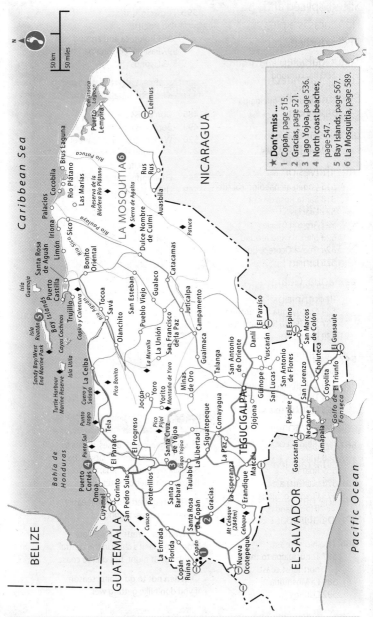

BELIZE

GUATEMALA

Caribbean Sea

Copán Ruinas
La Entrada
Florida
Copán
Cusuco
San Pedro Sula
Omoa
Cuyamel
Corinto
Puerto Cortés
Bahía de Honduras
El Paraíso
Punta Sal
Tela
Punto Izopo
Cuero y Calentura
Pico Bonito
La Ceiba
Trujillo
Cayos Cochinos
Puerto Castilla
Isla Guanoja
Isla Utila
Isla Roatán
Bay Islands
Sandy Bay/West End Marine Reserve
Turtle Harbour Marine Reserve
Capiro y Calentura
Santa Rosa de Aguán
Limón
Río Aguán
Savá
Tocoa
Bonito Oriental
Iriona
Sico
Río Sico
Palacios
Cocobila
Brus Laguna
Río Plátano
Las Marías
Reserva de la Biósfera Río Plátano
Puerto Lempira
Caratasca Lagoon
Leimus

LA MOSQUITIA

Potrerillos
El Progreso
Santa Bárbara
Santa Rosa de Copán
Gracias
Mt Celaque (2849m)
Celaque
Nueva Ocotepeque
Taulabé
Lago Yojoa
Santa Cruz de Yojoa
Pico Pijol
Jocón
Yorito
Montaña de Yoro
Yoro
La Muralla
Olanchito
La Unión
Pueblo Viejo
San Esteban
San Francisco de la Paz
Gualaco
Catacamas
Dulce Nombre de Culmi
Sierra de Agalta
Patuca
Río Patuca
Rus Rus
Auasbila

La Esperanza
Erandique
Nueva Ocotepeque
Siguatepeque
La Libertad
Comayagua
Minas de Oro
La Unión
Juticalpa
Campamento
Guaimaca
Talanga
San Antonio de Oriente
Danlí
El Paraíso
El Espino

EL SALVADOR

La Paz
Malcala
Marcala
Ojojona
Pespire
Guinope
San Lucas
San Antonio de Flores
San Lorenzo
Coyolita
Nacaome
Goascorán
Amapala
Golfo de Fonseca
Yuscarán
Choluteca
San Marcos de Colón
El Triunfo
El Guasaule

TEGUCIGALPA

NICARAGUA

Pacific Ocean

★ Don't miss ...
1 Copán, page 515.
2 Gracias, page 521.
3 Lago Yojoa, page 536.
4 North coast beaches, page 547.
5 Bay Islands, page 567.
6 La Mosquitia, page 589.

N
50 km
50 miles

Sliced, spliced and spread across a mountainous interior, Honduras is a pleasantly challenging surprise that has developed in curiously disconnected zones. In the heart of the mountains Tegucigalpa epitomizes the Latin city – a chaotic celebration of colonial architecture divided by steeply sloping cobbled streets. By contrast, the republic's second and more modern city, San Pedro Sula, on the coastal lowland plain, has a neat matrix of calles and avenidas that seem rather dull by comparison.

A world away, the Bay Islands bask under sunny skies. Utila thrives on a throw-it-together-and-see-if-it-works existence. It's easily the cheapest place to learn to dive in the western hemisphere.

Honduras is the second largest Central American republic after Nicaragua, but its population is smaller than that of neighbouring El Salvador, the smallest country. Bordered by Nicaragua, Guatemala, El Salvador and a narrow coastal Pacific strip, it is the northern Caribbean coast and beautiful Bay Islands that are a natural focus and a prime destination for visitors.

Inland, the mountainous terrain creates natural obstacles to easy, direct travel around the country. It also means that, for trekking and hiking, there are great swathes of beautiful hillside, much of which is dotted with small communities, largely disinterested in the comings and goings of the few travellers who venture so far off the beaten track.

In October 1998 Hurricane Mitch deluged Honduras with torrential rain leaving an estimated 10,000 people dead and damage to almost all parts of the country. While the physical damage has been cleaned up, 13 years on the economic and social impact continues to ripple through the country.

Essentials

Where to go

With the popularity of the Bay Islands as a diving destination, mainland Honduras is often missed in the frenzied rush towards the sea. And, while the beauty of the islands cannot be overstated, picking a route that takes in some of the smaller towns of Honduras gives a far better understanding of the country as a whole.

The capital, **Tegucigalpa**, has an old, colonial sector and a new section with modern hotels, shopping malls and businesses. Across the Río Choluteca is Tegucigalpa's twin city, **Comayagüela**, the working heart of the city with the markets and bus terminals. Around the capital, there are colonial villages, old mining towns, handicraft centres and good hiking areas, including **Parque Nacional La Tigra**, which will make ideal trips for a day or two.

West of Tegucigalpa, near the border with Guatemala, is Honduras' premier Maya archaeological site **Copán**, where new discoveries continue to be made, and some fine Maya art can be seen. A short distance from the site, the well-restored town of **Copán Ruinas** is a colonial gem and, nearby, the site of **El Puente** is beginning to reveal treasures hidden for centuries. Closer to the capital, quiet colonial towns such as **Gracias** and graceful **Santa Bárbara** are the site of opal mines, Lenca indigenous communities and the **national park** of **Mount Celaque**. There is lots of good hiking in the vicinity of the popular colonial city of **Santa Rosa de Copán**. A good way to explore this more traditional part of the country is to pick a route, travel in short distances and soak up the calm and tranquillity.

From Tegucigalpa a paved highway runs north to **San Pedro Sula**, the second city of the republic and the country's main business centre. The road passes the old colonial capital of Comayagua and beautiful Lago Yojoa. Northwest of San Pedro Sula, the **north coast** has a number of centres of interest to the visitor. The main port is **Puerto Cortés**, to the west of which is **Omoa**, an increasingly popular beach and fishing village with an old fort, from which an overland route enters Guatemala. East of San Pedro Sula are **Tela**, a more established resort, and **La Ceiba**, a good base for visiting the nearby national parks of Pico Bonito and Cuero y Salado, whitewater rafting trips on the Río Cangrejal and departure point for the Bay Islands and La Mosquitia. Further east, **Trujillo**, sitting at the southern end of a palm-fringed bay, was once the country capital.

Curving in an arc off the cost near La Ceiba, the **Bay Islands** of **Utila**, **Roatán** and **Guanaja**, plus the smaller **Hog Islands**, are some of Honduras' main tourist destinations. Travellers visiting just one part of Honduras often pick the islands. The diving is excellent and Utila is currently the cheapest dive centre in the Caribbean. The islands also have good beaches.

Northeast of Tegucigalpa is the province of Olancho, an agricultural and cattle-raising area that leads eventually to the Caribbean coast at Trujillo. Juticalpa and Catacamas are the main towns, and the mountains of the district have cloud forest, hiking trails and beautiful conservation areas. Beyond Olancho is **La Mosquitia**, most easily reached from La Ceiba, which is forested, swampy and very sparsely populated. Efforts are being made to promote sustainable development among the Miskito and the Pech. Small-scale ecotourism initiatives have been set up in some coastal communities and inland, making for adventurous and rewarding travel where the main ways of getting around are by boat, small plane or on foot.

Honduras' short **Pacific coast** on the Gulf of Fonseca is little visited, other than en route to Nicaragua and El Salvador. The main towns in the region are **Choluteca** and, in the gulf, **Amapala**, on the extinct volcanic Isla del Tigre. Another route to Nicaragua is that east of the capital through the town of **Danlí**, which passes the Panamerican Agricultural School at Zamorano and the old mining town of **Yuscarán**.

Suggested itineraries

The Honduran trail is pretty straightforward. Most people arrive from Guatemala and visit **Copán** with its nearby ruins and growing range of activities. From Copán it's a bus to San Pedro Sula and a quick change to continue to **Tela** or **La Ceiba**, both close to national parks. From La Ceiba the ferry leaves for **Roatán** and **Utila**, the budget travellers' choice for diving, snorkelling and island life. That trip will take about 10 days – add the flight or long bus journey to Tegucigalpa. From there, it's onwards to Nicaragua. If you have more time, a circular route goes to **Santa Rosa de Copán**, through **Gracias** to **Tegucigalpa**, and then from the capital to **Comayagua**, **Lago Yojoa** and **San Pedro Sula**. That will make your stay in Honduras close to three weeks – add one more if you want to visit **La Mosquitia**.

When to go

Climate depends largely on altitude. In Tegucigalpa, at 1000 m, temperatures range from 4°C (January-March) up to 33°C (April-May). In the lowlands to the north, temperatures in San Pedro Sula range from 20°C to 37°C with the coolest months being from November to February. On the Caribbean the dry season stretches from February to June, while the heaviest rains fall between August and December. Inland, rain falls throughout the year, with the drier months being from November to April. Some of the central highland areas enjoy a delightful climate, with a freshness that makes a pleasant contrast to the humidity and heat of the lowland zones.

What to do

Adventure tourism
Mountain biking is increasingly popular as is horse riding around Copán. Hardcore adventure can be found in the swamp wetlands and tropical forests of Mosquitia, usually by taking an organized tour.

Nature tourism
Nature trips take advantage of the wide variety of national parks. Birders have known about the treasures of the country for years, but hikers and trekkers are beginning to venture out through the valleys and across the hills that are often shrouded in cloud forest.

Scuba-diving
Diving off the Bay Islands has long been the number one attraction, with some of the best and most varied diving in Central America. PADI courses are among the cheapest in the world. Snorkelling is also excellent.

Whitewater rafting
Rafting is growing steadily in Honduras with the hotspot being the River Cangrejal, close to La Ceiba, where Grade II, III and IV rapids test both the novice and experienced paddler. The sport is relatively new to Honduras and more sites are sure to be found in the coming years.

Border essentials

Honduras–El Salvador
For crossings between Honduras and El Salvador (El Poy, El Amatillo, Perquín–Sabanetas), see page 420.

Honduras–Guatemala
For crossings between Honduras and Guatemala (El Florido, Entre Ríos–Corinto, Agua Caliente), see page 198.

Honduras–Nicaragua
Las Manos–Ocotal
Recommended as the best route between the capitals of Tegucigalpa and Managua. If driving, *tramitadores* will help you through the paperwork.
Currency exchange Better rates with money-changers on Nicaraguan side; best rates in Estelí.
Honduran immigration Open 0800-1600.
Nicaraguan immigration Open 24 hours. You must obtain a customs receipt for your luggage before presenting your passport and entry fees.
Onwards to Nicaragua Buses run every 30 minutes from Las Manos to Ocotal. From there, there are frequent connections to Estelí and Managua.
Onwards to Honduras Frequent direct connections with Tegucigalpa.

El Espino–Somoto
Border formalities are particularly tedious at this crossing. There are a few places to eat, but no hotels at the border itself.
Currency exchange Many money-changers; better rates in Nicaragua.
Honduran immigration Open 0800-1600, 100 m from the border.
Nicaraguan immigration Open 24 hours.
Onwards to Nicaragua Minibuses run from the border to Somoto every 30 minutes; taxis also run but may overcharge. Buses to Estelí depart hourly, two hours. There are also six daily buses direct to Managua, 3½ hours.

National parks → *See colour map 3, at the back of the book.*

The extensive system of national parks and protected areas provides the chance to enjoy some of the best scenery Honduras has to offer, much of it unspoilt and rarely visited. The National Parks' Office, **Conama** ① *next to the Instituto Nacional Agrario, 4 Av, Colonia Alameda, in Tegucigalpa*, is chaotic but friendly and a good source of information. **Cohdefor** ① *10 Av 4 Calle NO, San Pedro Sula, T2253-4959*, the national forestry agency, is also much involved with the parks. Parks have different levels of services – see individual parks for details. Natural reserves continue to be established and all support and interest is most welcome. Parks currently in existence are **La Tigra**, outside Tegucigalpa (page 503), and the **Río Plátano** (page 590). Underdevelopment since 1987 are **Monte Celaque** (page 522), **Cusuco** (page 539), **Punta Sal** (page 548), **Capiro y Calentura** (page 555), **Montaña Cerro Azul-Meámbar** (page 536), **Montaña de Yoro** (page 556) and **Pico Bonito** (page 552). These parks have visitor centres, hiking trails and primitive camping. The following have been designated national parks by the

Onwards to Honduras Taxis/minibuses shuttle passengers from the border to Choluteca. Alternatively, Empresa Esperanza runs a bus directly to Tegucigalpa, four hours; a taxi can take you to the bus stop, US$1.

Río Guasaule
Good roads at this crossing, the preferred route of international buses.
It might be worth using a 'helper' to steer you to the correct officials.
Fix price beforehand.
Currency exchange There is a Banco de Crédito Centroamericano by Nicaraguan immigration. Lots of money-changers. Beware children trying to distract you whilst you do business.
Honduran immigration Open 0800-1600.
Nicaraguan immigration Open 24 hours.
Onwards to Honduras Regular buses run Guasaule to Choluteca, 45 minutes. Connections to Tegucigalpa from there.
Onwards to Nicaragua Services to Chinandenga and León, every 30 minutes, one to two hours. Also direct services to Managua, four hours.

Leimus–Waspam
Possibly Central America's most remote border crossing, perched on the Río Coco in the heart of the Mosquitia. Lots of military in the area.
Currency exchange There are no banks or ATMs; bring all the cash you need. Shop-owners in Waspam or Puerto Lempira may change dollars or local currencies.
Honduran immigration Obtain your entry and exit stamps in Puerto Lempira, open Mon-Fri 0900-2300. Helpful office and a good source of information.
Nicaraguan immigration No known immigration in Waspam; the nearest may be in Bilwi (Puerto Cabezas), six gruelling hours away.
Onwards to Nicaragua Waspam has road connections to Bilwi and river connections to Miskito villages.
Onwards to Honduras Leimus offers road connections with Puerto Lempira.

government: **Montecristo-Trifinio** (page 524), **Santa Bárbara** (page 537), **Pico Pijol** (page 556), **Sierra de Agalta** (page 589) and **Montaña de Comayagua** (page 535). Wildlife refuges covered in the text are **Cuero y Salado** (page 553), **Las Trancas** (page 523) and **La Muralla-Los Higuerales** (page 587). For information on protected areas in the **Bay Islands**, see page 567.

Getting there

Air
Tegucigalpa, La Ceiba, San Pedro Sula and Roatán all have international airports. There are no direct flights to Tegucigalpa from Europe, but connecting flights can be made via Miami, then with **American Airlines** or **Taca**. There are flights to Tegucigalpa, San Pedro Sula and Roatán from Houston with **Continental** and services to Tegucigalpa from New York. **Taca** flies daily from Guatemala City and San Salvador, with connections throughout the region via El Salvador.

American Airlines fly daily from Miami, as do **Taca** and **Iberia**. There are also frequent services from San Pedro Sula. Services are also available with **Spirit Air** and **Delta**.

Road

There are numerous border crossings. With **Guatemala** to the west you can cross near Copán Ruinas at El Florido, on the Caribbean coast at Corinto or to the south at Agua Caliente. For **El Salvador** there are crossings at El Poy, leading to Suchitoto in the west, and Perquín leading to San Miguel and the east. For **Nicaragua**, the border post town of Guasale in the south leads 116 km on a very bad road to the Nicaraguan town of León, while the inland routes at Las Manos and El Espino guide you to Estelí and Matagalpa, in the northern hills. Crossing to Nicaragua through the Mosquitia coast is not possible – officially at least.

Taxes are charged on entry and exit at land borders, but the amount varies, despite notices asking you to denounce corruption. Entry is 60 lempiras and exit is 30 lempiras. Double is charged on Sunday. If officials make an excess charge for entry or exit, ask for a receipt. Do not attempt to enter Honduras at an unstaffed border. When it is discovered that you have no entry stamp you will either be fined US$60 or escorted to the border, and you will have to pay the guard's food and lodging; or you can spend a night in jail.

Sea

A regular weekly service departing Mondays at 1100 links Puerto Cortés with Mango Creek and Placencia, in Belize – see page 563 for details.

Getting around

Air

There are airstrips in all large towns and many of the cut-off smaller ones. Internal airlines include **Isleña**, www.flyislena.com (part of the Taca airlines group), **Sosa** and **Atlantic Air**. **Atlantic Air** serves La Ceiba, San Pedro Sula, Tegucigalpa, Roatán and Utila. **Sosa**, the largest domestic carrier, serves Roatán, Utila, Guanaja, San Pedro Sula, Tegucigalpa and other destinations in Honduras. La Ceiba is the main hub for domestic flights, especially for **Sosa** and **Atlantic**, and most flights to and from the islands stop there. Airport **departure tax** is US$37 (not charged if in transit less than nine hours). There is a 10% tax on all tickets sold for domestic and international journeys.

Road

Until recently, Honduras had some of the best roads in Central America. However, since the political crisis in 2009 many sections have become neglected and pitted with huge potholes, particularly between San Pedro Sula and Copán. Traffic tends to travel fast on the main roads and accidents are second only to Costa Rica in Latin America. If driving, take care and look out for speed bumps – *túmulos*, which are usually unmarked. Avoid driving at night; farm animals grazing along the verges often wander across the road. Total road length is now 15,100 km, of which 3020 km are paved, 10,000 km are all-weather roads and the remainder are passable in the dry season.

Bus There are essentially three types of service: local (*servicio a escala*), direct (*servicio directo*) and luxury (*servicio de lujo*). Using school buses, a *servicio a escala* is very slow, with frequent stops and detours and is uncomfortable for long periods. *Servicio directo* is faster, slightly more expensive and more comfortable. *Servicio de lujo* has air-conditioned European and Brazilian buses with videos.

Buses set out early in the day, with a few night buses running between major urban centres. Try to avoid bus journeys after dark as there are many more accidents and even occasional robberies.

If you suffer from motion sickness, the twisty roads can become unbearable. Avoid sitting at the back of the bus, take some water and sit by a window that will open. Minibuses are faster than buses, so the journey can be quite hair-raising. Pickups that serve out-of-the-way communities will leave you covered in dust (or soaked) – sit in or near the cab if possible.

Car Regular **gasoline/petrol** costs around US$3.60 per US gallon and US$3.25 for diesel. On entering with a car (from El Salvador at least), customs and the transit police give a 30-day permit for the vehicle. This must be renewed in Tegucigalpa (anywhere else authorization is valid for only one department). Charges for motorists appear to be: on entry, US$30 in total for a vehicle with two passengers, including provisional permission from the police to drive in Honduras, US$1 (official minimum) for car papers, fumigation and baggage inspection; on exit, US$2.30 in total. Motorcyclists face similar charges. These charges are changing all the time and differ significantly from one post to another (up to US$40 sometimes). They are also substantially higher on weekends and holidays. You will have to pass through Migración, Registro, Tránsito, Cuarentena, Administración, Secretaría and then a police vehicle check. At each stage you will be asked for money, for which you will not always get a receipt. On arriving or leaving with a vehicle there are so many checks that it pays to hire a *tramitador* to steer you to the correct officials in the correct order (US$1-2 for the guide). No fresh food is allowed to cross the border. The easiest border crossing is at Las Manos. The **Pan-American Highway** in Honduras is in bad condition in parts. One reader warns to "beware of potholes that can take a car. They suddenly appear after 20 km of good road without warning." If hiring a car, make sure it has all the correct papers and emergency triangles, which are required by law.

Cycling Bicycles are regarded as vehicles but are not officially subject to entrance taxes. Bicycle repair shops are difficult to find, and parts for anything other than mountain bikes may be very hard to come by. Some buses and most local flights will take bicycles. Most main roads have hard shoulders and most drivers respect cyclists. It is common for cars to blow their horn to signal their approach.

Hitchhiking Relatively easy. Travel is still on foot and by mule in many rural areas.

Taxi Widely available. Tuk-tuks have become very popular in Honduras, and are a quick and cheap way to move around in towns and cities.

Maps
The **Instituto Geográfico Nacional** produces two 1:1,000,000 maps (1995) of the country: one is a tourist map which includes city maps of Tegucigalpa, San Pedro Sula and La Ceiba, and the other is a good road map although it does not show all the roads. Both maps are widely available in bookshops in major cities and some hotels. **International Travel Maps (ITM)** has a 1:750,000 map of Honduras.

Sleeping

Accommodation in Honduras varies greatly. In Tegucigalpa and San Pedro Sula you will find the mix ranges from business-style hotels of international standards down to simple, but generally clean rooms. In popular tourist spots the focus is more on comfort and costs rise accordingly. Get off the beaten track and you'll find some of the cheapest and most basic accommodation in Central America – complete with accompanying insect life, it can be unbearable or a mind-broadening experience depending on your mood. There is a 4% extra tax on rooms in the better hotels.

Eating and drinking

The cheapest meals are the *comida corriente*, or the sometimes better prepared and more expensive *comida típica*, which usually contain some of the following: beans, rice, meat, avocado, egg, cabbage salad, cheese, bananas, potatoes or yucca, and always tortillas. *Carne asada* is charcoal-roasted meat and served with grated cabbage between tortillas; it is good, although rarely prepared hygienically. Make sure that pork is properly cooked. *Tajadas* are crisp, fried *plátano* chips topped with grated cabbage and sometimes meat; *nacatamales* are ground, dry maize mixed with meat and seasoning, boiled in banana leaves. *Baleadas* are soft flour tortillas filled with beans and various combinations of butter, egg, cheese and cabbage. *Pupusas* are thick corn tortillas filled with *chicharrón* (pork scratchings), or cheese, served as snacks with beer. *Tapado* is a stew with meat or fish, plantain, yucca and coconut milk. *Pinchos* are meat, poultry, or shrimp kebabs. *Sopa de mondongo* (tripe soup) is very common.

Fish is sold on the beaches at Trujillo and Cedeño; also freshly fried at the roadside by the shore of Lago Yojoa. While on the north coast, look out for *pan de coco* (coconut bread) made by Garífuna (Black Carib) women, and *sopa de camarones* (prawn soup) prepared with coconut milk and lemon juice. Honduras is now a major producer of tilapia with exports to the US and fresh tilapia available in many restaurants.

Drink

Soft drinks are called *refrescos*, or *frescos* (the name also given to fresh fruit blended with water, make sure you check that bottled water is used as tap water is unsafe); *licuados* are fruit blended with milk. Bottled drinking water is available in most places. *Horchata* is morro seeds, rice water and cinnamon. Coffee is thick and sweet. The main brands of **beer** are Port Royal Export, Imperial, Nacional, Barena and Salva Vida (more malty than the others). Local **rum** is cheap, try Flor de Caña white, or seven-year-old amber. Twelve-year-old Flor de Caña Centenario is regarded as the best.

Festivals and events

Most Roman Catholic feast days are celebrated.

1 Jan New Year's Day.
14 Apr Day of the Americas.
Mar/Apr Semana Santa (Thu, Fri and Sat before Easter Sun).

1 May Labour Day.
15 Sep Independence Day.
3 Oct Francisco Morazán.
12 Oct Columbus' arrival in America.
21 Oct Army Day.

Shopping

The best articles are those made of wood. Straw items, including woven ornaments, are also highly recommended. Leather is cheaper than in El Salvador and Nicaragua. As a single stopping point, the region around Santa Bárbara is one of the best places, with outlets selling handicrafts from nearby villages. In Copán Ruinas you can also get a wide range of products, including cigars and high-quality jewellery, as well as many Guatemalan handicrafts at similar prices. Alternatively you can explore the villages yourself and see the goods being made. Coffee is OK, but not great. Sales tax is 12%; 15% on alcohol and tobacco.

Essentials A-Z

Customs and duty free
There are no customs duties on personal effects..You are allowed to bring in 200 cigarettes or 100 cigars, or 500 g of tobacco, and 2 quarts of spirit.

Electricity
Generally 110 volts but, increasingly, 220 volts is being installed. US-style plugs.

Embassies and consulates
For a full list visit
http://hn.embassyinformation.com.
Belize, 114 Bella Vista, Belize City, T02-245-889.
Canada, 151 Slater St, Suite 805-A, Ottawa, Ontario K1P 5H3, T613-233-8900.
El Salvador, 89 Av Norte between 7 and 9 Calle Pte 561, Col Escalón, San Salvador, T2263-2808.
France, 8 rue Crevaux, 75116 Paris, T4755-8645.
Germany, Cuxhavener Str 14, D-10555 Berlín, T30397497-10.
Guatemala, 19 Av "A", 20-19, Zona 10, Guatemala City, T2363-5495.
Israel, 60, Medinat Hayehudim St, Entrance "A", 2nd floor, Herzlya Pituach 46766, Tel Aviv, T9957-7686.
Japan, 38 Kowa Bldg, 8F No 802, 12-24 Nishi Azabu 4, Chome Minato Ku, Tokyo 106-0031, T03-3409-1150.
Mexico, Alfonso Reyes 220, Col Condesa, México DF, T55-211-5747.

Netherlands, Nassauplein 17, 2585 EB, La Haya, T70-364-1684.
Nicaragua, Reparto San Juan del Gimnasio Hércules, Calle San Juan 312, Managua, T/F270-4133.
Spain, Paseo de la Castellana 164, 28046 Madrid, T91-579-0251.
UK, 115 Gloucester Place, London, W1H 3PJ, T020-7486-4880.
USA, 3007 Tilden St NW, Suite 4-M, Washington, DC 20008, T202-966-7702.

Health
Inoculate against typhoid and tetanus. There is cholera, so eating on the street or at market stalls is not recommended. There are hospitals and private clinics in Tegucigalpa, San Pedro Sula and larger towns. See page 38 for further information.

Identification
It is advisable to carry some form of identification at all times, because spot checks have increased, especially when entering or leaving major towns and near to international borders.

Internet
Internet cafés are widely available in the capital and in popular locations. Prices and connections vary greatly; in cities good speeds are at about US$1 per hr. On the islands, prices are a bit higher.

Language

Spanish is the main language, but English is often spoken in the north, in the Bay Islands, by West Indian settlers on the Caribbean coast, and in business communities.

Media

The principal newspapers in Tegucigalpa are *El Heraldo* and *La Tribuna*. In San Pedro Sula they are *El Tiempo* and *La Prensa*. Links on the net at www.honduras.com. The English weekly paper *Honduras This Week*, is now mainly online at www.hondurasthisweek.com. They're frequently looking for student interns.

There are 6 television channels and 167 broadcasting stations. Cable TV is available in large towns and cities.

Money → *US$1=18.89 lempiras (June 2011).* The unit of currency is the **lempira** (written Lps and referred to as lemps) named after a famous indigenous chief who lost his life while fighting the invasion of the Spanish. It is reasonably stable against the US dollar. Divided into 100 centavos, there are nickel coins of 5, 10, 20 and 50 centavos. Bank notes are for 1, 2, 5, 10, 20, 50, 100 and 500 lempiras. No one has change for larger notes, especially the 500. Any amount of any currency can be taken in or out of the country.

Credit cards and traveller's cheques

Acceptance of credit cards in Honduras is widespread but commissions can be as high as 6%. Some businesses may try to tack on a service charge to credit card purchases, which is illegal. Ask the manager to call **BAC** and check if the charge is permitted. It is advisable to have US$ cash, in smaller denominations, US$10-50.

MasterCard and Visa are accepted in major hotels and most restaurants in cities and larger towns. Amex is accepted in more expensive establishments. Cash advances are available from **BAC, Banco Atlántida, Aval Card** and **Honducard** throughout the country. BAC represents Amex and issues and services Amex credit cards.

TCs can be a hassle as most banks and business don't accept them.

Cost of living and travelling

Honduras is not expensive: 2 people can travel together in reasonable comfort for US$25 per person per day (less if on a tight budget), but prices for tourists fluctuate greatly. Transport, including domestic flights, is still the cheapest in Central America. Diving will set you back a bit, but at US$280 or so for a PADI course, it is still the cheapest in Central America.

Opening hours

Banks In Tegucigalpa Mon-Fri 0900-1500; on the north coast Sat 0800-1100.
Post offices Mon-Fri 0700-2000; Sat 0800-1200.
Shops Mon-Fri 0900-1200, 1400-1800; Sat 0800-1200.

Post

Airmail takes 4-7 days to Europe and the same for the USA. Expensive for parcels. Probably worth using a courier. 20 g letter to USA US$0.80, Europe US$1.30, rest of the world US$1.75. Parcel up to 1 kg to the USA US$18, Europe US$29, rest of the world US$35.

Safety

There are serious domestic social problems in Tegucigalpa and San Pedro Sula, including muggings and theft, but there is a Tourist Police service in place – in Copán Ruinas, Roatán, La Ceiba, Tela and San Pedro Sula – that has reduced the problem. Take local advice and be cautious when travelling alone or off the beaten track. The vast majority of Hondurans are honest, friendly, warm and welcoming, and the general perception is that tourists are not targeted by criminals.

Telephone → *Country code T+504.* Local operator T192; General information T193; International operator T197.

Hondutel provides international telephone services from stations throughout the country. The system has improved dramatically in recent years due to competition, with an increasing majority of Hondurans owning a cell phone. You can buy a cell phone for about US$10 from Tigo, Claro and Digicel, with phone cards from US$2 upwards.

Time
-6 hrs GMT.

Tipping
Normally 10% of the bill but more expensive places add a service charge.

Tourist information
Instituto Hondureño de Turismo, main office is at Edificio Europa, Av Ramón E Cruz and Calle República de México, Col San Carlos, Tegucigalpa, T2222-2124. Also an office at Toncontín Airport and several regional offices.

Useful websites
www.hondurastips.hn/ A reliable favourite with lots of information about Honduras and hotel, restaurant and transport listings (Spanish only). The biannual publication, *HONDURAS Tips*, edited by John Dupuis in La Ceiba, Edificio Gómez, Local No 2, 4 Calle, T/F2440-3383, is full of interesting and useful tourist information, in English and Spanish, free (available in Tegucigalpa from Instituto Hondureño de Turismo, and widely distributed around the country in major hotels).

www.hondurasweekly.com News, cultural features, travel tips, listings and links.
www.letsgohonduras.com The official Tourist Office (IHT) guide on the internet, with basic highlights.
www.netsys.hn Good business directory and useful links (in English).

Several regional guides are being developed – these are mentioned within the text.

Visas and immigration
Neither a visa nor tourist card is required for nationals of Western European countries, USA, Canada, Australia, New Zealand, Japan, Argentina, Chile, Guatemala, Costa Rica, Nicaragua, El Salvador, Panama and Uruguay. Citizens of other countries need either a tourist card, which can be bought from Honduran consulates for US$2-3, or a visa, and they should enquire at a Honduran consulate in advance to see which they need. The price of a visa seems to vary depending on nationality and where it is bought. Extensions of 30 days are easy to obtain (up to a maximum of 6 months' stay, cost US$5). There are immigration offices for extensions at Tela, La Ceiba, San Pedro Sula, Santa Rosa de Copán, Siguatepeque, La Paz and Comayagua, and all are more helpful than the Tegucigalpa office.

You will have to visit a country outside of Guatemala, Honduras and Nicaragua to re-enter and gain 90 days.

Weights and measures
The metric system is official.

Tegucigalpa and around

→ *Colour map 3, C2. Altitude: 1000 m. Population: 1.1 million.*

Genuinely chaotic, Tegucigalpa – or Tegus as it is called by locals – is cramped and crowded, but still somehow retains a degree of charm in what remains of the colonial centre. If you can bear to stay away from the Caribbean for a few days, it has much more history and charisma than its rival San Pedro Sula, to the north. Surrounded by sharp, high peaks on three sides, the city is built on the lower slopes of El Picacho. The commercial centre is around Boulevard

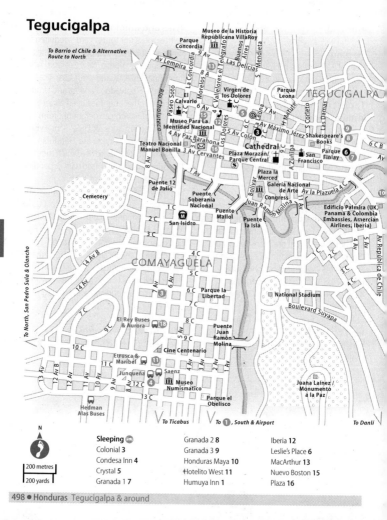

Tegucigalpa

Sleeping
Colonial 3
Condesa Inn 4
Crystal 5
Granada 1 7

Granada 2 8
Granada 3 9
Honduras Maya 10
†Hotelito West 11
Humuya Inn 1

Iberia 12
Leslie's Place 6
MacArthur 13
Nuevo Boston 15
Plaza 16

Morazán, an area known as 'zona viva', full of cafés, restaurants and shops. For contrast to the modern functional city, you can visit some of the centuries-old mining settlements set in forested valleys among the nearby mountains that are ideal for hiking. ▶▶ *For listings, see pages 505-512.*

Getting there

Toncontín international airport is 6.5 km south of the centre, US$4-5 in a taxi to the centre. The airport is in a narrow valley creating difficult landing conditions: morning fog or bad weather can cause it to close. The Carretera del Sur (Southern Highway), which brings in travellers from the south and from Toncontín Airport, runs through Comayagüela into Tegucigalpa. There is no central bus station and bus companies have offices throughout Comayagüela. On arrival it is very much easier – and recommended – to take a taxi to your hotel until you get to know the city.

Getting around

The winding of streets in the city means that moving around in the first few days is as much about instinct as following any map. There are cheap buses and taxis for city transport. The Tegucigalpa section of the city uses both names and numbers for streets, but names are used more commonly. In Comayagüela, streets designated by number are the norm. Addresses tend not to be very precise, especially in the colonias around Boulevard Morazán east and south of the centre of Tegucigalpa.

Tourist information

Instituto Hondureño de Turismo ⓘ *Edif Europa, Av Ramón E Cruz and Calle República de México, 3rd floor, Col San Carlos, T2238-3974, also at Toncontín Airport, open 0830-1530*, provides lists of hotels and sells posters and postcards. Information on cultural events around the country from **Teatro Nacional Manuel Bonilla** is better than at regional tourist offices. **El Mundo Maya** ⓘ *behind the cathedral next to the Parque Central, T2222-2946*, is a private tourist information centre.

San Pedro **18**

Eating 🍴
Duncan Maya **3**
Taiwan **6**

Best time to visit

The city's altitude gives it a reliable climate: temperate during the rainy season from May to November; warm, with cool nights in March and April; and cool and dry with very cool nights from December to February. The annual mean temperature is about 23°C (74°F).

Safety

Generally speaking, Tegucigalpa is cleaner and safer (especially at night) than Comayagüela. If you have anything stolen, report it to **Dirección de Investigación Criminal** (**DGIC**) ① *5 Av, 7-8 Calle (next to Edificio Palermo), T2237-4799.*

Background

Founded as a silver and gold mining camp in 1578, Tegucigalpa means silver hill in the original indigenous tongue; miners first discovered gold at the north end of the current Soberanía bridge. The present city is comprised of the two former towns of Comayagüela and Tegucigalpa which, although divided by the steeply banked Río Choluteca, became the capital in 1880 and are now united administratively as the Distrito Central.

Being off the main earthquake fault line, Tegucigalpa has not been subjected to disasters by fire or earthquake, unlike many of its Central American neighbours, so it has retained many traditional features. The stuccoed houses, with a single, heavily barred entrance leading to a central patio, are often attractively coloured. However, the old low skyline of the city has been punctuated by several modern tall buildings, and much of the old landscape changed with the arrival of Hurricane Mitch.

The rains of **Hurricane Mitch** in October 1998 had a devastating effect on the Distrito Central. But the damage caused by the Choluteca bursting its banks is hard to see these days, with the exception of the first avenue of Comayagüela, where abandoned homes and buildings remain empty. Bridges washed away by the floodwaters have now been replaced, power supplies are back and, in some respects, traffic is actually better now, since many routes were diverted from the heart of downtown. Today, Hurricane Mitch lives on as painful memory.

Sights

Crossing the river from Comayagüela by the colonial Mallol bridge, on the left is the old **Casa Presidencial** (1919), home to the National Archive. When this was a museum, visitors could see the President's office and the Salón Azul state room. Try asking – you may be lucky. (The new Palacio Presidencial is a modern building on Boulevard Juan Pablo II in Colonia Lomas del Mayab.)

Calle Bolívar leads to the Congress building and the former site of the University, founded in 1847. The site adjoining the church in Plaza La Merced is now the **Galería Nacional de Arte** ① *Tue-Fri 0900-1600, Sat 0900-1200, US$1.50,* a beautifully restored 17th-century building, housing a very fine collection of Honduran modern and colonial art, prehistoric rock carvings and some remarkable pre-Colombian ceramic pieces. There are useful descriptions of exhibits, and explanations of the mythology embodied in the prehistoric and pre-Colombian art.

Calle Bolívar leads to the main square, Plaza Morazán (commonly known as Parque Central). On the eastern side of the square are the **Palacio del Distrito Central**, and the domed and double-towered **cathedral**, built in the late 18th century but which have had a complete facelift. See the gilt colonial altarpiece, the fine examples of Spanish colonial art, the cloisters and, in Holy Week, the ceremony of the Descent from the Cross.

Avenida Miguel Paz Barahona, running through the north side of the square, is a key venue. To the east is the church of **San Francisco**, with its clangorous bells, and (on 3 Calle, called Avenida Cervantes) the old **Spanish Mint** (1770), now the national printing works.

From Plaza Morazán, heading west towards the river to Avenida Miguel Paz Barahona, opposite the post office is the **Museo Para La Identidad Nacional** ① *Tue-Sat 0900-1700, Sun 1000-1600, US$3.30*, a museum that is unashamedly about Honduras for Hondurans. Good multimedia presentation (with audio-guide, in Spanish only), and a well-thought-out trip through Honduran history, from plate tectonics to the present day. Its star attraction is 'Virtual Copán' – wide-screen CGI recreation of the Maya ruins; also occasional temporary exhibitions. Just enough detail without getting heavy. Every capital city in Central America should have a museum like this.

Head east a block, then left (north) along 5 Calle (Calle Los Dolores), is the 18th-century church of **Iglesia de Nuestra Señora de los Dolores**. Two blocks north and three blocks west of the church is the beautiful Parque Concordia with good copies of Maya sculpture and temples. On a hilltop one block above Parque Concordia, on Calle Morelos 3A, is **Museo de la Historia Republicana Villa Roy** ① *Mon-Sat 0800-16, US$1.10, www.ihah.hn*, the former site of the Museo Nacional and, in 1936, home of the former president, Julio Lozano. The building was restored, reconstructed and reopened in 1997. There are seven main rooms presenting Honduras' history from Independence in 1821 up to 1963, as well as cultural and temporary exhibits and a collection of graceful old cars.

Back on Avenida Miguel Paz Barahona, and further west, are the **Teatro Nacional Manuel Bonilla**, with a rather grand interior (1915) inspired by the Athenée Theatre in Paris and, across the square, the beautiful old church of **El Calvario**. Built in elegant colonial style, El Calvario's roof is supported by 14 pillars.

In Colonia Palmira, to the southeast of the city, is Boulevard Morazán, with shopping and business complexes, embassies, banks, restaurants, *cafeterías* and bars. You can get a fine view of the city from the **Monumento a La Paz** ① *open till 1700*, on Juana Laínez hill, near the Estadio Nacional (National Stadium), but don't walk up alone.

The backdrop to Tegucigalpa is the summit of **El Picacho**, with the Cristo del Picacho statue looming up to the north (see Valle de Angeles, below), although this can be hard to see at times. From Plaza Morazán go up 7 Calle and the Calle de la Leona to **Parque La Leona**, a small handsome park with a railed walk overlooking the city and safer than Monumento a La Paz. Higher still is the reservoir in El Picacho, also known as the **United Nations Park**, which can be reached by a special bus from the No 9 bus stop, behind Los Dolores church (in front of Farmacia Santa Bárbara, Sunday only, US$0.15); alternatively, take a bus to El Piligüin or Corralitos (daily at 0600) from the north side of Parque Herrera in front of the Teatro Nacional Manuel Bonilla.

Comayagüela

Crossing the bridge of 12 de Julio (quite near the Teatro Nacional Manuel Bonilla, see above) you can visit Comayagüela's market of San Isidro. In the Edificio del Banco Central, is the **Pinacoteca Arturo H Medrano** ① *12 Calle entre 5 y 6 Av*, which houses approximately 500 works by five Honduran artists and the **Museo Numismático** ① *Mon-Fri 0900-1200, 1300-1600*, which has a collection of coins and banknotes. Funds have been set aside to restore the older parts of Comayagüela, which should make the place more enjoyable to explore.

Heading north out of Tegucigalpa on the Olancho road, you come to **Talanga**, with a post office and Hondutel near the market on the main road. From Talanga it is a short trip to the historic and beautiful settlements of Cedros and Minas de Oro. From the Parque Central an unpaved road leads south to the Tegucigalpa–Danlí road making a triangular route possible back to the capital.

Cedros is one of Honduras' earliest settlements, dating from Pedro de Alvarado's mining operations of 1536. It is an outstanding colonial mining town with cobbled streets, perched high on an eminence amid forests. The festival of El Señor del Buen Fin takes place in the first two weeks of January. Buses to Talanga, Cedros and nearby San Ignacio leave from Reynita de San Ignacio in Mercado Zonal Belén, Comayagüela, T224-0066.

Santa Lucía → *Altitude: 1400-1600 m.*
About 14 km northeast of Tegucigalpa, on the way to Valle de Angeles, a right turn goes to the quaint old mining village of Santa Lucía which is perched precariously on a steep, pine forested mountainside overlooking the valley with Tegucigalpa below. The town has a colonial church with a Christ statue given by King Felipe II of Spain in 1592. There is a

Around Tegucigalpa

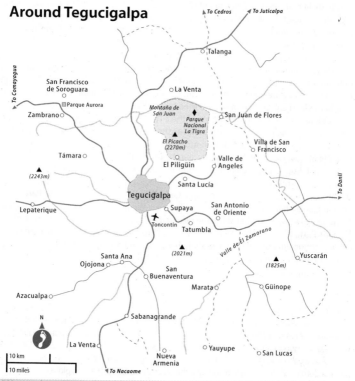

charming legend of the Black Christ, which the authorities ordered to be taken down to Tegucigalpa when Santa Lucía lost its former importance as a mining centre. Every step it was carried away from Santa Lucía it became heavier. When it was impossible to carry it any further they turned round, and by the time they were back in Santa Lucía, it was as light as a feather.

The town is lively with parties on Saturday night, and there is a festival in the second and third weeks of January, celebrating the 15 January Día de Cristo de las Mercedes. There are souvenir shops in the town, including **Cerámicas Ucles** just past the lagoon, second street on left, and another ceramics shop at the entrance on your right. On the way into the town from the capital the road is lined with many nurseries, selling flowers and plants for which the region is famous. There are good walks up the mountain on various trails, with fine views of Tegucigalpa.

A good circuit is to descend east from the mountain towards **San Juan del Rancho** through lovely landscapes on a good dirt road, then connect with the paved road to **El Zamorano**. From there continue either to El Zamorano, or return to Tegucigalpa (see below for opposite direction).

Valle de Angeles → *Altitude: 1310 m.*

About 30 minutes' drive from Tegucigalpa, Valle de Angeles is on a plain below **Monte San Juan**, with **Cerro El Picacho** (2270m) and **Cerro La Tigra** nearby. It is a popular spot for trips from the city, with a cool climate year round and is surrounded by pine forests. The town's shady little main plaza is decorated with brightly painted benches and bandstand, a pretty little twin-domed church and fringed by several restaurants with outdoor tables. The **tourist office** ① *Sat, Sun 0900-1200, 1330-1800*, is helpful but with limited information. There are tracks going through the forests, old mines to explore, a picnic area and a swimming pool; consequently it is crowded on Sundays. At the top of Cerro El Picacho there is a stunning view of the city and, if so inclined, you can visit the **zoo** ① *daily, 0800-1500, US$0.20*, of mostly indigenous animals including jaguar, spider monkeys and other animals and birds.

Parque Nacional La Tigra

① *US$10 entry. Go first to the Amitigra office, Edificio Italia, 6th floor, about 3 blocks southwest of Amex office on Av República de Panamá, Tegucigalpa, T2232-2660, www.amitigra.org; helpful. Book a visit here in advance.*

North of Tegucigalpa

Continue to San Juan de Flores (also called Cantarranas) and San Juancito, an old mining town. From here you can climb in the La Tigra cloud forest and even walk along the top before descending to El Hatillo and then to Tegucigalpa.

There are good climbs to the heights of Picacho and excellent hikes in the Parque Nacional La Tigra cloud forest. Only 11 km from Tegucigalpa, this cloud forest covers 238 sq km and is considered one of the richest habitats in the world with a great diversity of flora and fauna – bromeliads, orchids, arborescent ferns and over 200 species of bird. Single hikers must have a guide. There are two approach routes: go to **El Piligüin** (see below) for the Jutiapa entrance, from where you can start hiking, or to Gloriales Inn in El Hatillo. You can also walk 24 km from Tegucigalpa to the Jutiapa entrance. Then hike to the visitor centre of La Tigra at El Rosario (10 km, three hours, easy hiking, superb scenery). Alternatively, go to **San Juancito**, above which is the national park (well worth a visit, a stiff, one-hour uphill walk to El Rosario visitor centre, housed in the old mine hospital, with **park offices** ⓘ *daily 0800-1700*, friendly and helpful, with free park map/leaflet, dorms (**E** per person in basic but clean bunk rooms, with hot showers, breakfast available, extra) and starting point for six trails ranging from 30 minutes to eight hours, from 1800-2400 m above sea level (bring insect repellent).

Crumbling remains of the old mine buildings are dotted around the hillsides, some abandoned, others inhabited. Local resident Miguel Angel Sierra (T9648334) has some fascinating remnants, including an original gold mould and old photographs, all of which he is happy to show to visitors. The former US embassy at the Rosario mine has been renovated and turned into a museum and information centre, due to open soon, weekends only. The small **Pulpería-Cafetería El Rosario** sells snacks, coffee and groceries, useful for hiking in the park, and with lovely views from its tiny terrace and balcony.

A recommended hike is the **Sendero La Esperanza**, which leads to the road; turn right then take the **Sendero Bosque Nublado** on your left. The whole circuit takes about one hour 20 minutes. A few quetzal birds survive here, but you will need a good eye. In the rainy season (June, July, October and November) there is a spectacular 100-m waterfall (**Cascada de la Gloria**), which falls on a vast igneous rock. Do not leave paths when walking as there are steep drops. Also get advice about personal safety, as robberies have occurred.

From Parque Herrera in Tegucigalpa, buses throughout the day go to the village of **El Piligüin**, north of Santa Lucía. A delightful 40-minute walk down the pine-clad mountainside leads to **El Chimbo** (meals at *pulpería* or shop, ask anyone the way), then take bus either to Valle de Angeles or Tegucigalpa.

At Km 24 on the road to Danlí, there are climbs to the highest peak through the Uyuca rainforest. Information is available from the Escuela Agrícola Panamericana in the breathtaking **Valle del Zamorano**, or from the **Amitigra** office in Tegucigalpa (see above). The school has rooms for visitors. Visits to the school are organized by some tour operators. On the northwest flank of Uyuca is the picturesque village of **Tatumbla**.

Suyapa

Southeast of Tegucigalpa, the village of Suyapa attracts pilgrims to its big church, home to a tiny wooden image of the Virgin, about 8 cm high, set into the altar. A fiesta is held 1-4 February, see page 508. Take a bus to the University or to Suyapa from 'La Isla', one block northwest of the city stadium.

Sabanagrande

Further south (40 km) is Sabanagrande, just off the main highway. This typical colonial town, complete with cobbled streets, is a good day trip from Tegucigalpa. There is an interesting colonial church (1809), Nuestra Señora del Rosario 'Apa Kun Ka' (the place of water for washing), with the fiesta of La Virgen de Candelaria from 1-11 February. At 1000 m, it has a mild climate, beautiful scenery with pleasant walks, including views to the Pacific and the Gulf of Fonseca. The town is famous for its *rosquillas* (a type of biscuit).

Ojojona → *Altitude: 1400 m.*

Ojojona is another quaint, completely unspoiled, old village about 30 minutes (24 km) south of Tegucigalpa; turn right off the Southern Highway. The village pottery is interesting but make your selection carefully as some of it is reported to be of poor quality. **La Casona del Pueblo** offers the best handicrafts in town, including fine rustic ceramics. The local fiesta is 18-20 January. There are two well-preserved colonial churches in Ojojona, with fine paintings, plus two more in nearby **Santa Ana**, which is passed on the way from Tegucigalpa.

⊙ Tegucigalpa and around listings

Hotel and guesthouse prices		
LL over US$200	**L** US$151-200	**AL** US$101-150
A US$66-100	**B** US$46-65	**C** US$31-45
D US$21-30	**E** US$12-20	**F** US$7-11
G under US$7		
Restaurant prices		
₸₸₸ over US$15	₸₸ US$8-15	₸ under US$8
See pages 31-33 for further information.		

● Sleeping

Tegucigalpa *p498, map p498*
There is a 4% tax on hotel bills, plus 12% sales tax: check if it is included in the price.

AL Honduras Maya, Av República de Chile, Col Palmira, T2280-5000, www.hotelhonduras maya.hn. Spacious rooms and apartments, dated decor, casino, swimming pool, **Bar Mirador** with nightly happy hour 1700-1900, *cafeterías* (**Black Jack's Snack Bar**, **Cafetería 2000**), restaurant (**Rosalila**), very good buffet breakfast, conference hall and convention facilities for 1300, view over the city from upper rooms. Excellent travel agency in the basement. Expensive internet access.

A Humuya Inn, Col Humuya 1150, 5 mins from airport, T2239-2206, www.humuyainn.com. Rooms and service apartments, US owner. Recommended.

B MacArthur, Av Lempira 454 and Telégrafo, T2237-9839, www.hotelmacarthur.com. A/c, TV, private bath, cheaper without a/c, small pool. Recommended.

B Plaza, on Av Paz Barahona, in front of post office, T2237-2111, hotelplaza_centro@ yahoo.com. good location, friendly staff, hot water, cable TV, free internet in the lobby and breakfast included.

B-C Leslie's Place, Plaza San Martín, Col Palmira, T2220-5325. Close to good restaurants and bars in safe part of the city, a friendly little B&B with homely rooms and cosy lounge areas and garden, quiet and secure. Recommended.

C Crystal, 2nd floor, Máximo Jerez y S Mendieta, T2237-8980. TV, a/c, OK rooms.

C Nuevo Boston, Av Máximo Jerez 321, T2237-9411. Good beds, spotless, hot water, central. Good value, no credit cards, rooms on street side noisy, free coffee, mineral water and cookies in lounge, stores luggage, well run. Simple and recommended.

D Granada 1, Av Gutemberg 1401, Barrio Guanacaste, T2237-2381. Hot water on 2nd floor only, good, clean, safe, TV lounge. Internet café next door.

D Granada 2, T238-4438 and **D Granada 3**, T2237-0843, on the street leading uphill (to

Barrio Casamate) from northeast corner of Parque Finlay. Good beds, hot water, safe parking, can be noisy from passing traffic so try to get a room at the back. Recommended.
E-F Iberia, Peatonal Los Dolores, T2237-9267. Hot showers, clean, friendly and helpful owner happy to help guests get to know Tegus, refurbished, stores luggage, cheaper without fan.

Comayagüela *p501*
Convenient for buses to the north and west and there are many cheap *pensiones* and rooms. It is noisier and dirtier than Tegucigalpa, many places are unsuitable for travellers. If you are carrying luggage, take a taxi.
D Centenario, 6 Av, 9-10 Calle, T2222-1050. Safe parking. Recommended.
E Condesa Inn, 7 Av, 12 Calle. Clean, hot shower, a/c, TV, *cafetería*, very friendly, a bargain. Recommended.
E-F San Pedro, 9 Calle, 6 Av. With bath (cheaper without), or with private cold shower. Popular, restaurant.
F Hotelito West, 10 Calle, 6-7 Av. Towels and soap, hot water all day, very friendly, changes TCs. Recommended.

Santa Lucía *p502*
B La Posada de Dona Estefana, overlooking the church in the heart of the well preserved colonial town, T2779-0441, meeb@yahoo.com. Very pretty rooms, with cable TV and great views from balcony; lounge and pool; breakfast included.
C Hotel Santa Lucía Resort, 1.2 km before Santa Lucía, set among pine trees dripping with moss (*rigil*), T2779-0540, www.hotelsantaluciaresort.com. Spacious and comfy log cabins, with cable TV, lounge area, and balcony; pleasant grounds and ample parking space.

Valle de Angeles *p503*
B-D Villas del Valle, 500 m north of town, T766-2534, www.villasdelvalle.com. Selection of rooms, cabins and suites. Honduran and European food in the restaurant.

C Hotel y Restaurante Posada del Angel, northeast of centre, T2766-2233, hotelposadadelangel@yahoo.com. Swimming pool, indifferent service, moderate prices.

Parque Nacional La Tigra *p503*
E Eco Albergue La Tigra, in the old hospital of the mining company. Price per person. Rooms named after local birds, capacity for 50.
F Hotelito San Juan, San Juancito. 6 rooms with shared bathroom.

❷ Eating

Tegucigalpa *p498, map p498*
Take a walk down the pedestrianized stretch of Av Paz Barahona. In the evening, take a taxi to Blv Morazón. Most places close on Sun. There are good Chinese restaurants on Calle del Telégrafo in centre; huge servings at reasonable prices.
††† El Corral, 4a Av, opposite Hotel Clarión, Col Alameda, T2232-5066. Big, brash steakhouse, with excellent grilled meats and decent wine list. Lively at weekends, with live music, karaoke and dancing.
††† El Trapiche, Blv Suyapa, opposite National University. Colonial ranch atmosphere, good steaks and national dishes. Recommended.
††† Roma, Av Santa Sede, Calle Las Acacias 1601, 1 block off Av República de Chile. The oldest Italian restaurant in the city, good pizzas.
†† Casa María, Av Ramón E Cruz, Col Los Castaños, 1 block off Blv Morazán. Colonial building, good food.
†† El Crustáceo, Plaza San Martín y 3 Calle, Col Palmira. Seafood specialists in vaguely *cabaña*-style building with open-air terrace, popular with local rich kids.
†† Duncan Maya, Av Colón 618, opposite central Pizza Hut. Lively place, popular with locals, occasionally has live music. Good and reasonably priced.
†† El Gachupín, off Blv Morazán, Col El Castaño Sur. Superb, Mediterranean-style food, garden.

¶¶ **El Pórtico**, near Blv Morazán, T2236-7099. Good food but don't be in a hurry.

¶¶ **Mei-Mei**, Pasaje Midence Soto, central. Chinese. Recommended.

¶¶ **Rojo, Verde y Ajo**, 1 Av B, Col Palmira. Good food, reasonable price, closed Sun.

¶¶ **Tony's Mar**, Blv Juan Pablo II y Av Uruguay, Col Tepeyac, T2239-9379. Seafood, good, simple, New Orleans style.

¶ **El Patio 2**, easternmost end of Blv Morazán. Traditional food, good service and atmosphere, and generous portions. Recommended.

¶ **Taiwan**, round corner from **Hotels Granada 2 and 3**, on Av Máximo Jerez. Chinese food, huge portions, good value.

Bakeries

Antojitos, next door to **Hotel Granada 3**. Convenient for breakfast, closes at 1100, easiest place to eat in the area.

Basilio's Repostería y Panadería, Calle Peatonal between Los Dolores and S Mendieta. Good cakes, bread and pastries.

Salman's. Several outlets. Good bread/pastries.

Cafeterías

Al Natural, Calle Hipólito Matute y Av Miguel Cervantes. Some vegetarian, some meat dishes, huge fresh fruit juices, antiques, caged birds, nice garden atmosphere.

Café y Librería Paradiso, Av Paz Barahona 1351. Excellent coffee and snacks, good library, paintings and photos to enjoy, newspapers and magazines on sale, good meeting place.

Don Pepe's Terraza, Av Colón 530, upstairs, T2222-1084. Central, cheap, live music, but typical Honduran atmosphere. Recommended.

Comayagüela *p501*
Cafeterías

Bienvenidos a Golosinas, 6 Av, round corner from **Hotel Colonial**. Friendly, basic meals, beer.

Cafetería Nueva Macao, 4 Av No 437. Large portions, Chinese.

Comedor Tulin, 4 Av between 4 and 5 Calle. Good breakfasts.

Santa Lucía *p502*

¶¶ **Miluska**. A Czech restaurant serving Czech and Honduran food. Recommended.

¶ **Comedor**, next to the plaza/terrace of the municipality. On Sun food is available on the streets.

Valle de Angeles *p503*

¶¶ **Epocas**, Calle Mineral, opposite the Town Hall on the main plaza, T9636-1235. A wonderful ramshackle place, full of antiques and bric-a-brac, from old French horns to vintage cash registers (some items for sale); mixed menu of steak, chicken and fish as well as *típicos*; cheerfully talkative parrots in the backyard.

¶¶ **La Casa de las Abuelas**, 1 block north of Parque Central, T2766-2626. Pleasant courtyard with wine bar, café, library, satellite TV, email, phone, information and art gallery.

¶¶ **Las Tejas**, opposite the **Centro Turístico La Florida**. A Dutch-owned restaurant, serving traditional mix of meat and *típico* dishes.

¶ **Restaurante Papagaio**, Calle Peatonal, 1 block down from plaza, T9920-0714. Tue-Sun 0900-1800. Simple but friendly little place with large garden and kids' play area, serving breakfasts, steaks, pasta and *típicos*.

¶ **Restaurante Turístico de Valle de Angeles**, T2766-2148, on top of hill overlooking town, with rustic decor, cartwheel table tops and lovely views over forested valley Good meat and fish dishes but slow service.

Parque Nacional La Tigra *p503*

¶ **Grocery store**, next door to **Hotelito San Juan**, San Juancito. Sells fuel, drinks and can prepare *comida corriente*; same owners as hotel, T2766-2237.

¶ **Señora Amalia Elvir**, before El Rosario. Meals are available at Señora Amalia's house.

⊕ Entertainment

Tegucigalpa *p498, map p498*
Bars and clubs
In front of the Universidad Nacional on Blv Suyapa is **La Peña**, where every Fri at 2100 there is live music, singing and dancing, entrance US$1.40. Blv Morazán has plenty of choice in nightlife including **Taco Taco**, a good bar, sometimes with live mariachi music; next door **Tequila**, a popular drinking place only open at weekends. **Tobacco Road Tavern**, a popular gringo hang-out, in the downtown area on Calle Matute. **Iguana Rana Bar** is very popular with locals and visitors, similarly **La Puerta del Alcalá**, 3½ blocks down from Taca office on Blv Morazán, Col Castaño Sur. Pleasant open setting. Tierra Libre, Calle Casa de las Naciones Unidas 2118, 5 mins' walk from Plaza San Martín in Col Palmira, T3232-8923. Arty cinephile café/bar, with occasional screenings, small and friendly, with good cocktails and snacks (Mon-Sat, 1700-2400).

Cinemas
Plazas 1 to 5, in Centro Comercial Plaza Miraflores on Blv Miraflores. **Regis**, **Real**, **Opera**, and **Sagitario** at Centro Comercial Centroamérica, Blv Miraflores (for good US films). **Multiplaza**, Col Lomas del Mayab, 6-screens. In the city centre, **Lido Palace**, **Variedades** and **Aries**, 200 m up Av Gutemberg leading from Parque Finlay to Col Reforma.

⊛ Festivals and events

Suyapa *p504*
1-4 Feb Fiesta, with a televised *alborada* with singers, music and fireworks, from 2000-2400 on the 2nd evening.

Sabanagrande *p505*
1-11 Feb Fiesta of La Virgen de Candelaria.

Ojojona *p505*
18-20 Jan Fiesta.

⊙ Shopping

Tegucigalpa *p498, map p498*
Bookshops
Metromedia, Edif Casa Real, Av San Carlos, behind Centro Comercial Los Castaños, Blv Morazán, English books, new and second-hand, for sale or exchange. **Librería Paradiso** (see under Cafeterías, above). Books in Spanish. **Editorial Guaymuras**, Av Miguel Cervantes 1055. Second-hand bookstalls in **Mercado San Isidro** (6 Av y 2 Calle, Comayagüela), cheap.

Markets
Mercado San Isidro, 6 Av at 1 Calle, Comayagüela. Many fascinating things, but filthy; do not buy food here. Sat is busiest day. **Mercado de Artesanías**, 3 Av, 15 Calle, next to Parque El Soldado. Good value.
　Good supermarkets: **La Colonia**, in Blv Morazán; **Más y Menos**, in Av de la Paz. Also on Calle Salvador, 1 block south of Peatonal.

Photography
Kodak on Parque Central and Blv Morazán; **Fuji** by the cathedral and on Blv Morazán.

▲▲ Activities and tours

Tegucigalpa *p498 map p498*
Columbia, Calle Principal between 11 y 12 Av, Blv Morazán, T2232-3532, columbiatours@sigmanet.hn. Excellent for national parks, including Cusuco, Pico Bonito and Cuero y Salado, as well as Punta Sal and Bay Islands.
Explore Honduras Tour Service, Col Zerón 21-23 Av, 10 Calle NO, San Pedro Sula, T2552-6242, www.explorehonduras.com. Copán and Bay Islands tours.
Gloria Tours across from north side of Parque Central in Casa Colonial, T/F2238-2232. Information centre and tour operator.
Trek Honduras, Av Julio Lozano 1311, T2239-9827. Tours of the city, Bay Islands, Copán, San Pedro Sula, Valle de Angeles and Santa Lucía.

⊙ Transport

Tegucigalpa *p498, map p498*

Air
Toncontín Airport opens at 0530. Check in at least 2 hrs before departure; snacks, souvenir shops, several duty-free stores and internet. Buses to airport from Comayagüela, on 4 Av between 6 and 7 Calle, or from Av Máximo Jerez in downtown Tegucigalpa; into town US$0.19, every 20 mins from left-hand side outside the airport; yellow cabs, US$9-10, smaller *colectivo* taxis, US$6 or more.

Airline offices Atlantic Airline, T2220-5231; **Air France**, Centro Comercial Galería, Av de la Paz, T2237-0229; **Alitalia**, Col Alameda, 5 Av, 9 Calle No 821, T2239-4246; **American**, Ed Palmira, opposite Honduras Maya, 1st floor, T2232-1414; **British Airways**, Edif Sempe, Blv Comunidad Económica Europea, T2225-5101; **Continental**, Av República de Chile, Col Palmira, T2220-0999; **Grupo Taca**, Blv Morazán y Av Ramón E Cruz, T2239-0148 or airport T2233-5756; **Iberia**, Ed Palmira, opposite Honduras Maya, T2232-7760; **Isleña Airlines**, T236-8778, also at Toncontín Airport, T2233-2192, www.flyislena.com; **Japan Airlines**, Edif Galería La Paz, 3rd floor, Local 312, 116 Av La Paz, T2237-0229; **KLM**, Ed Ciicsa, Av República de Chile y Av República de Panamá, Col Palmira, T2232-6410; **Lufthansa**, Edif Plaza del Sol, No 2326, Av de la Paz, T2236-7560. **Sol Air** in Tegucigalpa on T2235-3737; **Sosa Airline**, at the airport, T2233-7351.

Bus
Local Fares are US$0.08-0.12; stops are official but unmarked.

Long distance To **San Pedro Sula** on Northern Hwy, 3¼-4 hrs depending on service. Several companies, including: Sáenz, Centro Comercial Perisur, Blv Unión Europea, T2233-4229, and **Hedman Alas**, 11 Av, 13-14 Calle, Comayagüela, T2237-7143, www.hedmanalas.com, US$18; both

recommended; **El Rey**, 6 Av, 9 Calle, Comayagüela, T2237-6609; **Viajes Nacionales (Viana)**, terminal on Blv de Las Fuerzas Armadas, T2235-8185. To **Tela** and **La Ceiba**, Viana Clase Oro, and Etrusca, 8 Av, 12 y 13 Calle, T2222-6881. To **Choluteca**, Mi Esperanza, 6 Av, 23-24 Calle, Comayagüela, T2225-1502. To **Trujillo**, Cotraibal, 7 Av, 10-11 Calle, Comayagüela, T2237-1666. To **La Esperanza**, Empresa Joelito, 4 Calle, No 834, Comayagüela. To **Comayagua**, most going to San Pedro Sula and **Transportes Catrachos**, Col Torocagua, Blv del Norte, Comayagüela. To **Valle de Angeles** and **Santa Lucía**, from stop on Av La Paz (near filling station opposite hospital). To **Juticalpa** and **Catacamas**, Empresa Aurora, 8 Calle, 6-7 Av, Comayagüela, T2237-3647. For **Danlí** and **El Paraíso**, for the Nicaraguan border at Las Manos, see page 490.

For travellers leaving Tegucigalpa, take the Tiloarque bus on Av Máximo Jerez, by Calle Palace, and get off in Comayagüela at Cine Centenario (Av 6) for nearby **Empresa Aurora** buses (for **Olancho**) and **El Rey** buses (for **San Pedro Sula**). 3 blocks northwest is Cine Lux, near which are **Empresas Unidas** and **Maribel** (8 Av, 11-12 Calle, T2237-3032) for **Siguatepeque**. Tiloarque bus continues to Mi Esperanza bus terminal (for **Choluteca** and **Nicaraguan border**). Take a 'Carrizal' or 'Santa Fe' bus ascending Belén (9 Calle) for **Hedman Alas** buses to **San Pedro Sula** and for Comayagua buses. The **Norteño** bus line to San Pedro Sula is alongside Mamachepa market, from where there are also buses for **Nacaome** and **El Amatillo** border with El Salvador.

International Ticabus, 16 Calle, 5-6 Av, Comayagüela, T2222-0590, www.ticabus. com, to **Managua** (US$32, 8 hrs), **San José** (US$52), **San Salvador** (US$20), **Guatemala City** (US$40, 12 hrs) and **Panama** (US$87) daily. Make sure you reserve several days ahead. **Hedman Alas** have a service to **Guatemala City** and **Antigua** that leaves

Tegucigalpa for San Pedro Sula, 0545, 12 hrs, US$52. Alternatively to **Nicaragua**, take Mi **Esperanza** bus to San Marcos de Colón, then taxi or local bus to El Espino on border. To **San Marcos**, 4 daily from 0730, direct to border at 0400, US$2.50, 5 hrs (0730 is the latest one that will get you into Nicaragua the same day). Or Mi **Esperanza** bus to Río Guasaule border, several daily, 4 hrs, US$2. To **San Salvador**, Cruceros del Golfo, Barrio Guacerique, Blv Comunidad Económica Europea, Comayagüela, T2233-7415, US$18, at 0600 and 1300, 6 hrs travelling, 1 hr or more at border. Connections to **Guatemala** and **Mexico**; direct bus to border at El Amatillo, US$2.50, 3 hrs, several daily; alternatively from San Pedro Sula via Nueva Ocotepeque and El Poy. To **San Salvador** and **Guatemala**, with King Quality from Tegucigalpa (T2225-5415) from **Cruceros del Golfo** terminal, 0600 and 1300 and San Pedro Sula (T2553-4547) at 0630. Alternatively, to Guatemala go to San Pedro Sula and take **Escobar**, **Impala** or **Congolón** to Nueva Ocotepeque and the border at **Agua Caliente**, or via **Copán** (see page 198).

Car
Car hire Avis, Edif Palmira and airport, T2232- 0088. **Budget**, Blv Suyapa and airport, T/F2235- 9531. **Hertz**, Centro Comercial Villa Real, Col Palmira, T2239-0772. **Maya**, Av República de Chile 202, Col Palmira, T2232-0992. **Molinari**, 1 Av, 2 Calle, Comayagüela and airport, T2237- 5335. **Thrifty**, Col Prados Universitarios, T2235-6077. **Toyota**, T2235-6694.

Car repairs Metal Mecánica, 1 block south of Av de los Próceres, Col Lara. Volkswagen dealer near Parque Concordia, good.

Taxi
About US$4-6 per person, but you can often bargain down to around US$3 for short distances within the city. More after 2200, cheaper on designated routes, eg Miraflores to centre.

Santa Lucía *p502*
Bus
To Santa Lucía from Mercado San Pablo, **Tegucigalpa**, Bus 101, every 45 mins, US$0.50, past the statue of Simón Bolívar by the Esso station, Av de los Próceres.

Valle de Angeles *p503*
Bus
To Valle de Angeles every 45 mins, US$0.50, 1 hr, leaves from San Felipe, near the hospital. To **San Juan de Flores** 1000, 1230, 1530.

Parque Nacional La Tigra *p503*
Bus
Buses leave from Mercado San Pablo, **Tegucigalpa**, for **San Juancito** from 1000, 1½ hrs, on Sat and Sun bus at 0800 packed with people visiting their families, US$1; passes turn-off to Santa Lucía and goes through Valle de Angeles. Return bus from San Juancito at 1500 from across the river and up the hill, opposite the park. On Sat, buses return at 0600 and 1200 from church, board early. For return journey double check local information. Alternatively, from behind Los Dolores church in Tegucigalpa you can take a bus to **El Piligüin/Jutiapa** at 0600; it passes through beautiful scenery by El Hatillo and other communities. From El Piligüin, it is a long, hot walk up to the park entrance.

Ojojona *p505*
Bus
Buses leave **Comayagüela** every 15-30 mins from Calle 4, Av 6, near San Isidro market, US$0.50, 1 hr. From same location, buses go west to **Lepaterique** ('place of the jaguar'), another colonial village, over 1-hr drive through rugged, forested terrain. Distant view of Pacific on fine days from heights above village.

● Directory

Tegucigalpa *p498 map p498*

Banks

There are many ATMs in the city centre. All banks have several branches throughout the city; we list the main offices. Branch offices are unlikely to change TCs, only US$ cash. **HSBC**, 5 Calle (Av Colón) in the centre and at 5 Calle in front of Plaza Morazán. **Banco Atlántida**, 5 Calle in front of Plaza Morazán (may agree to change money on Sat up to 1200). **Banco de Honduras** (Citibank), Blv Suyapa. **Banco del País**, Calle Peotonal in the centre, changes TCs. **Banco de Occidente**, 3 Calle (Cervantes) y 6 Av (S Mendieta) in the centre.

Visa, MasterCard and Amex cash advances (no commission) and TCs at **BAC**, Blv Morazán, and at **Honducard**, Av de la Paz y Ramón E Cruz, and at **Aval Card**, Blv Morazán. Banks are allowed to trade at the current market rate, but there is a street market along the Calle Peatonal off the Parque Central, opposite the post office and elsewhere. Exchange can be difficult on Sat, try **Coin**, a *casa de cambio* on Av de la Paz, inside **Supermercado Más y Menos**, same rates as banks, no commission, Mon-Fri 0830-1730, Sat 0900-1200, changes TCs but will photocopy cheques and passport; another branch of **Coin** on Calle Peatonal, good rates. Recommended.

Cultural centres

Alianza Francesa, Col Lomas del Guijarro, T2239-6163, cultural events Fri afternoon, French films Tue 1930. **Centro Cultural Alemán**, 8 Av, Calle La Fuente, T2237-1555, German newspapers, cultural events. **Instituto Hondureño de Cultura Interamericana (IHCI)**, Calle Real de Comayagüela,T2237-7539, has an English library and cultural events.

Embassies and consulates

Belize, T2220-5000, Ext 7770. **Canada**, Ed Financiero Banexpo, Local 3, Col Payaqui, Blv Juan Bosco II, T232-4551. **Costa Rica**, Col El Triángulo, 1a Calle, opposite No 3451, T2232-1768, bus to Lomas del Guijarro to last stop, then walk up on your left for 300 m. **Ecuador**, Av Juan Lindo 122, Col Palmira, T2236-5980. **El Salvador**, 2 Av Calzada República de Uruguay, Casa 219, Col San Carlos T2236-8045. **France**, Col Palmira, 3 Calle, Av Juan Lindo, T2236-6432. **Germany**, Ed Paysen, 3rd floor, Blv Morazán, T2232-3161. **Guatemala**, Col Las Minitas 4 Calle, Casa 2421, T2232-9704, Mon-Fri 0900-1300, take photo, visa given on the spot, US$10. **Italy**, Av Principal 2602, Col Reforma, T236-6391. **Japan**, Col San Carlos, between 4 and 5 Calle, 2 blocks off Blv Morazán and Av de la Paz, T2236-6828, behind Los Castaños Shopping Mall. **Mexico**, Av República de México, Paseo República de Brasil 2402, Col Palmira, T2232-6471, opens 0900, visa takes 24 hrs. **Netherlands** (Consulate), Edif Barahona, Col Alameda, next to INA, T2231-5007. **Nicaragua**, Av Choluteca 1130, bloque M-1, Col Lomas del Tepeyac, T2232-9025 daily, 0800-1200, US$25, visa can take up to 2 days. **Norway**, consular services in front of Residencial el Limonar, T2557-0856. **Panama**, Ed Palmira No 200, opposite Honduras Maya, 2nd floor, T2239-5508. **Spain**, Col Matamoros 801, T2236-6589, near Av de la Paz and US Embassy. **Sweden** (Consulate), Av Altiplano, Retorno Borneo 2758, Col Miramontes, T/F2232-4935. **UK**, Edif Banexpo, 3rd floor, Col Payaqu, T2232-0612. **USA**, Av La Paz, Mon-Fri 0800- 1700, take any bus from north side of Parque Central in direction 'San Felipe', T2236-9320.

Emergencies

Police 199; Red Cross 195; Fire 198.

Immigration

Dirección General de Migración, Av Máximo Jerez, next to Hotel Ronda, Tegucigalpa.

Internet

Café Don Harry, Av República de Chile 525, Edif Galerías TCB, T2220-6174. **@ccess Cyber**

Coffee, Centro Commercial La Ronda, Av Máximo Jerez next to Super Donuts, Mon-Sat 0800-1900, US$1.50 for 30 mins. **Cyberplace Center**, Av Máximo Jerez and Las Damas, Mon-Sat 0900-1900, US$1 per hr. **Cyberiada Internet Café**, Plaza Brezani, Av Máximo Jerez, Calle H Matute, open 24 hrs, US$1.80 per hr with free coffee. **Multinet**, on Barahona, also in Blv Morazán and Centro Comercial. Lots of machines with full services, 0830-1900, Sun 0900-1700. US$1.50 per hr. **Office Comp**, Av Cervantes, next to Hotel Excelsior, Mon-Sat 0830-1900. US$1 per hr. Small, but with high-speed connection. **PC Cyber**, Edif Paz Barahona, Calle Peatonal, Mon-Fri 0830-1700, Sat 0830-1400.

Laundry
La Cisne, 1602 Calle La Fuente/Av Las Delicias, US$2.50 up to 5 kg, same-day service. **Lavandería Italiana**, Barrio Guadalupe, 4 blocks west of Av República de Chile 300 block. **Lavandería Super Jet**, Av Gutemberg, 300 m east of Hotel Granada, US$0.20 per kg. **Mi Lavandería**, opposite Repostería Calle Real, 3 Calle, 2 Av, Comayagüela, T2237-6573, Mon-Sat 0700-1800, Sun and holidays 0800-1700.

Medical services
Dentist Dra Rosa María Cardillo de Boquín, Ed Los Jarros, Sala 206, Blv Morazán, T2231-0583. Recommended. **Dr Roberto Ayala**, DDS, C Alfonso XIII 3644, Col Lomas de Guijarro, T2232-2407. **Hospitals** Hospital y Clínica Viera, 11 y 12 Av, 5 Calle, Tegucigalpa, T2237-1365. **Hospital la Policlínica** SA 3 Av, 7 y 8 Calle, Comayagüela, T2237-3260. **Centro Médico Hondureño**, 3 Av, 3 Calle, Barrio La Granja, Comayagüela, T2233-6028. **Pharmacies** Farmacia Rosna, pedestrian mall off Parque Central, T2237-0605, English spoken. Recommended. **Regis Palmira**, Ed Ciicsa, Av República de Panamá, Col Palmira.

Post
Av Paz Barahona/C del Telégrafo, Lista de Correos (Poste Restante) mail held for 1 month, 20 g letter to US (US$0.80), Europe (US$1.30), rest of the world (US$1.75).

Telephone
Hondutel, Calle del Telégrafo y Av Colón, has several direct AT&T lines to USA, no waiting. Phone, fax and telegrams; open 24 hrs for phone services only. Also at 6 Av, 7-8 Calle, Comayagüela, with post office.

Work
Peace Corps, opposite Edif Ciicsa, on Av República de Chile, uphill past Hotel Honduras Maya.

Western Honduras

Close to the Guatemalan border, the serene ruins of Copán are Honduras' major Maya attraction. Treasured for its exceptional artistry when compared to other Maya sites, the ruins enjoy a calm and pleasant setting. The quiet town of Copán Ruinas nestles among hills nearby. In fact, the whole area is sprinkled with interesting towns and villages, mostly in delightful hilly surroundings; some with a colourful colonial history, others with their foundations in the Lenca communities, and many producing handicrafts. The ruins of Copán aside, one of the enjoyable aspects of western Honduras is that there are no 'must-sees' – just pick a route, take your time and enjoy the scenery and whatever else you may find. ▸▸ *For listings, see pages 525-533.*

Western Honduras

San Pedro Sula to Copán → *For listings, see pages 525-533.*

The Western Highway runs parallel to the border from San Pedro Sula southwest along the Río Chamelecón to Canoa (58 km), from where there is a paved road south to Santa Bárbara (a further 53 km). Continuing along the Western Highway, the road from Canoa towards Guatemala runs southwest to La Entrada (115 km from San Pedro), where it forks again left for Santa Rosa (see below) and right for an attractive 60-km road through deep green scenery to Copán Ruinas.

The regular bus is recommended rather than the dangerous minibus service, which can be a bit hair-raising. The road is paved throughout and in good condition.

La Entrada is a hot, dusty town and the place to change buses. Going south takes you to Santa Rosa and towards El Salvador, west to Copán and Guatemala.

El Puente ① *daily 0800-1600, US$5*, is a national archaeological park reached by taking a turn-off, 4.5 km west from La Entrada on the Copán road, then turning right on a well-signposted, paved road 6 km to the visitor centre. It is near the confluence of the Chamelecón and Chinamito rivers and is thought to have been a regional centre between AD 600 and 900.

Copán Ruinas → *For listings, see pages 525-533. Colour map 3, B1.*

→ *www.copanhonduras.org.*

A charming town set in the hills just to the east of the border with Guatemala, Copán Ruinas – to give the town its full name – thrives and survives on visitors passing through to visit the nearby ruins. Nevertheless, it is arguably the best-preserved and one of the most pleasant towns in Honduras. Close to the border with Guatemala, it's a good place to stop for a few days before heading straight to San Pedro Sula (172 km) and the Bay Islands or Tegucigalpa (395 km), with the impressive ruins of Copán, good hotels and restaurants, coffee plantation tours, hiking, caving, hot springs, horse riding, language schools and volunteer opportunities.

The **Museo Copán** ① *Mon-Sat 0800-1600, US$2*, on the town square has explanations in Spanish of the Maya empire and stelae. There is an interesting selection of artefacts, a burial site and a tomb that was unearthed during a road-building project. It is a good idea to visit the museum before the ruins. The completely restored Old Cuartel now houses the **Casa K'inich Interactive Children's Museum** ① *up the hill from Hotel Marina Copán, US$1.10, Tue-Sun 0800-1200, 1300-1700*, an interesting museum for everyone, not just for kids, and in a nice spot with great views of the town from towers in the perimeter wall. The **Enchanted Wings Butterfly House** ① *2 blocks west of the cemetery on the road to Guatemala, T2651-4133, daily 0800-1700, US$5.50*, is run by Bob 'The Butterfly Guy' Gallardo, specialist in Honduran butterflies. The garden, complete with restaurant, is beautiful and has exhibits of rare butterflies, an orchid garden and birdwatching tours can be arranged. Recommended. An excellent permanent **photography exhibition** ① *Mon-Fri, 0800-1600, free*, has opened at the Municipalidad on the main plaza. There are rare period photos and documentation from the first archaeological expedition to Copán at the turn of the 20th century, donated by Harvard University's Peabody Museum and archaeologists Barbara and Bill Fash.

Copán archaeological site

ⓘ *Daily, 0800-1600, US$15 entry to ruins and Las Sepulturas, admission valid for 1 day; US$7 to enter the museum with entrance to the tunnels an additional pricey US$15. Bilingual guided tours available (US$25, 2 hrs), recommended. The Copán Guide Association has a kiosk in the parking area where qualified bilingual guides can be hired at a fixed rate.*

Photographs of the excavation work and a maquette of the site are located in a small exhibition room at the visitor centre. There is a *cafetería* by the entrance to the ruins, and also a handicrafts shop, in the Parque Arqueológico, next to the bookshop, with local and country maps, and a Spanish/English guide book for the ruins, which is rather generalized. Useful books are: *Scribes, Warriors and Kings: City of Copán*, by William and Barbara Fash, and *History Carved in Stone*, a guide to Copán, by William Fash and Ricardo Argucía (3rd edition, 1998, US$3), published locally and available at the site. Luggage can be left for free.

The magnificent ruins of Copán are one of Central America's major Maya sites, certainly the most significant in Honduras, and they mark the southeastern limit of Maya dominance. Just 1 km from the village, there is a path beside the road from Copán to the ruins which passes two stelae en route. Get to the ruins as early as possible, or stay late in the day so you have a chance to be there without hordes of people.

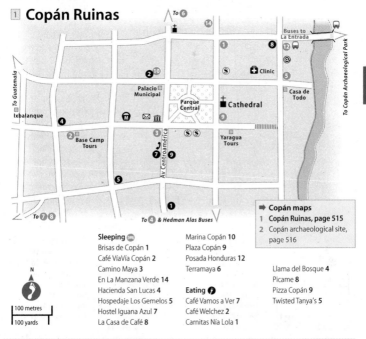

Copán Ruinas

Palacio Municipal

Parque Central

Ixbalanque

Base Camp Tours

Cathedral

Clinic

Casa de Todo

Yaragua Tours

To Guatemala

To Copán Archaeological Park

Buses to La Entrada

Av Centroamérica

To ④ *& Hedman Alas Buses*

N

100 metres
100 yards

➡ **Copán maps**
1 Copán Ruinas, page 515
2 Copán archaeological site, page 516

Sleeping
Brisas de Copán **1**
Café VíaVía Copán **2**
Camino Maya **3**
En La Manzana Verde **14**
Hacienda San Lucas **4**
Hospedaje Los Gemelos **5**
Hostel Iguana Azul **7**
La Casa de Café **8**

Marina Copán **10**
Plaza Copán **9**
Posada Honduras **12**
Terramaya **6**

Eating
Café Vamos a Ver **7**
Café Welchez **2**
Carnitas Nía Lola **1**

Llama del Bosque **4**
Picame **8**
Pizza Copán **9**
Twisted Tanya's **5**

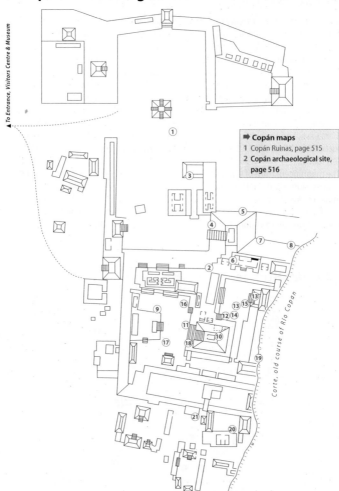

➡ **Copán maps**
1 Copán Ruinas, page 515
2 Copán archaeological site, page 516

N

50 metres
50 yards

Main Plaza with Stelae **1**
Acropolis **2**

Ball Court **3**
Hieroglyphic Stairway **4**
Structure 26 **5**
Council House,
  Temple 22A **6**
Temple of Meditation/
  Temple 22 **7**
House of Knives **8**
Structure 13 **9**

Structure 16 **10**
Altar Q **11**
Rosalila Building
  (within Structure 16) **12**
Entrance to Rosalila &
  Jaguar tunnels **13**
Hunal Building
  (beneath Rosalila)
  & Tomb of Founder **14**

East Court/Plaza
  de los Jaguares **15**
Plaza Occidental **16**
Altar I **17**
Altar H **18**
Temple 18 **19**
Structure 32 **20**
Zona Residencial **21**

Museo de Escultura Maya

ⓘ US$10, ticket from main ticket office not at the museum.

It is essential to visit the museum before the ruins. The impressive and huge two-storey Museum of Maya Sculpture and sculpture park houses the recently excavated carvings. In the middle of the museum is an open-air courtyard with a full-size reproduction of the Rosalila temple, found intact buried under Temple 16 with its original paint and carvings (see below). A reproduction of the doorway to Temple 16 is on the upper floor. The museum houses the original stelae to prevent weather damage, while copies will be placed on site. More than 2000 other objects found at Copán are also in the museum which has good explanations in Spanish and English. The exit leads to the ruins via the nature trail.

Archaeological site

When John Lloyd Stephens and Frederick Catherwood examined the ruins in 1839, they were engulfed in jungle. Stephens, a lawyer, and Catherwood, an architect, were the first English-speaking travellers to explore the regions originally settled by the Maya. They are credited with recording the existence of many of the ruins in the Maya area. Some of the finest examples of sculpture from Copán are now in London and Boston.

In the 1930s, the Carnegie Institute cleared the ground and rebuilt the Hieroglyphic Stairway, and since then the ruins have been maintained by the government. Some of the most complex carvings are found on the 21 **stelae**, or 3-m columns of stones on which the passage of time was originally believed to have been recorded. Under many of the stelae was a vault; some have been excavated. The stelae are deeply incised and carved with faces, figures and animals. There are royal portraits with inscriptions recording deeds and the lineage of those portrayed as well as dates of birth, marriage and death. Ball courts were revealed during excavation, and one of them has been fully restored. The **Hieroglyphic Stairway** leads up a pyramid; its upper level supported a temple. Its other sides are still under excavation. The stairway is covered for protection, but a good view can be gained from the foot and there is access to the top via the adjacent plaza. After Hurricane Mitch, the **Rosalila Temple**, in Temple 16, was opened to the public, as were other previously restricted excavations, in an effort to attract more visitors. The Rosalila and Jaguar tunnels below the site are now open to visitors at an additional cost (see above). Much fascinating excavation work is now in progress, stacks of labelled carved stones have been placed under shelters, and the site looks like it is becoming even more interesting as new buildings are revealed. The most atmospheric buildings are those still half-buried under roots and soil. The last stela was set up in Copán between AD 800 and 820, after less than five centuries of civilized existence. The nearby river has been diverted to prevent it encroaching on the site when in flood.

Also near the ruins is a **sendero natural** (nature trail) through the jungle to the minor ball court; take mosquito repellent. The trail takes 30 minutes and has a few signposts explaining the plants, animals and spirituality of the forest to the Maya. After 1600 is the best time to see animals on the sendero natural, which is open until 1700. About 4 km from the main centre is the ceremonial site known as **Los Sapos** *ⓘ entry US$2* (The Toads), a pre-Classic site with early stone carvings. The toad was a Maya symbol of fertility. East of the main ruins near Los Sapos is a stone, **Estela 12**, which lines up with another, **Estela 10**, on the other side of the valley at sunrise and sunset on 12 April every year.

One kilometre beyond the main ruins, along the road to San Pedro Sula, or connected by a stone path from the main site, is an area called **Las Sepulturas** *ⓘ entrance is almost*

2 km from the main site, entry to this site is included in the main Copán ticket, a residential area where ceramics dating back to 1000 BC have been found. Exhibits from the site are on display in the Copán Museum. It is a delightful site, beautifully excavated and well maintained, peaceful and in lovely surroundings.

Around Copán Ruinas

There are many caves around Copán to visit – some of which have unearthed Maya artefacts; ask locally. Also here, and in the neighbouring part of Guatemala, are a few remaining Chorti indigenous villages, interesting to visit, particularly on 1 November, Día de Los Muertos, when there are family and communal ceremonies for the dead.

After all the trekking has exhausted you, a trip to the thermal springs **Agua Caliente**, ① 20 km north from Copán, T2651-4746, daily 0800-2000, will be just what you need. Reached by a road through villages and beautiful scenery, it's a 45-minute journey by vehicle; pickups sometimes go for about US$25, shared between passengers. The cheapest option is local transport from beside the soccer field (three buses daily, US$1.50), though it's a very rough unpaved road, only advisable by 4WD in wet season. Best to use **Base Camp Adventures** for trips, US$15, plus entry to hot springs. Imaginatively designed as a Maya spiritual centre, complete with tunnel entry to a Xibalba 'underworld', Luna Jaguar offers a hedonistic treat, with 13 different hot pools, mud bath, hydrotherapy warm shower, DIY hot stone foot massage, nature trail and river bathing (US$10, plus extra for massage treatments), all set among the steamy lush forest with aloof Maya sculptures looking over the simmering bathers. Therapist on hand for advice; snacks and drinks served at the poolside. There are changing facilities, toilets, drinks and snacks in the park. Cold water pools before entrance to spa, US$3. Also on the road to Guatemala is the **Enchanted Wings Butterfly House** ① 0800-1700, US$3.

Nine kilometres east of Copán is **Santa Rita**, a small colonial town on the Copán River with cobblestones and red roofs (**Hospedaje Santa Rita** and unnamed outdoor restaurant recommended, off main road next to Esso; speciality tajadas, huge portions, cheap).

Also try the **Macaw Mountain** ① 10 mins from town centre, T2651-4245, www.macawmountain.com, US$10 (valid for 3 days), an ecotourism project incorporating Honduras' largest bird park with 130+ parrots, toucans and macaws, all locally rescued or donated, including some injured and sick birds. There are also some birds of prey, including tiny pigmy owls, all lovingly cared for in clean, spacious enclosures; some tamer birds are in an open area. There are tours of the coffee finca, with expert bilingual naturalist guides; riverside restaurant serving good, hearty food, including excellent coffee and freshly baked cakes, a visitor centre and river swimming. Highly recommended.

Santa Rosa de Copán → For listings, see pages 525-533. Colour map 3, B1. Altitude: 1160 m.

Santa Rosa is an important regional town with a colonial atmosphere of cobbled streets and some of the best colonial architecture in Honduras. Originally known as Los Llanos, it was made a municipality in 1812 and became capital of the Department of Copán when it was split from Gracias (now Lempira). The town is set in some of the best scenery in Honduras and the fine weather makes it ideal for hiking, horses and mountain biking.

Santa Rosa owes its wealth to the fact that it's an agricultural and cattle-raising area. Maize and tobacco are grown here, and visitors can see traditional hand-rolling at the **Flor de Copán cigar factory** ① 3 blocks east of the bus terminal, T2662 0185, Mon-Fri until 1700, closed 1130-1300, tours in Spanish at 1000 and 1400, US$2 per person – ask the guard *at the gate*. The central plaza and church are perched on a hilltop. There is a quieter plaza, the **Parque Infantil** ① *Calle Real Centenario y 6 Av SO*, a fenced playground and a nice place to relax. The main **market** ① *1 Calle and 3 Av NE*, has good leather items. **Farmers' markets** are held daily in Barrio Santa Teresa (take 4 Calle SE past 5 Avenida SE), and at 4 Calle SE and 5 Avenida SE on Sunday 0500 to 1000. ⟩⟩ *For further information, visit www.visitesantarosadecopan.org.*

Around Santa Rosa de Copán

Taking time to explore some of the forested hills around Santa Rosa will lead you through spectacular scenery and give an insight into the life of agricultural Honduras.

There are buses from Santa Rosa west to the small town of **Dulce Nombre de Copán** (US$0,55). There are rooms available next to the Hondutel office. Hikers heading for Copán and the border can continue west through the mountains to stay at **San Agustín** (buses and pickups from Santa Rosa), take a hammock or sleeping bag, continuing next day through Mirasol to reach the Ruinas road at El Jaral, 11 km east of Copán ruins (see above).

South of Santa Rosa, buses pass through **Cucuyagua**, with a scenic river, good swimming and camping on its banks, and **San Pedro de Copán**, an attractive village and an entry point into the Parque Nacional Celaque, see below.

Santa Rosa de Copán

Sleeping 🛏
Blanca Nieves 1
Continental 2
Elvir 4
Hospedaje Calle Real 5
Maya Central 10
Posada de Carlos y Blanca 7
Rosario 11
VIP Copán 3

Eating ✦
El Rodeo 2
Flamingos 3
Las Haciendas 4
Pizza Pizza 8
Weekends Pizza 9
Well 10

Walking from San Manuel Colohuete to Belén Gualcho

There is a well-defined, well-used and easy-to-follow mule trail linking these two villages, which makes a good one- or two-day hike. Maps are not essential as there are communities at many points along the way where advice can be sought. If required, a map of the area is available from the Lenca Cultural Centre in Gracias.

The path leading away from the village leaves from opposite the *pulpería* and *comedor* where the bus drops you, heading west and downhill into a valley. The path is used by 4WD vehicles and continues to San Sebastián. Just after the community of San José, after passing the last house, the path to Belén branches off. A smaller path leaves the 4WD track and climbs steeply up to your right and more northwest.

One hour Just after Peña Blanca, the path direction becomes unclear after it crosses an area of white chalky rocks. There are several other paths here. The main path heads north and steeply downhill at this point.

Two hours There is water all the year round in the Quebrada de Rogán.

Three hours All year round water in Río Gualmite, a short descent. After this there is a longish, steep ascent.

Four hours Just after this point the path branches on a large flat grassy area. Both paths lead to Belén Gualcho. The one to the left drops and crosses the river and then you are faced with a long, arduous and very steep ascent. We would recommend taking the path to the right, which exits to the far right of a grassy area by three small houses.

Five hours The path climbs as it skirts around the Cerro Capitán. Just after passing the steepest part, a small landslide forces the path into a descent almost to the river. From here, only 2 m above the river, you can walk steeply down off the path to the river bank where there is the most perfect camp site. Flat sandy soil in some shade on the edge of a coffee plantation and 2 m from the river.

Six hours From the camping site there is a long, continuous climb before dropping down sharply to cross the river. It is possible, but difficult, to cross the river at the point the path meets it. Take a small path off to the right just before the river, which leads to a suspension bridge. From the river it is a long continuous climb, not especially steep, to Belén Gualcho. It is between two small peaks that can be seen clearly after crossing the river. There are more houses after crossing the river and the odd *pulpería* where you can buy *refrescos* or food.

A mule trail (see box, above) connects **Belén Gualcho**, a Lenca village in the mountains and a good base for exploring the surrounding area, with **San Manuel de Colohuete** (1500 m), which has a magnificent colonial church whose façade is sculpted with figures of saints. Buses go to San Manuel from Gracias at 1300, four hours, and there's usually a pickup returning in the evening. There are no hotels so you must ask villagers about places to stay. There is an equally fine colonial church 30 minutes by 4WD vehicle to the southwest at **San Sebastián Colosuca** (1550 m). The village has a mild climate (two *hospedajes*; or try Don Rubilio; food at Doña Clementina García or Doña Alicia Molina). The Feria de San Sebastián is on 20 January. An hour's walk away is the Cueva del Diablo and 6 km away is Cerro El Alta with a lagoon at the top. From San Sebastián, a mule trail goes via the heights of **Agua Fría** to reach the route near the border at **Tomalá**.

One of the oldest settlements in Honduras, dominated by Montañas de Celaque, Puca and Opulaca – the country's highest peaks – Gracias is a charming, friendly town. Just 50 km from Santa Rosa, both the town and the surrounding countryside are worth a visit. Gracias was the

Gracias

To Santa Rosa de Copán

Río Arcagual

Cohdefor

C Principal

To Castillo San Cristóbal

Las Mercedes

Palacio Municipal

Parque Central

San Marcos

To Esperanza & Aguas Termales

San Sebastián

To Santa Lucía & Celaque

@

To La Campa

N

200 metres
200 yards

Guancascos **3**
Hospedaje Corazón
de Jesús **4**
Posada de Don Juan **5**
Rosario **6**
San Antonio **7**

Sleeping
Colonial **1**
Erick **2**

Eating
El Señorial **1**
La Fonda **2**

centre from which Francisco de Montejo, thrice Governor of Honduras, put down the great indigenous revolt of 1537-1538. Alonso de Cáceres, his lieutenant, besieged Lempira the indigenous leader in his impregnable mountain-top fortress at Cerquín, finally luring him out under a flag of truce, ambushed him and treacherously killed him. When the Audiencia de los Confines was formed in 1544, Gracias became for a time the administrative centre of Central America.

A helpful **tourist office** in the Parque Central can store luggage and arrange transport to Parque Nacional Celaque.

There are three colonial churches, **San Sebastián**, **Las Mercedes** and **San Marcos** (a fourth, Santa Lucía, is southwest of Gracias), and a restored fort, with two fine Spanish cannon, on a hill five minutes' walk west of the centre. The fort, **El Castillo San Cristóbal**, has been well restored, and at the foot of the northern ramparts is the tomb of Juan Lindo, President of Honduras 1847-1852, who introduced free education through a system of state schools.

Around Gracias
→ *For listings, see pages 525-533.*

Balneario Aguas Termales
ⓘ *Daily 0600-2000, US$2.50, rental of towels, hammock, inner tube, restaurant/bar.*
Some 6 km from Gracias along the road to Esperanza (side road signposted), are hot, communal thermal pools in the forest for swimming (one hour by a path, 1½ hours by road). To find the path, walk 2 km beyond the bridge over Río Arcagual to a second bridge before which turn right by a white house. Climb the hill and take the first path on the left (no sign), cross the river and continue for about 15 minutes to the pools. Good place to barbecue.

Parque Nacional Celaque

It takes at least a day to climb from Gracias to the summit of **Monte Celaque** (2849 m, the highest point in Honduras). Most people allow two days to enjoy the trip. The trail begins from behind the visitor centre of the Parque Nacional Celaque (1400 m), which is 8 km from Gracias, two hours' walk. There are several intersections, best to ask at each. You can also enjoy a day walk to **Mirador La Cascada** ① *entry fee US$3 plus US$3 per night camping in the mountain*, about three hours from the visitor centre, 1½ hours downhill going back. Transport can be arranged with the tourist office in the Plaza Central (US$10 per vehicle for up to four people). **Comedor Doña Alejandrina** just before the visitor centre, provides excellent breakfasts. Not much of the 8-km road from Gracias to the park is passable when wet, without a high-clearance or 4WD vehicle. Transport can be arranged through the Lenca Centre. **Armando Mondragón** (Texaco station, T2898-4002) does trips, including lunch. At the centre there are seven beds, shower and cooking facilities, drinks available, well maintained. There is another cabin nearby with 10 beds. Take a torch and sleeping bag. Behind the centre is a trail going down to the river where a crystal-clear pool and waterfall make for wonderful bathing. For guides to the park, contact **Dona Mercedes' Comedor** in Villa Verde (T2994-96681), **Don Luis Melgar**, or **Don Cándido** (T299715114), or one of their brothers; all recommended. Ask the guide the exact way or pay US$6 for the guide. There is a warden, Miguel, living nearby who can supply food and beer but it is safer to take supplies from Gracias. Contact **Cohdefor** or **CIPANAC** in Gracias before leaving for full information. There is a trail all the way to the summit (trees are marked with ribbons) which takes at least six hours: the first three are easy to a campsite at 2000 m (**Campamento Don Tomás**) where there is small hut, the rest of the way is steep. A better campsite if you can make it is **Campamento Naranjo**, with water, at about 2500 m – but you'll need a tent. Between these two sites, the climb is particularly steep and in cloud forest. Look out for spider monkeys. Above 2600 m quetzals have been seen. Many hikers don't bother with the summit as it is forested and enclosed; it's four hours down to the visitor centre. Don't forget good hiking boots, warm clothing, insect repellent and, given the dense forest and possibility of heavy cloud, a compass is also recommended for safety. Also, beware of snakes. There is a trail westward from the summit to Belén Gualcho which is steep towards Belén. It takes a couple of days, a guide might be a good idea.

Visiting the other peaks around Gracias is more complicated but interesting. Information, maps that you can photocopy, camping gear and guided tours can be found at the Lenca Cultural Centre.

Gracias to Erandique

After Gracias, the road runs 52 km to **San Juan del Caite** (a few *hospedajes*, Lempira, Sánchez, and the comfortable Hacienda, two restaurants nearby, helpful people and Peace Corps workers). From here a dirt road runs 26 km south to the small town of Erandique. Founded in 1560 and set high in pine-clad mountains not far from the border with El Salvador, it is a friendly town, and very beautiful. Lempira was born nearby, and was killed a few kilometres away. The third weekend in January is the local **Fiesta de San Sebastián**. Best time to visit is at the weekend. Market days are Friday and Sunday. Each of the three barrios has a nice colonial church. Ask around as there are lakes, rivers, waterfalls, springs and bathing ponds in the vicinity. Nearby is **San Antonio** where fine opals (not cut gems, but stones encased in rock) are mined and may be purchased. The many hamlets in the surrounding mountains are reached by roads that have been either resurfaced or rebuilt and the landscapes are magnificent.

There are several roads radiating from Erandique, including one to **Mapulaca** and the border with El Salvador (no immigration or customs or bridge here, at the Río Lempa), a road to San Andrés and another to Piraera (all passable in a car).

La Esperanza → *Colour map 1, C2. Altitude: 1485 m.*

Beyond San Juan del Caite the main, but still rough and stony, road winds through beautiful mountain pine forests to La Esperanza. It is 43 km from San Juan del Caite and another 98 km on a good road to Siguatepeque. Capital of Intibucá Department, La Esperanza is an old colonial town in a pleasant valley. It has an attractive church in front of the park. There is a grotto carved out of the mountainside west of the town centre, a site of religious festivals. There is a market on Thursdays and Sundays when the Lenca from nearby villages sell wares and food but no handicrafts. Nearby is the indigenous village of **Yaramanguila**. It's an excellent area for walking in forested hills, with lakes and waterfalls, although very cold December/January. You can hike to **Cerro de Ojos**, a hill to the northwest and visible from La Esperanza. It is forested with a clearing on top littered with many cylindrical holes; no one knows how they were formed, and they are a strange phenomenon. The turning to this hill is on the La Esperanza to San Juan road. Ask for directions.

Marcala and around → *For listings, see pages 525-533. Colour map 3, C2. Altitude: 1300 m.*

From La Esperanza, an unpaved road runs southeast to Marcala in the Department of La Paz (a paved road goes to La Paz). During the hotter months from March to May, a cooler climate can be found in the highlands of La Paz, with pleasant temperatures during the day and cold (depending on altitude) at night. Ideal for hiking and with beautiful scenery and dramatic waterfalls in the surrounding area, Marcala is a good base from which to visit Yarula, Santa Elena, Opatoro, San José and Guajiquiro. The Marcala region is one of the finest coffee-producing areas of Honduras and a visit to **Comarca**, at the entrance to town, gives an idea of how coffee is processed. Semana Santa is celebrated with a large procession through the main street and there is a **fiesta** in honour of San Miguel Arcángel in the last week of September.

Around Marcala

Near Marcala is **Balneario El Manzanal** ① *3 km on the road to La Esperanza, open weekends only*, which has a restaurant, two swimming pools and a boating lake. For panoramic views high above Marcala, follow this hike (one hour): head north past **Hotel Medina**, turn right (east) after the hotel and follow the road up into hills. After 2 km the road branches. Take the left branch and immediately on the left is a football field. A small path leaves from this field on the west side taking you through a small area of pine trees then out onto a ridge for excellent views. The track continues down from the ridge back to town, passing an unusual cemetery on a hill.

There are caves nearby on **Musula** mountain, the Cueva de las Animas in Guamizales and Cueva de El Gigante and El León near La Estanzuela with a high waterfall close by. Other waterfalls are El Chiflador, 67 m high, Las Golondrinas, La Chorrera and Santa Rosita. Transport goes to La Florida where there is good walking to the village of **Opatoro** and climbing **Cerro Guajiquiro**. Between Opatoro and Guajiquiro is the **Reserva las Trancas**, a heavily forested mountain where quetzales have been seen.

Yarula and Santa Elena are two tiny municipalities, the latter about 40 km from Marcala, with beautiful views (bus Marcala–Santa Elena 1230 returns 0500 next day, 2¾ hours, enquire at Gámez bus office opposite market; truck daily 0830 returns from Santa Elena at 1300). Sometimes meals are available at *comedores* in Yarula and Santa Elena. The dirt road from Marcala gradually deteriorates, the last 20 km being terrible, high clearance essential, 4WD recommended. In **La Cueva Pintada**, south of Santa Elena, there are pre-Columbian cave paintings (*pinturas rupestres*) of snakes, men and dogs; ask for a guide in Santa Elena. Ask also in this village about the **Danza de los Negritos**, performed at the annual **Fiesta de Santiago**, 24-25 March, in front of the church. A special performance may be organized, the dancers wearing their old wooden masks, if suitable payment is offered.

The village of **San José** (altitude: 1700 m) is a Lenca community where the climate can be cool and windy even in the hottest months. The scenery is superb, there's good hill walking (see box, page 520 for two examples; there are many others) and also rivers for swimming. Frequent pickups from Marcala, and two daily minibuses at about 0815 and 0900; from San José to Marcala minibuses depart at 0615 and 0645, one hour, US$1.

Nueva Ocotepeque → *For listings, see pages 525-533. Colour map 3, C1.*

Heading south from Santa Rosa, Nueva Ocotepeque gives access to good hiking and leads to the borders with Guatemala and El Salvador. The old colonial church of La Vieja (or La Antigua) between Nueva Ocotepeque and the border, is in the village of Antigua Ocotepeque, founded in the 1540s, but destroyed by a flood from Cerro El Pital in 1934.

The **Guisayote Biological Reserve** protects 35 sq km of cloud forest, about 50% virgin and is reached from the Western Highway, where there are trails and good hiking. Access is from El Portillo, the name of the pass on the main road north. El Portillo to El Sillón, the park's southern entrance, three to five hours. Twice daily bus from El Sillón to Ocotepeque. **El Pital**, 3 km east of Nueva Ocotepeque, at 2730 m is the third highest point in Honduras with several square kilometres of cloud forest. The park has not been developed for tourism.

The **Parque Nacional Montecristo** forms part of the Trifinio/La Fraternidad project, administered jointly by Honduras, Guatemala and El Salvador. The park is quite remote from the Honduran side, two to three days to the summit, but there are easy-to-follow trails. Access is best from Metapán in El Salvador. From the lookout point at the peak you can see about 90% of El Salvador and 20% of Honduras on a clear day. The natural resources office, for information, is opposite Texaco, two blocks from **Hotel y Comedor Congolón** at the south end of town. Raymond J Sabella of the US Peace Corps has written a very thorough description of the natural and historical attractions of the Department, including hikes, waterfalls and caves.

For Sleeping and Eating price codes and other relevant information, see Essentials pages 31-33.

● Sleeping

San Pedro Sula to Copán *p514*

C-E San Carlos, La Entrada, at junction to Copán Ruinas, T2898-5228. A/c, modern, cable TV, bar, swimming pool, restaurant (T/F2661-2187), excellent value.

E-F Central, by Shell, La Entrada. With 2 beds (cheaper with 1), bath, cold water, fans.

F Hospedaje Golosino Yessi, La Entrada. Parking, small rooms, OK.

F Hospedaje María, La Entrada. Good, limited food.

Copán Ruinas *p514, map p515*

L Hacienda San Lucas, south out of town, T2651-4495, www.haciendasanlucas.com. Great spot for calm and tranquillity. 8 rooms with hot water bath, restaurant, renovated hacienda home, lovely views of Copán river valley and hiking trails.

AL-B Marina Copán, on the plaza occupying almost an entire block, T2651-4070, www.hotelmarinacopan.com. Swimming pool, sauna, restaurant, bar, live marimba music at weekends, also caters for tour groups, large rooms with TV, a/c, suites, very tasteful and spacious, friendly atmosphere. Recommended.

A Camino Maya, corner of main plaza, T2651-4646, www.caminomayahotel.com. With bath, good restaurant, rooms bright and airy, cable TV, a/c, fans, rooms on courtyard quieter than street, English spoken, free internet, balconies on some upstairs rooms.

A Terramaya, 2 blocks uphill from main plaza, T2651 4623, www.terramayacopan.com. The town's first boutique-style hotel, with 6 small but tasteful rooms, glorious countryside views from those upstairs, leafy little garden with massage area and outdoor shower; lounge areas and library. Breakfast included. Owners of **Casa del Café** (see below) very

helpful and knowledgeable for local tours and activities.

A La Casa de Café, 4½ blocks west of plaza, T2651-4620, www.casadecafecopan.com. Renovated colonial home, with breakfast, coffee all day, library, expert local information, beautifully designed garden, lovely views over valley, friendly and interesting hosts, English spoken. Popular so best to reserve in advance, protected parking. **Bamboo Patio** massage pavilion offers 1-hr relaxation massage. Wi-Fi. Recommended.

B Brisas de Copán, T2651-4118. Terrace, modern rooms with bath, hot water, quiet, limited parking. Recommended.

B Plaza Copán, on southeast corner of main plaza, T2651-4508. Clean, bright rooms with kitschy decor, cable TV and a/c, restaurant facing plaza, pool, laundry, safe parking.

C Posada Honduras, central location, T2651-4059, www.laposadacopan.com. Private bath, ceiling fan and hot water.

D-E Café Via Via Copán, T2651-4652, www.viaviacafe.com. Great rooms, part of a worldwide Belgian network of cafés, breakfast US$2.75, special price for students with card and discounts for more than 1 night, hot water, good beds, bar and great vegetarian food.

D-E Hostel Iguana Azul, next to La Casa de Café and under same ownership, T2651-4620, www.iguanaazulcopan.com. Dormitory-style bunk beds in 2 rooms, shared bath, also 3 more private double rooms, hot water, free purified water, lockers, laundry facilities, garden patio, colonial decor, clean, comfortable, common area, books, magazines, travel guides (including Footprint), maps, garden, fans, safe box, English spoken. Good for backpackers.

E Hospedaje Los Gemelos, 1 block down from **Banco de Occidente**, T2651-4077. With shared bath, clean, fans, good value, friendly, pleasant patio. Recommended.

F En la Manzana Verde, T2651-4652, www.enlamanzanaverde.com. Great shared bunk rooms, shared bath, kitchen, same owners as Via Via. Good budget choice.

Apartments

Casa Jaguar Rental Home, just 5 blocks from Parque Central, T2651-4620, www.casa jaguarcopan.com. Comfortable village residence with 2 double bedrooms with a/c, fully equipped for self-catering. Available for the night, week or month. Contact La Casa de Café, see above.

La Casa de Don Santiago, T2651-4620, www.casadedonsantiagocopan.com. Same owners as Casa Jaguar, with 2 bedrooms, hot water bath, balconies with valley views, garden, fully equipped for self catering and available per night, week and month. Sparkling clean, comfortable and centrally located. Wi-Fi.

Santa Rosa de Copán p518, map p519

A Continental, 2 Calle NO y 2-3 Av, T6262-0801, on 2nd floor. Good value with bath, hot water, fan, cable TV, friendly management.

A Elvir, Calle Real Centenario SO, 3 Av SO, T/F2662-0805, hotelelvir@globalnet.hn. Safe, clean, quiet, all rooms have own bath, TV, hot water, drinking water; free internet in lobby good but pricey meals in *cafetería* or restaurant; gym and rooftop pool and bar.

B-C VIP Copán, 1 Calle, 3 Av, T2662-0265. With bath, TV, cheaper without, cell-like rooms but clean, safe, hot water in morning.

C Posada de Carlos y Blanca, Calle Centenario between 3 and 4 Av NO, T2662-4020, posadacarlosyb@yahoo.com. Cosy family-run B&B with 6 comfy rooms with firm beds and bath; homely lounge with internet use, pretty enclosed back garden, quiet and secure.

C-D Rosario, 3 Av NE No 139, T2662-0211. Cold water, with bath, cheaper without, friendly.

D Maya Central (not to be confused with Hospedaje Maya), 1 Calle NO y 3 Av NO, T2662-0073. With bath, cold shower, pleasant.

E Blanca Nieves, 3 Av NE, Barrio Mercedes, T2662-1312. Safe, shared bath with cold

water, laundry facilities. Going down hill but worth a look.

F Hospedaje Calle Real, Real Centenario y 6 Av NE. Clean, quiet, friendly, best of the cheaper places but sometimes water failures.

Around Santa Rosa de Copán p519

In Belén Gualcho hotels fill up quickly on Sat as traders arrive for the Sun market.

F Pensión, Corquín. Good *pensión* with a charming garden. Recommended.

G Hospedaje, east of Santa Rosa de Copán Lepaera, opposite market. Very basic.

G Hotelito El Carmen, Belén Gualcho, 2 blocks east down from the church in the plaza. Friendly, clean, good views. Recommended.

Gracias p521, map p521

AL-A Posada de Don Juan, Calle Principal opposite Banco de Occidente, T/F2656-1020, www.posadadedonjuanhotel.com. Good beds, great hot showers, nice big towels, laundry, some rooms have TV, a pool and parking. Recommended.

B Guancascos, at the west end of Hondutel road, T2656-1219, www.guancascos.com. Bath, hot water, TV, also rents 2-room cabin at Villa Verde adjacent to Monte Celaque visitor centre.

C Hotel Rosario, T2656-0694. Hot water, private bath, pool, clean and friendly.

D Colonial, 1 block south of Erick, T2656-1258. With bath, fan, bar, restaurant, very good.

D-E San Antonio, main street, 2 blocks from Texaco station, T2656-1071. Clean, pleasant, friendly, good.

E Erick, same street as bus office, T2656-1066. With bath, cheaper without (cold shower), TV, comfortable beds, fresh, bright, clean, good value with helpful, friendly owners. Laundry facilities, stores luggage, shop selling basic supplies and can arrange transport to Mt Celaque. Very convenient and recommended.

E Finca Bavaria, quiet place at the edge of town, T2656-1372. Good breakfasts. German/Honduran owned. Parking.

F Hospedaje Corazón de Jesús, on main street by market. Clean, OK.

La Esperanza *p523*
Simple but pleasant *pensiones*.

B Hotel Mina, 1 block south of east side of market, T2783-1071. Good beds, clean, very friendly, food available.

C La Esperanza, T2783-0068. With bath, cheaper without, warm water, clean, TV, friendly, good meals.

D Mejía Batres, ½ block from Parque Central, T2783-0051. With bath, clean, friendly, excellent value.

E El Rey, in Barrio La Morera, T2783-2083. Clean, friendly.

Marcala and around *p523*

D-E Medina, on main road through town, T2898-1866. The most comfortable, clean, modern with bath, *cafetería*, free purified water. Highly recommended.

E Hospedaje Edgar, main street, beginning of town. Clean, basic, no sheets.

E Hospedaje Jairo, 2 blocks east of main square. With bath.

E Unnamed hotel, San José. Run by Brit Nigel Potter ('Nayo'). Basic but comfortable and clean, with meals. He also takes groups to stay in Lenca villages, US$5 per person plus US$10 per person for accommodation in a village; ask for the house of Doña Gloria, Profe Vinda, Nayo or Ruth. At least one of these will be present to meet visitors.

Nueva Ocotepeque *p524*

C Maya Chortis, Barrio San José, 4 Calle, 3 Av NE, T2653-3377. Nice rooms with bath, double beds, hot water, fan, TV, minibar, phone, room service, quieter rooms at back, including breakfast, good restaurant, good value.

C Sandoval, opposite Hondutel, T2653-3098. Rooms and suites, breakfast included, private bath, hot water, cable TV, minibar, phone, room service, restaurant attached, good value.

E-F San Antonio, 1 Calle, 3 Av, T2653-3072. Small rooms but OK.

F Gran, about 250 m from town at the junction of the roads for El Salvador and Guatemala, just north of town, at Sinuapa. With bath, cold water, pleasant, clean, single beds only.

F Ocotepeque, by Transportes Toritos. Clean but noisy.

🍴 Eating

Copán Ruinas *p514, map p515*

🍴🍴🍴 **Café Welchez**, next to Hotel Marina Copán. Good cakes but expensive and coffee 'unpredictable'.

🍴🍴🍴 **Hacienda San Lucas**, south out of town, T2651-4106. Set menu by reservation, with 5-course meal, local ingredients, candlelight – great place for a special meal.

🍴🍴🍴 **Twisted Tanya's**, T2651-4182, www.twistedtanya.com. Mon-Sat 1500-2200. Happy hour 1600-1800. Lovely open-air setting, 2nd floor. Fine dining and quirky retro decor (ie mirrorballs) big portions, but overpriced and scatty service.

🍴🍴 **Café Vamos a Ver**, 1 block from plaza. Open daily 0700-2200. Lots of vegetables, good sandwiches and snacks, complete dinner US$5, pleasant, good value.

🍴🍴 **Café Via Via Copán** (see Sleeping, above). Food, fresh bread, bar, lodging.

🍴🍴 **Elisa's** at Camino Maya (see Sleeping, above). Excellent food at reasonable prices, pleasant, good service.

🍴🍴 **La Casa de Todo**, 1 block from Parque Central in a pleasant garden setting, www.casadetodo.com. Open 0700-2100. Restaurant, internet, craft shop, internet, book exchange. What more could you want?

🍴🍴 **Llama del Bosque**, 2 blocks west of plaza. Open for breakfast, lunch and dinner, pleasant, large portions of reasonable food, try their *carnitas típicas*. Recommended.

🍴🍴 **Pizza Copán**, locally known as Jim's, US expat Jim cooks up good old US of A fare: grilled chicken, BBQ steaks, burgers and good pizza.

¶ **Carnitas Nía Lola**, 2 blocks south of Parque Central, at end of road. Open daily 0700-2200. *Comida típica*, busy bar, relaxed atmosphere and book exchange.

¶ **Espresso Americano**, Parque Central location for a café serving great coffee, ideal for people-watching.

¶ **Picame** (see map). Good hearty food, good value, huge portions, popular with travellers. Recommended.

¶ **Pupusería y Comedor Mari**, ½ block from market. The best cheap, typical food in town. Clean, decent service, very popular with locals at lunchtime. Daily specials like seafood soup. Food is fresh, cheap and plentiful, popular with locals.

Santa Rosa de Copán *p518, map p519*

¶¶ **El Rodeo**, 1 Av SE. Good menu, specializes in steaks, nice atmosphere, plenty of dead animals on the walls, pricey.

¶¶ **Flamingos**, 1 Av SE, off main plaza, T2662-0654. Reasonably priced and good pasta and chop suey, popular with locals; upstairs lounge bar, painted flamingos on walls.

¶¶ **La Gran Villa**, on the *carretera*. Some of the tastiest meats and meals in Santa Rosa, run by Garífuna family. Recommended.

¶¶ **Las Haciendas**, 1 Av Calle SE. Steak and seafood, varied menu, filling *comida corriente*, and an attractive patio bar. Recommended.

¶¶ **Well**, 3 Calle 2 Av SE, Chinese, a/c, huge portions, good value and service.

¶ **Merendero El Campesino**, at the bus terminal. Good *comedor*.

¶ **Pizza Pizza**, Real Centenario 5 Av NE, 4½ blocks from main plaza. Good pizza and pasta, great coffee, but rather stark and soulless, US owned, book exchange.

¶ **Weekends Pizza**, 3 Av SO and 3C, T2662-4221. Downhill on edge of town but worth the walk for good-value pizzas, pastas and unusual extras like cheese straws; bright and colourful with lime green and marigold yellow walls. Home-made bread, local honey and coffee for sale. Wed-Sun 0900-2100. Recommended.

Around Santa Rosa de Copán *p519*

In Belén Gualcho there are 2 *comedores* on south side of plaza and east side on corner with store.

¶ **Comedor Mery**, Belén Gualcho. 1 block northwest of plaza. Good food in a welcoming family atmosphere.

¶ **Las Haciendas**, Belén Gualcho. Good.

Gracias *p521, map p521*

For breakfast, try the *comedores* near the market or, better, the restaurant at **Hotel Iris** (good *comida corriente* too) or **Guancascos**.

¶¶ **Comedor Graciano** and **Pollo Gracianito**, main street. Good value.

¶¶ **La Fonda** (see map). Good food, good value, attractively decorated, but no written menu – good practice for your Spanish. Recommended.

¶ **El Señorial**, main street. Simple meals and snacks, once house of former president Dr Juan Lindo.

¶ **Rancho de Lily**, 3 blocks west of Hondutel. Value for money, rustic cabin, bar service, good snacks.

La Esperanza *p523*

¶¶ **Pizza Venezia**, on edge of town towards Marcala. Good Italian dishes.

¶ **Cáfé El Ecológico**, corner of Parque Central. Home-made cakes and pastries, fruit drinks, delicious home-made jams.

¶ **Restaurant Magus**, 1 block east of plaza, Good food in a video bar atmosphere.

¶ **Unnamed restaurant** in front of church. Very good *comida corriente*.

Marcala and around *p523*

¶¶ **Riviera Linda**, opposite **Hotel Medina**. Pleasant atmosphere, spacious, a little pricey but good food.

¶ **Café Express**, beside Esso. Good breakfast and *comida corrida*. Recommended.

¶ **Darwin**, main street in centre. Cheap breakfasts from 0700. Recommended.

¶ **El Mirador**, on entering town by petrol station. Nice views from veranda, good food. Recommended.

¶ **Jarito**, opposite market entrance. Good.

Around Marcala p523
¶ **Comedor**, 500 m before plaza on main road. Good, clean and cheap.

Nueva Ocotepeque p524
¶¶ **Sandoval** and **Don Chepe**, at Maya Chortis. The best options. Excellent food, small wine lists, good value. Recommended. Comedor Nora (¶), Parque Central, and **Merendera Ruth** (¶), 2 Calle NE, just off Parque Central, both offer economical *comida corriente*, preferable to *comedores* around bus terminal.

⊕ Entertainment

Copán Ruinas p514, map p515
Barcito, one block down from SW corner of main square, small, cosy, laid-back bar on upstairs open terrace; 1700-1900 Happy Hour; also serves great and inexpensive gourmet snacks and tapas.
Papa Changos, located a few blocks from downtown. After hours spot, popular with young locals and traveller crowd. Gets going at midnight on Fri and Sat. The place to let loose and party till dawn.
Via Via, see Sleeping, every night till 2400. European chill-out lounge vibe, comfortable and popular, food until 2100.

Santa Rosa de Copán p518, map p519
Bars and clubs
Extasis, shows videos Mon-Thu night.
Luna Jaguar, at 3 Av, between 1 Calle SE and Calle Real Centenario, is the hottest disco in town, but proper dress required.
Manzanitas, is on the corner of 3 Av SE and Calle Real Centenario, if you fancy singing your heart out to a little karaoke.

Cinema
Plaza Saavedra, opposite Blanca Nieves, nightly at 1900.

⊛ Festivals and events

Santa Rosa de Copán p518, map p519
21-31 Aug Festival de Santa Rosa de Lima; the 'Tobacco Queen' is crowned at the end of the week.

La Esperanza p523
3rd week in Jul Festival de la Papa.
8 Dec Fiesta de la Virgen de la Concepción.

○ Shopping

Copán Ruinas p514, map p515
Selling all sorts of local crafts are **La Casa de Todo**, down the street from **Banco de Occidente**, is one of Copán's best crafts shop, with a popular café for light meals and snacks; **Yax Kuk Mo** on SW corner of plaza has biggest selection; **Mayan Connection**, opposite Barcito (see Entertainment, above) is a bit more expensive but better than average quality. **La Casa del Jade**, 1 block uphill from **Hotel Marina Copán** (with another branch in lobby) specializes in high-class designer jewellery.

Santa Rosa de Copán p518, map p519
Supermercado Manzanitaz, C Centenario.

▲ Activities and tours

Copán Ruinas p514, map p515
Animal and birdwatching
Birding guide and naturalist **Bob Gallardo** (T2651-4133, rgallardo32@hotmail.com) is the owner of the Butterfly Garden and an expert on Honduran flora and fauna. He leads birding trips, **natural history tours**, orchid and serpent tours around Copán and other parts of Honduras, including La Mosquitia. **Alexander Alvarado**, T9751-1680, alexander2084@hotmail.com, based in Copán Ruinas, also leads birdwatching and hiking tours around the country; knows his stuff and speaks good English.

Coffee tours

Copán Coffee Tour, Finca Santa Isabel, 40 mins' drive from Copán Ruinas, www.cafe honduras.com, T2651-4202. Run by family producers of high-quality Welchez coffee for 3 generations. 3- to 4-hr tour of grounds shows whole production process in lovely hillside setting, with terrace restaurant overlooking river; expert multilingual guides; US$25-30. Horse riding also available, through countryside rich with flora and fauna, including some 80 bird species and medicinal plants. The best tour of its kind in the area, highly recommended.

Horse riding

You will probably be approached with offers of horse hire, which is a good way of getting to nearby attractions. Riding trips are available to **Los Sapos** and **Las Sepulturas**, US$15 for 3 hrs. Watch out for taxi and on the street recommendations as the quality and price can be poor.

Finca El Cisne, T2651-4695, www.fincael cisne.com. Full-day tours to the coffee plantation high in the mountains including horse riding, lunch and transport. Also trips to hot springs on this working hacienda. Accommodation (**AL**). Good trip.

Tour operators

Base Camp Adventures, T2651-4695. Nature hikes US$8, treks, motocross tours US$40, horse riding US$15, expedition hikes US$20 and transport including shuttles to Guatemala City, Antigua US$12.

MC Tours, across the street from **Hotel Marina**, T2651-4453, www.mctours-honduras.com. Local and countrywide tours.

Copán Connections, T2651-4182, www.copanconnections.com. Tours, hotels, transport, specializing in Copán and Bay Islands. Run by Tanya of Twisted Tanya fame.

Santa Rosa de Copán *p518, map p519*
Tour operators

Lenca Land Trails, at Hotel Elvir, T/F2662-1375, www.lenca-honduras.com. Run by Max Elvir, who organizes cultural tours of the Lenca mountain villages in western Honduras, hiking, mountain biking, the lot; including a fascinating visit to a *purería* (cigar workshop), pilgrimage shrine and archaeological site at Quezailica, a village 38 km north of Santa Rosa. Excellent source of information about the region. Highly recommended.

Gracias *p521, map p521*
Tour operators

Celaque Aventuras Tours, based in Guancascos, T2656-1219. Run by Christophe Condor who organizes walking tours, visits to **La Campa**, the national park, thermal baths, horse hire, US$8, includes horse riding, visit to thermal pools day or night, visiting natural caves. Hot springs only, US$4.

Guancascos Tourist Centre, at the **Guancascos Hotel**, arranges tours and expeditions to Monte Celaque Parque Nacional, local villages and other attractions.

Marcala and around *p523*

For trips to visit Lenca villages see unnamed hotel in San José, under Sleeping, page 527.

⊖ Transport

Copán Ruinas *p514, map p515*
Bus

Heading inland you normally have to go to San Pedro Sula before heading for the coast or south to the capital.

There is a 1st-class direct service to **San Pedro Sula** with connections to **Tegucigalpa** and **La Ceiba** with Hedman Alas (T2651-4037, www.hedmanalas.com), 3 a day, 3 hrs to San Pedro. US$16, at 1030 and 1430, with connections in San Pedro for Tegucigalpa and La Ceiba. Also 0515 daily connection to **Tela**, 8 hrs, US$22 and **San Pedro Sula Airport, US$21. To Guatemala

City (US$35) and **Antigua** (US$42) at 1420 and 1800. To **San Pedro Sula** Casasola Express for San Pedro Sula (T2651-4078) at 0400, 0500, 0600, 0700 and 1400. Both services are comfortable, efficient, good value and with reclining seats.

If heading for **Santa Rosa de Copán** or **Gracias** get a bus to the junction at La Entrada and change there. Buses for **La Entrada** leave Copán Ruinas every 30 mins, 1 hr, US$1.80.

Plus+ Agency daily shuttle bus service (www.plustravelguate.com, T2651-4088), main office in Copán Ruinas, Comercial Handal, Calle Independencia, to many destinations around Honduras and to Guatemala City and Antigua (US$8). If travelling in a group, private express minibuses can be hired to **San Pedro Sula**, **Tela**, **La Ceiba**, and airport from **Hotel Patty** and **Yaragua Tours** – US$120 regardless of number of people. Numerous boys greet you on arrival to carry bags or offer directions for a small fee, while most are good kids, some will tell you hotels are closed when they aren't.

Tuk-tuk
As in much of Honduras, tuk-tuks have arrived, providing cheap, easy transport. Short trips around town cost US$0.50, **Macaw Mountain Bird Park** US$1.10, **ruins** US$0.80, **Hedman Alas** terminal US$1.10.

Santa Rosa de Copán and around
p518, map p519
Bus
Buses depart from the city bus station on Carretera Internacional.
Local 'El Urbano' bus to centre from bus station (on Carretera Internacional, 2 km below town, opposite Hotel Mayaland), US$0.15, 15 mins; taxi US$1.40.

Long distance If coming from the Guatemalan border at Nueva Ocotepeque, the bus will stop at the end of town near Av Centenario, 2 km below town, opposite Hotel Mayaland. To **Tegucigalpa**, Toritos leaves at 0400 from terminal Mon-Sat 0400 and 1000 Sun, US$6, 10 hrs; also **Empresa de Transportes la Sultana** (T2662-0940) has departures at 0500, 0700, and 0900. Alternatively, take an express bus to San Pedro Sula and an express bus on to Tegucigalpa (US$5, 6 hrs). To **Gracias**, Transportes Lempira, several 0630-1800, 1½ hrs, US$1.30. To **San Pedro Sula**, US$2.50, 4 hrs, every 45 mins 0400-1730, express service daily 2½ hrs, US$3.50 (**Empresa Torito**). Bus to **La Entrada**, 1 hr, US$1. To **Copán Ruinas**, 4 hrs on good road, US$2.90, several direct daily 1100, 1230 and 1400. Alternatively, take any bus to La Entrada, 1 hr, US$1, and transfer to a Copán Ruinas bus. South on paved road to **Nueva Ocotepeque**, 6 daily, US$1.80, 2 hrs. There you change buses for El Salvador and Guatemala (1 hr to border, US$1, bus leaves hourly until 1700).

Around Santa Rosa de Copán *p519*
Bus Numerous buses head south daily from Santa Rosa to **Corquín** (US$0.75, 2 hrs). **Belén Gualcho** to **Santa Rosa** daily at 0430 (Sun at 0930). To **Gracias** from main plaza at 0400, 0500 and 1330.

Gracias *p521, map p521*
Bus
A bus goes to **La Esperanza** at 0530 and 0730, or take bus to Erandique (they leave when full from La Planta) get off at San Juan from where frequent buses goes to La Esperanza (1 hr, US$2)There is a bus service to **Santa Rosa de Copán**, US$1.30, from 0530 to 1630, 5 times a day, 1½ hrs; beautiful journey through majestic scenery. Also to **San Pedro Sula** at 0500, 0800 and 0900, US$3, 4 hrs. Daily bus service to **Lepaera** 1400, 1½ hrs, US$1.50; daily bus to **San Manuel de Colohuete** at 1300. Cotral bus ticket office is 1 block north of Parque Central. **Torito** bus, a few metres from the main terminal, has buses to the Guatemalan border at **Agua Caliente**, one at 1000, change buses at Nueva Ocotepeque.

Gracias to Erandique p522
Bus

There are minibuses to Erandique from the bridge on the road to La Esperanza, 1100 daily, although most people go by truck from Gracias (there is sometimes a van service as far as San Juan) or La Esperanza (change trucks at San Juan intersection, very dusty). Return minibus to Gracias at 0500 daily, which connects with the bus to La Esperanza in San Juan. Trucks leave Erandique 0700 daily, but sometimes earlier, and occasionally a 2nd one leaves around 0800 for Gracias, otherwise be prepared for a long wait for a pickup.

La Esperanza p523
Bus

To **Tegucigalpa** several daily, 3½ hrs, US$5 (Cobramil, also to **San Pedro Sula**, and **Joelito**, 4 hrs, US$2.60). To **Siguatepeque** 0700, 0900, last at 1000, US$1.50, 1 hrs; also to **Siguatepeque**, **Comayagua** at 0600; and to the **Salvadorean border**; bus stops by market. Hourly minibuses to **Yaramanguila**, 30 mins. Daily bus to **Marcala**, 2 hrs at 1230 (but check), US$0.80 (truck, US$1.20, 2¼ hrs). Minibus service at 1130, US$1.50. Daily minibus service to **San Juan**, departs between 1030-1200 from a parking space midway between the 2 bus stops, 2½ hrs, pickups also do this journey, very crowded; for **Erandique**, alight at Erandique turn-off, 1 km before San Juan and wait for truck to pass (*comedor* plus basic *hospedaje* at intersection). If going to Gracias, stay on the La Esperanza–San Juan bus until the end of the line where a pickup collects passengers 15 mins or so later, 1 hr San Juan–Gracias. Buses to **Lake Yojoa** (see page 536), 2 hrs, US$2.50.

Marcala and around p523
Bus

To **Tegucigalpa** 0500, 0915 and 1000 daily via La Paz, 4 hrs, US$2.40 (bus from Tegucigalpa at 0800 and 1400, **Empresa Lila**, 4-5 Av, 7 Calle, No 418 Comayagüela,

opposite Hispano cinema); bus to **La Paz** only, 0700, 2 hrs, US$1; several minibuses a day, 1½ hrs, US$1.50. Bus also from Comayagua. Pickup truck to **San José** at around 1000 from market, ask for drivers, Don Santos, Torencio, or Gustavo. Bus to **La Esperanza** at about 0830, unreliable, check with driver, Don Pincho, at the supermarket next to where the bus is parked (same street as Hotel Medina), 1½-2 hrs, otherwise hitching possible, going rate US$1.20. Bus to **San Miguel**, El Salvador, **Transportes Wendy Patricia**, 0500, 1200, 7 hrs, US$3.50.

Nueva Ocotepeque p524
Bus

Transportes Escobar daily service **Tegucigalpa** to Nueva Ocotepeque/Agua Caliente, via La Entrada and Santa Rosa de Copán (12 Av entre 8 y 9 Calle, Barrio Concepción, Comayagüela, T2237-4897; **Hotel Sandoval**, T2653-3098, Nueva Ocotepeque). Buses to **San Pedro Sula** stop at La Entrada (US$1.70), 1st at 0030, for connections to Copán. There are splendid mountain views. From **San Pedro Sula** there are regular buses via Santa Rosa south (6 hrs, US$4.50); road is well paved.

⦿ Directory

Copán Ruinas p514, map p515
Banks Banco Atlántida with an ATM and Banco de Occidente are both on the plaza and take Visa. **BAC**, has similar services and an ATM for MasterCard and Amex. It is possible to change Guatemalan currency in Copán but not at the banks; try where buses leave for the border or with money changers behind Hotel Marina. **Internet** Yaragua Tours, off southeast corner of Parque Central, daily 0700-2200 per hr. Maya Connections, inside handicraft shop one block downhill from southwest corner of Parque Central US$1.50 per hr, daily 0730-1800. Casa de Todo, internet and much more. Open daily

0700-2100. **Language schools** Academia de Español Guacamaya, T/F2651-4360, www.guacamaya.com, classes US$140 a week, with homestay US$225, recommended. Ixbalanque, T/F2651-4432, www.ixbalanque.com, 1-1 teaching plus board and lodging with local family, US$210 for classes and 7 days homestay. **Post** Next to the market, Mon-Fri 0800-1200, 1300-1700, Sat 0800-1200, beautiful stamps available. Max 4 kg by airmail. **Telephone** Phone calls can be made from the office of Hondutel 0800-2100.

Santa Rosa de Copán *p518, map p519*
Banks Atlántida (has Visa ATM, maximum withdrawal US$30) and Banco de Occidente (has ATM), both are on main plaza. **Cultural centre** ½ block south of Parque Central with live music and singing, sculpture and picture galley. **Immigration** Av Alvaro Contreras y 2 Calle NO, helpful, extensions available. **Internet** Pizza Pizza, has email at US$4 per hr, good machines. Prodigy, C Centenario, US$1 per hr, also across the road from the Hotel Copán, US$2 per hr. **Laundry** Lavandaría Florencia, Calle Centenario. **Medical services** Dentist: Dr Wilfredo Urquía, at Calle Real Centenario 3-4 Av NE, speaks English. Recommended. Doctors: Clínica Médica Las Gemas, 2 Av NO, near Hotel Elvir, T2666-1428, run by Dr Soheil Rajabian (speaks English among other languages), 1st-class attention. Hospital:

Médico Quirúrgico, Barrio Miraflores, Carretera Internacional, T/F2662-1283, fast and efficient, but not cheap. **Post and telephone** The post office and Hondutel are on the park, opposite side to the cathedral. **Voluntary work** Hogar San Antonio, run by nuns across the street from the Parque Infantil (city playground), welcomes volunteers, as does the Cultural Centre.

Gracias *p521, map p521*
Banks Bancafé, Bancrecer and Banco de Occidente, but none take Visa yet. **Cultural centres** Music lessons including marimba, available from Ramón Alvarenga, 2 blocks west of Parque Central on the same side as Iglesia San Marcos. **Internet** plenty to choose from. **Post and telephone** Hondutel and post office 1 block south of Parque Central, closes 1100 on Sat.

La Esperanza *p523*
Banks Banco de Occidente, Banco Atlántida and Banadesa. **Internet** Couple of places, one near the cathedral, US$4 per hr.

Marcala and around *p523*
Banks Banco de Occidente and Bancafé.

Nueva Ocotepeque *p524*
Banks Banco de Occidente will change TCs. Banco Atlántida has Visa facilities.

Tegucigalpa to San Pedro Sula

The main road connecting Tegucigalpa and the country's second largest city, San Pedro Sula, heads north through beautiful scenery along the shore of Lago Yojoa, skirting villages of the Lenca communities. Although the tendency is to head north for the warmth and beauty of the beaches, a slow journey along the road is very rewarding. ▸▸ *For listings, see pages 539-546.*

Támara and Zambrano → *See Around Tegucigalpa map, page 502.*

The Northern Highway between Tegucigalpa and San Pedro Sula leaves the capital and enters the vast valley of Támara, with the village of the same name. A turning leads to the **San Matías waterfal**, in a delightful area for walking in cool forested mountains.

The road climbs to the forested heights of **Parque Aventuras** ⓘ *open at weekends*, at Km 33, good food, swimming pools, horses, bikes, then to **Zambrano** (altitude: 1450 m) at Km 34 and, at Km 36, midway between Tegucigalpa and Comayagua, **Parque Aurora** ⓘ *camping US$0.50 per person, admission US$0.70, food supplies nearby*. It has a small zoo, good swimming pools and a picnic area among pine-covered hills, a lake with rowing boats (hire US$1 per hour), a snack bar and lovely scenery. The birdwatching is good too.

Before descending to the Comayagua Valley, the Northern Highway reaches another forested mountainous escarpment. Stalls selling home-made honey and garish chunky pottery line the roadside. A track leads off to the right (ask for directions), with about 30 minutes' climb on foot to a tableland and the natural fortress of **Tenampua**, where the indigenous inhabitants put up their last resistance to the *conquistadores*, even after the death of Lempira. It has an interesting wall and entrance portal.

Comayagua and around → *For listings, see pages 539-546. Colour map 3, B2. Altitude: 550 m.*

Founded on 7 December 1537 as Villa Santa María de Comayagua on the site of an indigenous village by Alonzo de Cáceres, Comayagua is a colonial town in the rich Comayagua plain, 1½ hours' drive (93 km) north from the capital. On 3 September 1543, it was designated the Seat of the Audiencia de los Confines by King Felipe II of Spain. President Marco Aurelio Soto transferred the capital to Tegucigalpa in 1880.

There are many old colonial buildings in Comayagua, reflecting the importance of Honduras' first capital after Independence in 1821. The centre has had an impressive makeover recently, and is worth a visit for the impressive colonial architecture in and around the main square, Plaza León Alvarado. Comayagua was declared a city in 1557, 20 years after its founding. Within a couple of centuries a rash of civic and religious buildings were constructed. The former university, the first in Central America, was founded in 1632 and closed in 1842 (it was located in the Casa Cural, Bishop's Palace, where the bishops have lived since 1558). Others include the churches of **La Merced** (1550-1588) and **La Caridad** (1730), **San Francisco** (1574) and **San Sebastián** (1575). **San Juan de Dios** (1590 but destroyed by earthquake in 1750), the church where the Inquisition sat, is now the site of the Hospital Santa Teresa. **El Carmen** was built in 1785. The wealth of colonial heritage has attracted funds for renovation, which have produced a slow transformation in the town. The most interesting building is the **cathedral** in the Parque Central, inaugurated in 1711, with its plain square tower and façade decorated with sculpted figures of the saints, which contains some of the finest examples of colonial art in Honduras (daily 0700-1900). Of the 16 original hand-carved and gilded altars, just four survive today. The clock in the tower was originally made over 800 years ago in Spain and is the oldest working clock in the Americas. It was given to Comayagua by Felipe II in 1582. At first it was in La Merced when that was the cathedral, but it was moved to the new cathedral in 1715. You can climb the tower to see the clock and the old bells, with tour guides on hand in the cathedral (Ever Villanueva, T2994-77551, is knowledgeable and friendly). A huge floor mosaic of the cathedral façade has been built on the square, best seen from the tower. Half a block north of the cathedral is the **Ecclesiastical Museum** ① *daily 0930-1200, 1400-1700, US$0.60*. One block south of the cathedral, the **Museo de Arqueología** ① *at the corner of 6 Calle and 1 Av NO, Wed-Fri 0800-1600, Sat and Sun 0900-1200, 1300-1600, US$1.70*, housed in the former Palacio de Gobernación, is small scale but fascinating, with six rooms each devoted to a different period. Much of the collection came from digs in the El Cajón region, 47 km north of Comayagua, before the area was flooded for the hydroelectricity project. The **Casa Cultural** on a corner of the plaza, left of the cathedral, has permanent and temporary exhibitions of the city history and art, also **tourist information** ① *Tue-Thu 0900-1700, Fri and Sat 0900-2100, Sun 0900-1200, T2772-2028*, with a city map for sale, US$1.20. City tours are available in an open-topped tram from outside the Casa Cultural, daily every 30 minutes, US$1.50.

There are two colonial plazas shaded by trees and shrubs. A stone portal and a portion of the façade of **Casa Real** (the viceroy's residence) still survives. Built in 1739-1741, it was damaged by an earthquake in 1750 and destroyed by tremors in 1856. The army still uses a quaint old fortress built when Comayagua was the capital. There is a lively market area.

Parque Nacional Montaña de Comayagua is only 13 km from Comayagua, reached from the villages of San José de la Mora (4WD necessary) or San Jerónimo and Río Negro (usually passable). Contact **Fundación Ecosimco** ① *0 Calle y 1 Av NO in Comayagua, T772-4681*, for further information about the trails which lead through the cloud forest to waterfalls. The mountain (2407 m) has 6000 ha of cloud forest and is a major watershed for the area.

Siguatepeque → *Colour map 3, B2. Altitude: 1150 m.*

The Northern Highway crosses the Comayagua plain, part of the gap in the mountains which stretches from the Gulf of Fonseca to the Ulúa lowlands. Set in forested highlands 32 km northwest of Comayagua is the town of Siguatepeque, which has a cool climate. It is the site of the Escuela Nacional de Ciencias Forestales (which is worth a visit) and, being exactly halfway between Tegucigalpa and San Pedro Sula (128 km), is a collection point for the produce of the Intibucá, Comayagua and Lempira departments. The Cerro and Bosque de Calanterique, behind the Evangelical Hospital, is a 45-minute walk from the town centre. The Parque Central is pleasant, shaded by tall trees with the church of San Pablo on the north side and the cinema, **Hotel Versalles** and Boarding House Central on the east; **Hondutel** and the post office are on the south side.

Southwest from Siguatepeque, the route to La Esperanza is a beautiful paved road through lovely forested mountainous country, via **Jesús de Otoro**, where there are two basic *hospedajes* and **Balneario San Juan de Quelala** ① *US$0.30*, which has a *cafetería* and picnic sites. North from Siguatepeque, the highway goes over the forested escarpment of the continental divide, before descending towards Lago Yojoa. Just south of Taulabé on the highway are the illuminated **Caves of Taulabé** ① *daily, US$0.40, guides available*, with both stalactites and bats. North of Taulabé, and 16 km south of the lake is the turn-off northwest of a paved road to Santa Bárbara.

Lago Yojoa → *Colour map 3, B2. Altitude: 635 m.*

ⓘ *For local information contact Enrique Campos or his son at Hotel Agua Azul (see below). For more information, contact Proyecto Humuya, behind Iglesia Betel, 21 de Agosto, Siguatepeque (T2773-2426), or Proyecto de Desarrollo Río Yure, San Isidro, Cortés, Apdo 1149, Tegucigalpa.*

Sitting pretty among the mountains is the impressive Lake Yojoa, 22.5 km long and 10 km wide. To the west rise the Montañas de Santa Bárbara which include the country's second highest peak and the **Parque Nacional de Santa Bárbara** (see page 537). To the east is the **Parque Nacional Montaña Cerro Azul-Meámbar**. Pumas, jaguars and other animals live in the forests, pine-clad slopes and the cloud forest forming part of the reservoir of the Lago Yojoa basin. The national parks also have many waterfalls. The 50-sq-km Azul-Meámbar park is 30 km north of Siguatepeque and its highest point is 2047 m. To get to any of the entry points (Meámbar, the main one, Jardines, Bacadia, Monte Verde or San Isidro) a 4WD is necessary. A local ecological group, **Ecolago** ⓘ *Edificio Midence Soto, Parque Central (Tegucigalpa), T2237 9659*, has marked out the area and is to offer guided tours. **Ecolago** has guides who are expert in spotting regional birds; at least 373 species have been identified around the lake. At one time the lake was full of bass, but overfishing and pollution have decimated the stocks. Tilapia farming is now very important.

The Northern Highway follows the eastern margin to the lake's southern tip at **Pito Solo**, where sailing and motor boats can be hired. Frustratingly, there is no public access to the lakeshore, which is fenced off by farms and private properties. Lake excursions are also available at several of the waterfront hotels and restaurants (see pages 540 and 541), which also offer the best views.

On the northern shore of Lago Yojoa is a complex of pre-Columbian settlements called **Los Naranjos** ⓘ *US$5*, which are believed to have had a population of several thousand. It is considered to be the country's third most important archaeological site spanning the period from 1000 BC to AD 1000, and includes two ball courts. The site is slowly being developed for tourism by the Institute of Anthropology and History and has a visitor centre, small museum and coffee shop and a number of forest walking trails. Excavation work is currently in progress. The local office of the institute (T2557-8197) is at the **Hotel Brisas de Lago**. From the lake it is 37 km down to the hot Ulúa lowlands.

A paved road skirts the lake's northern shore for 12 km via Peña Blanca. A road heads southwest to **El Mochito**, Honduras' most important mining centre. A bus from 2 Avenida in San Pedro Sula goes to Las Vegas-El Mochito mine for walks along the west side of Lago Yojoa. Buses will generally stop anywhere along the east side of the lake. Another road heads north from the northern shore, through Río Lindo, to **Caracol** on the Northern Highway. This road gives access to the Pulhapanzak waterfall, with some unexcavated ceremonial mounds adjacent, and to Ojo de Agua, a pretty bathing spot near Caracol. **Peña Blanca** is, according to one reader, a "very ugly town" on the north side of the lake. Almost makes you want to stay.

Pulhapanzak waterfall

ⓘ *www.letsgopulha.com, T9995-1010, daily 0600-1800, US$2.80. The caretaker allows camping for US$0.85.*

The impressive 42-m waterfall at Pulhapanzak is on the Río Lindo. The waterfall is beautiful during, or just after the rainy season, and in sunshine there is a rainbow over the gorge. A path leads down to the foot of the falls, thick with spray, and very slippery; you can swim in river just before the edge – if you dare! There is a picnic area, a small *cafetería* and a good *comedor* 15 minutes' walk away down in the village, but the site does get crowded at weekends and holidays. There is also a large zip-wire course inside the grounds, with 13 sections, including one breathtaking stretch over the falls (US$32).

Santa Bárbara and around → *Colour map 3, B2. Altitude: 290 m.*

Santa Bárbara, surrounded by high mountains, forested hills and rivers, lies in a hot lowland valley 32 km west of Lago Yojoa. One of the nicest main towns in Honduras, it has little of architectural or historical interest compared with Gracias, Ojojona or Yuscarán, but it is here that you will find Panama hats and other goods made from junco palm. The majority of the population is fair-skinned (some redheads). In addition to being a pleasant place to stay, Santa Bárbara is also a good base for visiting villages throughout the Santa Bárbara Department. Nearby, the ruined colonial city of **Tencoa** has been rediscovered. A short local trek behind the town climbs the hills to the ruined site of **Castillo Bogran**, with fine views across the valley and the town. Heading south out of Santa Bárbara, the paved road joins the Northern Highway south of Lago Yojoa.

The Department of Santa Bárbara is called the Cuna de los Artesanos (cradle of artisans), with over 10,000 craftspeople involved in the manufacture of handicrafts. The main products come from the small junco palm, for example fine hats and baskets. The main towns for junco items are **La Arada**, 25 minutes from Santa Bárbara on the road to San Nicolás, and then branching off south, and **Ceguaca**, on a side road off the road to Tegucigalpa. Flowers and dolls from corn husks are made in Nueva Celilac. Mezcal is used to make carpets, rugs and hammocks, which are easy to find in towns such as **Ilama**, on the road to San Pedro Sula, which has one of the best small colonial churches in Honduras (no accommodation). People here also make *petates* (rugs) and purses.

Between Santa Bárbara and Lago Yojoa is the **Parque Nacional de Santa Bárbara** which contains the country's second highest peak, Montaña de Santa Bárbara at 2744 m. The rock is principally limestone with many subterranean caves. There is little tourist development as yet, with just one trail, and you can track down a guide in Los Andes, a village above Peña Blanca and Las Vegas. The best time to visit is the dry season, January-June. For information contact **Asociación Ecológica Corazón Verde** ⓘ *Palacio Municipal, Santa Bárbara*. There is a **Cohdefor** office just below the market (look for the sign) but they are not helpful.

San Pedro Sula and around

→ *For listings, see page 539-546. Colour map 3, B2. Altitude: 60-150 m. Population: 900,000.*

San Pedro Sula is the second largest and most industrialized city in the country and a centre for the banana, coffee, sugar and timber trades. It is a distribution hub for northern and western Honduras with good road links. Its business community is mainly of Arab origin, and it is considered the fastest-growing city between Mexico and Panama. By Central American standards, San Pedro Sula is a well-planned, modern city, but it's not a city you'll be inclined to stay in for long.

Ins and outs

Getting there San Pedro Sula is a more important international gateway than Tegucigalpa. Its airport, **Ramón Villeda Morales (SAP)** is 15 km from the city centre along a good four-lane highway. The **Gran Central Metropolitana** central bus terminal opened in March 2008. It's a short US$3 taxi from the centre of San Pedro Sula. ▸▸ *See Transport, page 544.*

Getting around The city is divided into four quadrants: Noreste (Northeast, NE), Noroeste (Northwest, NO), Sudeste (Southeast, SE) and Sudoeste (Southwest, SO), where most of the hotels are located, although newer hotels, shopping malls and restaurant chains are in the Noroeste. There are buses, minibuses and taxis for getting around town.

Best time to visit Although pleasant in the cooler season from November to February, temperatures are very high for the rest of the year. It is, nevertheless, a relatively clean city and the traffic is not too bad. The higher and cooler suburb of Bella Vista, with its fine views over the city, affords relief from the intense heat of the town centre.

San Pedro Sula

Sleeping		
Acrópolis **1**	Manhattan **11**	Terraza **19**
Ejecutivo **5**	Palmira **1 15**	
El Nilo **6**	Real Intercontinental	**Eating**
Gran Hotel Sula **2**	San Pedro Sula **3**	Bar El Hijo del Cuervo **2**
Internacional Palace **14**	San José **16**	Copa de Oro **1**
Jerusalem **10**	San Juan **17**	Gamba Tropic **3**
	San Pedro **7**	La Fortuna **5**

N
200 metres
200 yards

Background

The city was founded in 1536 by Pedro de Alvarado in the lush and fertile valley of the Ulúa (Sula) River, beneath the forested slopes of the Merendón mountains. There are many banana plantations.

Sights

The large neocolonial-style **cathedral** was completed in the 1950s. **Museo de Antropología e Historia** ⓘ *3 Av, 4 Calle NO, Mon, Wed-Sat 0900-1600, Sun 0900-1500, US$0.75, first Sun of the month is free,* has displays of the cultures that once inhabited the Ulúa Valley up to Spanish colonization and, on the first floor, local history since colonization. There is a museum café in the adjacent garden with fine stelae and a good set lunch. **Museo Jorge Milla Oviedo** ⓘ *3 Av 9 Calle NE, Barrio Las Acacias, T552-5060,* is run by the foundation that cares for the Cuero y Salado wildlife reserve.

Parque Nacional Cusuco

ⓘ *Entrance is US$15, which includes a guided trip; you cannot go on your own. Contact the HRPF at 5 Av, 1 Calle NO, San Pedro Sula, T552-1014. Also contact Cohdefor, 10 Av, 5 Calle NO, Barrio Guamilito, San Pedro Sula, T553-4959, or Cambio CA, who run tours. Permission from HRPF is required to walk through the park to Tegucigalpita on the coast. There is a visitor centre but bring your own food. You cannot stay or camp in the park, but camping is possible outside. Access by dirt road from Cofradía (Cafetería Negro, one block northwest of plaza, good food), on the road to Santa Rosa de Copán, then to Buenos Aires: 2 hrs by car from San Pedro Sula, 4WD recommended. See Transport, page 545.*

Parque Nacional Cusuco, 20 km west of San Pedro Sula, offers some excellent hikes, trails and birdwatching in cloud forest. Now managed by the Fundación Ecológica Héctor Rodrigo Pastor Fasquelle (HRPF), the park was exploited for lumber until the 1950s. It was declared a protected area in 1959 when the Venezuelan ecologist, Geraldo Budowski, reported the pine trees there were the highest in Central America. Cutting was stopped and the lumber company abandoned the site. It is a splendid location and well worth the effort. The area includes tropical rainforest and cloud forest with all the associated flora and fauna. It includes both **Cerro Jilinco**, 2242 m, and **Cerro San Ildefonso**, 2228 m. There are four trails, ranging from 30 minutes to two days. They use old logging roads traversing forested ridges with good views. HRPF produces a bird checklist that includes the quetzal.

⊙ Tegucigalpa to San Pedro Sula listings

For Sleeping and Eating price codes and other relevant information, see Essentials pages 31-33.

⊙ Sleeping

Támara *p534*
F Posada Don Willy, 500 m southwest of the toll station near Balneario San Francisco. With bath (electric shower), clean, quiet, fan, excellent value.

Zambrano *p534*
A-B Caserío Valuz, 1.5 km from the highway, 20 mins' walk on the road to Catarata Escondida, T9996-4294 (mob). 15 rooms with bath, most with balconies, 1- to 3-night packages including meals, also rooms for backpackers, with use of kitchen, volunteer work in exchange for room and board possible, a great place to relax, hike, read, paint.
A-C Casitas Primavera, Barrio La Primavera, 1.5 km west of main road, T2898-26625/

T2239- 2328. Cosy houses, lovely setting, sleeps 6 (arrangements can be made for 1-2 people, **E**).

Comayagua and around *p534*
A Santa María, Km 82 on the Tegucigalpa highway, T2772-7872. Private bath, a/c, cable TV. Best in town, although not in the centre.
B Quan, 8 Calle NO, 3 y 4 Av, T2772-0070, hquan@hondutel.hn. Excellent, with private bath, popular.
C América Inc, 2 Av y 1 Calle NO, T2772-0360. A/c, private bath, hot water, cheaper with fan.
D Norimax, Calle Central y 3 Av SO, Barrio Torondón, T2772-1210. Bath, a/c and TV, hot water, cheaper rooms available and car park.
E Libertad, south side of Parque Central, T2772-0091. Nice courtyard, much choice of room size, clean apart from the toilets, cold water shower outside, helpful, good restaurant 2 doors away.
F Galaxia, Miramar, Primavera, Terminal and **Tío Luis**, are *pensiones*, all within a couple of blocks of the bus stop on the *Panamericana*.

Siguatepeque *p535*
D Zari, T2773-2015. Hot water, cable TV, own generator, parking.
E-F Internacional Gómez, 21 de Junio, T2773-2868. With bath (cheaper without), hot water, clean, parking.
F Boarding House Central, Parque Central, T2773-2108. Very basic but good value; beware of the dog, which bites.
F Mi Hotel, 1 km from highway on road into town. With bath, parking, restaurant.
F Versalles, on Parque Central. Excellent, with restaurant, use of kitchen on request.

Lago Yojoa *p536*
L Gualiqueme, cottage at edge of lake, for information contact Richard Joint at Honduyate, T2882-3129. Has 4 bedrooms in main house, 2 in annexe. Daily, weekly, monthly rental, weekend packages include ferry and fishing boat.

C Brisas del Lago, close to Peña Blanca at the northern end of the lake, T2608-7229. Large, 1960s-era concrete hotel now looking a bit dated and mildewed, but with spacious rooms with a/c, cable TV and balcony, good value family suites; great lake views from gardens and pool. Good restaurant but overpriced, launches for hire and horse riding.
C-D Hotel Agua Azul, at north end of lake, about 3 km west from junction at Km 166, T/F2991-7244. Basic clean cabins for 2 or more persons, meals for non-residents, but food and service in restaurant is poor, beautiful gardens, manager speaks English, swimming pool, fishing, horse riding and boating, launches, kayaks and pedalos for hire, around US$6 for 30 mins; mosquito coils. Good reduction in low season. Recommended (except when loud karaoke is in full swing).
C-E Boarding House Moderno, Barrio Arriba, T643-2203. Rooms with fan better value than with a/c, with hot shower, quiet, parking. Recommended.
C-E Gran Hotel Colonial, 1½ blocks from Parque Central, T2643-2665. Fans in all rooms, some with a/c, cold water, sparsely furnished, friendly. Good view from roof. Recommended.
C-E Los Remos, Pito Solo, at the south end of the lake, T2557-8054. Has cabins and camping facilities (**G**). Clean, beautiful setting, good food, nice for breakfasts, no beach but swimming pool, boat trips, parking US$3.
E D&D Brewery and Guesthouse, T2994-9719, dndbrew@yahoo.com. Good rooms, with a garden with a small pool, book exchange and home brewed beer.

Santa Bárbara and around *p537*
F Ruth, Calle La Libertad, T2643-2632. Rooms without windows, fan.
G Pensión, near the church, Colinas. Basic.

San Pedro Sula and around *p537, map p538*
L Real Intercontinental San Pedro Sula, Blv del Sur at Centro Comercial Multiplaza,

T2545-2500, www.ichotelsgroup.com. Full service and the best in town.

A Ejecutivo, 2 Calle 10 Av SO, T2552-4289, www.hotel-ejecutivo.com. A/c, cable TV, café/bar, phone, own generator.

A Gran Hotel Sula, Parque Central, T2545-2600, www.hotelsula.hn. Rooms small and old-fashioned, but cosy, with all mod-cons. Good 24-hr restaurant, as well as bar, pool, gym and small shop. Charming and efficient service. Highly recommended.

B Acrópolis, 3 Calle 2 y 3 Av SE, T/F2557-2121. A/c, cable TV, parking, café, comfortable, friendly, good value.

C Hotel San Pedro, 3 Calle 2 Av SO, T2550-1513, www.hotelsanpedrosa.com. Private bath, a/c, cheaper with fan, popular, clean, good value, rooms overlooking street are noisy, stores luggage, secure parking.

C Internacional Palace, 3 Calle 8 Av SO, Barrio El Benque, T2550-3838. A/c, helpful, internet service, parking, pool, bar, restaurant OK.

D Palmira 1, 6 Calle 6 y 7 Av SO, T2557-6522. Clean, very convenient for buses, parking.

D Terraza, 6 Av 4-5 Calle SO, T2550-3108. Friendly, cheaper without a/c. Dining room dark.

E El Nilo, 3 Calle 2 Av SO, T2553-4689. Nice rooms, friendly.

E Manhattan, 7 Av 3-4 Calle SO, T2550-2316. A/c, a bit run-down.

F Jerusalem, 6 Calle 1 Av SE, T2946-8352. Safe, good value.

F San José, 6 Av 5 y 6 Calle SO, just round corner from **Norteños** bus station, T2557-1208. Friendly, clean, safe, cheap and cheerful.

F-G San Juan, 6 Calle 6 Av SO, T2553-1488. Modern, very noisy, clean, helpful, good value.

❶ Eating

Comayagua and around *p534*
Parque Central is surrounded by restaurants and fast-food establishments.

🍴🍴🍴 **Villa Real**, behind the cathedral, T2772-0101. Mixes colonial atmosphere with good international and Honduran cuisine.

🍴🍴🍴 **Hein Wong**, Parque Central. Chinese and international food, good, a/c, reasonably priced.

🍴🍴🍴 **Las Palmeras**, south side of Parque Central, T2772-0352. Good breakfasts, open for dinner and lunch, good portions, reasonable prices.

🍴 **Fruty Tacos**, 4 Calle NO, just off southwest corner of Parque Central. Snacks and *licuados*.

🍴 **Juanis Burger Shop**, 1 Av NO 5 Calle, near southwest corner of Parque Central. Friendly, good food, OK.

🍴 **Venecia**, Calle del Comercio, in front of **Supermercado Carol**, T2772-1734. Popular café-style restaurant.

Siguatepeque *p535*
🍴🍴🍴 **Granja d'Elia**, one of several restaurants on the Northern Hwy. Open all day, lots of vegetables, also meat, all-you-can-eat buffet, French chef, veg from own market garden and bread on sale outside.

🍴🍴🍴 **Juanci's**, main street. Open until 2300. US-style hamburgers, good steaks and snacks.

🍴 **Bicos**, southwest corner of Parque Central. Nice snack bar/patisserie.

🍴 **Cafetería Colonial**, 4 Av SE (behind church). Good pastries and coffee, outside seating.

🍴 **Pollos Kike**, next door. Pleasant setting, fried chicken.

🍴 **Supermercado Food**, south side of plaza. Has a good snack bar inside.

Lago Yojoa *p536*
Roadside stalls near Peña Blanca sell fruit.

🍴🍴🍴 **Brisas del Canal**, Peña Blanca, local food. Recommended, but small portions.

🍴🍴-🍴 **Comedores**, on the roadside. Serve bass fish caught in the lake, with **Atenciones Evita** being a popular choice.

🍴 **Comedor Vista Hermosa**, Peña Blanca. Has good, cheap food.

Cafés and bakeries
Panadería Yoja, 1 block from **Hotel Maranata**, Peña Blanca, good juices and pastries.

Santa Bárbara and around *p537*

Doña Ana, 1 block above Parque Central. No sign but restaurant in Ana's dining room, crammed with bric-a-brac, only meat, rice, beans and bananas, plentiful and good food if a little boring.

El Brasero, ½ block below Parque Central. Extensive menu of meat, chicken, fish, Chinese, good food, well prepared. Recommended.

Pizzería Don Juan, Av Independencia. Very good pizzas.

Comedor Everest, by bus stop on Parque Central. Friendly, good *comida corriente*.

Las Tejas, near Rodríguez. Friendly, good pizzeria.

McPollo, main street. Clean, smart, good.

Repostería Charle's, Parque Central. Excellent cakes, pastries, about the only place open for breakfast.

San Pedro Sula and around *p537, map p538*

International restaurants in all the top hotels.

Bar El Hijo del Cuervo, 13 Calle 7-8 Av NO, Barrio Los Andes. Mexican cuisine, informal setting of *champas* in tropical garden with fountain, à la carte menu, tacos, *quesadillas*.

La Huerta de España, 21 Av 2 Calle SO, Barrio Río de Piedras, 4 blocks west of Av Circunvalación. Daily until 2300. Supposedly the best Spanish cuisine in town.

Las Tejas, 9 Calle 16 y 17 Av, Av Circunvalación. Good steaks and fine seafood, as also at nearby sister restaurant La Tejana, 16 Av 19 Calle SO, Barrio Suyapa, T2557-5276.

Pamplona, on plaza, opposite Gran Hotel Sula. Pleasant decor, good food, strong coffee, excellent service.

Applebees, Circunvalación. Good food, service and prices. Highly recommended.

Chef Mariano, 16 Av 9-10 Calle SO, Barrio Suyapa, T2552-5492. Garífuna management and specialities, especially seafood, Honduran and international cuisine, attentive service, a/c, not cheap but good value, open daily for lunch and dinner.

Gamba Tropic, 5 Av 4-5 Calle SO. Delicious seafood, good wine, medium prices, a/c.

La Espuela, Av Circunvalación, 16 Av 7 Calle. Good grilled meats. Recommended.

La Fortuna, 2 Calle 7 Av NO. Chinese and international, very good, not expensive, smart, good service, a/c.

Sim Kon, 17 Av 6 Calle NO, Av Circunvalación. Arguably the best Chinese in town. Enormous portions. Try *arroz con camarones* (prawns with rice).

Copa de Oro, 2 Av 2 y 3 Calle SO. Extensive Chinese and Western menu, a/c, pleasant. Recommended.

Cafés

Café Nani, 6 Av 1-2 Calle SO. Good *pastelería*.

Café Skandia, ground floor, poolside at the Gran Hotel Sula. Open 24 hrs, best place for late night dinners and early breakfasts, good club sandwiches, good service.

Café Venecia, 6 Av 4-5 Calle. Good juices,

Espresso Americano, 2 branches, in Calle Peatonal, 4 Av, off southwest corner of Parque Central, and in Megaplaza shopping mall. Closed Sun, great coffee, cookies.

⊙ Entertainment

San Pedro Sula and around *p537, map p538*

Bars and clubs

A thriving nightlife exists beyond the casinos.
Mango's, 16 Av 8-9 Calle SO, Barrio Suyapa. Open 1900 onwards. Open terrace, pool tables, dance floor, rock music, snacks. An exclusive option is **El Quijote**, 11 Calle 3-4 Av SO, Barrio Lempira, cover charge.

Cinemas

There are 8 cinemas, all showing Hollywood movies, look in local press for details.

Theatre

The Círculo Teatral Sampedrano stages productions (see Cultural centres, page 546).

Proyecto Teatral Futuro, is a semi-professional company presenting contemporary theatre of Latin American countries and translations of European playwrights, as well as ballet, children's theatre, and workshops. Offices and studio-theatre at 4 Calle 3-4 Av NO, Edif INMOSA, 3rd floor, T2552-3074.

❀ Festivals and events

San Pedro Sula and around *p537, map p538*
End Jun Feria Juniana, the city's main festival.

○ Shopping

Siguatepeque *p535*
Leather goods A good leatherworker is Celestino Alberto Díaz, Barrio San Antonio, Casa 53, 2 Calle NE, 6 Av NE. 1 block north of Celestino's is a good shoemaker, leather shoes made for US$25.

San Pedro Sula and around *p537, map p538*
Bookshops La Casa del Libro, 1 Calle 5-6 Av SO. Comprehensive selection of Spanish and English-language books, good for children's books and game, just off Parque Central. **Librería Atenea**, Edif Trejo Merlo, 1 Calle 7 Av SO. Wide choice of Latin American, US and British fiction, philosophy, economics and so on. **Librería Cultura**, 1 Calle 6-7 Av SO. Cheap paperbacks, Latin American classics. **Librería Editorial Guaymuras**, 10 Av 7 Calle NO. Wide range of Hispanic authors.

Food **Supermercado Los Andes**, good supermarket at the intersection of Calle Oeste and Av Circunvalación.

Handicrafts Large artisan market, Mercado Guamilito Artesanía, 6 Calle 7-8 Av NO. Daily 0800-1700. Typical Honduran handicrafts,

cigars and 'gifiti' – local moonshine, at good prices (bargain), with a few imported goods from Guatemala and Ecuador; also good for fruit and vegetables, and baleada comedores. **Danilo's Pura Piel**, factory and shop 18 Av B/9 Calle SO. **Honduras Souvenirs**, Calle Peatonal No 7, mahogany woodcraft. The **IMAPRO Handicraft School** in El Progreso has a retail outlet at 1 Calle 4-5 Av SE, well worth visiting, fixed prices, good value, good mahogany carvings. The **Museum Gift Shop**, at the Museo de Antropología e Historia has lots of cheap *artesanía* gifts open during museum visiting hours.

▲ Activities and tours

Comayagua and around *p534*
Cramer Tours in Pasaje Arias.
Inversiones Karice's, 4 Av NO, very friendly and helpful.
Rolando Barahona, Av Central.
Comalhagua Tours, Plaza León Alvarado (entrance upstairs through Eskimo ice cream parlour), T9988-7101, city tours, and to El Rosario mine and Comayagua National Park; very informative and helpful.

San Pedro Sula and around *p537, map p538*
Maya Temple, www.mayatempletours.com, also offers travel services.

○ Transport

Zambrano *p534*
Bus From the capital take any bus going north to Comayagua, Siguatepeque or La Paz and tell the driver where you want to get off.

Comayagua and around *p534*
Bus To **Tegucigalpa**, US$1.10, every 45 mins, 2 hrs (**Hmnos Cruz**, Comayagua, T772-0850), and with Comalhuacan (T2772-3889), from 0440 to 1720. To **Siguatepeque**, US$0.55 with **Transpinares**.

To **San Pedro Sula**, US$1.50, 3 hrs, either catch a bus on the highway (very crowded) or go to Siguatepeque and change buses there. Incoming buses to Comayagua drop you on the main road outside town. From here you can walk or taxi into town. Buses depart from Torocagua: *colectivo* from Calle Salvador y Cervantes in town.

Siguatepeque *p535*
Bus To **San Pedro Sula**, from the west end of town every 35 mins, US$1.35. **Tegucigalpa** with **Empresas Unidas** or **Maribel**, from west plaza, south of market, US$1.50, 3 hrs. Alternatively take a taxi, US$0.50, 2 km to the highway intersection and catch a Tegucigalpa–San Pedro Sula bus which passes every 30 mins. To **Comayagua**, Transpinares, US$0.50, 45 mins. To **La Esperanza** buses leave from near Boarding House Central, 1st departure 0530, several daily, taxi from town centre US$0.50.

Lago Yojoa *p536*
Bus To lake from **San Pedro Sula**, US$1, 1½ hrs; bus from lake to **Tegucigalpa** with **Hedman-Alas**, US$3, 3-5 hrs, 185 km.

Pulhapanzak waterfall *p536*
Bus By car it's a 1½-hr drive from San Pedro, longer by bus. There is a bus from **Peña Blanca** every 2 hrs to the falls, or take a Mochito or Cañaveral bus from **San Pedro Sula** from the bus station near the railway (hourly 0500-1700) and get off at the sign to the falls, at the village of Santa Buena Ventura, US$0.95. Alternatively stay on the bus to Cañaveral (take identification because there is a power plant here), and walk back along the Río Lindo, 2 hrs past interesting rock formations and small falls. Last bus returns at 1630 during the week.

Santa Bárbara and around *p537*
Bus To **Tegucigalpa**, 0700 and 1400 daily, weekends 0900, US$3, 4½ hrs with Transportes Junqueños (passing remote villages in beautiful mountain scenery).

To **San Pedro Sula**, 2 hrs, US$1.90, 7 a day between 0500 and 1630. Bus to **San Rafael** at 1200, 4 hrs. Onward bus to **Gracias** leaves next day.

San Pedro Sula and around *p537, map p538*
Air
A taxi to the airport costs US$12 per taxi, but bargain hard. Yellow airport taxis cost US$18. Free airport shuttle from big hotels. Buses and *colectivos* do not go to the airport terminal itself; you have to walk the final 1 km from the La Lima road. Duty free, Global One phones, banks, restaurant on 2nd floor. Flights to **Tegucigalpa** (35 mins), **La Ceiba**, **Utila** and to **Roatán**. See page 491 for international flights.

Airline offices American, Ed Firenze, Barrio Los Andes, 16 Av 2-3 Calle, T2558-0524, airport T2668-3241. **Atlantic**, airport, T2668-7309. **Continental**, Plaza Versalles, Av Circunvalación, T2557-4141, airport T2668-3208. **Grupo Taca**13 Av NO corner of Norte de la Circunvalación, Barrio Los Andes, T2557-0525, airport T2668-3333. **Isleña**, Edif Trejo Merlo, 1 Calle 7 Av SO, T2552-8322, airport T2668-3333. **Sosa**, 8 Av 1-2 Calle SO, Edif Román, T2550-6548, airport 668-3128.

Bus
Local Local buses cost US$0.10, smaller minibuses cost US$0.20.

Long distance Central bus terminal opened in 2008. The Gran Central Metropolitana is clean, safe and a short US$3 taxi from the centre of San Pedro Sula. **Heading south**, buses pass **Lago Yojoa** for **Tegucigalpa**, very regular service provided by several companies, 4½ hrs, 250 km by paved road. Main bus services with comfortable coaches in the town centre are **Hedman Alas**, T2516-2273, 0830, 1330 and 1730, US$18; **Transportes Sáenz**, T2553-4969, US$7; **El Rey**, T2553-4264, or **Express**, T2557-8355; **Transportes Norteños**, T2552-2145, last bus at 1900; **Viana**, T2556-9261.

Heading west from San Pedro the road leads to **Puerto Cortés**, a pleasant 45-min journey down the lush river valley. With Empresa Impala, T2553-3111, from 0430 until 2200, US$1, or **Citul**, and also on to **Omoa** from 0600.

Heading east buses go to **La Lima**, **El Progreso**, **Tela** and **La Ceiba** (Tupsa and Catisa, very regular to El Progreso, hourly to La Ceiba from 0600 and 1800, 3 hrs, US$3), some with a change in El Progreso, others direct. Also 1st class to La Ceiba with **Viana** at 1030 and 1730, and with **Hedman Alas** at 0600, 1030, 1520 and 1820. US$16 To **Trujillo**, 3 per day, 6 hrs, US$5, comfortable.

Heading southwest buses go to **Santa Rosa de Copán** through the Department of Ocotepeque, with superb mountain scenery, to the **Guatemalan border**. Congolón, and Empresa Toritos y Copanecos, serve **Nueva Ocotepeque** (US$8) and **Agua Caliente** on the Guatemalan border with 7 buses a day; Congolón, T2553-1174.

To **Santa Rosa de Copán**, with connections at La Entrada for **Copán Ruinas**, with Empresa Toritos y Copanecos, T2563-4930, leaving every 20 mins, 0345-1715, 3 hrs, US$3.70. Take a bus to the junction of La Entrada and change for connection to Copán Ruinas if you're not going direct. 1st-class bus to **Copán Ruinas** with Hedman Alas, T2516-2273, daily at 1030 and 1500, 3 hrs, US$16 with a/c, movie and bathrooms. Also direct service with **Casasola-Cheny Express** at 0800, 1300 and 1400.

International Services available from Ticabus covering the whole of Central America from Mexico to Panama.

Car
Car rentals Avis, 1 Calle, 6 Av NE, T2553-0888; Blitz, Hotel Sula and airport (T2552-2405 or 668-3171); Budget, 1 Calle 7 Av NO, T2552- 2295, airport T2668-3179; Maya Eco Tours, 3 Av NO, 7-8 Calle, and airport (T2552-2670 or 2668-3168); Molinari,

Hotel Sula and airport (T2553-2639 or 2668-6178); Toyota, 3 Av 5 y 6 Calle NO, T2557-2666 or airport T2668-3174.

Car repairs Invanal, 13 Calle, 5 y 6 Av NE, T2552-7083. Excellent service from Víctor Mora.

Parque Nacional Cusuco p539
Bus **San Pedro Sula**–Cofradía, 1 hr, US$0.15, from 5 Av, 11 Calle SO (buses drop you at turn-off 1 km from town); pickup Cofradía-Buenos Aires 1½ hrs, US$1.75, best on Mon at 1400 (wait at small shop on outskirts of town on Buenos Aires road); the park is 12 km from Buenos Aires.

❶ Directory

Comayagua and around p534
Banks HSBC near Parque Central and others nearby include Banco Pro Credit Banco Atlántida, Banco de Occidente, Bancafé, Ficensa, Banadesa, Bamer and Banffaa All have ATMs, usually available 24/7 with security guard. **Immigration** Migración is at 6 Calle NO, 1 Av, good place to get visas renewed, friendly. **Medical services** Dentist: Dr José de Jesús Berlioz, next to Colegio León Alvarado, T772-0054.

Siguatepeque p535
Banks HSBC, Banco Atlántida and Banco de Occidente.

Santa Bárbara and around p537
Banks Banadesa, Bancafé, Banco Atlántida and Banco de Occidente.

San Pedro Sula and around p537, map p538
Banks HSBC, has a beautiful mural in its head office, 5 Av, 4 Calle SO and a branch at 5 Av, 6-7 Calle SO, changes TCs. Banco Atlántida, on Parque Central, changes TCs at good rates. Banco de Honduras (Citibank). Banco Continental, 3 Av, 3-5 Calle SO No 7.

Banco de Occidente, 6 Av, 2-3 Calle SO. **Bancafé**, 1 Calle, 1 Av SE and all other local banks. **BAC** for Visa, MasterCard and Amex is at, 5 Av y 2 Calle NO. These are also at **Aval Card**, 14 Av NO y Circunvalación, and **Honducard**, 5 Av y 2 Calle NO. **Cultural centres** Alianza Francesa, on 23 Av 3-4 Calle SO, T/F2553-1178, www.aftegucig alpa.com, offers French and Spanish classes, has a library, films and cultural events. Centro Cultural Sampédrano, 3 Calle, 4 Av NO No 20, T2553-3911, USIS-funded library, cultural events, concerts, art exhibitions and theatrical productions. **Embassies and consulates** Belize, Km 5 Blv del Norte, Col los Castaños, T2551-0124, 2551-0707. El Salvador, Edif Rivera y Cía, 7th floor, local 704, 5 y 6 Av 3 Calle, T/F553-4604. France, Col Zerón, 9 Av 10 Calle 927, T2557-4187. Germany, 6 Av NO, Av Circunvalación, T2553-1244. Guatemala, 8 Calle 5-6 Av NO, No 38, T/F2553-3560. Italy, Edif La Constancia, 3rd floor, 5 Av 1-2 Calle NO, T2552-3672. Mexico, 2 Calle 20 Av SO 201, Barrio Río de Piedras, T2553-2604.

Netherlands, 15 Av 7-8 Calle NE, Plaza Venecia, Local 10, T2557-1815. Nicaragua, Col Trejo, 23 Av A entre 11 Calle B y 11 Calle C No 145, T/F2550-3394. Spain, 2 Av 3-4 Calle NO 318, Edif Agencias Panamericanas, T2558-0708. UK, 13 Av 10-12 Calle SO, Suyapa No 62, T2557-2046. **Immigration** Calle Peatonal, just off Parque Central, or at the airport. **Internet** Internet cafés are found throughout town. Internet Café, Multiplaza centre, T2550-6077, US$1 per hr. Red Cybe Café, Calle 3, 1 block east of the Hedman Alas bus terminal, US$1per hr. **Laundry** Excelsior, 14-15 Av Blv Morazán. Lava Fácil, 7 Av, 5 Calle NO, US$1.50 per load. Lavandería Almich, 9-10 Av, 5 Calle SO No 29, Barrio El Benque. Rodgers, 4a Calle, 15-16 Av SO, No 114. **Medical services** Dentist: Clínicas Dentales Especializadas, Ed María Antonia, 3a Calle between 8 and 9 Av NO, apartamento L-1, Barrio Guamilito, T2558-0464. **Post** 3 Av SO between 9-10 Calle. **Telephone** Hondutel, 4 Calle 4 Av SO. Calls can be made from **Gran Hotel Sula**.

North coast

Honduras' Caribbean coast has a mixture of banana-exporting ports, historic towns and Garífuna villages. Working from west to east the main towns of interest are Omoa, Puerto Cortés, Tela, La Ceiba and Trujillo. In between the towns you will find isolated beaches and resorts, and national parks like Pico Bonito, which are perfect for hiking and whitewater rafting. The route west takes in the 'Jungle Trail' to Guatemala – which you can now do by bus.

Running parallel to the coast, a route from El Progreso runs south of the coastal mountain chain Cordillera Nombre de Dios leading to rarely visited national parks, pristine cloud forest and an alternative route to La Ceiba. ⟫ *For listings, see pages 556-566.*

Puerto Cortés → *Colour map 3, B2.*

Stuck out on the northwestern coast of the country and backed by the large bay of Laguna de Alvarado, Puerto Cortés is hot, tempered by sea breezes and close to many beautiful palm-fringed beaches. The success of the place is its location and most Honduran trade passes through the port, which is just 58 km from San Pedro Sula by road and rail, and 333 km from Tegucigalpa. It has a small oil refinery, a free zone and, being two days' voyage from New Orleans, is arguably now the most important port in Central America.

The Parque Central contains many fine trees but focuses on a huge Indian poplar, planted as a sapling in 1941, in the centre that provides an extensive canopy.

Getting there If entering Puerto Cortés by boat, go straight to immigration. Passports are often collected on the boat and returned as they are processed. The US$3 entry fee (make sure that you have the stamp) is the only official payment; if asked for more, demand a receipt.

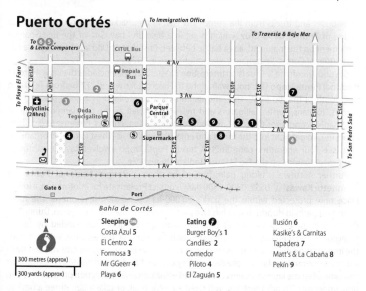

Puerto Cortés

Sleeping ⊖	Eating ⊙	Ilusión 6
Costa Azul 5	Burger Boy's 1	Kasike's & Carnitas
El Centro 2	Candiles 2	Tapadera 7
Formosa 3	Comedor	Matt's & La Cabaña 8
Mr GGeerr 4	Piloto 4	Pekín 9
Playa 6	El Zaguán 5	

N

300 metres (approx)
300 yards (approx)

Omoa → *Colour map 3, B2.*

Omoa, 18 km from Puerto Cortés, is set in the beautiful Bahía de Omoa where the mountains, lusciously carpeted in jungle, tumble towards the sea. You can watch fine purple sunsets from the quiet laid-back bars on the beach, and if you're lucky see dolphins in the bay. It has an 18th-century castle, **Fortaleza de San Fernando**, now renovated and worth a visit. It was built by the Spaniards in 1759 to protect the coast and shipments of silver, gold and cacao from British pirates. There is a **visitor centre** and a small, interesting **museum** ⓘ *Mon-Sun 0900-1600, US$1.40, tickets on sale at gate, guides available.*

During the week Omoa is a quiet, friendly fishing village, but at weekends it gets a little busier with Hondurans from San Pedro and the place becomes littered, followed by a grand clean-up on the Monday morning. Near Omoa are two waterfalls (**Los Chorros**), with lovely walks to each, and good hiking in attractive scenery both along the coast and inland.

It's a fair walk from the main road. Get a tuk-tuk for US$0.50 to the beach.

East of San Pedro Sula → *For listings, see pages 556-566.*

Tela → *Colour map 3, B2.*

Tela used to be an important banana port before the pier was partly destroyed by fire. Easily reached from San Pedro Sula with a bus service via El Progreso, it is pleasantly laid out with a sandy but dirty beach. Tela Viejo to the east is the original city joined by a bridge to Tela Nuevo, the residential area built for the executives of the American banana and farming company **Chiquita**. There is a pleasant walk along the beach east to Ensenada, or west to San Juan. More information is available at www.tela-honduras.com. **Note** Make sure you take a cab after midnight; Lps 30 per person at night.

Around Tela

Local buses and trucks from the corner just east of the market go east to the Garífuna village of **Triunfo de la Cruz**, which is set in a beautiful bay. Site of the first Spanish settlement on the mainland, a sea battle between Cristóbal de Olid and Francisco de Las Casas (two of Cortés' lieutenants) was fought here in 1524.

Beyond Triunfo de la Cruz is an interesting coastal area that includes the cape, **Parque Nacional Punta Izopo** (1½-hour walk along the beach, take water – 12 km from Tela) and the mouth of the Río Léan. This, and its immediate hinterland, is a good place to see parrots, toucans, turtles, alligators and monkeys as well as the first landing point of the Spanish conqueror Cristóbal de Olid. For information, contact **Prolansate** (see box, opposite). To get right into the forest and enjoy the wildlife, it is best to take an organized tour (see Tour operators, page 562). A trip to Punta Izopo involves kayaking through mangrove swamps up the Río Plátano, Indiana Jones style.

Further northwest, along palm-fringed beaches is **Parque Nacional Punta Sal 'Jeannette Kawas'** ⓘ *US$2, 0800-1500 daily,* contact **Prolansate** for information, a lovely place now protected within the park's 80,000-ha boundaries. It is one of the most important parks in Honduras and has two parts, the peninsula and the lagoon. During the dry season some 350 species of bird live within the lagoon, surrounded by forest, mangroves and wetlands. Once inhabited only by Garífuna, the area has suffered from the immigration of cattle farmers who have cleared the forest, causing erosion, and from a palm oil extraction plant on the Río San Alejo, which has dumped waste in the river and contaminated the lagoons. Conservation and environmental protection programmes are now underway. To get there you will need a motor boat, or take a bus (three a day) to

Tornabé and hitch a ride 12 km, or take the crab truck at 1300 for US$0.40 (back at 1700), on to Miami, a small, all-thatched fishing village (two hours' walk along beach from Tornabé), beer on ice available, and walk the remaining 10 km along the beach. There are also pickups from Punta Sal to Miami, contact Prolansate for information.

Jardín Botánico at Lancetilla ⓘ *T2448-1740, not well signposted – a guide is recommended, ask at the Cohdefor office; guide services daily 0800-1530, US$6; good maps available in English or Spanish US$0.30*, is 5 km inland, and was founded (in 1926) as a plant research station. Now, it is the second largest botanical garden in the world. It has more than 1000 varieties of plant and over 200 bird species have been identified. It has fruit trees from every continent, the most extensive collection of Asiatic fruit trees in the western hemisphere, an orchid garden, and plantations of mahogany and teak alongside a 1200-ha virgin tropical rainforest. But be warned, there are many mosquitoes.

To get to Lancetilla and the Jardín Botánico, take a taxi from Tela, US$4, but there are few in the park for the return journey in the afternoon, so organize collection in advance.

Northwestern coast

La Ceiba, the capital of Atlántida Department and the third largest city in Honduras, stands on the narrow coastal plain between the Caribbean and the rugged Nombre de Dios mountain range crowned by the spectacular Pico Bonito (2435 m) (see page 552). The climate is hot, but tempered by sea winds. Once the country's busiest port, trade has now passed to Puerto Cortés and Puerto Castilla, but there is still some activity. The close proximity to Pico Bonito National park, Cuero y Salado Wildlife Refuge and the Cayos

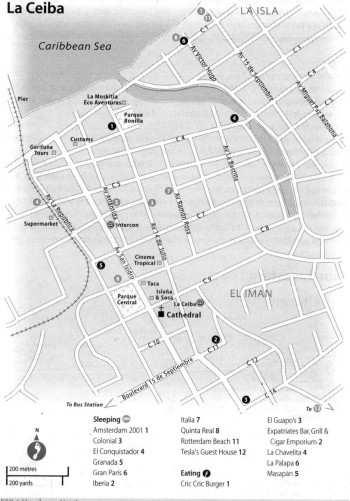

La Ceiba

Sleeping
Amsterdam 2001 **1**
Colonial **3**
El Conquistador **4**
Granada **5**
Gran París **6**
Iberia **2**

Italia **7**
Quinta Real **8**
Rotterdam Beach **11**
Tesla's Guest House **12**

Eating
Cric Cric Burger **1**

El Guapo's **3**
Expatriates Bar, Grill &
 Cigar Emporium **2**
La Chavelita **4**
La Palapa **6**
Masapán **5**

200 metres
200 yards

N

Cochinos Marine Reserve gives the city the ambitious target of becoming an important ecotourism centre. While the opportunities aren't immediately obvious, there is definitely a buzz about town – watch out for developments. The main plaza is worth walking around to see statues of various famous Hondurans including Lempira and a couple of ponds.

A **butterfly and insect museum** ① *Col El Sauce, 2a Etapa Casa G-12, T2442-2874, http:// butterflywebsite.com, Mon-Fri 0800—1600, closed Wed afternoon, Sat and Sun for groups only with advance reservation, US$1, student reductions*, has a collection of over 10,000 butterflies, roughly 2000 other insects and snakes. Good for all ages, you get a 25-minute video in both Spanish and English and Robert and Myriam Lehman guide visitors expertly through the life of the butterfly. There is also a **Butterfly Farm** ① *daily 0800-1530, entry US$6*, on the grounds of **The Lodge** at Pico Bonito.

Around La Ceiba → *See map, La Ceiba and the coast, below.*

Fig Tree Medical Centre ① *T2440-0041 (in La Ceiba), 25 km east of La Ceiba*, on the highway to Jutiapa, is a famous centre for alternative medicine. Operated by Dr Sebi, this facility is treating cancer and diabetes utilizing vegetarian diet, medications and the local hot springs. For more information or to visit call in advance. **Jutiapa** is a small dusty town with a pretty little colonial church. Contact Standard Fruit Company, Dole office in La Ceiba (off main plaza) to visit a local pineapple plantation. **Corozal** is an interesting Garífuna village near La Ceiba, at Km 209.5, with a beach, Playas de Sambrano and a hotel (see Sleeping, page 556). **Sambo Creek**, another Garífuna village, has nice beaches and a couple of hotels. Near the towns of **Esparta** and **El Porvenir**, thousands of crabs come out of the sea in July and August and travel long distances inland. The **Catarata El Bejuco** is a waterfall 7 km along the old dirt road to **Olanchito** (11 km from La Ceiba). Follow a path signposted to Balneario Los Lobos to the waterfall about 1 km upriver through the jungle. There is good swimming from a pebbly beach where the river broadens. Along this road is **El Naranjo** near **Omega Tours Jungle Lodge and Adventure Company**.

Yaruca, 20 km down the old road to Olanchito, is easily reached by bus and offers good views of Pico Bonito. **Eco-Zona Río María**, 5 km along the Trujillo highway (signposted path up to the foothills of the Cordillera Nombre de Dios), is a beautiful walk through the

La Ceiba and the coast

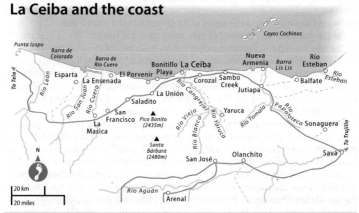

lush countryside of a protected area. Just beyond Río María is **Balneario Los Chorros** (signposted), a series of small waterfalls through giant boulders into a deep rock pool that is great for swimming (refreshments nearby). Upstream there is some beautiful scenery and you can continue walking through the forest and in the river, where there are more pools. Another bathing place, Agua Azul, with restaurant is a short distance away. The active can get on the **Río Cangrejal** for the exhilarating rush of Grade II, III and IV **whitewater rapids**, which can be combined with treks in to the wilderness of **Parque Nacional Pico Bonito** (see below).

Beaches around La Ceiba

Beaches in and near La Ceiba include **Playa Miramar** (dirty, not recommended), **La Barra** (better), **Perú** (across the Río Cangrejal at Km 205.5, better still, quiet except at weekends, deserted tourist complex, restaurant, access by road to Tocoa, 10 km, then signposted side road 1.5 km, or along the beach 6 km from La Ceiba) and **La Ensenada** (close to Corozal).

The beaches near the fishing villages of Río Esteban and Balfate are very special and are near Cayos Cochinos (Hog Islands) where the snorkelling and diving is spectacular. The Hog Islands (see page 573) can be reached by *cayuco* from Roatán, La Ceiba and **Nuevo Armenia**, a nondescript Garífuna village connected by road to Jutiapa. Take whatever you need with you as there is almost nothing on the smaller cayes. However, the Garífuna are going to and fro all the time.

Parque Nacional Pico Bonito

ⓘ *For further information on the park contact Leslie Arcantara at FUPNAPIB, at Calle 19, Av 14 de Julio, across from Suyapita Catholic church, Barrio Alvarado, T2442-0618. fupnapib@laceiba.com. Take care if you enter the forest: tracks are not yet developed, a compass is advisable. Tour companies in La Ceiba arrange trips to the park. A day trip, horse riding through the park, can be arranged through Omega Tours, see page 563. Trip includes food and guide, US$25. Recommended. Access to Public Trails in Pico Bonito is US$6. Go early in the morning for the best views, and to see birdlife and howler monkeys.*

Parque Nacional Pico Bonito (674 sq km) is the largest national park in Honduras and is home to Pico Bonito (2435 m). The Río Cangrejal, a mecca for whitewater rafting, marks the eastern border of the park. It has deep tropical hardwood forests that shelter, among other animals, jaguars and three species of monkey, deep canyons and tumbling streams and waterfalls (including Las Gemelas, which fall vertically for some 200 m).

Parque Nacional Pico Bonito has two areas open for tourism. The first is the Río Zacate area, located past the community of El Pino, 10 km west of La Ceiba; the second is on the Río Cangrejal, near the community of El Naranjo, about 7.5 km from the paved highway.

A hanging bridge over the Río Cangrejal provides access to the visitor centre and the **El Mapache Trail** up to the top of **El Bejuco** waterfall. Further up the road in **Las Mangas**, Guaruma (T2442-2693) there is a very nice trail with beautiful swimming holes in a pristine creek. The trail is well maintained and local guides are available.

For the Río Zacate area, access is just past the dry stream (*quebrada seca*) bridge on the main La Ceiba to Tela highway from where the road leads to the entrance through pineapple plantations to a steep trail leading up to the Río Zacate waterfall, about one hour 20 minutes' hiking. A good price range of accommodation is available in both areas.

Development of the park by **Curla** (Centro Universitario Regional del Litoral Atlántico) continues under the supervision of **Cohdefor**, the forestry office, and the **Fundación Parque Nacional Pico Bonito (FUPNAPIB)** ⓘ *Calle 19, Av 14 de Julio, La Ceiba, T2442-0618.*

Cuero y Salado Wildlife Reserve

ⓘ *US$10 to enter the reserve, which you can pay at Fucsa, keep the receipt, plus US$5 per person for accommodation. The reserve is managed by the Fundación Cuero y Salado (Fucsa) Refugio de Vida Silvestre, 1 block north and 3 blocks west of Parque Central (see map) to the left of the Standard Fruit Company, La Ceiba, T/F2443-0329, Apartado Postal 674. The foundation is open to volunteers, preferably those who speak English and Spanish.*

Near the coast, between the Cuero and Salado rivers, 37 km west of La Ceiba, is the Cuero y Salado Wildlife Reserve, which has a great variety of flora and fauna, including manatee, jaguar, monkeys and a large population of local and migratory birds. It extends for 13,225 ha of swamp and forest.

Nilmo, a knowledgeable biologist who acts as a guide, takes morning and evening boat trips for those staying overnight, either through the canal dug by Standard Fruit, parallel to the beach between the palms and the mangroves, or down to the Salado lagoon. Five kayaks are available for visitors' use. In the reserve are spider and capuchin monkeys, iguanas, jaguar, tapirs, crocodiles, manatee, hummingbirds, toucans, ospreys, eagles and vultures. A five-hour trip will take you to Barra de Colorado to see the manatees. Fucsa's administration centre, on the banks of the Río Salado, has photos, charts, maps, radio and a two-room visitors' house. There is also a visitor centre, with a full-service cafeteria and bilingual guides.

Getting there Take a bus to La Unión (every hour, 0600 until 1500 from La Ceiba terminus, 1½ hours, ask to get off at the railway line, ferrocarril, or Km 17), an interesting journey through pineapple fields. There are several ways of getting into the park from La Unión. Walking takes 1½ hours. Groups usually take a *motocarro*, a dilapidated train that also

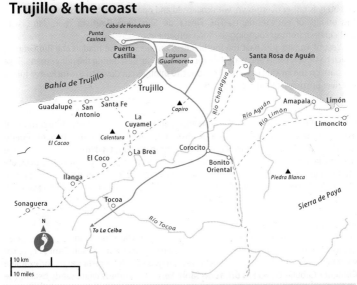

Trujillo & the coast

transports the coconut crop. From near Doña Tina's house (meals available), take a *burra*, a flat-bed railcar propelled by two men with poles (a great way to see the countryside) to the community on the banks of the Río Salado. To return to La Unión, it is another *burra* ride or a two-hour walk along the railway, then, either wait for a La Ceiba bus (last one at 1500), or ask for the short cut through grapefruit groves, 20 minutes, which leads to the main La Ceiba–Tela road, where there are many more buses back to town.

Trujillo and around → *For listings, see pages 556-566. Colour map 3, B3.*

→ *www.trujillohonduras.com.*

Once a major port and the former capital, Trujillo sits on the southern shore of the palm-fringed Bay of Trujillo. It is a quiet, pleasant town with clean beaches nearby and calm water that is ideal for swimming. Christopher Columbus landed close to the area on his fourth voyage to the Americas and the town was later founded in 1525 by Juan de Medina, making it the oldest town in Honduras. Hernán Cortés arrived here after his famous march overland from Yucatán in pursuit of his usurping lieutenant, Olid. Filibuster William Walker (see page 995) was shot near here in 1860; a commemorative stone marks the spot in the rear garden of the hospital, one block east of the Parque Central, and the old cemetery (near Hotel Trujillo) is his final resting place.

Fortaleza Santa Bárbara ① *US$1*, a ruined Spanish fortress overlooking the bay, is worth a visit. Most of the relics found there have been moved to the museum of Rufino Galán, but there are still a few rusty muskets and cannon balls. Twenty minutes' walk from Trujillo plaza is the **Museo y Piscina Rufino Galán Cáceres** ① *US$1, US$0.50 to swim*, which has a swimming pool filled from the Río Cristales with changing rooms and picnic facilities. Close by, the wreckage of a US C-80 aircraft that crashed in 1985 forms part of Sr Galán's museum. The rest of the collection is a mass of curios, some very interesting. The cemetery is rather overgrown, with collapsed and open tombs, but it does give a feel of the origins of early residents. The **Fiesta de San Juan Bautista** is in June, with participation from surrounding Garífuna settlements.

West of Trujillo, just past the football field on the Santa Fe road, is the **Río Grande**, which has lovely pools and waterfalls for river bathing, best during the rainy season. Take the path on the far side of river, after about 10 minutes cut down to the rocks and follow the river upstream along the boulders.

Beaches

Good beaches are found both on the peninsula and around Trujillo Bay. Before setting out ask which beaches are safe. Take a bus from near the Parque Central towards Puerto Castilla and ask the driver to let you off at the path about 1 km beyond the bridge over the lagoon. Other beaches around Puerto Castilla are separated by mangroves, are littered and have sandflies. The beaches in town tend to be less clean. If you're tempted to walk to find a cleaner stretch of sand don't walk alone; tourists here have been assaulted and robbed.

West of Trujillo

There are interesting Garífuna villages west of Trujillo. The road is rough, often impassable in wet weather, and jeeps are needed even in the dry season. **Santa Fe**, 10 km west of Trujillo, is a friendly place with several good Garífuna restaurants, for example **Comedor Caballero** and **Las Brisas de Santa Fe**, on the endless white sandy beach. The bus service continues to **San Antonio** (good restaurant behind the beach) and **Guadalupe**. Walk in the morning along the beach to Santa Fe and then get a bus back to Trujillo, taking plenty of water and sun block. This stretch of beach is outstanding, but watch out for *marea roja*, a sea organism that colours the water pink and can give irritating skin rashes to bathers. Also, be warned, local people consider this walk unsafe. It's best to go in a large group.

Santa Rosa de Aguán
One of the largest Garífuna communities, Santa Rosa de Aguán is an interesting coastal town, some 40 km east of Trujillo, with 7000 hospitable English- and Spanish-speaking inhabitants. The spreading settlement lies at the mouth of the Río Aguán, the greater part on the east of the bay. A white-sand beach stretches all the way to Limón, and the thundering surf is an impressive sight. Take drinking water, insect repellent, mosquito coils and high-factor sun screen.

If driving from Trujillo, turn left at Km 343, 20 km along the highway, where a good gravel road runs another 20 km to Santa Rosa. From where the road ends at the west bank, take a canoe ferry across to the east side.

Parque Nacional Capiro y Calentura
The Parque Nacional Capiro y Calentura encompasses these two mountains over-looking Trujillo. The four- to six-hour walk to the summit gives spectacular views and on a clear day Isla Roatán can be seen in the distance. The walk is best done early in the morning when the forest is alive with the sounds of birds, monkeys and other wildlife. The path can be reached by walking (or taking a taxi) up the hill past the **Villa Brinkley Hotel**. The road to the summit is in poor condition from the entrance of the park and can only be driven in a 4WD. Insect repellent is needed if you pause. As with all walks in this area, it's safest to go in a group. The park is run by the **Fundación Capiro Calentura Guaimoreto** (**FUCAGUA**) ① *Parque Central, Trujillo, Mon-Fri*. They have information on all the reserves in the area and also on hiking and tours. Until a new office is built in the park, entry tickets must be bought here before going to Capiro y Calentura. They are opening up trails, improving old ones and organizing guided tours through parts of the forest. The hike along the Sendero de la Culebrina uses the remnants of a colonial stone road used to transport gold from the mines in the Valle de Aguán. Halfway up the **Cerro de las Cuevas**, 7 km beyond Cuyamel, are impressive caves showing traces of occupation by pre-Columbian Pech people.

Refugio de Vida Silvestre Laguna de Guaimoreto (RVSLG)
FUCAGUA, see above, also administers the Refugio de Vida Silvestre, Laguna de Guaimoreto (RVSLG), northeast of Trujillo, where there is a bird island (Isla de los Pájaros), monkeys and good fishing. To visit, either arrange a trip with Fucagua, a tour agency such as Turtle Tours, or take a bus from Trujillo towards Puerto Castilla, get off just after the bridge which crosses the lagoon, then walk away from the lagoon for about 200 m to a dirt track on the left. Follow this and cross a low bridge and on the left is the house of a man who rents dug-out canoes. The Isla de los Pájaros is about 3 km up the lagoon, a bit too far for a dug-out. Another alternative is to go down to the wharf and hire out a motorized canoe or launch(price depends on the number of passengers and length of trip). There are no roads, paths or facilities in the area.

El Progreso and east → *For listings, see pages 556-566.*

El Progreso, an important but unattractive agricultural and commercial centre on the Río Ulúa, is 30 minutes' drive on the paved highway southeast of San Pedro Sula, en route to Tela. While most people make straight for the coast at Tela, heading east from El Progreso leads through mountain scenery up to the small town of Yoro, beyond to Olanchito and a link to La Ceiba. With everyone else rushing to the Bay Islands, you could well have the place to yourself.

Parque Nacional Pico Pijol → *Colour map 3, B2.*

This park protects the 2282-m summit of primary cloud forest that is home to many quetzales. It is 32 km from the town of **Morazán** in the Yoro Department, which is 41 km from Progreso (bus from Progreso or Santa Rita). In Morazán are **Hospedaje El Corazón Sagrado**, several restaurants and a disco. The lower slopes of Pico Pijol have been heavily farmed. Access by vehicle is possible as far as Subirana. A guide is needed from there to a large cave nearby; access is difficult. Another trail to the summit (2282 m) starts at **Nueva Esperanza** village (bus from Morazán, Parque Central); ask for the correct trail. The first day is tough, all uphill with no shade; the second is tougher and requires a lot of clearing. Take compass and topographical map. Also in the park is the waterfall at **Las Piratas** (bus Morazán–Los Murillos and then walk to El Ocotillo (ask for Las Piratas).

Yoro and around → *Colour map 3, B2.*

The paved highway to the prosperous little town of Yoro passes through pleasant countryside surrounded by mountains and dotted with ranches and farms. The **Parque Nacional Montaña de Yoro** is 8 km to the southeast (access from Marale), comprising 257 sq km of cloud forest, home to the Tolupanes people, also known as Xicaques. The **Asociación Ecológica Amigos de la Montaña de Yoro** has an office in the Parque Central in Yoro. From Yoro a dirt road continues to **Olanchito** via **Jocón**, through attractive country as the road snakes along the pine-forested slopes of Montaña Piedra Blanca and Montaña de la Bellota, with fine views of the surrounding valleys and distant mountain ranges.

◉ North coast listings

For Sleeping and Eating price codes and other relevant information, see Essentials pages 31-33.

● Sleeping

Puerto Cortés *p547, map p547*
Avoid 4 Calle between 1 and 2 Av and the area on 1 Av opposite the dockyards; it is unpleasant by day and dangerous at night.
AL Playa, 4 km west at Cienaguita, T2665-1105. Hotel complex, directly on beach, cable TV, good fish dishes in restaurant. Mountain bikes for rent, available to non-guests.

A Costa Azul, Playa El Faro, T2665-2260. Restaurant, disco-bar, billiards, table tennis, pool, horse riding, volley ball, good value.
C Mr GGeerr, 9 Calle, 2 Av E, T2665-0444. No hot water, very clean, a/c, bar, video, satellite TV. Recommended.
C-E El Centro, 3 Av 2-3 Calle, T2665-1160. With bath, a/c, hot water, cable TV, parking, garden, café, pleasant, well furnished.
D Frontera del Caribe, Playas de Camaguey, road to Travesía, T2665-5001. Very friendly, quiet, safe, on beach, restaurant on 1st floor, open, airy, good food, 7 rooms on 2nd floor, private bath, cold water, linen changed daily, fan. Recommended.

F Formosa, 3 Av 2 Calle E. With bath (some without), no towel, but soap and toilet paper provided, clean, fan, good value, friendly Chinese owner.

Omoa *p548*

B Sueño del Mar, T2658-9047, www.suenos demar.com. Newest hotel on the beach with a handful of rooms of differing sizes run by Canadian couple Karen and Mark. Great spot and the quiet end of the beach. Canadian breakfasts, laundry, Wi-Fi internet and a few steps from the beach. Recommended.

B Tatiana, on beach. With bath, clean and quiet.

B-C Fisherman's Hotel, great small hotel by the beach, clean, handy location, restaurant out front. A/c, cheaper with fan.

E Roli's Place, T/F2658-9082, http://yaxpactours.com. 80 m from beach, clean rooms with private bath and hot water, good information here of the region, bikes and kayaks for guests' use, games, shady garden and campground. Roli will change TCs, quetzals, euro and dollars. Quiet after 2200. Great, but not a party place.

Tela *p548*

During Easter week, the town is packed: room rates double; advance booking is essential.

AL Telamar, T2448-2196, www.hotel telamar.com. A large luxury resort of wooden bungalows, set on a palm-fringed, clean, white-sand beach. Rooms and villas available, also restaurants, bar, golf club, swimming pools, kids' activities and a conference centre.

A-B Maya Vista, top of hill, steep flight of steps starting opposite **Preluna**, T/F2448-1497, www.mayavista.com. Canadian-owned, French and English spoken, bath, a/c, hot water, bar, restaurant, delicious French-Canadian cuisine, fantastic views. Very highly recommended.

B Gran Central, just south of the centre of town, T/F448-1099, www.hotelgran central.com. French-owned, beautifully restored historic banana-port-era hotel. 1 suite, kitchen, hot water, cable TV, a/c,

security, safe box in each room. Local excursions available. Highly recommended.

C Mango B&B, 8 Calle, 5 Av, T2448-0338, www.mangocafe.net. A/c, hot water, TV, comfortable, well-furnished rooms, friendly, efficient; Spanish tuition, and bike hire. Recommended.

C Tela, 9 Calle, 3-4 Av NE, T2448-2150. Clean, airy, fans, hot water, will do laundry, with restaurant, but meagre breakfast, otherwise very good.

C-D Bertha's, 8 Calle, 9 Av NE, T2448-1009. Near bus terminal, with bath, a/c, cheaper with fan, clean. Recommended.

E Mar Azul, 11 Calle, 5 Av NE, T2448-2313. With fan and bath, charming helpful owner. Best backpacker place in town.

F Sara, 11 Calle, 6 Av, behind the restaurant Tiburón Playa, T2448-1477. Basic in a rickety old building, with bath, or without, poor sanitation. Cheapest in town, popular with backpackers, friendly, noisy especially at weekends from all-night discos.

Around Tela *p548*

There are cheap houses and *cabañas* for rent in Triunfo de la Cruz. There is a small hotel in Río Tinto, near Parque Nacional Punta Sal; accommodation is available in private houses.

A-B Caribbean Coral Inn, Triunfo de la Cruz, T2669-0224, www.globalnet.hn/caribcoralinn. With bath, fan.

A-B The Last Resort, Tornabé, T/F2984-3964. Has 8 bungalows for rent, some a/c, some fan, hot water, with breakfast, several cabins for different size groups.

D-F El Tucán, Triunfo de la Cruz. Backpacker place with *cabañas*.

La Ceiba *p550, map p550*

AL Quinta Real, Zona Viva, on the beach, T2440-3311, www.quintarealhotel.com. By far the best hotel in La Ceiba, with big, well-furnished rooms. Swimming pool, a/c, cable TV, beach, restaurant and bars, free Internet. (Taxi drivers sometimes confuse it with the **Hotel Quinta (A)** opposite the Golf Club on Tela–La Ceiba road, T2443-0223, which is modern and functional, also with pool, but not half as nice).

A-B Gran Hotel París, Parque Central, T/F2443-2391, hotelparis@psinet.hn. A/c, own generator, swimming pool, parking, good value.

B Iberia, Av San Isidoro, next door to Ceiba, T2443-0401. A/c, windows without screen. Recommended.

B Tesla's Guest House, Calle Montecristo 212, Col El Naranjal, opposite Hospital La Fe, T/F2443-3893. 5 rooms, private bathrooms, hot water, a/c, pool, phone, minibar, BBQ, laundry, friendly family owners speak English, German, French and Spanish, airport collection.

C Italia, Av Ramón Rosas, T2443-0150. Clean, a/c, good restaurant with reasonable prices, swimming pool, parking in interior courtyard.

C-E Posada Don Giuseppe, Av San Isidro at 13 Calle, T/F2442-2812. Bath, a/c (fan cheaper), hot water, TV, bar, restaurant. Comfortable.

D Colonial, Av 14 de Julio, between 6a and 7a Calle, T2443-1953. A/c, sauna, jacuzzi, cable TV, rooftop bar, restaurant with varied menu, nice atmosphere, tourist office, tours available. A bit run-down.

D El Conquistador, Av La República, T2443-3670. Cheaper with fan, shared bath, safe, clean, TV.

E Amsterdam 2001, 1 Calle, Barrio La Isla, T443-2311. Run by Dutch man Jan (Don Juan), good for backpackers, dormitory beds or rooms, with laundry, bit run-down, **Dutch Corner Café** for great breakfasts.

E Granada, Av Atlántida, 5-6 Calle, T2443-2451, hotelparis@psinet.hn. Bath, a/c, clean, safe, cheaper with fan.

E Rotterdam Beach, next door to Amsterdam 2001 at 1 Calle, Barrio La Isla, T2440-0321. On the beach, with bath, fan, clean, friendly, pleasant garden, good value. Recommended.

F Las 5 Rosas, Calle 8 near Av La Bastilla, opposite Esso. Clean, simple rooms, bath, fan, laundry, good value.

Around La Ceiba *p551*

B Coco Pando, Km 188, T969-9663, www.cocopando.com. On seafront a few kilometres west of La Ceiba, this palm-roofed building has great sunset views from upper deck; simple rooms with showers, a/c and TV (mixed reports about cleanliness and availability of hot water); free shuttle to town and airport; good value **Iguana** bar/restaurant and discotheque next door.

B Hotel Canadien, Sambo Creek, T2440-2099, www.hotelcanadien.com. With double suite. Can arrange trips to Hog Islands for US$80 per boat.

B Villa Rhina, near the turn-off from the main road, Corozal, T2443-1222. With pool and restaurant.

C Villa Helen's, Sambo Creek about 35 mins east of La Ceiba, T2408-1137, www.villa helens.com. Good selection of rooms from simple to luxury. Pool and on the beach, with a variety of activities in the quiet seclusion.

E Cabañas del Caribe, in Dantillo, 5 mins out of town on the road to Tela, T2441-1421, T2997-8746 (mob). 6 big cabins, some with jacuzzi, and 7 rooms on the beach, restaurant serving breakfast. Video screen in restaurant. Great place to relax. Call 1 day ahead to collect from town. Buses from La Ceiba for Dantillo every 30 mins.

E Hermanos Avila, Sambo Creek. Simple hotel-restaurant, clean; food OK.

E Finca El Edén, in Santa Ana, 32 km west of La Ceiba, bertiharlos@yahoo.de. Rooms, dorms, hammocks and mattresses. Good views to the sea and good food.

Beaches around La Ceiba *p552*

E Chichi, Nuevo Armenia. 3 small rooms, fan, mosquito net, clean, good food available.

Parque Nacional Pico Bonito *p552*
Río Cangrejo area

B-E Omega Tours Jungle Lodge and Adventure Company, El Naranjo, T2440-0334, www.omegatours.info. With wide range of options from simple rooms to comfortable *cabañas* and good food. Rafting and kayaking are available on the Río Cangrejal and trips to La Mosquitia (see page 589).

B-F Jungle River Lodge, on Río Cangrejal overlooking Pico Bonito, T2440-1268, www.jungleriverlodge.com. Private rooms and dorms, natural swimming pools, restaurant and breathtaking views. Rafting, canopy tours, zip-wires, hiking and mountain biking tours available. Activities include a free night's accommodation. Take Yaruka bus from main bus terminal, get off at Km 7; blue kayak marks entrance on river side of the road, call for arranged transport or join a tour.

D-E Cabañas del Bosque, up the road from Jungle River at Las Mangas. Nice rustic cabins with spectacular views in rooms and dorms.

Río Zacate area

LL-L The Lodge, Pico Bonito, 15 mins' drive west of La Ceiba, T2440-0388, T1-888-428-0221 (USA), www.picobonito.com. Honduras' 1st world-class ecolodge at the base of Parque Nacional Pico Bonito. Luxury wooden cabins – no TV, very peaceful – in 400 acres of grounds. Forest trails, with lookout towers, natural swimming holes and waterfalls; nature guides and tours, very popular with birders; butterfly farm and serpentarium; swimming pool and gourmet restaurant. Highly recommended.

D Natural View Ecoturism Center, in El Pino, T2386-9678. Very rustic cabins with access to trails in the vicinity. Cabins are built of adobe walls and thatched room, with a private bath, mosquito screens, but no power. Set in the middle of a plant nursery with a nice restaurant on premises. Efraín can help arrange several good trips nearby including a boat trip down the lower Río Zacate through mangroves to a farm located next to the beach, adjacent to Cuero y Salado.

D Posada del Buen Pastor, T2950-3404. Has 4 rustic rooms on the upper storey of a private home with private bath, cable TV and fan.

Cuero y Salado Wildlife Reserve *p553*

D-E Refuge, T/F2443-0329, Fucsa's administration centre, on the banks of the Río Salado. Has photos, charts, maps, radio and a 2-room visitors' house, sleeping 4 in basic bunks, electricity 1800-2100. No mosquito nets, so avoid Sep and Oct if you can. Don't wear open footwear as snakes and yellow scorpions can be found here. Book in advance. Food available. There's also tent space for camping at the refuge.

Trujillo and around *p554, map p553*

AL-B Christopher Columbus Beach Resort, outside town along the beach, drive across airstrip, T2434-4966. Has 72 rooms and suites, a/c, cable TV, swimming pool, restaurant, watersports, tennis, painted bright turquoise.

B Resort y Spa Agua Caliente Silin, Silin, on main road southeast of Trujillo, T2434-4247. *Cabañas* with cable TV, pool, thermal waters, restaurant, massage given by Pech Lastenia Hernández, very relaxing.

C O'Glynn, 3 blocks south of the plaza, T2434-4592. Smart, clean, good rooms and bathrooms, a/c, TV, fridge in some rooms. Highly recommended.

D Colonial, on plaza, T2434-4011. With bath, hacienda style, restaurant (**El Bucanero**, see Sleeping), a/c, safe and clean.

E Mar de Plata, up street west, T2434-4174. Upstairs rooms best, with bath, fan, friendly and helpful, beautiful view from room.

E-F Casa Kiwi, in Puerto Castilla, out of town, T/F2434-3050, www.casakiwi.com. A 5-km, 15-min bus journey from town in an isolated location. Private rooms and dormitories, with kitchen and restaurant facilities. On a secluded beach with the benefits of internet, book swap, boat rides, horse riding, local trips and perfect for true relaxation. Buses to Puerto Castilla from the bus station every couple of hours, US$0.40. Watch out when riding bikes in the area, especially at night.

E-F Catracho, 3 blocks south of church, then a block east, T2434-4439. Basic, clean, noisy, no water at night, wooden cabins facing a garden, camping space US$1.50, parking.

F Buenos Aires, opposite **Catracho**, T2434-4431. Monthly rates available, pleasant, clean, peaceful, but cabins damp and many mosquitos, organizes tours to national park.

Yoro and around *p556*
D Hotel Olanchito, Barrio Arriba, Calle La Palma, Olanchito, T2446-6385. A/c.
E Nelson, Yoro. Comfortable rooms with bath, fan, modern, good restaurant/bar and nice outdoor swimming pool on 3rd floor, bar/disco on roof with marvellous views. Warmly recommended.
E Valle Aguán y Chabelito, 1 block north of Parque Central, Olanchito, T2446-6718 (same management as **Hotel Olanchito**). Single rooms with a/c, doubles with fan, all rooms with cable TV, best in town, with best restaurant.
E-F Palacio, on main street, Yoro. All rooms with bath and fan and a good resaurant.
F Aníbal, corner of Parque Central, Yoro. Excellent value, private or shared bath, clean, pleasant, wide balcony, restaurant.
F Colonial, Calle del Presidio, Olanchito. Good value, bath, fan, cheaper with shared bath, restaurant, parking.
F Hospedaje, Jocón. Clean and basic.

❷ Eating

Puerto Cortés *p547, map p547*
❦❦ **Candiles**, 2 Av, 7-8 Calle. Good grills, reasonable prices, open-air seating.
❦❦ **Pekín**, 2 Av, 6-7 Calle. Chinese, a/c, excellent, good service, a bit pricey but recommended. Supermercado Pekín next door.
❦ **Burger Boy's**, 2 Av 8 Calle. Lively, popular with local teenagers.
❦ **Comedor Piloto**, 2 Av 1-2 Calle. Mon-Sat 0700-1800. Clean, satellite TV, fans, good value and service, popular.
❦ **El Zaguán**, 2 Av 5-6 Calle, closed Sun. Popular with locals, good for refreshments.
❦ **Ilusión**, 4 Calle E opposite Parque. Pastries, bread, coffee, nice for breakfast.
❦ **Kasike's Restaurant-Bar-Peña**, 3 Av y 9 Calle and **Carnitas Tapadera**, on same block. Recommended.

❦ **Matt's**, on same block as **La Cabaña**, a/c, nice bar, good food, not expensive.
❦ **Wendy's**, on the Parque. With inside play centre for children.

Cafés and ice cream parlours
❦ **Repostería y Pastelería Plata**, 3 Av and 2 Calle E, near Parque Central. Good bread and pastries, excellent cheap *almuerzo*, buffet-style, kids' playroom. Recommended.

Omoa *p548*
❦ **Cayuquitos**, on beachfront. Good-value meals all day, but service is very slow.
❦ **Fisherman's Hut**, 200 m to right of pier. Clean, good food, seafood, recommended. Don't expect early Sun breakfasts after the partying the night before.
❦ **Sunset Playa**, on beachfront at southern end of the beach. Good food, open all day.

Cafés and juice bars
❦ **Stanley**, on the beach next door to **Cayuquitos**. Good value, with good shakes and juices.

Tela *p548*
The best eating is in the hotel restaurants.
❦❦❦ **Casa Azul**, Barrio El Centro. Open till 2300. Run by Mark from Texas, subs, dinner specials, book exchange. Helpful.
❦❦❦ **Arecifes**. Calle Muelle de Cabotaje, on seafront road T441-4353. Open Tue-Sun. Best bar and grill in town.
❦❦ **César Mariscos**. Open from 0700. Nice location on the beach, serves good seafood, very good breakfast menu.
❦❦❦ **Iguana Sports Bar**, road between 2 town bridges leading out of town. Open-air, music.
❦❦❦ **Luces del Norte**, of Doña Mercedes, 11 Calle, 2 Av NE, towards beach from Parque Central, next to **Hotel Puerto Rico**. Delicious seafood and good typical breakfasts, very popular, also good information and book exchange.
❦❦❦ **Maya Vista**, in hotel (see Sleeping, above). Run by Québécois Pierre, fine cuisine, 1 of the best in Tela. Highly recommended.

♦♦ **Merendero Tía Carmen**, at the the Mango B&B (see Sleeping). Good food, Honduran specialities including *baleadas*, good *almuerzo*.
♦ **Bahía Azul**, good fresh food, excellent sea food.
♦ **Bella Italia**, Italian-owned serving pizza, on walkway by the beach.
♦ **El Pescador**, San Juan. On the beach, great seafood in a fine setting.
♦ **Sherwood**. Good food, popular, enjoy the view from the terrace, also opens 0700 and serves excellent breakfast.
♦ **Tuty's Café**, 9 Calle NE near Parque Central. Excellent fruit drinks and good cheap lunch specials, but slow service.

Cafés and ice cream parlours
Espresso Americano, in front of Parque Central. Best place in town for coffee, latte, cappuccino, with internet and international calls. Very popular.

La Ceiba *p550, map p550*
♦♦ **Cafetería Cobel**, 7 Calle between Av Atlántida and 14 de Julio, 2 blocks from Parque Central. Could be the best *cafetería* in the entire country, very popular with locals, always crowded, good fresh food, daily specials, highly recommended. Unmissable.
♦♦ **El Guapo's**, corner of 14 de Julio and 14 Calle. Open daily for dinner. US-Honduran owned, good combination of international and typical Honduran cuisine.
♦♦ **La Chavelita**, end of 4 Calle E, overlooking Río Cangrejal. Open daily for lunch and dinner. Seafood, popular.
♦♦ **La Palapa**, Av Víctor Hugo, next to **Hotel Quinta Real**. Giant, palm-roofed, wood-beamed 'palapa', serving juicy steaks, grills, fish, seafood and burgers; also sports bar with half a dozen TV screens, ice-cold beer. Good value for money though indifferent service.
♦♦ **La Plancha**, Calle 9, east of the cathedral. Open daily for lunch and dinner. Best steak house in La Ceiba, with good seafood dishes.
♦♦ **Toto's**, Av San Isidro, 17 Calle. Good pizzas.
♦ **Cric Cric Burger**, Av 14 de Julio, 3 Calle, facing attractive Parque Bonilla. Good fast

food, several branches. Recommended.
♦ **Expatriates Bar, Grill and Cigar Emporium**, Final de Calle 12, above **Refricón**, 3 blocks south, 3 blocks east of Parque Central. Thu-Tue 1600-2400. Honduran-American owners, very affordable, with good steak and shrimps. Free internet service for clients. Also have a branch at the Cangrejal River, Km 9.
♦ **Gallo Pinto**, Calle 9, east of the cathedral. Affordable typical Honduran cuisine in a pleasant informal setting.
♦ **Mango Tango**, on 1 Calle. The best Ceibeño cuisine in the Zona Viva. Open daily for dinner from 1730. Menu includes fish, pork, chicken and beef dishes, and the best salad bar in town! They also have a nice sports bar.
♦ **Masapán**, 7 Calle, Av San Isidro and Av República. Daily 0630-2200. Self-service, varied, well-prepared choice of dishes, fruit juices, good coffee. Recommended.
♦ **Palace**, 9 Calle, Av 14 de Julio. Large Chinese menu, surf 'n' turf. Recommended.
♦ **The Palm Restaurant**, centrally located, half a block from Parque Central in the **Banco de Occidente** building. American-style food open daily for breakfast, lunch and dinner. TVs with international news and sports. Free internet service for clients.
♦ **Paty's**, Av 14 de Julio between 6 and 7 Calle. Milkshakes, wheatgerm, cereals, donuts, etc, purified water, clean. Opposite is an excellent pastry shop. There are 2 more **Paty's**, at 8 Calle E and the bus terminal.

Around La Ceiba *p551*
♦♦ **Kabasa**, Sambo Creek. Seafood Garífuna-style, bar, delightful location.

Trujillo and around *p554, map p553*
Don't miss the coconut bread, a speciality of the Garífuna.
♦♦ **Galaxia**, 1 block west of plaza. Good seafood, popular with locals.
♦♦ **Oasis**, opposite HSBC. Outdoor seating, Canadian owned, good meeting place, information board, good food, bar, English books for sale, book exchange, local tours.
♦ **Bahía Bar**, T2434-4770, on the beach by

the landing strip next to **Christopher Columbus**. Popular with expats, also Hondurans at weekends, vegetarian food, showers, toilets.

† **Don Perignon**, uphill from Pantry. Some Spanish dishes, good local food, cheap.

† **El Bucanero**, on main plaza. A/c, video, good breakfast, *desayuno típico*.

† **Pantry**, 1½ blocks from the park. Garífuna cooking and standard menu, cheap pizzas, a/c.

☺ Entertainment

La Ceiba and around *p550, map p550*
Iguana Sports Bar Discoteque, in Coco Pando hotel (see Sleeping, above), is the place to go.
La Casona, 4a Calle. Thu-Sat 2000-0400. Most popular nightspot in town. Karaoke bar, good music.
Monaster, 1 Calle. Thu-Sat 2000-0400. Nice setting, good a/c. Several others along 1 Calle.

Trujillo and around *p554, map p553*
Head to **Rincón de los Amigos** or **Rogue's** if you're looking for drink at the end of the day. Also try the **Gringo Bar** and **Bahía Bar**. In **Barrio Cristales** at weekends there's *punta* music and lively atmosphere. Recommended.

The cinema shows current US releases (most in English with subtitles).

☀ Festivals and events

Puerto Cortés *p547, map p547*
Aug Noche Veneciana on 3rd Sat.

Tela *p548*
Jun Fiesta de San Antonio.

La Ceiba and around *p550, map p550*
15-28 May San Isidro La Ceiba's patron saint's celebrations continue for 2 weeks, the highlight being the international carnival on the 3rd Sat in May, when La Ceiba parties long and hard to the Afro-Caribbean beat of *punta* rock.

⊙ Shopping

Puerto Cortés *p547, map p547*
There is a souvenir shop, **Marthita's**, in the customs administration building (opposite Hondutel). The market in the town centre is quite interesting, 3 Calle between 2 and 3 Av. **Supertienda Paico** is on the Parque.

La Ceiba and around *p550, map p550*
Carrion Department Store, Av San Isidro with 7A Calle. **Deli Mart** late-night corner store on 14 de Julio, round corner from internet café, shuts at 2300. **El Regalito**, good-quality souvenirs at reasonable prices in small passage by large Carrión store. **T Boot**, store for hiking boots, Calle 1, east of Av San Isidro, T2443-2499. **Supermarket Super Ceibena**, 2 on Av 14 de Julio and 6A Calle.

Trujillo and around *p554, map p553*
Garí-Arte Souvenir, T2434-4207, in the centre of Barrio Cristales, is recommended for authentic Garífuna souvenirs. Owned by Ricardo Lacayo and open daily.
Tienda Souvenir Artesanía next to Hotel Emperador, handicrafts, hand-painted toys. 3 supermarkets in the town centre.

▲ Activities and tours

Puerto Cortés *p547, map p547*
Bahía Travel/Maya Rent-a-Car, 3 Av 3 Calle, T2665-2102.
Irema, 2 Av 3-4 Calle, T2665-1506.
Ocean Travel, Plaza Eng, 3 Av 2 Calle, T2665-0913.

Tela *p548*
Garífuna Tours, southwest corner of Parque Central, T2448-2904, www.garifunatours.com, knowledgeable and helpful with mountain bike hire, US$5 per day. Day trips to Punta Sal (US$31, meals extra), Los Micos lagoon (US$31) and Punta Izopo (US$24). La Ceiba–Cayos Cochinos (US$39), La Ceiba–Cuero Salado (US$68), Pico Bonito (US$33). Also

trips further afield to La Ceiba, Mosquitia (4 days, US$499) and a shuttle service between San Pedro Sula and La Ceiba, US$18 per person. Also La Ceiba–Copán, US$45. Good value. Highly recommended.
Honduras Caribbean Tours, T2448-2623, www.honduras-caribbean.com. Wide range of tours and treks throughout Honduras specializing in North coast.

La Ceiba and around *p550, map p550*
Ask around to find a tour that suits your needs and to verify credentials.
Caribbean Travel Agency, run by Ann Crichton, Av San Isidro, Edif Hermanos Kawas, Apdo Postal 66, T/F2443-1360, helpful, shares office with **Ríos Honduras**, see below.
Garífuna Tours, Av San Isidro 1 Calle, T2440-3252, www.garifunatours.com. Day trips into Pico Bonito National Park (US$34 per person), Cuero y Salado (US$49), rafting on the Cangrejal (US$34), trips out to Cayos Cochinos (US$49) and a shuttle service to Tela (US$1).
Junglas River Rafting, T2440-1268, www.jungleriverlodge.com.
La Ceiba Ecotours, Av San Isidro, 1st block, 50 m from beach, T/F2443-4207, hiking and riding in Parque Nacional Pico Bonito, visits to other nearby reserves, whitewater rafting, trips to La Mosquitia.
La Moskitia Eco Aventuras, Av 14 de Julio at Parque Manuel Bonilla, T/F2442-0104, www.lamoskitia.hn. Eco-adventure tours, run by Jorge Salaverri, extremely knowledgeable nature guide, enthusiastic and flexible. Specializes in trips to Mosquitia, including week-long expeditions to Las Marias and hikes up Pico Baltimore and Pico Dama. Highly recommended.
Omega Tours, T2440-0334, www.omega tours.info, runs rafting and kayaking trips on the Río Cangrejal, jungle hikes, and own hotel 30 mins upstream. Also tours to La Mosquitia ranging from easy adventure tours of 4 days up to 13-day expeditions. Prices drop dramatically with more than 2 people.

Ríos Honduras, T2443-0780, office@ rioshonduras.com, offering whitewater rafting, trips on the Río Cangrejal, spectacular, reservations 1 day in advance.

Cuero y Salado Wildlife Reserve *p553*
Although it is possible to go to the Salado and hire a villager and his boat, a qualified guide will show you much more. It is essential to bring a hat and sun lotion with you. Travel agencies in La Ceiba run tours there, but **Fucsa** arranges visits and owns the only accommodation in the reserve. Before going, check with **Fucsa** in La Ceiba. Although the office only has basic information, the people are helpful and there are displays and books about the flora and fauna to be found in the park. A guide and kayak for a 1-hr trip costs about US$10. Boatmen charge about US$20 for a 2-hr trip or US$40 for 5 hrs (6-7 persons maximum), US$6-7 for the guide.

Trujillo and around *p554, map p553*
Hacienda Tumbador Crocodile Reserve is privately owned, accessible only by 4WD and with guide, US$5 entry.

⊖ Transport

Puerto Cortés *p547, map p547*
Boat
To Guatemala Information from **Ocean Travel** at 3 Av, 2 blocks west of plaza.

To Belize Boats connecting to Belize leave from beside the bridge over the lagoon (Barra La Laguna), buy tickets at the blue wooden shack next to *joyería* near **Los Coquitos** bar just before bridge. Daily 0800-1700. The **Gulf Cruza** launch leaves Puerto Cortés on Mon at 1100, for **Mango Creek** and on to **Placencia**, 4 hrs arriving around 1340, US$50.

Remember to get your exit stamp. To be sure of getting an exit stamp go to Immigration in town (see Directory, below). If arriving from Belize and heading on straight away you don't need to go into town to catch a bus. Get on to the bridge, cross over the other side and keep walking 200 m to the main road. Buses going past are going to San Pedro Sula and beyond.

Bus

Virtually all buses now arrive and leave from 4 Av 2-4 Calle. Bus service at least hourly to **San Pedro Sula**, US$2.30, 45 mins, Citul (4 Av between 3 and 4 Calle) and **Impala** (4 Av y 3 Calle, T2255-0606). Expresos del Caribe, Expresos de Citul and Expresos del Atlantic all have minibuses to **San Pedro Sula**. Bus to **Omoa** and **Tegucigalpita** from 4 Av, old school bus, loud music, very full, guard your belongings. Citral Costeños go to the Guatemalan border, 4-5 Av, 3C E. Regular buses leave for **Omoa** (US$0.70) at 0730 to get to **Corinto** at the Guatemalan border.

Omoa *p548*
Boat

Boats leave for **Lívingston**, Guatemala, on Tue and Fri around 1000. Ask around to confirm. Ask at Fisherman's Hut for Sr Juan Ramón Menjívar.

Bus

Frequent buses to the Guatemalan border at 1000, 1400 and 1700. See page 198 for border-crossing information.

Tela *p548*
Bike

Hire from Garífuna Tours, 9 Calle y Parque Central (see page 562), and from Hotel Mango.

Bus

Catisa or **Tupsa** lines from San Pedro Sula to **El Progreso** (US$0.50) where you must change to go on to **Tela** (3 hrs in total) and **La Ceiba** (last bus at 2030 with Transportes Cristina). On **Catisa** bus ask to be let off at the petrol station on the main road, then take a taxi to the beach, US$0.50. Also 1st-class service with **Hedman Alas** at 1010, 1415 and 1810.

Bus from Tela to **El Progreso** every 25 mins; last bus at 1830, US$1.50. To **La Ceiba**, every 30 mins, from 0410 until 1800, 2 hrs, US$2. Direct to **Tegucigalpa**, Traliasa, 1 a day from Hotel Los Arcos, US$4.50, same bus to **La Ceiba** (this service avoids San Pedro Sula; 6 a day with **Transportes Cristinas** (US$9.20). To **Copán**, leave by 0700 via El Progreso and San Pedro Sula; to arrive same day. To **San Pedro Sula**, 1130 and 1715 with Diana Express (US$2.50), or 8 a day with **Transportes Tela Express**, last bus at 1700 (US$3). To **Trujillo** through Savá, Tocoa and Corocito.

Shuttle Garífuna Tours, see page 562, offers a shuttle service direct to **San Pedro**, US$18 and **Copán Ruinas**, US$45.

Around Tela *p548*
Bus

To **Triunfo de la Cruz**, US$0.40 (about 5 km, if no return bus, walk to main road where buses pass).

La Ceiba and around *p550, map p550*
Air

For La Mosquitia see page 589.

Golosón (LCE), 10 km out of town. See Getting there, page 491, for international services. For details of flights to Bay Islands, see page 567. Isleña (T2443-0179 airport), flies to **San Pedro Sula**, **Trujillo**, **Puerto Lempira**, **Roatán** and **Guanaja**; Taca fly to **Tegucigalpa** and **San Pedro Sula**. Sosa, the most reliable domestic airline flies to **Utila**, **Roatán**, **San Pedro Sula**, **Tegus** and others. Office on Parque Central, T2443-1399. **Atlantic Air**, T/F2440-2347. Sosa, **Atlantic** and **Isleña** all have flights. At weekends there are some charter flights that may be better than scheduled flights. Taxi to town US$8 per person or walk 200 m to the main road and share for US$2 with other passengers, also buses from bus station near Cric Cric Burger at end 3 Av, US$0.15. Intercity buses pass by the entrance.

Boat

Ferry schedules from the Muelle de Cabotaje, T445-1795 or T445-5056, with daily services as follows: La Ceiba–Utila 0815, 0930 and 1630, Utila–La Ceiba, 0630, 0945 and 1430, US$15. La Ceiba–Roatán, 1000 and 1600, Roatán–La Ceiba, 0700 and 1300, US$18. Boats leave from Muelle de Cabotaje. Too far to walk, about 15-min taxi ride from town, US$2-3 per person if sharing with 4 people, buses available from centre of town.

Trips to the **Hog Islands** can be arranged, call T441-5987 or through **Garífuna Tours** (see Activities and tours, page 562), US$65 for a boat load.

Bus

Taxis from centre to bus terminal, which is a little way west of town (follow Blv 15 de Septiembre), cost US$1 per person, or there are buses from Parque Central. Most buses leave from here. **Traliasa**, **Etrusca** and **Cristina** bus service to **Tegucigalpa** via Tela several daily, US$6, avoiding San Pedro Sula (US$1 to Tela, 2 hrs); also hourly service to **San Pedro Sula**, US$2 (3-4 hrs). Empresa Tupsa direct to **San Pedro Sula** almost hourly from 0530 until 1800. Also 1st class with **Hedman Alas** – take taxi to separate terminal. To **Trujillo**, 3 hrs direct, 4½ hrs local (very slow), every 1½ hrs or so, US$3; daily bus La Ceiba–Trujillo–Santa Rosa de Aguán. To **Olanchito**, US$1, 3 hrs; also regular buses to **Sonaguera**, **Tocoa**, **Balfate**, **Isletas**, **San Esteban** and other regional locations.

Car

Car rental Maya Rent-a-Car, Hotel La Quinta, T2443-3071. Dino's Rent-a-Car, Hotel Partenon Beach, T2443-0404. Molinari in Hotel París on Parque Central, T/F2443-0055.

Beaches around La Ceiba *p552*
Bus

To **Nuevo Armenia** from La Ceiba at 1100 US$0.75, 2½ hrs. At the bus stop is the office where boat trips are arranged to **Cayos Cochinos**, US$10, trips start at 0700.

Trujillo and around *p554, map p553*
Boat

Cargo boats leave for **Mosquitia** (ask all captains at the dock, wait up to 3 days, see page 589), the **Bay Islands** (very difficult) and Honduran ports to the west. Ask at the jetty. The trip to **Puerta Lempira** costs about US$15.

Bus

Trujillo can be reached by bus from **San Pedro Sula**, **Tela** and **La Ceiba** by a paved road through Savá, Tocoa and Corocito. From **La Ceiba** it is 3 hrs by direct bus, 4 hrs by local. 3 direct **Cotraibal** buses in early morning from Trujillo. Bus from **Tegucigalpa** (Comayagüela) with **Cotraibal**, 7 Av between 10 and 11 Calle, US$6, 9 hrs; some buses to the capital go via La Unión, which is not as safe a route as via San Pedro Sula. To **San Pedro Sula**, 5 daily 0200-0800, US$5. Public transport also to **San Esteban** and **Juticalpa** (leave from in front of church at 0400, but check locally, arriving 1130, US$5.20). Bus to **Santa Fe** at 0930, US$0.40, leaves from outside Glenny's Super Tienda. To **Santa Rosa de Aguán** and **Limón** daily.

Yoro and around *p556*
Bus Hourly bus service to **El Progreso**, several daily to **Sulaco**.

❶ Directory

Puerto Cortés *p547, map p547*
Banks Mon-Fri 0800-1700, Sat 0830-1130. HSBC, 2 Av, 2 Calle. Banco de Comercio cashes TCs. Banco de Occidente, 3 Av 4 Calle E, cashes Amex TCs, accepts Visa/ MasterCard. Banco Ficensa has ATM for MC and Amex only, 2 Av, 2C. Banks along 2 Av E, include **Atlántida** (2 Av, 3-4 Calle, has Visa ATM), **Bamer**, and HSBC.
Immigration Migración 5 Av y 3-4 Calle next to Port Captain's office, 0800-1800.
Internet Lema Computers, 5-6 Av, 2C, open Mon-Sat. **Medical services** Policlínica, 3 Av just past 1 Calle, open 24 hrs. **Post** Next door to Hondutel. **Telephone** Hondutel, dock entrance, Gate 6, fax and AT&T. Direct to USA.

Omoa *p548*

Banks Banco de Occidente does not take credit cards, but will cash TCs. Some shops will change dollars. Ask around. **Immigration** Migración office on the main road opposite Texaco. If you come from Guatemala by car you have to get a police escort from Corinto to Puerto Cortés. **Internet** Near the beach.

Tela *p548*

Banks Banco Atlántida (with ATM), HSBC, 9 C 3 Av, Visa and MasterCard cash advances and changes TCs. Also try Bamer and Atlántida. Casa de Cambio La Teleña, 4 Av, 9 Calle NE for US$, TCs and cash. Exchange dealers on street outside post office. **Immigration** Migración is at the corner of 3 Av and 8 Calle. **Internet** Service at the Mango Café. **Language classes** Mango Café Spanish School, US$115 for 4 hrs a day, Mon-Fri with a local tour on Sat, T2448-0338, www.mangocafe.net. **Laundry** El Centro, 4 Av 9 Calle, US$2 wash and dry. Lavandería Banegas, Pasaje Centenario, 3 Calle 1 Av. Lavandería San José, 1 block northeast of market. **Medical services** Centro Médico CEMEC, 8 Av 7 Calle NE, T/F2448-2456. Open 24 hrs, X-rays, operating theatre, smart, well equipped. **Post and telephone** Both on 4 Av NE. Fax service and collect calls to Europe available and easy at Hondutel.

La Ceiba and around *p550, map p550*

Banks HSBC, 9 Calle, Av San Isidro, and Banco Atlántida, Av San Isidro and 6-7 Calle, have ATM that accepts Visa. Cash advances on Visa and MasterCard from BAC on Av San Isidro opposite Hotel Iberia between 5 and 6 Calle; also Amex. **Honducard**, Av San Isidro for Visa, next to Farmacia Aurora. Better rates for US$ cash from *cambistas* in the bigger hotels (and at travel agency next door to Hotel Príncipe). Money exchange, at back of Supermercado Los Almendros, 7 Calle, Av San Isidro with Av 14 de Julio, daily 0800-1200, 1400-1800, T2443-2720, good rates for US$ cash and TCs. **Internet** Hondusoft, in Centro Panayotti, 7A Calle between San Isidro and Av 14 de Julio,

Mon-Fri 0800-2000, Sat 0800-1800, discount 1800-2000 when US$3 instead of US$6 per hr. La Ceiba Internet Café, Barrio El Iman, 9 Calle, T2440-1505, Mon-Sat 0900-2000, US$3 per hr. Iberia, next to Hotel Iberia, US$0.80 per hr. Intercon Internet Café, Av San Isidro, opposite Atlántida ATM. **Language schools** Best to do some research and look at the options. Worth considering are: Centro Internacional de Idiomas, T/F2440-1557, www.honduras spanish.com, provides a range of classes 5 days for US$150, with hotel option US$290, with branches in Utila and Roatán. Central America Spanish School, Av San Isidro No 110, Calle 12 y 13, next to Foto Indio, T/F2440-1707, www.ca-spanish.com, US$150 for the week, homestay also an option adding US$70, also have branches on Utila and Roatan. **Medical services** Doctors: Dr Gerardo Meradiaga, Edif Rodríguez García, Ap No 4, Blv 15 de Septiembre, general practitioner, speaks English. Dr Siegfried Seibt, Centro Médico, 1 Calle and Av San Isidro, speaks German. Hospital: Vincente D'Antoni, Av Morazán, T2443-2264, private, well equipped. **Post** Av Morazán, 13 Calle O. **Telephone** Hondutel for international telephone calls is at 2 Av, 5 y 6 Calle E.

Trujillo and around *p554, map p553*

Banks Banco Atlántida on Parque Central and HSBC, both cash US$, TCs and handle Visa. Banco de Occidente also handles MasterCard and Western Union. **Immigration** Opposite Mar de Plata. **Internet** Available in town. **Laundry** Next to Disco Orfaz, wash and dry US$2.50. **Libraries** Library in middle of square. **Medical services** Hospital on main road east off square towards La Ceiba. **Post and telephone** Post office and Hondutel, F2434-4200, 1 block up from church.

Yoro and around *p556*

Banks Banco Atlántida on Parque Central. **Post and telephone** Post office and Hondutel 1 block from Parque Central.

Bay Islands

A string of islands off the northern coast of Honduras, the Bay Islands are the country's most popular tourist attraction. Warm, clear Caribbean waters provide excellent reef diving – some of the cheapest in the Caribbean. Equally enjoyable are the white-sand beaches, tropical sunsets and the relaxed atmosphere which positively encourages you to take to your hammock, lie back and relax. The culture is far less Latino than on the mainland. English is spoken by many and there are still Black Carib – Garífuna – descendants of those deported from St Vincent in 1797. ▸▸ For listings, see pages 573-585.

Ins and outs

Getting there Transport to the Bay Islands is easy and there are regular flights with **Isleña**, **Sosa** and **Atlantic Airlines** from La Ceiba (T2440-2343) and San Pedro Sula (T2433-6016) to Utila and Roatán. **Taca** has an international service from Miami to Roatán. There is also a daily boat service from La Ceiba to Roatán and Utila. **Spirit Airlines** is going to provide direct flights from Fort Lauderdale (Miami) to La Ceiba from May 2009.

The islands → *www.caribbeancoast.com/bayislands/index.cfm.*

The beautiful Bay Islands (**Islas de la Bahía**), of white sandy beaches, coconut palms and gentle sea breezes, form an arc in the Caribbean, some 32 km north of La Ceiba. The three main islands are **Utila**, **Guanaja** and, the largest and most developed, **Roatán**. At the eastern end of Roatán are three smaller islands: **Morat**, **Santa Elena**, and **Barbareta**, with many islets and cayes to explore. Closest to the mainland are the small, palm-fringed **Hog Islands**, more attractively known as **Cayos Cochinos**.

The underwater environment is one of the main attractions and is rich and extensive; **reefs** surround the islands, often within swimming distance of the shore. **Caves** and caverns are a common feature, with a wide variety of **sponges** and the best collection of **pillar coral** in the Caribbean. There are many protected areas including the **Marine Parks** of Turtle Harbour on Utila, and Sandy Bay/West End on Roatán, which has permanent mooring buoys at the popular dive sites to avoid damage from anchors. Several other areas have been proposed as marine reserves by the Asociación Hondureña de Ecología: the Santuario Marino de Utila, Parque Nacional Marino Barbareta and Parque Nacional Marino Guanaja. The Bay Islands have their own conservation association (see under Roatán, page 569).

The traditional industry is fishing, mostly shellfish, with fleets based at French Harbour; but the supporting boat-building is a dying industry. Tourism is now a major source of income, particularly because of the scuba-diving attractions. English-speaking blacks constitute the majority of the population, particularly on Roatán. Utila has a population that is about half black and half white, the latter of British descent mainly from the settlers from Grand Cayman who arrived in 1830. Columbus anchored here in 1502, during his fourth voyage. In the 18th century the islands were the base for English, French and Dutch buccaneers. They were in British hands for over a century, but were finally ceded to Honduras in 1859. Latin Hondurans have been moving to the islands from the mainland in recent years.

The islands are very beautiful, but beware of the strong sun (the locals bathe in T-shirts), sandflies and other insects. Basic etiquette for snorkelling and diving applies. Snorkellers and divers should not stand on or even touch the coral reefs; any contact, even the turbulence from a fin, will kill the delicate organisms.

Utila is the cheapest and least developed of the islands and has a very laid-back ambience. Only 32 km from La Ceiba, it is low lying, with just two hills, Pumpkin and the smaller Stewarts, either side of the town known as **East Harbour**. The first inhabitants were the Paya and there is scant archaeological evidence of their culture. Later the island was used by pirates; Henry Morgan is reputed to have hidden booty in the caves. The population now is descended from Black Caribs and white Cayman Islanders with a recent influx from mainland Honduras. Independence Day (15 September) festivities, including boxing and climbing greased poles, are worth staying for. ⤃ *For more information, see www.aboututila.com.*

Around Utila

There are no big resorts on the island, although a couple of small, lodge-style, upmarket places have opened, otherwise the accommodation is rather basic. Sunbathing and swimming is not particularly good – people come for the diving. **Jack Neal Beach** has white sand with good snorkelling and swimming. **Chepee's White Hole** at the end of Blue Bayou peninsula has a beach for swimming. Snorkelling is also good offshore by the Blue Bayou restaurant, a 20-minute walk from town, but you will be charged US$1 for use of the facilities. There are hammocks and a jetty, which is great for fishing at sunset, and the only place to get away from the terrible sandflies. **Bandu Beach** is another option on the northern end of the island. Sunchairs, drinks and clean toilets are provided. Buy a drink or pay a US$2 charge. There is also sandfly relief at **Big Bight**, **Redcliff** and **Rocky Point**.

You can hike to **Pumpkin Hill** (about 4 km down the lane by HSBC, bikes recommended) where there are some freshwater caves with a beach nearby (watch out for sharp coral). It is also possible to walk on a trail from the airfield to Big Bight and the iron shore on the east coast, about 2 km, exploring tidal pools; nice views and beach but it is rocky so wear sandals.

Utila

Utila's dive sites

There are currently around 50 dive sites around Utila, where permanent moorings have been established to minimize damage to the coral reef. Although the reef is colourful and varied, there are not a lot of fish, and lobster have almost disappeared. The dive sites are close to shore at about 20 m depth but they are all boat dives. Diving off the north coast is more spectacular, with drop-offs, canyons and caves. Fish are more numerous, helped by the establishment of the Turtle Harbour Marine Reserve and Wildlife Refuge.

You can visit the **Iguana Station** ⓘ *Mon, Wed and Fri 1400-1700, T2425-3946, www.utila-iguana.de, US$2.20*, a short walk up hill from the fire station – follow the signs. Paying volunteer options possible. They also offer great trips through the mangroves to explore the more hidden parts of the island for around US$10.

Utila's cayes

A 20-minute motorboat ride from East Harbour are the cayes, a chain of small islands populated by fisherfolk off the southwest coast of Utila, which are known as the Cayitos de Utila. **Jewel Caye** and **Pigeon Caye** are connected by a bridge and are inhabited by a fishing community, which reportedly settled there to get away from the sandflies on Utila. Basic accommodation and food is available. **Diamond Caye** is privately owned, snorkelling offshore here is excellent. **Water Caye** is a coconut island with 'white hole' sandy areas and with wonderful bathing in the afternoons. It is the only place where you can camp, sling a hammock or, in an emergency, sleep in or under the house of the caretaker; take food and fresh water, or rent the caretaker's canoe and get supplies from Jewel Caye.

Roatán → *For listings, see pages 573-585. Colour map 3, A3/B3. Area:127 sq km.*

Roatán is the largest of the islands and has been developed quite extensively. But its idyllic charm is still apparent and quiet beaches are often just a short walk away. There is a paved road running from West End through to French Harbour, almost to Oak Ridge, continuing unpaved to Punta Gorda and Wilkes Point, as well as other unmade roads.

Tourist offices Bay Islands Conservation Association (BICA) ⓘ *Casa Brady, 1st floor, Sandy Bay, 200 m off road to Anthony's Key Resort, T2445-3117, www.bicaroatan.com, Irma Brady, director of BICA, which manages the Sandy Bay/West End Marine National Park and Port Royal National Park in eastern tip of island,* has lots of information about the reef and its conservation work; volunteers welcome. Local information maps are also available from **Librería Casi Todo**, West End. The **Voice Book** is a useful online directory of island services and businesses, as well as local news and reviews; monthly magazine edition available in most hotels: www.bayislandsvoice.com.

Coxen Hole

The capital and administrative centre of the department, Coxen Hole, or **Roatán City**, is on the southwest shore. Planes land and boats dock here and you can get transport to other parts of the island. It is a colourfully scruffy little town with not much of tourist interest but some souvenir shops are opening. Besides being the seat of the local government, it has immigration, customs and the law courts. There is a post office, supermarket, handicraft shops, restaurants, banks, travel agents, a bookshop and various other stores. Buses leave from outside the supermarket. All public transport starts or ends here. If taxis are shared, they are *colectivos* and charge the same as buses. A huge, swanky new cruise-liner dock has opened outside the western end of town, with the Town Center shopping mall, offering pricey cafés, gift shops, duty-free stores, and – probably unique on the island – free and spotless public toilets.

Sandy Bay

A short journey from Coxen Hole, en route to West End, is Sandy Bay, one of the quieter towns on the island. The **Carambola Botanical Gardens** ⓘ *opposite Anthony's Key Resort, www.carambolagardens.com, daily 0800-1700, US$10, guided tours (US$5) or self-guided nature trails*, created in 1985, contain many flowering plants, ferns and varieties of trees which can be explored on a network of trails – it is well worth a visit. The **Roatán Museum** ⓘ *T2445-3003, US$4*, has displays covering the history of the island, with plenty of information about the pirates who called Roatán home, and a collection of artefacts.

West End

Five minutes by road beyond Sandy Bay, the popular community of West End, at the western tip of the island, is the most popular place to stay. It's a narrow beach on a palm-fringed bay with a distinctly laid-back atmosphere. The **Sandy Bay/West End Marine Park** protects marine life in the area and large numbers of fish have flourished along the coast creating spectacular snorkelling. There are numerous good foreign and local restaurants with lots of pizza/pasta places, as well as hotels, *cabañas* and rooms to rent for all budgets. It is a stiff walk from Coxen Hole over the hills (three hours)to West End, or take the bus on the paved road (US$1; 20 minutes). ▸▸ *See www.roatan marinepark.com for more details.*

1 Roatán

➡ Roatán maps
1 **Roatán**, page 570
2 **Roatán – West End & West Bay**, page 571

West Bay

A beautiful clean beach with excellent snorkelling on the reef, particularly at the west end, where the reef is only 10-20 m offshore and the water is shallow right up to where the wall drops off 50-75 m out and scuba-diving begins. Biting sandflies – *jejenes* – can be

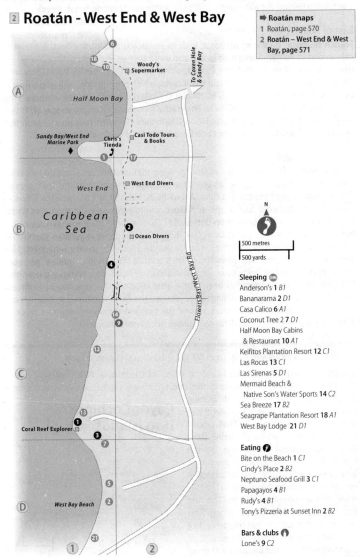

☑ Roatán - West End & West Bay

➡ **Roatán maps**
1 Roatán, page 570
2 **Roatán – West End & West Bay, page 571**

Woody's Supermarket

To Coxen Hole & Sandy Bay

Half Moon Bay

Sandy Bay/West End Marine Park

Chris's Tienda

Casi Todo Tours & Books

West End Divers

West End

Caribbean Sea

Ocean Divers

Flowers Bay/West Bay Rd

N

500 metres
500 yards

Coral Reef Explorer

West Bay Beach

Sleeping 🛏
Anderson's 1 *B1*
Bananarama 2 *D1*
Casa Calico 6 *A1*
Coconut Tree 2 **7** *D1*
Half Moon Bay Cabins & Restaurant 10 *A1*
Keifitos Plantation Resort 12 *C1*
Las Rocas 13 *C1*
Las Sirenas 5 *D1*
Mermaid Beach & Native Son's Water Sports 14 *C2*
Sea Breeze 17 *B2*
Seagrape Plantation Resort 18 *A1*
West Bay Lodge 21 *D1*

Eating 🍴
Bite on the Beach 1 *C1*
Cindy's Place 2 *B2*
Neptuno Seafood Grill 3 *C1*
Papagayos **4** *B1*
Rudy's **4** *B1*
Tony's Pizzeria at Sunset Inn 2 *B2*

Bars & clubs 🍸
Lone's **9** *C2*

a pest here at dusk, but since the hotel staff started raking the beach every day, which exposes their eggs to the sun and kills them, they are no longer such a nuisance. Developers have discovered the delights of West Bay and the atmosphere is changing fast. Apartments, hotels, bars and restaurants are springing up, though mostly low-rise, and hidden behind the palm trees, so it's still pretty quiet here during the week.

East of Coxen Hole

French Harbour, on the south coast, with its shrimping and lobster fleet, is the main fishing port of Roatán. There is no beach and there are two seafood-packing plants. The road passes Coleman's (Midway) Bakery, where you can buy freshly baked products. The bay is protected by the reef and small cayes, which provide safe anchorage. Roatan Dive and Yacht Club and Romeos Marina (at Brick Bay) offer services for visiting yachts. Several charter yachts are based here. There are a few cheap, clean places to stay, as well as expensive hotels and dive resorts. Eldon's Supermarket is open daily and has a range of imported US food. **Gios Restaurant** and **Casa Romeos** serve top-quality seafood.

Across the island

The main road goes across the mountain ridge along the island with side roads to Jonesville, Punta Gorda and Oak Ridge. You can take a bus on this route to see the island's hilly interior, with beautiful views from coast to coast. Alternatively, hire a small 4WD, which is almost as cheap if shared between four people and allows you to explore the dirt roads and empty bays along the island's northern tip. **Jonesville** is known for its mangrove canal, which is best reached by hiring a taxi boat in Oak Ridge. **Oak Ridge**, situated on a caye (US$1 crossing in a dory from the bus stop), is built around a deep inlet on the south coast. It is a sleepy little fishing port, with rows of dwellings on stilts built on the water's edge (a bus from Coxen Hole to Oak Ridge takes about one and a half hours, depending on passengers, US$1.70). Much of the town has been rebuilt after widespread destruction by Hurricane Mitch in 1998, but the new buildings have retained the same traditional stilt design and pastel colours. Boatmen offer tours around the bay and through mangroves to caves allegedly used by pirates; US$20 for 45 minutes, but it's worth bargaining.

Isla Guanaja → *For listings, see pages 573-585. Colour map 3, A3. Area: 56 sq km.*

Columbus called Guanaja the Island of Pines, but Hurricane Mitch swept most of them away. Since then, a great replanting effort has been completed and, until the pines have regrown, flowering and fruiting plants thrive on the island. The island was declared a forest reserve in 1961, and is now designated a national marine park. Good (but sweaty) clambering on the island gives splendid views of the jungle and the sea and there are several attractive waterfalls, which can be visited on the hills rising to the summit of 415 m. The first English settler was Robert Haylock, who arrived in 1856 with a land title to part of the island, the two cayes that now form the main settlement of Bonacca and some

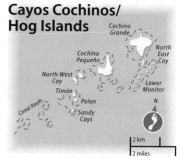

Cayos Cochinos/ Hog Islands

of the Mosquito coast. He was followed in 1866 by John Kirkconnell who purchased Hog Caye, where the Haylocks raised pigs away from the sandflies. These two families became sailors, boat builders and landowners, and formed the basis of the present population.

Much of Guanaja town, locally known as **Bonacca** and covering a small caye off the coast, is built on stilts above sea water, with boardwalks and concrete pathways, hence its nickname: the 'Venice of Honduras'. There are three small villages, **Mangrove Bight**, **Savannah Bight** and **North East Bight**, on the main island. Much of the accommodation is all-inclusive resorts, but you can visit independently as well. Sandflies and mosquitoes cannot be escaped on the island, and none of the beaches offer respite (coconut oil, baby oil or any oily suntan lotion will help to ward off sandflies).The cayes are better, including Guanaja town. South West Caye is especially recommended.

Cayos Cochinos (Hog Islands) → *For listings, see pages 573-585. Colour map 3, B3.*

The Hog Islands, 17 km northeast of La Ceiba, constitute two small islands and 13 palm-fringed cayes. **Cochino Grande** is the larger island, rising to an altitude of just 143 m, and **Cochino Pequeño** is the smaller. Both have lush tropical vegetation with primeval hardwood forests and there are fewer biting insects than in the Bay Islands. As part of a National Marine Reserve, Cayos Cochinos and the surrounding waters are protected. There is a fee to enter parts of the islands of US$10. There are Garífuna fishing villages of palm-thatched huts at Chachauate on Lower Monitor Cay, where you can organize basic accommodation, and East End Village on Cochino Grande. Transport to the Hog Islands can be sought on the supply *cayuco* from Nuevo Armenia (see page 552), or by boat from La Ceiba, Sambo Creek or Roatán. There is a small dirt airstrip. Dug-out canoes are the local form of transport. The islands are privately owned and access to most of the cayes is limited, being occupied only by caretakers.

◉ Bay Islands listings

For Sleeping and Eating price codes and other relevant information, see Essentials pages 31-33.

◓ Sleeping

Utila *p568, map p568*

L-AL Laguna Beach Resort, on point opposite Blue Bayou, T/F2668-68452, www.utila.com. Comfortable lodge, with bungalows each with own jetty, 8-day package includes meals and diving US$970, non-diver US$840. Fishing offered, can accommodate maximum of 40.

AL-B Mango Inn, La Punta, T2425-3326, www.mango-inn.com. With bath, cheaper without, fan, spotless, helpful, roof terrace, reduction for students with **Utila Dive Centre**. Pool, **Mango Café** and **La Dolce Vita Pizzeria** for brick-oven pizzas on premises. Recommended.

A-B Trudy's, 5 mins from airport, T/F2425-3103. Rooms with a/c and hot water. Also Trudy's Suites, with colour TV, fridge and microwave. Recommended. Underwater Vision dive shop on site.

B Jade Seahorse, T2425-3270, www.jadeseahorse.com. 5 great cabins, artistic, unusual and very funky, restaurant, bar, fantastic artistic gardens. Recommended.

C Bay View, 100 m from **Utila Lodge**, T2425-3114, bayviewinternet@yahoo.com. 2 apartments with kitchen, living and dining room. Located on the water. With or without bath, pier, family-run.

C-D Freddy's, off the boat and turn right, it's a long walk to just over the bridge, T2425-3142. Good rooms, kitchens, quiet end of town.

D-F Margaritaville, in a pleasant location just outside town near the beach,

T2425-3366. Very clean, big rooms with 2 double beds, private bathroom, friendly.
E Celena, main street, T2425-3228. With bath, clean with fan. Recommended.
E Countryside, 10 mins' walk out of town, T2425-3216. Shared bath, rooms and apartments, quiet, clean, friendly, fan, porch, ask in town for Woody and Annie.
E Harbour View, right on water, T2425-3159. Parrot's Dive on site, cheaper rooms with shared bathrooms upstairs, rooms with private bath downstairs, hot water, own generator, cleaning done only on arrival, TV, fans, run by Roger and Maimee.
E Seaside, opposite **Gunter's Dive School**, T2425-3150. Private and shared rooms, kitchen for use. Wi-Fi, nice place, clean, laundry service, hammocks, balcony. Popular with budget travellers. Recommended.
E Bavaria, up towards **Mango Inn**, offers clean, simple rooms.
E-F Cross Creek (see also Diving, page 580), T2425-3334, www.crosscreekutila.com. Good, clean rooms, with shower and shared toilets, discount for divers on courses.
F Loma Vista, up road opposite the dock, T2425-3243. Clean, fan, shared bath, very friendly, washes clothes cheaply.

Utila's cayes *p569*
All hotels are small family-run affairs (**D-F**).
F Hotel Kayla. Affiliated with **Captain Morgan's Dive Center** on Jewell Cay. Free accommodation at Jewell Cay with PADI courses. Jewell Cay and Pigeon Cay are linked by a bridge.
You can rent out **Little Cay** and **Sandy Cay** completely, details available from cayosutila@hotmail.com.

Roatán *p569, maps p570 and p571*
Coxen Hole
C Cay View, Calle Principal, T2445-1202. A/c, bath, TV, phone, laundry, restaurant, bar, dingy rooms, one with seaview, no breakfast, overpriced, but just about adequate if desperate.

C-E Mom, on main road into Coxen Hole, above pharmacy, next to hospital. Private or shared bath, modern, clean, a/c, TV.
E El Paso, next door to **Caye View**, T445-1367. Shared bath, restaurant.
F Naomi Allen, near the bus depot. Fan, clean, good.

West End
AL Half Moon Bay Cabins, Half Moon Bay, T445-4242. Bungalows and cabins with bath, restaurant with excellent seafood.
AL-B Coconut Tree, West End, T2445-4081, www.westbaycoconuttree.com. Private cabins (3 double beds) owned by Vincent Bush, a/c, kitchen, balcony, hot water, fan, fridge, clean, friendly, discounts in low season.
A-B Mermaid Beach, West End, T2445-4335, Clean, quiet, with bath, fan or a/c, dive shop next door.
A-C Keifitos Plantation Resort, on hillside above beach, T2978-4472, www.keifitos plantation.com. Bungalows in a beautiful setting, short walk from village, mosquitoes, bar, good breakfasts to 1300, champagne breakfasts Sun, horses for rent with guide, friendly owners, very quiet, very clean. Recommended.
B Casa Calico, north of Half Moon Bay, T2445-4231, www.casacalico.com. Comfortable, cable TV, videos, rooms and apartments, fan, 2 rooms with a/c, garden, huge balconies, apartments sleep 4 or more with kitchen, hot water, noisy in morning, friendly, helpful.
B Posada Arco Iris, Half Moon Bay, T2445-4264, www.roatanposada.com. Apartments with kitchen, hot water, fan, large balcony, friendly owners. Restaurant specializing in grilled meats. Highly recommended.
B Seagrape Plantation Resort, Half Moon Bay, T2445-4428, www.seagraperoatan.com. Cabins, rooms with private bath, hot water, family atmosphere, friendly, Visa accepted, nice location on rocky promontory, no beach, but snorkelling possible, full-service restaurant

and bar, inclusive packages available.
Fun drives for US$30 with equipment.

C Dolphin Resort, centre of Half Moon Bay, T2445-1280. Private bathroom, a/c and fan. Recommended.

C Sea Breeze, north of West End, T2445-4026, www.seabreezeroatan.com, Nice rooms, hot water, baths, a/c optional, suites and studios available with kitchens, windsurfers and kayaks for rent.

C-D Anderson's, behind Chris's Tienda, West End, T2455-5365. Basic rooms, shared bath, clean, fan, lower rates for longer stays.

C-D Chillies, Half Moon Bay, T2445-4003, www.nativesonsroatan.com/chillies.htm. Double rooms and dormitory, clean, fully equipped kitchen, lounge, big balcony, camping and hammocks available. Excellent value for money.

E Dora Miller (no sign), West End, 2 houses behind Jimmy's Lodge. Washing facilities, no fan, no mosquito nets, basic, noisy, friendly.

West Bay

LL-AL Island Pearl, on the beach, T2445-5005, www.roatanpearl.com. Double-storey apartments, a/c, hot water, tiled kitchen, handmade furniture, nicely decorated.

L Las Sirenas, midway along the beach, T2445-5009, www.hmresorts.com. Rooms, suites and enormous apartments, with a/c, flat-screen cable TV, and kitchen; small swimming pool; full board and shared amenities with adjacent HM resorts: Henry Morgan, Mayan Princess and Paradise Beach. Quiet, clean and well run. Recommended.

AL-A West Bay Lodge, south of West Bay beach, T2991-0694, www.westbay lodge.com. Cabins with hot water and fan, good breakfast.

AL-B Las Rocas, next to Bite on the Beach, T/F2445-1841, www.lasrocasresort.com. Duplex *cabañas*, very close together, hot water, balcony, smaller cabins sleep 3, larger

ones sleep 6, free boat transport to West End and back, dive shop and restaurant.

A-B Bananarama, centre of West Bay beach, T2992-9679. With bath, hot water, fan, PADI dive courses available, breakfast included for guests, good value. Recommended.

East of Coxen Hole

L Coco View Resort, French Harbour, T911-7371, www.cocoviewresort.com. Good shore diving, on lagoon.

L Reef House Resort, Oak Ridge, T2435-1482, www.reefhouseresort.com. Meals and various packages, including diving. Wooden cabins with sea-view balconies, seaside bar, private natural pool, dock facilities, good snorkelling from the shore.

A-B Executivo Inn, Mount Pleasant on the road to French Harbour opposite electricity plant, T2455-6708, www.executiveinn.org. Nice rooms, a/c, hot water, TV, pool, no beach.

C Palm Tree Resort, Brick Bay, T2445-1986. Cabins with bath, home cooking island style, quiet, diveshop, wall diving with boat.

E Dixon's Plaza, French Harbour, past the Buccaneer. Good.

E San José Hotel, Oak Ridge. With bath (2 rooms), cheaper without (3 rooms), clean, pleasant, good value, water shortages, good food, English-speaking owner, Louise Solórzano.

Elsewhere

B Ben's Restaurant, on coast road south out of Punta Gorda, T2445-1916. Nice cabins to rent, dive shop (US$35 per dive), limited equipment, disorganized, wooden deck over sea, local food, bar, friendly, safe parking.

Isla Guanaja *p572*

C-D Harry Carter, T2455-4303, ask for fan. Rooms are clean.

E Miss Melba, just before Hotel Alexander sign on left, house with flowers. 3 rooms in boarding house, run by friendly old lady with lots of island information, shared bathroom, cold water, great porch and gardens.

Cayos Cochinos (Hog Islands) *p573, map p572*
AL Plantation Beach Resort, Cochino Grande, T/F2442-0974. VHF 12. Rustic cabins on hillside, hot water, fans, diving offshore, yacht moorings, good steep walk up to lighthouse for view over cayes to mainland, music festival end Jul, local bands and dancers, they charge US$30 for the trip from La Ceiba.

E Cayo Timón (also known as **North Sand Cay**) can be visited from Utila, 1¼ hrs by boat; you can rent the caye (price per person), minimum 6, 8 is comfortable, A-frame, Polynesian style, do overnight diving trips, very basic, quiet, peaceful. Phone Roy and Brenda at **Thompson's Bakery**, Utila, T2425-3112, for information.

🅞 Eating

Utila *p568, map p568*
Menus are often ruled by the supply boat: on Tue and Fri restaurants have everything, by the weekend some drinks run out.
🍴🍴🍴 **Jade Seahorse**. Fri-Wed 1100-2200, closed Thu. A variety of seafood home-made style and *licuados*, coolest decor in town, includes the very popular **Treetanic** bar, high up in the trees 1700-2400.
🍴🍴-🍴🍴 **Mariposa Restaurant**. Lovely spot over the water, good views overlooking bay, nice atmosphere, bright, clean, airy. One of the nicest places in town. Offers fresh seafood. Expensive but good quality.
🍴🍴 **Bundu Café**. Fri-Wed, closed Thu. Regular typical menu. Mon is all-you-can-eat pizza and pasta. Broad selection of beach novels, romance and Western novels. Great spot to watch people on the street. Recommended.
🍴🍴 **Driftwood Café**. Texan BBQ-style place with good burgers. Airy setting above the water.

🍴🍴 **El Picante**, up towards **Mango Inn**. Upscale Mexican restaurant in a good location.
🍴🍴 **Indian Wok**, in front of **Tranquila Bar**. Open Mon, Wed and Fri. Variety of Asian dishes and home-made, good potato salad.
🍴🍴 **La Piccola**. Pastas, garlic bread, fish, pizza, great service. Upscale yet relaxed atmosphere offering lunch and dinner. One of the best places in town.
🍴 **Big Mamas**. Lovely place, the prettiest restaurant on Utila.
🍴 **Dave Island Café**. In front of Coco Loco. Tue-Sat, closed Sun and Mon. Very popular with locals and tourists. San Franciscan chef offers pork and chicken with a choice of sauces. Great curries and good vegetarian dishes. Great home-made chocolate cake. Big portions. Menu changes daily. Come early to get a seat.
🍴 **Howells's Restaurant**, near the UPCO building. Popular with locals, and often overlooked. Great lunch options with local dishes.
🍴 **Mermaid Restaurant**. Very nice building, airy, open, wood ceiling, buffet style, some of the quickest food on the island, economical prices, popular with divers and locals.
🍴 **Munchie's**. In a lovely restored historic building near the dock with a porch for people-watching. Nice snacks, good service. Daily specials. Also organize trips to the cayes.
🍴 **RJ's BBQ and Grill House**. Open Wed, Fri, Sun, 1730-2200. Great BBQ. Popular.
🍴 **Skidrow Bar and Restaurant**, in front of Ecomarine Dive shop. Great burritos, popular with expats. Mon night is pub quiz night.
🍴 **Thompsons Bakery**. Open 0600-1200. Very informal, friendly, good cakes, coconut bread, breakfasts, biscuits, cinnamon rolls, *baleadas*, cheap and with lots of information. Good lunch option.
🍴 **Zanzibar Café**. Funky ramshackle place typical of Utila. Breakfasts, shakes, burgers, sandwiches, pastas.

Utila's cayes *p569*
There are a few restaurants, a Sat night disco and little else.

Roatán *p569 maps p570 and p571*

Evening meals cost US$4-10. There is a good seafood restaurant on **Osgood Caye** a few mins by free water taxi from wharf.

Coxen Hole

⍥ **El Paso**, next to the **Caye View**. Good seafood soup.

⍥ **Le Bistro**, 10 mins' walk along seafront between Coxen Hole and West Bay, T9527-3136. Perched on a rocky outcrop on the beach. Thai and Vietnamese cuisine, with spicy seafood and curries. Beautiful spot with deck overlooking the sea; French owner François also takes snorkelling trips.

⍥ **Qué Tal Café**, on road to West End. Good coffee, herbal teas, sandwiches and pastries, shares space with bookstore.

⍥ **Hibiscus Sweet Shop**. Home-made fruit pies, cakes and biscuits.

⍥ **Pizza Rey**, opposite **Warren's**. Pizza slices.

West End

⍥ **Tong**. Asian and Middle East specialities, good location, salad buffet, expensive but worth it.

⍥ **Half Moon Bay Restaurant**, Half Moon Bay. Nice location to sit on terrace overlooking sea, more expensive than most, excellent food, service can be very slow.

⍥ **Belvedere's**, on water, West End. Fri-Sun 1900-2100. Nice setting, tasty Italian food. Recommended.

⍥ **Brick Oven**, about 15 mins out of West End (follow the signs). Good food and movies every night.

⍥ **Cannibal Café**, in the **Sea Breeze**. Open 1030 until 2200, closed Sun. Excellent Mexican food, large helpings, good value.

⍥ **Cindy's Place**, next to **Sunset Inn**. Local family breakfast, lunches and dinner in garden, fish caught same morning, also lobster and king crab. Recommended.

⍥ **The Cool Lizard**, Mermaid Beach. Seafood, vegetarian and chicken, home-made bread, salads, nice atmosphere, good.

⍥ **Keifito's Hangout**, West End. Good breakfast, champagne on Sun, well priced.

⍥ **Papagayos**, Half Moon Bay, on a jetty, T445-1008. Good atmosphere for pre-prandial tipple, reggae music, basic meals, no sandflies, great sundeck, Thu is band/dance/party night, also rooms to rent (**B**).

⍥ **Pinocchio's**, West End, along same path as the **Lighthouse**, www.roatan pinocchios.com. Excellent pasta, great stir fry and delicious salads, run by Patricia and Howard.

⍥ **Rick's American Café**, Sandy Bay. Open from 1700, except Wed. Tree-top bar, shows all sports events, best steaks on Roatán.

⍥ **Rudy's**. Open all day. Good pancakes and cookies for breakfast, sandwich combos, good atmosphere but pricey.

⍥ **Salt and Pepper Club**, entrance to West End. Supermarket, BBQ and live music.

⍥ **Tony's Pizzeria**, in the **Sunset Inn**. Fresh fish, good food, big portions.

⍥ **Velva's Place**, at the far end of Half Moon Bay. Island-style seafood and chicken dishes, try the conch soup, good prices.

⍥ **Sunset Playa** on the beach.

⍥ **Tartines and Chocolate**, Half Moon Bay. French bakery, good bread and pastries.

West Bay

⍥ **Bite on the Beach**, on the point over West Bay. Wed-Sun brunch, huge deck in gorgeous position, excellent, fresh food and great fruit punch. Nightly feeding of moray eels, which swim – or wriggle – up to the edge of the dock. A fun place, very friendly, recommended and very much what Roatán is about.

⍥ **Neptuno Seafood Grill**, between **Fosters** and **Coconut Tree 2**. Seafood, paella, barbecued crab, extensive bar, open daily for lunch and dinner.

⍥ **West Bay Lodge**, see Sleeping. Good breakfasts on a nice balcony with sea view.

East of Coxen Hole

There is a *taquería* close to HSBC on the main road in French Harbour serving good tacos, burritos and hamburgers.

⍥ **Gios**, French Harbour. Seafood, king crab speciality.

¶¶¶ **Roatan Dive and Yacht Club**, French Harbour. Daily specials, pizza, salads, sandwiches, usually very good.

¶¶ **BJ's Backyard Restaurant**, Oak Ridge, at the harbour. Island cooking, fishburgers, smoked foods, reasonable prices. There is a pizzeria and, next door, a supermarket.

¶¶ **Iguana Grill**, French Harbour. International cuisine and suckling pig.

¶¶ **Pirate's Hideaway**, at Calabash Bay, east of Oak Ridge. Seafood, friendly owner.

¶¶ **Romeo's**, French Harbour. Romeo, who is Honduran-Italian, serves good seafood, and continental cuisine.

¶¶ **Tres Flores**, French Harbour, on the hill. Good views, Mexican specialities, they pick up groups from West End, T2245-0007.

Isla Guanaja *p572*

¶¶ **Harbour Light**, through **Mountain View** nightclub. Good food, reasonably priced for the island.

⊙ Entertainment

Utila *p568, map p568*
Bars and clubs
Bar in the Bush is the place to go, 100 m beyond the **Mango Inn**, very popular, lots of dancing and always packed, Wed 1800-2330, Fri (Ladies Night) and Sun 1800-0300.

Coco Loco, on jetty at harbour front near **Tranquila Bar**, very popular with young divers, together, these 2 places are the anchors and reigning kings of late night Utila night life.

La Pirata Bar, at the dock. High up, great views, breezy.

Treetanic Bar, Inside **Jade Seahorse**. Hot spot on the island.

Cinema
Reef Cinema, opposite Bay Islands Originals shop, shows films at 1930 every night, at US$3 per person. Popcorn, hotdogs, a/c, comfortable seats, big screen. Also inside

the cinema is **Funkytown Books and Music**, an excellent bookshop to trade, sell and rent. Stock up here before you travel anywhere else. Also trades MP3s.

Utila Centre for Marine Ecology, opposite Trudy's, www.utilaecology.org. Offers free presentations on Tropical Marine Ecology, the 1st and 3rd Mon of each month, 1830-1930.

Roatán *p569, maps p570 and p571*
Most clubs come alive about midnight, play reggae, salsa, *punta* and some rock.

Coxen Hole
Harbour View, Thu-Sun nights, late, US$0.50 entrance, very local, usually no problem with visitors, but avoid local disputes. Hot and atmospheric.

Sundowners Bar, popular happy hour from 1700-1900, Sun quiz followed by BBQ.

West End
Bahía Azul, Fri is party night, DJ, dancing.

C-bar, fantastic location on beachfront near Seagrape Plantation.

Foster's, the late night hotspot, dance music Thu night as well as band nights.

Lone's Bar, Mermaid Beach, nightly BBQ, reggae music.

Sundowners Bar, popular happy hour from 1700-1900, Sun quiz followed by BBQ.

East of Coxen Hole
Al's, Barrio Las Fuertes, before French Harbour. Closed Sat night, salsa and plenty of *punta*.

⊛ Festivals and events

Utila *p568, map p568*
Aug Sun Jam on Water Caye at a weekend at the beginning of Aug, www.sunjam utila.com. Look out for details locally. They charge a US$2.50 entrance fee to the island; bring your own tent/hammock, food and water.

O Shopping

Utila *p568, map p568*
Arts and crafts
Bay Islands Original Shop sells T-shirts, sarongs, coffee, hats, etc. Mon-Fri 0900-1200 and 1300-1800, Sat and Sun 0900-1200.
Gunter Kordovsky is a painter and sculptor with a gallery at his house, good map of Utila, paintings, cards and wood carving.
Utila Lodge Gift Shop is also worth trying.

Roatán *p569, maps p570 and p571*
Supermarkets
Best to buy supplies in Coxen Hole.
Coconut Tree at West End is expensive.
Woods is cheaper. **Eldon** in French Harbour is also expensive. **Ezekiel**, West End, opposite church, sells fruit and veg.
Mall Megaplaza, French Harbour. New shopping mall by roadside east of town, with fast-food outlets.

▲ Activities and tours

Utila *p568, map p568*
The **Utila Snorkel Center**, for all those who do not want to dive, organizes trips. Inside Mango Tree Business building. See also **Bundu Café**, page 576.

Diving
Dive with care for yourself and the reef at all times; www.roatanet.com has plenty of information about Utila and its dive sites.

Utila is a very popular dive training centre. Learning to dive is cheaper here than anywhere else in the Caribbean, especially if you include the low living expenses. It is best to do a course of some sort; students come first in line for places on boats and recreational divers have to fit in. In recent years, Utila has developed a reputation for poor safety and there have been some accidents requiring emergency treatment in the recompression chamber on Roatán. Serious attempts have been made to change this by the diving community of Utila. The 3 or 4 accidents that happen annually are a result of cowboy divers and drug or alcohol abuse.

Instructors Choose an instructor who you get on with, and one who has small classes and cares about safety; follow the rules on alcohol/drug abuse and pay attention to the dive tables. There is a rapid turnover of instructors; many stay only a season to earn money to continue their travels, and some have a lax attitude towards diving regulations and diving tables. Check that equipment looks in good condition and well maintained. Boats vary, you may find it difficult to climb into a dory if there are waves. While a dive shop has a responsibility to set standards of safety, you also have a responsibility to know about diving times. If you don't, or are a beginner, ask.

Price There is broad price agreement across dive shops in Utila. Out of the revenues the **Utila Dive Supporters' Association** can budget for spending, facilities and eventually conservation. Whatever you may think of the idea, one benefit, is greater safety and better organized protection of the reef. Whether this works remains to be seen, but the price of saving a few dollars could end up costing lives. Dive insurance at US$3 per day for fun divers, US$9 for students (Advanced, or Open Water), US$30 for divemasters is compulsory and is available from the BICA office. It covers air ambulance to Roatán and the recompression chamber. Treat any cuts from the coral seriously, they do not heal easily.

PADI courses A PADI Open Water course costs US$320 (including certificate) with 4 dives, an Advanced course costs US$280 with 5 dives, US$256 if you do the Open Water course with the dive shop first. You can work your way up through the courses with rescue diver (US$350) and dive master (US$800). The Open Water usually comes with 2 free fun dives. Credit cards, if accepted, are 6% extra. Not permitted by credit cards but as all companies on the island do it you can't go elsewhere. Competition is fierce with over 15 dive shops looking for business, so you can pick and choose. Once qualified, fun dives are US$50 for 2 tanks. Dive shops offer free basic accommodation with packages. Most schools offer instruction in English or German; French and Spanish are usually available somewhere, while tuition handbooks are provided in numerous languages including Japanese. A variety of courses is available up to instructor level. If planning to do a diving course, it is helpful but not essential to take passport-sized photographs with you for the PADI card.

Dive operators
Altons Dive Center, T2425-3704, www.altons diveshop.com. Offers NAUI and PADI certification, weekly fish talk, recommended, popular, owned by the mayor of Utila.

Bay Islands College of Diving, on main street close to Hondutel tower, T425-3291, www.dive-utila.com. 5-star PADI facility, experienced and well qualified staff, good boats ranging from 50 ft, for large parties to skiff for smaller ones, environmentally sound. Only dive shop on the island with in-house pool and hot tub. The trauma centre and recompression chamber, shared by all dive shops, is located here. 5-star facility.

Captain Morgan's, T2425-3349, www.diving utila.com. Has been recommended for small classes, good equipment, friendly staff. The only dive shop that offers accomodation on nearby Pigeon Key. Popular with travelling couples.

Cross Creek, T2425-3397, www.crosscreek utila.com. 2 boats, maximum 8 people per instructor, 2-3 instructors, free use of kayaks, accommodation on site for students, 18 rooms, can also arrange transfers from the mainland.

Deep Blue Divers, T/F2425-3211, www.deep blueutila.com. One of the newer operators on

the island. The friendly owners are getting good feedback through word of mouth.

Gunter's Ecomarine Dive Shop, T/F2425-3350, http://ecomarinegunters. blogspot.com. Dive school with 4 divers per group maximum, 7 languages spoken. Most laid-back dive shop and the only dive school that does not hassle divers arriving at the ferry dock.

Paradise Divers, on the seafront, T2425-3148. Relaxed and friendly.

Parrot Aqua Adventures, T2425-3772, tatianaluna22@yahoo.com, run by a dynamic local couple. Good reviews by divers with small classes.

Underwater Vision Dive Center at Trudy's, T2425-3103, www.underwatervision.net. With accommodation. Very nice location at the Bay.

Utila Dive Centre, Mango Inn, PADI CDC, T/F2425-3326, www.utiladivecentre.com. Well-maintained equipment, daily trips to north coast in fast dory, recommended. All boats covered and custom-built, surface interval on cayes.

Utila Watersports, T/F2425-3264, run by Troy Bodden. 4 students per class. Troy also hires out snorkelling gear, photographic and video equipment and takes boat trips. Good reports.

Whale Shark & Oceanic Research Centre (WSORC), T2425-3760, www.wsorc.com. A professional scientific organization committed to education and preserving Utila's oceans, offers speciality courses including whale shark research, naturalist courses, research diver, fish ID, Coral ID. Free presentation 1930 Sun nights about whale sharks.

Roatán *p569, maps p570 and p571*
Boat trips
Kayak rentals and tours from **Seablades**, contact Alex at **Casi Todo**, 3- to 7-day kayak tours, US$150-250. Full and ½-day rental US$20 and US$12 (with instruction), kayaks available at **Tyll's**. From Rick's American Café, **Casablanca** charters on

yacht *Defiance III*, sunset cruises, party trips, full-day snorkelling, also can be arranged through **Casi Todo**. At West Bay beach is a glass-bottomed boat, **Caribbean Reef Explorer**, US$20 per 1½ hrs, unfortunately includes fish feeding, which upsets the reef's ecological balance. Glass-bottomed boat and 3-person submarine tours from the dock at Half Moon Bay, US$25 per person.

Diving

If you don't want to dive, the snorkelling is normally excellent. The creation of the Sandy Bay/West End Marine Park along 4 km of coast from Lawson Rock around the southwest tip to Key Hole has encouraged the return of large numbers of fish in that area and there are several interesting dive sites. Lobsters are still rare, but large grouper are now common and curious about divers. If the sea is rough off **West End** try diving around **French Harbour** (or vice versa) where the cayes provide some protection. There are more mangroves on this side, which attract the fish. **Flowers Bay** on the south side has some spectacular wall dives, but not many fish, and it is calm during the 'Northers' which blow in Dec-Feb. Few people dive the east end except the live-aboards (**Bay Islands Aggressor, The Aggressor Fleet, Romeo Tower**, French Harbour, T2445-1518) and people on camping trips to Pigeon Cay, so it is relatively unspoilt. Because fishing is allowed to the east, tropical fish are scarce and the reef is damaged in places. In addition to a few stormy days from Dec to Feb, you can also expect stinging hydroids in the top few feet of water around Mar and Apr which bother people who are sensitive to stings. Vinegar is the local remedy.

Courses As on Utila, the dive operators concentrate on instruction but prices vary (since Dec 1994 the municipal government has set minimum prices). You can normally find a course starting within 1 or 2 days. There is more on offer than in Utila; not everyone teaches only PADI courses. Prices for courses and diving vary with the season. In low season good deals abound. Open Water US$320, advanced US$280, fun dives US$40 (2-9 dives = US$35 each, 10+ = US$30 each). Despite the huge number of dive students, Roatán has a good safety record but it still pays to shop around and find an instructor you feel confident with at a dive shop which is well organized with well-maintained equipment. As in other 'adventure' sports, the cheapest is not always the best. Dive insurance is US$2 per day, and is sometimes included in the course price. If you do not have dive insurance and need their services, the hyperbaric chamber charges a minimum of US$800.

Dive operators

Anthony's Key Resort, Sandy Bay, T2445-3003. Mostly hotel package diving, also swim and dive with dolphins.
Aquarius Divers, West End. PADI courses, fun dives, excursions to the south walls in conjunction with Scuba Romance dive shop, Brick Bay.
Bananarama, West Bay, in centre of beach, next to **Cabaña Roatana**, T2445-5005. Small, friendly dive shop, run by young German family, boat and shore diving.
The Last Resort, Gibson Bight, T2445-1838 (in USA T305-893-2436). Mostly packages from the USA.
Native Son's Water Sports, next to Mermaid cabins, West End, T2445-4003. Run by Alvin, local instructor, PADI and PDSI courses and fun dives.
Ocean Connections at Sunset Inn, West End, T/F3327-0935, www.ocean-connections.com. Run by Carol and Phil Stevens with emphasis on safety and fun, good equipment, multilingual instructors, PADI courses, BSAC, the only shop with nitrox instruction, fast boats, also rooms and restaurant, dive/accommodation packages available. Recommended. Also at West Bay, entrance through Paradise Beach

Resort – though not attached to the resort – one of the few independent operators, T2445-5017. Very friendly and highly recommended.

Scuba Romance, Dixon Cove. Shop and equipment, large diesel boat and compressor, diving the south wall and the reef at Mary's Place, overnight trips to Barbareta, 6 dives, US$80, sleeping on the boat, work with Palm Cove Resort, cabin-style accommodation, home cooking.

Sueño del Mar Divers, T2445-4343. Good, inexpensive, American-style operation, tends to dive the sites closest to home.

Tyll's Dive, West End, T9698-0416, www.tyllsdive.com. Multilingual instructors, PADI, SSI courses. Accommodation also available.

West End Divers, West End, T2445-4289, www.westendivers.com. Italian owned, competent bilingual instructors, PADI Dive Centre.

Fishing

Trips can be arranged through Eddie, contact at **Cindy's** next to Ocean Divers, West End, small dory, local expert, good results, US$30 per hr, but prices can vary. Alternatively, go fishing in style from French Harbour, **Hot Rods** sports fisher, US$500 per day charter, T445-1862. Contact **Casi Todo**, T2445-1347, for fishing tours, ½- and full day. Fishing trips also available on **Flame**, contact Darson or Bernadette, T445-1616, US$20 per hr.

Submarine trips

Karl Stanley offers a probably unique opportunity with deep-sea submarine trips down to 2000 ft. At US$600 per person, a little on the pricey side, but then it's not an everyday option. **Stanley Submarines**, www.stanleysubmarines.com.

Tour operators

At **Belvedere's Lodge** on the headland at Half Moon Bay, Dennis runs snorkelling trips to secluded bays beyond Antony's Key in a glass-bottomed yacht. He also takes charters and sunset cruises all along the coast. Horse riding available from **Keifitos** or **Jimmy's** in West End. Alex does day trips to Punta Gorda and 2- to 3-day trips in his sailboat *Adventure Girl*, which is moored at **Ocean Divers** dock, contact here or at **Tyll's**. **Far Tortugas** charters, trimaran *Genesis*, does sailing trips with snorkelling and reef drag (snorkellers towed behind slow-moving boat), US$45 per day, US$25 per ½ day, contact **Casi Todo**, West End, T2445-1347. **Coconut Tree** have a rainforest tour to Pico Bonito, US$112 (guide, transport, lunch and snorkelling).

Travel agents

Airport travel agency has information on hotels, will make bookings, no commission. **Bay Islands Tour and Travel Center**, in Coxen Hole (Suite 208, Cooper Building, T2445-1585) and French Harbour. **Casi Todo 1** in West End or **Casi Todo 2** in Coxen Hole can arrange tours, locally and on the mainland, including fishing, kayaking, island tours, trips to Barbareta and Copán. Local and international air tickets also sold here as well as new and second-hand books, Mon-Sat, 0900-1630. **Columbia Tours**, Barrio El Centro, T2445-1160, good prices for international travel, very helpful. **Tropical Travel**, in Hotel Caye View, T2445-1146. **Carlos Hinds**, T2445-1446, has a van for trips, reasonable and dependable.

Zip-wire

High-wire canopy tour circuits are the latest craze on Roatán, with half a dozen sites strung around the island, including **Pirates of the Caribbean**, T2455-7576, **Mayan Jungle Canopy**,www.boddentours.com, and**South Shore Canopy Tour**, on West Bay Rd, T9967-1381, www.southshorezipline.com.

Isla Guanaja p572
Diving and sailing

The most famous dive site off Guanaja is the wreck of the *Jado Trader*, sunk in 1987 in about 30 m on a flat bottom surrounded by some large coral pinnacles which rise to about 15 m. Big black groupers and moray eels live here, as does a large shy jewfish and many other fish and crustaceans.

End of The World, next to **Bayman Bay Club**, T/F2402-3016, www.guanaja.com. Diving instruction, beachfront bar, restaurant, cabins, kayaks, canoes, hobie cats, white-sand beach, fishing. Highly recommended resort.

Jado Divers, beside **Melba's**, T2453-4326. US$26 for 2 dives, run by Matthew from US. Preston Borden will take snorkellers out for US$25 per boat load (4-6 people), larger parties accommodated with larger boat, or for customized excursions, very flexible.

⊖ Transport

Utila *p568, map p568*
Air
Sosa, T2452-3161, www.aerolineasosa.com, flies on Mon, Wed and Fri to **La Ceiba**, US$50. Also to **Roatán** (US$40), **San Pedro** (US$51) and **Tegucigalpa** (US$64). **Atlantic Air**, have 3 flights a week to La Ceiba. There is local transport between airport and hotels.

Boat
Ferry services on the Princess Utila, **La Ceiba**–Utila at 0930 and 1600, and Utila–La Ceiba at 0620 and 1400. Automatic ticketing US$21. Daily sailings Utila–**Roatán**, on Captain Vern's catamaran *Nina Elisabeth II*, T3346-2600 (mob), or ask at **Gunter's Dive Shop** on Utila and **Coconut Divers**, Half Moon Bay, Roatán. US$55 one way, no fixed schedule. Dock fee required when leaving Utila (US$1)

Cycling
Bike hire about US$5 per day. Try **Delco Bike**.

Roatán *p569, maps p570 and p571*
Air
The airport is 20 mins' walk from Coxen Hole, or you can catch a taxi from outside the airport for US$1.50. There is a hotel reservation desk in the airport, T2445-1930.

Change in Coxen Hole for taxis to West End. US$1 per person for *colectivos* to West End, US$2 to Oak Ridge. If you take a taxi from the airport they charge US$10 per taxi; if you pick one up on the main road you may be able to bargain down to US$5. **Isleña**, **Sosa** and **Atlantic Air** fly from **La Ceiba**, US$20 1 way (fewer Sun); flights also to and from **Tegucigalpa**, US$60, via **San Pedro Sula** (Isleña), US$50, frequency varies according to season. No other direct flights to other islands, you have to go via **La Ceiba** (to **Utila** US$38.50, to **Guanaja** US$51). Always buy your ticket in advance (none on sale at airport), as reservations are not always honoured.

From the USA, Taca flies on Sat from **Houston**, on Sun from **Miami**. From Central America, daily flights from **Belize City** (Isleña), Sat from **San Salvador** (Taca).

Airlines Taca, at airport T2445-1387; Isleña, airport T2445-1088; Sosa, airport T2445-1154. **Casi Todo**, T2445-1347, sells all flights within Honduras at same price as airlines.

Boat
Galaxy Wave catamaran sails twice daily from **La Ceiba** to Coxen Hole. Roatán–**La Ceiba** 0700 and 1400, La Ceiba–Roatán 0930 and 1630, T2445-1795 (Roatán), T2440-7823 (La Ceiba), US$52 return. No sailings in bad weather. At times the crossing can be rough, seasickness pills available at ticket counter, and steward gives out sick bags; smart modern ship, with café, and 2 decks, comfortable seating. Irregular boats from **Puerto Cortés** and **Utila**. Cruise ships visit from time to time, mostly visiting **Tabayana Resort** on West Bay.

Bus
From Coxen Hole to Sandy Bay is a 2-hr walk, or a US$1.70 bus ride, every 30 mins 0600-1700 from market, a couple of blocks in from Calle Principal. **Ticabus** buses go to French Harbour, Oak Ridge and Punta Gorda, daily every 45 mins from 0600-1630, US$1.75;

from parking lot opposite Centro Médico Euceda east end of Calle Principal.

Car

Car rental Captain Van, West End, vans, also mopeds and bicycles, good information about the islands; Roatan Rentals, West End, range of vehicles, pickups and vans for rent; Sandy Bay Rent-A-Car, US$42 per day all inclusive, jeep rental, T2445-1710, agency also in West End outside Sunset Inn; Toyota, opposite airport, have pickups, US$46, 4WD, US$65, Starlets US$35 per day, also 12-seater bus, US$56 per day, T2445-1166.

Cycling and mopeds

Captain Van's Rentals, West End; also from Ole Rentavan, T445-1819.

Taxi

If you take a private taxi, *privado*, negotiate the price in advance. The official rate from the airport to Sandy Bay/West End is US$15 per taxi regardless of the number of passengers; from ferry dock to West End is US$20. Luis (waiter at Bite on the Beach restaurant West End), runs taxi tours, very informative and knowledgeable, T9892-9846. Water taxis from West End to West Bay, every few minutes depending on passengers, US$3, from jetty next to Foster's Bar.

Isla Guanaja *p572*
Air

The airport is on Guanaja but you have to get a water taxi from there to wherever you are staying; there are no roads or cars; Sosa and Isleña (T2453-4208) fly daily from La Ceiba, 30 mins. Other non-scheduled flights available.

Boat

The *Suyapa* sails between Guanaja, La Ceiba and Puerto Cortés. The *Miss Sheila* also does this run and on to George Town (Grand Cayman). *Cable Doly Zapata*, Guanaja, for monthly sailing dates to Grand Cayman (US$75 1 way). Irregular sailings from Guanaja to Trujillo, 5 hrs.

① Directory

Utila *p568, map p568*
Banks Dollars are accepted on the island and you can pay for diving courses with dollars, TCs and credit cards, although the latter carry an 8-10% charge. Banco Atlántida Mon-Fri 0830-1530, Sat 0830-1130. HSBC Mon-Fri 0830-1530, Sat 0830-1130, changes dollars and gives cash against a Visa, but not MasterCard. There are now 2 ATM machines on the island. Thompson's Bakery and Henderson's Shack (next to La Cueva) will change dollars and TCs. Michel Bessette, owner of Paradise Divers, does Amex, Visa and MasterCard advances plus 8%.
Internet Annie's Internet, near the dock, 0800-1730, closed Sat, extortionate at US$0.15 per min. Seaside Internet, next to Seaside Inn, Mon-Fri 0900-1400 and 1600-1800. Also Internet Café on road to Mango Inn, Mon-Sat 0900-1700. Mermaids offers good internet service for reasonable prices. **Language schools** Central American Spanish School, T2425-3788, www.ca-spanish.com. 20 hrs per week instruction, 4 hrs per day, US$200, Accommodation US$160 per week. Also have schools on Roatan and La Ceiba. **Medical services** Utila Community Clinic (Mon-Fri 0800-1200), has a resident doctor. **Post** At the pier opposite Captain Morgan's Dive Centre, Mon-Fri 0800-1200, 1400-1600, Sat 0800-1100. **Telephone** Hondutel office, Mon-Fri 0700-1100 and 1400-1700, Sat 0700-1100, is near Utila Lodge. The main service is reported as unreliable. Hondutel sends (and receives) faxes. The REMAX office in the Mango Tree business building offers phone calls and most internet places offer Skype services.

Roatán *p569, maps p570 and p571*
Banks Banco Atlántida, Credomatic, and HSBC in Coxen Hole. There is also a BAC office where you can get a cash advance on your Visa/MasterCard, upstairs, before Caye

View Hotel on the main street. 5 banks in French Harbour; **HSBC** in Oak Ridge, T2245-2210, MasterCard for cash advances. No banks in West End. No exchange facilities at the airport. Dollars and lempiras can be used interchangeably for most services.

Emergencies Police, T9716-3837, Red Cross, T2445-0428. **Internet** Available at the Sunset Inn. The **Lucky Lemp**, opposite Qué Tal coffee shop, main street Coxen Hole, phone, fax and email services. **D & I Cyber Cafe**, Calle Principal, Coxen Hole, western edge of town, across river, Mon-Sat 0800-2100. **Cyber Planet**, Calle Principal, opposite Cay View Hotel, Coxen Hole, T2445-0194, US$3 per hr, daily 0800-2000. **Paradise Computer**, Coxen Hole, 10 mins' walk down road to West End. **Language School** West End Spanish School, T9927-44007. Weekly culture-based courses. **Medical services** Dentist: upstairs in the Cooper building for emergency treatment, but better to go to La Ceiba or San Pedro Sula. **Doctor:** Dr Jackie Bush has a clinic in Coxen Hole, no appointment necessary, for blood or stool tests, etc. **Ambulance and Hyperbaric Chamber**, Anthony's Key with full medical service. **Local hospital,** Ticket Mouth Rd, Coxen Hole, T2445-1499.

Post In Coxen Hole, stamps not always available, bring them with you or try **Librería Casi Todo** in West End. **Telephone and fax** Very expensive, you will be charged as soon as a call connects with the satellite, whether or not the call goes through. **Hondutel** in Coxen Hole, fax is often broken. **Supertienda Chris**, West End, T/F2445-1171, 1 min to Europe US$10, USA, Canada US$5. Both **Librería Casi Todo** and **Rudy's Cabins** in West End have a fax, US$10 per page to Europe, US$5 to USA. Rudy's charges US$2 a min to receive phone calls.

Isla Guanaja *p572*
Banks HSBC and Banco Atlántida.

The Northeast

Through the agricultural and cattle lands of Olancho State, a road runs near to the Parque Nacional Sierra de Agalta and beyond to Trujillo on the Caribbean coast. To the west, accessible only by air or sea, is the Mosquitia coast – a vast expanse of rivers and swamps, coastal lagoons and tropical forests filled with wildlife but with few people. From February to May you can taste the vino de coyol, which is extracted from a palm (a hole is made at the top of the trunk and the sap that flows out is drunk neat). With sugar added it ferments and becomes alcoholic (chicha); it is so strong it is called patada de burro (mule kick).

▶▶ For listings, see pages 592-595.

Eastern Honduras

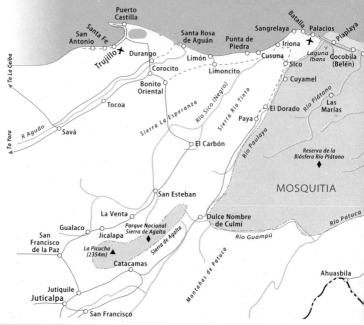

Tegucigalpa to the northeast coast → *For listings, see pages 592-595.*

The Carretera de Olancho runs from the capital northeast to the Caribbean coast. It passes through **Guaimaca** and **San Diego**, **Campamento**, 127 km, a small, friendly village surrounded by pine forests, and on to the Río Guayape, 143 km.

By the river crossing at **Los Limones** is an unpaved road north to **La Unión** (56 km), deep in the northern moutains passing through beautiful forests and lush green countryside. To the north is the **Refugio de Vida Silvestre La Muralla-Los Higuerales** ⓘ *US$1*, where quetzals and emerald toucanettes can be seen between March and May in the cloud forest. For those that have made the effort to get to this spot, if you're camping you may experience the frissonic pleasure of jaguars 'screaming' during the

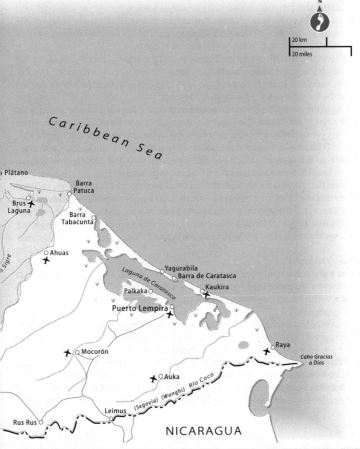

night. The park comprises the three peaks of **La Muralla**, 1981 m, **Las Parras**, 2064 m, and **Los Higuerales**, 1985 m. Cohdefor has an office on the main plaza for information, closed weekends. You are now required to take a guide with you on the trail. Cost is US$4, arrange in La Unión. Four trails range from 1-10 km and are recommended. There are two campsites in the forest (contact Cohdefor on T/F2222-1027 for prior arrangements), or there is accommodation for one or two at the visitor centre.

Juticalpa → *Colour map 3, B3. Altitude: 420 m.*
The main road continues another 50 km from Los Limones to Juticalpa, the capital of Olancho department, in a rich agricultural area for herding cattle and growing cereals and sugar cane. There is a paved road northeast through the cattle land of Catacamas, continuing to just beyond Dulce Nombre de Culmí.

Catacamas and around → *Colour map 3, B4. Altitude: 400 m.*
Catacamas lies at the foot of Agalta mountain in the Río Guayape valley in the Department of Olancho, 210 km from Tegucigalpa. The Río Guayape (named after an indigenous dress, *guayapis*) is famous for its gold nuggets.

The town was established by the Spaniards and the colonial church dates from the early 18th century. It is an agricultural and cattle-raising district. The National School of Agriculture (ENA) is based here, ask if you wish to visit their agricultural demonstration plots in the Guayape valley, 5 km south of the town.

Hiking in the mountains behind Catacamas is beautiful. From Murmullo there are trails to coffee farms. **Río Talgua**, 4 km east of Catacamas, is interesting with caves in which significant pre-Columbian remains have been found. The area and caves are worth a visit. Hiking to **El Boquerón**, stop off at the main road near Punuare, 17 km west of Catacamas, and walk up **Río Olancho**, which has nice limestone cliffs and a pretty river canyon. Through much of the canyon the stream flows underground.

Beyond Catacamas, a rough road continues northeast up the Río Tinto Valley to **Dulce Nombre de Culmí**. Further on is **Paya** where the road becomes a mule track but, in three to four days in the dry season, a route can be made over the divide (Cerro de Will) and down the Río Paulaya to Mosquitia (see below). Local police say that there is a path in the dry season from Dulce Nombre to San Esteban (about 30 km).

Juticalpa to Trujillo
There is a fine scenic road from Juticalpa to Trujillo. From Juticalpa head northeast and turn left where the paved road ends, to **San Francisco de la Paz**. Beyond San Francisco is **Gualaco**, which has an interesting colonial church (there are several places to stay, see Sleeping, page 592).

The town of **San Esteban** is 23 km from Gualaco. On the way you pass Agalta mountain, and some of the highest points in Honduras, and several waterfalls on the Río Babilonia.

After San Esteban the road continues to **Bonito Oriental** (via El Carbón, a mahogany collection point with the Paya communities in the vicinity). There are four hotels here. The final 38 km from Bonito Oriental to Trujillo are paved, through Corocito. There are many dirt roads between San Francisco and Trujillo. If driving, ask directions if in any doubt. Fuel is available in the larger villages but there is none between San Esteban and Bonito Oriental.

Parque Nacional Sierra de Agalta

Between the roads Juticalpa–Gualaco–San Esteban and Juticalpa–Catacamas–Dulce Nombre de Culmí lies the cloud forest of the Parque Nacional Sierra de Agalta, extending over 1200 ha and reaching a height of 2590 m at **Monte de Babilonia**, a massif with a number of interesting mountains. Several different ecosystems have been found with a wide variety of fauna and flora: 200 species of bird have been identified so far. There are several points of entry. Contact **Cohdefor** in Juticalpa, Culmí, Gualaco, San Esteban or Catacamas for information on access, maps, guides, mules and lodging. There is no infrastructure in the park, but a base camp is being built. A good trail leads to **La Picucha** mountain (2354 m). Access is from El Pacayal, 750 m, a short distance towards San Esteban from Gualaco (bus at 0700 which goes on to Tocoa). There are two campsites on the trail, the first at 1060m is just short of **La Chorrera** waterfall, which has a colony of white-collared swifts that nest in the cave behind the falls. Four to six hours above is the second campsite at 1900 m. The final section is mainly dwarf forest with low undergrowth on the summit. There is much wildlife to be seen and a good viewpoint 1 km beyond at the site of two abandoned radio towers. Hiking time is two days.

La Mosquitia → *For listings, see pages 592-595. Colour map 3, B4-5.*

Forested, swampy and almost uninhabited, Mosquitia is well worth visiting if you have the time and energy. In the the Central American Little Amazon, you can hope to see rainforest wildlife including monkeys and incredible birdlife as you drift through the varied habitat that includes lowland tropical rainforest, coastal lagoons, undisturbed beaches, mangroves, grasslands and patches of pine savannah. Home to members of the Miskito and Pech tribes as well as the Garífuna ethnic group who live in small communities on the coast and along the major rivers. The Río Plátano Biosphere Reserve, a UNESCO World Heritage Site, covers an area over 5200 sq km – one of the largest protected areas in Central America.

Ins and outs

While certainly a challenging environment, many backpackers visit the reserve either alone or with professional guides. For those travelling alone, as long as you have basic Spanish and are a reasonably confident traveller this is the cheapest option. With access by air, sea and road, you can visit any time of the year but it is usually best to avoid the heavy rains from November to January. The driest months are March to May and August to October.

What to take It's a tough environment and you should go prepared. Take a mosquito net and repellent, clothing for rain and also for cooler temperatures at night, good walking shoes and a first-aid kit. Also enough cash in small denominations for your stay (there are no banks in the area) and plastic bags to keep things dry.

For study of the region **MOPAWI (Mosquitia Pawisa**, www.mopawi.org) is the best source of information about the indigenous communities in Mosquitia. It is a non-profit-making, non-sectarian organization dedicated to the development of the region and the conservation of the biodiversity of its flora and fauna; volunteer opportunities available. There is a **head office** ① in Puerto Lempira, T898-7460, another **office** ① in Tegucigalpa, Residencias Tres Caminos 4b, lote 67, Apartado 2175, T235-8659, plus offices in several other villages.

MOPAWI is concerned with the protection of natural and human resources throughout Mosquitia and the Department of Gracias a Dios. Among its programmes is the conservation of marine turtles and the green iguana. The Reserva Biósfera Río Plátano (525,100 ha) with the Reserva Antropólogica Tawahka, the Reserva Nacional Patuca and together with Mosquitia Nicaragüense, constitute one of the largest forest reserves north of the Amazon.

Coastal villages

A narrow strand of land divides the inland waterway and Ibans lagoon from the Caribbean. Along this pleasant setting lie a number of small native villages starting with the Garífuna village of Plaplaya and continuing through the Miskito villages of Ibans, Cocobila, Raistá, Belén, Nueva Jerusalem and Kuri. Trails connect all of these villages making exploration easy with vast expanses of unspoiled, white-sand beaches providing an easy route for getting from place to place, with the sea providing a wonderful way to cool off during the heat of the day.

Apart from generally relaxing in the slow-paced life along the coast there are several interesting things to do in the area. In **Raistá**, the butterfly farm was a pilot project, focusing on raising the colourful butterfly species of the area to sell to live butterfly exhibition houses throughout the world (closed at end of 2010 through lack of funds).

In **Plaplaya**, a community-run Sea Turtle Project aims to protect the leatherback and loggerhead turtles that nest along the coast. Each night during the breeding season (March-June) members of the village patrol the beaches to find nesting turtles, carefully gathering the eggs and re-burying them in a guarded area where they are watched over until they hatch. The newborn turtles are then released into the sea. Visitors can accompany the beach patrols for a small donation to the program. There are two traditional dance groups in Plaplaya that can provide an interesting evening's entertainment for visitors.

The Miskito village of **Kuri**, 1½ hours along the beach from Belén, is worth a visit. Here the traditional wooden and thatch houses sit behind the beach, sheltered from the sea breezes by the 'Beach Grape' and palm trees along the sand dunes.

Reserva de la Biósfera Río Plátano

The reserve was established by the Honduran government in 1980 to protect the outstanding natural and cultural resources of the Río Plátano valley and its environs. In 1982 UNESCO declared the reserve a World Heritage Site. The tropical jungles here shelter a number of endangered birds, mammals and fish, among them **scarlet macaws** and **harpy eagles**, **jaguars** and **tapirs**, and the **cuyamel**, a prized food fish fast becoming extinct throughout Honduras. In addition, there are a number of **archaeological sites** about which little is known, and the fabled lost White City of the Maya is said to be hidden somewhere in the thick jungles of the Plátano headwaters.

The Miskito and the Pech living along the lower Plátano cultivate yuca, bananas, rice, corn and beans, and also feed themselves by hunting and fishing. The upper (southern) portion of the Plátano watershed is being quickly populated by mestizo immigrants from the poverty-stricken south of Honduras. These new settlers are cutting down the forest to plant crops and raise cattle, hunting wildlife mercilessly and dynamite-fishing. The government's intention officially to allow settlers into the Sico and Paulaya valleys, on the western edge of the reserve, was roundly criticized. It was feared that the agrarian reform programme would lead to the desertification of the Río Plátano. Added to the damage being done by the settlers, there are now disturbing reports that drug smugglers are cutting landing strips deep in the jungle. Given the pressure the reserve is under, it is recommended to visit it sooner rather than later.

Along the Río Plátano

For those in search of a little more rugged adventure you should find a boat to take you up the Río Plátano to Las Marías, a small Miskito and Pech village that is the last outpost of civilization in this part of the reserve. Local boatman are trying to organize themselves with a view to regulating minimum standards, a fair price for the passage and a rotation system to ensure the work is shared more evenly between them.

Most people stay the night in Raistá before and after visiting Las Marías. Gasoline is very expensive in La Mosquitia and this is reflected in the high cost of transportation. The ride to Las Marías costs about US$130 so put together a group of four or five people to share the cost. That price should get you a boat and boatman for three days to take you on the round trip (four to six hours each way) from the coast with a day in Las Marías to look around. If you stay longer you should negotiate a fair price with the boatman to cover his extra time. Bring food and water for the trip as well as other jungle gear. The journey upstream to Las Marías, although beautiful, can become very tedious and uncomfortable. Birdwatching can provide a diversion; there are three species of toucan as well as several species of parrot, tanagers, herons, kingfishers, vultures, hawk eagles and oropendolas. If you are lucky you might see crocodiles, turtles or iguanas. On arrival in Las Marías, arrange return at once.

An alternative route to Las Marías is by boat across Ibans Lagoon, 45 minutes by tuk-tuk, then 6½ hours' walk through jungle (rough path, hot, mosquitoes, take lots of water and insect repellent, and wear good hiking boots). This is only recommended for fit walkers in drier weather. Expect to pay around US$30 for the guide, and if returning from Las Marías by boat you'll probably still have to pay the return fare even if you're only travelling one way.

Las Marías

This Miskito-Pech village is the furthest limit of upstream settlement. Once in Las Marías you're normally met by a member of the *saca guía*, a representative of the Las Marías Ecotourism Committee who will let you know what trips are available in the area and help make arrangements on a rotation system that shares the work among the community. This group was set up with the help of MOPAWI and Peace Corps with the aim of developing and coordinating a system of ecotourism that benefits the local people, protects the reserve and also offers extraordinary experiences to tourists. A number of guides have been trained in Las Marías to deal with international visitors. They are coordinated by the Committee, have a set price structure with prices and rules posted on the walls of all the *hospedajes*.

Typical guided trips include day hiking on trails around the village, a three-day hike to scenic **Pico Dama** (very strenuous), a day trip by *pipante* upriver to see the **petroglyphs** at **Walpulbansirpi** left by the ancestors of the Pech or multi-day trips upriver to visit other petroglyph sites and view wildlife in the heart of the reserve. Note that it's harder to advance upriver during the rainy season from June to December. ➤ See Activities and tours, page 594.

Brus Laguna → *Colour map 3, B5.*

It is a 15-minute scenic flight from Puerto Lempira (see below) above Caratasca Lagoon and grassy, pine-covered savannahs to **Ahuas**, one-hour walk from the Patuca River (fabled for gold). There is a hospital here, four missions, some basic accommodation and a generally improving atmosphere. Irregular *cayucos* sail down to Brus Laguna for US$2.50, at the mouth of the Río Patuca, or US$12.50 (15 minutes) scenic flight in the mission plane. The airstrip is 4 km from village, take a lift for US$1. There is a disco at the riverside to the left of the bridge. Plagued by mosquitoes throughout summer and autumn.

Puerto Lempira → *Colour map 3, B5.*

Puerto Lempira is on the large Caratasca Lagoon. The main office of MOPAWI (see page 589) is here. The airstrip is only five minutes' walk from town. Regular tuk-tuks (motorized canoes) cross the lagoon to **Kaukira**, US$1.20 (a nice place, but nothing there), **Yagurabila** and **Palkaka**. The tuk-tuks leave Kaukira daily except Sunday at 0500, returning during the morning. In the afternoon the lagoon is usually too rough to cross.

Inland by road from Puerto Lempira are **Mocorón** and **Rus Rus**, which may be visited with difficulty (there is no public transport but any vehicle will give a lift) and is a beautiful, quiet village (accommodation at Friends of America hospital's house; meals from Capi's next door, ask Friends about transport out). A branch off this road leads southeast to **Leimus** on the Río Coco and the border with Nicaragua. Ask for Evaristo López (at whose house you can get breakfast) who can arrange transport to Leimus, most days, three to four hours for about US$3.50. He is also knowledgeable about area safety.

The road continues south to the small town of **Ahuashbila** on the upper river of the Río Coco, which marks the border with Nicaragua.

◉ The Northeast listings

For Sleeping and Eating price codes and other relevant information, see Essentials pages 31-33.

◉ Sleeping

Tegucigalpa to the northeast coast *p587*

F Hospedaje San Carlos, La Unión. Serves good vegetarian food.
F Hospedaje Santos, Campamento. Basic.
F Hotel, on plaza, Guaimaca, above restaurant Las Cascadas. Good value, clean and friendly.
F Hotelito Granada, Campamento. Basic.

Juticalpa *p588*

D El Paso, 1 Av NE y 6 Calle NO, 6 blocks south of Parque (on way to highway), T2885-2311. Quiet, clean, bath, fan, laundry facilities. Highly recommended.
D Las Vegas, 1 Av NE, T885-2700, central, ½ block north of Parque. Clean, friendly, with *cafetería*.
D-F Antúnez, 1 Calle NO y 1 Av NO, a block west of Parque Central, T2885-2250. With

bath (cheaper without), friendly, clean, also annex in same street.
F Familiar, 1 Calle NO between Parque and Antúnez. Bath, clean, basic. Recommended.
F Fuente, 5 mins from bus station on left side of main road to town centre. Basic but large and clean rooms.
F Regis, 1 Calle NO. Balcony, good value.

Catacamas and around *p588*

E Central, Barrio El Centro, T899-4276. With bath, cheaper without, big mango tree in front.
E Juan Carlos, Barrio José Trinidad Reyes, T2899-4212. Good restaurant. Recommended.
E La Colina, T2899-4488. With bath, hot water, fan, TV, parking.
F Hospedaje Tania, on the main street, Dulce Nombre de Culmí. Very basic.

Juticalpa to Trujillo *p588*

F Calle Real, Gualaco, near Parque Central. Basic, friendly, will store luggage.
F Centro, San Esteban. Very clean, nice family, best.

F Hotel Hernández, San Esteban. Cheapest.
F Hotel San Esteban, San Esteban.
Very friendly, clean.
F Hotelito Central, Gualaco. Similar to
Calle Real.

Coastal villages *p590*
Plaplaya
F Doña Yohana, close to the village centre.
F Doña Sede, east of village centre with
good meals.
F Basilia, traditional and the cheapest,
15 mins west of centre.

Raistá and Belén
Choose between **Eddie and Elma Bodden (F)**
on the lagoon and **Doña Cecilia Bodden (F)**,
just up from the lagoon towards the sea.
Try the food at **Elma's Kitchen (F)** in Raistá,
thought by some to be the best on the coast.
Near the lagoon between Raistá and Belén is
Doña Exe (F), and in Belén there is **Doña
Mendilia (F)**, near the grass airstrip.

Las Marías *p591*
Balancing the benefits of tourism are difficult
in such a sensitive area. Sharing the benefits
is one way of offsetting the negative impact
of tourism and, whenever possible, the
Ecotourism Committee tries to share tourists
between the 4 basic but clean *hospedajes*
(all **F**) of **Ovidio**, **Justa**, **Tinglas** or **Diana**,
with meals available for US$3. Very friendly
and with wonderful community atmosphere,
highly recommended (no electricity after
about 1900, bring torch).

Brus Laguna *p591*
D-E Estancia, T2433-8043 and **Paradise**,
T2433-8039. Rooms with a fan and
optional private bath.

Puerto Lempira *p592*
D Gran Hotel Flores. Some rooms with
bath. Recommended.
E Villas Caratascas. Huts with bath,
restaurant, disco.

F Charly's restaurant, Mocorón. Rooms
available. Price per person.
F Pensión Moderno. Good, friendly,
with electricity from 1800-2230.

🍴 Eating

Juticalpa *p588*
🍴 **Casa Blanca**, 1 Calle SE. Quite smart with
a good cheap menu, good paella.
🍴 **Comedor Any**, 1 Av NO. Good value
and friendly.
🍴 **El Rancho**, 2 Av NE. Specializes in meat
dishes, wide menu, pleasant.
🍴 **El Tablado**, 1 Av NE entre 3 y 4 Calle NO.
Good fish, bar.

Cafés
Helados Frosty, near Parque Central.
Ice creams.
La Galera, 2 Av NE. Specializes in *pinchos*.
Tropical Juices, Blv de los Poetas.
Good fruit juices.

Catacamas and around *p588*
In **Dulce Nombre de Culmí**, there are
several *comedores* on the main plaza.
🍴 **As de Oro**, Catacamas. Good beef dishes,
Wild West decor.
🍴 **Asia**, Catacamas. Chinese.
🍴 **Comedor Ejecutivo**, Catacamas. Buffet-
style meals US$2, local craft decorations.
🍴 **Continental**, Catacamas. Chicken dishes,
pizza, US beer.

Juticalpa to Trujillo *p588*
There are 3 nice *comedores* in **San
Esteban** near the Hotel San Esteban.
🍴 **Comedor Sharon**, Gualaco. One of
several places to eat.

Puerto Lempira *p592*
🍴 **Delmy**, 3 blocks north of main street.
Chicken and other dishes, noisy.
🍴 **Doña Aida**, north side of main road to
landing bridge. Fresh orange juice.

La Mosquitia, Centro Comercial Segovia in main street. Breakfasts and cheap fish.

⊕ Entertainment

Catacamas and around *p588*
Fernandos and **Extasis Montefresco** are bars outside town towards Tegucigalpa, pool (US$1.20), live music 2 evenings a week.
Cine Maya, Barrio El Centro, cinema.

Puerto Lempira *p592*
Hampu, is a bar by the landing bridge.

○ Shopping

Juticalpa *p588*
From 0600 on Sat, the market in Parque Central has a good selection of food, fruit, vegetables and souvenirs, said to be the best outdoor market in Olancho.

▲ Activities and tours

La Mosquitia *p589*
Several commercial guides organize trips into the Río Plátano Biosphere Reserve and may be a good option for those with limited Spanish. All-inclusive packages range from 3-14 days and cost about US$100 per day. In order to support ecotourism in the reserve you are encouraged to check the tour operator you are considering works with local people. For other options, see under San Pedro Sula, La Ceiba and Trujillo.
La Moskitia Eco Aventuras, with Jorge Salaverri, office in La Ceiba, T2442-0104, www.honduras.com/moskitia. Specializes in trips to La Mosquitia; excellent, possibly the best and most knowledgeable wildlife guide in all Central America.
Mesoamerica Travel (Col Juan Lindo, No 709, 8 Calle and 32 Av NO, San Pedro Sula, T2558-6447, www.mesoamerica-travel.com) and **Fundación Patuca** (Hauke Hoops)

(T236-9910), also specialize in travel in this region. **Mesoamerica** is the only company to run tours to the Zona Arriba of the Río Patuca (5 or 10 days).
Bob 'The Butterfly, Bird and Bug Guy' Gallardo, based in Copán Ruinas, rgallardo32 @hotmail.com. Highly regarded birding and other specialized nature trips to La Mosquitia.

Las Marías *p591*
The services of the *saca guía* are US$3.50. Guides are required even for day hikes due to the possibility of getting lost or injured on the faint jungle trails. The cost for a guide is US$6 per day for groups up to 5. Overnight hikes require 2 guides. River trips in a *pipante*, a shallow dug-out canoe manoeuvered with poles (*palancas*) and paddles (*canaletes*), require 3 guides plus US$4.20 for the canoe. 2 visitors and their gear will fit in each boat with the guides.

◎ Transport

Tegucigalpa to the northeast coast *p587*
Bus From **Comayagüela** to La Unión, daily, take 4 hrs. To get to the park, hire a truck from La Unión for about US$18. There's little traffic so it's difficult to hitchhike. If driving from **San Pedro Sula**, take the road east through Yoro and Mangulile; from **La Ceiba**, take the Savá–Olanchito road and turn south 13 km before Olanchito.

Juticalpa *p588*
Bus Bus station is on 1 Av NE, 1 km southeast of Parque Central, taxis US$0.50. Hourly to **Tegucigalpa** from 0330 to 1800; to **San Esteban** from opposite Aurora bus terminal at 0800, 6 hrs, US$2.25. To **Trujillo** 0400, 9 hrs, US$5.20. To **Tocoa** at 0500.

Catacamas and around *p588*
Bus From **Tegucigalpa** to Juticalpa/Catacamas, **Empresa Aurora**, 8 Av 6-7 Av,

Comayagüela, T237-3647, hourly 0400-1700, 3¼ hrs, US$2 to Juticalpa, 4 hrs US$2.75 to Catacamas. **Juticalpa**–Catacamas, 40 mins, US$0.60. To **Dulce Nombre de Culmí** (see below), 3 hrs, US$1.35, several daily.

Juticalpa to Trujillo *p588*
Bus To Juticalpa and to the north coast (Tocoa and Trujillo) buses are fairly frequent.

La Mosquitia *p589*
Air
Alas de Socorro fly to **Ahuas**, T2233-7025. This company charters planes for US$565, but per person it is US$60 1 way to Ahuas (see Medical services, below). **SAMi** flies to various villages from Puerto Lempira, eg **Ahuas**, **Brus Laguna**, **Belén**. There are expensive express flights to places like **Auka**, **Raya**, **Kaukira**.
    Airline offices Sosa, T898-7467.

Boat
Coastal supply vessels run between **La Ceiba** and the coastal villages of La Mosquitia. The *Corazón* and *Mr Jim* make the trip weekly and their captains can be found at the harbour east of La Ceiba. Prices vary (US$10-20); be prepared for basic conditions. There are no passenger facilities such as beds or toilets on board and the journey takes a good 24 hrs.

    Rivers, lagoons and inland waterways are the highways in the reserve and dug-out canoes provide the public transportation. Once in Palacios, you can catch *colectivo* boat transport at the landing near the **Río Tinto Hotel** to travel along the inland passage to coastal villages in the reserve such as Plaplaya, Raistá and Belén (about US$3.50 for a 1 or 2-hr trip). There is usually a boat to meet the planes that arrive in the morning and information on prices to different locations is posted in the airline offices. If you miss the *colectivo* you will usually have to pay extra for a special trip (about US$20).

Road
An upgraded road is the cheapest and most favoured route by locals. Take a bus from **La Ceiba** to Tocoa (US$2). From the market in Tocoa take a series of pickups (US$16 per person) along the beach to Batalla, crossing the various creeks that block the way in launches that wait to meet the cars. The journey to **Batalla** takes about 5½ hrs. From Batalla cross the lagoon in a boat to **Palacios** (US$0.70) and continue from there. The trip is not possible in the wetter months of the year (Jul, Oct and Nov).
Note Some may suggest the possibility of catching a truck from Limón to Sangrilaya then walking along the beach and wading across rivers for 1-2 days to get to Batalla. While this is possible it is not recommended because of the heat, bugs and general safety issues.

ⓘ Directory

Juticalpa *p588*
Banks HSNC (the only one that will change TCs), Banco Atlántida, Banco de Occidente. **Post** 2 blocks north from Parque Central, opposite Shell station. **Telephone** Hondutel on main street, 1 block from Parque Central.

Catacamas and around *p588*
Banks Banco Atlántida, Banco de Occidente, in Barrio El Centro. **Medical services** Dentist: Elvia Ayala Lobo, T2899-4129.

La Mosquitia *p589*
Medical services Hospitals: Alas de Socorro operates from Ahuas to collect sick people from villages to take them to Ahuas hospital. Contact the Moravian church (in Puerto Lempira Reverend Stanley Goff, otherwise local pastors will help).

Puerto Lempira *p592*
Banks Banco Atlántida.

Tegucigalpa to the Pacific

From the capital to the Golfo de Fonseca the route twists through mountain valleys down to the volcanic islands and Honduras' Pacific ports of San Lorenzo and Amapala. Near the coast the Pan-American Highway leads west to El Salvador and east though the hot plains of Choluteca to the quiet but popular beaches of Cedeña and Ratón and ultimately to Nicaragua. An alternative route to Nicaragua heads east, through the agricultural town of Danlí, to the border at Las Manos. Short detours from the highway lead to picturesque colonial villages and old mining centres in the hills. ▶▶ *For listings, see pages 598-600.*

Tegucigalpa to Goascarán

From the capital a paved road runs south through fine scenery. Beyond Sabanagrande (see page 505) is **Pespire**, a picturesque colonial village with the beautiful church of San Francisco, which has triple domes. Pespire produces small, delicious mangoes. At **Jícaro Galán** (92 km) the road joins the Pan-American Highway, which heads west through **Nacaome**, where there is a colonial church, to the border with El Salvador at **Goascarán**. At Jícaro Galán, Ticabus and other international buses from San Salvador, Tegucigalpa and Managua meet and exchange passengers.

San Lorenzo → *Colour map 3, C2.*

The Pan-American Highway continues south from Jícaro Galán, to the Pacific coast (46 km) at San Lorenzo, a dirty town on the shores of the Gulf of Fonseca. The climate on the Pacific litoral is very hot.

Amapala → *Colour map 3, C2.*

A 31-km road leaves the Pan-American Highway 2 km west of San Lorenzo, signed to Coyolito. It passes through scrub and mangrove swamps before crossing a causeway to a hilly island, around which it winds to the jetty at **Coyolito** (no *hospedajes* but a *comedor* and *refrescarías*).

The Pacific port of Amapala, on Isla del Tigre, has been replaced by Puerto de Henecán in San Lorenzo, and is reached by a road which leaves the Pan-American Highway at the eastern edge of San Lorenzo. The **Isla del Tigre** is yet another place reputed to be the site of hidden pirate treasure. In the 16th century it was visited by a number of pirates, including Sir Francis Drake. Amapala was capital of Honduras for a brief period in 1876 when Marco Aurelio Soto was president. Today, in addition to a naval base, Amapala is a charming, decaying backwater. The 783-m extinct Amapala volcano has a road to the summit where there is a US army unit and a DEA contingent. You can walk round the island in half a day. There is a ferry service from Coyolito, but fishermen will take you to San Lorenzo for a small fee, not by motor launch, and the trip takes half a day. The deep-sea fishing in the gulf is good. It is possible to charter boats to La Unión in El Salvador.

Choluteca and around → *For listings, see pages 598-600. Colour map 3, C3.*

Choluteca is expanding rapidly on the back of the local industries of coffee, cotton and cattle which flourish despite the hot climate. The town was one of the earliest settlements in Honduras (1535) and still has a colonial centre. The church of **La Merced** (1643) is being renovated and is due to be reconsecrated. The **Casa de la Cultura** and **Biblioteca**

Municipal are in the colonial house of José Cecilio del Valle on the corner of the Parque Central. A fine steel suspension bridge crosses the broad river at the entrance into Choluteca from the north (it was built in 1937). The social centre of **San José Obrero** ⓘ *3 Calle SO*, where handicrafts, in particular carved wood and chairs, can be bought. The **Mercado Municipal** ⓘ *7 Av SO, 3 Calle SO*, is on outskirts of town.

Cedeño beach, on the eastern side of the Gulf of Fonseca 40 km from Choluteca, is a lovely though primitive spot, with clean sand stretching for miles and often thundering surf. Avoid public holidays, weekend crowds and take a good insect repellent. Spectacular views and sunsets over the Gulf of Fonseca south to Nicaragua and west to El Salvador, and of the volcanic islands in the bay. Hourly bus from Choluteca (US$0.60, 1½ hours). A turn-off leads from the Choluteca–Cedeño road to Ratón beach, more pleasant than Cedeño. Bus from Choluteca at 1130; returns next morning.

East of Tegucigalpa → *For listings, see pages 598-600. Colour map 3, C3.*

A good paved road runs east from Tegucigalpa through the hills to Danlí, 92 km away in the Department of El Paraíso. There are no signs when leaving Tegucigalpa so ask the way. Some 40 km along, in the Zambrano Valley (see page 534), is the Escuela Agrícola Panamericana, which is run for all students of the Americas with US help: it has a fine collection of tropical flowers (book visits in advance at the office in Tegucigalpa).

Yuscarán → *Colour map 3, C3. Altitude: 1070 m.*

At Km 47.5, a paved road branches south to Yuscarán, in rolling pineland country preserved by the **Reserva Biológica de Yuscarán**, which protects much of the land around Montserrat mountain. The climate here is semi-tropical. Yuscarán was an important mining centre in colonial days and is a picturesque village, with cobbled streets and houses on a steep hillside. Ask to see the museum near the town plaza; you have to ask around to find the person who has the key, antiques and photographs are displayed in a restored mansion which belonged to a mining family. There is a **Casa de Cultura** ⓘ *in the former Casa Fortín, open Mon-Sat*. The Yuscarán **distilleries** ⓘ *one in the centre, the other on the outskirts, tours possible*, are considered by many to produce the best *aguardiente* in Honduras. The Montserrat mountain that looms over Yuscarán is riddled with mines. The old **Guavias mine** is close to Yuscarán, some 4 km along the road to Agua Fría. About 10 km further along, a narrow, winding road climbs steeply through pine woods to the summit of **Pico Montserrat** (1891 m).

Danlí → *Colour map 3, C3. Altitude: 760 m.*

Danlí, 102 km from Tegucigalpa, is noted for sugar and coffee production, a large meat-packing company (Orinsa), and is a centre of the tobacco industry. There are four cigar factories. The **Honduras-América SA factory** ⓘ *right-hand side of Cine Aladino, Mon-Fri 0800-1200, 1300-1700, Sat 0800-1200*, produces export-quality cigars at good prices. Also **Placencia Tabacos**, on the road to Tegucigalpa, where you can watch cigar-making. Better prices than at Santa Rosa. From Danlí to the north is **Cerro San Cristóbal** and the beautiful **Lago San Julián**.

El Paraíso → *Colour map 3, C3.*

A paved road goes south 18 km to El Paraíso, and beyond to the Nicaraguan border at Las Manos/Ocotal. El Paraíso is a pretty town in an area producing coffee, bananas and rice.

For Sleeping and Eating price codes and other relevant information, see Essentials pages 31-33.

● Sleeping

Tegucigalpa to Goascarán *p596*
There are very basic hotels with restaurants at the border in Goascarán.
C Oasis Colonial, Jícaro Galán, T2881-2220. nice rooms, good restaurant and pool and an unnamed basic guesthouse.
D Perpetuo Socorro, Barrio El Centro, Jícaro Galán, T2895-4453. A/c, TV.
F Intercontinental, in centre, Jícaro Galán. Basic, tap and bucket shower, friendly.
F Suyapa, Jícaro Galán. Basic, cheap.

San Lorenzo *p596*
C Miramar, Barrio Plaza Marina, T2781-2039. Has 26 rooms, 4 with a/c, good restaurant, overpriced, in rough dockside area, best not to walk there.
E-F Perla del Pacífico, on main street, T2781-3025. Fan, bath, comfortable, clean, friendly, central, charming. Recommended.

Amapala *p596*
Ask for **Doña Marianita**, who rents the 1st floor of her house.
B Hotel Villas Playa Negra, Aldea Playa Negra, T2898-8534. 7 rooms with a/c, 7 with fan, pool, beach, restaurant, isolated, lovely setting.
F Al Mar, above Playa Grande. Fan, scorpions, lovely view of mountains and sunset.
F Pensión Internacional on the harbour. Very basic, otherwise only local accommodation of low standard.

Choluteca and around *p596*
B La Fuente, Carretera Panamericana, past bridge, T2782-0253. With bath, swimming pool, a/c, meals.
D Camino Real, road to Guasaule, T2882-0610. Swimming pool, good steaks in restaurant. Recommended.

D Centroamérica, near La Fuente, T2882-3525. A/c, good restaurant, bar, pool, good value.
D Escuela de Español Mina Clavo Rico, El Corpus, Choluteca 51103 (east of Choluteca), T/F2887-3501. Price per person, US$90 per week, full board, living with local families, language classes (US$4 per hr), riding, craft lessons, work on farms, number of excursions.
D-E Pierre, Av Valle y Calle Williams, T2882-0676. With bath (ants in the taps), a/c or fan, TV, free protected parking, *cafetería* has good breakfasts, very central, credit cards accepted. Recommended.
E Brabazola, Barrio Cabañas, T2782-2534. A/c, comfy beds, TV, good.
E Pacífico, near Mi Esperanza terminal, outside the city. Clean, cool rooms, fan, cable TV, hammocks, quiet, safe parking, fresh drinking water, breakfast US$1.50.
F Hibueras, Av Bojórquez, Barrio El Centro, T2882-0512. With bath and fan, clean, purified water, *comedor* attached, good value.
F San Carlos, Paz Barahona 757, Barrio El Centro. With shower, fan, very clean, pleasant.
F Santa Rosa, 3 Calle NO, in the centre, just west of market, T2882-0355. Some with bath, pleasant patio, laundry facilities, clean, friendly. Recommended.

East of Tegucigalpa *p597*
B Escuela Agrícola Panamericana.
Rooms are available, but there is nowhere to eat after 1700.

Yuscarán *p597*
D-E Hotel, T2892-7213. Owned by Dutch man Freek de Haan and his Honduran wife and daughter, private or dormitory rooms, beautiful views of Nicaraguan mountains in the distance.
F Hotel Carol. 6 modern rooms with bath and hot water, annex to owner's fine colonial house, safe, family atmosphere, good value.

Danlí *p597*

C-D Gran Hotel Granada, T2883-2499. Bar, cable TV, accepts Visa. Restaurant and swimming pool, locals pay half price.

D-E La Esperanza, Gabriela Mistral, next to Esso station, T2883-2106. Bath, hot water, fan (more expensive with a/c), TV, drinking water, friendly, parking.

F Apolo, El Canal, next to Shell station, T883-2177. With bath, clean, basic.

F Danlí, El Canal, opposite **Apolo**. Without bath, good.

F Eben Ezer, 3½ blocks north of Shell station, T2883-2655. Basic, hot showers.

F Las Vegas, next to bus terminal. Noisy, restaurant, washing facilities, parking.

F Regis, 3 blocks north of Plaza Central. With bath, basic.

El Paraíso *p597*

E-F 5a Av Hotel y Restaurant, 5 Av y 10 Calle, T2893-4298. Bath, hot water, restaurant specializes in Mexican-American food. Parking.

F Lendy's, Barrio Nuevo Carmelo, by bus station, T2893-4461. Clean, prepares food.

🍴 Eating

San Lorenzo *p596*

🍴🍴 **Restaurant-Bar Henecán**, on Parque Central. A/c, good food and service, not cheap but worth it.

Amapala *p596*

🍴 **Mercado Municipal**. Several clean *comedores*.

🍴 **Restaurant-Bar Miramar** by the harbour. Overlooking the sea, pleasant, very friendly, good meals, hamburgers and *boquitas*, and you can hang your hammock.

Choluteca and around *p596*

🍴🍴 **Alondra**, Parque Central. Old colonial house, open Fri-Sun only.

🍴 **Comedor Central**, Parque Central. *Comida corriente* daily specials, *licuados*, sandwiches,

good for breakfast. Local specialities are the drinks *posole* and *horchata de morro*.

🍴 **El Burrito**, Blv Choluteca between 4 and 5 Av N. With good-value meals and fast service.

🍴 **El Conquistador**, on Pan-American, opposite **La Fuente**. Steaks, etc, outdoor seating but you have to eat inside, good but slow service. Will change money for customers. Recommended.

🍴 **Frosty**, on main street. Owned by **Hotel Pierre**, good food and juices.

🍴 **Tico Rico**, Calle Vincente Williams. Has been highly recommended.

Yuscarán *p597*

🍴 **Cafetería Colonial**, opposite **Banco de Occidente**. Serves excellent *desayuno típico* and *comida corriente*.

Danlí *p597*

🍴 **Comedor Claudio**. Good *comida corriente*, good information from locals.

🍴 **El Gaucho** and **España**, town centre. Good.

🍴 **El Paraíso de las Hamburguesas**. Cheap, good, owner very friendly.

🍴 **Pizzería Picolino**, 2 blocks southwest of Parque Central. Good pizzas.

🍴 **Rancho Típico**, El Canal, near Hotel Danlí. Excellent.

El Paraíso *p597*

🍴 **Comedor Edith**, on a small square on main road, after Parque Central towards border. US$0.85 for a meal.

🎉 Festivals and events

Choluteca and around *p596*

8 Dec The feast day of the **Virgen de la Concepción**, a week of festivities, followed by the **Festival del Sur**, 'Ferisur'.

Danlí *p597*

3rd week Aug Fiesta del Maíz lasts all week, with cultural and sporting events, all-night street party on the Sat; it gets very crowded with people from Tegucigalpa.

⊖ Transport

San Lorenzo *p596*
Bus Frequent *busitos* from **Tegucigalpa** to San Lorenzo (US$1) and **Choluteca** (US$1.50).

Amapala *p596*
Boat Motorized *lanchas* run between **Coyolito** and Amapala, US$0.35 per person when launch is full (about 10 passengers), about US$4 to hire a launch (but you will probably have to pay for the return trip as well). 1st boat leaves Amapala at 0700 to connect with 1st Coyolito–San Lorenzo bus at 0800; next bus from Coyolito at 0900.

Choluteca and around *p596*
Bus To **El Espino** (Nicaraguan border) from Choluteca, US$1.15, 1 hr, 1st at 0700, last at 1400. Also frequent minibuses to **El Amatillo** (El Salvador border) via San Lorenzo, US$1, from bus stop at bridge. Buses to Choluteca from Tegucigalpa with **Mi Esperanza**, **Bonanza** and **El Dandy**; Bonanza continues to San Marcos and departs Tegucigalpa hourly from 0530, 4 hrs to Choluteca, US$1.90. The municipal bus terminal is about 10 blocks from the municipal market, about 8 blocks from cathedral/Parque Central; Mi Esperanza has its own terminal 1 block from municipal terminal.

Yuscarán *p597*
Bus Frequent buses to **Zamorano** and **Tegucigalpa**; from the capital buses leave from Mercado Jacaleapa. For information, ask anyone in the Parque Central in Yuscarán.

Danlí *p597*
Bus From **Tegucigalpa**, US$2, from Blv Miraflores near Mercado Jacaleapa (from left-hand side of market as you face it), Col Kennedy, Tegucigalpa, hourly, 2 hrs, arrive 1½ hrs before you want to leave, long queues for tickets (take 'Kennedy' bus from C La Isla near the football stadium in central Tegucigalpa, or taxi, US$1.20, to Mercado Jacaleapa). Express bus from Col Kennedy, 0830, 1230 and 1700, US$2. One road goes east from Danlí to **Santa María** (several buses daily), over a mountain range with great views.

El Paraíso *p597*
Bus Minibuses from **Danlí** terminal to El Paraíso, frequent (0600 to 1740), US$0.40, 30 mins, don't believe taxi drivers who say there are no minibuses. **Emtra Oriente**, Av 6, Calle 6-7, runs 4 times a day from **Tegucigalpa** to El Paraíso, 2½ hrs, US$1.50. Buses from El Paraíso to **Las Manos**, about every 1½ hrs, US$0.35, 30 mins, or taxi US$4, 15 mins.

⊕ Directory

San Lorenzo *p596*
Banks Bancahorro (changes US$ cash and TCs), Banco Atlántida, and Banco de Occidente (no exchange); Chinese grocery gives good rates for US$ cash.

Amapala *p596*
Banks Banco El Ahorro Hondureño.

Choluteca and around *p596*
Banks Of the many banks in town, Banco Atlántida has a Visa ATM, and only Banco de Comercio changes TCs. Can be difficult to exchange money in Choluteca. **Embassies and consulates** El Salvador, to south of town, fast and friendly, daily 0800-1500. **Post** Mon-Fri 0800-1700, Sat 0800-1200, US$0.15 per letter for Poste Restante. **Telephone** Collect calls to Spain, Italy, USA only.

Danlí *p597*
Banks Banco Atlántida changes TCs without problems. Cash on Visa card, maximum US$50. Other banks as well. **Medical services** Dentist: Dr Juan Castillo, Barrio El Centro, T2883-2083.

El Paraíso *p597*
Banks Several branches in town including HSBC.

Contents

Nicaragua

At a glance

◉ **Getting around** Buses between large towns. Minibuses around the Managua, Masaya, Granada triangle. Boats out to the Corn Islands.

◉ **Time required** 2-3 weeks getting to know the country.

☼ **Weather** Dry season Dec-May. Wet from Jun-Oct. Always warm.

✖ **When not to go** Temperatures can be unbearably hot in May.

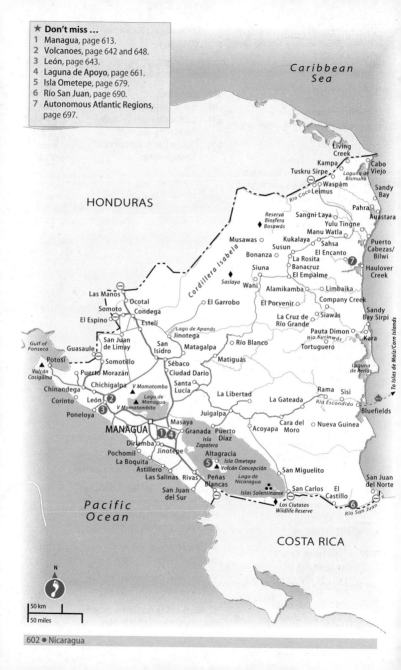

Caribbean Sea

Living Creek
Kampa
Tuskru Sirpe
Cabo Viejo
Laguna de Bismuna
Waspám
Sandy Bay
Río Coco Leimus
Pahra
Auastara

HONDURAS

Reserva Biosfera Bosawás
Sangni Laya
Yulu Tingne
Manu Watla
Musawas
Kukalaya
Sahsa
Puerto Cabezas/ Bilwi
Susun
El Encanto
Bonanza
La Rosita
Banacruz
Siuna
Saslaya
Wani
El Empalme
Haulover Creek

Las Manos
Ocotal
Condega
El Garrobo
Alamikamba
Limbaika
Company Creek
Somoto
El Porvenir
Sandy Bay Sirpi
El Espino
Estelí
La Cruz de Río Grande
Siawás
San Juan de Limay
Lago de Apanás
Jinotega
Pauta Dimon
Río Kurinwás
Kara
Guasaule
San Isidro
Matagalpa
Río Blanco
Tortuguero

Gulf of Fonseca
Potosí
Volcán Cosigüina
Somotillo
Puerto Morazán
Sébaco
Ciudad Darío
Santa Lucía
Matiguás
Laguna de Perlas

Chinandega
Chichigalpa
V Momotombo
La Libertad
La Gateada
Rama
Sisi
Río Escondido

Corinto
León
Lago de Managua
Juigalpa
Bluefields

Poneloya
V Momotombito
Cara del Moro
Nueva Guinea

MANAGUA
Masaya
Granada
Puerto Díaz
Acoyapa

Diriamba
Jinotepe
Isla Zapatera

Pochomil
Altagracia
Isla Ometepe
La Boquita
Volcán Concepción
San Miguelito

Astillero
Las Salinas
Rivas
Lago de Nicaragua
San Carlos
El Castillo
San Juan del Norte

San Juan del Sur
Peñas Blancas
Islas Solentiname
Los Ciutasos Wildlife Reserve
Río San Juan

Pacific Ocean

COSTA RICA

To Islas de Maíz/Corn Islands

N

50 km
50 miles

Nicaragua is a nation born out of poetry, fire and brazen revolutionary spirit. It is a land of tempestuous geological foundations and equally tempestuous history; a land where great heroism meets wild poetic struggle. The 1979 Sandinista revolution is indelibly etched on the Nicaraguan psyche and reminds the world that political destiny can and must be commandeered by the people. Sadly, years of counter-revolutionary violence have left their mark too. The notorious Contra War – sponsored and supported by the CIA – crippled the country's infrastructure and caused long-term damage to its international reputation. Today, Nicaragua is at peace and making a bold recovery. But in spite of burgeoning foreign investment, development is patchy. Power and water shortages are common, many towns lack paved roads, horse and cart are widely used, the black market reigns, and wood remains the principal source of fuel.

Travelling in Nicaragua is a challenging, intensive and irresistible adventure. It is at once beautiful, inspirational, amusing, saddening, grotesque and replete with endless anarchic charms. Through it all, the people – eternally decent and good humoured – are the country's finest asset. To the north, you'll find dark, entrancing mountains and an endearing countryside culture rooted in farming, ranching and horses. To the south, the vigorous Río San Juan courses through verdant rainforest reserves, offering some of the best wildlife viewing in Central America. To the west, the Pacific coast is enjoying a minor tourist boom thanks to its gorgeous, sandy beaches. To the east, a host of lesser-visited shores boast an English-speaking culture that is more Caribbean than Nicaraguan. Add the fine colonial towns of Granada and León, the magical island of Ometepe, the largest freshwater lake in Central America, remote indigenous villages, mysterious archaeological relics, and endless smoking volcanoes, and you have some compelling reasons to visit this captivating country, very much on its way up.

Essentials

Where to go

The largest of the Central American republics, Nicaragua is located at the junction of three continental plates. Earthquakes and volcanic eruptions frequently shake the country – at times, to its foundations. The people and most of the economic activity are concentrated, around the two great lakes of Managua and Nicaragua, and to the west of the Maribios volcanic chain that runs parallel to the Pacific shore. Stretching inland from the Caribbean coast, the largely unpopulated lowlands are challenging country for travelling and a nature paradise for those with the energy and time to spare.

Dramatic evidence of tectonic power can be seen in the capital, **Managua**, where the centre was destroyed by an earthquake in 1972. The old cathedral stands open to the skies, a crumbling testament to what the city could have been. Other sites in the old colonial centre, close to the shores of **Lago de Managua**, reflect Nicaragua's recent civil war. Within easy reach of the capital are the Pacific beaches of **Pochomil** and **Masachapa**.

Southeast of Managua is the colonial city of **Masaya**, a major centre for handicrafts in the region and a base for visits to the smoking crater of the **Santiago** volcano. The road continues to **Granada**, one of Nicaragua's major colonial cities, passing close to the crystal-clear waters of the beautiful Apoyo crater lake. Founded on the shores of **Lago de Nicaragua** in 1524, Granada is the oldest continually inhabited city on the mainland of the Americas. It promises a stunning setting, gorgeously restored Spanish buildings, hordes of camera-toting tourists and some of the best restaurants in the country. The lake also has an archipelago of 354 islands that are great for boat trips and nature watching. **Isla Zapatera**, an extinct volcano and pre-Columbian site, is accessible from Granada. **Ometepe**, easily reached from Granada and the lakeside town of **San Jorge**, near **Rivas**, is the largest island and a peaceful, popular destination with welcoming residents, indigenous petroglyphs and two forest-covered volcanoes ideal for climbing.

San Carlos marks the southeast corner of Lake Nicaragua at the outlet of the **Río San Juan**, which flows along the Costa Rican border to **San Juan del Norte**, and passes through some of Central America's most unspoilt forest; the potential for nature tourism is enormous. A short trip from San Carlos is the **Solentiname archipelago**, a group of forested islands and home to a community of artists. On the south Pacific coast, heading towards Costa Rica, the burgeoning resort town-cum-surfers' hang-out of **San Juan del Sur** provides beach life and fabulous sunsets. Close by is the country's most important turtle nesting ground at **La Flor**.

Two routes head round Lago de Managua from the capital, heading north to **Honduras**. The main route runs south of the lake shore arriving at the former capital of **León**, a feisty city of colonial houses, beautiful churches, students and captivating festivals. As the birthplace of Rubén Darío, one of Latin America's greatest poets, the city is rightly proud of its cultural heritage. Nearby are the Pacific beaches of **Las Peñitas** and **Poneloya**. Heading north is sweltering **Chinandega** and the national park of **Cosigüina** volcano, overlooking the Gulf of Fonseca. A second route goes east of Lake Managua through the refreshing highland towns of **Matagalpa**, **Jinotega** and **Estelí**, ideal country for walking and hiking.

On the Caribbean coast, **Bluefields** and **Bilwi** are port towns with an entirely different cultural flavour. Bluefields is a bumpy bus and boat journey from Managua, Bilwi makes for a long journey on a couple of buses. Out to sea, the **Corn Islands**, fringed with coral, are popular for bathing, snorkelling and diving. All can be reached by plane from Managua.

Suggested itinerary

If you're travelling through Central America, arriving from Honduras through Las Manos, you can stay a few days in **Estelí** and **León** to get the feel of the north. Drop in to **Managua** for a day or two to appreciate the capital's chaos if nothing else before spending a few days in the more attractive setting of **Granada**. From here you've got several options. Backtrack a bit for a few days in the isolated **Corn Islands**, or head round the southwest side of **Lake Nicaragua** and **Isla Ometepe**. **San Juan del Sur** on the Pacific coast is worth a stop before heading to Costa Rica. There are two options: straight down through **Peñas Blancas** to visit the Nicoya Peninsula, or more adventurously through **San Carlos**, which is a good base for visiting the Caños Negro Wildlife Reserve, Fortuna and Volcán Arenal.

When to go

The dry season runs from December to May, with temperatures becoming unbearably hot towards the end of the season, especially in the Pacific northwest. The wettest months are June to October. The most popular time to visit is just after the rainy season in November. The higher altitudes in the north are cooler year-round and chilly at night.

What to do

The national game is baseball, with a season running from November to February. There are five major league teams and Managua's Estadio Nacional stadium attracts crowds of up to 20,000. Football comes a poor second, breaking the trend of most Latin countries.

Opportunities for **nature tourism** are growing rapidly, with the lowlands of the Caribbean coast, the Río San Juan and the highlands around Matagalpa and Estelí attracting keen nature watchers. **Community tourism** is also developing in all parts of the country, allowing intrepid travellers to experience daily life in Nicaraguan communities and cooperatives. The northern highlands and the Maribios volcanoes of León and Chinandega are popular destinations for **trekking**. Granada is experiencing a steady rise in interest with activities such as **mountain biking**, hiking, zip-lining and kayaking. The Pacific coast has some good swimming beaches and there are excellent **surfing** opportunities to the south. Out on the Corn Islands, where the beaches are exquisite, **snorkelling** and **diving** are possible on nearby coral reefs.

Getting there

Air

There are no direct flights to Nicaragua from **Europe**. You will need to travel to a **US** city and catch a connecting service; the most common points of entry are Miami, Houston and Atlanta. Airlines with Managua-bound services include **American**, **Continental**, **Delta**, **Spirit** and **Taca**. From **Latin America** there are good connections with **Copa** and **AeroMéxico**.

Border essentials

Nicaragua–Honduras

For crossings between Nicaragua and Honduras (Las Manos–Ocotal, El Espino–Somoto, Río Guasaule, Leimus–Waspam), see page 490.

Nicaragua–Costa Rica
Peñas Blancas

The only Costa Rica–Nicaragua road crossing; often hectic on the Nicaraguan side. Lots of helpers around (and some unfriendly characters too). People may try to sell you forms and paperwork on the street or buses; you don't need to buy them. Be vigilant.

Currency exchange A branch of BCR in the customs building. No shortage of money-changers, but beware short change.

Nicaraguan immigration Open 0600-2200. If travelling on an international bus, processing can be lengthy and you must line up to have your bag searched by customs.

Costa Rican immigration Open Monday-Saturday 0600-2200, Sunday 0600-2000. Generally, faster processing than the Nicaraguan side.

Onwards to Costa Rica Several express buses daily to San José, five hours, departing 100 m north of Coca Cola terminal. To Liberia, 1½ hours.

Onwards to Nicaragua Buses to Rivas every 30 minutes, where you can catch connections to Granada, Managua, San Juan del Sur or Isla Ometepe. Direct express buses also run from Peñas Blancas to Managua, every 30 minutes, 3½ hours.

San Carlos–Los Chiles/Los Chiles–San Carlos

A very intriguing crossing used by adventurers and itinerant labourers travelling to and from Nicaragua's remote Río San Juan province. Quick and hassle-free, usually.

Currency exchange Banks in San Carlos on the Nicaraguan side, but you are strongly advised to bring some dollars and local currencies before setting out.

Nicaraguan immigration Open 0800-1600. If leaving Nicaragua, an exit stamp must be obtained in the San Carlos office, US$2, before embarking to Los Chiles.

Costa Rican immigration Open 0800-1600, closed for lunch. Entrance/exit stamps are available in the Los Chiles office, a few kilometres from the border.

Onwards to Costa Rica Good access to Fortuna.

Onwards to Nicaragua From Los Chiles, you need to catch a *lancha* up the river to San Carlos, 45 minutes, two daily, check schedule. From San Carlos you can travel east down the Río San Juan or take a ferry across Lake Nicaragua to Isla Ometepe or Granada.

San Juan del Norte–Barra del Colorado

This is not a regular border crossing and at last check there were no formal facilities on the Costa Rican side. Very interesting, but not practical if you are in a hurry.

Money exchange No banks or ATMs. Bring lots of cash and all the currency you need. Local stores may exchange at poor rates.

Nicaraguan immigration Stamps available at the new building on the dock. Ask around if it's unmanned.

Costa Rican immigration No formal facilities. Check in with the Guardia Civil in Barra del Colorado or Tortuguero if coming or going. Official entrance is in Puerto Limón.

Onwards to Costa Rica Twice-weekly boat service to Puerto Viejo de Sarapiqui and Tortuguero, Tuesday and Friday. Private boats expensive; cheaper to hitch with locals.

Onwards to Nicaragua A very bumpy *lancha* now connects San Juan del Norte with Bluefields, three to four hours, not for the faint-hearted. Regular boats also ply the Río San Juan as far as San Carlos, six to eight hours away.

Airport information International passengers arriving by air pay an entry tax of US$5; departing passengers pay an airport tax of US$32, payable in US dollars, often included in the price of your ticket. There is a sales tax of US$5 on tickets issued in and paid for in Nicaragua; a transport tax of 1% is levied on all tickets issued in Nicaragua. For information on Managua airport, see page 625.

River
In San Carlos there is an immigration post linking with the boat journey on the Río Frío connecting to Los Chiles in Costa Rica. There is also a border crossing at San Juan del Norte, at the mouth of the Río San Juan, but the region is very remote and the office may be manned infrequently. At the time of research, other immigration posts were planned for settlements along the Río San Juan – email a local hotel to find out the latest news.

Road
The main road links to the north are at El Guasaule and further inland on the Pan-American Highway at Las Manos with a third option at the border north of Somoto at El Espino in Honduras (see page 490). Crossing the border to Costa Rica in the south, the most commonly used crossing is at Peñas Blancas, although it is also possible to leave from San Carlos for Los Chiles (see page 606), connecting with Fortuna and Lake Arenal.

Getting around

Air
Nicaragua's sole domestic airline is **La Costeña**, T2263-2142, www.lacostena.com.ni, which operates a small fleet of single-prop Cessna Caravans and 2-prop Short 360s. In the Cessnas there is no room for overhead lockers, so pack light and check in all you can. For checked luggage on all flights there is a 15-kg (30-lb) weight limit per person for 1-way flight, 25 kg (55 lb) for round-trip tickets, any excess is payable on check-in. US$2 exit tax on domestic flights. Services depart from Managua to Bluefields, Corn Island, Minas (Bonanza/ Siuna/Rosita), Puerto Cabezas, San Carlos and Waspám. Domestic flights should be reconfirmed as soon as possible.

Road
The Pan-American Highway from Honduras to Costa Rica is paved the whole way (384 km) as is the shorter international road to the Honduran frontier via Chinandega. The road between Managua and Rama (for Bluefields) is also paved, and now continues in an unpaved way as far as Pearl Lagoon. Road directions are given according to landmarks (eg from the gas station, two blocks north, one block east), even where there are street names or numbers.

If arriving overland, there is an US$8 charge. Exit tax for foreigners is US$2 (US$5 at weekends). Always insist on a receipt and if in doubt, go to the Immigration Department in Managua to verify the charge. Officials in Las Manos may try to overcharge – be firm.

Bus Local buses are the cheapest in Central America and often the most crowded. Sometimes they are in very poor shape with holes in the floor and ceiling. Speedy minibuses are becoming more common, particularly on popular intercity routes; they are modern, comparatively comfortable and preferable to the battered old US school buses.

Baggage loaded on to the roof or in the luggage compartment may be charged for, usually at a flat fee of US$0.50. International **Ticabus** buses link Nicaragua with Central America from Panama to southern Mexico. Other international lines include Transnica, King Quality and Nica Expreso (León).

Car and motorcycle Motorists and motorcyclists pay US$20 in cash on arrival at the border (cyclists US$2, up to US$9 at weekends) in addition to the entry tax for other overland arrivals (see above). Do not lose the receipts, or you will have to pay again when you leave. Get the correct entry stamps or you will encounter all sorts of problems once inside the country. Vehicles not cleared by 1630 are held at customs overnight. Formalities can take up to four hours. On leaving, motorists pay five córdobas, plus the exit tax. Petrol is sold by the gallon. Regular petrol is US$2.61 per gallon – there are 24-hour service stations in the major cities, elsewhere they close at 1800. Be careful when driving at night, few roads are lit and there are people, animals and holes in the road. Crash helmets for motocyclists are compulsory.

Car hire costs around US$40 a day for a basic car, rising to US$100 for a jeep. Weekly discount rates are significant and if you want to cover a lot of sites quickly it can work out to be worthwhile. A minimum deposit of US$500 is required along with an international driving licence or a licence from your country of origin. Insurance costs US$10-30. Before signing up check insurance and what it covers and also ask about mileage allowance. Most agents have an office at the international airport and offices in other parts of Managua.

Cycling Several cyclists have said that you should take a 'proof of purchase' of your cycle or suggest typing out a phoney 'cycle ownership' document to help at border crossings.

Hitchhiking Hitching is widely accepted, but not easy because so many people do it and there is little traffic – offer to pay a small contribution.

Sea
The main Pacific ports are Corinto, San Juan del Sur and Puerto Sandino. The two main Atlantic ports are Puerto Cabezas and Bluefields.

Sleeping

Most hotels are run by independent operators with a few upmarket international chains beginning to arrive in popular areas. Standards vary greatly but there is plenty of competition in the mid- to low-budget range in most towns. In smaller towns, cheaper hotels tend to be better value.

Eating and drinking

Try *nacatamales* (cornflower dumplings stuffed with pork or chicken and vegetables, and boiled in banana leaves), an excellent value meal. *Gallo pinto* (rice and beans) is another tasty dish. Fizzy drinks are known as *gaseosas* in Nicaragua, as in neighbouring countries. Fresh fruit-based drinks and juices are *frescos*. Coffee can be terrible as most good Nicaraguan beans go for export and locals drink instant – ask for *café percolado* (filter coffee).

Festivals and events

Businesses, shops and restaurants all close for most of Holy Week; many companies also close down during the Christmas to New Year period. Holidays that fall on a Sun are taken the following Mon.

1 Jan New Year's Day.
Mar/Apr Holy Week 1200 Wed to Easter Sun.

1 May Labour Day.
19 Jul Revolution of 1979.
14 Sep Battle of San Jacinto.
15 Sep Independence Day.
2 Nov All Souls' Day (Día de los Muertos).
7-8 Dec Immaculate Conception (La Purísima).
25 Dec Christmas Day.

Shopping

Masaya is the centre for *artesanía*, selling excellent crafts, high-quality cotton hammocks, leather goods and colourful woven rugs often used as wall hangings and wicker furniture. Ceramics are produced in many parts of the country.

Essentials A-Z

Customs and duty free
Duty-free import of 500 g of tobacco products, 3 litres of alcoholic drinks and 1 large bottle (or 3 small bottles) of perfume is permitted.

Electricity
110 volts AC, 60 cycles, US-style plugs.

Embassies and consulates
Canada, contact embassy in USA
Costa Rica, Av Central 2540, Barrio La California, San José, T221-2924.
El Salvador, Calle El Mirador y 93 Av Norte, No 4814, Col Escalón, San Salvador, T263-2292.
France, 34 Av Bugeaud, 75116 Paris, T4405-9042.
Germany, Joachim-Karnatz-Allee 45 (Ecke Paulstr) 10557 Berlin, T206-4380.
Honduras, Col Tepeyac, Bloque M-1, No 1130, DC T239-5225.
Italy, Via Brescia 16, 00198 Roma, T841-4693.
Mexico, Prado Norte 470, Col Lomas de Chapultepec, esq Explanada, T5540-5625.
Spain, Paseo de la Castellana 127, 1-B, 28046 Madrid, T555-5510.
UK, Vicarage House, 58-60 Kensington Church St, London, W8 4DB, T020-7938-2373.
USA, 1627 New Hampshire Av NW Washington, DC 20009, T202-939-6570.

Health
Tap water is not recommended for drinking outside Managua, León and Granada and avoid uncooked vegetables and peeled fruit. **Intestinal parasites** abound; if requiring treatment, take a stool sample to a lab before going to a doctor. Note: Repeated tests may be required to catch a positive result. **Malaria** is prevalent; high risk areas are east of the great lakes, particularly in the northeastern lowlands, where you should take regular prophylaxis. **Dengue** fever is increasingly present; take precautions to avoid being bitten by mosquitoes. See also page 38.

Internet
Widely available in most towns and cities. Only the most remote settlements lacks connections.

Language
A basic knowledge of Spanish is essential for independent travel in Nicaragua. On the Caribbean coast a form of Creole English is widely spoken, but in the rest of the country

it's Spanish only. Nicaraguan Spanish is quite distinctive and initially tricky to grasp. Drop your 's's, roll your 'r's and turn your 't's to 'd's.

Media

All newspapers are published in Managua, but many are available throughout the country: **Dailies**: *La Prensa*, centre, the country's best, especially for coverage of events outside Managua; *El Nuevo Diario*, centre-left and sensationalist; *La Noticia*, right, government paper. **Weeklies**: *El Seminario*, left-leaning, well-written with in-depth analysis; *7 Días*, pro-Government; *Tiempo del Mundo*, owned by Rev Moon, good coverage of South America, not much on Nicaragua. **Monthlies**: *El País*, pro-government, good features. *Between the Waves*, tourist magazine in English.

Money → *US$1=22.35 córdobas (June 2011).* The unit of currency is the **córdoba (C)**, divided into 100 centavos. Any bank in Nicaragua will change US dollars to córdobas and vice-versa. US dollars are accepted as payment almost everywhere but change is given in córdobas. It is best to carry US$ notes and sufficient local currency away from the bigger towns. Take all the cash you need when visiting the Caribbean coast or Río San Juan. Carry small bills when travelling outside cities or using public buses.

ATMs and exchange

Bank queues can be very long so allow plenty of time, especially on Mon mornings and the 15th and 30th/31st of every month. When changing money take some ID or a copy. You cannot change currencies other than US dollars and euro (**BanCentro** only). Money changers on the street (*coyotes*) during business hours are legitimate and their rates differ little from banks.

Visa and MasterCard are accepted in many restaurants, shops and hotels in Managua, Granada and León. This applies to a lesser extent to Amex, Credomatic and Diners Club. But don't rely exclusively on credit cards. For cash advances the most useful bank is **Banco de América Central (BAC)**. **BAC** offers credit-card advances, uses the Cirrus debit system and changes all traveller's cheques (TCs). TCs often carry a commission of 5% so use your credit/debit card or cash if you can. TCs can only be changed in Managua at *Multicambios* in Plaza España and around the country at branches of **BAC** and **Banco de Finanzas** (Amex cheques only). Purchase receipts may be required when changing TCs in banks.

In Managua, ATM machines in the airport, at the Metrocentro and Plaza Inter shopping malls and in many gas station convenience stores. Outside the capital ATMs are becoming increasingly common in the main towns and at 24-hr gas stations. In remote areas, pack more cash than you need, including lots of small bills.

Cost of living and travelling

Nicaragua is not an expensive country as far as accommodation is concerned, and public transport is also fairly cheap. For food, a *comida corriente* costs about US$1.75 (restaurant meals US$4-13, breakfast US$2.50-3.50). However, on the islands or in out-of-the-way places where supplies have to be brought in by boat or air, you should expect to pay more. A tight daily budget would be around US$20-25 a day.

Opening hours

Banks Mon-Fri 0830-1200, 1400-1600, Sat 0830-1200/1300.
Businesses Mon-Fri 0800-1200, 1430-1730.

Post

Airmail to Europe takes 7-10 days, US$0.80; to USA, 18 days, US$0.55; to Australia, US$1.

Safety

Visitors must carry their passports with them at all times. A photocopy is acceptable, but make sure you also have a copy of your visa or entrance stamp. Pickpocketing and bag slashing occur in Managua, and on buses throughout the country. Apart from Managua at night, most places are generally safe. Reports of robberies and assaults in northern Nicaragua indicate that care should be taken in this area; ask about conditions before going, especially if proposing to leave the beaten track. Recently, there have been many disturbing reports of fake taxis or *piratas* targeting tourists for robbery, especially in Managua, Masaya and Rivas. Be careful who you befriend on buses and insist on private, not *colectivo* service.

Telephone → *Country code T+505.*

Phone lines are owned by the **Enitel**. If you are phoning from inside the prefix zone you need to dial the 8 digits, but if you are dialling a different zone you put '0' in front. For example, to call Managua from Masaya it would be T02266-8689. Phone cards are available from gas stations, supermarkets and shops.

International or national calls can be made at any **Enitel** office, 0700-2200. All calls paid for in córdobas. To the USA, US$3 for the 1st minute, US$1 for each following minute. Collect calls (*por cobrar*) to the USA and Europe are possible. For **SPRINT**, dial 171; **AT&T** 174 and **MCI** 166. To connect to phone services in Germany dial 169, Belgium 172, Canada 168, Spain 162, Netherlands 177, UK 175.

Time

- 6 hrs GMT.

Tipping

US$0.50 per bag for porters; no tip for taxi drivers. Restaurant bills include a 15% tax and 10% service is added or expected as a tip. In local *comedores*, some small change will suffice.

Tourist information

Tourist offices in Nicaragua are more concerned with internal development than public service. Tour operators and foreign-owned hotels are often better sources of information. However, the **Institute of Tourism** in Managua (see page 613) has a range of general brochures and information packs, www.visitanicaragua.com. In the USA, contact PO Box 140357, Miami, FL 33114-0357, T1-800-737-7253.

Useful websites

www.centramerica.com Has a search engine with news links and information.
www.nicanet.org For activist issues.
www.nicaragua.com Has an e-community.
www.toursnicaragua.com Has a good selection of photographs and images.
www.vianica.com Good on hotels, transport and itineraries.

Visas and immigration

Visa rules change frequently, so check before you travel, www.cancilleria.gob.ni. Visitors need a passport with a minimum validity of 6 months and may have to show an onward ticket and proof of funds in cash or cheques for a stay of more than a week. No visa is required by nationals of EU countries, the USA, Canada, Australia or New Zealand.

If you need a visa it can be bought before arriving at the border, it costs US$25, is valid for arrival within 30 days and for a stay of up to 30 days; 2 passport photographs are required. A full 30-day visa can be bought at the border, but it is best to get it in advance. Visas take under 2 hrs to process in the embassies in Guatemala City and Tegucigalpa, but may take 48 hrs elsewhere. Extensions can be obtained at the **Dirección de Migración y Extranjería**, Semáforo Tenderí, 2 1½ c al norte, Managua, T2244-3989 ext 3 (Spanish only), www.migracion.gob.ni. Arrive at the office before 0830. From the small office on the right-hand side you must obtain the *formulario* (10 córdobas). Then queue at the *caja* in the large hall to pay US$20 for your 30-day extension or US$60 for 90 days. In the absence of long queues, this is usually quick and straight-forward. There is a small, speedy *Migración* office in Metrocentro shopping mall where you can obtain a visa extension, recommended. Another possibility is to leave the country for 72 hrs and re-enter on a new visa.

Weights and measures
The metric system is official, but in practice a mixture is used of metric, imperial and old Spanish measurements, including the vara (about 1 m) and the manzana (0.7 ha). Petrol is measured in US gallons, liquids in quarts and pints, speed in kph, fabric in yards, with centimetres and metres for height, pounds for weight and Celsius for temperature.

Working and volunteering
Volunteer work in Nicaragua is not as common as it was during the Sandinista years. Foreigners now work in environmental brigades supporting the **FSLN**, construction projects, agricultural cooperatives and environmental organizations. Certain skills are in demand, as elsewhere in the developing world.

To find out about the current situation, try contacting non-governmental organizations in your home country, such as the **Nicaraguan Network**, 1247 East St, SE, Washington, DC 20003, T202-544-9355, www.nicanet.org; twin-town/sister-city organizations and Nicaraguan Solidarity Campaigns, such as **NSC/ENN Brigades**, 86 Durham Rd, London, N7 7DT, T020-561-4836, www.nicaraguasc.org.uk, or **Dutch Nicaragua Komitee**, Aptdo Postal 1922, Managua.

Casa Danesa, T2267-8126 (Managua), may be able to help find volunteer work, usually for 3 months. An excellent short-term non-profit volunteer experience can be had with **El Porvenir**, 1420 Ogden St, No 204, Denver, CO, 80218, T303-861-1499, www.elporvenir.org, an outgrowth of **Habitats for Humanity**. Work on drinking water, latrine and re-forestation projects.

Managua and around

→ *Colour map 4, A1. Population: 1,328,695. Altitude: 40-200 m.*
Managua, the nation's capital and commercial centre since 1852, was destroyed by an earthquake in March 1931 and then partially razed by fire five years later. Rebuilt as a modern, commercial city, the centre was again levelled by an earthquake in December 1972 when just a few modern buildings were left standing. Severe damage from the Revolution of 1978 to 1979 and flooding of the lakeside areas as a result of Hurricane Mitch in 1998 added to the problems. It's a tribute to the city's resilience that it still has the energy to carry on.
➻ *For listings, see pages 619-628.*

Ins and outs

Getting there

The airport is 12 km east of the city centre. Buses and taxis (US$15 to Barrio Martha Quezada, half the price if hailed from the main road) run from the airport to the city. International bus services arrive at several terminals throughout the city. **Ticabus** and **King Quality** are in Barrio Martha Quezada, close to most of the cheap hotels. **Transnica** is in Metrocentro. Provincial bus services have four main arrival/departure points. City buses and taxis serve the provincial terminals. ➻ *See Transport, page 625.*

Getting around

On foot Managua has nothing that even remotely resembles a city grid or urban planning and walking is a challenge and unsafe for those who are not familiar with the city's 600 barrios. The best bet is to get to Martha Quezada or Metrocentro and not travel more than 10 blocks on foot.

Bus Local bus routes are confusing as they snake around the city and you must know where you need to get off so you can whistle or holler when the destination grows near. It's best to avoid rush hours and sit near to the driver. Major routes include the **No 119** which passes the Centroamérica roundabout, travels through the heart of Metrocentro and past Plaza España. **Route 110** takes you from the northbound bus terminal of Mercado Mayoreo to La UCA where Express buses leave southwards.

Taxi This is the preferred method of transport for newcomers and although some drivers are grumpy or looking to make a week's pay in one journey, most Managua *taxistas* are very helpful and happy to share the city's hidden attractions.

Tourist information

The Nicaraguan Institute of Tourism, **INTUR** ① *T2254-5191, www.visitanicaragua.com, Mon-Fri 0800-1300,* is one block south and one block west of the Crowne Plaza Hotel (the old Intercontinental). They have maps, flyers and free brochures in English, but are generally not well equipped for public visits. The airport INTUR is just past the immigration check and has similar documents. Information on nature reserves and parks can be found at the Ministerio de Medio Ambiente y Recursos Naturales, **MARENA** ① *Km 12.5, Carretera Norte, T2263-2617, www.marena.gob.ni, Mon-Fri 0800-1300.*

Safety Nicaraguans are incredibly friendly but Managua is not the safest city in Central America. Never walk at night unless you are in a good area or shopping centre zone. Arriving in Managua after dark is not a problem, but it's best to book your hotel in advance and take a taxi. Long-distance buses are fine, but be careful in the market when you arrive to take the bus – there are many thieves and the atmosphere is generally confusing. When you arrive at the **Ticabus** station, make sure you know where you want to go before setting out. Note the roads between the terminal and Plaza Inter are now unsafe at all hours; enquire locally about the situation before walking anywhere. The **Mercado Oriental** (not to be confused with the Camino de Oriente which is safe and fun), said to be the largest informal market in Latin America, and its barrio, Ciudad Jardín, should be avoided at all costs. All travellers should exercise extreme caution when hailing a taxi in the street (see safety, page 610).

Sights

Lakefront and Old Centre
The old centre is a garden monument consisting of open spaces, ageing buildings and lakeside restaurants. Despite lying over 14 seismic faults and the warnings of seismologists, important new buildings have been built here including a presidential palace between the ruins of the cathedral and the lakefront, the epicentre of the 1972 earthquake. Much of the lakeside *malecón* was destroyed when Hurricane Mitch swept into town in 1998, but has since been rebuilt. It is now the site of a new touristic

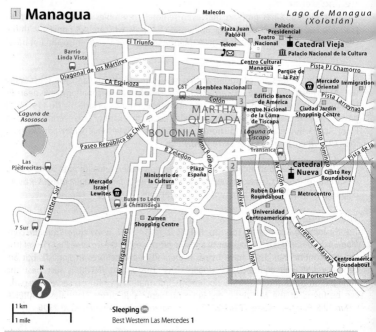

1 **Managua**

Sleeping
Best Western Las Mercedes 1

development, **Puerto Salvador Allende**, constructed by the FSLN and named after the famous Chilean Marxist. Although the port boasts *rancho*-style eateries and shops, the new marina was sadly washed away by floods in 2010.

Near the lake shore, the attractive neoclassical **Palacio Nacional de la Cultura**, previously the Palacio de los Héroes de la Revolución, has been beautifully restored and houses the **Museo Nacional de Nicaragua** ⓘ *T2222-4105, Tue-Sun 0900-1600, US$2 (guided tour only, sometimes available in English), US$2.50 extra charge to video, US$1 to photograph*, as well as the Archivo Nacional and the Biblioteca Nacional. The museum has a fine pre-Columbian collection, some of which is on permanent display in the Pacific and Northern archaeology display halls.

Damaged by earthquake, the **Catedral Vieja** (old cathedral) now has a roof of narrow steel girders and side-window support bars to keep it standing, the atmosphere is of a sad, old building past its prime, left in ruins, but hauntingly photogenic and worth a look. The **Centro Cultural Managua**, next to the Palacio Nacional de Cultura, has a good selection of before and after photos of quake-struck Managua in 1972. The centre is also home to the national art school and the national music school. There are some art exhibits in galleries downstairs.

The garishly painted **Palacio Presidencial** is in front of the Palacio de la Cultura on the opposite corner to the old cathedral. These buildings are situated on the **Parque Central** and provide a striking contrast with the modern **Teatro Rubén Darío** ⓘ *on the lake shore, www.tnrubendario.gob.ni, US$1.50-20 depending on show*, which hosts good plays, folkloric dances and musical events. There are usually temporary exhibitions in the theatre so, during the day, ask at the window to view the exhibit and you can probably look at the auditorium as well.

The **Parque de la Paz**, just southeast of the Parque Central, is part of the rebuilding programme for the old centre. The park is a graveyard for weapons and a few dozen truckloads of AK-47s are buried there, some seen sticking out of the cement; take care here, the neighbourhood on the other side is of bad repute. Three blocks south of the Parque Central are the offices of the **Asamblea Nacional** (Nicaraguan parliament), which include the city's only high-rise building, once the Bank of America, now the offices of the *diputados* (parliamentary members).

Tiscapa Hill and Metrocentro

From the hilltop south of the old centre, the **Parque Nacional de la Loma de Tiscapa** provides the best views of the capital and of the **Laguna de Tiscapa** on the south side of the hill. From the top, a giant black silhouette of **Sandino** stands looking out over the city. The spot has

Nuevo Diario

meter Maps

Carretera Norte

Bello Horizonte Shopping Centre

Ciudad Xolotlán

To Airport & ①

nicipalidad

Pista Portezuelo

Blvd Buenos Aires

To Mercado El Mayoreo Bus Station

Mercado Iván Montenegro

Pista Sábana Grande

oberto Huembes/ Mercado Central

Buses to Masaya, Granada & Rivas

⊣ Centro Comercial Managua

➡ Managua maps
1 Managua, page 614
2 Metrocentro, page 616
3 Martha Quezada and Bolonia, page 617

historical significance as it is the site of the former presidential palace; it was here that Sandino signed a peace treaty with Somoza and was abducted (and later killed) at the entrance to the access road. Underneath the park facing the *laguna* (now blocked by a fence) are the former **prison cells of the Somoza regime** ① *daily 0800-1630*, where inmates were said to have been tortured before being tossed into the lake. To get there, take the road behind the Crown Plaza to the top of the hill using an access road for the Nicaraguan military headquarters. Guards at the park are nervous about photography; ask permission and photograph only downtown and towards the stadium – do not take photos on the access road up to the park.

From Tiscapa hill, the **Catedral Nueva** (new cathedral), inaugurated in 1993, can be seen 500 m to the south of the lake. Designed by the Mexican architect Ricardo Legorreta, comments on the exterior range from 'strikingly beautiful' to 'sacreligious'. The interior, which is mostly unadorned concrete, has been described as 'post-nuclear, with an altar

② Metrocentro

Sleeping 😴
El Almendro **1**
Los Robles **2**
Managua Backpackers' Inn **3**
Real Intercontinental **4**
Royal Inn Bed & Breakfast **5**

Eating 🍴
Casa de Café **1**
Casa de las Nogueras **2**
El Muelle **3**
Garabato **4**
La Ballena que Cayó del Cielo **5**
La Cocina de Doña Haydée **6**

La Hora del Taco **7**
Las Brasas **8**
Marhaba **9**
María Bonita **10**

Bars & clubs 🍸
Hipa Hipa **11**
Santera **12**

➡ **Managua maps**
1 Managua, page 614
2 **Metrocentro, page 616**
3 Martha Quezada and Bolonia, page 617

200 metres
200 yards

resembling a futuristic UN Security Council meeting room'. Many visitors are fascinated by the Sangre de Cristo room, where a life-size bleeding Christ is encased in a glass and steel dome, illuminated by a domed roof with hundreds of holes for the sun to filter through. At night, the dome sparkles with the glow of lightbulbs in the holes. Pedestrian access is from the Metrocentro junction; vehicles need to approach from the east.

South of the Catedral Nueva lies the rotunda Rubén Darío and Managua's well-known Metrocentro area, popular with tourists and home to many upscale hotels. The district's principal artery is the **Carretera a Masaya**. This stretch of four-lane highway includes the **Metrocentro** shopping complex, numerous restaurants, the Pellas family business centre with the **BAC** and **Credomatic** headquarters, the cinema, disco and offices of **Camino de Oriente**, and now the swanky Galerías Santo Domingo shopping mall. You'll need to take a bus or taxi to get there or to the provincial bus terminals.

Plaza Inter, Barrio Martha Quezada and Bolonia

West of Tiscapa hill stands the **Hotel Crowne Plaza** (formerly the Hotel Intercontinental and still referred to as the '*viejo Intercontinental*'), a significant landmark that is reminiscent of a Mayan pyramid. Directly opposite lies the Plaza Inter, site of a shopping complex, cinema and US-style 'food court'. West of the Crowne Plaza, **Barrio Martha Quezada** is home to many mid-range and budget hotels, the Ticabus terminal and a mixture of well-to-do housing alongside poorer dwellings. South through the adjoining

Martha Quezada & Bolonia

Managua maps
1 Managua, page 614
2 Metrocentro, page 616
3 **Martha Quezada and Bolonia, page 617**

Sleeping
Casa de Huéspedes
  Santos **4**
Crowne Plaza **16**
El Conquistador **7**
El Molinito **10**
Europeo **6**
Hostal Real **13**
Hostal San Felipe **2**
La Posada del Angel **19**
Los Cisneros **20**

Los Felipe **21**
Mansión Teodolinda **1**
Posadita de Bolonia **11**

Eating
A La Vista Buffet **15**
Comida a la Vista Buffet **4**
El Churrasco **1**
La Casa de Los
  Mejía Godoy **2**
Mirna's **7**

Panadería Tonalli **9**
Rancho Tiscapa **3**
Rincón Cuscalteco **5**
Santa Fe **6**

Bars & clubs
Shannon Bar Irlandés **10**

N

200 metres
200 yards

and somewhat wealthy Bolonia district is **Plaza España**, next to the Rotondo El Güengüense roundabout, where you'll find a good supermarket, numerous shops, banks, travel agents, tour companies and many airline offices.

Museo Las Huellas de Acahualinca

ⓘ *Along the lake, 2 km due west of the Museo Nacional, T2266-5774, Mon-Fri 0800-1700, Sat and Sun 0900-1600, US$2.50; additional US$2 to take photographs, US$3 for video cameras; all explanations in Spanish; taxi recommended as it is hard to find and in an unsafe neighbourhood.*

These ancient prehistoric animal and human footprints, preserved in the sedimentary tufa and discovered when stone was being quarried, represent some of the oldest evidence of human occupation in Nicaragua. A museum has been created around the original site and the 6000-year-old footprints have been left as they were found in excavation. The museum also has a small display of ceramic artefacts found at the site and an illustration of the estimated height of the people who made the footprints. A must for lovers of archaeology and indigenous history.

Around Managua

Laguna de Xiloá

ⓘ *Sat and Sun only (US$0.35), US$1.60 for cars, US$0.30 for pedestrians; or take bus No 113 to Las Piedrecitas for Xiloá.*

There are several volcanic crater lakes close to Managua, some of which have become centres of residential development, with swimming, boating, fishing and picnicking facilities for the public. Among the more attractive of these lakes is Laguna de Xiloá, 16 km from Managua just off the new road to León. On Saturday and Sunday, the only days when buses run, Xiloá gets very crowded. It's quiet during the week and you can camp there, but without public transport you will have to walk or take a taxi. Other lakes within a 45-minute drive of Managua are **Laguna de Masaya** and **Laguna de Apoyo** (see pages 660 and 661).

Mateare and Momotombito

Thirty kilometres northwest of Managua, **Mateare** is a pleasant fishing and agricultural town with some of the finest lake fish in Lake Managua (eat at your own risk). Distanced from the capital by a large peninsula, the lake is much cleaner here than on the Managua side. The fishermen can take you to the small volcanic island of **Momotombito** (US$60 for a day trip). The best time of year to visit is during the rainy season, when the island is green and the swell on the lake small. Beware of snakes when hiking around the island. There are other small islands in the shadow of the smoking Momotombo volcano, which appears to loom over the lake from the mainland shore. Momotombito is a nature reserve, and has much bird and reptile life and a legendary family of albino crocodiles. There is a small military outpost on the calm side of the island. Stop there to check in if you wish to hike on the islands. Bring drinks or food as gifts for the (non-uniformed) guards, who are very friendly and usually quite bored. They might take you hiking for a small fee.

Pacific beaches near Managua

There are several beaches on the Pacific coast, about an hour's drive from Managua. Because of their proximity to the capital, they get very crowded during the high season (January to April). The nearest are Pochomil and Masachapa (54 km from Managua, bus service from terminal in Israel Lewites market every hour, US$1). **Pochomil** beach is deserted in the week out of season; it gets cleaner the further south you go, but there are rocks and strong waves here so swim with care. It is a tourist centre with a few hotels and many small family-owned restaurants. Don't sleep on the beach or the mosquitoes will eat you alive.

At the entrance to **Masachapa** is the access road to the **Montelimar Resort**. Just before the resort gates is the dirt road to the area's nicest public beach, **Montelimar Gratis** or **El Muelle de Somoza**, a long deserted stretch of clean sand from the Somoza pier to the rocky point that separates the resort from the rest of Masachapa. Take a bus to Masachapa and walk from main highway on the entrance road or drive to the pier, then walk north.

La Boquita is the nearest beach to the villages south of Managua and is visited by turtles from August to November. Just south of **Casares** (69 km from Managua) are further beaches. Access is a long hike or journey by 4WD and lodging is available.

Heading north from Managua, a visit to the broad sandy **El Velero beach** ① *US$3.50*, is recommended, despite the entry fee and poor road. Facilities are controlled by the **INSSBI (Instituto Nicaraguense de Seguridad Social y Bienestar)** for state employees and weekends are fully booked weeks in advance. The beach is beautiful and the sea is ideal for surfing and swimming. To get there, turn off at Km 60 on the old road to León and follow signs. **El Tránsito** is another lovely, undeveloped Pacific beach. Buses from Managua leave at 1200, 1315 and 1500 (from Terminal Lewites) and return at 0600 or 0700, US$0.70.

⊕ Managua and around listings

Hotel and guesthouse prices

LL over US$200	L US$151-200	AL US$101-150
A US$66-100	B US$46-65	C US$31-45
D US$21-30	E US$12-20	F US$7-11
G under US$7		

Restaurant prices

¶¶¶ over US$15	¶¶ US$8-15	¶ under US$8

See pages 31-33 for further information.

⊜ Sleeping

Managua *p613, maps p614, p616 and p617*
Accommodation is generally expensive in Managua. Martha Quezada has the most budget options, but it's unsafe in places. Note that the cheapest lodgings tend to charge per person, meaning some of the rates listed below will halve for single travellers.

Martha Quezada and around
LL-AL Hotel Crowne Plaza, 'el viejo Hotel Inter', in front of the Plaza Inter shopping centre, T2228-3530, www.crowneplaza.com. This is one of the most historic buildings in Managua, home to the foreign press for more

than a decade, Howard Hughes when he was already off the deep end, and the new Sandinista government briefly in the early 1980s. Some rooms have lake views, but are generally small for the price. Occasional good deals and discounts through the website.
A Mansión Teodolinda, INTUR, 1 c al sur, 1 c abajo, T2228-1060, www.teodolinda.com.ni. This hotel, popular with business people, has good quality, unpretentious rooms, all with private bath, hot water, safe, Wi-Fi, kitchenette, cable TV, telephone. There's also a pool, bar, restaurant, gym, vehicle rental agency, transportation to/from the airport and laundry service.
B El Conquistador, Plaza Inter, 100 m sur, 100 m abajo, T2222-4789, www.hotelel conquistador.info. 19 airy rooms with a/c, hot water, cable TV, telephone and Wi-Fi. There's a pleasant courtyard patio, and a range of services including tours, restaurant, parking, business centre and laundry. Prices include breakfast.
B-C Los Cisneros, Ticabus, 1c al norte, 1½ c abajo, T2222-3535, www.hotellos

cisneros.com. Comfortable apartments and rooms overlooking a lush garden with hammock space. All have cable TV, a/c, and Wi-Fi (at extra cost), but only the apartments have hot water. Los Cisneros can organize transit to the airport, tours all over the country, serves breakfast, offers legal advice and speaks English. Rooms and apartments are cheaper with fan (**C**). Recommended.

D Los Felipe, Ticabus, 1½ c abajo, T2222-6501, www.hotellosfelipe.com.ni. This hotel has a lovely garden, pool, restaurant, and many brightly coloured parrots. They're all caged, however, and in desperate need of stimulation. The 28 rooms have private bath, cable TV, Wi-Fi and telephone; cheaper (**E**) with fan. Almost a good deal for budget travellers, but can't really be recommended due to the cages.

D-E El Molinito, Ticabus, ½ c lago, T2222-2013. 14 small, basic rooms with private bath, TV and fan (**D**). Some ultra-cheap rooms have shared bath (**E**). Good value, simple, clean and hot during day. There's also a fridge available for clients. Friendly.

E Casa de Huéspedes Santos, Ticabus, 1 c al lago, 1½ c abajo, T2222-3713, www.casadehuespedessantos.com. Ramshackle cheapie with interesting (and slightly off-kilter) courtyard space and basic rooms. Some have bath, others have washbasins outside. There's a café, breakfast is served and internet is available (Wi-Fi or terminal). Friendly, popular, and a good place to meet travellers. They also do laundry.

E Hostal San Felipe, Ticabus, ½ c al lago, T2222-3178, hostalsanfelipe1@hotmail.com. Newish budget place near the bus station offering rooms with cable TV and fan. They come with or without private bath; some have hot water. There's also internet, parking, restaurant and laundry service.

Metrocentro

LL-AL Real Intercontinental Metrocentro, Metrocentro shopping plaza, T2276-8989, www.realhotelsandresorts.com. Nicaragua's finest international hotel, popular with business travellers. It has 157 rooms with hot water, a/c, telephone, Wi-Fi and cable TV. Facilities include pool, restaurant, bar and secretary service. Special weekend and multi-day rates with some tour operators. Certain rooms can be noisy on weekend nights. Recommended.

AL Hotel Los Robles, Restaurante La Marseillaise, 30 vrs al sur, T2270-1074, www.hotellosrobles.com. Managua's best B&B offers 14 comfortable rooms with classy furnishings, cable TV, a/c, hot water, Wi-Fi and luxurious bath tubs. The beautiful colonial interior is complimented by a lush, cool garden, complete with bubbling fountain. It's often full, so book in advance. Recommended.

B Hotel El Almendro, Rotonda Rubén Darío, 1 c sur, 3 c abajo (behind big wall, ring bell), T2270-1260, www.hotelelalmendro.com. 2 blocks from La UCA university, this private and secure hotel has comfortable, good quality rooms with hot water, a/c, cable TV, telephone and Wi-Fi. They also have a pool, pleasant garden space, private parking and studio apartments (**AL**) with kitchenette, cooking facilities and utensils. It's a decent choice, if University students aren't in annual protest (normally Nov-Dec). Breakfast included.

B Royal Inn Bed & Breakfast, Reparto San Juan, Calle Esperanza, No 553, T2278-1414, www.hroyalinn.com/en/. This intimate hotel has cosy rooms and good attention to detail. Services include hot water, a/c, cable TV, radio, Wi-Fi, garden, breakfast and very good coffee. The Nicaraguan touch.

F Managua Backpackers' Inn, Monte Los Olivos, 1 c al lago, 1 c abajo, ½ c al lago, Casa 55, T2267-0006, www.managuahostel.com. The only budget hostel in the Metrocentro area is kitted out with thrifty dorms (**E** with a/c) and simple private rooms (**D**). There's also a pool, hammocks and shared kitchen. They offer tourist information and are happy to help. Not bad.

Bolonia

A Hostal Real, opposite German Embassy, T2266-8133, www.hostalreal.com.ni. A very interesting and unusual hotel laden with exuberant antiques and art. Rooms vary greatly, and some of the interiors are exceptionally beautiful, particularly near the reception area. Very popular so book in advance. Wi-Fi and breakfast included.

A Hotel Europeo, Canal 2, 75 vrs abajo, T2268-2130, www.hoteleuropeo.com.ni. Each room is different, and some have interesting furnishings. The rooms out back are best. Features include a/c, private bath with hot water, cable TV and Wi-Fi. There's a restaurant, bar, business centre, secure parking, laundry service, guard and pool. Price includes continental breakfast. Staff are friendly and helpful. A quiet location.

A La Posada del Angel, opposite Iglesia San Francisco, T2268-7228, www.hotelposada delangel.com.ni. This hotel, filled with interesting art work and antique furniture, has lots of personality. Good, clean rooms have private bath, hot water, cable TV, a/c, minibar, Wi-Fi and telephone. There's a pool, restaurant, office centre and laundry service. Breakfast is included. Book in advance.

B Posadita de Bolonia, Canal 2, 3 c abajo, 75 m al sur, casa 12, T2268-6692, www.posadita debolonia.com.ni. This intimate hotel has 8 rooms with private bath, a/c, cable TV, telephone, Wi-Fi. It's in a quiet area, close to several galleries, and operates as a Costeña agent, selling plane tickets to the Corn Islands. The friendly owner speaks English and is helpful. Complete breakfast included.

Managua airport

A Best Western Las Mercedes, Km 11 Carretera Norte, directly across from international terminal of airport, T2255-9910, www.lasmercedes.com.ni. Conveniently located for flight connections, with large, tree-filled grounds, tennis court, pool and barber shop. Rooms are predictably comfortable, but check before accepting one. There can be noise and fumes from the airport during peak hours. Local phone calls can be made here when airport office is shut; the outdoor café is the best place to kill time while waiting for a plane.

Pacific beaches near Managua *p618*

LL Montelimar Resort, near Pochomil and Masachapa, T2269-6769, www.barcelomonte limarbeach.com. This expensive resort is becoming popular with package tours and is often booked solid Nov-Apr. It has a broad, unspoilt sandy beach ideal for bathing and surfing. The nearest public transport is 3 km away at Masachapa, taxi from Managua US$30 (70 km), or hire a car.

B Ticomo Mar, on the nicest part of Pochomil beach, T2265-0210. Best hotel in the region apart from Montelimar, but still poor value. Bungalows have private porches, kitchenettes, hot water, a/c, private bath.

C Hotel Palmas del Mar, La Boquita, centre of beach, T2552-8715. Beach front, private bath, a/c or fan, a bit noisy.

C Villas del Mar, just north of Pochimal centre, T2266-6661. Crowded, overpriced food, party atmosphere, use of swimming pool US$5 per person.

C-D Suleyka, Centro Turístico La Boquita, T8698-3355. Perched on the sand and overlooking the waves, **Hotel Suleyka** has a range of rooms, with or without a/c and sea views. Those downstairs are cheaper. Good restaurant attached. Friendly and recommended.

⊕ Eating

Managua *p613, maps p614, p616 and p617*
The Metrocentro shopping centre has lots of convenient fast food restaurants in its food court, including cheaper versions of good Nica restaurants like **Doña Haydée**, and **María Bonita**.

Martha Quezada

⊮ Rancho Tiscapa, gate at Military Hospital, 300 vrs sur, T2268-4290. Laid-back ranch-style eatery and bar. They serve traditional dishes like *indio viejo*, *gallo pinto* and *cuajada con tortilla*. Good food and a great, breezy view of new Managua and Las Sierras. Recommended.

†† La Casa de Los Mejía Godoy, Costado Oeste del Hotel Crowne Plaza, T2222-6110, www.losmejiagodoy.com. Mon-Tue 0800-1630, Wed-Sat 0800-1300. This famous terraced restaurant regularly hosts nationally renowned live music acts. They serve Nicaraguan cuisine, wholesome breakfasts and good, cheap lunch buffets (Mon-Fri only). Very popular and recommended.

† Comida a la Vista Buffet, Ticabus, 2 c abajo. Often packed out at lunchtime. Cheap buffet food.

† Mirna's, near Pensión Norma, 0700-1500. Good value breakfasts and *comidas*, lunch buffet 1200-1500 popular with travellers and Nicaraguans, friendly service. Recommended.

† Panadería Tonalli, Ticabus, 3 c arriba, ½ c al sur. Pleasant little bakery serving nutritious wholemeal breads, cakes, cookies and coffee. Proceeds go to social projects.

Metrocentro

††† Casa de las Nogueras, Av Principal Los Robles R 17, T2278-2506. A popular and often recommended high-class dining establishment serving fine international and Mediterranean cuisine on a pleasant colonial patio. The interior, meanwhile, boasts sumptuous and ornate decoration. A Managua institution.

††† María Bonita, Altamira, la Vicky, 1½ c abajo, T2270-4326. Mexican and Nicaraguan food, including a lunchtime buffet during the week. However, it's most popular on weekend nights, with live music and a noisy, happy crowd. Nice ambience and friendly staff.

†††-†† Marhaba, Hotel Seminole, 2 c sur, T2278-5725. Mediterranean cuisine served in an atmospheric setting. There are Turkish hookah pipes available for an after-dinner smoke, should you so desire. The kitchen is open late and the bar serves cocktails.

††† El Muelle, Intercontinental Metrocentro, 1½ c arriba, T2278-0056. Managua's best seafood. There's excellent *pargo al vapor* (steamed red snapper), *dorado a la parilla*, *cocktail de pulpo* (octopus), and great *ceviche*. It's a crowded, informal setting with outdoor seating. Highly recommended.

††† Garabato, Hotel Seminole, 2½ c sur, T2278-3156. A clean, popular restaurant serving classic Nicaraguan dishes to a mixed crowd of tourists and locals. Pleasant ambience, friendly service and charming rustic decor. There's occasional live music, souvenirs for sale and Wi-Fi too.

††† La Ballena que Cayó del Cielo, next to Camino de Oriente, T2277-3055. Good hamburgers, good grilled chicken, all in a laid-back open-air setting.

††† La Cocina de Doña Haydée, opposite Pastelería Aurami, Planes de Altamira, T2270-6100, www.lacocina.com.ni. Mon-Sun 0730-2230. Once a popular family kitchen eatery that has gone upscale. They serve traditional Nicaraguan food – try the *surtido* dish for 2, the *nacatamales* and traditional *Pío V* dessert, a sumptuous rum cake. Popular with foreign residents.

††† La Hora del Taco, Monte de los Olivos, 1 c al lago, on Calle Los Robles, T2277-5074. Good Mexican dishes including *fajitas* and *burritos*. A warm, relaxed atmosphere.

††† Las Brasas, in front of Cine Alhambra, Camino Oriente, T2277-5568, www.restaurantelasbrasas.com. This restaurant is the best value in town, serving decent, traditional Nicaraguan fare in an outdoor setting. It's a good place to come with friends and order a half bottle of rum; it comes with ice, limes, coke and 2 plates of food. Great atmosphere.

† Casa de Café, Lacmiel, 1 c arriba, 1½ c sur, T2278-0605. Mon-Sun 0700-2200. The mother of all cafés in Managua, with airy upstairs seating area that makes the average coffee taste much better. Good turkey sandwiches, desserts, pies and *empanadas*. There's another branch on the 2nd level of the Metrocentro shopping plaza, but it lacks the charm and fresh air. Popular and recommended.

El Guapinol, Metrocentro, www.restaurante elguapinol.com. The best of the food-court eateries with very good grilled meat dishes, chicken, fish and a hearty veggie dish (US$5). Try *Copinol* dish with grilled beef, avocado, fried cheese, salad, tortilla and *gallo pinto* US$4, from 1100 daily.

Bolonia

El Churrasco, Rotonda El Güegüence. This is where the Nicaraguan president and parliamentary members decide the country's future over a big steak. Try the restaurant's namesake which is an Argentine-style cut with garlic and parsley sauce. Recommended.

Santa Fe, across from Plaza Bolonia, T2268-9344. Tex-Mex style with walls covered in stuffed animal heads. It does a pretty good beef grill and *taco* salad, but bad *burritos*. Noisy and festive at lunchtime.

A La Vista Buffet, Canal 2, 2 c abajo, ½ c lago (next to Pulpería América). Lunch only 1130-1430. Nicaragua's best lunch buffet. They do a staggering and inexpensive variety of pork, chicken, beef, rice dishes, salads and vegetable mixers, plantains, potato crêpes and fruit drinks. Popular with local television crews and reporters, as well as local office workers, who are often queuing down the street at midday. Highly recommended.

Rincón Cuscatleco, behind Plaza Bolonia, T2266-4209. Daily 1200-2200. Good cheap *pupusas salvadoreñas*, also *vigorón* and *quesillos*. Cheap beer and very relaxed.

⊕ Entertainment

Managua p613, maps p614, p616 and p617
Bars and clubs
Bar Chamán, Porton Principal de la UCA, 1 km abajo, ½ c sur, T2272-1873, www.chamanbar.com US$3 entrance which includes US$1.50 drink coupon. A young, devout dancing crowd sweats it out to salsa, rock and *reggaeton*.

Hipa Hipa, Km 7.5 Carretera Masaya, Plaza Familiar, www.elhipa.com. Dress smartly for this popular disco, a favourite among Managua's rich kids. The best action is on Wed, Fri and Sat night, cover includes a few beverages.

La Casa de los Mejía Godoy, Costado Oeste del *Hotel Crowne Plaza*, T2222-6110, www.losmejiagodoy.com. This is a chance to see 2 of Nicaragua's favourite sons and most famous folk singers. A very intimate setting, check with on-line programme to make sure either Carlos or Luis Enrique is playing. Fri is a good bet, entrance US$10.

La Ruta Maya, Montoya, 150 m arriba, www.rutamaya.com.ni. Entrance US$5. Good bands play Thu-Sun, with reggae often on Thu, fine folk concerts and political satirists. Often features nationally and internationally renowned performers; check the website for programmes.

Santera, Costado Este de BAC, T2278-8585. In addition to live poetry, theatre and music performances, Santera features an eclectic mix of musical genres, including jazz, pop, reggae and salsa, The general ambience is low-key, relaxed, bohemian and friendly. Snacks and national beers are served.

Shannon Bar Irlandés, Ticabus, 1 c arriba, 1 c sur. Fabled Irish pub serving fast food, whisky and expensive Guinness. A Managua institution and popular with an international crowd.

Cinema
If possible, see a comedy; the unrestrained laughter of the Nicaraguan audience is sure to make the movie much funnier.

Alianza Francesa, Altamira, Mexican Embassy, ½ c norte, T2267-2811, www.alianzafrancesa.org.ni. French films every Wed and Sat at 2000, free admission, art exhibits during the day.

Cinemas Galerías 10, 2nd floor, Galerías Santo Domingo, Carretera a Masaya, T2276-5065, www.galerias.com.ni. Plush, modern and thoroughly a/c cinema in Managua's swankiest mall.

Cinemas Inter, Plaza Inter, T222-3828, www.cinemas.com.ni. 8 screens showing American films, subtitles in Spanish, buy weekend tickets in advance.
Cines Alhambra, 3 screens, Camino de Oriente, T2278-7278, www.cinesalhambra.com. Mostly US films with Spanish subtitles, occasional Spanish and Italian films, US$3, icy a/c. You'll find a second branch at Multicentro Las Americas, Bello Horizonte.
Metrocentro Cinemark, Metrocentro. T2271-9042, www.cinemarkca.com. 6 screens, small theatres with steep seating, very crowded so arrive early.

Dance and theatre
Ballet Tepenahuatl, folkloric dances at the Teatro Rubén Darío.
Doña Haydée, opposite **Pastelería Aurami**, Planes de Altamira, T2270-6100. Folkloric dance on Tue.
Intermezzo del Bosque, Colegio Centro-americano 5 km al sur, T8088-30071. On Wed, food, dances, US$40, check with **Delicias del Bosque**, or **Grayline Tours**, www.graylinenicaragua.com.
Teatro Nacional Rubén Darío, Frente al Malecón de Managua, T2222-7426.

⊛ Festivals and events

Managua *p613, maps p614, p616 and p617*
1-10 Aug The Festival de Santo Domingo (Managua's patron saint) is held at El Malecón church: ceremonies, horse racing, bullfights, cockfights, a lively carnival; proceeds go to the General Hospital. **1 Aug** (½ day) and **10 Aug** are local holidays.
7 Dec La Purísima, is held nationwide and is particularly celebrated in Managua. Altars are erected to the Virgin Mary, with singing, processions, fireworks and offerings of food.

○ Shopping

Managua *p613, maps p614, p616 and p617*
Handicrafts
Mercado Oriental is not recommended, see Safety, page 614.
Mercado Ricardo Huembes (also called **Mercado Central**), Pista Portezuelo, take bus No 110 or 119. The best place to buy handicrafts, and just about anything else. Artesanía from all parts of the country at the northeast end of the parking lot.
Mi Pueblo at Km 9.5 on Carretera Sur, T8882-5650. Handicrafts and plants and there's also a good restaurant.
Takesa, del Intercontinental 2 c al sur, ½ abajo, Edif Bolívar 203, T2268-3301. A smart shop selling Nicaraguan arts and crafts, high quality and high prices.

Shopping malls
In increasing order of prestige, the 3 big shopping malls are the **Plaza Inter**, **Metrocentro** and **Galerías Santo Domingo**.

▲ Activities and tours

Managua *p613, maps p614, p616 and p617*
Canopy tour
Tiscapa Canopy Tour, T8886-2836, www.canopytoursnicaragua.com. Tue-Sun 0900-1630, US$15. A breathtaking zip-line ride that is operated using 3 long metal cables and 4 platforms to traverse Tiscapa lake, at times more than 70 m in the air.

Spectator sports
The national sport and passion is **baseball**, with games on Sun mornings at the Estadio Denis Martínez. The season runs Nov-Feb and tickets cost US$1-5.

Tour operators
Careli Tours, Planes de Altamira, opposite the Colegio Pedagógico La Salle, T2278-6919, www.carelitours.com. One of Nicaragua's oldest tour operators with a professional

service, very good English-speaking guides and traditional tours to all parts of Nicaragua. **Gray Line Tours**, Lotería Nacional, 1c abajo, 1c sur, T2277-2097, www.graylinenicaragua. com. Good, professional company with a range of tours including good-value 1-day tours, night tours of Managua and folkloric performances. Manager Marlon speaks French and English.

Schuvar Tours, Plaza España Edif Bamer No 4, T2270-1010, www.schuvartours.com. Various cultural and adventure tours, transportation, car rental and flights.

Tours Nicaragua, Centro Richardson, contiguo al Banco Central de Nicaragua, T2265-3095, www.toursnicaragua.com. One of the best, offering captivating and personalized tours with a cultural, historical or ecological emphasis. Guides, transfers, accommodation and admission costs are included in the price. English-speaking, helpful, professional and highly recommended. All tours are private and pre-booked; no walk-ins.

⊖ Transport

Managua *p613, maps p614, p616 and p617*
Air
For **Managua International Airport (MGA)** Be early for international flights – formalities are slow and thorough. Artisan stalls and cheap food in between arrivals and departures. Duty free shops, café, toilets through immigration. You are not allowed to stay overnight. There are ATMs and money-changing facilities.

Domestic flights Tickets can be bought at the domestic terminal, which is located just west of the exit for arriving international passengers, or from travel agents or tour operators. Fuel and ticket prices are rising, and schedules are subject to change at any time. To **Bilwi**, 0630, 1030, 1430, US$97 one-way, US$148 return, 1½ hrs. To **Bluefields**, La Costeña, 0630, 1000, 1400, US$83 one-way, US$128 return, 1 hr. To **Corn Islands**, 0630, 1400, US$107

one-way, US$165 return, 1½ hrs; To **Minas**, 0900, US$92 one-way, US$139 return, 1 hr. To **San Carlos**, 1330, US$82 one-way, US$120 return, 1 hr. To **Waspam**, 1000, US$155 return, 1½ hrs. For return times see individual destinations.

Airline offices AeroCaribbean, Monte de los Olivos 1 c arriba, 15 vrs al lago. T2277-5191, aerocar@cablenet.com.ni. **AeroMéxico**, Optica Visión, 75 vrs arriba, 25 vrs al lago, T2266-6997, www.aero mexico.com. **American Airlines**, Rotunda El Güegünse 300 vrs al sur, T2255-9090, www.aa.com. **Continental Airlines**, Edificio Ofiplaza, segundo piso edificio 5, T2278-7033, www.continental.com. **Copa Airlines**, Carretera a Masaya Km 4.5 edificio CAR 6, T2267-0045, www.copaair.com. **Delta Airlines**, Hotel Seminole, 350 vrs sur, Casa 58, T2270-0535, www.delta.com. **Spirit Airlines**, International airport, T233-2884, www.spirit air.com. **Taca Airline**, Edificio Barcelona, Plaza España, T2266-6698, www.taca.com.

Bus
Local Due to safety concerns, crowded local buses are not recommended. Beware of pickpockets, particularly on tourist routes. City buses run every 10 mins 0530-1800, every 15 mins 1800-2200, when last services begin their routes; buses are frequent but routes are difficult to fathom. Tickets cost about US$0.20.

Long distance *Bus Expresos* are much faster than regular routes. Payment is required in advance and seat reservations are becoming more common. Stay focused and alert at the bus stations, and once on board, check the going fare with a fellow passenger to avoid extra charges. All fares and schedules below are subject to change.

La UCA (pronounced La 'OO-ka'), close to the Metrocentro, serves just a few destinations. The microbuses are cheap, fast and highly recommended if travelling to Granada, León or Masaya.

To **Granada**, every 15 mins or when full, 0530-2100, US$0.95, 1 hr. To **Diriamba**, every 30 mins or when full, 0530-2000, US$1.10, 45 mins. To **Jinotepe**, every 20 mins or when full, US$1.10, 1 hr. To **León**, every ½ hr, 0730-2100, US$1.90, 1½ hrs. To **Masaya**, every 15 mins or when full, 0530-2000, US$0.60, 40 mins.

Mercado Roberto Huembes, also called Mercado Central, is used for destinations southwest. To **Granada**, every 15 mins, 0520-2200, Sun 0610-2100, US$0.60, 1½ hrs. To **Masaya**, every 20 mins, 0625-1930, Sun until 1600, US$0.35, 50 mins. To **Peñas Blancas**, every 30 mins or when full, US$2.40, 2½ hrs; or go to Rivas for connections. To **Rivas**, every 30 mins, 0600-1900, US$1.90, 1¾ hrs. To **San Juan del Sur**, every 30 mins, 1000-1600, US$2.60, 2½ hrs; or go to Rivas for connections to **San Jorge** (ferry to Ometepe), every 30 mins, 0600-2100, US$1.90, 2 hrs; or go to Rivas for connections.

Mercado Mayoreo, for destinations east and then north or south. To **Boaco**, every 30 mins, 0500-1800, US$1.50, 2 hrs. To **Camoapa**, every 40 mins, 0630-1700, US$2.00, 3 hrs. To **El Rama**, 8 daily, 0500-2200, US$8, 8 hrs; express bus 1400, 1800, 2200, US$9.50, 6 hrs. To **Estelí**, every 30 mins, 0400-1800, US$2.20, 3½ hrs; express buses, hourly, 0600-1700, US$3.10, 2½ hrs. To **Jinotega**, hourly, 0400-1730, US$3.50, 3½ hrs; or go to Matagalpa for connections. To **Juigalpa**, every 20 mins, 0500-1730, US$2.50, 2½ hrs. To **Matagalpa** every 30 mins, 0330-1800, US$2, 2½ hrs; express buses, 12 daily, US$2.50, 2 hrs. To **Ocotal**, express buses, 12 daily, 0545-1745, US$4.50, 3½ hrs. To **San Rafael del Norte**, express bus, 1500, US$5, 4 hrs. To **San Carlos**, 0500, 0600, 0700, 1000, 1300, 1800, US$9, 7-10 hrs. To **Somoto**, hourly, 0400-2000, US$3.10, 3½ hrs.

Mercado Israel Lewites, also called Mercado Boer, for destinations west and northwest. Some microbuses leave from here too. To **Chinandega**, express buses, every 30 mins, 0600-1915, US$2.50, 2½ hrs. To **Corinto**, every hour, 0500-1715, US$3.50, 3 hrs. To **Diriamba**, every 20 mins, 0530-1930, US$1.10, 1 hr 15 mins. To **El Sauce**, express buses, 0745, 1445, US$3.25, 3½ hrs. To **Guasaule**, 0430, 0530, 1530, US$3.25, 4 hrs. To **Jinotepe**, every 20 mins, 0530-1930, US$0.50, 1 hr 30 mins. To **León**, every 30 mins, 0545-1645, US$1.25, 2½ hrs; express buses, every 30 mins, 0500-1645, US$1.50, 2 hrs; microbuses, every 30 mins or when full, 0600-1700, US$1.90, 1½ hrs. To **Pochomil**, every 20 mins, 0600-1920, US$0.80, 2 hrs.

International buses The cheap and efficient international buses are often booked up many days in advance and tickets will not be sold until all passport/visa documentation is complete. The best known is Ticabus, which parks in Barrio Martha Quezada, from Cine Dorado, 2 c arriba, T2222-6094, www.ticabus.com, with services throughout Central America. Other operators include **King Quality**, end of Calle 27 de Mayo, opposite Plaza Inter, T2228-1454, www.king-qualityca.com and Transnica, Rotonda de Metrocentro 300 m al lago, 50 m arriba, T2277-3133, www.transnica.com.

To **Costa Rica** Ticabus, 0600, 0700, 1200, US$23, executive class US$36, 8 hrs; King Quality, 1330, US$43, 8½ hrs; Transnica, 0530, 0700, 1000, 1200 (executive), US$23, executive service US$46, 8½ hrs.

To **El Salvador** Ticabus, 0500, US$35, executive class US$49, 11 hrs; King Quality, 0330 (quality), 0530 (cruceros), 1130 (King), 'Cruceros class', US$30, 'Quality Class' US$49, 'King Class' US$74, 11 hrs.

To **Guatemala** Ticabus, 0500, US$52, executive class US$67, 30 hrs including an overnight stay in El Salvador; King Quality, 0230 (cruceros), 1530 (quality/king), 'Cruceros class' US$63, 'Quality Class' US$70, 'King Class' US$96, 15 hrs.

To **Honduras (Tegucigalpa)** Ticabus, 0500, US$23, 8 hrs, then continues to San Pedro Sula, US$37, 10 hrs; King Quality,

0330 (king), 1130 (quality), 'Quality Class' US$41, 'King Class' US$68, 8½ hrs.

To **Mexico (Tapachula)** Ticabus, 0500, US$74, executive class US$89, 36 hrs, including overnight stay in El Salvador; **King Quality**, 'Quality Class' US$78, 'King Class' US$100.

To **Panama** Ticabus, 0600, 0700, 1200, US$63, executive class US$87, 28-32 hrs, including a 2- to 6-hr stopover in Costa Rica.

Car

All car hire agencies have desks at the international airport arrivals terminal. It is not a good idea to rent a car for getting around Managua, as it is a confusing city and fender benders are common and an injury/accident means you could go to jail, even if not at fault. Outside the capital main roads are better marked and a rental car means you can get around more freely.

For good service and 24-hr roadside assistance, the best rental agency is **Budget**, with rental cars at the airport, T2263-1222, and **Holiday Inn**, T2270-9669. Their main office is just off Carretera Sur at Montoya, 1 c abajo, 1 c sur, T2255-9000. Average cost of a small Toyota is US$50 per day while a 4WD (a good idea if exploring) is around US$100 per day with insurance and 200 km a day included; 4WD weekly rental rates range from US$600-750. Check website for details: www.budget.com.ni.

Taxi

Taxis (the best method of transport for foreigners) can be flagged down on the street. Fares range from US$1.50-2 for a short trip, US$2-3.50 across town, US$7-15 to airport. Due to safety concerns, avoid shared *colectivos*. Once a destination is agreed with the driver, ask how much (*¿por cuánto me lleva?*) before getting in. Street names and numbers are not universal and the driver may not know your destination; have the telephone number of your hotel with you. Taxis from the airport are 50% cheaper from the main road beyond the car park.

Radio taxis are recommended for early flights or late-night transport. Companies include: **Co-op 25 de Febrero**, T2222-4728, or **Co-op 2 de Agosto**, T2263-1512, get price quote on the phone (normally 80-100% more expensive).

⊙ Directory

Managua *p613, maps p614, p616 and p617*
Banks
Any bank in Nicaragua will change US$. TC purchase receipts may be required in banks when changing TCs. The best 2 banks for foreigners are **Banco de América Central (BAC)** and **Banco de Finanzas (BDF)**. BAC offers credit card advances, uses the Cirrus debit system and changes all TCs with a 5% commission. **BDF** changes Amex TCs only, also with a 5% commission. In Managua ATM machines are found in the airport, at the Metrocentro and Plaza Inter shopping malls and in many gas station convenience stores ('Red Total'). There are also money changers, but take care, some of them are tricksters. See page 610 for more details.

Embassies and consulates
Austria, Rotonda El Güegüense, 1 c al norte, T2266-3316. **Argentina**, Las Colinas C Prado Ecuestre 235B, T2276-2654. **Brasil**, Km 7.5 carretera sur, T2265-0035. **Canada**, Bolonia Los Pipitos, 2 c abajo, T2264-2723. Mon-Thu 0900-1200. **Costa Rica**, Las Colinas II Entrada, 1 c al lago, 1 c arriba, T2276-0115. 0900-1500. **China**, Altamira 3a etapa, Panadería Sampsons 50 m al lago, T2267-4024. **Colombia**, Las Colinas 2nd entrance, 1 c arriba ½ c al lago No 97, T2276-2149. **Denmark**, Bolonia Salud Integral, 2 c al lago, 50 vrs abajo, T2254-5059. **Finland**, Edificio El Centro, 2nd floor, rotonda El Güegüense, 600 m al sur, T2278-1216. 0800-1200, 1300-1500. **France**, Iglesia El Carmen, 1½ c abajo, T2222-6210, 0800-1600. **Germany**, Plaza España, 200 m lago, T2266-3917. Mon-Fri 0900-1200. **Guatemala**, just after Km 11 on Carretera a Masaya,

T2279-9835. Fast service, 0900-1200 only.
Honduras, Las Colinas No 298, T2276-2406.
Italy, Rotonda El Güegüence, 1 c lago,
T2266-6486. 0900-1200. Japan, Rotonda el
Güegüence 1 c abajo, 1 c al lago, T2266-1773.
Mexico, Km 4.5, Carretera a Masaya, 1 c arriba,
T2278-1859. **Netherlands,** Colegio Teresiano,
1c sur, 1 c abajo, T2276-8630. **Panamá,** Col
Mantica, el Cuartel General de Bomberos,
1 c abajo, No 93, T/F2266-8633. 0830-1300,
visa on the spot, valid 3 months for a 30-day
stay, US$10, maps and information on the
Canal. **Russia,** Frente Colegio Dorís María 164,
T2276-2005. **Spain,** Av Las Colinas, Central
No 13, T2276-0966. **Sweden,** Plaza España,
1 c abajo, 2 c lago, ½ c abajo, Apdo Postal
2307, T2255-8400. 0800-1200. **Switzerland,**
Banpro Las Palmas, 1 c abajo, T266-3010. **UK,**
La Fise, 40 vrs abajo, T2278-0014. 0900-1200.
USA, Km 4.5, Carretera del Sur, T2266-6010.
0730-0900. **Venezuela,** Km 10.5, Carretera
a Masaya, T2276-0267.

Emergencies
Police: T118 in an emergency; the local police
station number will depend on what *distrito*
you are in. Start with the Metrocentro area
number, T2265-0651. **Fire:** T115 in an
emergency; the central number is T2265-
0162. **Red Cross:** T128 in an emergency.

Immigration and customs
See Essentials, page 611.

Internet
Lots of places, especially in and around Plaza
Inter, María Quezada and Metrocentro. Most
internet cafés are open daily, charge around
US$0.60 per hr and also offer internet calls.

Language schools
Casa Nicaragüense de Español, Km 11.5
Carretera Sur, Spanish classes and a thorough
introduction to Nicaragua, accommodation
with families. **Huellas,** Col Centroamérica,
Callejón El Ceibo G-414, T2277-2079, intensive
classes, private classes and regular classes
(0880-1200). **Nicaragua Spanish School,**

Rotonda Bello Horizonte, 2 c al sur, 2 c arriba,
T2244-4512, regular and private classes.
Universidad Americana, Centro de Idiomas
Extranjeros, T2278-3800 ext 301, open course
with flexible hours and regular 5-month
course. **Universidad Centroamericana (UCA),**
Centro de Idiomas Extranjeros, T2278-3923,
ext 242-351, 5-week regular classes of all levels
and open classes with flexible hours.

Medical services
Dentists Dr Claudia Bendaña, T2277-1842
and **Dr Mario Sánchez Ramos,** T2278-1409,
T2278-5588 (home). **Doctors** Internal
medicine, **Dr Enrique Sánchez Delgado,**
T2278-1031; **Dr Mauricio Barrios,** T2255-
6900. **Hospitals** The best are Hospital
Metropolitano Vivian Pellas, Km 9.5 Carretera a Masaya, 250 vrs abajo, T2255-6900,
www.metropolitano.com.ni; **Hospital
Bautista,** near Mercado Oriental, T2264-
9020, www.hospitalbautistanicaragua.com;
Hospital Militar, T2222-2763 (go south from
Hotel Crowne Plaza and take 2nd turn on
left); and **Hospital Alemán-Nicaragüense,**
Km 6 Carretera Norte Siemens, 3 blocks south,
T2249-0611, operated with German aid,
mostly Nicaraguan staff. Make an appointment by phone in advance if possible.

Post
21 locations around Managua, the main
post office for the country is 1 block west of
Parque Central. Wide selection of beautiful
stamps. **Poste Restante** (*Lista de Correos*)
keeps mail for 45 days, US$0.20 per letter.
There is another post office in the Centro
Comercial Managua and at the airport.

Telephone
Inside the Edificio Enitel, **Claro** has telephone,
mobile, fax and internet services, T2222-7272,
www.claro.com.ni. **Movistar,** Km 6.5
Carretera a Masaya, Edificio Movistar,
T2277-0708, www.movistar.com.ni, is the
main competitor. Many cybercafés facilitate
national and international calls, as well as
Skype (internet calls).

Northern Highlands

Nicaragua's ruggedly beautiful northern mountains and valleys have staged much of the history that has given the country its dubious international reputation. This is where Sandino fought the US occupation of Nicaragua from 1927 to 1933 and where the rebel Sandinistas launched their first attacks against the Somoza administration in the 1960s. Then, in the 1980s, the Contras waged war against the Sandinista government in these mountains. Today, most visitors would be hard pressed to see where all this aggression came from. Most of the northern ranges and plains are full of sleepy villages with ancient churches, rustic cowboys and smiling children. Nothing is rushed here and many of the region's villages are evidence that time travel is indeed possible, with the 21st century in no danger of showing itself any time soon. ▶▶ *For listings, see pages 634-641.*

North from Managua

The Pan-American Highway leaves Managua just north of the international airport and runs into Nicaragua's most beautiful non-volcanic mountains all the way to Honduras. The Pan-American Highway forks at the junction of **Sébaco**, where delicious fresh vegetables and other local produce are sold. To the east, the Carretera a Matagalpa rises through the charming village of Chaguitillo, eventually arriving in **Matagalpa** and **Jinotega** – the heart of coffee-growing country. To the northwest, the highway continues on a 134-km journey to the Honduran border, passing numerous historic locales, including **La Trinidad**, an attractive mountain village set in a canyon, and the popular city of **Estelí**. Roughly 10 km northwest of Sébaco on the Pan-American Highway, near **San Isidro**, a reasonable road branches west to join the Pacific Highway near León (110 km). Buses run from Estelí to San Isidro every 30 minutes (1½-two hours, US$0.50), and San Isidro to León every 30 minutes (three to four hours, US$1.50).

Matagalpa and around → *For listings, see pages 634-641. Colour map 3, C4. Altitude: 672 m.*

Set in a broad valley circled by green mountains, including the handsome Cerro de Apante at 1442m, Matagalpa appears quite attractive at a distance, but less so close up. The city has prospered in recent years, thanks not only to increased coffee production, but also the fact that it boasts a high percentage of high-quality shade-grown coffee and has developed organic growing practices, which bring the highest prices. The local festival and holiday on 26 September celebrates the **Virgen de las Mercedes**.

Although the main attraction of Matagalpa is the sublime beauty that lies just outside it, the **Catedral de San Pedro de Matagalpa** (1897) is worth a visit and there are two other city churches that are pleasant: the late-19th-century **Templo de San José de Laborio** in front of the Parque Darío and the primitive Nicaraguan baroque **Iglesia de Molagüina**, which is the oldest church in Matagalpa, believed to date from 1751. The city and region's most unique artisan craft is the beautiful *cerámica negra* (black pottery), and it is possible to visit one of the city's ceramic cooperatives. The **Coffee Museum** ① *on the main avenue, Parque Morazán, 1½ c sur, 0800-1230, 1400-1900*, exhibits photographs and antique objects used in the early days of coffee production in Matagalpa.

For tourist information, **INTUR** ① *alcaldía, 1 c arriba, ½ c al sur, T772-7060*, has limited, patchy details on local attractions. **Matagalpa tours** ① *Banpro, ½ c arriba, T772-0108*, *www.matagalpatours.com*, are an excellent source of information, with a thorough knowledge of the city and the surrounding mountains; they speak Dutch and English.

Around Matagalpa

A 32-km road runs from Matagalpa east to the Tuma Valley and the largely indigenous town of **San Ramón**, founded by a friar from León, José Ramón de Jesús María, in 1800. Beyond Ramón is **Yacúl**, a place made famous in recent years by its well-managed ecolodge and

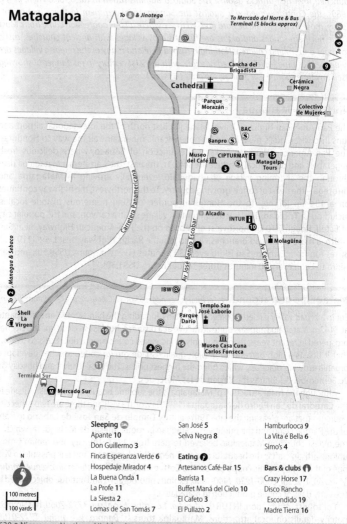

Matagalpa

To 8 & Jinotega

To Mercado del Norte & Bus Terminal (5 blocks approx)

To 6 6 7

Cancha del Brigadista

Cathedral

Cerámica Negra

Parque Morazán

Colectivo de Mujeres

BAC

Banpro $

Museo del Café

CIPTURMAT

Matagalpa Tours 15

Alcadía

INTUR 10

Molagüina

Carretera Panamericana

Av. José Benito Escobar

Av. Central

To 2, Managua & Sébaco

IBW

Shell La Virgen

Templo San José Laborio

Parque Darío

17 10

19

2

4

16

4

11

Museo Casa Cuna Carlos Fonseca

Terminal Sur

Mercado Sur

N

100 metres
100 yards

Sleeping
Apante **10**
Don Guillermo **3**
Finca Esperanza Verde **6**
Hospedaje Mirador **4**
La Buena Onda **1**
La Profe **11**
La Siesta **2**
Lomas de San Tomás **7**

San José **5**
Selva Negra **8**

Eating
Artesanos Café-Bar **15**
Barrista **1**
Buffet Maná del Cielo **10**
El Cafeto **3**
El Pullazo **2**

Hamburlooca **9**
La Vita é Bella **6**
Simo's **4**

Bars & clubs
Crazy Horse **17**
Disco Rancho
  Escondido **19**
Madre Tierra **16**

Café Nicaragüense: from German to gourmet

Large-scale coffee growing in Nicaragua is directly tied to German immigration, promoted by 19th-century Nicaraguan governments that offered 500 *manzanas* (350 ha) of land to any investor who would plant 25,000 coffee trees, bringing migrant planters from Germany, US, England, France and Italy.

The pioneer of Nicaragua coffee planting was Ludwing Elster, originally from Hanover, and his wife Katharine Braun, from Baden Baden who settled in Matagalpa in 1852. In 1875, Wilhelm Jericho arrived and founded the Hacienda Las Lajas, promising to lure 20 more German families to Nicaragua. When the Nicaraguan government started offering the 500 *manzanas* free to inspire production, more than 200 foreign families settled and began growing coffee in Matagalpa and neighbouring Jinotega.

At the time, Colombia had yet to become a coffee producer and the Nicaraguan product was considered among the world's best, along with coffee from Costa Rica and Guatemala. The international coffee price was US$8 for a 100 pound sack of coffee.

Today Nicaraguan coffee is planted on more than 160,000 *manzanas* by 30,000 different farms with country-leader Jinotega producing around 680,673 100-lb bags of coffee a year, followed by Matagalpa at 624,818 bags, and the province of Nueva Segovia with 193,435 bags. The country's best coffee export customers are the USA, Spain, Belgium and France.

The push for high-quality organic shade coffee has lifted Nicaragua to sixth place in the world in gourmet coffee production, with an annual output of organic coffee three times greater than Costa Rica, and Nicaragua's organic coffee now draws frequent international acclaim. In a survey by *Coffee Review*, two of the top four ranked brews in the world were Nicaraguan. Matagalpa organic coffee grower Byron Corrales is now charging US$200 for his 100-lb sacks (above an average market price US$75 per sack) after the industry magazine *Coffee Review* gave his coffee 94 out of 100 points ranking it number two in the world. They raved that the Matagalpa-grown coffee was a "fruity and richly floral coffee – papaya, lemon, coffee fruit, hints of dusk-blooming flowers and chocolate, all ride a strong, balanced structure: good body, smooth, supple, sweet acidity."

private nature reserve, **Esperanza Verde** ① *office in San Ramón, from the Catholic church, 1½ c al este, T2772-5003, www.fincaesperanzaverde.com*. There are few finer places in Nicaragua for birdwatching and enjoying the nature of the northern mountains. The award-winning reserve has a butterfly-breeding project, organic shade-grown coffee, hiking trails and great views. Buses to Yucul run from Matagalpa's north terminal.

North from Matagalpa, a rough road spirals to Jinotega, rising out of the valley and into one of the most scenic paved highways in the north, lined by highland farms, virgin cloud forest and breathtaking views of the surrounding valleys and mountains. At Km 139.5, an old Somoza-era tank destroyed by rebels marks the entrance to **Selva Negra** ① *T2772-3883, www.selvanegra.com*, a private rainforest reserve and organic coffee *finca* with hiking trails, interesting Germanic cottages and good birdwatching. **Disparte de Potter** ① *Km 143, T2612-6228*, is a famous restaurant named after a local English eccentric. Futher north, at Km 145.5, lies the entrance to the **Reserva Natural Arenal**, one of the finest cloud forest reserves in Nicaragua. It promises great birdwatching, particularly on the **Sendero Los Quetzales**.

Jinotega and around → *Colour map 3, C4. Population: 33,000. Altitude: 641 m.*

Jinotega is a pleasant, friendly town which has famous images in the church; if it's closed, ask around. The jail, which was used in the years of the Somoza dictatorship, has been converted into a youth centre. There are several banks near the main plaza. **Alianza Turística** ① *Alcaldía, 2 c arriba, 1½ al sur, Spanish only*, has good information on the town. **INTUR**① *Texaco, 1 c norte, T2782-2166*, is also worth a try. A beautiful hike, which starts from behind the cemetery, leads up to the cross above the city (1½-hour round trip). As with Matagalpa, excellent coffee is grown in the region. One road leads from Jinotega to El Tuma power station (18 km); another, unpaved and picturesque, goes to Estelí, through La Concordia, but there's very little transport between La Concordia and Estelí.

Around Jinotega

Eight kilometres east of Jinotega is the beautiful **Lago de Apanás** (buses every hour from Jinotega, 20 minutes, US$0.35), an artificial lake created by the damming of the Río Tuma. The lake is used to produce energy in a hydroelectric plant and is great for fishing, full of *guapote* (perch) and *tilapia*. Small enterprises lining the lake will fry fish for visitors and it's possible to rent a small boat and fish on the lake; ask the locals.

The paved highway north of Jinotega leads to **San Rafael del Norte**. There are some good murals in the local church, and a chapel on the hill behind, at Tepeyak, built as a spiritual retreat. The town was involved in the Sandinista struggle and its recent history is very interesting. The **Museo General Sandino** ① *in the Casa Museo Ejército Defensor de La Soberanía Nacional; if locked, ask for the key at the mayor's house across the street*, is where Sandino used to send off telegrams to his troops in different parts of the northern hills. The young woman to whom he dictated his messages became his wife and the town has claimed him as their native son ever since.

Estelí → *For listings, see pages 634-641. Colour map 3, C3. Population: 73,000. Altitude: 844 m.*

Estelí is a rapidly developing departmental capital, heavily damaged during the Revolution of 1978 to 1979. It's not especially attractive, but it is dynamic, with a large student population injecting life into an otherwise humdrum agricultural centre. Worth visiting is the **Casa de Cultura**, which has a small exhibition of petroglyphs found in the area and of military memorabilia, and the **Galería de los Héroes y Mártires**, next door, with mementoes and photographs of those killed defending the Revolution and moving paintings on the outside walls. Many cooperatives and support organizations were developed in the aftermath of the Revolution. One of them, the **Asociación de Ex-combatientes Históricos 18 de Mayo** ① *Calle Principal, ½ c south of the Plaza de la Cathedral*, is good and has some crafts and a café with posters all over the walls. The **Ministry of Health Information Centre** ① *Calle Principal, 4 blocks from the Plaza*, is involved with projects to revive traditional medicine and healing and offers advice on a wide range of herbal remedies. Estelí is known as the capital of cigars, with the finest tobacco in Central America grown in the surrounding hills. The town is full of factories, some of which produce the best *puros* in the world and allow visitors to observe the rolling process. **Treehuggers Tourism office** ① *inside Hospedaje Luna, catedral, 1 c al norte, 1 c arriba, T8441-8466, www.cafeluzyluna.com*, can help arrange visits and is the best source of travel information in Estelí. Alternatively, head to the **INTUR office** ① *southwest corner of Parque Central, ½ c abajo, 2nd floor, T2713-6799, 0800-1300*.

Estelí

To Somoto & Honduras

To Cigar Factory
(Segovia Cigars)

Crafts

@Computer
Soluciones
Parque
Central

Cathedral

Shell

Artesanía
Sorpresa

Amnlae
Women's
Centre

Supermercado
Palí

El Salvador
Cooperative

Ministry of Health
Information Centre

Cenac
Language School

Craft

Parque
Infantil

Shell

Bus Station
North

Gran Vía Bolívar

Principal

To 6

Carretera Panamericana

C 4 NE
C 2 NE
C 1 NE
C Perú
C 1 SE
C 2 SE
C 3 SE
C 5 SE
C 7 SE
C 9 SE
C 11 SE

To 11 15 16 10, Buses
South & Managua

N

100 metres
200 yards

Sleeping
Casa Nicarao 7
Don Vito 1
El Mesón 3
Hospedaje Luna 4
Hospedaje
  San Francisco 11
Hostal Tomabu 5
Los Arcos 12
Moderno 6

Eating
Ananda 1
Café Luz 2
Cafetería El Rincón
  Pinareño 7
Cohifer 3
Koma Rico 8
La Casita 10
Pullaso's Ole 4
Sopas El Carao 6
Vuela Vuela 9

Bars & clubs
Cigarzone 11
El Chamán 15
Semáforo Rancho 16

Around Estelí → For listings, see pages 634-641. Colour map 3, C3.

Reserva Miraflor → Altitude: 800-1500 m.

Miraflor is a 5675-ha nature reserve 28 km northeast of Estelí in the Department of Jinotega. It contains the **Laguna de Miraflor** and has a wide range of flora and fauna (including the quetzal). The **Unión de Cooperativas Agropecuarias (UCA) Miraflor** ① *costado noreste de la catedral 2 c arriba, ½ c sur, T2713-2971, www.miraflor. org*, manages the reserve, but ecotourism is now handled by the **Treehuggers Tourism office** (see page 632), which you should approach before visiting the reserve. The cooperative can provide wooden huts, basic facilities and accommodation (E), meals, horse hire (US$7 per day) and guided walks (US$15 for one to three people).

El Sauce and around

A very poor gravel road just north of Estelí runs to El Sauce where there is a large 16th-century church (burnt down in 1997 and refurbished in 2002). It's a place of pilgrimage and people come from all over Central America to visit the black **Christ of Esquipulas**, celebrated in a giant festival that culminates 15-18 January. After 20 km, an equally rough road branches north to **Achuapa**, beyond which an unmade road continues through the *artesanía* town of **San Juan de Limay** (one *hospedaje*), famous thoughout Nicaragua for its great **soapstone carvings**. The artists are happy to invite you into their house to watch them carve (average sculpture costs US$8 or less). Further on, **Pueblo Nuevo** (two basic *hospedajes*) is near an archaeological site. From here the road goes on to join the Pan-American Highway just east of Somoto.

Condega → Population: 8000. Altitude: 561 m.

From Estelí, the Pan-American goes north to Condega, a quiet town. Its name means 'pottery makers' and the indigenous village was once known for its ceramics. Some of the country's most beautiful pottery is still made here and visitors are welcome at the **Ducuale Grande Ceramic Cooperative** ① *opposite Colegio Ana Velia de Guillén, T2752-2374,* a women's co-op that makes attractive red-clay earthenware; there's a small shop attached. Condega has a small and well-kept **archaeological museum** ① *Casa de Cultura de Condega, Plaza Central, Julio C Salgado, opposite the Policía Nacional, T2752-2221, Tue-Sun 0800-1200, 1400-1800,* with permanent expositions of discoveries from the region.

Somoto → *Population: 14,000. Altitude: 700 m.*

Continuing along the highway you reach Somoto, a pleasant town in a lovely setting. Recent excavations have uncovered unusual pre-Columbian remains which are on display at the **Museo Arqueológico de Somoto** ① *on the Parque Central, Mon-Fri 0800-1200.* The town is famous for the best *rosquillas* (a traditional toasted food, dry but tasty, made of egg, cheese, cornmeal and butter) in Nicaragua. Try the *viejita*, which also has pure cane sugar in the centre. Some 15 km north of Somoto is one of Nicaragua's most impressive canyons, a national monument well worth visiting. It's a moderate and slippery 3-km hike from a highway exit, best reached by taxi (US$4). A guide is recommended, but not essential.

Ocotal → *Colour map 3, C3. Population: 27,000. Altitude: 606 m.*

From Somoto a road turns off right to Ocotal (18 km), a clean, cool, whitewashed town on a sandy plain and well worth a visit. The Parque Central is lush, verdant and one of Nicaragua's most attractive plazas. Ocotal is near the Honduran border, to which a road runs north (bus marked Las Manos), and the scenery is wonderful. From Ciudad Sandino – formerly Jícaro – 50 km east from Ocotal, you can get to **San Albino**, where there are many gold mines and the nearby Río Coco is used to wash the gold.

⦿ Northern Highlands listings

For Sleeping and Eating price codes and other relevant information, see Essentials pages 31-33.

⦿ Sleeping

Matagalpa and around *p629, map p630*
Many places shut their doors by 2200-2300. The town has an erratic water supply and possible shortages Mar-Apr.
B Lomas de San Tomás, Escuela Guanuca 400 m este, T2772-4189, snthomas2006@ yahoo.com. The most luxurious hotel in the region. 26 spacious rooms have private bath and hot water, cable TV, telephone, Wi-Fi and minibar. Attractive grounds and great views, but not very central. Good reports.
C Don Guillermo, Enitel, 25 vrs oeste, T2772-3182. A new, tastefully attired hotel with 7 big, clean, comfortable, good-value

rooms. Each has cable TV, hot water and Wi-Fi. Breakfast is included and there's a night guard on the door. Recommended.
D Hotel San José, behind Iglesia San José, T2772-2544, hotelsnjose2009@yahoo.es. 12 comfortable, clean rooms with able TV, fan and hot water (**C** with a/c). On the small side but not bad. There's a pleasant garden and services include Wi-Fi, laundry and parking.
E Hotel Apante, west side of Parque Darío, T2772-6890. 14 simple rooms with private bath, hot water and cable TV. The management's friendly, there's Wi-Fi and free water and coffee 24 hrs. OK.
E Hotel La Profe, Shell el Progreso, 20 vrs norte, T2772-2506. A pleasant, family-run place. Simple, tidy rooms have cable TV, fan, private bath and hot water (**F** with shared bath). Not bad.

E Hotel La Siesta, Texaco, 1½ oeste, T2772-2476. A clean, tidy, friendly hotel. Rooms have hot water, cable TV and fan. Cheaper with shared bath (**F**). There's internet facilities, international call centre and a café too.

F La Buena Onda, El Brigadista, 2½ c este, T2772-2135, www.hostelmatagalpa.com. This great new hostel has a range of clean, comfortable dorms, each with private bath. There's also some spacious private rooms (**D**), a library, TV room, DVDs, free coffee, laundry service and a good restaurant attached (see below). For longer-term stays there's an apartment available at US$400/month. Friendly and helpful with good connections to **Matagalpa Tours**. Recommended.

G Hospedaje Mirador, Parque Darío, 1½ c abajo, T2772-4084. 27 simple, bare-bones rooms around a courtyard, all have shared bath and no fan. Ramshackle and ultra-basic, but the price can't be beaten.

Around Matagalpa

A-B Selva Negra, T2772-3883, www.selva negra.com. A range of rooms (**B**), and Germanic cottages (**A**) on the edge of the rainforest. Large 4-person units for families too (**L-AL**). See also page 631.

B Finca Esperanza Verde, office in San Ramón, Iglesia Católica, 1½ c este, T2772-5003, www.fincaesperanzaverde.org. This famous ecolodge has a range of hand-some wood and brick cabins with covered patios, solar power, private bath and bunk beds. Various packages are available; consult the website for more. There's also camping at US$6 per person. See also page 631.

C Hacienda San Rafael, on the road to La Dalia, T2612-2229. This lovely organic coffee farm is the producer of the fine **Café de los Reyes**. Lodging is in an attractive wooden lodge that affords some spectacular views of surrounding mountains above well-manicured gardens. The 270-ha farm has short nature paths, 1 leading to a small waterfall. Rooms have 1 shared bath, meals are available, reservations only.

Jinotega and around *p632*
Most hotels and restaurants lock their doors at 2200, Fri-Sun 2300.

A-D El Jaguar Cloud Forest Reserve, T2279-9219 (Managua), www.jaguarreserve. org. 2 wood cabins **A** at the edge of the forest with spectacular views if clear, private baths, small kitchens and living space and a biological station with dorm rooms **D**.

B Hotel Café and Restaurant Borbon, Texaco, 1 c abajo, ½ c norte, T2782-2710. The best hotel in the province has 25 very nice, comfortable rooms with private bath, hot water, a/c, Wi-Fi, cable TV. Elegant, quiet and friendly with a good restaurant attached (♛♛-♛♛) serving traditional dishes.

D Hotel Sollentuna Hem, Esso, 1 c arriba, 2½ c norte, T2782-2334, sollentuna.hem@ gmail.com. This clean, safe, family hotel has 16 rooms, all with private bath, cable TV, fan and hot water. The owner lived in Sweden for many years, and offers a range of beauty treatments including massage and pedicure. Pleasant and professional.

D La Quinta, Parque Central, 7 c norte, over the bridge, T2782-2522, becquerfernandez@ yahoo.ca. This Nicaraguan mini-resort has a pleasant setting among the pine trees. There's a range of rooms and cabins (**B**), all comfortable and well-equipped with cable TV, private bath and hot water. Amenities include Wi-Fi, parking, a pool, restaurant, karaoke bar and disco. Helpful English-speaking management. Recommended.

E Hotel Central, catedral, ½ c norte, T2782-2063, abrahaniarivera@yahoo.com. 20 plain, simple, newly renovated rooms of varying quality. Rooms upstairs have private bath, cable TV and a great mountain views. Convenient central location, as the name might suggest.

Estelí *p632, map p633*
B Hotel Los Arcos, northeast corner of the Cathedral, ½ norte, T2713-3830, www.familiasunidas.org/hotelosarcos.htm. This brightly painted, professionally managed and comfortable hotel has 32 clean, spacious

rooms with private bath, a/c or fan, and cable TV. The attached restaurant, **Vuela Vuela**, is also reputable, and profits go to social projects. Breakfast included.

C Hotel Don Vito, Parque Infantil, 1½ c arriba, T2713-4318, www.hoteldonvito esteli.com. A comfortable new business hotel with 26 clean, generic, well-appointed rooms. Most have hot water, a/c and cable TV, but there a few cheaper ones have fan (**D**). Other services include restaurant, laundry and Wi-Fi.

D Casa Hotel Nicarao, central plaza, 1½ c sur, T2713-2490. 9 clean, comfortable rooms with fan and private bath, all set around a relaxing, sociable courtyard filled with plants, paintings and sitting space. Very friendly management and a nice atmosphere, but the walls are a bit thin. There are cheaper rooms without bath (**E**).

D El Mesón, Av Bolívar, central plaza, 1 c norte, T2713-2655, hotelelmeson-esteli.com. Clean, comfortable rooms at this friendly, helpful hotel, all with hot water and cable TV. There's also Wi-Fi, parking and a restaurant, as well as a good travel agency next door and an *artesanía* shop over the road. Recommended.

D Hostal Tomabú, Opposite the Parque Infantil, T8914-3963, hostaltomabu.esteli@ gmail.com. Friendly, family-run hotel whose name means 'place of the sun'. They have 15 good, clean rooms with hot water, fan and cable TV. Bright colours and potted flowers. Lots of connections with tour operators and professional, personal attention. Recommended.

E Moderno, catedral, 2½ c sur, T2713-2378. Clean and comfortable rooms with a/c, hot water and cable TV (cheaper with fan). There's a restaurant for guests and breakfast is included. Friendly desk staff and Wi-Fi. Not bad, recommended.

F Hospedaje Luna, catedral, 1 c al norte, 1 c arriba, T8441-8466, www.cafeluzyluna.com. This popular hostel is part of an excellent non-profit social enterprise. Facilities include 2 dorms, 2 private rooms (**E**), hammock space, an activities board, tourist information, DVDs, lockers, tours and drinking water.

Volunteer work in Miraflor can be arranged here – 3 months commitment and Spanish speakers preferred. Discounts for longer stays and groups. Highly recommended.

F Hospedaje San Francisco, next to Parque Infantil. Just one of a handful of cheapies in this area. Rooms are basic and clean with outside bathroom. The hotel is friendly and pleasant enough. Shabby, but the price is right.

Condega *p633*

F Hospedaje Framar, on main plaza next to Casa de Cultura, T2715-2393. With 14 very clean and pleasant rooms, cold showers, nice garden, safe, friendly, owner speaks English, excellent value. Safe parking for motorbikes.

Somoto *p634*

E Hotel Colonial, iglesia, ½ c al sur, T2722-2040. An attractive, professionally managed hotel with decent rooms; all have private bath, cable TV and fan. Popular with businessmen and NGOs.

E Hotel Panamericano, on north side of Parque Central, T2722-2355. Good-value rooms at this interesting hotel, where you'll find an orchid collection, a craft shop and a menagerie. The annexed section, a few roads away has a lovely garden and recreation area. The owners run trips to the canyon and surrounding countryside. Highly recommended.

F Hospedaje La Provedencia, Intel, 2½ c norte, T2722-2089. Offers 6 simple rooms with 2 shared baths inside a house. Friendly, family-run and basic.

Ocotal *p634*

B Hotel Frontera, behind the Shell station on the highway to Las Manos, T2732-2668, hosfrosa@turbonett.com. This is the best hotel in town, even if it looks like a prison compound from outside. It has an inviting swimming pool, bar, restaurant and events room. The rooms are clean and comfortable, if uninspiring, and cheaper without a/c (**D**). They also offer Wi-Fi, laundry service and international call facility.

C-D Casa Huesped 'Llamarada del Bosque', Parque Central, T2732-2643, llamaradadelbosque@hotmail.com. Conveniently located on the central plaza, this reasonably priced hotel has a wide range of rooms, but those upstairs are more spacious, modern and comfortable (**C**). Services include Wi-Fi, cable TV, fan, hot water and conference room. They also own the popular restaurant on the corner of the plaza.

F Hostal Canada, Instituto Nacional de Segovia, 2 c oeste, T2732-0309. Quiet, friendly hotel with 7 simple rooms, all equipped with private bath and fan. Good kitchen and a comfortable sitting room with TV. Breakfast is offered but not included.

⦿ Eating

Matagalpa and around *p629, map p630*

♥♥ Artesanos Café-Bar, Banpro, ½ c arriba. This pleasant café-bar has a wooden, rancho-style interior. They do breakfasts, light lunches, and hot and cold drinks including *licuados*, iced coffee and really excellent cappucinos. Popular with locals and tourists.

♥♥ La Buena Onda, see Sleeping, above, T2772-2135, www.hostelmatagalpa.com. Wed-Mon for lunch and dinner. Bohemian café ambience and flavourful fare like coconut curry, chicken with mango and filet mignon. Also light snacks, including sweet salads and sandwiches. Recommended.

♥♥ La Vita é Bella, Col Lainez 10, from Buena Onda, ½ c north, then right down an alleyway to an unmarked house, T2772-5476. An Italian-run restaurant, which has received strong praise from several readers.

♥♥ Restaurante El Pullazo, on the highway just south of town, T2772-3935. Has a famous and tasty dish with the same name as the establishment: a very lean cut of beef cooked in a special oven and smothered with tomatoes and onions, served with fresh corn tortillas, *gallo pinto* and a fruit juice.

♥♥-♥ El Cafeto, southeast corner of Parque Morazán, 1 c sur, ½ c oeste. A clean, modern café that's good for salads, sandwiches and other snacks. On the pricey side but not bad. Light and airy.

♥ Buffet Maná del Cielo, Iglesia Molaguina, ½ c norte, T2772-5686. Daily 0700-2100. Variety of typical Nicaraguan buffet food. Cheap and filling. Not bad.

♥ Hamburlooca, La Cancha del Brigadista, 3 c arriba, T2772-7402. Rough 'n' ready burger joint. They do home deliveries too.

Cafés

Barrista, northwest corner of Parque Darío, 2½ c norte. Excellent Americanos, cappuccinos, espressos and other locally sourced caffeinated fare. There's also Wi-Fi, cakes and snacks to go with your cup of the black stuff. A proper coffee house and recommended.

Simo's, southwest corner of Parque Darío, ½ c oeste. Good, strong coffee at **Simo's**. They also serve light meals and can get quite busy with diners in the evenings. Try the cheesecake if it's in stock. Also has Wi-Fi.

Jinotega and around *p632*

♥♥ Roca Rancho, Esso, 1 c sur, 2½ c arriba. Tue-Sun 1200-0000. This fun, friendly restaurant looks like a beach bar. They serve *comida típica*, shrimps, burgers, *bocas*, beer and liquors. There's live music on Thu.

♥♥-♥ Soda Buffet El Tico, Esso, 2½ c sur. Reputable buffet restaurant serving good Nicaraguan food. Clean, professional and popular with tourists.

♥ Chaba's Pizza, Esso, 2 c sur, 2½ arriba, T2782-2692. When you've had enough of *pollo frito* and *gallo pinto*, try these pizzas.

♥ Las Marías, Esso, 2½ c sur. Good locals' lunch buffet with pork-, chicken- and beef-based Nica dishes. Family-run and friendly. Recommended.

Cafés

Soppexcca, Ferretería Blandón Moreno, 1 c abajo, www.soppexcca.org/en. The best coffee in town, produced by an environmentally aware and progressive cooperative. Highly recommended.

Estelí p632, map p633

Pullaso's Olé, Casa de la Mujer, 1 c abajo, T2713-4583, www.pullasosole.com. Delicious steaks grilled to your taste and impeccably served in a pleasant garden setting. The best restaurant in town, carnivores will be pleased. Not cheap, but highly recommended.

Cohifer, catedral, 1 c arriba, ½ c al sur. A very decent establishment that promises a fulfilling gastronomic experience. They serve a range of excellent steaks, chicken and fish dishes, as well as some lighter, more economical fare, including burgers and sandwiches. Well established.

Vuela Vuela, Parque Central, 1 c norte, in Hotel Los Arcos. A pleasant interior and a nice place for an evening meal. They serve meat, chicken and fish dishes, tempting specials like stuffed prawns, and snacks, like tacos and sandwiches. Some dishes, like the export-quality steak and paella, are tasty but also on the pricey side ().

Cafetería El Rincón Pinareño, Enitel, ½ c sur. Cuban and Nicaraguan dishes and home-made pastries, try *vaca frita* (shredded fried beef with onions and bell peppers), *sandwich cubano*, good service and food, crowded for lunch.

Café Luz, catedral, 1 c al norte, 1 c arriba. This English-owned café is part of a non-profit enterprise that supports communities in Miraflor. They serve a range of breakfasts, including fruit salads with yogurt and granola, pancakes with honey, and – for those homesick Brits – egg and bacon buttie. They also sell *artesanías* and light lunches. Recommended.

Koma Rico, Enitel, 1 c norte, 1½ c arriba. Some of the best street food in the city. They serve tasty grilled meats and chicken. Very popular with locals.

Sopas El Carao, Almacén Sony, 1 c sur, 1 c abajo, T2713-3678. Daily 0900-2000. Chicken, crab and iguana soups, grilled meats, bull balls consommé. Authentic and recommended.

Cafés, juice bars and bakeries

Ananda, Enitel, 10 vrs abajo. Chilled out yoga centre with a plethora of happy-looking plants. They serve delicious and healthy fresh fruit *licuados* – the perfect nutrient boost. Highly recommended.

La Casita, opposite la Barranca, at south entrance to Estelí on Panamericana, T2713-4917, casita@sdnnic.org.ni. Nicaragua's best home-made yogurt in tropical fruit flavours. Very cute place with pleasant outdoor seating underneath trees on back patio. Recommended.

Condega p633

La Cocina de Virfrank, Km 191, Carretera Panamericana, T2715-2391. Daily 0630-2000. Very cute roadside eatery set in a little garden with excellent food and economical prices.

Somoto p634

Restaurante Almendro, Iglesia, ½ c al sur. Famous for its steaks, good *comida corriente*. Big tree in the centre gives the restaurant its name and is a famous Mejía Godoy song.

Restaurante Somoteño, Parque Central, 2 c abajo, 75 vrs al norte, on Carreterra Panamericana, T2722-2518. Cheery outdoor seating with bamboo walls, great beef grill with friendly service and monumental portions: *corriente* (normal), semi à la carte (too big) and à la carte (way too big), Recommended.

Cafetería Bambi, Enitel, 2½ c sur, T2722-2231, Tue-Sun 0900-2200. Surprisingly no deer on the menu, just sandwiches, hamburgers, hot dogs, tacos and fruit juices.

Ocotal p634

Llamarada del Bosque, south side of Parque Central, T2732-2643. Popular locals' joint that serves tasty and economical buffet food and *comida típica*.

¶┩ Restaurante La Cabaña, next to Hotel Benmoral, T2732-2415. Daily 1000-2300. Good steak dishes like *filete a la cabaña* or *jalapeño*. Lovely garden setting with banana trees and separate gazebos for the tables.

┩ Comedor la Esquinita, Esso, 1 c al sur. Clean, pleasant *comedor* with tables set around a leafy courtyard. They serve economical Nica fare.

● Entertainment

Matagalpa and around *p629, map p630*
Bars and clubs
Artesanos Café-Bar, Banpro, ½ c arriba. A popular place that draws a diverse crowd of locals and expats. Cocktails, rum and beer, in addition to coffee. Recommended.
Madre Tierra, southwest corner of Parque Darío, ½ c sur. Adorned with political photos, peace flags and iconic, revolutionary portraits, this café-bar has an alternative feel. They serve light meals and cold beer. The action hots up at night, with regular live music and occasional documentary films.

Estelí *p628, map p633*
Bars and clubs
Cigarszone, Carretera Panamericana, southern entrance to the city. Estelí's most modern and popular disco. Also features live music and boisterous young things.
Café Luz, catedral, 1 c al norte, 1 c arriba. Most evenings at Café Luz see an eclectic mix of expats, Nicas, volunteers and travellers gathering together to drink beer, coffee or rum, or otherwise engage in relaxed conversation. Friendly and cosy.
El Chamán, Hospital San Juan de Dios, 200 m sur. Lively place that's attracts a young, energetic crowd.
Semáforo Rancho Bar, Hospital San Juan de Dios, 400 m sur. Don your dancing shoes for Estelí's quintessential night spot. It hosts some of the best live music in the country, with nationally and internationally renowned acts performing regularly.

● Shopping

Matagalpa and around *p629, map p630*
Cerámica Negra, Parque Darío. This kiosk, open irregularly, sells black pottery in the northern tradition – a style found only in parts of Chile, Nicaragua and Mexico. For more information contact Estela Rodríguez, T2772-4812.

Estelí *p632, map p633*
Artesanía Sorpresa, opposite Enitel. A new shop with locally produced handicrafts.
Casa Estelí, Monumento centenario, 20 m al sur, T713 2584, www.asdenic.org. On the Panamerican highway, this information centre displays arts and crafts by local talent and cooperatives.
La Esquina, costado oeste de catedral, 1 c norte. Owned by **Hotel El Mesón**, opposite, they have a decent and interesting stock of crafts.

▲ Activities and tours

Matagalpa and around *p629, map p630*
Tour operators
Matagalpa Tours, Banpro, ½ c arriba, T2772-0108, www.matagalpatours.com. This reputable agency runs tours to the north and further afield. Trekking, hiking, birdwatching and rural community tours are among their well-established repertoire. Also offers excellent mountain bike tours, from 2 hrs to several days. Dutch and English speaking, helpful and friendly. The best agency in town – for all your adventuring needs. Highly recommended.

Estelí *p632, map p633*
Cigars
Estelí's famous cigar factories can be toured with independent guides or agencies. **Leo Flores Lovo**, T8415-2428, tourdeltabaco@ gmail.com, leads popular 1-hr tours that include a chance to roll your own. Also recommended are **Tree Huggers** (see

below). Alternatively, you can contact the factories directly (a comprehensive list is available from INTUR).

Tour operators

Tisey, Apdo Postal No 63, T2713-2655, next to **Hotel El Mesón** and run by same management as the hotel. Good for plane tickets.

Tree Huggers Tourism Office, catedral, 1 c al norte, 1 c arriba, inside **Hospedaje Luna**, T8441-8446, www.cafeluzyluna.com.The best tour operator in town and a great source of information. They offer a wide range of options, include cigar factory tours, city tours, hiking, cultural excursions and community visits. Also acts as booking agent for **UCA Miraflor**. Highly recommended.

⊖ Transport

North from Managua *p629*
Sébaco is a major transportation hub with northbound traffic to **Matagalpa** and **Jinotega** and northwest to **Estelí**, **Ocotal** and **Somoto**. Buses pass every 15 mins to/from **Estelí** US$1.20, **Matagalpa** US$1.10 and **Managua** US$1.50. Buses between Matagalpa and Sébaco pass the highway just outside **Chagüitillo** every 15 mins.

Matagalpa and around *p629, map p630*
Terminal Sur (Cotransur), is located near Mercado del Sur and used for all destinations outside the department of Matagalpa.
To **Jinotega**, every ½ hr, 0500-1900, US$1.40, 1½ hrs. To **Managua**, every ½ hr, 0335-1805, US$2.20, 3-4 hrs; express buses, every hour, 0520-1720, US$2.75, 2½ hrs. To **Estelí**, every ½ hr, 0515-1745, US$1.40, 2-3 hrs; express buses, 1000, 1630, US$1.50, 1½ hrs. Express bus to **León**, 0600, US$2.75, 3 hrs. Express bus to **Masaya**, 0700, 1400, 1530, US$2.75, 4 hrs.
Terminal Norte, by Mercado del Norte (Guanuca), is for all destinations within the province of Matagalpa including **San Ramón** and **El Tuma**. Taxi between terminals US$0.50.

Jinotega and around *p632*
Most destinations will require a change of bus in Matagalpa. To **Matagalpa**, every ½ hr, 0500-1800, US$1.50, 1½ hrs. To **Managua**, express buses, 10 daily, 0400-1600, US$4, 3½ hrs. To **San Rafael del Norte**, 10 daily, 0600-1730 US$1, 1 hr. Taxis in Jinotega are available for local transport, average fare US$0.50.

Estelí *p632, map p633*
Estelí has 2 terminals, both located on the Pan-American Hwy. The north terminal deals with northern destinations like Somoto and Ocotal. The south terminal, a short distance away, deals with southern destinations like Managua. A handful of Managua express buses also stop at the Shell station, east of the centre on the Pan-American Hwy.
   North station For northern destinations. To **Somoto**, every hour, 0530-1810, US$1.10, 2½ hrs, use this service to connect to El Espino border bus. To **Ocotal**, every hour, 0600-1730, US$1.40, 2 hrs, use this for bus to Las Manos crossing. To **Jinotega**, every hour, 0445, 0730, 0830, 1330, 1600, US$2.25, 2 hrs. To **El Sauce**, 0900, US$1.25, 3 hrs. To **San Juan de Limay**, 0530, 0700, 1000, 1215, 1400, 1500, US$2.25, 3 hrs. To **Miraflor**, take a bus heading towards **San Sebastián de Yalí** (not one that goes to Condega first), 3 daily 0600, 1200, 1600, US$2, 1½ hrs. Return bus passes at 0700, 1100 and 1620. You can also come in 4WD; there are 2 rental agencies in Estelí.
   South station Express bus to **León**, 0645, 3 hrs, US$2.75 To **Managua**, every ½ hour, 0330-1800, US$2, 3 hrs; express buses, roughly every hour, 0545-1515, US$2.75, 2 hrs. To **Matagalpa**, every ½ hour, 0520-1650, US$1.40, 2 hrs; express buses, 0805, 1435, US$1.50, 1½ hrs.

Ocotal p634

The bus station for Ocotal is on the highway, 1 km south of the town centre, 15-20 mins' walk from Parque Central. Buses to **Las Manos/Honduras border** every 30 mins, 0500-1645, US$0.80, 45 mins (for border essentials, see page 490). To **Somoto**, every 45 mins, 0545-1830, US$0.75, 2½ hrs. Express bus to **Managua**, 10 daily, 0400-1530, US$4.50, 4 hrs. To **Ciudad Antigua**, 0500, 1200, US$1.25, 1½ hrs. To **Estelí**, leaves the city market every hour, 0445-1800, US$1.30, 2½ hrs; express buses are Managua-bound, 2 hrs, US$1.65, they will drop you off at the Shell station, just east of central Estelí.

ⓘ Directory

Matagalpa and around p629, map p630
Banks Banco de América Central (BAC and Credomatic), Parque Morazán, 1 c al sur, on Av Central, changes all TCs and cash on Visa and MC and has ATM for most credit and debit cards with Cirrus logo. **Banpro**, opposite **BAC**, offers similar services. **Internet** Many internet places around town, particularly along Av José Benito Escobar, most charge US$0.50 per hr.

Estelí p632, map p633
Banks Almost every bank in the city is located in 1 city block. If you go 1 block

south and 1 block west from southwest corner of the central park you will find the 2 banks that change TCs, **Banco de América Central (BAC)**, T2713-7101, which changes all brands of TCs. **Internet** Cafés all over town, most charge US$0.50 per hr. **Language schools** Centro Nicaragüense de Aprendizaje y Cultura (CENAC), Apdo 40, Estelí, T2713-5437, 2 offices: Texaco, 5 c arriba, ½ c sur, and De los Bancos 1 c sur, T2713-2025, ½ c arriba. 20 hrs of Spanish classes, living with a family, full board, travelling to countryside, meetings and seminars, opportunities to work on community projects, US$140 per week. Also teaches English to Nicaraguans and others and welcomes volunteer tutors. **Los Pipitos- Sacuanjoche Escuela de Español**, Costado Noreste Catedral, 1 c norte, ½ c abajo, T2713-3830, www.lospipitosesteli. org.ni. Social projects are a part of the course and all profits go to disabled children and their families. Excursions to local cooperatives and homestay available. US$50-175, flexible options. Contact **Treehuggers tourism office**, see pages 632 and 640, for more information on Spanish schools.

Ocotal p634
Bank Bancentro, Parque Central, 1 c norte, 1 c abajo, has a Visa ATM and money-changing facility; as does **Banco Procredit**, Parque Central, 1 c abajo.

León and the west

An alternative route to Honduras leaves the capital heading through the Pacific lowlands to the Gulf of Fonseca, passing under the shadow of Los Maribios – a chain of volcanoes that runs from Momotombo on Lake Managua to Cosigüina on the gulf. This route takes in León, a city influential in shaping Nicaraguan history since colonial times. On the Pacific coast are the beaches at Poneloya and Las Peñitas. From León, 88 km from Managua, the Pacific Highway continues north to the industrial town of Chinandega. From here, routes lead west to the port of Corinto, north to the Gulf of Fonseca and east to Guasaule and the Honduran border. For the adventurous traveller, León is a good base to climb one of the volcanoes of Los Maribios: Momotombo is known for its perfect shape and incredible views from the top; Cerro Negro is the youngest volcano in Central America, erupting every four to five years; Volcán Telica has bubbling mudholes at the base and glowing lava in the crater; San Cristóbal is the tallest volcano in Nicaragua and highly active; while Cosigüina is surrounded by beautiful nature and famous for its huge crater lake and spectacular views. ➤➤ For listings, see pages 650-657.

Towards León

The old paved road to León crosses the Sierra de Managua, offering fine views of the lake. It is longer than the new Pacific Highway and not in good condition. About 60 km down the new road to León lies the village of **La Paz Centro**, with several truck-stop restaurants and accommodation. There is a good range of cheap, handmade pottery here, and you can ask to see the potters' ovens and production of bricks. Try the local speciality *quesillo* (mozzarella cheese, onions and cream wrapped in tortilla), available all along the highway. From here you can reach **Volcán Momotombo**, which dominates the Managua skyline from the west. It is possible to camp on the lakeside with great views of the volcano.

You need a permit to climb Momotombo from the south as a geothermal power station has been built on the volcano's slopes. At the time of writing, no permit was required to climb the volcano from the north but one reader has reported it as being a gruelling 11-hour climb. Take local advice and use a professional guide – ask at **Va Pues** or **Quetzaltrekkers** in León. ➤➤ See Tour operators, page 655.

León Viejo
ⓘ *US$2 entrance fee includes Spanish-speaking guide.*
At the foot of the volcano lies León Viejo, destroyed by earthquake and volcanic eruption on 31 December 1609 and now being excavated. It was here that the brutal first Spanish governor of Nicaragua Pedrarias and his wife were buried in La Merced church next to Francisco Hernández de Córdoba, the country's founder who had been beheaded under order of Pedrarias. Archaeological excavations have revealed the **cathedral**, the **Convento de la Merced**, the **Casa del Gobernador**, as well as the bodies of Hernández de Córdoba and Pedrarias, which have been placed in a special tomb in the Plaza Mayor. The ruins themselves are little more than low walls and probably only of serious interest to archaeologists, but you can see the ground plan of the old Spanish town and from the ruins of the old fortress there are breathtaking views of Volcán Mombotombo, Lake Managua and Momotombito Island and the Maribios Volcanoes range. To get to León Viejo, take a Managua bus and get out in La Paz Centro, US$1, 45 minutes. Catch a second bus (or taxi) to Puerto Momotombo, US$0.50, 30 minutes, and walk 10 minutes to the site from there.

León has a colonial charm unmatched elsewhere in Nicaragua, except perhaps by Granada. It is typified by narrow streets, red-tile roofs, low adobe houses and time-worn buildings. Founded by Hernández de Córdoba in 1524 at León Viejo, 32 km from its present site, it was moved here after the devastating earthquake of 1609. The existing city was founded in 1610. In recent years, economic factors have taken precedence over the cleaning up of old buildings, but the work continues slowly.

As the capital, León was the dominant force in Nicaragua until Managua took control in 1852. Today, it is still thought of as the 'intellectual' capital, with a university (Universidad Nacional Autónoma de Nicaragua, UNAN) founded in 1804, religious colleges, the largest cathedral in Central America, and several colonial churches. It is said that Managua became the capital, although at the time it was no more than an indigenous settlement, because it was halfway between violently Liberal León and equally violently Conservative Granada.

Ins and outs

Getting there Regular buses to León run from Managua and Chinandega, with frequent routes from Estelí and Matagalpa. International buses will drop you off, if asked, at the entrance to town. The bus terminal is at the northeastern end of town, a 20-minute walk, or short taxi ride from the centre.

Getting around Most attractions are within a few blocks of the centre so choosing a fairly central hotel will make it an easy city to explore on foot. Local buses will take you to the terminal and a network of *colectivos* work as cheap taxis (US$0.20). Taxis cost US$0.75 during the day, US$1 at night.

Tourist information **INTUR** ① *Parque Rubén Darío 2½ c al norte, T2311-1325, www.leononline.net*, has maps for sale, reference books and friendly staff.

Sights

Legend has it that the plans for the **Basílica de la Asunción** (the **cathedral**) ① *to see inside, visit between 0700-0900 or 1600-1800*, were switched with those of Lima (Peru) by mistake. However, the enormous size of the building, designed by Guatemalan architects, may be explained by the need to withstand the area's heavy seismic activity. Construction was begun in 1746 and was not completed for 113 years. Its famous shrine – 145 cm high, covered by white topazes from India given by Felipe II of Spain – is, sadly, kept in a safe in the vestry, to which the bishop holds the key. The cathedral also houses a very fine ivory Christ, the consecrated Altar of Sacrifices and the Choir of Córdoba, the great Christ of Esquipulas (in bronze with a cross of very fine silver) and statues of the 12 Apostles. At the foot of one of these statues is the tomb of Rubén Darío, the 19th-century Nicaraguan poet, and one of the greatest in Latin America, guarded by a sorrowful lion. All the entrances to the cathedral are guarded by lions said to come alive after midnight to patrol the old church.

The old Plaza de Armas, in front of the cathedral, is now **Parque Jerez**, but is usually referred to as **Parque Central**. It is the social heart of the city, home to many street vendors and a statue of General Jerez, a mid-19th-century Liberal leader. On the plaza's east side you'll find the new **Museo de la Revolución** ① *Mon-Sat 0900-1600, US$1.50*, with modest photographic exhibits and fine views from the roof of the building;

León

To Chinandega & San Jacinto

To Bus Terminal (3 blocks) & Market

6 C NE

TSA Tours Travel

San Juan
Bautista

Parque
San Juan

Mercado
San Juan

Museo
Entomológico   Quetzaltrekkers

Western
Union

2 C NE

@

La Unión
Supermarket

Cinemas   1 C NE

El Calvario

1 C SE

2 C SE

3 C SE

Cimac

4 C SE

(5)   (6)

Spanish-language tours are led by FSLN comrades.

León has the finest **colonial churches** in Nicaragua, more than 12 in all, and they are the city's most significant attraction. **La Recolección**, with a beautiful baroque Mexican façade, built in 1786, has a neoclassical interior with mahogany woodwork. **La Merced**, which was built in 1615 and burned by pirates in 1685, is notable for its seven different altars. It is one of the oldest churches in León and has fine woodwork inside and a restored exterior. **San Felipe** was built at the end of the 16th century for the religious services of the black and mulatto population of the city. It was rebuilt in the 18th century in a manner true to its original form, a mixture of baroque and neoclassical. **El Calvario**, constructed during the same period, is notable for its neoclassical façade attributed to the growing French influence in Spain at the time. The **Iglesia y Convento de San Francisco** ⓘ *US$1.50*, founded in 1639, is the oldest convent with a church in León. It still has two plateresque altars from Spain and its original pillars. In 1830, after the expulsion of the Franciscans from Nicaragua, it was used by various civic organizations and is now a gallery. The **Iglesia de San Nicolás de Laborío**, was founded in 1618 for the local indigenous population, and is the most modest of the León churches, constructed of wood and tiles over adobe walls with an unostentatious façade and a simple altar, 10 m tall. The celebration for San Nicolás is 10 September. The **Iglesia de Nuestra Señora Pilar de Zaragoza** was built from 1884-1934 and has two unusual octagonal turrets and an arched doorway with tower above. There is a pleasant walk south across the bridge, past the church of **Guadalupe**, to the cemetery.

The house of poet Rubén Darío, the famous 'Four Corners' in Calle Rubén Darío, is now the **Museo-Archivo Rubén Darío** ⓘ *Tue-Sat 0900-1200, 1400-1700,*

Comedor Lucía **11** *C5*
El Mississippi **12** *D6*
El Sesteo **6** *D4*
La Casa Vieja **13** *C2*
La Mexicana **4** *B3*
Mediterráneo **8** *C3*
Pan y Paz **7** *C5*
Pure Earth Café **9** *C3*

Terraza M **10** *B3*

Bars & clubs 🌔
Camaleón **14** *C4*
Don Señor **21** *C3*
Olla Quemada **15** *D1*
Oxygen 2 **16** *D3*

Rubén Darío: the prince of Spanish letters

The great Chilean poet Pablo Neruda called him "one of the most creative poets in the Spanish language" when, together with the immortal Spanish poet Federico García Lorca, he paid tribute to Rubén Darío in Buenos Aires in 1933. In front of more than 100 Argentine writers, Lorca and Neruda delivered the tribute to the poet they called "then and forever unequalled".

Darío is without a doubt the most famous Nicaraguan. He is one of the greatest poets in the history of the Spanish language and the country's supreme hero. Born Felix Rubén García Sarmiento in Metapa, Nicaragua in 1867, Rubén Darío was raised in León and had learnt to read by the age of four. By the time he was 10, little Rubén had read *Don Quixote*, *The Bible*, *1001 Arabian Nights* and the works of Cicero. When he was 11, he studied the Latin classics in depth with Jesuits at the school of La Iglesia de La Recolección. In 1879, at the age of 12, his first verses were published in the León daily newspaper *El Termómetro*. Two years later he was preparing his first book. Later, he became the founder of the Modernist movement in poetry, which crossed the Atlantic and became popular in pain. His most noted work, *Azul*, revolutionized Spanish literature, establishing a new mode of poetic expression with innovation in form and content.

As well as being a poet, Darío was a diplomat and a journalist. He wrote for numerous publications in Argentina, the United States, Spain and France. In 1916 he returned to the city of León, and, despite several attempts at surgery, died of cirrhosis on the night of 6 February. After seven days of tributes he was buried in the Cathedral of León. Darío gave Nicaraguan poetry a worldwide projection and solidified it into the national passion that continues to flourish today.

Ox that I saw in my childhood, as you steamed
in the burning gold of the Nicaraguan sun,
there on the rich plantation filled with tropical
harmonies; woodland dove, of the woods that sang
with the sound of the wind, of axes, of birds and wild bulls:
I salute you both, because you are both my life.

You, heavy ox, evoke the gentle dawn
that signaled it was time to milk the cow,
when my existence was all white and rose;
and you, sweet mountain dove, cooing and calling,
you signify all that my own springtime, now
so far away, possessed of the Divine Springtime.

'Far Away'. From *Selected Poems* by Rubén Darío, translated by Lysander Kemp, University of Texas, Austin, 1988.

Sun 0900-1200, entry and guided tour free but donations accepted. It has an interesting collection of personal possessions, photographs, portraits and a library with a wide range of books of poetry in Spanish, English and French. Darío died in 1916 in another house in the northwest sector (marked with a plaque). **Alfonso Cortés** – another of Nicaragua's finest poets who wrote a famous poem while chained to the bars in front of Rubén's old bed – went insane while living in Darío's house in 1927 and spent the rest of his years in a Managuan asylum until his death in 1969.

Two blocks west of La Merced church is the **Centro Popular de la Cultura** which has frequent exhibitions and events, and is a good place to see live folk concerts (schedule on the front door). The **Museo de Leyendas y Tradiciones** ⓘ *Parque Central, 3 c sur, Tue-Sat 0800-1200, 1400-1700, US$0.50*, has handcrafted life-size models depicting the rich legends of León. The **Museo Ortiz Guardián** ⓘ *Mon- Fri 1100-1900, US$2.50*, is a colonial home and art museum; it showcases national and international talent and is well worth a look. **CIMAC** ⓘ *Costado sur del Puente Martínez, ½ c arriba, 1 c al norte, T2311-0752, cimac@ibw.com.ni, Mon-Fri 0800-1100, 1400-1700, Sat 0800-1100, US$2*, which used to be a garbage plant, has been transformed into a centre for urban environmental initiatives, with a short self-guided trail and further information available at site. The shady trees supply a welcome break from the dust and heat of the city. Insect-lovers should head to the **Museo Entomológico** ⓘ *ENEL, 30 vrs arriba, opposite Western Union, T2311-6587, Thu-Tue 0900-1200, 1400-1600, US$1*.

Sutiava

The western end of the city is the oldest, and here is the oldest of all the churches, the parish church of **San Juan Bautista** in Sutiava (1530). Las Casas, the Apostle of the Indies, preached here several times. It has a fine façade, the best colonial altar in the country and an interesting representation of *El Sol* (the sun), carved in wood on the ceiling. The church has been beautifully reconstructed. Just south of the church on the dirt plaza is a **museum** ⓘ *daily 0800-1100, 1400-1700, Sat 0800-1000, US$0.50*, housing many colonial relics.

On the main street north of the church is a small **Museo de la Comunidad Indígena Sutiava** or **Museo Adiac** ⓘ *T2311-5371, Mon-Fri 0800-1200, 1400-1700, Sat 0800-1200, donations greatly appreciated*, with an anthropological and historical museum. The ruins of the nearby parish churches of Vera Cruz and Santiago are both crumbling and unapproachable. Also in the suburb of Sutiava is the **Casa de Cultura** with several interesting murals adorning the walls. Inside there are a few cafés, information about prominent Nicaraguan cultural figures and the offer of a free history and cultural lesson on Thursdays (1500) in basic Spanish.

Around León → *For listings, see pages 650-657.*

Poneloya and Las Peñitas beaches

A newly paved road from León heads 19 km west to Poneloya and Las Peñitas, a couple of relaxed and friendly beach communities. Both contain long beautiful stretches of sand and a mixture of humble houses and rich vacation homes. During the week you will have the beaches to yourself, but at weekends people come from León, and in Semana Santa it's sardine time. In general, Poneloya tends to be frequented by Nicas, whilst Las Penitas is preferred by gringos. Most of the coast has big waves and strong currents (swim here with great caution – there are drownings every year). The south end of Las Peñitas and Puerto Mántica, at the north end of Poneloya, are the best for swimming, with good surfing in between; board rental from **Hotel Oasis** and **Surfing Turtle Lodge**. At **Hostel Barca de Oro** in Las Peñitas you can hire kayaks for exploring the mangroves of the Reserva Natural Isla Juan Venado, an area rich in crocodiles, iguanas and other wildlife.

San Jacinto

On the road to Estelí, 12 km north of the intersection with the Chinandega–León road, is San Jacinto. About 200 m to the west of the road is a field of steaming, bubbling **mud**

holes, which is worth visiting. You should approach carefully, the ground may give and scald your legs; follow other footmarks for safety, avoiding walking on the crystallized white sulphur, and listen for hissing. It is recommended to hire a guide (ask tour operators in León) or trust one of the local children (US$0.50 tip) to show you where it is safe to walk. A visit can be combined with a hike to the edge of the spectacular crater of Telica with glowing lava inside. The climb is fairly easy but trails can be hard to find. It's best to use a professional guide and make an excursion from León – ask at Tierra Tours, **Va Pues** or **Quetzaltrekkers**. ▶ *See Tour operators, page 655.*

Chinandega → *Colour map 3, C3. Population: 137,940. Altitude: 70 m.*

About 40 km beyond León, Chinandega is one of the hottest, driest towns in Nicaragua. Agriculturally, this is one of the richest areas in Central America producing bananas, peanuts, sugar cane and shrimps. There's a good market by the bus terminal and you can hire horse-drawn cabs. The local fiesta is on 26 July. The **tourist office** ⓘ *opposite BAC, T2341-1935*, has a helpful representative who speaks English and Italian.

Chichigalpa

Not far away, near Chichigalpa, is the **Ingenio San Antonio**, the largest sugar mill in Nicaragua, with a railway between the town and the mill (five trains a day each way May-November, passengers taken, US$0.10; also bus US$0.30). While there are no official tours of the installations, you can apply at Gate (*Portón*) 14 to be shown around. On the edge of Chichigalpa itself is the **Flor de Caña distillery**, maker of what many believe to be the finest rum in the world, aged up to 21 years and made in over 15 flavours. On leaving you will recognize the picture on the bottle labels, a palm-shaded railway leading towards Chichigalpa with volcanoes in the background.

León & Los Maribios volcanic chain

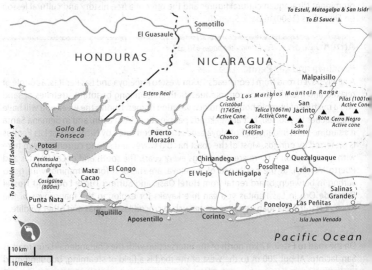

Corinto → *Colour map 3, C3. Population: 17,414. Altitude: 3 m.*

Twenty-one kilometres from Chinandega, Corinto is the main port in Nicaragua and the only one at which vessels of any considerable size can berth. About 60% of the country's commerce passes through here. The town itself is on a sandy island, **Punto Icaco**, connected to the mainland by long railway and road bridges. There are beautiful old wooden buildings with verandas, especially by the port. Entry to the port is barred to those without a permit.

On the Corinto–Chinandega road is **Paseo Cavallo beach** (Restaurante Buen Vecino). The sea is treacherous here and people drown every year. There are no facilities in Corinto's barrier islands, but they are beautiful with crashing surf on one side, calm and warm swimming water on the other. The journey can be negotiated with any fisherman. A *panga* can be rented for the whole day for US$60 so you can explore the numerous islands and mangroves. You'll see lots of birdlife but also lots of sandflies, so be sure to bring repellent.

North of Chinandega

The road north to Puerto Morazán passes through the village of **El Viejo**, US$0.20 by bus from Chinandega, 5 km, where there is an old church, **La Basílica del Viejo**, famous throughout the country for its celebration on 6 December called **La Lavada de la Plata**, which consists of devotees washing all silver parts of the altar. The basilica has la Virgen del Hato, which leaves the altar every December in a major pilgrimage to visit Corinto, Chinandega, León and Managua.

From Chinandega there are six buses a day to **Potosí** (at least three hours, US$1.20). In the centre of the village there are warm thermal springs in which people congregate to relax each afternoon. There are also pleasant black-sand beaches; the sea, although the colour of coffee, is clean. The passenger ferry from Potosí to La Unión (El Salvador) has been suspended. Ask around for an ad hoc service or ask in Chinandega before setting out to the peninsula. Rumours suggest that there may be a service from Corinto to La Unión.

It is a four-hour hike to the cone of **Volcán Cosigüina**. The path is overgrown and very difficult to follow, so you need a guide (see Tour operators, page 655). There is plenty of wildlife in the area, including poisonous snakes. On 23 January 1835, one of the biggest eruptions in history blew off most of the cone, reducing it from 3000 m to its present height of 800 m, throwing ash as far as Colombia, and leaving an enormous crater lake. From the cone there are beautiful views of the Golfo de Fonseca shared by Nicaragua, Honduras and El Salvador. The volcano and the surrounding dry tropical

forest are a Reserva Natural, administered by the Ministry of the Environment and Natural Resources in Managua.

   Jiquilillo beach is an increasingly popular destination, 42 km from Chinandega and reached by a mostly paved road branching off the El Viejo–Potosí road. Lying on a long peninsula, there are a few tranquil lodgings and small restaurants. From Chinandega a rough paved road goes to the Honduran border on the **Río Guasaule** near **Somotillo** (where the road improves) heading to Choluteca, Honduras. The bus from Chinandega takes 1¾ hours (US$1.25).

◉ León and the west listings

For Sleeping and Eating price codes and other relevant information, see Essentials pages 31-33.

◉ Sleeping

León p643, map p644

AL La Perla, Iglesia La Merced, 1½ c norte, T2311 2279, www.laperlaleon.com. This handsome 19th-century building has been carefully remodelled and now boasts a plethora of elegant a/c rooms, some with bath tubs, several suites, a bar, restaurant, casino, and pool. Spacious and grand.

AL-A Hotel El Convento, connected to Iglesia San Francisco, T2311-7053, www.el conventonicaragua.com. This intriguing hotel is decorated with elegant antique art, including an impressive gold leaf altar and sombre religious icons. Rooms are comfortable and there's a very good restaurant.

B Hostal La Casa Leonesa, catedral, 3 c norte, 15 vrs arriba, T2311-0551, www.lacasaleonesa.com. This typical León house has a lovely elegant interior, Wi-Fi, a swimming pool and 10 rooms of varying size, all with private bath, hot water, cable TV, telephone. Breakfast included. Rooms upstairs are cheaper (**C**).

B Los Balcones, Esquina de los Bancos, 1 c arriba, T2311-0250, www.hotelbalcones.com. A handsome colonial building with an attractive courtyard, bar and restaurant. The 20 rooms have private bath, hot water, a/c and cable TV; some have a have good view. Wi-Fi and laundry service available; breakfast included. Tasteful, professional and comfortable.

C Europa, 3 C NE, 4 Av, T311-6040, www.hoteleuropaleon.com. A reasonable business hotel, although some rooms are much better than others. Expect Wi-Fi, safe, telephone, a/c and hot water as a minimum. Elsewhere there's pleasant patios and quiet enclaves. Other services include restaurant, bar and parking. Cheaper with fan (**D**).

C La Casona Colonial, Parque San Juan, ½ c abajo, T2311-3178. This pleasant colonial house has 7 good-value, simple, homely rooms with attractive antique furniture, private bath and a/c. Management is friendly and hospitable, and there's a lovely green garden too. Cheaper with fan (**D**). Recommended.

C-D San Juan de León, Costado norte del Parque San Juan, T2311-0547, www.hsanjuandeleon.com. Located on the attractive San Juan plaza, this hotel has 20 clean, comfortable rooms on 2 floors, all with private bath, cable TV and a/c (**C** with fan). Wi-Fi, laundry service, lawn, pleasant roof-top patio and kitchen available. Continental breakfast included.

C-F Hostel Iguana, Iglesia La Merced, 1½ c norte, T2311-4643, www.hosteliguana.com. A lot of love has gone into **Hostel Iguana**, a colourful place with pleasant chill-out spaces and a fine restaurant attached (try the Italian pasta). The good-value rooms (**C** with a/c, **E** with fan) are clean and comfortable. The dorm (**F**) has only a few beds so it won't get overcrowded. A quiet, attractive and friendly lodging. Recommended.

D-F Lazybones Hostel, Parque de los Poetas, 2½ c norte, T2311-3472, www.lazybones.com. Managed by a friendly English/Colombian couple, this excellent hostel has a refreshing pool and lots of extras. Clean dorms (**F**) and private rooms; some have private bath (**D**), cheaper without (**E**). Check out the mural by one of Managua's best graffiti artists.

D-G Via Via, Banco ProCredit, ½ c sur, T2311-6142, www.viaviacafe.com. Part of a worldwide network of Belgian cafés, this excellent and professionally managed hostel offers clean dorm beds (**G**) and a range of private rooms (**D-E**), some with TV. There's a tranquil garden and popular restaurant-bar. In the manager's words, 'a meeting place for cultures'. Recommended.

D-G Tortuga Booluda, southwest corner of Parque Central, 3½ c abajo, T2311-4653, www.tortugabooluda.com. A very pleasant, friendly hostel with clean dorms (**F**), private rooms (**D** with bath, **E** without), and 1 a/c suite with views (**C**). Internet, Wi-Fi, pancake breakfast, organic coffee, kitchen and more. Relaxed and recommended.

E Calle de los Poetas, Calle Rubén Darío, Museo Darío 1½ c abajo, T2311-3306, rsampson@ibw.com.ni. This comfortable, good-value guesthouse has a relaxed home ambience, spacious rooms with private and shared bath, a beautiful garden and friendly hosts. It's also the base for **Sampson Expeditions** (see page 656). Often full, so arrive early. Discounts for longer stays. Recommended.

E Hostal Clínica, 1 Av NO, Parque Central, 1½ c sur, T2311-2031, roxyprincesscutie@hotmail.es. Family-run and very Nicaraguan. Simple single and double rooms have fan and private (**E**) or shared bathroom (**F**). There's an ultra-cheap dorm too (**G**). Washing facilities, terrace with hammock space, breakfast and drinks are available. Very friendly, good reports.

E-G Albergue de León, Gasolinera Petronic, ½ c abajo, T8894-1787, www.hostal elalberguedeleon.com. A very colourful, if slightly grungy, bare-bones hostel with plant-filled courtyards, ultra-cheap dorms (**G**) and private rooms (**E**). Amenities include kitchen, Wi-Fi, DVD, book exchange, coffee,

bikes and lockers. Reportedly a good place to pick up volunteer work.

E-G Sonati Hostel, Iglesia la Recolección, 1c norte, ½ c arriba, T2311-4251, www.sonati.org. Owned by a biologist and tied to an environmental education organization, **Sonati** is a tranquil new hostel with hammock space and a 'hummingbird garden'. Clean dorms (**G**) and private rooms (**E**) are available with the usual hostel amenities like laundry, free organic coffee, book exchange, kitchen, Wi-Fi, internet and water refill. Reforestation and other volunteer opportunities are offered, as well as interesting tours (see **Sonati Trekking**, page 656).

E-G Bigfoot Hostel, Banco ProCredit, ½ c sur, T8917-8832, www.bigfootnicaragua.com. Sociable, buzzing and popular with the whipper-snappers. This hip backpackers' joint has lots of economical dorm space, a handful of private rooms (**E**), pool, volcano-boarding tours, TV, pool table, bar, lockers, and a popular restaurant (see **Pure Earth Café**).

Poneloya and Las Peñitas beaches *p647*
Most of the best restaurants are found at the hotels and hostels.

B Rise Up Surf Camp, Salinas Grandes, T8917-8832, www.riseupsurftours nicaragua.com. A comfortable and professionally maintained surf camp some 30 mins from León. Good access to the world-class waves of Puerto Sandino. Meals, tours, yoga and massage available. Book beds and transport through **Bigfoot Hostel** or **Green Pathways** in León.

B Suyapa Beach Hotel, in Las Peñitas, T2317-0217, www.suyapabeach.com. A well-kept and professional hotel with a small pool and 24 clean rooms, all with a/c and private bath; a few cheaper ones have fan (**C**). Rooms on 2nd and 3rd floor have ocean views and a breeze. Often full with groups and popular with moneyed Nicas.

C Samaki, overlooking the bay, Las Peñitas, T8640-2058, www.LaSamaki.net. 4 tasteful rooms with good mattresses, mosquito nets, running water, Wi-Fi and private bath. Canadian-owned, very relaxed, friendly and hospitable, and home to Nicaragua's only kite-surfing operation. Currently for sale at a reasonable price and highly recommended.

C-D Surfing Turtle Lodge, Isla Los Brasiles, transport from Poneloya, T8640-0644, www.surfingturtlelodge.com. This solar-powered surfers' lodge is located right on the beach. It has comfortable wooden cabins (**C**, own bath), double rooms (**D**, shared bath) and an economical dorm (**F**). Options include surf lessons, board rental, massage, yoga, Spanish lessons, fishing and salsa. Protects the turtles who visit the island. Good reports.

D El Oasis, Las Peñitas, T8839-5344, www.oasislaspenitas.com. Right on the beach, El Oasis has 7 large rooms with poor mattresses; some have phenomenal views. There's also several chill-out spaces with hammocks and gringo day-trippers like to hang-out here. The restaurant has great views but the restrooms are sometimes unclean. Tours to Isla Juan Venado available, US$15 per person. Surf board rental available.

D-F Barca de Oro, Las Peñitas, at the end of the beach facing Isla Juan Venado Wildlife Refuge, www.barcadeoro.com.ni, T2317-0275. Friendly, funky hotel and day-trip hang-out with dorm beds (**F**) and private rooms (**D**), all with fan and bath. Bamboo 'eco-cabañas' are also available; they sleep 4 (**C**). Services include kayaking, horse riding, body boarding and many more.

Chinandega p648

A Los Volcanes, Km 129.5, Carretera a Chinandega, at southern entrance to city, T2341-1000. Very pleasant, comfortable rooms with private bath, hot water, a/c, cable TV. There's a smart restaurant and bar, service is professional.

B Los Balcones, Esquina de los Bancos, 75 vrs norte, T2341-8994, www.hotelbalcones.com. Same owners as the reputable Los Balcones in León. 18 clean, comfortable rooms with cable TV, hot water and a/c. Wi-Fi and breakfast included. Good and professional.

C Hotel Pacífico, Iglesia San Antonio, 1½ c sur, T2341-3841, www.hdelpacifico.com. Comfortable, friendly hotel with decent, modern rooms, all have a/c, cable TV, private bath, Wi-Fi and hot water. Breakfast included and laundry service available. Recommended.

D Don Mario's, Enitel, 170 vrs norte, T2341-4054. Great-value rooms and friendly hosts at this homely lodging. Rooms have a/c, private bath and cable TV; cheaper with fan (**E**). Chill-out space and tables overlook the plant-filled courtyard and the kitchen is available if you wish. The owners speak excellent English, 'anything you want, just ask'. Relaxed family atmosphere and highly recommended.

North of Chinandega p649

E Rancho Esperanza, Jiquilillo, 200 m behind Disco ONVI, www.rancho-esperanza.com, T8879-1795. This friendly and relaxed 'low-impact' rancho has a good location on the beach. Various bamboo *cabañas* are available, as well as dorms for the thrifty (**F**). 3 meals a day costs US$10. Activities include surfing, kayaking, hiking and community tours. Volunteer opportunities are also available. Good reports.

E Rancho Tranquilo, near Pulpería Tina Mata, Los Zorros, 10 mins from Jiquilillo, T8968-2290, www.rancho-tranquilo-nica.com. For people looking to escape the 'Lonely Planet Gringo trail', **Rancho Tranquilo** is a relaxed backpacker place with cabins and ultra-cheap rooms (**G**). There's also hammocks, vegetarian food and volunteer opportunities. Managed by Tina, a friendly lady from California and the only gringa in the village.

Eating

León p643, map p644

¶ **Bárbaro**, Parque de los Poetas, 1 c sur. Efficient and often buzzing bar-restaurant where moneyed Nicas like to be seen. The surroundings are clean and the service is fast.

A range of meat and chicken dishes are available, all reasonably tasty and filling, but nothing special. An army of staff is on hand.

¶¶ Cocinarte, costado norte Iglesia de Laborío. Quality vegetarian restaurant and intriguing international menu of Eastern, Middle Eastern and Nicaraguan cuisine. They use a lot of fresh and organic produce and host a monthly organic market. Fri evenings are music nights and Sun afternoon sees chess matches and free coffee. Recommended.

¶ El Sesteo, next to cathedral, on Parque Central. The place for watching the world go by, particularly in the late afternoon. Good pork dishes, *nacatamales*, fruit drinks and *cacao con leche*, although everything on the menu is grossly overpriced. Begging can be frequent if you sit outside.

¶¶ Mediterráneo, Parque Rubén Darío, 2½ c norte. This popular restaurant serves French and Mediterranean cuisine, fresh fruit juices and Italian wines. They offer a wide range of meat and chicken dishes (the steaks are excellent) and takeaway pizzas too. Relaxed, candlelit ambience and an attractive colonial building. Recommended.

¶¶-¶ La Casa Vieja, Iglesia San Francisco, 1½ c norte. Mon-Sat 1600-2300. Lovely, intimate restaurant-bar with a rustic feel. Serves reasonably tasty meat and chicken dishes, beer and delicious home-made lemonade. Popular with Nicas.

¶¶-¶ La Terraza M, Parque Rubén Dario, 2½ c norte. Intimate little eatery and bar with much the same menu as its more upmarket neighbour, **El Mediterráneo**. The fresh fruit juices are good, as are steaks and sandwiches (try the cholesterol-rich Mozza). Breakfasts are economically priced. There's a also bakery attached where they sell fresh bread, croissants, *pan de chocolate* and cakes. The garden looks great at night when its lit up with candles and fairylights. Generally good, but a bit inconsistent.

¶¶-¶ Pure Earth Café, Banco Procredit, ½ c sur. Intimate non-profit café that's best on Wed and Sun evenings when you can get a pizza and 2 *mojitos* for US$7 (pizza feeds 2).

Otherwise they offer a simple vegetarian menu with good juices, natural teas and organic ingredients grown on-site. Some of the café's proceeds go to reforestation and conservation projects. Open for breakfast, lunch and dinner. Closed Tue.

¶¶-¶ Via Via, Banco Procredit ½ c sur. A popular place, although hit and miss with the food. Breakfasts are reliable, economical and worth a go – try 'el macho', which comes with a cigarette and shot of rum. *Papas fritas* are also good, including Belgian and Dutch variations. Otherwise there's a range of so-so *platos típicos* from Mexico and Central America.

¶ Cafetín San Benito, northwest corner of the Parque Central, 1 c abajo, ½ c norte. Open for lunch and dinner, Mon-Sat, San Benito serves up cheap, wholesome, high-carb Nica grub with a Chinese twist. Get there 1130 and 1730 for fresh servings (later is not so good). Popular with students and budget travellers.

¶ Comedor Lucía, Banco Procredit, ½ c sur. Reputable *comedor* serving good but slightly pricey *comida típica* and buffet food, popular with locals. Dinners are much simpler and cheaper than lunch, Mon-Sat.

¶ El Mississippi, southeast corner of the cathedral, 1 c sur, 2½ c arriba. Also known as, perhaps unfortunately, '**La Cucaracha**'; everyone is raving about the bean soup here. Simple, unpretentious dining at this locals' haunt. Tasty, energizing and highly recommended.

¶ La Mexicana, La Iglesia Merced, 2 c norte, ½ c abajo. Economical, no-frills Mexican grub, but tasty and completely authentic. The *chilaquiles* and *burritos de res* are the best offerings, particularly after a cold beer or 2. Popular with the locals, greasy and recommended.

Cafés and bakeries

Pan and Paz, northeast corner of the cathedral, 1 c norte, 1½ c arriba. This excellent French bakery serves what is probably the best bread in Nicaragua. They also offer great-value sandwiches, delicious quiches and scintillating fresh fruit juices. Highly recommended.

Café La Rosita, northwest corner of Parque Central, ½ c abajo. A pleasant colonial building with chequered floors and a tranquil courtyard. They serve good, if pricey, coffee, cappuccino, cakes, sandwiches, salads and all-day breakfasts. The chocolate brownies are very tasty. Wi-Fi enabled and recommended.

Chinandega *p648*

♈ **Buenos Aires**, Plaza Colonial, 2½ c sur. A good place for an evening meal. This jaunty, brightly coloured restaurant serves meat, chicken and fish dishes under a thatched palapa roof. Specialities include a range of *enchiladas*, beef steaks and breaded shrimp dishes. Not bad.

♈ **Corona de Oro**, Iglesia San Antonio, 1½ c arriba, T341-2539. Chinese food with flavour. The chicken curry and shrimp skewers are especially tasty. Often recommended by the locals.

♈ **El Paraíso**, Plaza Colonial, 3 c arriba, on the Guasule highway. A large outdoor restaurant with a vast *palapa* roof. New and professional, serving the usual meat, chicken and fish fare. Seemingly a favourite of lunchtime business-men and moneyed Nicas.

♉ **Las Tejitas**, Parque Central, 7 c arriba. Cheap and cheerful. They serve buffet food, grilled meats and *comida típica*. Very popular and always packed out. A Chinandega institution.

⊙ Entertainment

León *p643, map p644*
Bars and clubs
León has a vibrant nightlife, owed to its large student population.

Bárbaro, Parque de los Poetas, 1c sur. Popular with visiting foreigners and Nicas who like to show they have cash to burn. Barbaro serves wine and cocktails in addition to the usual beer and rum tipple. Some people, however, may find the lights a little too bright.

Camaleón, Iglesia La Recolección, 35 vrs abajo. **Camaleón** is a hot and sweaty after-party and something of a León institution. It's best enjoyed in a state of absolute inebriation. Things don't start rocking until well after 2300.

Don Señor, opposite Parque La Merced. Tue-Sun. Roof-top bar that's popular with students and young Nicas on Fri nights, with liberal doses of karaoke, dancing and beer. A good place to catch some cool breezes and see the locals cut loose. The bar downstairs, **El Alamo**, promises some interesting experiences too.

Olla Quemada, Museo Rubén Darío, ½ c abajo. Popular on Wed nights with live music acts and lots of beer; salsa on Thu. Great place, friendly atmosphere.

Oxygen 2, Teatro Gonzales, 75 vrs abajo. Darkened disco that plays everything from R&B to salsa, reggae to techno, rock to pop. Popular with gringos and Nicas alike, so don your dancing shoes and dress to impress. Open Tue-Sun; ladies night Fri.

Via Via, Banco ProCredit, ½ c sur. Good on most nights, but best on Fri when there's live music. Salsa on Sat, free pool on Tue and quiz night on Mon. Good, warm atmosphere. Popular with foreigners and locals and often praised.

Cinema
There is a cinema with 3 screens in the Plaza Nuevo Siglo, next to the La Unión supermarket. It shows mostly US movies with Spanish subtitles, US$2.50.

⊛ Festivals and events

León *p643, map p644*
Mar/Apr Holy Week ceremonies are outstanding with sawdust street-carpet, similar to those in Guatemala, especially in Sutiava on Good Fri after 1500.
20 Jun Liberation by Sandinistas.
1 Nov All Saints' Day.
Dec Santa Lucía is celebrated in Sutiava; there are processions, religious and cultural events, sports and Pepe Cabezón (a giant

head on legs) accompanies La Gigantona (an impossibly tall princess) through the city.
7 Dec Día de la Concepción, festivities including singing, dancing and fireworks.

O Shopping

León p643, map p644
Crafts and markets
If you're looking for crafts, try the street markets on the north side of the cathedral. Additionally, **Flor de Luna**, Iglesia San Fransisco, 75 vrs abajo, Mon-Sat 0900-1900, stocks Nicaraguan artesanías, whilst **Kamañ**, southwest corner of the Parque Central, 20 vrs abajo, sells an assortment of handicrafts, bags and simple jewellery.

The best market is in the pale green building behind the cathedral which sells meat, fruit and veg inside, and shoes, fans and stereos in the street stalls outside. The inside market is a good place to find out what tropical fruits are in season. There's another market near the Iglesia San Juan, which stocks mostly stationery, bags and school supplies; and one at the bus terminal, which sells everything from vegetables to furniture. Both are dirty and hot.

Supermarkets
La Unión supermarket, catedral, 1 c norte, 2 c arriba, is modern and well-stocked; there is another good supermarket, Salman, behind Hotel El Convento. There's also an inexpensive but dimly lit Palí northeast of the centre, near the bus station and market. A convenient mini-mart can be found just south of Via Via and Bigfoot.

▲ Activities and tours

León p643, map p644
Tour operators
Bigfoot Adventure, Banco ProCredit, ½ c sur, www.bigfootnicaragua.com. The original and most professional Volcano boarding outfit in

town will kit you out with a board and safety gear, and transport you to the top of Cerro Negro. The fastest boards have been clocked at 70 kph. Tours depart daily, US$23, plus park entrance fee, around US$5.
Green Pathways, Banco Procredit, ½ c sur, T2315-0964, www.greenpathways.com. Green pathways aspires to carbon-neutral sustainability and donates proceeds towards environmental projects. They offer the usual range of local tours, but also specialize in alternative 'adventure in nature' trips further afield. These include whale-watching expeditions, tours of the Atlantic coast, bird-watching and tours of the northern highlands.
Nicasí Tours, southwest corner of Parque Central, ½ c abajo, T8414-1192, www.nicasi tours.com. The best cultural and community tours in town. Nicasí offers a diverse range of activities including rooster fights, cooking, cowboy, city and historical tours. Promises unique insights into the Nica way of life. Recommended.
Tierra Tour, La Merced, 1½ c norte, T2315-4278, www.tierratour.com. This Nicaragua travel specialist is Dutch-Nicaraguan owned and they are famed for their popular volcano boarding tours. They also offer good information and affordable tours of León, the Maribios volcanoes and Isla Juan Venado reserve. English, Dutch, Spanish, German and French spoken. Also domestic flights and trips all over the country, as well as shuttles direct to Granada and other places. Well established and reliable.
Va Pues, north side of El Laborío Church, inside **Cocinarte** restaurant, T2315-4099, www.vapues.com. Popular tours include sand-boarding on Cerro Negro, cultural trips to León Viejo, night turtle tours, kayaking, mangrove tours, tours of Sutiava's work-shops, horse riding, visits to San Jacinto's mud fields or Pacific coast salt factories, and city tours. English, French, Dutch and Spanish spoken. Well-established and professional.

Trekking

Quetzaltrekkers, Iglesia Recolección, 1½ c arriba, T2311-6695, www.quetzal trekkers.com. An ethical non-profit organization with proceeds going to street kids. Multi-day hikes to Los Maribios US$20-70 including transport, food, water, camping equipment. Quetzaltrekkers is volunteer-led and the team is always looking for new additions. They prefer a 3-month commitment and will train you as a guide. Nice guys and recommended.

Sampson Expeditions, Calle Rubén Darío, 1½ c abajo, inside **Hostal Calle de Los Poetas**, T2311-3306, rsampson@ibw.com.ni. Kayaking in Juan Venado and Laguna El Tigre, volcano expeditions, poetry tours. Rigo Sampson comes from a family of devout hikers and climbers and is Nicaragua's foremost expert on climbing the Los Maribios Volcanoes. He also works closely with educational organizations. Professional and highly recommended.

Sonati Trekking, Iglesia la Recolección, 1c norte, ½ c arriba, T2311-4251, www.sonati.org. Affiliated to an environmental education NGO, Sonati offers ecology-focused tours of the volcanoes, forests, mangroves and nature reserves. There is a particular emphasis on flora and fauna. Birdwatching in dry forest and mangrove swamps is also offered.

☉ Transport

Towards León *p642*
Bus
Frequent bus service to **La Paz Centro** from Managua, Terminal Lewites, every 30 mins.

León *p643, map p644*
Bus
Buses to Estelí and Matagalpa leave only if there are enough passengers; travel on Fri if possible, or simply go to San Isidro for connections. To **Managua**, express bus, every 30 mins, 0500-1600, US$1.90, 1 hr 45 mins. To **Chinandega**, express bus, every

15 mins, 0500-1800, US$1, 1 hr 45 mins. To **Corinto**, every 30 mins, 0500-1800, US$1, 2 hrs. To **Chichigalpa**, every 15 mins, 0400-1800, US$0.75, 1 hr. To **Estelí**, express bus, 0520, 1245, 1415, 1530, US$2.50, 3 hrs. To **Matagalpa**, express bus, 0420, 0730, 1445, US$2.50, 3 hrs. To **San Isidro**, every 30 mins, 0420-1730, US$1.50, 2½ hrs. To **El Sauce**, every hour, 0800-1600, US$1.50, 2½ hrs. To **El Guasaule**, 0500, US$2, 2½ hrs. To **Salinas Grandes**, 0600, 1200, US$0.40, 1½ hrs.

Buses and trucks for **Poneloya** and **Las Peñitas** leave from Sutiava market, every hour, 0530-1735, US$0.60, 25 mins. Service can be irregular so check to see when last bus will return. There are more buses at weekends.

International buses Contact individual agencies for schedules and costs; **Ticabus**, San Juan church, 2 c norte, in the Viajes Cumbia travel agency, T2315-2027, www.ticabus.com. **Transnica**, Colegio Mercantil ½ c abajo, T2311-0821, www.trans nica.com. **Nica Expresso**, Agencia Benitours, north side of Iglesia San Juan, 25 vrs norte, T2315-2349, www.nicaexpresso.com. **King Quality**, corner of 2a Calle NE and 3a Av NE, T2311-2426, www.king-qualityca.com.

Taxis
There are many taxis in the centre, at the bus terminal and on the bypass road. Day-time fares are US$0.75 per person to any destination in the city; US$1 at night.

Poneloya and Las Peñitas beaches *p647*
Buses to León pass hourly, 0530-1730, 20 mins, US$0.60.

Chinandega *p648*
Bus
Most buses leave from the new market at southeast edge of town. To **Corinto**, every 20 mins, 0430-1800, US$0.40, 30 mins. To **Somotillo**, every 3 hrs, 0900-1500, US$2, 2 hrs. To **Guasaule**, every 2 hrs, 0400-1700,

US$2, 2 hrs. To **Managua**, every 30 mins, 0430-1700, US$2.50, 3 hrs. To **León**, every 10 mins, 0430-1800, US$1, 1 hr. Buses for **Potosí, El Viejo**, Jiquilillo and **Puerto Morazán** leave from the Santa Ana Mercadito northwest of town every 15-40 mins, 0730-1600. A bus links Terminal, Mercado and Mercadito.

⊙ Directory

León *p643, map p644*

Banks Banks are clustered on the streets immediately north of the cathedral. A block west of La Unión Supermarket is **BAC** (Banco de América Central), the best bank for TCs and cash withdrawals from credit/debit cards, including maestro and cirrus networks. Other banks offer withdrawals on Visa cards only. If you need to change currency, it's often quicker and easier to use the cash-waving 'coyotes' who hang around outside. **Consulates** Spain, María Mercedes de Escudero, Av Central 405, T2311-4376. **Fire** T2311-2323. **Hospital** catedral, 1 c sur, T2311-6990. **Internet** At nearly every hotel and almost every street in León; head for Via Via or Bigfoot, where you'll find at least three cybers in the same street. **Language schools** León Spanish School, Casa de Cultura, Iglesia La Merced, 1½ c abajo, T2311-2116, www.leonspanishschool.org. Flexible weekly or hourly one-on-one tuition with activities, volunteering and homestay

options. Pleasant location inside the casa de cultura. **Metropolis Academy**, northwest corner of the Cathedral, ½ c norte, T8932-6686, www.metropolisspanish.com. A range of programmes from simple hourly tuition to full-time courses with daily activities and family homestay. **UP Spanish School**, Parque Central, 3½ c norte, www.upspanish schoolleon.com, T8878-3345. Flexible one-on-one classes with experienced and dedicated teachers. Options include homestay, volunteering and activities. Good reports and highly recommended. **Via Via**, Banco ProCredit, ½ c sur, T2311-6142, www.viaviacafe.com. This growing cultural centre has good ties to local communities and a popular hostel-restaurant-bar on site. A convenient, sociable option. **Laundry** Lavamático, northeast corner of Parque Central, 4 c norte. Wash and dry, quick service but not economical. **Medical services** Plenty of clinics, thanks to the university. For blood tests and others, including parasites, **Clínica Metropolitana**, Colegio Mercantil, 25 vrs norte, T2311-2750. They also have general doctors and specialists for consultation, US$15-25. There are many other labs and clinics in the area, including some low-cost ones. **Police** T2311-3137. **Post** Correos de Nicaragua, Iglesia La Merced, 2 c abajo, 3½ c norte. **Red Cross** T2311-2627. **Telephone** Enitel, on Parque Central at the west side, T2311-7377. Also at bus terminal.

Towards Granada

The journey from Lago de Managua to Lago de Nicaragua passes several volcanoes including Volcán Santiago whose crater spews out tonnes of sulphurous gases over Parque Nacional Volcán Masaya. Nearby, the town of Masaya is a centre for handicrafts in a coffee-growing zone. The blasted remains of Mombacho are near the historical city of Granada. The perfect cone of Concepción, on Isla de Ometepe, rises out of the waters of Lago de Nicaragua, which has a number of other islands that can be visited by boat. ▶▶ *For listings, see pages 666-675.*

Parque Nacional Volcán Masaya → *Colour map 4, A1.*

ⓘ *Daily 0900-1700, US$4. The visitor centre is 1.5 km from the entrance at Km 23 on the road from Managua. There are picnic facilities, toilets and barbecues nearby. It's possible to camp, but there are no facilities after the centre closes. Soft drinks, bottled water and sometimes fresh coconut water are available at the visitors' centre. Ask the bus driver to drop you off at Km 23 on the Managua–Masaya route. It's easy to hitchhike from either city, especially on Sun. At the entrance, park rangers might be available to drive you up to the summit for US$1.50.*

Created in 1979, Parque Nacional Volcán Masaya is the country's oldest national park. It covers an area of 54 sq km, and contains 20 km of trails leading to and around two volcanoes rising to around 400 m. **Volcán Nindirí** last erupted in 1670. The more active **Volcán Masaya** burst forth in 1772 and again in 1852, forming the Santiago crater between the two peaks; this in turn erupted in 1932, 1946, 1959 and 1965 before collapsing in 1985, and the resulting pall of sulphurous smoke made the soil uncultivable in a broad belt to the Pacific. Take drink, a hat and hiking boots if you're planning on doing much walking. If walking to the summit, leave early as there is little shade along the road. You should spend no more than 20 minutes at the crater's edge, as the air is toxic and smoke-filled; asthma-sufferers should avoid it altogether.

Santiago's most recent eruption was on 23 April 2001. Debris pelted the parking area of the park with flaming rocks at 1427 in the afternoon, shooting tubes of lava onto the hillside just east of the parking area and setting it ablaze. Today the cone remains highly irregular with large funnels of sulphuric acid being followed by periods of little or no smoke. On 4 October 2003 Santiago emitted an eruption cloud 4.6 km in length, but no actual eruption is forthcoming. A real eruption is expected soon.

Although research into the activity of Volcán Masaya is limited, gaseous emissions range from 500 to 3000 tonnes a day, making the volcano one of the largest natural polluters in the world.

Volcán Masaya was called *Popogatepe* or 'mountain that burns' by the Chorotega people who believed that eruptions were a sign of anger from the goddess of fire, Chacitutupe. To appease her they made sacrifices to the lava pit, which often included children and young women. In the 16th century Father Francisco de Bobadilla planted a cross on the summit of Masaya to exorcize the *Boca del Infierno* (Mouth of Hell); the cross visible today commemorates the event.

The biggest natural heroes of the park are the unique **parakeets** (*chocoyos*) who nest in the active Santiago crater. These orange- or crimson-fronted parakeets are best spotted just before the park closes between March and October. They lay two to four eggs per nest in the interior cliffs of the crater in July and after incubation and rearing lasting roughly three months, leave their highly toxic home for the first time.

From the visitor centre, a short path leads up to Cerro El Comalito, with good views of Mombacho, the lakes and the extraordinary volcanic landscapes of the park; longer trails continue to Lake Masaya and the San Fernando crater.

Masaya → For listings, see pages 666-675. Colour map 4, A1. Population: 140,000. Altitude: 234 m.

Masaya lies 29 km southeast of Managua, and is the folkloric and crafts centre of Nicaragua, home to more artisans than any other place in the country. The town is in almost constant celebration with religious festivals, including Central America's longest

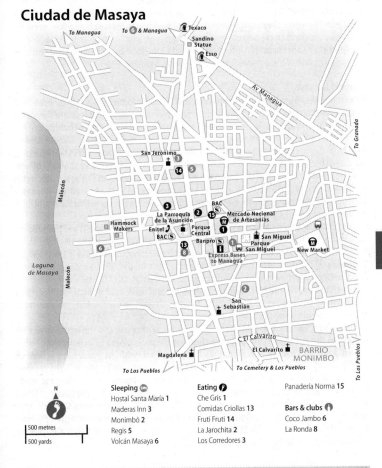

Ciudad de Masaya

Sleeping 🛌
Hostal Santa María **1**
Maderas Inn **3**
Monimbó **2**
Regis **5**
Volcán Masaya **6**

Eating 🍴
Che Gris **1**
Comidas Criollas **13**
Fruti Fruti **14**
La Jarochita **2**
Los Corredores **3**
Panadería Norma **15**

Bars & clubs 🍸
Coco Jambo **6**
La Ronda **8**

party, the **San Jerónimo** festival. Running for three months from 30 September, the festival includes traditional dancing, music and countless processions.

Every Thursday the **Jueves de Verbena** is a smaller festival with dancing, eating and drinking late into the night. It takes place at the 'new' artisan market or **Centro de Artesanías** (closed Sundays) (also called the **Centro Cultural Antiguo Mercado de Masaya**), which is the best place to see one of Masaya's more than 30 professional folkloric dance troops. The 19th-century market was ruined during the Revolution but is today restored and very popular with Nicaraguans. It sells excellent hammocks, leather work, colourful woven rugs and furniture. The 'old' market, close to the bus park, is marginally cheaper but crowded, dirty and recommended only for its visceral atmosphere.

The best place to buy local craftwork directly from the artisans is the indigenous barrio of **Monimbo**. On Avenida los Leones you find several **guitar shops**, where you can order a tailor-made guitar. Try a little shop (in the backyard) 75 m east of Parque los Leones (T2522-2479), where they charge US$40-50 for a new guitar. Masaya is also the centre for Nicaraguan rocking chairs and other wooden furniture, which can be bought packed for transporting by air. For tourist information head to the local branch of **INTUR** ① *Banpro, ½ c sur, just south of the artisan market, T2552-7651, Mon-Fri 0900-1300.*

Around Masaya

Fifteen minutes from Masaya is **Nindirí**, named after its former chief represented by a statue in the Parque Central. Known as the city of myths and legends, it is one of the oldest settlements in Nicaragua with evidence of over 3000 consecutive years of habitation. It is so rich in ceramic history that its small museum, the privately owned **Museo Nindirí** ① *1 block north of the Rubén Darío library, Tue-Sat, donation of US$1-2 requested,* has one of the country's most impressive pre-Columbian collections and Spanish colonial relics. It is run by the wife of the founder who will show you around. The town suffered in the Revolution of 1978 to 1979 and in Masaya you can visit the **Museo de Héroes y Mártires** ① *open daily.* Another museum, 45 minutes' walk from Plaza Central (ask directions), is that of **Camilo Ortega**, which has exhibits on recent history.

The small **Laguna de Masaya** is at the foot of Volcán Masaya; water is too polluted for swimming, but there is a good view of the town. **Volcán Santiago** is also nearby.

Just outside Masaya to the north, on the road from Managua, is an old hilltop fortress, **Coyotepe** ① *US$0.50,* also called La Fortaleza, built in the 19th century to protect Masaya. Once a torture centre used first by the Somozistas, later by the Sandinistas, it is now a clubhouse for the boy scouts. It is deserted and eerie (take a torch, or offer a boy scout US$1-2 to show you around). Even if you don't want to see the fort, the view from the top of the hill is spectacular.

The nearby village of **Niquinohomo** is Sandino's birthplace, and the house where he lived from the age of 12 is opposite the church in the main plaza.

San Juan de Oriente is a charming colonial village with an interesting school of pottery (products are for sale). Nearly 80% of the inhabitants are engaged in the ceramic arts. To visit an artisan family workshop walk from north entrance of the village towards the church. Just before the church and next to the women's co-op is the house of Dulio Jiménez, who is very happy to show visitors his operation. Buses from Granada cost US$0.30. It is a short walk to neighbouring **Catarina** (famous for ornamental plants), and a 1-km walk or drive uphill to **El Mirador**, with a wonderful view of Laguna de Apoyo (Granada and Volcán Mombacho too on a clear day).

El Güegüence: comedy and identity

In Nicaragua the name is omnipresent. The play *El Güegüence* is about humour, it is about corruption, the power of language and the clever art of revenge and it defines the very essence of what it means to be Nicaraguan.

Although the play's author is anonymous, it was almost certainly first written down between 1683-1710 in a mixture of Náhuatl and Spanish. The author was a master of languages and colonial law and had a sharp sense of humour. The play is both hilarious and profound in its use of language and comic timing. It is laced with double meanings, many to insult the Spanish colonial ruler who plays the sucker. The humour is often vulgar and all the characters in the play are targets. The great José Martí called it a "master comedy" and León's vanguard poet, Salomón de la Selva, said it was, "as good as or better than what we know of Greek comedy before Aristophanes". The work has been analysed by just about every Nicaraguan intellectual of any note who all have their own conception of the play's deeper meaning. However, they agree it to be a master play of American indigenous theatre, a source of cultural pride for Nicaragua.

The plot is simple. *El Güegüence* is an Indian trader in goods, some contraband, all of great variety, some of high value. He is called in by the local colonial chief of police for a bribe. He first plays semi-deaf, then stupid to avoid the subject of payment in a very funny "who's on first?" type of skit. Eventually he is brought in to meet with the governor and he befriends him with his cleverness, his humour and brilliantly funny lies. *El Güegüence* then manages to marry off one of his boys to the daughter of the governor by changing his reality from that of abject poverty (to avoid the bribe) to feigning immense wealth.

El Güegüence is the need of the Nicaraguan sense of humour to maintain pride, combat state corruption, salvage a seemingly hopeless situation with wit and break the chains of class structure. The use of laughter and irony to face difficult situations and the capacity to laugh at oneself are essential to the Nicaraguan character.

The sapphire blue crater lake of **Laguna de Apoyo** is very clean, beautiful for swimming and well worth a visit. The waters are kept warm by underwater vents and the sulphur content keeps mosquitos away. It's quiet during the week but busy at weekends. Without your own transport it's probably easiest to visit the lagoon from Granada with transport provided by the **Bearded Monkey**, see Shuttles, page 674. There is good hiking and birdwatching in the surrounding hills and accommodation on the lake shore.

Granada → *For listings, see pages 666-675. Colour map 4, A1. Population: 111,506. Altitude: 60 m.*

Situated on the northwest shore of vast Lake Nicaragua, and at the foot of Volcán Mombacho, Granada is increasingly popular and currently the place to hang out in Nicaragua. Founded in 1524 by Hernández de Córdoba on the site of the indigenous village of Xalteva, it is the oldest city to be continually inhabited and in its original location in continental Latin America. The prosperous city was attacked on at least three occasions by British and French pirates coming up the San Juan and Escalante rivers, and much of old Granada was burnt by filibuster William Walker in 1856. Despite its turbulent history, Granada – the third largest city of the republic – still retains many beautiful buildings and has preserved its Castilian traditions.

Granada

Sleeping 🛏
Alhambra **1** *C3*
Backpackers Inn **9** *C2*
Bearded Monkey **2** *B2*
Casa San Francisco **11** *B3*
Casa San Martín **4** *B3*
Colonial **5** *B3*
Con Corazón **10** *B3*
El Club **6** *C2*
Granada **14** *B5*
Hospedaje Cocibolca **8** *B4*
Hospedaje La
  Libertad **12** *C2*
Hostal Esfinge **16** *D3*
La Calzada **18** *B4*
La Casona de los
  Estrada **3** *B3*
La Gran Francia **7** *C3*
Patio del Malinche **13** *C4*
Plaza Colón **17** *C3*
Terrasol **15** *C2*

Ins and outs

Getting there There are very regular and quick bus and minibus services between Managua and Granada, making it a good base even if your main interest is the capital. International buses pass the western side of town.

Eating

Café Blue **2** C3
Café Isabella **3** B2
Coyote Grill **4** B4
Doña Conchi's **5** C2
El Garaje **6** B4
El Zaguán **7** C3
Garden Café **1** B3
Imagine **8** B3
Kathy's Waffle House **27** B3
Los Bocaditos **11** C3
Los Portales **12** B3
Maverick Reading
  Lounge **13** B3
Mediterráneo **14** C3
Mona Lisa **30** B4
Panadería Luna **9** C2
Querube's **31** C3
Roadhouse **18** B4
TelePizza **15** B3

Bars & clubs

Centralito **10** B4
Kelly's Bar **16** C4
Nuestro Mundo **17** C3
Zoom **19** B4

Getting around Small and manageable on foot, the focal point of the town is the Parque Central. Heading east takes you to the popular tourist drag of Calle Calzada, Lake Nicaragua and the Complejo Turístico (tourist centre). South of the Parque is the working heart of the city with the market and many bus departure points. East, west and north of the park, the streets are a bit quieter. Horse-drawn carriages available for hire if you want to rest your feet.

Tourist information **INTUR** ① *Iglesia San Fransisco, ½ c al sur, on Calle Arsenal, T2552-6858.* A reasonably helpful INTUR office with maps, flyers and information on local and national sites. Sometimes there are English-speaking staff.

Sights

The centre of the city, about 10 blocks from the lake, is the **Parque Central**, with many trees and food stalls selling Granada's famous *vigorón*, a popular dish of fried pork skins, yucca, and cabbage salad served on a big banana leaf. Bordering the park are many civic buildings, the landmark **Hotel Alhambra** and the cathedral. In between the red house of the bishop and the cathedral is the century cross with a time capsule of belongings from 1899 buried underneath in the hope of a peaceful 20th century. This practice was repeated in 1999 with another cross and time capsule in front of the La Merced church in the hope of a peaceful 21st century. The **cathedral**, rebuilt in neoclassical style, is simpler in design and ornamentation than the church of **La Merced**, two blocks west, which was built in 1781 to 1783, half destroyed in the civil wars of 1854, restored in 1862 and is currently undergoing another restoration. Its interior is painted in pastel shades, predominantly green and blue, and you can ascend the bell tower for interesting views, US$1. Another two blocks west beyond La Merced, is the church of **La Jalteva** (or *Xalteva* – the indigenous name of Granada), which faces a park with ornate ponds. Not far from La Jalteva is **La Pólvora** ① *donations to the caretaker,* an old fortress that has been partially restored and opened to the public. It has a pleasant rooftop with views of the church and volcano east from the turrets. The chapel of **María Auxiliadora** ① *open to public at 1600,* where Las Casas, Apostle of the Indies, often preached, is hung with local lace and needlework. Heading southwest from Jaltega, the cemetery is worth a visit as the resting place of key figures from Nicaraguan history. Heading towards the Managua bus terminal from Jaltega, you pass the beautiful, now-dilapidated **hospital**, which was built in 1886. It makes for great photography, but check the guard is around before entering.

Directly north of Parque Central is the restored **Casa de Los Leones** ① *T2552-4176, www.c3mundos.org, free during the day, check bulletin board for events,* restored and run by the international foundation **Casa de los Tres Mundos**. It is a beautiful colonial house, with good art exhibits and concerts. Heading west is the fortress-church of **San Francisco**, Nicaragua's oldest, though burned many times and now only the front steps are from 1524. There are some wonderful sculptures inside. Next door is the **Museo del Convento de San Francisco** ① *0800-1800, US$3, US$2.50 extra for photography.* Originally a convent (1524), it was then a Spanish garrison, William Walker's garrison, a university and more recently an institute. The cloister surrounds about three dozen tall palms. Restoration is now complete and it is the country's most interesting pre-Columbian museum, housing 28 sculptures from Isla Zapatera in the lake, dating from AD 800-1200. Note especially the double sculptures of standing or seated figures bearing huge animal masks, or doubles, on their heads and shoulders (including lizard, tortoise, jaguar). The museum also contains several galleries with changing exhibits of Nicaraguan art and there's a snack bar.

Lake Nicaragua – El Mar Dulce

A lake so vast the Spanish conquistadors dubbed it the 'freshwater sea' (*mar dulce*), Lago de Nicaragua, also known as Cocibolca, covers 8264 sq km. In a little country like Nicaragua, this truly is massive. The lake is fed by numerous rivers in Nicaragua and northern Costa Rica and its waters drain into the Caribbean Sea, via the Río San Juan. Lago de Nicaragua is punctuated by more than 450 volcanic islands: this is the earth as it was being formed millions of years ago, for Cocibolca is actually a 160 km by 65 km flood plain with the earth rising up around it and inside it. Its average depth is 20 m with some deep sections near Ometepe at 60 m. The two continents were finally connected on the lake's west coast, some four or five million years ago, blocking off the Caribbean from the Pacific and forming a land bridge that allowed the wildlife and vegetation of the two great continents to mix.

For an estimated 30,000 years, the bridge has been used by people too.

The indigenous name for the lake was Ayagualo and some of its islands were important religious sites, places of organized worship, human sacrifice and ritual cannibalism. Indeed, getting to the islands in canoes must have been a religious experience in itself: due to its shallow floor, Cocibolca's waves change by the hour and the lake surfaace can change from calm to rough in no time at all.

Lake Nicaragua is unique in its freshwater sawtooth fish, sharks, sardines and the prehistoric gar fish and a trip to Nicaragua without visiting its freshwater sea is like touring Egypt without visiting the pyramids. And yet it is still free of big resorts, pleasure yachts, and commercial fishing boats. Latin America's second biggest lake, remains as it has been for thousands of years: a place of volcanoes, mysteries and murmurs from the past; a huge body of clean, fresh water, teeming with fish, asleep under an endless sky.

Calle Calzada is lined with touristy restaurants and runs from the Parque Central to Plaza España by the dock on Lake Nicaragua, passing the church of Guadalupe en route. From the dock, ferries depart once a week for Isla Ometepe and the Río San. It is a five-minute walk along the lakeshore to the **Complejo Turístico** ① *US$0.12*, an area with restaurants, bars, paths and benches. The lake beach is popular at weekends and on national holidays, having been cleaned up and built into a pleasant park; marimba bands stroll the beach and play a song for you for a small fee. At night everyone decants to the club and bars of the *complejo*, but you should always use taxis to get here and back as it is unsafe to walk after dark.

Horse-drawn carriages are available for hire and are used here as taxis by the locals. The drivers are happy to take visitors around the city (US$4.50 for 30 minutes, US$9 per hour). You can see most of the city's sites in a half-hour rental. A recommended walk, or carriage ride, starts from La Pólvora and continues down Calle Real, past La Capilla María Auxiliadora, La Jalteva, La Merced to Parque Central. From the cathedral you can then continue to La Virgen de Guadalupe and to the lake front along La Calzada.

Around Granada

Reserva Natural Volcán Mombacho

ⓘ *Thu-Sun 0800-1700, US$8 including transport to the summit. To get there, take a bus towards Nandaime or Rivas from Granada or Masaya and get off at the Emapalme Guanacaste, from where it's 1 km to the entrance. You can continue hiking to the summit, passing attractive coffee fincas, but it's long, brutal and strenuous towards the end. Trucks to the summit depart 0830, 1000, 1300, 1500.*

Volcán Mombacho is the dark, eternally brooding backdrop to Granada's pretty, colonial streets. Its green slopes are home to *fincas* (farms) at the lower reaches and a small but attractive cloud forest reserve higher up. Hardcore hikers may be disappointed by the three trails, sometimes inundated with tourists. Guides are obligatory on the hardest trail (US$10). An interesting possibility is a night hike to view the salamanders unique to the region. Three canopy tours also offer high-speed experiences of the volcano; **Mombotour**, and **Mombacho Canopy Tour** are located well below the cloud forest zone.
▶▶ *See Activities and tours, page 672.*

Archipiélago Las Isletas

Scattered like a broken necklace over the waters of Lake Nicaragua, Las Isletas are a chain of 354 tiny, jewel-like islands. Formed by a violent volcanic eruption, the islands are fertile havens for arboreal and avian species, and some are inhabited by fishermen and small communities. Some have also been snapped up by local real estate agents and are now 'for sale' to rich foreigners. You can visit the Isletas as part of a tour, with boats departing from the lake shore or at Puerto Asese, 3 km from the entrance to the Complejo Turístico. (see page 672). Perhaps the best way to experience the rich aquatic wildlife of the islands is at dawn, in a kayak. ▶▶ *See Activities and tours, page 672.*

Parque Nacional Archipiélago Zapatera

Home to the country's most important pre-Columbian sites, the 11 islands of this archipelago contain mysterious petroglyphs, a crater lake and wonderfully active ecosystems, including tropical dry and wet forests. Zapatera is the largest and most important site. A number of massive basalt statues have been recovered there and are now on exhibition in Granada's San Fransisco convent. It's best to visit the islands as part of a tour as **MARENA** are reportedly turning away unsolicited visitors. Use an agency in Granada or Managua.

◉ Towards Granada listings

For Sleeping and Eating price codes and other relevant information, see Essentials pages 31-33.

◉ Sleeping

Parque Nacional Volcán Masaya *p658*
B Hotel Besa Flor, Km 19.8 Carretera a Masaya, 200 m sur, 500 m oeste, T2279-9845, www.hotel-besa-flor.de. Lovely hotel located close to Volcán Masaya national park. 5 rooms have private bath with hot water, Wi-Fi and free local calls. There's also a lush garden and access to a private nature reserve. Spanish, English and German are spoken. Recommended.
C Hotel Volcán Masaya, Km 23, Carretera a Masaya, T2522-7114, hotelvolcan@hotmail.com. Great location in front of the volcano park, with spectacular views from the shared patio. Rooms have private bath, a/c, fridge and cable TV. The lobby area is good for relaxing.

Masaya *p659, map p659*

B Hotel Monimbó, Plaza Pedro Joaquín Chomorro, 1 c arriba, 1½ c norte, T2522-6867, hotelmonimbo 04@hotmail.com. 7 clean, comfortable rooms with private bath, hot water, a/c and cable TV. There's a pleasant patio and garden space with relaxing hammocks. Other services include Wi-Fi, laundry, restaurant-bar, tours and transportation. Breakfast included.

B-C Hostal Santa María, Banpro, 1 c arriba, ½ c sur, info@hostalsantamarianic.com, T2552-2411. This centrally located hotel has a range of clean, comfortable rooms with private bath and cable TV (**B** with a/c, **C** with fan). There's a small pool in the garden.

C Maderas Inn, Bomberos, 2 c sur, T2522-5825, www.hotelmaderasinn.com. A friendly little place with a pleasant family ambience and a variety of rooms kitted out with private bath, a/c, cable TV. Continental breakfast is included, but there are also cheaper rooms without breakfast or a/c (**E**). Services include

medical consultations, Wi-Fi, tours, parking, laundry service and airport transfer. There's also hammock space for chilling out.

F Hotel Regis, La Curacao, 40 vrs norte, T2522-2300, hotelregismasaya@hotmail.com. Very friendly and helpful owner. Rooms are clean and basic, with shared bath and fan. The price is right, but there are at least 3 other economical options on the same block. Ultra-cheap (**G**) for single travellers.

Around Masaya *p660*

B San Simian, south of Norome Resort, T8813-6866, www.sansimian.com. A peaceful spot with 5 great *cabañas* with Balinese-style outdoor shower or bathtubs – perfect for a soak under the starry sky. Facilities include restaurant, bar, dock, hammocks, kayaks and a catamaran (US$15 per hr). Day use US$5. Yoga, massage, Spanish classes and manicure/pedicure can be arranged. Recommended.

E Estación Ecológico (FUNDECI-GAIA), north shore of lake, follow signs for **Apoyo**

Spanish School, T8882-3992, www.gaia nicaragua.org. Friendly low-key hostel managed by biologist Dr Jeffry McCrary. Accommodation is in simple dorms and rooms with tasty home-cooked meals served 3 times daily. Activities include reforestation (volunteers receive discounts), Spanish school, diving, kayaking and birdwatching. The research station also offers biology courses and is a great place to learn about conservation generally. Highly recommended.

Granada p661, map p662

AL La Gran Francia, southeast corner of Parque Central, T2552-6002, www.lagran francia.com. This traditional colonial building has handsome rooms with private bath, hot water, cable TV, a/c, minibar and internet access. Standard rooms are dark and face a wall, junior suites (**L**) have big wooden doors that lead on to small balcony with a lovely view and lots of light; worth the extra money. There's a pool, hotel staff are friendly and the rates include a stingy breakfast.

AL-A Hotel Alhambra, Parque Central, T2552-4486, www.hotelalhambra.com.ni. Granada's landmark hotel has a stunning location on the plaza. Rooms vary dramatically in quality and price. They include 'classic rooms' (**A**) with a/c, cable TV and hot water; 'superior rooms' (**A**) with king- or queen-size beds and minibar; and luxury 'suites' (**AL**).

AL-A Plaza Colón, frente al Parque Central, T2552-8489, www.hotelplazacolon.com. Atmospheric colonial grandeur at this long-established hotel. Comfortable rooms are well equipped with a/c, minibar, cable TV, hot water and internet, but those with balconies (**AL**) also have fantastic views over the square. There's a pool, restaurant and a small army of staff to care for your needs. Recommended.

A Casa San Francisco, Corrales 207, T2552-8235, www.casasanfrancisco.com. This attractive, tranquil hotel is composed of 2 colonial houses with 13 lodgings that vary greatly. One house has 2 suites and 2 comfortable rooms with private bath, cable

TV, a/c, pool and a modern kitchen. The other has 8 rooms and 1 suite, a pool and restaurant. The friendly and helpful staff speak English.

A Hotel Colonial, Calle La Libertad, Parque Central, 25 vrs al norte, T2552-7581, www.hotelcolonialgranada.com. This centrally located, colonial-style hotel has a range of pleasant, comfortable lodgings, including 27 heavily decorated rooms with 4-poster beds and 10 luxury suites with jacuzzi (**AL**); all have hot water, a/c, cable TV, safe and Wi-Fi. There are 2 pools, a conference center, a tour agency, and the restaurant serves breakfast only.

A Patio del Malinche, Calle El Caimito, de Alcaldía, 2½ c al lago, T2552-2235, www.patiodelmalinche.com. This beautiful and tastefully restored colonial building has 15 clean, comfortable rooms overlooking an attractive garden and pool. There's a bar and tranquil patio space in which you can have breakfast or simply relax. Rooms are equipped with a/c, cable TV, fan, hot water, safe and Wi-Fi. Tidy and elegant.

A-B Hotel Granada, opposite Iglesia Guadalupe, T2552-2974, www.hotelgranada nicaragua.com. **Hotel Granada** has been renovated and offers 3 classes of room. The standards (**B**) are reasonably sized, comfortable and equipped with cable TV, Wi-Fi, a/c and hot water. The colonial rooms (**A**) are smaller but more attractive, adorned with bureaus and other wooden furniture. The suites (**AL**) are large and much more expensive. The hotel grounds are rambling and boast the largest swimming pool in town.

A-B La Casona de los Estrada, Iglesia San Francisco, ½ c abajo, T2552-7393, www.casona losestrada.com.ni. Decorated with fine furnishings, this small, homely hotel has 6 pleasant, well-lit rooms with private bath, hot water, a/c, Wi-Fi and cable TV. There's a pleasant plant-filled courtyard, English and French are spoken, and prices include breakfast.

B Casa San Martín, Calle La Calzada, catedral, 1 c lago, T2552-6185, www.hcasasan martin.com. 7 clean, cool, spacious rooms in a beautiful colonial home. All have cable

TV, private bath, Wi-Fi, a/c or fan. Nice decor and garden terrace, very authentic Granadino feel. Staff speak English.

B Hotel Con Corazón, Calle Santa Lucía 141, T2552-8852, www.hotelcon corazon.com. As the name suggests, this 'hotel with heart' strives to be ethical and donates its profits to social causes. Rooms are simple, minimalist and comfortable; all are fitted with a/c, cable TV and fan. There's a pleasant colonial patio, bar, pool, hammocks, and a restaurant serving international food (♥♥). Often recommended by former guests.

C Terrasol, Av Barricada, T2552-8825, www.hotelterrasol.com. Rooms at the Terrasol are comfortable, modern and adorned with good artwork. Each has cable TV, private bath and a/c (cheaper with fan). Some have balconies with views of the street. The restaurant downstairs has had good reports, thanks to the managers who have a background in the food industry. **Terrasol** also offers tours, laundry service, car rental and transit to/from the airport.

C-D El Club, Parque Central, 3 c abajo, T2552-4245, www.elclub-nicaragua.com. This Dutch-owned hotel has 2 suites with mezzanine floors, as well as several small, windowless, fading rooms with private bath, a/c, cable TV and Wi-Fi. The cheapest (**D**) are quite cramped. The bar lays on a loud party on Thu, Fri and Sat nights, when you won't get much peace. Prices include breakfast.

D Backpackers Inn, Calle Real Xalteva y Av Barricada, 25 m sur, T2552-4609, www.backpackers-inn.com. A very clean and attractive hostel for sensible independent travellers. There's a colonial courtyard, traditional art work, good hammocks, well-tended garden, cafe, business centre and restaurant. Other services include Wi-Fi, laundry and tours.

E Hospedaje Cocibolca, Calle La Cazada, T2552-7223, www.hospedajecocibolca.net. A friendly, family house with 24 clean, simple rooms. There's Wi-Fi, a kitchen, free coffee in the morning and plenty of chess sets. A few rooms have cable TV and a/c (**C**).

Very nice owners, and they have a slightly more comfortable and upmarket hotel (**C**) a block away.

E La Calzada, Calle Calzada, near Iglesia Guadalupe, T2552-7684, www.hospedajela calzadanica.blogspot.com. This family-run guesthouse has 8 big, simple rooms with fan and private bath; cheaper with shared bath. Authentically Nicaraguan, but has seen better days. Internet terminal available.

E-F Hostal Esfinge, opposite market, T2552-4826, esfingegra@hotmail.com.ni. Lots of character at this friendly old hotel near the market. They offer a variety of simple rooms, including those with bath (**E**), shared bath (**F**) and a/c (**C**). There's a shared kitchen, washing area, ping-pong table, lockers, fridge and a leafy garden with pleasant hammocks and seating. Nica-owned and highly recommended for down-to-earth budget travellers.

E-G Bearded Monkey, Calle 14 de Septiembre, near the fire station, T2552-4028, www.thebeardedmonkey.com. A sociable, popular hostel with dormitories (**G**), private rooms (**E**), and hammocks for seriously impoverished backpackers. Runs transport to Laguna de Apoyo, see page 661.

E-G Hospedaje La Libertad, Av 14 de Septiembre, T2552-4087, www.la-libertad. net. Managed by the friendly Chepe, this relaxed and sociable hostel offers economical dorm beds (female only or mixed, **G**) and simple private rooms (**E-F**). There's a well-stocked bar, leafy courtyard, good hammocks, internet terminals, Wi-Fi, free coffee and large lockers. La Libertad also offers a range of tours with 'Jimmy the Man' and supports local artists. Pleasant atmosphere.

🍴 Eating

Masaya *p659, map p659*

♥♥ **La Jarochita**, Costado Este del Parque Central, 50 vrs norte, T2522-2186. Daily 1100-2200. The best Mexican in Nicaragua; some drive from Managua just to eat here. Try *sopa de tortilla*, and chicken *enchilada* in *mole* sauce, *chimichangas* and Mexican beer. Recommended.

¶¶ Restaurante Che Gris, Esquina Sureste del Mercado de Artesanía, T2552-0162. Very good food in huge portions, including excellent *comida típica*, *comida corriente* and à la carte dishes like steaks, chicken and pork.

¶¶-¶ Los Corredores, Iglesia Parroquia La Asunción, 1 c norte, ½ c abajo, T2552-2291. A big, new colonial-style building with a well-fitted interior. They serve burgers, club sandwiches, grilled meats and other meaty fare. Economical lunch-time deals (¶) Mon-Fri, 1100-1500, but dinner is served all nights of the week too. Occasionally hosts live music.

¶ Comidas Criollas, Parque Central, Costado Sur. This large, clean, buffet restaurant serves up healthy portions of Nica fare.

Cafés, juice bars and bakeries

Fruti Fruti, northeast corner of Parque Central, 3½ c norte. Tasty, sweet, fresh fruit smoothies, including delicious *piña coladas*.

Panadería Norma, northwest corner of the artisan market, ½ c norte. Good, fresh-brewed coffee, bread, cakes and pastries.

Granada *p661, maps p662*

¶¶¶ Imagine, Calle La Libertad, del Parque Central, 1 c al lago, T8842-2587, www.imagine restaurantandbar.com. A very decent and creative restaurant that utilizes fresh and organic ingredients to produce dishes like seared sushi tuna, 100% grain-fed lamb chops, flaming breast of duck and mango bread with chocolate fondue. Not cheap, but there's a modest bar menu (¶¶) for tight or impoverished travellers. Recommended.

¶¶¶ Mediterráneo, Calle Caimito, T2552-6764. Daily 0800-2300. Mediterranean cuisine served in a Spanish-owned colonial house with an attractive and tranquil garden setting. Mixed reviews; good seafood but bad paella. Popular with foreigners.

¶¶¶-¶¶ Doña Conchi's, Calle La Libertad, north-west corner of the Parque Central, 2½ c abajo. Wed-Mon 1100-2300. A beautiful restaurant, illuminated by candles and adorned with rustic decorations. They serve quality dishes like grilled salmon, seabass and lobster (¶¶¶), as well as slightly cheaper, reasonably good (if very garlicky) pasta (¶¶). Lovely garden seating and pleasant service. Recommended.

¶¶¶-¶¶ El Zaguán, on road behind cathedral (east side), T2552-2522. Mon-Fri 1200-1500 and 1800- 2200, Sat and Sun 1200-2200. Incredible, succulent grilled meats and steaks, cooked on a wood fire and served impeccably. Undoubtedly the best beef cuts in Granada, if not Nicaragua. Meat-lovers should not miss this place. Highly recommended.

¶¶ Coyote Grill, Parque Central, 3 c al lago, La Calzada, T2252-2457. Same owner as **Pizza Luca** next door. They serve burgers, chicken, steak, salads, *fajitas*, fries and American-style fare. Some outdoor seating, but indoors is comfortable too.

¶¶ El Garaje, Calle Corrales, del Convento de San Fransisco, 2½ c al lago, T8651-7412. Mon Fri 1130-1900. A wonderfully under-stated Canadian-owned restaurant and undoubtedly one of Granada's best dining options. The menu changes weekly and includes tasty specials like Jamaican curry, roast turkey, Mediterranean salad and Szechuan steak wrap. Fresh, healthy, beautifully presented home-cooking. Good vegetarian options too. Highly recommended.

¶¶ Kathy's Waffle House, opposite Iglesia San Francisco. 0730-1400. The best breakfasts in Granada. It's always busy here in the morning, especially weekends. You'll find everything from waffles to pancakes to *huevos rancheros*, with free coffee refills. Highly recommended.

¶¶ Mona Lisa, Calle La Calzada, 3½ c al lago, T2552-8187. Undoubtedly the best pizzas in Granada; stone-baked, tasty and authentic. Friendly and recommended.

¶¶ Roadhouse, Calle La Calzada, 2 c al lago. Popular with Nicaraguans, this American-style restaurant serves lots of beer and a range of wholesome burgers. Their fries, flavoured with cajun spices, are the best thing they do. Inside tends to be rowdier than outside.

¶¶-¶ Café Isabella, 108 Calle Corrales, Bancentro, 1 c norte, ½ c abajo. Open for breakfast and lunch, this café has a large terrace overlooking the street and interior garden. They serve some vegetarian dishes.

†¶-¶ **Los Portales**, opposite Cafemail on Plaza de los Leones, T2552-4115. Daily 0700-2200. Simple Mexican food, sometimes overpriced but there are good people-watching opportunities to make up for it.

¶ **Café Blue**, southwest corner of Parque Central, 1½ c sur. Mon-Sat. Cosy little restaurant with a casual café ambience. They serve a range of cheapish breakfasts, including fruit, pancakes, bacon and eggs, as well as economical lunches, which mainly consist of meat and chicken fare.

¶ **Los Bocaditos**, Calle el Comercio. Mon-Sat 0800-2200, Sun 0800-1600. A bustling, but clean locals' joint with buffet from 1100-1500, breakfast and dinner menu.

¶ **Restaurant Querube's**, Calle el Comercio, opposite Tiangue 1. Clean and popular locals' joint near the market. They serve greasy, high-carb Nicaraguan and Chinese fare from a buffet, and do set lunches and breakfasts.

¶ **TelePizza**, Bancentro, 1½ c al lago, T552-4219. Daily 1000-2200. Good, tasty pizzas; but not outstanding. Popular with Nicaraguan families, if you've had enough of the gringo places. They deliver too.

Cafés, bakeries and juice bars

Garden Café, Enitel, 1 c al lago. A very relaxed, breezey café with a lovely leafy garden and patio space. They do breakfasts, sandwiches, coffees, muffins and cookies. They have a small book collection and Wi-Fi. Friendly and pleasant.

Maverick Reading Lounge, Telepizza, 1 c abajo. Fair trade gourmet coffee, hot tea, good selection of magazines in English and Spanish, second-hand books, cigars.

Panadería Luna, Calle Xalteva, Lotería Nacional 100 vrs al lago. The best bakery in town with a good selection of European-style white and brown bread, cookies, cakes and other treats. They serve sandwiches and coffee too, and there's a second branch on the popular Calle La Calzada.

⊕ Entertainment

Masaya *p659, map p659*
Bars and clubs
Coco Jambo, next to the *malecón*, T2522-6141. Fri-Sun from 1900. US$2, very popular disco, mixed music, lots of fun. A couple of other discos in the area.

La Ronda, south side of Parque Central, T2522-3310. Tue-Thu 1100-2400, Fri-Sun 1100-0200. Music and drinks, beautiful building with a young festive crowd.

Dance
Every Thu folkloric dances are performed behind the Mercado Artesanía in Masaya.

Granada *p661, maps p662*
Bars and clubs
The action tends to gravitate towards Calle La Calzada with a kind of thronging carnivalesque atmosphere Fri-Sun evenings. This can be rather grim or quite jolly, depending on your level of inebriation.

Centralito, Calle La Calzada, Parque Central, 2½ c al lago. Popular with Nicas as well as foreigners, Centralito often sees spirited (and well-oiled) crowds gathered at its outdoor tables on Calle La Calzada. A good place to meet the locals, get loud and ridiculous, and soak up the local ambience.

El Club, northwest corner of Parque Central, 3 c abajo. A modern bar with a European ambience, pumping dance music and a mixture of locals and foreigners. Stylish and a cut above the rest. Most popular Thu-Sat, when parties run late into the night.

Kelly's Bar, Calle el Caimito, 1 c al lago. Feisty boozer that's popular with a young beer-swilling crowd. Happy hour is every day 1600-1800, Texas Hold'em is Mon at 1800, and live music Wed at 2100. They show sports on TV, have a selection of games, and play rock from the 70s, 80s and 90s. There's also a kitchen and they boast over 30 types of cocktail.

Nuestro Mundo, southeast corner of Parque Central, next to the Alcaldía. A large space with 2 floors of diversions. Featured entertainment include billiards, live music, table football, Nintendo, karaoke and cable TV. **Zoom Bar**, Calle Calzada, Parque Central, 3 c lago, across from Hospedaje Cocibolca, www.zoombargranada.com. A very North American sports bar with a big-screen TV and American football memorabilia. Very popular with beer-soaked gringos and older gentlemen expats (who are invariably accompanied by much younger Nica women). The burgers, contrary to the sign outside, are only average.

Cinema
1 block behind **Hotel Alhambra**, 2 screens, but open irregularly.

⊛ Festivals and events

Granada *p661, maps p662*
Mar Folklore, Artesanía and Food Festival for 3 days (check locally for dates).
Mar/Apr Holy Week.
14-30 Aug Assumption of the Virgin.
Aug La Hípica takes place 2nd weekend of Aug. The Sun preceding La Hípica is **La Fiesta de Toros** with bulls running in the streets of Granada.
25 Dec Christmas celebrated with masked and costumed performers.

○ Shopping

Granada *p661, maps p662*
El Mercado de Granada, Parque Central, 1 c abajo, then south on Calle Atravesada, is a large green building surrounded by many street stalls. It's dark, dirty and packed. Just west of the market is **Supermercado Palí**, also dark and dirty, with a selection of low-price goods. The best (and most modern) supermarket is **La Colonia**, on the highway to Masaya, from the Esso at the end of Av Elena Arellano, 1½ c al lago.

▲ Activities and tours

Granada *p661, maps p662*
Boating, kayaking and windsurfing
Mombotour, Centro Comercial Granada No 2, next to BAC, T2552-4548, www.mombo tour.com. Having acquired the reputable 'Island Kayaks' agency, Mombotour offer kayak lessons and guided tours of the Isletas, which can be combined with longer birding expeditions. A 2½-hr kayak tour costs US$30 including guide, transportation and entrance fees; book in advance.
NicarAgua Dulce, Marina Cocibola, Bahía de Asese, T2552-6351, www.nicaraguadulce. com. An ecologically aware outfit that contributes to local communities. They offer kayak rental by the hour or day to explore the lesser-visited Asese Bay, which can be done with or without a guide, or additional bicycle rental if you wish to explore the peninsula.
Zapatera Tours, Calle Palmira contiguo a la Cancha, T8842-2587, www.zapatera tours.com. This long-established company specializes in lake tours with trips to Las Isletas, Zapatera, Ometepe and the Solentiname archipelago. They also offer biking, hiking and windsurfing.

Canopy tours
See also page 666.
Mombacho Canopy Tour, T8997-5846, canopy@cablenet.com.ni (book at least 24 hrs in advance). Daily 0900-1700, is located on the road up to the Mombacho cloud forest reserve. US$30, US$10 student discount. It combines well with a visit to the cloud forest reserve which is on this side of the volcano.
Mombotour, Centro Comercial Granada No2, next to BAC, T2552-4548, www.mombo tour.com. US$38 per person. Cost includes transfers by 4WD up and down the mountain from Granada; transfers normally leave at 0830 and 1330 daily and you must book in advance.

Cycling
Cycling is a great way to explore the area, particularly the peninsula de Asese. Many

agencies rent out bikes, but these are some specialists:

Bicimaximo, east side of the Parque Central, next to Va Pues, T8387-6789, info@bici maximo.com. Cycle rentals at US$4 for a half day, US$6 for an 8- to 12-hr day.

Detour, Alcaldía, 150 vrs al lago, Calle Caimito. Good bicycles with shock absorber, locks, maps, helmets, tips and repair kit at US$2/hr, US$5 for a half day, US$8 for a full 24 hrs.

Cultural and community tourism

UCA Tierra y Agua, Shell Palmira, 75 vrs abajo, T2552-0238, www.ucatierrayagua.org. Daily 0830-1630. This organization will help you organize a visit to rural communities around Granada including La Granadilla, Nicaragua Libre and Aguas Agrias. Very interesting and highly recommended for a perspective on local life and the land.

Health and spa

Pure Natural Health and Fitness Center, Calle Corrales, from Convento San Fransisco, 1½ c al lago, T8481-3264, www.purenica. com. A range of well-priced packages and therapies including excellent massage, reiki and beauty treatments. Professional, friendly and highly recommended (especially for yoga).

Seeing Hands, inside EuroCafe, off the north-west corner of Parque Central. This excellent organization offers blind people an opportunity to earn a living as masseurs. A range of effective, professional massages are available, from a 15-min back, neck and shoulder massage, US$3, to a 1-hr table massage, US$12.50.

Tour operators

The following list is not exhaustive, but includes some of the more well-established companies.

De Tour, Alcaldía,150 vrs al lago, T2552-0155, www.detour-ameriquecentrale.com. This relatively new operator offers a range of interesting cultural and historical tours, including unique trips to the gold mines of Chontales. Other possibilities are coffee tours, horse riding, kayaks, community tourism and bicycle rental. Different and worth a look.

Oro Travel, Convento San Francisco, ½ c norte, T2552-4568, www.orotravel.com. Granada's best tour operator offers quality, specialized tours and trips, many including transfers and hotels. Owner Pascal speaks French, English and German. Friendly and helpful. Recommended.

Tierra Tour, Calle la Calzada, catedral, 2 c lago, T0862-9580, www.tierratour.com. This well-established Dutch-Nicaraguan agency offers a wide range of affordable services including good-value trips to Las Isletas, cloud forest tours, birding expeditions and shuttles. Helpful and friendly.

Va Pues, Parque Central, blue house next to the cathedral, T552-8291, www.vapues.com. This award-winning agency offers canopy tours, turtle expeditions, Zapatera cultural heritage tours, car rental, domestic flights and a 'romantic getaway' tour to a private island. They work closely with a sister company, **Agua Trails**, www.aguatrails.com, which operates out of Costa Rica and specializes in the Río San Juan region on the border.

⊖ Transport

Masaya p659, map p659

Bus The regular market or Mercado Municipal is where most buses leave from, it is 4 blocks east of the south side of the artisan market. Express bus to **Managua (Roberto Huembes)**, every 20 mins, 0500-1900, US$0.60, 50 mins. To **Jinotepe**, every 20 mins, 0500-1800, US$0.50, 1½ hrs. To **Granada**, every 30 mins, 0600-1800, US$0.50, 45 mins. To **Matagalpa**, 0600, 0700, US$2.75, 4 hrs.

From Parque San Miguelito, between the artisan and regular markets on Calle San Miguel, express buses leave for La UCA in **Managua**, every 30 mins, 0530-1900, US$0.80, 40 mins. You can also board any bus on the Carretera a Masaya to **Managua** or towards **Granada**. Note the sign above front windshield for destination and flag it down. For **Parque Nacional Volcán Masaya** take any Managua bus and ask to step down at park entrance. Buses to **Valle de Apoyo** leave twice daily, 1000, 1530, 45 mins, US$0.70, then walk down the road that drops into the crater.

International bus North and south-bound Transnica (reservations T2552-3872), and King Quality buses stop at the Texaco staion on the highway. Ticabus, agency, in front of the Old Farmacia Aguilar, Ciber Centro, T2552-0445, stops at the Esso.

Taxi Fares around town are US$0.40 per person anywhere in the city. Approximate taxi fares to: **Granada** US$15, **Laguna de Apoyo**, US$7, **Managua** US$20, **airport** US$25. Horse-drawn carriages (*coches*) are for local transport inside Masaya, US$0.50.

Granada p661, maps p662
Boat and ferry
For short expeditions, you can easily find boats by the lakeside *malecón* and in the Complejo Turístico. Otherwise try **Marina Cocibolca**, www.marinacocibolca.net. Check the Marina's administrative offices for information on costs and schedules for visits to the Isletas, Zapatera, and nearby private reserves.

For long-distance ferry, services depart from the *malecón* and schedules are subject to change, www.epn.ni. The ferry to **San Carlos** leaves the main dock on Mon and Thu at 1400, and stops at **Altagracia, Ometepe** after 4 hrs (US$4 1st class, US$2 2nd class), **Morrito** (8 hrs, US$5 1st class, US$3, 2nd class), **San Miguelito** (10 hrs, US$5.50 1st class, US$3 2nd class) and finally **San Carlos** (14 hrs, US$9.50 1st class, US$4 2nd class). This journey is slow, take your own food and water, pillow and a sleeping bag if you have them. The first class deck is much more comfortable than the crowded and noisy 2nd-class deck below – worth the extra dollars. The ferry returns from San Carlos on Tue and Fri following the same route. For **Altagracia** you can also take a cargo boat with passenger seats on Wed and Sat (1200, 4½ hrs, US$2). It is faster to go overland to **San Jorge** and catch a 1-hr

ferry to **Ometepe**, see San Jorge, page 679, for more details.

Bus
Intercity bus For the border with **Costa Rica** use **Rivas** bus to connect to **Peñas Blancas** service or use international buses.

Express minibuses to La UCA in **Managua** from a small lot just south of Parque Central on Calle Vega, every 20 mins, 0500-2000, 45 mins, US$0.95. Another express service departs from a different terminal, shell station, 1 c abajo, 1 c norte, which goes to the sketchy **Mercado Oriental**, US$0.95. Either can drop you on the highway exit to **Masaya**, US$0.60, from where it's a 20-min walk or 5-min taxi ride to the centre. Buses to Mercado Roberto Huembes, Managua, US$0.60, also leave from a station near the old hospital in Granada, west of centre, but they're slower and only marginally cheaper.

Leaving from the Shell station, Mercado, 1 c al lago: to **Rivas**, 7 daily, 0540-1510, 1½ hrs, US$1.50, most depart before midday; to Nandaime, every 20 mins, 0500-1800, 20 mins, US0.70; to **Niquinohomo**, every 30 mins, 0550-1800, 45 mins, US$1, use this bus for visits to **Diriá, Diriomo, San Juan de Oriente, Catarina**; to **Jinotepe**, 0550, 0610, 0830, 1110, 1210 and 1710, 1½ hrs, US$0.80, for visits to **Los Pueblos**, including **Masatepe** and **San Marcos**. There's a second terminal nearby, Shell station, 1 c abajo, 1 c norte, serving **Masaya**, every 30 mins, 0500-1800, 40 mins, US$0.50.
International bus To **San José**, Costa Rica, daily. See individual offices for schedules: **King Quality**, Av Arellano, from Shell Guapinol, 1½ c al sur, www.king-qualityca.com; **Ticabus**, Av Arellano, from the old hospital, 1½ c al Sur, T2552-8535, www.ticabus.com; **Transnica**, Calle Xalteva, Frente de Iglesia Auxiliadora, T2552-6619, www.transnica.com.

Shuttles to **Laguna Apoyo**, Mon, Wed, Fri, 1030, from the Bearded Monkey Hostel, when there is sufficient demand, ½ hr, US$2. They return at 1800.

Paxeos, Parque Central, blue house next to cathedral, T2552-8291, www.paxeos.com. Daily shuttles to **Managua airport**, US$12; **León,**US$20; **San Juan del Sur**, US$23; and **San Jorge**, US$18. Also try **Tierra Tour** (see Tour operators, above) for competitive rates.

Car hire
Budget Rent a Car, at the Shell station near the north city entrance, T2552-2323, provides very good service. Also try **Dollar**, in Hotel Plaza Colón, T2552-8515; or **Alamo**, in Hotel Colonial, T2552-2877. If you rent a car in Managua you can leave it here, or you can hire it in Granada and drop it off in Managua or other northern destinations. However, cheaper rates can be found in Managua with other companies.

Taxi
Granada taxi drivers are useful for finding places away from the centre, US$0.50 during the day, US$1 at night. To **Managua** US$25, but check taxi looks strong enough to make the journey.

● Directory

Masaya *p659, map p659*
Banks All banks will change dollars. The **BAC**, opposite the northwest corner of the artisan market, has an ATM; as does **Banpro**, opposite the southwest corner. There's a **Bancentro** on the west side of the plaza with a Visa ATM. You'll also find street changers around the plaza. **Internet** Intecomp, is south of the main plaza. Also try **Mi PC a colores**, on Sergio Delgadillo.

Around Masaya *p660*
Language schools Apoyo Intensive Spanish School, Laguna de Apoyo, T8882-3992, www.gaianicaragua.org, groups of 4, 5 hrs' tuition per day. 5-day programme, US$220 for a week including accommodation and food or US$710 per month, family stays available. It is also possible to stay in the lodge without enrolling in the school, from

US$16 plus meals, contact the school for more information.

Granada *p661, map p662*
Banks Banco de Centro América (BAC) Parque Central, 1 c abajo, on Calle La Libertad, has an ATM and will change TCs and US$. ATM at Esso Station (15-min walk from town centre) accepts Cirrus, Maestro, MasterCard as well. **Banpro**, BAC, 1 c al sur, has a less reliable ATM and money-changing facilities. Bancentro, BAC, 1 c al norte, has a Visa ATM. **Western** Union, from fire station ½ block south, Mon-Sat 0800-1300, 1400-1700. **Internet** Internet cafés can be found all over town, while most *hostales* and hotels also offer internet access, including international calls. **Language schools** APC Spanish School, west side of Parque Central, T2552-4203, www.spanish granada.com. Flexible immersion classes in this centrally located language school. There are volunteer opportunities with local NGOs. **Casa Xalteva**, Iglesia Xalteva, ½ c al norte, T2552-2436, www.casaxalteva.com. Small Spanish classes for beginners and advanced students, 1 week to several months. Home stays arranged, and voluntary work with children, recommended. **Nicaragua Mía Spanish School**, inside Maverick's reading lounge, Calle Arsenal, behind hotel Colonial, T2552-2755, www.nicaragua-mia-spanish school.com. An established and professional language school with various learning options, from hourly to weekly tuition. The school takes an ethical approach and contributes to local causes. **Laundry** Mapache Laundry Service, Calle Calzada and El Cisne, from the Parque Central 2 c al lago, ½ c norte, T2552-6711, open 0900-1800, fast service, US$5 for a medium load; and **La Lavandería**, almost opposite, Calle La Libertad, good lads, similar rates. **Medical services** Red Cross, T2552-2711. **Police** T2552- 2929. **Post** Calle El Arsenal, from Convento San Fransisco, ½ c al lago, DHL, next to Casa de los Tres Mundos, T2552-6847. **Telephone** Claro (Enitel) on northeast corner of Parque Central. Movistar, from the northeast corner of the Parque Central, ½ c norte. ●

Rivas Isthmus and Ometepe Island

The slender isthmus of Rivas, bordered by Costa Rica to the south, is a well-travelled agricultural department served by the Pan-American Highway. The department capital is a pleasant, if uninteresting transportation hub with connections to some of the country's finest attractions. To the west lie burgeoning Pacific resorts, fantastic waves and famous turtle-nesting sites. To the east lies the port of San Jorge, Lake Nicaragua and the tranquil island of Ometepe, rising mysteriously with twin volcanoes. To the south, the Pan-American Highway continues its journey into Costa Rica and beyond, making Rivas an exciting department of diverse scenery, transition and international frontiers. ▸▸ *For listings, see pages 681-689.*

Managua to Rivas → *For listings, see pages 681-689.*

Approximately 26 km from Managua, the Pan-American Highway climbs to 900 m at Casa Colorada. Further on, at El Crucero, a paved branch road goes through the Sierra south to the Pacific beaches of Pochomil and Masachapa. The highway continues through the beautiful scenery of the sierras to **Diriamba**, in a coffee-growing district 42 km from Managua. In the centre of the town is the **Museo Ecológico de Trópico Seco** ① *Tue-Sat 0800-1200, 1400-1700, Sun 0800-1200, US$1,* with displays of local flora and fauna, including coffee and turtles, and a section on volcanoes. The local fiesta is on 20 January. There is a 32-km dirt road direct to the beach at **Masachapa** (no buses).

Five kilometres north of Diriamba a paved road branches off the main highway and runs east through **San Marcos**, Masatepe (famous for wooden and rattan furniture) and Niquinohomo to Catarina and Masaya. A road also leads to **La Concepción**, a small industrious village in the highlands, very typical of this part of Nicaragua, where few travellers go. The area is rich in pineapple, pitaya, coffee, mandarins and oranges and the people are welcoming. Access is by bus from Jinotepe, every 20 minutes, US$0.50, or from Managua's Roberto Huembes terminal, every half an hour, US$0.75.

Five kilometres beyond Diriamba is **Jinotepe**, capital of the coffee-growing district of Carazo. It has a fine neoclassical church with modern stained-glass windows from Irún, in Spain. 'Liberation Day' is celebrated on 5 July here, while the fiesta in honour of St James the Greater runs from 24-26 July.

From **Nandaime**, 21 km south of Jinotepe, a paved road runs north to Granada (bus US$0.50). Nandaime has two interesting churches, El Calvario and La Parroquia (1859-1872). The annual fiesta, 24-27 July, features masked dancers.

At Km 85 a signed turn-off leads down a long dirt road to the private reserve and lodge of **Domitila** (see Sleeping, page 681). About 45 km beyond Nandaime (US$0.40 by bus) is Rivas.

Rivas → *For listings, see pages 681-689. Colour map 4, A2. Population: 41,764. Altitude: 139 m.*

The Costa Rican national hero, drummer Juan Santamaría, sacrificed his life here in 1856 when setting fire to a building captured by the infamous William Walker. On the town's Parque Central is a lovely old basilica. In the dome you can see the fresco of the sea battle against the ships of Protestantism and Communism. The Parque has some old, arcaded buildings on one side, but also some new buildings.

Rivas is a good stopping place if in transit by land through Nicaragua. The bus station, adjacent to the market, is on the northwest edge of town about eight blocks from the main highway. The road from the lake port of San Jorge joins this road at Rivas; 11 km beyond Rivas, at La Virgen on the shore of Lake Nicaragua, it branches south to San Juan del Sur. The **tourist office (INTUR)** ⓘ *75 m west of the Texaco station (in front of Hospedaje Lidia), T2453-4914 (ask for Sr Francisco Cárdenas)*, has good maps of Nicaragua and general information.

Refugio de Vida Silvestre Río Escalante Chacocente
ⓘ *US$0.70, www.chacocente.info.*
Between Nandaime and Rivas are various turnings south that lead eventually to the Pacific coast (all are rough; high clearance is more important than 4WD). One of these turnings (89 km from Managua if going via Diriamba and Jinotepe; 61 km from Peñas Blancas), just south of the Río Ochomogo bridge, is signposted to the **Refugio de Vida Silvestre Río Escalante Chacocente**. This 4800-ha reserve of forest and beach is the second most important turtle nesting site in the country and one of the biggest tracts of tropical dry forest in the Pacific basin. The forest is full of mammal, reptile and birdlife and the beach is long and empty. Bring your own hammock and shade. The rough dirt road to the coast (45 km) goes to Las Salinas. Turn right here to **Astillero**, which has a fishing cooperative, and continue to the reserve. You will probably have to ask directions several times and cross a number of rivers, the last of which is impassable after rain without a very strong 4WD). Camping is safe and you can buy fish from the co-op. At **Chacocente**, there is a **Marena** office, a government-sponsored **turtle sanctuary** (signs say 'authorized personnel only'; don't be put off, they welcome visitors). The **Marena** wardens protect newly hatched turtles and help them make it to the sea (a magnificent sight from November to December). Unfortunately, turtle eggs are considered to have aphrodisiac properties and are used as a dietary supplement by the locals. **Marena** is virtually powerless to prevent egg theft, although for two months a year the reserve is protected by armed military personnel.

San Juan del Sur → *For listings, see pages 681-689. Colour map 4, A2.*

San Juan del Sur on the Pacific coast has a beautiful bay which is rapidly developing. A few years ago this was a humble fishing village, now tourists, expats and estate agents are transforming it into an expensive Costa Rican-style development. Still, the sunsets have to be seen to be believed, and the village has retained its small-town feel, for now at least. You'll find it 28 km from Rivas, south along the Pan-American Highway and then right to the coast along a road which is in good condition. There is also a direct dirt road from Rivas going through beautiful countryside, but it is only good when dry.

The town beach is cleaned daily, but at weekends and on holidays, especially Semana Santa, San Juan is busy; otherwise the beaches are quiet during the week. The **INTUR tourist office** ⓘ *between the beach and the market in front of Joxi, www.sanjuandelsur.org.ni, Mon-Fri 0900-1200, 1300-1700, Sat 0900-1200*, is helpful, sells maps and a guide of San Juan del Sur. Alternatively, try www.sanjuandelsurguide.com.

North of San Juan del Sur
There is an unpaved access road to beaches north of San Juan del Sur at the entrance to the town. **Playa Marsella** is a slowly growing resort set on a pleasant beach, but not one of the most impressive in the region. North of here, **Los Playones** is playing host to ever-increasing crowds of surfers with a scruffy beer shack and hordes of daily shuttle trucks. The waves are good for beginners, but are often heavily oversubscribed. **Maderas** is the next

beach along, where many shuttles claim to take you (they don't, they drop you at the car park at Los Playones). This is a pleasant, tranquil spot, good for swimming and host to some affordable lodgings, best booked in advance. **Bahía Majagual** is the next bay north, a lovely white-sand beach tucked into a cove. On the road to Majagual before reaching the beach is the private entrance to **Morgan's Rock** a multimillion-dollar private nature reserve, reforestation project and the most expensive hotel in Nicaragua. Much further north is the legendary surf spot of **Popoyo**, which is starting to get crowded with international surfers.

San Juan del Sur

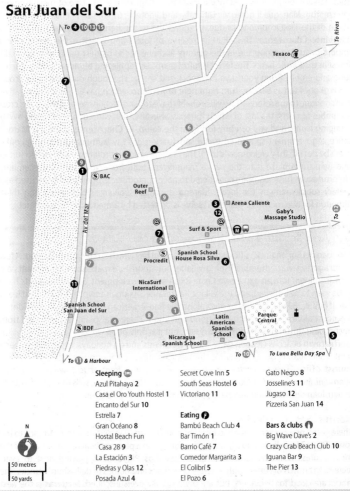

Sleeping
Azul Pitahaya **2**
Casa el Oro Youth Hostel **1**
Encanto del Sur **10**
Estrella **7**
Gran Océano **8**
Hostal Beach Fun
  Casa 28 **9**
La Estación **3**
Piedras y Olas **12**
Posada Azul **4**

Secret Cove Inn **5**
South Seas Hostel **6**
Victoriano **11**

Eating
Bambú Beach Club **4**
Bar Timón **1**
Barrio Café **7**
Comedor Margarita **3**
El Colibrí **5**
El Pozo **6**

Gato Negro **8**
Josseline's **11**
Jugaso **12**
Pizzería San Juan **14**

Bars & clubs
Big Wave Dave's **2**
Crazy Crab Beach Club **10**
Iguana Bar **9**
The Pier **13**

South of San Juan del Sur

You can take a boat to more pristine beaches such as **Playa del Coco** on the poor road to Ostional, or simply ask around for a bus leaving to Ostional (1300 at the market, two hours). The surfing on nearby beaches is good, **Playa Remanso** and Yankee are current hotspots but you should not walk to them under any circumstances; use a taxi or the colectivos provided by hotels, hostels and surf shops. ▸▸ *See Transport, page 688.*

Refugio de Vida Silvestre La Flor ① *US$10, US$2.50 student discount, access by 4WD or on foot*, covers 800 ha of tropical dry forest, mangroves, estuary and beach. A beautiful, sweeping cove with sand and many trees, it is the most important and most visited beach by nesting sea turtles from August to November. During the high season, armed guards protect the arrival of the turtle (sometimes in their thousands and usually lasting a period of three days). The rangers are very happy to explain the creatures' reproductive habits. Many birds live in the protected mangroves at the south end of the beach. Camping is provided during the turtle arrivals, US$25 per night, first come, first served. Bring a hammock and mosquito netting as insects are vicious at dusk. The ranger station sells soft drinks. To get there, the exit for the dirt path south is 200 m before the entrance to San Juan del Sur, 21 km from the highway. Several rivers, most of which have firm beds, must be crossed.

On the southwestern shore of Lake Nicaragua close to Rivas, **San Jorge**, is the main departure point for Ometepe Island, but on Sundays in summer the town itself is very lively with music, baseball, swimming and lots of excursion buses.

Isla Ometepe → *For listings, see pages 681-689. Colour map 4, A2.*

The largest freshwater island in the world, Ometepe is a highlight of any trip to Nicaragua. It has two volcanoes, one of them, **Concepción**, a perfect cone rising to 1610 m; the other, **Volcán Maderas**, rising to 1394 m. There are two main villages, on either side of Volcán Concepción: Moyogalpa and Altagracia, which are connected by bus. **Moyogalpa** is the main port and island gateway, the usual arrival point and now home to an embroynic travellers' scene. **Altagracia** is smaller and more charming, with ferry connections to Granada and the Río San Juan. The people of Ometepe are said to be the kindest in Nicaragua, partly because the Revolution and Civil War were never waged here. There are many indigenous **petroglyphs** on the island, the best being near **Finca Magdalena**.

Safety Several hikers have fallen to their death trying to summit Ometepe's volcanoes unguided. Always use professional and qualified guides, and beware local scammers. In recent years, motorbikes have taken over the island and some tourists have been in nasty and expensive accidents. Clarify all insurance issues before hiring a vehicle.

Altagracia → *Colour map 4, A2.*

If arriving by ferry from Granada or San Carlos, pickups provide transport for the 2-km ride into town. In the main plaza there is a **sculpture park** of pre-Columbian-style ceramics with some large basalt statues, similar to those housed in the San Francisco museum in Granada. The **Museo de Ometepehas** ① *opposite the Parque Central, US$1, guide in Spanish*, has displays covering local ethnographic and environmental themes. Ask for the birdwatching site about 3 km from Altagracia; birds fly in the late afternoon to nest on offshore islands.

You can stroll to the base of **Volcán Concepción** (last major eruption in 1954), for good views of the lake in the company of many birds and howler monkeys. A full ascent takes about five hours (take water), with alpine vegetation, heat from the crater and howler monkeys as attractions. It gets very steep near the summit and visibility is often restricted by clouds. Recommended guides include Eduardo Manzanares or Berman Gómez from **Ometepe Expeditions**. There is an alternative route up Volcán Concepción from behind the church in Moyogalpa. The walk takes eight hours; a machete is useful. Camping is possible near the top. South of Volcán Concepción is Laguna Charco Verde (see below).

Around Isla Ometepe → *Colour map 4, A2.*

For **Volcán Maderas**, take an early bus (0430 or 0530) from Altagracia to Balgües (or stay overnight) and ask for **Finca Magdalena** (20 minutes' walk). From here it's a 2½-hour walk through banana plantations and forest to the beautiful lagoon in the crater (the path can be very muddy, boots recommended). This is one of the country's finest Pacific basin cloud forests with howler monkeys accompanying you on your way to the volcano summit. The climb is not technical, but a guide is highly recommended. They can be found at the coffee cooperative in Balgües, **Finca Magdalena** and in Moyogalpa at **Ometepe Expeditions**. On the southwest flank of Volcán Maderas is **Salto San Ramón**, a 110-m waterfall, accessible from the settlement of San Ramón. Take water on all hikes and climbs.

Other activities on the island include the **Laguna Charco Verde** (ask around for the legend on Chico Largo who is still said to watch the lagoon), the popular beach of **Santo Domingo**,

Ometepe

To Granada ▶

To San Carlos

To Granada

San Marcos · · San Mateo ○ San José del Norte ○ Puerto de Gracia

La Flor ○

Altagracia

El Chipote ○

Moyogalpa

Volcán Concepción (1610m)

La Primavera ○

Urbaite ○

Playa Santo Domingo

Punta Jesús María

Esquípulas ○

Los Angeles ○

San José del Sur

La Unión ○

Isthmus of Istián

Socorro Balgües

Bona Fide

To San Jorge

Sinacapa

Santa Cruz

El Porvenir

La Palmera

Charco Verde ○ Quiste

Lago de Nicaragua

San Antonio ○

Mérida ·

San Ramón Waterfall

Volcán Maderas (1394m)

San Pedro

San Ramón

Tichuna

N

5 km
5 miles

Sleeping 🛏
Albergue Ecológico
  Porvenir **22**
American & Café **14**
Caballito Mar **4**
Central **5**
Charco Verde Inn **6**
Chico Largo Hostel **19**
Costa Azul **18**

El Encanto **20**
Finca del Sol **8**
Finca Ecológica El
  Zopilote **23**
Finca Magdalena **13**
Finca Playa Venecia **15**
Finca Santo Domingo **2**
Hacienda Mérida **7**
Hospedaje Ortiz **9**

Island Landing **10**
Istiam **1**
Little Morgan's **11**
Totoco **12**
Villa Paraíso **3**

Petroglyphs ∴

and a swimming hole, '**Ojo de Agua**' ⓘ *close to Santo Domingo, US$1*. The village of **Mérida** is a good departure point for kayak trips up the Río Istiam and, near San José del Sur, a new museum houses the island's best collection of pre-Columbian artefacts, **El Ceibo** ⓘ *0800-1200, 1300-1700, US$6*; look out for signs on the Moyogalpa– Altagracia highway. The island does not offer a lot in terms of entertainment besides some local dancing at weekends. Every month there is the **Fiesta de Luna Llena** (full-moon party) at Charco Verde (ask around for directions and times). **Fiestas patronales** are held year-round in different villages, the festivities 22-26 July in Moyogalpa and 12-18 November in Altagracia include both religious processions and bull riding.

◉ Rivas Isthmus and Ometepe Island listings

For Sleeping and Eating price codes and other relevant information, see Essentials pages 31-33.

● Sleeping

Managua to Rivas *p676*
B Domitila, Km 85, T8881-1786, www.
domitila.org. This tropical dry forest reserve near the shores of Lake Nicaragua and Isla Zapatera has some fine, simple, rustic lodgings with private bath and sawdust toilets. Hiking trails are charged at high rates; visits to Isla Zapatera can be arranged and are better value.

Rivas *p676*
B Nicarao Inn Hotel, northwest corner of Parque Central, 2 c abajo, T2563-3836, www.hotelnicaroinn.com.ni. The finest hotel in Rivas has 18 tastefully decorated, comfortable rooms, all with a/c, cable TV, hot water and Wi-Fi. Polite and professional. Breakfast included.
D Español, across from the southeast corner of Iglesia San Pedro, T2563-0006. Dusty old cheapie with 5 basic rooms, each has bath and fan. Clean but faded. Restaurant attached.
E-F Hospedaje Hilmor, across from the northeast corner of Iglesia San Pedro, T2563-5030. A range of economical rooms. Some have private bath and TV (**E**), others are ultra-basic with shared bath (**F**). Shared kitchen is available and breakfasts are cooked on request at extra cost. The owner is friendly.

San Juan del Sur *p677, map p678*
Hotel prices in San Juan del Sur double for Semana Santa, Christmas and New Year.

LL Piedras y Olas, Parroquia, 1½ c arriba, T2563-7000, www.pelicaneyesresort.com. Beautiful, peaceful, luxurious houses and hotel suites with private bath, a/c, cable TV, sitting area, great furnishings and views of the bay. Sailing trips on the *Pelican Eyes* boat can be arranged. Recommended.
AL Victoriano, Paseo Marítimo, costado norte Enitel, T2568-2005, www.hotel victoriano.com.ni. This gorgeous clapboard mansion almost looks like it belongs on the Caribbean. It is actually a restored English Victorian-era family house. Rooms are simple, stylish and elegant with a/c, cable TV, DVD, Wi-Fi and all the usual amenities. One of the best in town and a place to be seen.
A La Estación, Mercado, 2 c al mar, T2568-2304, www.laestacion.com.ni. Built on the ruins of the old railway station, although you would never have guessed from looking at this modern building. La Estación has 18 rooms in total, including suites with sea views, various doubles and singles, all clean, comfortable and well-tended. Services include restaurant-bar, Wi-Fi, a/c and hot water.
A Posada Azul, BDF, ½ c arriba, T2568-2698, www.laposadaazul.com. La Posada Azul is a tranquil and intimate lodging with a handful of comfortable, well-furnished rooms. There's a lush garden, self-service bar and a modest pool. An attractive wooden building with lots of history and character. Full breakfast included.
B Gran Océano, northwest corner of Parque Central, 1½ c al mar, T2568-2219, www.hotel granoceano.com.ni. A popular hotel that also specializes in sports fishing expeditions.

They have 22 rooms with private bath, a/c, hot water and cable TV. The top-floor rooms are much more spacious and comfortable. Breakfast included.

C Hotel Azul Pitahaya, mercado, 1 c al mar, T2568-2294, www.hotelazulsanjuan.com. Comfortable rooms with good mattresses, hot water, cable TV and a/c. There's Wi-Fi in the café downstairs, which serves familiar gringo food. Tours, surf board rental and transportation available. Breakfast included.

C Hotel Encanto del Sur, iglesia, 100 m sur, T2568-2222, www.hotelencantodelsur.com. One of the best deals in town. This hotel has 18 clean, modern, comfortable rooms with private bath, cable TV, Wi-Fi and a/c, cheaper with fan (**D**). Quiet and away from the action. Recommended.

D Secret Cove Inn, Mercado, 2 c sur, ½ c abajo, T8672-3013, info@thesecretcovenicaragua.com. Intimate and friendly bed and breakfast lodging with a handful of clean, comfortable, well-appointed rooms. They offer tours and information, use of kitchen, hammocks, Wi-Fi and a chilled out communal area. Very relaxed, welcoming and helpful. Nice owners. Recommended.

D-E Hostal Beach Fun Casa 28, mercado, 1 c al mar, 1 c norte, T2568-2441, javieralara@hotmail.com. Long-standing budget favourite with a range of simple economical private rooms, with (**D**) or without (**E**) bath and TV. A few have a/c (**C**). Services include free Wi-Fi, use of computer terminal and shared kitchen. Tours, transport to/from the beaches and ATV rental offered. English spoken.

E Estrella, mercado, 2 c sur, T2568-2210. Weathered and fading old cheapie with simple rooms, partitioned walls, good breezes, sea views and shared bath. Overlooks the beach and is equipped with Wi-Fi, computer terminals. Famously discourteous staff and management, but an old favourite that is now a SJDS institution.

E South Seas Hostel, Texaco, 1½ c al mar, T2568-2084, www.southseasnicaragua.com. A pleasant Nica-owned budget lodging with a relaxed family atmosphere. They have

clean, comfortable, simple rooms with fan and shared bath (**C** with a/c), and there's also a great kitchen for your own cooking, a pool and a sun terrace. Discounts for longer stays. Recommended.

F Casa el Oro Youth Hostel, Hotel Colonial, 20 vrs sur, T2568-2415, www.casaeloro.com. A very popular hostel with clean, economical dorms (**F**, the ones upstairs are better), simple but pleasant private rooms (**D**), and a plethora of services including Wi-Fi, computer terminals, shuttles, tours and surf lessons (see Tour operators, below). Youthful, fun and buzzing.

North of San Juan del Sur

LL Morgan's Rock Hacienda & Ecolodge, Playa Ocotal, sales office is in Costa Rica, T506-8670-7676, www.morgansrock.com. Famous 'ecolodge' with precious wood bungalows and unrivalled views of the ocean and forest. The cabins are built on a high bluff above the beach and are connected to the restaurant and pool by a suspension bridge. Highly recommended if you've got the dosh.

AL Buena Vista Surf Club, Playa Maderas, www.buenavistasurfclub.com, T8863-4180. The **Buena Vista** boasts several attractive (but rustic) treehouses up on the cliffs, each with private bath, fan and mosquito nets. The communal 'rancho', where guests gather to eat and drink, has superb views of the ocean. Breakfast and dinner included; minimum 2 night stay. Board rental and tours available.

D-G Camping Matilda, Playa Maderas, T2456-3461. The best cheap lodgings in the area. They have 8 rooms with private bath (**D**), 2 small dormitories (**F**), and some funny little houses that look just like dog kennels (**G**). Very friendly, relaxed and pleasant. Often full.

South of San Juan del Sur *p679*

LL-AL Parque Marítimo El Coco, 18 km south of San Juan del Sur, T8999-8069, www.playaelcoco.com.ni. Differently sized apartments and houses right on the sand and close to La Flor Wildlife refuge. Suits 4-10 people, most have a/c, all have baths, TV and cleaning service included. Rates vary according to season, weekday nights less expensive. Interesting rural excursions are offered.

B Latin Latitudes, Playa Yankee, T8671-9698, www.latinlatitudes.com. B&B that's received good reports from former guests. This great-looking house, 10 mins from the beach, has just a few rooms and suites (book in advance), all comfortable, clean and well appointed. Plenty of hammocks to chill out in and Wi-Fi access too. Full breakfast included.

Isla Ometepe *p679, map p680*

Moyogalpa

C-G Island Landing, muelle municipal, 20 vrs arriba, almost next to the port. A very new, comfortable and attractive hotel with a range of options. For the impoverished there are hammocks (**G**) and dorms (**F**). For the better off there are private rooms (**E**), well-equipped apartments (**C**) and comfortable *casitas*. Island Landing has breezy views of the lake, volcano and the bustling port. Friendly and hospitable. Recommended.

D American Café and Hotel, muelle municipal, 100 vrs arriba, a white building on the right, T8645-7193, simonesantelli14@gmail.com. Excellent value, handsome, comfortable, spacious, well-furnished and immaculately clean rooms. Hosts Bob and Simone are very friendly and hospitable. Italian, German, Spanish and English spoken. A good source of information. Recommended.

Moyogalpa to Altagracia

B-C Hotel Charco Verde Inn, almost next to the lagoon, San José del Sur, T8887-9302, www.charcoverde.com.ni. Pleasant *cabañas* with private bath, a/c, terrace (**B**), and doubles with private bath and fan (**C**). Services include restaurant, bar, Wi-Fi, tours, kayaks, bicycles, horses and transportation. An Ometepe favourite with good reports.

C-E Finca Playa Venecia, 250 m from the main road, San José del Sur, T8887-0191, www.fincavenecia.com. Very chilled out, comfortable lodgings and a lovely lakeside garden. They have 4 rooms (**D**) and 15 *cabañas* (**C**), some with lake view and some

cheaper ones with fan (**D**). There's a good restaurant in the grounds, Wi-Fi, horses, tours, motorcycles, transportation and English-speaking guides. Recommended.

E-G Chico Largo Hostel, next to Finca Playa Venecia, T8886-4069, www.chicolargo.net. 2 economical dorms, 1 with lake views (**F**), 1 without (**G**). They also have a few private rooms with bath and fan (**F**). Services include ATV rental, a camping area and a grill for cooking. Boat tours offered. Friendly and relaxed.

Altagracia

E-F Hotel Central, Iglesia, 2 c sur, T2552-8770, doscarflores@yahoo.es. 19 rooms and 6 *cabañas*, most with private bath and fan. There's a restaurant and bar, bicycle rental, tours, laundry service, parking, and hammocks. They've got a stash of games to keep you entertained in the evening. Credit cards accepted. Friendly and recommended.

F Hospedaje y Restaurante Ortiz, del Hotel Central, 1 c al arriba, ½ c al sur, follow signs near entrance to town, T8923-1628, www.hospedajeortiz.com. A friendly, relaxed hotel managed by the hospitable Don Mario. They offer a range of pleasant budget rooms with shared bath (rooms with private bath are also in the works, **E**). An amiable family atmosphere. Highly recommended for budget travellers.

Playa Santo Domingo

A-D Villa Paraíso, beachfront, T2569-4859, www.villaparaiso.com.ni. One of Ometepe's longest-established and most pleasant lodgings. A beautiful, peaceful setting with 25 stone *cabañas* (**B**) and 5 rooms (**D**). Some of the cabins have a patio and lake view (**A**). Often fully booked, best to reserve in advance.

B-D Finca Santo Domingo, Playa Santo Domingo, north side of Villa Paraíso, T2569-4862, www.hotelfincasantodomingo.com. Friendly lakeside hotel with a range of rooms (**C-D**) and a handful of bungalows across the road (**B**), all with private bath. The rooms are generally clean and brightly coloured, but reports are sometimes mixed. The restaurant serves *comida típica* and has good views.

C-D Hotel Costa Azul, Villa Paraíso, 50 vrs sur, T2569-4867, www.hotelcostaazul.com.ni. The **Costa Azul** has 12 big, clean, well-lit rooms with good solid furniture, a/c, private bath and TV with DVD. There's also a restaurant serving *comida típica* and breakfasts. Bike and motorbike rental, tours and guides available. Cheaper with fan (**D**).

Santa Cruz

C Finca del Sol, from the fork in the road, 200 m towards Balgües, T8364-6394, www.finca delsol.blinkweb.com. A lovely natural place with comfortable and ecologically designed *cabañas*. They grow their own organic fruit and veg and also farm sheep. A maximum of 8 guests are permitted at any one time and you will definitely need to book in advance. Great, friendly hosts and recommended.

D El Encanto, 100 m north of Santa Cruz, on the beach road, T8867-7128, www.goel encanto.com. A very tranquil and well-tended *finca* with beautiful views and lots of sleepy, breezy porches. The rooms are good, clean and comfortable, and there's fine volcanic vistas. Various tours and dorm beds (**F**) are also available. Friendly. Highly recommended.

E Albergue Ecológico Porvenir, Santa Cruz, T2552-8782, doscarflores@yahoo.es. Stunning views at this tranquil, secluded lodge at the foot of Maderas. Rooms are clean, comfortable and tidy, with private bath and fan. Scores of petroglyphs are scattered throughout the grounds, making it one of the island's most important archaeological sites. Nearby trails run to the crater lake and miradors. Recommended.

E Hotel Istiám, Villa Paraíso, opposite the beach, 1 km north of Santa Cruz, T8844-2200, ometeptlng@hotmail.com, reservations through Ometepetl in Moyogalpa. Basic and often seemingly abandoned, this friendly, family-run place has a wonderfully isolated location on the beach road. Rooms are simple but clean, with fan and bath, cheaper shared (**F**). A few rooms now have a/c (**D**). Restaurant, tours, kayaks, horses, wind-surfing and bike rental available. Recommended.

E-G Finca Ecológica El Zopilote, from the fork in the road, 300 m towards Balgües, T8369-0644, www.ometepezopilote.com. El Zopilote is a funky organic finca that's popular with backpackers, hippies and eco-warrior types. They offer dorm beds (**G**), hammocks (**G**) and *cabañas* (**E**), but are often full so it's best to book in advance. Offerings include full moon parties, voluntary work placements, use of kitchen, tours and horse riding. Tranquil and alternative.

F-G Little Morgan's, from the fork in the road, 200 m towards Balgües, T8949-7074, www.littlemorgans.com. A fun, popular place with hospitable Irish management, a pool table and a well-stocked bar. They offer rustic dormitories (**F**), hammocks (**G**) and 2 *casitas* (**D**), as well as guided tours, kayaks (there's access to a good sheltered bay), fishing, bicycles, horses and massages. Some of the hotel's structures are artfully reminiscent of *Lord of the Rings*.

Balgües and around

A Totoco Eco-Lodge, Balgües, sign from the road, 1.5-km steep climb uphill, T8425-2027, www.totoco.com.ni. **Totoco** is an ethically oriented and ecologically aware project that includes a permaculture farm, ecolodge and development centre. They have 4 very comfortable custom-designed *cabañas* (more in the works) with solar power, hot showers and compost toilets. A very honest and professional business that has earned its eco-credentials. Highly recommended.

C-G Finca Magdalena, Balgües, signs from the road, 1.5-km steep climb uphill, T8498-1683, www.fincamagdalena.com. Famous cooperative farm run by 26 families, with accommodation in a small cottages, *cabañas* (**C**), doubles (**F**), singles, dorms (**G**) and hammocks. You can work in exchange for lodging, 1 month minimum. Locally produced coffee and honey available for sale.

Mérida

C-G Hacienda Mérida, el Puerto Viejo de Somoza, T8868-8973, www.hmerida.com.

Popular hostel with a beautiful setting by the lake. Lodgings have wheelchair access and include a mixture of dorms (**G**) and rooms (**D**), some with views (**C**). There's a children's school on-site where you can volunteer, also kayak rental, good quality mountain bikes, internet and a range of tours available, including sailing.

F Caballitos Mar, Mérida, follow signs from the road, T8842-6120, www.caballitosmar.com. Great new Mérida alternative that has the best access to the Río Istiam and good kayaks for day or night tours. Fernando, the Spanish owner, is friendly and helpful and cooks a decent paella. Rooms are basic and there are only a few of them at present (if they're full the neighbour also has cheap beds). There are hammocks. Recommended.

❶ Eating

Rivas *p676*

¶ Rancho Coctelera Mariscazo, Estadio de Rivas, 800 vrs sur, on the Panamericana. One of the best seafood restaurants in Nicaragua, with great fish dishes *a la plancha*, excellent *sopa de mariscos* (seafood soup). Simple decor, friendly service, very good value. Highly recommended.

¶¶-¶ Vila's Rosti-Pizza, south side of Parque Central, T2563-0712. A grand old building that looks almost too elegant to house the fast-food joint that it does. Vila's offers roast chicken, tacos, pizza and other wholesome grub. Locals seem to rate it.

¶ Guajiros, northwest corner of Parque Central, 1 c norte, 1½ c abajo. Good, clean, unpretentious dining at this intimate little Cuban restaurant. They serve national dishes, buffet fare and *comida a la carta*.

San Juan del Sur *p677, map p678*

There are many popular, but overpriced restaurants lining the beach, where your tourist dollars buy excellent sea views and mediocre food. Only the better ones are listed below.

¶¶¶ Bambú Beach Club, Malecón Norte, 200 m from the bridge, www.thebambubeachclub.com. Conceived and executed by a German-Austrian-Italian trio, the Bambu Beach Club is one of San Juan's finest dining options and often recommended. Mediterranean-inspired seafood with a hint of Nica.

¶¶¶-¶¶ Bar Timón, across from Hotel Casablanca. Probably the best of the beachfront eateries, serving lobster, prawns and a host of other seafood dishes. No plastic furniture here. Popular and Nicaraguan.

¶¶¶-¶¶ El Colibrí, mercado, 1 c este, 2½ sur. The best restaurant in town, with an excellent and eclectic Mediterranean menu, great decor and ambience, fine wines and really good food, much of it organic. Pleasant, hospitable and highly recommended.

¶¶¶-¶¶ El Pozo, mercado, ½ c sur. Smart and stylish, with a robust international menu and an attractive, young clientele. Food and atmosphere is decidedly Californian. Lots of good reports.

¶¶ Josseline's, on the beach. One of the better beachside eateries, offering the usual seafood fare like shrimps, fillets and lobster. Some limited meat and chicken dishes too.

¶¶ Jugaso, Mercado, 5 vrs norte, opposite Arena Caliente. Breezy little café that serves flavourful daily specials like Mediterranean salad and mango chicken. Also does tasty sandwiches, omelettes, coffee and juices. Friendly and recommended.

¶¶ Pizzería San Juan, southwest corner of Parque Central, ½ c al mar. Tue-Sun 1700-2130. Often buzzing with ex-pats and visitors, this restaurant serves excellent and authentic Italian pizzas – one is large enough to satisfy two people. Recommended, but perhaps not for a romantic evening meal.

¶ Comedor Margarita, mercado, ½ c norte. *Comida típica* and other cheap fare. Unpretentious, wholesome and good value daily specials. A nice change. Recommended.

Cafés

Barrio Café, Mercado, 1 c al mar, www.barriocafesanjuan.com. Familiar café food for homesick Westerners, including pancakes, bagels, coffee, burgers, sandwiches, wraps and cakes. A good place for breakfast and checking emails on the Wi-Fi.

Gato Negro, mercado, 1c al mar, 1 c norte. Popular gringo café with good, if slightly pricey, coffee, a reading space, breakfasts and snacks. This is also one of the best bookshops in the country, with the largest collection of English-language books in Nicaragua, and plenty of fiction too. Chocolate chip and banana pancakes are great for sweet teeth. Recommended.

◉ Entertainment

San Juan del Sur *p677, map p678*
Bars and clubs
Big Wave Dave's, Texaco, 200 m al mar, T2568-2203, www.bigwavedaves.net. Tue-Sun 0830-0000. Popular with foreigners out to party and hook up with others. Wholesome pub food and a busy, boozy atmosphere.

Crazy Crab Beach Club, Malecón Norte, at the end of the road. The only thing in San Juan del Sur that passes for a disco, **Crazy Crab** sees a good mix of locals and foreigners, most of them under 30 years old. A great place to let loose on the dance floor.

Iguana Bar, Malecón, next door to Timón, www.iguanabeachbar.com. Also known as Henry's Iguana, a very popular hang-out with tourists, often buzzing and a good place to knock back rum and beer. They also do food, including sandwiches, burgers, beer and cheese-drenched nachos. Various happy hours and events, check the website for the latest.

The Pier, Malecón norte. Popular beachfront hang-out with an eclectic international crowd, live music and DJs. A relaxed, friendly ambience inside and bonfires on the sand outside. Happy hour 1900-2100 every night. Everything from rock to world music. Recommended.

▲ Activities and tours

San Juan del Sur *p677, map p678*
ATV rental
Hostal Beach Fun Casa 28, mercado, 1 c al mar, 1c norte, T2568-2441, javieralara@hotmail.com. A wide range of ATVs available for an hour, half day or full day.

Canopy tour
Da' Flying Frog, just off road to Marsella, T8613-4460. US$30. 17 platforms, 2.5-km of zip-line and great views from the canopy. One of Nicaragua's longest, promising adrenalin-charged thrills.

Diving
The waters around San Juan del Sur are home to a wrecked Russian trawler and a plethora of sea creatures including rays, turtles and eels.
Neptune Watersports, www.neptunenicadiving.com. This PADI centre offers 2-tank dives, Open Water certification and training to Dive Master level. They also do fishing and snorkelling tours.

Fishing
Depending on the season, the waters around San Juan harbour all kinds of game fish, including marlin, jack and dorado. Many hotels and surf shops offer fishing packages, including **Gran Oceano**. Otherwise try:
Super Fly Sport Fishing, advance reservation only, T8884-8444, www.nicafishing.com. Fly fishing and light tackle, deep-sea fishing, Captain Gabriel Fernández, fluent in English with lots of experience, also fishes north Pacific Coast and Lake Nicaragua.

Paintballing
El Gran Nelson, Km 127.5 Carretera San Juan del Sur, T2560-0122, karenr1828@yahoo.com. If you fancy some SAS-style action head to this recreation centre on the highway. Then shoot your friends and family, with paint-balls, of course. Fun and different.

Sailing

Pelican Eyes Sailing Adventures, Parroquia
1½ c arriba, T2563-7000, www.pelicaneyes
resort.com. Sails to the beach at Brasilito,
US$90 per person full day, US$60 per person
half day, discount for hotel guests, minimum
10 people, leaves San Juan at 0900.

Surfing

The coast north and south of San Juan del
Sur is among the best in Central America for
surfing, access to the best areas are by boat
or long treks in 4WD. Board rental costs
US$10 per day; lessons US$30 per hr.
Although the town is quite inundated with
surf shops, only the most established and
reputable of them are given below:
Arena Caliente, mercado, ½ c norte,
T815-3247, www.arenacaliente.com.
Friendly Nica-run surf shop with board rental,
surfing lessons and transport to beaches.
Affordable accommodation (**G**) is available
in town along with various 'surf camp'
packages. Other options include snorkelling,
spear-fishing, canopy tours and horse riding.
Recommended.
Good Times Surf Shop, mercado, 1 c al mar,
½ c norte. Also known as 'Outer Reef SA'.
This well-established and professional surf
shop specializes in quality and customized
surfboard rentals, lessons, and tours. Tours
include day trips as well as multi-day and
boat trips to surf hard-to-reach waves.
Friendly, helpful and highly recommended.
Dave claims he "will never piss on your
leg and tell you it's raining."

Tour operators

Casa el Oro, Hotel Colonial, 20 vrs sur,
T2568-2415, www.casaeloro.com.
Casa el Oro runs a popular surf school with
economically priced instruction, new boards
and experienced teachers. Additionally, they
offer sea turtle tours, horse-riding trips on the
beach, sailing, fishing and canopy tours.
Works with local communities. Professional
and well established.

Isla Ometepe *p680, map p680*
Archaeology

Professor Hamilton Silva, Altagracia, north
side of the Catholic church, or enquire in the
town's museum, T8905-3744. A resident
expert and writer on Ometepe's history and
archaeology, Professor Hamilton Silva speaks
a little English and leads very interesting and
good-value tours to the island's petroglyph
sites. At weekends he can be found at his
home in Mérida, from **Margarita's** bar
70 m south, an archaeological site in itself.
Recommended.

ATVs, biking and motorbiking

Bikes and motorbikes are now ubiquitous on
Isla Ometepe (see Safety, page 679) and are
a great way to get around. Most hotels have
units for rent and charge US$5-7 per day for
bicycles, US$20-30 for motorbikes or mopeds.
In Moyogalpa, enquire at the bars near the
dock, or try **Robinson**, who has many new
cycles, motorbikes and a few ATVs (US$50 per
day), find him 4 blocks uphill from the port,
then one block south, T8691-5044,
robinson170884@gmail.com. Ensure your
unit is robust if aiming to cross the rough
dirt-roads on the north side of Concepción
or on the east side of Maderas.

Kayaking

At the time of press, **Island Landing**, close to
the dock, was planning to offer kayak rental
in addition to bikes and motorbikes.
Caballitos Mar, Mérida, follow signs from the
road, T8842-6120, www.caballitosmar.com.
The best starting point for kayak excursions
down the Río Istiam, where you might spot
caiman and turtles if you're lucky. Rentals are
available for US$5 per hr, negotiable. Dawn
is the best time for wildlife viewing, pack
sunscreen and check lake conditions before
setting out. For the brave, there are also
night tours. Recommended.

Organic farming

Bona Fide, Balgües, www.projectbonafide.
com. Also known as Michael's farm, **Bona**

Fide offers innovative courses in perma-culture as well as volunteer opportunities for those wishing to learn more about the science and work of organic farming. An interesting project.

Tour operators
Ometepe Expeditions, 75 m from the port, behind the white fence and in front of **Hotel Ometepetl**, T8363-5783, ometepexpeditions@ hotmail.com. A highly reputable agency that worked with the BBC to guide a group of disabled people to the summit of Concepción. They offer a range of tours including half- and full-day hikes to the volcanoes and cloud forests. Experienced, knowledgeable, English-speaking and helpful. One of the best and highly recommended.

Windsurfing
Hotel Istiám, Villa Paraíso, opposite the beach, 1 km north of Santa Cruz, T8844-2200, ometeptlng@hotmail.com. Ideally positioned to catch the strong winds hitting Playa Santo Domingo, **Hotel Istiam** has a small windsurfing operation. Kayaks are available too, but conditions on this exposed part of the island can be rough and challenging.

⊖ Transport

Rivas p676
To **Managua**, every ½ hr, 0630-1700, US$2, 2½ hrs; express buses, US$2.50, 2 hrs; microbuses, US$3, 1½ hrs. To **Granada**, every 45 mins, 0530-1625, US$1.50, 1¾ hrs. To **Jinotepe**, every ½ hr, 0540-1710, US$1.50, 1¾ hrs. To **San Juan del Sur**, every ½ hr, 0600-1830, US$1, 45 mins. To **Peñas Blancas**, every ½ hr, 0500-1600, US$0.75, 1 hr.

International buses Ticabus, Pulpería El Diamante, de la Estacion Texaco, 150 vrs norte T8847-1407, www.ticabus.com, and Transnica, Shell, 4 c al lago, T8898-5195, www.transnica.com,have buses bound for Costa Rica and Honduras stopping at the Texaco station on the highway.

Taxi From centre of Rivas to the dock at **San Jorge**, US$1 colectivo (US$4 private). To **San Juan del Sur**, US$1.75 colectivo (US$7.50 private). To **Peñas Blancas**, US$1.50 colectivo (US$6 private). In all cases beware overcharging and exercise caution (see Safety, page 679).

San Juan del Sur p677, map p678
Bus To **Managua** express bus 0500, 0530, 0600, 1730, 2½ hrs, ordinary bus every hour 0500-1530, US$2.50, 3½ hrs. Or take a bus/taxi to Rivas and change here. To **Rivas**, every ½ hr, 0500-1700, US$1, 40 mins. For **La Flor** or **Playa El Coco** use bus to **El Ostional**, 1600, 1700, US$ 0.70, 1½ hrs. Return from El Coco at 0600, 0730 and 1630.

Shuttles Several companies run shuttles to the beaches north and south of San Juan del Sur, including **Casa Oro Youth Hostel** and **Arena Caliente**. Both have at least 3 daily departures to **Los Playones**, next to Maderas, and 1 daily departure to Remanso, US$5. Note schedules are affected by tides and may not operate in inclement weather.

Boat Rana Tours, kiosk opposite Hotel Estrella on the seafront, T8877-9255. Runs transport to the northern beaches like **Michal**, **Marsella** and **Maderas**. They depart at 1100 and return at 1630, US$10 per person.

Taxi Colectivo is a very feasible way to get to Rivas and slightly quicker than the bus. They depart from the market, US$1.75 per person, or US$7.50 for the whole taxi.

4WD You can usually find a 4WD pickup to make trips to outlying beaches or to go surfing. You should plan a day in advance and ask for some help from your hotel. Prices range from US$20-75 depending on the trip and time. You can also hire 4WDs, contact Alamo Rent a Car, inside hotel **Casa Blanca**, T2277-1117, www.alamonicaragua.com.

South of San Juan del Sur *p679*

San Jorge

Boat To **Ometepe**, ferry and boats, 12 daily, 0730-1830, 1 hr, US$2-3. Return journeys 0530-1600. Services are greatly reduced on Sun.

Taxi From San Jorge a road runs from the shore through Rivas to the port of San Juan del Sur.

Taxi to **Rivas**, US$1.50 (per person), beware overcharging, *colectivos* US$0.50. Direct from San Jorge to **San Juan del Sur** costs US$15. It is a lot cheaper to take a taxi to Rivas and another one from Rivas to San Juan.

Isla Ometepe *p680, map p680*

Boat The lake can have very big swells. The best access route to the island is from San Jorge on the lake's southwest shore to Moyogalpa. The ferry and boat offer regular services. Cars are transported with the ferry.

From Moyogalpa to **San Jorge**, 12 daily boats and ferries, hourly 0530-1600, US$2. Reduced services on Sun, 3 ferries only.

The port of Altagracia is called San Antonio and is 2 km north of the town; pickups meet the boat that passes between Granada and San Carlos. To **San Carlos**, Mon and Thu 1800-1900, US$8, 11 hrs. To **Granada**, Tue and Fri, around 0000, US$4, 3½ hrs.

Bus Buses wait for the boats in Moyogalpa and run to **Altagracia** hourly, 0530-1830, US$1, 1 hr. To **San Ramón** 0830, 0930, US$1.25, 3 hrs. To **Mérida**, 0830, 1445, 1630, US$2, 2½ hrs. To **Balgües**, 1030, 1530, US$2, 2 hrs. For **Charco Verde**, take any bus to Altagracia that uses the southern route.

---

❶ Directory

Rivas *p676*

Banks The plaza has 2 banks: a **Banpro** on the west side, and a **Banco Procredit** with a Visa ATM on the northwest corner. There's

also a BAC ATM, plaza, 2 c oeste. **Internet** Gaby Cyber, from bus terminal 5 blocks south, ½ block east, US$1 per hr, Mon-Sat 0800-2000, Sun 0900-1900.

San Juan del Sur *p677, map p678*

Banks Banco Procredit, mercado, 1 c al mar, has a Visa ATM and will change dollars; BDF, Mercado, 2c al mar, 1c sur, has a Visa ATM; BAC (ATM only, all networks), Malecón, next to Hotel Casablanca. Some hotels might change dollars too. **Internet** Several places in town, Leo's, daily 0800-2100, US$1 per hr, and **Super-Cyber Internet Service**, 0800-2200, US$1 per hr, internet calls as well). **Fire** T8993-4797. **Language schools** Playas del Sur, Enitel, 50 vrs norte, opposite the beach, T8668-9334, www.playasdelsur spanishschool.com. Operated by a women's collective and one of the oldest schools in Nicaragua. They offer flexible programmes of 1-to-1 tuition, homestays, activities and voluntary work. All teachers have 8-12 years of experience. Spanish School San Juan del Sur, T2568-2432, www.sjdss panish.com. Regular morning classes, tutoring with flexible hours. Spanish Ya, Texaco, 100 vrs norte T8898-5036, www.learnspanishya.com. 1-to-1 classes, accommodations, activities and volunteer opportunities. DELE courses and diplomas. **Laundry** Various around town. Try: Lavandería Gaby, mercado, ½ c arriba, around US$3 for a medium-sized load. **Police** T2568-2382. **Post** 150 m left (south) along the seafront from the main junction.

Isla Ometepe *p680, map p680*

Banks Banco Procredit, pier, 500 vrs uphill, with Visa ATM and dollar changing facility. There's a Western Union attached. You can also change money (no TCs) in the 2 biggest grocery stores (1 opposite Hotel Bahía) or in hotels. Best to bring all the cash you need from Rivas. **Internet** Limited services on the island, try up the road from the port in Moyogalpa, or at the Hotel Castillo in Altagracia.

Río San Juan and the Solentiname Archipelago

The Río San Juan, running through deep jungles, drains Lake Nicaragua from its eastern end into the Caribbean at San Juan del Norte. Over 190 km long and with more than 17 tributaries, it runs the length of the southern border of the Indio Maíz Biological Reserve and connects Lake Nicaragua to the Atlantic Ocean. It is the best area in Nicaragua to spot wildlife. This great river has played an integral part in Nicaragua's colonial and post-colonial history and is one of the most accessible of the country's many pristine nature-viewing areas. Disputes with Costa Rica over ownership and navigation rights are on-going – the last flare-up was in 2010.

The department's capital, San Carlos, is perched on the shores of Lake Nicaragua, providing access to the wonderful Solentiname archipelago. These idyllic islands are home to various artistic communities, where families practise a type of primitivist art that has reached galleries in New York and Paris. The archipelago has a fascinating history, and was the subject of a famous social experiment in Utopianism. ▶▶ *For listings, see pages 693-696.*

Background

First sailed by the Spanish in 1525, the complete length of the river was navigated on 24 June 1539, the day of San Juan Bautista, hence its name. In colonial times it was a vital link between the Spanish Caribbean and the port of Granada. After three attacks by Caribbean pirates on Granada, the Spanish built a fortress at El Castillo in 1675. The English tried to take the fort twice in the 18th century, failing the first time thanks to the teenage Nicaraguan national heroine Rafaela Herrera, and then succeeding with Lord (then Captain) Nelson, who later had to withdraw owing to tropical diseases. Later it became the site of many aborted canal projects. It is still a most rewarding boat journey.

San Carlos → *See map, page 691. Colour map 4, A2. Altitude: 39 m.*

Like a ragged vulture, San Carlos is perched between several transportation arteries. It is the jumping-off point for excursions to the Islas Solentiname, along the Río Frío to Los Chiles in Costa Rica and the Río San Juan itself, with irregular launches to the river from the lakeside. It's a reasonably ugly town, but not overly offensive. Nearby are the two great nature reserves of Los Guatusos and Indio Maíz. In the wet season it is very muddy. At San Carlos there are the ruins of a fortress built for defence against pirates.

Solentiname Archipelago → *Colour map 4, A2.*

On **Isla San Fernando**, many locals carve and paint balsa wood figures. The diet on the island is somewhat limited but there is lots of fresh fruit. Ask for Julio Pineda or his sister Rosa, one of the local artists. The island has a new **museum** ⓘ *US$1*, with a variety of natural and cultural history exhibits as well as a spectacular view of the archipelago, especially at sunset; if closed ask in the village if it can be opened. Apart from at the hotel, there is no electricity on the island, so take a torch.

Isla La Venada, named for its plentiful population of *venado* (deer), is also home to artists, in particular the house of Rodolpho Arellano who lives on the south side of the island. He is one of the region's best painters and his wife, daughters and grandson all paint tropical scenes and welcome visitors to see and purchase their works. On the north side of the island is a series of semi-submerged caves with some of the best examples of petroglyphs from the pre-Columbian Guatuso tribe.

Isla El Padre is privately owned and the only island inhabited by howler monkeys. If you circle the island in a boat they can usually be spotted in the trees.

Isla Mancarrón is the largest in the chain, with the highest hill at 250 m. This is where the famous revolutionary/poet/sculptor/Catholic priest/Minister of Culture, Ernesto Cardenal, made his name by founding a school of painting, poetry and sculpture, and even decorating the local parish church in naïve art. He preached a kind of Marxist liberation theology, where the trials of Christ were likened to the trials of poor Nicaraguans. There is a monument to the Sandinista flag outside the church. Hiking is possible on the island where many parrots and *Moctezuma oropendolas* make their home. The island's hotel of the same name is part of the local folklore as its founder Alejandro Guevara was a hero of the Sandinista Revolution; his widow Nubia and her brother Peter now look after the place.

Los Guatusos Wildlife Reserve

Known as the cradle of wildlife for Lake Nicaragua, Los Guatusos is home to many exotic and varied species of bird and reptile. It is also heavily populated by monkeys, especially howlers. The reserve is crossed by three rivers, Guacalito, Zapote and Papaturro, which are popular for boat touring. It is essential to be at the park for sunrise to see the best of

San Carlos

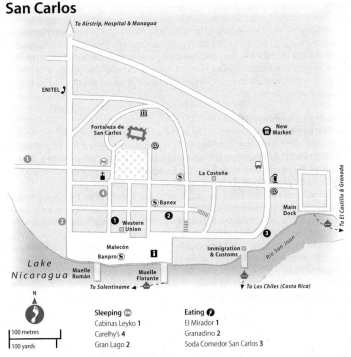

Sleeping	Eating
Cabinas Leyko **1**	El Mirador **1**
Carelhy's **4**	Granadino **2**
Gran Lago **2**	Soda Comedor San Carlos **3**

the wildlife. After 1030 the river often becomes busier with the immigration traffic of labourers heading to Costa Rica. A new **research centre** ⓘ *explanations in Spanish only, US$4, ask for Armando who is an enthusiastic expert on orchids*, built by Friends of the Earth and the Spanish Government, has a collection of over 90 orchids native to the region and a butterfly farm. Visitors are welcome. Lodging is also possible in the research centre. There is a public boat from San Carlos to Papaturro (Monday to Saturday 1100 and 1400, US$1, 1½ hours; check the return schedule locally).

El Castillo to the Caribbean

Some 60 km downriver is **El Castillo**, built around the restored ruins of the 18th-century Spanish fort called **La Fortaleza de la Inmaculada Concepción**. The old fort has a good history **museum** ⓘ *closes at 1200 for lunch, US$1.50*. The **tourist office** on the quay has a leaflet about the fort and town. It was here that Nelson did battle with the Spanish forces. There are great views of the river from the fortress. The town is on a wide bend in the river where some shallow but tricky rapids run the whole width. Horse riding is possible (about US$6 per hour). El Castillo is a good place to pick up food on the river.

Reserva Biológica Indio Maíz

A few kilometres downstream is the Río Bartola and the beginning of the Reserva Biológica Indio Maíz, 3000 sq km of mostly primary rainforest and home to more than 600 species of bird, 300 species of reptile and 200 species of mammal including many big cats and howler, white-faced and spider monkeys. Sleeping is possible in **Refugio Bartola**, a research station and training ground for biologists; it has a labyrinth of well-mapped trails behind the lodge. The hotel guides are very knowledgeable. They will also take you down the Río Bartola in canoe for great wildlife viewing and birding. Neglect in recent years has made turning up without booking a bit of a gamble, so make sure you book in advance. Camping is possible; ask the park ranger (his house is across the Río Bartola from the **Refugio Bartola** lodge).

Bartola and further east

The river past **Bartola** becomes more beautiful and the Costa Rican border reaches to the south bank of the river. The Costa Rican side is partially deforested; the Nicaraguan side with the Indio Maíz Reserve is almost entirely intact. Watch out for turtles, birds and crocodiles. Two hours downriver is the **Río Sarapiquí** and immigration check-points for both Costa Rica and Nicaragua (no stamps available though).

If coming from the Río San Juan to Río Sarapiquí you will need to check in with the Costa Rican guard station if you want to spend the night, or even if you want to pick up something at the store. If continuing down the river without stopping you only need to check in at the Nicaraguan station on the Río San Juan.

Past the Sarapiquí, the San Juan branches north, and both sides of the river (heavily forested) become part of Nicaragua again as the Río Colorado heads into Costa Rica. Two hours or so later, the San Juan reaches the Caribbean via a series of magnificent forest-wrapped lagoons. The Río Indio must be taken to reach the isolated but surprisingly wealthy village of San Juan del Norte.

San Juan del Norte and around → *Colour map 4, A3.*

One of the wettest places on the American continent with more than 5000 mm of rain each year, San Juan del Norte (also called Santa Isabel) is also one of the most beautiful, with primary rainforest, lagoons, rivers and the Caribbean Sea. It is settled by a small population, though it was once a boom town in the 19th century, when the American industrialist Cornelius Vanderbilt was running his steamship line between New York and San Francisco. Then called Greytown, San Juan del Norte was the pickup point for the steamship journey to the Pacific via the Río San Juan, Lake Nicaragua to La Virgen and then by mule overland to San Juan del Sur. This service was quite popular during the 'gold rush' of San Francisco and a young Mark Twain made the crossing, later recounting his journey in the book *Travels with Mr Brown*. The town remained in its location on the Bahía San Juan del Norte, actually a coastal lagoon, until the 1980s, when fighting caused its population to flee. Re-established in its current location on the the east bank of the Río Indio, the village is separated from the Caribbean Sea by 400 m of rainforest. The population is a mix of Miskito, Creole, Rama and Hispanic. A new thrice-weekly boat services connects San Juan del Norte with Bluefields, US$30, quite rough and not for the faint of heart.

If in your own boat (chartered), a trip further down the **Río Indio** is recommended, with lots of wildlife, virgin forest and Rama (please respect their culture and privacy). A visit to the ruins of old **Greytown** is also interesting, with a well-marked trail that leads through various cemeteries buried in the forest and to the town centre where only foundations and the church bell remain. It has been described as 'incredibly atmospheric' with amazing wildlife and is great for birding in the morning. Note the names on some of the tombstones, which include sailors from around the world. Most of the year the entrance is underwater so rubber boots are of great use here as for the rest of the region. Swimming is best in the **Blue Lagoon**; as there are many sharks in the Caribbean. If coming on the public boat from San Carlos, Melvin can arrange tours with one of his *pangas* (expect to pay around US$15-20 for a boat).

◉ Río San Juan and the Solentiname Archipelago listings

For Sleeping and Eating price codes and other relevant information, see Essentials pages 31-33.

◉ Sleeping

San Carlos *p690, map p691*
C Gran Lago Hotel, Caruna, 25 vrs al lago, T8823-3488. This hotel has views of the lake and serves fruit breakfast in the mornings. The rooms are comfortable enough, with private bath, a/c, cable TV and 24-hr water. Purified water and coffee available throughout the day.

E Cabinas Leyko, Policía Nacional, 2 c abajo, T2583-0354. One of the better places in town, with clean, comfortable rooms, good mattresses, private bath and a/c. Cheaper with fan and shared bath (**F**).

E Carelhy's Hotel, iglesia católica, ½ c sur, T2583-0389. 15 clean and simple rooms; 5 have a/c (**D**). Each room has 2 beds and can sleep 3. Can help arrange tours or transportation. Internet in the works. Discount for longer stays or groups.

Solentiname Archipelago *p690*
It's possible to stay in basic but generally very clean private homes.
C Hotel Celentiname or **Doña María**, T2276-1910, Isla San Fernando. This laid-back place is the most traditional of the hotels here. The rustic cabins have private bath and nice decks. Generated power, all meals included. Lush garden and friendly owners.
C Hotel Mancarrón, up the hill from the cement dock and church, T2277-3495,

hotelmancarrun@gmail.com, Isla Mancarrón. Great birdwatching around this hotel that has access to the artisan village. Rooms are airy, screened, equipped with mosquito netting and private bath. The managers are personal and friendly. Prices include 3 great home-cooked meals per day. Recommended.

Los Guatusos Wildlife Reserve *p691*
C La Esquina del Lago, at the mouth of the Río Frío, T2849-0600, www.riosanjuan.info. Surrounded by vegetation and visited by 61 species of bird, this tranquil and hospitable lodge on the water is owned by former newspaper-man Philippe Tisseaux. A range of tours available, including birdwatching and world-class sports fishing. Free transport from San Carlos, a 5-min ride away (speak to **Restaurant El Güegüense** near the Malecón to arrange transit to the hotel). Recommended.

El Castillo to the Caribbean *p692*
Río Sábalo
C Hotel Sábalos, on confluence of San Juan and Sábalo rivers, T2271-7424, www.hotelsabalos.com.ni. This simple and friendly hotel has a good location, with views up and down the river, great for watching locals pass in canoes. 9 wooden rooms have private bath and fan. The best resting spot on upper San Juan. Recommended.

El Castillo
Few hotel rooms have private bathrooms.
C Hotel Victoria, el muelle, 400 vrs arriba, at the end of the end road, T2583-0188, www.hotelvictoriaelcastillo.com. This friendly and hospitable hotel has 9 wood panelled rooms with cable TV, a/c and private bath (**E** with shared bath). The best place in town. Recommended.
D Albergue El Castillo, next to fortress above city dock, T8924-5608. Comfortable, if simple, wooden rooms and great views from a shared balcony overlooking the river. Only 1 room has a private bath. Noisy early morning as the public boats warm up (0500) motors. 25 mins of internet and breakfast included.

E-F Nena Lodge, el muelle, 350 vrs arriba, T8821-2135, www.nenalodge.com. This new hotel has a range of simple budget rooms equipped with mosquito nets, soap and towels. Many of them open onto a communal balcony slung with hammocks. The most expensive (**E**) have their own bathroom.

Reserva Biológica Indio Maíz *p692*
A Refugio Bartola, confluence of Río San Juan and Río Bartola, T8376-6979, refugiobartola@yahoo.com. Simple wooden rooms with private bath, high ceilings and solid beds. Prices include 3 meals, juice and coffee. There's a research station on site and a private reserve with a labyrinth of trails. You need a guide as it's easy to get lost. Recommended.

San Juan del Norte and around *p693*
LL Río Indio Lodge, Bahía de San Juan, between Indio and San Juan rivers, near San Juan del Norte, T506-2231-4299, www.rioindiolodge.com. Multi-million dollar lodge, designed for upscale fishing packages but excellent for wildlife safaris, birdwatching and rainforest walks. Recently named one of the top 10 jungle lodges in the world.
D Cabinas El Escondite, San Juan del Norte, behind the military base north of the pier, T8414-9761 ask for Rasta. Spacious wooden cabinas with bunk beds, private bath and a pleasant garden. The owner, Rasta, speaks English and cooks the best Caribbean food in town (ƮƮ-Ʈ). Great host and relaxed vibe. Recommended.
E Cabinas Monkey, San Juan del Norte, el muelle, 150 vrs norte on Calle Principal, T8407-6757. Nice little budget cabins with fan, mosquito net, hard beds, sporadic plumbing, private bath, lots of hummingbirds in the garden and complimentary condoms in the rooms. Good value.

🍴 Eating

San Carlos *p690, map p691*

🍴🍴-🍴🍴 Granadino, opposite Alejandro Granja playing field, T2583-0386. Daily 0900-0200. Considered the best in town, with a relaxed ambience and pleasant river views, *Camarones en salsa*, steak and hamburgers. Not cheap.

🍴 El Mirador, Iglesia Católica, 1½ c sur, T2583-0367. Daily 0700-2000. Superb view from patio of Lake Nicaragua, Solentiname, Río Frío and Río San Juan and the jumbled roofs of the city. Decent chicken, fish and beef dishes starting at US$3 with friendly service. Recommended, though it closes if the *chayules* are in town.

🍴 Soda Comedor San Carlos, muelle principal, 100 m sur. One of many cheap and popular places in the area serving economical Nica food.

El Castillo *p692*

🍴🍴-🍴🍴 Bar Cofalito, on the jetty. Has a great view upstairs overlooking the river and serves excellent *camarones de río*, considered by many the best in town, with fresh fish most evenings.

🍴🍴-🍴🍴 Borders Coffee, next to the dock. Good but pricey pasta in organic tomato sauce, vegetarian fare, curries, shrimps, and fresh organic cappuccinos at this friendly little café. Nice views of the river and a good place to wait for your boat. They can also arrange stays at a nearby *finca*.

🍴🍴-🍴 El Chinandegano, el muelle, 300 vrs arriba. Fish, chicken and other Nica fare. Reasonable and well presented, but the flavours aren't stunning. Overlooks the water and has economical rooms for rent.

San Juan del Norte *p693*

🍴🍴-🍴 Doña Marta's, el muelle, 350 m sur along the waterfront, the building with the blue tin roof. Doña Marta's serves very tasty, reasonably priced fish and shrimp. It has a great waterfront setting and is the best restaurant in town.

🍴🍴-🍴 Soda Tucán, el muelle, 150 m sur on the main street. Small, clean *comedor* serving economical Nica fare. Various tours offered by the owners.

⛰ Tours and activities

San Carlos *p690, map p691*
Tour operators
San Carlos Sport Fishing, La Esquina del Lago hotel, at the mouth of the Río Frío, T2849-0600, www.riosanjuan.info. Operated Phillipe Tisseaux, who has many years of experience fishing the Río San Juan, where plenty of tarpon, snook and rainbow bass can be caught. He also offers birdwatching, kayaking and cultural tours. Recommended.

El Castillo *p692*
Tour operators
'The First Step' Adventure and Eco-Tours, inside Cofalito's restaurant, next to the dock, T8432-8441, www.firststepecotours.com. Kayaking, fishing, hiking and custom-made adventures. Popular tours include a 3-day adventure to Boca San Carlos to explore waterfalls and jungle, and a 5-day trip to San Juan del Norte (for the experienced). Fun and recommended.

San Juan del Norte *p693*
Tour guides
Edgar 'Rasta' Coulsen, Cabinas el Escondite, behind the military base north of the pier, T8414-9761. Born in old Greytown, Rasta is one of Nicaragua's best guides and important community figure. He offers trips to Greytown, US$65; Caimain watching, US$100; Night walks, US$100; Mangrove tours, US$120; and 3-day trips into the Indio Maíz reserve to visit Rama communities and basalt rock formations. Highly recommended.

❂ Transport

San Carlos *p690, map p691*
Air To **Managua**, La Costeña, 1425, US$82
one-way, US$120 return, 1 hr. Sit on the left
for the best views. There is a maximum
weight for flights – you will be asked your
body weight. Flights land and take off
within 5 mins, so early arrival is advised.
Taxi from airstrip to dock US$1.

Boat *Pangas* are small motor boats; *botes*,
long, narrow ones; *planos*, big broad ones.
Arrive at least 30 mins in advance to ensure
a seat on a short ride; allow 1 hr or more for
long trips. All schedules are subject to
random changes; check locally before setting
out. To **Solentiname**, Tue, Fri, 1230, US$4,
2½ hrs, stopping at islands **La Venada**, **San
Fernando**, **Mancarrón**. To **Los Guatuzos**,
stopping at **Papaturro**, Tue, Wed, Fri, 0700,
US$5, 3½ hrs. To **Los Chiles**, Costa Rica, daily
1030, 1330, US$4, 2 hrs. To **El Castillo** (and
Sábalos), 0800, 1015 (express), 1200 (slow
boat), 1430, 1530, 1630 (express), 1½ hrs
(express), 2½ hrs, US$5 (express), US$4, US$2
(slow boat), reduced services on Sun when
only first two boats run. Avoid the slow boat
if you can, it's a gruelling 6-hr ride. To **San
Jan del Norte**, Tue, Thu, Fri, 0600, 12-14 hrs,
US$14; express services run Tue and Fri in the
wet season, 7-9 hours, US$30. The ferry to
Granada leaves from main dock in San
Carlos, Tue and Fri 1400, US$9.50 1st class,
US$4 2nd class, 14 hrs. 1st class has a TV,
nicer seats and is usually less crowded; it's
worth the extra money. Bring a hammock if
you can and expect a challenging journey.

Bus To **Managua**, daily, 0800, 1145, 1430,
1800, 2000, 2200, US$9, 6-8 hrs. This was
once a notoriously brutal ride, but is gradually
improving thanks to the paving of the
highway. Until it is complete, you may get
stuck in bogs Sep-Nov. Ask locally for the
latest news.

Solentiname Archipelago *p690*
Boat Private transfers from San Carlos to
Solentiname 1-1½ hr, US$55-85 per boat.
Public boat to **San Carlos**, Tue and Fri, 0430,
2-3 hrs, US$4.

El Castillo *p692*
Boat All schedules are subject to change;
check times locally.
To **San Carlos**; 0500 (slow boat), 0520
(express), 0700, 1130 (express), 1400, 1530
(express) US$2.75 (US$3.75 express, US$2
slow boat), 1½-2½ hrs, reduced services on
Sun when only first 2 boats run. Avoid the
slow boat if you can. To **San Juan del Norte**,
Tue, Thu, Fri, 0900, US$12.50, 8-9 hrs. In the
west season, express services run Tue and
Fri, 0800, 5-6 hrs, US$25.

San Juan del Norte *p693*
To **San Carlos**, stopping at **El Castillo**, Thu
and Sun, 0430, US$12.50 (US$25 express).
To **Bluefields**, Sun, Wed, Fri, 0800, US$30,
3-4 hrs, with stops at Monkey Point and
others. A bumpy ride that should not be
attempted by pregnant women or anyone
with a bad back.

❶ Directory

San Carlos *p690, map p691*
Banks BDF, Fortaleza San Carlos, 1 c sur,
1 c arriba, T583-0144. There is a **Banpro** with
a Visa ATM on the *malecón*, as well as a
Banex, 1 block south of the plaza, and a
BDF, Fortaleza San Carlos, 1 c sur, 1 c arriba,
T2583-0144. You are advised to bring as
much cash as you need. No TC changes,
but you can change dollars, córdobas or
colones with the *coyotes* at the entrance
to immigration and customs.

Caribbean Coast lowlands

→ *Colour map 4, A3.*

Nicaragua's eastern tropical lowlands make for a striking change from the rest of the country. Gone are the volcanoes, hills and valleys, and in their place is lush, tropical rainforest drenched between May and December with heavy rainfall. Most of the population are the African-influenced Miskito people who live in the northern lowlands, mainly around Puerto Cabezas. Their economy is based on timber, fishing and mining. To reach the Caribbean port of Bluefields, you can fly or travel down the Río Escondido from the river port of El Rama. English is widely but not universally spoken. ▶▶ *For listings, see pages 700-706.*

Background

This area, together with roughly half the coastal area of Honduras, was never colonized by Spain. From 1687 to 1894 it was a British Protectorate known as the Miskito Kingdom. It was populated then, as now, by the Miskito, whose numbers are estimated at 75,000. There are two other indigenous groups, the Sumu (5000) and the Rama, of whom only a few hundred remain, near Bluefields. Also near Bluefields are a number of Garífuna communities. Today's strong African influence has its roots in the black labourers brought in by the British to work the plantations and in Jamaican immigration. The Afro-Nicaraguan people call themselves *criollos* (Creoles). The largest number of inhabitants of this region are Spanish-speaking *mestizos*. The Sandinista Revolution, like most other political developments from the Spanish-speaking part of Nicaragua, was met with mistrust. Although the first Sandinista junta recognized the indigenous peoples' rights to organize themselves and choose their own leaders, many of the programmes failed to encompass their social, agricultural and cultural traditions. Relations deteriorated and many engaged in fighting for self-determination. A low point was reached when the Sandinista Government ordered forced resettlement of many Miskito villages, burning to the ground what was left behind. About half the Miskito population fled as refugees to Honduras, but most returned after 1985 when a greater understanding grew between the Sandinista Government and the people of the east coast. The Autonomous Atlantic Region was given the self-governing status in 1987; it is divided into Región Autonomista Atlántico Norte (RAAN) and Región Autonomista Atlántico Sur (RAAS). In Nicaragua, the Caribbean coast is almost always referred to as the Atlantic coast.

Managua to Rama → *For listings, see pages 700-706.*

At **San Benito**, 35 km from Managua on the Pan-American Highway going north, the Atlantic Highway branches east, paved all the way to Rama on the Río Escondido. Shortly after Teustepe, a paved road goes northeast to Boaco. A turn-off, unpaved, goes to **Santa Lucía**, a village inside a crater, with a women's handicraft shop. There is also a cooperative here with an organic farming programme (information from **Unag** in Matagalpa). **Boaco** (84 km from Managua) is called the city of two floors because of its split-level nature. The upper floor has a nice square with good views of the countryside.

Juigalpa → *Colour map 4, A2. Population: 41,000.*

The Atlantic Highway continues through Juigalpa, a pleasant town with one of the best museums in Nicaragua, **Museo Gregorio Aguilar Barea** ① *Mon-Fri, US$0.25, T8812-0784,* housing a collection of idols resembling those at San Agustín, Colombia. The bus terminal is in the town centre near the market, up the hill. Banks accept dollars in cash only.

Rama

The main road continues east to **Santo Tomás** and smaller villages (including La Gateada, connected by air from Managua via San Carlos on Friday with **La Costeña**, T2285-0160), then to **Cara de Mono**, on the Río Mico, and finally to **Rama**, 290 km from Managua. From Rama, you can take a boat to Bluefields or the daily bus to Pearl Lagoon. This is on a new road, and is an alternative way to travel to the coast. From Pearl Lagoon, *pangas* sail to Bluefields.

Bluefields → *For listings, see pages 700-706. Colour map 4, A3. Population: 42,665.*

Dirty, chaotic yet curiously inviting, Bluefields, the most important of Nicaragua's three Caribbean ports, gets its name from the Dutch pirate Abraham Blaauwveld. It stands on a lagoon behind the bluff at the mouth of the Bluefields River (Río Escondido), which is navigable as far as Rama (96 km). In May there is a week-long local festival, **Mayo-Ya!** with elements of the British maypole tradition, local music, poetry and dancing. The local **Fiesta de San Jerónimo** is on 30 September. Limited tourist information is available from INTUR ⓘ *Punta Fría, opposite the police station, Mon-Fri, 0800-1700.* There are bars, a couple of reggae clubs, *comedores*, restaurants and an **Almacén Internacional**. Prices are about the same as in Managua. Be prepared for frequent power and water cuts.

Laguna de Perlas

The lagoon itself is some 50 km long with mostly Creole villages round its shores, such as Pearl Lagoon, Haulover, Brown Bank, Marshall Point and San Vicente. **La Fe** and **Orinoco** are Garífuna (of African descent) villages, while **Raitipura** and **Kakabila** are indigenous villages. In Raitipura there is a Danish housing project, run by Mogens Vibe who takes on volunteers for a minimum of one week (recommended). Within walking distance is the swimming beach of **Awas** (basic accommodation).

Outlying areas of the Región Autonomista Atlántico Sur

The **Río Kurinwás** area north of Bluefields is a fascinating, largely uninhabited jungle area, where it is possible to see monkeys. It might occasionally be possible to get a boat to **Tortuguero** (also called Nuevo Amanecer) a *mestizo* town that will really give you a taste of the frontier. Tortuguero is about a six-hour speedboat ride from Bluefields up the Kurinwás River; several days by regular boat. The **Río Grande** is the next river north of the Kurinwás, connected to the Pearl Lagoon by the Top-Lock Canal. At its mouth are five interesting villages: the four Miskito communities of **Kara**, **Karawala**, **Sandy Bay Sirpi** and **Walpa**, and the Creole village of **La Barra**. Sandy Bay Sirpi is situated on both the river and the Caribbean and has a pleasant beach.

Travelling upriver, the Río Grande is noticeably more settled than the Río Kurinwás. After some distance (about a six-hour speedboat ride from Bluefields, several days by regular boat), you reach the *mestizo* town of **La Cruz de Río Grande**. It was founded in about 1922 by Chinese traders to serve workers from a banana plantation (now disused) further upriver. La Cruz has a very pretty church. The adventurous can walk between La Cruz and Tortuguero; it takes about 10 hours each way in the dry season, 12 hours in the rainy season.

Islas de Maíz/Corn Islands → *For listings, see pages 700-706. Colour map 4, A4.*

The Corn Islands are two small islands fringed with white coral and slender coconut trees, perfect for relaxation. **Little Corn**, the smaller of the two and far more idyllic, escaped serious damage in the 1988 hurricane and can be visited by boat from the larger island, **Big Corn**, a one-hour ride by *panga*. On Little Corn Island there is no electricity and no phones, just pristine white-sand beaches and some of the Caribbean's finest undisturbed coral reefs. Big Corn is a popular Nicaraguan holiday resort (the best months are March and April). The nicest beaches on Big Corn are on **Long Bay** (walk across the island from Playa Coco)and **Brig Bay**, by the dock.

If you climb the mountain, wear long trousers as there are many ticks. On Little Corn you can climb the lighthouse for fantastic views of the whole island (not recommended if you are uncomfortable with heights). The language of the islands is English. The islanders are very friendly but petty thievery has been reported. Be wary of touts who greet you at the airport, posing as impartial guides; they may charge you for their services. Make sure you take enough money with you to the island as credit cards are not accepted and everything is more expensive than on the mainland; dollars are widely used.

Northeast Nicaragua → *For listings, see pages 700-706.*

Puerto Cabezas → *Colour map 3, B6. Population: 50,941.*

Puerto Cabezas, capital of the Región Autonomista Atlántico Norte, has a distinctly different atmosphere from Bluefields. It is principally a large Miskito village and offers an excellent introduction to the Miskito area. You can arrange to stay in small Miskito villages, for example near Haulover, a few hours by boat south of Puerto Cabezas. There are significant minorities of *mestizos* (referred to on the coast as *españoles* or the Spanish) and Creoles, many of whom came to 'Port' by way of Las Minas. Spanish is a second language for the majority of residents; many speak at least some English, and for some, English is their native language. The local name for Puerto Cabezas is **Bilwi**, although the name is of Sumo origin. The Miskitos conquered the Sumos to obtain the town some time in the last century. There are two main roads, the only paved streets, which run parallel to each other and to the sea. At the southern end of the town is the port area; a walk along the pier at sunset is highly recommended. The airport is at the northern end. The main market occupies the central part of town.

Waspám and the Río Coco → *Population: 38,701.*

The Coco River (called *Waspán* in Spanish and *Wanghi* in Miskito) is the heart of Miskito country. There is a road from Puerto to Waspám; during the dry season the 130-km trip should take about three hours by 4WD vehicle, several hours longer by public bus (leaves Puerto at 0700, Monday to Saturday and, with luck, returns from Waspám at 1200). The bus can be boarded at several points in Puerto along the road out of town, US$5 to Waspám. The trip takes you through the pine forests, red earth, and north of Puerto towards the Coco River (the border with Honduras, see page 491), and you will pass through two Miskito villages, **Sisin** and **Santa Marta**. Hitching is possible; if you cannot get all the way to Waspám, make sure you are left at Sisin, Santa Marta or La Tranquera. You can take lifts from the military; never travel at night.

Parque Nacional Saslaya → *Colour map 3, B5.*

Saslaya was the first national park in Nicaragua, located within the **Reserva Biósfera Bosawás**, and contains the largest tropical cloud forest in Central America. The **Proyecto Ecoturístico Rosa Grande**, supported by Nature Conservancy and the Peace Corps involves the community of **Rosa Grande**, 25 km from Siuna, near an area of virgin forest with a trail, waterfall on the River Labú and lots of wildlife including monkeys and large cats. One path leads to a lookout with a view over the **Cerro Saslaya**; another circular path to the northwest goes to **Rancho Alegre Falls**. Guides can be hired for US$7 a day plus food. Excursions cost US$13 per person for guide, food and camping equipment. You may have to pay for a camp guard while hiking. Tourism is in its infancy here and you may find little things 'added on' to your bill. Be certain you have enough supplies for your stay. Contact Don Trinidad at the *comedor* in Santa Rosa. In Siuna, contact **Proyecto Bosawás** ① *200 m east of airstrip; Mon-Fri 0800-1700*. Groups of five or more must reserve in advance; contact the **Amigos de Saslaya** ① *c/o Proyecto Bosawás, Siuna, RAAN*, by post or telegram.

◉ The Caribbean Coast lowlands listings

For Sleeping and Eating price codes and other relevant information, see Essentials pages 31-33.

◉ Sleeping

Bluefields *p698*

Many hotels in Bluefields are quite basic and run-down.

A Hotel Oasis, 150 m from Bluefields Bay, T2572-2812, www.oasishotelcasino.net. The best hotel in town with spacious modern rooms, comfortable furnishings, Wi-Fi, cable TV and professional service. There's lots of slot machines downstairs, should you fancy a low-key punt. Breakfast included.

D Caribbean Dreams, Barrio Punta Fría, Pescafrito, ½ c sur, T2572-1943. 27 rooms with private bath, a/c or fan, and cable TV. Services including restaurant with home cooking and à la carte menu, Wi-Fi (US$2 per day) and laundry. Clean and often booked, call ahead. Owners helpful.

D Mini Hotel Central, Barrio Punta Fría, opposite Bancentro, T2572-2362. 14 simple and fairly uninspiring rooms with private bath, a/c, TV. Cheaper with fan (**E**), although the cheapest rooms are very no frills and those downstairs may be noisy. There's mediocre restaurant attached. OK for the budget traveller, but not fantastic.

E La Isleña, Barrio Central, next to Joyería Isamar, T2572-0706. New, friendly place with reasonably priced rooms, most with fan, cable TV and private bath, a few with a/c. Some reports of loud music in the evening, so ask for a quiet room if this bothers you. There's also a garden and pleasant restaurant attached. Not bad.

E Los Pipitos, Barrio Central, next to the Oficina Direción General de Ingreso, T2572-1590. 4 simple rooms with TV, private bath and a/c, cheaper with fan (**F**). There's a bakery on the premises that serves good coffee and cake. Friendly.

F Hostal Doña Vero, Barrio Central, opposite Mercadito Mas x Menos, T2572-2166. New, clean, well-attended budget lodgings and without doubt the best deal in town. Rooms on the top floor are large, comfortable and great value. Those downstairs are smaller. Some ultra-cheap quarters have shared bath. Very secure and pleasant, with good attention to detail. Thoughtful and friendly. Highly recommended.

Laguna de Perlas *p698*

C Casa Ulrich, muelle principal, 300 vrs norte, at the end of the paved road, T8603-5173, casaulrich@hotmail.com. The only hotel in town with a waterfront location and swimming off the terrace out back. They have 10 comfortable rooms with a/c, cable TV and private bath (a few cheaper rooms have fan, **D**). Nice, hospitable owners. A happy place. Recommended.

C-D Hotelito Casa Blanca, in May 4 sector, T2572-0508, www.casablancapearllagoon. fortunecity.com. One of the best hotels in town, with a range of clean, light rooms; 5 have private bath (**C**), 6 have shared bath (**D**). The owners, Sven and Miss Dell, are very hospitable and friendly. Advance reservations preferred. A nice family house, recommended.

E Hotel Slilma, Enitel tower, 50 vrs sur, 75 vrs arriba on the left-hand turn, T2572-0523, rondownleiva@hotmail.com. Also known by its Spanish name, 'Las Estrellas', **Hotel Slilma** is a friendly, helpful lodging, highly recommended for budget travellers. They have 20 rooms, most with shared bath, cable TV and fan, but a few new ones also have private bath and a/c (**D**).

Islas de Maíz/Corn Islands *p699*
Big Corn
AL Casa Canada, South End, T8644-0925, www.casa-canada.com. Sophisticated, luxurious rooms with ocean views. Each is splendidly equipped with a DVD player, minibar, coffee-maker, leather chairs and mahogany furniture. There's free Wi-Fi for guests and a beautiful infinity pool over-looks the waves. Friendly and hospitable management. Recommended.

A-B Hotel Paraíso, Brig Bay, T2575-5111, www.paraisoclub.com. A professional, friendly hotel, managed by 2 Dutch gentlemen, Mike and Ton, who contribute to local social projects. They have 9 doubles (**B**) and 5 bungalows (**A**), all clean, comfortable and well fitted with a/c, hammocks and mosquito nets. Prices include breakfast at their restaurant, which has free Wi-Fi and an internet terminal. Tours and snorkelling offered. Highly recommended.

B Martha's Bed & Breakfast, Southwest Bay, just south of Picnic Centre, T8835-5930. This

hotel has lovely landscaped grounds and 8 clean, unpretentious rooms with private bath, a/c and cable TV. Comfortable enough, but the value isn't great.

C Vientos del Norte, North End, T2575-5112, www.bigcornisland.com/ vientosdelnorte.html. Also known as Ike's place, **Vientos del Norte** offers a range of well-equipped quarters (**C**) with fridge, coffee machine, microwave and toaster. Those overlooking the ocean or with a/c cost slightly more. They also have an annex with well-furnished family-sized lodgings and some economy rooms (**D**). Friendly and recommended.

E Silver Sand, Sally Peaches, south of rocky point, T8948-1436. Managed by the colourful Ira Gómez, who could well be a character from a *Pirates of the Caribbean* movie. His rustic fishermen's cabins have seen better days, but their secluded setting near the beach is tranquil and pleasant.

F Nautilus, Brig Bay, T2575 5055. This friendly hostel evokes the old school travel spirit of the 1960s and 70s. They have 12 dorm beds and extras including lockers, kitchen, fridge, cable TV, Wi-Fi and garden. A little cramped and grungy, but OK. Recommended for budget wanderers.

Little Corn
The north end is the greenest, wildest area, but somewhat isolated and difficult to reach at night. The cheapest lodgings are clustered on the south side of the island, although these are becoming increasingly poor value.

A Peace and Love Farm, north end of the island, www.farmpeacelove.com. Not a hotel, Peace and Love farm has one cottage and one 'suite', both with fully equipped kitchens and enough space for 3 adults, or 2 adults and 2 children under 10 (sharing a bed). This is the place for people who wish to self-cater and get away from it all. Book your stay well in advance, as they are often full.

A-C Casa Iguana, on southeastern bluff, www.casaiguana.net. This is a famous, popular lodging, beautifully located with stunning views of the beaches. They have 4 'economy' *cabañas* with shared bath (**C**), 9 *casitas* with private bath (**A**), and 2 'luxury' *casitas* (**A**). They grow their own food in lush, attractive gardens. Book in advance, especially in high season (note prices drop by US$10 in low season).

A-C Little Corn Beach and Bungalows, on the east coast, north of Sunrise Paradise, T8333-0956, www.littlecornbb.com. A new place on the beach with a mixture of smart bunkhouses (**C**), rooms (**B**) and bungalows (**A**). All come with fan and sleep up to 4 (US$5 extra for each additional person). The bungalows are particularly comfortable and have good views, wooden floors and decent showers. Restaurant attached.

B Derek's, at northeastern tip, www.dereksplacelittlecorn.com. Attractive wooden cabins on stilts, faintly reminiscent of Southeast Asia. All are equipped with renewable energy, mosquito nets, orthopaedic mattresses, hammocks, porches and sea views; showers and toilets are shared. The restaurant serves flavourful and interesting food. Derek's place is a tranquil, social spot by the beach, and Derek is a friendly host. Prices drop by US$10 in low season.

B-D Ensueños, Otto Beach, www.ensuenoslittlecornisland.com. Trippy, rustic cabins with sculpted *Lord of the Rings*-style interiors; some have electricity, some don't. The grounds are wonderfully lush and filled with exuberant fruit trees, and naturalist owner Ramón Gil is an interesting and friendly host. There are comfortable houses too (**B**), and good meals are also available. Recommended.

E-F Elsa's, north along beach from **Casa Iguana** (see above). The long-established Elsa's offers simple wooden cabins with sea views and own bath (**E**), as well as cheaper lodgings without either (**F**). The restaurant serves lobster, fish and vegetarian food for US$6-10 a plate. Snorkels, tours, hammocks and beer available. Hospitable, friendly, safe and relaxed. 'Everyone welcome'. Many other cheap lodgings in the area.

Puerto Cabezas *p699*

D Casa Museo, next to Centro de Computación Ansell, T2792-2225. Also known as Miss Judy's, this lovely house has lots of interesting art and artefacts in the attached museum and gallery. Rooms are spacious and comfortable and have private bath, TV and a/c (cheaper with fan, **E**). Friendly and interesting, with lots of family history. Highly recommended.

F Hotel Tangny, Enitel, 1 c arriba, 50 m norte. Clean and simple. They offer a range of cost effective rooms including some with TV and own bath, others with no TV and own bath, and some ultra-cheap quarters with no TV and shared bath. A reasonable economical choice.

Parque Nacional Saslaya *p700*

E Chino, Siuna. The best and most expensive place in town.

F Bosawás Field Station, on the River Labú. Has hammocks but not many, clean but simple, locally produced and cooked food about US$1.25.

F Costeño, Siuna, 100 m east of airstrip. Basic.

⑦ Eating

Bluefields *p698*

♔♔♔ **Chez Marcel**, alcaldía, 1 c sur, ½ c abajo, T2572-2347. This long-established 'fine dining' seafood restaurant is the best that Bluefields has to offer. The fading red curtains speak of better days, but the food is still tasty and the service attentive. Often recommended by the locals.

♔ **Bella Vista**, Barrio Punta Fría, T2572-2385. Daily 1000-2300. On the water's edge, overlooking the tired old boats and bay, this seafood restaurant serves shrimp, lobster, meat and *comida económica*.

♔ **Pelican**, Barrio Pointeen, La Punta, at the end of the road. Evenings here are often buzzing with drinkers and diners. Great breezes from the balcony, comfortable interior, friendly service and average food, including seafood and meat. Not a bad place to spend an evening. Good for rum and beer at least.

La Loma, Barrio San Pedro, opposite University BICU, T2572-2875. An open air ranch with a great view from the top of a hill. They serve a wide range of pricey food including meat, chicken and fish dishes. A good spot for a beer, breezes and occasional live music. Nice atmosphere.

Irie Food and Honey Sweet's, Obelisco, 25 vrs sur. An intimate, unpretentious little place that serves great shrimps and fish fillet in coconut sauce. Excellent value and often frequented by locals at both lunch and dinner time. A pleasant, colourful interior and service with a smile. The best restaurant in town. Highly recommended.

Comedor Vera Blanca, Barrio Central, opposite ADEPHCA. A simple comedor offering simple high-carb food, including obligatory chicken and fish dishes. Often packed with locals for lunch and dinner.

Laguna de Perlas p698

Queen Lobster, muelle principal, 200 vrs norte, T8662-3393, www.queenlobster.com. Owned by Nuria Dixon Curtis, the queen lobster is possibly the best place in town. This ranch-style eatery on the water's edge serves good seafood, including lobster and crab in red or coconut sauce. Order 'Mr Snapper' and you'll get a whole pound of fish. Good views and recommended.

Islas de Maíz/Corn Islands p699

Steer clear of baby lobsters as the harvesting threatens the local population.

Big Corn

Doña Lola's, Also known as Casa Oro del Negro, Sally Peaches, access road is signed. Loud, occasional outrageous and thoroughly hospitable seafood restaurant overlooking the waves. Here, the irrepressible Doña Lola cooks up a tasty range of local and Ecuadorian dishes, including wholesome lobster and fish recipes. Belting atmosphere driven by country and western tunes at top volume.

Fisherman's Cave, next to dock. This great little seafood restaurant overlooks the water and fishing boats. Usually a relaxing spot, although it's sometimes loud with inebriated fishermen. Open for breakfast, lunch or dinner, and good for a coffee or beer whilst awaiting the boat to Little Corn.

Nautilus Restaurant, North Point, open 0800-2200. Fabulously eclectic menu with Caribbean curry and classic dishes like rondon soup, containing vegetables, coconut milk and seafood. They also do pizza and will deliver. Generally tasty, but gringo prices mean it's not great value.

Seva's Place, 500 m east of Anastasia's in Sally Peaches. One of the island's best and longest-established restaurants. They serve great seafood, meat and chicken from a fine location with rooftop seats and ocean views. Try the lobster *a la plancha*.

Little Corn

Dining options on Little Corn are slowly improving. You'll find various cheap and cheerful *comedores* around the port. Most hotels have restaurants too.

Habana Libre, just north of boat landing. Really tasty, flavourful dishes including succulent veal, fish and lobster served with interesting sauces. There's terraced seating, good music and amiable staff. Cuban specialities are available on request and in advance. Be sure to try a *mojito* – they're outstanding.

Café Tranquilo, the port, 100 m south. Tranquilo serves a range of snacks and light dishes, including bruschetta, ceviche, cheeseburgers, chicken filets, sandwiches, tacos, quesadillas and cookies. Very popular with the gringos, quite tasty but a bit pricey. Wi-Fi available at US$6 an hr. Gift shop attached. Breakfast and lunch only.

Doña Rosa's, the port, 175 m south, 100 m east, on the path to **Casa Iguana**. Reasonably priced for the island, you can get a 3-course meal for US$6 or so, including fish and shrimp dishes. The portions are on the small side though.

Miss Bridgette's, the dock, 20 m south, then slightly east, off the path. A lovely little *comedor* serving wholesome, home-cooked fare. Service is very Caribbean, so be prepared to wait.

Puerto Cabezas *p699*
Crisfa, enitel, 2½ c sur, 1 c oeste. Tasty *comida típica*, meat, seafood and chicken dishes. Not bad, one of the better ones.
Kabu Payaska, hospital, 200 vrs al mar. Often recommended by the locals, this restaurant overlooking the water serves some of the best seafood and *comida típica* in town.

▲ Activities and tours

Laguna de Perlas *p698*
Tour operators
Many hoteliers are able to arrange guides or transportation to the Pearl Keys or Pearl Lagoon communities, including Casa Blanca, one of the best. Otherwise try:
Queen Lobster, muelle principal, 200 vrs norte, T8662-3393, www.queenlobster.com. The most organized and forward-thinking outfit in town. They offer cooking classes, including a fishing expedition and trip to the market; sportsfishing to the rich waters of northern lagoon (own equipment necessary), where homestay on a *finca* is possible; community and rural tourism, including camping, farming, fishing and living the Miskito life; trips to Wawasha Reserve; bicycle rental; and transport to the Pearl Keys. Recommended.

Islas de Maíz/Corn Islands *p699*
Big Corn
Diving Nautilus Resort & Dive Centre, North Point, T2575-5077, www.nautilus-dive-nicaragua.com. Diving and snorkelling tours to see the cannons of the old Spanish Galleon, Blowing rock and coral reefs, as well as trips further afield. PADI Open-Water certification from US$280,

advanced certification from US$230, night dives and 2-tank dives US$65 per person (Little Corn and Blowing Rock, US$95), snorkelling trips and glass-bottom boat tours at US$20 per person.

Little Corn
Diving Little Corn island is one of the best and cheapest places in the world to get diving qualifications. The island's 2 dive shops charge the same for their services. Excluding manuals, an Open Water certificate costs US$305; advanced Open Water US$225. A 1-tank dives cost US$35; 2 tanks US$65.
Dive Little Corn, boat landing in village, T8823-1154, www.divelittlecorn.com. There's a strong PADI ethos at this 5-star, gold palm centre, with training right up to assistant instructor level. They also offer night dives, single and 2-tank dives, snorkelling tours, and 5 or 10 dive packages – trips leave several times daily. There's a 10% discount if you stay with Casa Iguana in the high season; consult their website for more details.
Dolphin Dive, in the village, south of the dock, T8690-0225, www.dolphindivelittlecorn.com. **Dolphin Dive** offers PADI instruction to dive master level, and a range of customized trips for diving, fishing or snorkelling. Underwater digital camera rental costs US$20 including a CD. Various dive packages are available, including discounts at **Hotel Delfines** next door. Groups are kept small.

Puerto Cabezas *p699*
Cultural and community tourism
AMICA, supermarket Monter, 2½ c sur, T2792-2219. This women's organization can arrange tours and transportation to communities around Bilwi. The all-inclusive packages are expensive for individuals, so it's best to organize a group. They can also provide contacts and lodgings if you want to arrange your own transport.

⊖ Transport

Rama *p698*

Bus From Managua, buses leave for Rama from the Mercado Mayoreo every hour, 0400-1130, 8 hrs, US$7. To **Managua**, hourly 0400-1130. To/from **Juigalpa**, hourly 0800-1500, 6 hrs, US$3.75. To **Pearl Lagoon**, 1600, 3 hrs, US$7.50; from Pearl Lagoon to Rama, 0600.

Boat To **Bluefields**, pangas depart when full, several daily, 0530-1600, US$10, 2 hrs. The ferry is slightly cheaper and much slower. It departs Mon, Wed and Fri in the early morning (around 0800 when the bus has arrived), US$8, 5-8 hrs.

Bluefields *p698*

Air The airport is 3 km south of the city centre, either walk (30 mins) or take a taxi US$0.75 per person. **La Costeña** office, inside the terminal, T2572-2500. All schedules are subject to random and seasonal changes. It's best to get your name on the list several days in advance, if possible, and especially if travelling to Bilwi.

To **Managua**, daily 0840, 1110, 1310, 1610, US$83 one-way, US$128 return, 1 hr. To **Corn Islands**, daily 0730, 1510, US$64 one-way, US$99 return, 20 mins. To **Bilwi**, Mon, Wed, Fri, 1110, US$96 one-way, US$148 return, 1 hr.

Boat Motorboats (*pangas*) depart when full. The early ones are more reliable, and services on Sun are restricted. Note all schedules below are subject to almost constant change; confirm departure times at the port well in advance of your trip. If the Corn Island ferry is grounded no replacement will be made available.

To **Pearl Lagoon**, from 0830, several daily, US$7.50, 1-1½ hrs. To **El Rama**, 0530-1600, several daily, US$10, 2 hrs. To San Juan del Norte, Mon, Thu, Sat, 1000, US$30, 3-4 hrs, with stops at El Bluff and Monkey Point. To

Corn Islands, *Bluefields Express*, Wed 0900, US$11; 'Captain D' (departs from El Bluff) Wed 1700, US$12.50; Island Express (departs from El Bluff), Fri 0900, US$12.50.

Islas de Maíz/Corn Islands *p699*

Air La Costeña flies from Big Corn to **Managua** with a stop in **Bluefields**, daily at 0810 and 1540, US$165 round trip, 90 mins with stop. Re-confirm seats before travelling. La Costeña airline office is on Big Corn, T2575-5131.

Boat **Big Corn** to **Little Corn**, daily 1000, 1630, US$6.50, 40 mins. Little Corn to Big Corn, daily 0700, 1400, US$6.50, 40 mins. Boats leave from main dock, first come, first served. US$0.20 charge to get into the dock area. Buy big blue trash bags to keep luggage dry at shop across from dock entrance, best to sit near the back.

Mainland boats: Subject to change, check locally; Corn Islands to **Bluefields** leaves Tue, 0900, US$12, 5-6 hrs; and Fri and Sun 1200. To **Bilwi**, daytime departure, once per month, US$30, 3 days.

Bus Buses and *colectivos* travel clockwise and anti-clockwise round Big Corn. US$0.70 per person regardless of distance all day.

Puerto Cabezas *p699*

Air The newly renovated airport is 3 km north of town, from where taxis charge US$1 to anywhere in Bilwi. If flying to Bluefields, try to get your name on the list several days in advance. To **Bluefields**, Mon, Wed, Fri, 1210, US$96 one-way, US$148 return, 1 hr. To **Managua**, La Costeña, daily 0820, 1220, 1610, US$97 1-way, US$148 round-trip; Frequent cancellations so it's best to make reservation and pay just before plane leaves. Bring your passport: there are 'immigration' checks by the police in Puerto, and sometimes in the waiting lounge in Managua; also, there is a customs check when returning from the coast by air to Managua.

Bus Public bus service is available between Puerto and **Waspám** and from **Matagalpa** (14 hrs). Furthermore, Puerto is connected by road to **Managua**; however, this 559-km trip should only be attempted in the dry season (early Jan to mid-May) in a 4WD vehicle. With luck, it will take only 2-3 days (the road, almost all of it unpaved, is not bad from Managua to Siuna, but becomes very difficult after that); do not drive at night. If you drive back from Puerto to Managua, take the road out of town and turn left at the sign, SW Wawa.

Car It is not possible to rent a vehicle or bicycle in Puerto, but arrangements for a car and driver can be made (ask a taxi or at your *hospedaje*).

Parque Nacional Saslaya *p700*
Air La Costeña flies daily to **Siuna**, reservations in Siuna, T2263-2142.

Bus Daily from Siuna market to the park at 0500 and 0730, sometimes at 1100, US$2.25.

Car There are 2 road links from **Managua**: 1 through Matagalpa and Waslala; the other through Boaco, Muy Muy, Matiguás and Río Blanco, a very scenic 330-km drive, about 7 hrs by 4WD in the dry season; check on the security situation before starting out.

La Rosita is 70 km east of Siuna, and it is also possible to drive on through to **Puerto Cabezas**, although the road is in poor shape.

⊙ Directory

Bluefields *p698*
Banks There are banks for money changing, some ATMs. Internet is widespread around town.

Puerto Cabezas *p699*
Banks There is Banpro for changing dollars, one ATM. **Hospital** On the outskirts of town.

Contents

Footprint features

At a glance

○ **Getting around** Mostly by bus; boats to Tortuguero and Bahía Drake.

◎ **Time required** Ideally 4-5 weeks.

☀ **Weather** Dec-Apr is best.

✕ **When not to go** Wet season.

Costa Rica

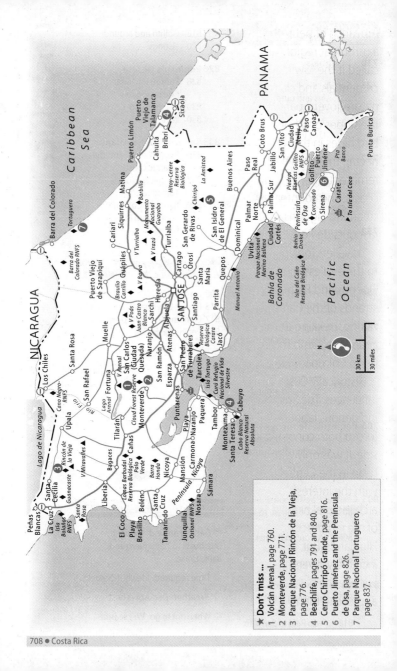

★ **Don't miss ...**
1 Volcán Arenal, page 760.
2 Monteverde, page 771.
3 Parque Nacional Rincón de la Vieja,
  page 776.
4 Beachlife, pages 791 and 840.
5 Cerro Chirripó Grande, page 816.
6 Puerto Jiménez and the Península
  de Osa, page 826.
7 Parque Nacional Tortuguero,
  page 837.

A beacon of neutral democratic ideals, Costa Rica stands out in a turbulent region; as far back as the 1930s one commentator called it the "Switzerland of Central America". Whatever its political credentials and claims to neutrality, this country is undeniably a nature-lovers' paradise: you'll find moss-draped cloud forest on the slopes of Monteverde, where the red and green sacred quetzal bird hides in the treetops and hummingbirds busy round drinking nectar; there's rainforest wilderness on the Osa Peninsula and remote turtle-nesting beaches on the north Atlantic and Pacific coasts. The country's volcanic peaks range from the gentle steaming lagoons of Irazú and Poás to the explosive Arenal, just outside Fortuna, where red-hot lava lights up the night sky.

Travellers looking to combine nature and comfort should head to the endless sand and surf beaches of the Nicoya Peninsula, Quepos and Parque Nacional Manuel Antonio, or to the off-beat strands of the Caribbean. For adrenalin junkies there's whitewater rafting, trekking and coast-to-coast mountain biking, and the chance to climb the barren *páramo* savannahs to the peak of Cerro Chirripó.

Historically Costa Rica has avoided the extremes of external influences. The Spanish found no mineral wealth here or compliant indigenous labour to work the land. Hard conditions and poverty forced both conquerors and conquered to work and live side by side. It was only with the arrival of wealth from the magic coffee bean in the Central Highlands that a landed gentry arose to conflict with the interests of a liberal merchant class. As a result, Costa Rica's architectural highlights are somewhat limited compared to much of the region, concentrated in the churches that dot the Central Highlands. But, just like the country's natural nuances that host incredibly diversity, the architectural differences are subtle. And just like the natural wonders, you'll have to look harder to truly appreciate them.

Essentials

Geographically Costa Rica is the smallest but two of the Central American republics (after El Salvador and Belize) and only Panama and Belize have fewer inhabitants. Despite these diminutive tendencies, the 'Rich Coast' has carved out a niche market as the nature destination in Central America with a well-developed network of national parks and biological reserves protecting large tracts of unspoilt tropical wilderness. Adventure activities are an option to sap untapped adrenalin and there are plenty of glorious beaches for lazing around and soaking up the perfect climate. Known throughout Latin America as the continent's purest democracy, Costa Rica celebrated a centenary of democracy in 1989. For Ticos, as the citizens are known, the country has the highest standard of living in Central America, the highest literacy rate (95%), the second lowest birth rate (after Panama) and the greatest degree of economic and social advancement.

Where to go

Costa Rica's main attractions are its countryside, nature and wildlife. Although the country has a colourful history, most of the colonial heritage has been lost in earthquakes over the centuries. **San José**, the capital, is a lively city, and worth enjoying for a couple of days, visiting museums and cultural attractions while organizing trips to other parts of the country.

Surrounding San José is the **Meseta Central** draped in the quirky charms and graceful air of **Zarcero**, **Sarchí**, **Heredia** and **Alajuela** in the heart of this agricultural and coffee-producing region. Just 57 km from the capital, the impressive crater and easily reached summit of **Volcán Poás** steams and puffs in a national park with a sprinkling of wildlife and a few trails. To the east, the former capital Cártago is overshadowed by **Volcán Irazú**, with spectacular views from the summit. Nearby the **Orosí Valley** leads to the hidden beauty of Costa Rica's newest reserve **Parque Nacional Tapantí**. Further east on the Caribbean slope, **Turrialba** is a prime site for world-class **whitewater rafting** on the scenic Reventazón and Pacuare rivers, staying in secluded lodges offering comfortable nature tourism and guided tours.

North to San Carlos the route leads to **Fortuna** and **Lake Arenal**, the backdrop to the most spectacular of Costa Rica's volcanoes – the active **Arenal**. A perfect cone, it is best watched at night when, with luck, the red hot lava can be seen spewing out of the top before rolling and crashing down the mountainside. In addition to being the starting point for volcano trips, **Fortuna**, at the foot of Arenal, is a good base for boat trips to the wetlands of **Caño Negro Wildlife Refuge**, a birdwatcher's paradise near **Los Chiles**, and a route between Costa Rica and Nicaragua.

South of Lake Arenal is **Monteverde Forest Reserve**, a private reserve and a guiding light in the world of conservation. Difficult to reach, the epiphyte-laden cloud forest spans the continental divide, protecting the habitat of the resplendent quetzal and many other tropical birds. Nearby **Santa Elena** and several other private reserves offer nature visits and dramatic canopy tours for visitors.

Continuing north the Pan-American Highway leads towards the Nicaraguan border. **Guanacaste**, in the northwest, is drier with open plains once used for cattle ranching inspiring a distinctive regional music, dance and culture. From the town of **Liberia**, trips to **Parque Nacional Rincón de la Vieja** reveal an array of geothermal curiosities including mud pots and hot springs. Close to the Nicaraguan border, **Parque Nacional Santa Rosa** protects rare dry tropical forest and Pacific beaches used by nesting turtles. These two parks, along with the adjacent Parque Nacional Guanacaste, encompass the Guanacaste Conservation Area, declared a World Heritage Site by the United Nations in 1999. Beach lovers should head for the **Nicoya Peninsula**, with miles of white-sand beaches. Resorts are springing up if you want parties, dancing and services, but smaller towns exist for solitude, sun loving and surf.

On the southern Pacific, beautiful beaches fringe the coast from the transport hub of **Puntarenas** through the surf hangout of **Jacó**, to the justifiably popular **Quepos** with treasured **Parque Nacional Manuel Antonio** nearby, and the quieter spots around **Dominical** and **Playa Hermosa**. In the far south, the **Osa Peninsula** draws naturalists to the beauty of **Parque Nacional Corcovado**'s protected primary rainforest. It's tough, hot, sweaty and not for the faint hearted, but you won't regret the effort.

The Pan-American Highway travels down the southern spine of the country from San José to Panama through the spectacular mountain scenery of the Cordillera Talamanca. The country's highest mountain, **Cerro Chirripó** (3820 m), is climbed from **San Gerardo** near **San Isidro de El General**. Throughout the area, lodges catering for all budgets offer birdwatching and guided tours in the mountains, where the **Parque Nacional Chirripó** and neighbouring **Parque Internacional La Amistad** protect the country's largest area of virgin forest with the greatest biological diversity.

Puerto Limón is the main town on the Caribbean with a vibrancy and rhythm that shines through at carnival each October. While much of the region is used for banana cultivation, on the coast towards the Nicaraguan border is **Parque Nacional Tortuguero**, reached through a network of inland canals and waterways full to bursting with tropical birdlife, basking crocodiles, noisy monkeys and beaches used by nesting turtles.

South of Puerto Limón the road leads to Panama through the towns of **Cahuita**, **Puerto Viejo** and **Manzanillo**. Strong local cultures, a proud expatriate community and protected tropical rainforest attract backpackers and the discerning traveller to this forgotten corner of Costa Rica. It's also the best route to Bocas del Toro in Panama.

Suggested itinerary

All traffic goes through San José so your visit will inevitably involve a few days in the capital. If travelling from Nicaragua, you have two options. Cross by land at Peñas Blancas to travel down the **Nicoya Peninsula** for a few days on the beach, or to **Liberia** to spend time clambering around the volcanic **Rincón de la Vieja**. The second option is to cross to Los Chiles for a trip to **Caño Negro Wildlife Reserve** before moving on to **Fortuna** and the explosive **Arenal**. The next stop might be a few days in Santa Elena to visit **Monteverde Cloud Forest**. From here, you could spend 10 days travelling down the Pacific coast, stopping at **Manuel Antonio National Park** and the **Osa Peninsula** in the south before heading to Panama. Alternatively, head to **San José** and after a few days, continue east to **Tortuguero** before heading south to **Cahuita**, **Puerto Viejo de Talamanca** and the border with Panama. At a push you would need two or three weeks in Costa Rica; four to five weeks would be much more relaxing.

When to go

In general, the best time to visit is December to February. This is during the dry season (December to April), but before the temperatures really rise (March and April). Two main factors contribute to the local climatic conditions: altitude and location. The climate varies from the heat and humidity of the Caribbean and Atlantic lowlands, usually around the mid-20°Cs, falling to the warm temperate Meseta Central with chilly temperatures at greater heights – in the Cordillera Talamanca, the average temperature is below 16°C. On the Pacific side there is a well-defined wet season (May-November). The wetter Atlantic side has no specific dry season but there is less rainfall between March and September. Festivals are spread throughout the year, but the two biggest are Independence Day (September) and Día de la Raza (October).

What to do

Ballooning and bungee jumping

If you're looking for a last big-spending celebration, hot-air-balloon rides take you over the trees near Arenal Volcano and also the Turrialba region. Contact **Serendipity Adventures**, T2558-1000, www.serendipity adventures.com. The final suggestion is to jump off a bridge. Bungee jumping, that is, off the Colorado bridge, close to Grecia in the Meseta Central (see page 735).

Diving, snorkelling and swimming

There is swimming on both Atlantic and Pacific coasts. Offshore, sea kayaking is increasingly popular. Snorkelling and scuba-diving are offered by several hotels and most beach tour offices, but you have to pick your spot carefully. Anywhere near a river will suffer from poor visibility and the coral reef has died in many places because of agricultural pollutants washed downstream, particularly on the Caribbean coast. Generally, on the Caribbean side, you can see wrecks and coral reefs, particularly in the southeast towards the Panamanian border, while on the Pacific side you see large pelagics and sportfish. Liveaboard dive boats head for the islands of Caño and Isla del Coco. Divers are not permitted in national parks or reserves, nor within 500 m of the protected sea turtle zone north of Parque Nacional Tortuguero.

Fishing

For sport fishing, sailfish and marlin are targeted off the Pacific; snook and tarpon are caught in the Caribbean, the largest snook being found in Sep and Oct, mostly north of Limón (where there are fishing

lodges), but also towards Panama. Exciting it may be, cheap it is not. Anglers can save money in groups, since it is usually the same cost to rent a boat for 1 or 4.

Nature tourism

Tourists particularly enjoy the many well-kept and well-guarded national parks and nature reserves that protect some samples of the extraordinarily varied Costa Rican ecosystems. In the north the variety is daunting and includes some of the last patches of dry tropical forest in the **Parque Nacional Santa Rosa**, the cloud forest of **Monteverde** and the **Talamanca Mountains**, and 9 active volcanoes including **Rincón de la Vieja**, **Poás**, **Irazú** and of course **Arenal**. There is a standard entrance fee of US$10 for all national parks. **Manuel Antonio** is closed on Mon; **Cabo Blanco** is closed on Mon and Tue.

Birdwatchers and butterfly lovers have long flocked to Costa Rica to see some of the 850 or so species of bird and untold varieties of butterfly. All of these can best be seen in the parks, together with monkeys, deer, coyotes, armadillos, anteaters, turtles, coatis, raccoons, snakes, and, more rarely, wild pigs, wild cats and tapirs.

Although the national parks and other privately owned reserves are a main tourist attraction, many are in remote areas and not easy to get to on public transport; buses or coaches that do go tend to stay for a short time. There is a tendency for tour companies to dominate the National Park 'market' to the exclusion of other public transport. For tight budgets, try making up a party with others and sharing taxis or hiring a car.

Asociación de Voluntarios (ASVO), Paseo Colón, Toyota, 250 m north, T2258-4430, www.asvocr.org. Contact if you want to work as a volunteer in the parks, at US$12 per day for lodging and food. Bilingual tourist information and/or telephone numbers for individual national park offices is available by dialling T192. AVSO's Nature Hostel (**D-E**) hostel@asvocr.org, provides an option for supporting the ongoing work of **AVSO**, complete with free internet.

Fundación de Parques Nacionales (FPN), Av 15, San José, T2257-2239, Mon-Fri 0800-1200, 1300-1700, 300 m north and 150 m east of Santa Teresita Church, Barrio Escalante, between Calles 23-25. Contact for information and permits to visit and/or camp or conduct research in the parks. Check in advance if your trip depends on gaining entrance.

Sistema Nacional de Areas de Conservación (SINAC), T2283-8004, PO Box 10104-1000, San José, www.costarica-nationalparks.com, administers the National Park System (write in advance or call).

Rafting, kayaking and canoeing

The rivers of Costa Rica have proved to be highly popular for whitewater rafting, kayaking and canoeing, both for the thrill of the rapids and the wildlife interest of the quieter sections. The 5 most commonly run rivers are the **Reventazón** (and the Pascua section of it), **Pacuare, Corobicí, Sarapiquí** and El General. You can do a day trip but to reach the Grade IV and V rapids you usually have to take 2-3 days. The Reventazón is perhaps the most accessible but the Pacuare has been recommended as a more beautiful experience. The Corobicí is slower and popular with birdwatchers. **Ríos Tropicales** (see page 735) has been recommended. For reasons of safety heavy rain may cause cancellations, so make sure your plans are flexible.

Surfing and windsurfing

Windsurfing is good along the Pacific coast, particularly in the bay close to La Cruz and world class on Lake Arenal, particularly the west end where hotels have equipment for hire. Surfing is popular on the Pacific and southern Caribbean beaches, attracting professionals who follow storm surges along the coast. Beginners can take classes in some resorts like Tamarindo, Jacó and Dominical, and proficient surfers can get advice on waves from surf shops in these areas.

Other sports

Football (soccer) is the national sport (played every Sun at 1100, Sep-May, at the Saprissa Stadium). **Mountain biking** is popular throughout most parts of the country with options to simply rent the bike and push out on your own, or join a guided trip. There are several **golf** courses close to the capital, and a growing number on the Nicoya Peninsula and at Los Sueños Marriott, near Jacó. The Meseta Central is good country for **horse riding**; horses can be hired by arrangement directly with owners. Most fiestas end with **bullfighting** in the squares, with no horses used. Bullfights are held in San José during the Christmas period. There is no kill and spectators are permitted to enter the ring to chase, and be chased by, the bull.

Getting there

Air

The main international airport is at San José (see page 723). Departure tax is a flat rate of US$26 per person, regardless of nationality or immigration status, when leaving by air. Exit taxes, by air or land, and legislation regarding visa extensions, are subject to frequent change and travellers should check these details as near to the time of travelling as possible.

From Europe From most European cities flights connect in the US at Miami, Houston, Dallas and many others with **American Airlines**, **Continental** and **Grupo Taca**. **Iberia** have daily flights between Madrid and San José. There are direct charter flights in season from several European cities including Frankfurt (**Condor**).

From North America Flights from North America are many and varied (more than 20 each week), again some stop in Miami so check if a direct flight is important. Departure points include: Atlanta, Boston, Chicago, Dallas, Houston, Los Angeles, Miami, New York, Orlando, San Francisco, Toronto, Washington DC. **Daniel Oduber International Airport**, near Liberia, is increasingly popular, conveniently located just 30 minutes from some of Guanacaste's finest beaches. Charter specials available from time to time.

From South America Flights from South American cities include Bogotá (**Copa**, **Grupo Taca**), Cali (**SAM**, **Grupo Taca**), Caracas (**Grupo Taca**), Cartagena (**SAM**), Guayaquil (**Grupo Taca**), Lima (**Grupo Taca**), Quito (**Grupo Taca**) and Santiago (**Grupo Taca**).

From Central America The **Grupo Taca** alliance provides connections with all capitals and several of the more popular tourist destinations including Cancún, Guatemala City (also **United** and **Copa**), Managua (**Copa**), Mexico City (also **Mexicana, United**), Panama City (**Copa**), San Pedro Sula, San Salvador (**Copa**) and Tegucigalpa.

From the Caribbean There are a couple of flights a week to Havana (**Cubana, Grupo Taca**) and regular charters to San Andrés, Colombia (**SAM**). Also flights to Santo Domingo (**Copa**).

Road
Road links to the north are on the Pan-American Highway at Peñas Blancas with immigration services and buses connecting to and from Nicaragua. It is possible to cross the northern border close to Los Chiles, making the journey by land or boat to San Carlos. Crossing the border on the North Pacific is possible but immigration services are non-existent and transportation is irregular.

The main crossing to Panama at Paso Canoas is straightforward and problem-free. On the Caribbean coast, Sixaola links with the Panamian town of Guabito over the old banana bridge. Immigration services on both sides but only during normal office hours.

Sea
The main ports for international cargo vessels are **Puerto Limón**, with regular sailings to and from Europe, and **Caldera**, on the central Pacific coast. Contact shipping agents, of which there are many, in Puerto Limón and San José for details. Cruise vessels arrive at Caldera, Puntarenas and Puerto Limón, normally stopping for little more than 24 hours.

Getting around

Air
There are domestic airports, with scheduled services provided by **Sansa** or **NatureAir** at Barra Colorado, Carate, Carrillo-Sámara, Coto 47, Drake Bay, Golfito, Liberia, La Fortuna, Limón, Nosara Beach, Palmar Sur, Puerto Jiménez, Punta Islita, Quepos, Tamarindo, Tambor and Tortuguero. Several charter companies also operate out of San José.
➸ *See Transport, page 736.*

Border essentials

Costa Rica–Nicaragua

For crossings between Costa Rica and Nicaragua (Peñas Blancas, San Carlos–Los Chiles, San Juan del Norte–Barra Colorado), see page 606. **Note** Panama is an hour ahead of Costa Rica.

Costa Rica–Panama
Paso Canoas

Busy, well-plied crossing on the Pan-American Highway. Painless, unless travelling on an international bus when you can expect long queues. Lots of amenities, but generally insalubrious. International bus tickets and car insurance available.

Currency exchange Plentiful money-changers. Try Banco Nacional de Panama for TCs and ATM.

Costa Rican immigration Open 0600-2200 (Costa Rica time).

Panamanian immigration Open 24 hours.

Onwards to Panama Local bus connections with David and the Chiriquí highlands. For Volcán/Cerro Punta, change in La Concepción. Buses to Panama City with Padafront, 11 daily, every 1½ to two hours; or go to David and change.

Onwards to Costa Rica Connections with the central Pacific coast and San José, as well as the Burica peninsula.

Sixaola–Guabito

Straightforward and interesting crossing divided by an old United Fruit Company railway bridge over the Río Sixaola. Basic hotel accommodation available but undesirable; if stuck try Imperio or Cabinas Sánchez, T2754-2105. Best access to Caribbean destinations.

Currency exchange No banks; try money-changers or the supermarket. Poor rates.

Costa Rican immigration Open 0700-1700 (Costa Rica time); shut for lunch for one hour on Saturday and Sunday. Office is just before the bridge.

Panamanian immigration Open 0700-2300 (Panama time); often closes an hour early.

Onwards to Panama To reach the Bocas del Toro archipelago, take a bus from Guabito to Almirante, 1½ hours, then a boat to Isla Colón, 20 minutes. If there are no direct buses, change in Changuinola.

Onwards to Costa Rica Regular connections to Puerto Limón and the Caribbean coast. Four direct buses daily from Sixaola to San José, 5½ hours.

Río Sereno

A minor crossing in the Chiriquí highlands. Quiet and cool, although some reports of lengthy bureaucratic treatment. Vehicle formalities cannot be completed.

Currency exchange Bank with ATM, but no exchange; bring currency or ask locally who might change it.

Costa Rican immigration Open 0800-1600, Sunday till 1400 (Costa Rican time). In the white building, overstays will be redirected for processing in Paso Canoas.

Panamanian immigration Open 0500-1700. Visas/tourist cards are reportedly unavailable; only those who require neither may enter.

Onwards to Panama Dawn to dusk services from Río Sereno to Volcán, La Concepción and David.

Onwards to Costa Rica Frequent buses run to San Vito via Sabilito.

Road

Costa Rica has a total of 35,700 km of roads of which 7500 km are paved. The Pan-American Highway runs the length of the country, from the Nicaraguan to the Panamanian borders. A highway has been built from Orotina to Caldera, a port on the Gulf of Nicoya, which has replaced Puntarenas as the principal Pacific port. There is also a highway from Orotina to Ciudad Colón. Another road goes from Orotina as far as Quepos greatly improving access to the Pacific beaches. Beyond Quepos, it's a dirt road down to Dominical, but continuing further south from Dominical to Ciudad Cortés, the road is generally good. All four-lane roads into San José are toll roads. It is illegal to ride in a car or taxi without wearing seatbelts.

Bus The good road network supports a regular bus service that covers most parts of the country. Frequency declines with popularity but you can get to most places with road access eventually. San José is the main hub for buses, although you can skip down the Pacific coast by making connections at Puntarenas. Coming from Nicaragua, direct to Arenal, requires cutting in and travelling through Tilaran.

Two shuttle bus companies offer transport from the capital to dozens of beach and tourism destinations in comfortable air-conditioned minibuses; they're quicker but more expensive. ▸▸ *See Transport, page 738.*

Car Driving in Costa Rica allows for greater flexibility when travelling. Many of the nature parks are in remote areas; 4WD and high-clearance is recommended and sometimes essential; in the wet season some roads will be impassable. Always ask locals or bus drivers what the state of the road is before embarking on a journey. Do not assume that if the buses are running, a car can get through too.

Tourists who enter by car or motorcycle pay US$10 road tax, including mandatory insurance, and can keep their cars for an initial period of 90 days. This can be extended for a total period of six months, for about US$10 per extra month, at the **Instituto Costarricense de Turismo**, or at the **Customs office** ① *Av 3, Calle 14*, if you take your passport, car entry permit, and a piece of stamped paper (*papel sellado*) obtainable at any bookshop. Cars are fumigated on entry. If you have an accident while in the country do not move the vehicle and immediately contact **Policía de Tránsito** ① *San José, T2222-9330 or T2222-9245*.

Car hire Renting a car can be a surprisingly economical way to travel if you can form a group and split the costs. As with all rentals, check your vehicle carefully as the company will try to claim for the smallest of 'damages'. Most leases do not allow the use of a normal car off paved roads. Always make sure the spare tyre is in good order, as potholes are frequent. You can have tyres fixed at any garage for about US$2 in 30 minutes. Guideline prices: smallest economy car US$38-48 per day includes unlimited mileage or US$250-310 per week; 4WD vehicle costs US$60-120 per day, US$440-770 per week, including unlimited mileage. Driver's licence from home and credit card are generally required. Loss damage waiver (LDW) insurance is mandatory and costs an extra US$11-14 per day; excess is between US$750 and US$1500. Cash deposits or credit card charges range from US$800 to US$1800, so check you have sufficient credit. Discounts for car hire are available during the 'Green Season' (May to November). If you plan to drop off a hired car somewhere other than where you picked it up, check with several firms for their charges: **Elegante**, **Ada** and **National** appear to have the lowest drop-off fees. Insurance will not cover broken windscreens, driving on unsurfaced roads or damaged tyres.

Safety Never leave anything in a hired car and never leave your car on the street, even in daylight. Secure parking lots are available in most cities. Regular reports of break-ins at national parks and other popular tourism areas. Driving at night is not recommended.

Fuel Main fuel stations have regular (unleaded) US$1.17 and diesel US$0.85 per litre; super gasoline (unleaded) is available throughout the country, US$1.21 per litre. Prices are regulated by the government.

Road tolls Costa Rica has a road toll system, with charges of between US$0.35 to US$0.55 for some of the busiest routes in the Central Highlands.

Cycling Cycling is easier in Costa Rica than elsewhere in Central America; there is less heavy traffic and it is generally more 'cyclist friendly'. However, paving is thin and soon deteriorates; look out for cracks and potholes, which bring traffic to a crawl. The prevailing wind is from the northeast so, if making an extensive tour, travelling in the direction of Panama is slightly more favourable.

Recommended reading for all users: Baker's *The Essential Road Guide to Costa Rica*, with detailed strip maps, kilometre by kilometre road logs, motoring information plus San José map and bus guide (Bill Baker, Apdo 1185-1011, San José). Cycle shops have sprung up around the country offering parts and repair services.

Hitchhiking Generally easy and safe by day, but take the usual precautions.

Sea

Ferries serve the southern section of the Nicoya Peninsula from Puntarenas. The Osa Peninsula has a regular ferry service linking Golfito and Puerto Jiménez, and Bahía Drake is reached on boats from Sierpe. Boats travel to Tortuguero from Moín, close to Puerto Limón, and from Cariari, north of Guápiles.

Maps

The **Instituto Geográfico Nacional** ① *Calle 9, Av 20-22, open 0730-1600*, at the Ministry of Public Works and Transport in San José, supplies good topographical maps for walkers. **ITM** has a 1:500,000 travel map of Costa Rica, available at bookstores throughout the country. Maps are also available in San José at **7th Street Books** ① *Calle 7, Av 1 and Central, T2256-8251*; **Universal** ① *Av Central and Calle 1, T2222-2222*; and **Lehmann** ① *Av Central, Calle 1-3, T2223-1212*.

Sleeping

Accommodation in Costa Rica favours couples and groups – the price of a single room is often the same as a double, and the price of a room for four is often less than double the price for two. So if you can get in a group, the cost per person falls considerably. Accommodation prices during the 'green' season (May to November), are generally much lower. A 13% sales tax plus 3.39% tourism tax (total 16.39%) are added to the basic price of hotel rooms. A deposit is advised at the more expensive hotels in San José, especially in the high season (December to April), to guarantee reservations. If you arrive late at night in the high season, even a guaranteed reservation may not be kept.

The **Costa Rica Bed & Breakfast Group**, which has 300 bed and breakfast inns and small hotels around the country in its membership, helps with reservations. The **Costa Rican Chamber of Hotels** ① *T2220-0575, www.costaricanhotels.com*, provides information about its members (mostly larger hotels) and an online reservation system. The **Costa Rican Tourist Board** ① *T2291-5740, www.turismo-sostenible.co.cr*, has an eco-rating system for hotels, an encouraging indicator of progress.

Camping opportunities in Costa Rica are limited with few official campsites. It is possible to camp in some national parks. Contact the Fundación de Parques Nacionales in San José for details (see Nature tourism, page 712).

Eating and drinking

Local cuisine

Sodas (small restaurants) serve local food, which is worth trying. Very common is *casado*, a cheap lunch which includes rice, beans, stewed beef or fish, fried plantain and cabbage. *Olla de carne* is a soup of beef, plantain, corn, yucca, *ñampi* and *chayote* (local vegetables). *Sopa negra* is made with black beans, and comes with a poached egg in it; *picadillo* is another meat and vegetable stew. Snacks are popular: *gallos* (filled tortillas), *tortas* (containing meat and vegetables), *arreglados* (bread filled with the same) and *empanadas*. *Pan de yuca* is a speciality, available from stalls in San José centre. For breakfast, try *gallo pinto* (rice and beans) with *natilla* (a slightly sour cream). The best ice cream can be found in *Pops* shops.

In general, eating out in Costa Rica is more expensive than elsewhere in Central America. A sales tax of 13% plus 10% service charge are added to restaurant bills.

Drink

There are many types of cold drink made either from fresh fruit or milk drinks with fruit (*batidos*) or cereal flour whisked with ice cubes. Drinks are often sugared well beyond North American or European tastes (ask for *poco azúcar*). The fruits range from the familiar to the exotic; others include *cebada* (barley flour), *pinolillo* (roasted corn), *horchata* (rice flour with cinnamon), *chan*, which according to Michael Brisco is "perhaps the most unusual, looking like mouldy frogspawn and tasting of penicillin". All these drinks cost the same as, or less than, bottled fizzy products. The coffee is excellent. Local beers are Bavaria, Pilsen, Imperial, Rock Ice and Kaiser (which is non-alcoholic).

Festivals and events

1 Jan New Year's Day.
19 Mar St Joseph.
Mar/Apr Easter. Nearly everyone is on holiday; everywhere is shut on Thu, Fri and Sun, and many shops close on Sat and most of the previous week as well.
11 Apr Battle of Rivas.
1 May Labour Day.
Jun Corpus Christi.
29 Jun St Peter and St Paul.
25 Jul Guanacaste Day.
2 Aug Virgin of Los Angeles.

15 Aug Mothers' Day.
15 Sep Independence Day.
12 Oct Día de la Raza (Columbus Day). The main festival is **Carnival in Puerto Limón**, the week before and after Columbus Day. There's music, dance, street processions and general festivities. Hotels book up, but it's definitely worth making the effort to go.
8 Dec Immaculate Conception.
25 Dec Christmas Day.
28-31 Dec San José only.

Shopping

The best buys are wooden items, ceramics and leather handicrafts. Many wooden handicrafts are made of rainforest hardwoods and deforestation is a critical problem. Coffee should have 'puro' on the packet or it may contain sugar or other additives.

Essentials A-Z

Accident and emergency
Police: T117/127. **Fire:** T118. **Medical (Red Cross):** T128.

For Police, Fire, Red Cross emergencies/ bilingual operators: T911.

Customs and duty free
Duty-free allowances are 500 g of manufactured tobacco, 2 kg of chocolate and 5 litres of liquor. Any amount of currency may be taken in or out, but amounts over US$10,000 must be declared. Cameras, binoculars, camping equipment, laptop computers and other portable items of personal/ professional/leisure use are free of duty.

Electricity
110 volts AC, 60 cycles, US-style plugs.

Embassies and consulates
Australia, De la Sala House, 11th floor, 30 Clarence St, Sydney NSW: 2000, T9-261-1177.
Belize, Room 3, 2nd floor, Capital Garden Plaza, Belmopan, T822-1582.
Canada, 325 Dalhouise St, Suite 407, Ottawa, ON, K1N 7G2, T613-562-2855.
El Salvador, 85 Av Sur y Calle Cuscatlán, 4415 Col Escalón, SS, T2264-3865.
France, 78 Av Emile Zola, 75015 Paris, T4-578-9696.
Germany, Dessauerstrasse 28-29 D-10963 Berlin, T30-2639-8990.
Guatemala, 15 Calle 7-59, Zona 10, Guatemala City, T2366-9918.
Honduras, Residencial El Triángulo Lomas del Guijamo, Calle 3451, Tegucigalpa, T232-1768.
Israel, Abba Hillel Silver St, 14 Mail Box, 38 Beit Oz, 15th floor, Ramat Gan, 52506, T3-613-5061.

Italy, Viale Liegi 2, Int 8, Roma, T4425-1046.
Japan, Kowa Building, No 38, 9th floor, 901 4-12-24 Nishi Azabu Minato, Ku Tokio, 106-0031, T3-486-1812.
Mexico, Calle Río Poo 113, Col Cuauhtémoc between Río Pánuco and Lerma, México DF, T5525-7765.
Netherlands, Laan Copes van Cattenburch 46, 2585 GB, Den Haag, T70-354-0780.
Nicaragua, de la Estatua de Montoya, 2 c al lago y ½ c arriba (Callejón Zelaya), Managua, T266-2404.
Norway (covers **Sweden** and **Denmark**), Skippergat 33, 8th floor, 0154 Oslo, Noruega, T2233-0408.
Panama, Calle Samuel Lewis Edificio Plaza Omega, 3rd floor, Contiguo Santuario Nacional Panamá, T264-2980.
Spain, Paseo de la Castellana 164, 17-A, 28046 Madrid, T91-345-9622.
Switzerland, Schwarztorstrasse 11, 3007 Berna, T031-372-7887.
UK (covers **Portugal**), Flat 1, 14 Lancaster Gate, London, W2 3LH, T020-7706-8844.
USA, 2114-S St, North West Washington DC 20008, T202-234-2945.

For more embassies, see www.rree.go.cr.

Health
Drinking water is safe in all major towns; elsewhere it should be boiled. Bottled water is widely available.

Intestinal disorders are prevalent in the lowlands. Malaria is on the increase: malaria prophylaxis is advised for visitors to the lowlands, especially near the Nicaraguan and Panama border. Dengue fever has been recorded throughout the country, mostly in coastal cities. Having said all that, the standards of health and hygiene are among the best in Latin America. For further information, see page 38.

Internet
Internet cafés are popular and connections in the towns tend to be good. Prices vary but a rough guide is US$1-2 for 1 hr in the Central Valley; up to US$5 in beach towns and tourism areas. Rates are lower around colleges and universities.

Language
Spanish is the first language, but you will find someone who can speak some English in most places. In the Caribbean the Afro-Caribbean population speak a regional Creole dialect with elements of English.

Media
The best San José morning papers are *La Nación* (www.nacion.co.cr) and business-orientated *La República* (www.larepublica.net); there is also *Al Día*, *El Heraldo*, *Diario Extra* (the largest circulating daily) and *La Prensa Libre* (www.prensalibre.co.cr). *La Gaceta* is the official government daily paper. The *Tico Times* (www.ticotimes.net) is out on Fri, and there is the *San José*, which is great for news in English with classifieds.

There are 6 local TV stations, many MW/FM radio stations throughout the country. Local **Voz de América** (VOA) station. **Radio Dos** (95.5 FM) and **Rock Radio** (107.5 FM) have English-language DJs and music. Many hotels and private homes receive 1 of the 4 TV stations offering direct, live, 24-hr satellite TV from the USA. All US cable TV can be received in San José.

Money → *US$1= 502 colones (June 2011).*
The unit is the **colón**, which in most years devalues slowly against the dollar. There are 5, 10, 25, 50, 100 and 500-colon coins. Notes in use are for 1000, 2000, 5000 and 10,000 colones. US dollars are widely accepted but don't depend on being able to use them.

ATMs and exchange
US dollars can be exchanged in most banks. Most tourist and 1st-class hotels will change dollars and traveller's cheques (TCs) for guests only; the same applies in restaurants and shops if you buy some-thing. Hardly anyone will change damaged US dollar notes. All state-run banks and some private banks will change euro, but it is almost impossible to exchange any other major currency in Costa Rica. For bank drafts and transfers commission may be charged.

Banks are starting to stay open later and several open on Sat. Most banks will process cash advances on Visa/MasterCard. ATMs that accept international Visa and/or MasterCard are widely available at most banks, and in shopping malls and at San José airport. Credomatic handles all credit card billings; they will not accept a credit card charge that does not have the imprint of the borrower's card plus an original signature. This is the result of fraud, but it makes it difficult to book tours or accommodation over the phone.

If your card is lost or stolen, ring T0800-011-0184 (MasterCard/Visa) or T0800-012-3211 (AMEX).

Cost of living and travelling
Costa Rica is more expensive than countries to the north. While transport is reasonably cheap, you get less for your money in the hotels. You will be able to survive on US$30 a day, but that does not allow for much in the way of activities. A more realistic budget is US$50-70.

Opening hours
Banks Mon-Fri 0900-1500.
Businesses Mon-Fri 0900-1200, 1400-1730 (1600 government offices), Sat 0800-1200.
Shops Mon-Sat 0800-1200, 1300-1800 (most stay open during lunch hour).

Post

Airmail letters to Europe cost 180 c, postcards 165 c; to North/South America, letters 155 c, 135 c for postcards; to Australia, Africa and Asia, letters 240 c, postcards 195 c. Expreso letters, 140 c extra, several days quicker to USA and North Europe. Registered mail, 400 c. Airmail takes 5 to 10 days. All parcels sent out of the country by foreigners must be taken open to the post office for clearance. **Lista de Correos**, charges 75 c per letter and will keep them for 4 weeks. For information call Correos de Costa Rica, T800-900-2000.

Safety

Generally speaking, Costa Rica is very safe but, as ever, there are some problem areas. Look after your belongings in hotels – use the safe. If hiring a car do not leave valuables in the vehicle and leave nothing unattended on beaches or buses. Theft (pickpocketing, grab-and-run thieves and mugging) is on the increase in San José, especially in the centre, in the market, at the Coca Cola bus station, in the barrios of Cuba, Cristo Rey, México, 15 de Setiembre and León XIII. Keep away from these areas at night and on Sun, when few people are around, as we have received reports of violent robberies. Street gangs, known as *chapulines*, are mostly kids. The police do seem to be trying to tackle the problem but help yourself by avoiding potentially dangerous situations.

You are advised to carry your passport (or a photocopy) with you at all times.

Tax

Departure tax US$26 per person.
Road tax US$10, when entering Costa Rica by car or motorcycle.
Sales tax 13%.

The sales tax plus 3.39% tourism tax is added to hotel room prices.

Telephone → *Country code T+506.*

There are no area codes in Costa Rica, the **international direct dialling** code (to call out of Costa Rica) is T00. Dial T116 for the operator. In Mar 2008, Costa Rica changed telephone numbers from 7 to 8 digits. All landlines now have a 2 in front of the old 7-digit number and all mobile phones now have an 8 in front of the old 8-digit number. Nationwide phone changes are taken up by organizations and people at different rates. A few websites are still quoting the old 7-digit numbers. Be prepared when using phones and taking down numbers.

Long-distance telephone services are handled by the state-run **Instituto Costarricense de Electricidad** (ICE) and its subsidiary **Radiográfica Costarricense SA** (RACSA), Telecommunications Centre, A 5, Calle 1, San José, Mon-Fri 0800-1900, Sat 0800-1200, closed Sun.

Standard rates to US, Canada, Mexico and South America are US$0.45 per min; Panama is US$0.40 and Europe and the rest of the world (except Central America and Belize) US$0.60 a min if you dial direct; operator-assisted calls cost up to US$3.12 per min. Only variable rates are to Central America: standard rates between 0700 and 1900 (US$0.40 per min), reduced between 1900 and 2200 (US$0.35) and reduced again between 2200 and 0700 and during the weekend (US$0.28). Add 13% sales tax.

Public phones are maddening to use, various kinds are available: some use 10 and 20 colón silver coins, others use 50 colón gold coins, and still others employ at least 2 types of calling cards, but not interchangeably. The 199 cards are recommended, but it's often easiest to call collect inside (T110) and outside (T116) the country: Assistance for hearing impaired (Spanish only) is T137.

Phone cards with 'Personal Identification Numbers' are available for between US$0.80 and US$10. These can be used for national and international direct dialling from a private phone. Calls abroad can be made from phone booths; collect calls abroad may be made from special booths in the RACSA office, or from any booth nationwide if you dial T116 for connection with the international operator (T175 for collect calls to the USA). Phone cards can be used. Dial T124 for international information. Country Direct Dialling Codes to the USA are: **MCI/World Phone** 0800-012-2222, **AT&T** 0800-0114-114, **Sprint/GlobalOne** 0800-013-0123, **Worldcom** 0800-014-4444.

Time
-6 hrs GMT.

Tipping
A 10% service charge is automatically added to restaurant and hotel bills, as well as the 13% sales tax.

Tourist information
Instituto Costarricense de Turismo (ICT), underneath the Plaza de la Cultura, Calle 5, A Central-2, T2223-1733, www.visitcosta rica.com. Daily 0900-1700. All tourist information is given here along with a good free map of San José and the country. See page 723 for more details. Student cards give reductions in most museums.

Useful websites
www.centralamerica.com Costa Rica's Travelnet, contains general information on tourist-related subjects.
www.infocostarica.com A Yahoo-style search engine with information, links and maps for all things Costa Rican.

Visas and immigration
Nationals of most EU nations, the US, Canada, Israel and Japan do not need visas for visits of up to 90 days. Nationals of the Republic of Ireland, Australia and New Zealand do not need a visa, but visits are limited to 30 days. For more information, check www.migracion.go.cr.

If you overstay the 30- or 90-day permitted period, you must report to immigration before leaving the country. For longer stays ask for a Prórroga de Turismo at Migración (Immigration) in San José. For this you need 4 passport photos, an airline or bus ticket out of the country and proof of funds (for example TCs); you can apply for an extension of 1 or 2 months, at 300 colones per month. The paperwork takes 3 days. If you leave the country, you must wait 72 hrs before returning, but it may be cheaper and easier to do this to get a new 30-day entry. Travel agents can arrange all extension and exit formalities for a small fee.

Monetary fines for overstaying your visa or entry permit have been eliminated; if you plan to stay longer, be aware that immigra-tion officials have said that tourists who overstay their welcome more than once will be denied entry into the country on subsequent occasions – part of government efforts to crack down on 'perpetual tourists'.

An onward ticket (a bus ticket, which can be bought at the border immigration office or sometimes from the driver on Tica international buses, or a transatlantic ticket) is asked for, but can be refunded in San José with a loss of about US$3 on a US$20 ticket. Cashing in an air ticket is difficult because you may be asked to produce another ticket out of the country. Also, tourists may have to show at least US$300 in cash or TCs before being granted entry (especially if you have no onward ticket).

Weights and measures
Metric.

San José

→ Colour map 4, B3. Altitude: 1150 m.
Nestled in a broad, fertile valley producing coffee and sugar-cane, San José was founded in 1737 and became capital in 1823 after struggles for regional ascendency between competing towns of the Central Valley. Frequent earthquakes have destroyed most of the colonial buildings and the modern replacements do little to inspire. But, like any city, the mix of museums and general attractions make it worth a couple of days' stay. ▶▶ *For listings, see pages 729-741.*

Ins and outs

Getting there
Aeropuerto Internacional Juan Santamaría is 16 km from the centre along a good *autopista*. A taxi from the pre-payment booth costs US$15 and efficient buses running every 10 minutes leave from outside the terminal building for San José city centre. Long-distance buses have their terminals scattered round town (see map, page 724) but the majority are close to the Coca Cola Terminal, in the central west of the city. Bus connections in Costa Rica and with other Central American countries are very good.

Getting around
For the most part the city conforms to a grid systems – *avenidas* run east–west; *calles* north–south. Avenidas to the north of Avenida Central are given odd numbers; those to the south even numbers. Calles to the west of Calle Central are even-numbered; those to the east are odd-numbered. The three main streets, Avenida Central, Avenida 2 and the intersecting Calle Central, encompass the business centre. The main shops are along Avenida Central, a pleasant downtown stroll in the section closed to traffic.

Some people find the narrow streets too heavily polluted with exhaust fumes preferring to stay in the suburbs of Escazú, Alajuela or Heredia and using regular bus services to make the journey to town. It's probably a good choice if you've already visited San José, but if it's your first time in the capital you should give it a try for a couple of days at least. A circular bus route travels along Avenida 3 out to La Sabana and back making a useful circuit and an impromptu city tour. Taxis can be ordered by phone or hailed in the street; they are red and are legally required to have meters and to use them. Traffic is congested especially between 0700 and 2000, so driving in the city centre is best avoided. If you do drive, watch out for no-parking zones. Seven blocks of the Avenida Central, from Banco Central running east to Plaza de la Cultura, are closed to traffic and most of the downtown streets are one-way.

Tourist information
Instituto Costarricense de Turismo ① *under Plaza de la Cultura, Calle 5, Av Central-2, T2223-1733, Mon-Fri 0900-1700.* Can also be found at Juan Santamaría airport (very helpful, will check hotels for you), the main post office and at borders. Free road maps of Costa Rica, San José and the metropolitan area and public transport timetables available. **OTEC** ① *Calle 3, Av 1-3, Edif Ferenz, San José, T2523-0500, www.otecviajes.com,* the youth and student travel office, is extremely helpful with good special discounts for ISTC and FIYTO members.

Best time to visit

The climate is comfortable, with temperatures between 15° and 26°C, though the evenings can be chilly. The rainy season lasts roughly from May to November; the rest of the year it's mainly dry.

Sights

Many of the most interesting public buildings are near the intersection of Avenida Central and Calle Central. The **Teatro Nacional** ① *just off Av 2, on Calle 3, T2221-1329 (tours), T2221-5341 (event and ticket information), Mon-Sat 0900-1600, www.teatronacional.go.cr, from US$5*, built in 1897, has marble staircases, statues, frescoes and foyer decorated in gold with Venetian plate mirrors. It has a coffee bar run by **Café Britt** and guided tours. Nearby is **Plaza de la Cultura** ① *Av Central, Calle 3-5*, which, in addition to being a great place for people-watching, hosts public concerts. The **Museo de Oro Procolombino** ① *entrance is off Calle 5, T2243-4202, www.museosdelbancocentral.org, daily 0915-1700, US$11*, has a booty of golden treasure buried beneath the Plaza de la Cultura. Fine golden figures of frogs, spiders, raptors and other creatures glisten in this spectacular pre-Columbian gold museum sponsored by the **Banco Central**. Also here is the **Museo Numismático** with an exhibition on the history of Costa Rican money.

1 San José

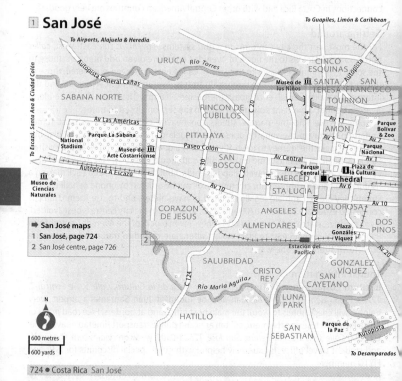

➡ San José maps
1 San José, page 724
2 San José centre, page 726

The **Museo Nacional** ⓘ *Calle 17, Av Central-2, T2257-1433, www.museocostarica.go.cr, Tue-Sat 0830-1630, Sun 0900-1630, US$8, children and students with ID free*, east from the Plaza de la Cultura, has interesting displays on archaeology, anthropology, national history, some gold and ex-President Arias' Nobel Peace Prize. Information is in Spanish and English. Facing it is the **Plaza de la Democracia**, a concrete cascade built to mark the November 1989 centenary of Costa Rican democracy. The **Palacio Nacional** ⓘ *Av Central, Calle 15*, is home of the Legislative Assembly; any visitor can attend debates, sessions start at 1600.

Two blocks north of the Museo Nacional is the **Parque Nacional**, with a grandiloquent bronze monument representing the five Central American republics ousting the filibuster William Walker (see the Nicaragua History section) and the abolition of slavery in Central America. There is also a statue donated by the Sandinista Government of Nicaragua to the people of Costa Rica. To the north of the park is the **Biblioteca Nacional**. East of the library is the **Museo de Formas, Espacio y Sonidos** ⓘ *Calle 17, Av 3-7, T2222-9462, Tue-Fri 0930-1600, US$1, students and children free, wheelchair accessible, signs in Braille*, housed in the old Atlantic Railway Station. In the old liquor factory west of the Biblioteca Nacional, now the Centro Nacional de la Cultura, is the **Museo de Arte y Diseño Contemporáneo** ⓘ *Av 3, Calle 15-17, T2257-7202, Tue-Sat 1000-1700, US$3, students with ID US$0.50*.

One of the best museums in the city is the **Museo del Jade Fidel Tristan** ⓘ *INS building 11th floor, Av 7, Calle 9-13, T2287-6034, Mon-Fri 0830-1530, Sat 1100-1600, US$8*, with the largest collection of jade carvings in Central America, pottery and sculpture. With explanations in Spanish and English, and topped off with a beautiful view over the city, it's a fascinating museum and shouldn't be missed.

Along Calle Central, west of the Teatro Nacional, is **Parque Central**, with a bandstand in the middle among trees, again with occasional performances. East of the park is the monumental architecture of the **Catedral Metropolitana**; to the north is the **Teatro Melico Salazar** ⓘ *see press for details or call T2221-4952*, which has a good mix of performances throughout the year.

Further west, in **Parque Braulio Carrillo**, opposite the eclectic neo-Gothic design of **La Merced** church, is a huge carved granite ball brought from the Diquís archaeological site near Palmar Norte. There are other such designs at the entrance to the Museo de Ciencias Naturales.

At the end of Paseo Colón, at Calle 42, **Parque La Sabana** was converted from the former city airport in the 1950s; the old airport building on the east side is now the **Museo de Arte Costarricense** ⓘ *T2222-7155, Tue-Sun 0900-1600, www.musarco.go.cr, free*, with a small but interesting display of paintings and sculptures. At the west end of the park is the **Estadio Nacional**, with seating for 20,000 spectators at (mainly) football matches, basketball, volleyball and tennis courts, a running track, lake and swimming pool.

2 San José centre

To Airports

Av 13
Av 11
Av 5
Av 5
Av 3

Centro Colón (Embassies etc)
Av 1
Av 3

Museo de Arte
Paseo Colón

Parque La Sabana
Av 2
Av 4

To San Antonio Escazú

Parque Braulio Carrillo
Ministerio de Salud
La Merce

Av 6
Av 8

Av 10 San Martín

Cemetery

Av 10
Av 12

➡ **San José maps**
1 San José, page 724
2 San José centre, page 726

Av 18
Av 20
Av 20 Bis

N

300 metres (approx)
300 yards (approx)

Sleeping
Aurola Holiday Inn **2** *B5*
Avenida Segunda **3** *C5*
Bienvenido **5** *B3*
Boston **6** *C4*
Britannia **7** *A5*
CACTS **8** *B2*
Casa Ridgway **9** *C6*
Casa Yoses **12** *C6*
Centroamericano **10** *B4*
Cinco Hormigas Rojas **11** *B6*
Costa Rica Backpackers **13** *C6*

Del Rey **14** *B5*
Diana's Inn **15** *B5*
Don Carlos **17** *B5*
Fleur de Lys **20** *C5*
Galileo Hostel **22** *B1*
Gaudy's Backpackers' Hostel **23** *A1*
Gran Imperial **25** *B4*
Grano de Oro **26** *B2*
Green House Hostel **4** *D5*
Hostal Toruma **27** *C6*
Hostel Pangea **28** *A5*

Joluva **29** *A5*
Otoya **33** *B4*
Pensión Boruca **35** *B3*
Pensión de la Cuesta **36** *B5*
Pensión Musoc **37** *B3*
Rialto **39** *B4*
Rincón de San José **40** *B6*
Rosa del Paseo **42** *B2*
Santo Tomás **1** *B5*
Tica Linda **44** *C5*
Tranquilo Backpackers **45** *A5*

Opposite the southwest corner of Parque Sabana are the impressive natural displays of the **Museo de Ciencias Naturales** ⓘ *Colegio La Salle, T2232-1306, Mon-Sat 0730-1600, Sun 0900-1700, US$1.50, children US$1*, next to the Ministry of Agriculture; take 'Sabana Estadio' bus from Avenida 2, Calle 1 to the gate.

Eating 🍴
Ana Italiana **1** *B2*
Café La Bohemia **4** *B4*
Café Mundo **2** *B6*
Café Parisienne **3** *B5*
Churrería Manolo **4** *B4*
El Chicote **12** *A1*
El Cuartel de la Boca del Monte **19** *B6*
Gran Diamante **5** *B4*
Jurgen's **20** *C6*
La Bastille **6** *B2*

La Esquina del Café **7** *A5*
La Puriscaleña **8** *B4*
La Vasconia **9** *B5*
Lubnan **10** *B2*
Machu Picchu **11** *B2*
Pollo a la Leña **13** *B5*
Soda Tapia **14** *B1*
Tin Jo **15** *C5*
Vishnu **16** *B5*

Bars & clubs 🍸
Chelle's **17** *B5*

Disco Salsa 54 **18** *B5*
Nashville South **20** *B5*
Risas **21** *B4*

Buses 🚌
Alajuela & Airport Buses **1** *B3*
Heredia Buses **2** *B3/B4*
Liberia Buses **3** *B3*
Panaline Bus **4** *B3*
San Isidro Buses **5** *D4*
Ticabus **6** *C5*

Transnica Bus **7** *B3*
Terminal Alfaro **8** *A3*
Terminal Atlántico Norte **9** *A3*
Terminal Caribe (Sixaola) **10** *A4*
Terminal Cartago **11** *D5*
Terminal Coca Cola **12** *B3*
Terminal Los Santos **13** *D6*
Terminal Puntarenas **14** *C3*
Terminal Turrialba **15** *C5*

North of Avenida Central, on Calle 2, is the **Unión Club**, the principal social centre of the country. Opposite is the **Correo Central**, general post and telegraph office which also houses an internet café, pastry shop and the **Museo Postal, Telgráfico y Filatélico** ① *upstairs, Mon-Fri 0800-1700, free.*

A couple of blocks to the west is the hustle and bustle of the **Mercado Central**, dating back to 1881, rich with the shouts, cries, smells and chaos of a fresh produce market. Good cheap meals for sale as well as some interesting nick-nacks for the passing tourist. Often crowded; watch for thieves.

The Disneyesque building on the horizon to the north of the city is the **Centro Costarricense de Ciencias y Cultura** (Scientific and Cultural Centre) in the old city penitentiary with the **Galería Nacional**, **Biblioteca Carlos Luis Sáenz**, the **Auditorio Nacional** and **Museo de Los Niños** ① *Calle 4, Av 9, T2258-4929, Tue-Sat 0830-1630, Sun 0900-1630, US$8, children free.* Interesting as much for the well-restored building as for the exhibits using former prison cells and spaces to good effect.

Along Avenida 3, north of the Plaza de la Cultura, are the four gardens of the remodelled **Parque Morazán**, with another bandstand at the centre. A little to the northeast, **Parque España**, cool, quiet, and intimate, has for neighbours the **Casa Amarilla** (Yellow House), seat of the Ministry of Foreign Affairs, and the **Edificio Metálico**, imported from Europe to become one of the country's first schools.

To the north of Parque Morazán is **Parque Simón Bolívar**, now a recreation area, with **Simón Bolívar National Zoo and Botanical Gardens** ① *Av 11, just east of Calle 7 (go down Calle 7 about 3 blocks from Av 7), T2233-6701, daily 0900-1630, US$4.20.* It's been remodelled and much improved, with all native plants numbered and listed in a brochure; although the animal cages are small. There's also a restaurant and souvenir shop.

To the north of town, a reasonable walk or a short taxi ride, is **Spirogyra** ① *100 m east, 150 m south of Centro Comercial El Pueblo (near Hotel Villa Tournón), T2222-2937, daily 0800-1700, guided tours for more than 10 people (reservations required), US$8, US$6 students, US$4 children,* a fascinating butterfly farm close to the city but filled with life. To get there, take 'Calle Blancos' bus from Calle 3 and Avenida 5 to El Pueblo.

Around San José → *For listings, see pages 729-741.*

San José is a good base for excursions into the beautiful Meseta Central. Excursions to the spectacular **Orosí Valley** and **Irazú Volcano** are given under Cártago (see page 752). **Volcán Poás** gently simmers and steams from its elevated position at the northern limit of the Central Highlands and can be visited from San José (**TUASA** bus departs from Avenida 2, Calle 12-14 at 0830, returns 1430, US$4.75 round trip, T2442-6900), Heredia or Alajuela (see page 742). To reach **Volcán Barva** in Parque Nacional Braulio Carrillo, take a bus to San José de la Montaña (see page 746). Enquire first about the likely weather when planning a visit to Poás, Irazú or Barva as cloud will limit the views; early morning visits recommended.

San Antonio de Escazú, a western suburb of San José popular with the expatriate community, hosts the **Día del Boyero** (National Oxcart Drivers' Day) on the second weekend in March. Festivities culminate on the Sunday in a colourful oxcart parade from the school to the centre, accompanied by typical *payasos* (clowns). Open-air dancing in the evening to music played on a marimba. ►► *See Festivals and events, page 734.*

In La **Guácima**, 35 minutes west of San José, 20 minutes south of Alajuela, is a **Butterfly Farm** ① *open daily 0830-1700, US$20 adults, under 11s US$12.50, includes guided tour, with four between 0830 and 1500,* dedicated to rearing and exporting over 120 species of butterfly. The first such farm in Latin America, now with over 100 associated farmers throughout Costa Rica, it is believed to be one of the second largest exporters of farm-bred butterflies in the world (the largest is in Taiwan). Created by Joris Brinckerhoff, a former Peace Corp volunteer and his wife in 1984, the farm opened to the public in 1990. All visitors receive a two-hour guided tour. Visit in the morning as butterflies require heat from the sun for the energy to fly so when it is cool or cloudy, there may be less activity.

The Butterfly Farm offers round trip minibus transportation from San José hotels. The public bus for La Guácima, leaves from Calle 10, Avenida 2-4, behind La Merced Church in San José (0800, 1100 and 1400, returns at 1230, 1530 and 1730, one hour, US$0.55); at the last stop walk 300 m from the school south to the butterfly sign. From Alajuela take a bus marked 'La Guácima abajo', which departs 100 m south, 100 m west of **Tikal Supermarket** (40 minutes, at 0620, 0900, 1100 and 1300; returning at 0945, 1145, 1345, 1545 and 1745).

From San José you can take a tour of **Café Britt's coffee farm** ⓘ *near Barva de Heredia, T2277-1600, www.coffeetour.com, 1100, 1½ hrs, US$20*, where you can see the processing factory, tasting room and a multi-media presentation using professional actors of the story of coffee. You can arrange to be picked up at various points and hotels in San José. **Teatro Dionisio Chaverría** at **Café Britt** hosts weekend theatre and a children's show on Sunday afternoons.

◉ San José listings

Hotel and guesthouse prices

LL over US$200   **L** US$151-200   **AL** US$101-150
A US$66-100   **B** US$46-65   **C** US$31-45
D US$21-30   **E** US$12-20   **F** US$7-11
G under US$7

Restaurant prices

♦♦♦ over US$15   ♦♦ US$8-15   ♦ under US$8
See pages 31-33 for further information.

◉ Sleeping

San José *p723, maps p724 and p726*
There are cheap hotels between the Mercado Central, Mercado Borbón and the Coca Cola terminal. Cheaper hotels usually have only wooden partitions for walls, making them noisy. Hotels in the red-light district, Calle 6, Av 1-5, near Mercado Central, charge on average US$10 with toilet and shower for a night.
LL-L Grano de Oro, Calle 30, Av 2-4, T2255-3322, www.hotelgranodeoro.com. Exquisite converted 19th-century mansion, 40 rooms and suites, beautiful terrace gardens, renowned restaurant. Friendly, good value.
AL Aurola Holiday Inn, Av 5 between Calle 5-7, T2523-1000, www.aurolahotels.com. Mainly business clientele, casino, good view of city from casino.

AL-A Britannia, Calle 3, Av 11, T2223-6667, www.hotelbritanniacostarica.com. 1910 Spanish-style beautifully restored mansion, high standard, antique furniture, very good service, excellent restaurant, worth the money.
AL-A Fleur de Lys, Calle 13, Av 2-6, T2223-1206, www.hotelfleurdelys.com. Restored Victorian mansion house, good restaurant, bar. Stylishly elegant. Recommended.
AL-A Hotel del Rey, Av 1, Calle 9, T2257-7800, www.hoteldelrey.com. Nice single, double, triple rooms, standard or deluxe, suites. Landmark hotel, centre of casino and upmarket red-light district, not recommended for families, walls a bit thin. Has a restaurant.
A Don Carlos, Calle 9, Av 7-9, T2221-6707, www.doncarloshotel.com. 33 rooms, interesting traditional building, much artwork and statuary, sun deck, free coffee, Annemarie's giftshop with good selection, credit cards accepted, airport shuttle.
A Rosa del Paseo, Paseo Colón, Calle 28-30, T2257-3225, www.rosadelpaseo.com. Beautifully restored mansion, breakfast included. Good location for access to the city centre but not in the heart of town.

A Santo Tomás, Av 7, Calle 3-5, T2255-3950, www.hotelsantotomas.com. French Victorian mansion, 20 rooms, pool, garden, internet access, secure parking, Restaurant El Oasis next door, tours arranged.

B Cinco Hormigas Rojas, Calle 15, Av 9-11, T2255-3412, www.cincohormigasrojas.com. Nice decor, small house. Prices includes taxes.

B Rincón de San José, formerly Edelweiss, Av 9, Calle 13-15, 100 m east of Condovac offices, T2221-9702, www.hotelrincondesanjose.com. English, Dutch and Spanish spoken, comfortable, native hardwood furniture and carved doors. Pleasant courtyard bar, helpful, friendly.

B-C CACTS, Av 3 bis, Calle 28-30, 3 blocks north of Pizza Hut, Paseo Colón, T2221-2928, www.hotelcacts.com. Safe, good service, breakfast and taxes included, TV, friendly, pets allowed. Recommended.

C Diana's Inn, Calle 5, Av 3, Parque Morazán, near Holiday Inn, T2223-6542, dianas@racsa.co.cr. An old building formerly used by the president, now restored, includes breakfast and taxes, discounts available, a/c, TV, hot water, noisy, free luggage storage, safe box.

C-D Hostal Toruma, Av Central, Calle 29-31, T2234-9186. Completely revamped, a good mid-range 'luxury' budget option with free internet and good security.

C-E Casa Ridgway, Calle 15, Av 6-8, T2233-6168, www.amigosparalapaz.org. 1-4 beds in room, shared bath, use of kitchen, very helpful, friendly, laundry possible, group rates and facilities.

C-E Green House Hotel, Plaza González Víques, Calle 11, Av 16 y 18, T2258-0102, www.greenhousehostel.altervista.org. Very clean, both private and shared rooms come with hot water bath, free breakfast, communal kitchen, Wi-Fi, cable TV, not close to the centre, but great spot otherwise.

D Centroamericano, Av 2, Calle 6-8, T2221-3362. Includes taxes, private bath, clean small rooms, very helpful, will arrange accommodation in other towns, free shuttle (Mon-Fri) to airport, laundry facilities.

D Pensión de la Cuesta, Av 1, Calle 11-15, T2256-7946, www.pensiondelacuesta.com. A little off the wall in style, with artwork all over this old colonial home. Shared bath, use of the kitchen and internet, includes breakfast.

D-E Hostel Pangea, Av 11, Calle 3 bis, T2221-1992, www.hostelpangea.com. Friendly, clean, use of kitchen. Good local information, with free coffee, internet, breakfast and reportedly the only hostel in Central America with heated pool, jacuzzi, licensed bar and wet bar. Good spot.

D-F Costa Rica Backpackers, Av 6, Calle 21-23, T2221-6191, www.costaricabackpackers.com. Top billing at these prices with a pool, good dormitory and private rooms, kitchen and laundry services, free coffee and internet. Parking possible.

D-F Tranquilo Backpackers, Calle 7, Av 9-11, T2223-3189, www.tranquilobackpackers.com. Dormitory and private rooms with great, relaxed atmosphere, but not very helpful.

E Avenida Segunda, Av 2 No 913, Calle 9-11, T2222-0260, acebrisa@racsa.co.cr. Includes taxes, shared or private bath, friendly, stores luggage.

E Bienvenido, Calle 10, Av 1-3, T2233-2161. Clean, hot shower, near centre and airport bus, best hotel near Coca Cola bus terminal.

E Boston, Av 8, Calle Central-2, T2221-0563. With or without bath, good, very friendly, but noisy, will store luggage.

E JC Friends Hostel, Calle 34 y Av 3, Casa Esquinera, Paseo Colón. Owned by an extremely well-travelled Tico who has bucketfuls of local information to impart. Communal kitchen, lockers, a/c and internet access. Tuasa bus stops opposite. Also have a *hostal* in Tamarindo.

E Otoya, Calle 1, Av 3-5, T2221-3925, erickpensionotoya@24horas.com. Close to the centre, cleanish, friendly and quite popular, you're allowed to use the telephone (free local calls). Hot water throughout and some rooms with private bath, includes taxes. Luggage store, laundry service, English spoken.

E Pensión Musoc, Calle 16, Av 1-3, T2222-9437. With or without private bath, very clean, hot water, luggage stored, will do laundry. Friendly, near bus stations so somewhat noisy, but recommended.

E-F Casa Yoses, Av 8, Calle 41, 25 mins west from **Spoon** in Los Yoses, T2234-5486, www.casayoses.com. Popular hostel in restored mansion, located near the trendy San Pedro Mall, breakfast and internet are gratis, relaxing gardens, quiet area.

E-F Gaudy's Backpackers' Hostel, Av 5, Calle 36-38, T2258-2937, www.back packer. co.cr. Good backpacker choice, with dorm accommodation, kitchen, communal areas and internet access. Good location and quieter than the other cheap options.

E-F Gran Imperial, on the western side of the Central Market, Calle 8, Av 1-Central, T2222-8463, www.hostelgranimperial.com. Mixed reports, small rooms, thin walls, clean, sometimes noisy, with or without private bath, limited hot showers, includes taxes, restaurant with good prices, best to reserve. Good for meeting other travellers, with balcony overlooking Central Market. A great spot for relaxing, locked luggage store, TV.

F Galileo Hostel, 100 m east of **SodaTapia**, T2248-2094, www.hostelgalileo.com. Friendly place, charming property with dorm beds and free internet.

F Pensión Boruca, Calle 14, Av 1-3, near Coca Cola terminal, T2223-0016. Shared bath, hot water, laundry service, rooms a bit dark but friendly owner.

F Rialto, Av 5, Calle 2, 1 block north of Correos, T2221-7456. Shared or private bath, hot water, safe, friendly but can be very noisy.

G Tica Linda, Av 10, Calle 7-9. Dormitory accommodation, use of kitchen, hot water and laundry, TV in communal area. Will store luggage, popular with travellers. No sign, just a notice on the front. Moves often which makes finding the place a problem, but popular. Ask locally.

Near the airport
See Alajuela, page 747.

Around San José *p728*
B Costa Verde Inn, 300 m south of the 2nd San Antonio de Escazú cemetery, T2228-4080, www.costaverdeinn.com. A secluded and charming country home with 14 imaginatively decorated rooms – a popular choice away from the centre of town.

B Pico Blanco Inn, San Antonio de Escazú, T2228-1908, www.hotelpicoblanco.com. All rooms with balconies and views of Central Valley, several cottages. English owner, restaurant with English pub, airport pickup can be requested. It's recommended.

Camping
Belén, San Antonio de Belén, 2 km west of intersection at Cariari and San Antonio, 5 km from airport, turn off Hwy 1 on to Route 111, turn right at soccer field then 1st left for 1 km, T2239-0421. US$10 per day, American-owned trailer park, shade, hot showers, laundry, friendly, recommended, good bus service to San José.

🍴 Eating

San José *p723, maps p724 and p726*
Traditional dishes, feasting on a steady supply of rice and beans, tend to be a little on the heavy side but are definitely worth trying.

At lunchtime cheaper restaurants offer a set meal called a *casado*, US$1.50-2.50, which is good value. There are several cheap Chinese places along Av 5. For reliable and seriously cheap places, try the **Mercado Central**, around the Coca Cola bus terminal and the area to the southwest of **Parque Central**. *Autoservicios* do not charge tax and service and represent the best value. There are plenty of fast-food outlets dotted throughout the city.

TTT Ana Italiana, T2222-6153, Paseo Colón, Calle 24 y 26. Closed Mon. Good Italian food and friendly.

TTT Café Mundo, Av 9, Calle 13-15, opposite Hotel Rincón de San José, T2222-6190. Old mansion tastefully restored, good salads, great pasta, wonderful bread, a stylish joint.

℣℣℣ El Chicote, on north side of Parque Sabana, T2232-0936. Reliable favourite, country style, good grills.

℣℣℣ El Cuartel de la Boca del Monte, Av 1, Calle 21-23, T2221-0327. Live music at night but a good and popular restaurant by day.

℣℣℣ Jurgen's, Calle 41 and Paseo Rubén Darío, Barrio Dent in Los Yoses, T2224-2455. Closed Sun. 1st-class service, excellent international menu, sophisticated atmosphere.

℣℣℣ La Bastille, Paseo Colón, Calle 22, T2255-4994. Closed Sun. Stylish French food in elegant surrounds.

℣℣℣ La Cocina de Leña, north of the centre in El Pueblo, Barrio Tournón, T2255-1360. Excellent menu, the very best in Tico cuisine, upmarket, but warm, friendly ambience.

℣℣℣ La Esquina del Café, Av 9, Calle 3b. Daily 0900-2200. Speciality coffee roasters with good restaurant, souvenir shop, live music twice a month.

℣℣℣ Lubnan, Paseo Colón, Calle 22-24, T2257-6071. Authentic Lebanese menu, vegetarian selections, great service.

℣℣℣ Marbella, out beyond San Pedro mall, T2224-9452. Fish, paella specialities, packed on Sun, very good.

℣℣℣ Tin Jo, Calle 11, Av 6-8, T2221-7605. Probably the best Asian cuisine in town.

℣℣ Café La Bohemia, Calle Central, Av 2, next to Teatro Melico Salazar. Pastas and meats as well as light lunches such as quiches and crêpes.

℣℣ Gran Diamante, Av 5, Calle 4-6. Basic Chinese with a 'lively kitchen' where you can watch the food being prepared.

℣℣ La Vasconia, corner of Av 1, Calle 5. Great little restaurant combining a passion for football and food. Basic in style, good traditional dishes.

℣℣ Los Antojitos, on Paseo Colón, on Pavas Hwy west of Sabana, in Tibás, San Antonio de Escazú and in Centro Comercial Cocorí (road to suburb of San Pedro), T2232-2411. Serves excellent Mexican food at fair prices.

℣℣ Machu Picchu, Calle 32, Av 1-3, T2222-7384. Open from 1700, closed Sun. Great Peruvian food, good service in homely atmosphere.

℣℣ México Bar, north of the Coca Cola district in Paso de la Vaca, T2221-8461. Dead by day, comes alive at night with a flurry of music and good Mexican food.

℣℣ Vishnu, Av 1, Calle 1-3, also on Calle 14, Av 2. Daily 02800-2000. Best known vegetarian place in town, good quality, cheap and good *plato del día*. Try their soya cheese sandwiches and ice cream, sells good wholemeal bread.

℣ Chicharronera Nacional, Av 1, Calle 10-12. Self-service and very popular.

℣ China Bonita at Av 5, Calle 2-4. One of the cheapest Chinese options in town.

℣ Corona de Oro, Av 3, Calle 2-4 (next to Nini). An excellent *autoservicio*.

℣ Don Sol, Av 7b No 1347. Excellent 3-course vegetarian lunch, run by integral yoga society (only open for lunch).

℣ El Merendero, Av 6, Calle Central-2. *Auto-servicio* serving cheap local food, popular with Ticos.

℣ La Puriscaleña, on the corner of Calle Central and Av 5. A good, local *comedor*. The *menú del día* is a tasty bargain.

℣ Pollo a la Leña, Calle 1, Av 3-5, which has seriously cheap chicken, popular with locals.

℣ Whapin, Calle 35, Av 13, Excellent Caribbean restaurant with extensive menu, authentic rice and beans and fried plantains, live music occasionally.

Cafés, sodas and ice cream parlours
Café del Teatro, Av 2, Calle 3, in foyer of National Theatre. Open Mon-Sat. Pricey but worth it for the sheer style and sophistication of the belle époque interior.

Café Parisienne on the Plaza de la Cultura, the street café of the **Gran Hotel Costa Rica**. Food a little overpriced, but have a coffee and watch the world go by.

Churrería Manolo, Av Central, Calle Central-2 (restaurant upstairs). Open 24 hrs. Simple, quick food with takeaway options on the street, good sandwiches and hot chocolate.

Helados Boni, Calle Central, Av 6-8. Home-made ice cream.

Helados Rena, Calle 8, Av Central. Excellent.

La Esquina del Café, Av 9, Calle 3b, Barrio Amón, T2257-9868. Daily 0900-2200. Speciality coffee roasters with beans from 6 different regions to taste, also a good restaurant with a souvenir shop. Live music twice a month.

La Nutrisoda, Edif Las Arcadas. Daily 1100-1800. Home-made natural ice cream.

Macrobiótica, Calle 11, Av 6-8. Health shop selling good bread.

Ruiseñor, Paseo Rubén Darío and Calle 41-43, Los Yoses, T2225-2562. The smart place to take coffee and snacks in east San José.

Soda El Parque, Calle 2, Av 4-6. Open 24 hrs. A popular spot for business people by day and relaxing entertainers by night.

Soda La Luz, Av Central, Calle 33, east towards Los Yoses. Good filling and cheap meals.

Soda Nini, Av 3, Calle 2-4. Cheap and cheerful.

Soda Tapia, Calle 42, Av 2-4, east side of Parque Sabana. Classic stopping place for Josefinos, with good food, served quickly.

Soda Vegetariana, next to Librería Italiana. Vegetarian with good juices and food.

Spoon has a central bakery at Av Central, Calle 5-7. Good coffee and pastries to take out or eat in, also light lunches.

⦿ Entertainment

San José *p723, maps p724 and p726*
Bars and clubs
The *Tico Times* has a good listings section.
Beatles, Calle 9, Av Central. Good music, popular with ex-pats.

Calle de la Armagua, San Pedro. Happening street for young Ticos from 2230 onwards.

Centro Comercial El Pueblo, north of town in Barrio Tournón, with a cluster of fine restaurants, bars and discos. This is where Ticos party the night away until dawn. **Cocoloco** is the liveliest of the discos, **Infinito** gets a slightly older crowd and **La Plaza** outside the centre, is often not as busy.

Chelle's, Av Central, Calle 9, T2221-1369. Excellent 24-hr bar and restaurant which changes its mood and clientele through the day. Great snacks and people-watching.

Disco Salsa 54, Calle 3, Av 1-3. The place to go for salsa.

El Cuartel de la Boca del Monte, Av 1, Calle 21-23, T2221-0327. Live music at weekends, popular with students, hip young things but without the flashy dress. Recommended.

Key Largo, Parque Morazán. Live music, very popular with the **Hotel del Rey** crowd and all the stuff they get up to!

La Avispa, Calle 1, Av 8-10, and **Déjà vu**, Calle 2, Av 14-16. Both are gay-friendly discos, but not exclusively so.

Nashville South, Calle 5, Av 1-3. A popular Country and Western-style gringo bar.

Risas, Calle 1, Av Central, T2223-2803. Bars on 3 floors, good, popular with locals.

Terrau, Calle de la Armagua, San Pedro. The most popular of many clubs along this street. The area gets going around 2300 and keeps going till dawn. You'll need photo ID to get into the clubs.

Cinemas
Excellent modern cinemas showing latest releases are located throughout the metropolitan area, see *La Nación* for listings.

Cine Universitario at the UCR's Abelardo Bonilla law school auditorium in San Pedro, T2207-4717, shows good films at 1700 and 1900 daily, US$5.

El Semáforo in San Pedro shows films made in Latin America and Spain.

Sala Garbo, Av 2, Calle 28, T2222-1034, shows independent art house movies.

Variedades, Calle 5, Av Central-1, T2222- 6108. Others can be found in **Los Yoses**, T2223-0085, San Pedro, T2283-5716, **Rohrmoser**, T2232-3271 and **Heredia**, T2293-3300.

Theatre
More than 20 theatres offer live productions in the San José area; check the *Tiempo Libre* entertainment supplement every Thu in *La Nación* for show times, mostly weekends.

Teatro del Angel, Av Central, Calle 13-15, T2222-8258. Has 3 modern dance companies.
Teatro Nacional, Av 2, Calle 3-5 T2221-5341 (recommended for the productions, the architecture and the bar/café), US$6 for guided tour, T2221-1329, www.teatro nacional.go.cr, behind it is La Plaza de la Cultura, a large complex.
Teatro Melico Salazar, Parque Central, T2233-5424, www.teatromelico.go.cr, for popular, folkloric shows.

⊛ Festivals and events

San José *p723, maps p724 and p726*
Dec-Jan Christmas/New Year. Festivities last from mid-Dec to the first week of Jan, with dances, horse shows and much confetti throwing in the crowded streets. The annual El Tope horse parade starts at noon on 26 Dec and travels along the principal avenues of San José with a **carnival** the next day.
Mar The International Festival of Culture assembles musicians from throughout Central America in a week of performances in the Plaza de Cultura around the 2nd week of Mar, although concern over the future of the event exists due to lack of funding.
2nd Sun in Mar Día del Boyero (Day of the Oxcart Driver) is celebrated in San Antonio de Escazú. Parades of ox-drawn carts, with music, dancing and blessings from the priesthood.
Mar/Apr Street parades during Easter week.
Sep 15 Independence Day. Bands and dance troupes move through the streets, although activities start to kick-off the night before with the traditional nationwide singing of the National Anthem at 1800.

Around San José *p728*
San Antonio de Escazú
2nd weekend of Mar Día del Boyero (National Oxcart Drivers' Day). Festivities culminate on the Sun in a colourful oxcart parade from the school to the centre. Dancing in the evening to marimba music.

⊙ Shopping

San José *p723, maps p724 and p726*
Bookshops
Casa de la Revista, Calle 5, Av 1-3, T2256-5092. Mon-Fri 0900-1800, Sat 0800-1700. Good selection of maps, newspapers, magazines and some books (mostly paper-backs) in English. For other locations and information, call main office of Agencia de Publicaciones de Costa Rica, T2283-9383.
Librería Lehmann, Av Central, Calle 1-3, T2223-1212, has a large and varied selection of Spanish and English books and magazines. They also stock maps including the 1:50,000 topographical maps produced by the Instituto Geográfico Nacional de Costa Rica (IGN).
Mora Books, Av 1, Calle 3-5, T2255-4136, www.morabooks.com, in Omni building above Pizza Hut, Mon-Sat 1100-1900. Large selection of used books, reasonable prices.
7th Street Books, Calle 7, Av Central, T2256-8251, marroca@racsa.co.cr. A wide range of new and used books covering all topics of interest to visitors to Costa Rica, including Footprint. Mon-Sat 0900-1800, Sun 1000-1700.

Crafts and markets
Market on Av Central, Calle 6-8, 0630-1800 (Sun 0630-1200), good leather suitcases and wood. **Mercado Borbón**, Av 3-5, 8-10, fruit and vegetables. *Artesanía* shops include: **Canapi**, Calle 11, Av 1 (a cooperative, cheaper than most), **Mercado Nacional de Artesanía**, Calle 11, Av 4, T2221-5012, Mon-Fri 0900-1800, Sat 0900-1700, a good one-stop shop with a wide variety of goods. **La Casona**, Calle Central, Av Central-1, daily 0900-1900, a market of small *artesanía* shops, is full of interesting little stalls. **Galería Namu**, opposite the Alianza Francesa building on Av 7 and Calle 5-7, Mon-Sat 0900-1630, T2256-3412, www.galerianamu.com, is the best one-stop shop for home-grown and indigenous art, with the distinctly bright-coloured ceramics of Cecilia Figueres. Items can be shipped if required and online shopping is possible. At the **Plaza de la Democracia** in front of the

National Museum, tented stalls run the length of a city block, great place to buy hammocks, arts and crafts at competitive prices. Don't be afraid to negotiate. **Centro Comercial El Pueblo**, near the Villa Tournón Hotel, also has a number of stalls but is mainly upmarket, built in a traditional 'pueblo' style.

In **Moravia** (8 km northeast of San José with stops often included on city tours) the block-long **Calle de la Artesanía** includes souvenir stores, including well-known **La Rueda**, T2297-2736, good for leatherworks.

Photography

Taller de Equipos Fotográficos, 120 m east of kiosk Parque Morazán, Av 3, Calle 3-5, T2223-1146. Authorized Canon workshop.
Tecfot, Av 7, Calle Central, T2221-1438. Repairs all cameras, authorized Minolta dealer, good service and reasonable rates.

Shopping malls

Shopping malls are popping up in different parts of town including San Pedro, on the eastern ring road, complete with cinema. The expanded **Multiplaza Mall**, near Camino Real, Escazú, has great shops and lots of cinemas.

▲ Activities and tours

San José *p723, maps p724 and p726*
Long-term visitors can see the Calendar pages of the *The Tico Times* for clubs and associations.

Bungee jumping

After Rafael Iglesias Bridge (Río Colorado), continue on Pan-American Hwy 1.5 km, turn right at Salón Los Alfaro, down the track to Puente Colorado. **Tropical Bungee**, T2248-2212, www.bungee.co.cr, operates 0900-1600 daily in high season, US$65 1st jump, US$30 for the 2nd (same day only) includes transport from San José, reservations required.

Cycling

Coast to Coast Adventures, T2280-8054, www.ctocadventures.com, run trips in the local area.

Nature tours

ACTUAR, T2248-9470, www.actuarcostarica.com. An association of 26 community-based rural tourism groups.
Aguas Bravas, T2292-2072, www.aguas-bravas.co.cr. Whitewater rafting on rivers around the Central Valley, also horse riding, biking, hiking and camping.
Costa Rica Expeditions, Av 3, Calle Central 3, T2257-0766, www.costaricaexpeditions.com. Upmarket wildlife adventures include whitewater rafting (US$95 for 1-day trip on Río Pacuare, includes lunch and transport; other rivers from US$69-95) and further options. They own **Tortuga Lodge**, **Corcovado Lodge Tent Camp** and **Monteverde Lodge**. Daily trips, highly recommended.
Ecole Travel, lobby of Gran Hotel, T2253-8884, www.ecoletravel.com. Chilean-Dutch, highly recommended for budget tours to Tortuguero, Corcovado and tailor-made excursions off the beaten track.
Green Tropical Tours, Calle 1, Av 5-7, T2229-4192, www.greentropical.com. Options outside the norm including tours to Guayabo National Monument, Los Juncos and cloud forest.
Horizontes, Calle 28, Av 1-3, T2222-2022, www.horizontes.com. A big operator in Costa Rica, high standards, educational and special interest, advice given and arrangements made for groups and individuals.
Mitur, T2296-7378, www.mitour.com. A range of tours, including Ilan Ilan in Tortuguero US$199, 3-days, 2 nights.
Ríos Tropicales, Calle 38, between Paseo Colón and Av 2, 50 m south of Subway, T2233-6455, www.riostropicales.com. Specialists in whitewater rafting and kayaking (sponsors of the World Rafting Championships in Turrialba, Oct 2011), good selection, careful to assess your abilities, good food, excellent guides, US$285 for 2-day trip on Río Pacuare, waterfalls, rapids, including camping and food. Many other options throughout the country.
Typical Tours, Las Arcadas, next to the Gran Hotel Costa Rica, T2233-8486. City tours, volcano tours, nature reserves, rafting, cruising.

Several companies focus on trips to Tortuga Island. Try **Bay Island Cruises**, T2258-3536, www.bayislandcruises.com. Daily tours to Tortuga Island, US$79 includes lunch and transport from San José area.

Night tours

Costa Rican Nights Tour, La Uruca, T2290-3035, www.puebloantiguo.co.cr. This 3-hr dinner show incorporates fireworks, marimba music, a show and a guided tour through San José in Pueblo Antiguo. Takes place Wed, Fri, Sat 1900-2200.

Swimming

The best public pool is at **Ojo de Agua**, 5 mins from the airport in Alajuela, 15 mins from San José. Daily 0600-1600, US$1.30, T2441-0655. Direct bus from Calle 10, Av 2-4 (behind La Merced Church) in San José or take bus to Alajuela and then another to San Antonio de Belén. There is also an open-air pool at **Plaza González Víquez**, in the southeast section of San José, crowded. Weekends only, US$1, T2256-6517.

Tour operators

Aventuras Naturales, Av Central, Calle 33-35, T2225-3939, www.adventurecostarica.com. Specialists in whitewater rafting with their own lodge on the Pacuare, which has a canopy adventure tour. Also several other trips.
COOPRENA (Simbiosis Tours), San José, T2290-8646, www.turismoruralcr.com. A group supporting small farmers, broadly working to the principle of sustainable tourism. Offers tours and accommodation around the country.
Costa Rican Trails, 325 Curridabat de la Pops, 300-m al Sur y 250 al Este, T1 888-803-3344 (USA), T1866-865-7013 (Canada), www.costaricantrails.com. Travel agency and tour operator, offering 1-day and multi-day tours and packages, selected and resorts, reliable local ground and air transport.
LA Tours, PO Box 492-1007, Centro Colón, T2221-4501. Kathia Vargas is extremely helpful in rearranging flights and reservations.

Super Viajes, American Express representative, Oficientro Ejecutivo La Sabana, Edif 1 Sabana, PO Box 3985, T2220-0400.
Swiss Travel Service, is one of the biggest tour operators with branches in many of the smarter hotels, T2282-4898, www.swisstravelcr.com. Can provide any standard tour, plus several specialist tours for birdwatchers. Good guides and warmly recommended.

Transport

San José *p723, maps p724 and p726*
Air
The much-improved **Aeropuerto Internacional Juan Santamaría (SJO)** is at El Coco, 16 km from San José along the Autopista General Cañas (5 km from Alajuela). Airport information, T2443-2622 (24 hrs). The **Sansa** terminal for domestic flights is next to the main terminal. **Sansa** runs a free bus service to the airport for its passengers. Bank at the airport 0800-1600, with ATM available as well. **ICT**, open in the day time, has a helpful tourist office in the main terminal for maps, information and hotel reservations. Another terminal, 1 km west of the main terminal, is used by charter flights and private planes. **Buses** to city centre from main street outside ground-floor terminal. Buses to airport, continuing on to Alajuela from Av Central-2, Calle 10, every 10 mins from 0500-2100; 45 mins, US$0.50 (good service, plenty of luggage space). **Taxi** to and from airport, US$15. Taxis run all night from the main square. For early flights you can reserve a taxi from any San José hotel the night before. All taxi companies run a 24-hr service.

Internal flights Sansa and Nature Air (from Tobias Bolaños, 8 km west of San José, in Pavas) operate internal flights throughout the country. **Sansa** check-in is at office on Av Las Américas and Calle 42, free bus to and from airport. Check schedules on **Nature Air**, T2299-6000, www.natureair.com. If you made reservations before arriving in Costa Rica, confirm and collect tickets as soon as possible after arrival. Book ahead, especially for the beaches. In Feb and Mar, planes can be fully booked 3 weeks ahead. On all internal scheduled and charter flights there is a baggage allowance of 12 kg. Oversized items such as surfboards or bicycles are charged at US$15 if there is room in the cargo hold.

From San José you can fly to **Barra del Colorado**, **Coto 47**, **Drake Bay**, **Golfito**, **Liberia**, **Limón**, **Nosara**, **Palmar Sur**, **Puerto Jiménez** (with a connecting flight to **Carate**, on the border of Corcovado National Park), **Punta Islita**, **Quepos**, **Carrillo-Sámara**, **Tamarindo**, **Tambor**, **Tortuguero** and **Granada** in Nicaragua and **Bocas del Toro** in Panama.

Airline offices
International carriers   Air France, Condominio Vista Real, 1st floor, 100 m east of POPs, Curridabat, T2280-0069; **Alitalia**, Calle 24, Paseo Colón, T2295-6820; **American**, Sabana Este, opposite Hotel TRYP Meliá, T2257-1266; **Avianca**, Edif Centro, p 2, Colón, Paseo Colón, Calle 38-40, T2233-3066; **British Airways**, Calle 13, Av 13, T2257-8087; **Condor Airlines**, Calle 5, Av 7-9, T2256-6161; **Continental**, Oficentro La Virgen No 2, 200 m south, 300 m east and 50 m north of American Embassy, Pavas, T2296-4911; **Copa**, Av 5, Calle 1, T2223-2672; **Delta**, 100 m east of Toyota and 50 m south, T2257-2992; **Grupo Taca**, see Sansa above; **Iberia**, Paseo Colón, Calle 40, T2257-8266; **KLM**, Sabana Sur, behind Controlaría General Building, T2220-4111; **Lloyd Aéreo Boliviano**, Av 2, Calle 2-4, upstairs, T2255-1530; **LTU International Airways** (German charter airline), Condominio da Vinci, Oficina No 6, Barrio Dent, T2234-9292; **Lufthansa**, Calle 5, Av 7-9, T2243-1818; **Martinair**, Dutch charter airline – subsidiary of KLM, see above; **Mexicana**, Paseo Colón Torres Mercedes, T2295-6969, Mexican Tourist Card available here; **SAM**, Paseo Colón, Calle 38-40, Edif Centro Colón, 2nd floor, T2233-3066; **Singapore Airlines**, Edificio Isabela San Pedro,

T2234-2223; **Servivensa**, Edif Centro Colón, 2nd floor, Paseo Colón, Calle 38-40, T2257-1441; **Swissair**, Calle Central, Av 1-3, T2221-6613; **United Airlines**, Sabana Sur, behind Controlaría General Building, T2220-2027; **Varig**, Sabana West 150 m south of Canal 7, T2290-5222.

National and charter airlines
Aerobell, T2290-0000, www.aerobell.com, at Pavas; Alfa Romeo Aéreo Taxi, in Puerto Jiménez, T2735-5112; Nature Air (see above); Paradise Air, T2296-3600, www.flywith paradise.com, based in Pavas; Sansa, T2223-4179, www.flysansa.com.

Bus
Local   Urban routes in San José cost US$0.50 or less. Hand baggage in reasonable quantities is not charged. A cheap tour of San José can be made on the bus marked *periférico* from Paseo Colón in front of the Cine Colón, or at La Sabana bus stop, a 45-min circuit of the city. A smaller circuit is made by the 'Sabana/ Cementerio' bus, pick it up at Av 2, Calle 8-10.

Regional   In the majority of cases, buses start or finish their journey at San José so there are services to most towns; see under relevant destination for details of times and prices. Check where the bus stops at your destination, some routes do not go to the centre of towns, leaving passengers some distance away.

Bus stations are scattered around town: **Alajuela** (including airport) from Av 2, Calle 12-14; **Cahuita**, **Limón**, **Manzanillo**, **Puerto Viejo de Talamanca**, **Sixaola** all served from **Gran Terminal del Caribe** (**Guapileños**, **Caribeños**, **Sixaola**); **Jacó**, **Carará**, **Quepos**, **Manuel Antonio**, **Uvita** all depart from from **Terminal Coca Cola**; **Santa Cruz** (½ block west), **Peñas Blancas** (100 m north) from outside **Terminal Coca Cola**; **Cártago** from **Terminal Cártago** during the day, after 2030 from **Gran Hotel Costa Rica**, Av 2, Calle 3-5; **Cd Quesada** (**San Carlos**), **Fortuna**, **Guápiles** (**Braulio Carrillo**),

Los Chiles, Caño Negro, Monteverde (outside terminal), **Puerto Jiménez** (outside terminal), **Puerto Viejo Sarapiquí**, **Tilarán** (½ block north) from Terminal Atlántico Norte at Av 9, Calle 12; **Playa del Coco**, **Liberia** from Calle 14, Av 1-3; **Golfito**, **Nicoya**, **Nosara**, **Palmar Norte**, **Paso Canoas**, **Sámara**, **San Vito**, **Tamarindo** from Terminal Alfaro; **San Isidro de El General** (2 companies, Musoc and **Tuasur**), terminal down on Av 22-24, Calle Central, **Heredia** from Terminal Heredia or a minibus from Av 2, Calle 10-12; **Volcán Irazú** from Av 2, Calle 1-3, opposite Gran Hotel Costa Rica; **Volcán Poás** from Av 2, Calle 12-14; **Puntarenas** from Terminal Puntarenas, Calle 16, Av 10-12; **Santa María de Dota** from Terminal Los Santos; **Turrialba** from Terminal Turrialba.

Shuttle bus 2 companies, Interbus, T2283-5573, www.interbusonline.com, and **Fantasy Tours/GrayLine**, T2220-2126, www.graylinecostarica.com, offer transport from the capital to dozens of beach and tourism destinations in comfortable a/c minibuses, bilingual drivers, hotel pickup, tickets US$30-80 one-way, with a good weekly pass.

International If the timing of your journey is important, book tickets: in Dec-Jan, buses are often booked 2 weeks ahead, while at other times of the year outside holiday seasons there are plenty of spaces.

Ticabus terminal at Calle 9-11, Av 4, T2221-8954, www.ticabus.com, office open Mon-Sun 0600-2200. Ticabus to **Guatemala City**, 3 daily, 60 hrs, US$68, with overnight stay in Managua and San Salvador. To **Tegucigalpa**, 3 daily, 48 hrs, US$42, overnight stay in Managua. To **Managua** 3 daily, US$21, 10 hrs including 1 hr at Costa Rican side of border and another 2 hrs on Nicaraguan side while they search bags. To **Panama City** 1200 daily, US$37 1 way, 18 hrs (book in advance). To get a Panamanian tourist card you must buy a return ticket – you can get a refund in Panama but with a discount of 15%. **Transnica**, Calle 22, Av 3-5,

T2223-4242, www.transnica.com, runs buses with TV, video, a/c, snacks, toilet, to **Managua** 4 daily, US$23 return. Before departure have your ticket confirmed on arrival at the terminal; when buying and confirming your ticket, you must show your passport. When boarding the bus you are given an immigration form.

Expreso Panaline goes to **Panama City** daily at 1200 from the Terminal de Empresarios Unidos de Puntarenas Calle 16, Av 10-12, T2221-7694, www.expreso panama.com, US$35 1 way, US$70 return, reduction for students, arrives 0300; a/c, payment by Visa/MasterCard accepted. They are modern, comfortable buses, although there is not much room for long legs, but they have the advantage of covering a scenic journey in daylight. A bus to **Changuinola** via the Sixaola–Guabito border post leaves San José at 1000 daily, 8 hrs, from opposite Terminal Alfaro, T2556-1432 for info, best to arrive 1 hr before departure; the bus goes via Siquirres and is the quick route to **Limón**.

Car

Car hire Most local agencies are on or close to Paseo Colón, with a branch or drop-off site at or close to the airport and other locations around the country.

International companies with services include **Adobe**, **Alamo**, **Avis**, **Budget**, **Dollar**, **Economy**, **Hertz**, **Hola**, **National**, **Payless**, **Thrifty**, **Toyota** and **Tricolor**.

Solid, T2442-6000, www.rentacarcosta rica.com, are a local company with several offices around town including **Hostal Toruma**, most competively priced in town; **Wild Rider Motorcycles**, also rents cheap 4WD vehicles (see below).

Motorcycle and bike

Rental Wild Rider Motorcycles, Paseo Colón, Calle 32 diagonal Kentucky, next to Aventuras Backpackers, T2258-4604, www.wild-rider.com, Honda XR250s, Yamaha XT600s and Suzuki DR650SE available for rent from US$55-80 a day, US$700-1200 deposit required. 4WD vehicles also available, US$240-410 per week, monthly discounts.

Cycle repairs Cyclo Quiros, Apartado 1366, Pavas, 300 m west of US Embassy. The brothers Quiros have been repairing bikes for 20 years, good place for general information and repairs, highly recommended.

Taxis

Minimum fare US$0.57 for 1st km, US$0.31 additional km. Taxis used to charge more after 2200, but that rule has been rescinded. Taxis are red and have electronic meters called *marías*, if not, get out and take another cab. For journeys over 12 km, price should be negotiated between driver and passenger. Radio cabs can be booked in advance. To order a taxi, call **Coopeguaria**, T2226-1366, **Coopeirazu**, T2254-3211, **Coopemoravia**, T2229-8882, **Coopetaxi**, T2235-9966, **Taxi San Jorge**, T2221-3434, **Taxis Guaria**, T2226-1366, **Taxis Unidos SA**, which are the official taxis of the Juan Santamaría International Airport and are orange instead of red, T2222-6865, or look in the classified adverts of *The Tico Times* for car and driver hire.

❶ Directory

San José *p723, maps p724 and p726*
Banks

Queues in state-run banks tend to be long; using privately run banks is recommended. The 15th and end of the month (pay day for government employees) are especially bad. Visa and MasterCard ATMs are widespread and the best option in the capital. Queues tend to be shorter outside San José. Money can be sent through **Banco de San José** or **Banco de Costa Rica** at 4%. Credit card holders can obtain cash advances from **Banco de San José** (Visa, MasterCard) and **Credomatic Los Yoses** in colones (Master Card ATM) and **Banco Popular** (Visa ATM) minimum cash advance: US$50 equivalent. ATMs which will accept international Visa/MasterCard are available at most banks,

shopping malls and San José airport. **Banco Crédito Agrícola de Cártago**, state-run, 9 branches, also makes advances on Visa, no commission, no limits. **Banco de Costa Rica**, Av 2, Calle 4, state-run, changes TCs, open 0830-1500, long queues, 1% commission. **Banco de San José**, Calle Central, Av 3-5, private, commission 2.5%. **Banco Nacional**, head office, Av 1-3, Calle 2-4, state-run, will change TCs into dollars but you pay a commission, accepts Visa credit cards as do most of the bigger banks in San José and other major towns. Many private banks are open late and Sat, including **Banco Cuscatlán**, with 12 branches around the country, Mon-Fri 0800-1800, Sat 0800-1200, T2299-0299.

An alternative to the banks for getting money are money-transfer services: **Western Union**, T2283-6336, www.westernunion. com, operates out of many pharmacies and other locations. Quicker than banks but you pay a price premium. **Interbank**, transfers are cheaper and you don't need an account, but take several days or more. Ask at a bank's information desk for details.

Cultural centres

Alianza Francesa, Av 7, Calle 5, French newspapers, French films every Wed evening, friendly; **Centro Cultural Costarricense Norteamericano**, Calle 37, Av 1-5, Los Yoses, T2207-7500, www.centrocultural.cr, open daily until 1930, free, shows good films, plays, art exhibitions and English-language library.

Embassies and consulates

Belgium, Barrio Dent, T2280-4435, 0800-1330; **Canada**, Building 5 (3rd floor) of Oficentro Ejecutivo La Sabana, Sabana Sur, T2242-4400, Mon-Thu 0800-1630, Fri 0800-1330; **El Salvador**, Paseo Colón, from Toyota 500 m north and 25 m west, T2257-7855; **France**, Curridabat, 200 m south, 25 m west of Indoor Club, T2234-4167, 0830-1200; **Germany**, Rohrmoser, 200 m north and 75 m east of Oscar Arias' house, T2232-5533, 0900-1200; **Guatemala**, 500 m south, 30 m east of POPs, Curridabat, T2283-2557, 0900-1300; **Honduras,** Rohrmoser, T2291-5143, 0900-1230; **Israel,** Edificio Colón, 11th floor, Paseo Colón, Calle 38-40, T2221-6444, 0900-1200; **Italy,** Los Yoses, Av 10, Calle 33-35, T2234-2326, 0900-1200; **Japan,** Oficentro building No 7, La Sabana, T2296-1650; **Mexico,** Consulate, Av 7, Calle 13-15, T2225-7284, 0830-1230; **Netherlands,** Oficentro Ejecutivo La Sabana, Sabana Sur, T2296-1490, Mon-Fri 0900-1200; **Nicaragua,** Av Central, Calle 25-27, opposite Pizza Hut, T2222-2373, 0830-1130 and 1330-1500, 24-hr wait for visa, dollars only, passport photo; **Norway,** Centro Colón, 10th floor, T2283-8222. Mon-Thu 1400-1700; **Panama,** San Pedro, T2281-2442, strict about onward ticket, 0900-1400, you need a photograph and photocopy of your passport, visa costs US$10 cash and takes up to 24 hrs; **Spain,** Paseo Colón, Calle 32, T2222-1933; **Sweden,** honorary consul at Almacén Font, 100 m east of La Pozuelo, La Uruca, T2232-8549; **Switzerland,** Centro Colón, p 10, Paseo Colón, Calle 38, T2221-4829, 0900-1200; **UK,** Centro Colón, p 11, end of Paseo Colón with Calle 38, T2258-2025, 0900-1200; **USA,** in the western suburb of Pavas, opposite Centro Comercial, catch . a ruta 14 bus to Pavas, Zona 1 from Av 1 and Calle 16-18, T2220-3939, 0800-1630; **Venezuela,** Los Yoses, de la 5a entrada, 100 m south, 50 m west, T2225-8810, 0830-1230, visa issued same day, US$30, helpful.

Immigration
The immigration office is on the airport highway, opposite Hospital México. You need to go here for visas extensions, etc. Queues can take all day. To get there, take bus No 10 or 10A Uruca, marked 'México', then cross over highway at the bridge and walk 200 m along highway – just look for the queue or ask the driver. Better to find a travel agent who can obtain what you need for a fee, say US$5. Make sure you get a receipt if you give up your passport.

Internet
Cybercafé, in the basement of Edificio Las Arcadas, next to the Gran Hotel Costa Rica, is central and open daily 0700-1900, charging US$1.80/hr. **Internet Café,** 4th floor, Av C, Calle 4, 0900-2200. A better way to spend less money as it is just 400 colones for full or part hr, but not a café. Several branches around town including at the western end of Paseo Colón in Edifico Colón, Calle 38-40, and if you want to type all night there is a 24-hr café in San Pedro, close to Banco Popular.

Language schools
The number of schools has increased rapidly. Listed below are just a selection recommended by readers. Generally, schools offer tuition in groups of 2-5 for 2-4 weeks. Lectures, films, outings and social occasions are usually included and accommodation with families is encouraged. Many schools are linked to the university and can offer credits towards a US course. Rates, including lodging, are around US$1000-1100 a month. **Academica Tica de Español,** in San Rafael de Coronado, 10 km north of San José, T2229-0013, www.academiatica.com; **AmeriSpan,** 1334 Walnut St, 6th floor, Philadelphia, PA 19107, T215-751-1100, www.amerispan.com, has affiliated schools in Alajuela, Heredia, San José and 6 others locations; **Costa Rican Language Academy,** Barrio California, T2280-5834, www.spanish andmore.com, run by Aída Chávez, offers language study and accommodation with local families, and instruction in Latin American music and dancing as well; **Costa Rica Spanish Institute,** Zapote in San Pedro district, T2234-1001, www.cosi.co.cr, also branch in Manuel Antonio; **Instituto Británico** in Los Yoses, 1000 San José, T2225-0256, www.institutobritanico.co.cr, teaches English and Spanish; **Instituto de Español Costa Rica,** A 1, Calle Central – Calle 1, Apartado 1405-2100, Guadalupe, TT2280-6622, www.costaricaspanishschool.com. Close to the centre of San José, and complete with its own B&B. English, French and German

spoken; **Universal de Idiomas**, in Moravia, T2223-9662, www.universal-edu.com, stresses conversational Spanish; **Intercultura**, Heredia, T2260-8480, www.intercultura costarica.com. Intensive courses with excursions to beaches, volcanoes, rainforest and a volunteer programme.

Laundry
Washing and dry cleaning at **Centro Comercial San José**, 2000, daily 0730-2000, US$3.75 for large load; **Lavandería Costa Rica**, Av 3, Calle 19-21, US$5 for a large load; **Lavandería Lavamex**, below Hotel Gran Imperial at Calle 7, Av 1-Central, US$4 to wash, US$4 to dry, quick service and very friendly. Book swap, very popular with travellers, much more than a laundry thanks to the helpful owners Karl and Patricia.

Libraries
Biblioteca Nacional, opposite Parque Nacional, Mon-Fri 0830-1630, also has art and photography exhibitions; **Centro Cultural Costarricense Norteamericano**, C 37, Av 1-5, www.centrocultural.cr, T2207-7500, has a good English-language library.

Medical services
Dentists Clínica Dental Dr Francisco Cordero Guilarte, Rohrmoser 300 m east of Plaza Mayor, T2223-8890; **Dra Fresia Hidalgo**, Uned Building, San Pedro, 1400-1800, English spoken, reasonable prices, recommended, T2234-2840; **Fernando Baldioceda** and **Silvia Oreamuno**, 225 m north of Paseo Colón on the street that intersects at the Toyota dealership: both speak English; **Alfonso Villalobos Aguilar**, Edif Herdocía, p 2, Av 3, Calle 2-4, T2222-5709.
Doctors Dr Jorge Quesada Vargas, Clínica Internacional, Av 14, Calle 3-5, speaks German.
Hospitals and clinics Social Security hospitals have a good reputation (free to social security members, few members of staff speak English), free ambulance service run by volunteers: Dr Calderón Guardia, T2257-7922, **San Juan de Dios**, T2257-6282,

México, T2232-6122; **Clínica Bíblica** Calle 1, Av 14, 24-hr pharmacy, T2257-5252, frequently recommended and the one most used by the local expatriate community and offers 24-hr emergency service at reasonable charges with staff who speak English, better than the large hospitals, where queues are long; **Clínica Católica**, northeast of San José, another private hospital with 24-hr pharmacy, T2246-3000; **Hospital CIMA**, T2208-1000, on the highway toward Escazú, country's newest and most modern private hospital, bilingual staff, expensive rates, 24-hr pharmacy, T2208-1080.

Police
Thefts should be reported in San José to **Recepción de Denuncias**, Organismo de Investigación Judicial (OIJ), Calle 19, Av 6-8, T2295-3643. Call for nearest OIJ office in outlying areas.

Post
Calle 2, Av 1-3, open for sale of stamps Mon-Fri, 0700-1700, Sat-Sun 0700-1800. Stamp vending machine in main post office. Lista de Correos, Mon-Fri 0800-1700, quick service. **Couriers** DHL, Pavas, Calle 34, T2209-6000, www.dhl.com; Fed Ex, Paseo Colón, 100 m east of León Cortés' statue, T2293-3157, www.fedex.com; UPS, 50 m east of Pizza Hut central office, Pavas, San José, T2239-0576, www.ups.com.

Telephone
Faxes and internal telegrams from main post office. Fax abroad, internet access and email from **RACSA**, Av 5, Calle 1, 0730-2200 (see also Essentials, page 721). ICE (Instituto Costarricense de Electricidad), Av 2, Calle 1, for phone calls (phone card only), and fax service, 0700-2200, 3-min call to UK US$10, friendly service (cheaper than **Radiográfica**, but check). Collect/reverse charge telephone calls can be made from any public telephone. English-speaking operators are available. See also page 721.

Meseta Central West

Hilly and fertile with a temperate climate, the Central Highlands is a major coffee-growing area. Fairly heavily populated, picturesque and prosperous towns sit in the shadows of active volcanoes. Exploring the towns and villages of the region – each with its own character and style – gives good insight into the very heart of Costa Rica.

From San José, the Pan-American Highway heads north east through the Meseta Central for 332 km along good roads to the Nicaraguan border. While CA1 will take you north, by sticking to it you'll miss visiting the remnants of colonial architecture found in Alajuela, Heredia and the countless smaller towns that enjoy the spring-like temperatures of the highlands. Although it's easier to explore the region in a private vehicle, frequent public buses and short journeys make hopping between towns fairly straightforward – if stepping out from San José it's probably worth dumping most of your luggage in the city and travelling light. ⟩⟩ *For listings, see pages 747-751.*

Northwest of San José → *For listings, see pages 747-751.*

Alajuela → *Colour map 4, B3. Altitude: 952 m.*
The provincial capital of Alajuela has a slightly milder climate than San José, making it a popular weekend excursion for Josefinos. Famous for its flowers and market days (Saturday market is good value for food), regular buses from San José make it an easy day trip. Alternatively, stay in Alajuela, and use the regular buses to visit the capital. It is 5 km from the international airport, and is handy for early flights and late arrivals.

The town centres on the Parque Central with the 19th-century domed church on the eastern side. The unusual church of La Agonía, five blocks further east, is an interesting mix of styles. One block to the south, Juan Santamaría, the national hero who torched the building in Rivas (Nicaragua) in which William Walker's filibusters were entrenched in 1856, is commemorated by a monument. One block north of the Parque Central, the **Museo Histórico Juan Santamaría** ① *Av 3, Calle 2, Tue-Sun 1000-1800, www.museojuan santamaria.go.cr*, tells, somewhat confusingly, the story of this war.

Parque Nacional Volcán Poás → *Colour map 4, B3.*
① *Daily 0800-1530, 1 hr later Fri-Sun, Dec-Apr, US$10, good café next door, and toilets further along the road to the crater. If you wish to get in earlier you can leave your car/taxi at the gates, walk the 3 km up the hill and pay on your way out. The volcano is very crowded on Sun so go in the week if possible. Arrive early as clouds often hang low over the crater after 1000, obstructing the view. Wear good shoes, a hat and suncream.*
Volcán Poás (2708 m) sits in the centre of the Parque Nacional Volcán Poás (6506 ha), where the still-smoking volcano and bubbling turquoise sulphur pool are set within a beautiful forest. The crater is almost 1.5 km across – the second largest in the world. The park is rich with abundant birdlife given the altitude and barren nature of the terrain and home to the only true dwarf cloud forest in Costa Rica.

From Alajuela two paved roads head north for 37 km to the volcano. The first through San Pedro de Poás and Fraijanes, the second follows the road to San Miguel, branching left just before the town of Vara Blanca. In the park, trails are well marked to help guide you from the visitor centre to the geysers, lake and other places of interest. The main crater is 1 km along a road from the car park. There is a visitor centre by the car park with explanations of the recent changes in the volcano. There is also a good café run by **Café Britt**; alternatively, bring your own food and water.

From **Vara Blanca** the road runs north past the popular La Paz waterfall, round the east side of the volcano through Cinchona and Cariblanco. **La Paz Waterfall Gardens** ⓘ *5 km north of Vara Blanca, T2482-2720, www.waterfallgardens.com, US$35*, has forest trails past five huge falls and one of the world's largest butterfly and hummingbird gardens, a restaurant with buffet lunch and the **Peace Lodge Hotel** (**LL**). The road is twisty, winding through lush forest, with several waterfalls down to the lowlands at **San Miguel**. Here the road leads either northeast heading to La Virgen and eventually Puerto Viejo de Sarapiquí (see page 835), or northwest to Venecia (see below).

La Virgen
Ten kilometres northeast of San Miguel is La Virgen, near the Río Sarapiquí, a good spot for Grade I, II and III rafting, which is organized by the hotel **Rancho Leona**. From San José, take the Río Frío bus which passes through San Miguel, or a bus from San Carlos, and ask to get off at **Rancho Leona**. Juan Carlos in La Virgen has been recommended as a guide for rafting, T2761-1148, from US$30 per person.

Venecia and around
Heading west from San Miguel, Venecia (two buses daily from San José, 4½ hours, US$3) has an interesting church. Near Venecia are the pre-Columbian tumuli of **Ciudad Cutris**.

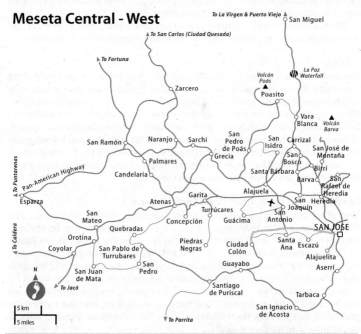

Meseta Central - West

A good road goes to within 2 km of Cutris, from where you can walk or take a 4WD vehicle; get a permit to visit from the local *finca* owner.

West of Venecia is Aguas Zarcas, where the road splits. Heading directly north, the roads descends into the jungle lowlands, following the Río San Carlos towards the Nicaraguan border, passing through several small towns. After about 40 km, in Boca Tapada, is **La Laguna del Lagarto Lodge** (see page 748).

Grecia

The road from Alajuela north east to San Carlos (see page 758) passes through Grecia and several towns of the Meseta Central, with good paved roads leading to others. The hills are covered with green coffee bushes, interspersed with other plants for shade. Grecia is also a major pineapple producer, and has an interesting church made entirely of metal. A short distance along the road to Alajuela is **El Mundo de las Serpientes** ① *T2494-3700, snakes@ racsa.co.cr, 0800-1600, US$4, children US$1.50, reductions for biology students*, a snake farm with more than 50 species. On the old road about 10 km towards Tacares is **Los Chorros Recreational Park** ① *US$4*, with two massive waterfalls and picnic spots.

Sarchí and Naranjo → *Colour map 4, B3.*

Heading west is the town of Sarchí, the country's artisan centre, where you can visit the *fábricas* that produce the intricately geometric and floral designs painted on ox-carts, which are almost a national emblem. The town is divided in two, Sarchí Norte and Sarchí Sur, separated by some 4 km. The green church (until they paint it again) in Sarchí is especially attractive at sunset. Travel agents in San José charge around US$40 for a day trip to Sarchí usually combined with a trip to Volcán Poás.

The road continues north to Naranjo, a quiet agricultural town with an exquisite bright white church, and a shocking post-modern pyramidal structure in the main square.

Zarcero

Frequent bus services from San José/Alajuela pass through Zarcero, on the lip of the continental divide, en route to San Carlos (Ciudad Quesada). The town is famous for vegetable farming, dairy products and notable for the topiary creations of Evangelista Blanco Breves that fill the main plaza. Bushes are clipped, trimmed and shaped into arches leading up to the white church with twin towers, with shapes of animals, dancing couples, a helicopter, many designs of Henry Moore-like sculptures and a small grotto. The interior of the quaint church, overshadowed somewhat by the plaza, is made entirely of wood, even the pillars, painted cream and pale grey with patterns in blue, brown, green and pink; cartouches, emblems and paintings.

San Ramón and Los Angeles Cloud Forest Reserve

West of Naranjo along the Pan-American Highway is the town of San Ramón, 76 km from San José. A clean town, known locally as the City of Poets, with an attractive Parque Central, and a street market on Saturday mornings. The **Museo de San Ramón** ① *opposite the park, Tue-Fri 1300-1700, T2437-9851*, records the history and culture of the local community. There's good walking in the surrounding area. You can visit the coffee processing plant (in season) at the **Cooperativa de Café** ① *US$15-39*, in San Ramón.

Heading north the road forks, left to Zarcero. The right fork heads north to La Tigra and Fortuna, passing the Los Angeles Cloud Forest Reserve (20 km from San Ramón). The private 800-ha reserve (see **Hotel Villablanca**, page 748) offers hiking, guided tours, horse riding and canopy ascents. The local fiesta is around the day of San Ramón, 30 August, when local saints are carried on litters to the town's church.

Palmares and Atenas → *Colour map 4, B3.*

Palmares, 7 km southeast of San Ramón, has a pretty central park with lovely tall trees, where sloths are occasionally spotted. The quiet town comes alive in January for the annual **Fiestas de Palmares**, with food, carnival rides, concerts and parades.

After Palmares you can pick up the Pan-American Highway and head to the coast or return to San José, or continue south to Atenas. The church and main plaza in Atenas lie on an earthquake fault. The local speciality, *toronja rellena*, is a sweet-filled grapefruit. Atenas is reputed to have the best climate in the world, with stable temperatures of between 17 and 32°C year round.

North of San José → *For listings, see pages 747-751.*

Heredia → *Colour map 4, B3. Altitude: 1200 m.*

Ten kilometres north of San José, Heredia is capital of the province of the same name and an important coffee centre. It is a convenient and pleasant place to stay, away from the pollution of San José but close to the capital and the airport, and with good public transport. The town is mostly new with only the main square maintaining a colonial atmosphere in its architecture. The short squat **Basílica de la Inmaculada Concepción**, built in 1797, has survived countless earthquakes. To the north of the central plaza, with a statue to the poet Aquileo Echeverría (1866-1909), is the solitary defensive structure of **El Fortín**. Across the street the **Casa de la Cultura** is a fine colonial home that now hosts concerts and exhibitions. The School of Marine Biology at the Universidad Nacional campus has a **Museo Zoológico Marino**.

Around Heredia

One of the largest coffee *beneficios* is **La Meseta**. The bus from Heredia to Santa Bárbara will drop you at the gate and you can ask for a guided tour. A more popular tour is of **Café Britt's coffee farm** ⓘ *US$20, tours 1100, 1½ hrs, includes lunch and show, T2277-1500, www.coffeetour.com*, near Barva de Heredia where you can see the processing factory, tasting room and multimedia presentation of the story of coffee. You can be picked up from Heredia or at various points in San José. The **Teatro Dionisio Chaverría** at Café Britt hosts weekend theatre, and a children's show on Sunday afternoons.

North of Heredia is the historic town of **Barva**, on the slopes of Volcán Barva; there frequent buses to/from Heredia. At Barva, the **Huetar Gallery** is recommended for arts, crafts and delicious food. There is also a **Museo de Cultura Popular** ⓘ *Mon-Fri 0900-1600, US$1.50*, 500 m east of the Salón Comunal de Santa Lucía de Barva. North of Heredia through San Rafael, above Los Angeles, is **Galería Octágono** ⓘ *T2267-6325 www.galeria octagono.com*, an arts gallery with handmade textiles by a women's community cooperative, and also a B&B, see page 749. Beyond Barva, to the west, is **Santa Bárbara**, good seafood at the **Banco de los Mariscos** (T2269-9090), 500 m west from the central plaza. Five kilometres west of Heredia is **San Joaquín de Flores**, a small rural town with views of Barva and Poás volcanoes.

A short distance south of Heredia on the road to **Santo Domingo** is **INBio Parque** ⓘ *T2507-8107, www.inbio.ac.cr, Fri 0800-1700, Sat-Sun 0900-1730, US$44*, an educational and recreational centre that explains and gives insight into Costa Rica's biological diversity. In a small area you can visit the ecosystems of central highland forest, dry forest and humid forest, with trails set out for bromelias and *guarumo*.

Volcán Barva

Parque Nacional Braulio Carrillo ① *park entry US$10, no permit needed* (see page 833), to the north of Heredia, includes Volcán Barva, at 2906 m. This section of the park is ideal for hiking with a good trail leading up to the summit with three lagoons nearby, and excellent views and wildlife encounters for the few that make the effort. The really enthusiastic can hike all the way down to the lowlands arriving close to La Selva Biological Station near Puerto Viejo de Sarapaqui, but careful planning is required. There is a ranger station and camp site near the entrance, 4 km north of Sacramento, from where it's a 3-km easy climb to the top – still a treasure and, amazingly, a well-kept secret from the hordes.

San José de la Montaña to Sacramento

From San José de la Montaña it is four hours' walk to Sacramento but some buses continue towards Sacramento halving the walk time (otherwise walk, hitchhike, or arrange a ride with the park director). A taxi between Heredia and Sacramento costs US$10.

South of San José

Aserrí to San Pablo de Turrubares

Ten kilometres south of San José is Aserrí, a village with a beautiful white church. On Friday and Saturday evenings, street bands begin the fiesta with music from 2000, followed by marimbas. Extremely popular among locals, the dancing is fabulous, with *chicharrones*, tortillas and plenty of other things to eat and drink. Further along the same road is **Mirador Ram Luna**, a restaurant with a fine panoramic view. At the end of the road is **San Ignacio de Acosta**, again with a good church containing life-size Nativity figures. Buses from San José (Calle 8, Avenida 12-14 in front of the Baptist church) via Aserrí hourly from 0500 to 2230, return 0430 to 2100, one hour. The unpaved road continues to **Santiago de Puriscal**, which was the epicentre for many earthquakes in 1990. Although the church is now closed as a result, there are excellent views from the town and the road. From here it is possible to take a dirt road to the Pacific coast, joining the coastal road near Parrita (see page 805). Alternatively, take the road to **San Pablo de Turrubares**, from where you can either head west for Orotina, via an unpaved road through San Pedro and San Juan de Mata, or for Atenas via Quebradas, then east to Escobal, next stop on railway, then 4WD necessary to Atenas.

For Sleeping and Eating price codes and other relevant information, see Essentials pages 31-33.

● Sleeping

Alajuela *p742*

The 2 **Hampton Inns** and the **Garden Court** are the closest place to stay near the airport, 2 km east of Juan Santamaría on the main highway.

LL Xandari, T2443-2020, www.xandari.com. Once an old coffee *finca* overlooking the Central Valley, this architectural treasure has 21 private villas, health restaurant, organic gardens, trails and waterfalls, spa treatments and many facilities. One of the best hotels in Costa Rica.

AL Garden Court Hotel, T2443-0043, www.gardencourtairporthotel.com. Good comforts, including pool in this Holiday Inn Express. You're here for the proximity to the airport.

AL Hampton Inn Airport, T2436-0000, www.hamptoninn.com. 100 rooms, double glazing, a/c, free-form outdoor pool, bar, fast-food places nearby, children free and discounts for 3 or 4 adults sharing.

AL Hampton Inn and Suites, T2442-3320, www.grupomarta.com. Luxury suites and facilities for business travellers.

A-B Hotel 1915, Calle 2, Av 5-7, 300 m north of Parque Central, T2440-7163, www.1915 hotel.com. Old family home smartly refurbished with stylish garden patio café. Very good service. Rooms have cable TV, mini fridge, telephone, some with a/c, price includes breakfast. Best in town for the price.

B Viña Romántica, up in the hills near Alajuela on road to Poás volcano, T2430-7621, www.vina romantica.com. Great spot, gourmet meals, minimum 3 days.

C Hotel Mi Tierra, Av 2, Calle3-5, T2441-1974, www.hotelmitierra.net. Offers pool, adventure tours and parking. Popular with travellers.

C Islands B&B, Av 1, Calle 7-9, 50 m west of La Agonía church, T2442-0573, islandsbb@

hotmail.com. A small family-run Tico-owned B&B with 8 comfortable rooms. Some rooms have cable TV, free local calls. Airport pickup available, very secure and 24-hr parking.

C-D Hotel Alajuela, on corner across from central park at Av Central and Calle 2, T2441-1241, alajuela@racsa.co.cr. 28 generally good rooms and apartments all with private bathrooms. Helpful staff, garden patio for relaxing.

C-D Pensión Alajuela, Av 9, Calle Central-2, opposite the court house, T2443-1717, www.pensionalajuela.com. Mixed bag of 12 simple rooms, some with private bath, some without. Small bar downstairs, laundry and fax service. 24-hr parking next door.

C-E Charly's Place, a couple of blocks north of the central park on Av 5, Calle Central-1, T2440-6853, www.charlysplacehotel.com. Popular place, with 14 rooms most with private bathrooms, cheaper without, some with TV. Also cheap backpackers' area. Credit cards accepted.

D Mango Verde Hostel, Av 3, Calle 2-4, T2441-6330, mifloresbb@hotmail.com. 6 clean rooms with private bath and hot water, close to the centre of town. Court-yard, kitchen and communal area, relaxing atmosphere. Parking.

E-F Cortez Azul, Av 3, Calle 2-4, 100 m west of Museo Juan Santamaría, T2443-6145, hotelcortezazul@gmail.com. Popular spot with a handful of good, clean rooms.

E-G Central Alajuela, Av Central, Calle 8, close to the bus terminal, T2443-8437. Basic rooms, shared bathrooms have cold water but it is reasonably clean. Popular with Ticos arriving from out of town.

Parque Nacional Volcán Poás *p742*

Camping in the park is not permitted but there are several places advertising cabins on the road up to Poás and nearby.

L-AL Poás Volcano Lodge, west of Poasito, 500 m from Vara Blanca junction on road to Poasito, at El Cortijo farm, sign on gate, 1 km to house, T2482-2194, www.poas

volcanolodge.com. English-owned, includes breakfast, dinner, wholesome food, rooms in converted buildings with bath, or in farmhouse with shared bath, jungle trail, good walking, horseback riding 25 mins to volcano by car, 1½ hrs from San José.

D Albergue Ecológico La Providencia, near Poás NP (2 km from green entrance gate to volcano), T2232-2498. Private reserve, beautiful horse-riding tour US$25-30 including lunch.

La Virgen p743

AL La Quinta de Sarapiquí Lodge, Bajos de Chilamate on the Río Sardinal, T2761-1052, www.laquintasarapiqui.com. Costa Rican-owned, family-run lodge, 23 rooms with bath and fan, bar and restaurant overlooking the rainforest, tubing down rivers, popular with birdwatchers (bird list available). Also a frog and butterfly garden.

C Albergue Ecológico Islas del Río, T2292-2072 in San José, T2766-6524, in Chilamate, www.aguas-bravas.co.cr. Price per person. The operational centre of Aguas Bravas close to Puerto Viejo de Sarapiquí, includes meals, rooms with private and shared bathroom, ideal for groups, canopy tour, hiking. Río Sarapiquí trips arranged.

D-F Finca Pedro y el Lobo, T2761-1406, www.fincapedro.com. Beautiful rustic accommodation, also options for camping, kayaking, rafting and exploring waterfalls.

E Rancho Leona, T2761-1019, www.rancholeona.com. Private rooms, kayaking, meals available also jungle tours.

Venecia and around p743

B-C La Laguna del Lagarto Lodge, Boca Tapada, T2289-8163, www.lagarto-lodge-costa-rica.com. 12 rooms with bath, 6 with shared bath, friendly, 500 ha of forest, good for watching animals, boat trips down Río San Carlos to Río San Juan.

D Recreo Verde, Marsella, near Venecia, T2472-1020. A good choice in a recreational and ecological conservation park. There are hot springs, primary forest, a few trails going to nearby caves and helpful, friendly staff.

Grecia p744

A Posada Mimosa, Costa Rica, T2494-5868, www.mimosa.co.cr. B&B, rooms, suites and cabins set in beautiful tropical gardens, pool. Uses solar energy.

Sarchí and Naranjo p744

B Rancho Mirador, on the *Panamericana*, 1 km west of the turn-off for Naranjo, T2451-1302. Good-value *cabañas*, restaurant with local food, a spectacular view of coffee *fincas* and San José in the distance. Owner Rick Vargas was formerly a stunt pilot in the US.

C Cabinas Daniel Zamora, Sarchí, T2454-4596. With bath, fan, hot water, very clean and extra blankets if cold at night.

C Hotel Villa Sarchí Lodge, 800 m north of Sarchí, T2454-5000. Has 11 rooms with private bath, hot water, cable TV and pool.

G La Bamba, Naranjo, down the hill by the football pitch. May muster up enough energy to let you stay in 1 of their simple rooms.

Zarcero p744

C-D Don Beto, by the church, T2463-3137. With bath, very friendly, clean.

San Ramón and Los Angeles Cloud Forest Reserve p744

L Hotel Villablanca, north of town set in the 800-ha Los Angeles Cloud Forest Reserve, T2461-0300, www.villablanca-costarica.com. Naturalist hikes, some up to 8 hrs, canopy tour, horse riding, night walks, birdwatching, coffee plantation tour and the famous La Mariana Chapel with handpainted ceiling tiles – you don't have to stay to visit.

A-B La Posada, T2445-7359, www.posada hotel.net. 400 m north of the cathedral. 34 good rooms, with private bath, hot water, use of kitchen, laundry. Parking and small patio.

D San Ramón, 100 m east, 25m south of Banco de Costa Rica, T2447-2042. 35 spotless rooms (but pretty garish decor), with private bathroom, hot water and cable TV. Parking.

E Hotel Nuevo Jardín, 5 blocks north of the central park, T2445-5620. Simple, clean and friendly.

E Gran Hotel, 150 m west of post office, T2445-6363. Big rooms, private bathrooms, hot water, friendly, communal TV area.

Palmares and Atenas p745
A El Cafetal Inn, out of Atenas, in St Eulalia, 4.7 km towards Grecia, T2446-5785, www.cafetal.com. Nice setting on a coffee plantation, private house, large pool, 10 rooms, airport transport, recommended.

Heredia p745
A Valladolid, Calle 7, Av 7, T2260-2905, www.hotelvalladolid.net. 11 spacious rooms and suites, all with a/c, private bath, telephone and cable TV. 5th floor has sauna, jacuzzi and **Bonavista Bar** with fine views overlooking the Central Valley.
B-C Apartotel Vargas, 800 m north of Colegio Santa Cecilia and San Francisco Church, T2237-8526, www.apartotelvargas. com. 8 large, well-furnished apartments with cooking facilities, hot water, laundry facilities, TV, internet, enclosed patio with garage and nightwatchman, English-speaking staff. Sr Vargas will collect you from airport. Excellent choice if taking language classes and in a group. Best option in town.
C-D Hotel Heredia, Calle 6, Av 3-5, T2238-0880. Has 12 rooms, some quite dark, but all have private bath and hot water, parking.
D Las Flores, Av 12, Calle 12-14, T2261-8147. With bath, clean, quiet, parking. Recommended.
G Colonial, Calle 4-6, Av 4, T2237-5258. Clean, friendly and family-run, will park motorcycles in restaurant.
G El Verane, Calle 4, Av 6-8, next to central market, T2237-1616. Rooms on street side are slightly better, close to bus terminal.

Around Heredia p745
LL Finca Rosa Blanca, 1.6 km from Santa Bárbara de Heredia, T2269-9392, www.fincarosablanca.com. Deluxe suites in an architectural explosion of style and eloquence, romance and exclusivity at the extremes of imagination. Spa facilities for comfort. Quality restaurant and bar.

L-AL Bougainvillea de Santo Domingo, just west of Santo Domingo, T2244-1414, www.hb.co.cr. Excellent service, pool, sauna, spectacular mountain setting, free shuttle bus to San José. Highly recommended.
E Galería Octágono, T2267-6325, www.galeriaoctagono.com. An arts gallery and B&B; other meals and transport available at additional cost, wonderful cypress cabin, hikes, and friendly and informative owners.

● Eating

Alajuela p742
Finding something to eat in Alajuela is not difficult, most restaurants, cafés and sodas are within 1 or 2 blocks of the Parque Central and down Calle Central.
℗ La Mansarda, Plaza Central. Good, wholesome Tico dishes.
℗ Café Almibar, Av Central, Calle 1-3. Another snacking stop popular with locals.
℗ Jalapeño's, Central T2430-4027. Great Mexican food, friendly, 50 m south of the post office.
℗ La Cocina de Abuelita, Av Central, Calle 1-3. Simple lunchtime, buffet menu.
℗ Trigo Miel, Av 2, Calle Central-2. One of a couple of patisserie cafés in Alajuela serving divine snacks and good coffee.

Venecia and around p743
℗ El Parque, near church, Venecia. Good local food.

Zarcero p744
The town is known for cheese and fruit preserves.
℗ Soda/Restaurant El Jardín, 1st floor, overlooking the plaza. Local lunches and breakfasts. Good view of topiary.

San Ramón and Los Angeles Cloud Forest Reserve p744
℗ Tropical, near northwest corner of the Parque. Excellent ice cream parlour.

Heredia p745

☗☗-☗ La Rambla, Calle 7, Av 7. Services a good mix of *comida típica* and international dishes.

☗ Cowboy Restaurant, T2237-8719 Calle 9, Av 5. Grill option where the Mid-West meets Costa Rica. Lively bar in the evenings. Credit cards accepted.

☗ El Gran Papa, Calle 9, Av 3. Open for dinner, good range of *bocas*, pastas and cocktails.

☗ La Luna de Valencia, a few kilometres north of Barva, T2269-6665. Authentic paella restaurant, vegetarian options, friendly service, recommended.

☗ Le Petit Paris, Calle 5 and Av Central-2, T2262-2564. Closed Sun. A little piece of France simply oozing style. The ambience shifts between the bar, restaurant and patio café. Divine food, live music on Thu.

☗-☗ Baalbek Bar & Grill, San Rafael de Heredia on the road to Monte de la Cruz, T2267-6482. Good Mediterranean food, live music Fri /Sat.

☗-☗ Bulevar Bar, Av Central, Calle 5-7. One of the happening places with a lively balcony bar upstairs and fast food and *bocas* available.

☗-☗ Fresas, Calle 7, Av 1, T2262-5555. Diner-style restaurant serving snacks, sandwiches, breakfast, full meals, fresh fruit juices and strawberries; bar upstairs.

☗-☗ Las Espigas, corner of Parque Central. Good coffee, pastries and lunch specials.

☗ Entrepanes, upstairs from **Pop's** diagonal to Parque Central. Fine coffee and pastries.

☗ Vishnu Mango Verde, Calle 7, Av Central-1, T2237-2526. Good wholesome vegetarian served fast-food-style.

☻ Festivals and events

Alajuela p742

11 Apr Juan Santamaría Day, a week of bands, concerts and dancing in celebration of the life of the town's most famous son.

Mid-Jul The fruitful heritage comes to the fore with a **Mango Festival** of parades, concerts and an arts and crafts fair.

○ Shopping

Alajuela p742

Goodlight Books, Calle 1-3, T2430-4083. Quality used books, mostly English, espresso and pastries. Internet available.

Sarchí and Naranjo p744

One of the largest *artesanías* is **Fábrica de Chaverri** in Sarchí Sur. **Taller Lalo Alfaro**, the oldest workshop, is in Sarchí Norte and worth a visit to see more traditional production methods. Both sell handmade furniture, cowhide rocking chairs and wooden products as well as ox-carts, which come in all sizes.

● Transport

Alajuela p742

Bus Service to **San José**. Depart Alajuela from main bus terminal Calle 8, Av Central-1, or Av 4, Calle 2-4 every 10 mins, 30 mins, US$0.90, with both services arriving on Av 2 in the capital. To **Heredia** from 0400 until 2200, 30 mins, US$0.70. Buses to the Butterfly Farm at **La Guácima** marked 'La Guácima abajo' leave from Av 2 between Calle 8-10, US$0.40. 1 block south of the terminal buses depart for several small villages in the area including **Laguna de Fraijanes** and **Volcán Poás**.

Parque Nacional Volcán Poás p742

The volcano can be reached by car from **San José**. A taxi for 6 hrs with a side trip will cost about US$50-60. There is a daily excursion bus from the main square of Alajuela right up to the crater, leaving at 0915 (or before if full), connecting with 0830 bus from San José (from Av 2, Calle 12-14); be there early for a seat; although extra buses run if necessary, the area gets very crowded, US$4 return. The bus waits at the top with time to see everything (clouds permitting), returning 1430. For **Poasito** organize a taxi, hitch or take the 0600 or 1600 bus from Alajuela to **San Pedro de Poás**, hitch/ taxi to Poasito and stay overnight, hiking or hitching up the mountain next morning.

Sarchí and Naranjo *p744*

Express bus from **San José** to Sarchí, Calle 16, Av 1-3, 1215, 1730 and 1755, Mon-Fri, returning 0530, 0615, 1345, Sat 1200, 1½ hrs, US$1.80. **Tuan T2441-3781** buses every 30 mins, 0500-2200 from Alajuela bus station, 1½ hrs, US$1.30.

Transportes Naranjo, T2451-3655, run buses to/from **San José's** Coca Cola terminal every 40 mins, US$1.25. Buses connect other towns and villages in the area.

San Ramón and Los Angeles Cloud Forest Reserve *p744*

San Ramón is a transport hub. A regular service from **San José Empresarios Unidos**, T2222-0064, at Calle 16, Av 10-12, go to **Puntarenas**, 10 a day, every 45 mins or so, US$2.30. There is also a regular service to **Fortuna** and **Alajuela**. Buses run to surrounding villages and towns.

Palmares and Atenas *p745*

The library on the plaza in Atenas also serves as the bus office, **Cooptransatenas**, T2446-5767. Many daily buses to **San José**, either direct or via **Alajuela**, US$1.40.

Heredia *p745*

Buses from **San José**, from Av 2, Calle 12-14, every 10 mins daily, 0500-0015, then every 30 mins to 0400, 25-min journey, US$0.70. Return buses from Av 6, Calle 2-1.

Local buses leave from Av 8, Calle 2-4, by the market.

Volcán Barva *p746*

Accessible from **Heredia**, there is no route from the San José–Limón Hwy. Buses leave from the market at 0630, 1230 and 1600, returning at 0730, 1300, 1700. Arriving at

Porrosati (a town en route to Volcán Barva). Some continue as far as Sacramento, otherwise walk 6 km to park entrance, then 4 km to lagoon. Be careful if leaving a car; there are regular reports of theft from rental cars.

---

❶ Directory

Alajuela *p742*

Banks No shortage of banks, all within 3 blocks of each other and most with ATM, including **Banco Nacional**, Calle 2, Av Central-1, facing central park, **Scotiabank**, next door, **Banco Crédito Agrícola de Cártago**, Calle 2, Av Central-2, and **Banco de Santa Cruz**, Calle 2, Av 3, which is also the office of **Credomatic**. **Emergency** T911. **Internet** Southside of main plaza, Mon-Sun 0900-2200, US$0.60 per hr. Also with pool tables. **Interplanet**, across from La Agonía church on Av Central and Calle 9, daily 0830-2200. **Medical services** Hospital San Rafael, 200m southeast of the airport autopista intersection, T2436-1000, can help in a crisis. **Post** Corner of Av 5 and Calle 1, Mon-Fri 0730-1700, Sat mornings.

Sarchí and Naranjo *p744*

Banks Banco Nacional has branches in Sarchí Sur and Sarchí Norte, and on the north side of the plaza in Naranjo, with Visa and MasterCard ATM. **Post** Services are found in both villages.

Heredia *p745*

Language schools Centro Panamericano de Idiomas, San Joaquín de Flores, T2265-6306, www.cpi-edu.com. Accommodation with local families. **Intercultura Language and Cultural Center**, Heredia, T2260-8480, www.interculturacostarica.com. Small classes, also with a campus at Playa Samara.

Meseta Central East

The eastern Central Highlands offer relative quiet, despite being close to San José. The former capital and pilgrimage site of Cártago sits meekly at the bottom of the fuming Irazú volcano before the meseta falls away to the beautiful Orosí Valley. The thundering Río Reventazón leads the next step down the Atlantic slope, beginning its journey to the Caribbean, passing Turrialba, a good base for whitewater adventure. Meanwhile, the slopes of nearby Turrialba volcano hide the country's main archaeological site of Guayabo with good hiking opportunities to its summit. ▶▶ *For listings, see pages 755-757.*

Cártago and around → *For listings, see pages 755-757. Colour map 4, B3. Altitude: 1439 m.*

Cártago, at the foot of the Irazú Volcano and 22.5 km from San José on a toll road (US$0.75), is encircled by mountains. Founded in 1563, it was the capital of Costa Rica for almost 300 years until San José assumed the role in 1823. Since then the town has failed to grow significantly and remains small, though densely populated. Earthquakes in 1841 and 1910 destroyed many of the buildings and ash from Irazú engulfed the town in 1963. While colonial-style remnants exist in one or two buildings, the town feels as if it is still reeling from the impact of so much natural devastation and is keeping quiet, waiting for the next event.

The most important attraction in town, and the focal point for pilgrims from all over Central America, is the **Basílica de Nuestra Señora de Los Angeles**, the patroness of Costa Rica, on the eastern side of town. Rebuilt in 1926 in Byzantine style, it houses the diminutive **La Negrita**, an indigenous image of the Virgin under 15 cm high, worshipped for her miraculous healing powers. The basilica houses a collection of finely made silver and gold images, no larger than 3 cm high, of various parts of the human anatomy, presumably offered in the hope of being healed. The most important date in the pilgrims' calendar is 2 August, when the image of La Negrita is carried in procession to churches in Cártago with celebrations throughout Costa Rica.

Also worth seeing is **La Parroquia** (the old parish church), roughly 1 km west of the basilica, ruined by the 1910 earthquake and now converted into a delightful garden retreat with flowers, fish and hummingbirds.

Around Cártago

Aguas Calientes, 4 km southeast of Cártago and 90 m lower, has a warm-water *balneario* ideal for picnics. On the road to Paraíso, 8 km from Cártago, is an orchid garden, the **Jardín Botánico Lankester** ① *10 mins' walk from the main road, T2552-3247, daily 0830-1630, US$7.50*, run by the University of Costa Rica. The best displays are between February and April. While off the beaten track, the gardens are worth a visit. The Cártago–Paraíso bus departs every 30 minutes from the south side of central park in Cártago (15 minutes); ask the driver to let you out at Campo Ayala. Taxi from Cártago, US$5.

Volcán Irazú → *Colour map 4, B3. Altitude: 3432 m.*
① *US$10, 0800-1530 most of the year.*

Irazú's crater is an impressive half-mile cube dug out of the earth, surrounded by desolate grey sand, which looks like the surface of the moon. President Kennedy's visit in 1963 coincided with a major eruption and, in 1994 the north wall of the volcano was destroyed by another eruption that sent detritus down as far as the Río Sucio, within sight of the the San José–Limón Highway. The views are stupendous on a clear day and the main reason for the trip. But the clouds normally move in enveloping the lower peaks and slopes by 1300 (sometimes even by 0900 or 1000 between July and November), so get there as early as you can to have a greater chance of a clear view of the mountains and the sun shining on the clouds in the valleys below. There's little wildlife other than the ubiquitous Volcano Junco bird and the few plants which survive in the barren landscape, but ongoing colonization is attracting more birds.

It's definitely worth the trip and an early start. As one traveller wrote: "In the afternoon the mountain top is buried in fog and mist or drizzle, but the ride up in the mist can be magical, for the mountainside is half displaced in time. There are new jeeps and tractors, but the herds of cattle are small, the fields are quilt-work, handcarts and ox-carts are to be seen under the fretworked porches of well-kept frame houses. The land is fertile, the pace is slow, the air is clean. It is a very attractive mixture of old and new. Irazú is a strange mountain, well worth the ride up."

Orosí Valley

Further east from Cártago a trip round the Orosí Valley makes a beautiful circular trip, or a fine place to hang out for a while in a valley that is often overlooked as the crowds rush to the more popular spots on the coast. The centrepiece of the valley is the artificial Lake Cachí used for hydroelectric generation. Heading round the lake counter-clockwise, the road passes through Orosí, clips the edge of Parque Nacional Tapantí, continuing to the Cachí Dam and completes the circuit passing through Ujarrás. Along the way there are several miradors which offer excellent views of the Reventazón Valley. For transport, see each destination. Day trips can be easily arranged from San José.

In **Orosí** there is an 18th-century **mission** ⓘ *closed Mon*, with colonial treasures, and just outside two **balnearios** ⓘ *US$2.50*, with restaurants serving good meals at fair prices. It's a good place to hang out, take some low-key language classes, mixed with mountain biking and trips to the national park and other sites of interest.

Parque Nacional Tapantí-Macizo de la Muerte
ⓘ *Daily 0700-1700, US$10.*

Twelve kilometres beyond Orosí is the Parque Nacional Tapantí-Macizo de la Muerte, one of the wettest parts of the country (some parts reportedly receiving as much as 8 m of rain a year). From June to November/December it rains every afternoon. Approached from Orosí, and just 30 km from Cártago, the national park is suprisingly easy to reach and packs in the interest.

Covering 58,000 ha, Tapantí-Macizo includes the former Tapantí National Park and much of the Río Macho Forest Reserve. The park protects the Río Orosí basin which feeds the Cachí Dam hydro power plant. Strategically, the southern boundary of the park joins with Chirripó National Park, extending the continuous protected area that makes up La Amistad Biosphere Reserve. The park incorporates a wide range of life zones with altitudes rising from 1220 m to over 3000 m at the border with Chirripó. The diverse altitudes and relative seclusion of the park has created an impressive variety of species – 260 bird species, 45 mammals, lizards, snakes – a list which is currently incomplete due to the relatively recent creation of the park. There are picnic areas, a nature centre with slide shows (ask to see them) and good swimming in the dry season (November-June), and trout fishing season (1 April-31 October).

Cachí

Continue around the lake to Cachí and the nearby **Casa del Soñador** (Dreamer's House) which sells wood carvings from the sculpture school of the late Macedonio Quesada. The road crosses the dam wall and follows the north shore to Ujarrás, then back to Cártago. The **Charrarra tourist complex** ① *30-mins' walk from Ujarrás*, has a good campsite, restaurant, pool, boat rides on the lake and walks. It can be reached by direct bus on Sunday. Buses leave from Cártago one block north of the Cártago ruins.

Ujarrás

Ujarrás (ruins of a colonial church and village) is 6.5 km east of Paraíso, on the shores of the artificial Lago Cachí. There is a bus every 1½ hours from Paraíso that continues to Cachí. Legend has it that in 1666 English pirates, including the youthful Henry Morgan, were seen off by the citizens of Ujarrás aided by the Virgin. The event is now celebrated annually in mid-March when the saint is carried in procession from Paraíso to the ruined church.

Turrialba and around → *For listings, see pages 755-757. Colour map 4, B3. Altitude: 646 m.*

Turrialba (62 km from San José) connects the Central Valley highlands and Caribbean lowlands, and was once a stopping point on the old Atlantic railway between Cártago and Puerto Limón. The railway ran down to Limón on a narrow ledge poised between mountains on the left, and the river to the right, but no longer operates. The **Centro Agronómico Tropical de Investigación y Enseñanza (CATIE)** ① *about 4 km southeast of Turrialba, T2558-2000 ext 2275, www.catie.ac.cr, botanical garden open daily 0700-1600, T2556-2700, US$6*, covers more than 800 ha of this ecologically diverse zone (with many fine coffee farms). It has one of the largest tropical fruit collections in the world and houses an important library on tropical agriculture; visitors and students are welcome for research or birdwatching. Past CATIE on the south side of the river, a large sugar mill makes for a conspicuous landmark in Atirro, the centre for macadamia nuts. Nearby, the 256-ha **Lake Angostura** has now flooded some of the whitewaters of the Río Reventazón.

Around Turrialba

Many whitewater rafting companies operate out of Turrialba, with trips to the **Río Reventazón** and **Río Pacuare**. The rafting is excellent; the Pascua section of the Reventazón can be Grade V at rainy times. The Pacuare is absolutely perfect with divine scenery. By contacting the guides in Turrialba you can save about 30% on a trip booked in San José, provided they are not already contracted.

Volcán Turrialba (3329 m) may be visited from Cártago by a bus from Calle 4 y Avenida 6 to the village of San Gerardo. From Turrialba take a bus to Santa Cruz. From both, an unpaved road meets at **Finca La Central**, on the saddle between Irazú and Turrialba.

Monumento Nacional Guayabo

① *T2559-1220, Tue-Sun 0800-1530, US$10, local guides available, water, toilets, no food.*

About 19 km north of Turrialba, near Guayabo, is a 3000-year-old ceremonial centre excavated with paved streets and stone-lined water channels. The archaeological site, 232 ha and 4 km from the town of Guayabo, is now a national monument, and dates from the period 1000 BC-AD 1400. There are excellent walks in the park, where plenty of birds and wildlife can be seen. Worth a trip to see Costa Rica's most developed ancient archaeological site but small in comparison to the great sites of the Maya. There is also a camping area.

For Sleeping and Eating price codes and other relevant information, see Essentials pages 31-33.

● Sleeping

Cártago *p752*
B-C Los Angeles Lodge B&B, near the Basílica at Av 4, Calle 14-16, T2591-4169. Clean, nice rooms, restaurant.
E Dinastia, Calle 3, Av 6-8, close to the old railway station, at the Las Ruinas end of town, T2551-7057. Slightly more expensive with private bath. The rooms are small although better with a window. Safe hotel but in lively area north of the central market. Credit cards accepted.

Volcán Irazú *p752*
E Hotel Gestoria Irazú, on the slopes of Irazú on the way up, in San Juan de Chicúa, T2253-0827. Simple rooms with private bath, hot water and extra blankets to get you through the cold winter nights.

Orosí Valley *p753*
B Orosí Lodge, T2533-3578, www.orosi lodge.com. 6 rooms and a house with balcony overlooking the valley towards Volcán Irazú each with private bath, hot water and kitchenette. Just about everything you could want; divine home-baked cookies, mountain bikes, kayaks and horses for rent, and an internet service. Credit cards accepted. Excellent value.
C Hotel Reventazón, T2533-3838, hotelreventazon@gmail.com. Rather stark and characterless rooms, with telephone, TV, fridge, internet. Clean and friendly service, good local knowledge. Credit cards accepted.
C-G Montaña Linda, T2533-3640, www.montanalinda.com. A classic and well-run backpackers' place, with a range of options. Dormitory rooms, camping, and B&B service if you just can't get out of bed! There is also a language school, with package deals for lodgers. Great spot with a very friendly, knowledgeable team.

E Río Palomo, in Palomo, just south of Orosí, T2533-3128. Cabins, pool, laundry facilities, good restaurant.

Parque Nacional Tapantí-Macizo de la Muerte *p753*
B Monte Sky Mountain Retreat, near Tapantí, T2228-0010. Cabins with shared bath, cold water, includes meals, hiking trails through forest. Camping platforms also available. In addition to the price there is a US$8 per person entrance fee to the 300-ha private reserve.
C Kiri Lodge, 1.5 km from the park entrance, T2533-2272, www.kirilodge.net. Excellent lodging and food, breakfast included. Peaceful, trout fishing, very friendly, good trails on 50-ha property.

Camping
No camping is allowed at the park. See **Monte Sky Mountain Retreat**, above.

Turrialba *p754*
AL-A Wagelia, Av 4, entrance to Turrialba, T2556-1566, www.hotelwageliaturrialba.com. 18 rooms, bath, some a/c, restaurant. Overpriced, but not much else to choose from at this level.
C-D Interamericano, facing the old railway station on Av 1, T2556-0142, www.hotel interamericano.com. Price per person. Very friendly place, family-run, popular with kayakers. Clean, private or shared bath. Safe for motorbikes. Internet service, bar and communal area with TV and books.
D Alcázar, Calle 3, Av 2-4, 25 m north of Banco Norte. Small terrace upstairs, each room has cable TV, telephone, fan and a private bath with hot water. Small, cheap bar/restaurant downstairs with frightening colour schemes.
D-E Central, next to Interamericano, T2556-0170. Price per person, with bath, restaurant, basic.
E Hotel Turrialba, Av 2, Calle 2-4, T2556-6654. Clean simple rooms with private bath,

hot water and TV. There are also a couple of pool tables and drinks for sale.

F Laroche, north of Parque Central on Calle 1. Simple and basic rooms but friendly with comfortable beds. Small bar downstairs.

G Whittingham, Calle 4, Av 0-2, T2550-8927. Has 7 fairly dark but OK rooms, some with private bath – an option if other places are full.

Around Turrialba *p754*

LL-L Casa Turire, 14 km southeast of Turrialba, follow the signposts, T2531-1111, www.hotelcasaturire.com. Overlooking Lake Angostura, 12 luxury rooms with bath, 4 suites, cable TV, phone, restaurant, pool, library, games room, in the middle of a 1620-ha sugar, coffee and macadamia nut plantation. Virgin rainforest nearby, trails, horses, bike rental, excursions.

A-B Turrialtico, on road to Siquirres, T2538-1111, www.turrialtico.com. On top of hill with extensive views. Rooms are clean with private bath, comfortable, friendly. Going northeast from Turrialba, the main road follows the Río Reventazón down to Siquirres (see page 835).

B Albergue Mirador Pochotel, Pavones, T2538-1010. 10 basic cabins, restaurant, a popular spot.

F San Agustín, Vereh, some 25 km southeast of Turrialba (take bus via Jicotea). Truly isolated for a real rural Costa Rica experience. Candlelight camping, river bathing, hiking and horse riding in surrounding area – basic, and a very pure rainforest experience.

Monumento Nacional Guayabo *p754*

E Albergue y Restaurant La Calzada, T2559-0023. Call in advance to make a reservation and check they're open.

🍴 Eating

Cártago *p752*

⊺ **Auto 88**, east of public market. Cafetería-style, with beer-drinking room adjoining dining room.

⊺ **Soda Apollo**, northwest corner of parque, opposite **La Parroquia**. 24-hr snack option.

Volcán Irazú *p752*

⊺⊺-⊺ **Restaurante Linda Vista**. Spectacular views, as you'd expect from Costa Rica's highest restaurant, serving good food and drinks. But most people stop to post, stick, pin or glue a business card, or some other personal item, to the wall.

Turrialba *p754*

⊺⊺-⊺ **Pizzería Julián**, on the square. Popular.

⊺ **La Garza**, main square. Cheap, local good food.

⊺ **Nuevo Hong Kong**, just east of the main square. Good, reasonable prices.

⊺ **Soda Burbuja**, a block south of square on Calle Central. Local dishes, excellent portions, very good value.

🔺 Activities and tours

Cártago *p752*

Mercatur, next to Fuji at Av 2, Calle 4-6, provides local tourist information.

Around Turrialba *p754*

See also the companies in San José (eg **Ríos Tropicales**, page 735).

Serendipity Adventures, T2558-1000, www.serendipityadventures.com. Canyoning rappelling and hot-air ballooning. Recommended.

Tico's River Adventures, T2556-1231, www.ticoriver.com. With recommended local guides.

⊖ Transport

Cártago *p752*

Bus To **San José** every 10 mins from Av 4, Calle 2-4. Arrives and departs San José from Calle 5, Av 18-20 for the 45-min journey, US$0.90. After 2030 buses leave from Gran Hotel Costa Rica, Av 2, Calle 3-5. **Orosí/Río Macho**, for **Parque Nacional Tapantí** every 30 mins from Calle 6, Av 1-3, 35-55 mins, US$0.95. **Turrialba**, every hour from Av 3,

Calle 8-10, 1 hr direct, US$1.40, 1 hr 20 mins *colectivo*. **Cachí**, via **Ujarrá** and **Paraíso** from Calle 6, Av 1-3, every 1½ hrs, 1 hr 20 mins. **Paraíso**, every 5 mins from Av 5, Calle 4-6. **Aguacalientes**, every 15 mins from Calle 1, Av 3-5. **Tierra Blancas** for Irazú, every 30 mins from Calle 4, Av 6-8, US$2.

Closest bus for **Irazú** rides to San Juan de Chichua, still some 12 km from the summit. The bus leaves Cártago from north of the central market, Av 6, Calle 1-3, at 1730, returning at 0500 the next day, so you have to spend at least 2 nights on the volcano or in a hotel if you can't get a ride. To visit **Volcán Turrialba** take a bus from Calle 4 y Av 6 to the village of San Gerardo.

Volcán Irazú *p752*
Bus It is possible to get a bus from Cártago to Tierra Blanca (US$0.33) or San Juan de Chicúa (which has 1 hotel) and hitch a ride in a pickup truck. Or you can take a Cártago–Sanatorio bus. Ask the driver to drop you at the crossroads outside Tierra Blanca. From there you walk 16 km to the summit. If you're looking for a day trip from San José, a yellow 'school' express bus (Buses Metropoli SA, T2530-1064), runs from Gran Hotel Costa Rica, **San José**, daily 0800. It stops at Cártago ruins 0830 to pick up more passengers, returns 1230 with lunch stop at Restaurant Linda Vista, US$3.90.

Taxi From **Cártago** is US$32 return. A taxi tour from **Orosí** costs US$10 per person, minimum 3 people, and stops at various places on the return journey, eg Cachí dam and Ujarrás ruins. Since it can be difficult to find a decent hotel in Cártago, it may be easier to take a guided tour leaving from **San José**, about US$44, 5½ hrs includes lunch, transport from San José. If driving from San José, take the turn-off at the Ferretería San Nicolás in Taras, which goes directly to Irazú, avoiding Cártago.

Orosí Valley *p753*
Bus From **Cártago** to Orosí/Río Macho from Calle 6, Av 1-3, every 30 mins, journey time of 35-55 mins, US$0.90.

Parque Nacional Tapantí-Macizo de la Muerte *p753*
Bus The 0600 bus from Cártago to Orosí gets to Puricil by 0700, then walk (5 km), or take any other Cártago–Orosí bus to Río Macho and walk 9 km to the refuge. Alternatively take a taxi from **Orosí** (US$7 round trip, up to 6 passengers), or **San José**, US$50.

Turrialba *p754*
Bus From **San José** every hour 0530-2200 from Terminal Turrialba, Calle 13, Av 6-8, 1½ hrs, US$2.40 from **Cártago**, 1 hr, US$1.40, runs until about 2200. Service to **Siquirres**, for connections to Caribbean lowlands, hourly, 40 mins, US$2.

Monumento Nacional Guayabo *p754*
Bus From **Turrialba**, there are buses at 1100 (returning 1250) and 1710 (returning 1750), and on Sun at 0900, return 1700 (check times, if you miss it is quite difficult to hitch as there is little traffic), US$0.95 to Guayabo. Several daily buses pass the turn-off to Guayabo; the town is a 2-hr walk uphill (taxi US$10, easy to hitch back). **San José** tour operators offer day trips to Guayabo for about US$65 per person (minimum 4 people), cheaper from Turrialba.

Directory

Cártago *p752*
Banks Most banks have ATMs. Banco de Costa Rica, Av 4, Calle 5-7. Banco Scotiabank, Park Central at Av 2, Calle 2. Banco Nacional, Av 2, Calle 1-3. **Emergencies** Call T911. **Internet** Café Línea, Av 4, Calle 6-8, the only internet place in town, looks decidedly temporary. **Medical services** Dr Max Peralta, entrance on Calle 3, Av 7. The pharmacy is along Av 4 between Calle 1-6.

Orosí Valley *p753*
Language schools Montaña Linda Language School, T2533-3640, see Sleeping. Uses local teachers with a homestay option if you want total submersion. Recommended.

Northern Costa Rica

The Cordillera de Tilarán and the Cordillera de Guanacaste stretch to the Nicaragua border. Tucked in the eastern foothills is the vast artificial Lago Arenal, resting calmly beneath the highly active Volcán Arenal. A number of quieter spots can be found in the area with fine opportunities for fishing and wildlife spotting, while the more active can go rafting, windsurfing, horse riding and trekking. ➤➤ *For listings, see pages 762-767.*

San Carlos and around → *Colour map 4, B3.*

Also known as **Ciudad Quesada**, San Carlos is the main town of the northern lowland cattle and farming region and is a hub of communications. True to form, the town has a frontier feel with an air of bravado and a pinch of indifference. Situated on the downside of the northern slopes of the central highlands mountain region, the temperature rises and the speed of life slows down. In a town without major sights, the huge church overlooking the main plaza stands out. The cavernous interior is matched for style by modern stained-glass windows and an equally massive sculpture of Christ above the altar. As a regional centre San Carlos is served by frequent buses from San José, and has good connections to La Fortuna and Los Chiles. The bus terminal, about 1 km north of town, is close to a shopping centre and cinema. From San Carlos a paved road runs northwest to **Florencia** (service station). At Platanar de San Carlos, there are a couple of sleeping options, see page 762.

Los Chiles and Refugio Natural de Vida Silvestre Caño Negro → *Colour map 4, B3.*

ⓘ *Caño Negro park administration, T2471-1309, for information and reservations for food and lodging; US$10 entrance to the park.*

Heading through the northern lowlands, a good road carves through rich red laterite soils in an almost straight line for 74 km through flat land where the shiny leaves of orange and citrus fruit plantations have replaced forest. Just short of the Nicaraguan border is Los Chiles, where boat trips head through some remaining dense, tropical vegetation into the 10,171-ha Caño Negro Natural Wildlife Refuge and Caño Negro Lake, spanning about 800-ha in the rainy season. Birdwatchers flock to the northern wetlands to see the amazing variety of birdlife which feasts at the seasonal lake created by the flood waters of the Río Frío. The lake slowly shrinks in the dry season (January to April). The variety of habitats in the refuge makes a rewarding trip for anyone interested in seeing alligators, turtles and monkeys. Fishing trips for snook and tarpon are easily arranged.

Los Chiles is a small town on the banks of the Río Frío, a few hundred metres west of Highway 35. The central plaza doubles as a football pitch, and most places of interest are within a block or two. The days pass slowly as children chuck themselves off the dockside in the heat of the afternoon sun. Ask about guides at **Restaurant Los Petates**, **Restaurant El Parque** or **Rancho Eco-Directa**. A three-hour tour with Esteban, Oscar Rojas (T2471-1090) and Enrique, who have all been recommended, costs about US$60. Alternatively, **Aventuras Arenal in Fortuna** run trips to Caño Negro (see below), approximately US$63. It's cheaper to get a boat from **Los Chiles** to the park (US$60 for a boat, up to four people) rather than taking a tour from elsewhere (eg Fortuna) and convenient if you are going on to Nicaragua, but there are not always boats available nor sufficient numbers to fill one.

Fishing trips are likely to be beyond the budgets of many, but then what price do you put on catching a 2-m-long tarpon. A full day's fishing on the Río Frío, Río San Juan or

Lago de Nicaragua (boat, rods and drinks included) can range from US$95 to US$500 with **No Frills Fishing Adventures** (see page 762), depending on the boat and destination.

Fortuna → *Colour map 4, B3. Altitude: 254 m.*

The small town of Fortuna is an ideal base for exploring the Arenal region with the ominous silhouette of the active Volcán Arenal looming above the town. Reached on a paved road running west from San Carlos/Ciudad Quesada or along the northern shore of Lake Arenal from Tilaran, it's worth a few days of your travels. Once a quiet town that shuddered in the shadow of the volcano's power, it has grown rapidly to accommodate the steady increase in visitors keen to see the active volcano and an ever-increasing range of activities.

Getting there Transport between Fortuna and Santa Elena is time consuming by bus as it requires traveling to Tilarán for a connecting bus on the bumpy road up to Santa Elena. Alteratives are to get a jeep, boat, and jeep leaving Fortuna at 0830 and 1230, US$25, or horse riding to Monteverde (US$85). It is also becoming possible to get transfers to Tortuguero – ask locally for details.

Around Fortuna

About 6 km south of Fortuna are the impressive **Río Fortuna Waterfalls** ① *US$7, drinks available at the entrance*, plunging 70 m into the cloud of swirling mist and spray. It's a pleasant walk down the road for a couple of kilometres before turning off to head uphill through yucca and papaya plantations. From the entrance, a steep and slippery path leads to the falls, so take shoes with a good tread. Bathing is possible, so take swimming clothes, but it's safer 50 m downstream. If you don't want to walk, there are several options. You can drive, but 4WD is necessary. Bicycle hire (US$3 per hour, US$15 per day) is one option and hard work, or you can hire a horse for the day at around US$50. Two to three hours' climb above the falls is the crater lake of Cerro Chato. The top (1100 m) is

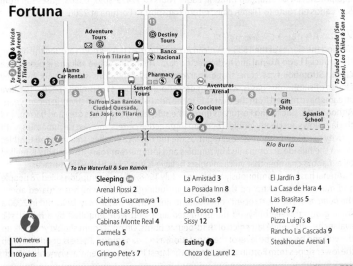

Fortuna

Sleeping 🛏	La Amistad 3	El Jardín 3
Arenal Rossi 2	La Posada Inn 8	La Casa de Hara 4
Cabinas Guacamaya 1	Las Colinas 9	Las Brasitas 5
Cabinas Las Flores 10	San Bosco 11	Nene's 7
Cabinas Monte Real 4	Sissy 12	Pizza Luigi's 8
Carmela 5		Rancho La Cascada 9
Fortuna 6	**Eating 🍴**	Steakhouse Arenal 1
Gringo Pete's 7	Choza de Laurel 2	

reached through mixed tropical/cloud forest, with a good view (if you're lucky) but beware of snakes on the path. Organized trips from Fortuna US$75.

Safari river floats down the Río Peñas Blancas (US$49) and **whitewater rafting**, best in the wet season (from US$85 for a one-day trip including all food and transport), are available through several tour operators. **Horse riding** through the forest to Monteverde costs around US$85 per person for the day trip. Luggage is taken on pack animals or by vehicles. Some operators seem to change the route once underway due to some 'unforeseen problem', so agree the route and try to arrange compensation if there are major changes. Due to competition for business, many horses are overworked on this route. Although difficult when on a budget, try not to bargain down the price, and do ask to see the horses before beginning the journey. The journey is also possible via jeep-boat-jeep (US$25-30).

A small **snake farm** ① *a few kilometres west of Fortuna, US$2*, with 40 specimens is a good opportunity to get up close and personal with these rather cool creatures.

Almost 5 km north of Fortuna is the **Baldi Thermae complex** ① *T2479-9651, daily 1000-2200, US$26*, with four thermal pools ranging from 37° up to 63°C – the limits of endurance without being poached. It's a great experience and there are poolside drinks available. A taxi from town costs US$4, a bus is US$1.

Ten kilometres northwest of Fortuna is **Balneario Tabacón** ① *T2460-2020, daily 1000-2200, day guests welcome, entry from US$75*, a kitsch complex of thermal pools, waterfalls and (for residents) beauty treatments, with three bars and a restaurant. The water is hot and stimulating; there are a pools at descending heights and temperatures as well as water slides and a waterfall to sit under. The food is good and the fruit drinks thirst quenching. The resort (L) is popular with evening coach tours from San José. Taxi from Fortuna to Tabacón US$6. Cheaper are the hot waters about 4 km further along the road at **Quebrada Cedeña**, which are clean and safe. There is no sign but look for four parked cars.

Also near Fortuna are the limestone **Cavernas del Venado**. Tours from Fortuna with all equipment can be arranged through **Eagle Tours** ① *T2479-9091, US$65*. Buses run from San Carlos en route to Tilarán daily; return transport to Fortuna at 2200.

Volcán Arenal → *Colour map 4, B3.*

Skirting the slopes of the 1633-m Volcán Arenal, the road travels north around the base to the artificial **Lago Arenal** and hydroelectric dam. The highly active volcano is beautiful, a classic Stromboli-type cone shape characterized by explosions sending out hot grey clouds of sulphurous gases, which can descend the slopes at alarming speeds. The lava streams have moved from the west side to the northeast following activity in recent years. Although the side facing Fortuna is green, the side facing the lake is grey and barren, and the lava flows are clearly visible. There are three active craters and several fumaroles, with activity particularly impressive at night, as the red hot lava crashes, smashes and tumbles down the hillside accompanied by rumbles and intermittent roars. The activity is fuelled by a magma chamber that vulcanologists believe is just 5 km below the surface.

Arenal has been continuously active since July 1968, when an eruption killed 78 people and more or less destroyed three villages including Tabacón, which is situated above the *balneario*. The most recent continuous major activity was in May 1998, but in 2000 a small group travelled beyond the permitted area, and were engulfed by a pyroclastic avalanche – the guide later died of third-degree burns. On no account should you walk up the volcano beyond the level of the vegetation, as it's dangerous. There is good hiking on the lower slopes from Fortuna. You can see the latest images of Arenal at www.arenal.net.

If you are visiting between May and December you may not see much as the volcano is usually obscured by clouds and rain and there can be bad weather for weeks on end. Clouds and rain are common in the afternoons all year round, but the clouds do break and you may be lucky. If you can hire a taxi for a trip at about 0400-0500, and you can get up, the sky is often clearer.

To the east, the vast Lago Arenal reflects the moods of the volcano perfectly: smooth and calm from a distance, but whipped up to a waved frenzy by strong easterlies which are squeezed by the hills on either side. The surrounding area offers a multitude of opportunities for hiking, mountain biking, windsurfing and many other activities. There is also access to Santa Elena and Monteverde on foot or horseback.

Park information Much of the area surrounding the volcano is a national park which most people visit as part of a tour. The most common entrance is through **Hotel Los Lagos**, see page 764), which offers night tours at 1700 for hotel guests, if the sky is clear. **Aventuras Arenal** can provide dependable advice.

Tour operators offer trips to view the volcano at night followed by a visit to the thermal baths; a typical four-hour tour, costing US$59 per person, leaves Fortuna at about 1530 and returns by 1930. Make sure the entry fee to the baths is included.

You can also visit the park on your own. The entrance is on the western flank of the volcano, on the other side to Fortuna, 2 km down a bumpy road signposted to Arenal Observatory Lodge. Four interesting trails, taking up to 1½ hours each, lead through the national park going through a mixture of terrains, that flourish in the microclimate of heavy rainfall bought on by the volcano.

North to Upala

A quiet route north leads from Fortuna to **San Rafael de Guatuso**. There is a 'voluntary' toll of US$1 between Jicarito and San Rafael for reconstruction work on this road. You can come back to the lake either by turning off before San Rafael through **Venado** (where there are caves), or from San Rafael itself, where there are a couple of basic hotels. If you continue along the road from San Rafael northwest towards the Nicaraguan border you come to **Upala** and a poor road east to **Caño Negro**. There is a direct bus from San José to Upala, T2221-3318 (from Avenida 3-5, Calle 10 at 1000 and 1700, four hours).

Around Lago Arenal

A mostly paved road twists and winds round the northern shore of Lake Arenal, leading to Tilarán via Nuevo Arenal. Whether travelling by bus or car, you can get from Fortuna to Monteverde via Tilarán in a day, but set out early to make your connection with the 1230 bus in Tilarán or to avoid driving after dark. The lakeside road has improved greatly in recent years, but some sections are still unpaved. The main hazard is the winding road and some seriously pot-holed sections.

There is plenty of good accommodation around the lake shore, much of it in the higher price brackets. With only a couple of buses a day, and limited traffic, getting off the bus for a look will almost certainly delay you for a day.

If you do stop, an excellent café for a meal and drink with great views over the lake is **Toad Hall** ① *T2692-8020*, towards the northeastern end, which has an excellent souvenir shop with a good mix of Costa Rican crafts, some modern, some traditional, most desirable.

(**Nuevo**) **Arenal** is a small town (population 2500) with not much to see. It's new, because it moved from its original location which now lies deep below the surface of the lake.

Continuing west towards Tilarán, the western side of the lake is popular with **windsurfers** throughout the year, and between December and April the conditions are world class. A batch of hotels cater for windsurfers of all levels; there are many other options in the area so take your pick if you want to stop.

Tilarán → *Colour map 4, B2.*

Tilarán would not appear on the list of destinations for travellers were it not for its role as a small regional transport hub for people journeying between Fortuna, Santa Elena/Monteverde and Cañas on the Pan-American Highway. In town there is pretty much nothing to do, and with luck, the connecting buses will be timed perfectly to avoid you having to wait too long. But if you do, there are several places to catch a bite to eat, and several good places to stay if you need a bed for the night.

◉ Northern Costa Rica listings

For Sleeping and Eating price codes and other relevant information, see Essentials pages 31-33.

● Sleeping

San Carlos and around *p758*

A Hotel La Garza, Platanar de San Carlos, 8 km from Florencia, T2475-5222, www.hotel lagarza.com. 12 charming bungalows with bath and fan, overlooking river. Idyllic spot with good views of Arenal. Guided tours,boat trips, fishing, 230 ha of forest and cattle ranch.
A Tilajari Resort Hotel, Muelle San Carlos, 13 km north of Platanar de San Carlos, T2462-1212, www.tilajari.com. Luxury rooms, and suites, a/c, private bath, tennis courts, 2 pools, sauna, bar, restaurant, horses and excursions available. Popular with luxury groups.
C La Central, on west side of park, San Carlos, T2460-0301, www.hotellacentral.net. Private bath, hot water, fan, TV and phone in room.
D Don Goyo, San Carlos, T2460-1780. 20 clean, well-lit rooms, with private bath rooms, fans, cable TV – best value in town.
E Hotel del Valle, Av 3, Calle 0-2, San Carlos, T2460-0718. Nothing special but friendly and secure, a good deal at this price.
E-F El Retiro, on the north side of the park, San Carlos, T2460-0463. Bath, hot water, clean and comfortable, popular with local business people.
E-F Fernando, Av 1 Calle 2-4, around corner from **Banco Popular**, T2460-3314. Probably

the best of several basic *pensiones* if you can get one of the new rooms.
F Cabinas Kimbara, on the main road 800 m north of Muelle gas station, T2469-9100. Basic rooms, private bath, fan, includes taxes, pool.

Los Chiles *p758*

B Rancho Tulipan, 1 block west of the Parque Central opposite the immigration offices, T2471-1414, www.rancho tulipan.com. Good restaurant, 10 clean well-appointed rooms with a/c, TV, bath and hot water, breakfast and taxes included. Can arrange a wide variety of tours in the area including river safaris and fishing trips. The manager Carlos Sequera is useful for information on travelling to Nicaragua.
D Hotel Carolina, close to main highway, T2471-1151. Clean and well maintained – the best of the budgets. Accommodation ranges from small, fairly dark rooms with shared bath to a/c cabins with TV.
E No Frills Fishing Lodge, on the main highway just before town, T2471-1410. Set on a 40-ha property, clean modern rooms, restaurant and bar, 8 boats for fishing expeditions (see page 759).
E-F Cabinas Jabirú, 100 m from the bus stop, a few blocks from the central park, T2471-1496. Cheaper price for Youth Hostel members. Good, but simple rooms, with private bathrooms, fan, some with TV and parking. Postal service, fax and laundry and a

range of interesting tours. Cheapest to Caño Negro (US$20 per person, minimum 3) and to El Castillo de la Concepción in Nicaragua. **G Onassis**, southwest corner of main plaza, T2471-1447. Your best bet of the strip facing the football pitch. Basic rooms, clean, shared bath, meals upon request.

Fortuna *p759, map p759*

As one of the most popular destinations for all visitors to Costa Rica, accommodation tends to be quite pricey in high season. Conversely, generous discounts in the green/low season are common.
AL-A Arenal Country Inn, south of town, T2479-9670, www.arenalcountryinn.com. A former working hacienda with 20 large, fully equipped *cabinas* set in pleasant tropical gardens. After eating in the dining room – once a holding pen – you can rest by the pool before heading out to explore.
AL-A Las Cabañitas, 1.5 km east of town, beyond **Villa Fortuna**, T2479-9400. 43 cabins with private baths, a couple of pools, observatory for viewing Arenal volcano, restaurant. Recommended.
A Fortuna, 1 block southeast of the central park, T2479-9197. One of the newest places in town, with 44 rooms (12 wheelchair accessible), all fully accessible. Price includes breakfast.
A-B Albergue Ecoturístico La Catarata, 2 km from town, rough road, T2479-9522, www.cataratalodge.com. Price per person. Reservations essential for the 21 rooms and cabins in this cooperative with organic garden, home-made soaps and shampoos, good fresh food, butterfly farm, taxi US$2, hot water, laundry, all meals. Run by community association and supported by WWF Canada and CIDA Canada.
A-B Cabinas Monte Real, 1 block from the main plaza, T2479-9357, www.montereal hotel.com. Close to the centre, quiet and friendly, big rooms with private bath and hot water, swimming pool, internet, next to the river and also close to centre. Parking.

A-B San Bosco, town centre, T2479-9050, www.arenal-volcano.com. All rooms with private bath, quiet, signs on main road, clean, friendly, nice gardens with terrace, pool and view of the volcano, excellent service and attention to detail, slightly less without a/c.
B Hotel Arenal Rossi, T2479-9023, www.hotelarenalrossi.com. 1 km west, towards the volcano, with breakfast, friendly owner, hot water, fan, watch the volcano from the garden, horses for rent, good value.
B Hotel Carmela, on the south side of the church, www.hotelarenalcarmela.com. 26 rooms with private bath, floor and ceiling fans, some with fridge. Very central, hot showers, can arrange tours. Apartment sleeping 5 available (**E** per person).
B-C Las Colinas, southeast of the central park, T2479-9305, www.lascolinasarenal.com 20 tidy rooms, with private bathroom, some with incredible views. Friendly management, good discounts in the low season. Internet access with Wi-Fi. Recommended.
B-F Arenal Backpacker's Resort, T2479-7000, www.arenalbackpackersresort.com. Good hostel a short distance north out of town. Dorm and private rooms. Great spot with a pool in the garden with view of Arenal for relaxing when you want to relax.
C Cabinas Guacamaya, town centre, T2479-9393. 8 good-sized rooms sleeping 3 or 4, all with private bath and hot water, fridge and a/c. Clean and tidy, with plenty of parking.
C Cabinas Las Flores, west of town, 2 km on road towards the volcano, T2479-9307. Clean, basic, but a little overpriced, restaurant.
C-D Hotel Villa Fortuna, 500 m south of the bridge, 1 km east from the central plaza, T2479-9139. Has 12 bright and tidy cabins, with neat bathrooms, fans or a/c, nice pool and simple gardens.
D Hotel La Amistad, central, www.hotel laamistadarenal.com, T2479-9364. Clean, friendly, hot water, firm beds.
E La Posada Inn, a couple of blocks east of the Parque Central, T2479-9793, laposadainn@yahoo.com. Price per person. 8 simple, but spotless rooms, bath with hot

water, fans but mosquitoes reported. Small communal area out front, communal kitchen and the friendly owner Thadeo is very helpful. **E Sissy**, office is 100 m south and 100 m west of church, T2479-9256. Quiet spot beside the river, basic rooms with private bathroom; others have shared bath, and there's access to a kitchen and camping spaces (US$3 per person); simple but friendly. Recommended. **G Gringo Pete's**, east end of town, T2479-8521, gringopetes2003@yahoo.com. Great place, dormitory and private rooms, clean and tidy. Kitchen facilities and communal area for relaxing. Good notice board and tours arranged. Recommended. Another, bigger and better **Gringo Pete's** opening across town soon, expected to be **D-E**.

Volcán Arenal p760

Fortuna is the easiest place to stay if you don't have your own transport, but the whole area from Fortuna all along the shores of the lake is littered with hotels and eating options. Hotels on the southern side of the lake are slightly cut off but have fantastic views.
LL-AL Montaña de Fuego, T2479-1220, www.montanadefuego.com. 66 bungalows and rooms, with the stylish (and pricey) **Acuarelas** restaurant, canopy tour.
L-AL Los Lagos, T2479-1000, www.hotellos lagos.com. 94 comfortable cabin rooms sleeping up to 4, day visits US$20, excellent food and spectacular views of the volcano over the lake, good facilities and small café. New spa, canopy tour and frog farm. There are 3 marked footpaths towards the lava fields and lakes through the forest.
L-AL Arenal Paraíso Resort & Spa, 7.5 km from Fortuna, T2479-1100, www.arenalparaiso.com. 124 rooms, good views of the volcano.
L-A Arenal Observatory Lodge, north-western side of the volcano, 4 km after El Tabacón, a turn towards the lake down a (signposted) gravel road, T2290-7011, www.arenalobservatorylodge.com. 4WD recommended along this 9-km stretch (taxi-jeep from Fortuna, US$30). Set up in 1973, the

observatory was purely a research station but it now has 42 rooms varying from cabins with bunk beds and bath, to newer rooms with queen-size beds. There are stunning views of the volcano (frighteningly close), Lake Arenal, and across the valley of Río Agua Caliente. The lava flows on the other side of the volcano, but the trails are beautiful and the service excellent.
AL Volcano Lodge, 6 km from Fortuna, T2460-6080, www.volcanolodge.com. 65 rooms with open-air restaurant good for viewing the volcano.
AL-A Arenal Vista Lodge, T2692-2079. Has 25 rooms with bath, arranges boat trips, riding and hiking, close to hanging bridges and canopy tour, also butterfly garden.
AL-A Linda Vista del Norte Lodge on the gravel road, taking the right fork (not to the **Arenal Observatory Lodge**), near **Arenal Vista Lodge**, T2479-1551, www.hotellinda vista.com. Nice views, several good, unspoilt trails in the area, horse riding tours, hot water. Recommended.

Camping

There is a small campsite just before the park entrance with hook-ups for vehicles, US$2.50 per person. Great views of the volcano and a good spot for walking.

Camping is also possible on the edge of the lake, no services, but good view of volcano at night.

North to Upala p761

AL Magil Forest Lodge, 3 km from Col Río Celeste, near San Rafael de Guatuso, T2221-2825. Set in 240 ha on the foothills of the 1916-m **Volcán Tenorio** (now a national park of 12,871 ha with thermal waters, boiling mud and unspoilt forest). 7 rooms with private bath, price includes meals.
G Pensión Buena Vista, Upala. Basic, food available.

Around Lago Arenal p761

LL La Mansión Marina and Club, T2692-8018, www.lamansionarenal.com. On the lake, beautiful pool, very relaxing.

L-A Arenal Lodge, travelling round the lake from Fortuna, just north of the dam wall up 2.5-km steep road, T2460-1881, www.arenal lodge.com. Stunning views to the north and south. Rooms, suites, excellent restaurant.

AL-B Hotel Los Héroes (Pequeña Helvecia), 10 km from Arenal towards Tilarán, T2692- 8012, www.hotellosheroes.com. Delightful Swiss owners with inspiring energy. A superb hotel, complete with Swiss train service.

AL-B Hotel Tilawa, 8 km north of Tilarán, T2695-5050, www.hotel-tilawa.com. With great rooms, restaurant, tennis and excellent opportunities for wind surfing, kayaking and birdwatching. Equipment for rent at US$55 a day. Guaranteed beginner lesson – if it's not fun it's free; try not to laugh and you've got a good deal. Good discounts off season.

A Chalet Nicholas, west end of lake, T2694-4041, www.chaletnicholas.com. Bed and breakfast (a speciality), run by friendly retired North Americans. Non-smokers only, children under 10 discouraged. Recommended.

A-B La Ceiba, 6 km from Arenal, T2692-8050, www.ceibatree-lodge.com. Overlooking Lake Arenal, Tico owned and run, good, helpful, great panoramic views, good breakfast.

B Rock River Lodge, on the road skirting the lake, T2692-1180, www.rockriverlodgecr.com. Rooms and bungalows, with bathroom, good restaurant. Excellent activity spot with day options for surfing, fishing and good mountain biking. Bikes available for hire.

C Aurora Inn B&B (Nuevo) Arenal, T2694-4590. Private bath, pool and jacuzzi, art gallery, wedding receptions overlooking Lake Arenal.

C La Alondra, west of La Mansión Marina and Clubs, T2692-8036. With simple, basic rooms sleeping up to 4 and great Tico restaurant from US$5.

Tilarán *p762*

D Cabiñas El Sueño, 1 block north of bus terminal/central park, T2695-5347. Clean rooms around central patio, hot water, fan, TV, friendly and free coffee. Good deal.

D Naralit, on the south side of the church, T2695-5393. Clean, with a restaurant.

E Hotel Restaurant Mary, south side of church, T2695-5479. Bath, small pleasant rooms, the upstairs is recommended.

E-F Central, round the back of the church, 1 block south, T2695-5363. With shared bath (more with own bath), noisy.

● Eating

San Carlos and around *p758*

Variety of sodas in the central market offer *casados*, check out the great sword collection displayed at La Ponderosa.

♥♥♥ Coca Loca Steak House, next to Hotel La Central, T2460-3208. Complete with Wild West swing door.

♥♥ Los Geranios, Av 4 and Calle. Popular bar and restaurant serving up good *bocas* and other dishes.

♥♥ Restaurant Crystal, on the western side of the plaza. Sells fast food, snacks, ice cream and good fruit dishes.

Los Chiles *p758*

♥ El Parque on the main plaza. With good home cooking.

♥ Los Petates, on road running south of the central park. Has good food, cheap with large portions but check the bill.

Fortuna *p759, map p759*

♥♥♥ La Vaca Muca, out of the town on the way to Tabacón, T2479-9186. Typical Latino food, steak house.

♥♥♥ Las Brasitas, at west end of town (see map), T2479-9819. Open-air restaurant serving abundant authentic Mexican fare with a laid-back European-café style.

♥♥ Choza de Laurel, west of the church, T2479-7063. Typical food in a rustic setting, serving breakfast, lunch and dinner, US$2-4.50, occasionally greeted by passing hummingbirds.

♥♥ Coco Loco, south of town, T2468-0990. Coffee, smoothies and fruit drinks, gallery and souvenirs.

¶¶ **El Jardín**, on the main street opposite the gas station, T2479-9360. Good menu with a mix of local and fast food, pizza, good place to watch the world go by.

¶¶ **Nene's**, 1½ blocks east of the main square, T2479-9192. Good food, pleasant service, not expensive. Recommended.

¶¶ **Pizza Luigi's**, west end of town (see map), T2479-9898. Formal, open-air restaurant with distinctly Italian pretensions toward pizza and pasta. Good wine list for Fortuna.

¶¶ **Rancho La Cascada**, corner of Parque with high conical thatched roof, T2479-9145. Good *bocas*, films sometimes shown in evenings.

¶¶ **Steakhouse Arenal** next to Hotel Las Flores. Mid-priced steak house with Texan tendencies.

¶¶ **Vagabondo**, west end of town, T2479-8087, www.vagabondocr.com. Reasonably priced pizza and pasta, also has rooms (**A**) with breakfast.

¶ **La Casa de Hara**, round the side of Hotel Fortuna. Very good local food, fast service and normal prices – where the locals eat.

Around Lago Arenal *p761*

¶¶¶-¶ **Caballo Negro**, a couple of kilometres west of (Nuevo) Arenal, T2694-4515. The best restaurant for miles, serving vegetarian, Swiss and seasonal fish dishes with organic salads. Warm family atmosphere.

¶¶ **Maverick's Bar & Restaurant** (Nuevo) Arenal, T2694-4282. Grilled meat, pizza, excellent food, salad bar and very friendly.

¶¶ **Restaurante Lajas** (Nuevo) Arenal, T2694-4385. Tico and vegetarian fare.

¶¶ **Típico Arenal** (Nuevo) Arenal, T2694-4159. Good local dishes with seafood and vegetarian options. Large room upstairs (**C**) with private bath and hot water, the best cheap place in town.

¶¶ **Toad Hall**, northeast of the lake, T2692-8020. Café, restaurant and gift shop.

Tilarán *p762*

¶¶ **Restaurant La Carreta**, at the back of the church, T2695-6593. The place to go and relax if you have time to kill. Excellent break-

fast and lunch only, North American food, pancakes, coffee and good local information.

¶ **Stefanie's**, out of the bus station to the left on the corner of the main plaza. Good and quick if you need a meal between buses.

▲ Activities and tours

Fortuna *p759, map p759*
Tour operators
Arenal Bungee, town centre, T2479-7440. Bungee, water touchdowns, rocket launcher and big-swing adventures US$50 each.
Arenal Canopy Tour, east down the main street, T2479-9769, www.canopy.co.cr. Offer a short horse-riding journey from Fortuna, US$55, as well as quad tours, mountain bike rental and general tours.
Aventuras Arenal, main street, T2479-9133, www.arenaladventures.com. Provides all tours in the area, and has been around for many years. Can help with enquiries about other parts of Costa Rica.
Desafío, just off main square by thatched restaurant, T2479-9464, www.desafio costarica.com. Full range of tours, and with office in Monteverde.
Eagle Tours, T2479-9091, www.eagle tours.net. Helpful, with usual tours.
Sunset Tours, T2479-9800, www.sunset tourcr.com. Reliable, long-standing company with a selection of tours. Recommended.

● Transport

San Carlos and around *p758*
Bus Direct bus from Terminal Atlántico Norte, **San José**, hourly from 0645-1815, 2¼ hrs, US$2.90, return 0500-1930. From San Carlos buses go northwest to **Tilarán** via **Fortuna** and **Arenal** (0630 and 1400, US$1 to Fortuna, US$4 to Tilarán), other buses go to **Fortuna** through El Tanque, 6 daily, 1½ hrs, **San Rafael de Guatuso** and **Upala**, north to **Los Chiles**, hourly, 3 hrs, US$4, northeast to towns on the Río San Carlos and Río Sarapiquí, including

Puerto Viejo de Sarapiquí (5 a day, 3 hrs), and east to the Río Frío district.

Los Chiles *p758*
Bus Going into Costa Rica, there are direct buses to **San José** daily 0500, 1500, 5 hrs, from San José Atlántico Norte Terminal, Calle 12, Av 7-9, to Los Chiles at 0530, 1530, US$4.20 with **Auto Transportes San Carlos**, T2255- 4318. Alternatively take one of the hourly buses from the same terminal in San José to **San Carlos**, US$4 (**Cd Quesada**) from where there are hourly services to the capital. From **Fortuna**, take the bus to San Carlos, get off at Muelle and wait for a connection.

Fortuna *p759, map p759*
Bus From **San José** there are daily returning buses hourly from 0500-1930 from Terminal Atlántico Norte, with **Auto Transportes San José–San Carlos**, T2255-4318, 4½ hrs, via San Carlos, US$4.20. From **San Carlos**, 6 buses daily, 1 hr, US$1. To **Tilarán** there are 2 buses daily at 0800 (connecting to 1230 bus Tilarán–Santa Elena/Monteverde and 1300 bus Tilarán–Puntarenas) and 1730, US$2.90, 4 hrs. Shuttle bus services to **Monteverde** and **Tamarindo** (US$35 per person, minimum 6). Leaving Fortuna, there are frequent buses to **San Ramón** with buses to San José every 30 mins, and good connections to Puntarenas. Also regular service to **Cd Quesada**.

Car hire Alamo, T2479-9090, has an office in town; Poás T2479-8027. **Taxi** Taxis in the area overcharge. Agree on price before travelling.

Tilarán *p762*
Bus If heading for Santa Elena and Monte-verde see page 769. Direct bus from **San José**, 4 daily, 4 hrs, from Terminal Atlántico Norte. 2 daily buses to **San Carlos** via Fortuna at 0700 and 1230. To **Fortuna**, 3 hrs, US$2.00. Daily bus to **Santa Elena** (for Monteverde), 1230, 2½ hrs, US$1.65, return 0700 daily. Tilarán–Puntarenas 0600, 1300, 3 hrs, US$3. 5 daily buses to **Cañas** (at 0500, 0730, 1000, 1230 and 1530, 40 mins, US$1.25), where

buses head north and south along the Pan-American. If you get the 1230 Tilarán–Liberia bus you can reach the Nicaraguan border before it closes.

ⓘ Directory

San Carlos and around *p758*
Banks Banco Nacional, Av Central, west of the church, T2461-9200. Banco de Costa Rica, east side of park and another near the market, T2461-9006, both have ATMs. Others nearby, include Banco Popular, T2460-0534. **Internet** Ask around or try Café Internet, Av 5, Calle 2-4, 400c per hr, Mon-Fri 0800-2100, Sat 0800-1800. **Post** Av 5, Calle 2-4.

Los Chiles *p758*
Banks Banco Nacional, with ATM, on central park. **Post** Services provided by Cabiñas Jabirú, 25 m north of market.

Fortuna *p759, map p759*
Banks Banco Nacional de Costa Rica, T2479-9022, will change TCs, ATM. Banco Popular, T2479-9422, Visa ATM. Coocique, open Sat mornings 0800-1200, Visa ATM. **Internet** Prices in Fortuna are quite expensive. Try Eagle Tours, T2479-9091, or Destiny Tours. **Laundry** Lavandería La Fortuna, Mon-Sat 0800-2100, US$5 wash and dry 4 kg. **Pharmacy** Farmacia Dr Max, east down the main street, Mon-Sat 0730-2030, Sun 0800-1200. **Post** Down main street, shares building with the police.

Around Lago Arenal *p761*
Banks Banco Nacional (Nuevo) Arenal, beside the football pitch.

Tilarán *p762*
Banks Banco Cootilaran, a couple of blocks north of Parque Central, has a Visa and MasterCard ATM, and there's a Banco de Costa Rica in town. **Internet** Café across from bus station.

Northwest Costa Rica

The route of the Pan-American Highway heads north passing near the world-renowned Monteverde Cloud Forest in the Cordillera de Tilarán, the marshes of the Parque Nacional Palo Verde, the active Volcán Rincón and the dry tropical forest of the Parque Nacional Santa Rosa on the Pacific coast, as it crosses the great cattle haciendas of Guanacaste before reaching the Nicaraguan border.» For listings, see pages 778-785.

San José to Esparza and Barranca

The Pan-American Highway from San José descends from the Meseta Central to Esparza, an attractive town with a turbulent early history, as it was repeatedly sacked by pirates in the 17th century, belying its peaceful nature today.

The stretch of the highway between San Ramón and Esparza (31 km) includes the sharp fall of 800 m from the Meseta Central, often shrouded in mist and fog making conditions treacherous for road users. Beyond Esparza is the **Bar/Restaurant Mirador Enis**, a popular stopping place for tour buses breaking the journey at a service station with fruit stalls nearby, before a left turn at Barranca for Puntarenas, 15 km.

Puntarenas and around → *Colour map 4, B3.*

Puntarenas fills a 5-km spit, thrusting out into the Gulf of Nicoya, east to west, but no wider than six avenues. Although popular with locals, most visitors pass through, using it as a transport hub with links to the southern Nicoya Peninsula or to get a bus north or south to other parts of the country without returning to San José. If heading for Nicoya, see page 786. If heading to Santa Elena/Monteverde see below, and page 783. It is also the Pacific destination for the bright white, cruise palaces that float through the Central American ports, and dock at Muelle de Cruceros on the Calle Central.

Once the country's main Pacific port with rail links to the Central Highlands, it has since been superseded by Caldera a few kilometres to the south. The northern side of the peninsula, around Calle Central with the market, banks, a few hotels and the fishing docks, is run-down and neglected, typical of small tropical ports. The southern side is made up of the **Paseo de los Turistas**, drawing crowds to the hot, sometimes dirty beach, especially at weekends. There are several hotels along the strip, as well as restaurants, bars and a general seafront beach atmosphere. There is a public swimming pool at the western end of the point (US$1 entrance), close to the ferries, and good surfing off the headland. There is a **Museo de la Historia Marina** ① *T2661-5036, Tue-Sun 0945-1200, 1300-1715, US$1.80*, in the Cultural Centre by the main church and tourist office. Across the gulf are the hills of the Nicoya Peninsula. **Puntarenas Marine Park** ① *T2661-5272, www.parquemarino.org, daily 0900-1700, US$5 children US$3.50*, offers 28 large aquariums showing Costa Rica's marine life. In the gulf are several islands including the **Islas Negritas**, a biological reserve reached by passenger launches.

Monteverde and Santa Elena → *For listings, see pages 778-785.*

Monteverde Cloud Forest Reserve is one of the most precious natural jewels in Costa Rica's crown, and an opportunity to see plants, insects, birds and mammals in grand profusion – in theory, at least. Protected by law, this private preserve is also protected by appalling access roads on all sides (the nearest decent road is at least two hours from the town). Santa Elena and Monteverde, although separate, are often referred to as the same place; most sites of interest are between the town of Santa Elena at the bottom of the hillside and Monteverde Cloud Forest Reserve at the top.

Ins and outs
From the Pan-American Highway northwest to Km 149, turn right (just before the Río Lagarto). Continue for about 40 km on mostly gravel road (allow 2½ hours) to Santa Elena. Parts of the road are quite good, but in wet weather 4WD is recommended for the rough parts. If driving, check that your car rental agreement allows you to visit Monteverde. A 33-km shorter route is to take the Pipasa/ Sardinal turn-off from the Pan-American Highway shortly after the Río Aranjuez. At the park in Sardinal, turn left, then go via Guacimal to the Monteverde road.

Buses come from Puntarenas via the Km 149 route. There are also buses from Tilarán to the north with connections to Fortuna/Volcán Arenal, and Cañas on the Pan-American Highway. There are two daily buses from San José.

Travelling between Fortuna and Santa Elena, you can travel overland by horse, jeep, boat or combinations of the three. It's adventurous, challenging and enjoyable depending on the weather conditions at the time. Travel agents in either location can advise and organize.

Santa Elena and around
Santa Elena is a rugged and busy place, often packed with visitors exploring options or just passing time. It is cheaper to stay in town rather than along the single, unpaved road that twists and turns for 5 km through the village of Monteverde, with hotels and places of interest situated along the road almost to the reserve itself. **Santa Elena Reserve**, **Sky Trek** and **Sky Walk** are to the north of Santa Elena, all other places of interest are east, heading up the hill.

Five kilometres north of Santa Elena, off the road to Tilarán, is **Sky Trek** ⓘ *T2645-5238, www.skytrek.com, daily 0700-1500, US$60, student US$48, child US$38*, a popular and breathtaking zip-wire experience, as you fly through the air on a network of cables strung out from giant forest trees. On clear days the view from the highest tower is unbelievable. Night-time zip-wires have recently been introduced. Included in the package is **Sky Tram**, which involves travelling through the canopy in six-seater cable cars.

Very close to Santa Elena, at the start of the climb to Monteverde, is the **Serpentarium** ⓘ *T2645-6002, daily 0900-2000, US$8, US$6 students*, with specimens of snakes and amphibians found in the nearby cloud forest. Other natural history places of interest include the **Frog Pond** ⓘ *TT2645-6320, daily 0900-2030, US$12*, with 25 species of frog, and the **Bat Jungle** ⓘ *daily 0900-2000, T2645-5052, www.batjungle.com, US$8*, where you can learn about the nocturnal habits of over 40 bats.

Just 100 m beyond **Hotel Sapo Dorado** is the **Orchid Garden** ⓘ *T2645-5510, daily 0800- 1700, US$5, US$3 students*, with about 400 species collected by Gabriel Barboza.

A dirt road opposite the **Hotel Heliconia** leads to the **Monteverde Butterfly Garden** ⓘ *T2645-5512, daily 0930-1600, www.monteverdebutterflygarden.com, US$9, US$7 students, including guided tour, best time for a visit 1100-1300*, a beautifully presented large garden planted for breeding and researching butterflies. Near the Butterfly Garden is **Finca Ecológica** ⓘ *T2645-5869, 0700-1730 daily, US$10, night tours US$15, free map*, with three trails totalling around 5 km with bird lists for birdwatching and varied wildlife in this transitional zone between cloud and tropical dry forest, guides available. Good night tours. Down the same path is **Aerial Adventures** ① *daily 0800-1600, US$10, T2645-5960*, a ski-lift-style ride travelling slowly through the treetops. Ideal for birdwatching.

Monteverde & Santa Elena

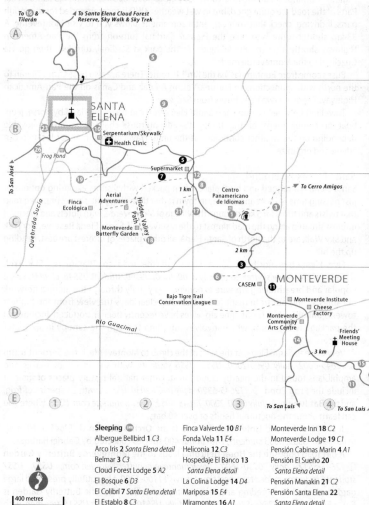

To ⑯ & Tilarán

To Santa Elena Cloud Forest Reserve, Sky Walk & Sky Trek

SANTA ELENA

Serpentarium/Skywalk
Health Clinic

Frog Pond

To San José

Supermarket

To Cerro Amigos

1 km

Centro Panamericano de Idiomas

Quebrada Sucia

Aerial Adventures

Finca Ecológica

Hidden Valley Path

Monteverde Butterfly Garden

2 km

MONTEVERDE

CASEM

Bajo Tigre Trail Conservation League

Monteverde Institute
Cheese Factory

Río Guacimal

Monteverde Community Arts Centre

Friends' Meeting House

3 km

To San Luis

To San Luis

Sleeping

Albergue Bellbird **1** *C3*	Finca Valverde **10** *B1*
Arco Iris **2** *Santa Elena detail*	Fonda Vela **11** *E4*
Belmar **3** *C3*	Heliconia **12** *C3*
Cloud Forest Lodge **5** *A2*	Hospedaje El Banco **13**
El Bosque **6** *D3*	*Santa Elena detail*
El Colibrí **7** *Santa Elena detail*	La Colina Lodge **14** *D4*
El Establo **8** *C3*	Mariposa **15** *E4*
El Sapo Dorado **9** *B2*	Miramontes **16** *A1*
	Montaña Monteverde **17** *C3*

Monteverde Inn **18** *C2*
Monteverde Lodge **19** *C1*
Pensión Cabinas Marín **4** *A1*
Pensión El Sueño **20**
Santa Elena detail
Pensión Manakin **21** *C2*
Pensión Santa Elena **22**
Santa Elena detail

N

400 metres
400 yards

Santa Elena Cloud Forest Reserve

ⓘ *0700-1600, entrance US$14, students US$7, T2645-5390, www.reservasantaelena.org, for information. It is a long, steep hike from the village; alternatively hire a taxi, US$6.50.*

One kilometre along the road north from Santa Elena to Tilarán, a 5-km track is signposted to the reserve, managed by the **Centro Ecológico Bosque Nuboso de Monteverde**. It is 83% primary cloud forest and the rest is secondary forest at 1700 m, bordered by the Monteverde Cloud Forest Reserve and the Arenal Forest Reserve. There is a 12-km path network and several lookouts where, on a clear day, you can see and hear Volcán Arenal. The 'canopy tour' is recommended: you climb inside a hollow strangler fig tree then cross between two platforms along aerial runways 30 m up, good views of orchids and bromeliads, then down a 30-m hanging rope at the end. There are generally fewer visitors here than at Monteverde. The **Centro Ecológico Bosque Nuboso** is administered by the local community and profits go to five local schools. It was set up by the Costa Rican government in 1989 with collaboration from Canada. The rangers are very friendly and enthusiastic. There is a small information centre where rubber boots can be hired and a small café open at weekends. Hand-painted T-shirts are for sale.

Santa Elena detail

Monteverde and around → *Colour map 4, B3.*

Strung out along the road to the cloud forest, the settlement at Monteverde – between Santa Elena and the reserve – was founded by American Quakers in the 1950s. Without a centre as such, it started life as a group of dairy farms providing milk for a cooperative cheese factory. The **cheese factory** ⓘ *shop closes 1600*, now privately owned, still operates selling excellent cheeses of various types, fresh milk, ice cream, milkshakes\ to die for and *cajeta* (a butterscotch spread).

Today, Monteverde maintains an air of pastoral charm, but tourism provides more revenue for the town than dairy produce ever could. It was the vision of the dairy farmers that led to the creation of the reserve to protect the community watershed. When George Powell and his

Sleepers Sleep Cheaper
  Hostel **26** *B1*
Tina's Casitas **23** *B1*
Trapp Family Lodge **24** *E5*
Villa Verde **25** *E4*

Eating ❼
Chunches **1** *Santa Elena detail*
El Bosque **3** *C3*

Johnny's Pizza **5** *B2*
Lucía's **7** *C2*
Marisquería El Márquez **8**
  Santa Elena detail
Morphos **9** *Santa Elena detail*
Pollo Asado El Campesino **10**
  Santa Elena detail
Stella's Bakery **11** *D3*

wife spent time in the region studying birds they realized the importance of protecting the area. Working with local residents they created the reserve in 1972 – foresight that has spawned the creation of many other natural attractions locally and throughout the country.

The best way of getting the full low-down on the place is at the **Museum of Monteverde History** ⓘ *daily 0930-1930, US$5.* A spacious museum that records the history of Monteverde, beginning with the creation of the Central American isthmus three million years ago to its settlement by indigenous people – then the arrival of the Ticos, followed by the Quaker settlers, and then biologists, conservationists and ecotourism.

Reserva Sendero Tranquilo ⓘ *daily, T2645-5010, entry restricted to 12 people at any one time,* is a private 200-ha reserve near the Monteverde cheese factory. Reservations and guides should be arranged through **El Sapo Dorado** hotel, which also offers night tours for US$25 per person.

Just before the entrance to Monteverde Cloud Forest is the **Hummingbird Gallery** ⓘ *T2645-5030, daily 0700-1700,* where masses of different hummingbirds can be seen darting around a glade, visiting feeding dispensers filled with sugared water. Outside the entrance is a small shop/photo gallery that sells pictures and gifts, as well as **Bromeliads Nature Bookstore and Café**. There is also a slide show at **Hotel Belmar**, **The Hidden Rainforest** ⓘ *1930 daily except Fri,* by Bobby Maxson.

Adjoining the Monteverde Cloud Forest is **El Bosque Eterno de los Niños (Children's Eternal Rainforest)** ⓘ *T2645-5003, www.acmcr.org,* established in 1988 after an initiative by Swedish schoolchildren to save forests. Currently at 22,000 ha, the land has been bought and is maintained by the **Monteverde Conservation League** with children's donations from around the world. The **Bajo Tigre** trail takes 1½ hours, parking available with notice, a guide can be arranged, but no horses are allowed on the trail. Groups can arrange trips to the **San Gerardo** and **Poco Sol Field stations** ⓘ *0800-1600, entrance US$6, students US$2, contact the Monteverde Conservation League for reservations at San Gerardo or Poco Sol, T2645-5003, www.acmcr.org, US$50 a night.*

Monteverde Cloud Forest Reserve

ⓘ *www.cct.or.cr. The reserve entrance is at the field station at the top of the road. Bus from Santa Elena heads up the hill leaving at 0600 and 1100 returning at 1400 and 1700. The total number of visitors to the reserve at any one time is 150, so be there before 0700 to make sure of getting in during high season (hotels will book you a place for the following day). Tour buses come in from San José daily. Entrance fee US$17 (students with ID US$9) valid for multiple entry during the day, cannot be purchased in advance. Office open daily 0700-1630; the park opens at 0700 and closes at 1700. A small shop at the office sells various checklists, postcards and APS film, gifts and excellent T-shirts, the proceeds of which help towards the conservation project.*

Straddling the continental divide, the 10,500-ha Monteverde Cloud Forest Reserve is privately owned and administered by the Tropical Science Centre – a non-profit research and educational association. The reserve is mainly primary cloud forest and spends much of the year shrouded in mist, creating stunted trees and abundant epiphytic growth. The best months to visit are January to May, especially February, March and April. It contains more than 400 species of bird, including the resplendent quetzal, best seen in the dry months between January and May, especially near the start of the Nuboso trail; the three-wattled bellbird with its distinctive 'bonk' call; and the bare-necked umbrella bird. There are more than 100 species of mammal, including monkeys; Baird's tapir; six endangered cats (jaguar, jaguarundi, margay, ocelot, tigrillo and puma); reptiles; and amphibians. But be warned, travellers frequently report there is little chance of seeing much wildlife. The reserve also includes an estimated 2500 species of plant and more than 6000 species of insect. The entrance is at 1500 m, but the maximum altitude in the reserve is over 1800 m. Mean temperature is between 16° and 18°C and average annual rainfall is 3000 mm. The weather changes quickly and wind and humidity often make the air feel cooler.

The commonly used trails are in good condition and there are easy, short and interesting walks for those who do not want to hike all day. Trail walks take from two hours but you could easily spend all day just wandering around. Trails may be restricted from time to time if they need protection. There is a trail northwards to the Arenal volcano that is increasingly used, but it is not easy. There are three refuges for people wishing to spend the night within the reserve boundaries, see Sleeping, page 780. Free maps of the reserve are available at the entrance. Follow the rules, stay on the paths, leave nothing behind, take no fauna or flora out; no radios/CD players/iPods, etc are allowed.

Guides Natural history walks with biologist guides, every morning and afternoon, three to four hours, US$17, US$14 for children; advance reservations at the office or through your hotel are strongly recommended. If you use a private (non-reserve) guide you must pay his entrance fee too. An experienced and recommended guide is **Gary Diller** ① T2645-9916, he also does night tours. There are 25 others operating, of varying specialization and experience. Excellent night tours in the reserve are available normally with **Ricardo Guindon** or call **Monteverde Reserve** ① T2645-5112, US$17, at 1900 sharp. Day or night, a guide is recommended if you want to see wildlife, since the untrained eye misses a lot.

Donations and volunteer work Donations are welcomed for purchasing additional land and maintaining and improving existing reserve areas. If you are interested in volunteer work, from non-skilled trail maintenance to skilled scientific assistance work, surveying, teaching or studying on a tropical biology programme, contact the reserve (US$14 per person, board and lodging, two weeks minimum). The Conservation League works with schools in the area on education regarding conservation. Donations can be made at the **Monteverde Cloud Forest Reserve** office or **Tropical Science Centre** ① San José, T2253-3267, www.cct.or.cr, or the **Monteverde Conservation League** ① Apdo Postal 124-5655, San José, Costa Rica, T2645-5003, www.acmcr.org.

North to Guanacaste Province → For listings, see pages 778-785.

North of Barranca, the Pan-American Highway heads towards the province of Guanacaste – the cultural heartland of Costa Rica, home to the *sabanero* cowboy and the rolling plains of the northern ranches. The province also includes the Peninsula of Nicoya and the lowlands at the head of the gulf. Rainfall is moderate; 1000-2000 mm per year. The long dry season makes irrigation important, but the lowlands are deep in mud during the rainy season.

Guanacaste, with its capital Liberia, has a distinctive people, way of life, flora and fauna. The smallholdings of the highlands give way here to large haciendas and great cattle estates. The rivers teem with fish; there are all kinds of wildlife in the uplands.

The people are open, hospitable and fun-loving, and are famed for their music and dancing, and in fact, the Punto Guanacasteco has been officially declared the national dance. There are many fiestas in January and February in the local towns and villages, which are well worth seeing.

Heading northwest on the Pan-American Highway, turn right just after the Río Aranjuez at Rancho Grande (or just south of the Río Lagarto at Km 149) to access a dramatic and at times scenic route to Santa Elena-Monteverde.

Some 43 km north of Barranca is the turn-off for **Las Juntas**, an alternative route to Monteverde for those using the Tempisque ferry or arriving from Guanacaste; a third of it is paved. After Las Juntas, there is a mining ecomuseum at **La Sierra de Abangares** ① *daily 0600-1800, US$1.80*, with mining artefacts from a turn-of-the-20th-century gold mine.

Four kilometres north, the long-awaited bridge over the Tempisque River finally opened in April 2003, ending the long waits for the car ferry. After about 6 km, a road to the right at San Joaquín leads to the **Hacienda Solimar Lodge** (see Sleeping, page 780), a 1300-ha cattle farm with dry tropical virgin forest bordering Parque Nacional Palo Verde (see below) near Porozal in the lower Tempisque River basin. The freshwater Madrigal estuary on the property is one of the most important areas for waterbirds in Costa Rica (only guests staying at the Hacienda can visit). Also surrounded by gallery forest, it is recommended for serious birdwatchers. Reservations essential, contact **Birdwatch** ① *T2228-4768, www.birdwatchcostarica.com*.

Sixty-seven kilometres north of Barranca, **Cañas** has little to keep the visitor for long. There are a number of interesting sights nearby and, for the traveller arriving from the north, this is the cut-through to Tilarán and connecting buses to Arenal or Fortuna. **Las Pumas** ① *behind Safaris Corobicí, Cañas, free but donations welcome and encouraged*, is a

Guanacaste Conservation Area

Sleeping 🛌
Hacienda Lodge
Guachipelín 1
Rincón de la Vieja
Lodge 3

20 km
20 miles

small, private, Swiss-run animal rescue centre which specializes in looking after big cats, including jaguar. It's an unmissable if rather sad experience.

Parque Nacional Palo Verde

At the south of the neck of the Nicoya Peninsula is Parque Nacional Palo Verde, currently over 18,650 ha of marshes with many water birds. Indeed, in the *laguna* more than 50,000 birds are considered resident. The views from the limestone cliffs are fantastic. **Palo Verde Biological Station** ① *T2661-4717, Reservations on T2524-0607, www.ots.ac.cr*, is a research station run by the Organization for Tropical Studies. It organizes natural history walks and basic accommodation; US$89 with three meals and one guided walk per stay, cheaper for researchers, make advance reservations. Turn off the Pan-American Highway at **Bagaces**, halfway between Cañas and Liberia. There is no public transport. The **Palo Verde Administration offices** ① *T2661-4717*, are in Bagaces, next to the service station. Park entrance US$10. There are two ranger stations, Palo Verde and Catalina. Check roads in wet season.

Liberia and around → *For listings, see pages 778-785. Colour map 4, B2.*

→ *Population: 40,000.*

Known as the 'White City', Liberia is a neat, clean, cattle town with a triangular, rather unattractive modern church, and single-storey colonial houses meticulously laid out in the streets surrounding the central plaza. The town is at the junction of the Pan-American Highway and a well-paved branch road leads southwest to the Nicoya Peninsula.

There is a helpful **tourist office** ① *3 blocks south of the plaza on Calle 1, Av 6, T2666-1606*, English is spoken; leave a donation as the centre is not formally funded (the information is not always accurate). In the same building is the **Museo del Sabanero (Cowboy Museum)** ① *museum and tourist office Mon-Sat 0800-1200, 1300-1600, US$0.45*, a poorly presented display of artefacts. You can also get some tourist information across the plaza from the church.

Africa Mia animal park ① *T2661-8165, www.africamia.net, US$65 entry, US$55 child*, a short distance south of town near Salto, features animals from Africa, including ostriches, zebra and giraffes, and has picnic areas, a restaurant and offers tours. Further north is the turn-off northeast to **Quebrada Grande**.

Parque Nacional Rincón de la Vieja

ⓘ *Park entry US$10. There are 2 ways into the park: the southern route, which has less traffic, goes from Puente La Victoria on the western side of Liberia and leads, in about 25 km, to the Santa María sector, closest to the hot springs. In this part, you can hike 8 km to the boiling mud pots (Las Pailas) and come back in the same day; the sulphur springs are on a different trail and only one hour away. The northern route turns right off the Pan-American Highway 5 km northwest of Liberia, through Curubandé (no public transport on this route). Beyond Curubandé, you cross the private property of Hacienda Lodge Guachipelin (US$2 to cross), beyond which is Rincón de la Vieja Lodge, see Sleeping. Day trips are possible to all areas, US$15 for Rincón de la Vieja, US$40 for Santa Rosa and US$50 for Palo Verde. Minimum of 4 required, prices per person. Park is closed Mon for maintenance.*

Most easily visited from Liberia, Parque Nacional Rincón de la Vieja (14,161 ha) was created to preserve the area around the Volcán Rincón de la Vieja, to the northeast of the town. It includes dry tropical forest, mud pots, hot sulphur springs and several other geothermal curiosities. The volcanic massif reaches to 1916 m and can be seen from a wide area around Liberia when not shrouded in clouds. The area is cool at night and subject to strong, gusty winds and violent rains; in the day it can be very hot, although always windy. These fluctuations mark all of the continental divide, of which the ridge is a part. From time to time the volcano erupts, the last eruption being in November 1995, when it tossed rocks and lava down its slopes.

Liberia

200 metres
200 yards

Sleeping 🛏
Anita **1**
Boyeros **2**
Cabinas Sagitarios **3**
Daysita **4**
Del Aserradero **13**
Guanacaste **5**
Hostal Ciudad Blanca **6**
La Casona **7**
La Posada del Tope **9**
La Siesta **10**
Liberia **12**

Eating 🍴
Copa de Oro **4**
El Bramadero **1**
Hong Kong **2**
Los Comales **3**
Marisquería Paso Real **4**
Panymiel **5**
Pronto Pizzería **6**

The park is home to over 350 recorded species of bird, including toucans, parrots, three-wattled bellbirds and great curassows, along with howler monkeys, armadillos and coatis, ticks and other biting insects. It also has the largest density of Costa Rica's national flower the *guaria morada* or purple orchid. Horses can be rented in the park from some of the lodges. If you want to climb the volcano you will need to camp near the top, or at the warden's station, in order to ascend early in the morning before the clouds come in. Trails through the park lead to most sights of interest, including beautiful waterfalls and swimming holes. There are several accommodation options in or near the park, and shorter trips easily arranged from Liberia.

Parque Nacional Santa Rosa

About halfway to the Nicaraguan border from Liberia, is Parque Nacional Santa Rosa (38,673 ha). Together with the Murciélago Annex, the peninsula to the north of the developed park, it preserves some of the last dry tropical forests in Costa Rica, and shelters abundant and relatively easy-to-see wildlife. During the dry season, the animals depend on the water holes and are thus easy to find until the holes dry up completely. Conservation work in the area is also trying to reforest some cattle ranches in the area – helped by the fact that cattle have not been profitable in recent years.

Close to the park headquarters and research buildings, the historically important **La Casona** was an essential visit for every Tico child as it is from here that the patriots repelled the invasion of the filibuster Walker in 1856, who had entrenched himself in the main building. Unfortunately the old hacienda building, once the Museo Histórico de Santa Rosa, was almost completely destroyed by fire in May 2001. Rebuilt, La Casona reopened in 2002. There are several good trails and lookouts in the park, the easiest of which is close to La Casona. Lasting a couple of hours, it leads through dry tropical forest with many Indio Desnudo (naked Indian) trees, which periodically shed their red flaky bark.

Deeper in the park, **Playa Naranjo** (12 km, three hours' walk or more, or use 4WD, park authorities permitting) and **Playa Nancite** (about the same distance from the entrance) are major nesting sites of **leatherback** and **olive ridley sea turtles**. The main nesting season is between August and October (although stragglers are regularly seen up to January) when flotillas of up to 10,000 Ridley turtles arrive at night on the 7-km long Playa Nancite. Females clumsily lurch up the beach, scoop out a deep hole, deposit and bury an average of 100 ping-pong-ball sized eggs before returning exhausted to the sea. Playa Nancite is a restricted-access beach; you need a written permit to stay plus US$2 per day to camp, or US$15 in dormitories. Permits from **SPN** in San José, and the **Park Administration building** ⓘ *Santa Rosa, T2666-5051, make sure you have permission before going*. Research has been done in the Playa Nancite area on howler monkeys, coatis and the complex interrelation between the fauna and the forest. Playa Naranjo is one of the most attractive beaches in the country. It is unspoilt, quiet and very good for surfing. There is good camping, drinking water (although occasionally salty) and BBQ facilities.

La Cruz and Isla Bolaños → *Colour map 4, B2.*

The last town before the border, La Cruz has a bank (for cash, traveller's cheques or credit card transactions), a handful of hotels and absolutely incredible sunsets from the hilltop overlooking the Bahía de Salinas. Down in the bay the Islas Bolaños Wildlife Refuge and some of the best conditions for windsurfing in Costa Rica.

Isla Bolaños is a 25-ha National Wildlife Refuge protecting the nesting sites of the brown pelican, frigate bird and American oystercatcher. The island is covered with dry forest and you can only walk round the island at low tide. The incoming tidal surge is very dangerous, be off the island before the tide comes in. No camping is allowed.

◉ Northwest Costa Rica listings

For Sleeping and Eating price codes and other relevant information, see Essentials pages 31-33.

◉ Sleeping

San José to Esparza and Barranca *p768*
AL-A Hotel Vista Golfo, 14 km off the Inter-American Hwy at Miramar, T2639-8303. Wildlife, canopy tour, horse riding, waterfalls and spring-fed pool on 27 ha in what is now an adventure park.
D Hotel Castanuelas, close to the highway, T2635-5105. A/c, quiet, cooler alternative to Puntarenas.
D Hotel Río Mar, Barranca, T2663-0158. With bath and restaurant. Good.

Puntarenas and around *p768*
Accommodation is difficult to find from Dec-Apr, especially at weekends.
L-AL Tioga, on the beach front with Calle 17, T2661-0271, www.hoteltioga.com. 54 rooms; those with balconies are much better, with views. Private bath, a/c, TV and telephone. Restaurant, swimming pool, very good.
B-C La Punta, Av 1, Calle 35, T2661-0696. Good spot 1 block from car ferry, with bath, hot water, secure parking, good pool. American-owned, big rooms, friendly, clean.
B-C Las Hamacas on beach front between Calle 5-7, T2661-0398. Rooms are OK, but noisy when the bar is in full flow. Small pool. Could do with a lick of paint; for now it is overpriced.
C-D Cayuga, Calle 4, Av Central-1, T2661-0344. Has 31 rooms with private bathroom, a/c, pretty dark rooms, restaurant. There is a small garden patio but it's hardly paradise.
C-D Gran Hotel Chorotega, on the corner of Calle 1, Av 3 near the banks and market, T2661-0998. Clean rooms with private bath, cheaper with shared. Efficient and friendly service. Popular with visiting business people. A good deal.

D Gran Imperial, on the beach front, in front of the Muelle de Cruceros, T2661-0579. Pleasant rooms, although a little dark, but clean with private bath and fan. Small garden patio, and a very chilled atmosphere, restaurant. Good spot and handy for buses.
E Cabezas, Av 1, Calle 2-4, T2661-1045. Has 23 rooms, some with private bath, cheaper without. Simple rooms with no frills but bright and clean. Good deal.
E-F Río, Av 3, Calle Central-2 near market, T2661-0331. Private bath, fans, good rooms. Friendly Chinese owners keen to help, lively, sometimes noisy, but popular place.
G Monte Mar, Av 3, Calle 1-3. Very basic, some rooms with fan, but bearable on a budget.

Santa Elena *p769, map p770*
AL-A Arco Iris, southeast of Banco Nacional, T2645-5067, www.arcoirislodge.com. Rooms with bath, restaurant with good healthy breakfast, horses for rent, plenty of parking.
AL-A Finca Valverde, 300 m east of Banco Nacional up hill on road to the reserve, T2645-5157, www.monteverde.co.cr. Rooms with bath, nice gardens for birdwatching, bar and restaurant.
B Miramontes, leading into Santa Elena from the north, T2645-5152, www.swisshotel miramontes.com. 8 comfortable rooms in a quiet spot, Swiss-run, wonderful restaurant.
C Pensión El Sueño, T2645-5021, www.hotel elsuenocr.com. Very friendly, hot shower, small but nice rooms, clean, pricey meals, car park. Run by Rafa Trejos who does horse-riding trips into the mountains to see quetzals.
C-G Pensión Santa Elena, T2645-5051, www.pensionsantaelena.com. Good range of rooms of varying standards and quality – all good value for the money. Very popular, clean, good food, kitchen available.
D El Colibrí, T2645-5682. Clean, friendly, timber built, with balconies.

D Hospedaje El Banco, see map. Price per person. Family-run, friendly, hot shower, clean, good information, English spoken.

E Tina's Casistas, T2645-5641, www.tinas casitas.de. 4 cabins with 9 rooms with private or shared bath. In a quiet part of Santa Elena and worth a look if you want a little more comfort.

G Pensión Cabinas Marín, 500 m north of the centre past the Agricultural College. Spacious rooms (room 8 has a nice view), good breakfasts, friendly.

G Sleepers Sleep Cheaper Hostel, T2645-6204, www.sleeperssleepcheaperhostels. com. Cheap budget accommodation with dorm rooms. Kitchen and internet access too.

Monteverde *p771, map p770*

LL El Establo, next to **Heliconia**, T2645-5110, www.elestablo.com. 155 carpeted rooms with private bathroom, restaurant, 50-ha farm with 50% cloud forest, own nature guide, good birdwatching, riding stables, 35 horses, family-run, very accommodating. Recommended.

LL-L Monteverde Lodge, T2645-5057, www.costaricaexpeditions.com. With restaurant, jacuzzi, daily slide shows US$5 at 1800. Recommended.

L El Sapo Dorado, T2645-5010, www.sapo dorado.com. 30 suites, 10 with fireplaces, good but expensive restaurant (0700-2100).

L Fonda Vela, T2645-5125, www.fonda vela.com. Private bathroom, hot water, 40 beautiful rooms and suites spread around 5 buildings. A 25-min walk, 5-min drive to the reserve, on a 14-ha farm with forest and trail system, good birding, 2 excellent restaurants (open to public), bar, TV room, art gallery and conference room.

L Heliconia, T2645-5109, www.hotel heliconia.com. Private bathrooms, restaurant, very comfortable, excellent food, private reserve and nature rails. Highly recommended.

AL-A Belmar, 300 m behind service station, T2645-5201, www.hotelbelmar.net. Swiss chalet style, beautiful views of Nicoya, restaurant, good.

A Cloud Forest Lodge, 300 m north of Sapo Dorado, T2645-5058, www.cloudforest lodge.com. 20 rooms with bath. Restaurant, beautiful views and tours available here with **Canopy Tours**, see Activities and tours.

A Hotel de Montaña Monteverde, T2645-5046, www.monteverdemountainhotel.com Comfortable, set meals, good, wholesome food, sauna, jacuzzi, good views of Nicoya, excellent birdwatching on 15-ha reserve, transport from San José available. Recommended.

A Trapp Family Lodge, closest to the reserve, T2645-5858, www.trappfam.com. Tidy rooms, upstairs with balconies, downstairs with terraces. Restaurant and friendly, helpful hosts.

A-B Villa Verde, 1 km from reserve, T2640-4697, www.villaverdehotel.com. Rooms with hot showers, others with shared bath, some with kitchenette, includes breakfast. Clean, nice, with restaurant and excellent views. Good package rates for students.

B El Bosque, next to restaurant of same name, T2645-5158, www.bosquelodgecr.com. Has 26 comfortable rooms with hot showers. Clean, fine views, beautiful gardens and short trail, safe parking.

B La Colina Lodge, between Monteverde and reserve, T2645-5009. Private bath, balconies with some rooms, cheaper in dormitory, helpful, luggage stored, small area for camping, one of the original houses of Monteverde with some nice touches. Marvin Rockwell, the former owner and one of the original Quaker settlers, pops in to give talks when requested.

C Mariposa, T2645-5013. Has 3 rooms in a single block sleeping up to 3 people, with private bath. A family atmosphere with breakfast included in the price.

C Pensión Manakin, just beyond El Establo, along a short road on the right, T2645-5080. Offers 10 simple rooms, a few with private bath, cheaper with shared bath, also fully equipped cabins. Filling breakfast and evening meals are available, in a family atmosphere great for sharing stories with other guests. A small balcony at the back makes a calm place to sit and relax. The Villegas are very knowledgeable about the area, and will help arrange tours and transport up to the reserve if required.

D-E Albergue Bellbird, just before the gas station, T2645-5518. There are 6 rooms in mainly dorm-style accommodation, shared bathrooms, restaurant with typical food.

E Monteverde Inn, down track opposite Heliconia, T2645-5156. Private bathroom, quiet, breakfast included. Run-down, price per person.

Monteverde Cloud Forest Reserve *p772*
Shelter facilities throughout the reserve cost US$3.50-5 a night, reserve entry fee for each night spent in the park, plus key deposit of US$5. Bring sleeping bag and torch. You can make your own meals. Dormitory-style accommodation for up to 30 people at entrance, **Albergue Reserva Biológica de Monteverde**, T2645-5122, US$40 full board only, includes park entrance fee. Reservations only for all reserve accommodation (usually booked up by groups).

North to Guanacaste Province *p773*
B Capazuri B&B, 2.5 km north of Cañas, T2669-6280. Also camping US$7 per person.

B Hacienda Solimar Lodge, solimar@racsa.co.cr. 8 rooms with private or shared bathroom, includes meals, minimum 2 nights, transport on request, local guide, horse riding. Recommended for serious birdwatchers, contact **Birdwatch**, T2228-4768, www.bird watchcostarica.com, see page 774. Reservations essential.

C El Corral, Pan-American, Cañas, T2669-1467. With bath.

D Cañas, Calle 2, Av 3, Cañas, T2669-0039. With bath, clean, pleasant.

F Cabinas Corobicí, Cañas, T2669-0241. Has 11 good rooms with bath and parking available. Price per person.

Liberia and around *p775, map p776*
B Las Espuelas, 2 km south of Liberia, T2666-0144, www.bestwestern.com. Good,

a/c, satellite TV, swimming pool, round trip bus service from San José.

C Boyeros, on Pan-American Hwy with Av Central, T2666-0722, www.hotel boyeros.com. Pool, bath, restaurant.

C Hostal Ciudad Blanca, Av 4, Calle 1-3, from Gobernación 200 m south, 150 m east, T2666-3962. Has 12 nice but dirty rooms, a/c, hot water, TV, restaurant/bar, parking, rooster wake up call.

C Hotel del Aserradero, Pan-American Hwy and Av 3, T2666-1939. Has 16 big rooms with bath, parking and fans.

C Santa Clara Lodge, 4 km from Quebrada Grande, T2666-4054. Has 4 rooms with shared bath, 1 room with bath, cattle farm, horse riding, dry forest.

D Guanacaste, Calle 12, Av 3, just round corner from bus stations, T2666-0085, www.higuanacaste.com. Clean, bath, friendly, restaurant, safe parking, money exchange, Ticabus agency offers transfers and tours here. Camping area, English spoken, group discount, 15% student discount, affiliated youth hostel. Recommended.

D La Siesta, Calle 4, Av 4-6, T2666-0678. Clean, with bath, restaurant, swimming pool, helpful owner who speaks English.

D-F Hotel Daysita, Av 5, Calle 11-13, T2666-0197. Restaurant, pool, quiet, not central. Cheaper to share 6-bedded room with bath.

D-F La Posada del Tope, Rafael Iglesias, 1½ blocks south from church, T2666-3876. Clean, friendly, helpful, with shower, laundry facilities, parking, bike rentals, baggage storage. The owner Dennis has a telescope for star gazing. Price per person.

E-F La Casona, Av 6, Calle Central, T2666-2971. Rooms for up to 4 people, shared bath, washing facilities, rooms facing street get very hot; more expensive in annex with private bath.

E-F Liberia, ½ block south of main square, T2666-0161. Cheaper with shared bath, fans, clean, friendly, good information board and breakfast, laundry facilities. Recommended.

F Cabinas Sagitarios, Av 11, Calle 2, T2666-0950. With bath, run by Dutchman

and Costa Rican, breakfast and dinner available on request, friendly.
G Anita, Calle 4 y Av 8, T2666-1285. Bath, clean, family-run, friendly, café, shop, parking, best of the range.

Parque Nacional Rincón de la Vieja
p776, map p774
LL-A Hacienda Lodge Guachipelin, accessed through the northern route, T2666-8075, www.guachipelin.com. Meals available, 50 rooms, internet, canopy tour, naturalist guides, riding, hot springs, sulphur springs, mud pools, waterfalls (transport from Liberia arranged, US$50 per person round trip).
A Buena Vista Mountain Lodge, accessed through the Santa María sector, T2661-8158, www.buenavistalodgecr.com. Rooms, waterslide, canopy tour, spa, internet, restaurant/bar.
D Miravieja Lodge, accessed through the Santa María sector, T8383-6645. Rustic lodge in citrus groves, meals, transport and tours.

Parque Nacional Santa Rosa *p777*
Camping
There is a pleasant campground at Park Administration, T2679-9692, about 7 km from the entrance with giant strangler figs that shade your tent from the stupendously hot sun, and very adequate sanitary facilities, picnic tables, and so forth for US$2.15 per person per night. There is a small *comedor* for meals (breakfast 0600-0630, lunch 1100-1200, evening 1700-1800, good) and drinks near the campground but it is advised that you bring some of your own supplies; a tent is useful and essential in the wet season. You may be able to sleep on the veranda of one of the scientists' houses. Bring a mosquito net and insect repellent. If the water is not running, ask Park Administration.

La Cruz and Isla Bolaños *p777*
AL-A Ecoplaya Beach Resort, Bahía Salinas, T2228-7146, www.ecoplaya.com. All-inclusive resort, well maintained with nice restaurant.

AL-A Hotel La Mirada, on road out to the Pan-American Hwy, T/ F2679-9084. Clean, tidy rooms, ample parking.
B-C Amalia's Inn, 100 m south of Parque Central. Stunning views, small pool, very friendly and excellent local knowledge. Extra person US$5, and 1 room sleeps 6. Excellent value for groups and recommended.
D-E Cabinas Santa Rita, 150 m south of Parque Central, T2679-9062. Nice, clean, secure with good parking. Cheaper with fan. Would be great in any other town not competing with **Amalia's**.
E Hotel Bella Vista, ½ block northwest of the plaza, T2679-8060. Rooms, restaurant/ bar, great view.

Camping
Playa Morro Trailer Park y Cabinas, west of La Cruz, on Bahía Salinas looking over to Isla Bolaños. Drinking water, showers, toilets, tennis, barbecue, fishing boats and horses to rent, 1-km beach.

🍴 Eating

Puntarenas and around *p768*
There are many bars and a couple of discos along the Paseo de los Turistas. A number of Chinese restaurants on Av Central and Calle 1 and there is good, cheap food from market stalls, eg *sopa de carne* (meat soup).
🍴 **Aloha**, on the seafront on Calle 17. Worth checking out.
🍴 **Casa de Mariscos**, Calle 7-9, T2661-1666, closed Wed. On the beach front, good seafood, reasonable prices.
🍴 **Jardín Cervecero Bierstube**, on the seafront at Calle 23-25, T2661-5293. Good for sandwiches, hamburgers and a beer.
🍴 **Kayte Negro**, north side of the peninsula on Av Badillo, Calle 17. Good local food.
🍴 **La Yunta**, on the beachfront at Calle 19, T2661-3216. A popular steak house, open all night.
🍴 **Mariscos Kahite Blanco**, near launch. Excellent and locally renowned seafood.

♥ **Soda Brisas del Mar**, on Calle Central, Av 2-4. Good for a snack.
♥ **Soda Macarena**, opposite the Muelle de Cruceros (dock). Handy while waiting for buses.

Around Puntarenas
♥ **María Vargas**, Roble, 10 km east of Puntarenas. Bar and restaurant, friendly, good food, reasonable prices.

Santa Elena p769, map p770
♥♥♥ **Chunches**, opposite Pensión Santa Elena, T2645-5147, closed Sun. A very useful place with good espresso bar and snacks, used books, magazines, laundromat, fax service.
♥♥ **Marisquería El Márquez** (see map), T2645-5918, closed Sun. Seafood and *casados*.
♥♥ **Morphos** (see map), T2645-5607. Typical and international fare, recommended, with a good atmosphere, but not cheap.
♥ **Pollo Asado El Campesino** (see map). Tico soda, early breakfast special.

Monteverde p771, map p770
♥♥♥-♥♥ **Johnny's Pizza**, on main road between Santa Elena and Monteverde, T2645-5066. Good wood oven-cooked pizzas in a relaxed atmosphere, café, souvenir shop. Tables outside give extra chance to see wildlife.
♥♥♥-♥♥ **Restaurant Lucía's**, down road opposite **Heliconia**, T2645-5337. Tasty lasagne, international and vegetarian fare.
♥♥ **Restaurant El Bosque**, on road to reserve, next to **Casem**, open from 0630. Shop, good food, clean.
♥ **Stella's Bakery**, opposite Casem, T2645-5560. Excellent wholemeal bread, cakes and good granola – there's a café if you want to eat in.

North to Guanacaste Province p773
♥♥♥ **Rincón Corobicí**, next to **La Pacífica**, Cañas, T2669-6191. Clean and pleasant, with a small zoo and offers rafting down Río Corobicí.
♥♥ **Central**, main square. Good Chinese restaurant.
♥♥ **Restaurant Panchitos**, main square, Cañas. Good and inexpensive.

Liberia and around p775, map p776
♥♥♥ **Marisquería Paso Real**, south side of main square. Great ceviche and seafood.
♥♥ **Chop Suey**, Calle Central. Chinese, big helpings.
♥♥ **Copa de Oro**, next to Hotel Liberia. Chinese, huge servings, good value.
♥♥ **El Bramadero**, part of **Hotel Bramadero** on the Pan-American Hwy. Popular, breakfast from 0630, lively bar in the evenings.
♥♥ **Jardín de Azúcar**, just off plaza, T2666-3563. Self service, good variety and tasty.
♥♥ **Pronto Pizzería**, Calle 1, Av 4. Good food (not just pizzas) in a charming colonial house.
♥♥-♥ **Hong Kong**, 1½ blocks east of church. Chinese, cheap and cheerful.
♥ **Los Comales**, Calle Central, Av 5-7. 0630-2100. Traditional Guanacaste dishes prepared with maize, run by women's cooperative.
♥ **Panymiel**, Av Central, Calle 8-9, and Av 3, Calle 2. Bakery, snacks and drinks, good value.

La Cruz and Isla Bolaños p777
♥ **La Orchidea**, La Cruz, T2679-9316. Seafood, cheap. Daily 0630-2200.
♥ **Restaurant Telma**, La Cruz, T2679-9150. Tico food, cheap.
♥ **Soda Marta**, La Cruz, T2679-9347. Cheap Tico fare.

⊛ Festivals and events

Puntarenas and around p768.
Jul Fiesta de la Virgen del Mar, on the Sat closest to the 16 Jul, with a week of festivities leading to a carnival and regatta of decorated fishing boats and yachts.

Monteverde p771, map p770
Dec-Mar Monteverde Music Festival, T2645-5053. Classical and jazz concerts at sunset, local, national and international musicians. Programme from local hotels.

Liberia and around p775, map p776
25 Jul, Guanacaste Day sees dancing, parades and cattle related festivities.

○ Shopping

Monteverde *p771, map p770*
Casem, a cooperative gift shop, is located just outside Monteverde on the road to the reserve next to **El Bosque** restaurant, T2645-5190. It sells embroidered shirts, T-shirts, wooden and woven articles and baskets. Next door, there's a shop selling Costa Rican coffee.

Liberia and around *p775, map p776*
Mini Galería Fulvia, on the main plaza, sells *Tico Times*, English papers and books. English spoken and helpful.
Tiffany's, Av C-2, Calle 2, general gifts, cigars.

▲ Activities and tours

Puntarenas and around *p768*
See under San José Tour operators, page 735, for Gulf of Nicoya cruises.

Monteverde *p771, map p770*
Canopy Tours, at Cloud Forest Lodge, T2645-5243. Offer tours of 5 platforms, connected by steel cables, to explore the forest canopy, US$45 per person, US$35 for students at **Cloud Forest Lodge**.

North to Guanacaste Province *p773*
Tour operators
CATA Tours, Cañas, T2296-2133, full-day tours to Parque Nacional Palo Verde.
Safaris Corobicí is 4 km past Cañas on the Pan-American Hwy, 25 m before the entrance to **Centro Ecológico La Pacífica**, T2669-6191. Float tours down the Río Tenorio, US$37 per person for 2 hrs' rafting, US$60, ½-day, under 14 yrs ½-price.

Liberia and around *p775, map p776*
Tour operators
Hotel Liberia can organize tours, rent out bikes and assist with enquiries. A recommended guide for the nearby national parks is **Alejandro Vargas Rodríguez**, who lives in front of the Red Cross, T2666-1889.

⊖ Transport

San José to Esparza and Barranca *p768*
Bus If going from **San José** to Monteverde it is possible to change buses in Barranca, rather than going all the way to Puntarenas, if you leave the capital before 1230.

Puntarenas and around *p768*
Bus Terminal for San José is at Calle 2, Av 2-4. Buses every 40 mins, 0415-1900 to **San José**, 2 hrs, US$4.30. Buses from San José leave from Terminal Puntarenas Calle CB16, Av 10-12, T2222-0064, 0600-1900. Daily bus to **Santa Elena** for Monteverde, T2222-3854 0630 and 1430, US$2.50, 5 hrs. Buses south to **Quepos** from main bus station, 6 daily via **Jacó**, US$$2.00, 4 hrs, return 0430, 1030, 1630. To **Liberia** with Empresa Pulmitan, first at 0600, last 1500, 4 hrs, US$1.50. To **Tilarán** via **Cañas** at 1130 and 1630, US$2. Good café at bus terminal where you can wait for your bus.

Ferry Check which dock your ferry leaves from. For the **Nicoya Peninsula** see page 786. To southern Nicoya Peninsula from the dock at Calle 35. To **Playa Naranjo** at 1000, 1420,and 1900, returning at 1250, 1700 and 2100, 1½ hrs. T2661-1069 for exact times. Pedestrians US$1.60, motorbikes US$3, cars US$12. The ferry dock is about 1 km from Puntarenas bus station, local buses run between the two, otherwise walk or get a taxi. Buses meet the ferry for **Nicoya** (through Carmona, 40 km unpaved, 30 km paved road, crowded, noisy, frequently break down, US$1.25, 2¼ hrs), **Sámara** (US$1.30), **Coyote**, **Bejuco** and **Jicaral**.
From the same dock a car ferry goes to **Paquera** at 0830, 1330, 1830 and 2230, returning at 0500, 1100, 1700 and 2030, 1½ hrs, T2641-0118 to check the times. On arrival, get on the bus (which waits for the ferry) as quickly as possible (to **Cóbano**, 2-3 hrs, US$1.25, bad road, to **Montezuma** US$2.60, 1½ hrs at least), pay on the bus, or get a taxi. **Hotel Playa Tambor** also runs a

car ferry to **Paquera** 7 times daily leaving Paquera 0500, 0700, 1000,1145,1500, 1630 and 2000. A bus to **Tambor** will be waiting at Paquera on your arrival. T2661-2084 for information.

Launch **Paquera**-Puntarenas leaves from behind the central market, directly north of the bus stop at 0600, 1100 and 1515, returning at 0730, 1230 and 1700. Pedestrians US$1.50, motorbikes US$1.80, Tickets are sold when the incoming boat has docked.

Santa Elena p769, map p770
Bus From **Puntarenas**, Terminal Empresarios Unidos, daily at 1415, occasionally at 1315 as well, 2½-4 hrs, returns 0600, US$2.20. This bus arrives in time to catch a bus to **Quepos** for Manuel Antonio. See Monteverde Transport, below, for buses from **San José**.

To **Tilarán** the 0700 (US$1.80, 3 hrs) connects with the 1230 bus to **Fortuna** and others to **Cañas** for the Pan-American Hwy, Liberia and Nicoya Peninsula.

Car There is a service station, Mon-Sat 0700-1800, Sun 0700-1200.

Horse Several places rent horses; look for signs between Santa Elena and Monteverde or ask at your hotel. Try not to hire horses that look overworked.

Taxi Santa Elena to Monteverde, US$6, and Monteverde to the reserve, US$5.75 (hunt around for good prices). Not so easy to find a taxi for return trip, best to arrange in advance.

Monteverde p771, map p770
Bus From **San José** a direct bus runs from Av 9, Calle 12, just outside Terminal Atlántico Norte daily at 0630 and 1430, 4½ hrs, US$4. Leaves Monteverde from **Hotel Villa Verde** also at 0630 and 1430, picking up through town, stopping at Santa Elena bus stop (be early). Check times in advance, Sat bus does not always run in low season (T2645-5159 in Santa Elena, T2222-3854, in San José). This service is not 'express', it stops to pick up

passengers all along the route, and is not a comfortable ride. Keep your bag with you at all times; several cases of theft reported. Alternatively, get a bus to **Puntarenas** and change there for Santa Elena, see above.

North to Guanacaste Province p773
Bus The Cañas bus station is 500 m north of the centre, where all buses depart from except for those to San José, which leave from the terminal 300 m west of Parque Central on the Pan-American Hwy.
To **San José**, Transportes La Cañera, T2669-0145, 8 daily from 0400, 3½ hrs, arriving and departing from Calle 16, Av 1-3. To **Liberia**, 10 daily from 0530. To **Puntarenas**, 8 daily from 0600. To **Upala**, for Bijagua and Volcán Tenorio, 7 daily from 0500, 1¾ hrs, US$1.50. To **Tilarán**, 7 daily from 0600. Buses to Tilarán for **Nuevo Arenal**, past the volcano and on to **Fortuna**, or for connections to **Santa Elena** and **Monteverde**. If going by road, the turn-off for Tilarán is at the filling station, no signs.

Liberia and around p775, map p776
Air The Aeropuerto Internacional Tomás Guardia, about 13 km from Liberia (LIR) on the road to the Nicoya Peninsula was reopened in 1992, revamped in 1995 and renamed **Aeropuerto Daniel Oduber Quirós**, after the former president who came from Guanacaste. The runway can handle large jets and charter flights, and direct daily flights to **Miami**. Lacsa, T2666-0306; Sansa, T2221-9414; Nature Air, T2220-3054. There is a direct weekly flight to **New York** arriving Sat, through **Air-Tech**, www.airtech.com, Wed, Sat and Sun. Delta flights from **Atlanta**. American flights from **Miami**, Continental from **Houston**.

Bus To **San José** leave from Av 5, Calle 10-12, with 14 a day, US$4.25, 4 hrs. Other buses leave from the local terminal at Calle 12, Av 7-9. Liberia to **Playa del Coco**, hourly, 0500-1800, **Playa Hermosa** and **Panama**, 5 daily 0730- 1730, 1½ hrs, **Puntarenas**, 7 a day, 0500-1530, **Bagaces/ Cañas**, 4 a day,

0545-1710, **Cañas Dulces**, 3 a day, 0600-1730, **La Cruz/ Peñas Blanca**, 8 a day 0530-1800. **Filedefia–Santa Cruz–Nicoya**, 0500-2020, 20 a day.

Car Car rental **Sol** and **Toyota** car rental agencies (see map) offer same prices and allow you to leave the vehicle at San José airport for US$50.

Parque Nacional Rincón de la Vieja p776, map p774
A taxi costs US$30 1-way from Liberia. Most hotels will arrange transport for US$15 per person, minimum 6 passengers. Departure at 0700, 1 hr to entrance, return at 1700; take food and drink. You can also hitch; most tourist vehicles will pick you up. If you take your own transport a 4WD is best, although during the dry season a vehicle with high clearance is adequate.

Parque Nacional Santa Rosa p777
Parque Nacional Santa Rosa is easy to reach as it lies west of the Pan-American Hwy, about 1 hr north of Liberia. Any bus going from Liberia to Peñas Blancas on the Nicaraguan border will drop you right at the entrance (US$0.70, 40 mins), from where it's a 7-km walk, but you may be able to hitch a ride. Last bus returns to Liberia about 1800. Coming from the border, any bus heading south will drop you off at the entrance.

La Cruz and Isla Bolaños p777
Bus Regular buses to **San José** from 0545 until 1630, 5½ hrs. To **Liberia**, 5 daily 0700-1730, 1½ hrs. To **Peñas Blancas**, 5 daily 0730-1730, 1 hr. To **Playa Jobo** in Bahía Solanos, at 0530, 1030 and 1500, from main plaza.

ⓘ Directory

Puntarenas and around p768
Banks Banco Nacional and Banco de Costa Rica, on Av 3, Calle 1-3 near the Central Market, changes TCs, and with ATM.

Internet Millennium Cyber Café, on the beach front with Calle 15, only one in town so popular, 1000-2200, 600c per hr. Free coffee if you're lucky. **Post** Av 3, Calle Central-1, close to Central Market. **Telephone** ICE and Radiográfica, Av C, Calle 2-4.

Santa Elena p769, map p770
Banks Banco Nacional, daily 0900-1500, to change TCs with commission and advance cash against Visa. ATM machine for Visa in the supermarket opposite the post office. **Internet** Several places are opening up, but with poor communication links are charging exorbitant prices. Try **Treehouse Cafe**, T2645-5751 US$3 per hr 0700-2200 and Pura Vida.

Monteverde p771, map p770
Cultural centres Galería Extasis, 250 m south of La Cascada, T2645-5548, exhibits sculptures by the Costa Rican artist, Marco Tulio Brenes. **Language schools** A branch of the **Centro Panamericano de Idiomas**, in Heredia, has opened a school on the road up to the reserve, T2645-6306. Accommodation is with local families.

Liberia and around p775, map p776
Banks Banco Popular and Bancrecer both have Visa ATMs. **Banco de Costa Rica** is on the main plaza. **Credomatic**, Av Central, MasterCard ATM. For money exchange, try *casa de cambio* on Calle 2 or ask around, eg **Restaurant Chun San**, behind the cathedral. **Internet** Planet, ½ block south of the church, cheap, with good machines, Mon-Sat 0800-2200, Sun 0900-2100. Ciberm@nia, north side of main plaza, T2666-7240, US$1.25 per hr. **Medical services** Enrique Baltodano Hospital, T2666-0011. Pharmacies close to the main plaza.

Península de Nicoya

Fringed by idyllic white-sand beaches along most of the coastline, the Nicoya Peninsula is hilly and hot. There are few towns of any size and most of the roads not connecting the main communities are in poor condition. While several large hotel resorts are increasingly taking over what were once isolated coves, they are generally grouped together and there are still many remote beaches to explore. A few small areas of the peninsula are protected to preserve wildlife, marine ecosystems and the geological formations of Barra Honda. ▶▶ *For listings, see pages 792-802.*

Ins and outs

Getting there There are several ways of getting to the Nicoya Peninsula. From Liberia head west along the Highway 21 towards Santa Elena. The **Taiwan Friendship Bridge** over the Tempisque, leaving the Pan-American Highway roughly halfway between Puntarenas and Liberia, provides a short cut, saving time and gas money getting to the

Península de Nicoya

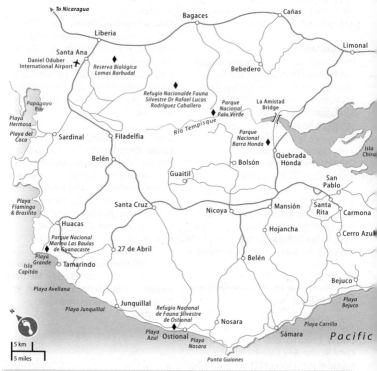

peninsula, eliminating the ferry. Just across the river is **Hotel Rancho Humo** ⓘ *T2255-2463*, with boat trips on the Tempisque and Bebedero rivers, visits to Palo Verde and Barra Honda national parks.

A third route uses ferries from Puntarenas. The **Salinero car ferry** crosses the Gulf of Nicoya to Playa Naranjo. Buses meet the ferry for Nicoya (US$1.25, 2¼ hours), Sámara (US$1.30), Coyote, Bejuco and Jicaral. A fourth route also departs from Puntarenas to Paquera from the dock at Calle 35. On arrival, get on the bus (which waits for the ferry) as quickly as possible (to Cóbano, two to three hours, US$1.25, bad road, to Montezuma US$2.60, 1½ hours at least), pay on the bus, or get a taxi. **Hotel Playa Tambor** also runs a ferry service, **Naviera–Tambor SA**, between Puntarenas and Paquera, with a bus running between Paquera and the hotel in Tambor.

Getting around All the beaches on the Nicoya Peninsula are accessible by road in the dry season. Most places can be reached by bus from Nicoya. However, the stretch from Paquera to Montezuma and the Cabo Blanco Reserve is connected to Playa Naranjo and the north only by very poor roads. There is no bus connection between Playa Naranjo and Paquera and the road is appalling even in the dry season.

Beaches Even in high season, you will be able to find a beautiful beach that is uncrowded. There are so many of them, just walk until you find what you want. You will see plenty of wildlife along the way, monkeys, iguanas and squirrels as well as many birds. There can be dangerous undertows on exposed beaches; the safest bathing is from those beaches where there is a protective headland, such as at Playa Panamá in the north.

Santa Cruz and around

Heading from Liberia by road, the first town you reach is Santa Cruz, known as Costa Rica's National Folklore City for its colourful fiestas, dancing and regional food. January is the month for the fiesta dedicated to Santo Cristo de Esquipulas, when it can be difficult to find accommodation. There is also a rodeo fiesta in January. But for the rest of the year, it's a quiet little town, with a charming modern church, providing supplies for the beach tourism industry. If you need to buy food, Santa Cruz is a good place to stock up.

In **Guaitil**, 9 km east of Santa Cruz and 19 km north of Nicoya, local artisans specialize in reproductions of indigenous Chorotegan pottery. They work with the same methods used by the indigenous long ago, with minimal or no use of a wheel and no artificial paints. Ceramics are displayed at the local *pulpería*, or outside houses. At **San Vicente**, 2 km southeast of Guaitíl, local craftsmen work and sell their pottery.

West coast beaches → For listings, see pages 792-802.

A number of beaches are reached by unpaved roads from the Santa Cruz–Liberia road. Many can be accessed by bus from the Liberia bus station, others may require you to change buses at Santa Cruz. Each of the beaches has its appeal – Tamarindo and Playa del Coco for partying, Flamingo to the north and Junquillal for their greater seclusion, and Grande for nesting turtles and surfing.

Playa del Coco and around

After the town of **Comunidad**, a road leads east to Playa del Coco and Playa Hermosa, and the ever-pending resort development of Playa Panamá, see below.

Playa del Coco is a popular resort some 8 km from the highway, set in an attractive islet-scattered bay hemmed in by rocky headlands. It's a good place to chill out, with a mix of good services without being too developed. The best beaches are to the south. All activities concentrate on the beach and fishing. Coco is the starting point for surf trips to Santa Rosa spots by boat, such as **Witch's Rock**. Snorkelling and diving are nothing special, but for a diving expedition to the **Islas Murciélago**, see page 800. Sightings of manta rays and bull sharks are common around Islas Catalinas and Islas Murciélago.

There are bars, restaurants and a few motels along the sandy beach. It is too small to get lost. To reach it, leave the road at Comunidad (road paved). Be wary of excursions to secluded Playa Verde, accessible by boat only, as some boatmen collaborate with thieves and reap the rewards later. A 2.5-km road heads southwest from Playa del Coco to **Playa Ocotal**.

Playa Hermosa and Playa Panamá

A spur road breaks from the main road to Playa del Coco heading north to Playa Hermosa. This is one of the nicest resorts and served by a paved road. Accommodation is mixed, but it's a good quiet alternative to other beaches in the region. Walking either to the left or the right you can find isolated beaches with crystal-clear water. The big **Papagayo** tourist complex near Playa Panamá, which once planned to provide as many as 60,000 hotel rooms, started years ago. Objections have delayed construction, but the project continues.

Playa Tamarindo and around

South of Filadefia, close to Belén, a mostly paved but poor road heads east to the beach and popular surf spot of Playa Tamarindo (www.tamarindobeach.net) and other beaches. The sunsets are incredible and while most make their way to the beach for that magic moment, the strong beach culture makes this a popular place to hang out.

Either side of the sunset, Tamarindo is a flurry of activity, easily the liveliest beach resort on the Nicoya Peninsula and development is quickly changing the place. The beach is attractive with strong tides in places so take care if swimming. Three good breaks provide a variety of options for the surf crowd. Beyond surf and sun, the most popular excursion is an evening trip to Playa Grande and the leatherback turtle nesting sights from October to March. There's a good blend of hotels and bars to make it a good beach stop – not too busy, but not dead.

Close to Tamarindo, **Playa Avellanas** is a quiet beach with good surfing for those who want to get away from the service culture of Tamarindo. Shuttle buses run from Tamarindo and there are a handful of accommodation options.

Playa Grande

North of Playa Tamarindo is Playa Grande and the **Parque Nacional Marino Las Baulas de Guanacaste** (485 ha terrestrial, 22,000 ha marine), well known as a nesting site for **leatherback turtles** (October-February). Organized trips only available from Tamarindo or hotels in Playa Grande. Also in town is **El Mundo de La Tortuga** ① *T2653-0471*, an unusual turtle museum. The road from the main highway at Belén leads directly to Playa Grande, a sleepy town with almost no transport and no way of getting around.

Playa Flamingo and beaches to the north

North of Tamarindo and Playa Grande are the beaches of **Conchal**, **Brasilito**, **Flamingo** and **Potrero**. It's a collection of beaches with subtle changes of atmostphere. Conchal is a beautiful 3-km beach full of shells, but with only luxury accommodation; most budget travellers stay at Brasilito and walk along the beach. Further north, the bay around Playa Flamingo has white sand, although the actual beach has some fairly intrusive developments with a grab-all approach to beachfront properties; in fact, the beach is now polluted and not as beautiful as it was. Several smaller beaches retain a relaxed atmosphere where life is governed by little more than the sunrise and beautiful sunsets. Further north is the isolated beach of Potrero with pockets of visitors.

Playa Junquillal → *Colour map 4, B2.*

South of Tamarindo, Playa Junquillal is one of the cleanest beaches in Costa Rica and is still very empty. Completely off the beaten track with almost no tourist facilities, it does have a selection of stylish hotels, most of which are quite pricey, but there is also camping if you have a tent.

Nicoya → *Colour map 4, B2.*

Nicoya, at the heart of the peninsula, is a pleasant little town distinguished by possessing the country's second oldest church, the 17th-century church of San Blas. Damaged by an earthquake in 1822 it was restored in 1831, and is currently undergoing renovations. The Parque Central, on Calle and Avenida Central, is leafy and used for occasional concerts. Buses arrive at Avenida 1, Calle 3-5. Most hotels and banks are within a couple of blocks of the central park. The area **Conservation Offices** (**ACT**) are on the northern side of central park. There is no general information for visitors, but they can assist with specific enquiries.

Parque Nacional Barra Honda → *Colour map 4, B2.*

① *Entry US$10, no permit required.*

A small park in the north of the Nicoya Peninsula (2295 ha), Barra Honda National Park was created to protect a mesa with a few caves and the last remains of dry tropical forest in the region. The park office is near Barra Honda at **Santa Ana**, at the foot of the mesa, and there are two different trails to the top; two hours' hiking.

Sámara and Playa Carrillo → *Colour map 4, B2.*

Sámara (www.samarabeach.com) is a smallish Tico village that has maintained some of its regular way of life alongside tourist development. The beautiful beach, 37 km from Nicoya on a paved road, is probably the safest and one of the best bathing beaches in Costa Rica. Playa Carrillo is 5 km away at the south end of the beach. The litter problem is being tackled with rubbish bins, warning signs, refuse collections and bottle banks. Both places have airstrips served by scheduled services from San José.

Nosara → *Colour map 4, B2.*

Nosara (www.nosara.com) is a small village about 26 km north of Sámara without much to see or do in it – which makes it ideal if you like lying around on beaches. Indeed most come for the three unspoiled beaches which are not particularly close to the village.

Playa Nosara is north of the village across the Río Nosara where you may see turtles (see below); Peladas is the prettiest and smallest, south of the river, and Guiones is safe for swimming and good for surfing. Expatriates have formed the Nosara Civic Association to protect the area's wildlife and forests and prevent exploitation.

Playa Ostional

North of Nosara is Playa Ostional where **Olive Ridley turtles** lay eggs July-November along the coastal strip of the Refugio Nacional de Vida Silvestre Ostional. The turtles arrive for nesting at high tide. The villagers are allowed to harvest the eggs in a designated area of the beach, the rest are protected and monitored. Outside the egg-laying period it is very quiet. Contact the MINAE (Ministry of Environment and Energy) ranger station for details (T682-0470).

Southern Península de Nicoya → *For listings, see pages 792-802.*

The southern Nicoya Peninsula is almost completely cut off from the north. Roads are appalling and those that exist are frequently flooded in part. For this reason most access the region by ferry from Puntarenas. Arriving at **Playa Naranjo** there are several expensive eating places by the dock and a gas station. Beaches and stopping points are dotted along the southern shore of the peninsula passing through low key coastal centres of Tambor, Montezuma, Cabuya, Mal País and Playa Santa Teresa.

Paquera

Paquera is a small village 22 km along the coast from Playa Naranjo. There are a few shops and some simple lodgings, for example **Cabinas Rosita** on the inland side of the village. It is separated from the quay by 1 km or so; apart from a good soda, a restaurant, a public telephone and a branch of **Banco de Costa Rica**, there are no facilities.

Tambor, Curú National Wildlife Refuge and Cóbano

The small village of **Tambor**, 19 km from Paquera, has a dark sand beach, some shops and restaurants. The beach is beautiful, 6 km long with rolling surf; 1½ hours on a bone-shaking road from the ferry. However cruise ships from Puntarenas come here, and part of the beach has been absorbed by the large and controversial **Hotel Playa Tambor**. Built around a cattle farm by the Barceló group of Spain, the resort is alleged to have encroached on the public beach and drained a swamp that was a wildfowl habitat. A second stage is planned at Punta Piedra Amarilla, with a 500-boat yacht marina, villas and a total of 1100 rooms. Buses travelling from Paquera to Montezuma, pass through Tambor, connecting with the car ferry arriving from Puntarenas, US$2.60, two hours.

North of Playa Tambor is the **Curú National Wildlife Refuge** ① *T2661-2392, in advance and ask for Doña Julieta*. Only 84 ha, but with five different habitats and 110 species of bird. Access is through private land.

Cóbano, near Montezuma, can be reached by bus from Paquera ferry terminal, and buses for Tambor, Cóbano and Montezuma meet the launches from Puntarenas (there is an airstrip with flights from San José). Roads north, west and south out of Cóbano, require 4WD. Cóbano has a petrol/gas station.

Montezuma → *Colour map 4, B2.*

No longer a sleepy hamlet, Montezuma is a very popular small village on the sea. It is a well-liked backpacking destination and at busy periods hotels fill up every day, so check in early. Although it gets crowded, there are some wonderful beaches; many are rocky, with strong waves making it difficult to swim, but it's very scenic. There are beautiful walks along the beach – sometimes sandy, sometimes rocky, always lined with trees – that visit impressive waterfalls. The village can be reached in four hours from Puntarenas if you get the early launch. There is a tourist office at **Aventuras Montezuma**, which is very helpful and often knows which hotel has space; ask here first before looking around. The once-popular **Cabinas Karen** are now closed. Prior to her death in 1994, Doña Karen donated her land to the National Parks in memory of her late husband, creating what was to become Reserva Natural Absoluta Cabo Blanco (see below). **Cabinas Karen** now houses park guards.

Around Montezuma

Close to the village, 20 minutes up the Río Montezuma, is a beautiful, huge **waterfall** with a big, natural swimming hole, beyond which is a smaller waterfall. Intrepid walkers can carry on up to further waterfalls but it can be dangerous and accidents have been reported. There's another waterfall, 6 km north of Montezuma, with a pool right by the beach – follow the road out to the beach at the north end of town and keep going past three coves for about half an hour until you reach the trail off to the left (you can't miss it).
▶ *See Tour operators, page 800.*

You can use Montezuma as a base for exploring the **Reserva Natural Absoluta Cabo Blanco** ① *Wed-Sun 0800-1600, US$6, jeep/taxi from Montezuma US$7, first at 0700, returns 1600*. The 1172-ha reserve is 11 km from Montezuma. The marine birds include frigate birds, pelicans and brown boobies; there are also monkeys, anteaters, kinkajou and collared peccary. You can bathe in the sea or under a waterfall. At the beautiful **Playa Balsitas**, 6 km from the entrance, there are pelicans and howler monkeys.

At **Cabuya**, 2 km from Cabo Blanco Reserve, the sea can be cloudy after rough weather. Cabuya Island can be visited on foot at low tide. On the road west out of Cabuya, **Cafetería El Coyote** specializes in local and Caribbean dishes. On the west coast of the peninsula is the fast-growing village of **Mal País**. The coast here is virtually unspoilt with long white beaches, creeks and natural pools, and the facilities stretch north up the beach to blend with **Santa Teresa**. The surfing appeal of the area is growing with Mal Pais best suited for beginners, and the more experience crowd going up to Santa Teresa. It's a fast-changing area.

You can also arrange tours to **Isla Tortuga**. Many businesses rent horses; check that the horses are fit and properly cared for. Recommended for horses are **Cocozuma Traveller** and **Aventuras Montezuma**.

For Sleeping and Eating price codes and other relevant information, see Essentials pages 31-33.

⊜ Sleeping

Santa Cruz *p787*

C Diria, on the main road, T2680-0080. Bath, restaurant, pools.

C-D La Pampa, 25 m west of Plaza de los Mangos, T2680-0586. A/c, cheaper without, near parque, good, clean.

E-F Anatolia, 200 m south, 100 m west of plaza, T2680-0333. Plywood partitions, dirty bathrooms.

G Pensión Isabel, behind the church, T2680-0173. Price per person, simple box rooms.

Playa del Coco and around *p788*

Good discounts (up to 40%) in green season. At Playa Ocotal, only top-end accommodation, but good diving services.

AL El Ocotal Resort Hotel, Playa Ocotal, T2670-0321, www.ocotalresort.com. Rooms, suites and bungalows, PADI dive shop on beach, sport fishing, surfing, tennis, 3 pools, car hire, excursions.

AL-A Villa Casa Blanca, Playa Ocotal, T2670-0518, www.hotelvillacasablanca.com. 15 idyllic rooms, with breakfast, friendly and informative, family atmosphere, small pool. Pricey but very good.

A-B La Puerta del Sol, north of Playa del Coco, T2670-0195. Great little family-run hotel. Good food in Italian restaurant, small pool and gym, friendly atmosphere and free scuba lesson in hotel pool.

B Villa del Sol, at northern end of Playa del Coco, T2670-0085, www.villadelsol.com. Canadian-owned (from Quebec), with pool, clean, friendly, safe, big garden with parrots. Recommended.

C Coco Palms, Playa del Coco, beside football pitch, T2670-0367, www.hotelcocopalms.com. German-run, large pool, gringo bar and parking.

C Pato Loco Inn, Playa del Coco, T2670-0145. Airy rooms, Italian restaurant, internet for guests.

C-E Cabinas Chale, north of Playa del Coco, T2670-0036. Double rooms and villas, with private bath. Pretty quiet, small resort-style spot, small pool, 50 m from beach. Good deal, especially villas which sleep up to 6.

D Cabinas El Coco, just north of the pier right on the beach, T2670-0110. With bath and good reasonable restaurant.

D Witch's Rock Surf Camp, Playa del Coco, T2670-1138. Simple rooms.

D-E Luna Tica, Playa del Coco, south of the plaza, T2670-0127. Also with an annex over the road (friendly, clean). Both usually full at weekends.

Playa Hermosa and Playa Panamá *p788*

The Playa Panamá area has several all-inclusive resort-style hotels (**L**).

L Hotel Playa Hermosa, southern end of Playa Hermosa, T2672-0046, www.hotelplayahermosa.com. Italian-run, 22 clean rooms, better prices for groups, very good Italian restaurant overlooking gardens. Recommended.

L-A Villa del Sueño, southern end of Playa Hermosa, T2672-0026, www.villadelsueno.com. Canadian-owned, with big rooms, good restaurant, pool and live music. Apartments for longer stays.

AL-A El Velero, Playa Hermosa, T2672-1017, www.costaricahotel.net. With an airy villa feel, nice rooms with a/c and bathrooms, pool, clean, good restaurant.

C Iguana Inn, 100 m from the beach, T2672-0065. Has 9 rooms, some with kitchen. Relaxed, laid-back spot, with use of kitchen, and laundry.

Playa Tamarindo and around *p788*

Plenty of accommodation – best in each budget range listed. Book in advance at Christmas and New Year.

L Capitán Suizo, a long way south of the centre towards Playa Langosta, T2653-0075, www.hotelcapitansuizo.com. 8 bungalows, 22 rooms with patio or balcony, a/c, pool, restaurant, kayaking, scuba-diving, surfing, sport fishing available, riding on hotel's own horses, Swiss management. One of Costa Rica's distinctive hotels.

L-A Tamarindo Diria, near centre of town, T2653-0032, www.eldiria.com. Full range of services, good restaurants, beautiful pool, expensive tours offered with good guide, now with a golf course nearby.

AL VOEC, on the beach, T2653-0852, www.voecretreats.com. A women's retreat, offering 6-night package that includes accommodation, meals, daily surf and yoga lessons, 1 private surf lesson, 2 spa treatments at Coco Spa, a surf excursion to remote waves and the use of surfing equipment. Price per person.

A-B Cabinas Hotel Zullymar, southern end of town, T2653-0140, www.zullymar.com. Rooms with a/c and cheaper cabins, good beach bar. Recommended.

B-C Cabinas Marielos, near the bus stop, T2653-0141, www.cabinasmarieloscr.com. Clean basic rooms, with bath, use of kitchen, popular, book ahead.

C Pozo Azul, at the northern entrance to town, T2653-0280. Cabins, a/c, cheaper in low season, cooking facilities, clean, good, swimming pool.

D Frutas Tropicales, just south of Tamarindo Vista Best Western, T2653-0041. Has 3 simple, spotless and quiet rooms.

C-D Villas Macondo, 1 block back from the beach, T2653-0812, www.villasmacondo.com. Rooms with shared kitchen, and apartments. Swimming pool, washing machine, safety boxes, fridge and friendly people too.

E Botella de Leche, at the southern end of town, T2653-0189, www.labotelladeleche.com. Hostel rooms, very clean, use of kitchen, big communal lounge. Good choice.

F Rodamar, 50 m from Tamarindo Vista, T2653-0109. No a/c or fan, no mosquito nets, but clean, helpful, kitchen, shared bath. Family atmosphere and cheapest good deal.

G Tsunami, at the northern end of town. Basic, tidy rooms, private bath and use of the kitchen. Turn up and see if there's space, it's probably full of surfers more interested in water than comfort. Great value.

Playa Avellanes

E Casa Surf, T2652-9075, www.casa-surf.com. Friendly, good place, with helpful owners who produce marvellous food from their own bakery.

Playa Grande *p789*

A-B Hotel Las Tortugas, right on the beach in the centre of town, T2653-0423, www.lastortugashotel.com. 11 rooms with bathroom, pool, restaurant, meals included, tours arranged.

B-C Playa Grande Inn, T2653-0719, www.playagrandeinn.com. Formerly Rancho Diablo. 10 rooms with fan, good set up for surfers.

F Cabinas/Restaurante Playa Grande, 500 m before beach at the entrance to town, T8354-7661 (mob). 8 cabins with bath and kitchen, also has camping. Price per person.

Playa Flamingo and beaches to the north *p789*

A Mariner Inn, Playa Flamingo, T2654-4081. Has 12 rooms with bath, a/c, free camping on the beach.

B Bahía Potrero Beach Resort, Playa Potrero, T2654-4183. Bar, pool, 10 rooms with bath.

B-C Cabinas Bahía Esmeralda, Playa Potrero, T2654-4480. Garden, pool, hot water, roof ventilator, Italian restaurant.

B-C Cabinas Isolina, Playa Potrero, T2654-4333, www.isolinabeach.com. 250 m from beach, nice garden, roof ventilator.

B-D Hotel Brasilito, Playa Brasilito, close to beach on plaza, T2654-4237, www.brasilito.com. Good rooms. Horses, kayaks and bikes to rent. Los Arcades Restaurant, run by Charlie and Claire, mixing Thai and local dishes, closed Mon.

D Cabinas Mayra, Playa Potrero, T2654-4213. On beach, friendly, with pretty, basically equipped cabins. Camping on the beach.

D Ojos Azules, Playa Brasilito, T2654-4343. Run by Swiss couple, 18 cabins, good breakfasts with home-baked bread, nightmare decor.

F-G Brasilito Lodge, Playa Brasilito, right on the beach, T2654-4452, www.brasilito-conchal.com. Big rooms, good beds, bit of a bargain really. Internet service, several tours available. Also camping. Price per person.

Playa Junquillal *p789*

A-B Iguanazul, T2658-8124, www.iguanazul.com. 24 different sizes of tiled-roof cabins on a cliff, great spot, hot water, fan or a/c, pool, restaurant, bar, sport fishing on 27-ft *Marlin Genie*, close to good surfing.

B El Lugarcito, T2658-8436, ellugarcito@racsa.co.cr. B&B, ocean views, restaurant/bar, tours, diving, boutique.

B Tatanka, T2658-8426, www.hoteltatanka.com. 10 cabins with a pool. Good restaurant serving Italian, French and Tico dishes.

B-D Guacamaya Lodge, T2658-8431, www.guacamayalodge.com. Immaculate bungalows and 1 fully equipped house with pool, ocean views, Swiss cuisine.

C El Castillo Divertido, T2658-8428, www.costarica-adventureholidays.com. Castle rooms, restaurant, gardens, rooftop star-gazing deck, music.

C Playa Junquillal, on the beach, T2653-0432. Sleeping 2-4. Ideal for surfers and beach lovers.

C-D Hibiscus, close to the beach, T2658-8437. Big rooms with big windows, seafood restaurant with German specialities, garden, 50 m to beach, German-run.

Camping

Camping Los Malinches, after Iguanazul at the northern entrance to town off main road down a dirt track. Spectacular location, clean bathroom provided. Worth the effort, but bring all your own food.

Nicoya *p789*

A-B Hotel Turístico Curime, 500 m south of the centre on road to Sámara, T2685-5238. Fully equipped bungalows, 3-m-deep pool.

E Jenny, or **Yenny** as the sign says, on the corner of Calle 1, Av 4, T2685-5050. Spotless, with bath, a/c, towels, soap and TV. Cavernous rooms – book in with a friend and play hide and seek. Recommended.

E Las Tinajas, opposite Liberia bus stop on Av 1, T2685-5081. With bath, modern, clean, good value.

E-F Pensión Venecia, opposite old church on square, T2685-5325. Squidgy beds but good value for the price. Recommended.

F-G Chorotega, Calle Central, Av 4-6, T2685-5245. With bath (cheaper without), very good value, clean, quiet. Rooms at back have windows. Clothes-washing facilities (good Chinese soda opposite).

Sámara *p790*

A Hotel Fénix, on beach about 2 km east of the village, T2656-0158, www.fenixhotel.com. 6 slightly cramped double units with fans, kitchenettes, hot water, small pool, friendly. Internet for guests.

A Mirador de Sámara Aparthotel, rising up the hill above the village, T2656-0044, www.miradordesamara.com. Very friendly, German-owned. 6 large, cool and comfortable suites with bath and kitchen. Recommended.

B-C Belvedere, sloping up the hill, T2656-0213. Very friendly German owners. A cosy hotel with 10 small rooms, very clean. Recommended.

C Marbella, inland, road going south, T2656-0362. German-run, beautiful grounds, pool, good service, close to beach. Recommended.

C-D Casa Valeria, on the beach near the supermarket, T2656-0511. Friendly and good value, especially for 3 sharing, breakfast included, various different rooms, some with sea view, all nicely decorated, most with bath, hot water. Kitchen and laundry available, small bar, tours, tickets and car rental arranged. Recommended.

E Arenas, at the western end of town, T2656-0320. Comfortable, cheaper for longer stays, good restaurant opposite, pleasant bar next door.

Camping

Camping Coco, near the beach, T2656-0496. With toilets, electricity until 2200. The same family own **Camping San Martín**, T2656-0336, same deal, also offer **La Tigre Tours** kayak, snorkel, diving and trips to see dolphins. **Camping Los Mangos**, slightly further from the beach.

Nosara *p790*

B Villaggio, Punta Guiones de Garza, close to Nosara, 17 km north of Sámara, T2654-4664, www.flordepacifico.com. An upmarket very simply furnished beach hotel with vacation ownership plan, 30 bungalows, international restaurant, club house, bars, pool, disco, good packages arranged in San José, T2233-2476.
B Rancho Suizo Lodge, Playa Pelada, T2682-0057, www.nosara.ch. Swiss-owned bungalows, restaurant, credit cards accepted, whirlpool, hiking, riding, bird and turtle watching.
D Casa Río Nosara, on the road to the airstrip, T2682-0117. Rancho-style house with cabins and nice garden, clean, friendly, camping, canoe tours and horse riding arranged, German owners.
E Cabinas Agnell, in the village, T2682-0142. With bath, good value.
F Cabinas Chorotega, in the village near the supermarket, T2682-0129. Has 8 simple, clean rooms, shared or own bath. Bar and restaurant downstairs, so can be noisy.

Playa Ostional *p790*

You can camp on the beach.
G Cabinas Guacamaya, T2682-0430. With bath, clean, good food on request. Price per person.
G Cabinas Ostional, next to the village shop. Very basic accommodation in cabins with bath, clean, friendly.

Southern Península de Nicoya *p790*

B-C Oasis del Pacífico, on beach, Playa Naranjo, T2661-0209. A/c, old building, clean, quiet, with pool, good restaurant and free transport from ferry. Recommended.

D El Paso, north of ferry, Playa Naranjo, T2641-8133. With bath, cheaper without, cold water, clean, restaurant and pool.
F Cabinas Maquinay, 1.3 km towards Jicaral, Playa Naranjo, T2661-1763. Simple rooms with a pool and the attached **Disco Maquinay**.

Tambor, Curú National Wildlife Refuge and Cóbano *p790*

LL-L Tango Mar, 3 km from Tambor, T2683-0001, www.tangomar.com. All services including golf course and its own waterfall.
D Dos Lagartos, Tambor, T2683-0236. Cheap, clean, good value.
D-E Cabinas Cristina, on the beach, Tambor, T2683-0028. With bath, cheaper without, good food.

Montezuma *p791*

Montezuma is a very small place; hotels furthest from the centre are a 10-min walk.
A El Tajalín, T2642-0061, www.tajalin.com. Very smart hotel, spotlessly clean, rooms come with private hot water shower and a/c, located in a quiet out of the way spot and yet moments from the high street. Hammock terrace for relaxing.
AL-B Amor de Mar, T2642-0262, www.amordemar.com. This well-loved hotel has the feeling of a special place. Rooms are pristine with private bath and hot water. Breakfast and brunch is served on a very pretty terrace that joins well-manicured gardens, where visitors can recline in hammocks and stare out to sea.
A-B El Jardín, T642 0074, www.hotelel jardin.com. 15 rooms and 2 fully equipped villas located on the hill overlooking the town and ocean beyond. Shower, hot water, a/c, private terraces and hammocks. In the grounds is a pool with a little waterfall, very restful and great views, superb spot.
A-C Los Mangos, a short walk south of the village, T2642-0076, www.hotellosmangos.com. Large site comprising 9 bungalows, each accommodating 3 people, with bath, hot water and fan. Also 10 rooms, some

with shared bath, some for 4 people. Yoga classes run from an open-sided pagoda on the grounds. Different and fun and lots of free mangos (when in season).

B Horizontes, on road to Cóbano, T2642-0534, www.horizontes-montezuma.com. Language school, restaurant, pool, hot water. Highly recommended.

C Cabinas Mar y Cielo, on the beach, T2642-0261. Has 6 rooms, sleeping 2-5 people, all with bath, fan and sea view. Recommended.

C Montezuma Paradise, 10 mins' walk out of town, on the road to Cabuya, past the waterfall entrance, T2642-0271. Very friendly owners have rooms with shared bath and 1 with private, overlooking the ocean and minutes from a secluded beach cove.

C Pargo Feliz, T2642-0065, elpargofeliz@costarricense.cr. Cabins with bath. Serves good food in a peaceful atmosphere – something the owners are keen on.

C-D La Cascada, 5 mins' walk out of town, on the road to Cabo Blanco, close to the entrance to the waterfalls, T2642-0057. Lovely hotel with pretty, well-kept rooms and a wide hammock terrace overlooking the ocean for relaxing. Restaurant serves local food for breakfast, lunch and dinner.

C-D Montezuma Pacific, 50 m west of the church, next to El Tajalin, T2642-0204. With private bath, hot water and a/c.

E Lucy, follow road south past **Los Mangos**, T2642-0273. One of the oldest hotels in town and one of the most popular budget options, due to its location on the sea. 10 rooms with fans, some with sea view. Shared bath, pleasant balcony. Ultra-friendly Tica owner. Restaurant next door opens during high season. Recommended.

E-G El Tucán, at the top of the road down to the beach, T2642-0284. Wooden hotel on stilts, clean, small wood-panelled rooms, shared shower and toilet, fan, mosquito net on window. Recommended.

F Hotel El Capitán, on the main street, T2642-0069. Old wooden house with an endless variety of rooms, most with shared

cold water bath, but some with private. Very friendly owners and good location, can get a little noisy, good for backpackers.

F Pensión Arenas, on the beach, T2642-0308. Run by Doña Meca, rustic small rooms, with fan, shared bath, no frills but pleasant balcony and sea view. Free camping. Laundry service.

F Pensión Jenny, at the end of the track by the football field, T2642-0306. Basic lodging with shared bath, cheap and clean, nice out of the way location. Laundry service.

Around Montezuma *p791*

LL Milarepa, Playa Santa Teresa, on beach, T2640-0023, www.milarepahotel.com. Nice bamboo bungalows, open-air bathroom.

A Celaje, Cabuya, on beach, T2642-0374, www.celaje.com. Very good Italian restaurant. Pool, rooms with bath, hot water, good.

A-B Los Caballos, 3 km north on road to Cóbano from Montezuma, T2642-0124. Has 8 rooms with bath, pool, outdoor restaurant, ocean views, gardens. 5 mins from beach. Great horse-riding trips.

A-D Funky Monkey Lodge, Santa Teresa, T2640-0317, www.funky-monkey-lodge.com. The same very friendly and hospitable owners have extended their relaxed and very attractive resort. They now have one bungalow sleeping 8 people, 3 private bungalows and 2 apartments, sleeping 2-4 and a suite with a large balcony overlooking the ocean. They also have a rather upmarket dormitory with individual beds. The apartments have a/c, ocean view, access to the kitchen and face the swimming pool. They have a restaurant, bar, TV, DVD, ping-pong table, surfboard rental and organize surf lessons, local tours, car or ATV rental. Recommended.

A-D Mal País Surf Camp, Mal País, T2640-0031, www.malpaissurfcamp.com. Restaurant, pool, also has camping.

B-C Cabañas Playa Santa Teresa, Playa Santa Teresa, 150 m from beach, T2640-0137. Surfboard rental, horses, German-run.

B-D Cabinas Las Rocas, 20 mins south of Montezuma, T2642-0393, www.caboblanco park.com. Good but quite expensive meals, small, seashore setting, isolated.
B-F Frank's Place, Mal País, the road junction, T2640-0096. Set in tropical gardens. Wide variety of rooms with private or shared bath, and self-catering options available. Good range of services and local advice.
C-D Cabañas Bosque Mar, Mal País, T2640-0074. Clean, large rooms, hot water shower, attractive grounds, good restaurant on beach nearby, 3 km to Cabo Blanco Reserve.
D Cabinas Mar Azul, Mal País, T2642-0298, Run by Jeannette Stewart, camping possible, delicious fried fish, shrimp, lobster.
D Linda Vista, on the hill over Montezuma, T2642-0274. Units sleep 6, with bath (cold water) and fan, ocean views.
D Mochila Inn, 300 m outside Montezuma, T2642-0030. *Cabinas* from US$30, also houses and apartments for around US$350 per month.
D-F Cabinas y Restaurante El Ancla de Oro, Cabuya, T2642-0369. Some cabins with bath, others shared bathroom, seafood restaurant, lobster dinners US$10, filling breakfasts, owned by Alex Villalobos, horses US$20 per day with local guide, mountain bike rental, transport from Paquera launch available. El Delfín restaurant at crossroads, friendly, good-value local food.
E Casa Zen, Santa Teresa. Smart, budget accommodation with shared bath and one fully furnished apartment. Camping area also available. Close to the beach, restaurant on site.
F-G Cabañas Playa El Carmen, Playa Santa Teresa, T2683-0281. Basic cabins and camping, shared bath and kitchen. Jungle Juice, vegetarian restaurant, serves smoothies and meals from US$4.

Camping
Rincón de los Monos, 500 m along the beach from the centre of Montezuma, T2643-0048. Clean, well organized, lockers for rent. Lots of monkeys around.

Eating

Santa Cruz *p787*
⁋ **Coopetortilla**, 3 blocks east of the church. A local institution– a women's cooperative cooking local dishes. Cheap and enjoyable.

Playa del Coco and around *p788*
⁋⁋⁋ **Mariscos la Guajira**, on southern beach. Popular and beautiful beach-front location.
⁋⁋⁋ **Papagayo**, near the beach, T2670-0298. Good seafood, recommended.
⁋⁋ **Bananas**, on the road out of town. The place to go drinking and dancing until the early hours.
⁋⁋ **Cocos**, on the plaza, T2670-0235. Bit flashy and pricey for the area, but good seafood.
⁋⁋ **El Roble**, beside the main plaza. A popular bar/disco.
⁋⁋ **Playa del Coco**, on the beach. Popular, open from 0600.
⁋ **Jungle Bar**, on the road into town. Another lively, slightly rougher option.

Playa Tamarindo and around *p788*
⁋⁋⁋ **Fiesta del Mar**, on the loop at the end of town. Large thatched open barn, good food, good value.
⁋⁋⁋ **Ginger**, at the northern end of town, T2672-0041. Tue-Sun. Good Thai restaurant.
⁋⁋⁋ **Iguana Surf** restaurant on road to Playa Langosta. Good atmosphere and food.
⁋⁋ **Coconut Café**, on beach near **Tamarindo Vista**. Pizzas, pastries and good fish. Check for good breakfasts and cheap evening meals.
⁋⁋ **El Arrecife**, on roundabout. Popular spot to hang out, with Tico fare, good chicken and pizzas.
⁋⁋ **The Lazy Wave**, on road leading away from the beach, T2653-0737. Menu changes daily, interesting mix of cuisine, seafood.
⁋⁋ **Portofino**, at end of road by roundabout. Italian specialities and good ice cream.
⁋⁋ **Stellas**, on road leading away from the beach. Very good seafood, try dorado with mango cream. Recommended.
⁋ **Arco Iris**, on road heading inland. Cheap vegetarian, great atmosphere.

¶ Frutas Tropicales, near Tamarindo Vista. Snacks and breakfast.

Playa Flamingo and beaches to the north *p789*

¶¶ La Casita del Pescado, Playa Brasilito. Some reasonably priced fish dishes which you have to eat quickly because the stools are made of concrete.

¶¶ Marie's Restaurant, Playa Flamingo, T2654-4136. Breakfast, seafood, *casados* and international dishes.

¶¶ Pizzeria Il Forno, Playa Brasilito. Serves a mean pizza.

¶¶ Restaurant La Boca de la Iguana, Playa Brasilito. Good value.

¶¶-¶ Las Brisas, at the northern end of Playa Potrero. A great spot for a beer and a snack, and surprisingly popular for its cut-off location.

¶ Costa Azul, Playa Potrero, by the football pitch. One of several restaurants in the area, popular with locals.

¶ Cyber Shack, Playa Brasilito. Internet, coffee, breakfast and UPS service.

Playa Junquillal *p789*

¶¶¶ La Puesta del Sol, T2658-8442. The only restaurant along the strip, but then nothing could compete with the dishes from this ittle piece of Italy. Spectacular setting. Very popular so reservations required.

Nicoya *p789*

¶¶ Café de Blita, 2 km outside Nicoya towards Sámara. Good.

¶¶ Soda El Triángulo, opposite Chorotega. Good juices and snacks, friendly owners.

¶¶ Teyet, near Hotel Jenny. Good, with quick service.

¶ Daniela, 1 block east of plaza. Breakfast, lunches, coffee, *refrescos*, good.

Sámara *p790*

There are several cheap sodas around the football pitch in the centre of town.

¶¶¶ Restaurant Delfín, on the beach. Very good value and French-owned. They also have *cabinas*.

¶¶¶ El Ancla Restaurant, on the beach, T2656-0716. Seafood.

¶¶ Las Brasas, by the football pitch, T2656-0546. Spanish restaurant and bar.

¶¶ Restaurant Acuario, on the beach. Serves Tico and other food.

¶ Soda Sol y Mar, on the road to Nosara. Costa Rican and International food.

Nosara *p790*

¶¶¶ Gilded Iguana, Playas Guiones. Gringo food and good company.

¶¶¶ La Dolce Vita, south along the road out of town. Good but pricey Italian food.

¶¶ Casa Romántica, Playas Guiones. The European restaurant.

¶¶ Corky Carroll's Surf School, T2682-0385. Surf lessons and a good Mexican/Thai restaurant (closed Sun).

¶¶ Giardino Tropicale, in the middle section. Pizza.

¶¶ Hotel Almost Paradise, Playas Guiones, T2682-0173. Good food with a great view.

¶¶ La Luna, slightly up the hill. Good food and ambience.

¶¶ Olga's, Playa Peladas. Seafood on the beach.

¶ Soda Vanessa, Playas Guiones. One of several sodas in the village. Good, very cheap.

Playa Ostional *p790*

¶¶-¶ Mirador de los Tortugueros, 1 km south of Cabinas Guacamaya. Good restaurant with coffee and pancakes. Great atmosphere. Recommended.

Montezuma *p791*

¶¶¶ Playa de Los Artistas/Cocina Mediterránea, about 5 mins south of town on the road to Cabuya. Best restaurant in town.

¶¶ Bakery Café, north end of town. Great for breakfast, with bread, cakes and excellent vegetarian food.

¶¶ Brisas del Mar, just south of the soccer ground in Santa Teresa. Offers great local seafood – tuna or *mahi mahi* straight from the boats at Mal País. Great service and atmosphere. Highly recommended.

Chico's Playa Bar, on the beach. Popular hangout, great sushi. They stop serving food in the low season.

Cocolores, on the beach behind **El Pargo Feliz**, T2642-0096. Closed Mon. Good for seafood and nice veggie options.

El Pulpo Pizzeria, Santa Teresa, good-value pizzeria that also delivers.

El Sano Banano, on the road to the beach. Health-food restaurant, good vegetarian food, large helpings, daily change of menu, milkshakes, fresh fruit and yoghurt, owned by Dutch/Americans, free movies with dinner.

Pizza Romana, opposite **El Capitán**. Good Italian food cooked by Italians, pizzas, pesto, fresh pastas, etc.

Tayrona, behind **Taganga**. Great pizza, Italian owned, attractive restaurant off the main street.

Soda El Caracol, located by the football field. One of several sodas around town serving good Tico food, very cheap.

Soda Monte Sol, on the road to Cabo Blanco. Recommended for good Mexican burritos, good value, big helpings.

Taganga, located at the top of the high street, opposite El Tucan hostel. Argentine grills, chicken and meat.

Entertainment

Playa Tamarindo and around *p788*
With a long beachside strip, it's a question of exploring town until you find something that works. Call it bar surfing if you like.

Sámara *p790*
Bar La Góndola is popular and has a dart board. Opposite is **Bar Colocho**. **Dos Lagartos** disco is on the beach near **Al Manglar** and the disco at **Isla Chora** is the place to be during the season if you like resort discos.

Nosara *p790*
Some of the nightlife is in the village as well – **Bambú**, **Disco Tropicana** and various others line the football pitch.

Montezuma *p791*
Bar Moctezuma, usually open the latest, but not as loud as the others.
Chico's Bar and **Chico's Playa Bar**, a relaxing cocktail by the beach, or late night salsa dancing ad very loud reggaeton parties.
Congo Azul Bar, reggae nights Thu and Sat.

Around Montezuma *p791*
New bars are opening up every year along the beach front at Mal País. For a treat, try a *mojito* on the terrace at the exclusive resort of **Flor Blanca** at the northern edge of Santa Teresa.
Bar Tabu, Santa Teresa. Probably the most popular bar in the area, great location on the beach; good music, always lively, open late.
La Llora Amarilla, Santa Teresa. Now very popular, large venue that hosts regular disco and party nights.
Mal País Surf Camp, Mal País. Bar open every night, live jam night on Wed.

O Shopping

Playa Tamarindo and around *p788*
The town is increasingly a retail outlet selling everything you need for the beach, as well as general living with a couple of general stores in the centre of town.

Sámara *p790*
The **supermarket**, near **Casa del Mar**, is well stocked and you can get fresh bread and croissants from **Chez Joel**. **Free Radical** super/soda on main road, 1 km east of town centre, offers fresh *ceviche*, delightful pastries, beer, wine, natural juices, local honey and unusual hand-blown glass products.

Montezuma *p791*
There are now a number of rather pricey, boutique-style souvenir and clothes shops in Montezuma, most sell a very similar range.
Librería Topsy, T2642-0576. Mon-Fri 0800-1400, Sat 0800-1200. Sells books and maps and will take postcards and small letters to the post office for you.

▲▲ Activities and tours

Playa del Coco and around *p788*
Agua Rica Charters, T2670-0473, or contact them through the internet café. Can arrange transport to Witch's Rock for surfers, approximately US$400 for up to 10.
Deep Blue Diving, beside **Hotel Coco Verde**, T2670-1004, www.deepblue-diving.com, has diving trips to Islas Catalinas and Islas Murciélago, where sightings of manta rays and bull sharks are common. 2-tank dive from US$79. Will also rent gear.
Rich Coast Diving, TT2670-0176, www.richcoastdiving.com.

Playa Hermosa and Playa Panamá *p788*
Diving Safari, based at the **Sol Playa Hermosa Resort** on Playa Hermosa, T2453-5044, www.billbeardcostarica.com. One of the longest-running diving operations in the country, offering a wide range of options in the region.

Playa Tamarindo and around *p788*
Diving
Try the **Pacific Coast Dive Center**, T2653-0267, or **Agua Rica Dive Center**, T2653-0094.

Surfing and yoga
VOEC, on the beach, T2653-0852, www.voecretreats.com. A woman's retreat that offers 6-night packages, which include surf and yoga lessons. See Sleeping, page 793.

Tour operators
There are many tours on offer to see the turtles nesting at night in Playa Grande.
Hightide Adventures and Surfcamp, T2653-0108, www.tamarindoadventures.net, offers a full range of tours.
Iguana Surf Tours, T2653-0148, rent surfboards, they have one outlet near the beach, opposite the supermarket, the other in the restaurant of the same name.

Sámara *p790*
Most hotels will arrange tours for you. You can rent bikes from near the *ferretería* on the road to Cangrejal. Recommended, though are:
Tip Top Tours, T2656-0650, run by a very nice French couple, offering dolphin tours (from US$45 per person), mangrove tours (US$43 per person) and waterfall tours (US$20 per person). Naturalist guided tours to Barra Honda and Isla Chora (US$70 per person), as well as slightly more unusual trips like *Journée Cowboy* where you spend a day on the ranch roping cattle and eat with a Tico family.
Wing Nuts Canopy Tour, T2656-0153 US$40, kids US$25, family-run, friendly service, spectacular ocean views from the treetops, with 12 platforms, lots of wildlife close up, great photo opportunity, 1st-class equipment.

Nosara *p790*
Casa Río Nosara for horse or river tours, and **Gilded Iguana** for kayaking and fishing. For turtle tours, try **Rancho Suizo**, T2682-0057, or **Lagarta Lodge**, T2682-0035, who are both sensitive to the turtles and don't exploit or bother them.

Montezuma *p791*
Aventuras en Montezuma, T2642-0050. Offers a similar range, snorkelling to Tortuga Island, canopy, sunset and wildlife tours for similar prices, also taxi boat to Jacó, US$35, minimum 5 people. Ivan and his staff are also very helpful as a tourist office and can advise on hotels and other matters locally and nationally. They also book and confirm flights.
Cocozuma Traveller, T2642-0911, www.cocozumacr.com. Tico-owned company, now one of the best in Montezuma. Runs all the usual tours including horse rides and Isla Tortuga. Their boat taxi now runs to Jacó (US$40), Sámara (US$40) and Tamarindo (US$40). They will also arrange hotels, transfers, car rental and have quadbikes

for hire. Very helpful staff are happy to give information about the area.

Montezuma Eco Tours, T2642-1000, www.montezumaecotours.com on the corner opposite **Soda Monte Sol**. Offer a wide range of tours, including shuttle to Cabo Blanco (US$3), kayaking/snorkelling at Isla Cabuya (US$25 per person), day trip to Isla Tortuga (US$40 per person), horse rental (US$25) and bike rental (US$5 per day). Also boat/road transfers to Jacó/Tamarindo for around US$150 for up to 6 people.

Montezuma Expeditions, top of the high street, T2642-0919, www.montezuma expeditions.com. Very efficient set up – organize private and group transport around the country, trips between US$35 and US$48 per person, these include, San José, Fortuna (Arenal), Monteverde and Jacó.

Zuma Tours, Cóbano, T8849-8569, www.zumatours.net. Lots of information available on their website.

⊖ Transport

Santa Cruz *p787*

Bus Buses leave and arrive from terminals on Plaza de los Mangos. From **San José**, 9 daily, 0700-1800, 4½ hrs, US$8, Calle 18-20, Av 3, ½ block west of Terminal Coca Cola, return 0300-1700. To **Tamarindo**, 2030, return 0645, US$0.80, also to **Playa Flamingo** and nearby beaches, 0630, 1500, return 0900, 1700, 64 km. To **Liberia** every hour, US$1.60, 0530-1930. To **Nicoya** hourly 0630-2130, US$0.70.

Taxi To **Nicoya**, US$10.50 for 2 people.

Playa del Coco and around *p788*

Bus From **San José** from Calle 14, Av 1-3, 0800, 1400, 5 hrs, return 0800, 1400 US$7. 6 buses daily from **Liberia**, 0530-1815, return 0530-1800.

Playa Hermosa and Playa Panamá *p788*

Bus From **Liberia**, Empresa Esquivel, 0730, 1130, 1530, 1730, 1900, return 0500, 0600, 1000, 1600, 1700, US$1.20.

Playa Tamarindo and around *p788*

Air Several daily flights from **San José** with Sansa (US$71 1 way) and **NatureAir** (from US$83 to US$111) from **San José**. Daily flight from **Fortuna** with Sansa.

Bus From **Santa Cruz**, 0410, 1330, 1500 daily. To Santa Cruz first bus at 0600, US$0.70. Express bus from **San José** daily from Terminal Alfaro, 1530, return 0600 Mon-Sat, 0600, Sun 1230, 5½ hrs. Bus back to San José, can be booked through Hotel Tamarindo Diria, US$9.60.

Playa Flamingo and beaches to the north *p789*

Bus From **San José** to Flamingo, Brasilito and Potrero, daily from Av 3, Calle 18-20, 0800, 1000, 6 hrs, from US$9.50, return 0900, 1400. From **Santa Cruz** daily 0630, 1500, return 0900, 1700, 64 km to Potrero.

Playa Junquillal *p789*

Bus Daily from **Santa Cruz** departs 1030, around US$9.80, returns to Santa Cruz at 1530.

Nicoya *p789*

Bus From **San José**, 8 daily from Terminal Alfaro, 6 hrs, US$6.70-9; from **Liberia** every 30 mins from 0430-2200; from **Santa Cruz** hourly 0630-2130. To **Playa Naranjo** at 0500 and 1300, 2¼ hrs, US$3. 12 buses per day to **Sámara**, 37 km by paved road, 1 to **Nosara**.

Sámara *p790*

Air Daily flights from **San José**, Sansa US$71, **Nature Air**, US$83-111.

Bus From **Nicoya**, 45 km, 1½ hrs, US$2.20, 0800, 1500, 1600, return 0530, 0630, 1130, 1330, 1630. Express bus from Terminal Alfaro, **San José** daily at 1230, return Mon-Sat 0430, Sun 1300, 5-6 hrs. School bus to **Nosara**

around 1600; ask locally for details. It is not possible to go from Sámara along the coast to Montezuma, except in 4WD vehicle; not enough traffic for hitching.

Taxi Official and others stop outside bus station (US$20 to **Nosara**, US$10 to **Nicoya**).

Nosara *p790*
Air Sansa has daily flights to **San José**, US$71, **Nature Air**, US$83-111.

Bus Daily from **Nicoya** to Nosara, Garza, **Guiones** daily from main station, 1300, return 0600, US$3, 2 hrs; from **San José** daily from Terminal Alfaro at 0600, 6 hrs, return 1245.

Playa Ostional *p790*
Bus 1 daily at 0500 to **Santa Cruz** and **Liberia**, returns 1230 from Santa Cruz, 3 hrs, US$1.75.

Montezuma *p791*
Bus To **Paquera** daily at 0530, 0815, 1000, 1215, 1400 and 1600, connecting with the car and passenger ferry to **Puntarenas** central docks. Tickets available in advance from tourist information centre; be at bus stop outside **Hotel Moctezuma**, in good time as the bus fills up quickly, US$2.60, 1 hr (the road has been paved). To **Cabuya** US$1, buses run 4 times a day. Change at Cóbano for **Mal País** – 2 buses run daily from Cóbano, 1100 and 1400 (check as times can change).

Taxi To **Cóbano** US$5. To **Paquera** US$20.

① Directory

Santa Cruz *p787*
Banks Banco Nacional, with ATM, on main road. **Post** 400 m west of Plaza de los Mangos.

Playa del Coco and around *p788*
Banks Banco Nacional, closed Sat.

Internet Café Internet 2000, on road out of town, also try E-Juice Bar, T2670-05563 and **Leslie Café**.

Playa Tamarindo and around *p788*
Banks Banco Nacional, opposite Hotel Diria. **Internet** Tamarindo Internet, T2653-0404.

Nicoya *p789*
Banks With ATMs on main square and Calle 3, with very welcome a/c. **Post** On corner of main square.

Sámara *p790*
Banks There is no bank in Sámara, although hotels may change money. **Internet** Tropical Latitudes Internet Café in centre of town, and hotels may offer access. **Post** Almost on the beach.

Nosara *p790*
Internet and telephone Nosara Office Centre, offering email, fax, photocopies and international calls. **Language schools** Rey de Nosara language school is in the village, T2682 0215, www.reydenosara. itgo.com. Classes from US$25 per hr. They can often advise about other things to see and do in the area and arrange tours and homestays.

Montezuma *p791*
Banks Change money at Hotel Moctezuma, Aventuras en Montezuma and Cocozuma Traveller (otherwise go to the Banco Nacional in Cóbano, T2642-0210). **Internet** There is an internet café in Pizz@net next to the Hotel Moctezuma, US$2 per hr. Sano Banano has an all-Mac internet, a little pricey at US$3 per hr and can be slow. Another is located behind El Parque Hotel. **Laundry** Laundrette in Pensión Jenny and Hotel Arenas (on the beach). **Medical services** If you need a pharmacy, you will have to go to Cóbano.

Central Pacific coast

West of the Central Highlands lies a slim lowland strip of African palm with just the occasional cattle ranch. But, for the visitor, it is the miles of beaches stretching from Jacó almost continuously south to Uvita that are the real attraction. Parque Nacional Manuel Antonio is a major destination with developed services. Further south, the beaches are quieter and the Parque Nacional Marino Ballena, which is harder to get to, is barely developed; but it's of interest to divers and whalewatchers. ▸▸ For listings, see pages 808-814.

Esparza to the Pacific coast

From Esparza on the Pan-American Highway a road runs 21 km southeast to **San Mateo** (from where a road runs northeast to Atenas and the Central Highlands – see page 745). Just before San Mateo, at Higuito de San Mateo, is **Las Candelillas** ① T2428-9157, a 26-ha farm and reforestation project with fruit trees and sugar cane. There is a day use recreational area with showers, pool and riding, trails and bar/restaurant.

From San Mateo a road runs south to **Orotina**, which used to be an important road/rail junction on the San José–Puntarenas route. Today the area is home to **Original Canopy Tour** at **Mahogany Park** ① T2257-5149, which charges US$45 to fly through the trees; transportation is available.

West of Orotina the road forks northwest to the port of **Caldera**, via Cascajal, and southwest to the Pacific coast at Tárcoles.

The Costanera to Quepos → For listings, see pages 808-814.

The Costanera or coastal road passes through Jacó, Manuel Antonio and Quepos and on to Dominical before heading inland to San Isidro de El General or continuing south to Palmar Norte. If you want a popular beach, pick somewhere before Manuel Antonio. Beyond Manuel Antonio, although not deserted, you'll find things a lot quieter. If driving yourself, check the state of the roads and bridges before setting out to San Isidro. Just because buses are getting through, it doesn't mean cars can. Leave nothing of value in your vehicle; thefts, robberies and scams are regularly reported in the area. The road is paved as far as Quepos and with few potholes. Thereafter it is a good, but dusty, gravel road, paved in villages until Paquita, just before Quepos. After Quepos, the road is unpaved to Dominical. From Dominical the road inland through Barú to San Isidro is paved but landslides can make this section hazardous. High clearance is needed if a bridge is down. South from Dominical, the Costanera drifts through small expat communities that are only just being explored by visitors. They cover a range of budgets, but all are for people seeking solitude while it lasts.

Reserva Biológica Carara

① Daily 0700-1600, US$7.

Between Orotina and Jacó the Carara Biological Reserve (5242 ha) is rich in wildlife. Three trails lead through the park: one lasting a couple of hours leaves from close to Tarcoles bridge; the others lasting a little over one hour from the ranger station to the south. The reserve protects a transitional zone from the dry north coast of the country to the very humid region of the southeast. Spider monkeys, scarlet macaws and coatis can all be seen in the reserve.

One of the most popular free experiences in Costa Rica is to peer over the side of the Río Tárcoles bridge to see the opaque sediment-filled waters broken by the bony backs of the somnolent crocodiles below. It's easy to find the spot to stop, as cars cram the roadside, especially at dawn and dusk when scarlet macaws can be seen returning to their roosts from Carara Biological Reserve on the southern banks of the river.

You can get a closer look by taking a boat tour with **Jungle Crocodile Safari** ① *T2241-1853*, or **Crocodile ECO Tour** ① *T2637-0426, US$25 per person from the dock in Tárcoles, US$35 round trip from Jacó.*

Next to Carara is **La Catarata** ① *T2236-4140, 0800-1500, 15 Dec-15 Apr, US$7.50*, a private reserve with an impressive waterfall with natural pools for bathing. Take the gravel road up the hill beside **Hotel Villa Lapas**: it's 5 km to the entrance, and a 2.5-km hike to falls and pools, but it's worth the effort. There are signs on the main road. **Bijagual Waterfall Tours** ① *T2661-8263*, offer horse riding or 4WD to the falls.

Jacó

A short distance from Carara is Jacó, a large stretch of sandy beach, with a lively and youthful energy. It is popular with surfers and weekenders from San José, and comes with a rough'n'ready, earthy commercial appeal. If you want to learn to surf, this is as good a

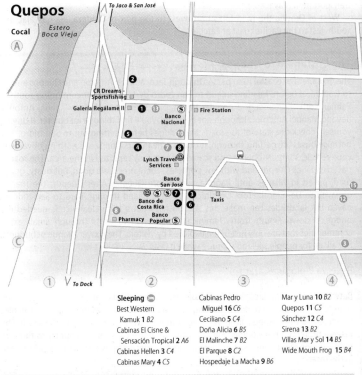

Sleeping 🛏
Best Western
   Kamuk **1** *B2*
Cabinas El Cisne &
   Sensación Tropical **2** *A6*
Cabinas Hellen **3** *C4*
Cabinas Mary **4** *C5*

Cabinas Pedro
   Miguel **16** *C6*
Ceciliano **5** *C4*
Doña Alicia **6** *B5*
El Malinche **7** *B2*
El Parque **8** *C2*
Hospedaje La Macha **9** *B6*

Mar y Luna **10** *B2*
Quepos **11** *C5*
Sánchez **12** *C4*
Sirena **13** *B2*
Villas Mar y Sol **14** *B5*
Wide Mouth Frog **15** *B4*

place as any, with several surf shops offering courses and boards for rent. If you want to party with crowds on their annual holiday, it's a great spot. If you're looking for peace and quiet, go elsewhere.

Jacó to Quepos

From Jacó the potholed road runs down the coastline with lovely views of the ocean. The beaches are far quieter and, if you have a car, you can take your pick. A few kilometres south is **Playa Hermosa**, which is right on the main road and has a popular surfing beach. If travelling by car, 20 km further and a few kilometres off the road is **Playa Bejuco**, **Esterillos Centro** and **Playa Palma**, near Parrita; definitely worth exploring. Beyond **Parrita** (Banco Nacional, Banco de Costa Rica, a gas station and a few stores) the road travels through a flat landscape of endless African palm plantations. Many of the plantation villages are of passing interest for their two-storey, balconied houses laid out around a central football pitch, a church of some denomination and the obligatory branch of AA. The carriageway narrows to single track on bridges along this road so take care if you're driving, especially at night.

Quepos → Colour map 4, B3.

Developed as a banana exporting port by United Brands, Quepos was forced to reinvent itself following the devastation of banana plantations in the region overwhelmed by Panama disease, in the early 1950s. Endless rows of oil-producing African Palm have replaced the bananas and Quepos has long since shrugged off the portside image, to the extent that few even bother to explore the dock at the southern end of town.

Southeast of Quepos, a winding road, lined with hotels, bars, restaurants and stores rises and falls for 7 km before reaching the beautiful coastline of Parque Nacional Manuel Antonio (see below) and nearby beautiful beaches. Quepos plays an important role as a service town for local and foreign tourists. It is cheaper than the Manuel Antonio road, there is no shortage of restaurants, bars and shops, and regular buses make the journey to the national park. Tell the bus driver where you are going and you'll be dropped at your chosen hotel.

Eating ●
Basarno's **1** *B2*
Café Milagro **2** *A2*
Dos Locos **3** *C2*
El Banco Sports Bar **4** *B2*
El Gran Escape **5** *B2*
Escalofrío **6** *C2*

Gardin Gourmet **9**
L'Angolo **7** *C2*
Pan Aldo **10** *C5*
Pizza Gabriels **8** *B2*

Parque Nacional Manuel Antonio

ⓘ *Tue-Sun 0700-1600, closed Mon, US$10. Guides available, but not essential, at entrance. Early and late are the best times to see the wildlife. Breakfast and other meals available from stalls just before the river, where cars can be parked and minded for US$1 by the stallholders. Basic toilets, picnic tables and drinks available by the beaches, cold-water showers at Manuel Antonio and Espadilla Sur beaches.*

From the southeastern corner of Quepos, a road winds up, over and round the peninsula of Punta Quepos, passing the flourishing hotels, restaurants, bars and stores along the length of this rocky outcrop. Travelling the road for the first time, you can't fail to be impressed by the beauty of the views. And at night, you can't help being blinded by the neon lights that speckle the hillside – evidence of the vibrant tourist trade. At times it is difficult to believe a national park flourishes on the other side of the watershed. The impact on what was once an attractive stretch of jungle-clad coastline is indisputable. For some it is an environmental catastrophe, for others it is a demonstration of the importance of planning to protect.

With 683 ha of mangrove swamps and beaches, home to a rich variety of fauna and flora, Manuel Antonio National Park can rightly claim to be one of Costa Rica's most popular protected areas – second only to Volcán Poás. Just 7 km south of Quepos on a paved road, three beautiful, forest-fringed beaches stretch along the coastline and around the headland of Punta Catedral: **Espadilla Sur**, **Manuel Antonio** and **Puerto Escondido**. Iguanas and white-faced monkeys often come down to the sand.

In addition to enjoying the beaches, hiking is also good in the park. A 45-minute trail, steep in places, runs round the Punta Catedral between Espadilla Sur and Manuel Antonio beaches. If you're early, and quiet, it is possible to see a surprising amount of wildlife. A second walk to Puerto Escondido, where there is a blow hole, takes about 50 minutes. The map sold at the entrance shows a walk up to a mirador, with good views of the coastline.

Manuel Antonio has been a victim of its own success with some of the animals becoming almost tame. But for all the criticism of recent years, it is still beautiful and highly enjoyable. Overdevelopment outside the park and overuse within has led to problems of how to manage the park with inadequate funds. In 1992 the National Park Service (SPN) threatened to close it and a number of tour operators removed it from their itineraries. You are not allowed to feed the monkeys but people do, which means that they can be a nuisance, congregating around picnic tables expecting to be fed and rummaging through bags given the chance. Leave no litter and take nothing out of the park, not even seashells.

The range of activities in the area outside the park is slightly bewildering. Sea kayaking is possible, as is mountain biking, hiking, canopy tours, canyoning, deep-sea fishing and even quad biking. Most hotels will assist with booking trips, and there are agencies in Quepos that can also advise. The beaches in the park are safer than those outside, but rip tides are dangerous all along the coast. Beaches slope steeply and the force of the waves can be too strong for children.

Quepos to Palmar Norte

Playa Matapalo

Beaches, beaches, endless stretches of sandy beaches. Thirty kilometres southeast from the congestion of Quepos towards Dominical the unpaved coastal road drifts almost unnoticed through Playa Matapalo, where you'll find an expansive, beautiful sandy beach recommended for surfing, relaxing and playing with your ideas of paradise. Other activities, in an overwhelmingly Swiss community, include fishing, horse riding and hiking to mountain waterfalls.

Dominical → Colour map 4, B2.

Twelve kilometres further on, at the mouth of the Río Barú, is Dominical (www.dominical.biz), a small town with a population of a few hundred. No more than 500 m from one end to the other it's popular with surfers and often busy. It's a great spot for surfing. Hotel prices soar in high season and most hotels are close to noisy bars. Treks and horse riding trips to waterfalls are possible if the beach is too much to bear. Just north of the town **Hacienda Barú** has a **national wildlife preserve**, with activities like abseiling, canopy tours and nature walks (see below). If you want to touch up your Spanish try the **Adventure Education Center** ① T2787-0023, www.adventurespanishschool.com, with an immersion Spanish school. They have schools in Arenal and Turrialba as well. Most people come here for the surfing; if you want to learn visit the **Green Iguana Surf Camp** ① T8825-1381, www.greeniguanasurfcamp.com, who provide board hire, group lessons, individual lessons and package deals.

Punta Dominical is 4 km south of town (no transport). A poor dirt road follows a steep path inland up the Escaleras (stairs) to some secluded accommodation blending beach and rainforest.

Uvita

If you get the impression the southern Pacific coast is about beaches, you'd be right. The village of Uvita, 18 km south of Dominical, has beautiful beaches all along the coastline. You can walk in the nearby forests, swim in nearby waterfalls or at the beach, take a boat trip and watch birds. Ballena Marine National Park (see below) protects over 5000 ha of Pacific coral reef, and humpback whales can be sighted at nearby Isla Ballena between December and April.

The road south from Uvita is being repaved as far as Ciudad Cortés, and access to the beaches of Playa Ballena and Playa Bahía is getting easier with consequent development of the area.

Parque Nacional Marino Ballena

The vast majority of Ballena (Whale) Marine National Park is coastal waters – 5161 ha against 116 ha of protected land – which may go some way to explaining why there isn't a lot to see at this least-developed national park. The underwater world is home to coral reefs and abundant marine life that includes common and bottle-nosed dolphins as well as occasional visits from humpback whales at times seen with their calves.

Although there is a rarely staffed **rangers station** ① T2786-7161, in Bahía, and signposts line the Costanera, the infrastructure in the park is non-existent. There is a nominal entrance fee of US\$6 which is rarely collected. Along the beach at Bahía is a turtle-nesting project administered by the local community. As with the park itself, the organization is very ad hoc – visitors and volunteers are welcome. Beachcombing is good, as is snorkelling when the tides are favourable. Boat trips to the island can be arranged from Bahía, and diving is starting up with the most recommended local being Máximo Vásquez, or Chumi as he is known. The coastal road continues south beside **Playa Tortuga**, passing small communities of foreigners hiding and enjoying one of the quietest spots near a beach in Costa Rica, to join the Pan-American Highway at Palmar Norte (see page 818).

For Sleeping and Eating price codes and other relevant information, see Essentials pages 31-33.

⊙ Sleeping

Esparza to the Pacific coast p803

A El Rancho Oropéndola, San Mateo, T2428-8600. Cabins with private bath or rooms with shared bath, rustic and peaceful, pool, nature trails.

D Cabinas Kalim, Orotina, near plaza, T2428-8082.

Reserva Biológica Carara p803

LL Villa Caletas, Punta Leona, to the south of the reserve, T2637-0505, www.hotelvilla caletas.com. One of the distinctive hotels of Costa Rica. French-owned, divine rooms and 14 villas atop a mountain with amazing views, spectacular sunsets, lush gardens, pool, restaurant, boat and nature tours.

Jacó p804

Accommodation in Jacó is overpriced; look for discounts May-Nov.

L-AL Cocal, on beach near the centre of town, T2643-3067, www.hotelcocaland casino.com. 2 pools, hammocks, German-owned, restaurant. Highly recommended.

AL-B Pochote Grande, northern end of town, T2643-3236, www.hotelpochote grande.net. Beautiful, German-owned hotel with bar and restaurant. Good rooms, free-form pool and a superb 500-year-old *pochote* tree shading the grounds. Good value.

A-C Cabinas Las Palmas, northern end of town, T2643-3005. Neat rooms, some with kitchenette, all with bath and fan, clean. Pretty gardens.

B Hotel Paraíso Escondido, 150 m east of the Catholic church on calle Los Cholos, T2643-2883, www.hoteljaco.com. All rooms with a private bath, patio and a/c, rooms cheaper with fan. Swimming pool and

laundry service. The owner often meets arriving buses. Good spot and worth the price.

B-C Alice, south of centre, T2643-3061. Tidy rooms with private bath, small terrace and pool.

B-C Los Ranchos, central and close to the beach, T2643-3070. 4 bungalows and 8 rooms sleeping 4-8 people, lively spot.

C Cabinas La Cometa, central, T2643-3615. With fan and hot water, very clean.

C El Jardín, at northern end of town, close to the beach, T2643-3050. Has 10 rooms in quiet spot, friendly with small pool.

C-E Hotel Kangaroo, at the southern end of town, T2643-3351, www.hotelkangaroo.info. Mix of dorms and private rooms, but it's the atmosphere that keeps people happy and recommending this place.

D Bohío, central and near beach, T2643-3017. Private bath, cold water, fan, camping.

E Cabinas Gipsy Italiano, near beach at northern end, T2643-3448. With bath and hot water.

E Cabinas Wahoo, behind the restaurant of the same name not far from buses, T2643-3513. Simple rooms, with private bath and fan. Good value.

F Hotel de Haan, at the beach end of Calle Bohío, T2643-1795, www.hoteldehaan.com. Popular backpacker spot, with pool, laundry, kitchen facilities, Good choice.

Camping

Camping El Hicaco, slightly south of the centre, T2643-3226, and **Restaurant Los Hicacos** are both down same access route to the beach.

Camping Madrigal, at the southern end of the beach, T2643-3329. A quiet spot.

Jacó to Quepos p805

AL-A Beso del Viento, Playa Palo Seco, 5 km, T2779-9674, www.besodelviento.com. Swimming pool, French owners, stylish rooms.

A Hotel El Delfín, Esterillos Centro and Playa Bejuco, T/F2778-8054. Completely renovated with swimming pool, all rooms with breezy balcony, secluded, clean, good restaurant, considered by many to be one of the best beach hotels in Costa Rica. Recommended.

A La Isla, Playa Palo Seco, T2779-9016. Bar, pool, horse and canoe trips, hot water, a/c.

A-B Auberge du Pelican, Esterillos Este, T2778-8105, www.pelicanbeachfront hotel.com. Café, French/Canadian owners, restaurant. Great spot, private airstrip out back, beach out front.

B La Felicidad Country Inn, Esterillos Centro and Playa Bejuco, T2778-6824, www.lafelicidad.com. Oceanfront, pool and restaurant.

B Vista Hermosa, Playa Hermosa, T2643-3422. Pool, simple rooms with a/c, restaurant, secure parking.

B-C Hotel Sandpiper Inn, T2643-7042, www.sandpipercostarica.com. Spacious cabins, pool, restaurant, sportfishing.

C-D Cabinas Maldonado, Playa Palma, T2227-5400. Rooms sleeping 4, with bath, cold water, kitchen.

E Finca Don Herbert, Playa Palma. With bath, clean, parking.

E Rooms/Restaurant Alex, Playa Palma, T2779-6667. 2.6 km south, with bath, fan. Recommended.

E-F Jungle Surf Café, Playa Hermosa. Basic cabins with a Tex-Mex burger bar.

F Rancho Grande, Playa Hermosa, T2643-3529. Large wooden house with communal kitchen, popular with surfers, great atmosphere. Small store for supplies.

G Las Brisas, Playa Palma. Simple rooms near beach.

Quepos *p805, map p804*

It's difficult to find accommodation on Sat Dec-Apr, and when schools are on holiday.

B Best Western Kamuk, central, near the bus terminal, T2777-0811, www.kamuk.co.cr. Shower, TV, a/c, some ocean views, bar and restaurant with large-screen videos.

B Cabinas Pedro Miguel, towards Manuel Antonio, T2777-0035, www.cabinaspedro miguel.com. Simple rooms, small and very friendly Tico owners. Next door is Centro de Idiomas del Pacífico.

B Hotel Sirena, near bus station, T2777-0528. Has 14 quite good rooms with private bathroom, a/c. Restaurant and pool.

C Cabinas El Cisne and Sensación Tropical, 75 m north of Catholic church and football pitch, T2777-0719. Safe, family-run, secure parking, bigger rooms on left. Recommended.

C-D El Malinche, close to bus station, T2777-0093. Has 27 clean and good rooms, simply decorated, some with a/c much cheaper without.

C-F Wide Mouth Frog, short distance from the bus terminal, T2777-2798, www.widemouthfrog.org. Private rooms and dorms.

D Villas Mar y Sol, towards the eastern side of town, T2777-0307. Has 8 rooms with private bath and hot shower. Relaxed spot, parking.

D-E Ceciliano, towards the eastern side of town, on the road leading to Manuel Antonio, T2777-0192. Family-run, quiet, small rooms, with bath, hot.

D-E Hotel Quepos, eastern side of town, T2777-0274. With bath, cheaper without, simple, recommended.

E Cabinas Hellen, eastern side of town, T2777-0504. Quite small rooms with private bath and fan, but clean and plenty of parking.

E Cabinas Mary, by football pitch close to Iguana Tours, T2777-0128. Clean, friendly, OK.

E-G Hospedaje La Macha, next to post office on walkway by the football pitch, T2777-0216. Includes the cheapest beds in town. Very basic but clean.

F Doña Alicia, on walkway by football pitch, T2777-0419. Big cabin with bath, friendly, quiet, parking, can wash clothes.

F El Parque, on waterfront road, T2777-0063, Price per person, friendly, clean, a bit run-down but good value, private bath, fan.

F Mar y Luna, central, T2777-0394. With or without bath, quiet, clean, friendly, popular.

F Sánchez, a couple of blocks east of the bus terminal, T2777-0491. Without bath, OK.

Parque Nacional Manuel Antonio *p806*

There are hotels all along the road from Quepos to Manuel Antonio, many of them expensive. Many shut in the low season; in high season, it's best to book ahead. The area is full to bursting at weekends with locals camping on the beach. The parked Second World War plane – decked out as a bar – marks the start of the downhill to the beach.

LL Makanda by the Sea, down a dirt road leading to Punta Quepos from opposite **Café Milagro**, T2777-0442, www.makanda.com. 11 villas and studios with superb open design. An idyllic and romantic paradise spot.

LL Sí Como No, T2777-0777, www.sicomono.com. A superb hotel with beautiful touches of design using stunning stained glass, all the comforts you would expect, and service par excellence plus a cinema.

LL-A Costa Verde, at the train carriage restaurant and reception, T2777-0584, www.costaverde.com. Apartments for 2-4 people, with kitchenette and bath, 2-bedroom villas available, well-appointed, pool and a couple of restaurants. Several nature trails out the back. Recommended.

AL-A Karahé, along the main road towards the beach, on private road, T2777-0170, www.karahe.com. Includes breakfast, cabins on a steep hillside with lovely view, sleep 3-4, recommended, fridge, bath, a/c or fan, good restaurant, swimming pool across the road, access to beach, walk to park along the beach.

A Villa de la Selva, overlooking the bay, T2777-0434. Has 5 simple rooms, some with kitchenettes. Up above most of the activity, this is a charming spot away from the mêlée. Recommended.

A-B La Arboleda, T2777-1056, www.hotel-arboleda.com. Cabins on hillside leading down to beach sleep 2-3, bath, fan, Uruguayan restaurant, 8-ha wood. Beware snakes, crabs and monkeys in the yard at night. Recommended.

B Hotel Manuel Antonio, T2777-1237. Good breakfast, camping possible nearby, ask in the restaurant. Handy, just minutes from the national park and the beach.

B Vela Bar, T2777-0413, www.velabar.com. Large rooms with bath, fans, safes, very good restaurant, fishing and other trips, also has a fully equipped house to rent.

B-C B&B Casa Buena Vista, T2777-1002. Offers a breathtaking view and wonderful breakfast terrace, friendly owner.

B-C Mono Azul, T2777-1954, www.hotelmonoazul.com. 20 rooms, conference rooms, library, internet, 2 nightly movies, international headquarters of **Kids Saving the Rainforest** and souvenir store with profits going to save the rainforest. Friendly place with a couple of pools, and a good restaurant.

D Cabinas Ramírez, towards the end of the road, T2777-5044. With bath, food and bar, free hammocks and camping, guests can help with cooking in exchange.

D-F Vista Serena Hostel, at the start of the road, T2777-5132, www.vistaserena.com. Good quality budget option on the Manuel Antonio strip. Good rooms, private or dorms, and balconies with hammocks looking out to the coast.

F Costa Linda, up the side road just before the park, T2777-0304. Double rooms or 4-bedded room, fan, water shortage, watch out for racoons raiding the outdoor kitchen in the night, good breakfasts; dinner rather pricey.

Dominical *p807*

Booking hotels is slightly easier in the Dominical and Uvita area using regional specialists and booking service **Selva Mar**, T2771-4582, www.exploringcostarica.com.

LL-A Diuwak, back from the beach, T2787-0087, www.diuwak.com. Rooms and suites, sleeping up to 4 people, with private bath. Mini supermarket and internet service, pool.

A Hotel/Restaurant Roca Verde, on the beachfront about 1 km south of Dominical, T2787-0036, www.rocaverde.net. Tropical rooms with a/c. Small balcony or terraces, with a pool. Big bar and restaurant. Recommended.

A-B Hacienda Barú, about 2 km north of Dominical, T2787-0003, www.hacienda baru.com. A 332-ha reserve that began life as a private reserve in 1972. Cabins sleeping 3 or more with private bath, hiking, riding. So much to see and do in such a small area. There is a canopy observation platform, tree climbing, night walks in the jungle and several self-guided trails and a butterfly garden.

A-B Villas Río Mar Jungle and Beach Resort, out of town, 500 m from beach, T2787-0052, www.villasriomar.com. 40 bungalows with bath, fridge and fan, pool, jacuzzi, tennis court, trails, riding, all inclusive.

A-C Hotel Pacífico Edge, Punta Dominical, T2771-4582, www.exploringcostarica.com. **Selva Mar** service. 4 large cabins with great views of ocean and rainforest.

C Bella Vista Lodge, Punta Dominical, T2388-0155 or T2771-4582 (through the **Selva Mar** reservation service). Great view, good large meals, owned by local American Woody Dyer, organizes trips in the area. There are also houses to rent.

C Posada del Sol, 100 m from beach, T2787-0085. Owned by local historian Mariela Badilla, 20-odd rooms, bath, fan, patio with hammocks, also 2-bedroom apartment with kitchen for US$150 per week. Rooms vary.

C-D Río Lindo, at the entrance to town, T2787-0028. Clean, tidy rooms with a balcony or terrace. Private bath with fan or a/c. Pool and bar area.

C-D Tortilla Flats, formerly Cabinas Nayarit right on the sea front, T2787-0033. Rooms sleeping up to 3 people, with private bath and hot water. A bit overpriced if just for 2.

C-F Cabinas San Clemente, on beach, T2787-0026. Clean, with or without a/c, friendly, US-owned, restaurant, also cheaper, basic dorm rooms, shared bath, fan; **San Clemente Bar and Grill**, under same ownership, good, big portions.

D-F Cabinas El Coco, at end of main street, T2787-0235. With or without bath, negotiate price, unfriendly, noisy, a last option. Camping possible.

Uvita *p807*

The central booking service **Selva Mar**, T2771-4582, www.exploringcostarica.com, makes booking a hotel in this area easier.

A Canto de Ballenas, 6 km south of Uvita, close to Parque Nacional Marino Ballena, T2248-2538, www.hotelcantoballenas.com. Rustic, but fine, wooden cabins in a simple land- scaped garden. Great spot in a quiet location.

A Villa María Luisa Lodge, Bahía Uvita, T2743-8094. Simple cabins sleeping up to 6.

C Cabinas El Chamán, 2 km south on the beach, T2771-2555. Nice location, 8 simple *cabinas* with private bathroom, camping US$4 per person.

C-D Cascada Verde, Uvita village, up the hill, www.cascadaverde.org. *Hostal*, educational retreat and organic farm, German-run, vegetarian food, yoga and meditation workshops available. Pay for a bed, hammock or camp, or work for your lodgings. Long-term lodgings preferred, great spot if you take to the place.

C-G The Tucan Hotel, Uvita village, just off the main road, T2743-8140, www.tucan hotel.com. Low-key and pleasant spot in Uvita. Dormitory and private rooms, kitchen available, advice on local travel options and Wi-Fi.

D-E Coco Tico Ecolodge, Uvita village, T2743-8032. 6 clean *cabinas*, sleep 3, with private bathroom and trails outback.

E Cabinas Las Gemelas, Playa Bahía Uvita, T2743-8009. Simple rooms, with showers and bathrooms. Quiet spot with gardens for camping.

E Cabinas Los Laureles, Uvita village, 200 m turn on the left from the main road, T2771-8008. Nice location, 3 *cabinas* with private bathroom, simple and quite good.

E Roca Paraíso, near Cabinas El Chamán, T2220-4263 for information. Basic.

F Cabinas Punta Uvita, opposite Restaurant Los Almendros close to the beach. Simple, basic *cabinas* with private bathroom.

Parque Nacional Marino Ballena *p807*

A Hotel Villas Gaia, Playa Tortuga, 200 m to the beach, T2244-0316, www.villasgaia.com. 12 spacious cabins with private bathrooms (hot water), fan and terrace. Swimming pool and restaurant serving Swiss, international and vegetarian dishes. Ocean view, diving school, horses. Several other quiet secluded options opening up.

B Posada Playa Tortuga, Playa Tortuga, T2384-5489, www.hotel-posada.com. Run by Gringo Mike, a great spot and place to stay, and Mike knows everything there is to know about the area.

❼ Eating

Jacó *p804*

There are lots of *sodas* in Jacó.

🍴🍴🍴 **Sunrise Grill Breakfast Place**, centre of town. Breakfast from 0700, closed Wed.

🍴🍴🍴 **Wishbone**, on the main street. Big plates of Mexican food, from US$6.

🍴🍴🍴 **Chatty Cathy's**, on the main drag. A popular dining spot.

🍴🍴 **La Ostra**, centre of town. Good fish in this pleasant open-air restaurant open all day.

🍴🍴 **Wahoo**, just within the centre to the north. Good Tico food, mainly fish.

Jacó to Quepos *p805*

🍴 **Doña María's Soda**, small central market, Parrita, T8842-3047. Tasty *casados*.

Quepos *p805*, map *p804*

There are many good restaurants along the road towards Manuel Antonio.

🍴🍴 **Basarno's**, near the entrance to town. Bar, restaurant and club. Daily 1000-0100. A good mix of snacks and a lively spot later in the night.

🍴🍴🍴-🍴🍴 **El Gran Escape**, central, T2777-0395. Lively collection of restaurants and bars offering Tex Mex, pizza and sushi. Good food and service, recommended.

🍴🍴 **Dos Locos**, central, T2777-1526. Popular with Mexican and Tico fare, open to the street, occasional live music.

🍴🍴 **El Banco Restaurant and Sports Bar**, near El Gran Escape, T2777-0478. Remodelled long bar with bright neon, good Tex Mex food and will cook your catch.

🍴🍴 **Escalofrío**, next to Dos Locos. Pizza, pasta and ice cream to die for from US$4.

🍴🍴 **Gardin Gourmet**, opposite Escalofrío. Great deli with lots of imported treats.

🍴🍴 **Pizza Gabriels**, central, T2777-1085. Popular little spot with a lively undercurrent. Fine pizza and pasta from US$6.

Cafés, snacks and bakeries

The municipal market (for fruit and bread) is at the bus station.

Café Milagro, on the waterfront, T2777-0794, www.cafemilagro.com. Best espresso, cakes, pies, Cuban cigars, souvenirs, freshly roasted coffee for sale; another branch on the road to Manuel Antonio.

L'Angolo, opposite Dos Locos. Serves a mix of breads, olives, hams and everything you'd need for self-catering or picnicking in style.

La Buena Nota, on road near the beach in Manuel Antonio, T2777-1002. Sells English-language newspapers. A good place to seek local information, run by Anita Myketuk, who has initiated publicity on rip tides.

Pan Aldo, right in front of the soccer pitch, T2777-2697. Italian specialities, wholewheat sourdough, great bread and pastries.

Dominical p807

♥ **Jazzy's River House**, down the main street. More an open-house cum cultural centre, occassionally have meals followed by an open-mic set up on Wed.

♥ **Restaurant El Coco**, in town. Serves good food and rents budget rooms.

♥ **San Clemente**, in town. A good mix of Tex Mex with big servings.

♥ **Thrusters**, in town. A hip spot for the surf crowd, with sushi in the front restaurant.

♥ **Soda Nanyoa**, in town, offers Costa Rican specialities.

◉ Entertainment

Jacó p804

Discos in town include **Central**, close to the beach, T2643-3076, **Los Tucanes**, **El Zarpe Sports Bar**, T2643-3473, **Club Olé**, T2643-1576, restaurant, bar, disco and games.

▲ Activities and tours

Quepos p805, map p804

Amigos del Río, opposite the football pitch, T2777-0082, www.amigosdelrio.net. River rafting, kayaking, canopy and horse riding tours, good guides.

Iguana Tours, close to the church on the football pitch, T2777-2052, www.iguana tours.com. Excellent local knowledge with many tours available. Friendly and helpful.

Lynch Travel Services, right in the centre of town, T2777-0161, www.lynchtravel.com.

◉ Transport

Jacó p804

Bus

From **San José** Coca Cola bus station, 3 daily, 3½ hrs, US$3.90, arrive at Plaza Jacó-Complex terminal at north end of town, next to Pizza Hut. Also several buses to **Quepos**.

Quepos p805, map p804

Air

There are several daily flights from **San José**, with Sansa (US$63-79) and Nature Air (US$40 1 way). The Sansa office is under Hotel Quepos, T2777-0683.

Bus

There are 3 express buses a day leaving **San José** Coca Cola bus station, T2223-5567, at 0600, 1200 and 1800, returning at 0600, 0930, 1200 and 1700, 3½ hrs, US$7, book a day in advance, 6 regular buses, 4½ hrs, US$6. There are buses northwest along the coast to **Puntarenas**, 3½ hrs, 0430, 1030, and 1500, return 0500, 1100, 1430, US$3.30. 2 daily buses via **Dominical** to **San Isidro de El General**, T2771-4744, 0500, and 1330, 3½ hrs, US$4, connections can be made there to get to the Panamanian border, return 0700, 1330.

Taxi

Taxis congregate opposite the bus terminal, just up from **Dos Locos** restaurant. Minibuses meet flights.

Parque Nacional Manuel Antonio p806

Bus

There are 3 express buses a day, direct from **San José**, 4 hrs, US$7.60. At weekends buy your ticket the day before; buses fill to standing room only very quickly. Roads back to San José on Sun evening are packed. A regular bus service runs roughly ½-hourly from beside **Quepos** market, starting at 0545, to Manuel Antonio, last bus back at 1700, US$0.35.

Car

If driving, there is ample guarded parking in the area, US$6.

Taxi

From **Quepos**, approximately US$10. Minibuses meet flights from San José to the airport at Quepos (see above), US$2.25.

Dominical *p807*

Bus

To **Quepos** 0545, 0815, 1350 (Sat and Sun) and 1450, US$3.20. To **San Isidro**, 0645, 0705, 1450, 1530, 1 hr, US$2.50. To **Uvita** at 0950, 1010, 1130 (weekends) 1710 and 2000, US$1.10. To **Cd Cortés** and **Cd Neily** 0420 and 1000. To **San José**, 0545, 1340 (Sat and Sun), 7 hrs.

Uvita *p807*

Bus

From **San José** Terminal Coca Cola, Mon-Fri 1500, Sat and Sun 1500, 1500, return Mon-Fri 0530, Sat and Sun 0530, 1300, 7 hrs, US$8.90. From **San Isidro** daily 0800, 1600, return 0600, 1400. From **Dominical**, last bus 1700 or 1800, US$1,10.

---

❶ Directory

Jacó *p804*

Banks Banco Nacional in centre of town. **Internet** Iguana Mar, Centro de Computación and Mexican Joe's Internet Café. **Language schools** City Playa

Language Institute, T2643-4023, service@costaricareisen.com, offers Spanish classes with or without homestay, and the novel option of free surfing lessons. **Post** Near Municipalidad offices.

Quepos *p805, map p804*

Banks Several branches in town including Banco Nacional, which has a Visa ATM as does Banco Popular and Banco San José. The best place to exchange TCs or US$ cash is at Distribuidora Puerto Quepos, opposite Banco de Costa Rica, 0900-1700, no paperwork, no commission, all done in 2 mins, same rate as banks. **Immigration** On the same street as the Banco de Costa Rica. **Internet** Access available from Internet Quepos, fast machines, good service, US$1.50 per hr. Several others in town, including Arte Net, Quepos Diner & Internet Café, Internet Tropical, CyberLoco and Internet Cantina. **Language schools** Escuela D'Amore, in a great setting overlooking the ocean, halfway between Quepos and the national park, T2777-1143, www.escueladamore.com. Believes in the immersion technique, living with local families. Costa Rica Spanish Institute, T2234-1001, www.cosi.co.cr. **Laundry** Lavanderías de Costa Rica, near the football pitch, good. **Medical services** The hospital is out of town, T2777-0922. Red Cross, T2777-0118. **Police** T2777-0196. **Post** On the walkway by the football pitch, 0800-1700.

San José to Panama

Heading through the Talamanca mountains, the Pan-American Highway reaches its highest point at Cerro de la Muerte (Peak of Death) and passes El Chirripó, Costa Rica's highest peak at 3820 m, as the scenic road drops down through the valley of the Río de El General to the tropical lowlands of the Pacific coast and the border with Panama. Private reserves along the route are ideal for birdwatching – here the resplendent quetzal enjoys a quieter life than his Monteverde relations – and mountain streams are stocked with trout providing both sport and food. Lodges and hotels are usually isolated, dotted along the highway. Towards Costa Rica's most southerly point, the Península de Osa is a nature haven of beautiful pathways, palm-fringed beaches and protected rainforest – well worth the effort if you have the time.
▸▸ *For listings, see pages 820-825.*

Travelling the Pan-American Highway → *For listings, see pages 820-825.*

From San José the Pan-American Highway runs for 352 km to the Panama border. It's a spectacular journey along a generally good road but challenging if you're driving, with potholes, occasional rockslides during the rainy season, roadworks and generally difficult conditions.

From Cártago, the route heads south over the mountains, beginning with the ascent of **Cerro Buena Vista** (3490 m), a climb of almost 2050 m to the continental divide. A little lower than the peak, the highest point of the road is 3335 m at Km 89, which travels through barren *páramo* scenery. Those unaccustomed to high altitude should beware of mountain sickness brought on by a too rapid ascent. For 16 km the road follows the crest of the Talamanca ridge, with views of the Pacific 50 km away, and on clear days of the Atlantic, 80 km to the east.

Some 4.5 km east of Km 58 (Cañón church) is **Genesis II**, a privately owned 40-ha cloud forest National Wildlife Refuge, at 2360 m, bordering the **Tapantí–Macizo de la Muerte National Park**. Accommodation is available here and at several other places along the way. At Km 78 is **Casa Refugio de Ojo de Agua**, a historic pioneer home overlooked but for a couple of picnic tables in front of the house. At Km 80 a steep, dramatic road leads down the spectacular valley of the Río Savegre to **San Gerardo de Dota**, a birdwatchers' paradise. The highest point is at Km 89.5, where temperatures are below zero at night.

San Isidro de El General → *Colour map 4, B3. Altitude: 702 m.*

The drop in altitude from the highlands to the growing town of San Isidro passes through fertile valleys growing coffee and raising cattle. The huge **cathedral** on the main plaza is a bold architectural statement, with refreshing approaches to religious iconography inside. The **Museo Regional del Sur** ⓘ *Calle 2, Av 1-0, T2771-5273, Mon-Fri 0800-1200, 1330-1630, free,* is in the old marketplace, now the Complejo Cultural. The 750-ha **Centro Biológico Las Quebradas** ⓘ *7 km north of San Isidro, T2771-4131, Tue-Fri 0800-1400, Sat and Sun 0800-1500, closed Oct,* has trails and dormitory lodging for researchers. San Isidro de El General is also the place to stock up for a trip into Parque Nacional Chirripó and to climb Cerro Chirripó Grande (3820 m), see page 817.

Parque Nacional Chirripó

ⓘ *US$15 plus US$10 per night, crowded in season, make reservations through the Oficina de los Parques Nacionales (OPN) in San Gerardo, T2742-5083, open 0630-1200, 1300-1630. Get the latest information from www.sangerardocostarica.com. If you want to walk or climb in the park, get food in San Isidro and book accommodation at the OPN. The bus to San Gerardo leave from the bus station in the market south of the cathedral plaza. The blue and white bus marked San Gerardo leaves at 0930, 1400 and 1845, taking 1½ hrs, US$1.60. Return buses at 0515, 1130 and 1600.*

San Isidro de El General is west of Costa Rica's highest mountain **Cerro Chirripó Grande** (3820 m) in the middle of Parque Nacional Chirripó (50,150 ha). Treks starts from San Gerardo de Rivas (see below). The views from the hilltops are splendid and the high plateau near the summit is an interesting alpine environment with lakes of glacial origin and diverse flora and fauna. The park includes a considerable portion of cloud forest and the walk is rewarding.

Parque Nacional Chirripó neighbours **Parque Internacional La Amistad** (193,929 ha), established in 1982, and together they extend along the Cordillera de Talamanca to the Panamanian border, comprising the largest area of virgin forest in the country with the greatest biological diversity.

San Gerardo de Rivas

In a cool, pleasant spot, San Gerardo de Rivas is at the confluence of the Río Blanco and the Río Pacífico Chirripó. Close to Parque Nacional Chirripó entrance, it is the starting point for the climb up **Cerro Chirripó Grande** (3820 m). If you haven't booked accommodation at the refugio in San Isidro you can try booking at the MINAE office (see box, opposite).

As interest in this quiet area grows, new tours are appearing including trips to local waterfalls (US$40) and nature tours.

Handy for weary legs after the climb, there are **hot springs** ⓘ *daily 0700-1800, entrance US$5*, in the area. Before crossing the concrete bridge turn left to 'Herradura' for 10 minutes then look for the sign after Parque Las Rosas; go down to the suspension bridge, cross the river and continue for 10 minutes to the house where you pay. Full information about the town, including accommodation, at www.sangerardocostarica.com.

Buenos Aires to Paso Real

Continuing southeast, a good road sinks slowly through the Río General valley where the Talamanca Mountains dominate the skyline. At Km 197 (from San José), the change from coffee to fruit is complete; at the junction for **Buenos Aires** is the huge **Del Monte** cannery. The town, a few kilometres off the Pan-American Highway, has some simple accommodation.

Heading 17 km east towards the mountains is the **Reserva Biológica Durika**, a privately owned reserve of roughly 800 ha, aiming to create a self-sustained community in the Talamanca mountains. Accommodation is available in some rustic cabins.

South along the highway, the small towns of Térraba and Boruca are the most prominent remains of the nation's indigenous population. The community of **Boruca**, with a small *hostal* (**F**), has a small, poorly maintained museum, but every year the **Fiesta de los Diablitos** on the last day of December and first two days of January, and the last day of January and the first two days of February in **Rey Curre**, see the culture come alive in a festival of music, dance and costume. There is a daily bus to Boruca from Buenos Aires at 1130 (1½ hours).

Climbing the Chirripó peaks

The early morning climb to the summit of Cerro Chirripó, Costa Rica's highest mountain, is a refreshing slog after the relative comforts often encountered in Costa Rica. The hike takes you through magnificent cloud forest draped in mosses and ephiphytes before entering a scorched area of *paramo* grasslands with incredible views to the Pacific and Atlantic coastlines on clear days. The widlife – birdlife in particularly – is incredible and, even if you don't see it, you will certainly hear it. The trek itself is not difficult but it is tiring being almost consistently uphill on the way and a knee-crunching, blister-bursting journey down.

From the *refugio* inside the park, you can also explore the nearby Crestones, a volcanic outcrop that has been etched on to the minds of every Costa Rican, and the creatively named Sabana de los Leones and Valle de los Conejos. There are useful orientation maps on www.sangerardocostarica.com.

If you wish to climb the 3820 m Cerro Chirripó, Costa Rica's highest mountain, you must make advance reservations by calling the MINAE park service office in San Gerardo (T2771-5116), the access town to Chirripó, around 12 km northeast of San Isidro de El General. After phoning for reservations you are given a couple of days to pay by bank deposit to guarantee your space. Visitors are not allowed into the park without reservations at the *refugio*. During the dry season it's often full, so it's a good idea to make arrangements as soon as possible. Start in the early morning for the 8- to 10-hour hike to the *refugio*. The cost is US$15 entry for each day spent in the park, plus US$10 shelter fee per night. Guides are available. The *refugio* has simple but adequate accommodation, with space for about 80 people and a large kitchen area.

The cold – often frosty in the morning – is a bit of a shock in contrast to the rest of Costa Rica, but you can rent blankets and sleeping bags from the *refugio*. Gas cookers are also available for hire (US$2). There are sufficient water supplies en route although you will need to carry your food supplies. Electrical power at the *refugio* is only for a couple of hours each night, so be sure to bring a flashlight. The top of Chirripó is located a further 5.1 km beyond the Crestones base camp.

In addition to the high camp there is a shelter about halfway up, **Refugio Llano Bonito** (2500 m), which is simple and occasionally clean, with wooden floor, two levels to sleep on, no door but wind protection, drinking water and toilet. It's about four hours' walk from San Gerardo and three hours' walk on to **Refugios Base Crestones**. Plan for at least two nights on the mountain – although you can do it with only one night if you're tight for time, rising very early to summit on the second day in time to go all the day down in one hit. While nights can be cold, daytime temperatures tend to be warm to hot, so go prepared with sunscreen and hat. In the rainy season, trails up the plateau are slippery and muddy, and fog obscures the views. Time your descent to catch the afternoon bus back to San Isidro.

For a general update on San Gerardo and climbing Chirripó, visit www.sangerardocostarica.com.

At **Paso Real** the highway heads west to Palmar Norte, with a turn heading towards San Vito (see below) and the Panamanian border.

Palmar Norte and Palmar Sur

Taking a sharp turn at Paso Real (straight on for San Vito – see below), the Pan-American Highway heads west to Palmar Norte (Km 257 – with gas station) from where a paved road leads to Ciudad Cortés. A road heads northwest to Dominical (see page 807).

Crossing the Río Grande de Terraba leads to Palmar Sur, which is 90 km from the Panamanian border. There are several very large stone spheres in the area. A banana plantation close to town has stone spheres – 1.5 m in diameter and accurate within 5 mm – of pre-Columbian manufacture, though their use is a matter of conjecture. Recent theories are that they were made to represent the planets of the solar system, or that they were border markers.

From Palmar Sur the Pan-American Highway heads southeast to Chacarita (33 km) where a road turns off to the Osa Peninsula, to Río Claro (another 26 km) where a road leads to Golfito, another 15 km leads to Ciudad Neily which is 16 km from the border at Paso Canoas.

Sierpe

Through a matrix of cooperative banana and African plantations, a road leads to Sierpe, on the Río Sierpe, where there are several small hotels and the departure point for boats to Bahía Drake, see page 827.

Paso Real to San Vito → *For listings, see pages 820-825. Colour map 4, B4.*

The road from Paso Real to San Vito is now paved and has lovely views. **La Amistad International Park** has few facilities for visitors at present, but one secluded lodge is found way up in the hills beyond Potrero Grande, just south of the Paso Real junction on the way to San Vito. Near the border is **San Vito**. Originally built by Italian immigrants among denuded hills, it is a prosperous but undistinguished town.

On the road from San Vito to Ciudad Neily at Las Cruces are the world-renowned **Wilson Botanical Gardens** ① *T2773-4004, www.ots.ac.cr*, owned by the **Organization for Tropical Studies**, 6 km from San Vito. In 360 ha of forest reserve are over 5000 species of tropical plants, orchids, other epiphytes and trees with 331 resident bird species. It is possible to spend the night here if you arrange it first with the **OTS** ① *T2240-6696, in San José (L per person all-inclusive), US$32 per person for day visits with lunch*. On the same road is **Finca Cántaros** ① *T2773-3760*, specializing in local arts and crafts, owned by Gail Hewson Gómez. It's one of the best craft shops in Costa Rica – worth a look even if you don't buy anything.

Border with Panama–Sabalito

The road south from San Vito to Ciudad Neily is paved, in good condition and offers some of the best coastal views in the country as the road rapidly falls through the hills. Heading east from San Vito, a good gravel road, paved in places, runs via Sabalito (Banco Nacional) to the Panama border at Río Sereno. There are buses from Sabalito to San José. See page 715, for details of this border crossing.

Golfito and around → *For listings, see pages 820-825. Colour map 4, B4.*

Thirty-one kilometres north of the border a road branches south at Río Claro (several *pensiones* and a fuel station) to the former banana port of Golfito, a 6-km-long linear settlement bordering the Golfo Dulce and steep forested hills. While elements of hard sweat and dock labour remain, Golfito's prominence today comes from being Costa Rica's only free port, set up in 1990, selling goods tax free at about 60% of normal prices. Popular with shoppers from throughout the country, it can be difficult to get a hotel room at weekends. Check out www.golfito-costarica.com for information on lodging and activities in the area.

Golfito also provides boat and ferry access to Puerto Jiménez and the Osa Peninsula, and popular fishing and surfing beaches to the south of the town.

Entering the town from the south heading north there are a few hotels where the road meets the coast. In 2 km is the small town centre of painted buildings with saloon bars, open-fronted restaurants and cheap accommodation – probably the best stop for budget travellers. Nearby is the dilapidated *muellecito* used by the ferries to Puerto Jiménez and water taxis. A further kilometre north are the container port facilities and the **Standard Fruit Company**'s local HQ, though many of the banana plantations have been turned over to oil palm and other crops. Beyond the dock is the free port, airstrip and another set of hotels.

The **Refugio Nacional de Fauna Silvestre Golfito**, in the steep forested hills over-looking Golfito, was created to protect Golfito's watershed. Rich in rare and medicinal plants with abundant fauna, there are some excellent hikes in the refuge. Supervised by the University of Costa Rica, they have a field office in Golfito.

Thirty minutes by water taxi from Golfito, you can visit **Casa Orquídeas** ① *T2775-1614, tours last about 2½ hrs, US$5 per person, US$20 minimum, closed Fri*, a family-owned botanical garden with a large collection of herbs, orchids and local flowers and trees, that you can see, smell, touch and taste.

To the north of Golfito is the **Parque Nacional Piedras Blancas** tropical wet forest. The area was being exploited for wood products, but has been steadily purchased since 1991 with help from the Austrian government and private interests, notably the classical Austrian violinist Michael Schnitzler. All logging has now ceased and efforts are devoted to a research centre and ecotourism, concentrated in an area designated **Parque Nacional Esquinas**. Near the village of **La Gamba** a tourist lodge has been built (see Sleeping, below). La Gamba is 6 km along a dirt road from Golfito, or 4 km from Briceño on the Pan-American Highway between Piedras Blancas and Río Claro.

Beaches around Golfito

Playa de Cacao is about 6 km (1½-hour walk) north of Golfito round the bay, or a short trip by water taxi. Further north is the secluded beach of **Playa San Josecito** with a couple of adventure-based lodges.

About 15 km by sea south of Golfito, and reached by water taxi or a long bus journey (US$2 by *colectivo* ferry from the small dock; 0600 and 1200, return 0500, 1300), **Playa Zancudo** is a long stretch of clean golden sound, dotted with a few rustic hotels ideal for relaxing and lazing away the days. Still further south is **Pavones**, where a world record left-hand wave has elevated the rocky beach to the realm of surfing legend. South of Pavones, towards the end of the peninsula and at the mouth of the Golfo Dulce is **Punta Banco**.

Ciudad Neily, Paso Canoas and the Panama border

Ciudad Neily is an uninspiring town providing useful transport links between San Vito in the highlands and the coastal plain, and is roughly 16 km from Paso Canoas on the border with Panama. Paso Canoas is a little piece of chaos with traders buying and selling to take advantage of the difference in prices between Costa Rica and Panama. With little to hold you, there is little reason to visit unless heading to Panama. If misfortune should find you having to stay the night, there are some reasonable options.

San José to Panama listings

For Sleeping and Eating price codes and other relevant information, see Essentials pages 31-33.

Sleeping

Travelling the Pan-American Highway *p815*
L-AL Hotel de Montaña Savegre, San Gerardo de Dota, T2740-1028, www.savegre.co.cr. Waterfalls, trout fishing, prices include meals.
B-C Trogón Lodge, San Gerardo de Dota, T2740-1051, www.grupomawamba.com. 23 fine wooden cabins with private bathroom, set amongst beautiful gardens connected by paths used by dive-bombing hummingbirds.
C Finca Eddie Serano Mirador de Quetzales, Km 70, T2381-8456. A 43-ha forest property at 2650 m. Eddie Serrano has passed away, but one of his sons will show visitors quetzals (almost guaranteed, but don't tell anyone at **Monteverde Cloud Forest**) and other endemic species of the highlands. 10 cabins, sleeping 2-5, with wonderful views, private bath, price per person includes breakfast, dinner and guided hike.
E Hotel and Restaurant Georgina, Km 95, T2770-8043. At almost 3300 m, Costa Rica's highest hotel, basic, clean, friendly, good food (used by southbound **Tracopa** buses), good birdwatching; ask owners for directions for a nice walk to see quetzals.

Camping
Los Ranchos, San Gerardo de Dota, at the bottom of the hill, T2771-2376. Camping in perfect surroundings. No transport down here, but pickups from the highway can be arranged.

San Isidro de El General *p815*
B Rancho La Botija, out of town on the road to San Gerardo, T2770-2147, www.rancho labotija.com. Restaurant, pool, hiking to nearby petroglyphs, open 0900 at weekends, great restaurant littered with fragments of *botijas*. Recommended.
C Talari Mountain Lodge, 10 mins from San Isidro on the road to San Gerardo, T2771-0341, www.talari.co.cr. 8-ha farm, with bath, riverside cabins, known for birdwatching, rustic.
C-D Hotel Los Crestones, in town, T2770-1200, www.hotelloscrestones.com. Big rooms, complete with TV, swimming pool. Wheelchair accessible.
D-E Astoria, on north side of square, T2771-0914. Tiny but clean rooms.
E El Valle, Calle 2, Av Central-2, T2771-0246. Cleanish, one of the better cheapies.
E Hotel/Restaurant Amaneli, in town, T2771-0352. Has 41 quite good rooms with private bathroom, fan, some noisy.
E Hotel Iguazu, Calle Central, Av 1, T2771-2571. Hot water, cable TV, clean, safe with parking.
E-F Hotel Chirripó, south side of Parque Central, T2771-0529. Private or shared bath, clean, very good restaurant, free covered parking, recommended.
F Lala, Calle Central, Av 1, T2771-0291. Basic and simple.

San Gerardo de Rivas *p816*
All accommodation is on the road up to the park.
D Pelícano, T2742-5050, www.hotel pelicano.net. 11 rooms sleeping between 2 and 5 people, with great views, a bar and restaurant. Beautiful setting with countless birds. Also has a swimming pool.

D-E El Urán, at the very top, closest to the park entrance, T2742-5003, www.hotel uran.com. Simple, clean rooms, lots of blankets and a restaurant that will feed you early before setting out.

D-E Roca Dura, opposite the football pitch, T2742-5071, rocadurasangerardo@ hotmail.com. Built on a huge boulder, 7 rooms with hot showers, good *comedor*, nice view, shop next door, friendly owners.

E Marín, next to MINAE office, T2742-5099. Basic but friendly and good value.

F Cabinas El Descanso, T2742-5061. 7 bunks, bathroom, hearty meals available, gas stove for hire, horses for rent and guide services offered, recommended. Price per person.

F Cabinas/Restaurant Elimar, 500 m out of village. Swimming pool, simple restaurant, 4 quite good *cabinas* with private bathroom, hot water.

F El Bosque, T2742-5021, elbosque@ gmail.com. With a small bar and restaurant. Looks a bit scruffy from the outside, but spotless rooms and great views over the valley from some rooms.

Camping

You can camp at Roca Dura and El Bosque, or near the park office, in San Gerardo near the bus stop. Check in first and pay US$0.30.

Buenos Aires to Paso Real *p816*

C-D Cabañas, Durika Biological Reserve, T2730-0657, www.durika.org. Rustic cabins. Includes 3 vegetarian meals a day, with a wide range of activities including walks, hikes to the summit of Cerro Durika and cultural tours. Around US$10 per person on top of the daily rate.

F Cabinas Violeta, Buenos Aires, next to the fire station, 200 m west of the plaza, T2730-0104. Clean, simple, central and OK if you're stuck for the night.

G Cabinas Mary, Buenos Aires, 800 m south of the centre close to the **Aridikes** office, T2730-0187. Quiet spot which tries to be clean.

Palmar Norte and Palmar Sur *p818*

D-F Hotel y Cabinas Casa Amarilla, 300 m east of bus station on the plaza, T2786-6251. With fan, cabins are more expensive than the hotel rooms, rooms at back quieter, rooms over restaurant noisy but cheaper.

E Cabinas Tico-Alemán, on the highway near the gas station, T2786-6232. 25 *cabinas* with private bathroom. Best in town.

G Hotel Xinia, 150 m east from bus station, T2786-6129. 26 rooms, very basic but OK, shared bathroom.

Sierpe *p818*

B Río Sierpe Lodge, T2384-5595, www.rio sierpelodge.com. All- inclusive plan with an emphasis on fishing.

C Oleaje Sereno, T2786-7580, www.hotel oleajesereno.com. Good rooms, with restaurant on river bank.

F-G Margarita, T2786-7574. Has 13 good rooms. Friendly owners and good value.

Paso Real to San Vito *p818*

C El Ceibo, just down from main plaza, T2773-3025. With bath, hot water and TV, good restaurant.

D-E Cabinas Rino, right in the centre of town, T2773-3071. Clean and well maintained. Good deal.

E Cabinas Las Huacas, near Cabinas Firenze, T2773-3115. Has 13 OK cabinas with private bathroom, hot water, TV, which were looking very run-down when last visited.

F Las Mirlas, 500 m out of town on road to Sabalito, T2773-3714. In same location as **Hotel Pitier**, but more attractive.

G Cabinas Firenze, close to the gas station, on the road from San Isidro, T2773-3741. Has 6 basic *cabinas*, sleep 5, with private bathroom.

G Colono, plaza area, T2773-4543. Cheap and central.

G Hotel Pitier, 500 m out of town on road to Sabalito, T2773-3027. Clean, with bath.

Golfito p818

AL Esquinas Rainforest Lodge, near La Gamba, 6 km from Golfito, T2741-8001, www.esquinaslodge.com. Full board, private baths, verandas overlooking the forest, tours, all profits to the local community.

C Las Gaviotas, next to El Gran Ceibo, T2775-0062, www.hotelmarinalasgaviotas.com. 21 cabins and rooms, with bath, a/c and with excellent restaurant looking out over the waterfront.

C Sierra, at the northernmost part of town, near the airport and free zone, T2775-0666. 72 double rooms, a/c, a couple of pools, restaurant. Rooms are better than the place looks from the outside.

D Golfo Azul, T2775-0871. Has 20 large, comfortable rooms, with bath and a/c, good restaurant.

D La Purruja Lodge, 4 km south of Golfito, T2775-5054, www.purruja.com. 5 duplex cabins with bath, plus camping US$2 per tent.

E Delfina, town centre, T2775-0043. Shared bath, fan, friendly, basic. Some rooms with private bath much better. Rooms on street are noisy, parking available.

E Mar y Luna, T2775-0192. Has 8 rooms sleeping 2-4, with bath, fan, restaurant on stilts above the sea, quiet spot, good deal.

E Melissa, behind Delfina, T2775-0443. Has 4 simple rooms, with private bath, clean and quiet, great spot overlooking bay. Parking available. Recommended.

E-F Del Cerro, close to the docks, T2775-0006. Offering 20 simple rooms sleeping 1-6, private bathroom, laundry services, fishing boat rentals.

E-F Golfito, central, T2775-0047. Quiet, with a couple of rooms overlooking the bay and an apartment at US$30. A little run-down but OK.

F Costa Rica Surf, T2775-0034. Has 25 dark rooms, most with private bath. Big bar downstairs. Not the best in town, but OK.

G El Uno, above Chinese restaurant of same name, T2775-0061. Very basic and mildly amusing if you fancy pretending to be a banana in a packing case, but friendly.

Beaches around Golfito p819

AL Tiskita Jungle Lodge, Punta Banco, T2296-8125, www.tiskita-lodge.co.cr. A 162-ha property including a fruit farm, with excellent birdwatching, 14 cabins overlooking ocean. Overlooks beach, cool breezes, waterfall, jungle pools, trails through virgin forest – great spot.

AL-B Cabinas La Ponderosa, Pavones, T8824-4145 (T954-771-9166 in USA), www.cabinaslaponderosa.com. Owned by 2 surfers, large cabins, fan or a/c, with bath (hot water), walking, horse riding, fishing, diving and surfing; also house for rent (sleeps 6), restaurant.

B Latitude 8, Playa Zancudo, T2776-0168, www.latitude8lodge.com. A couple of secluded, tranquil cabins with full kitchen and hot water.

B Los Cocos, Playa Zancudo, Golfito, T2776-0012, www.loscocos.com. Beach front cabins at the ocean with private bathroom, hot water, mosquito net, fan, kitchenette, refrigerator, veranda. Also provide boat tours and taxi service. Discounts for longer stays. Heavenly.

C Pavones Surf Lodge, Pavones, T2222-2224 (San José). Includes meals, 2 cabins with bath, 6 rooms with shared bath.

C-D Coloso Del Mar, Playa Zancudo, T2776-0050, www.coloso-del-mar.com. Great little spot with 4 simple cabins overlooking the beach and a Tico/Caribbean restaurant.

C-D Mira Olas, Pavones, T2393-7742, www.miraolas.com. Cabins with kitchen and fan, low monthly rates, jungle trail.

C-D Sol y Mar, Playa Zancudo, T2776-0014, www.zancudo.com. 4 screened cabins, hot water, fan, 3-storey rental house (US$700 per month), 50 m from ocean, bar/restaurant, meals 0700-2000, home-baked bread, great fruit shakes, volleyball with lights for evening play, badminton, paddleball, boogie boards, library. Highly recommended.

E-F The Yoga Farm, Punta Banco, www.yogafarmcostarica.org. A laid-back retreat, set on a mountainside surrounded by primary rainforest and near the beach.

A great place to get back to nature, it offers a range of activities (see Activities and tours, page 824). Price includes accommodation, food and yoga. Price per person.

F Pensión Fin del Mundo, Playa Zancudo, over **Restaurant Tranquilo**. 6 simple rooms with fan, mosquito net, clean, shared bathroom. English book exchange at **Tienda Buen Precio**.

F Rancho Burica, Pavones. With thatched cabins, horse riding, fishing, tours to Guaymí indigenous reserve.

Ciudad Neily, Paso Canoas and the Panama border p819
Ciudad Neily

D Cabinas Andrea, T2783-3784. 18 clean *cabinas* with private bathroom, a/c or fan, TV. Popular with Ticos coming through town, handy for main bus terminal.

E-F El Rancho, just off the highway, T2783-3060. Has 50 resort-style cabins with bath, TV (cheaper without). Restaurant open 1600.

F Cabinas Heileen, north of plaza, T2783-3080. Simple *cabinas* with private bathroom, fan.

F Hotel Musuco, just off the Pan-American Hwy, T2783-3048. With bath, cheaper without, fan, clean and quiet. Good deal.

G Hotel Villa, north of **Hotel Musoc**, T2783-5120. Cheapest and last option in town.

Paso Canoas

E Cabinas Interamericano, T2732-2041. With bath and fan, some with a/c, good value upstairs, restaurant.

F Cabinas Jiménez, T2732-2258. Quite good *cabinas* with private bathroom, fan. Very clean, good deal.

F Hilda, south of town, T2732-2873. Good rooms, very clean, restaurant over the road. Recommended.

G Cabinas El Paso, T2732-2740. OK rooms with shower.

🍴 Eating

San Isidro de El General p815
🍴 **La Cascada**, Av 2 and Calle 2, T2771-6479. Balcony bar where the bright young things hang out.

🍴 **Restaurant Crestones**, south of the main plaza, T2771-1218. Serves a good mix of snacks, drinks and lively company.

🍴 **Restaurant El Tenedor**, Calle Central, Av Central-1, T2771-0881. Good food, friendly, big pizzas, recommended.

🍴 **Soda Chirripó**, south side of the main plaza. Gets the vote from the current gringo crowd in town.

🍴 **La Marisquería**, corner of Av 0 and Calle 4. Simple setting but great *ceviche*.

🍴 **Soda J&P**, indoor market south of the main plaza. The best of many.

Paso Real to San Vito p818
🍴 **Lilianas**, San Vito. Still showing homage to the town's Italian heritage with good pasta dishes and pizza.

🍴 **Restaurant Nelly**, San Vito, near **Cabinas Las Huacas**. Good wholesome truck-drivers' fare.

Golfito p818
Many seafood places along the seafront.
🍴 **Cubana**, near post office. Good, try *batidos*.

🍴 **El Uno**, near Cubana. Good, reasonably priced seafood.

🍴 **La Dama del Delfín Restaurant**, downtown. Breakfast from 0700, snacks, home-baked goods, closed for dinner and Sun.

🍴 **Le Eurekita**, centre. Serves a mean breakfast of *huevos rancheros*.

Beaches around Golfito p819
🍴 **Bar y Restaurant Tranquilo**, Playa Zancudo. A lively spot between **Zancudo Beach Club** and **Coloso del Mar**.

🍴 **Macondo**, Playa Zancudo. Italian restaurant which also has a couple of rooms.

🍴 **Soda Katherine**, Playa Zancudo, T2776-0124. From US$4, great Tico fare; also simple cabins.

▲ Activities and tours

San Isidro de El General *p815*
Ciprotur, Calle 4, Av 1-3, T2771-6096, www.ecotourism.co.cr. Good information on services throughout the southern region.
Selvamar, Calle 1, Av 2-4, T2771-4582, www.exploringcostarica.com. General tours and the main contact for out-of-the-way destinations in the southern region.

Golfito *p818*
Land Sea Tours, T2775-1614, landsea@racsa.co.cr. Know everything there is to know about the area. They can organize almost anything including national and international flights, and can advise on crewing on yachts heading up and down the coast.

Beaches around Golfito *p819*
The Yoga Farm, Punta Banco, www.yogafarmcostarica.org. Yoga, horse riding and hikes through the rainforest. Also organize homestay with an indigenous family.

⊖ Transport

San Isidro de El General *p815*
Bus Terminal at Av 6, Calle Central-2 at the back of the market and adjacent streets but most arrive and depart from bus depots along the Pan-American Hwy. From **San José** (just outside Terminal Coca Cola), hourly service 0530-1730, US$4.20, 3 hrs (buses to the capital leave from the highway, Calle 2-4). To **Quepos** via **Dominical** at 0500 and 1330, 3 hrs, US$4. However, **Tracopa** buses coming from **San José**, going south go from Calle 3/Pan-American Hwy, behind church, to **Palmar Norte**, US$5.20; **Paso Canoas**, 0830-1545, 1930 (direct), 2100; **David** (Panama) direct, 1000 and 1500; **Golfito** direct at 1800; **Puerto Jiménez**, 0630, 0900 and 1500. Waiting room but no reservations

or tickets sold. **Musoc** buses leave from the intersection of Calle 2-4 with the Pan-American Hwy.
    Most local buses leave from bus terminal to the south of the main plaza. Buses to **San Gerardo de Rivas** and **Cerro Chirripó** leave 0500 and 1400, return 0700 and 1600.

Taxi A 4WD taxi to San Gerardo costs about US$20 for up to 4 people.

Palmar Norte and Palmar Sur *p818*
Air Daily flights with Sansa (from US$65) and Nature Air, **San José**–Palmar Sur (from US$101 1 way).

Bus Express bus to **Palmar Norte** from Terminal Alfaro, with Tracopa from **San José**, 7 daily 0600-1800, 5 hrs, US$9.70, via **San Isidro de El General**, 5 buses return to the capital 0445-1300. 5 buses daily to **Sierpe** for the boat to **Bahía Drake** (page 827) 45 mins, US$0.30. Also buses north to **Dominical**, and south to the **Golfito** and the Panamanian border.

Sierpe *p818*
Bus and boat 5 buses daily to **Palmar Norte**, 0530-1530, 45 mins, US$0.30. Boats down Río Sierpe to **Bahía Drake**, 1½ hrs, US$70 per boat. Many hotels in Drake have boats, may be able to get a lift, US$15 per person.

Paso Real to San Vito *p818*
Bus Direct buses **San José** to San Vito, 4 daily, 0545, 0815, 1130 and 1445, from Terminal Alfaro, Calle 14, Av 5; direct bus San Vito–San José 0500, 0730, 1000, 1500, 6 hrs, corriente buses take 8 hrs, US$11. Alternative route, not all paved, via Cd Neily (see below); from San Vito to **Las Cruces** at 0530 and 0700; sit on the left coming up, right going down, to admire the wonderful scenery; return buses pass Las Cruces at 1510.

Golfito *p818*
Air Several daily flights to **San José**, with **Sansa** (US$71 one-way). Runway is all-weather, tight landing between trees; 2 km from town, taxi US$0.50.

Bus From **San José** 0700 (8½ hrs) and 1500 (6 hrs express) daily from Terminal Alfaro, return 0500 (express), 1300, US$12.40; from **San Isidro de El General**, take 0730 bus to Río Claro and wait for bus coming from Cd Neily. To **Paso Canoas**, US$1.30, hourly from outside Soda Pavo, 1½ hrs. To **Pavones** at 1000 and 1500, and return at 0430 and 1230, 3 hrs, US$1.80. A spit of land continues south to Punta Burica with no roads and only a couple of villages.

Sea There is a boat service between Golfito and **Puerto Jiménez**, leaving the dock in Golfito at 1130, US$2.50, 1½ hrs, returning at 0600, or chartering a water taxi for US$60, up to 8 passengers, is possible.

Water taxis in and around Golfito, **Froylan Lopez**, T8824-6571, to **Cacao Beach**, **Punta Zancudo**, **Punta Encant**o or to order, US$20 per hr up to 5 persons.

Docks Land Sea Tours (see above) and Banana Bay Marina (T2775-0838, www.bananabaymarina.com) accommodate boats up to 150 ft – either of these places might be an option if heading south on a boat, but you'll need to ask nicely and be a bit lucky.

Ciudad Neily, Paso Canoas and the Panama border *p819*
Bus The terminal in Cd Neily is at the northern end of town, beside the Mercado Central. Daily bus to **San José**, with **Tracopa**, from main square (6 daily, US$12.40, 7 hrs, on Sun buses from the border are full by the time they reach Cd Neily). Buses arrive at Av 5 and Calle 14 in San José. Services to **San Vito** inland, and to **Palmar**, **Cortés** and **Dominical** (0600 and 1430, 3 hrs). Also to **Puerto Jiménez** at 0700 and 1400, 4 hrs.

Bus for **Golfito** leaves from the centre of town every 30 mins. The Pan-American Hwy goes south (plenty of buses, 20 mins, US$0.65) to Paso Canoas on the Panamanian border. *Colectivo* US$1.80, very quick.

San José–Paso Canoas, 8 hrs, US$13 from Terminal Alfaro at 0500, 1100 (direct), 1300, 1800, return 0400, 0730, 0900, 1500 (T2223- 7685). Not all buses go to the border. International buses that reach the border after closing time wait there till the following day. Hourly buses to Cd Neily, ½ hourly to Golfito.

⊙ Directory

San Isidro de El General *p815*
Banks Banco Nacional, on north side of plaza, Mon-Fri, 0830-1545. **Internet** Bruncanet, on north side of plaza, and MS Internet Café. **Post** 3 blocks south of the church. **Telephone** ICE office on Calle 4, Av 3-PAH.

Paso Real to San Vito *p818*
Banks There are branches of Banco Nacional and Banco Popular in San Vito. **Post and internet** Post office at the northern end of town.

Golfito *p818*
Banks Banco Nacional near dock, Mon-Fri 0830-1535, T2775-1622. **Internet** Internet café, on ground floor below Hotel Golfito.

Ciudad Neily, Paso Canoas and the Panama border *p819*
Banks In Cd Neily, there are branches of Banco Nacional and Banco de Costa Rica. At Paso Canoas, banks on either side of border close at 1600 local time. Slightly better dollar rate for colones on the Costa Rican side. **Internet** Planet Internet at the northern end of Cd Neily.

Península de Osa

Across the Golfo Dulce is the hook-shaped appendage of the Osa Peninsula. Some distance from most other places of interest in the country, the journey is worthwhile as the peninsula is world famous for the diversity of flora and fauna in Parque Nacional Corcovado, with some of the best rainforest trekking and trails in the country. ►► *For listings, see pages 830-832.*

Ins and outs

Getting to the peninsula is becoming easier. There is a daily ferry service from Golfito arriving at the small dock in Puerto Jiménez; bus services run from San José, passing through San Isidro de El General, Palmar North, and from the south at Ciudad Neily; and boats ply the coastal route from Sierpe to Bahía Drake. You can also fly from San José.

Puerto Jiménez → *Colour map 4, B4.*

Getting there To reach Puerto Jiménez from the Pan-American Highway (70 km), turn right about 30 km south of Palmar Sur; the road is paved to Rincón, thereafter it is

Puerto Jiménez

To Golfito

Golfo Dulce

To Dos Brazos, Rincón & San José

Osa Natural

Football Pitch

Bus to Carate

Café El Sol

Tonsa Tours

To Playa Platanares

MINAE National Park Office

Sansa   Banco Nacional

To Matapalo, Carate & Corcovado

N

100 metres
100 yards

Sleeping
Agua Luna **1**
Cabinas Bosque Mar **2**
Cabinas Marcelina **3**
Cabinas Puerto
  Jiménez **4**
Cabinas Thompson **5**

Iguana Iguana **7**
La Choza del Manglares **8**
Oro Verde **9**
Parrot Bay Village **10**
Pensión Quintero **11**

Eating
Agua Luna **1**
Carolina &
  Escondido Trex **2**
Il Giardino **3**
Juanita's Mexican
  Bar & Grille **4**

Península de Osa – rain, snakes and mosquitoes

Avoid the rainy season. Bring umbrellas (not raincoats, which are too hot), because it will rain, unless you are hiking, in which case you may prefer to get wet. There are a few shelters, so only mosquito netting is indispensable. Bring all your food if you haven't arranged otherwise; food can only be obtained at Puerto Jiménez and Agujitas in the whole peninsula, and lodging likewise. The cleared areas (mostly outside the park, or along the beach) can be devastatingly hot. Chiggers (*coloradillas*) and horseflies infest the horse pastures and can be a nuisance, similarly sandflies on the beaches; bring spray-on insect repellent. Another suggestion is vitamin B1 pills (called thiamine, or *tiamina*). Mosquitoes are supposed to detest the smell and leave you alone. Get the Instituto Geográfico maps, scale 1:50,000. Remember finally that, as in any tropical forest, you may find some unfriendly wildlife like snakes (fer-de-lance and bushmaster snakes may attack without provocation), and herds of peccaries. You should find the most suitable method for keeping your feet dry and protecting your ankles; for some, rubber boots are the thing, for others light footwear that dries quickly.

driveable with many bridge crossings. There is a police check point 47 km from the Pan-American Highway.

Once a gold-mining centre, Puerto Jiménez still has the feel of a frontier town although most miners were cleared from the Parque Nacional Corcovado area over 20 years ago.

Today, Puerto Jiménez is a popular destination with its laid-back, occasionally lively atmosphere, reasonable beaches nearby and, of course, the beautiful national park on the Pacific side of the peninsula. Look out for *El Sol de Osa*, www.soldeosa.com, an up-to-date community-information service. A particular charm of Puerto Jiménez, barely five blocks square, is its relative freedom from road traffic; scarlet macaws can be seen roosting in the trees around the football pitch. There are good local walks to the jungle, where you will see monkeys and many other birds, and to beaches and mangroves. There is a seasonal migration of humpbacks between October and March.

Geological treasures can be seen at the gold mine at **Dos Brazos** about 15 km west of town; ask for the road that goes uphill beyond the town, to see the local gold mines. Several *colectivo* taxis a day to Dos Brazos, last bus back at 1530 (often late); taxi US$7.25. You can also take a long walk to **Carate** (see below), which has a gold mine. Branch to the right and in 4 km there are good views of the peninsula. A topographical map is a big help, obtainable from Instituto Geográfico in San José. At **Cabo Matapalo** on the tip of the peninsula, 18 km south of Puerto Jiménez, are several expensive sleeping options.

Bahía Drake

Arriving by boat from Sierpe, Bahía Drake provides a northern entrance point to the Osa Peninsula and Parque Nacional Corcovado. In March 1579, Sir Francis Drake careened his ship on Playa Colorada in Bahía Drake. There is a plaque commemorating the 400th anniversary of the famous pirate's nautical aberration in **Agujitas**. Life in the bay is not cheap, and combined with transport, costs can quickly mount up. Bahía Drake, which continues south merging seamlessly with Agujitas, is a popular destination for divers with Isla Caño nearby. Open Water PADI courses (US$340) are available at **Cabinas Jinetes de Osa** or through **Caño Divers** at Pirate Cove.

Parque Nacional Corcovado → *For listings, see pages 830-832. Colour map 4, C4.*

Corcovado National Park, including **Reserva Biológica Isla del Caño** (84 ha), comprises over 42,469 ha – just under half the Osa Peninsula. Consisting largely of tropical rainforest, swamps, miles of empty beaches, and some cleared areas now growing back, it is located on the Pacific Ocean at the western end of the peninsula. An ideal spot for just walking along endless beaches, the park is also filled with birds, mammals and six species of cat.

Ins and outs

If short of time and/or money, the simplest way to the park is to take the pickup truck from outside **Tonsa Tours** in Puerto Jiménez to Playa Carate (most days at 0600 and 1400, 2½ hours, US$7 one way, returning at 0800 and 1600, ask in advance about departure). Or call **Cirilo Espinosa** (T2735-5075), or **Ricardo González** (T2735-5068), for a 4WD jeep taxi. It is possible to book a flight from Puerto Jiménez to Carate or La Sirena in the park for US$99 per person, minimum five people. Ask at the airstrip or call T2735-5178.

The **MINAE office** ⓘ *Puerto Jiménez, near the airport, T2735-5036, daily 0830-1200, 1300-1700*, will give permits for entering the park (US$7) and will book accommodation at **La Sirena**, see page 832. Hiking boots and sandals are useful if you are walking in the park.

Southern Costa Rica & the Osa Peninsula

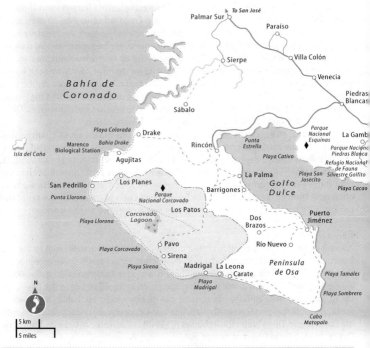

Around the park

At **Carate** there is a dirt airstrip and a store, run by Gilberto Morales and his wife Roxana (they rent rooms, but they are often full of gold miners; they also have a tent for hire, but take a sleeping bag). There are several luxury options here and a couple more lodges 30 minutes' walk west along the beach.

Five minutes' walk further down the beach is **La Leona** park wardens' station and entrance to the park. To go beyond here costs US$7 per day, whether you are walking along the beach to La Sirena (18 km, six hours, take sun protection), or just visiting for the day. Beyond here to the end of **Playa Madrigal** is another 2½ hours' walk, partly sandy, partly rocky, with some rock pools and rusty shipwrecks looking like modern sculptures. The shore rises steeply into the jungle, which grows thickly with mangroves, almonds and coconut palms. Check with wardens about high tide so you don't get stuck. There are a couple of rivers along the beach, the first, Río Madrigal, is only about 15 minutes beyond La Leona (lovely and clear, deep enough for swimming about 200 m upstream, a good place for spotting wildlife). The best place for seeing wildlife, though, is La Sirena, where there are paths inland and the terrain is flatter and more isolated.

You can head inland from Sirena on a trail past three conveniently spaced shelters to **Los Patos**, after passing several rivers full of reptiles (20 km, six to nine hours depending on conditions). The wooden house is the ranger station with electricity and TV, and four beds available at US$1.75 per night; meals possible if you don't bring your own food. Its balcony is a great observation point for birds, especially the redheaded woodpecker. From Los Patos you can carry on to the park border then, crisscrossing the Río Rincón to **La Palma** (small *hostal*), a settlement on the opposite side of the peninsula (13 km, six more hours), from which there are several 'taxis' making the one-hour trip to Puerto Jiménez (see above). An offshoot of this trail will lead you to a raffia swamp that rings the **Corcovado Lagoon**. The lagoon is only accessible by boat, but there are no regular trips. Caymans and alligators survive here, sheltered from the hunters.

From Sirena you can walk north along the coast to the shelter at **Llorona** (plenty of waterfalls), from which there is a trail to the interior with a shelter at the end. From Llorona you can proceed north through a forest trail and along the beach to the station at **San Pedrillo** on the edge of the park. You can stay here, camping or under roof, and eat with the rangers, who love company. From San Pedrillo you can take the park boat (not cheap) to Isla del Caño; a lovely (staffed) park outpost.

Isla del Coco

This has to be one of the world's most distant island destinations: the steep-sided and thickly wooded island and national park of 24 sq km lies 320 km off the Osa Peninsula, on the Cocos Ridge, which extends some 1400 km southwest to the Galápagos Islands. There is virtually nothing on the island, apart from a few endemic species, but you can visit for some of the world's best diving. The BBC/Discovery Channel shot some dramatic silhouetted images of tiger sharks here for their *Blue Planet* series. Historically, though, it was a refuge for pirates who are supposed to have buried great treasure here, though none has been found by the 500 or so expeditions looking for the 'x' that marked the spot. Travel by chartered boat can be made in Puntarenas, after a government permit has been obtained, or you can take a scuba-diving cruise on the **Okeanos Agressor** ① *T2232-0572 ext 60 (in US: PO Drawer K, Morgan City, LA 70381, T504-385-2416)*. The twice-monthly 10-day trips are understandably expensive (about US$4235 for 10 days).

◉ Península de Osa listings

For Sleeping and Eating price codes and other relevant information, see Essentials pages 31-33.

● Sleeping

Puerto Jiménez *p826, map p826*
There is a website covering Jiménez hotels: www.jimenezhotels.com.

LL Iguana Lodge, 5 km southeast of Puerto Jiménez behind the airstrip, T8829-5865, www.iguanalodge.com. 4 cabins, good swimming and surfing.

AL Parrot Bay Village, left from the pier, T2735-5180, www.parrotbayvillage.com. Fully equipped wooden cabins sleeping 1-5, restaurant, beautiful spot, almost private beach. Cheaper in groups.

A-B Cabinas Puerto Jiménez, on the gulf shore with good views, T2735-5090, www.cabinasjimenez.com. Remodelled big rooms, many with private decks looking out to the gulf, spotless. Wi-Fi internet access.

A-B La Choza del Manglares, right beside the mangrove on the river, T2735-5002, www.manglares.com. Clean, well-maintained cabins with private bath. In the day regular visits from monkeys, scarlet macaws and the occasional crocodile in the grounds by the river. Completely renovated.

B-C Agua Luna, facing pier, T2735-3593. Rooms sleeping 2-4 with bath, good, although pricey; restaurant next door.

C-D Cabinas Marcelina, down main street, T2735-5007. With bath, big clean, friendly, nice front yard, totally renovated, small discount for youth hostelling members.

E Cabinas Bosque Mar, T2735-5681. Clean, large rooms and restaurant.

E Hotel Oro Verde, main street, T2735-5241. Run by Silvia Duirós Rodríguez, 10 clean, comfortable rooms, with bath and fan, some overlooking the street.

E Iguana Iguana, on road leading out of town, T2735-5158. Simple rooms with private bath, restaurant, small bar, pool.

F Pizzería Cabinas Mariel, T2735-5071. Simple cabins.

G Cabinas Thompson, 50 m from the centre, T2735-5910. With bath, fan, clean but dark.

G Pensión Quintero, just off main street, T2735-5087. Very simple wooden building, but clean and good value; will store luggage. Ask for Fernando Quintero, who rents horses and has a boat for up to 6 passengers, good value; he is also a guide, recommended. Price per person.

Cabo Matapalo

LL Lapa Ríos Wilderness Resort, T2735- 5130, www.laparios.com. The cream of the crop. Includes meals. 14 luxury palm-thatched bungalows on private 2400-ha reserve (80% virgin forest, US owners Karen and John Lewis), camping trips, boats can be arranged from Golfito. Idyllic, fantastic views, recommended.

LL-L El Remanso Rainforest Beach Lodge, Cabo Matapalo, T2735-5569, www.elremanso.com. Houses and cabins for rent, all fully equipped and with ocean views, an oasis of peace.

Bahía Drake p827

LL Aguila de Osa Inn, the normal landing point, T2296-2190, www.aguiladeosa.com. Includes meals; fishing, hiking, canoeing and horse riding available, comfortable cabins made with exotic hardwoods. Recommended.

LL Drake Bay Wilderness Camp, opposite Aguila de Osa Inn, T2770-8012, www.drake bay.com. Price per person, with meals, cabins, tents available, pleasant family atmosphere, pool, 2 restaurants. Great views. Wide range of tours available.

LL La Paloma Jungle Lodge, T2239-0954, www.lapalomalodge.com. Price per person includes meals. 9 cabins with bath, guided tours with resident biologist. Packages.

A Cabinas Jinete de Osa, T2236-5637, www.costaricadiving.com. Good hotel, run by 2 brothers from Colorado. Diving a speciality, PADI courses offered. Spacious and airy rooms, all with bath, hot water, fan. Recommended.

A Rancho Corcovado Lodge, in the middle of the beach, T2786-7059. www.ranchocorcovado.com. Price per person. Simple, rustic rooms, many with view, all with bath. Friendly Tico owners, nice open-air restaurant on beach serves *comida típica*. Camping permitted.

A-B Pirate Cove, northern end of the beach, T2786-7845, www.piratecove.com. Very nice tent-like cabins emulate an

outdoor experience minus the mud. US$55 per person shared bath, US$70 with bath, 3 meals included.

E Bella Vista Lodge, on the beach at the southern end of town, T2770-8051. The only budget option in town and disappointing. Basic rooms, 2 with bath, 3 shared (even more basic), meals (US$3-5) not included.

Camping

Camping is allowed outside **Rancho Corcovado** (use of electricity and bathrooms included) or outside **Pirate Cove** (north end of beach), no fixed price, small charge for baths.

Parque Nacional Corcovado p828

MINAE office, facing the airstrip, Puerto Jiménez, T2735-5036. For booking dormitory accommodation and camping facilities in Corcovado National Park.

L Casa Corcovado Jungle Lodge, along the coast from San Pedrillo, T2256-3181, www.casacorcovado.com. Outside the park in the forest, but with 500 m of beach more or less opposite Isla del Caño, 14 bungalows, many facilities, packages from 2 nights full board with boat transport (2 hrs) from Sierpe.

AL-A Corcovado Lodge, 30 mins' walk west of Carate along the beach, T2257-0766, www.costaricaexpeditions.com. 20 walk-in tents with 2 campbeds in each, in a beautiful coconut grove with hammocks overlooking the beach; to be sure of space book through **Costa Rica Expeditions** in San José, see page 735. Clean showers and toilets; good food, take a torch. Behind the camp is a trail into the jungle with a great view of the bay; many birds to be seen, plus monkeys and frogs.

AL-A La Leona Eco-Lodge, 30 mins' walk west of Carate along the beach, T2735-5705, www.laleonaecolodge.com. Rustic tent cabins, crocodile spotting, rappelling, yoga and night hikes. Price per person.

E La Leona park wardens' station, at entrance to the park. Maximum 12 people in basic rooms or camping, meals available. Book in high season through SINAC.

E La Sirena, book through **MINAE**, Puerto Jiménez, near the airport, T2735-5036. In dorms, maximum 20 people (reservation essential), take sheets/sleeping bag. Also camping, no reservation needed, 3 meals available. Bring mosquito netting.

❶ Eating

Puerto Jiménez *p826, map p826*
¶¶¶ **Agua Luna**, on the seashore near the dock, T2735-5033. Stylish setting, beautifully presented but pricey.
¶¶¶ **Il Giardino**, just off the main street. Quiet little Italian, intimate setting, and good food.
¶¶¶-¶¶ **Carolina**, down the main street, T2735-5185. Highly recommended for fish (everything actually), good prices. **Escondido Trex** office at back of restaurant.
¶¶ **Juanita's Mexican Bar and Grille**, central, T2735-5056. Happy hour, crab races, good Mexican fare, seafood from US$4.
¶ **Pollo Frito Opi Opi**, north end of town, T2735-5192. Fried chicken, hamburgers, fries.
¶ **Soda Bosquemar**, on main street, T2735-5681. Good food at good prices.

▲ Activities and tours

Puerto Jiménez *p826, map p826*
Aventuras Tropicales, opposite the football pitch, T2735-5195, www.aventuras tropicales.com. Can book accommodation and has a couple of computers with internet.
Escondido Trex, in the back of **Carolina**, T2735-5210, www.escondidotrex.com. Excellent local information, treks, kayaking and jungle trips.
MINAE office, facing the airstrip, T2735-5036, for booking dormitory lodging and camping facilities in Corcovado National Park.
Tonsa Tours, see map. Run by the quiet Jaime, provides many of the normal tours, and also jungle treks across to Carate.

Not for the faint-hearted, but certain to be fascinating.

❷ Transport

Puerto Jiménez *p826, map p826*
Air
There are daily flights to Puerto Jiménez and **Golfito** with Sansa (US$71) and **Nature Air** (from US$114 one-way) from **San José**.

Bus
1 block west of the main street. A café by the bus terminal is open Sat 0430 for a cheap and reasonable breakfast. From **San José**, just outside Terminal Atlántico Norte (C 12, Av 9-11), there are 2 buses daily to Puerto Jiménez at 0600 and 1200 via San Isidro, US$12.60, 8 hrs, return 0500, T2735-5189. There are also buses from **San Isidro**, leaving from the Pan-American Hwy at 0930 and 1500, US$8, returns at 0400 and 1300, 5 hrs. To **Cd Neily** at 0500 and 1400, 3 hrs, US$3.80. A few *colectivos* to **Carate** depart from outside **Restaurant Carolina** daily 0530 and 0600, cost US$7. Service may be restricted in the wet season. Local bus is US$1.80.

Sea
There is a boat service between **Golfito** and Puerto Jiménez, leaving the dock in Golfito at 1130, US$2.50, 1½ hrs, returning at 0600, or chartering a water taxi for US$60, up to 8 passengers, is possible.

❸ Directory

Puerto Jiménez *p826, map p826*
Banks Branch of Banco Nacional, T2735-5155. **Internet** Café El Sol, on main street, 0700-1900, US$8 per hr. **Post** Opposite the football pitch.

San José to the Atlantic

Heading east from San José, the Central Highlands quickly fall away to the sparsely populated flat Caribbean lowlands. The tropical rainforest national parks of Tortuguero and Barra del Colorado, leading through coastal canals and waterways, are a nature lover's paradise with easily arranged trips, normally from San José, into the rainforest. South of the distinctly Caribbean city of Puerto Limón, coastal communities have developed to provide comfortable hangouts and laid-back beach life for all budgets. ▸▸ *For listings, see pages 842-856.*

There are two routes from San José to Puerto Limón on the Atlantic coast. The newer main route goes over the Cordillera Central, through the Parque Nacional Braulio Carrillo down to Guápiles and Siquirres. This highland section is prone to fog and if driving yourself, requires extra care. The second, more scenic but considerably longer route follows the old Atlantic railway to Cártago, south of Irazú volcano to Turrialba, joining the main highway at Siquirres.

Parque Nacional Braulio Carrillo → *Colour map 4, B3.*

The third largest of Costa Rica's national parks Parque Nacional Braulio Carrillo was created to protect the high rainforest north of San José from the impact of the San José–Guápiles–Puerto Limón highway. It extends for 47,583 ha, and encompasses five different types of forest with abundant wildlife including hundreds of species of bird, jaguar, ocelot and Baird's tapir. Various travel agencies offer naturalist tours, approximately US$65 from San José. San José to Guápiles and Puerto Limón buses go through the park.

The entrance to the **Quebrada González centre** ⓘ *daily 0800-1530 US$7*, is on the highway, 23 km beyond the Zurquí tunnel, just over the Río Sucio at the Guápiles end and has an administration building. To get there, take any bus to the Atlantic and ask to be dropped off. There are three trails: **Las Palmas**, 1.6 km (you need rubber boots); across the road are **El Ceibo**, 1 km, circular; and **Botarrama**, entry 2 km from Quebrada González. The trail has good birdwatching and the views down the Río Patria canyon are impressive. The Zurquí centre near the tunnel has been closed but may open again soon so ask at headquarters. It has services and the 250-m Los Jilqueros trail to the river.

Beyond Quebrada González (1.5 km) is **Los Heliconios** ⓘ *entry US$7*, butterfly garden with an insect museum and amphibians. Adjoining it, **Reserva Turística El Tapir** ⓘ *entry US$7*, has a 20-minute trail and others of one to two hours.

An ingenious **Rainforest Aerial Tram** ⓘ *Tue-Sun 0630-1600, Mon 0900-1530, 90 mins' ride costs US$55, students with ID and children half price, children under 5 are not allowed; office in San José, Av 7, Calle 7, behind Aurola Holiday Inn, T2257-5961*, lifts visitors high into the rainforest, providing a fascinating up-close and personal view of the canopy life. The price includes a guided nature walk. It's best to go as early as possible for birds. Tourist buses arrive from 0800. There's also a zip-wire, trekking tour, birding tour and serpentarium. US$104 covers everything. There's a guarded car park for private vehicles and restaurant for meals in the park. It can be difficult to get reservations during the high season. The San José office organizes an all-inclusive package leaving around 0800 daily, with pickups at most major hotels.

Further on, at the Soda Gallo Pinto is the **Bosque Lluvioso** ⓘ *T2224-0819, daily 0700-1700, entry US$15*, a 170-ha private reserve. It is at Km 56 on the Guápiles highway (**Rancho Redondo**), with a restaurant and trails in primary and secondary forest.

The turn-off at Santa Clara to Puerto Viejo de Sarapiquí is 13 km before Guápiles. At the junction is **Rancho Robertos** (T2711-0050), a good, popular and reasonable roadside restaurant). For Guápiles, see below. Nearby is a **Tropical Frog Garden**, an interesting short stop if you have the time.

Parque Nacional Braulio Carrillo & Puerto Viejo loop

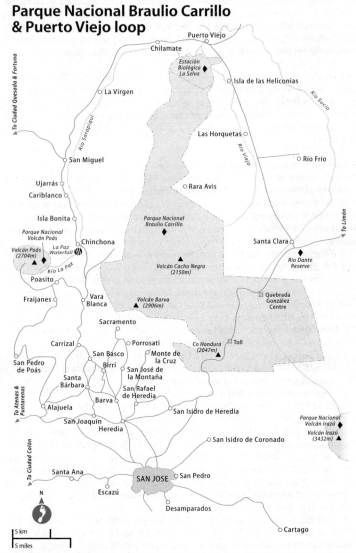

There is a private reserve bordering the Parque Nacional Braulio Carrillo called **Río Danta**, with 60 ha of primary rainforest and short limited treks (US$4) arranged with meals (US$6-9). For information contact **Mawamba Group** ⓘ *T2223-2421, must be pre-arranged, no drop-ins.*

Puerto Viejo de Sarapiquí → *Colour map 4, B3.*

Puerto Viejo de Sarapiquí is 40 km north of the San José–Limón highway and 20 km from La Virgen to the southwest. Once an important port on the Río Sarapiquí, only occasionally do launches ply the Río Colorado to the Canales de Tortuguero. There is reported to be a cargo boat once a week to Barra del Colorado (no facilities, bring your own food, hammock, sleeping bag), and on to Moín, about 10 km by road from Puerto Limón. There is little traffic, so you will need luck and a fair amount of cash. There is good fishing on the Río Sarapiquí.

In the neighbourhood is **La Selva Biological Station** ⓘ *T2766-6565, www.ots.ac.cr, 3½-hr guided natural history walk with bilingual naturalists daily at 0800 and 1330-1600, US$30 per person,* on the Río Puerto Viejo, run by the **Organization for Tropical Studies**. The floral and faunal diversity is unbelievable. Several guided and self-led walks, including a **Sarapiquí River Boat Tour**, are available but to visit it is essential to book in advance. Accommodation is also available.

The Río Sarapiquí flows into the San Juan, forming the northern border of Costa Rica. The Río San Juan is wholly in Nicaragua, so you technically have to cross the border and then return to Costa Rica. This will cost US$5 and you will need a passport and visa. Trips on the **Río Sarapiquí** and on the **Río Sucio** are beautiful (US$15 for two hours); contact William Rojas in Puerto Viejo (T2766-6108) for trips on the Río Sarapiquí or to Barra del Colorado and Tortuguero. There is a regular boat service to Tortuguero on Monday and Thursday, returning on Tuesday and Friday, costing US$55 per person.

Las Horquetas de Sarapiquí

Seventeen kilometres south of Puerto Viejo, near Las Horquetas de Sarapiquí, is **Rara Avis** ⓘ *T2764-1111, www.rara-avis.com,* rustic lodges in a 600-ha forest reserve owned by ecologist Amos Bien. This admirable experiment in educating visitors about rainforest conservation takes small groups on guided tours (rubber boots provided), led by biologists. You must be prepared for rough and muddy trails, lots of insects but great birdwatching and a memorable experience.

South Caribbean coast

Guápiles, Guácimo and Siquirres → *Colour map 4, B3/4.*

One hour from San José (bus costs US$1.45), Guápiles is the centre of the Río Frío banana region. It is another 25 km from Guácimo to Siquirres, a clean, friendly town and junction for roads from Turrialba with the main highway and former railways.

Matina → *Colour map 4, B4.*

Twenty-eight kilometres beyond Siquirres, heading north at the 'techo rojo' junction is Matina, a small, once-busy town on the railway but off the highway. Today, it is an access point to Tortuguero and the less well-known private **Reserva Natural Pacuare**, 30 km north of Puerto Limón, which is accessible by canal from Matina. Run by Englishman John Denham, it has a 6-km stretch of **leatherback turtle nesting beach**, protected and guarded by the reserve. Volunteers patrol the beach in May and June, measuring and tagging these magnificent marine turtles (US$50 per person per week, includes good meals and accommodation). For volunteer work, contact Carlos Fernández, **Corporación de Abogados** ⓘ *Av 8-10, Calle 19, No 837, San José, T2233-0508, fdezlaw@racsa.co.cr, organization information at www.turtleprotection.org.*

Puerto Limón and the Atlantic coast → *For listings, see pages 842-856.*

On a rocky outcrop on an almost featureless coastline, Puerto Limón is the country's most important port. Between Puerto Limón and the Río San Juan on the Nicaraguan border, the long stretch of Atlantic coastline and its handful of small settlements is linked by a canal system that follows the coastline. The region encompasses Parque Nacional Tortuguero, famed for its wildlife and turtle-nesting beaches, and Refugio Nacional de Fauna Silvestre Barra del Colorado. The Río San Juan forms the border between Costa Rica

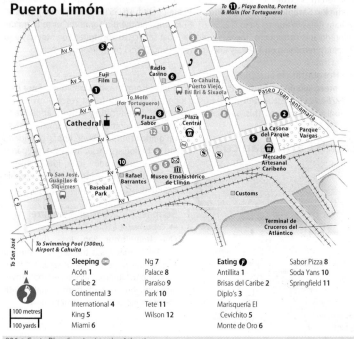

Puerto Limón

Sleeping		Eating	
Acón **1**	Ng **7**	Antillita **1**	Sabor Pizza **8**
Caribe **2**	Palace **8**	Brisas del Caribe **2**	Soda Yans **10**
Continental **3**	Paraíso **9**	Diplo's **3**	Springfield **11**
International **4**	Park **10**	Marisquería El	
King **5**	Tete **11**	Cevichito **5**	
Miami **6**	Wilson **12**	Monte de Oro **6**	

and Nicaragua; however, the border is not mid-river, but on the Costa Rican bank. English is widely spoken along the coast.

Puerto Limón → *Colour map 4, B4.*

Built on the site of the ancient indigenous village of Cariari, Columbus dropped anchor at Punta Uvita, the island off the coastline, on his fourth and final voyage. The climate is very humid and it rains almost every day. With a mainly black population and a large Chinese contingent, the town has a distinctly Caribbean feel, expressed particularly during carnival but in most bars every weekend.

Parque Vargas and the seafront promenade at the rocky headland are popular places for social gatherings and killing time, making for ideal people-watching territory, especially in the evening. Parque Vargas, sadly rather run-down, has an impressive botanical display with a colourful mural depicting the history of Limón and a bandstand.

On the upside, the nightlife is good, particularly for Caribbean music and dancing, culminating in carnival every October, Costa Rica's largest festival. There is a small **Museo Etnohistórico de Limón** ① *Calle 2, Av 2, Mon-Fri 0900-1200, 1300-1600*, featuring material relating to Columbus' arrival in Limón. The cargo docks are still active with international crews making regular journeys, as well as being the landing point for pristine floating palaces cruising the Caribbean. The **carnival**, which takes place just before 12 October, is Costa Rica's biggest; it's crowded and prices rise, but it's definitely worth seeing.

Around Puerto Limón

Playa Bonita and **Portete** have pleasant beaches about 5 km along the coastal road from Puerto Limón. **Moín**, a further 1.5 km east along the road, is the sight of the international docks, which exports some 2.8 million bunches of bananas annually. The docks are also the departure point for barges to Tortuguero and Barra del Colorado (eight hours). Boats also run from Moín to Tortuguero (see below) and may be hired at the dockside. Buses run to Moín every 40 minutes from 0600-1740, 30 minutes, US$0.10. If shipping a vehicle, check which dock. Some simple accommodation options are available if you end up waiting here.

Parque Nacional Tortuguero → *For listings, see pages 842-856. Colour map 4, B4.*

① *Tortuguero Information Centre, T8833-0827, safari@racsa.co.cr.*

Tortuguero is a 29,068-ha national park, with a marine extension of over 50,000 ha, protecting the Atlantic nesting sites of the green and leatherback turtle and the Caribbean lowland rainforest inland. As with much of Costa Rica, getting the timing right to see this natural phenomenon is essential. The green turtles lay their eggs at night on the scrappy, rather untidy beach from June to October, with the hatchlings emerging from the depths of their sandy nests until November at the latest. Leatherbacks can be seen from March to June. Hawksbill and loggerheads also nest at Tortuguero but numbers are minimal. Trips to look for nesting turtles are carefully monitored and you must be accompanied by a licensed guide at all times. ►► *For details, see Tour operators and Transport, pages 852 and 855.*

While your visit may not coincide with those of the turtles, the canals of jungle-fringed waterways behind the beach, teeming with bird and insect life, are always a pleasure.

A **visitor centre**, close to the village of Tortuguero, has information on the park and the turtles. Round the back of the headquarters there is a well-marked and recommended 1.4-km nature trail. In the centre is a small gift shop. To the northern end of the village is the **Caribbean Conservation Corporation**, which has played a fundamental role in the creation and continued research of the turtle nesting grounds. There's an interesting and very informative **Natural History Museum** ⓘ *T2224-9215 (San José), www.cccturtle.org, daily 1000-1200, 1400-1730, donation US$1.* Information about all this and more can be found on the village website, www.tortuguerovillage.com.

A guide is required for trips along the beach at night and recommended for trips through the waterways. Do not swim at Tortuguero as there area sharks. If travelling with a lodge, tours will be arranged for you. If organizing independently, contact the information kiosk in the village for instructions and to link up with a registered guide. To visit the turtles at night you must pay US$7 park entrance fee, and US$5 each for a guide. A guide and tour in no way guarantees you will see a turtle or hatchlings.

Tours through the water channels are the best way to see the rainforest, ideally in a boat without a motor. The canal, bordered with primary rainforest, gives way to smaller channels, and, drifting slowly through forest-darkened streams, the rainforest slowly comes

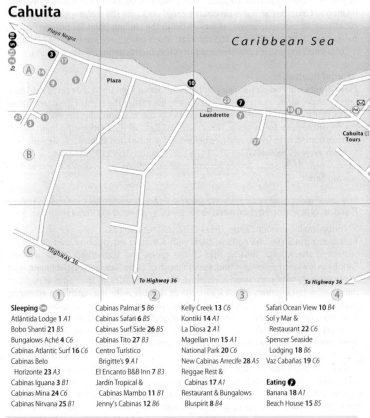

Cahuita

Sleeping 🛏	Cabinas Palmar **5** *B6*	Kelly Creek **13** *C6*	Safari Ocean View **10** *B4*
Atlántida Lodge **1** *A1*	Cabinas Safari **6** *B5*	Kontiki **14** *A1*	Sol y Mar &
Bobo Shanti **21** *B5*	Cabinas Surf Side **26** *B5*	La Diosa **2** *A1*	Restaurant **22** *C6*
Bungalows Aché **4** *C6*	Cabinas Tito **27** *B3*	Magellan Inn **15** *A1*	Spencer Seaside
Cabinas Atlantic Surf **16** *C6*	Centro Turístico	National Park **20** *C6*	Lodging **18** *B6*
Cabinas Belo	Brigitte's **9** *A1*	New Cabinas Arrecife **28** *A5*	Vaz Cabañas **19** *C6*
Horizonte **23** *A3*	El Encanto B&B Inn **7** *B3*	Reggae Rest &	
Cabinas Iguana **3** *B1*	Jardín Tropical &	Cabinas **17** *A1*	**Eating** 🍴
Cabinas Mina **24** *C6*	Cabinas Mambo **11** *B1*	Restaurant & Bungalows	Banana **18** *A1*
Cabinas Nirvana **25** *B1*	Jenny's Cabinas **12** *B6*	Bluspirit **8** *B4*	Beach House **15** *B5*

alive with wildlife including birds – over half of those found in Costa Rica – monkeys, sloths and, for the lucky, alligators, tapirs, jaguars, ocelots, peccaries, anteaters and even manatees. You can hire a canoe and guide for about US$6 per hour per person in a boat without motor, or US$12 with a motor, minimum of four people. Night tours cost US$15 per person per hour. Fishing tours, with all equipment included, cost US$35 per person, with a minimum of two people. Take insect repellent. ▸▸ *See Tour operators, page 852.*

Barra del Colorado → *For listings, see pages 842-856.*

The canals are part artificial, part natural; originally they were narrow lagoons running parallel to the sea separated by a small strip of land. Now the lagoons are linked, and it is possible to sail as far as Barra del Colorado, in the extreme northeast of Costa Rica, 25 km beyond Tortuguero. They pass many settlements. The town is divided by the river, the main part being on the northern bank. Secluded and difficult to get to, the **Refugio Nacional de Fauna Silvestre Barra del Colorado** (81,213 ha) is a national wildlife refuge. The reserve and the Parque Nacional Tortuguero share some boundaries, making for a far more effective protected zone. The fame of the region's fauna extends to the waters, which are world-renowned for fishing.

Once across the Río Colorado (which in fact is the south arm of the Río San Juan delta), you can walk to Nicaragua (see under Nicaragua, San Juan del Norte, page 693) along the coast, but it is a long 30-km beach walk, take food and lots of water. Most hikers overnight en route. Seek advice before setting out.

N
100 metres
100 yards

School

Laundrette

& Willies Tours

Roberto's Tours

To Coastal Path

Parque Nacional Cahuita

Cha Cha Cha **2** *B5*
Chao's Paradise **3** *A1*
Coral Reef **1** *B5*
La Casa Creole **5** *A1*
Le Fe **8** *B5*
Mango Tango Pizzeria **17** *B5*
Miss Edith's **6** *A4*
Palenque Luisa **4** *B5*
Pastry Shop **7** *B3*
Relax & Rikki's Bar **13** *B5*

Sobre las Olas **10** *A2*
Soda Priscilla **16** *C6*

Bars & clubs
Cocos **14** *B5*

South from Puerto Limón
→ *For listings, see pages 842-856.*

Penshurst
South of Limón, a paved road shadows the coastline normally separated by little more than a thin line of palms. Beyond Penshurst is the **Hitoy Cerere Biological Reserve**. If you have time, camping is easy in the hills and there are plenty of rivers for swimming. Further south the road leads to Cahuita, Puerto Viejo and on towards Manzanillo – all sleepy beach towns, with lively centres, comfortable hideaways, and coastal and nature opportunities to explore. If heading for the border, heading inland just north of Puerto Viejo takes you through Bribri and on to Sixaola.

From Penshurst it is 11.5 km to Cahuita; this stretch of the road is paved to the edge of Cahuita.

Cahuita and Parque Nacional Cahuita → *Colour map 4, B4.*
ⓘ *Entry to the park US$10. The official entrance to the park is at Puerto Vargas, about 5 km south of Cahuita, where the park headquarters, a nature trail, camping facilities and toilets are situated. Take the bus to Km 5, then turn left at the sign. You can enter the park for free from the southern side of Cahuita, which is ideal for relaxing on the beach, but leave a donation. If you have the option, visit during the week when it is quieter. There is a tourist complex in the area, and the restaurant Marisquería, at Puerto Vargas park entrance, is an Italian, with a jovial host who also has rooms.*

The small town of **Cahuita** hides 1 km back from the main road, and enjoys a sleepy feel. A laid-back community, it's a good place to hide away in one of the secluded spots or to party in the centre of town. North of the town is **Playa Negra**, a beautiful black-sand beach ideal for swimming or just lazing about in a hammock, while to the south is the national park. Most people stay in Cahuita to explore the park.

Cahuita National Park (1068 ha) is a narrow strip of beach protecting a coral reef off shore and a marine area of 22,400 ha. The length of the beach can be walked in about three hours, and passes endless coconut palms and interesting tropical forest, through which there is also a path. It is hot and humid, so take drinking water, but a wide range of fauna can be seen, as well as howler monkeys, white-faced monkeys, coatis, snakes, butterflies and hermit crabs. Over 500 species of fish inhabit the surrounding waters and reef tours are available. An old Spanish shipwreck can be seen and reached without a boat. Snorkellers should take care to stay away from the coral, which is already badly damaged by agricultural chemicals and other pollutants. The park extends from the southern limit of Cahuita town southeast to Puerto Vargas.

Note Cahuita and Puerto Viejo have suffered from what locals believe is a lack of support and investment from central government. An undercurrent of problems, partially based on the perception that everyone on the Caribbean coast takes drugs, does mean that you may be offered drugs. If you are not interested, just say no.

Puerto Viejo de Talamanca → *Colour map 4, B4.*
Puerto Viejo is a good base and a quietly happening party town, with a number of good beaches stretching out to the south. Activities in the area are numerous and you could spend many days exploring the options. There is reef diving nearby, or you can head south to Mandoca for lagoon diving from canoes. Surfers seek out the glorious **Salsa Brava** wave, which peaks from December to February. Away from the beach, nature trips range from tough treks in Gandoca–Manzanillo Wildlife Refuge (see below) through to gentle strolls around the self-guided botanical gardens to the north of town. There are also several cultural trips to KeKöLdi and Bribri indigenous reserves and options to take dug-outs to the inland town of Yorkin. The **Asociación Talamanqueña de Ecoturism y Conservación** ⓘ *ATEC, T2750-0191, www.ateccr.org*, provides tourist information, sells locally made crafts and T-shirts, and also offers guide services, rainforest hikes, snorkelling and fishing trips. The **South Caribbean Music Festival** takes place in the lead up to Easter.

Around Puerto Viejo

There are a number of popular beaches southeast along the road from Puerto Viejo. Traffic is limited, buses occasional, but it is walkable. About 4 km away is **Playa Cocles**, which has some of the best surfing on this coast, and 2 km further on is **Playa Chiquita**, with many places to stay. Next is **Punta Uva**, beyond which, after another 5 km, you arrive in **Manzanillo**, followed by white-sand beaches and rocky headlands to **Punta Mona** and the **Gandoca-Manzanillo Wildlife Refuge** ① *ANAI, T2224-6090*, a celebration

Puerto Viejo de Talamanca

Caribbean Sea

To ⑫

Manuel León's **6**
Reef Runner Divers
Atlántico Tours
17
Money Exchange
⑫ ⑨ ⑱ ⑲
10
18
22
14 **15** **19**
3
Salsa Brava Surf Shop
ATEC ℹ
8
25
Jungle Café
@ Laundrette
13
Baptist
21
1
14
20
22
24
Terraventuras
Pharmacy
@
Banco de Costa Rica
20
7 **16**
5
23
7
11

To Playa Negra

To ⑥   To ⑤

N

50 metres
50 yards

Sleeping
Bull Inn **20**
Cabinas Casa Verde **2**
Cabinas Grant **3**
Cabinas Lika **21**
Cabinas Los Almendros **1**
Cabinas Popular **17**
Cabinas Soda Mitchell **16**
Cabinas Tropical **4**

Cabinas Yucca **19**
Cashew Hill **5**
Coco Loco Lodge **6**
Fortaleza **14**
Guaraná **13**
Jacaranda **7**
Las Olas Camping & Cabinas **18**
Los Sueños **8**
Maritza **9**
Puerto Viejo **10**
Pura Vida **11**
Rocking J's **12**
Tamandua Lodge **22**

Eating
Amimodo **9**
Bread & Chocolate **1**
El Parquecito **3**
Hot Rocks **14**
Jammin Juices & Jerk Chicken **17**
La Terraza **15**
Lidía's Place **5**
Monchies **23**
Pan Pay **6**
Peace & Love Coffee **22**
Pizza Boruca **21**
Pizzeria Rusticone **13**
Pollo Frito **18**

Red Stripe Café **20**
Salsa Brava **12**
Soda Miss Sam **7**
Soda Palmer **19**
Stanford's **10**
Tamara **8**

Bars & clubs
Baba Yaga **25**
Sunset **24**

of Costa Rican diversity largely left alone by prospectors and tourists alike. Among other projects, marine scientists are interested in the protection of the giant leatherback turtle. Volunteer work is possible.

Bribri

At **Hotel Creek**, north of Puerto Viejo, the paved road heads through the hills to the village of Bribri, at the foot of the Talamanca Range Indigenous Reserve. Halfway between is **Violeta's Pulpería**. From Limón, **Aerovías Talamaqueñas Indígenas** fly cheaply to **Amubri** in the reserve (there is a *casa de huéspedes* run by nuns in Amubri). Villages such as Bribri, Chase, Bratsi, Shiroles and San José Cabécar can be reached by bus from Cahuita. Several buses daily to Bribri from Limón. Continuing south is Sixaola, on the border with Panama (see page 715).

◉ San José to Atlantic listings

For Sleeping and Eating price codes and other relevant information, see Essentials pages 31-33.

◉ Sleeping

Puerto Viejo de Sarapiquí *p835*
A Selva Verde Lodge, out of town, heading west a few kilometres towards La Virgen, T2766- 6800, www.holbrooktravel.com. On over 200 ha of virgin rainforest reserve, 40 double rooms, 5 bungalows for 4, includes meals, caters mainly for tour groups. Sensitively set in among the rainforest, evening lectures by biologists, excellent for birdwatchers and naturalists with extensive trail system, rafting, canoeing and riding through property; tours with biologists organized.
A-B El Gavilán Lodge, on the southern bank of the Río Sarapiquí, reached by taxi, T2234-9507, www.gavilanlodge.com. Includes breakfast, set in 100-ha private reserve by the river pier, good restaurant, good jungle paths, riding and river tours, 12 rooms private bath, garden jacuzzi, special group and student/researcher rates, day trips and overnight trips from San José.
B El Bambú, in centre north of park, T2766-6359, www.elbambu.com. Bath, fan, TV, pool, gym, including breakfast, very pleasant.
B Posada Andrea Cristina, just out of town near the main road junction, T2766-6265, www.andreacristina.com. Comfortable small cabins, set amongst tropical gardens. Good local knowledge.
D Mi Lindo Sarapiquí, overlooking park, T2766-6074. Has 6 spotless rooms with bath, fan, hot water and restaurant downstairs. Recommended.
F Cabinas Monteverde, next to El Bambú, T2766-6236. Bath, restaurant, but pretty dirty.
F Hospedaje Gonar, on road to the dock above hardware store (*ferretería*) without signpost, T8844-4677. Basic rooms, ones with windows slightly better. Shared bath, pretty dirty.

Las Horquetas de Sarapiquí *p835*
AL River-Edge Cabin and **Waterfall Lodge**, T2764-3131, www.rara-avis.com. Accommodation at Rara Avis, the lodge is a beautiful 8-room jungle lodge in an idyllic setting, the cabin is deeper in the rainforest for even more seclusion. There is also treetop accommodation and rates for backpackers at **Las Casitas**.

Guápiles, Guácimo and Siquirres *p835*
B Casa Río Blanco, Guápiles, about 6 km west of Guápiles look out for the big yellow road sign on, take first right before the Río Blanco bridge and follow signpost for 1 km, T2710-4124, www.casarioblanco.com. Accommodates 12 guests in comfortable cabins, with breakfast, run by Herbie and Annette from Amsterdam. Beautiful gardens

and a great spot for people interested in the environment. Recommended.

C Río Palmas, Guácimo, 1 km past EARTH School, T2760-0330. Has 30 rooms, private bathroom, pool, restaurant. The 200-ha property includes ornamental plant farm and rainforest.

D Cabinas Car, Guápiles, 50 m west of church, T2710-0035. Has 10 clean, tidy rooms, with private bath, hot water, fan and TV.

D Centro Turístico Pacuare, Siquirres, T2768-6482. Renovated, with large pool.

D Centro Turístico Río Blanco, Guápiles, on main road at entrance to town, T2710-7857. With bath, fan. Recommended.

E Alcema, Siquirres, 50 m east of market, T2768-6004. Some dark rooms, with fan, clean, shared bath.

E Cabinas de Oro, Guápiles, northeast of bus terminal, T2710-6663. Clean rooms, private bath with hot water, cheaper without. Restaurant nearby.

E Don Quito, 3.5 km towards Siquirres, T2768-8533. Pleasant, good restaurant.

F Hotel Alfaro (El Tunél), Guápiles, 50 m west of bus terminal, T2710-6293. Simple rooms, no frills, but clean. Open 24 hrs, with a rather funky aluminium stairway. Good value.

Puerto Limón *p837, map p836*
Beware of theft at night, and remember it is a port; there are a lot of drunks roaming the streets.

B-C Park, Av 3, Calle 1-2, T2798-0555. Neat little hotel with 34 rooms, sea-facing rooms, quiet and cool, restaurant good.

C-D Acón, on corner of main square, Calle 3, Av 3, T2758-1010. Big rooms with private bath, a/c, clean, safe, good restaurant, a bit run-down, popular daily disco **Aquarius** except Mon.

C-D Caribe, facing Parque Vargas, Av 2, Calle 1-2, T2758-0138. Big, immaculate rooms with private bath, hot water and big fan. Good deal.

D-E Miami, next to **King** on Av 2, Calle 4-5, T2758-0490. Has 35 rooms, all with private

bath, some with a/c, others with fans. Secure and efficient. Credit cards accepted.

D-E Tete, 1 block west of main square, Av 3, Calle 4-5, T2758-1122. Clean rooms, bright and good beds. Some rooms sleeping up to 6 and some with balconies overlooking the square.

E Palace, 1 block north of bus stops, Calle 2-3, Av 2. Family-run hotel, with 33 mostly big rooms. Pretty clean, balcony overlooking street, popular with travellers and good place to make up groups for Tortuguero.

E-F International, opposite the Continental, Av 5, Calle 2-3, T2758-0434. Private bath, some with a/c other with fan, good deal.

F Continental, a little north of the centre, Av 5, Calle 2-3, T2798-0532. Has 25 big, good and clean rooms with ceiling fans.

F King, next to post office near main square on Av 2, T2758-1033. Simple rooms, pretty dark, but clean and secure.

G Hotel Wilson, on street west of main square, Av 3, Calle 4-5, T2758-5028. Clean, tidy and central, OK.

G Ng, Calle 4, Av 5-6, T2758-2134. Has 15 basic rooms some with bath, cheaper without. Basic and a bit untidy, but friendly. Price per person. Good for the price.

G Paraíso, Av 2, Calle 4-5. Plyboard partitions divide a once-beautiful house into tiny, dark, box rooms. Hard-core roughing it and a little sad.

Parque Nacional Tortuguero *p837*
Top-end hotels normally target package deals; walk-in rates given where available. There are many cheap *cabañas* in town; the boatmen or villagers will help you find them. Staying in town is better for the local economy.

In town
B-C Casa Marbella, in front of the Catholic church, T2709-8011, http://casamarbella. tripod.com. B&B with 4 small rooms, with private bath. Run by local guide Daryl Loth. Good source of information and in the centre of the village.

C Miss Junie's, T2709-8102. Has 12 good cabins at the north end of town.

D Cabinas Tortuguero, T2709-8114, tinamon@racsa.co.cr. 5 little cabins, each sleeping 3 with private bath, pleasant garden with hammocks. Nice spot.

E Yoruki Lodge, T2709-8068. Clean, simple rooms looking over the river.

E-F Cabinas Sabina's, T2709-8069. Winding down, the end of an era, with just 16 rooms remaining. Good views looking out over to the Caribbean.

E-F Mary Scar, T2711-0671. Basic stuff: foam mattresses, but friendly enough if things elsewhere are full.

Out of town

Places out of town, best visited as part of a package, include:

LL Mawamba Lodge, T2293-8181, www.grupomawamba.com. Comfortable cabins with fans, pool, walking distance to town. Turtle beaches are behind property.

LL-AL Pachira Lodge, across the canal from town, T2223-1682, www.pachiralodge.com. 3-day/2-night package includes transport, food, tours with bilingual guide, US$269.

AL Tortuga Lodge, T2257-0766 (San José), www.costaricaexpeditions.com. Price per person includes meals. Very comfortable accommodation, in big rooms each with veranda or balcony.

AL Turtle Beach Lodge, T2248-0707, www.turtlebeachlodge.com. 2- to 7-day packages from US$210 in 48 ha of beautifully landscaped tropical grounds.

B Laguna Lodge, T2225-3740, www.laguna tortuguero.com. 50-odd cabins, with bath and fan, restaurant, bar, beautiful gardens, pool and conference room.

C Caribbean Paradise, 1 channel back from Tortuguero, T2223-0238 (difficult to reach, try going direct when you arrive). Run by Tico Carlos and his wife Ana, includes 3 meals. 16 simple rooms, no set itinerary, personal service, activities as you want them. A refreshing change from the general offering and very enjoyable.

C El Manati, T2534-7256. Tico family-run, simple rooms with a terrace. Relaxing spot, work with **Ecole Travel** in San José. Price includes breakfast, good value.

C-F Tortuguero Caribe Lodge, near Ilan Ilan, T2385-4676. Offers 10 simple cabins, friendly Tico-run and owned. Book direct or as package through **Ecole Travel** in San José. More expensive price includes breakfast and dinner.

E Ilan Ilan, through the **Agencia Mitur** in San José, T2296-7378, www.ilan-ilan lodge.com. All-inclusive packages, simple rooms in a line, with small terrace. Pool, jacuzzi and riverside bar. 2-day pacakage US$160. Recommended.

G Caño Palma Biological Station, 6 km north of Tortuguero, administered by the **Canadian Organization for Tropical Education and Rainforest Conservation** (in Canada T905-683-2116). Basic rooms for volunteer staff. Price per person, includes meals. A good place for serious naturalists or just for unwinding, accommodation for up to 16 in wooden cabin, freshwater well for drinking and washing. Minimum stay 2 weeks.

Camping

You can sometimes camp at the national park office for US$2.50.

Barra del Colorado *p839*

L-AL Silver King Lodge, T2711-0708, www.silver kinglodge.com. Price per person. Deluxe sport-fishing hotel, 5-night packages includes flights, meals, rooms with bath, a/c, swimming pool.

E Tarponland Lodge, T2710-2141. Cabins, run by Guillermo Cunningham, very helpful and knowledgeable. If you have a tent you may be able to camp at **Soda La Fiesta**, lots of mosquitoes.

Penshurst *p839*

AL Los Aviarios del Caribe, 30 km south of Limón just north of Penshurst, T2750-0775, www.slothrescue.org. A sloth rescue sanctuary with a small nature reserve.

The friendly owners offer canoe trips in the Estrella river delta and there's a volunteer programme if you have time to spare. They also have a number of comfortable rooms. Recommended.

AL Selva Bananita Lodge, 20 km from Puerto Limón at Cerro Mochila heading inland at Bananito, T2253-8118, www.selvabananito.com. 7 cabins on secluded farm, solar heating, primary rainforest tours, tree climbing, horses and bikes to rent.

Cahuita and Parque Nacional Cahuita *p840, map p838*

Beware of theft on the beach and drug pushers who may be undercover police.

A El Encanto Bed and Breakfast Inn, Playa Negra, T2755-0113, www.elencanto bedandbreakfast.com. Attractive place built by very stylish French owners, among shady gardens with pool. 3 bungalows with private bath, hot water, fan, mosquito net, terrace and hammocks and 1 3-bedroom apartment. Yoga and massage are available.

A La Casa de las Flores, Cahuita, T2755-0326, www.lacasadelasfloreshotel.com. Centrally located, 200 m north of park entrance, this Italian-run hotel is modern and very clean. The black and white minimalism is quite harsh in the bedrooms.

A-B La Diosa, Playa Grande, past Playa Negra, T2755-0055, www.hotelladiosa.net. Colourful bungalows with luxury jacuzzi, a/c, private hot water bath, hammocks, pool, gym, massage, games room, internet, surf/kayak equipment – all this and on the beach. Cheaper out of season.

A-B Magellan Inn, 2 km north of Cahuita, T2755-0035, www.magellaninn.com. Includes breakfast, 6 beautifully decorated rooms with bath and fan, and 10,000-year-old pool (honestly) set in peaceful gardens and with renowned French Creole restaurant.

A-C Kayas Place, Playa Negra, T2750-0690, www.kayasplace.com. Beautifully hand built with reclaimed wood, each room is a little different and accommodation ranges from simple to more luxurious *cabinas*. Opposite the beach, a nice chilled spot.

B Atlántida Lodge, Playa Negra, north of Cahuita, on the main road, T2755-0115. With private bath and ceiling fan. Pleasant gardens, pool, jacuzzi, massage, safe parking for cars and motorcycles. Bar and restaurant onsite.

B Kelly Creek, within a couple of blocks of the centre of town, by entrance to national park, T2755-0007, www.hotelkellycreek.com. Large rooms with veranda, ceiling fan to assist fresh sea breezes, good service and great spot.

B-C Bungalows Aché, by the entrance to the national park, T2755-0119, www.bunga lowsache.com. A little off the beaten track in a very tranquil and attractive location. Well-kept bungalows with private hot water bath, mosquito nets, coffee maker, fridge and hammocks, friendly owners.

C-D Cabinas Iguana, 800 m north of Cahuita, T2755-0005. Swiss-owned, very friendly, cabins or houses to rent, kitchen, fan, mosquito netting, balcony, clean, waterfall-fed pool, nice location. Big 2-for-1 book swap. Very good value. Recommended.

C-D Jardín Tropical and Cabinas Mambo, Playa Negra, north of Cahuita, T2755-0033, http://jardintropical.ch. 2 decent bungalows sleeping 2-4, or a house with kitchen for 5. Poison dart frogs in the gardens.

C-D Jenny's Cabinas, heading to the beach, T2755-0256, www.cabinasjenny.com. Balconies with view, Canadian-owned, bath, fan, breakfast available, running water, close to the sea but surrounding area a bit scruffy.

D Cabinas Palmar, down a little road from the bus stop which goes straight to the seafront, T2755-0243. Tico-run, clean, good, friendly and very helpful. Internet café.

D Cabinas Tito, Playa Negra, north of Cahuita, T2755-0286. Clean, quiet cabins sleeping 2-3, good for families, good value.

D Spencer Seaside Lodging, on beach close to Jenny's Cabinas, T2755-0027. Beachfront basic rooms, internet, community kitchen. Price per person.

D-E Cabinas Atlantic Surf, south end of town near the beach, T2755-0116, www.cabinasatlanticsurf.com. Wooden hotel with communal balconies and hammocks and relaxed vibe. Rooms come with private hot water bath, fan and mosquito nets.

D-E Centro Turístico Brigitte's, Playa Negra, north of Cahuita, down a small track, T2755-0053, www.brigittecahuita.com. Friendly, quiet, Swiss-run, good restaurant, wildlife, 2 small cabins sleeping 2 – one with kitchen, excellent local information, internet, laundry service, bike rentals, horse riding and many different tours. Recommended.

D-E Hotel National Park, opposite Kelly Creek, by entrance to national park, T2755-0244. Bright rooms, fan, just about friendly, the beach-front restaurant makes it a good spot.

D-E Reggae Rest and Cabinas, near Chao's Paradise in Play Negra, T2755-0515. Basic *cabinas* all with private bath in nice location by the beach.

D-E Restaurant and Bungalows Bluspirit, just out of town on the road to Playa Negra. Gorgeous split-level bungalows with private bath, hot water and hammocks, by the beach. Run by a very friendly couple who also serve fresh fish and Italian home-cooked meals in their bar and restaurant.

D-E Safari Ocean View, towards Play Negra, T2755-0393. 5 decent *cabinas* with private bath and hot water, also terrace and hammocks, great location a short amble to the shore and good value for the price.

E Cabinas Belo Horizonte, Playa Negra, north of Cahuita, T2755-0206. A couple of good rooms, quite simple but on the beach, rent for US$200 per month or US$20 per day.

E Cabinas Mina, main street. Very friendly owners offer very basic rooms with private bath and cold water.

E Cabinas Nirvana, towards Playa Negra, T2755-0110, nirvana99@racsa.co.cr. Wooden rooms in a very tranquil spot, hot water private bath, swimming pool in gardens.

E Cabinas Safari, opposite Cabinas Palmar, T2755-0405. Simple rooms with fan and shared bath and hot water, friendly owner Wayne Palmer, clean, price per person, good value.

E Cabinas Surf Side, facing the school, T2755-0246. Clean, good value. Parking.

E New Cabinas Arrecife, right on the coast close to **Miss Edith's**, T2755-0081. OK rooms, but great spot and view from restaurant.

E Sol y Mar, on the road to parque nacional, T2755-0237. Friendly owners have rooms that sleep 2-6 people, with private hot-water bath. Rooms are a little tatty, but fine and some very spacious. Their local restaurant is good for breakfast.

E Vaz Cabañas, towards the park entrance, T2755-0218. Friendly, cold shower, some fans, quite clean, good restaurant, safe parking. Recommended. Same owners have now opened more *cabañas* (**E**), under the same name, in front of the bus station. Clean and bright with private hot-water showers.

E Villa Delmar, close to national park entrance, T2755-0392. Rooms with private shower, cold and hot water. Bicycle rental, laundry service and parking.

E-F Bobo Shanti, around the corner from Cabinas Safari. Colourfully painted in red, green and gold. Rooms have private bath, hot and cold water. Chilled vibes.

E-F Cabinas Margarita, Playa Negra, north of Cahuita, down a 200-m path, T2755-0205. Simple rooms, quiet spot, nice atmosphere, clean.

Camping

It's possible to camp in Cahuita National Park. **Colibrís Paradise**, out of village close to Playa Negra.

Kontiki, near Playa Negra, T2755-0261. With laundry, showers and toilets, also a few cabins.

Puerto Viejo de Talamanca *p840, map p841*

Discounts are often available May-Nov. **AL-A Samasati Lodge & Retreat Center**, near Hone Creek on junction between Cahuita and Puerto Viejo, T2750-0315, www.samasati.com. Beautiful mountain location with 100-ha reserve, vegetarian restaurant, meditation courses, reservation recommended.

A Escape Caribeño, 500 m along road to Punta Uva, T2750-0103, www.escape caribeno.com. German-run, well-furnished cottages, fully equipped, some a/c.

A-B Cabinas Los Almendros (see map), T2750-0235, www.cabinaslosalmendros.com. 3 fully equipped apartments and a complex of conventional rooms with private hot water bath, a/c and cable TV in the more expensive ones. None of the Caribbean charm but good facilities, especially for families. Cash exchange, credit card advances, tour advice, good, friendly service.

B Lizard King, out of town, heading north, T2750-0614/0630. Smart *cabinas* located upstairs at their Mexican restaurant, not always open. Swimming pool.

B-C Cabinas Casa Verde, central, T2750-0015, www.cabinascasaverde.com. Comfortable rooms with hammocks, private bath, cracked tile showers in beautiful gardens. A pool and open-air jacuzzi add to the relaxation. The owner collects Central American poison dart frogs and keeps them in tanks dotted around the grounds; ask to take a look, even if you are not a guest. Very nice owners and staff, recommended.

B-D Cashew Hill, south of town, T2750-0256, www.cashewhilllodge.co.cr. Re-developed in the last few years, although retaining rustic charm. 6 family-orientated rooms, with both private and shared bath, fans and mosquito nets. Set in 1 ha of beautiful gardens on the rolling hills above the town, mirador looks out over the jungle tops to the sea. Yoga massage retreats and classes available. Quiet, very chilled atmosphere.

B-D Coco Loco Lodge, south of town, T2750-0281, www.cocolocolodge.com. Quiet spot in expansive garden south of town, nice thatched wooden and stone cabins, some fully equipped with kitchen and cable TV. Popular. English, German and Spanish spoken.

C Bungalows Calalú, on the road to Cocles, T2750-0042, www.bungalowscalalu.com.

Bungalows with and without kitchen, also swimming pool and beautiful butterfly garden in the grounds.

C Guaraná, opposite Lulu Berlu Gallery, T2750-0244, www.hotelguarana.com. Very attractive hotel if a little pricey, well kept. All rooms with private, hot water bath, fans, mosquito nets, private balconies and hammocks. They also have a communal kitchen and parking space.

C Jacaranda, a few blocks back (see map), T2750-0069, www.cabinasjacaranda.net. A very relaxed spot away from the beach set in beautiful gardens, with coloured mosaic pathways and private areas to read and relax. Rooms are fixed with colourful throws and side lights, showers are spacious. Very attractive place, hot water throughout, fans, mosquito nets. Communal kitchen. Massages can be booked to take place in a pagoda in their flower garden.

C Maritza, central, T2750-0003. In cabins, with bath, clean, clean, friendly. Affiliated to International Youth Hostel Association, English spoken. A map in the bar shows all the hotels and *cabinas* in the area. Highly recommended.

C-D Cabinas David, just out of town past Lizard King, T2750-0542, cabinas_david@ yahoo.com. *Cabinas* with private, hot water shower, individual terrace with hammocks.

D Cabinas Grant, on the road out of town (see map), T2752-0292. Local ownership, large clean rooms, with private bath and fan. Each with a small terrace. Restaurant upstairs is now a seafood eatery.

D Cabinas Tropical, close to the coast, T2750-0283, www.cabinastropical.com. 8 spotless rooms, some with fridges, with good mattresses, private bath and hot water. Pleasant gardens with shaded garden house for relaxing, small bar/café. The German owner, Rolf Blancke, is a tropical biologist and runs tours. Recommended.

D Cabinas Yucca, north of town, T2750-0285. Has 5 *cabinas* with private hot water showers, good value and great spot, nice beach garden, parking, friendly, German-run.

D Hotel Fortaleza, on main street in the middle of town, T2750-0028. Rooms with private hot water bath, not a particularly special building, but fine, clean and a very relaxed friendly atmosphere with communal terrace for watching street life.

D-E Cabinas Soda Mitchell, close to Soda Lidia. 3 sparkling rooms sleeping 2-3 people, with private shower and (usually) hot water. Very pleasant owner and quiet out-of-the-way location.

D-E Café Rico, north end of town. Coffee shop with a couple of rooms with private shower and hot water. Very friendly English owner and probably the best coffee in town.

D-E Pura Vida, a few blocks back from the main street (see map),T2750-0002, German-Chilean run, friendly, very clean, hammocks. Sadly lacking in character but recommended.

D-F Puerto Viejo, just off the main street (see map), T2750-0620. Great management make the place the most chilled in town. 78 beds in basic rooms sleep 1 to 5, 3 have private hot-water bath, the rest are shared hot and cold water showers. There is a communal kitchen and large areas to eat, chat and be social. 1 fully equipped apartment for monthly rental (approximately US$500). Owners are all surfers and they offer board rental, buy and sell, also wave info. Scooter rental available. Popular with surfers.

D-G Las Olas Camping and Cabinas, next to Salsa Brava Restaurant. Basic for the price – camping from US$6, rooms from US$25 – rooms with private bath and hot water, but great spot on the beach and friendly local owners. Showers and toilet facilities for campers.

E Bull Inn, first left after Harbor Supermarket. Locally owned, very clean and bright rooms with private bath, hot water, and a communal balcony.

E Los Sueños, main steret (on map), T2750-0369, www.costaricaguide.info/lossuenos.htm. Laid-back and very relaxing, just 4 colourful and bright rooms.

E-F Cabinas Popular, opposite the back entrance of Casa Verde. Nicely located at the back of the town – very peaceful with rural backdrop – rather basic rooms and a little dark, but extremely good value, private shower, but cold water.

E-G Rocking J's, on the beach out of town, towards Cocles, T2750-0657, www.rockingjs.com. A sprawling multi-coloured campers' paradise. Huge covered hammock hotel and area for tents – bring your own or rent one of theirs. They also have a 'tree house' room, with double bed under a retractable ceiling so you can watch the stars, also a music system and fridge (you need never come down) and the 'King Suite', an open-sided, colourful room, with private bath. Coloured mosaic murals, communal kitchen, toilets and restaurant, all done by guests. They also offer kayak, surfboard and bike rentals, and the occasional full moon party.

F Cabinas Lika, southern end of town (see map). Friendly backpackers set-up with private rooms, dorms and hammocks, shared kitchen and laid-back vibe.

F Cabañas Yoli, 250 m from bus stop. Clean, basic, fan, OK – one of the last Tico-owned places.

F Sol y Sombre, at entrance to town, with the style of the French. 5 clean rooms, with fan and mosquito nets. Small restaurant downstairs.

G Tamandua Lodge, behind Cabinas Dolce Vida. Very basic budget accommodation, with shared rooms, shared bathroom and shared kitchen.

Around Puerto Viejo *p841*

L-B Aguas Claras, 4.5 km from Puerto Viejo on road to Manzanillo, T2750-0131, www.aguasclaras-cr.com. 5 beautiful cottages each painted a different colour with pretty white wooden gables and balconies. All fully equipped and very close to the beach. Restaurant Miss Holly serves gourmet breakfast and lunch. Recommended.

AL Tree House Lodge, Punta Uva, T2750-0706, www.costaricatreehouse.com. Dutch owner Edsart has 3 apartments – 2 of which are the most unusual in Costa Rica: the treehouse and the beach suite (there is also a beach house). All are fully equipped with kitchen facilities and hot water, and all are equally luxurious.

AL-A Shawandha, Playa Chiquita, T2750-0018, www.shawandhalodge.com. Beautiful bungalows in the jungle with a calm and private feel and fantastic mosaic showers. Massages now available. Very stylish restaurant serving French-Caribbean fusion, pricey.

A Hotel Kasha, Playa Chiquita, T2750-0205, www.costarica-hotelkasha.com. 14 bungalows in lush gardens on the beach, beautiful pool, jacuzzi and restaurant.

A Hotel Las Palmas, Playa Uva, T2759-0303, www.laspalmashotel.com. Cabins, 26 rooms, pool, snorkelling, rainforest, tours, transport from San José on Wed, Fri, Sun, US$30 return, US$20 1 way.

A-B Banana Azul Guest House, Playa Negra, T2750-2035, toll free T1-800-821-5352, www.bananaazul.com. Neat and comfortable rooms with private bath as well as beach houses. Breakfast included.

A-B Cariblue Bungalows, Playa Cocles, T2750-0035, www.cariblue.com. Nice natural complex with palm roofs, set in beautiful garden. Restaurant and bar on site along with a games room and library.

B Almonds and Corals Tent Camp, Playa Uva, T2272-2024, www.almondsandcorals.com. Luxury camping with bath and hot water in tents on platforms in the forest, pool, restaurant, trips arranged to Punta Mona, snorkelling, bike hire, breakfast and dinner included. Sleeping in the wild, with some comfort thrown in.

B Playa Chiquita Lodge, Playa Chiquita, T2750-0408, www.playachiquitalodge.com. The lodge labels itself a beach jungle hotel and that's exactly what it feels like. They have 11 rooms and 3 houses (monthly rentals accepted) all with hot water, hammocks and plenty of space, easy beach access and breakfast included.

B Totem Cabinas, Playa Cocles, T2750-0758, www.totemsite.com. Surf-orientated hotel heavy on the bamboo furniture. Luxury

rooms with lounge areas, private shower, hot water, cable TV and private balconies overlooking Playa Cocles. Italian bar and restaurant, internet room and swimming pool. Surf board rental and surf and kite school.

B-C La Costa de Papito, Playa Cocles, T2750-0080, www.lacostadepapito.com. 11 beautifully designed bungalows with all the style you'd expect from Eddie Ryan (**Carlton Arms Hotel**, New York). Rooms with fan and bath. Great owners who love to make their guests happy, recommended. Costa de Papito now host **Pure Jungle Spa**, T2750-0536, www.purejunglespa.com, Tue-Sat, or by appointment. Treatments are organic and handmade and sound good enough to eat … They range from chocolate facials to banana body wraps.

B-C Miraflores Lodge and Restaurant, Playa Chiquita, T2750-0038, www.miraflores lodge.com. 10 rooms (2 with kitchen), a/c, breakfast included, with bath, fan, gardens, lots of wildlife. English and French spoken. Cheaper rates in low season.

C Azania, Playa Cocles, T2750-0540, www.azania-costarica.com. Beautiful thatched-roof bungalows with great facilities in garden setting, restaurant, pool and jacuzzi, parking.

C Cabinas Pangea, Manzanillo, behind **Aquamor**, T2759-9012, www.greencoast. com/aquamor.htm. 2 nice rooms with bath, also house on beach with kitchen.

D-E Cabinas Something Different, T2759-9014, Manzanillo. 10 very clean rooms, 6 with a/c, all with private bath and hot water, big parking area and kitchen use available, friendly local people.

F Cabinas Las Veraneras, Manzanillo. Rooms with shared bath.

F Cabinas/Restaurant Maxi, Manzanillo, T2754-2266. Basic rooms, highly respected seafood restaurant.

F Selvin Cabins and restaurant, Playa Uva. With room and dormitory accommodation.

🍴 Eating

Puerto Limón *p837, map p836*
Cheap food is available in and around the Central Market. *Casados* in market in the day, outside it at night, good, cheap food. Try *pan bon*, spicy bread from Creole recipe, sold near bus stop for San José.

🍴🍴🍴 **Springfield**, north of town opposite the hospital. Stylish with a mix of Tico and international dishes. Best restaurant in town.

🍴🍴 **Antillita**, Calle 6, Av 4-5. Caribbean rice and beans, meat, open evenings only.

🍴🍴 **Brisas del Caribe**, facing Parque Vargas, Av 2, Calle 1, T2758-0138. Cheap noodles, meat, seafood, and good service.

🍴🍴 **Marisquería El Cevichito**, Av 2, Calle 1-2, T2758-1380. Good fish, steaks and *ceviche* and good spot for people-watching.

🍴🍴 **Monte de Oro**, Av 4, Calle 3-4. Serves good local dishes, in a rough and ready atmosphere.

🍴🍴 **Park Hotel**, Av 3, Calle 1-2 (see Sleeping). Does good meals overlooking the sea.

🍴🍴 **Sabor Pizza**, corner of Av 3 and Calle 4. Good pizza.

🍴🍴 **Soda Yans**, Av 2, Calle 5-6. Popular spot.

🍴 **Diplo's**, Av 6, Calle 5-6. The best, and cheapest, Caribbean food in town.

🍴 **Milk Bar La Negra Mendoza**, at the central market. Good milk shakes and snacks.

🍴 **Samkirson**, Calle 3, Av 3-4. One of several Chinese restaurants. Good value.

🍴 **Soda Mares**, overlooking market square. Daily 0700-1400. Good food.

Parque Nacional Tortuguero *p837*
🍴🍴 **Café Caoba**, Tortuguero village. Cheap and has excellent pizza, sandwiches and shrimp.

🍴🍴 **Miss Junie's**, north end of Tortuguero village. Very popular, has good local dishes, reservation necessary.

🍴🍴 **The Vine**, Tortuguero village. Pizzas and sandwiches.

🍴 **El Dolar**, Tortuguero village. Simple restaurant, small menu, good *casado*.

🍴 **Restaurant El Muellecito**, Tortuguero village, T2710-6716. Also 3 simple cabins.

Cahuita and Parque Nacional Cahuita *p840, map p838*
If the catch is good restaurants have lobster.

🍴🍴🍴 **La Casa Creole**, Playa Negra, by the Magellan Inn, 2 km north of Cahuita, T2755-0104 (for reservations). Mon-Sat 0600-0900. A culinary feast of French and Creole creations, from US$8. Recommended.

🍴🍴 **Cha Cha Cha**, Cahuita, T2755-0191. Opens at 1700, closed Mon International menu, great food and service, refreshing chic decor, very good pasta from US$4.

🍴🍴 **Chao's Paradise**, T2755-0421, Playa Negra. Typical Caribbean food and seafood specials, good little reggae bar, with oropendula nests overlooking the beach.

🍴🍴 **Coral Reef**, next to Coco's Bar, Cahuita. Very accommodating local management can cook to your tastes, great local food with seafood specialities.

🍴🍴 **Mango Tango Pizzeria**, Cahuita. Great home-made pasta with a wide variety if Italian sauces, quite a rarity in these parts, good pizza, good restaurant.

🍴🍴 **Miss Edith's**, Cahuita, T2755-0248. Open daily until 2130. Almost legendary. Delicious Caribbean and vegetarian food, nice people, good value, no alcohol licence, take your own, many recommendations for breakfast and dinner, but don't expect quick service.

🍴🍴 **Pizz n' Love**, Cahuita. Excellent restaurant run by a Dutch hippy, pizzas named after celebrities with loads of good toppings such as ricotta, parmesan and ginger prawns, served on tables painted with slogans such as 'give pizza a chance'. Recommended.

🍴🍴 **Restaurant Banana**, top of Playa Negra. A good restaurant and bar away from the crowds. Recommended.

🍴🍴 **Restaurant Palenque Luisa**, Cahuita. Has the distinctly tropical feel with split-bamboo walls, sand floors and a good *menú típico*.

🍴🍴 **Restaurant Relax**, Cahuita, over Rikki's Bar. Fantastic pizzas, pastas, some Mexican and fish, good Italian wines.

¶¶ **Sobre las Olas**, Playa Negra, T2755-0109. Closed Tue. On the beach serving Tico and Italian, popular bar in the evening.

¶¶ **Sol y Mar**, Cahuita. Open 0730-1200, 1630-2000, need to arrive early and wait at least 45 mins for food. Red snapper and volcano potato especially wicked, US$5; also good breakfasts, try cheese, egg and tomato sandwich, US$2. Good value.

¶¶-¶ **100% Natural Coffee Shop**, Cahuita. Snacks, tapas and cocktails, and of course, natural coffees. Internet.

¶¶-¶ **The Beach House**, Cahuita. Bar and restaurant, cocktails served, laid-back establishment on the high street. Surf lessons and information available.

¶¶-¶ **Rest Le Fe**, opposite **Coco's Bar**, Cahuita. Large variety of dishes all centred round rice and beans, good typical food.

¶ **Ice Cream Shop**, high street, Cahuita. Ice cream and juice kiosk.

¶ **The Pastry Shop**, Playa Negra, T2755-0275. Delicious breads, brownies and pies.

¶ **Soda Priscilla**, opposite **Sol y Mar**, Cahuita. Good budget breakfast *pinto*, eggs and fresh juices.

Puerto Viejo de Talamanca *p840, map p841*

¶¶¶ **Amimodo**, north end of town, overlooking the beach, beyond **Standord's**. Fine Italian restaurant with prices to match. Reputedly fantastic. Weekend Latin nights. Doesn't always come with a smile.

¶¶¶-¶ **Stanford's**. Upstairs restaurant has a rather pricey, but good menu in arty surroundings.

¶¶ **Chili Rojo**, is east of town, past **Stanford's**. Thai, Eastern and vegetarian food including humous and falafel platters and coconut curries and delicious home-made ice cream.

¶¶ **El Parquecito**, facing sea in the centre. Nice breezy atmosphere, specializes in pizza and Italian dishes.

¶¶ **Grant Seafood**, located over **Cabinas Grant** (see Sleeping). Seafood restaurant.

¶¶ **Jammin Juices and Jerk Chicken**, by the coast. Roast chicken with a variety of

home-made sauces and salsas, also great vegetarian selection, open for breakfast, lunch and early dinners. Recommended.

¶¶ **La Terraza**, main street, above **Frutería Ivone**. Lovely Italian owner and chef, will cook to your requirements – ravioli, lasagne, pastas and seafood and tiramisu for afters.

¶¶ **Pizzeria Rusticone**, 1 block back from main street (see map). Best pizzas in town cooked in original ovens, excellent pastas including home-made ones, all at good prices, recommended.

¶¶ **Salsa Brava**, north end of town (see map). Spanish food, closed Sun. Recommended.

¶¶ **Tamara**, on main street, T2750-0148. Open 0600-2100. Local good fish dishes, popular throughout the day and packed at weekends.

¶¶-¶ **Bread and Chocolate**, centre of town (see map). A breakfast café well-known for its home baking and the morning menu is filled with good, home-made choices, ranging from eggs, bacon and fresh bread to oatmeal with apple and cinnamon. Breads and cakes, mint and nut brownies and divine chocolate truffles are home-made and the café is well recommended.

¶¶-¶ **Hot Rocks**, main street. American joint that serves steak, nachos and pizzas, cocktails and beers served in front of cinema-size movie screen – they show 3 films a night, free with dinner or drinks.

¶ **Carlos Pool Bar**, 1 block from the main street, behind **Pollo Frito** (see below). Locally owned bar that serves cheap and large *casados*, soda included in the price. Pool tables and sometimes a movie showing.

¶ **Lidia's Place**, south of centre. Good typical food and to-die-for chocolate cake that does not hang round.

¶ **Peace and Love Coffee**, south end of town. Ex-**Bambú** owners. Italians making fantastic home-made breads and pizzas, lasagnes and other mouth-watering delicatessen items at surprisingly reasonable prices.

¶ **Pizza Boruca**, opposite the church (see map). Best pizza slices in all Costa Rica, cheap and delicious – this man is always busy.

Pollo Frito, north end of town, opposite Stanford's (see map). Affectionately named the 'fried chicken place' – no one ever remembers its real name. A late-opening café, perfect for late-night snacking, serves mainly (as you would guess) fried chicken and yucca, but also rice and beans, *casados* and sandwiches.

Red Stripe Café, south end of town (see map). Snacks and smoothies.

Soda Miss Sam, south of the centre, good local food piled high, good value.

Soda Palmer, north end of town (see map). Cheap Chinese food, big plates, nice people.

Cafés and bakeries

Monchies, 2 blocks off the main street (see map). Delicious baked goods.

Pan Pay, beachfront. Good bakery. Also serve great breakfasts: eggs with avocado, fresh bread and tomato salsa, omelettes, pastries, etc. A good place to read the paper and nod at the locals – a very popular spot in the morning.

Around Puerto Viejo *p841*

El Living, Playa Cocles. Pizza, drinks and music, very laid back, and good prices.

La Isla Inn, Playa Cocles. Serves Japanese Caribbean fusion, including sushi, soups, salads, and stir-fry.

Magic Ginger, Hotel Kasha, Playa Chiquita. Restaurant and bar serving gourmet French cooking, seafood specials and exotic salads.

Rest Maxi, Manzanillo. Reggae-style restaurant serving typical Caribbean food and seafood specials.

Aguas Dulce, Playa Cocles. Ice creams, pastries and sandwiches.

Coffee Bar, on the shore near Cabinas Jenny, is a good reggae spot.

Puerto Viejo de Talamanca *p840, map p841*

Puerto probably has the most lively nightlife on Costa Rica's entire Caribbean coast and has always run on an unspoken rota – each bar having a particular night, and this is still (loosely) the case. Various bars have bid for Bambu's Mon and Fri reggae nights, which now run between **Sunset Bar** (by the bus stop) and **Baba Yaga** (next to Hotel Puerto Viejo). (**Bambu** was a bar that burnt down several years ago.) **Sunset** has live events and pool tables; they have also taken over **Jam Night** on Wed (that used to be held at **Tesoro** in Cocles). **Baba Yaga** is smaller and more intimate; and they run the occasional dance music event.

Jhonny's Bar (or **Mike's Playground**, depending on how local you are – **Jhonny's** is the original) is perhaps the best night now in town on Thu, Sat and Sun. Right on the beach, with Puerto's reggae/dancehall best.

Stanford's Disco, tends to be the quietest, despite being one of the originals. **Dubliner Irish Bar** is past Salsa Brava. Don't get too excited, they're apparently often out of Guinness and there's nothing in the way of traditional ale, but there's a flag on the wall and lots of Irish music, so if you fancy something not very tropical. **Bar In and In**, over Rest Tamara in the high street is a much more laid-back reggae bar for pre-party drinks and cocktails. There is a small bar at **Café Puerto Viejo**, with olives and expensive cocktails – ambient and chilled music makes a change from the reggae everywhere else.

🌐 Entertainment

Cahuita and Parque Nacional Cahuita *p840, map p838*

Rikki's Bar and **Cocos Bar** in the centre of Cahuita; the latter is the livelier of the 2 and hosts reggae nights on Fri and live music.

⛰ Activities and tours

Parque Nacional Tortuguero *p837*
Tour operators
Most people visit Tortuguero as part of a tour from San José flying into the airport, or catching an agency bus and boat from

Matina. It is possible to travel to Tortuguero independently (see Transport, below). Tours from San José include transport, meals, 2 nights' lodging, guide and boat trips for US$215-330 per person (double occupancy). **Caño Blanco Marina**, 2 Av, 1-3 C, San José, T2256-9444 (San José), T2710-0523 (Tortuguero). Runs a daily bus-boat service San José–Tortuguero at 0700, US$50 return, Book in advance – if you miss the boat, there is nothing else in Caño Blanco Marina. **Mawamba**, T2223-2421, www.grupoma wamba.com. Minimum 2 people, 3 days/ 2 nights, daily, private launch so you can stop en route, with launch tour of national park included. Accommodation at the very comfortable **Mawamba Lodge**, 3-day/ 2-night package, Tue, Fri, Sun US$330. Other accommodations have very similar packages, with the difference being the level of comfort in the hotel. **Ilan Ilan Lodge**, T2255-3031, www.ilan-ilanlodge.com is one of the more affordable at US$215 for 2 nights, US$160 for one night (but not really worth it). **OTEC** (see page 723) runs 3-day/2-night tours for US$180, with small student discount; a trip to see the turtles in Jul-Sep costs extra. Tours from Puerto Viejo de Sarapiquí, including boat trip to Tortuguero, meals, 2 nights' lodging, guide and transport to San José cost US$275-400 per person (double occupancy). *Riverboat Francesca*, T2226-0986, www.tortuguero canals.com, costs US$200-220 per person 2 day-1 night trips exploring the canals for exquisite wildlife, sportfishing. Longer packages are also available.

Organizing a package trip from **Puerto Limón** is more difficult. **Viajes Tropicales Laura**, T2795-2410, www.viajestropicales laura.net, have been highly recommended, daily service, open return US$60 if phoned direct, more through travel agencies; pickup from hotel, will store luggage, lunch provided, excellent for pointing out wildlife on the way. An inclusive 2-day, 1-night package a from Puerto Limón with basic accommodation, turtle-watching trip

and transport (no food) costs from US$99 per person.

Guides Several local guides have been recommended, including **Johnny Velázquez**; **Alberto**, who lives next to Hotel Mary Scar; **Rubén Bananero**, who lives in the last house before you get to the National Park office, sign on pathway, recommended for 4-hr tour at dusk and in the dark; **Chico**, who lives behind Sabina's Cabinas, US$2 per hr, and will take you anywhere in his motor boat; **Ernesto**, who was born in Tortuguero, and has 15 years' experience as a guide, contact him at Tropical Lodge or through his mother, who owns Sabina's Cabinas; **Rafael**, a biologist who speaks Spanish and English (his wife speaks French), and lives 500 m behind Park Rangers' office (ask rangers for directions); he also rents canoes. **Ross Ballard**, a Canadian biologist who can be contacted through Casa Marbella.

Daryl Loth lives locally and runs **Tortuguero Safaris**, T8833-0827, safari@racsa.co.cr. **Barbara Hartung** of **Tinamon Tours**, T2709-8004, www.tinamon tours.de, a biologist who xspeaks English, German, French and Spanish, is recommended for boat, hiking and turtle tours in Tortuguero (US$5 per person per hr; all-inclusive trips from Limón 3-days, 2-nights, US$140 per person). Both Daryl and Barbara are strong supporters of using **paddle power**, or at most electric motors. Provide the latest details of how to get to Tortuguero yourself.

There are several **boats for rent** from Tortuguero, ask at the *pulpería*. The use of polluting 2-stroke motors is outlawed in Tortuguero, and the use of 4-stroke engines is limited to 3 of the 4 main water channels.

Cahuita and Parque Nacional Cahuita *p840, map p838*
Snorkelling equipment and **surfboards** available for rent. **Horses** can be hired, but try to ensure they are in good shape.

Bicycles can be hired for about US$7 per day and you can cycle to Puerto Viejo and the Panamanian border through some beautiful scenery.

Tour operators
Wide range of activities available including water sports and nature tours.
Cahuita Tours, T2755-0232, exotica@racsa. co.cr, excursions by jeep and glass-bottomed boat tours over the reefs, bike, diving and snorkelling equipment rental, international telephone service (ICE) and Western Union money transfer. **GrayLine** bus travel can be arranged here.
Roberto's Tours, office located at his restaurant (**Roberto's**) on the main street. Very nice people run all the usual tours of the area including snorkelling and diving.
Willies Tours, T2755-0267, www.willies-costarica-tours.com. Willie is most helpful and knows everything about Cahuita and surrounding areas. He runs tours to Tortuguero, Panama, Bribri indigenous reserve and whitewater rafting in the Pacuare river. The office is located opposite Restaurant Palenque on the main street, where he also runs an internet café.

Puerto Viejo de Talamanca p840, map p841
Tours in Puerto Viejo include canopy, snorkelling, boat trips and diving in Cahuita and Manzanillo, trips to an indigenous reserve, rafting in Pacuare, kayaking, birdwatching, etc.
ATEC is the easiest source of information (www.ateccr.org) and the original provider of information and tours combining eco-tourism and conservation but you can also try **Canopy Tour** and **Terraventuras**, T2750-0750, www.terraventuras.com; **Exploradores Outdoors**, T2750-6262, www.exploradoresoutdoors.com; **Atlántico Tours**, T2750-0004, offer several trips; **Reef Runner Divers**, T2750-0480, www.reefrunner divers.com; **Yuppi and Tino**, T2750-0621 in Puerto Viejo; **Aguamar Adventures**, in

Manzanillo, have been operating since 1993, and offer diving courses and local trips. Snorkel tours from US$35, tank dives from US$50.

⊙ Transport

Puerto Viejo de Sarapiquí p835
Bus
Buses stop on north side of park. From **San José** 7 daily from Gran Terminal del Caribe, 1½ hrs, US$3.45, through PN Braulio Carrillo, or through Heredia, 4 daily, 3½ hrs, US$4.20. From **Cd Quesada**, 5 daily, 2½ hrs.

Car
To get there by car from **San José**, after passing through the PN Braulio Carrillo take Route 4, a paved road which turns off near Santa Clara to Puerto Viejo; it bypasses Río Frío and goes via Las Horquetas. A more scenic but longer route leaves from Heredia via San Miguel and La Virgen, and on to Puerto Viejo.

Guápiles, Guácimo and Siquirres p835
Bus
In Guápiles, buses leave from a central terminal a block to the north of the church. Regular buses to **San José** and **Puerto Limón**. Buses to **Puerto Viejo de Sarapiquí** ever 2½ hrs, and to **Río Frío** every 1½ hrs.
For Siquirres, at least 1 bus per hour leaves Gran Terminal del Caribe in **San José**, 2½-hr journey, US$2.90.

Puerto Limón p837, map p836
Bus
Town bus service is irregular and crowded. Service from **San José** with CoopeLimón, T2233-3646 and **Caribeño**, T2222-0610, at least every hour, 0500-2000, daily. Arrive and depart from Calle 2, Av 1-2, 2½ hrs, US$5.30. Also services to **Guápiles** and **Siquirres**, US$1.30. From same stop buses to Siquirres/ Guápiles, 13 daily, 8 direct. Near Radio Casino on Av 4, Calle 3-4, buses leave for **Sixaola**,

first 0500, last 1800, US$5.30, stopping at **Cahuita**, **Puerto Viejo** and **Bribri** en route. To **Manzanillo**, at 0600, 1430, returning 1130, 1900, 1½ hrs, US$4.20. To **Moín** from Calle 5, Av 3-4, every 30 mins between 0600-2200, US$0.40.

Parque Nacional Tortuguero p837
Air
Daily flights from **San José** with **Nature Air** (US$91).

Boat
It is quite possible to travel to Tortuguero independently, but more challenging than the all-inclusive packages. There are a couple of options. From **Limón**, regular vessels leaves from the Tortuguero dock in **Moín**, north of Limón, US$50 return. It is a loosely run cooperative, with boats leaving at 1000. There is also a 1500 service that runs less frequently. If possible, book in advance through the Tortuguero Information Centre (check the times; they change frequently). If you are in a group you may be able to charter a boat for approximately US$200.

An alternative route is between Puerto Veijo de Sarapiqui and Tortuguero. Boats leave Puerto Viejo on Mon and Thu, returning on Tue and Fri. US$55 per person.

Bus and boat
From **San José**, the bus/boat combination is the cheapest option and a mini-adventure in itself. Take the 0900 bus to Cariari from the Terminal Gran Caribe, arriving around 1045. Walk 500 m north to the ticket booth behind the police station where you can buy you bus/boat ticket to Tortuguero. Take the 1200 bus to **La Pavona**, arriving around 1330. Take 1 of the boats to Tortuguero, which will arrive about 1500. The journey is about US$10 1-way. Don't be talked into a package if you're not interested – there are plenty of services to choose from in Tortuguero. The return service leaves at 0830 and 1330 giving you 1 or 2 nights in Tortuguero. (There appears to be an attempt to monopolize this service but for the time being at least, there are a couple of boats in operation.)

Alternative routes include the 1030 bus from San José to Cariari, changing to get the 1400 bus to La Geest and the 1530 boat to Tortuguero. Or 1300 bus San José–Cariari, 1500 bus Cariari to La Pavona, 1630 boat La Pavone to Tortuguero.

It is also possible to take a bus from Siquirres to **Freeman** (unpaved road, US$1.70), a Del Monte banana plantation, from where unscheduled boats go to Tortuguero; ask around at the bank of the Río Pacuare, or call the public phone office in Tortuguero (T2710-6716, open 0730-2000) and ask for **Johnny Velázquez** to come and pick you up, US$57, maximum 4 passengers, 4 hrs. Sometimes heavy rains block the canals, preventing passage there or back. Contact **Willis Rankin** (T2798-1556) an excellent captain who will negotiate rampaging rivers. All riverboats for the major lodges (see below) leave from Hamburgo or Freeman. If the excursion boats have a spare seat you may be allowed on.

Penshurst p839
Bus
Small buses leave **Limón** (Calle 4, Av 6) for **Valle de Estrella/Pandora**, 7 a day from 0500, at 2-hourly intervals, last at 1800, 1½ hrs (returning from Pandora at similar times).

Cahuita and Parque Nacional Cahuita p840, map p838
Bus
Service direct from **San José**'s Terminal del Caribe, to **Cahuita** at 0600, 1000, 1200, 1400 and 1600, return 0700, 0800, 0930, 1130 and 1630, 3½ hrs, US$7.90, T2257-8129, **Trans Mepá**, 4 hrs, US$4.50, and from **Puerto Limón**, in front of Radio Casino, 0500-1800, return 0630-2000, 1 hr, US$2, T2758-1572, both continuing to Bribri, and Sixaola (dirt road) on the Panamanian border (US$1, 2 hrs). The bus drops you at the crossing of the 2 main roads in Cahuita.

Puerto Viejo de Talamanca
p840, map p841
Bus
Daily services from **San José** from Gran Terminal del Caribe at 0600, 1000, 1200, 1400 and 1600, return at 0730, 0900, 1100 and 1600, 4 hrs, US$9; from **Limón** daily from Radio Casino, 0500-1800, return 0600-2000, 1½ hrs; 30 mins from **Cahuita**, US$0.80. To **Manzanillo** at 0700, 1530, 1900, returning 0500, 0830, 1700, ½ hr, US$0.80. To **Sixaola** 5 daily, 0545 until 1845, 2 hrs, US$2.

Around Puerto Viejo *p841*
Bus
Express bus to **Manzanillo** from Terminal Sixaola, **San José**, daily, 1600, return 0630. From **Limón** daily 0600, 1430, return 1130, 1900, 1½ hrs.

⊙ Directory

Puerto Limón *p837, map p836*
Banks Usual hours and services, all with ATMs at Banco de Costa Rica, Av 2, Calle 1, Mon-Fri 0900-1400; Banco Nacional, Av 2, Calle 3, with ATM; Banco Popular, Calle 3, Av 1-2, with ATM. Banco de San José, Av 3, Calle 3-4, with ATM. **Internet** Edutec Internet, on 2nd level above Plaza Caribe, US$2.30 per hr. Also 24-hr access at Internet, 1 block from Mas X Menos, US$1 per hr. **Laundry** Av 2, Calle 5-6, price per item, not that cheap, but 2-hr turnaround. **Medical services** Red Cross, Calle 3, Av 1-2, T2758-0125. Hospital, on road to Moin, T2758-2222. **Post** Opposite central

for international calls at Av 2, Calle 5-6 and at Calle 3, Av 4-5, Mon-Thu 0800-1700, Fri 0800-1600.

Cahuita and Parque Nacional Cahuita *p840, map p838*
Banks None. Money exchange is difficult except occasionally for cash dollars (**Cahuita Tours** changes dollars and TCs). Take plenty of colones from Limón. Nearest banks are in **Puerto Viejo** and **Bribri** (20 km) but several places accept credit cards. **Internet** Cyberbet, part of Cabinas Safari, US$1.60 per hr. **Willies Tours** has internet, opposite the bus station. **Post** Next to police station at northern end of town.

Puerto Viejo de Talamanca *p840, map p841*
Banks Banco Nacional is 3 blocks south of ATEC, with ATM machine, but only take Visa or Plus (not MasterCard or Cirrus). The bank in Bribri does accept MasterCard credit card. You can change TCs and cash at **Manuel León's general store** on the beach. **Cabinas Los Almendros** changes TCs, euro and US dollars, and give credit card advance. **Internet** From ATEC, US$2.50 per hr. Also Jungle Café, fastest internet in town, but pricey and pre-pay cards only. **Books, Librería & Bazar Internet**, also fast, US$2.50 per hr. Internet next to Hot Rocks, slow, but open late. **Medical services** Chemist at the shopping area by the bank. **Police** On sea front. **Post** At the shopping area by the bank. US$2 to send, US$1 to receive. **Telephone** There is a public telephone outside the ATEC office.

Contents

Footprint features

Panama

At a glance

◉ **Getting around** Buses up to a point; flights at times; taxis best in Panama City and cheap for groups.

◉ **Time required** 2-3 weeks.

☼ **Weather** From Dec-Apr, the dry season, temperatures are in the high 20°Cs .

✖ **When not to go** The wettest months are Oct and Nov.

COSTA RICA

COLOMBIA

Caribbean Sea

Pacific Ocean

DARIÉN

PANAMA CITY

Puerto Obaldía

Boca de Cupe

Yaviza

Paya

Darién

Serranía del Darién

Serranía del Sapo

Serranía de Majé

Canazas

La Palma

Santa Fe

Golfo de San Miguel

Cordillera de San Blas

Lago Bayano

Chepo

Pacora

Golfo de Panamá

Pearl Islands

Kuna Yala

El Porvenir (San Blas Islands)

Nombre de Dios

Isla Grande

Portobelo

Colón

Cristóbal

Fuerte San Lorenzo

Lago Gatún

Isla Barro Colorado

Pueblo Nuevo Huesital

La Chorrera

Punta Chame

Isla Tabogo

San Carlos

Santa Clara

El Valle

Antón

Aguadulce

Golfo de Parita

Sarigna

Los Santos

Las Tablas

Pedasí

Cañas

Tonosí

Cambutal

Cerro Hoya

Azuero Peninsula

Macaracas

Chitré

La Atalaya

Nata

Penonomé

Santiago

Calobre

Santa Fe

Gatuncito

Omar Torrijos

Cordillera Central

Golfo de los Mosquitos

Guabalá

La Mesa

Soná

El Tigre de San Lorenzo

Isla de Coiba

Golfo de Chiriquí

Boca Chica

Isla Boca Brava

Golfo de Chiriquí National Marine Park

Las Lajas

Chiriquí Grande

Parque Nacional Marino Isla Bastimentos

Laguna de Chiriquí

Península de Valiente

Bocas del Toro

Isla Colón

Almirante

Changuinola

Guabito

La Amistad

Cordillera de Talamanca

Río Sereno

Cerro Punta

Volcán Barú

Volcán

Boquete

La Concepción

David

Pedregal

Puerto Armuelles

Punta Burica

Paso Canoas

50 km

50 miles

N

★ Don't miss...

1 Panamá Viejo, page 881.
2 The Canal, page 899.
3 San Blas islands, page 913.
4 Isla de Coiba, page 923.
5 Chiriquí, page 930.
6 Bocas del Toro, page 947.
7 Darién, page 960.

The isthmus of Panama owes much to its fortuitous geographic position. Over 900 species of bird, 10,000 species of plant and scores of rare animals make their home on this sinuous, snake-like land mass, a vital biological corridor between the Americas. At its most slender point, less than 80 km of land separates the Atlantic and Pacific oceans, making Panama an inevitable meeting point for global cultures. European, Afro-Caribbean, Chinese, North and South American influences are strongly evident, but it is the nation's indigenous peoples who supply the most colour and intrigue.

Today, Panama is a place of great dynamism and change, fast emerging as one of Latin America's most powerful nations. No single element has been more critical in driving the nation's development than the Panama Canal, a key component in the world trade system. Plans to expand the 'big ditch' are well underway and signal an evermore prominent role for this tiny nation. Panama's fate as the crossroads of the world is sealed. Fortunately, the mood is optimistic. Panameños are proud of their country and its accomplishments and some politicians are boasting, perhaps over-optimistically, that Panama will achieve First-World status in a single generation.

But all this development comes at a price and the integrity of Panama's fragile natural environment is in peril. Rainforests are being cleared for gated communities and foreign-owned housing projects; ancient tribal lands face obliteration from grandiose mining and hydroelectric schemes; and many of the country's most beautiful coastal habitats have already been wrecked by luxury hotels hoping to profit from tourism. But as the world awakens to Panama's intense natural beauty, there's increased pressure to protect it. National parks, nature reserves and conservation projects are springing up everywhere. Panama may just choose sustainability yet.

Essentials

For thousands of years, people and animals have used the Panamanian corridor as a channel of communication. At the time of conquest, the Spaniards used it as a crossing point between the Atlantic and Pacific Oceans and forays north and south along the coast. In part Panama owes its creation to this positioning (the outcome of a squabble between Colombia and the United States in 1903), and the make-up of its population and their distribution has been affected by this corridor ever since. Today, over 40% of Panamanians live in two cities – Panama City and Colón – which control access to the canal. International control continued until 31 December 1999, when the Canal Area, formerly the US Canal Zone, was returned to Panamanian jurisdiction.

Where to go

Panama City is a modern city, spread round the Bahía de Panamá. From the hilltop lookouts Parque Natural Metropolitano and Cerro Ancón, visitors enjoy spectacular views of the banks and high-rise buildings of the capital with the Canal in the distance. The rubble and ruins of Panamá Viejo lie to the east, the city's original location sacked by the pirate Henry Morgan. The younger replacement of Casco Viejo dates from 1673 and is slowly being restored to its former glory.

The city lies at the Pacific end of the **Panama Canal**, a feat of engineering that lifts ocean-going liners 26 m to Lago Gatún on the 67.5-km voyage between the Caribbean Sea and the Pacific Ocean. The financial cost of the canal was staggering; the price in human terms was over 22,000 lives. The Canal is surprisingly beautiful, consisting of the river-fed **Lago Gatún**, which is reached by a series of locks on the Pacific and Caribbean sides. Within the lake is **Reserva Biológica de la Isla Barro Colorado**, to which animals fled when the basin flooded. **Parque Nacional Soberanía**, which forms part of the watershed of Lake Gatún, is an easier trip, just 30 minutes from the capital.

At the Caribbean end of the Canal is **Colón**, the country's major port for container traffic, shipping and, for the dedicated shopper, the second largest tax-free zone in the world. To the east is **Portobelo**, the site of flamboyant 16th- and 17th-century markets, where warehouses filled with Peruvian gold and silver were guarded against pirate raids. Off the coast lies the marine burial site of the British buccaneering seaman Sir Francis Drake. Quiet, beautiful beaches await the visitor today. Further east, the 365-island **Archipiélago de San Blas** of crystalline waters and palms continues its autonomous existence under the guidance of the Kuna nation. The islands can be visited and hotels, lodges and simple cabinas are opening to cater for the growing tourist interest.

The Pan-American Highway runs almost parallel to the Pacific coastline from Panama City to Costa Rica, running through agricultural zones, Pacific beaches, colonial towns and mountain landscapes. The **Península de Azuero** is dotted with old colonial towns, beaches perfect for surfing, and nature reserves of wetland birds, nesting turtles and quiet solitude. Open pastures and savannahs give way to sugar plantations on approach to **David**, the hot and humid third city of the Republic. It is a place with good services and communications, and a gateway to the mountain resorts of **Boquete** and **Volcán**. Up in the cool **Chiriquí Highlands** dominated by **Volcán Barú**, there is good hiking, horse riding, river rafting and other adventure sports.

North of the **Talamanca Mountains**, banana plantations stretch across the northern Caribbean lowlands that surround **Laguna de Chiriquí**. The offshore islands of **Bocas del Toro** and the **Parque Nacional Marino Isla Bastimentos** are home to nesting turtles, birds and other wildlife. Once cut off and difficult to reach, the islands are growing in popularity. If lying around relaxing on idyllic beaches isn't appealing enough, the snorkelling and diving on the unspoilt reefs is excellent.

Darién in the east is the most inhospitable part of Panama where all roads, including the Pan-American Highway, eventually just peter out. The fit and adventurous are tempted to cross one of the world's last great wildernesses on foot, but sadly this has not been possible for many years due to safety concerns. Luckily, not all of the Darién is off limits and with careful planning it's possible to experience the region's immense tropical forests and intriguing indigenous communities, very much off the beaten track.

Suggested itinerary

Most people arrive in Panama overland from Costa Rica and head straight for **Bocas del Toro** – it's chilled, relaxed and there's a lot going on. From there it's a long haul to **Panama City**. You can break the journey, with a rather circuitous but rewarding detour stopping off at David for a trip into the mountains at Boquete for trekking, whitewater rafting and exploring. When you get to Panama City, the short trip to see or to travel the **Panama Canal** is essential. A trip out to the indigenous **Comarca Kuna Yala** and its blissful archipelago over 400 islands is a memorable end to any trip. A couple of weeks should cover the main areas.

When to go

The most popular time to visit is in the dry season from mid-December to mid-April. Temperatures vary little throughout the country ranging year-round temperatures from 30-32°C (85-90°F) in the day dropping to 21-22°C (70-72°F) at night. Above 500 m, temperatures fall, making the highland towns attractive spots to cool off.

Rainfall, however, varies greatly. The Caribbean side of the central Cordillera is soaked with around 4000 mm annually. On the Pacific slope, it is much lighter with an average of 1700 mm. Both areas have pronounced seasonal variations. Rainfall begins to taper off some time in December for the dry season. At this time rainfall on the Pacific side is scarce, or absent altogether, though on the Atlantic side you can expect a downpour 365 days a year. Even in the rainy season, however, the downpours, though heavy, usually last only an hour or two, and almost always come in mid-afternoon. The driest months in Bocas del Toro are February to April and August to October.

What to do

Panama's tourism potential for special interest travel is only now being truly appreciated. It is a paradise for fishermen and birdwatchers alike; there are fine beaches and beautiful islands along both Atlantic and Pacific coasts; several indigenous as well as colonist communities provide considerable cultural interest; ecotourists can find a variety of challenging activities in Panama's superb national parks, and there are few places as demanding – or rewarding – to seasoned travellers as the Darién (get local advice on levels of safety). Visitor facilities in Panama are well developed for those engaged in international commerce, off-shore banking and for bargain-hunting shoppers, and many other aspects of tourism are developing quickly.

Birdwatching
Birdlife is abundant and varied in Panama and the country is an important destination for many birdwatchers. The Darién jungle, both coastlines, the forest fringe along the Canal, and the Chiriquí (where quetzals, among many other species, may be seen) all provide their own special attractions for the birder. Those interested are referred to *A Guide to the Birds of Panama*, by R S Ridgely and J A Gwynne Jr (Princeton University Press, 1992.)

Community tourism
Panama is home to 8 indigenous groups – Naso, Bribri, Ngöbe, Buglé, Bokota, Emberá, Wounaan and Kuna – and many of them are now opening their doors to responsible tourism. From the Caribbean islands of Kuna Yala to the jungles of the Naso Kingdom and the highland villages of the Comarca Ngöbe-Buglé, a host of worthy community-run projects promise fascinating cultural encounters and the opportunity to explore some of the most unspoilt and visually arresting land in the country.

Diving
Diving is the best locally developed sport. The Caribbean coral reefs are similar to those of Belize and Honduras, extending southeast for 100 km along from the Costa Rica border and then from Colón 300 km to the border with Colombia. For information on these areas, see under Bocas del Toro, Portobelo and the San Blas islands.

The Pacific has quite different ecosystems owing to the much greater tidal ranges, differing water temperature and density. Places to go include Taboga, the Pearl Islands, Iguana Island and Parque Nacional Coiba. A third, and perhaps unique experience, is diving in the lakes of the Panama Canal, mainly to visit wrecks, submerged villages and the odd train left behind by the filling of the canal.

Scuba Panama has a good website, www.scubapanama.com.

Hiking
Volcán Barú, Panama's highest peak at 3475 m, and nearby Cerro Punta are the 2 best climbs in the country but there are several excellent long walks. The hike from Cañita on the Darién road over the continental divide to Cartí is an alternative to flying to San Blas. The Camino de Cruces and Camino Real are jungle walks that follow in the steps of the Conquistadors crossing the continental divide and, if combined into an ocean-to-ocean hike, take 8 days. A good range for hiking is the Serranía de Majé east of Panama City, visiting Embera villages and its howler monkey population. Closer is the Parque Nacional Chagres and a 3-day walk from Cerro Azul to the coast.

Nature tourism
Some 43% of Panama remains forested and a quarter of the land has protected status, which includes 14 national parks, wildlife refuges and forest reserves that are home to over 900 recorded bird species – including the endangered great green macaw and the harpy eagle, the national bird. Most national parks can be visited without hindrance if you can get there – there is supposed to be a US$3 entry fee but it is rarely charged. Transport can be very difficult and facilities non-existent; the largest, Darién National Park, is a good example. Slowly the value of the National Park system to tourism is being realized and some parks now have accommodation in huts for US$5 a bed.
Asociación Nacional de Conservación de la Naturaleza (ANCON), Amelia Denis de Icaza, Edif No 153, Cerro Ancón, Quarry Heights, Apdo 153, T314-0052, www.ancon.org.
ANAM, Edif 804, Albrook, Balboa, Ancón, near the domestic terminal at Albrook, T500-0855, www.anam.gob.pa.

Rafting, tubing and river running

Whitewater rafting is best in the Chiriquí river system near David – Grades III to IV on the Río Chiriquí (all year round) – and the Chiriquí Viejo Palón section (Dec-Apr) when the river is not in full speight. Also in the Parque Nacional Chagres area, north of Panama City, with Grades II and III, which some consider better for tubing – floating down river on an inflated inner tube (generally best Aug- Dec). There are a selection of operators in Boquete, see page 944.

Surfing

Surfing is best at Isla Grande, Playa Venado on the Azuero Peninsula, Santa Catalina on the Pacific coast of Veraguas and Bocas del Toro. In the capital, **Kenny Myers**, T6671-7777, www.panamasurftours.com, offers tours to the more out-of-the-way beaches. Also check out Playa Río Mar near San Carlos, just 1.5 km from Panama City, and **Río Mar Surf Camp**, T6516-5031, www.riomar surf.com. Options range from turn-up-and-surf to rooms, boards, classes and transport.

Getting there

Air

Tocumen International Airport is 27 km east of the city centre. Taxis (US$25) and buses run to Panama City. For a lower price, take a shared cab (compartido), and while you may wait a little longer, the price becomes US$10-15 for two or three people respectively. Ensure you have an onward ticket on arrival in Tocumen (bus or air should suffice, do not let Copa intimidate you). There is now a whopping airport departure tax of US$40, payable in cash only but often already included in the cost of a ticket. There is a US$4 tax on air tickets over US$100 purchased in Panama.

From Europe At the time of research, **British Airways** was rumoured to be planning direct flights from the UK to Panama; check for the latest. Meanwhile, **KLM** offers direct flights from Amsterdam, Netherlands, and **Iberia** provides direct services from Madrid, Spain. All other flights include a stop-over in the USA, but Tocumen's expansion plans mean that could change soon.

From the USA **Continental**, **Iberia**, **Copa** and **American Airlines** fly out of Miami, which is the main connection hub for flights to Panama, along with Newark and Houston. **Delta** exclusively serves Atlanta. No frills **Spirit Airlines** serves the widest range of US destinations at the cheapest prices.

From Central America
Copa, **Avianca** and **Grupo Taca** offer numerous connections with major cities in Mexico and Central America. **Nature Air** flies out of Costa Rica to various destinations, including Bocas del Toro.

From South America **Gol Transportes Aéreos** offers numerous flights out of Argentina and Brazil. Aires offers connections with Colombia. Other major airlines flying out of South America include **Lloyd Aéreo Bolivano**, **Copa** and **Avianca**.

From the Caribbean **Copa** has flights from Havana, Kingston, Port-au-Prince, San Juan and Santo Domingo.

Border essentials

Panama–Costa Rica
For border crossings between Panama and Costa Rica, see page 715.

Panama–Colombia
For information on sailing to Colombia via the San Blas islands, see page 914.

Road

Overland passage to Panama from Costa Rica on the Pacific side is at Paso Canoas, where crossing is straightforward, simple and fast. International buses make the journey from Costa Rica to David and on to Panama City stopping one to three hours for paperwork, depending on time of day and queues (see page 715). It is also possible to cross into Panama at Río Sereno in the Talamanca mountains, and at Sixaola/Guabito on the Caribbean coast. Passengers and vehicles (car or motorcycle) are given 90 days at the border.

Sea

The Panama Canal is on the itineraries of many shipping services from Europe and the USA that take passengers, but charges are high. Cruise ships frequently call into Panama and Colón, January-March.

It is not hard to find yachts or sailboats plying the Caribbean sea between Colombia and Panama. Most depart from Cartagena and drop passengers in Kuna Yala (San Blas islands) from where you'll need to arrange boat or plane connections to the mainland. The trip takes around three days, US$350-450, including food. To find a captain, enquire at Cartagena's yacht club, or look out for adverts posted in youth hostels. Always check the seaworthiness of the vessel (and trustworthiness of the crew) before agreeing passage. Find out how many other passengers will be joining you and avoid any boat that looks old or overcrowded.

Getting around

Air

Local flights cover most part of the country. There are two major airlines: **Aeroperlas** ⓘ T378-6000, www.aeroperlas.com, the **Grupo Taca** subsidiary; and **Air Panama** ⓘ T316-9000, www.flyairpanama.com, with a more modern fleet. Charters are possible but less common. Try **Mapiex** ⓘ T315-0344, www.mapiex.com.

On internal flights passengers must present their identity documents and have their luggage weighed. As excess baggage charges are frequent, ask if it is cheaper to ship excess as air freight (*carga*) on the same flight.

Road

The main highway crossing the isthmus runs from Colón to Panama City. Alternatively, a well-maintained scenic road traverses the isthmus from Gualaca in Chiriquí to the town of Chiriquí Grande in Bocas del Toro, crossing the Swedish-built Fortuna hydroelectric dam. The road continues to Almirante and the regional centre of Changuinola, opening up a beautiful route along the Caribbean. The Pan-American Highway, usually called the

Interamericana in Panama, runs east from Panama City to Chepo and into the province of Darién, and west to the Costa Rican border. It is paved throughout (as far east as Yaviza in the Darién) and is being improved. There is a modern toll road between Panama City and La Chorrera, and the section between David and La Concepción is a modern, four-lane highway. There are expressways in and around Panama City.

Bus The bus network covers the entire country, generally with efficient, timely services. Many of the long-distance buses are small minibuses, normally modern and comfortable, but large, modern air-conditioned buses cover the seve-hour trip between Panama City and David. Services are more expensive than elsewhere in Central America. Slower 'regular' buses run in some areas of the countryside. 'Express' buses with air conditioning operate between Panama City and Colón and to David and the border with Costa Rica.

Car Average **car hire** rates range from US$24 per day for a small saloon to US$70-100 for 4WD jeep, free mileage, insurance US$8 per day, 5% tax, US$500 deposit (can be paid by credit card), minimum age 23, home driver's licence acceptable. If you require a 4WD it is better to book a few days in advance. If planning to rent from an international company, consult them before leaving home. Sometimes deals are available that cannot be made in Panama. Rental cars are not allowed out of the country; these are marked by special licence plates.

Super grade gasoline (called *super*) costs about US$3.50 per US gallon (3.78 litres); unleaded is available in larger towns. Low octane (*regular* or *normal*) costs about US$3.30; diesel is about US$3.15. For motorcyclists, note that a crash helmet must be worn.

Taking a car with Panamanian plates to Costa Rica requires a permit from the Traffic Police (*Tránsito*) obtainable on presentation of the ownership certificate and a document from the Judicial Police (*PTJ*) indicating that the vehicle has not been reported stolen. A travel agency, for example **Chadwick's** in Balboa, will arrange this for you for US$30.

Sea
Boats and comfortable yachts provide tours all or part way through the canal. Contact tour operators in Panama City or Colón for details. It is also possible to travel through offering linehandling services, if you have sailing experience and turn up at the right time.

Shipping a vehicle Taking a vehicle out of Panama to Colombia, Venezuela or Ecuador is not easy or cheap. The best advice is to shop around the agencies in Panama City or Colón to see what is available when you want to go. Both local and international lines take vehicles, and sometimes passengers, but schedules and prices are very variable.

To Panama: The recommended agency is **Panalpina** ① *Los Andes 2, Ojo de Agua, Vía Transmística, Panama City, T273-7066, www.panalpina.com*. Jürgen Lahntaler speaks German, English and Spanish. Panalpina can also arrange shipment of vehicles to Ecuador, Venezuela and Chile.

To Colombia: Agents include **CSAV** ① *PO Box: 0832-2775, Edificio Frontenac, Local 2-B, Calle 50 y esq 54 Este, Panama City, T269-1613, www.csav.com*, who also sail to other countries in South America on both the Atlantic and Pacific side.

To **Barranquilla**, **Vicente Simones' Colón** ⓘ *T195-1262, beeper 270-0000, code 700283*, will arrange all paperwork for US$25: car passage US$800, motorcycle US$50, plus US$50 per passenger, no accommodation on ship other than hammock space, take food and drink for a week (even though voyage should be three days).

To **Cartagena**, **Captain Newball** ⓘ *Edificio Los Cristales, Piso 3, Calle 38 y Av Cuba, Panama City*. On the same route, **Central American Lines** ⓘ *agent in Panama, Colón T441-2880, Panama City T236-1036*, sail once a week. Also **Géminis Shipping Co SA** ⓘ *Apdo Postal No 3016, Zona Libre de Colón, República de Panamá, T441-6269, F441-6571*. Mr Ricardo Gil is helpful and reliable. Another agent, **Barwil** ⓘ *Galerías Balboa Suite 35, Av Balboa, Panama City, T263-7755, www.barwil-panama.com*, arranges shipments to Colombia (Cartagena) and elsewhere in Latin America from Balboa or Cristóbal.

Customs formalities at the Colombian end will take up to three days to clear (customs officials do not work at weekends). Cartagena is the best port because it is privately run, more secure and more efficient. Go first to customs: **DIAN** ⓘ *Manga CL27 A 24-83, Diagonal DIAN, Jefe División de Servicio al Comercio Exterior*. Here you will receive, for free, the necessary documents to enter the port (this takes about 24 hours).

To Ecuador: Weekly (sometimes more often) sailings with combined services of **Maersk Line** ⓘ *Blv Costa del Este, Complejo Business Park, Edificio Norte, piso 5, Panama City, T206-2200, www.maerskline.com*, visit the website to find your nearest office. **Hapaglloyd** agents are **AGENCO** ⓘ *Edif Eurocentro, PB, Av Abel Bravo, Urbanización Obarrio, Panama City, T300-1400, www.hapag-lloyd.com*, about US$900 for a 6-m container. Shipping to Guayaquil from Panama's container port of Manzanillo, next to Colón, is the best choice, preferable to Colombia or Venezuela. **TNE (Transportes Navieros Ecuatorianos)** ⓘ *T269-2022*, ship vehicles to Guayaquil; agent in Cristóbal, Agencia Continental SA, T445-1818. Another agent recommended in Cristóbal is **Associated Steamships** ⓘ *Balboa, T211-9400, www.shipsagent.com*. Customs agents cost US$60 in Colón, US$120 in Guayaquil; 12 days from starting arrangements in Panama to leaving Guayaquil docks. Seek advice on paperwork from the Ecuadorean consul in Panama. **Barwil** (see above for Colombia) will ship vehicles to Arica, Chile.

To Venezuela: In addition to those mentioned above, agents include: **Cia Transatlántica España** ⓘ *T269-6300*, to La Guaira. **Vencaribe** (a Venezuelan line), agent in Cristóbal: **Associated Steamship** (Wilford and McKay, see above), T252-1258 (Panama), T445-0461 (Cristóbal). There are several agencies in Colón/Cristóbal. Formalities before leaving can be completed through a travel agency – recommended is **Continental Travel Agency** ⓘ *at the Hotel Continental, T263-6162*. In Venezuela there are customs complications (without carnet) and this route is not really recommended.

Maps

Topographic maps and aerial photos are sold by the **Instituto Geográfico Nacional Tommy Guardia (IGNTG)** ⓘ *Vía Simón Bolívar, opposite the National University (footbridge nearby, fortunately), T236-2444, www.ignpanama.gob.pa, take Transístmica or Tumba Muerto bus, Mon-Fri 0800-1530*. Maps from 1:500,000 to 1:50,000 available. **ITM** (www.itmb.com) have a 1:800,000 travel map of Panama.

Sleeping

The very best in five-star luxury is available in Panama City and several comfortable lodges are found in the larger towns and mountain and jungle hideaways. If travelling further afield, accommodation in the **D** category and below is available in most towns of interest. Camping is generally tolerated.

Eating

In Panama City the range of food available is very broad with a profusion of restaurants and well-stocked supermarkets. In the interior tastes are simpler and available ingredients less varied. Most food is boiled or fried in vegetable oil (usually soybean oil). Virtually every restaurant will have a *comida corriente* (meal of the day), which will include a serving of meat, chicken or fish, white rice and a salad, a dish of boiled beans garnished with a *tajada* (slice) of fried ripe plantain. It will cost about US$2 in towns, perhaps more in the city, less in villages. A bowl of *sopa de carne* (beef broth with vegetables) or *sopa de pescado* (fish chowder) is usually available as a first course for US$0.50. Breakfast normally consists of eggs, a small beefsteak or a slice of liver fried with onions and tomatoes, bread and butter and some combination of *frituras*.

The staple of Panamanian food is white rice, grown not in paddies but on dry land, and usually served at every meal, often with the addition of chicken, shrimp, vegetables, etc. Meat is usually fried (*frita*) or braised (*guisada*), rarely grilled except in the better restaurants. Beef is common; pork, chicken and the excellent fish are usually a better choice.

The national dish is *sancocho de gallina*, a stew of chicken, yuca, *ñame* (dasheen), plantain, cut-up pieces of corn on the cob, potatoes and onions and strongly flavoured with *culantro*, an aromatic leaf similar in flavour to coriander (*cilantro*). *Ropa vieja* ('old clothes') is beef boiled or steamed until it can be shredded, then sautéed with onions, garlic, tomatoes and green or red peppers, often served with yellow rice (coloured with *achiote*). Piquant *ceviche*, eaten as a first course or a snack with cold beer, is usually raw corvina or shellfish seasoned with tiny red and yellow peppers, thin slices of onion and marinated in lime juice; it is served very cold with crackers (beware of the bite). A speciality of the Caribbean coast is *sao*, pigs' feet pickled with lime and hot peppers. Also try *arroz con coco*, coconut rice, or the same with *tití*, tiny shrimp; also *fufú*, a fish chowder with coconut milk. *Mondongo* is the stewed tripe dish called *menudo* in Mexico; the Panamanian version is less spicy, but very well seasoned.

Most *panaderías* sell good pastries: in Panama City most of the European standards are available; in the country, try *orejas*, *costillas* or *ma'mellena* ('fills me up more', a sweet bread-pudding with raisins); *dulces* (of coconut, pineapple, etc), are cakes or pastries, not sweets/candies as elsewhere (the latter are *confites*). Among the items sold at the roadside you may see bottles stopped with a corncob, filled with *nance*, a strong-flavoured, yellow-green fruit packed with water and allowed to ripen and ferment slightly; *pifá/pixbae*, a bright orange fruit which, when boiled, tastes much like sweet potato (two or three will see you though to your next meal); *níspero*, the tasty, acidic yellow fruit of the chicle tree.

There are dozens of sweetened fruit drinks found everywhere in the country, making excellent use of the many delicious tropical and temperate fruits grown here: *naranja* (orange), *maracuyá* (passion fruit), *guayaba*, *zarzamora* (blackberry), *guanábana*, etc. The generic term is *chicha dulce*, which also includes drinks made with rice or corn. Most common carbonated canned drinks are available. Panamanian beer tends to be low in alcohol, *Panamá* and *Soberana* are the most popular locally. *Chicha fuerte* is the alcoholic form of corn or rice drink fermented with sugar, brewed mostly in the countryside. Sample with care. The local rum, for example *Carta Vieja*, is not bad. *Seco*, a harsh brand of 'white lightning' made from the juice of sugar cane, brand name *Herrerano*, deserves respect.

Festivals and events

1 Jan New Year's Day.	**3 Nov** Independence Day.
9 Jan Martyrs' Day.	**4 Nov** Flag Day.
Feb/Mar Shrove Tuesday Carnival.	**5 Nov** Independence Day
Mar/Apr Good Friday.	(Colón only).
1 May Labour Day (Republic).	**10 Nov** First Call of Independence.
15 Aug Panama City only.	**28 Nov** Independence from Spain.
1 Nov National Anthem Day.	**8 Dec** Mothers' Day.
2 Nov All Souls' Day.	**25 Dec** Christmas Day.

The school holidays are December to March, and during these times the popular tourists spots are busy so make reservations in advance.

The fiestas in the towns are well worth seeing. Panama City at **Carnival** time, held on the four days before Shrove Tuesday, is the best. During carnival, women who can afford it wear the voluminous *pollera* dress, a shawl folded across the shoulders, velvet slippers, tinkling pearl and polished fish-scale hair ornaments (called *tembleques* from their quivering motion) in spirited shapes and colours. The men wear a *montuno* outfit: round straw hats, embroidered blouses and trousers sometimes to below the knee only, and carry the *chácara*, or small purse.

At the **Holy Week** ceremonies at Villa de Los Santos the farces and acrobatics of the big devils – with their debates and trials in which the main devil accuses and an angel defends the soul – the dance of the 'dirty little devils' and the dancing drama of the Montezumas are all notable. The ceremonies at **Pesé** (near Chitré) are famous all over Panama. At **Portobelo**, near Colón, there is a procession of little boats in the canals of the city. **Bullfights**, where the bull survives, are an important part of rural fairs, as are rodeo events.

The indigenous Ngöbe-Bugle (Guaymí) of Chiriquí province meet around 12 February to transact tribal business, hold feasts and compete for brides by tossing balsa logs at one another; those unhurt in this contest, known as *Las Balserías*, are viewed as heroes.

Shopping

More traditional Panamanian crafts include the colourful *molas* embroidered by the Kuna people of the San Blas islands. Masks, costumes, ceramics and woven hats can be found in several small villages dotted around the Azuero Peninsula. These are on sale in many places. Straw, leather and ceramic items are also available, as are carvings of wildlife made from wood, nuts and other natural materials. And of course, don't forget the quintessential **Panama hat**. Good ones are expensive. Duty-free imported goods including stereos, photographic equipment, perfume and clothes are cheap in the Colón Free Zone on the Caribbean coast. Most items are cheaper than at point of origin.

Customs and duty free

Panamanian Customs are strict; drugs without a doctor's prescription may be confiscated. Cameras, binoculars, etc, 500 cigarettes or 500 g of tobacco and 3 bottles of alcoholic drinks for personal use can be taken in free of duty. However, passengers leaving Panama by land are not entitled to any duty-free goods.

Electricity

110 volts AC, 60 cycles, US-style plugs. 220 volts is occasionally available in homes and hotels.

Embassies and consulates

Embassies/consulates can be checked at www.mire.gob.pa.
Australia, 1/234 Slade Rd, Bexley North, Sydney NSW 2207, T9150-8409.
Austria, Elisabethstr 4/5/4/10, A-1010 Vienna, T587-2347.
Belgium, Blvd Général Jacques 18, 1050 Brussels, T649-0729.
Canada, 130 Albert St, Suite 300 Ottawa, ON, Kip 564, T236-7177.
Costa Rica, Barrio La Granja, San Pedro, de la bomba de gasolina Higuerón, 200 m sur y 25 m al este, San José, T2281-2103.
France, 145 Av de Suffren, 75015 Paris, T4566-4244.
Germany, Wichmannstrasse 6, D-10787 Berlin, T302-260-5811.
Israel, 10 Hei Be'lyar, 3rd floor Apt 3, Kikar Hamedina, Tel Aviv 62093, T695-6711.
Italy, Piazza del Viminale No 5 – Piano 5 – Interno 16, 00184 Rome, T4425-2173.
New Zealand, Level 7, 300 Queen St, Auckland 1010, T379-8550.
Nicaragua, del Cuartel de Bomberos 1 c abajo, casa 93, Managua, T2266-8633.
South Africa, 229 Oliver St, Brooklyn, Pretoria, 0181, T460-6677.
Spain, Claudio Coello 86, 1° 28006, Madrid T576-5001.

Sweden, Ostermalmsgatan 59, 114 50, 102 04 Stockholm, T662-6535.
UK, 40 Hertford St, London, W1Y 7TG, T020-7409-2255.
USA, 2862 McGill Terrace NW, Washington DC 20008, T202-483-1407, www.embassyofpanama.org.

Health

Water in Panama City, David, Boquete, Colón and most major towns and cities is safe to drink. Drink bottled water in Bocas del Toro where the expanding water system is not as clean as desired. In smaller towns, it is best to drink bottled or boiled water to avoid minor problems. **Yellow fever** vaccination is recommended before visiting Darién. Travellers to Darién Province and Kuna Yala (including the San Blas islands) should treat these as **malarial areas** in which there is resistance to chloroquine. Treatment is expensive; insurance underwritten by a US company would be helpful.
See page 38 for further information.

Internet

Internet access is available throughout the country. Charges average out at about US$1-2 per hr.

Language

Spanish is the national language, but English is widely understood. The older generation of West Indian immigrants speak Wari-Wari, a dialect of English incomprehensible to most other English speakers. In rural areas, indigenous people use their own languages and many are bilingual.

Media

La Prensa, www.prensa.com, is the major local daily newspaper. Others are *La Estrella de Panamá*, *El Universal de Panamá*, *El Panamá América*, www.epasa.com, and 2 tabloids, *Crítica Libre*, www.critica.com.pa, and *El Siglo*. *Colón News* is a weekly

publication in Spanish and English.
In English is the bi-weekly *Panama News*, www.thepanamanews.com.

The international edition of the *Miami Herald* is printed in Panama; many other US newspapers are widely available in the capital.

Money → *US$1=1 balboa (June 2011).*
The unit of currency in Panama is the balboa, but Panama issues no paper money; US banknotes are used exclusively, and US notes and coins are legal tender. There are 'silver' coins of 50c (called a *peso*), 25c (called *cinco reales* or *cuara*, from US 'quarter'), 10c, nickel of 5c (called a *real*) and copper of 1c. All coins are used interchangeably with US equivalents, which are the same in size and composition. There is great reluctance in Panama to accept US$50 and US$100 notes because of counterfeiting. Do not be offended if asked to produce ID and sign a register when spending them. You can take in or out any amount of currency. If travelling north, remember that US dollar notes, especially smaller denominations, are useful in all Central American countries and may be difficult to obtain in other republics. Stocking up on a supply of US$5 and US$1 notes greatly facilitates border crossings and traffic problems in Central America where 'fees' and 'instant fines' can become exorbitant if you only have a US$20 note.

ATMs and credit cards
ATMs are widespread in Panama and can be found in all but the most remote locales. Visa ATMs are available at branches of **Telered**, call T001-800-111-0016, if card is lost or stolen. MasterCard/Cirrus ATMs are available at **Caja de Ahorros** offices and others in the Pronto system. **MasterCard** emergency number is T001-800-307-7309; **Western Union** is T269-1055. See Panama City Directory, page 896.

Cost of living and travelling
Prices are somewhat higher than in the rest of Central America, although food costs much the same as in Costa Rica. The annual average increase in consumer prices fluctuates in line with US trends. A tight budget would be US$20-25 per day; more comfortable and realistic is US$35-50.

Opening hours
Banks Open at different times, but are usually open all morning, and often on Sat.
Government departments Mon-Fri 0800-1200, 1230-1630.
Shops Mon-Sat 0700/0800-1200, 1400-1800/1900.

Post
When sending mail, great care should be taken to address all mail as 'Panama' or 'RP' (Republic of Panama). Airmail takes up to 10 days, sea mail 3-5 weeks from Europe. Example rates for airmail (up to 15 g) are as follows: Central, North and South America and Caribbean, 35c; Europe, 45c up to 10 g, 5c for every extra 5 g; Africa, Asia, Oceania, 60c. Parcels to Europe can only be sent from the post office in the El Dorado shopping centre in Panama City (bus from Calle 12 to Tumba Muerto). Post offices, marked with blue and yellow signs, are the only places permitted to sell stamps.

Tax
US$5 arrival tax in addition to the airport departure tax of US$40, payable by all passengers (cash only). US$4 tax on air tickets over US$100 purchased in Panama. There is a 10% tax on all hotel prices.

Telephone → *Country code T+507.*
The **international direct dialling** code (to call out of Panama) is T00; **Telecarrier** T088+00; **Clarocom** T055+00. Dial T102 for the local operator and T106 for an international operator. Collect calls are permitted, 3 mins minimum, rates are higher than direct, especially to USA. **Cable & Wireless** now run the telephone system and have offices in most towns. Cost of direct dialled calls, per min, are US$1-3.20. Calls are roughly 20-30% cheaper for most,

but not all destinations from 1700-2200. Lowest rates apply Sun all day. Many cheap international call centres in Panama City, check the the internet cafés on Vía Veneto, off Vía España for best offers.

Public payphones take 5, 10 and sometimes 25 cent coins. Phone cards are available in denominations of US$3, 5, 10, 20 and 50, for local, national and international calls. There are prepaid *Aló Panamá* cards – dial 165 for connection in US$10, US$20, US$30 and US$50 denominations, but they are 50% more expensive than payphone cards. For **AT&T** dial T109. For **SPRINT** (collect calls only) T115 and for **MCI** T108. **BT Chargecard** calls to the UK can be made through the local operator.

Time
-5 hrs GMT.

Tipping
In mid-range restaurants, tip 10% of the bill, often already included. Porters expect US$1 for assistance at the airport. Taxi drivers don't expect tips. Leave small change in local cafés and cheap restaurants.

Tourist information
Instituto Panameño de Turismo (IPAT) toll-free T011-800-SIPANAMA from the US or Canada, www.visitpanama.com, or contact your nearest embassy. Once in country, IPAT have an office in Panama City (see page 872).

Useful websites
www.businesspanama.com Economic, political and business information.
www.panamainfo.com An excellent site in English with good general information on Panama and links to several other national sites including newspapers, government organizations and tourist services.
www.panamatours.com A pure tourism site with a good overview of the country.
www.stri.org The Smithsonian Tropical Research Institute, whose headquarters are in Panama.

Visas and immigration
Visitors must have a passport valid or a minimum of 6 months, and in most cases a tourist card or a visa. Tourist cards are available at borders, from Panamanian consulates, **Ticabus** or airlines. To enter Panama officially you must have an onward flight or bus ticket, travel agent confirmation of the same, and must be able to demonstrate that you have sufficient funds (US$500 in cash, credit card or valid traveller's cheques) to cover your stay and departure; generally officers will not check your funds unless they fear you may be destitute.

Citizens of most European (including the United Kingdom) and Central American countries do not need a tourist card or a visa. Citizens of the United States, Canada, most Caribbean, South American and some Asian countries need a tourist card (US$5). Citizens of Egypt, Peru, Dominican Republic, many African, Eastern European and Asian countries require a visa – check with Panama's Migración office, www.migracion. gob.pa, for more information.

At the time of press, there was some confusion and inconsistency concerning the number of days you will be granted on entry. Presidential decree states visitors with without tourist cards are entitled to a maximum stay of 180 days, no renewals (visas 90 days). However, the actual law postulates a 90-day maximum, renewable by up to a further 90 days at a migration office (check on-line for requirements, www.migracion.gob.pa). In practice, many border officials are falling in line with Presidential decree and granting visitors 180 days, but if you plan on staying longer than 3 months in Panama, you'd be wise to double-check. If your stamp/tourist card fully expires you can renew it by leaving the country for 72 hrs and re-entering.

Weights and measures
Metric and imperial systems are both used.

Panama City

→ *Colour map 5, B1.*

Panama City is a curious blend of old Spain, US-style mall developments and the bazaar atmosphere of the east. Hardly surprising then that it has a polyglot population unrivalled in any other Latin American city. Beyond the new developments and skyscrapers that mushroomed along the southern end of the Canal, the palm-shaded beaches, islands in the bay and encircling hills still constitute a large part of Panama City's charm. And its cabarets and nightlife are an added attraction for any self-respecting hedonist. ▸▸ *For listings, see pages 885-898.*

Ins and outs

Getting there **Tocumen International Airport** is 27 km from the city centre. For flights, see page 863. Set-price taxis (US$25), cheaper if shared (*compartido*) and buses are available for getting into Panama City. The bus journey should take one hour but can take up to three in rush hour. Car rental companies also have offices at the airport. The city is well served by international buses from countries throughout Central America, with offices in the centre of town. ▸▸ *See Transport, page 894.*

Getting around The old part of the city, Casco Viejo, can easily be toured on foot. There are old, usually crowded and very cheap buses for getting to other districts, although these are slowly being replaced by modern Metrobuses. An underground Metro system is also in the works. The taxis charge on a zone system and can be shared if you wish to economize; overcharging is common. Many *avenidas* have both names and numbers, although locals are most likely to use the names, so asking for directions can be a bit complicated. Also, few buildings display their numbers, so try to find out the nearest cross street.

The wider metropolitan area has a population of approximately 720,000. Adjacent to the city, but constituting a separate administrative district, is the town of San Miguelito, a residential area for over 330,000 people. Once a squatter community, every available square inch of hillside has been built on and it is increasingly considered to be a part of greater Panama City.

Tourist offices **Instituto Panameño de Turismo (IPAT)** ⓘ *Av Samuel Lewis y Calle Gerardo Ortega, Edif Central, T526-7000, www.ipat.gob.pa,* have good lists of lodgings and other services. There are other **IPAT kiosks** ⓘ *Tocumen Airport in Panamá Viejo, Tue-Sun 0800-2200; on the pedestrian mall on Av Central, Mon-Fri 0900-1700; and opposite Hotel Continental on España,* and in all regions of the country.

Safety Tourist police are present in the downtown areas, but few speak English. Panamanians are generally very friendly and helpful, however, certain areas of the capital can be dangerous after dark. Attacks have been reported in Casco Viejo (although this area is now well patrolled by police during the daytime) and Panamá Viejo. Marañón, San Miguelito (on the way in from Tocumen Airport) and Calidonia can all be dangerous; never walk there at night and take care in daylight, too. Poor districts like Chorillo, Curundú and Hollywood are best avoided altogether. Probably the safest district for budget travellers to stay is Bella Vista, although it can be deserted after dark. Taxis are the safest way to travel around the city and drivers will give you good advice on where not to go.

Background

Modern Panama City was founded on its present site in 1673. The capital was moved from Old Panama (Panamá Viejo), 6.5 km to the east, after Henry Morgan looted the South American treasure chest depot of Golden Panama in 1671. Today, it is a thoroughly modern city complete with congested streets and noisy traffic. Uncollected trash mouldering in the tropical heat and the liberal use of razor-wire are other eyesores but, despite its blemishes, the city does possess considerable charm. The old quarter, called Casco Viejo or San Felipe, massively fortified by Spain as the era of widespread piracy was coming to an end, lies at the tip of the peninsula at the eastern end of the Bay of Panama.

Sights

Perched on the Pacific Ocean, Panama City's shifting barrios supply intriguing insights into the nation's historical development. In Casco Viejo and Santa Ana, you'll find scores of colonial mansions, beautified plazas and canal-era monuments. Nearby, the district of Calidonia is replete with commerce, traffic and proud civic structures dating to the early Republic. Further north, in the district of Bella Vista – an area comprised of numerous neighbourhoods including Obarrio and El Cangrejo – there's a slew of bold new skyscrapers reaching unrestrained into the 21st century.

Casco Viejo

Casco Viejo (the 'Old Compound' or San Felipe), which occupies the narrow peninsula east of Calle 11, is an unusual combination of beautifully restored public buildings, churches, plazas, monuments and museums alongside inner-city decay which, after decades of neglect, is now gradually being gentrified. Several budget hotels are found here, some very badly run-down but not without their faded glory. Created in 1673 after the sacking of Panamá Viejo, Casco Viejo is a treasure trove of architectural delights, some restored, others in a desperate state of repair, but most demanding a gentle meander through the shady streets. In 1992 local authorities began reviving some of the area's past glory by painting the post-colonial houses in soft pastels and their decorations and beautiful wrought-iron railings in relief. New shops and restaurants are moving into restored buildings in an attempt to make Casco Viejo a tourist attraction.

At the walled tip of the peninsula is the picturesque **Plaza de Francia**, with its bright red poinciana trees and obelisk topped by a cockerel (symbol of the Gallic nation), which has a document with 5000 signatures buried beneath it. Twelve large narrative plaques and many statues recall the French Canal's construction history and personalities; the work of Cuban doctor Carlos Finlay in establishing the cause of yellow fever is commemorated on one tablet. Facing the plaza is the French Embassy, housed in a pleasant early 20th-century building; it stubbornly refused to relocate during the years when the neighbourhood declined and is now one of the main focus points in the area's renaissance. Built flush under the old seawalls around the plaza are **Las Bóvedas** (The Vaults), the thick-walled colonial dungeons where prisoners in tiny barred cells were immersed up to their necks during high tides. Nine 'vaults' were restored by the Instituto Panameño de Turismo (IPAT) in 1982 and converted into a so-so art gallery – **Galería Las Bóvedas** ① *Tue-Sun 1100-1900. The French restaurant Las Bóvedas occupies another 2 'vaults' next to the former Palacio de Justicia, partly burned during 'Operation Just Cause' and now housing the Instituto Nacional de Cultura (INC), with an interesting mural by Esteban Palomino on the ground floor.*

Steps lead up from the Plaza de Francia to the **Paseo de las Bóvedas** promenade along the top of the defensive walls surrounding the peninsula on three sides. This is a popular place for an evening stroll; it is ablaze with bougainvillea and affords good views of the Bahía de Panamá, the Serranía de Majé on the Panama/Darién provincial border (on a clear day), Calzada Amador (known during the Canal Zone era as the Causeway) and the islands beyond.

Two blocks northwest of the Plaza (Avenida A and Calle 3) are the restored ruins of the impressive **Church and Convent of Santo Domingo** (1673, later destroyed by fires in

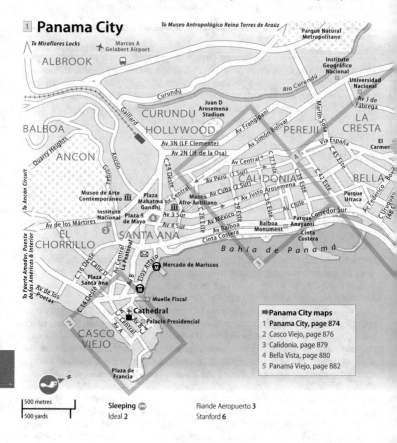

1 Panama City

To Museo Antropológico Reina Torres de Arauz
Parque Natural Metropolitano

To Miraflores Locks
Marcos A Gelabert Airport

ALBROOK

Instituto Geográfico Nacional

Río Curundú

Universidad Nacional

Curundú

Av J de Fábrega

CURUNDU

Juan D Arosemena Stadium

Gaillard

HOLLYWOOD

Av Frangipani

Av Simón Bolívar

Martín Sosa

LA CRESTA

BALBOA

Av 3N (LF Clemente)

PEREJIL

Via España

El Carmer

Quarry Heights

Av 2N (JF de la Osa)

Gorgas

ANCON

Av Central

BELLA

Av Perú (1 Sur)

CALIDONIA

Museo de Arte Contemporáneo

Av Cuba (2 Sur)

Av Justo Arosemena

Plaza Mahatma Gandhi

Museo Afro-Antillano

Parque Uraca

Instituto Nacional

Av 3 Sur

Av Chile

Plaza 5 de Mayo

Av 4 Sur

Av México

Parque Corredor Sur

EL CHORRILLO

Av de los Mártires

SANTA ANA

Av Balboa

Balboa Monument

Parque Anayansi

Cinta Costera

La Peatonal

Av Central

Cinta Costera

Bahía de Panamá

To Fuerte Amador, Puente de las Américas & Interior

Plaza Santa Ana

Eloy Alfaro

Mercado de Mariscos

Av de los Poetas

Muelle Fiscal

Cathedral

➡ Panama City maps
1 Panama City, page 874
2 Casco Viejo, page 876
3 Calidonia, page 879
4 Bella Vista, page 880
5 Panamá Viejo, page 882

CASCO VIEJO

Palacio Presidencial

Plaza de Francia

500 metres
500 yards

Sleeping 😴
Ideal 2

Riande Aeropuerto 3
Stanford 6

1737 and 1756), both with paired columns and brick inlaying on their façades. The famous 15-m-long flat arch, **Arco Chato**, which formed the base of the choir, was built entirely of bricks and mortar with no internal support. When the great debate as to where the Canal should be built was going on in the United States Congress, a Nicaraguan postage stamp showing a volcano, with all its implications of earthquakes, and the stability of this arch – a supposed proof of no earthquakes – are said to have played a large part in determining the choice in Panama's favour. In 2003, it finally collapsed and today's arch is a reconstruction. A chapel on the site has been converted into the interesting

Museo de Arte Colonial Religioso ① *Tue-Sat 0830-1630, admission US$0.75, students and seniors US$0.25, T228-2897,* whose treasures include a precious Golden Altar, a delicate snail staircase, silver relics and wooden sculptures from Lima and Mexico, 19th-century engravings of the city, and the skeleton of a woman found during excavation of the church.

Not far from Santo Domingo, across Avenida Central, the neoclassical **Teatro Nacional** ① *T262-3525, Mon-Fri 0800-1600, US$0.50,* with 850-seat capacity, opened in 1908 with Verdi's *Aida* being performed in what was then considered the state of the art in acoustics. French-influenced sculptures and friezes enliven the façade, while Roberto Lewis' paintings depicting the birth of the nation adorn the theatre's dome. The ballerina Dame Margot Fonteyn, who married a member of the prominent Arias family and was a long-time resident of Panama until her death in 1991, danced at the theatre's re-inauguration in 1974.

Diagonally opposite the Teatro Nacional (Avenida B and Calle 3) is the peaceful **Plaza Bolívar**, with a statue of the liberator Simón Bolívar, draped in robes, standing below a large condor surrounded by plaques of his deeds. Around the square are the former **Hotel Colombia**, the **Church of San Felipe Neri**, and many 19th-century houses still displaying roofs of red-clay tiles bearing the stamp 'Marseilles 1880'. On the east side stand **San Francisco Church** ① *Mon-Sat 1430-1800, Sun all day,* colonial but 'modified' in 1917 and modernized in 1983, and the **San Francisco Convent** (1678), the largest of all the religious buildings, which was restored by Peruvian architect Leonardo Villanueva. The Bolivarian Congress of June 1826, at which Bolívar proposed a United States of South America, was also held in the Chapter Room of the Convent, now known as the **Salón Bolívar**, and the 1904 Constitution was also drafted here. This northern wing was dedicated as the **Instituto Bolívar** in 1956; its wood panelling, embossed leather benches and paintings (restored in part by the government of Ecuador) may be viewed with an authorized guide from the Bolivarian Society (T262-2947). The adjacent Colegio Bolívar, built on a pier over the water, is due to become the new Cancillería (Ministry of Foreign Affairs).

Another long block west of Plaza Bolívar, and one block north on the seafront (Avenida Eloy Alfaro) between Calles 5 and 6, is the **Palacio Presidencial**, the most impressive building in the city, built as an opulent residence in 1673 for successive colonial auditors and governors. It was enlarged and restored under President Belisario Porras in 1922. Note the road to the palace has a security checkpoint; bring your passport if you wish to pass for a closer look.

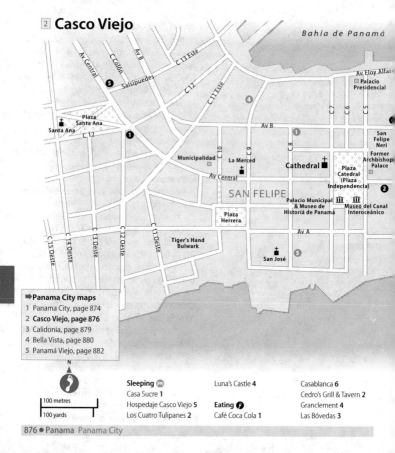

2 Casco Viejo

Bahía de Panamá

➡ Panama City maps
1 Panama City, page 874
2 Casco Viejo, page 876
3 Calidonia, page 879
4 Bella Vista, page 880
5 Panamá Viejo, page 882

100 metres
100 yards

Sleeping
Casa Sucre 1
Hospedaje Casco Viejo 5
Los Cuatro Tulipanes 2
Luna's Castle 4

Eating
Café Coca Cola 1

Casablanca 6
Cedro's Grill & Tavern 2
Granclement 4
Las Bóvedas 3

Two blocks south of the Palacio Presidencial is the heart of the old town, the **Plaza Catedral** or **Independencia**, with busts of the Republic's founders, and surrounding public buildings. On the west is the **cathedral** (1688-1794, refurbished in 1999), with its twin towers, domes, classical façade encrusted with mother-of-pearl and three of the tower bells brought from the Old Panama Cathedral. To the right of the main altar is a subterranean passage that leads to other *conventos* and the sea. On the southwest corner with Calle 7 is the neoclassical **Palacio Municipal** (City Hall), on the first floor of which is the **Museo de Historia de Panamá** ① *Mon-Fri 0800-1600, US$1*, which covers the nation's history since European landfall, and includes highlights of the treaty between Panama and the USA which led to the construction of the Canal. The former post office next door, originally built in 1875 as the **Grand Hotel** ("the largest edifice of that kind between San Francisco and Cape Horn" according to a contemporary newspaper), is the city's best example of French architecture. It became de Lesseps' headquarters during Canal excavations in the 1880s and was sold back to Panama in 1912. It has been entirely gutted and converted into the **Museo del Canal Interoceánico** ① *Plaza Catedral, T/F211-1650, Tue-Sun 0900-1700, US$2, concessions US$0.75, www.museodelcanal. com, photography not allowed, English- and French-speaking guides are available, other languages available if booked in advance, hand-held English audio commentaries cost US$5.* It has interesting displays relating to the history and construction of the canal, including a detailed section on life in the US-controlled canal zone. Note nearly all the signs are in Spanish. Recommended.

The east side of the Plaza is dominated by the former **Archbishop's Palace.** Later occupied by a university, this was a shelter for runaway kids and then spent a period as the **Central Hotel** (1884), once the most luxurious in Central America. The interior featured a palm garden, restaurants, barber shop, 100 rooms with private baths and a wooden staircase imported from New York, and it was the centre of Panama's social life for decades. After falling into complete disrepair, it is now being restored.

There are a number of other interesting religious structures within two or three blocks of the cathedral, but the most-visited is the **Church of San José** ① *Av A and Calle 8, 1 block west and 2 south of the Plaza Catedral, T228-0190,* with its famous Altar de Oro, a massive baroque altar carved from mahogany and, according to common belief, veneered with gold. This was one of the few treasures saved from Henry Morgan's attack on Old

Monolo Caracol **8**
Mostaza **7**
Panadería Azukitar **5**
Tequila **9**

Panama in 1671 and legend records different versions of how it was concealed from the buccaneers: whitewashed by the priest, or even covered in mud by nuns.

A block to the south on Calle 9 is the run-down **Plaza Herrera**. French influence is evident in the windows and flower-filled cast-iron balconies of the green and pale pink houses and *pensiones*. This area is one Casco Viejo's last surviving bastions of authentic street life. Behind Plaza Herrera are the ruins of the **Tiger's Hand Bulwark**, where the defensive wall ended and the landward-side moat began. The strongpoint held a 50-man military post and 13 cannon; it was demolished in 1856 as the town expanded but restored in 1983. Portions of the moat can still be detected.

Avenida Central and Santa Ana

From Calle 10 heading north, Avenida Central, Panama City's main commercial street, enters the 'mainland', curves northeast into the commercial working class district of Santa Ana, then runs parallel to the Pacific coast. En route its name changes to Vía España – although signs reading 'Avenida Central España' exist in parts – until eventually concluding at Tocumen Airport.

At the Avenida's crossing with Calle B, close to Casco Viejo, is the small **Plaza Santa Ana** with its colonial church (1764). The square is a favourite among shoe-shiners and elderly gentlemen; many buses depart from here to all parts of the city. Nearby, running between Avenida Central and Calle B (officially known as Carrera de Chiriquí), is an exotic, narrow alley called **Salsipuedes** – 'get out if you can' – where crowded stalls sell everything from fruit to old books and medicinal plants. Over 75% of the street's residents in 1892 were Chinese merchants, but the city's Chinatown (**Barrio Chino**) is now largely confined to nearby Calle Juan Mendoza and adjacent Calle B with a typical Chinese archway at the entrance; Chinese restaurants and spice-filled shops.

Plaza 5 de Mayo and around

The next section of Avenida Central is a pedestrian precinct called **La Peatonal**, with trees and decorations, cut-price department stores and wandering street vendors. It emerges at **Plaza 5 de Mayo**, Calle 22 Este, an important and busy road intersection from where buses leave for the Canal. In the centre of the Plaza is an obelisk honouring the firemen who died in a gunpowder magazine explosion on the site in May 1914. A block north lies a large monument called 'The Allegoric Frieze of Justice'. It is dedicated to the assassinated President José Antonio Remón Cantera and features various brass figurines and fountain. Directly behind it stands the Palacio Legislativo, also known as the National Assembly, often bustling outside with groups of protestors. East of the monument lies the **Museo Afro-Antillano** ① *Justo Arosemena and Calle 24 Este, T262-5348, Tue-Sat 0830-1530, US$1*, which features an illustrated history of Panama's West Indian community and their work on the Canal. There's a small library.

Calidonia

As Avenida Central continues north, it enters the district of Calidonia and grows hectic with shops, stalls, kiosks and street vendors. There are many economical hotels in the surrounding grid of streets, but the area is sleazy after dark. Towards the northern end of Calidonia lies a stately neighbourhood known as La Exposición, named after an important 1916 international science and agriculture fair. It has two pleasant plazas, Porras and Arias. There are also two museums: **Museo de Ciencias Naturales** ① *Av Cuba y Calle 30, T225-0645, Tue-Sat 0900-1530, Sun 1300-1630, US$1, students and seniors US$0.25*, which has good sections on geology, palaeontology, entomology and marine biology, and **Museo Casa del Banco Nacional** ⓘ *Calle 34 between Av Cuba and Av Justo Arosemena, Mon-Fri 0800-1230, 1330-1630, free,* which, although not widely known, is worth a visit. It contains a large numismatic and stamp collection and a history of banking from the 19th century.

Cinta Costera

The new oceanfront Cinta Costera (coastal belt) runs parallel to Avenida Central. Completed in 2009 at a cost of US$189 million, the project included the reclamation of some 25 ha of land. The Cinta roars alongside the Pacific Ocean with no less than 10 lanes of traffic, engulfing a statue of Vasco Núñez de Balboa that once occupied a more commanding position at the water's edge. Fortunately, the builders of the highway saw fit to compliment their thoroughfare with plenty of park space. Complete with flourishing palm trees, green grass, cycle lanes, basket ball courts and restaurants, the Cinta is as popular with joggers, walkers and rollerbladers as it is with motorists. Sunday evening is a good time to stroll and soak up the family atmosphere, or simply admire the skyscrapers illuminated against the night sky.

Bella Vista and the Banking district

Bella Vista lies northeast of Calidonia, once a very pleasant residential district and now home to the glass and steel towers of 'New Panama'. This sizeable district includes the neighbourhood of **Perejil** (parsley), originally called Perry Hill, and at the point where Vía España passes the Iglesia del Carmen, **El Cangrejo** (the crab) – a popular apartment and restaurant quarter with many upmarket stores and boutiques. The University City is nearby on the Transisthmian Highway. All these areas are evidence of Panama City's

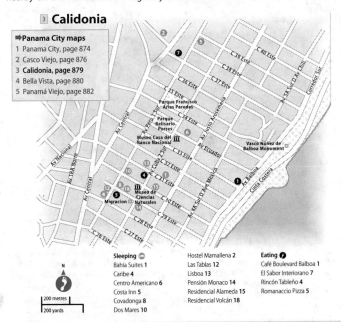

3 Calidonia

➡**Panama City maps**
1 Panama City, page 874
2 Casco Viejo, page 876
3 **Calidonia, page 879**
4 Bella Vista, page 880
5 Panamá Viejo, page 882

Parque Francisco Arias Paredes
Parque Belisario Porres
Museo Casa del Banco Nacional ▥
Vasco Núñez de Balboa Monument
Museo de Ciencias Naturales
Migración

N
200 metres
200 yards

Sleeping 🛏
Bahía Suites **1**
Caribe **4**
Centro Americano **6**
Costa Inn **5**
Covadonga **8**
Dos Mares **10**

Hostel Mamallena **2**
Las Tablas **12**
Lisboa **13**
Pensión Monaco **14**
Residencial Alameda **15**
Residencial Volcán **18**

Eating 🍴
Café Boulevard Balboa **1**
El Sabor Interiorano **7**
Rincón Tableño **4**
Romanaccio Pizza **5**

Bella Vista is an empty hill where hunting was practised as recently as the 1960s.

sensational growth since the post-war economic boom and the spread of the centre northeastwards; the attractive residential suburb of Punta Paitilla was an empty hill where hunting was practised as recently as the 1960s.

4 Bella Vista

To 1 5 12

➡Panama City maps
1 Panama City, page 874
2 Casco Viejo, page 876
3 Calidonia, page 879
4 Bella Vista, page 880
5 Panamá Viejo, page 882

Sleeping
California 2 D1
El Panamá 3 B2
Euro 4 D1
Hostal La Casa
 de Carmen 5 A3
La Jungle House 11 B1
Miramar
 Intercontinental 9 D2
Vía España 7 D1

Eating
Athens 2 C2
Café La Musa de Chai 1 A1
Caffé Pomodoro 4 B2
El Burger Bar 5 B2
El Patio Mexicano 6 A3
Grand Deli Gourmet 7 B3
Greenhouse 9 A2
Habibi's 8 D2
Italian Pasta 10 A3

Las Tinajas 13 D2
Madame Chang 14 D3
Niko's Café 17 B3
Noel 12 A3
Ozone Café 18 D2
Parillada Martín Fierro 19 A2
Pavo Real 20 A2

N

200 metres
200 yards

Parque Natural Metropolitano and around

ⓘ *Between Av Juan Pablo II and the Camino de la Amistad, west of El Cangrejo along the Río Curundú, T232-5552, www.parquemetropolitano.org, visitor centre open Tue-Sun, US$2. To get there, take the bus marked 'Tumba Muerto', from Av Central, and ask to be dropped at the Depósito, from where it signposted; or a taxi, US$3.*

The 265-ha Parque Natural Metropolitano has a mirador (150 m) with a great view over the city and a glimpse of the Canal, as well as various interpretive walking trails from which *tití* monkeys, agoutis, coatis, white-tailed deer, sloths, turtles and up to 200 species of bird may be glimpsed (go early morning for best viewing). The **Smithsonian Institute** (see page 883) has installed a construction crane for studying the little-known fauna in the canopy of this remnant of tropical semi-deciduous lowland forest; contact the Smithsonian Institute if you would like to make an ascent.

The **Museo Antropológico Reina Torres de Araúz** ⓘ *Av Juan Pablo II and Calle Curundú, T232-7644, Tue-Sun 0900-1600,* lies a short walk from the park and is home to the country's finest anthropology collection. Sadly, however, there have been on-going issues with the building's ambient conditions, which are apparently unsuitable for displaying archaeological items. At the time of research, uninspired displays on Panama's national heroes had replaced the interesting historical exhibits. They are working on a solution; check locally for an update.

Panamá Viejo

ⓘ *Tue-Sun 0900-1700, US$3, T226-8915, www.panamaviejo.org, US$4 for the cathedral lookout, US$6 for museum and lookout. Getting there: taxi from the city centre, US$5-7; buses from Vía España or Avenida Balboa, US$0.80. Panamá Viejo also makes a good excursion for passengers with a little time to kill at nearby Tocumen Airport; taxis can be as much as US$5 but still reasonable, especially if this is the only chance you'll have to see Panamá. Alternatively, take any bus marked Vía España, get off at Vía Cincuentenario, then take a bus to Panamá Viejo.*

A wander among the ruins of Panamá Viejo still gives an idea of the site's former glory, although many of the structures have been worn by time, fungus and the sea. The narrow **King's Bridge** (1620) at the north end of the town's limits is a good starting point; it marked the beginning of the three trails across the isthmus and took seven years to build. Walking south brings you to the **Convento de San José**, where the Golden Altar originally stood (see page 875); it was spared by the great fire that swept the town during Morgan's attack (which side started the fire is still debated). Several blocks further south is the main plaza, where the square stone tower of the **cathedral** (1535-1580) is a prominent feature (US$4 extra). In the immediate vicinity are the Cabildo, with imposing arches and columns, the remnants of **Convento de Santo Domingo**, the **Bishop's Residence**, and the **Slave Market** (or House of the Genovese), whose gaol-like structure was the hub of the American slave trade. There were about 4000 African slaves in 1610, valued at about 300 pesos apiece. Beyond the plazas to the south, on a rocky eminence overlooking the bay, stand the **Royal Houses**, the administrative stronghold including the **Quartermaster's House**, the **Court** and **Chancellery**, the **Real Audiencia** and the **Governor's Residence**.

Further west along the Pacific strand are the dungeons, kitchens and meat market (now almost obliterated by the sea); a store and refreshment stands cluster here on the south side of the plaza, and handicrafts from the Darién are sold along the beach. Across

Calle de la Carrera stands another great complex of religious convents: **La Concepción** (1598) and the **Compañía de Jesús** (1621). These too were outside the area destroyed by the 1671 fire but are today little more than rubble. Only a wall remains of the Franciscan **Hospital de San Juan de Dios**, once a huge structure encompassing wards, courtyards and a church. Another block west can be seen part of the **Convento de San Francisco** and its gardens, facing the rocky beach. About 100 m west is the beautiful **Convento de La Merced**, where Pizarro, Almagro and their men attended Mass on the morning they sailed on their final and momentous expedition to Peru. Decades later Morgan stored his plunder here until it could be counted, divided up and sent back to the Atlantic side. At the western limit of Panamá Viejo stands **La Navidad Fort** (1658). Its purpose was merely to defend the **Matadero (Slaughterhouse) Bridge** across the Río Agarroba but its 50-man garrison and half-dozen cannon were no match for the determined force of privateers; it is also known as Morgan's Bridge because it was here that the attack began.

There is a **visitor centre** ⓘ www.panamaviejo.org, with exhibitions in Spanish, as well as maps, pictures and models of how Panama's first city would have looked. There are also opportunities for students to volunteer in future excavations. By the ruins is **Museo de Panamá Viejo** ⓘ *Vía Cincuentenario, T226-89156, Mon-Sun 0900-1700, US$2.*

The whole area (unfenced) is attractively landscaped, with plenty of benches to rest on, and floodlit at night. Late afternoon when the sun is low is an especially nice time to visit, although at least two hours should be allowed to appreciate the site fully. The main ruins are patrolled by police and reasonably safe. **Dame Margot Fonteyn**, the ballerina, is buried alongside her husband Roberto Arias Guardia in the Jardín de la Paz cemetery

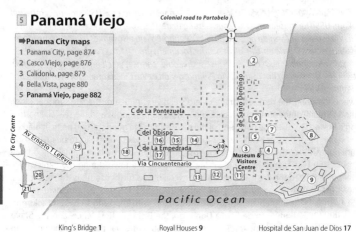

5 **Panamá Viejo**

➡**Panama City maps**
1 Panama City, page 874
2 Casco Viejo, page 876
3 Calidonia, page 879
4 Bella Vista, page 880
5 Panamá Viejo, page 882

King's Bridge **1**
Convento de San José **2**
Main Plaza **3**
Cathedral **4**
Cabildo **5**
Convento de Santo Domingo **6**
Bishop's Residence **7**
Slave's House/
House of the Genovese **8**

Royal Houses **9**
Emperor's Bridge **10**
Dungeons **11**
Kitchens **12**
Meat Market **13**
Convento de Compañía
de Jesús **14**
Convento La Concepción **15**
Church of La Concepción **16**

Hospital de San Juan de Dios **17**
Convento de San Francisco **18**
Convento de la Merced **19**
La Navidad Fort **20**
Matadero/
Slaughterhouse Bridge **21**

Not to scale

behind Panamá Viejo. IPAT organizes free folklore events and local dance displays on Saturdays in the dry season (*verano*), which are worth seeing. The tourist office in Panama City (T226-7000) has a list of programmes and can supply professional guides if required.

Ancón Hill

Formerly part of the US-controlled canal zone, the verdant slopes of Ancón Hill overlook the capital with shady trees and chattering wildlife – a welcome refuge from the city's smog-choked avenues. There are good chances of spotting tamarinds, agoutis, sloths and a variety of birds in the surrounding vegetation. From the summit, the expansive Bay of Panama, Amador causeway, Casco Viejo and financial district are all clearly visible in the east. The Panama railroad, canal, locks and port operations can be seen in the west. The road to the top starts in Quarry Heights, from where much of the stone to build Miraflores and Pedro Miguel locks was mined. The walk, best accomplished in the clean morning light, takes around 30 minutes. En route, you will pass many US-style houses, including the offices of the environmental organization ANCON.

The lower slopes of the hill are dotted with numerous important buildings, including the headquarters of the **Smithsonian Tropical Research Institute** ① *Tupper Building, Roosevelt Av, Mon-Fri 0900-1700, Sat 0900-1200, café Mon-Fri 1000-1630, T212-8000, www.stri.org*, an English-language scientific research centre where applications to visit Barro Colorado Island are made. The café/bookshop sells environmental books and nature guides, including national park maps. Nearby, along Calle Culebra, is the former **Gorgas Army Community Hospital**, named after William Crawford Gorgas, the physician who is credited with clearing the Canal Zone of its most malignant tropical diseases. Today it functions as the National Oncology Hospital. On Avenida de los Mártires, look out for the sign to the **Museo de Arte Contemporáneo** ① *Av de los Mártires, entrance on Av San Blas, T262-8012, Tue-Sun 0900-1700, US$1*. Housed in a former Masonic Lodge (1936), the permanent collection of national and international modern paintings and sculptures has special exhibitions from time to time, and a library of contemporary visual art open to students. The stately **Instituto Nacional** also stands on the four-lane Avenida de los Mártires. At **Mi Pueblito** ① *north of Av de los Mártires, east of the Quarry Heights entrance, 0900-2100, US$1*, you'll find nostalgic replicas of three different villages: one colonial from the Central Provinces, one Afro-Antillian and one indigenous. It's on a busy road so best to take a taxi.

Balboa → *Colour map 5, B1.*

The town and docks of Balboa are just over 3 km west of Panama City (10 minutes by taxi, US$5) and stand between in the former canal zone between the quays and Ancón Hill. The district is ordered, planned and sterile – a typical American answer to the wilfulness and riot of the tropics. The impressive Canal administration building has fine murals depicting the trials and dramas of the canal construction. Behind it, steps lead to a small park, a reflecting pool and marble monolith commemorating George Washington Goethals, the canal's chief engineer. A long palm-flanked parkway known as the Prado leads southwest of the monument and concludes at a modest fountain dedicated to John Stevens and various amenities including a theatre, post office, bank and fast food café. Continue southeast along Avenida Arnulfo Arias Madrid and you will soon arrive at the Antiguo YMCA which houses a small artesanía market. A much larger **Centro de Artesanías** is located directly behind it.

Calzada Amador

Before the Puente de las Américas crosses the Panama Canal, the long peninsula of Fuerte Amador stretches into the Pacific, formerly the HQ of the Panamanian Defence Force, seized by US forces in 1989 and returned to Panama in 1994. Beyond Fuerte Amador are the formerly fortified islands of Naos, Perico and Flamenco, linked by the 4-km causeway (**Calzada Amador**) built of rubble excavated from the Canal. There are many interesting buildings in this area bearing the marks of the conflict, and some attractive lawns and parkland. The Calzada has been extensively developed over recent years and now includes a cruise-ship terminal. As you enter the Causeway you pass the **Figali Convention Centre**, built and inaugurated in 2003 for the Miss Universe competition and centennial celebrations. The Figali Centre now hosts major music and sports events. It has fine views of the Puente de las Américas and the ships lined up to enter the Canal. There are small charges for entry and for swimming at Solidaridad beach on **Naos** (crowded at weekends and the water is polluted – not recommended). At Punta Culebra on Naos is the **Marine Exhibition Center** ① *T212-8793, Tue-Fri 1300-1800, Sat-Sun 1000-1800, US$2* (of the Smithsonian Tropical Research Institute), with interesting aquaria and exhibitions on marine fauna. As the road reaches **Isla Perico**, there is a block of restaurants, bars and some shops underneath what is set to be an apartment-style hotel. A 'mega resort' is in process at Naos Harbour – a 300 room hotel, 114 room apartment-hotel, casino, shops, condos and new beach, and there is a proposal for a cable car to the Causeway descending from the top of Ancón Hill – an addition vehemently opposed by many locals. **Flamenco**, the last of the islands, is the headquarters for the **National Maritime Service** and home to the **Flamenco Yacht Club**, a large duty-free store and a pristine mall of boutiques, expensive souvenir shops and lively range of restaurants, bars and clubs. Most popular between Wednesday and Saturday nights.

The **Bridge of Life Biodiversity Museum** ① *T314-1395, www.biomuseopanama.org*, currently being developed on the Causeway, is designed by architect Frank Gehry with botanical gardens designed by New York specialist Edwina von Gal. Labelled a learning centre and 'hub of an interchange of nature, culture, the economy and life' the museum is an impressive and modern testament to Panama's location as a major ecological rossroads.

Isla Taboga

Tobaga island – dubbed 'Island of Flowers' – is a favourite year-round resort. It produces delicious pineapples and mangoes, and has one of the oldest churches in the Western hemisphere. Admission to the beach at **Hotel Taboga** is US$10, redeemable in tokens to buy food and drink (covered picnic huts cost extra). There are other good places to swim around the island, but its south side is rocky and sharks visit regularly.

Calypso Queen (T314-1730) provide ferry services to Taboga island from Isla Naos Pier on Amador Causeway. The trip outis very interesting. You pass the naval installations at the Pacific end of the Canal, the great bridge linking the Americas, tuna boats and shrimp fishers in for supplies, and visiting yachts from all over the world. Part of the route follows the channel of the Canal, with its busy traffic. Taboga itself, with a promontory rising to 488 m, is carpeted with flowers at certain times of year. There are few cars in the meandering, helter-skelter streets and just one footpath as a road. All items are expensive on the island, so make sure you bring plenty of cash as there is no bank.

Islas Perlas

Some 75 km southeast of the city are the Islas Perlas (Pearl Islands), where you will find beautiful beaches with crystal-clear water, good snorkelling, diving and sailing, and lots of sharks. The islands are so-named for the prolific pearl fishing in colonial days; today, these waters are rich in Pacific mackerel, red snapper, corvina, sailfish, marlin and other species, drawing lots of sea anglers. High mountains rise from the sea, and there is a little fishing village on a shelf of land at the water's edge. **Contadora**, one of the smallest Pearl Islands, has become quite famous since its name became associated with a Central American peace initiative. It was also where the last Shah of Iran, Mohammed Rezá Pahlaví, was exiled, in a house called 'Puntalara', after the Iranian Revolution. Contadora is popular with Canadian, Spanish and Italian holidaymakers and is becoming crowded, built-up and consequently not as peaceful as it once was.You'll find no less than 13 powdery white beaches flanking its shores and a growing number of luxury hotels.

Nearby, **Isla San José** is a private island with waters rich in marine life, particularly black marlin, drawing sports fishers keen to snag a catch, and perhaps a world record – no less than 16 have been bagged here already. This is the second largest island in the archipelago, home to exceptionally fertile soils and abundant plant species. **Isla Viveros** is a particularly idyllic spot filled with turquoise lagoons and white sand beaches. It's a good place to watch flocks of great frigates, but unfortunately you'll also have to share the paradise with a hideous new housing development (www.islaviveros.com). One of the more pristine islands in the archipelago is **Isla San Telmo**, the site of lush primary forests, prolific bird species and nesting turtles. Whales also visit the region is great numbers during the month of September.

◉ Panama City listings

Hotel and guesthouse prices
LL over US$150 **L** US$100-150 **AL** US$66-99
A US$46-65 **B** US$31-45 **C** US$21-30
D US$12-20 **E** US$7-11 **F** under US$7
Restaurant prices
♦♦♦ over US$15 **♦♦** US$8-15 **♦** under US$8
See pages 31-33 for further information.

● Sleeping

Tocumen International Airport *p872*
LL-AL Riande Aeropuerto, near Tocumen Airport (5 mins), T290-3333, www.hoteles riande.com. Conveniently located for fliers, with free transport to the airport. Rooms are dated and in some cases, shabby. Amenities include pool (loud music all day), tennis courts and casino. Poor value. Mixed reports.

Casco Viejo *p873, map p876*
LL-L The Canal House, Av A and Calle 5, T228-1907, www.canalhousepanama.com.

Housed in an handsome 19th-century town house, this exclusive boutique hotel has received praise in *The New York Times* and other international press. It has 3 crisp, elegant suites, all immaculately presented. Private, professional and personalized service. Not cheap.
LL-AL Casa Sucre Hotel, Calle 8 and Av B, T6679-7077, www.casasucreboutique hotel.com. This restored 1873 guesthouse is another reliable boutique option. It has 4 bedrooms and 3 apartments, all well-equipped with Wi-Fi, cable TV, fridge, microwave and balcony. Apartments have fully fitted kitchens and great stone work. A reasonable deal for groups.
D-E Luna's Castle, 9a este, between Av B and Av Alfaro, T262-1540, www.lunascastle hostel.com. A very popular backpacker hostel in a beautiful old colonial mansion. You'll find a wealth of amenities here including comfortable communal spaces, Wi-Fi, table

tennis, guitars, book exchange and a kitchen. Dorms (**E**) and private rooms (**D**) available, rates include pancake breakfast. Book ahead.

F Hospedaje Casco Viejo Calle 8, in front of San José church, T211-2027, www.hospedajecascoviejo.com. A mix of simple rooms (**D**) at this backpackers' hostel, with private and shared bathrooms, and dorms (**F**) too. A safe, quiet spot with outdoor terrace, kitchen and internet access.

Apartments

LL-L Los Cuatro Tulipanes, Casa las Monjas Apt 2A, Av Central between Calle 3a y 4a (above **Granclement Ice Cream**) T211-0877, www.loscuatrotulipanes.com. Several taste-fully attired apartments in the heart of Casco Viejo, including studios, 1- and 2-bedroom properties. Well-equipped, charming, comfortable and often recommended.

Avenida Central and Santa Ana *p878, maps p874 and p876*

C Stanford, Plaza 5 de Mayo, T262-4933, hotelstanford@cwpanama.net. Formerly **Hotel Internacional**, this tower on the plaza has spacious rooms with hot water, a/c and cable TV. Although a little tatty for the price, the views of the city and ocean are almost worth it.

D Ideal, Calle 17 Oeste, off Av Central, between Plaza Santa Ana y Plaza 5 de Mayo, T262-2400. This faded old hotel – complete with gaudy decor – certainly hasn't forgotten its heyday in the 1970s. Rooms are clean and tidy with hot water, a/c and cable TV. There's a pool. Hectic location and brusque management.

Calidonia *p878, map p879*

A Bahía Suites, Calle 31, between Av Cuba and Av Justo Arosemena, T225-8578, www.hotelbahiasuites.com. A new hotel with 74 clean, comfortable rooms, each with a/c, cable TV, safe and telephone as standard; suites have jacuzzi. There's also a pool on the roof, gym, restaurant and breakfast included.

A Costa Inn, Av Perú y Calle 39, T225-1522, www.hotelcostainn.com. A sparklingly clean

and comfortable hotel right on the edge with Bella Vista. Double rooms feature 2 bathrooms, and the rooftop pool has great views of the city. Scheduled transport to the airport and other places. Breakfast included. Helpful, pleasant.

B Caribe, Av Perú y Calle 28, T225-0404, www.caribehotel.net. One of the city's older hotels, with 153 very large rooms, rooftop pool and bar, casino, Wi-Fi, parking, events room and restaurant. In the heart of Calidonia.

B Centro Americano, Av Justo Arosemena y Av Ecuador, T227-4555, www.hotelcentro americano.com. The 61 rooms here are very clean, smart and well appointed, with Wi-Fi, hot water, plasma screen cable TV. Some have balconies and views of the bay. Restaurant, business centre and parking available. Recommended.

C Dos Mares, Calle 30 between Perú and Cuba, T/F227-6149, dosmares@cwpanama. net. This hotel has a good rooftop pool with views across the city. Some rooms are more 'renovated' than others, so ask to see a few. Otherwise generally clean and comfortable, with a/c, hot water, cable TV and phone as standard. There's internet service a restaurant. Popular with Ticos.

C Lisboa, Av Cuba y Calle 31, T227-5916. The rooms at this hotel are nice and big, but avoid those overlooking the main road below. The usual amenities include a/c, hot water and cable TV, with a restaurant downstairs. Well-established. An old favourite.

C Residencial Alameda, Calle 30 Este, Av Cuba, T225-1758, residencialalameda@hot mail.com. A big, modern building. Rooms here are comfortable, with ill-matching furniture, a/c, clean bathrooms, hot water, cable TV and telephone. Wi-Fi throughout. Not bad.

C Covadonga, Calle 29, Av Perú, T225-5275, marit@sinfo.net. This hotel has a good rooftop terrace with a pool and views over the city. Rooms are clean and comfortable, with cable TV, sometimes noisy a/c, and powerful, hot showers.

D Pensión Monaco, Av Cuba y Calle 29, T225-2573. This large, echo-filled place has big, comfortable rooms; some have good views. Cable TV, hot water and a/c are standard, private parking available.

D Residencial Volcán, Calle 29 and Av Perú, T225-5263, opposite Migración, next to Museo de Ciencias Naturales. A very good option for budget travellers. Rooms have a/c or fan, and cable TV. Guests have access to the rooftop pool at **Covadonga**, next door. Friendly, clean and recommended.

D-E Hostel Mamallena, Casa 7-62, Calle Primera, Perejil, T6676-6163, www.mama llena.com. A backpacker hostel with private rooms (**D**) and dorms, kitchen and plenty of places to hang out. Often full. They've done their research, and have details about sail boats to Colombia on the website.

E Las Tablas, Av Perú y Calle 29 Este. Rooms here are equipped with fan and national TV. They're a good deal for budget travellers, although the hotel interior is a bit dark and gloomy. Opposite is **El Machetazo** super-market, food for cheap meals. Chatty owner.

Bella Vista and the Banking District
p879, map p880

LL Miramar Intercontinental, Av Balboa, T250-3000, www.miramarpanama.com. Former guests of this classy hotel include President Bush, who hired 120 rooms here during his visit to Panama. This illustrious lodging has a wealth of amenities, including 3 restaurants, a huge pool, gym, Wi-Fi and exclusive marina.

LL-AL El Panamá, Vía España 111, T215-9182, www.elpanama.com. Built in 1951, this famous hotel sports a tropical art deco style, huge rooms, good pool and a vast Vegas-style casino. A bit inefficient, but generally good.

B California, Vía España y Calle 43, T263-7736, www.hotelcaliforniapanama.net. A good, clean, professional hotel with friendly, English-speaking staff. Rooms are modern, with a/c, cable TV, Wi-Fi and hot water. There's a restaurant attached and gym upstairs.

B Euro Hotel, Vía España 33, opposite the Bella Vista, T263-0802, www.eurohotel panama.com. Located on a busy street, this

hotel has large, comfortable rooms with a/c, hot water and cable TV. There's also a pool, restaurant and bar.

B Hotel Vía España, Calle Martín Sosa (on the corner of Vía España), T264-0800, www.hotel-viaespana.com. This large hotel has clean rooms with comfy beds, a/c, private bath, telephone, Wi-Fi, fridge, TV with cable. A few suites have a jacuzzi for a very good price. Restaurant on-site, breakfast included and free transport to the airport. Friendly and recommended.

C-E Hostal La Casa de Carmen, Calle 1a El Carmen Casa 32 (from Vía Espana and Vía Brasil, 1 block north, 1 block east), T263-4366, www.lacasadecarmen.net. 3 friendly Panamanian ladies run this good-value option close to the action. Rooms have a/c and come with or without private bath. Dorms are also available (**E**). Lovely relaxing garden. Popular and highly recommended.

C-E La Jungla House, Calle 49a Oeste and Vía Argentina 11, 5th floor RINA building, T214-8069, www.lajunglahouse.com. Clean, simple, down-to-earth hostel with 3 dorms, 5 private rooms (**C**), 2 lounges and a kitchen. Wi-Fi throughout. Same owners as **Hostel Nomba** in Boquete.

Isla Taboga *p884*

You may be able to find locals to stay with.

A Cerrito Tropical, north end of town, T390-8999, www.cerritotropicalpanama.com. Small B&B overlooking the bay leading to the Canal. It has 6 comfortable rooms, all with a/c, as well as a vacation apartment that sleeps 4 (**L**). Price includes breakfast.

B Taboga, T250-2122, htaboga@sinfo.net. Apdo 550357, Paitilla, Panamá, 300 m east of wharf. Rooms here have a/c, and cable TV. There's also a restaurant, café, pool and beach.

D Chu, on main street, 200 m left of wharf, T250-2036. A wooden colonial-style building with beautiful views, own beach and terraced restaurant serving traditional fish and chicken dishes. The walls are thin and bathroom is shared.

Islas Perlas *p885*
L Contadora Resort, T214-3719, www.
hotelcontadora.com. Same ownership as
El Panamá in Panama City, this chalet
complex has a nice location on beach,
but it's a little run-down.
A Contadora Island Inn, T6699-6414,
www.contadoraislandinn.com. A selection
of rooms here, all with private bath and
B&B service. There's also a good range of
relaxation and adventure acitivities.

🍴 Eating

Casco Viejo *p873, map p876*
As Casco Viejo slowly gentrifies, more and
more good restaurants are popping up.
There are few economical options.
¶¶¶-¶¶ Casablanca, Plaza Bolívar. Long-
established restaurant with tables al
fresco in the picturesque plaza. The food
is reasonable, but not fantastic. They serve
meat, pasta, salad and seafood.
¶¶¶-¶¶ Las Bóvedas, Plaza Francia. Located in
the converted dungeons at the seaward end
of Casco Viejo, this atmospheric restaurant
serves up French cuisine beneath intimate,
arched stone ceilings. An interesting spot,
with an adjoining art gallery and live jazz
Fri-Sat. Closed Sun.
¶¶¶-¶¶ Monolo Caracol, Av Central, across
from Palacio Nacional de Gobierno y Justicia.
This widely respected restaurant serves
excellent tapas and seafood, uses the freshest
ingredients and is often recommended. It is
popular and can get noisy. Closed Sun.
¶¶¶-¶¶ Mostaza, Calle A opposite Arco
Chato. This is one of the best restaurants in
Casco Viejo, often visited by the president.
It's an intimate spot with an Argentine-
inspired menu of excellent beef cuts, steaks
and grilled fish. Live music at the weekends.
¶¶ Cedro's Grill and Tavern, Av Central,
Between Calle 4 and 5. American-style grill
house serving burgers and other wholesome
fare. The pizzas are very tasty, recommended
and best washed down with a cold beer or two.

¶¶ Tequila, Av A and Calle 3. A popular
tourist joint serving fish tacos, burritos
and other seasoned fare from Mexico.
Some outdoor seating on the corner that's
good for people-watching.

Cafés, bakeries and ice cream parlours
Granclement, Calle 3 between Av Central
and Roberto Chiari. Fantastic gourmet ice
cream to take your taste buds to another
level. Not cheap, but delicious.

Avenida Central and Santa Ana *p878,
maps p874 and p876*
Cafés and bakeries
Café Coca Cola, Av Central and Plaza
Santa Ana. A bustling, interesting little locals'
haunt with reasonably priced set lunches.
Panadería Azukitar, Av Central, near
Plaza Santa Ana. Big, clean place with lots
of sweet rolls, cakes and other sugary treats.

Calidonia *p878, map p879*
Dining in Calidonia isn't fantastic, but it is
economical. Most hotels have passable
restaurants, otherwise eateries here are
mostly simple affairs, geared towards locals.
¶¶-¶ Café Boulevard Balboa, Calle 33 and
Av Balboa. One of the few bay-side eateries
that hasn't been demolished for new
skyscrapers. This Panamanian diner has been
around since the 1950s and continues to
serve good breakfasts, lunches and dinners.
Popular with Panamanians. Closed Sun.
Recommended.
¶¶-¶ Romanaccio Pizza, Calle 29, between
Av Cuba and Av Peru. Good, tasty Italian-
style pizzas with authentic crusts. Forget
the burgers. Closed Sun.
¶ El Sabor Interiorano, Calle 37, between
Av Central and Av Perú. A cosy, unassuming
little locals' haunt serving affordable staples
and Panamanian fare.
¶ Rincón Tableño, Av Cuba No 5 y Calle 31.
Panamanian fare. Several locations, this
popular restaurant serves good *comida
criolla* and is always bustling with working-
class Panamanians. Lunchtimes only.

Bella Vista and the Banking District
p879, map p880

The best restaurants in town are clustered in the neighbourhoods of Bella Vista, especially along Vía Argentina. There are few economical eateries, however – head for bakeries and supermarkets.

₩₩₩ **Madame Chang**, Av 5 Sur, between Calle 48 and Calle 49. Some claim this is the best Chinese restaurant in Latin America. It's a well-established haunt, with a calm, clean interior and a menu sporting Peking duck and other tasty fare. Recommended.

₩₩₩ **Parrillada Martín Fierro**, Calle Eusebio A Morales, T264-1927. Carnivores will delight at the excellent beef cuts, Argentine steaks and other fine meat dishes served at this reputable steak house.

₩₩₩-₩₩ **El Patio Mexicano**, Av 1a B Norte, off Vía Argentina. Excellent Mexican cuisine from this authentic and atmospheric restaurant that serves delicious *mole*-renched peppers, tasty enchiladas and tequila cocktails. The best Mexican in the city, and reassuringly creative. Closed Mon.

₩₩ **Athens**, corner of Av Uruguay and Av 4 Sur. A lively restaurant specializing in Greek and Middle Eastern cuisine, including stuffed pittas, kebabs and salads. Good atmosphere and cheapish, average grub.

₩₩ **Café La Musa de Chai**, Vía Argentina, northwest end, opposite the HSBC and upstairs from the cyber. A friendly, intimate restaurant with a bohemian vibe and superb Puerto Rican specialities. Try one of the combo plates – the *monfogo* is particularly tasty. Reasonable prices and highly recommended.

₩₩ **Caffé Pomodoro**, Av Eusebio A Morales, north of Calle 55. Tasty and affordable Italian cuisine from renowned local restaurateur Willy Diggelmann. Fresh, simple and served in hearty portions, the way Italian food should be.

₩₩ **El Burger Bar**, Mini-mall, Av Eusebio Morales. Bright and bold sports themed joint where you can enjoy gourmet burgers, sugary drinks and occasionally discounted beer and cocktails. Racy music and icy a/c.

₩₩ **Greenhouse**, Vía Argentina and Av 4a B Norte. Swamped in swathes of green foliage, this trendy café-lounge serves burgers, wraps and sandwiches and overlooks the Vía Argentina.

₩₩ **Habibi's**, Calle Uruguay. Tasty, full-flavoured Middle Eastern food served in a converted colonial mansion. Good hummus and kofta kebabs. There's outdoor seating on the patio where you can also soak up the Calle Uruguay vibe. Not bad.

₩₩ **Las Tinajas**, on Calle 51, near Ejecutivo Hotel, T263-7890. Panamanian cuisine and traditional entertainment, including dance, music and costumes (Tue and Thu-Sat from 2100). A little touristy, but the food is very good and authentic. There's also a craft shop attached. Closed Sun.

₩₩ **Ozone Café**, Calle Uruguay. Busy, noisy, but intimate little restaurant in the Marbella district. They serve international food to a young crowd, including very good Middle Eastern dishes like kebabs, hummus and Turkish pizza. The sandwiches were only so-so during our visit.

₩₩ **Pavo Real**, Vía Argentina and Calle José Martí. This upmarket English pub and restaurant serves wholesome British fare for homesick expats, including fish and chips, and international food such as steak, burgers and salads. There's darts too.

₩ **Niko's Café**, with 4 locations at Vía España near El Rey supermarket, T264-0136; El Dorado Shopping Centre, T260-0022; Paitilla, past old airport T270-2555; and behind the former Balboa High School in the Canal Zone T228-8888. Cheap, reliable fast food, including burgers, subs and sodas.

Bakeries and delis

Noel, Vía Porras, between Av 1a C Norte and Av 2ac Norte, El Carmen. One of the city's best bakeries and great for a cheap lunch of fresh pizza or empanadas. Highly recommended.

Grand Deli Gourmet, Av Samuel Lewis. Swish deli in the swanky neighbourhood of Obarrio. They sell cheese, cooked meats, coffee, salads, tasty empanadas and fresh bread.

Italian Pasta, Vía España. A favourite lunchtime haunt among office workers. They sell cheap, filling pasta from a buffet, as well as good frozen green pesto for uncomplicated creations back at the hostel.

Calzada Amador *p884*

♥♥ **Crêpes and Waffles**, located upstairs at the Flamenco Mall and other branches in Marbella and Albrook. Pleasant, light dishes, including crêpes and waffles, as the name suggests. Don't forget to check out the amazing ice-cream menu.

♥♥ **Pencas**, Amador Causeway, in front of Plaza Iberoamericana, T211-3671, www.pencas.com. Panamanian food and live 'Panamanian Expressions' – folkloric nights with music and dancing on Wed nights. Call ahead and make a reservation as it gets busy.

⊙ Entertainment

Panama City *p872, maps p874, p876, p879 and p880*

Bars and clubs

Many late night haunts are concentrated in the Marbella district, particularly along and around Calle Uruguay (Calle 48).
La Chiva Parrandera. Is an open-sided bus that tours the hot-spots from 2000-2400. Call T263-3144, for information, US$25 per person.
Café Bolívar, Plaza Bolívar, Casco Viejo. Small, snug bar with outside tables.
Casablanca, Plaza Bolívar, Casco Viejo. Fancy, hip bar and restaurant offering Provençale/Thai cuisine. Mixed reports on the food.
Deep Room, Calle Uruguay area of Bella Vista. An excellent club. Tribal house and electronica. Late start, sometimes 0400.
La Parrillita, Av 11 de Octubre, Hato Pintado. Restaurant/disco in a railway carriage.
Las Bóvedas, Plaza de Francia, Casco Viejo, T228-8068. Jazz on the weekends from 2100-0100.
Liquid, Calle 50 and Calle José de la Cruz. A popular dance club that hosts electronic events and late night dance parties. If there's

any big pop music names in town, they're likely to be playing here.
Moods, Calle Uruguay. Reggae, reggaeton, salsa and other Latin music. A slightly older crowd and occasional live music.
Next, Av Balboa, T265-8746. One of the biggest commercial discos in the city – sweaty, pricey and popular.
Oz Bar and Lounge, Calle 53 Este, Marbella. Well established chill-out lounge bar with house nights and good DJs. Ladies drink free on Fri.
Panamá Viejo, T221-1268. Colombian restaurant, bar and disco. Open 24 hrs.
Unplugged, Calle 48, Bella Vista. Mon-Sat, rock 'n' roll club.
Voodoo Lounge, Plaza Pacífica, Punta Pacífica, T215-1581. Fri house music, live DJs Sat electronic music.
Wasabi Sushi Lounge, Marbella, T264-1863, Electronic music, live DJs, occasional retro and sushi. Wed is ladies nights, when the sangria flows for free.

Cabarets, casinos and gambling

Panamanians are big gamblers and there are more than 20 state-managed casinos in Panama City, some in the main hotels. If you fancy a punt, most offer blackjack, baccarat, poker, roulette and slot machines. Winnings are tax-free and paid without deductions.

Cinema and theatre

La Prensa and other newspapers publish daily programming (*cartelera*) of cultural events. Good range of cinemas including **Cine Balboa** near Steven's Circle, **MultiPlaza Mall** at Punta Pacífica, modern multi-screen **Albrook Mall**, www.albrookmall.com, and **Multi Centro** in Paitilla, have large multi-screen cinemas.
Anayansi Theatre, in the Atlapa Convention Centre, Vía Israel, San Francisco. Has a 3000-seat capacity, good acoustics, regular recitals and concerts.
Balboa Theatre, near Steven's Circle and post office in Balboa. Folkloric groups and jazz concerts sponsored by National Institute of Culture.

Cine Universitario, in the National University, T264-2737. US$1.50 for general public, shows international and classic movies, daily (not holidays) at 1700, 1900 and 2100.
Guild Theatre, in the Canal Area at Ancón. Amateur productions mainly in English.
Teatro Nacional, see page 875, occasionally has shows and performances. There are regular folklore sessions every other Sun and monthly National Ballet performances when not on tour. Check press for details.

O Shopping

Panama City *p872, maps p874, p876, p879 and p880*

Duty-free imported luxuries of all kinds are an attraction at the Zona Libre in Colón, but Panama City is a booming shopping centre where anything from crystal to cashmere may be cheaper than at their point of origin.

The smartest shops are along **Calle 50** (Av 4 Sur) in Campo Alegre, and **Vía España** in Bella Vista and El Cangrejo, but **Av Central** is cheaper and more popular.

Of the various commercial centres, with banking, entertainment and parking facilities, the largest is **Los Pueblos**, on Vía Tocumen, with buses leaving from 5 de Mayo, or take a taxi for US$5. It's a huge complex of mega-stores. **Multi Plaza** is a new mall located at Punta Pacífica, close to Atlapa, with department stores, shops, restaurants, banks and an 8-screen cinema. **Multi Centro** is at Punta Paitilla and easily accessible from the centre of town. **Albrook**, by the national bus terminal, has a very large mall that includes a cinema and food courts.

Arts and crafts

Traditional Panamanian *artesanía* includes *molas*; straw, leather and ceramic items; *chunga nawala* (palm fibre) canasters; the *pollera* circular dress, the *montuno* shirts (embroidered), the *chácara* (a popular bag or purse), the *chaquira* necklace made by Ngöbe-Buglé people, and jewellery.

Indigenous Darién (Embera) carvings of jungle birds and animals from cocobolo wood or *tagua* nut (small, extremely intricate, also *tagua* necklaces) make interesting souvenirs (from US$10 up to US$250 for the best, museum-quality pieces). The tourist office has a full list of *artesanía* shops, including those in the main hotels.

Artesanías Nacionales, indigenous co-ops selling a good selection direct from open-air outlets, can be found in Panamá Viejo, Canal Area at Balboa and along road to Miraflores Locks at Corozal (daily if not raining).

Flory Salzman on Vía Venetto at the back of El Panamá Hotel, T223-6963. The best place outside San Blas islands for *molas*, huge selection, sorted by theme, ask for discounts.

La Ronda, Calle 1a, Casco Viejo, www.pana malaronda.com. An attractive little store that sells a range of Panamanian *artesanías*. Convenient if you can't get out to the markets.

Mercardo Artesanal de Cinco de Mayo, behind the old Museo Antropológico Dra Reina. Stalls selling Kuna, Ngöbe-Buglé and Embera crafts as well as local Panamanian work. They also have a range of hammocks and artefacts from neighbouring countries.

Reprosa, Av Samuel Lewis y Calle 54, T269-0457. A unique collection of pre-Columbian gold artefacts reproduced in sterling silver vermeil; David and Norma Dickson make and sell excellent reproductions (**Panamá Guacas**, T266-6176).

Books and music

Exedra Books, Vía España and Vía Brasil. A small selection of English-language books, including numerous travel guides, but alas no Footprint. Pleasant coffeeshop inside.

Gran Morrison, Vía Espana, T269-2211, and 4 other locations around the city. Books, travel guides and magazines in English.

Legends, Calle 50, San Francisco, diagonal to the Iglesia de Guadalupe de Panamá, T270-0097. A cultural oasis – CDs, books, T-shirts and posters.

Librería Argosy, Vía Argentina north of Vía España, El Cangrejo, T223-5344. Very good selection in English, Spanish and French, also sells tickets for musical and cultural events. Recommended.

Librería Cultural Panameña, SA, Vía España y Calle 1, Perejil, T223-5628, www.libreria cultural.com. Mon-Fri 0900-1800, Sat 0900-1700. Excellent, mostly Spanish bookshop with obscure Panamanian prints as well as regular titles and very helpful staff.

National University Bookshop, on campus between Av Manuel Espinosa Batista and Vía Simón Bolívar, T223-3155. For an excellent range of specialist books on Panama, national authors, social sciences and history, Mon-Fri 0800-1600. Highly recommended. **Simón Bolívar Library** on campus has extensive Panamanian material, only for registered students but visitors engaged in special research can obtain a temporary permit from the director, Mon-Fri 0800-2000, Sat 0900-1300. **Smithsonian Tropical Research Institute** (see page 883), Edif Tupper, Av de los Mártires (opposite National Assembly), has a book-shop and the best English-language scientific library in the city, Mon-Fri 0800-1600.

Markets and supermarkets
Bargain hard as prices are extremely competitive. The **municipal market** is located in Santa Ana on Av B and Calle 15 Este. It is large, busy, well-stocked and reasonably ordered. Separate halls sell meat, vegetables, dried goods and cooked meals. For fish, head to the **Mercado de Mariscos**, nearby on Av Balboa, where you'll find an excellent restaurant upstairs.

Supermercado El Rey has a branch on Vía España just east of Hotel Continental, at El Dorado, and at several other locations. **Super 99**, **Farmacias Arrocha**, **Casa de la Carne** (expensive) and **Machetazo**, also a department store (on Av Central, Calidonia), are said to be the city's best.

Newspapers and magazines
The international edition of the *Miami Herald* is widely available at news stands and hotels, as are leading US papers and magazines. Spanish and English magazines at branches

of **Farmacias Arrocha**, **Super 99** and **Gago** supermarkets/drugstores.

▲ Activities and tours

Panama City *p872, maps p874, p876, p879 and p880*
Birding and wildlife
Advantage Tours, T6676-2466, www.advantagepanama.com. Founded by a group of biologists, this reputable operator offers a range of birding and wildlife tours, including expeditions to Darién. The guides are experienced and well trained and often have a background in biology or tourism. Sponsors of the Audubon Society.

Ancon Expeditions, Calle Elvira Méndez, next to **Marriott Hotel**, T269-9415, www.ancon expeditions.com. This is the tour operator for the environmental agency ANCON. Excellent guides and service, with especially recommended programmes in the Darién region (Cana Valley and Punta Patiño). They can also arrange programmes to most of Panama's wilderness areas. Darién treks and specialist birding programmes available.

Panama Audubon, Casa 2006-B, Llanos de Curundu, T232-5977, www.panamaaudubon. org. The excellent Panama Audubon Society is the country's foremost avian authority. They have been involved in the study, protection and promotion of Panama's birds for 35 years. They host regular events including lectures, workshops, field trips and tours.

Diving
See also individual listings for Bocas del Toro and Veraguas, both with excellent sites.
Panama Dive Adventure, Miguel Brostella Av, Edif Don Manuel 2a, opposite TGI Fridays, El Dorado, T279-1467, www.webpty.com/dive. Diving and technical courses, including deep diver. Tours to both coasts and sites including Portobelo, Bocas del Toro, Coiba and Isla Iguana. Equipment sales, rental, repair and service. They also have offices at **Coco Plum lodge** in Portobelo.

Panama Divers, T448-2293, www.panama divers.com. A very reputable dive operator that offers custom-made tours and promises 'Discovery Channel quality' underwater experiences. They travel to both Pacific and Caribbean coasts, including premier sites such as Isla Coiba. PADI certification to Divemaster level, with special photography and videography courses offered.

Scubapanama, Urbanización El Carmen, Av 6 Norte y Calle 62a No 29-B, T261-3841, www.scubapanama.com. Respected local dive operator. Offer dives in the Caribbean (near Portobelo), Pacific and the Canal. 1 option includes all 3 areas in 1 day. Longer trips can be arranged on request, including options in Islas Perlas and Isla Coiba. Given sufficient numbers all-inclusive multi-day trips to Isla Coiba start at around US$450-500. Certification courses available. Additional offices in Portobelo.

Fishing
Panama Canal Fishing, T6678-2653, www.panamacanalfishing.com. Fishing trips on Lago Gatún, where you can catch world-class peacock bass and snook. They claim to reel in 20-30 per person, as peacock bass is not native to the lake and their numbers are presently out of control.

Sailing
Panama Yacht Tours, T263-5044, www.panamayachttours.com. Private charters, canal transit, sunset cruises, parties and fishing trips, including services to both coasts.

San Blas Sailing, T314-1800, www.sanblas sailing.com. The first and oldest San Blas sailing charter offers crewed yacht tours of the Kuna Yala archipelago lasting from 4 to 21 days. They have an impressive fleet of monohulls and catamarans.

Tour operators
Adventuras Panama, Edificio Celma, oficina 3, El Paical, T260-0044, www.aventuraspanama.com. Specialist in hiking, rock climbing and canyoning. Very knowledgeable about Darién and the old colonial roads, and very active on looking for new opportunities. Many trips focus on the nearby Chagres National Park including the 'Jungle Challenge' which involves rappelling off a series of waterfalls.

Arian's Tours, Vía España, Plaza Concordia, oficina 143A, T213-1172, www.arianstours pty.com. This agency offers a wide range of cultural and ecological tours including birdwatching, visits to indigenous communities, night tours of Panama City, hiking in national parks and dolphin observation.

EcoCircuitos, Hotel Country Inn and Suites, ground floor, Amador, T314-0068, www.ecocircuitos.com. Expertly run with conservation and sustainability an utmost priority. Good range of creative tours include hiking, diving, cultural exchange and educational programs. Close ties to Panama's

only ecotourism organization, APTSO. One of the best and highly recommended. **EcoMargo Tours**, Punta Paitilla Mall (Paitilla Business Plaza), Av Italia, T264-8888, www.margotours.com. Specializes in ecotourism for small groups with an emphasis on using local guides. Professional and well-established with over 30 years' experience. They can also book various lodges and excursions.

Panama Pete Adventures, Av Miguel Brostella, Plaza Camino de Cruces No 35, near Country Inn & Suites El Dorado, T231-1438, www.panamapeteadventures.com. All the adventure options available in Panama, including biking, hiking, caving, fishing and kayaking.

Panama Star Tours, Vía España 120, T265-7970, www.panamastar.com. Arranges itineraries and books accommodation throughout the country. Well-established and professional.

⊖ Transport

Panama City *p872, maps p874, p876, p879 and p880*

Air

International flights Tocumen International Airport (PTY), 27 km, www.tocumenpanama.aero. Official taxi fare is US$25 to or from Panama City, maximum 2 passengers in same party, US$14 each sharing with 1 other, or US$10 per person if you share making it a *colectivo*. US$2 extra if you go by the toll road – much quicker. Bargaining is possible with regular cabs but not with tourist taxis at the airport.

From airport to city, walk out of the terminal and across the main road to the bus shelter. Another option is to walk 300 m to the traffic circle where there is a bus shelter (safe but hot during the day). For about US$3 (should only be US$1.20) driver takes you by Panamá Viejo, just off the main airport road.

Buses to the airport are marked 'España-Tocumen', 1 hr, US$0.35, but if going at a busy time, eg in the morning rush hour, allow 1½-3 hrs. Express buses leave from Av Justo Arosemana, just off Plaza 5 de Mayo.

There is a 24-hr **left-luggage** office near the **Budget** car rental desk for US$1 per article per day (worth it, since theft in the departure lounge is common). The official IPAT tourist office at the airport remains open to meet late flight arrivals. There are duty-free shops at the airport with a wide selection and good prices. Most facilities are found in upper level departure area **Banco Nacional de Panamá**, **Cable & Wireless** office for international phone, fax and internet access); car rental is downstairs at Arrivals.

Airline offices Aerolíneas Argentinas, Vía Brasil y Av Ramón Arias, T269-3815; **AeroMéxico**, Av 1BNorte, El Cangrejo, T263-3033; **Air France**, Calle Abel Bravo y 59 Obarrio T269-7381; **Alitalia**, Calle Alberto Navarro, T269-2161; **American Airlines**, Calle 50 Plaza New York, T204-8999; **Avianca**, Calle 50, Edificio Solendeg, 263-3060; **Aviatur**, T315-0311; **Cathy Pacific**, Av 1-B Norte, El Cangrejo, T263-3033; **Continental**, Av Balboa y Av 4, Ed Galerías Balboa, Planta Baja, T263-9177; **Copa**, Av Justo Arosemana y Calle 39, T217-2672; **Cubana**, Av Justo Arosmena, T227-2291; **Delta**, Edif World Trade Centre, Calle 53E, Marbella, T214-8118; **Grupo Taca**, Centro Comercial Camino de Cruces, Local 2, Vía Ricardo J Alfaro, T360-2093; **Iberia**, Av Balboa y Calle 43, T227-2322; **KLM**, Av Balboa y Calle Uruguay, Edif Plaza Miramar, T264-6395; **LAB**, Calle 50 No 78, Ed Bolivia, T263-6771; **LanChile**, Calle 72, San Francisco, T226-7119; **Lufthansa**, Calle Abel Bravo y 59 Obarrio, Ed Eurocentro, T269-1549; **Mapiex Aéreo**, T315-0344; **United Airlines**, Bella Vista, L-1, T225-6519.

Domestic flights These operate from Marcos A Gelabert airport at Albrook in the Canal Area. There is no convenient bus service, taxis charge US$2-3. Good self-service café especially for fried breakfast before early flight to San Blas. **Aeroperlas**, reservations T315-7500, www.aeroperlas.com, operates daily flights to 17 destinations throughout the country. **Air Panama**, T316-9000, www.flyair panama.com, have flights to 22 destinations, including San José in Costa Rica. **Mapiex Aéreo**, sales T315-0344, www.mapiex.com, operates private charters to several destinations throughout the country including many Darién outposts. Rodolfo Causadias of **Transpasa**, T226-0842, is an experienced pilot for photographic work.

Bus

Local Most buses in urban areas are second-hand US school buses brightly painted in fanciful designs, but in poor condition. They are known as *diablos rojos* (red devils) and are notorious for roaring engines and aggressive drivers. For better or worse, they are gradually being replaced by modern Metrobuses. Most outbound (east) buses travel along Av Perú, through Bella Vista, before fanning out to their various destinations. Inbound (west) buses travel along Vía España and Av Central through the Calidonia shopping district. The basic fare is US$0.25, usually paid to the driver upon descending; if there is a fare box, deposit upon entering. To stop at the next authorized stop, call out '*parada*' to the driver.

Long distance All buses apart from the Orange buses leave from the clean and efficient bus terminal in Albrook, near the domestic airport. Taxi US$3 to centre. Facilities at the vast terminal include ATMs, internet access, clothes shops, luggage shops, bakeries and basic restaurants.

Most long-distance buses are fairly modern and in good condition. Except for the longest routes, most are 24-seater 'Coaster'-type minibuses. Offices are arranged in a long line from right to left in the terminal.

Orange buses to all **Canal Area** destinations (Balboa, Miraflores, Paraíso, Kobbe, etc) leave every 1-2 hrs from SACA terminal near Plaza 5 de Mayo; from the Plaza, walk past the National Assembly tower and turn left.

From the **Gran Terminal de Transporte**, Albrook (T232-5803): **Bocas del Toro**, 0800 (Mon, Fri, Sat, Sun) and 2000, 12 hrs, US$24, or go to David and change; Chame/San Carlos, every 15 mins, 0530-2000, US$2.70; **Chitre**, hourly, 0600-2300, 3½ hrs, US$7.50; **Colón**, every 30 mins, 0330-2130, 2 hrs, US$2-2.50; **David**, hourly, 0530-0000, US$12.50-15; Darién, 4 daily, US$14; El Valle, every ½ hr, 0445-2100, 2 hrs, US$3.50; **Las Tablas**, hourly, 0600-1900, 5 hrs, US$8; **Paso Canoas (border with Costa Rica)**, 10 daily, 8 hrs, US$14; **Penonomé**, every 15 mins, 0445-2245, 2¼ hrs, US$4.50; **Santiago**, every ½ hr, 0600-2300, 3½ hrs, US$7.50.

International Buses going north through Central America get booked up so reserve a seat in advance and never later than the night before departure. **Ticabus**, in the Gran Terminal de Transporte, Albrook, T314-6385, www.ticabus.com, run a/c buses to **San José**, daily at 1100, arriving at 0200 the next day, US$35 one-way (but check times and prices which change at regular intervals); continuing to **Managua**, US$55; **Tegucigalpa**, US$75, and on as far as **Tapachula** on the Mexico–Guatemala Pacific coast border, US$124, via **Guatemala City**, US$105 (3½ days, overnight in Managua and El Salvador). Tickets are refundable; they pay on the same day, minus 15%. **Panaline** to **San José** from the Albrook Gran Terminal, T314-6383, leaves daily at 2200 arriving at 1530 the following day, US$25. You can also travel with **Padafront**, T314-6263, www.padafront.com, Panama City–Paso Canoas then change to **Tracopa** or other Costa Rican buses for San José and other destinations en route to the Costa Rican capital.

Car

Several major downtown arteries become one-way during weekday rush hours, eg Av 4 Sur/Calle 50, one-way heading west

0600-0900, east 1600-1900. The Puente de las Américas can be used only to go into or out of town depending on time and day, mostly weekends; these directions are not always clearly signed.

Car rental At the airport: Avis, T238-4056; Budget, T238-4068; Dollar, T238-4032; Hertz, T238-4081 and National, T238-4144.
In El Cangrejo: Avis, Vía Venetto, T264-0722; Barriga, Edif Wonaga 1 B,.Calle D, T269-0221; Budget, T263-9190; Dollar, T269-7542. Gold, Calle 55, T264-1711; Hertz, Hotel Sheraton, T226-4077 ext 6202, Calle 50, T264-1111; El Cangrejo T263-6663; International, Vía Venetto, T264-4540.

Taxi
Service is generally good, but drivers can be scarce during peak hours and otherwise temperamental. Many have little clue where many streets are – it's good to have a rough idea of the address location. Voluntary sharing is common but not recommended after dark. If a taxi already has a passenger, the driver will ask your destination to see if it coincides with the other passenger's. If you do not wish to share, waggle your index finger or say 'No, gracias'. Similarly, if you are in a taxi and the driver stops for additional passengers, you may refuse politely. Unfortunately, overcharging is very common and official fares are based on an elusive zone system. You should pay around US$2 to travel from Bella Vista to San Felipe, but they will ask for more if you look like a tourist. Panamanians rarely tip. Hourly hire, advised for touring dubious areas, US$10 per hr. Radio taxis summoned by telephone are highly recommended. They are listed in yellow pages under 'Taxis'. Add US$0.40 to fare for pickup. 'Tourist taxis' at major hotels (aged, large American cars with 'SET' number plates) have a separate rate structure: they are more expensive than those you flag down.

Train
A train runs daily from Corozal Passenger Station in Panama City to **Colón** US$22 one way, US$44 return, 0715, returns 1715, 1¼ hrs. Turn up on the day or book in advance through tour operators. More details available at www.panarail.com. A cab to the station from Panama City costs about US2.50.

Isla Taboga p884
Boat
Taboga is reached in 1-1½ hrs with **Calypso Queen** services departing from Isla Naos on the Amador Causeway (check the times in advance, T314-1730); taxi from Panama City about US$7. From Panama City to Taboga: Mon, Wed, Fri, 0830 and 1500; Tue and Thu, 0830; Sat and Sun, 0800, 1030 and 1600. From Taboga to Panama City: Mon, Wed, Fri 0930 and 1630; Tue and Thu 1630; Sat and Sun, 0900, 1500 and 1700. Return fare US$12.

Islas Perlas p885
Air
Aeroperlas and Air Panama operate daily services between **Contadora** and **Panama City** (see Domestic flights, above).

ⓘ Directory

Panama City p872, maps p874, p876, p879 and p880
Banks
See also Money, page 870. Try to avoid 15th and last working day of the month – pay days. Panamanian banks' hours vary, but most open Mon-Fri 0800-1500, Sat 0800-1200. Visa T264-0988; MasterCard T263-5221; Diners T263-8195. Algemene Bank Nederland changes Thomas Cook TCs. American Express, Agencia de Viajes Fidanque, Av Balboa, Torre Banco BBVA, Piso 9, T225-5858, Mon-Fri 0800-1715, does not exchange TCs. International Service Center, T001-800-111-0006. ATM for withdrawals at Banco Continental near hotel of same name. Banistmo, Calle 50, Mon-Fri 0800-1530, Sat

0900-1200, changes TCs, no commission on AMEX, US$5 per transaction for other TCs. **Banco General** takes American Express, Bank of America and Thomas Cook TCs, 1% commission, minimum US$2 per transaction. Branch at Av Central y 4 Sur (Balboa) can be used for cash advances from ATMs on Visa. **Bank of America**, Vía José de la Cruz Herrera, Calle 53 Este, no commission on own TCs, US$0.10 tax. You can buy AMEX TCs at **Banco Mercantil del Istmo** on Vía España (they also give cash advances on MasterCard). **Banco Nacional de Panamá**, Vía España opposite the Hotel Continental, T205-2000, changes AMEX TCs with 1% commision. **Banco Sudameris** will also change Thomas Cook TCs. **Chase Manhattan Bank**, US$0.65 commission on each TC, Visa advances. **Citibank** has plenty of ATMs for cash withdrawals for its own debit or credit card holders, also Visa cash advances. **Lloyds Bank**, Calle Aquilino de la Guardia y Calle 48, Bella Vista, T263-6277, T263-8693 for foreign exchange, offers good rates for sterling (the only bank which will change sterling cash, and only if its sterling limit has not been exhausted). It is possible to change South American currencies (poor rates) at **Panacambios**, ground floor, Plaza Regency, behind Adam's Store, Vía España, near the Banco Nacional de Panamá and opposite Hotel Riande Continental (it also has postage stamps for collectors).

Embassies and consulates
Canada, World Trade Center, Galería Comercial, 1st floor, Calle 53e, Marbella, T264-9731; **Chile**, Vía España, Edif Banco de Boston, T223-9748, 0900-1200, 1400-1600; **Colombia**, World Trade Center, Calle 53e, Marbella, T264-9266, 0800-1300; **Costa Rica**, Calle Samuel Lewis, T264-2980, 0900-1600; **El Salvador**, Av Manuel Espinoza Batista, Edif Metropolis 4A, T223-3020, 0900-1300; **France**, Plaza de Francia, Zona 1, T211-6200; **Germany**, Edif Bank of America, Calle 50 y 53, T263-7733, 0900-1700; **Guatemala**, Edif Altamira, 9th floor, 9-25, Vía Argentina,

T269-3475, 0800-1300; **Honduras**, Av Balboa, Bay Mall, T264-5513, 0900-1400; **Israel**, Edif Grobman, Calle MM Icaza, 5th floor, PO Box 6357, T264-8022; **Italy**, Av Balboa Edif Banco Exterior, T225-8948, 0900-1200; **Mexico**, Edif Credicorp, Calle 50, T263-4900, 0800-1200; **Netherlands**, Altos de Algemene Bank, Calle MM Icaza, 4, T264-7257, 0830-1300, 1400-1630; **Nicaragua**, Edif de Lessep's, 4th floor, Calle Manuel María Icaza, T264-8225; **Norway**, Calle La Boca, Balboa, T228-1103, 0900-1230, 1430-1630; **Spain**, Plaza Porras, entre Av Cuba y Av Perú, Calle 33A, T227-5472, 0900-1300; **Sweden**, consulate at Av Balboa y Calle Uruguay, T264-3748, 0900-1200, 1400-1600; **Switzerland**, Av Samuel Lewis y Calle Gerardo Ortega, Edif Banco Central Cancellería, 4th floor, T390-6330, PO Box 499 (Zona 9A), 0845-1145; **UK**, MMG Tower, Calle 53, Zona 1, T269-0866; **USA**, PAS Building 783, Demetrio Basilio Lakas Av Clayton, T207-7000, http://panama.us embassy.gov ; **Venezuela**, Edif HSBC, 5th floor, Av Samuel Lewis, T269-1244, 0830-1100.

Immigration
Migración y Naturalización, Av Cuba (2 Sur) y Calle 29, T225-8925; visa extensions and exit permits issued Mon-Fri 0800-1530. **Ministerio de Hacienda y Tesoro**, Av Perú/ Calle 36, T227-4879, for tax compliance certificate (*paz y salvo*) required for exit visa (*permiso de salida*) if you stay more than 30 days. **Customs** for renewal of permits and obtaining exit papers for vehicles at Paitilla airport.

Internet
Internet cafés are everywhere in Panama City, but are especially concentrated in Vía Veneto and the commercial centre around Vía España. Rates can be as low as US$0.50 per hr. New places are constantly opening, with many offering perks to clients, such as free coffee.

Language schools
ILERI, 42G Vía La Amistad, El Dorado T/F392-4086, www.ileripanama.com. Small school

offering homestays, US$450 per week 1-to-1 tuition. **Spanish Panama School**, Vía Argentina, T213-3121, www.spanish panama.com. Group instruction in the heart of Cangrejo. Mostly good reports, but ensure you are placed at the correct level.

Laundry
Lavamático Lavarápido, Calle 7 Central No 7-45, ½ block from Plaza Catedral, Mon-Sat 0800-2000, Sun 0900-1400. Many around Plaza Catedral; wash and dry US$2. **Lavandería y Lavamático América**, Av Justo Arosemana and Calle 27. Self service wash and dry only US$1.50. Very convenient for the Calidonia hotels.

Medical services
Dentist Balboa Dental Clinic, El Prado, Balboa, T228-0338, good, fair price. **Dr Daniel Wong, Clínica Dental Marbella**, Edif Alfil (ground floor), near Centro Comercial Marbella, T263-8998. Dr D Lindo, T223-8383, very good but fix price before treatment.

Hospitals and clinics The US Gorgas Army Community Hospital has closed and US medical facilities have moved to the Howard Air Force Base, across the Puente de Las Américas. Private clinics charge high prices; normally visitors are treated at either the **Clínica San Fernando**, T305-6300, or the **Clínica Paitilla**, T265-8800, which both have hospital annexes. For inoculations buy the vaccine at a chemist and ask them to recommend a clinic; plenty in La Exposición around Parque Belisario Porras.

Post
There is no home postal delivery service in Panama. Recipients either have a post office box (*apartado*), or receive mail via General Delivery/Poste Restante (*Entrega General*).

The new main post office is close to Casco Viejo at the west end of Av Balboa at Av B, opposite the Mercado de Mariscos, Mon-Fri 0700-1745, Sat 0700-1645; 'Poste Restante' items are held for a month. Official name and zone must be included in the address: **Main Post office**: 'Zona 1, Central, Av Balboa opposite Mercado de Mariscos'; **Calle 30 East/Av Balboa**: 'Zona 5, La Exposición'; **El Dorado Shopping Centre**, Tumba Muerto: 'Zona 6A, El Dorado'; **Vía España, Bella Vista** (in front of Piex store): 'Zona 7, Bella Vista'. Parcels sent 'poste restante' are delivered either to **Encomiendas Postales Transístmicas** at the El Dorado Centro Comercial or the main post office if there is no duty to pay on the goods. The post office operates a courier system called **EMS** to most Central and South American countries, Europe, US and some Asian countries. Packages up to 20 kg: 2 to 3 days to USA (500 g documents to Miami US$13); 3 to 4 days Europe US$20; Asia US$25. Also private courier services, eg **UPS**, Edif Fina, Calle 49, El Cangrejo, to London or Paris, 3-4 days, US$30; **Jet Express (Federal Express)**, Edif Helga, Vía España y Av 4 Sur/Calle 50, 500 g to Miami, 2 days, US$19.

Telephone
Cable & Wireless has its main office in Vía España, on the ground floor of Banco Nacional building. They offer excellent but expensive international telephone, telex, fax and modem (use Bell 212A type) facilities. Collect calls to 21 countries, dial T106. For cost of phone cards and international calls, see Essentials, page 45. Local calls in Panama City, US$0.10 for 3 mins, US$0.05 for each additional min; anywhere else in the country, US$0.15 per min.

Panama Canal area

→ Colour map 5, B1.

Whether travelling through the Canal, or just standing at its side, watching the vast ocean-going vessels rise and fall as they pass through the locks, it's hard not to be impressed. Most Panameños will insist that you visit Miraflores Locks, with good reason, for the viewing platform here supplies unrivalled views of the colossal canal operations. But if it's scale you're after, the Gatún Locks near Colón are truly gigantic, with ships passing directly under the viewing platform. Traversing the canal by boat is another option for experiencing the scale of this world wonder. But the canal isn't all ships and locks. The immense quantities of water required for its day-to-day operation are supplied by the vast, verdant rainforests skirting its banks. Awesome rivers, fascinating indigenous tribes and scores of colourful birds find their home in these protected forests, some of the most accessible wilderness in the Americas.
▸▸ For listings, see pages 903.

Background

The Panama Canal was created from the artificial, river-fed Lago Gatún, 26 m above sea level, which supplies the water for the lock system to function. Ships sail across the lake after having been raised from sea level by a series of locks on either the Atlantic or the Pacific approach. They are then lowered by the locks on the opposite side. As the crow flies, the distance across the isthmus is 55 km. From shore to shore the Canal is 67.5 km, or 82 km (44.08 nautical miles) from deep water to deep water. It has been widened to 150 m in most places. The trip normally takes eight or nine hours for the 30 to 40 ships passing through each day. On the Atlantic side there is a normal variation of 30 cm between high and low tides, and on the Pacific of about 380 cm, rising sometimes to 640 cm.

From the Pacific, the Canal channel goes beneath the Puente de las Américas and passes the port of Balboa. The waterway has to rise 16.5 m to Lago Miraflores. The first stage of the process is the Miraflores Locks, 1.5 km before the lake. A taxi to the locks from the city costs US$10. At the far end of the lake, ships are raised another 9.5 m by the single-step Pedro Miguel Locks, after which the 13 km Gaillard, or Culebra Cut is entered, a narrow rock defile leading to Lago Gatún. Opposite Miraflores Locks, there is a swing bridge. Gaillard Cut can be seen from Contractor's Hill, on the west side, reached by car (no buses) by turning right 3 km past Puente de las Américas, passing Cocolí, then turning as signed. The road beyond Cocolí goes on to Posa, where there are good views of the locks, the cut and former Canal Zone buildings.

Panama Canal Railway

ⓘ *Corozal One West, T317-6070, www.panarail.com.*

The Panama Canal Railway first opened in 1855 under auspices of the Panama Rail-Road company. Its function was to carry California gold rush prospectors to the Pacific Coast. Today the railway runs parallel to the canal, carrying tourists and Free Zone executives between Panama City and the Caribbean port of Colón. This is a great way to experience the misty early morning canal. You'll traverse the isthmus in just one hour, but the return service from Colón doesn't depart until several hours later, giving you time to briefly explore the coast. ▸▸ *See Transport, page 903.*

Parque Nacional Camino de Cruces

Skirting the eastern banks of the Panama Canal, the Parque Nacional Camino de Cruces, on the Gaillard Highway (www.anam.gob.pa) was established in 1992 to consolidate the protected areas of the Parque Nacional Soberanía to the north and the Parque Metropolitano to the south. The park derives its name, 'Way of Crosses', from the fragments of old Spanish gold trails hidden within its forest enclaves. Some of these old cobblestone paths are now partially restored and trails here are generally well maintained. They include the famous Las Cruces Trail, which travels north into Parque Nacional Soberanía and as far as the Río Chagres, where plundered treasure was once loaded onto boats and steered to the Caribbean. The park is particularly resplendent during the flowering months of April and May. The landscape rises and falls with gentle hills, home to oak, cotton and palm trees.

Miraflores Locks

Miraflores Visitor Centre ① *Mon-Sun, 0900-1630, www.pancanal.com, US$8 entrance to the museum and Canal viewing platform, US$5 for platform only*, was constructed as part of Centenial celebrations at a cost is US$6 million. The large observation deck supplies superb views of transiting vessels and enthusiastic commentary in English and Spanish. The museum is spread over four floors with captivating exhibitions on global trade, local ecology, engineering and the history of the canal. The entrance price also includes a documentary film in English and Spanish, and there is a café and restaurant. This is the easiest and most popular way to experience the canal. To get there from Panama City, take the Gamboa bus from the SACA terminal (see transport). A taxi will cost around US$10 one-way from the city.

Pedro Miguel Locks

These locks lie several kilometres north of Miraflores and offer a poor man's experience of the canal. It's free to watch the ships at these one-chamber locks, but you won't get anything like the views at Miraflores. A taxi from Panama City costs US$12 one-way.

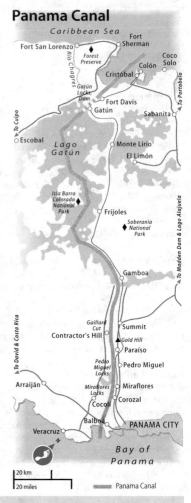

Panama Canal

Caribbean Sea

Fort San Lorenzo
Fort Sherman
Forest Preserve
Coco Solo
Colón
Cristóbal
Río Chagres
Gatún Locks, Dam
Fort Davis
Gatún
Sabanita
To Cuipo
To Portobelo
Escobal
Lago Gatún
Monte Lirio
El Limón
Isla Barro Colorado National Park
Frijoles
Soberanía National Park
To Madden Dam & Lago Alajuela
Gamboa
To David & Costa Rica
Gaillard Cut
Contractor's Hill
Summit
Gold Hill
Paraíso
Pedro Miguel Locks
Pedro Miguel
Arraiján
Miraflores Locks
Miraflores
Cocolí
Corozal
Balboa
PANAMA CITY
Veracruz
Bay of Panama
20 km
20 miles
Panama Canal

Parque Municipal Summit

ⓘ *Carretera Gaillard towards Gamboa, 20 mins from Panama City, T232-4854, 0900-1700, US$1.*

Parque Municipal Summit is home to an impressive botanical collection with 150 species from Asia, Africa and the Americas, including the world's finest palm collection. Their zoo shelters 40 species of animals, all endemic to Panama, including the majestic harpy eagle – Panama's national bird. The park has been actively involved in conservation for many years, working closely with organizations such as the Smithsonian Tropical Research Institute and Houston zoo. They sometimes need volunteers for environmental education and other tasks.

Parque Nacional Soberanía

ⓘ *Carretera Gaillard, T232-4192, www.anam.gob.pa, 0600-1700, US$3.*

The exuberant rainforest habitat of the Parque Nacional Soberanía contains over 1300 species of plant, 100 species of mammal, 55 species of amphibian, 79 species of reptile and over 500 species of bird. Resident fauna include deer, agoutis, jaguars, peccaries, monkeys, sloths, snakes, caimans and abundant vociferous frogs. It is one of the finest bird observation areas in the world. The park has several fabulous trails. The **Plantation Trail** begins at the turn-off for the Canopy Tower (on the highway to Gamboa) and follows an old plantation road built in 1910. It's a moderate, 6.5-km trail that concludes at the intersection for the **Camino de Cruces Trail**. The park's most famous and popular trail, however, is the **Pipeline Road**, accessed from the Carretera Gaillard running along the canal, just north of Gamboa, the old American dredging port. The now-abandoned coast-to-coast pipeline was built during the Second World War by the US and hidden in the jungle as a guarantee of oil supply should the canal be sabotaged. Birdlife here is very prolific, particularly early in the morning. A well-qualified guide will really bring your experience of this world-class trail to life. Some 1.6 km from the entrance to the Pipeline Road you'll pass the **Rainforest Discovery Centre** ⓘ *premium hours 0600-1000, US$20 entrance; normal hours 1000-1600, US$15*, which has a superb observation tower with views over the canopy.

Parque Nacional Chagres

The Parque Nacional Chagres is particularly wild and rugged, punctuated by dramatic valleys, rocky mountains, rivers and dense tracts of vegetation, including rare elfin forests at the higher altitudes. The park is also home to Lago Alajuela, formerly Madden Lake, an artificial reservoir formed by the damming of the Río Chagres. It is used to generate electricity as well as maintain the level of Lago Gatún, vital for the functioning of the canal. The entire Chagres area has great potential for jungle adventure. Multi-day trekking trips into wildlife rich parts of the forest can be arranged with companies in Panama City, as can tubing, rafting and abseiling within the watershed – see Tour operators, page 893. The park can be reached by bus from Panama City, first go to Las Cumbres and then take a second bus to **Caimitillo**. After that it is a 3½- to four-hour walk to **Nuevo Caimitillo**. Dugout canoes offer transportation to Emberá indigenous villages at Parara Puru (15 minutes) and Embera Drua (30-40 minutes). The Emberá in this area are friendly and seem to be coping well with the impacts of tourism – they also make excellent quality crafts which are sold at very reasonable prices. It may be possible to stay within the village of Parara Puro for a small fee and with the permission of community, giving a greater insight into village life. Also consider employing Emberá guides/assistants to spread the benefits of tourism. The Camino Real passes through the park if you want to follow in the footsteps of the old Spanish colonists.

Barro Colorado Nature Monument
ⓘ *Smithsonian Tropical Research Institute, Tupper Building in Ancón, US$70, T212-8000, www.stri.org. Trips last 4-6 hrs, including boat, audio-visual display and lunch, but take water. Prior booking is absolutely essential. Make arrangements a few weeks in advance with the Institute in Ancón (bring ID). Boats depart from Dredging Division dock at Gamboa (be on time, they won't wait).*

Lago Gatún was created with the damming of the Río Chagres at Gatún and now supplies the water necessary for the day-to-day functioning of the canal. Inside the lake is **Barro Colorado Island**, to which many animals fled as the basin slowly filled. The island is a formally protected area called the Barro Colorado Nature Monument and has been a site of scientific research for over 70 years. The **Smithsonian Tropical Research Institute** (see page 883) accept limited numbers of visitors to their research facilities. The excursion is highly recommended for seeing wildlife, especially monkeys, and includes transportation to the island, a lecture, buffet lunch and walk around a guided trail with over 50 points of interest. You must reserve your place at least two weeks in advance. Visitors without permits will be turned away on arrival.

Gatún Locks
On the Caribbean side of the canal, 10 km southwest of Colón, are the Gatún Locks (*Esclusas de Gatún*) with their neat, attendant town. The **observation point** ⓘ *daily 1000-1630*, is perhaps the best spot in the Canal area for photographing the passage of ships. The most magnificent of the Canal's locks, Gatún integrates all three lock 'steps' on the Atlantic side, raising or lowering ships to or from 26 m in one operation. The flights are in duplicate to allow ships to pass in opposite directions simultaneously. Passage of the locks takes about one hour. A bus from Colón to Gatún Locks costs US$1.

◉ Panama Canal area listings

For Sleeping and Eating price codes and other relevant information, see Essentials pages 31-33.

⊜ Sleeping

LL-L Canopy Tower Ecolodge, signposted from just beyond Summit Gardens on the Transisthmus Hwy, T264-5720, www.canopy tower.com. A hotel and ecolodge that rises to the rainforest canopy in a converted old communications tower. 7 quirky rooms with private bath, price includes meals and guided walks. Some cheaper rooms available off season. Excellent for wildlife and highly recommended.

LL-L Gamboa Rainforest Resort, on the hill above Gamboa overlooking the Chagres River, T314-5000, www.gamboaresort.com. This looming green and white resort is built on old American golf course. There is an ancient tree dividing the complex. Cheapest rooms are in apartments formerly occupied by US dredging engineers. An aerial tramway runs silently through the canopy to a mirador with good views. Tour available to non-residents.

▲ Activities and tours

Canal tours

Several agencies in Panama City offer boat tours of the canal. Most find that a partial transit through Miraflores and Pedro Miguel locks is enough to appreciate the operation.

Canal and Bay Tours, T209-2000, www. canalandbaytours.com. Full transit of the canal on the first Sat of the month, 0730, adults US$165, children US$75. Partial transit every Sat, 0930, adults US$115, children US$75. They also run various tours to Panama Bay, including an evening tour with bar and calypso.

Panama Marine Adventures, T226-8917, www.pmatours.net. Full transit of the canal once a month, adults US$165, children US$75, call for schedule. Partial transit Thu, Fri and Sat, Jan-Mar; and Sat, Apr-Dec; adults US$115, children US$65.

⊖ Transport

Bus

All the major Panama Canal destinations including Miraflores Locks, Summit, Gamboa and the Parque Nacional Soberanía are served by orange buses from **Panama City**, which traverse the Gaillard highway. They depart from the **SACA** terminal next to Plaza 5 de Mayo, every 2 hrs, 0500-2230, US$0.35-1. For Miraflores, ask the drive to drop you at 'Las Esclusas de Miraflores', from where it's a 10-min walk. A taxi to the locks is US$10.

Car

A good way to experience the Panama Canal area is to rent a car. See rental agencies, page 896.

Train

The famous Panama Canal Railway runs daily from Corozal Passenger Station in Panama City to **Colón**, US$22 one way, US$44 return, departs 0715, returns 1715, 1 hr. Turn up on the day or book in advance through tour operators. More details available at www.panarail.com. A cab to the station from Panama City costs about US$3. The outdoor viewing platform is great for feeling the rush of wind and jungle.

Central Caribbean coast

Panama's central Caribbean coast has always been a vital port of call for goods and persons moving between the Old World and New. Waves of Spanish conquistadors, colonialists, gold prospectors and canal workers have all passed through this transitory and historically fascinating region. Tourism on the Central Caribbean coast is nascent. Economically, the region is far less developed than its Pacific cousin and few visitors venture beyond its colonial ruins. Press on, though, and you'll discover a swathe of protected forests and dive sites. The beaches are scant but pleasant nonetheless.

The ramshackle slum of Colón, with its attendant port of Cristóbal, forms the northern terminus of the Panama Canal and railroad, where tax-free goods are traded in an enormous Free Zone – just like the great gold fairs of colonial times. East and west of Colón, a string of handsome fortifications recall the era of piracy, when buccaneers such as Sir Francis Drake were drawn to the great wealth that passed through on its way to Spain. They include the UNESCO World Heritage Site of San Lorenzo, and the enigmatic Portobelo, with its old canons pointing wistfully over the sea. The central Caribbean coast has a strong Afro-Caribbean flavour, with interesting communities of Congos – the descendants of escaped African slaves – inhabiting the towns and villages along its shores. The population of Isla Grande are particularly welcoming and lay on a good party at the weekend.
▶▶ *For listings, see pages 909-912.*

Colón and Cristóbal → *For listings, see pages 909-912.*

Landfall on the Caribbean side for the passage of the Canal is made at the twin cities of Cristóbal and Colón, the one merging into the other almost imperceptibly and both built on Manzanillo Island at the entrance of the Canal in Bahía Limón. The island has now been connected with the mainland. Colón was founded in 1852 as the terminus of the railway across the isthmus; Cristóbal came into being as the port of entry for the supplies used in building the Canal.

Avenida del Frente is the main commercial street and is quite active but has lost its past splendour: the famous Bazar Francés closed in 1990, the curio shops are not noteworthy and the railway station stands virtually deserted except for the movement of a few freight trains. Nevertheless, there is talk of declaring the whole of Colón a free zone (the Zona Libre being the city's main attraction), the authorities are moving to give the city new housing and employment (residential estates such as 'Rainbow City' and 'Puerto Escondido' are being extended on the landward side to relocate entire neighbourhoods of slums), and the demands on Cristóbal's busy port facilities (200 million tons of cargo a year) continue to increase. It is to be hoped that, if these plans are realized, Colón may become a pleasant place again.

Ins and outs

Safety Mugging, even in daylight, is a real threat in both Colón and Cristóbal. The situation has improved now that the two main streets and some of the connecting ones are guarded by police officers; you are still strongly recommended not to stray too far from their range of sight. Keep a few dollars handy for muggers if the worst happens.

Sights

The French-influenced **cathedral** ⓘ *C 5 y Av Herrera, 1400-1745 daily*, has an attractive altar and good stained-glass windows. The **Washington Hotel** ⓘ *on the seafront at the north end of the town*, is the town's most historic structure and is worth a look. The original

Colón

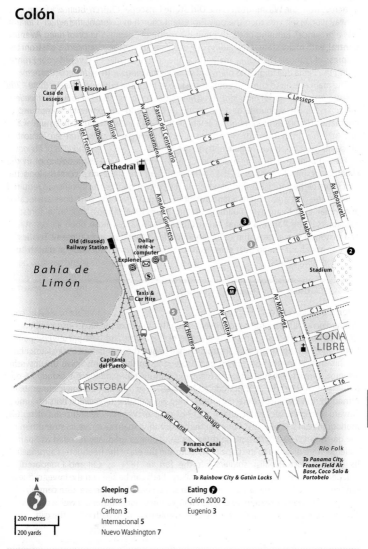

Casa de Lesseps

Episcopal

C1

C2

C3

C4

C5

C6

C7

C Lesseps

Cathedral

Av del Frente

Av Balboa

Av Bolívar

Av Justo Arosemena

Paseo del Centenario

Amador Guerrero

Old (disused)
Railway Station

Dollar rent-a-computer

Explonet

C8

C9 ❸

❸

C10

Av Santa Isabel

Av Roosevelt

Bahía de Limón

Taxis &
Car Hire

❺

Av Herrera

Av Central

Av Meléndez

C11

C12

C13

Stadium ❷

❷

Capitanía
del Puerto

CRISTOBAL

Calle Canal

Calle Tobago

Panama Canal
Yacht Club

C14

ZONA
LIBRE

C15

C16

Río Folk

To Rainbow City & Gatún Locks

To Panama City,
France Field Air
Base, Coco Solo &
Portobelo

N

200 metres

200 yards

Sleeping 🛏
Andros **1**
Carlton **3**
Internacional **5**
Nuevo Washington **7**

Eating 🍴
Colón 2000 **2**
Eugenio **3**

wooden hotel was built in 1850 for employees of the Railroad Company. President Taft ordered a new fireproof hotel to be built in 1912 and the old one was later razed. Although remodelled a number of times, today's building, with its broad verandas, waving palms, splendid chandelier, plush carpets and casino, still conjures up a past age, while the café provides an excellent view of ships waiting to enter the Canal.

Across from the **Washington** is the **Old Stone Episcopal Church**, built in 1865 for the railway workers; it was then the only Protestant church in Colombia (of which Panama was a province). Running north through the centre of Colón is the palm-lined **Avenida Central**, with many statues (including one of *Columbus and the Indian Girl*, a gift from the Empress of France). The public market is at the corner of Calle 11. **Avenida del Frente**, facing the Bahía de Limón, has many old wooden buildings with wide verandas.

The main reason to come to Colón is to shop at the **Zona Libre** ⓘ *Mon-Fri 0800-1700 (a few places retail on Sat morning), if you have a car, pay a minder US$1 to watch it while in the zone.* It's the second-largest free zone in the world, an extensive compound of international stores and warehouses established in 1949 and surrounded by a huge wall – pick up a free map from hotels or tourist office showing who sells what. A passport or official ID must be shown to gain entry to the zone.

The 30-minute beach drive around Colón's perimeter is pleasant and cool in the evening; despite the slums at the south end there are some nice homes along the east shore of the peninsula. Permission from the Port Authority security officer is required to enter the port area, where agents for all the world's great shipping lines are located in colonial Caribbean-style buildings dating from 1914. Almost lost in a forest of containers is the **Panama Canal Yacht Club** ⓘ *T441-5882*, whose open-air restaurant and historically decorated bar offer very good food (seafood and Chinese). This is the place to ask about sailing boat charters to the Kuna Yala (see page 913) or shorter trips aboard visiting yachts.

West of Colón → *For listings, see pages 909-912.*

Fuerte San Lorenzo

Perched on a cliff-top promontory overlooking the mouth of the Río Chagres with great views of the coast, Fort San Lorenzo is one of the oldest and best-preserved Spanish fortifications in the Americas. Construction had begun the year before Drake launched a 23-ship attack on the post (1596) and proceeded up the Chagres in an unsuccessful attempt to reach Panama City. The following century, Morgan fought a bloody 11-day battle to take the fort as a prelude to his decisive swoop on Panamá Viejo in 1671. Although new defences were then built, they were unable to prevent British Admiral Edward Vernon's successful attack in 1740 (one of Vernon's cannon with the 'GR' monogram can still be seen). Engineer Hernández then spent seven years strengthening the garrison (1760-1767), but the threat to San Lorenzo gradually receded as Spanish galleons were diverted to the Cape Horn route and the era of the freebooters approached its end. The last Royalist soldiers left the fort in 1821 as Colombia declared its Independence from Spain. The earliest artillery sheds can be seen on the lower cliff level but most of the bulwarks, arched stone rooms and lines of cannon are 18th century. The site has undergone an extensive UNESCO renovation programme and is well worth a visit. There is a picnic area and a tiny beach is accessible by a steep path down the cliff.

Costa Abajo

There is no crossing of the Chagres at San Lorenzo. To continue down the Costa Abajo you have to return to the Gatún Dam and take the gravel road along the west side of the river, which winds its way through pristine forest to the coastal village of **Piña** and its kilometre-long beach. The road runs west along a steep and rocky shore to **Nuevo Chagres** and **Palmas Bellas**, quiet fishing resorts in coconut palm groves, but with few facilities. You'll need a 4WD to continue to **Río Indio** and **Miguel de la Borda**, where the road comes to an end. The villages beyond, including historic **Río Belén** where one of Columbus's ships was abandoned in 1502, are still only accessible by sea.

Portobelo and around → *For listings, see pages 909-912.*

Parque Nacional Portobelo

The Parque Nacional Portobelo is a large protected area north of the Parque Nacional Chagres. It encompasses the Costa Arriba all the way from Buena Ventura to Isla Grande, including a strip of teeming protected water that can be dived. Two dive shops serve the area and both are located in **Buena Ventura**, nothing more than a handful of buildings and a few kilometres west of Portobelo. This is also the site of the best lodgings in the area. The national park can be hiked, with two forested hills – Cerro Cross and Cerro Brujas – and a trail that adjoins the famous Camino Real, which you'll need a few days to follow in entirety. You shouldn't venture into the forests without a trustworthy guide. There are no tour operators in the region, but any agency in Panama City should be able to set you up. Alternatively, enquire locally – your hotel will probably have contacts.

Portobelo

East of Colón along the Caribbean coastline is Portobelo, founded in 1519 on the protected bay in which **Columbus** sought shelter in 1502. Researchers believe they have now located the wreck of the *Vizcaína*, abandoned by Columbus, in shallow waters somewhere off the coast of Portobelo. Now little more than a large village, the 'Beautiful Port' was once the northern terminus of the **Camino Real**, where Peruvian treasure, carried on mule trains across the isthmus from Panama City, was stored in fortified warehouses. The gold moved on when the periodic arrival of the Spanish Armada created famed fairs where the wealth of the New World was exchanged for goods and supplies from Europe. The fair of 1637 saw so much material change hands that, according to the Englishman Thomas Gage, it took 30 days for the loading and unloading to be completed. In the **Royal Contaduría**, or Customs House, bars of gold and silver were piled up like firewood. Such riches could hardly fail to attract foreign pirates. Portobelo was one of **Francis Drake**'s favourite targets but it was also his downfall; he died here of dysentery in 1596 and was buried in a lead-lined coffin in the bay off Isla Drake. Divers are currently attempting to discover the exact spot, intending to return Drake's body to his home city of Plymouth. By the beginning of the 17th century several *castillos* (Santiago, San Gerónimo and San Fernando) had been built of coral stone quarried nearby to protect the harbour. Attacks continued, until in 1740 the treasure fleets were rerouted around the Horn and the Portobelo Fairs ended. The fortifications were rebuilt after Vernon's attack in 1744 but they were no longer seriously challenged, leaving the fortresses visible today. The largest, the aptly named 'Iron Castle', was largely dismantled during Canal construction. But there are many other interesting ruined fortresses, walls, rows of cannon and remains of the town's 120 houses and public buildings still to be seen standing along the foreshore amid the present-day village. In 1980 the remains of the colonial structure, known as the **Monumental Complex** ⓘ *US$1, closed Sun*, was declared a World Cultural Heritage Monument by UNESCO. The Contaduría (1630) has been restored, with similar plans for the Plaza, Hospital Chapel and the Fernández House. There is a small museum with a collection of arms.

In **San Felipe Church** (1776) is the 17th-century cocobolo-wood statue of the Black Christ, about whose origin there are many legends. One tells of how fishermen found it floating in the sea during an epidemic of cholera in the town. It was brought ashore and immediately the epidemic began to wane. Another says that the life-size image was on its way to Cartagena when the ship put in to Portobelo for supplies. After being thwarted five times by rough weather to leave port, the crew decided the statue wished to remain in Panama. It was thrown overboard, floated ashore and was rescued by the locals.

The **tourist office (IPAT)** ⓘ *just west of the square behind the Alcadía, T448-2073, Mon-Fri 0830-1630*, can provide guides, schedules of Congos and other performances, as well as comprehensive information about the many local points of interest, including the surrounding 34,846-ha **Portobelo National Park**, which has 70 km of coast line with beautiful beaches, superb scuba-diving sites and boat rental to visit secluded beaches nearby, such as **La Huerta**. Services in town are limited with no bank or post office and just one minimart.

East to Isla Grande
A paved road continues northeast from Portobelo to Isla Grande, and another heads east to Nombre de Dios (25 km) and Palenque. Scuba-diving is offered at several places along the way. The road passes through **Garrote** and **La Guaira**, from where *lanchas* (motor boat) can be hired (US$1.50) at the car park to cross to Isla Grande.

Isla Grande
This island is a favourite on account of its dazzling white palm-fringed beaches, the fishing, scuba-diving, snorkelling and windsurfing, and the relaxed way of life. The best beaches are enclosed in front of the two expensive hotels, but you should be able to use them. A good, more public beach, is on a spit before Hotel Isla Grande. The island's 300 black inhabitants make a living from fishing and coconut cultivation. A powerful French-built lighthouse crowns the small island's northern point, where there is a mirador, reached by steep path. There are a number of colourful African-tinged festivals held here throughout the year. The part of the village to the right of the landing stage is more lively with competing salsa sounds.

Nombre de Dios and beyond
The beautiful, deserted mainland beaches continue as the 'road' heads east to Nombre de Dios. The historic town (1520) near the present village was once the thriving trading port which first hosted the famed fairs, located at the end of the stone-paved Camino Real from the capital. By the 1550s more than half the trade between Spain and its colonies was passing through its lightly defended harbour, but in 1594 the decision was made to move operations to the more sheltered site of Portobelo. The Camino Real was diverted and Nombre de Dios was already dying when Drake captured and burnt it two years later, so that William Dampier could describe the site some years later as "only a name ... everything is covered by the jungle with no sign that it was ever populated". Excavations

have taken place revealing the Spanish town, parts of the Camino Real, a broken cannon and other objects, most of which are now in the National Museum.

The modern village is built on either side of a freshwater channel, a footbridge links the two. The church is built on a plaza on the west side, the main square is on the east. It has few facilities, one hotel and a restaurant on the square, but there's a beautiful beach for the few who get this far. A *cayuco* (US$3 per person, 12 minutes) can be taken to **Playa Damas**, an unusual beach where alternating patches of red and white sand resemble a chess board. The beach is owned by an amateur ecologist who has built some rustic huts and a campsite, **Costa El Oro** (T263-5955), on a small island here; he also offers expert guidance on local fishing and diving spots. Buses come into the centre en route to Portobelo or Cuango; while most go as far as the main square before coming back the same way, some turn round before this at the little plaza beside the police station.

The track staggers on for another 25 km linking the peaceful fishing villages of the **Costa Arriba**. Locals eagerly await the paved road's eventual extension through the succession of seaside villages to the Golfo de San Blas opposite El Porvenir, the capital of the Kunas' self-governed area of Kuna Yala ('Kuna Earth').

Not far beyond Nombe de Dios, near **Viento Frío**, is **Diver's Haven**, which, as the name suggests, is recommended for diving tours. The next village is **Palenque**, unspoilt, with a good beach and very rudimentary huts for visitors. **Miramar** is the cleanest of all the *pueblitos* along this coastline. The occasional smuggling boat puts in here and a few Panama City tourists come to stay in the three houses on the tiny **Isla Bellavista** (ask Niano at **Bohio Miramar** bar/restaurant) – US$70 for house with three double beds, no beach but you can swim off the jetty). Boats can take you on to **Santa Isabel** (beyond the reach of the dirt road), US$35 for the boat, or to **Kuna Yala** US$25 each, minimum eight people. The village at the end of the road is **Cuango**, a bit run-down and dusty between rains, with a littered beach.

For Sleeping and Eating price codes and other relevant information, see Essentials pages 31-33.

⊜ Sleeping

Colón and Cristóbal *p904, map p905*
There are plenty of dirt-cheap *pensiónes* in Colón, but safety is definitely an issue and none of them have been recommended here.
A Nuevo Washington, Av del Frente Final, T441-7133, newwashingtonhotel@eveloz.com. An interesting old hotel with lots of history and character. The art deco-style building has a garden with good views of ships entering the canal. There's a restaurant, bar and casino on site.
B Andros, Av Herrera, between Calle 9 y 10, T441-0477, www.hotelandros.com. This hotel is modern, clean and comfortable. It has 60 rooms with TV, a/c, hot water and Wi-Fi. Good restaurant attached.
C Carlton, Calle 10 y Av Meléndez, T447-0111, www.elhotelcarlton.com. Clean, professional and comfortable enough Rooms have a/c, telephone, cable TV and hot water. There's also a restaurant, internet and laundry service. A good choice and one of the better hotels.
C Internacional, Av Bolívar, y Calle 11, T445-2930. Rooms here are clean, bright and tidy. The usual amenities include a/c, hot water, cable TV, free internet, restaurant, bar and garden terrace. Simple but comfortable.

Portobelo and around *p907*
Accommodation is limited in and around Portobelo.
B Coco Plum Cabañas, Buena Ventura, 5 km west on road to Colón, T448-2102, www.cocoplum-panama.com. Colourful, nautically themed cabins adorned with fishing nets and shells. There's a small dive shop attached and they offer snorkelling tours and transit to the beaches. A pretty, relaxing spot.

B Scuba Portobelo, Buena Ventura, T261-3841, www.scubapanama.com. Clean, pleasant, nautically themed rooms and cabins with a/c, fan and hot water. There's a common room for reading, restaurant-bar, and tours in *lancha* (motor boat) offered. Owned by **Scuba Panama**, who also do dive trips from here. Rates rise slightly at the weekends.
F Hospedaje Sangui, T448-2204, on the highway in Portobelo, close to the church. Economical and basic quarters with shared bath and cold water. For the impoverished traveller.

Isla Grande *p908*
During holidays and dry season weekends, make reservations in advance; prices often double during high season. All hotels have bars and simple restaurants.
LL-AL Bananas Village Resort, north side of the island, usually accessed by boat but also by path over the steep hill, T263-9510, www.bananasresort.com. Relatively discreet luxury hotel, on the best beach on the island, with a good but expensive bar. Day use costs US$35 and includes a welcome cocktail.
B Isla Grande, T225-2798 (reservations), west of the main pier, at the end of the path, www.islagrande.com. Colourful, if slightly run-down cabins overlooking the beach, popular with Panamanians. There are rooms too, slightly cheaper than the cabins. Rates rise over the weekend (**A**).
C Villa Ensueño, east of the main pier, T448-2964, www.hotelvillaensueno.com. Big lawns (big enough to play football), colourful cabins and picnic tables overlooking the water. There are also hammocks, ping-pong and *artesanías*. Friendly and pleasant.
D Cabañas Jackson, immediately behind main landing stage, T441-5656. Clean, friendly and economical lodgings. Rooms have fan, cold water and spongy beds. Grocery shop attached.

Nombre de Dios and beyond *p908*
AL Jimmy's Caribbean Dive Resort, about
4 km east of Nombre de Dios, T6682-9322,
www.caribbeanjimmysdiveresort.com.
Cabins on the beach with a restaurant and
dive school. All-inclusive packages are
available for divers, but conditions and
visibility vary with the seasons. Check
before heading out.

🍴 Eating

Colón and Cristóbal *p904, map p905*
Hotels **Carlton** and **Washington** have
good restaurants (🍴). There are also
several fast-food outlets.
🍴 **Colón 2000**, Calle 11 and Av Roosevelt.
Big, clean restaurant at the ferry terminal.
They serve reliable breakfasts and lunches.
🍴 **Hotel Andros**, Av Herrera and Calle 9,
T441-0477. Modern self-service outlet,
open till 2000, except Sun – check out
the mirrors.
🍴 **Eugenio**, Calle 9 and Av Meléndez. Bustling
locals' haunt with lots of cheap eats and
wholesome home-cooking.

Portobelo and around *p907*
A number of small *fondas* serve coconut
rice with fresh shrimps, spicy Caribbean food
with octopus or fish, or *fufú* (fish soup cooked
with coconut milk and vegetables).
🍴 **La Ancla**, Buena Ventura, 5 km west on
the road to Colón. **Coco Plum**'s restaurant is
pleasant, brightly decorated and overlooks
the waves. They serve breakfasts, lunches
and seafood dinners.
🍴 **Los Cañones**, in Buena Ventura, 5 km west
on the road to Colón. Good food in a lovely
setting by the water, but not cheap.
🍴 **La Torre**, T448-2039, in La Escucha, 3 km
west on the road to Colón. Large wooden
structure serving good seafood.

Isla Grande *p908*
You'll find lots of good fresh fish at a host
of places on the waterfront.
🍴 **Kiosco Milly Mar**, just west of landing
pier. A cute little place serving excellent
fish dishes at moderate prices.
🍴-🍴 **Bar-Restaurant Congo**, west of the
pier. This restaurant juts out over the water
on its own small pier. They serve up the
usual Caribbean treats, rum, beer and
fresh fish.

⊛ Festivals and events

Portobelo and around *p907*
21 Oct The miraculous reputation of the
Black Christ is celebrated annually; purple-
clad pilgrims come from all over the country
and the statue is paraded through the town
at 1800 on a flower- and candle-covered
litter carried by 80 men (who take 3 steps
forward and 2 steps back to musical
accompaniment); feasting and dancing
till dawn.
Jan-Mar/Apr Other fiestas in the Portobelo
region – for example **Carnival**, **Patron
Saint's Day** (20 Mar) – are opportunities
to experience the congos. Unlike the dance
of the same name found elsewhere on the
Caribbean coast, the congo here is the name
given both to the main, male participants
and a slowly unfolding ritual which lasts
from the **Día de los Reyes** (6 Jan) to **Easter**.
Among the various explanations of its
symbolism are elements of the people's
original African religions, their capture into
slavery, their conversion to Catholicism and
mockery of the colonial Spaniards. Members
of the audience are often 'imprisoned' in a
makeshift palisade and have to pay a
'ransom' to be freed.

⊖ Transport

Colón and Cristóbal *p904, map p905*
Air
Former US France Field AFB has replaced Colón's old airstrip as the busy local airport, on the mainland east of the city, taxi under US$1 but bargain. **Aeroperlas** have daily flights Mon-Thu to **Panama City**, T430-1038. Flights are hectic with Free Zone executives; no reservations so allow plenty of time or plan to stay the night in Colón.

Boat
For **San Blas** try asking at Coco Solo pier, T430-7327, or in Miramar, but be aware that services are less frequent than they were. The ride is rough and not particularly recommended.

Bus
Bus station on Av del Frente and Calle 12. To **Panama City**, every 20 mins, express (a/c) US$2.50, regular buses, US$2, about 2 hrs; to **La Guaira**, 5 daily, 2 hrs, US$2.85; to **Portobelo**, hourly, US$2.50, 1 hr (note that Portobelo can be visited from Panama City in a day without going into Colón by taking an early bus to the Sabanitas turn-off (US$1) and waiting for a Colón–Portobelo bus (US$1.50)).

Taxi and car rental
Tariffs vary, US$0.75 in Colón, US$1.25 to outskirts, US$8-10 per hr. Taxis (and car rental) on Av del Frente facing Calle 11; most drivers speak some English and can advise on 'no-go' areas. You are advised to take a taxi between the train and bus stations.

Train
US$22, one way, US$35 return, to **Panama City**, leaves 1715, station on west side of town just off the centre.

Portobelo and around *p907*
Boat
Launch to **Santa Isabel** (beyond reach of Costa Arriba road), 2 hrs, to **San Blas** 3 hrs, but these services are increasingly infrequent.

Bus
To **Colón**, hourly, 0700-1800, 1 hr, US$2.50; to **María**, **Chiquita**, 40 mins, US$0.80; to **La Guaira**, 5 daily, US$1.25, 45 mins (taxi is also a possibility). To villages further east, take buses marked 'Costa Arriba' from stop at back of square: **Nombre de Dios**, 45 mins US$1; **Palenque**, 70 mins, US$1.50; **Miramar**, 80 mins US$3, **Cuango**, 1½ hrs, US$3.50. Road paved until just beyond Nombre de Dios.

Isla Grande *p908*
Buses drop you at **La Guaira** on the mainland from where *lanchas* (motor boat) nip across to the island, US$1.50. Tell the boatman if you need a particular locale, **Bananas Resort**, for example. From La Guaira 5 buses per day go to Colón, hourly, 0530-0830, the last at 1300, US$2.85. There may be later buses on Sun and you should expect crowding at such times. Hitching with weekend Panamanians is also possible, all the way to **Panama City** if you're lucky!

❶ Directory

Colón and Cristóbal *p904, map p905*
Banks Banco Nacional de Panamá. Caja de Ahorros. Chase Manhattan Bank. Citibank. Lloyds Bank agency in Colón Free Zone, at Av Santa Isabel y Calle 14, T445-2177. Mon-Fri 0800-1300. **Internet** Explonet, Frente, between Calle 9 y Calle 10, Mon-Sat 0800-2300, Sun 1300-2000, US$2.50 per hr. Dollar Rent-a-Computer, Calle 11 Y Av Guerrero, above Café Nacional, T441-7632, US$2.50 per hr, net phones US$0.61 per min to England. **Post** In Cristóbal Administration Building, on corner of Av Bolívar and Calle 9. **Telephone** Cable & Wireless in Cristóbal.

Isla Grande *p908*
Telephone There are 2 pay phones: 150 m to the left of the landing jetty, on a small plaza, to the right beside the basketball court.

Kuna Yala (San Blas islands)

→ *Colour map 5, B2.*
The Archipiélago de San Blas (or Las Mulatas) is a broad string of 365 islands ranging in size from deserted islets with just a few coconut palms to inhabited islands, about 50 in total and home to hundreds of Kuna people. Lying off the Caribbean coast east of Colón, the archipelago stretches along the coast for over 200 km from the Gulf of San Blas to the Colombian border. The islands' distance from the mainland ranges from 100 m to several kilometres. ▸▸ *For listings, see pages 916-917.*

Ins and outs
There are about 20 basic airstrips in the San Blas islands and province. They include: El Porvenir, Cartí, Río Sidra, Río Azúcar, Narganá, Corazón, Río Tigre, Playón Chico, Tupile, Tikantiki, Ailigandi, Achutupu (also known as Uaguitupu), Mamitupu, Ogobsucum, Ustupu, Mansucum, Mulatupu, Tubuala, Calidonia and Puerto Obaldía. You can be dropped off at any island or village and picked up later, subject to negotiations with the pilot but, though this may sound appealing, it is probably not wise since there is no drinking water or food. One of the best islands to visit from the Porvenir area is **Dog Island** with a superb beach and great snorkelling on a wreck just 20 m offshore. Hotel prices usually include a trip here. There is a 'local' tax of US$1 per island. Any travel agent in Panama can book a San Blas tour.

An alternative route to San Blas is via the paved highway to Darién (see page 963).

The most common point of entry into the San Blas, **El Porvenir** is taken up with an airstrip, customs and immigration. On a sailing journey this is the place to obtain your final exit stamp from Panama, or to check in if coming from Colombia. El Porvenir has a rustic hotel and is not unattractive, with a palm-fringed beach at the north end. Reef systems around the island invite snorkelling but intensive fishing means large marine life is scarce.

Background
The Kuna (Cuna or Tule) are the most sophisticated and politically organized of the country's seven indigenous groups (Kuna, Embera, Waounan, Ngobe, Bugle, Naso and Bribri). They run the San Blas Territory virtually on their own terms after a rebellion in 1925, with internal autonomy and, uniquely among Panama's indigenous groups, they send their representative to the National Assembly. Each community is presided over by a *sáhila* (chief). Land is communally owned but coconut trees may belong to individuals. The Kuna have their own language, although Spanish is widely spoken. The women wear gold noserings and earrings, costumes with unique designs and *molas* (see box, page 915), based on local themes, geometric patterns, stylized fauna and flora and pictorial representations of current events or political propaganda. They are outside the Panamanian tax zone and have negotiated a treaty perpetuating their long-standing trade with small craft from Colombia. Photographers need to have plenty of cash when they visit, as the set price for a Kuna to pose is US$1 per photo.

Wichub-Huala and Nalunega
Just south of Porvenir, Wichub-Huala and Nalunega are heavily inhabited labyrinths of huts and alleys and are culturally fascinating. Both have communal halls where the

Sailing to Colombia via the San Blas islands

With the price of a plane ticket to Cartagena costing around US$200, an alternative, more adventurous route to Colombia could be spending several days travelling by boat. It's adventurous, a true travel experience and a chance to see part of the world normally reserved for those with very big budgets.

Two types of boat can take you to Colombia. The first are local trading vessels, which occasionally head to Colombia stopping at many of the more inhabited Kuna islands and settlements along the coast. These are usually around US$200 per person, all the way to Cartagena, Barranquilla or Santa Marta. You may be able to track one down at the Colón port.

A second option is recreational yachts, often foreign-owned and travelling between Panama and Cartagena, Colombia. Some boats are on round-the-world trips, but a small number make it their business to ferry adventurous travellers to and from Colombia. Price is between US$300-400, including basic food. These boats usually leave from Portobelo or Isla Grande; you'll often find them advertised in hostels – try **Hostel** Mamallena (www.mamallena.com) or **Hostel Wunderbar** (www.hostel wunderbar.com), or contact Sr Burgos at Hotel San Blas. If coming from Cartagena in Colombia visit **Casa Viena**, www.casaviena.com.

Sailing vessels usually head along the coast using the most northerly islands of the San Blas, such as Cayos Holandés as overnight stops before the two- to three-day sail across the open sea to Colombia. Prevailing winds and currents make it a rougher ride from Panama to Colombia.

Choosing a boat and captain is important. Sailing is not a risk-free business as demonstrated by the multitude of wrecks in the San Blas area. Talk to your captain about previous experience and look at the boat. If in doubt, listen to your instincts. Bear in mind there is no set schedule for departures – you may have to wait to get enough people together. And as ever, when leaving a country, paperwork is important. Make sure you've completed exit formalities as directed by your captain.

---

political decisions of the villages are made, and both have simple accommodation and general stores. The shop on the south side of Wichub-Huala (the island closer to Porvenir) seems to be better stocked; it's a good place for last-minute supplies.

Cayos Chichime

Not more than a couple of hours sail to the east lie the idyllic islands of the Cayos Chichime, also known as Wichudup or Wichitupo in the Kuna language. The deep-water channel entering the harbour is only 30 m wide with reefs on both sides, and requires care even from experienced captains. Both islands are beautiful and inhabited by only a handful of Kuna who survive through a combination of fishing, harvesting coconuts and selling *molas* to passing boats. The Kuna are friendly, easy-going people and interesting to talk to. Many of the Kuna who live on the islands only do so for four to five months per year before returning to the more inhabited islands or moving on to another island. One of the islands' more permanent residents seems to be Umburto who, if he has space, will let you stay in a hut for US$5 per night – he might even throw in some food. And for a small fee the family will also cook locally caught seafood (through don't accept lobster or

La mola

You might not know what it is until you see one, but the *mola* – literal translation a 'blouse' – is the most colourful artistic expression of Kuna Yala – the San Blas archipelago. A mola is a reverse appliqué, or 'cut-out', decorative textile made by Kuna women. First created in the mid-19th century it is still worn daily on the front and back of a blouse.

Usually measuring 40 by 33 cm, *molas* are made out of up to seven (but on average three to four) superimposed, differently coloured materials. Each layer is cut to make up a design element constituted by the unveiled layer beneath it. The ragged hem is folded over and sewn down with concealed stitching. This careful craftwork and step-by-step process slowly reveals a design of a bird, aquatic creature, monster, a generic scene such as fishing or even perhaps a protecting spirit or a wild dance of colours, but always something personal to the creator's imagination.

The traditional *mola*, the 'serkan' design, with its small range of totemic objects, has been added to by the Kuna encounter with modern Panama and you are as likely to see a mola depicting an aeroplane, map, flag, political leanings, or an American invasion, which can be just as interesting. Another development is machine-made *molas* with simplistic motifs and gaudy colours.

As gifts and souvenirs, *molas* make great miniature wall-hangings and have the advantage of being light and small, so they don't take up too much precious space in the backpack. It's worth seeking out a good quality one. Don't worry about exact symmetry, but do look for fine and even outlines, the narrower, the better. The larger pattern should come out of the top layer, often black or maroon, and the detail mainly from lower layers. Some *molas* have appliqué – sewn on, as opposed to cut away, motifs – and they can create additional depth and enliven the surface, but try to avoid those with fill-in – dots and triangles and small circles roughly applied to fill up space. Stitching should be even and usually hidden, never substituted with tape, and where there is decorative surface stitching it shouldn't compete with the more graphic cut-away. Check the quality of the material in the lower layers and run your hand across the surface of the *mola* to make sure the layers are not scrunching up.

crab due to over-fishing, and certainly not the meat or eggs of sea turtles, which are sometimes caught). Umburto has a boat with a motor and will take you to Porvenir for a negotiated price.

The Kuna will try and sell you *molas*, one of their few methods of obtaining cash income – if you're not interested, it will be sufficient to decline politely.

Cayos Holandés

To the east of Chichime lies a long chain of sparsely inhabited islands known as Cayos Holandés or Dutch Keys. Some of the islands have no permanent residents, but most have at least one family of Kuna harvesting coconuts. These *cayos* are the furthest from the mainland in Kuna Yala and have a rugged, remote feel. Washed by strong Caribbean swells, the Cayos Holandés harbor abundant marine life along the barrier reef and in the deepwater channels at either end of the group – in these areas Caribbean reef sharks, tarpon and rays are often seen. Even on the sheltered southern side there exist some pristine patch reefs only metres from islands themselves. Toward the eastern end of the chain is an excellent protected anchorage known to local yacht types as 'the swimming pool', due to its clear, calm water and location surrounded on all sides by islands. As with Chichime, caution and good navigational charts are required when entering this area.

◉ Kuna Yala (San Blas islands) listings

For Sleeping and Eating price codes, and other relevant information, see pages 31-33.

● Sleeping

It's a very good idea to book ahead. Camping is possible on some of the islands, but you'll need permission; speak to the *sáhila* (the local chief) first. Point of entry is specified below but you may still require sea connections (these should be provided by the hotel, assuming you've booked ahead). All rates are per person and usually include meals, transport and excursions.

LL Sapibenega Kuna Lodge, 5 mins from Playón Chico, T215-1406, www.sanblasthe kunalodge.com. Widely acknowledged as one of the best (and most expensive). Lodgings consist of beautiful, cane-and-thatch *cabañas* on stilts, all solar-powered with private baths, balconies and hammocks.

L Uaguinega Ecoresort, Isla Uaguitupu (point of entry: Mamitupo), T832-5144, www.uaguinega.com. Also known as **Dolphin Island Lodge**. A range of upmarket wooden cabins and cane-and-thatch *cabañas*. Amenities include bar-restaurant, hammocks and volley ball.

AL Cabañas Wailidup, Isla Wailidup (point of entry: El Porvernir), 25 mins from El Porvenir, T259-9136 (Panama City) or T6709-4484, www.kuna-niskua.com. Very exclusive *cabañas* on a private island, all powered by solar energy. Guests enjoy their own personal beach, bar-restaurant and pier. Sandflies may be an issue during certain months.

AL Kwadule, Isla Kwadule (point of entry: Corazon de Jesús). An exclusive private island with attractive *cabañas* on stilts overlooking the water. There's a very nice restaurant/bar and a nearby coral reef too. Rooms have private bath.

A Cabañas Coco Blanco, Isla Ogobsibu (point of entry: El Porvernir), 15 mins from El Porvenir, T6706-7316, cabanascoco blanco@yahoo.it. Secluded private island with a handful of traditional cane-and-thatch *cabañas* right on the beach. Interestingly, they prepare a lot of Italian food.

B Kuanidup, Isla Kuanidup (point of entry: Río Sidra), 25 mins from Río Sidra, T6635-6737, kuani9@hotmail.com. An idyllic, isolated spot with rustic *cabañas*, swaying hammocks, lovely coral reef and achingly picturesque white-sand beaches. The perfect castaway desert island.

B Kuna Niskua, Isla Wichub-Huala (point of entry: El Porvernir), 5 mins from El Porvenir, T259-9136 (Panama City) or T6709-4484, www.kuna-niskua.com. Owned by the friendly and knowledgeable Sr Juan Antonio Martínez. These are some of the most attractive rooms in the area. Most rooms have private bath and shower, but some cheaper ones have shared bath (**C**). Recommended.

B Cabañas Ukuptupu, Isla Ukuptupu (point of entry: El Porvernir), 5 mins from El Porvenir, T293-8709 (Panama City) or T6746-5088, www.ukuptupu.com. Housed in the former Smithsonian Institute Research Station, these wooden cabins are built on platforms over the water. The owner, Don Juan García, speaks some English and is very hospitable.

B Hotel El Porvenir, El Porvenir, T221-1397 (Panama City) or T6692-3542, hoteleporvenir@hotmail.com. Managed by the friendly Miss Oti. Simple, solid rooms close to the airstrip, with a handy grocery store attached. Rates include 3 meals, but lobster is extra. All rooms have a private bathroom. For large groups, call the Panama City number.

B Hotel San Blas, Isla Nalunega (point of entry: El Porvenir), 5 mins from El Porvenir. T344-1274 (Panama City) or T6749-9697. Located inside a Kuna community. The traditional cane-and-thatch *cabañas* here are more interesting than the solid brick wall rooms upstairs, which are simple and smallish.

D Alberto Vásquez's, Nalunega, 5 mins from El Porvenir, T6772-5135. If you would like the experience of staying in a Kuna house, Alberto Vásquez has 2 rooms, each with a 2-person capacity, shared bath, bucket-and-barrel shower. Reasonable rates include 3 meals. Alberto works for Juan García (**Cabañas Ukuptupu**) and is a good guide.

⊛ Festivals and events

All the following fiestas are traditional and involve dances, games, meals and speeches. Those on Narganá have a stronger Western element (but also typical dancing and food).
Feb Anniversary of the Tule Revolution, at Playón Chico, Tupile, Ailigandi and Ustupu.

19 Mar Fiesta patronal on Narganá.
8 Jul Anniversary of Inakiña on Mulatupo.
29-31 Jul Fiesta patronal on Fulipe.
20 Aug Charles Robinson anniversary on Narganá.
3 Sep Anniversary of Nele-Kantule on Ustupo.
11 Sep Anniversary of Yabilikiña on Tuwala.

○ Shopping

Molas ('reverse appliqué' blouses, see box, page 915) cost upwards of US$10 each. You can also try the San Blas perfume *Kantule*. Both *molas* and *Kantule* are also obtainable in many Panama City and Colón shops.

⊖ Transport

Air
Both **Air Panama** and **Aeroperlas** fly to Kuna Yala, serving all of the major destinations. El Porvenir is the entry point for most visitors, US$37.50 one-way plus taxes. All flights leave between 0600 and 0630, Mon-Sat, returning 0700-0830. Evening and Sun flights must be booked privately. Baggage over 15 kg is charged at US$0.50 per kg, so wear your heavy stuff.

The Interior

→ *Colour maps 4, C5/6 and 5, B1.*

Cross the Puente de las Américas from Panama City and you enter the most densely populated rural quarter of the country, a Panama that is in great contrast to the cosmopolitan capital and the Canal: colonial towns, varied agriculture, traditional crafts and music, Pacific beaches and beautiful mountain landscapes with good walking options. The Pan-American Highway crosses the region known as 'El Interior' (though the term can refer to any area outside the capital), en route to Costa Rica. Particularly striking are the colonial villages of the Azuero Peninsula – Panama's folkloric heartland and a bastion of traditional music, crafts, festivals and dance. ➡➡ *For listings, see pages 924-929.*

Panama City to Costa Rica

The Pan-American Highway, also known as the *Interamericana*, heads westwards along a well graded and completely paved road from Panama City through Concepción to the Costa Rican border for 489 km. Leaving Panama City, the Pan-American Highway crosses the **Puente de las Américas** over the Canal at the Pacific entrance (if on a bus, sit on the right-hand side – north – for the best views). The bridge was built between 1958 and 1962 by the USA to replace the ferry crossing. It is 1653 m long and, with a road surface to seaway distance of 117 m, there is ample room for all ships to pass below. The bridge, which has three lanes, is the only vehicular crossing on the Pacific side of the canal. There is also a pedestrian walkway for the length of the bridge, but muggings have occurred on the bridge even in broad daylight so take care. Buses run to a mirador on the far side of the bridge from the city.

La Chorrera → *Colour map 5, B1.*
The first place you reach, 13 km from Panama City, is the small town of **Arraiján**. Another 21 km by four-lane highway (toll US$0.50) takes you to La Chorrera with an interesting store, **Artes de las Américas**, filled with wooden carvings. A branch road (right) leads 1.5 km to **El Chorro**, the waterfall from which the town takes its name. At Km 20, among hills, is the old town of **Capira** (good food is on offer next to the Shell station, Chinese-run). Just west of Capira is a sign indicating the turn-off to **Lídice**, 4 km north of the highway, at the foot of Cerro Trinidad (which local tradition calls 'the end of the Andes'). The town was the home of Czech immigrants who in 1945 succeeded in having the name changed from Potero to commemorate Lídice in their homeland, which suffered heavily in the Second World War.

The highway passes through the orange groves of Campana, where a 4-km road climbs to **Parque Nacional Altos de Campana**. Created in 1966, the 4816-ha park – the first in Panama – protects humid tropical forest growing on mountainous volcanic rock that forms picturesque cliffs ideal for walking and hiking.

San Carlos and beaches → *Colour map 5, B1.*
At Bejuco, 5 km east of Chame, the road stretches down a 28-km peninsula to **Punta Chame**, with a white-sand beach, a few houses, and just one hotel/restaurant. At low tide, the sand is alive with legions of small pink crabs. There is a splendid view northeast to Taboga Island and the entrance to the Canal in the distance. Food is prepared by the

beach, there are several bars and a pickup running between the highway and the beach costing US$1 is your link to the outside world.

Beyond Chame are two beaches: **Nueva Gorgona**, 3-4 km long, waves increasing in size from west to east, and a well-stocked grocery store. A little further along the Pan-American is **Playa Coronado**, the most popular beach in Panama, but rarely crowded. Homeowners from Playa Coronado have installed a checkpoint at the turning, unaffiliated with the police station opposite. Be polite, but do not be deterred from using the public beach.

Opposite the turning to Playa Coronado is a road inland to Las Lajas and beyond to the hills and **Lagunas del Valle**, about one hour from the highway. Ten kilometres beyond Playa Coronado is the town of **San Carlos**, where there's good river and sea bathing (beware of jelly fish and do not bathe in the estuarine lake). There are not many restaurants in San Carlos, but there are plenty of food shops.

El Valle

Five kilometres on, a road to the right leads, after a few kilometres, to a climb through fine scenery to the summit of **Los Llanitos** (792 m) (direct bus from Panama City US$3.50, or US$1 from San Carlos), and then down 200 m to a mountain-rimmed plateau (7 km by 5.5 km) on which is the comparatively cool, summer resort of El Valle. Four kilometres before El Valle is a parking spot with fine views of the village and a waterfall nearby. Soapstone carvings of animals, straw birds, painted gourds (*totumas*), carved wood tableware, pottery and *molas* are sold in the famous Sunday market, which is very popular with Panamanians and tourists. There is also a colourful flower market. The orchid nursery has a small zoo and Panama's best-known **petroglyphs** can be seen near the town. This is one of many good walks in the vicinity (ask directions); another is to the cross in the hills to the west of town.

Beyond El Valle is the **Canopy Adventure** ① T983-6547 (in El Valle, Spanish only), T264-5720 (in Panama City) http://adventure.panamabirding.com, daily 0600-1700, US$50, with a series of cables and wires whizzing you through the forest; the last stage swoops across the face of a waterfall. It's good for all ages and the whole experience takes about 1½ hours and includes a short hike through the forest. To get there from El Valle take a bus to El Chorro Macho or taxi to La Mesa.

Santa Clara and Antón→ *Colour map 5, B1.*

Santa Clara, with its famous beach, 115 km from Panama City, is the usual target for motorists. The beach is about 20 minutes from the Pan-American Highway, with fishing, launches for hire and riding. About 13 km beyond is Antón, which has a special local *manjar blanco* (a gooey fudge) and a crucifix reputed to be miraculous.

Penonomé → *Colour map 4, B6.*

A further 20 km is the capital of Coclé province, Penonomé, an old town even when the Spaniards arrived. An advanced culture which once thrived here was overwhelmed by volcanic eruption. Objects revealed by archaeologists are now in Panama City, in the American Museum of Natural History in New York, and in the local **Museo Conte de Penonomé** ① Tue-Sat 0900-1230, 1330-1600, Sun 0830-1300. The local university and the **Mercado de Artesanato** on the highway are worth a visit. There is a delightful central plaza with the air of a tiny provincial capital of times past. The town is often a lunch stop for motorists making the trip from Panama City to the western border.

Balneario Las Mendozas and Churuquita Grande

Just under 1 km northwest of Penonomé is Balneario Las Mendozas, on a street of the same name, an excellent, deep river pool for bathing in. Further down the Río Zaratí, also known as the Santa María, is **La Angostura** where the river dives down a canyon. The dirt access road is usually suitable for ordinary cars. There are copper- and gold-mining activities in this area and further north, beyond La Pintada, where a 35-km road has been built to **Coclecito** on the Caribbean side of the Continental Divide. The mining company is also involved in conservation work including reforestation near La Angostura. Northeast of Penonomé is **Churuquita Grande** (camping is possible near the river with a waterfall and swimming hole). There's a **Feria de la Naranja** (orange festival) held on the last weekend of January. From Penonomé you can visit **La Pintada** (buses every 30 minutes), a mountain village that makes a quiet stopping-off point for hiking and horse riding.

El Caño, El Copé and Natá → *Colour map 4, B6.*

El Caño is 24 km west of Penonomé, and 3.5 km from the main road is the **Parque Arqueológico del Caño** ① *Tue-Fri 0900-1600, Sat-Sun 1030-1300, US$1,* which has a small museum, some excavations (several human skeletons have been found in the burial site) and standing stones.

From El Caño (the ruins) you can take a *chiva* up into the mountains, changing to another at Río Grande, to the village of **El Copé** (direct buses from Panama City), which gives access to the **Parque Nacional Omar Torrijos** a protected forest of rubber trees with some good trails.

A further 7 km along the Pan-American Highway is **Natá**, one of the oldest towns in Panama and the Americas (1520). The early colonists fought constant attacks led by Urracá. The Iglesia de Santiago Apóstol (1522) is impressive, with interesting wood carvings. It is sady run-down now; donations gratefully received for restoration work.

Aguadulce → *Colour map 4, B6. Population: 14,800.*

Some 10 km beyond is Aguadulce, a prosperous supply centre (bus from Panama, US$6), with local pottery for sale and *salinas* (saltworks) nearby.

Another 17 km further on, just after the large Santa Rosa sugar plantation, a road leads off right to the mountain spa of **Calobre** (31 km). The hot springs are, however, a good hour's drive away, on a very rough road, through great mountain scenery.

Azuero Peninsula → *Colour map 5, C1.*

The small town of Divisa, 61 km beyond Penonomé, is the crossroads for a major paved road that branches south into the Azuero Peninsula, one of the earliest parts of Panama to be settled. Despite road paving in the south and east, many of the peninsula's small towns are still remote and preserve much of their 400-year-old colonial traditions, costumes and a number of white churches. In addition to its tranquillity, the region's cleanliness and prosperity are a welcome change from Panama City. Most towns of any size on the peninsula have annual carnivals (the four days before Ash Wednesday) but the one in Las Tablas is especially picturesque and popular with visitors. Accommodation is in short supply at this time throughout the region. ➤➤ *For listings, see pages pages 924-929.*

Chitré and around → *For listings, see pages 924-929. Colour map 5, C1.*

Passing through **Parita**, with a church dating from 1556, the road reaches the cattle centre of Chitré (37 km), capital of Herrera Province and the best base for exploration. The **cathedral** (1578) is imposing and beautifully preserved. The small **Museo de Herrera** ① *C Manuel Correa, Tue-Sat 0900-1230, 1330-1500, Sun 0900-1200, US$1*, has historical exhibits, a few archaeological artefacts, and some local ethnographic displays. The town is known primarily for its red clay pottery, especially its roofing and floor tiles, which are exported, and for its woven mats and carpets.

There are some nice beaches close to Chitré served by local buses, for example **Playa Monagre** and **El Rompio** ① *take the Santa Ana bus from Chitré terminal, frequent services during the day, 30 mins, US$1 to Monagre*, which are busy at weekends and holidays. It is a 30-minute walk south along the beach from Monagre to El Rompío, where you can catch a bus back to Chitré or head further south at low tide for mangroves and solitude. There are a few restaurants at Monagre, but no accommodation.

At **Puerto Agallito**, 15 minutes by bus from Chitré, many migratory birds congregate and are studied at the **Humboldt Ecological Station**. Along the swampy coast just to the north is the 8000-ha **Parque Nacional Sarigua**, established in 1984 to preserve the distinctive tropical desert and mangrove margins of the Bahía de Parita. Ancient artefacts have been unearthed within the park's boundaries. The pre-Columbian site of **Monegrillo** is considered very significant but there is little for the non-specialist to appreciate.

La Arena, the centre for Panamanian pottery, is 2 km west of Chitré. The Christmas festivities here, 22-25 December, are worth seeing if you're in the area. To get there, take a bus from Chitré (US$0.30; taxi US$1.50). Alternatively, tour operators in Panama City can arrange shopping tours here.

Los Santos, only 4 km across the Río La Villa from Chitré in Los Santos province, is a charming old town with a fine 18th-century church (San Anastasio) containing many images. The first call for Independence came from here, recognized in the interesting **Museo de la Nacionalidad** ① *Plaza Bolívar, Tue-Sat 0900-1600, Sun 0900-1200, US$1*, set in a lovely house where the Declaration was signed on 10 November 1821. **Azuero regional IPAT office** ① *T966-8072, Mon-Fri 0830-1630*, is next door.

The main road continues 22 km southeast through agricultural country to the tiny town of **Guararé**, notable only for its folkloric museum, the **Museo Manuel Zárate** ① *2 blocks behind the church, T996-2535*, where examples of Azuero's many traditional costumes, masks and crafts are exhibited in a turn-of-the-20th-century house. There is also a wealth of traditional dance, music and singing contests during the annual National Festival of **La Mejorana** (24 September).

Las Tablas and around → *Colour map 5, C1.*

Las Tablas (6 km further) is capital of Los Santos province and the peninsula's second largest city, 67 km from the Divisa turn-off. The central **Iglesia de Santa Librada** with its gold-leaf altar and majestic carvings is one of the finest churches in this part of Panama and is now a National Historic Monument. **El Pausilipo**, former home of thrice-President Porras – known to Panamanians as 'the great man' – is in the process of being turned into a museum. Las Tablas is widely known for its **Fiesta de Santa Librada**, 19-23 July, see page 927).

The lovely and unspoilt beach of **El Uverito** is located about 10 km to the east of town but has no public transport (taxi US$4.50). A paved road runs to **Mensabé**.

Smaller paved roads fan out from Las Tablas to the beaches along the south coast and the small villages in the hills of the peninsula. A circular tour around the eastern mountain range can be done by continuing south to **Pocrí** and **Pedasí** (42 km), then west to **Tonosí**, all with their ancient churches and lack of spectacular sights, but typical of the Azuero Peninsula. Another 57 km of paved road runs directly over the hills from Tonosí to Las Tablas.

Pedasí → *Colour map 5, C1.*

Pedasí is a peaceful little town and the municipal library near the church has many old volumes. The local festival, on 29 June is **Patronales de San Pablo**. President Mireya Moscoso was born in Pedasí and the family figures prominently in the town's history. Beautiful empty beaches (**Playa del Toro**, **Playa La Garita** and **Playa Arena**) and crystal-clear seas are 3 km away, but beware of dangerous cross-currents when swimming. There is no public transport to the beaches but it is a pleasant walk early in the morning. You can also walk along the seashore from one beach to another, best at low tide. The local fishing craft are based at **Playa Arena** (also the safest for swimming) and boats can be hired for sport fishing, whale watching and visits to **Isla Iguana**, a wildlife sanctuary 8 km offshore, protecting the island's birdlife, reptiles (including turtles) and forest. Locally hired boats cost about US$40 for half a day. The **IPAT** office in Los Santos arranges tours with knowledgeable naturalist René Chan who lives locally.

Playa Venado and Tonosí

About 31 km from Pedasí, and 12 km before Cañas, a small sign points to the black-sand beach of **Playa Venado**, a surfers' paradise. There are five *cabañas* for rent here. The road onwards goes to **Cañas** (no hotel), running near the Pacific coast for a short distance, with a string of lovely coves and sandy beaches accessible by rough tracks.

From Tonosí a branch road goes a few kilometres further south to **Cambutal**, west of which begins **Parque Nacional Cerro Hoya**, where sea turtles come ashore to lay their eggs from July to November. There is also a 20-km long beach at Guánico Abajo, 20 minutes' drive from Tonosí, but no public transport.

An alternative to the main road returning to Las Tablas takes the inland road north following the Río Tonosí. Crossing a saddle between the two mountain ranges that occupy the centre of the Peninsula (picturesque views of forested Cerro Quema, 950 m), the road arrives at **Macaracas**, another attractive but unremarkable colonial town, from where two paved roads return to Los Santos and Chitré (35 km).

Ocú

About 45 km west of Chitré is Ocú, an old colonial town, whose inhabitants celebrate a few notable fiestas during the year with traditional dress, music, masks and dancing. Ocú is also known for its woven hats, which are cheaper than elsewhere in Panama.

The central mountains effectively cut off the western side of the peninsula from the more developed eastern half. There is only one road down from the highway, a gruelling gravel/dirt ribbon that staggers from near Santiago down the western coastline of the Peninsula as far south as the village of Arenas (80 km) before giving up in the face of the surrounding scrubby mountain slopes. Eastward from here the Peninsula reaches its highest point at Cerro Hoya (1559 m). No roads penetrate either to the coast or into the mountains, ensuring solitude for the **Parque Nacional Cerro Hoya**, which protects most of the southwest tip. The 32,557-ha park protects four life zones in a region that has been devastated by agriculture, over-grazing, season burning and human population pressure. More than 30 species of endemic plant have been recorded in the park and it is one of the last known sites to see the red macaw. One research trip in 1987 even found an endemic species of howler monkey. Turtles also use the coastal beaches for nesting from July to November. There are no refuges.

Santiago and around → *For listings, see pages 924-929. Colour map 4, C6.*

Back on the Pan-American Highway, from the junction at Divisa the roads enters the Province of Veraguas – the only one with seaboards on both oceans – and arrives after 37 km in Santiago. Capital of the province, Santiago is one of the oldest towns in the country, in a grain-growing region that is very dry in summer. Very good and cheap *chácaras* – macramé bags used by male *campesinos* as a convenient holdall for lunch and other necessities in the fields – are sold in the market here. Heading north for 18 km is **San Francisco**; which has a wonderful old church with wooden images, altarpieces and pulpit. The swimming pool is adjacent to the church.

East of Santiago is the turn-off to **La Atalaya**, site of a major pilgrimage and festival in honour of a miraculous statue of Christ, and home of the **Instituto Jesús Nazareno** ⓘ *open to visitors on Sun*, an important agricultural school for rural boys. West of Santiago is **La Mesa** (turn-off at Km 27), with a beautiful, white colonial church. The old rough road heads south through **Soná** and rejoins the Pan-American at **Guabalá**. The paved highway from Santiago to Guabalá saves a couple of hours.

Santa Catalina, accessible from Santiago and then the small town of Soná, a route served by a few local buses per day, is a relaxed but fast-developing coastal village. Santa Catalina's main claim to fame has been as the location of some of Central America's best surfing breaks. **ScubaCoiba** ⓘ *on the main street, T202-2171, www.scubacoiba.com*, provides access to Coiba's unique submarine world. Numerous hotels in Santa Catalina cater to a wide range of budgets. There's also a surf school. It may be possible to arrange an independent trip to Coiba for US$50-60 by chartering a local boat.

Isla de Coiba

Some 80 km to the southeast is Isla de Coiba, which, at 503 sq km, is the largest island within Panamanian territory. A former penal colony, the limited interaction has ensured the protection of the plant, animal and marine life in the area which has been protected since 1992 as **Parque Nacional Coiba**. The park itself covers over 2700 sq km and includes areas of rich open ocean, Coiba and outlying islands and the second largest coral reef in the Eastern Pacific. On land the mostly untouched rainforest supports Panama's largest surviving colony of scarlet macaws, along with 146 other avian species. The marine environment, which in terms of pelagic life can only be rivalled by islands such as Cocos and the Galapagos, boasts 23 recorded species of whale and dolphin, including humpback, sperm and killer whales, some of which can spotted on dive trips to the island. Marine life of the fishy kind includes whitetip, bull, hammerhead and whale sharks in addition to manta and eagle rays.

◉ The Interior listings

For Sleeping and Eating price codes and other relevant information, see Essentials pages 31-33.

● Sleeping

San Carlos and beaches *p918*
A Río Mar, beyond San Carlos on the Río Mar beach, T223-0192. Has a good seafood restaurant.
B Cabañas de Playa Gorgona, San Carlos, T269-2433. Cheaper, with kitchenettes, BBQ, pool, shade, hammocks, on the ocean.
B Gorgona Hayes, San Carlos, T223-7775. With pleasant pool, fountain, tennis court, restaurant. Good.

Camping
Camping is possible on Palmar Beach.

El Valle *p919*
The town has no real centre, although the market marks El Valle's commercial heart. Accommodation is hard to find at weekends.
L-AL Canopy Lodge, on the road to Chorro el Macho, T264-5720, www.canopy lodge.com. This is the sister hotel of the famous Canopy Tower near Gamboa and popular among birders. Very comfortable and highly recommended by former guests, including Sir David Attenborough. Packages are available and reservations required. Recommended.
A Hotel Campestre, at the foot of Cara Coral Hill, T983-6146, www.hotelcampestre.com. This hotel has 20 comfortable rooms, all with fan, Wi-Fi, hot water and TV. It has a dramatic location at the foot of a mountain and there's a short nature walk that begins in the grounds. Prices include breakfast.
C Hotel Don Pepe, Av Principal, T983-6425, www.hoteldonpepe.com. Owned and operated by the gregarious Don Pepe, who can often be found in the well-stocked *artesanía* store below. Rooms are clean and comfortable with hot water and TV. Friendly and recommended.

D-E Pensión Niña Dalia, Av Central, T983-6425. Spartan quarters for backpackers and budget travellers. The restaurant lays on a popular weekend lunch buffet – all you can eat for US$7. Private houses nearby may rent cheaper rooms.

Santa Clara and Antón *p919*
AL Cabañas Las Sirenas, Santa Clara, T223-0132, www.lasirenas.com. Clean, comfortable and well-equipped *cabañas* for 5 or 8 people. The landscaped environment is swathed in colourful flowers and backs onto the beach, making this a very attractive and relaxing lodging.
D Hotel Rivera, Antón, Km 131, T987-2245. Clean, simple lodgings with bath and a/c or fan, located on the Interamericana. Cheaper without bath.

Penonomé *p919*
C Guacamaya, on the Interamericana, east side of town, T991-0117, www.hotelsuitesguacamaya.com.pa. Clean, comfortable and tidy rooms with hot water, a/c and cable TV. There's a restaurant, bar and casino too. Pleasant enough, if fairly unremarkable.
D Dos Continentes, Av Juan D Arosemena, T997-9325, www.hoteldoscontinentes.net. Large, comfortable rooms with hot showers, cable TV and a/c. There's a good little restaurant downstairs, pool and an internet terminal. Clean and functional. Not bad.

Balneario Las Mendozas and Churuquita Grande *p920*
AL Posada Cerro La Vieja, Chiguirí Arriba, T983-8905, www.posadalavieja.com. An excellent purpose-built lodge for walkers and ecotourists. It offers guided treks on foot or mule, including through the mountains to petroglyphs, waterfalls and organic farms.

Aguadulce p920

D El Interamericano, on the Interamericana, T997-4363. Clean rooms with bath, a/c, TV and balcony. Also has a swimming pool.

E Pensión Sarita, T997-4437. Spartan quarters for the budget traveller.

Chitré p921

Prices can rise by 50-100% during festivals.

B Hotel Los Guayacanes, Vía Circunvalación, T996-9758, www.losguayacanes.com. A large, comfortable 'country-club'-style hotel with generous grounds, casino, pool, tennis court, restaurants and artificial lagoon. Perhaps not as sophisticated as it pretends to be, but reasonably good value and quite secluded.

C Versalles, Paseo Enrique Grensier, near entry to Chitré, T996-4422, www.hotelver salles.com. An unsightly box-like exterior gives way to a rather pleasant interior complete with a cool, lush gardens and pool. Not bad, a little bland but good value. It's a 5- to 10-min walk from the city centre.

D Rex, Calle Maliton Matín by main plaza, T/F996-4310, hotelrex6@hotmail.com. An excellent location on the plaza, with great views from a shared balcony. Rooms are smallish, have a/c and cable TV. Breakfast is included in the price. Internet available. Recommended.

E Pensión Central, Av Herrera next to **Hotel Bali Panama**, T996-0059. Clean and basic with soft beds, but OK. Get a quieter room at the back. Rooms have a/c and cable TV but are a few dollars cheaper with fan.

E Santa Rita, Calle Manuel Correa y Av Herrera, T996-4610. Very simple, functional rooms with cable TV, a/c and hot water. The cheaper rooms have fan and no hot water. Friendly and clean, with restaurant attached.

Las Tablas p921

C-D Piamonte, Av Belisario Porras, T994-6372, hotelpiamonte@hotmail.com. A friendly, helpful hotel. Rooms are clean and comfortable with modern a/c units;

the junior suites have big baths. The sign outside says 'Monolo'. Restaurant attached. Recommended.

D Pensión Mariela, Av Belisario Porras, opposite **Piamonte**, T994-6473. Small, functional rooms, but comfortable and spotlessly clean.

Pedasí p922

C Dim's Hostel, Av Principal, T995-2303. A lovely hostel with a peaceful leafy garden, hammocks, restaurant, internet and good clean rooms. Transport to Playa Venado and Isla Iguana available. Very friendly and recommended.

D Hotel Residencial Pedasí, Av Central, at the entrance to town, T995-2490, info@ residencialpedasi.com. This attractive terracotta building has comfortable rooms with hot water, a/c and cable TV. Friendly.

Playa Venado p922

E There are 5 *cabañas* for rent here (no electricity, very basic, overpriced), and plenty of idyllic **camping** spots (camping free, showers cost US$0.25), as well as a combined open-air restaurant.

Santiago and around p923

C Gran David, Santiago, on the Interamericana, T998-4510. A good deal for budget travellers. Rooms here are clean and functional with private bath, a/c and hot water (cheaper with fan and without TV, **D**). There's a pool and lots of weird walkways. The attached restaurant is OK – economical, but portions are stingy.

C Piramidal, Santiago, on the Interamericana, T998-3123. A rather cold, grey building, but friendly inside, and conveniently located for the Panama City–David bus, which stops right by it. Rooms have a/c, TV, and shower. There's a good pool. Recommended.

D La Qhia Hostel, Santa Fe, 52 km north of Santiago, T954-0903, www.panama mountainhouse.com. This ecologically aware hostel is operated by a Belgian/Argentine couple and offers access to the surrounding

natural attractions, including Santa Fe National Park and various waterfalls. There are dorms (**F**) and private rooms.
E Santiago, Calle 2, near the cathedral, Santiago, T998-4824. Quite shabby and run down, but friendly and economical. Rooms have a/c and private bath, but no TV. Rooms with fan are even cheaper (**F**).

Camping
Campamento Evagélico 'La Buena Esperanza', some 28 km west of Santiago, off the road to Canazas, T999-6237, www.elcampamento.net. A beautiful setting on a lake with a few cabins.

Isla de Coiba *p923*
Santa Catalina
C Oasis Surf Camp, Playa Estero, 15 mins from town. Comfortable, colourful *cabañas* on the beach. Amenities include restaurant, tours, surf lessons and board rental.

🍴 Eating

El Valle *p919*
You'll find a handful of functional eateries close to the market, otherwise most dining takes place in the hotels.
††† La Casa de Lourdes, Calle El Ciclo, T983-6450, www.lacasadelourdes.com. This is the place for that special evening meal, where you'll find Panamanian cuisine at its finest. Interesting, exotic dishes include Yucca croquets, blackened fish in a tamarind sauce, and cashew fruit and nut tart. A real treat.
††-† Don Pepe Wholesome, economical fare and a wide range of dishes to choose from, including burgers, chicken and Chinese.
††-† Pensión Niña Dalia, Av Central, has an open-air eatery which lays on a good weekend lunch buffet popular with the locals.

Penonomé *p919*
††-† Jin Foon, on the Interamericana, inside **Hotel Guacamaya**. Fairly good Chinese food and the usual meat, chicken and fish staples, for those who prefer less exciting flavours.

Chitré *p921*
†† El Mesón, in the **Hotel Rex**, on the plaza. Good national and international dishes, including a barbeque platter of various grilled meats. The portions are generally quite generous and tasty, apart from the sandwiches which are poor. Recommended.
††-† Pizza Monolo, Paseo Enrique Geenzier. Pizza joint that's popular with Panamanian families and quite buzzing on a Sat evening. Small bakery attached.
† El Aire Libre, on the plaza. Popular little locals' place that's always busy at breakfast time.
† El Chitreano, Calle Antonio Burgos. Charming little locals' haunt with checkered table cloths and *comida típica* served in large portions.
† La Estrella, on the plaza, opposite the cathedral. Buffet fare and other economical eats.

Pedasí *p922*
††† Turístico JR's, T995-2176. Owner was formerly head chef at **El Panamá** in Panama City (see page 887). Swiss/French dishes, good quality and variety, expensive. Recommended.
† Angela. Local fare, good.

Santiago *p923*
†††-†† Mar del Sur, Av Central. One of Santiago's finest restaurants, serving Peruvian-style seafood.
††-† Los Tucanes, on the Interamericana. Large, clean, buffet place that's economical and popular with the locals. There's a smarter, more expensive restaurant with the same name next door, and a bakery, too, for a cheap breakfast or snack.

✪ Festivals and events

Some of Panama's most fascinating and raucous festivals are celebrated in the Azuero Peninsula, giving you the chance to experience the region at its most expressive. Expect hotel rates to double during Carnaval, Semana Santa or the Feast of Corpus Christi. Some dates change annually and you should check with the tourist board to see what's on when. There are many settlements across the peninsula, each with a patron saint and a corresponding festival; ask around to see what's happening locally.

Chitré and around *p921*
16-22 Jan San Sebastían, the district's patron saint, is celebrated in Ocú with costumed folklore groups.
Mar/Apr Villas de Los Santos and Guararé are particularly renowned for their **Semana Santa** celebrations.
End Apr The Feria de Azuero. 'Little devil' (*diablito*) and other masks featuring in the fiestas are the local handicraft speciality and may be purchased from stalls or workshops around Los Santos and in Parita.
May/Jun Corpus Christi (40 days after Easter) is a 4-day feast celebrated in Los Santos with one of the country's most famous and popular festivals, a glorious distillation of the peninsula's strong Spanish roots and well worth attending.
24 Jun Chitré's patrion saint is honoured in the **Fiesta de San Juan Bautista**. Also in the preceding week.
3-6 Aug The town of Parita's patron saint, **Santo Domingo**, has a well-attended festival with lots of bullfighting.
Aug Festival del Manito and El Matrimonio Campesino is a 3-day festival in Ocú straight from medieval Spain and well worth witnessing. Dramatic performances include the Duelo del Tamarindo and the Pentiente de la Otra Vida.
18 Aug Processions commemorate Parita's founding in 1558.

23-28 Sep The Feria de la Mejorana is an important folk music festival that attracts great crowds to Guararé. A 'mejorana' is a type of string instrument, much like a guitar.
19 Oct Chitre's founding (1848) is celebrated with colourful performances and historically themed parades.
10 Nov Villa de Los Santos. Celebrations commemorate Panama's Independence from Spain.

Las Tablas *p921*
Feb Commencing the Sat before Ash Wed, **Carnaval** is celebrated all over the Azuero Peninsula with great gusto, but Las Tablas takes the crown. Expect 4 days of spirited celebrations, with lots of dancing, drinking and water fights. Calle Arriba and Calle Abajo famously compete for the best floats and beauty queens.
19-23 Jul Fiesta de Santa Librada and incorporated **Fiesta de la Pollera**. Las Tablas is widely known for this festival. The *pollera* is a ruffled, intricately embroidered in a single colour, off-the-shoulder dress based on colonial fashions and is now the national costume of Panama; *polleras* are made in villages near Las Tablas, the most beautiful coming from Santo Domingo (5 km east).

Pedasí *p922*
29 Jun Celebrations with folkloric dancing honour the **patron saint of Pedasí**.
16 Jul Playa El Arenal, near Pedasí, is the site of an annual **fishing tournament**.
25 Nov More music and dancing in honour of the town Pedasí's patron saint.

▲ Activities and tours

Isla de Coiba *p923*
Diving and snorkelling
Excellent but expensive package trips to Coiba can be arranged with good dive centres in Panama City (see Panama City Activities and tours, page 892). More

economically, book with a local dive shop such as: **Scuba Charters**, Santa Catalina, T6565-7200, www.scuba-charters.com; or **Scuba Coiba**, Santa Catalina, T6575-0122, www.scubacoiba.com.

⊖ Transport

El Valle *p919*
Bicycle
The preferred mode of transport for the locals and a good way to get around. Various places rent them out. Try Don Pepe's, US$2 per hr, US$8 per day.

Bus
To **Panama City**, hourly, 0700-1600, 2½ hrs, US$3.50.

Santa Clara, Antón, Penonomé and Aguadulce *p919 and p920*
Bus
Frequent and efficient buses travel in both directions along the Interamericana, passing through and between all the above towns. Locate a concrete bus shelter when you want to catch one and shout 'parada' when you want to get out.

From **Penonomé**, buses to **Panama City** pass every 15 mins, US$4.50, 2½ hrs. For **David**, go to Santiago and change.

Chitré and around *p921*
Bus
Chitré is the transport hub of the peninsula. There is a bus terminal just outside town, take city bus **Las Arenas**.

To **Panama City** (250 km), hourly, 0600-2300, 4 hrs, US$7.50. To **Santiago**, every ½ hr, 0600-1800, 1½ hrs, US$2.50. There is no direct service to **David**, change at Santiago. To **Divisa**, 30 mins, US$1.30; same fare and time to **Las Tablas** (buses leave when full). To **Tonosí**, 3 hrs, US$4.50.

Las Tablas and around *p921*
Bus
To **Panama City**, hourly, 0600-1630, 5 hrs, US$8; to **Santo Domingo**, every ½ hr, 0600-1630, 10 mins, US$0.40; to **Tonosí**, every 45 mins, 0800-1600, 2½ hrs, US$4.25; to Pedasí, every 45 mins, 0500-1800, 1 hr, US$2; to Playa Venado,1400, 2 hrs, US$3.20.

Pedasí *p922*
Bus
To **Las Tablas**, every 45 mins, 0500-1700, 1 hr, US$2.

Playa Venado and Tonosí *p922*
Bus
1 a day to Playa Venado from **Las Tablas** at 1400, about 2 hrs, US$3.20, return at 0700. No direct bus Pedasí–Tonosí.

Pedasí–Cañas around 0700 and 1500, US$2; **Cañas–Tonosí** 1 a day. **Tonosí–Las Tablas**, 4 a day between 0700 and 1300, US$3, 1 hr, leave when full.

A milk truck leaves Tonosí at 0700 for **Chitré**, via Cañas, Playa Venado, Pedasí and Las Tablas, takes passengers, returns 1230.

Tonosí–**Chitré** via Macaracas, 4 a day before 1100, 3 hrs, US$4, mostly paved road.

Hitchhiking
Hitching is difficult as there is little traffic.

Ocú *p922*
Bus
Several buses a day from Chitré, 1 hr, US$1.75, and buses on to **Panama City**, US$7.

Those with limited time can get a glimpse of the peninsula and villages by taking a bus from Chitré to **Pesé**, **Los Pozos** or **Las Minas**, all in the foothills of the western range, and then another to **Ocú**; staying the night and taking another bus on to Santiago to return to the Panama City–David Highway.

Car

Ocú can be reached directly from the
Interamericana (19 km) by a paved turn-off
south just past the Río Conaca bridge
(11 km west of Divisa); *colectivos* run from
here for US$0.80. Alternatively, a mostly
gravel road runs west from Parita along the
Río Parita valley, giving good views of the
fertile landscapes of the northern peninsula.

Santiago and around *p923*

Bus To **Panama City**, every ½ hr, 0600-
2300, 3½ hrs, US$7.50; for **David**, buses stop
outside the **Hotel Piramidal**, hourly, 3½ hrs,
US$7.50; to **Chitré**, every ½ hr, 0600-1700,
1½ hrs, US$3; to **San Fransisco**, every ½ hr,
0700-1600, 1 hr, US$1.75; to **Santa Fe**, every
hour, 0700-1600, ½ hrs, US$2.50; to **Palmilla**,
10 daily, 0600-1730, 2 hrs, US$3.50; for **Santa
Catalina** first go to Soná, then take connecting a bus, 0515, 1200, 1600, 2 hrs, US$4.

For the Parque Nacional Cerro Hoya,
there's a service **Palmilla**–Santiago,
10 daily, 0530-1630, 2 hrs, US$3.50.

Santa Catalina

Bus Despite its burgeoning tourism
infrastructure, Santa Catalina remains
relatively remote and can only be reached via
Soná. From **Soná**, infrequent buses connect
with the coast, 0515, 1200, 1600, 2 hrs, US$4.

⊙ Directory

Chitré and around *p921*

Internet Econoútiles stationary store,
Av Herrera 1 block from cathedral, US$3
per hr. Also at **Abacus**, Belarmino Urriola,
US$2.50 per hr.

Chiriquí

The land rises sharply as it enters Chiriquí Province and the Cordillera de Talamanca – a spine of rugged, alpine-like mountains that reach west into Costa Rica and east into the Cordillera Central. The rich volcanic soil of the highlands supports a scattering of diminutive farming communities, rambling fincas and crops of coffee, vegetables, strawberries and citrus fruit. The mingling of Atlantic and Pacific winds creates the so-called bajareque, *a fine mist that shrouds the area and supplies it with a year-round spring-like climate. Chiriquí's wilderness of fog-drenched peaks are a great setting for outdoor adventures. You can hike between flower-festooned villages, bike through the hills, explore indigenous villages or brave ferocious whitewater rapids. But descend into the steamy lowlands and you'll find yet more diversions: remote windswept beaches, dazzling coral reefs and utterly unspoilt islands. Chiriquí has it all, just as its inhabitants like to boast.* ▸▸ *For listings, see pages 939-946.*

David and the lowlands

David, capital of Chiriquí Province, is a hot and humid city, rich in timber, coffee, cacao, sugar, rice, bananas and cattle. Founded in colonial times as San José de David, it is the second city of the republic and has prospered thanks to international trade with Costa Rica, a mere hour away. Although lacking aesthetic charm, David is safe and friendly and an important gateway to the Chiriquí highlands and the Caribbean province of Bocas del Toro. It's also home to a wide selection of hotels and restaurants, making it a good place to break the trip from Costa Rica and become acquainted with Panama and its people.

Ins and outs

Getting there David is located on the Interamericana highway, where international buses bound for Panama City drop their passengers. Most provincial and long-distance buses with a final destination of David arrive in the city's downtown bus station, Paseo Estudiante, a five-minute walk from Plaza Cervantes. David's airport is **Aeropuerto Internacional Enrique Malek (DAV)** ① *Vía Aeropuerto, T721-1072.* Taxis to centre US$3-4.

Getting around David presents a significant navigational challenge to the visitor. It is perfectly flat with no prominent landmarks, the central plaza is not central, there are no street signs, some streets have two names and the locals use neither, preferring nostalgic points of reference (eg across the street from where the old oak used to be) to genuinely useful guidance. City bus routes are circuitous and generate additional confusion. When you get hopelessly lost take a taxi – for US$1-2 it's not such a bad idea.

Information The **IPAT tourist office** ① *Av 3 Este y Calle A Norte on Parque Cervantes, T775-4120, Mon-Fri, 0830-1630,* is friendly and helpful.

Sights

Although geographically off-centre, Parque Miguel de Cervantes Saavedra is the social and commercial heart of David, known by most locals as 'el parque'. At its centre stands a blue-grey diamond-like fountain, designed by Osmeida Ferguson and inaugurated in 2007. On the northwest side stands the functional and wholly unremarkable blue and white Iglesia de la Sagrada Familia.

Barrio Bolívar, known in former times as Barrio El Peligro, occupies a few square blocks southeast of Plaza Cervantes and is the site of the original settlement of David. Today, there's not much to see beyond a handful of historic buildings. The neighbourhood's geographic centre is marked by the sedate Plaza Bolívar. On its northwest side, the Catedral de San José is a modern structure with a separate and beautifully textured stone bell-tower built by Italian architect José Belli in 1892. A block northwest of Plaza Bolívar, on Av 8a Este, you'll find one of the city's oldest and most aesthetically pleasing buildings – the former 19th-century home of Chiriquí's 'founder', José de Obladía Orejuela. The building, complete with a rustic red-tile roof and attractively landscaped garden, was undergoing restoration at the time of research. It is hoped that it will soon return to its long-running function as a museum of archaeology, religious art and local history.

The diminutive port of Pedregal, 8 km south of the city centre, is perched on the serpentine Río Platanal, close to the estuary of the mighty Río Chiriquí, whose waters empty into the Pacific ocean. Along with Boca Chica, it is a popular starting point for

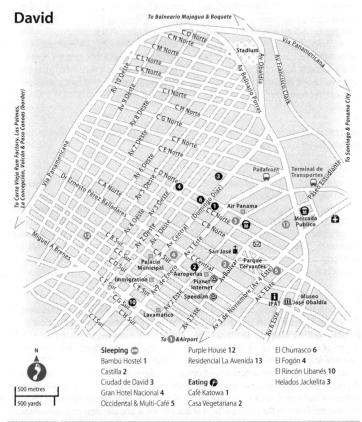

David

N
500 metres
500 yards

Sleeping 😴
Bambú Hostel 1
Castilla 2
Ciudad de David 3
Gran Hotel Nacional 4
Occidental & Multi-Café 5
Purple House 12
Residencial La Avenida 13

Eating 🍴
Café Katowa 1
Casa Vegetariana 2
El Churrasco 6
El Fogón 4
El Rincón Libanés 10
Helados Jackelita 3

Riding the rapids: whitewater rafting in Chiriquí

Chiriquí's rugged, mountainous terrain is home to some of the most accessible and challenging whitewater rapids in Central America. The **Río Chiriquí** and **Río Chiriquí Viejo** offer experiences of differing ferocity, from relatively gentle Grade II jaunts to adrenalin-charged encounters with violent Grade V monsters.

The **Río Chiriqui Viejo** offers the best year-round rafting in the province, although this fantastic river is currently under threat from new plans for a hydroelectric dam. Grade III and IV rapids course through the **Palon section**; Grade II and III rapids in the tamer **Sabo section**. The **Jaguar section** is a Grade IV stretch with 73 rapids and 16 km of canyons and waterfalls. There are other more technical Grade V and VI rapids that require experience and preparation to reach, most notable the **Puma section**, near Volcán.

All of the Río Chiriquí rapids become more difficult in the rainy season, June to December, rising a grade or even two grades during the especially wet months of October and November. The wet season also supplies enough water for some more subdued rapids, including the Grade III **Witches section** of the Río Chiriquí. Beyond here, the Río Gariche, Río Majagua and Río Esti have Grade II and III rapids, suitable for beginners, families and children.

Be sure to discuss your options thoroughly with your chosen tour operator and check your insurance cover before embarking. Two very reputable and long-standing whitewater specialists can be found in Boquete: **Chiriquí River Rafting**, Avenida Central, next to Lourdes, T720-1505, www.panama-rafting.com; and **Panama Rafters**, just below the square on Avenida Central, T/F720-2712.

sports fishing trips and other expeditions to the Gulf of Chiriquí's emerald isles, including the fabled Parídas archipelago.

Dolega

The small town of Dolega, whose name means 'place of winter', lies 13 km north of David on the highway to Boquete. Few tourists ever visit. The town is known principally for its hydroelectric plant, its church, its orchids, and the **Bookmark Secondhand Bookshop** ⓘ *David–Boquete highway, T776-1688, Tue-Sun 0900-1700*, which contains one of the country's best collections of second-hand English language books. Roughly 4 km south of town on the highway you'll find the entrance to the refreshing El Majagua waterfall, part of a popular resort complex that opens only during high season (off season it's abandoned and best avoided).

Pacific Coast

You'll find the scorching black-sand beaches of **Playa Barqueta**, 30 minutes west of David, good for surfing and replete with wealthy vacation homes. It also plays host to the **Refugio de Vida Silvestre de Playa La Barqueta**, a turtle-nesting site that's close to the resort of **Las Olas**. To reach Playa Barqueta from David, head west along the Interamericana then south along the turning to Alanje.

East of David, the Interamericana advances into the interior, flanked by mountains to the north and by tangled mangroves, estuaries, marshland, tropical forests and swamps to the south. Human settlements are sparse. Around 38 km from the city, the turning at Horconcitos leads to the fishing village of Boca Chica, a popular destination with sports fishermen, birders and surfers. The tranquil island of Boca Brava lies just across a narrow channel, five to 10 minutes in water taxi, US$3, from where it is easy to arrange trips to the unspoilt and highly recommended paradise atolls of the **Parida Archipelago**. The islands are part of the stunning **Parque Nacional Marino Golfo de Chiriquí**, a protected area of coral reefs where there is excellent diving on offer; contact Carlos Spragge of **Boca Brava Divers** ⓘ *T775-3185, www.scubadiving-panama.com*. Whale watching is also an option, August-December, when humpbacks migrate through the area. Most eastbound buses can drop you at the Horconcitos turning, from where taxis, US$5-10, and irregular buses, US$2-3, ply the paved road south to the coast.

Much further east of Horconcitos, some 70 km from David, lies the Pacific beaches of **Las Lajas**. Facilities are limited with a couple of small, sparse restaurants, so remember to bring your own food and drink from town. Watch out for strong waves and sharks. To get there, take the southbound turn-off at San Félix, or take a morning bus from David to Las Lajas, US$4. From there it's a short taxi trip, US$3, to the beach.

David to Costa Rica

La Concepción lies 25 km west of David on the Interamericana highway; roughly halfway between David and the border crossing of Paso Canoas. Sometimes referred to as Bugaba, after the district of which it is capital, La Concepción is an important agricultural shipping point, widely known for its handmade saddles. It is also the gateway to the town of Volcán and the western section of the Chiriquí highlands, from where it's possible to reach the far-flung and lesser visited border crossing of Río Sereno (see box, page 715). The town's Fiesta de la Candelaria builds up from the end of January to 2 February.

Further west, **Paso Canoas**, 52 km from David, is Panama's most important border crossing. It's a busy town with many places to eat and shop. Informally crossing back and forth between stores and business areas is easy, but travellers intending to leave one country for the other must submit to formalities before proceeding (see box, page 715). At Gariche, a few kilometres east of Paso Canoas, there is a secondary checkpoint where cars and buses coming from Costa Rica are checked. Have passport, tourist card, vehicle permit and driver's licence handy in case they are asked for (usually hassle free).

Boquete and around

Nestled in the verdant valley of the Río Caldera, the highland town of Boquete has always been an important centre of commerce and agriculture. At 1060 m, the cool climate allows for the production of orchids, strawberries, root vegetables and most importantly, coffee. The surrounding mountains are green and rugged, thickly forested in parts, home to thunderous rivers, piping hot springs, cool waterfalls and abundant bird-life. Widely peddled as a retirement destination, an influx of foreign baby-boomers have been arriving on the scene since the 1990s. Increasingly, Boquete looks and feels like a well-heeled North American suburb. The region's changing demographic, along with rock bottom coffee prices, mean many locals are turning to tourism as a new, alternative source of income.

Ins and outs

Getting there Boquete lies 38 km north of David on a well-plied paved highway. Buses depart from David's main bus terminal every 20 minutes, 0525-2125, US$1.45, and reach Boquete's main plaza roughly one hour later.

Getting around Boquete is small and easily navigated on foot. The town's principal artery is Avenida Central, where you'll find most shops, hotels, restaurants and the plaza.

Tourist information The stunningly positioned **CEFATI centre** ① *1 km south of downtown Boquete on the highway, T720-4060, Mon-Fri 0900-1700*, provides local information and has a coffeeshop attached.

Sights

Boquete is a slow-paced, predominantly wood-built town with several attractive landscaped parks, including the main plaza and the nearby Parque de las Madres. The fairground east of the river is the site for the annual **Feria de las Flores y del Café**, usually held mid-January. In April, a **Feria de las Orquídeas** is held with many varieties of local and exotic orchids. Outside of the *ferias*, flower-lovers should head to **Mi Jardín es su Jardín** ① *Av Central, roughly 500 m north of the plaza, T720-2040, 0900-1800, free*, Boquete's most famous and striking botanical garden. Home to over 200 species of flowers, some two acres of imaginatively landscaped grounds contain colourful plant beds, bubbling creeks, teeming carp ponds and surreal ornaments like plastic flamingos and giant psychedelic cows.

Boquete has gained international recognition as a producer of fine coffees and a tour of one of the area's many *fincas* will guide you through the processes of planting, harvesting and roasting to a tasting of the final product. **Café Ruiz** ① *T720-1000, www.caferuiz.com*, is recommended as a convenient option, although there are many other reputable growers and too many to list here.

There are numerous hiking trails that snake the mountains around town, including the strenuous but rewarding **Pianista Trail**, on the Alto Lino loop north of Boquete, famed for its cloud forests and birdlife. Whitewater rafting is another highly recommended activity (see Tour operators, page 944), whilst the adrenalin-charged zip-line thrills of the

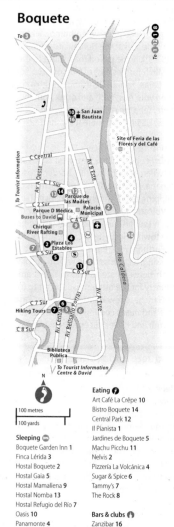

Boquete

100 metres
100 yards

Sleeping 🛏
Boquete Garden Inn 1
Finca Lérida 3
Hostal Boquete 2
Hostal Gaia 5
Hostal Mamaliena 9
Hostal Nomba 13
Hostal Refugio del Río 7
Oasis 10
Panamonte 4
Pensión Topas 6
Rebequet 8
Riverside Inn 12

Eating 🍴
Art Café La Crêpe 10
Bistro Boquete 14
Central Park 12
Il Pianista 1
Jardines de Boquete 5
Machu Picchu 11
Nelvis 2
Pizzería La Volcánica 4
Sugar & Spice 6
Tammy's 7
The Rock 8

Bars & clubs 🍸
Zanzibar 16

Boquete Tree Trek ⓘ *Los Establos Plaza, T720-1635, www.adventurist.com*, never fail to excite. Boquete's ultimate outdoor experience is an ascent of Volcán Barú, Panama's highest peak.

Volcán Barú

At 3474 m, Volcán Barú is Panama's highest peak and the views from the summit can be astounding. On an exceptional day, you can glimpse both Pacific and Atlantic oceans. Although dormant for the last 600 years, Volcán Barú – which is composed of seven different craters – is technically active. In 2006, significant seismic activity was detected beneath it, causing some scientists to warn of an imminent eruption.

Since 1976, the volcano has been protected as part of the 14,322 ha Parque Nacional Volcán Barú. The park shelters a variety of life zones, including humid mountain forest, mountain rainforest, and in the upper echelons, cloud and dwarf forest. Ten different rivers course through the area, including the Río Caldera and Río Chiriquí, both vital to local agricultural activities. The local fauna is diverse with some 40 endemic species, five species of big cat, numerous bats, endangered mammals, amphibians, reptiles and over 400 species of bird, such as black and white hawk eagles, volcano juncos (a type of sparrow) and, between January and May, numerous resplendent quetzals. Average temperatures in the park range from a subtropical 20°C on the lower slopes to a distinctly chilly 10°C higher up. During the dry season, frost is not unusual on the summit, or even the occasional flurry of snow. On average, the park receives 4000 mm of rain per year. The highest parts can receive as much as 6000 mm.

The park can be accessed from Boquete on Barú's east slopes, or Volcán, Cerro Punta and Guadalupe on the west. It is easier to summit from the east side, whilst the famous Sendero Los Quetzales (see page 938) is best followed from the west. It is 21 km from Boquete to the summit, a six- to eight-hour ascent (and a five- to six-hour descent) best accomplished in the dry season. The first 7 km consist of a paved road lined with aromatic pines and coffee groves, which concludes at an ANAM station where you must pay an entrance fee of US$5. From there, the road climbs through cloud forest draped with creepers, lichen and bromeliads. There are good views of the valley, the Río Caldera and Pacific beyond. Some 9 km from the park entrance there's a sign 'La Nevera' – a small side trail leads to a cool mossy gully with a stream for water, but no flat ground to camp.

At the summit there is a forest of TV and radio aerials in a fenced enclosure. A small path leads to a cross and trigonometric point. The best views of the craters from here. Sometimes, through the haze, you can see rainbows formed by the *bajareque* drizzle. You may see both oceans on a very clear day (rare), but you have a better chance if you camp overnight (ANAM rangers station available) and climb to the summit at dawn. You can also drive to the summit but you will need a 4WD and a winch, two hours. From the summit it's possible to climb down the west side and on to Volcán. A trail begins 50 m before the cross, descending steeply over sand and scree before entering the forest. It takes eight to 12 hours to reach Volcán, and there's no water until you are halfway down. A guide is recommended if descending from the summit to Cerro Punta. Pack waterproofs and warm clothing.

Pozos de Caldera

ⓘ *Daily, 0800-1900, US$2.*

The hot springs of Caldera are the perfect antidote to weary limbs and bones. Four thermally heated pools of differing temperatures, most of them enclosed by foliage and rustic walls of rocks, are said to alleviate rheumatism, arthritis and skin problems. Wandering peacocks and a cheeky spider monkey add an exotic flavour to the site, and the owner offers horse tours and buffalo rides. You can access the village of Caldera from either Boquete or David, four or five buses daily. Alternatively, hike 7 km from the Caldera turning (marked Chiriquitos), located 11 km south of downtown Boquete on the David highway. From the village, follow the signs to the springs, 45-60 minutes.

Comarca Ngöbe-Buglé

The rolling mountains east of Chiriquí province belong to the semi-autonomous Comarca Ngöbe-Buglé, a self-administered indigenous reservation belonging to two distinct but not dissimilar groups: the Ngöbe and the Buglé. The community of Soloy (www.comarcangobebugle), 90 minutes from David, has recently opened its doors to tourism and is highly recommended for first-hand encounters with day-to-day Ngöbe life. You can stay with a family or in simple lodgings (outdoor toilet, no electricity) whilst learning about local cultural traditions, or take to the hills for some first-class outdoor adventures. Hikes, horse riding and water rafting can all be organized locally through Medo (www.medoawardspace.com) or Destino Besiko (www.destinobesiko.com). Don't miss the stunning **Cascada Kiki** – the highest waterfall in the country.

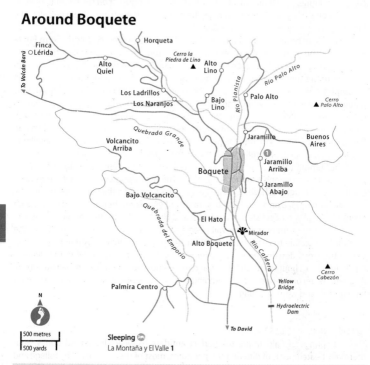

Around Boquete

Sleeping
La Montaña y El Valle 1

The western section of the Tierras Altas (highlands) de Chiriquí is bounded on the north by the Cordillera and on the west by the Costa Rican border, a prosperous and dynamic agricultural region renowned for vegetables, flowers, superb coffees and the brown Swiss and Holstein dairy herds that thrive in the cool highland pastures. The area is a birdwatchers' mecca and is also popular with residents of Panama City wishing to cool off for a few days.

Heading away from La Concepción there is a very good paved road north, rising 1200 m in 32 km to Volcán. From Cuesta de Piedra, a turning to the right will take you to the canyons of the **Macho de Monte**, a rather small river that has worn deep, narrow gorges. Further on, to the left, is the **Mirador Alan Her** ① *US$0.10*, with good views from the purpose-built tower to the sea, and on a clear day, the Punto Burica peninsula that marks the Panama–Costa Rica border. Local cheeses on sale are very good, especially the mozzarella. Near Volcán, you can get excellent wood carvings at **Artes Cruz** where Don Cruz, who speaks English, will make charming souvenirs to order and have them ready on your return trip.

Volcán and around → *Colour map 4, B5.*

Volcán sits on a broad 1450-m-high plateau formed by an ancient eruption of Volcán Barú. The pumice soil is extremely porous and dries within minutes of the frequent torrential downpours in the rainy season; in summer the area is tinder dry.

The town is very spread out. The centre (with police station, gas station, supermarket and bakery) clusters around the crossroads to Cerro Punta and Río Sereno. Volcán is a rapidly growing farming town, with nurseries cultivating ferns for export, the **Beneficio Café Volcán Barú** (interesting tours during the October-February harvest season), and a small factory owned by the Swiss Bérard family producing excellent European-style sausages. San Benito school is noted for hardwood furniture, woodcarvings using *cocobolo* hardwood and hand-painted ceramics sold for the benefit of the school. Brother Alfred will let you browse through his warehouse full of English books from the now-closed Canal Zone libraries and you can take away what you will. **Cerámica Beija-Flor** is run by local women who market their own wares.

Southwest of town is the **Las Lagunas de Volcán** nature reserve, with two beautiful lakes, abundant aquatic and other birdlife. High vehicles or 4WDs are required in the wet season. **Sitio Barriles**, 6 km from town on the road to Caizán (several buses daily, US$0.50), has interesting petroglyphs; also past Finca Palo Santo, 5 km from town on the road to Río Sereno. **La Fuente Park** ① *US$0.25* (signed from the main road) has playing fields and a spring-fed swimming hole (source of Río Gariché) that's excellent for children.

Volcán is a good jumping-off place for the ascent of **Volcán Barú**. It is possible to climb the west side in one or two days, camping about halfway by a small spring (the only reliable water in the dry season) or in a crater near the top (no water), descending the following day to Boquete on the vehicle road (see page 935). The trail is beautiful, climbing gently at first through lush cloud forest (many birds, butterflies, and orchids), then scrambling steeply over loose volcanic sand and scree – a challenging but rewarding hike. Guides can be arranged in Volcán; climbers sometimes get lost. For **tourist information**, Angel Rodríguez at **Hotel Don Tavo** speaks fluent English and is very knowledgeable about the area.

The road divides at the police station in Volcán. The right branch continues north to tiny **Bambito** and **Cerro Punta** (22 km), following the Chiriquí Viejo river valley up the northwest foothills of Volcán Barú. Cross the dry plain known as **Paso Ancho**, with coffee farms in the hill to the west.

Cerro Punta → *For listings, see pages 939-946. Colour map 4, B5. Altitude: 2130 m.*

Heading north from Volcán, at the end of the road is Cerro Punta Set in a beautiful valley, it is at the heart of a vegetable- and flower-growing zone, and a region of dairy farms and racehorse stables. It is sometimes called 'Little Switzerland' because of its Alpine-style houses and the influence of Swiss and former-Yugoslav settlers (there is a settlement called **Nueva Suiza** just south of town). The countryside, full of orchids, is beautiful, though economic pressures push the potato fields ever higher up the hillsides, to the cost of the wooded areas, and sadly encourage the extensive use of agro-chemicals. There are many fine walks in the crisp mountain air. Continue through Cerro Punta to follow the main street as it curves to the left. **Haras Cerro Punta** (topiary initials clipped in the hedge) and **Haras Carinthia** (name visible on stable roof) are well-known thoroughbred farms who will usually receive visitors and show them round. Further on is the small bridge at Bajo Grande. The right fork leads to **Respingo**, where there is a small forest ranger station.

Hikes and nature trails

Sendero Los Quetzales Continuing along the main road in Cerro Punta through town is the starting point of the easy six-hour hike, mostly downhill after an initial climb, to Boquete. The track is clear in places and there are a few signs showing the direction and time to Boquete, with the last section following the Río Caldera canyon. It is easier in the dry season (December-April), but can be enjoyed throughout the year. Take food, insect repellent and rain gear. This hike is also recommended for birdwatching; quetzales and many other species may be seen. Take a taxi (4WD) from Cerro Punta to the Respingo ranger station, US$10. You can stay overnight here in the rangers' quarters (**F** per person), clean, shared bath and kitchen. The Camino Los Quetzales leads to **Bajo Mono**, from which there are irregular local buses to Boquete (20 minutes, US$1). The walk can also be done in the opposite direction (uphill). It is possible to set out from and return to Boquete in one (very long) day.

Parque la Amistad ① *7 km from the centre of Cerro Punta (signposted at road junction, entrance fee US$1, payable at Las Nubes)*, has been open since 1991, with two trails, good for birdwatching, including quetzals. Nature buffs should also visit **Los Quetzales Reserve** inside Parque La Amistad. See Sleeping, page 942.

Volcán to the border → *For listings, see pages 939-946. Colour map 7, B5.*

From the fork at the police station in Volcán, the left branch loops 48 very scenic kilometres west, climbing over the Cerro Pando, and passing through beautiful cattle country and coffee plantations on a well-paved, little-travelled, winding road to the Costa Rican border. **Los Pozos**, an area of small thermal pools beside a rushing river, is a good campsite, but only accessible by 4WD vehicles and hard to find as the turn-off from Volcán–Río Sereno road is unmarked. Enquire at **Panadería Mollek** (good espresso and pastries), opposite the police station in Volcán. Sr Juan Mollek has a farm at Los Pozos and can provide information. At **Río Colorado**, 15 km from Volcán, **Beneficio Café Durán**, a coffee processing plant whose delicious aroma of fermenting pulp and drying beans will announce its proximity from kilometres away, is hospitable to visitors. At **Santa Clara**, 25 km from Volcán, is the **Finca Hartmann**, 1300-1800 m, where the US **Smithsonian Tropical Research Institute** maintains a biological research station devoted to ecological studies. Enter the unmarked drive 50 m west of petrol station, next to a green house with 'Ab Santa Clara No 2' sign and proceed 1 km on a dirt road. Latest birdwatching checklist compiled by researchers lists 277 species observable on the densely wooded coffee and cattle farm which borders La Amistad International Park to the north. Biologists and the Hartmann family welcome visitors and have information in Spanish and English.

Border with Costa Rica – Río Sereno → See box, page 715.

The village of Río Sereno has the air of a cowboy town. The Panamanian businesses are centred around the plaza (including **Banco Nacional** – changes traveller's cheques), and the Costa Rican businesses along a street right on the border. Approaching the village from Volcán, abandoned installations from the era of military government are visible on the right. The bus station is just to the right of the *alto* (stop) sign. Follow the main street left along the plaza to where it ends at a steep road crossing diagonally. This is the border with Costa Rica, otherwise unmarked. Numerous vendors' stalls, especially Sunday during coffee harvest (October to December or January). It is safe to park (and lock) your vehicle in the open area of **Almacén Universal**. Costa Rican shops selling leather goods, a few crafts, clothing, gladly accept US dollars at current rates. Do not miss the upper floor of **Super Universal** and **Supermercado Xenia**. If crossing into Panama, sell your colones here; it will be much more difficult in Volcán or David and rates are worse in Panama City.

Río Sereno to Paso Canoas

A paved winding road runs 50 km south along the Panama side of the border to Paso Canoas, about two to two and a half hours by bus. At Km 41 an impressive cascade over 100 m high pours over a cliff on the left of the Río Chiriquí Viejo below. For information on whitewater rafting on the Río Chiriquí Viejo from Breñón during the dry season, see Boquete, Activities and tours, page 944. There is a good view of the river valley at Km 47, with Volcán Barú visible to the northeast.

◉ Chiriquí listings

For Sleeping and Eating price codes and other relevant information, see Essentials pages 31-33.

David *p930, map p931*

L Ciudad de David, Calle D Norte and Av 2a Este, T774-3333, www.hotelciudadde david.com. This slick new business hotel has 103 impeccable and tastefully attired rooms, pool, gym, spa, restaurant and business centre. Rack rates are high, but they often offer discounts of nearly 50%. The best in town. Recommended.

A Gran Hotel Nacional, Av Central and Calle Central, T775-2221, www.hotelnacional panama.com. A long-running upmarket option and landmark David hotel. Rooms are comfortable, generic and overpriced. New rooms and pool-side rooms cost extra (**AL**). The amenities are generally excellent, including garden, pool, casino and 3 restaurants. The lunch buffet isn't bad, US$7.25.

B Castilla, Calle A Norte, between Av 2a Este and Av 3a Este, T774-5260, www.hotelcastilla panama.com. A clean, quiet hotel with an attractive lobby and 68 well-appointed rooms. Services include Wi-Fi, parking, a/c, cable TV and hot water. The restaurant serves Spanish and Panamanian food. Friendly, helpful staff and discounts off-season. Recommended.

C-D Occidental, Calle 4a on Parque Cervantes, T755-4068. This old budget favourite overlooking the plaza is on the musty side, but rooms are good and comfortable. They come equipped with a/c, cable TV and hot water. Some rooms are exceptionally large and excellent value – ask to see a few.

E Residencial La Avenida, Av 3a Este and Calle D Norte, T774-0451, residenciala venida@hotmail.com. One of David's best budget hotels. It has clean, pleasant rooms with lots of space and natural light. They come equipped with a/c, cable TV, phone and Wi-Fi. Cheaper quarters have fan. Quiet, relaxed and good value. Recommended.

F Bambú Hostel, Calle de la Virgencita, San Mateo Abajo, T730-2961, www.bambu hostel.com. A friendly, sociable hostel with a pleasant landscaped garden, pool and 'Mayan-style' rancho bar. Small dorms (**F**) and a few well-equipped double rooms are available (**C** with private bath, **D** without). Located in the suburbs; take a taxi to get there.

F The Purple House, Calle C Sur and Av 6a Oeste, T774-4059, www.purplehouse hostel.com. Hostel close to the town centre with private rooms (**C-D**) and dorms (**F**), all equipped with orthopaedic mattresses. A wealth of amenities includes book exchange, artesanías, DVD, kitchen, Wi-Fi and stacks of travel information. Helpful, but reports are mixed. Located away from the centre; take a taxi.

Boquete and around *p933, map p934*
Accommodation is difficult to find during the *feria*.

LL Riverside Inn, Palo Alto, T720-1076, www.riversideinnboquete.com. One of Boquete's most exclusive lodgings, complete with beautifully decorated rooms and an especially handsome master suite with a

4-poster bed and jacuzzi. 'Standard' rooms have superb mattresses and Egyptian cotton linen. Luxurious, but not cheap.

L Finca Lérida, T720-2285, www.finca lerida.com. One of Boquete's most famous and elegant 'ecolodges' and a destination in itself. Finca Lérida offers a diverse range of rooms and suites, many in classic Scandinavian style, after the lodge's original owners. The grounds are vast and rambling and a birders' delight.

AL Boquete Garden Inn, Palo Alto, T720-2376, www.boquetegardeninn.com. Perched on the banks of the Río Palo Alto, the hospitable **Boquete Garden Inn** has received consistently good reviews, and for good reason. Its 5 *cabañas* are spacious, tastefully decorated and well equipped. Beautiful, tranquil, flowery grounds and fantastic, friendly owners. Highly recommended.

AL Panamonte, Av 11 de Abril, Bajo Boquete, T720-1324, www.panamonte.com. Built in 1919, this highly attractive hotel is today managed by the Collins family (Swedish/American). The rooms here are elegant and comfortable, while the garden is home to over 200 varieties of orchid. Spa facilities available. Charming and recommended.

A Hotel Oasis, Av Buenos Aires, just over the bridge, Bajo Boquete, T720-1586, www.oasis boquete.com. This attractive hotel overlooks the Río Caldera close to the flower fair. They have 11 clean, decent rooms and 6 stylish suites (**AL**). Pleasant gardens and good views over the valley. The restaurant is recommended.

B Rebequet, Calle 7 Sur and Av B Este, Bajo Boquete, T720-1365, www.rebequet.com. Excellent spacious rooms and a handful of comfortable cabins around the garden. The rooms are well equipped with tasteful furniture, and hammocks. Breakfast included and 50% reduction in low season. Popular, friendly and helpful. Recommended.

C Hostal Boquete, just off Calle 4 Sur to left of bridge, Bajo Boquete, T720-2573, www.hostalboquete.com. This lovely hostel has great views of the river and a pleasant, sociable atmosphere. Various brightly coloured rooms are available, all with private bath, Wi-Fi and cable TV. Recommended.

C Pensión Topas, Av Belisario Porras, Bajo Boquete, T720-1005, www.pension-topas.com. Brightly coloured hotel run by the Schöb family. The garden has views of Volcán Barú, a small pool, volley ball court, patio and an inquisitive toucan. There's also a handful of cheaper rooms with shared bath (**E**). Friendly.

C-D Hostal Refugio del Río, from Plaza Los Establos, 1 block west, ½ block north, Bajo Boquete, T720-2088, www.refugiodelrio.com. The friendly **Refugio del Río** has comfortable annexed private rooms (**C-D**) with pleasant riverside porches, cable TV, private bath and hot water. For budget travellers, there are 2 dorms (**F**) complete with communal kitchen. Motorbike, cycle and ATV rental available. Recommended.

D Hostal Mamallena, Parque Central, Bajo Boquete, T720-1260, www.mamallena boquete.com. A new and popular back-packers' joint with a convenient central location on the plaza. Opened by the same team who own **Mamallena** in Panama City, the hostel boasts 17 private rooms (**D**) and 5 dorms of different sizes (**F**). Plenty of amenities. Friendly, helpful and English-speaking.

D-F Hostal Nomba, 100 m west of Parque Central, behind **Bistro Boquete**, Bajo Boquete, T720-2864, www.nombapanama.com. Sociable self-styled 'adventure hostel' that's very popular with backpackers. They offers simple but comfortable dorms (**F**) and private rooms (**D**), communal kitchen, library and more. Their on-site tour agency can organize a range of excursions.

F Hostal Gaia, Av Central, behind Sugar and Spice bakery, Bajo Boquete, T720-1952, www.hostalgaia.com. Friendly, intimate little *hostal* with small dorms for 4-6 persons, fully equipped kitchen, games, books, laundry, lockers and free coffee. 2 private rooms are also available (**C**). New, clean, pleasant and recommended.

Comarca Ngöbe-Buglé p936
G Medo, on top of the hill near the main bus stop, www.medo.awardspace.com. Medo offers 2 rustic rooms and can help organize stays with families, guides, horses, whitewater rafting and other activities. They are one of the main tourism operators in town and they always need volunteers. Highly recommended.

Volcán and around p937
Hotels are often fully booked during holidays. Price categories shown for cottages are for 1 or 2 people, but most for larger groups for the same price or slightly more.

AL Bambito Camping Resort, Bambito, T771-4265, www.hotelbambito.com. 47 rooms with all expected comforts in a fine country setting.

AL-A Hostal Cielito Sur B&B, 9 km from Volcán, past **Hotel Bambito** but before town of Cerro Punta, T/F771-2038, www.cielitosur.com. A lovely place to stay, personal attention, each room is decorated with artwork from Panama's indigenous groups, delicious country-style breakfast is included.

AL-A Las Huacas, main street at west end of Volcán, T771-4363, www.huacascabins.com. 5 pleasant cottages with hot water, club-house, elaborate gardens, interesting aviaries, English spoken.

A Cabañas Dr Esquivel, on the road behind **Supermercado Bérard**, Volcán, T771-4770, www.cabanasdresquivel.com. Several large houses in a compound, friendly.

A Dos Ríos, Volcán, T771-4271, www.dos rios.com.pa. Older wooden building (upper-floor rooms quieter), restaurant, bar, garden with stream, private baths. Mixed reports.

C Cabañas Las Reinas, Volcán, signed from main road, T771-4338. Self-contained units with a kitchen in lawn setting.

C Don Tavo, main street, Volcán, T/F771-5144. Comfortable, garden, private baths, hot water, restaurant, clean, friendly. Recommended.

D La Nona, Calle La Fuente, El Valle, T771-4284. Cabins for up to 5, friendly, good value.
D Motel California, on main street, Volcán, T771-4272. Friendly Croatian owner (Sr Zizic Jr) speaks English, clean private baths, hot water, parking, larger units for up to 7, restaurant, bar, quiet, good but check beds, some are very old and soft.

Cerro Punta p938
L-C Los Quetzales Lodge & Spa, T771-2182, www.losquetzales.com, at Guadalupe. A true forest hideaway with self-contained cabins inside Parque Amistad. A multitude of animals and birds, including quetzals, can be seen from the porches. Back in town, there are dormitories, chalets and some economical rooms, all comfortable and pleasant. Spa facilities and restaurant are excellent. Very special and highly recommended.
C Hotel Cerro Punta, T720-2020. With 9 simple rooms and a quite good restaurant, just before the turning to La Amistad.

Volcán to the border p938
A The Hartmanns, 1 km beyond the end of the dirt road, Santa Clara, T775-5223, www.fincahartmann.com, have comfortable wooden cabins available in the woods, no electricity but with bath and hot water on a working coffee *finca*. Also some bunks (**D**).

Border with Costa Rica p939
D Hotel Los Andes, Río Sereno. Good.

⊙ Eating

David p930, map p931
⊪ El Churrasco, Av Central, between Calle C Norte and Calle D Norte. This popular restaurant serves a decent lunch buffet with a broad selection of wholesome, economical Panamanian fare. In the evening there are stone-baked pizzas, as well as the restaurant's namesake, beef *churrasco*. Recommended.
⊪ El Fogón, Calle D Norte and Av 2a Oeste. A popular, brightly decorated David institution.

They serve Panamanian and international food like ceviche, burgers, whole chicken and pasta. The seafood menu is particularly extensive with a range of lobster, prawn, filet, octopus dishes.
⊪ El Rincón Libanés, Calle F Sur, between Av Central and Av 1a Este. Arabic and Lebanese cuisine, including kebabs and other grilled meat, tasty hummus and tsasiki. They have water pipes and molasses tobacco, if you fancy an after-dinner smoke. Recommended.
⊦ Casa Vegetariana, Av 2a Este and Calle Central. A great little vegetarian buffet serving economical Chinese fare. Fill your plate with noodles and other grub for US$1.50 or less. Open for lunch only. Recommended.
⊦ Multi-Café, Plaza Cervantes, Av 4a. Economical breakfasts, lunches and dinners served from a buffet. Cheap and filling, but pick something that looks fresh and hot. OK for a quick meal, but nothing special. Popular with locals.

Cafés, bakeries and juice bars
Café Katowa, Plaza Real, Calle D Norte, between Av Central and Av 1a Este. Pricey but good coffees, cappuccinos and espressos. Western coffeehouse ambience.
Helados Jackelita, Calle E Norte, between Av Central and Av 1a Oeste. Very good fresh fruit ice creams and smoothies. Recommended.

Boquete and around p933, map p934
⊪⊪ The Rock, Av 11 de Avril, Palo Alto, inside the Riverside Inn, www.therockboquete.com. The Rock enjoys a reputation as one of Boquete's finest restaurants. Their gourmet offerings include delicious onion soup, trout fillet, pork ribs, Thai chicken and steak. Great service, pleasant setting and recommended.
⊪⊪-⊪ Art Café La Crêpe, Av Central, near San Juan Batista. A range of French crêpes are served at this jazzy, continental eatery, including some very creative ones. Province cooking is the house speciality. The attached art gallery displays work by international artists. Recommended.

ⵟⵟⵟ-ⵟⵟ Oasis, Av Buenos Aires, just over the bridge, Bajo Boquete, T720-1586, www.oasisboquete.com. Gourmet dining in a vibrant and sophisticated setting. Tasty offerings include ceviche, king prawn cocktail, Waldorf salad, and tricolour mousse. Good service, but mixed reports on the lamb.

ⵟⵟ Antojitos Mexicanos, Av Central, Bajo Boquete. One of a handful of Mexican restaurants in town, but this one is undisputedly the best. They serve tasty, home-cooked fare including tacos, burritos and chilaquiles. The interior is brightly painted in typical Mexican style. Authentic and recommended.

ⵟⵟ Bistro Boquete, Av Central, Boquete. US owner Loretta once cooked for a US president in her previous establishment in Colorado. Her bistro here is renowned for excellent filet mignon at reasonable prices. Recommended.

ⵟⵟ Il Pianista, Palo Alto, near Boquete Paradise. Located on a hill close to the entrance of the Pianista hiking trail, this oft-praised restaurant serves large, tasty Italian dishes like pizza and calzone. Good for a lunch stop after completing the hike. Romantic and cosy setting, friendly service and reasonable prices. Recommended.

ⵟⵟ Machu Picchu, Av Belisario, Porras. Fantastic Peruvian food cooked by a very friendly Peruvian. Pleasant interior, impressive menu, mostly meat, fish and seafood, and overall this restaurant is heartily recommended by locals as one of the best in town.

ⵟⵟ-ⵟ Tammy's, at the entrance to the cemetery, opposite the Texaco on Av Central, Bajo Boquete, www.tammysboquete.com. Firewood-roasted chicken, kebabs, falafels, hummus, wraps, sandwiches, pizza and flame-grilled burgers are just some of the offerings at **Tammy's**. Popular with ex-pats.

ⵟ Central Park, Parque Central, Bajo Boquete. Intimate but casual little restaurant and coffeeshop on the plaza. They offer economical fare, including hearty breakfasts and set lunches, as well as *comida típica* like stewed meat, grilled pork and pan-fried fish.

ⵟ Jardines de Boquete, Calle 5 Sur, opposite Plaza Los Establos, Bajo Boquete. Cheap and cheerful Panamanian fare, including a variety of meat and chicken dishes. Lunchtime specials are ultra-economical. Great for budget wanderers.

ⵟ Nelvis, Av A Oeste, behind Plaza Los Establos, Bajo Boquete. Very popular with locals at lunch-time, cheap and cheerful **Nelvis** sees crowds queue up for the economical Panamanian buffet. The fried chicken is reportedly the best in town.

ⵟ Pizzería La Volcánica, Av Central, ½ block from main plaza. Good pizzas and pasta at reasonable prices. Economical and popular.

Bakeries

Sugar and Spice, Av Central, Bajo Boquete. Excellent café-bakery on the edge of town. They serve delicious breads, pies and cakes, as well as sandwiches, and in the colder months, soup. Recommended.

Volcán and around *p937*

ⵟⵟ La Hacienda Restaurant, Bambito, T771-4152. Fresh trout, barbecued chicken. Recommended.

ⵟ Hotel Don Tavo, Volcán. Restaurant in hotel, serving pizza and local dishes.

ⵟ La Luna, 4 km on the road to Cerro Punta in Paso Ancho. Good Chinese food.

ⵟ Lizzy's, near post office, Volcán. Fast food, English spoken.

ⵟ Lorena, on road to Río Sereno. Tables on porch. Good fish brought from coast daily.

ⵟ Marisquería El Pacífico, main road east of main intersection, Volcán. Recommended.

Border with Costa Rica *p939*

ⵟⵟ Bar Universal, Río Sereno. Recommended for fried chicken with plantain chips (family atmosphere during the day, more raucous Sat evenings and on pay day during the coffee harvest).

ⵟⵟ Sr Eli, top end of the Costa Rican street. Unnamed restaurant, serving good food, friendly and helpful.

😎 Entertainment

Boquete and around *p933, map p934*
Not renowned for nightlife Boquete is
usually a ghost town after 2200, however,
the recent influx of tourists and ex-pats are
having some impact. African-themed
Zanzibar, Av Central, is open till midnight
and serves cocktails (closed Mon).

Volcán and around *p937*
Weekend discos at **Eruption** and **Kalahari**,
rustic, good places to meet young locals.

⚙ Festivals and events

David *p930, map p931*
Mid-Mar, Fería Internacional de David. A
major 10-day festival that sees over 300,000
visitors and over 500 diverse exhibitors in the
fields of industry, commerce and agriculture.

Boquete and around *p933, map p934*
Jan Feria de las Flores y del Café is a
2-week-long festival (starts 2nd week of Jan)
highlighting Boquete's abundance of exotic
and colorful flowers. This time of year coffee
harvesting season is in full swing and the fair
exhibits coffee and coffee-based products.
Vendors come from all over Central America
to sell their wares. Lodgings fill up, so make
reservations in advance.
28 Nov Independence from Spain. Boquete
erupts in a day-long parade hosting marching
bands of schools from all over Panama.

Volcán and around *p937*
Dec Feria de las Tierras Altas is held
during the 2nd week of Dec in La Fuente
Park. Rodeo, dancing, crafts fair and many
other attractions.

⛰ Activities and tours

David *p930, map p931*
Travesías, Calle B Norte between Av 5 and 6
Este, T774-5352, www.travesiaspanama.com.
Reputable, offering a good selection of
local tours.

Boquete and around *p933, map p934*
River rafting
Chiriqui River Rafting, Av Central, next to
Lourdes, T720-1505, www.panama-
rafting.com. Open 0830-1730. Bilingual
father-and-son team Héctor and Ian Sánchez,
offer 2- to 4-hr Grade II, III and IV trips with
modern equipment, US$85-105 per person.
Recommended.
Panama Rafters, just below the square
on Av Central, T/F720-2712, www.panama
rafters.com. Good, solid rafting operation
with quality gear, guides and a strong
emphasis on safety. Kayak and multi-day
trips are available, but most trips are run
on the excellent Río Chiriquí Viejo.

Tour operators
Boquete Mountain Safari Tours, Plaza
Los Establos, Av Central, T6627-8829,
www.boquetemountainsafari tours.com.
Good selection of ½- and full-day tours, from
hikes to full-on adventures. Uses distinctive
vintage Landrovers. Helpful and friendly.
Boquete Outdoor Adventures, Plaza
los Establos, Av Central, T720-2284,
www.boqueteoudooradventures.com.
Various 1-day and multi-day adventure
packages in Chiriqui and beyond. Specializes
in whitewater kayaking and also offers rafting
and sea kayaking.
Boquete Tree Trek, Plaza los Establos,
Av Central, www.aventurist.com, T720-1635.
High-speed zip-line tours of the forest
canopy. They also offer hiking, biking
and diving.
Explora Ya, Plaza Los Establos, Av Central,
T730-8344 Excellent and well-presented new
outfit that offers a diverse range of local
adventures including hiking, rafting, hot

springs, horse riding, rock climbing and ascents of Volcán Barú. Affiliated with the popular **Habla Ya Spanish School**. Recommended.

Feliciano Tours, T6624-9940, provides tours and transport of the area US$20-60. Good for those needing guidance on trails of the area, some English spoken.

Hiking/Birdwatching Tours, T720-3852. Run by Terry Van Niekerk, who speaks English, Spanish and Dutch, and provides hiking and birdwatching tours of the area surrounding Boquete. Highly recommended for the **Los Quetzales** hike (5 hrs). Prices from US$47.50.

⊖ Transport

David *p930, map p931*

Air

David airport is being expanded and will soon handle long-haul international flights. To **San José** (Costa Rica), **Air Panama**, 1030, US$125 one-way. To **Panama City**, Air Panama, 0800, 1400, 1800, US$80 one-way; **Aeroperlas**, 0755, 1325, 1725, US$80 one-way. All fares exclude tax. **Aeroperlas** flights to Bocas del Toro and Changuinola were suspended at the time of research. You can acquire tickets at the airport, or downtown: **Air Panama**, Av 2a Este and Calle D Norte, T775-0812, www.flyairpanama.com; **Aeroperlas**, Calle Central, between Av 2a Este and Av 3a Este, www.tacaregional.com.

Bus

Long-distance David's long-distance bus station is located at Av 2 Este, 1 block north of Av Obaldía. Taxi to city centre, US$1. Padafront have their own terminal at AV 2 Este and Av Obaldía. To **Almirante**, every ½ hr, 0300-1900, 4-5 hrs, US$7. To **Boquete**, every 20 mins, 0525-2125, 1 hr, US$1.45. To **Caldera**, every 1-2 hrs, 0610-1915, 1 hr, US$2. To **Changuinola**, every ½ hr, 0300-1900,

5-6 hrs, US$8. To **Cerro Punta**, every 15 mins, 0445-2030, 2 hrs, US$2.90. To **Dolega**, every 10 mins, 0520-2330, ½ hr, US$0.80. To **Panama City**, Terminales David–Panama, 16 daily, 0300-0000, 7-8 hrs, US$12.50; Express 2245 and 0000, 5-6 hrs, US$15; Padafront, 5 daily, 0500-2000, US$12.60. To **Paso Canoas**, every 15 mins, 0600-2130, 1 hr, US$1.75. To **Río Sereno**, every 40 mins, 0430-1800, 2½ hrs, US$4.25. To **Soloy**, hourly, 0800-1200 and 1400-1700, 1½ hrs, US$2.50. To Tolé, every 40 mins, 0700-1945, 1½ hrs, US$2.50. To **Volcán**, every 15 mins, 0445-2030, 1½ hrs, US$2.50.

International Panaline and Ticabus services travelling from **San José** (Costa Rica) to **Panama City** drop off passengers on the Interamericana in David, but there is no way to board a bus. The quickest and cheapest way of reaching Costa Rica is to take a bus to **Paso Canoas**, cross the border on foot and pick up a bus on the other side. If you don't want to change buses, **Tracopa** offer services David–San José, 0830, US12, 8 hrs, but you will be queuing for immigration and customs along with your fellow passengers.

Car hire

Alamo, Aeropuerto Enrique Malek, T721-0101, www.alamopanama.com. **Express rent-a-car**, Calle 3a and Av F Sur, T777-3200, www.expressrentpanama.com. **Hertz**, Aeropuerto Enrique Malek, T721-8471, www.rentacarpanama.com. **Nacional**, Aeropuerto Enrique Malek, T721-0000, www.nationalpanama.com.

Boquete and around *p933, map p934*

Bus

Local buses depart from the southeast corner of the main plaza, called El Parque, old fashioned and pretty, every 20 mins to **Volcán** US$1, **David** US$0.75, and **Paso Canoas** US$1.25.

❶ Directory

David *p930, map p931*

Banks David has scores of banks. On Plaza Cervantes, **Banco Nacional** has ATM facilities and changes travellers' checks. Other options include **HSBC**, Calle C Norte, between Av 3a and 4a; **Banco General**, Calle B Norte and Av 1a Este; and **Banco Universal**, Calle B Norte and Av 1a Este; many more branches around town including some on the Interamericana highway. **Cultural centres** Culturama, Av 6a Este, between Calle Central and Calle A Norte, T730-4010, www.semanario culturama.com. **Dentist** Clínica Spiegel, Av Belisario Porras, T775-2683, good reports. **Hospitals** The best private hospital is Hospital Mae Lewis, Carretera Inter-americana, T755-4616, www.maelewis.net. Several laboratories for blood and stool tests, including **Clínco Bio Médica**, Av 3a Este and Calle D Norte. **Immigration** Immigration office, Calle C Sur, between Av Central and 1a Este, Mon-Fri 0800-1500. **Internet** Cybers are widespread in the downtown area, most charging US$0.50-1/hr. Try **Planet Internet**, Av 3a Este and Calle Central. **Laundry** A few *lavamáticos* are clustered on Av 2a Este, between Calle F Sur and Calle D Sur. **Libraries** Biblioteca Publica Santiago Anguizola, Calle A Sur, between Av 1a and 2a Este. Small collection, but housed in the old train station. **Post** Main post office on Calle C Norte, between Av 3a Este and 4a Este. **Telephone** Banks of pay-phones can be found on Plaza Cervantes. Main offices of Cable and Wireless, Av 2a Este and Calle C Norte.

Boquete and around *p933, map p934*

Banks Global Bank, Mon-Fri, 0800-1500, Sat 0800-1500 changes TCs with a commission of US$1 per cheque and has an ATM. Same hours at **Banco Nacional** and Banolar, on the main street, who will both cash TCs. **Internet** Kelnix, beside Chiriquí River Rafting, T720-2803, daily 0800-2000, US$1.80 per hr. **Language schools** Habla Ya, Plaza Los Establos, Av Central, T720-1294, www.hablaya panama.com. Very good, professional outfit that receives good reviews from formers students. Class sizes are small and teachers are well trained. Recommended. Spanish by the River, Alto Boquete, T720-3456, www.spanishatlocations.com. A little out of town but has also received good reviews. **Laundry** Lavomático Las Burbujas, just south of church, very friendly, US$1 to wash. **Post** In the Palacio Municipal.

Volcán and around *p937*

Banks Banco Nacional and Banco de Istmo, Mon-Fri 0800-1500, Sat 0800-1200, both change dollar TCs. **Internet** Sinfonet, in Hotel Don Tavo, US$1 per hr, friendly and helpful. Hardware store Ferremax, main road opposite police station, T771-4461, sends and receives international faxes, 0700-1200, 1400-1800, US$1.50 per page plus telephone charge, English spoken. **Laundry** Lava-mático Volcán, main road opposite Jardín Alegría dancehall. Service only US$2.50, wash, dry and fold, reliable, Doña Miriam will have washing ready when promised.

Bocas del Toro province

Panama's Caribbean banana-growing region has historical links with Columbus' fourth voyage and with the black slaves imported to work the plantations. Ports of varying age and activity lie on the Laguna de Chiriquí, providing an alternative land route to Costa Rica. This region is subject to heavy rainfall, which may take the form of daily afternoon downpours or violent tropical storms. Only from January to March is there much respite from the regular soakings. ▸▸ *For listings, see pages 952-959.*

Towards Laguna de Chiriquí

From Chiriquí on the Pan-American Highway, 14 km east of David, there is a road north over the mountains to Chiriquí Grande (98 km). Beyond Gualaca the road passes the Fortuna hydroelectric plant, the Cricamola Indigenous Reservation and descends through virgin rainforest to the Caribbean. On the way up the hill, just north of Valle de la Mina is **Mary's**, a simple restaurant. If travelling under your own steam you can stop to admire the views across Lago Fortuna resevoir, from where the road is a tough, steep and twisting climb to the the the continental divide, 62 km from the Pan-American Highway, and marked by nothing more than an altitude marker sign.

There is a 10-m waterfall 2.5 km north of the divide. Going north from the continental divide to Chiriquí Grande is a cyclist's delight – good road, spectacular views, little traffic and downhill all the way, but nowhere to eat until Punta Pena, just outside Chiriquí Grande. The road reaches the sea at **Chiriquí Grande**, once the embarkation point for travellers catching the ferry to Almirante and beyond, but now, with the new road heading north, rarely visited.

Banana coast

Fifty kilometres north of Chiriquí Grande, one of Central America's most important banana-growing regions extends from **Almirante** northwest across the border to Costa Rica. Today Almirante is a small commercial port, usually just a transit point for tourists heading to or from the Bocas archipelago. The banana railway starts/ends here. In the 1940s and 50s, disease virtually wiped out the business and plantations were converted to *abacá* and cacao. With the development of disease resistant strains of banana, the *abacá* and cacao have been all but replaced, and banana plantations once again thrive. The main players in the industry are large multinational companies. **Cobanat**, who export through **Chiquirí Land Company** (a subsidiary of **Chiquita Brands**) and **Dole** (a subsidiary of **Standard Brands**), who export bananas to Europe and the US from Almirante. In April 1991 a devastating earthquake struck northwest Panama and southeast Costa Rica. An island in the bay which sank during the earthquake now shows as nothing more than a patch of shallow turquoise water.

Isla Colón and Bocas del Toro → *For listings, see pages 952-959. Colour map 4, B5.*

Across the bay are the rainforest, reefs and beaches of the **Bocas Islands**, the most important of which is **Isla Colón**. The protected bay offers all forms of watersport and diving, beautiful sunrises and sunsets. All the islands harbour plenteous wildlife but especially those east of Colón where tropical birds, butterflies, red, yellow and orange frogs and a great variety of other wildlife abounds. For some, this is being called the new

Galápagos, but, as in that fragile paradise, attraction and concern walk hand in hand. Formerly a major banana producer, the industry failed to revive alongside the mainland plantations and the main sources of income are now fishing and tourism. Bocas del Toro town, where most visitors stay, is on the southeast tip of the island. Most activity takes place around the broad main street – Calle 3a – and the leafy square. The **Feria del Mar** is at the end of September/early October, but for most of the rest of the year it is peaceful and quiet, although more hotels are appearing each year. English is spoken by most of the black population. At the **tourist office** ① *on the seafront, T757-9642, www.bocas.com, Mon-Fri 0830-1630*, there is an informative permanent exhibit, with English translations, about Columbus' landfall, indigenous peoples in the province, the fire at Bocas in 1904 and the United Fruit Company years. Keep an eye on local issues with the monthly *Bocas Breeze*, also online at www.thebocasbreeze.com.

Islands and island trips

Trips can be made to the islands of the archipelago (Bastimentos – see below, **Caranero** and **Solarte** – also known as Nancy); to the bird sanctuary of **Swan Cay** (Isla del Cisne); and to the beautiful **Islas Zapatillas**, for beaches and fishing. Do not go to deserted stretches of beach alone and if you do go, be wary of strong ocean currents – rip tides have caused numerous deaths here. Many of the island names relate to Columbus' landfall here on his fourth voyage in October 1502 (Caranero was where he careened his ships, Bastimentos where he took on his supplies). The islands also have a rich buccaneering history.

1 **Bocas del Toro Archipelago**

➡️ **Bocas del Toro maps**
1 **Bocas del Toro Archipelago, page 948**
2 Bocas del Toro, page 949

On Isla Colón there are some attractive beaches: **Playa Bluff**, 8-9 km northwest of Bocas, is one hour by bike; take the paved road out of town past the cemetery until it runs out and then carry straight on following the shoreline; **Playa Boca del Drago**, on the northwest point, is reached by a newly improved road across the island. Regular buses head over to **Boca del**

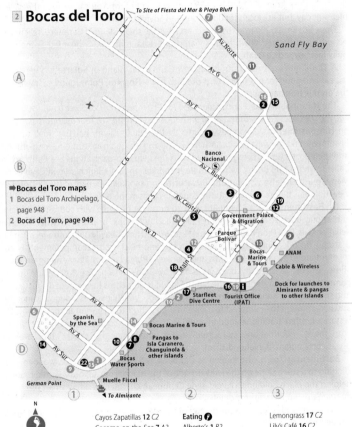

2 Bocas del Toro

To Site of Fiesta del Mar & Playa Bluff

Sand Fly Bay

➡ **Bocas del Toro maps**
1 Bocas del Toro Archipelago, page 948
2 Bocas del Toro, page 949

Banco Nacional

Government Palace & Migration

Parque Bolívar

Bocas Marine & Tours

ANAM

Cable & Wireless

Dock for launches to Almirante & pangas to other Islands

Starfleet Dive Centre

Tourist Office (IPAT)

Spanish by the Sea

Bocas Marine & Tours

Pangas to Isla Caranero, Changuinola & other islands

Bocas Water Sports

German Point

Muelle Fiscal
To Almirante

N

100 metres
100 yards

Sleeping
Angela/Sol y Sombra 5 A2
Bahía 1 D1
Bocas del Toro 2 C2
Bocas Inn Lodge 3 B3
Casa Amarilla 4 A2
Casa Verde/
  La Mama Loca 9 D1

Cayos Zapatillas 12 C2
Cocomo-on-the-Sea 7 A2
Del Parque 8 C2
El Limbo 10 C2
Gran Kahuna Hostel 14 D2
Heike 11 C2
Lula's B&B 17 A2
Mondo Taitu 18 A3
Olas de la Madrugada 6 D1
Palma Royale 15 D1
Sagitarius 24 C2
Tropical Suites 19 C2

Eating
Alberto's 1 B2
Bocas Blended 2 A3
Buena Vista Bar
  & Grill 17 C2
Casbah 15 A3
Chitre 18 C2
El Lorito 3 B2
El Pecado 4 C2
El Ultimo Refugio 14 D1
Gringos 5 C2
La Ballena 6 B3
La Buguita 7 D2

Lemongrass 17 C2
Lily's Café 16 C2
Natural Mystic 10 D1
Om Café 12 B3
Panadería Dulcería
  Alemana 19 B3
Starfish Coffee 8 D2
Super Gourmet 22 D1

Bars & clubs
Barco Hundido 9 C3
Rip Tide 11 A3
Toro Loco 13 C3

Drago daily, leaving from the main square in town. This is a little-visited part of the island. Behind the beach there's a good restaurant and a cheap hostel. A local conservation project has an office here and it might be possible to hire dive and snorkel gear.

Colón also has **La Gruta del Drago**, a cave occupied by long-beaked white bats, which fly out at dusk (tour US$10 plus US$5 for lunch on beach). You can walk to the cave, a pleasant day, but ask locals for directions and advice on safety.

Opposite Bocas, 200 m across the channel, is the small island of **Caranero**, reached by *panga* either flagged down from a waterfront restaurant/bar, or boarded at the small quay just beyond **Le Pirate**.

A 15-minute boat ride from Bocas town, the quiet island of **Solarte** is a very quiet retreat and good for day trips. For those into frogs, **Hospital Point** (good snorkelling) is the orange frog hangout.

The **National Marine Park** ① *tours US$15-20 per person, US$75 per boat, 0900-1600, entry to the Cayos Zapatillas section of the park is US$10 extra, see Tour operators, page 958,* on **Isla Bastimentos** encompasses virtually the whole island, bar the small town of Bastimentos on the western tip. Both this island and Isla Colón are turtle-nesting grounds and their protection is being improved with the help of organizations like **Caribaro**, on Calle 3, who set up beach patrols. There is snorkelling and a lunch stop at Cayo Crawl. Many tour boats also visit **Laguna Bocatorito** (no snorkelling), part of Isla Cristóbal, to view dolphins before going on to the Zapatillas Cays in the park.

On **Bastimentos** it's a 30-minute walk to northern beaches with soft off-white sand and strong undertow; ask directions, take food and drink, or ask if anywhere is open selling meals. **Red Frog Beach** is the best known and now heavily built into a resort; it has a strong rip tide, but **Polo's Beach** (with red-and-black frog accompaniment) is also recommended – look out for sloths and monkeys. **Playa Larga**, halfway along the north shore, is best reached by boat, as is nearby Polo's Beach. The Ngobe indigenous community of Bahía Honda on the South Side of Bastimentos have opened a restaurant and small ecotourism project the 'Trail of the Sloth', which involves a dugout canoe trip and hike through the rainforest to a cave that plays host to an important bat colony. The restaurant offers traditional food in addition to the more common Panamanian dishes. For more information call T6669-6269 (mobile), or check the website bocas.com/indians/bahiahonda.htm.

Bastimentos Town, also known as Old Bank, is a stilted, ramshackle, wooden affair clinging to a steep slope on the leeward side of the island. Tourism once skirted round it, helping the place hold on to its old-style Caribbean charm; now a few smart places are opening up, but it is still very quiet.

Cayos Zapatillas Norte is the quieter of the two Zapatillas because the tour boats do not generally stop here.

Isla Popa and **Cayo Agua**, the other main islands in the area, are sparsely settled, heavily forested and have no beaches.

Diving

Several places throughout the archipelago are popular for diving. The joy of diving in Bocas lies in the details, with some wonderful intact coral gardens (74 out of 79 Caribbean coral species exist here) that seem to play host to a multitude of little gems. Brittle stars, spotted morays, arrow crabs, toadfish and squid are just some of the inhabitants you can expect to see, along with most of the common Caribbean reef fish. Occasionally larger grouper, rays and nurse sharks also put in an appearance.

Good dive sites include: **Tiger Rock** with stronger currents, deeper dives, larger fish and sometimes nurse and whitetip reef sharks; dolphin and wash rocks with rock pinnacles, overhangs and caverns and **La Gruta Polo** with good coral, canyons and caverns. **Hospital Point** is popular for both day and night dives. Several good locations near the resort for scuba-diving and for snorkelling in the clear waters around **Mangrove Point**.

Cavern diving at **Polo's Beach**, only in calm sea, **Punta Vieja** on the northeast shore of Bastimentos and boat dives at **Cayos Zapatillas**.

The best **snorkelling** sites are **Hospital Point** on Cayo Nancy, **Punta Vieja**, **Islas Zapatillas**, but only outside the reef – tour boats will just drop you off at North Cay for snorkelling off the beach (points en route on tours are also disappointing – **Cayo Crawl** has two great sites with very colourful coral, known as Cayo Crawl Inside and Outside, referring to reefs several hundred meters offshore to the east and west – the area directly around the island is seagrass only; hire a boat and guide from one of the dive shops to see the best of the reef. Some areas, such as the islands around the entrance to **Laguna Bocatorito**, harbour habitats where large coral and sponge colonies run right up to the edges of the mangroves creating the unique and fascinating ecosystem. These areas are as a beautiful as they are fragile and require great caution to avoid damaging the reef and its inhabitants, so if not experienced and confident with your snorkelling ability it's best to leave these areas alone and stick to corals in deeper water.

Surfing

The break on the point of Bastimentos where the island curves away from Carenero to meet First Beach (or Playa Wizard) is the renowned and occasionally terrifying (reaching up to 25 ft) **Silver Back**, which attracts surfers from around the globe (peaks December to February).

Playa Bluff is a good beach break, **Playa Paunch** is mostly reef, both are excellent breaks on Colón, and the northeast point of **Caranero**, a full reef, and the most popular of the island breaks. ➤➤ For board rental, see Activities and tours, page 958.

Towards Costa Rica → For listings, see pages 952-959.

Changuinola

Between Almirante and the Costa Rica border is sprawling Changuinola, the main commercial centre in the region which, although architecturally not attractive, has an airport and lively nightlife with sketchy local bars. Changuinola is good for shopping (the food markets are great), there are also several banks where you can change traveller's cheques and use ATMs. Visitors should take care going out at night here; women alone will almost certainly be approached if they enter bars, and maybe also on the street.
→ For border information, see page 715.

The Naso Kingdom

The Río Teribe, known as Tjer Di or 'Grandmother Water' in Naso, is the central axis and spiritual heart of the Naso Kingdom – a remote and thickly forested territory governed by one of indigenous America's last remaining monarchies. The 3500-strong Naso, who occupy 11 communities on or around the riverbanks, consider themselves guardians and heirs to their natural environment. Ancient Naso ancestral lands encompass vast swathes of the Amistad Biosphere Reserve and the Parque Nacional Palo Seco, home to over 400 brilliant bird species, scores of rare mammals, reptiles and amphibians, and more plant and tree species than can be found in the entire European continent. Unsurprisingly, the Naso are masters of bush-craft and jungle medicine. To get to the Río Teribe, first catch a bus from Changuinola to El Silencio, every 20 minutes, US$0.65, taking half an hour. From El Silencio you can hire a boatman to take you upstream, US$35-50, or more economically (and less scenically), catch a truck on the new road as far as Bonyic or Weckso, every half hour, US$1, 20 minutes.

Humedal San San Pond Sak

Established as a protected area in 1994, the Humedal San San Pond Sak encompass 16,125 ha of vitally important wetlands. The park is home to an impressive array of wildlife, including a large population of critically endangered manatees, who dwell all year long among the brackish waters and tangled roots of the mangrove swamps. The reserve is managed by ANAM, but you are advised to organize your visit 24 hours in advance through the **Asociación de Amigos y Vecinos de la Costa y la Naturelza (AAMVECONA)** ⓘ *offices at the reserve's entrance, 5 km north of Changuinola on the highway to Guabito, T6666-0892, www.aamvecona.com.* To get there, catch a bus bound for Las Tablas, US$0.70, 10 min, and ask to be let out at the entrance; or take a taxi, US$4.

⚫ Bocas del Toro province listings

For Sleeping and Eating price codes and other relevant information, see Essentials pages 31-33.

⚫ Sleeping

Towards Laguna de Chiriquí *p947*
For nature lovers and those looking for a fantastic location, the Cloudforest Jungle Lodge can be found just inside the Fortuna Forest Reserve.
B Finca La Suiza, on the southern side of the Fortuna Reserve, Quadrifoglio, T6615-3774 (in David), www.panama.net.tc. To get there from Gualaca: pass the sign to Los Planes (16.4 km) and the turning to Chiriquicito; 300 m after this junction is the sign for the Fortuna Reserve, 1 km beyond the sign is the gate to the *finca* on the right Owned by a Swiss couple, Herbert Brüllmann and Monika Kohler, excellent for bird-watching on 20 km of forest trails, very good food, comfortable accommodation with bath and hot water, breakfast US$5, dinner US$14.50.

Isla Colón and Bocas del Toro *p947, map p949*
LL Punta Caracol, western side of the island, T757-9410, www.puntacaracol.com. An

exclusive and famous eco-resort consisting of a string of thatched luxury bungalows arcing over the water on their own private pier. Very secluded, first-class and attentive.
LL-AL Bocas del Toro, Calle 2a, T757-9771, www.hotelbocasdeltoro.com. This attractive 'boutique' hotel on the seafront has been constructed with 11 types of hard wood. Clean, comfortable rooms with flatscreen TVs, a/c, orthopaedic mattresses and a complimentary bag of organic coffee.
LL-AL Tropical Suites, Calle 1a, T757-9880. Boutique hotel located in the heart of downtown Bocas. A range of suites boast fully equipped kitchens, attractive wood furnishings, Wi-Fi, a/c, flat screen TVs, and in some cases, jacuzzis. Rates vary with views and season. Sometimes good internet rates are available. Breakfast included.
L-A El Limbo, Calle 2a, T757-9062, www.ellimbo. com. This 'boutique' hotel has a great location overlooking the channel between Isla Colón and Caranero. The business-like rooms have nice wooden floors and walls. Those with balconies and sea views are better, and more expensive (**L**). They also have a place on Isla Bastimientos (**A**).

AL Bocas Inn Lodge, north end of Main St, Bocas, T757-9600, bocasinn@ancon expeditions.com. Run by tour operator **Ancon Expeditions** (see page 892). Comfortable and simple with pleasant, spacious bar and terrace, communal veranda upstairs and platform for swimming. Prices include breakfast. Good reviews.

A Bahía, south end of main street, Bocas del Toro, T757-9626, www.ghbahia.com. Built in 1905, this interesting historic building was the former HQ of the **United Fruit Company**. All rooms have hot water, TV, a/c, and the remodelled rooms are more expensive. Ask to see a room before accepting.

A Cocomo-on-the-Sea, Av Norte y Calle 6a, T757-9259, www.cocomoonthesea.com. A lovely place on the seafront with a lush tropical garden, sundeck and 4 clean, simple rooms with a/c and private bath. A huge 'all you can eat' breakfast is included and lots of amenities. US owner Douglas is a superb fellow and very helpful. Nice place and recommended.

A Palma Royale, Main St, www.palma royale.com. A new condo-style establishment that's received good reviews from guests. They offer a range of designer suites (**A**), studios (**LL**) and a penthouse (**LL**) with handsome hand-crafted wood furniture, flat screen TVs, Wi-Fi and all the usual amenities.

B Casa Amarilla, Calle 5a and Av G, T757-9938, www.casaamarilla.org. 4 large airy rooms with good beds, a/c, fridge, digital safe, laptops, Wi-Fi and large flat-screen cable TVs. Owner Dennis Fischer is helpful and interesting to chat to. Free coffee and tea all day. A good place and recommended. Best to book in advance.

B Hotel Olas de la Madrugada, Av Sur, T757-9930, www.hotelolas.com. This popular hotel built over the water has 24 clean, bright rooms, all with a/c, cable TV and private hot water shower. Wakeboard rental available. Wi-Fi and breakfast included. Friendly, with good attention.

B Lula's B&B, Av Norte, across street from **Cocomo-on-the-Sea**, T757-9057,

www.lulabb.com. Old style, family-run place with a kitchenette and deck upstairs and a living area downstairs. Owners Bryan and Jana Hudson are friendly and helpful. Homely, clean, quiet, safe and very secure.

C Del Parque, Calle 2a, on the plaza, T757-9008, hdelparque.webs.com. Well-kept old town house with light wooden rooms and good beds, a/c, pleasant shared balconies, good views, hammocks, hot water, use of kitchen, Wi-Fi, free coffee and fruit. Dorm beds are also now available (**F**), discounts in low season, and can help arrange tours. Much better upstairs.

C Hotel Angela, Av Norte and Calle 6a, T757-9813, www.hotelangela.com. Managed by Claudio from Memphis, who is a true gentleman and very helpful. **Hotel Angela** has 12 rooms with a/c, private bath, hot water and Wi-Fi. TVs and ortho-paedic mattresses were planned for the near future. There is also a comfortable apartment with a full kitchen and jacuzzi (**AL**). Recommended.

D Hotel Cayos Zapatillas, Calle 3a, on the plaza, T757-9844. This popular cheapie has a handy central location. It offers scores of simple, occasionally scruffy rooms with private hot water shower, cable TV and fan. Rooms with a/c cost more (**C**). Simple and economical, although noise may be an issue at times. Wi-Fi and kitchen are available for guests.

D Sagitarius, Calle 4a, T757-9578, hsagitario@cwpanama.net. Simple, reasonably priced wooden rooms with hot water, bath, TV and a/c (cheaper with fan). Locally owned, clean and good for budget wanderers.

D-E Casa Verde, Av Sur, T6633-8050, www.bocaswaterfrontrentals.com. This small, friendly hostel has a range of simple private rooms (**D**), all kitted with a/c, fridge, electronic safe and shared bath with hot water. Various economical dorm beds (**E**) are also available, including some doubles (**D**). General amenities include a communal kitchen, Wi-Fi, internet terminal, a sea deck for swimming, inner tubes, and a buzzing little bar-restaurant. Recommended.

E-F Gran Kahuna Hostel, Calle 3a, T757-9038, www.grankahunabocas.com. A large, popular surf hostel located at the heart of the action on main street, Gran Kahuna offers a range of economical dorms, Wi-Fi, games, communal TV, surf board rental, classes, transportation to the breaks and various surf and stay packages. Clean, well-established and sociable.

E-F Mondo Taitu, Bocas del Toro, T757-9425, www.mondotaitu.com. Ramshackle party hostel that vaguely resembles a ship wreck. A good place to hang out and get groups for trips. The bar is busy (and noisy) in the evenings, happy hour 1900-2000. A handful of 'tree house rooms' (**D**) and various dorms available (**E-F**). Friendly and popular with surfers, backpackers and whippersnappers.

F Heike, Calle 3a, on the plaza, T757-9708, www.hostelheike.com. A friendly, inexpensive backpackers' hostel with 2 private rooms (**D**), 6 dorms (**F**), shared bathrooms, kitchen, communal veranda, coffee all day and a cosy sun terrace complete with hammocks, internet terminals, good breezes and sofas. Surfboards are available for rent. Recommended for surfers.

Islands and island trips *p948, map p948*

LL Al Natural, Old Point, Isla Bastimentos, T/F757-9004, www.alnaturalresort.com. Belgian-owned ecolodge bungalows using traditional techniques and native fallen trees. Price includes transport from Isla Colón, 3 lovingly prepared meals with wine, use of kayaks and snorkelling gear. Email reservations in advance. Highly recommended.

AL-C Careening Cay Resort, Isla Caranero, north side of the island, T757-9157, www.careeningcay. com. Attractive wooden *cabañas* in a tranquil, well-manicured location, some are equipped with stove, microwave and fridge, all have a/c, TV, DVD and bath. Recommended.

A Buccaneer Resort, Isla Caranero, east side, T757- 9042, www.bocasbuccaneer.com.

Situated close to good surf breaks, swimming areas and coral reef, Bucaneer's offers a range of simple, wooden lodgings to suit families, groups and couples. Wi-Fi available and breakfast included. Friendly, helpful management.

C The Point, Old Bank, Isla Bastimentos, at the end of the road, northern tip of the island, T757-9704, sloopj4@yahoo.com. The Point boasts superb views, breezes and great access to local reef breaks. Rooms are modest, comfortable and equipped with fridge, coffee-maker, fan and bath. Clients may also use surf boards. The balcony is a great spot to relax in a hammock. Friendly and recommended.

D Tío Tom's Guesthouse, Old Bank, Isla Bastimentos, T757-9831, www.tiotoms guesthouse.com. Dutch adventurer Tío Tom is a Bastimentos institution. He offers rustic wooden rooms on the water, all with private bath, and a pleasant bungalow with its own terrace (**C**). Lots of interesting extras, very knowledgeable about Panama and the islands. Recommended.

D Yellow Jack, Old Bank, Isla Bastimentos, T6908-3621, www.yellow-jack.com. A very cool, secluded budget hotel with 4 simple private rooms (**D**) and a small house with a 5-person capacity (**A**). Amenities include use of the fridge, dive school and a pleasant communal area built over the water. Friendly Argentine management, chilled out atmosphere and recommended.

D-F Hostel Bastimentos, Old Bank, Isla Bastimentos, T757-9053, www.hostal bastimentos. This long-established budget hostel has an elevated position overlooking the town. Lodgings include ultra-cheap dorm beds (**F**) and a wide range of double rooms (**D**), cheaper without private bath (**E**) and more expensive with hot water and fridge (**C**). Amenities include 2 shared kitchens, Wi-Fi, internet terminal and free *cayucos*.

F Aqua Lounge Hostel and Bar, T6456-4659, Isla Caranero, www.bocasaqualounge. info. A very cool and popular hostel that flies in great DJs for their famous twice weekly parties. Lodgings consist of large dorms (**F**) and 6 simple private rooms (**D**) with shared bath. Highly recommended for discerning revellers.

Changuinola p951

C Alhambra, Calle 17 de Abril, T758-9819. A range of 32 rooms, some are large, all are equipped with bath, hot water, a/c, telephone and TV. Those overlooking the street may be noisy.

D Semiramis, Calle 17 de Abril, diagonally opposite the **Alhambra**, T758-6006. Offers 29 dark rooms with outstandingly kitsch pictures, a/c, hot water, TV, and Wi-Fi in the lobby. The restaurant serves seafood. Parking available. Friendly.

The Naso Kingdom p951

D OCEN, Bonyic, T6569-3869, www.ocen.bocas.com. Managed by Raul Quintero, this community tourism project offers 2 separate facilities with a total capacity for 18 persons. The concrete house has a living room, bathroom and working area. The 'blue house' is wooden and much more simple. The cost of 3 meals is US$13 per person per day.

D Weckso Eco-Lodge, across the river from Bonyic, T6574-9874, www.weckso.org. Built in the grounds of a former Pana-Jungla military training camp, Weckso offers both concrete and traditional wooden lodgings, all with mosquito nets, limited electricity and shared bath. Meals cost extra, US$4-5. Attractive, peaceful grounds on the edge of the rainforest, good attention and personalized service. Highly recommended.

⑦ Eating

Isla Colón and Bocas del Toro p947, map p949

🍴🍴🍴 **La Ballena**, Av E, next to **Swan Cay Hotel**. Delicious Italian seafood pastas and cappuccinos, good for breakfast with tables outside. On the pricey side but has a good reputation.

🍴🍴🍴 **La Casbah**, Av G. Popular and intimate evening restaurant with seating inside and out. Dishes are fresh, creative and tasty with both local and Mediterranean inspiration. Catch of the day is good.

🍴🍴-🍴🍴 **El Pecado**, Calle 3a, under **Hotel Laguna**. Panamanian and international food including Lebanese. Great drinks and good wines worth splashing out on, also try their early evening hummous with warm Johnny Cakes (coconut bread). Recommended.

🍴🍴 **Alberto's Restaurant**, Calle 5a. Authentic Italian cuisine including great pizza, pasta and lasagne. There's also BBQ meat and fish. Wine is served. Reasonable prices.

🍴🍴 **Buena Vista Bar and Grill**, Calle 2a. Long-standing restaurant-bar run by a very friendly Panamanian and his American girlfriend. Good menu for both bar snacks and main meals, grills, tacos, fish and veggie options. Nice spot over the water to relax and chat with a beer or cocktail.

🍴🍴 **El Ultimo Refugio**, Av Sur and Calle 5a. A ramshackle and romantic setting on the water with lots of candlelight and a plant-covered wooden deck. Creative dishes include Peruvian ceviche, marlin filet, pork tenderloin, pineapple and ginger shrimp. Popular and recommended.

🍴🍴 **Gringos**, Calle 4a, behind **Golden Grill**. Authentic Tex-Mex menu with some classic recipes imported from Baja California. The nachos and salsa are excellent, the burritos rich and filling. Wholesome comfort food, popular with expats and recommended.

🍴🍴 **Lemongrass**, Calle 2a, next to **Buena Vista**, upstairs. One of the best in Bocas. English-owned, friendly, buzzing and recommended. They serve seafood and thai curries. Views over the bay and excellent bar for cocktails.

🍴🍴 **Natural Mystic**, Calle 3a. As the name might suggest, mystically themed with oriental artwork and a decidedly bohemian vibe. The changing menu often features affordable fish and shrimp dishes. Sometimes there are live music acts too.

🍴🍴 **Sol y Sombra**, Av Norte y Calle 6a, inside **Hotel Angela**. This relaxed waterside restaurant has a fine local reputation. The changing menu includes specials like ceviche, prawn cakes, prime ribs and passion fruit crème brûlée. The filet mignon is to die for. Only open for dinner at the time of research, but planned to open for lunch too. Highly recommended.

♥-♥ La Buguita, Calle 3a, attached to La Buga dive shop. Popular with backpackers and divers, this little café on the water serves fish tacos, deli sandwiches, breakfast burritos, smoothies and mini-pizzas.

♥-♥ Lili's Café, Calle 1a, next to Tropical Suites Hotel. Chilled out and friendly café on the water serving Caribbean cuisine with a health food twist. A good range of breakfasts and mains, including pastas, soups, salads and sandwiches. Open for breakfast and lunch only.

♥ El Lorito, Calle 3a. Most popular – and oldest – local café in town, serving cheap, wholesome buffet food and cakes. Ask for the pudding – unique to Bocas – and their malted milkshakes.

♥ Om Café, Av E. Closed Wed and Thu. Excellent, home-made Indian food served in very relaxing and ambient surroundings. Tables are available on the balcony or private rooms for larger parties. Om also serves good breakfasts. Recommended.

♥ Restaurant Chitre, Calle 3a. Long-running *fonda* serving cheap and cheerful buffet fare. Nice owners, and a good spot for watching street traffic.

Cafés, bakeries, delis and juice bars

Bocas Blended, Calle Norte, on the corner opposite Casa Max. Quirky old bus converted into a juice bar. There's conspicuous seating on the roof where you can watch the world go by. Juices are good and rich in vitamins, but not cheap. They also do wraps and other snacks.

Panadería Dulcería Alemana, Calle 2. This small German bakery does tasty cakes, delicious fresh bread, good coffee and light snacks. Very good, but not cheap, and service is sometimes inattentive.

Starfish Coffee, Calle 3, just before Bocas Water Sports, Bocas del Toro. Cappuccino, pastries, croissants and brownies. Excellent breakfast deals at reasonable prices. Recommended.

Super Gourmet, Calle 1, near the ferry for Almirante. Deli and gourmet supermarket that does very good, if pricey, sandwiches, pastas and salads. You'll also find tasty local produce and plenty of foreign imports here.

Islands and island trips *p948, map p948*

♥♥♥-♥♥ Cosmic Crab Café, Isla Caranero, north side of the island, facing Isla Colón. Managed by a friendly American couple, Joan and Steve, who offer a creative menu with diverse international influences including Greek, Thai, Indian and Caribbean. They also have an entire menu devoted just to Martinis.

♥♥ Bibi's on the Beach, Isla Caranero, part of Bucaneer's Resort, east side of the island near Black Rock, T6785-7984, www.bibison thebeach.com. Managed by friendly Argentine Luis Bertone. Fresh, tasty, Creole-style seafood. Open for breakfast, lunch and dinner every day except Tue. Good ambience. Recommended.

♥♥ Island Time, Isla Bastimentos, on the hill, 5-10 mins from Old Bank, follow the path next to the police station. Excellent, authentic Thai curries, soups and noodles served on a pleasant deck overlooking the jungle and ocean. The best restaurant on the island. Very satisfying and highly recommended.

♥ Puntai Pizza, Old Bank, Isla Bastimentos, south of the police station. Run by Nicole, Puntai serves sandwiches, coffee, breakfasts, juices, and of course, fresh baked pizza. Good local reports and worth a look. Breakfast and dinner only.

♥ Up in the Hill, 15 mins from Old Bank, Isla Bastimentos, follow the path next to the police station. Intimate and ramshackle café attached to an interesting cacao and coconut farm. They serve hot coffee, fresh herbal teas, juices, brownies and exquisite truffles.

☺ Entertainment

Isla Colón and Bocas del Toro *p947, map p949*

Barco Hundido, Calle 1a, next to Cable & Wireless office. The **Wreck Deck** (its original name) is built over a wrecked, sunken boat. Once very popular, there have been some negative reports lately. Watch your back and your wallet.

La Mama Loca, inside **Casa Verde Hostel**. A nice little crowd at the time of research. Beer, cocktails, shooters and shots by the waters' edge, and usually live music from 1800, including reggae. Friendly and recommended.

Mondo Taitu, Av G, T757-9425. Busy and often buzzing bar in a backpackers' hostel. Good for beer, cocktails, hukka pipes and meeting other travellers. A young, image-conscious crowd.

Rip Tide, A famous and popular expat bar built into a big old boat on the water. Good for a beer and a laugh, but not for innocents. They also do filling grub, including chicken wings, should you get peckish.

Toro Loco, Av Central, between Calle 1a and 2a. A US-style grill and bar with loud music, sports TV, dart board and various dark little corners. Popular with expats and praised as one of the best watering holes in town.

Islands and island trips *p948, map p948*

Every Mon anyone who wants to party heads over to Isla Bastimentos to **Blue Mondays**, a largely local event with live Calypso music and the full Caribbean vibe. Hugely popular. Also check out:

Aqua Lounge, Isla Caranero. An estimated 300-400 people attend the legendary parties at the **Aqua Lounge**, hosted every weekend and on an additional night in the week. Highly recommended.

▲ Activities and tours

Isla Colón and Bocas del Toro *p947, map p949*

Diving and snorkelling

Sep-Oct and Mar-Apr are the best months for diving and snorkelling. Bocas is a good place for beginners and courses are competitively priced during low season. A 2-tank dive costs US$50-60.

Bocas Watersports, Calle 3a, T757-9541, www.bocaswatersports.com. Dive courses, waterskiing and kayak rental. They offer a day-long snorkelling tour to Dolphin Bay, Crawl Cay, Red Frog and Hospital Point, snacks included, US$20. Training from Open Water Diver to Dive Master.

La Buga Dive Center, Calle 3a, T757-9534, www.labugapanama.com. An expanding and popular outfit. They offer training from Open Water to Dive Master. They claim to have the biggest, fastest boat in the area, and know special dive sites their competitors don't. Also offers surf lessons.

Starfleet, Calle 1a, next to Buena Vista, T757-9630, www.starfleetscuba.com. A very professional, PADI Gold Palm IDC centre, managed by Tony and Georgina Sanders from England. They offer training from Open Water Diver right up to Instructor level. A 2-tank dive is US$60, a day-long snorkel tour, US$20. Dive-master internships also available. Highly recommended.

Health and Spa

Bocas Yoga, Calle 4a, the big purple building, www.bocasyoga.com. Dedicated Yoga studio with daily classes in Hatha, Vinyasa and Anusara-inspired yoga. Drop-in rates US$5 per class, multi-class packages also available.

Sailing

Catamaran Sailing Adventures, Av Sur y Calle 6a, next to Hotel Dos Palmas, T757-9710 or T6464-4242, www.bocassailing.com. Owner Marcel offers popular day sailing tours on his 12-m catamaran around the Bocas Islands for US$44, including lunch and snorkelling gear. Trips leave daily at 0930, but you will need advance reservation.

Surfing
You can rent boards from hostels like Gran Kahuna, Mondo Taitu and Heike. **Tropix**, on Calle 3a (T757-9415) make custom boards for sale. **Bocas Surf School** operates from **Lula's B&B**, Av H, T6482-4166, www.bocassurfschool.com.

Tour operators
There are numerous tour operators, most have maps and photos to help plan your own day if you have a big enough group. Usual tours visit either Dolphin Bay, Hospital Point, Coral Cay and Red Frog Beach (Bastimentos), or Boca del Drago and Swans Cay (Bird Island). For a little extra you can add Cayos Zapatilla to the first tour. You are advised to use reputable operators rather than street touts.
Jampan, Calle 1a, T757-9619, www.jampan tours.com. A professional, safe and well-established operator with quiet, fuel-efficient 4-stroke motors and knowledgeable bilingual captains. They visit all the usual haunts and some unusual ones too. Recommended.
Transparente Tours, Calle 3a, beside The Pirate, T757-9915, transparentetours@ hotmail.com. A long-running and reputable operator that offers boat tours of the islands and major sights. An interesting and original option is to the far flung and very beautiful island of Escudo de Veraguas.

Island and island trips *p948, map p948*
Diving and snorkelling
Scuba 6 Dive Center, Old Bank, inside Tio Tom's Guesthouse, T6793-2722, www.tiotomsguesthouse.com. An enthusiastic new outfit managed by experienced and adventurous divers. Groups are kept small and course materials are available in German, English, Dutch or Spanish. Recommended.

Surfing
Escuela del Mar, part of Bucaneer's Resort, east side of the island near Black Rock, T6785-7984, luisbertone@gmail.com. Passionate surf instructor Luis Bertone has 20 years' experience riding waves. His surf school is perfectly positioned next to Black Rock, an ideal break for learners. Recommended.

⊖ Transport

Towards Laguna de Chiriquí *p947*
Boat
Water taxi from Almirante to **Bocas** US$4. To get to the *muelle* from the bus station, cross over railway line, bear left following far side of fence across scrub land to road, head left along road 2 blocks to the quay; or take a taxi, US$1. Take care, sketchy area.

Bus
From Almirante to **David**, every 40 mins, 4 hrs, US$7; **Changuinola**, 30 mins, US$1.50.

Isla Colón and Bocas del Toro *p947, map p949*
Air
Fares and schedules are subject to changes and tax. Always confirm departure times 24-48 hrs before departure. To **Panama City**, Aeroperlas, 1130, 1430, US$80; Air Panama, 0800, 1630, US$80, 1 hr. To **Changuinola**, Aeroperlas, 1030, US$8, 10 mins. Nature Air (Costa Rica, www.nature air.com) now operate flights between Bocas del Toro and **San José** (Costa Rica), from US$140 1 way, promotions sometimes available.

Boat
Water taxis To and from **Almirante** run every ½ hr, 0630-1830, 30 mins, US$4. From Isla Colón to the other islands, including **Caranero**, **Bastimentos** and **Solarte**, water taxis depart from various points along the waterfront. Fares are US$1-3 one-way, and always rising with the cost of petrol. From

Caranero or Bastimentos Town it's easy to flag down a passing boat. If you're going to remote beaches, don't forget to arrange a time to be picked up. If hiring a boat, try to arrange it the day before, at least US$60 per day, depending on the boatman (4 hrs minimum, can take 9 people or more, depending on boat size).

Towards Costa Rica *p951*
Bus
If going on to Costa Rica from Bocas, get the first water taxi for connections at Sixaola. A bus leaves Changuinola direct for **San José** at 1000, however, if you are simply going to **Puerto Viejo** or **Cahuita**, you can leave anytime before lunch. The border closes at 1700 and Costa Rica is 1 hr behind Panama. Immigration at the Sixaola border crossing requires you to have proof of a return flight out of the country or back to Panama and will ask to see it. Currently you can buy bus tickets at the border that are sufficient.

Changuinola *p951*
Air
Fares and schedules are subject to changes and tax. Always confirm departure times 24-48 hrs before departure. To **Bocas del Toro**, Aeroperlas, 1100, 1400, US$8, 10 mins. To **Panama City**, Air Panama, 0715, 1600, US$80, 1 hr.

Bus
To **Almirante**, every 30 mins till 2000, 30 mins, US$1.50. To **San José** 1 daily, 1000 (no office, pay on bus) US$8, 6-7 hrs, 1 stop for refreshments in Limón, but many police checks (this bus may not always run). Alternatively, catch a Las Tablas bus to Guabito, every 20 mins till 2000, 30 mins, US$0.80, cross the border on foot and catch a service from Sixaloa onto Limón. Buses to **David**, depart from Terminal Urracá, every 30 mins, 4 hrs, US$7.

Boat
At the time of research, the Snyder canal was closed due to flood damage and services between Changuinola and Bocas del Toro were suspended; enquire locally for an update.

ⓘ Directory

Isla Colón and Bocas del Toro *p947, map p949*
Banks Banco Nacional de Panamá, Calle 4 and Av E, T757-5948, Mon-Fri 0800-1500, Sat 0900-1200, 24-hr ATM. **Immigration** Migración office, at the back of the Palacio, is for visitors arriving by air or boat. Officials are at the airport to stamp passports of those arriving nationals covered by the '*convenio*' and to provide tourist cards for others (eg US citizens arriving from Costa Rica; see page 871). Those requiring visas must go to the Banco Nacional to purchase the relevant documentation (US$10) and then go to the office in the Palacio. This office does not renew tourist cards or visas. **Internet** Bocas Internet Café, next to the M/S Isla Colón Supermarket on main street, US$2 per hr; Don Chicho's Internet, next to El Lorito restaurant, US$2 per hr. **Language schools** Spanish by the sea, T757-9581, www.spanishatlocations.com. A wide range of intensive courses that can be combined with adventure activities. **Laundry** Lavamático, on the right, just beyond Hostal Ancón at north end of town, US$3 per load, pick up following day.

Changuinola *p951*
Bank Bancistmo Mon-Fri 0800-1500, Sat 0900-1200, changes AMEX TCs. Cash advances on Visa and MasterCard. **Immigration** Oficina de Migración, renewal of visas and tourist cards.

Darién

→ Colour map 5, B3.

Having traversed the entire north American continent from Alaska, the Panamerican highway promptly ends in the Darién. Beyond it, a wilderness of dark and impenetrable rainforests reaches across the frontier into Colombia – the so-called Darién Gap, currently a favourite haunt of smugglers and paramilitaries. Notoriously difficult and dangerous to navigate, many travellers have vanished in the consuming jungles of the Darién. A particularly tragic episode in the region's history recalls the Scottish colony of New Edinburgh. Founded in 1698 on the Darien's Caribbean coast, the colony descended into starvation, violence and disease before collapsing into ruin entirely. More successful endeavours include those of Vasco Núñez de Balboa, who crossed the Darién in 1513 and became the first European to lay eyes on the Pacific coast. Today, the Darién enjoys a dark reputation as a 'no-go' zone. This is certainly true of some areas, including the classic

Darién

overland route into Colombia, which should not be attempted. Equally, there are areas that can be visited safely, including parts of the sublime Parque Nacional Darién, the provincial capital, settlements along the Panamerican highway, and the fascinating Emberá and Wounaan villages along the Río Sambú. Successful navigation of the region does require travelling experience savvy, and if you don't have plenty of money to fund your trip, you should have plenty of time. A strong constitution helps too ... and lots of insect repellent.
▶ *For listings, see pages 967-968.*

Ins and outs

Getting there
The cheapest way into the Darién is by road, but non-existent infrastructure means flying may be the only safe way to reach your final destination. Plan thoroughly before setting out. By bus, there are eight daily departures from Panama City to Yaviza (six to eight hours, US$16). By plane, **Aeroperlas** flies from Panama City to Bahía Piña and Jaqué; **Air Panama**

flies from Panama City to Garachiné, Jaqué, Puerto Obaldia and Sambú. **Ancon Expeditions** (see page 892) runs charter flights from Panama City to their field station in Cana, included in their tour packages.

Getting around
Independent exploration of the Darién is impossible without reasonable Spanish – you will need to talk to locals to secure private vehicles or otherwise glean up-to-date information on public transport, which is often infrequent, casual and without any fixed schedule. Most river travel is conducted on motorized longboats called *piraguas*. They are hired privately with a captain and pole-man, US$10-20 per day, but gasoline is extra and extremely expensive. How much you use depends on the horse-power and type of engine, the total cargo/passenger weight, distance covered and type of boat – US$150-200 per day is a rough estimate. If possible, buy your gasoline separately and ensure your boatman uses yours and yours only, returning any unused quantities at the end of the trip (you can easily sell any you don't use). If travelling long distances, always enquire about the availability of gasoline en route and pack a barrel or tank for the return leg if necessary. It's possible to hitch rides on cargo boats but arrange a fee before boarding. River travel is always

The harpy eagle

The wildest and most remote forests of Panama still play host to one of Latin America's most magnificent predators, the harpy eagle (*Harpia harpyja*). Standing 1 m tall and with 5-cm talons that rival the claws of a grizzly bear, the harpy is the world's most powerful bird of prey. In comparison to its huge body size, the eagle's wingspan (around 2.1 m) is not large, an adaptation that allows it to glide between the trees with exceptional stealth and agility, searching for its favoured prey of monkeys and sloths.

Harpy eagles need huge territories with good wildlife populations in order to survive. Massive deforestation in Panama and elsewhere in Latin America has resulted in its disappearance from vast swathes of its former habitat. Due to its rarity, and the fact that the harpy does not often soar, this bird is tough to track down. But Panama is perhaps the harpy's greatest stronghold in Central America, and several nest sites have been identified in the Darién and Canal areas. Agencies in Panama City can arrange trips to these nest sites.

speedier in the wet season when water levels are higher. Hiking between destinations is very common but subject to important safety concerns (see below). Always use a guide and be aware the going is rough and muddy in the wet season. There are very few roads in the Darién – paved or otherwise. A car is largely redundant, but you'll need a good 4WD with high clearance if you do want to drive cross-country (not recommended in the wet season when tracks are washed out). The highway to Yaviza is now paved.

Safety and precautions

The Darién is a dangerous wilderness populated by drug-runners, bandits, paramilitaries and other on-the-edge characters. It pays to be cautious. By the same token, many people travel safely to the region each year by following common-sense guidelines and not visiting areas deemed 'no-go'. The forests east of Yaviza, with a few exceptions, are considered dangerous for foreign visitors, particularly beyond the last-stop frontier town of Boca de Cupe, where you may be arrested if you attempt to go any further. Note it has not been safe to cross the Darién Gap into Colombia for many years and you will risk kidnapping and murder if you try. The destinations detailed in this section were 'safe' at the time of research, but it is important to realize that the situation in the Darién is constantly changing. Seek up-to-date information before setting out.

For your safety, it is a legal requirement to present identification at frequent security checkpoints throughout the region. Keep your passport handy and make the local police station your first port of call upon arrival anywhere. A guide is absolutely obligatory if trekking in the rainforest – even if you have years of wilderness experience, the police will demand you hire one. Choose your guides carefully and consult the local ANAM office or other trustworthy persons in the community. Due to banditry, do not discuss your journey or destination with people you don't know. Using an established tour operator will probably not work out cheaper than using your own guides and hired transport, but it will certainly be safer and hassle-free. **Ancon Expeditions** and **EcoCircuitos** are particularly recommended for their Darién expeditions (see pages 892 and 893).

Conditions in the Darién are generally extreme and you should pack for wet weather, blazing sun, high humidity and blood-thirsty bugs. Malaria is endemic. Take medication in advance of setting out and use nets and lashings of repellent to protect against other insect-borne diseases. If trekking, it is recommended you sleep in a zipped tent to avoid unpleasant night-time encounters with vampire bats, which are sometimes infected with rabies. If bitten, a course of vaccination shots must be administered within 24 hours and there is no guarantee they will work. Venomous snakes pose a further threat, especially at night. If you require antivenin, hospitals can be found in Yaviza, La Palma and Real, along with a string of health centres in smaller settlements. As a precaution, wear boots until you need to sleep and always, always shake them out in the morning. Tap water is not potable in the Darién, so you will need a purifier or purification tablets. Blackouts are common – torches, matches, candles and batteries are a wise idea. There are no banks beyond Yaviza and La Palma, so bring lots of cash and never allow stocks to run out. In all other cases, pack for survival ...

Panama City to Yaviza → *For listings, see pages 967-968.*

The Interamericana is now paved as far as Yaviza and passes through a string of sleepy towns en route to its conclusion in the jungle. Until the 1970s, everything east of Chepo, 50 km from Panama City, was thickly forested and part of the Darién Gap. Not so today. Actually located in Panamá province, Chepo itself is a reasonably large town and has modern amenities including an ATM, stores and a hospital. About 18 km east of Chepo, you'll pass the 30-km-long El Llano–Cartí highway, which crosses over the continental divide and into Kuna Yala. It is also recently paved and offers access to the reputable **Burbaya Lodge**, an upmarket but pleasantly rustic ecolodge with good forest trails and some of the world's best birding (see Sleeping, page 967).

Lago Bayano
Back on the Interamericana, the town of Cañita, 10 km further east, has good, if not better provisions than Chepo. Expansive Lago Bayano lies another 12 km ahead. Created in 1976 with the damming of the Bayano river, the 350-sq-km lake displaced thousands of Kuna and Emberá, many of whom relocated to the banks of the Río Chagres in what is today the Parque Nacional Chagres. On the south side of Lake Bayano, which is named after a famous Cimarron (escaped African slave) warrior, are the atmospheric, bat-filled **Bayano Caves**. To visit, you need to charter a boat, US$50. Once inside, cover your mouth to avoid inhaling nasty particles and do not swim in the water – it is reportedly home to crocodiles and carnivorous fish.

Ipetí
Beyond Bayano, the highway rolls east towards the provincial border with Darién, closely flanked by the folded ridges of the **Serranía de Majé** to the south. The settlement of Ipetí, which is composed of three ethnically distinct Kuna, Emberá and Latino townships, is worth a stop if you have time. The Emberá contingent have established a community tourism project where you can experience village life, hike in the surrounding forests, swim in waterfalls, take canoe trips or get beautified with *jagua* temporary tattoos. Continuing east on the highway, you'll pass the towns of **Tortí** and **Cañazas**, both with basic amenities, including hotels in Tortí, before crossing into Darién at **Agua Fría No 1**.

Santa Fe

The 6000-strong town of Santa Fe lies 3 km off the Interamericana, roughly 25 km east of the Panamá-Darién border. In former times, the settlement prospered thanks to its river connections with the Pacific ocean. Today, there's not much to see beyond some basic stores and small hotels. About 10 km east of the Santa Fe turn-off lies **Quebrada Honda**. If you have a 4WD, you can turn south here and head 11 km on a bumpy track to the excellent community tourism project of **Puerto Lara**, www.puertolara.com. This friendly Wounaan village offers a host of fun activities including body painting, traditional dancing, hiking and fishing. Taxi pick-up available, book in advance.

Metetí

It's another 26 km on the Interamericana until you arrive at Metetí, a major town and stopover just 50 km from the end of the highway. It is home to convenience stores, restaurants, hotels and many colonists from other parts of the country, mostly from Chiriquí province in the west. Many people pass through Metetí on their way to La Palma, the capital of the Darién (see below). Public boats depart from Puerto Quimba, 20 km away on the Río Iglesias (0730-1830, 30 minutes, US$3). To get to the port, catch a local bus (US$1.50) or a taxi (US$10). Should you need to stay overnight in Metetí, there are a few cheap, basic hotels and one outstanding option – the **Filo de Tallo** ecolodge ⓘ *www.panamaexoticadventures.com* (see Sleeping, page 967). In nearly every way, Metetí is a preferable place to Yaviza, which is insalubrious at the best of times.

Yaviza

Rough-and-ready Yaviza is the end of the road. Like many frontier towns, it throngs with barely concealed criminal undertones. There are numerous cheap hotels, stores, restaurants and seedy bars, along with a police station where you must check in immediately. If you intend to visit the Parque Nacional Darién, you must also register with ANAM and pay park entrance fees. From Yaviza, it's possible to hire a boat to **El Real** (one hour, US$60-80). You can hitch on a public cargo boat too (US$5-10), but finding one is a matter of luck and persistence. If you find yourself stuck, the sights are modest. On the banks of the Río Chucunaque you'll find the crumbling remains of the **Fuerte San Jerónimo de Yaviza**, an old Spanish fort used to protect gold shipments from the mines at Cana. The port, too, makes a worthy distraction. Otherwise, the best thing you can do is start drinking.

Parque Nacional Darién

ⓘ *Park entrance fees US$5. It is not possible to visit the park alone ; you will require a guide and the permission of ANAM before you proceed.*

The Parque Nacional Darién encompasses 579,000 ha of pristine wilderness along the Panama-Colombia border. It is the largest protected area in Central America and a UNESCO Biosphere Reserve since 1983. The park is punctuated by diverse natural features including vast lowland rainforests, cloud forests, mountain ranges, rambling coastline, rugged ravines and gorges. Dispersed Kuna, Emberá and Wounaan settlements lie within the park, mostly along the banks of river systems such as the Tuira, Balsas, Sambú and Jaqué rivers. Unsurprisingly, the Parque Nacional Darién is one of the world's premier nature and wildlife destinations. Some 450 bird species are known to inhabit the park, including harpy eagles, macaws, parakeets, quetzals and the virtually ubiquitous toucans.

Resident mammals include rare jaguars, peccaries, bush dogs, tapirs, capybaras, anteaters, agoutis, coatis, deer and scores of different monkeys. Botanists, too, will find plenty to inspire them in the primeval forests, which are home to towering virgin trees and untold species of orchid.

Pirre Field Station (Rancho Frío)

The Pirre Field station is managed by ANAM (T299-6965 in El Real) and offers very rustic accommodation on fold-out cots (F), a simple dining area and cooking facilities. Camping and hammocks (G) are an option if you bring your own gear. There are a couple of good trails in the vicinity, including a forested loop trail that passes some waterfalls (do not scale them, highly dangerous!) and the more strenuous **Cerro Pirre Trail**, which ascends a stiff mountain ridge (guide essential). **Note** You will not be able to buy food at the station, so bring enough for yourself and the guide who leads you there, if he's staying overnight. A little extra will sweeten the guards too, and they might cook for a small fee.

Pirre Field Station is located at Rancho Frío, 13 km south of the town of **El Real** – a fairly large frontier settlement that's best accessed from Yaviza (see above). Be aware that El Real is your last chance to pick up supplies, including anti-malarial medicine if you're running low. If you get stuck, there's a rustic *pensión* (F) and a few *fondas* for cheap meals. From El Real, you need to hire a guide for the two- to three-hour trek to Rancho Frío, ANAM charges US$20-30 but other guides may be cheaper. In the wet season the trip can take four hours and you will certainly need rubber boots. If you don't want to walk, you can take a boat up the Río Pirre as far as the Emberá village of **Piji Baisal** (US$75) and hike from there (guide still necessary), one hour.

Cana Field Station

Cana Field Station is managed by the ANCON, an environmental NGO based in Panama City. The station occupies a former mining camp in the foothills of the Pirre mountain ridge. Years ago, over 20,000 people lived in the area, most of them employed in the local gold mine, but today there's little evidence of that beyond old equipment rusting in the undergrowth. Cana is one of the most isolated places in Central America and one of the most lauded birdwatching sites in the world. Getting there isn't cheap. In the past, it was possible to follow an old railway line from **Boca de Cupe**, 30 km away – the highly policed and edgy last outpost of 'civilization'. However, the two-day hike to Cana through the lawless Darién Gap is now considered dangerous and must not be attempted. That leaves the landing strip. Flights to Cana are chartered by Ancon Expeditions (see page 892) and are included in their reputable Darién package tours. Costs are high but the facilities, which include a stunning cloud forest camp up in the mountains, are certainly a cut above the poor man's shack at Rancho Frío.

La Palma and around

La Palma, the diminutive capital of the Darién, is perched on the gulf of San Miguel at the place where the first European, Vasco Núñez de Balboa, emerged to 'discover' the Pacific coast of the Americas. Perched on the water's edge, it's a hot, grubby, indolent place that's not exactly friendly or inviting, but is interesting to experience. Although comprising little more than a few roads, La Palma has the best amenities for miles, including a bank, airstrip, simple hotels, bars, eateries and general stores. If you have time to kill, charter a boat to visit **El Fuerte de San Carlos de Boca Chica** – a ruined fortress on the Island of Boca Chica. Built in the mid-19th century, it formed part of the defences for the Cana gold mine.

Reserva Natural Punta Patiño

Managed by ANCON, the Reserva Natural Punta Patiño encompasses 263 sq km of primary and secondary forests, black-sand beaches and extensive Ramsar-listed wetlands, including red and black mangroves around the mouth of the Río Mogué. It is the largest private nature reserve in Panama. Scores of birds can be spotted along the waterways, including kingfishers, waders, herons and duck, with scores more in the forests, including harpy eagles. You can also observe large colonies of capybaras, a few crocodiles and, if you're exceptionally lucky, jaguars. The reserve has good trails, including a two-hour loop known as the **Sendero Piedra de Candela** (the Flintstone trail), so-named for the reddish quartz littered on the trail (it sparks if you strike it with a machete). ANCON manage a very pleasant lodge on a hill inside the park and ferry guests from La Palma as part of their packages. Otherwise you will have to charter your own vessel (one hour, US$60-80); the ride can be choppy.

Mogué

Perched between jungle and riverbank, the colourful Emberá village of Mogué is a popular excursion for guests of ANCON's Punta Patiño lodge. Around 60 families live in the village, definitely geared towards tourism. Traditional dances, crafts and tattoos are among the offerings, along with trips to find harpy eagles. If you want to stay overnight, bring a tent or hammock. There's a large wooden shelter and communal kitchen for guests, but it's best to book your visit through a tour operator. Mogué is about 1½ hours from La Palma, or half an hour from Punta Patiño.

Río Sambú

A journey up the jungle-shrouded Río Sambú – home to several authentic Emberá and Wounaan communities – is one of the most interesting river journeys in Panama. The largest and most important village in the region, **Sambú**, has an airstrip, medical centre, hotels and payphone. It makes a good base for exploring destinations further upstream, including **Puerto Indio** and **Pavarandó**. The best place to stay in town is Sambú Hause, see Sleeping, below, operated by a friendly American expat who knows the best guides and destinations. Sambú can be reached by thrice weekly *panga* from La Palma (US$20, schedules vary). Expect to pay around US$100 round-trip to travel from Sambú to the furthest communities upstream.

Bahía Piña

Bahía Piña on the Pacific coast is known for its superb fishing – more International Game Fish Association records have broken here than anywhere else in the world. Marlin, sailfish, dorado, tuna and snapper all populate the waters, which are carefully protected from commercial exploitation. The bay owes its large fish population to the **Zane Grey Reef** – a seamount that gathers plankton and attracts large predators. Flush fishermen like to stay at the **Tropic Star Lodge** (see Sleeping, below), a very upmarket destination that sees Hollywood filmstars and wealthy politicians among its clientele. Around 8 km from the Tropic Star, lies the very small community of **Jaqué**, home to indigenous refugees who fled the fighting in Colombia. It's possible to catch a boat from Jaqué to Buenaventura in Colombia, US$100, but it's a rough trip and you may have to wait five days for an available passage.

For Sleeping and Eating price codes and other relevant information, see Essentials pages 31-33.

⊜ Sleeping

Panama City to Yaviza *p963*
L Burbayar Lodge, Llano–Cartí highway, T236-6061, www.burbayar.com. Rustic and highly regarded ecolodge with 7 secluded wood cabins, restaurant, hammocks and tranquil, leafy grounds. Can arrange tours to indigenous communities, surrounding forests and Bayano lake. At the heart of a world-class birdwatching zone. Rates are per person and include 3 meals.
L Filo de Tallo, Metetí, T314-3013 (Panama City booking office), www.panamaexoticadventures.com. High-end, rustic accommodation with a natural, peaceful setting and expansive views over the valley. French-run and ecologically aware. Tours of communities and forests available. Rates are per person, book in advance.
D Hotel 3Americas, Yaviza, T299-4439. Run-down local lodgings that have been serving stranded travellers for decades. Rooms are plain and simple.

Parque Nacional Darién *p964*
LL Cana Field Station, Santa Cruz de Cana, T269-9415 (Panama City booking office), www.anconexpeditions.com. Formerly the headquarters of the gold mine and now a world-class birding lodge and biological research centre managed by ANCON. The wooden field station has 12 simple, screened bedrooms with battery-powered lamps and single semi-orthopaedic beds. Shared bathrooms have hot water. Limited electricity. If you want to stay, you must purchase an expensive 5- or 8-day tour package.
F Pirre Field Station, Rancho Frío, T299-6965 (ANAM in El Real). Simple jungle lodgings with cooking facilities and camping space. Basic amenities include cold showers, flush

toilets and limited electricity. Consult ANAM, who manage the station, before setting out. Rates are per person.

La Palma and around *p965*
LL Punta Patiño Lodge, Reserva Natural Punta Patiño, T269-9415 (Panama City booking office), www.anconexpeditions.com. An excellent and very comfortable wildlife lodge managed by ANCON. Cabins are well appointed with a/c, private bath, hot water and sublime views. The complex also includes an early 20th-century chapel. Guests stay as part of all-inclusive packages, not cheap.
D Sambú Hause, Sambú, T6687-4177, www.sambuhausedarienpanama.com. A friendly, comfortable bed-and-breakfast in the jungle. American-owned and very knowledgeable about the area. Rates are per person and include breakfast. Recommended.
E Hotel Biaquiru Bagara, La Palma, T299-6224. Plain and simple, but comfortable enough. Cheaper with shared bath. There's also a market nearby for supplies.

Bahía Piña *p966*
LL Tropic Star Lodge, 800-682-3424 (US booking), www.tropicstar.com. Possibly the world's finest fishing resort. Luxury facilities include bar, restaurant and pool. The preferred haunt of moneyed sportsmen. Stays are part of expensive all-inclusive fishing packages.

▲ Activities and tours

Tour operators
Ancon Expeditions, Calle Elvira Méndez, Edificio Dorado 3, Panama City, T269-9415, www.anconexpeditions.com. One of the best tour operators in Central America. They run a variety of tours to the Darién, including a 2-week birding expedition that concludes in Cana Field Station and a comprehensive 2-week 'Darien Explorer Trek' that goes

almost everywhere. Very specialized and high quality, but not cheap either.

Eco Circuitos, Pelican Av, Amador Causeway, Hotel Country Inn and Suites, ground floor, Suite 3 (Panama City) T314-0068, www.ecocircuitos.com. A highly reputable agency with good green credentials and an emphasis on sustainable tourism. They offer specialized tours to the Darién as part of their cultural and wildlife packages.

⊖ Transport

Panama City to Yaviza *p963*
Bus
Several daily departures from Panama City's main bus terminal to Yaviza, 0330-0700, 6-8hrs, US$16, stops at all towns en route, breaks for meals and snacks.

Metetí *p964*
Bus
To **Puerto Quimba**, every ½ hr, 0600-2100, ½ hr, US$1.50.

Boat
From Puerto Quimba to **La Palma**, depart when full, 0730-1830, ½ hr, US$3. Only the first of the day is guaranteed. Interesting journey through tropical rainforest and mangrove thickets.

Yaviza *p964*
Bus
To **Panama City**, several daily, 6-8 hrs, US$16.

Boat
To **El Real** (for Pirre Station/Rancho Frío), private charter, US$60-80; cargo boat, no schedule, US$5-10 per person.

La Palma *p965*
Boat
To **Puerto Quimba**, depart when full, 0730-1830, ½ hr, US$3. Only the first of the day is guaranteed. To **Reserva Punta Patiño**, 1 hr, organize through ANCON. To **Mogué**, 2½ hrs, private charter US$100-150 (bring extra fuel for the return). To **Sambú**, 3-4 hrs, private charter US$150-200; or thrice weekly private boat, schedules vary, US$20.

Río Sambú *p966*
Air
From Sambú to **Panama City**, Air Panama, Tue and Thu, 1 hr, US$60.

Boat
To **La Palma**, 3-4 hrs, private charter US$150-200; or thrice weekly private boat, schedules vary, US$20.

Bahía Piña *p966*
Air
Tropic Star Lodge includes charter flight to the region as part of their packages. Alternatively: Jaqué to **Panama City**, Aeroperlas, Tue and Thu, 1½ hrs, US$79.51 one-way; Bahía Piña/**Jaqué**, Air Panama, Mon and Fri, US$65 one-way.

Contents

Background

Regional history

Arrival of the American people

While controversy continues to surround the precise date humans arrived in the Americas, the current prevailing view suggests the first wave of emigrants travelled between Siberia and Alaska across the Bering Strait ice bridge created in the last Ice Age, approximately 15,000 years ago. Small hunter-gatherer groups quickly moved through the region, and in fertile lands they developed agriculture and settled. By 1500 BC sedentary villages were widespread in many parts of the Americas, including Central America, where stone-built cities and complex civilizations also began to emerge.

Pre-Columbian civilizations

Despite the wide variety of climates and terrains that fall within Central America's boundaries, the so-called Mesoamerican civilizations were interdependent, sharing the same agriculture based on maize, beans and squash, as well as many sociological traits. These included an enormous pantheon of gods, pyramid-building, a trade in valuable objects, hieroglyphic writing, astronomy, mathematics and a complex calendar system. Historians divide Mesoamerican civilizations into three broad periods, the **pre-Classic**, which lasted until about AD 300, the **Classic**, until AD 900, and the **post-Classic**, from AD 900 until the Spanish conquest.

Olmecs

Who precisely the Olmecs were, where they came from and why they disappeared is a matter of debate. It is known that they flourished from about **1400-400 BC**, lived in the **Mexican Gulf coast** region between Veracruz and Tabasco, and that all later civilizations have their roots in Olmec culture. They are particularly renowned for their carved **colossal heads**, jade figures and altar. They gave great importance to the jaguar and the serpent in their imagery and built large ceremonial centres such as **San Lorenzo** and **La Venta**. The progression from the Olmec to the Maya civilization seems to have taken place at Izapa on the Pacific border of present-day Mexico and Guatemala.

Maya

The best known of the pre-Conquest civilizations were the Maya, thought to have evolved in a formative period in the **Pacific highlands** of Guatemala and El Salvador between **1500 BC** and about **AD 100**. After 200 years of growth it entered what is known today as its Classic period, when the civilization flourished in Guatemala, El Salvador, Belize, Honduras and southern Mexico. The height of the Classic period lasted until AD 900, after which the Maya resettled in the Yucatán, possibly after a devastating famine, drought or peasant uprising. They then came under the influence of the central Mexican Toltecs, who were highly militaristic, until the Spanish conquest in the 16th century.

Throughout its evolution, Mayan civilization was based on independent city states that were governed by a theocratic elite of priests, nobles and warriors. Recent research has revealed that these cities, far from being the peaceful ceremonial centres once imagined, were **warring adversaries** striving to capture victims for sacrifice. This change in perception of the Maya was largely due to a greater understanding of Mayan hieroglyphic writing, which appears both on paper codices and on stone monuments. Aside from a gory preoccupation with sacrifice, Mayan culture was rich in **ceremony, art, science, folklore** and **dance**. Their cities were all meticulously designed according to strict and highly symbolic geometric rules: columns, figures, faces, animals, friezes, stairways and temples often expressed a date, a time or a specific astronomical relationship. Impressively, the Mayan calendar was so advanced that it was a nearer approximation to sidereal time than either the Julian or the Gregorian calendars of Europe; it was only .000069 of a day out of true in a year. The Maya also formulated the concept of 'zero' centuries in advance of the Old World, plotted the movements of the sun, moon, Venus and other planets, and conceived a time cycle of more than 1800 million days.

Conquest

It was only during his fourth voyage, in 1502, that **Columbus** reached the mainland of Central America. He landed in **Costa Rica** and Panama, which he called **Veragua**, and founded the town of Santa María de Belén. In 1508 Alonso de Ojeda received a grant of land on the Pearl coast east of Panama, and in 1509 he founded the town of San Sebastián, later moved to a new site called Santa María la Antigua del Darién (now in Colombia). In 1513 the governor of the colony at Darién was **Vasco Núñez de Balboa**. Taking 190 men he crossed the isthmus in 18 days and caught the first glimpse of the Pacific; he claimed it and all neighbouring lands in the name of the King of Spain. But from the following year, when **Pedrarias de Avila** replaced him as Governor, Núñez de Balboa fell on evil days, and he was executed by Pedrarias in 1519. That same year Pedrarias crossed the isthmus and founded the town of Panamá on the Pacific side. It was in April 1519, too, that **Cortés** began his conquest of Mexico. Central America was explored from these two nodal points of Panama and Mexico.

Settlement

The groups of Spanish settlers were few and widely scattered, a fundamental point in explaining the **political fragmentation** of Central America today. Panama was ruled from Bogotá, but the rest of Central America was subordinate to the Viceroyalty at Mexico City, with Antigua, Guatemala, as an Audiencia for the area until 1773, and thereafter Guatemala City. Panama was of paramount importance for colonial Spanish America for its strategic position, and for the trade passing across the isthmus to and from the southern colonies. The other provinces were of comparatively little value.

The small number of **Spaniards intermarried** freely with the locals, accounting for the predominance of mestizos in present-day Central America. But the picture has regional variations. In Guatemala, where there was the highest native population density, intermarriage affected fewer of the natives, and over half the population today is still purely *indígena* (**indigenous**). On the Meseta Central of Costa Rica, the natives were all but wiped out by disease and, as a consequence of this great disaster, there is a community of over two million whites, with little *indígena* admixture. **Blacks** predominate along the Caribbean coast of Central America. Most were brought in as cheap labour to work as railway builders and banana planters in the 19th century and canal cutters in the 20th. The **Garífuna** people, living between southern Belize and Nicaragua, arrived in the area as free people after African slaves and indigenous Caribbean people intermingled following a shipwreck off St Vincent.

On 5 November 1811, **José Matías Delgado**, a priest and jurist born in San Salvador, organized a revolt with another priest, Manuel José Arce. They proclaimed the Independence of El Salvador, but the Audiencia at Guatemala City suppressed the revolt and took Delgado prisoner. Eleven years later, in 1820, the revolution of Spain itself precipitated the Independence of Central America. On 24 February 1821, the Mexican **General Agustín de Iturbide** announced his **Plan de Iguala** for an independent Mexico. Several months later, the Central American *criollos* followed his example and announced their own **Declaration of Independence** in Guatemala City on 15 September 1821. Iturbide invited the provinces of Central America to join with him and, on 5 January 1822, Central America was annexed to Mexico. Delgado, however, refused to accept this decree and Iturbide, who had now assumed the title of **Emperor Agustín I**, sent an army south under Vicente Filísola to enforce it. Filísola had completed his task when he heard of Iturbide's abdication, and at once convened a general congress of the Central American provinces. It met on 24 June 1823, and thereafter established the **Provincias Unidas del Centro de América**. The Mexican Republic acknowledged their Independence on 1 August 1824, and Filísola's soldiers were withdrawn.

The United Provinces of Central America

In 1824, the first congress, presided over by Delgado, appointed a provisional governing *junta* which promulgated a constitution modelled on that of the United States. The Province of Chiapas was not included in the Federation, as it had already adhered to Mexico in 1821. Guatemala City, by force of tradition, soon became the seat of government.

The first president under the new constitution was **Manuel José Arce**, a liberal. One of his first acts was to **abolish slavery**. El Salvador, protesting that he had exceeded his powers, rose in December 1826. Honduras, Nicaragua and Costa Rica joined the revolt, and in 1828 **General Francisco Morazán**, in charge of the army of Honduras, defeated the federal forces, entered San Salvador and marched against Guatemala City. He captured the city on 13 April 1829, and established that contradiction in terms: a liberal dictatorship. Many conservative leaders were expelled and church and monastic properties confiscated. Morazán himself became President of the Federation in 1830. He was a man of considerable ability; he ruled with a strong hand, encouraged education, fostered trade and industry, opened the country to immigrants, and reorganized the administration. In 1835 the capital was moved to San Salvador.

These reforms antagonized the conservatives and there were several uprisings. The most serious revolt was among the *indígenas* of Guatemala, led by Rafael Carrera, an illiterate mestizo conservative and a born leader. Years of continuous warfare followed, during the course of which the Federation withered away. As a result, the federal congress passed an act which allowed each province to assume the government it chose, but the idea of a federation was not quite dead. Morazán became President of El Salvador. Carrera, who was by then in control of Guatemala, defeated Morazán in battle and forced him to leave the country. But in 1842, Morazán overthrew Braulio Carrillo, then dictator of Costa Rica, and became president himself. At once he set about rebuilding the Federation, but a popular uprising soon led to his capture. He was shot on 15 September 1842 and with him perished any practical hope of Central American political union.

The separate states

The history of **Guatemala, El Salvador, Honduras** and **Nicaragua** since the breakdown of federation has been tempestuous in the extreme (**Costa Rica**, with its mainly white population and limited economic value at the time, is a country apart, and **Panama** was Colombian territory until 1903). In each, the ruling class was divided into pro-clerical conservatives and anti-clerical liberals, with constant changes of power. Each was weak, and tried repeatedly to buttress its weakness by alliances with others, which invariably broke up because one of the allies sought a position of mastery. The wars were mainly ideological wars between conservatives and liberals, or wars motivated by inflamed nationalism. Nicaragua was riven internally by the mutual hatreds of the Conservatives of Granada and the Liberals of León, and there were repeated conflicts between the Caribbean and interior parts of Honduras. Despite the permutations and combinations of external and civil war there has been a recurrent desire to re-establish some form of **La Gran Patria Centroamericana**. Throughout the 19th century, and far into the 20th, there have been ambitious projects for political federation, usually involving El Salvador, Honduras and Nicaragua; none of them lasted more than a few years.

Regional integration

Poverty, the fate of the great majority, has brought about closer economic cooperation between the five republics, and in 1960 they established the **Central American Common Market** (CACM). Surprisingly, the Common Market appeared to be a great success until 1968, when integration fostered national antagonisms, and there was a growing conviction in Honduras and Nicaragua, which were doing least well out of integration, that they were being exploited by the others. In 1969 the 'Football War' broke out between El Salvador and Honduras, basically because of a dispute about illicit emigration by Salvadoreans into Honduras, and relations between the two were not normalized until 1980. Hopes for improvement were revived in 1987 when the Central American Peace Plan, drawn up by President Oscar Arias Sánchez of Costa Rica, was signed by the presidents of Guatemala, El Salvador, Honduras, Nicaragua and Costa Rica. The plan proposed formulae to end the civil strife in individual countries, achieving this aim first in Nicaragua (1989), then in El Salvador (1991). In Guatemala, a ceasefire after 36 years of war led to the signing of a peace accord at the end of 1996. With the signing of peace accords, emphasis has shifted to regional, economic and environmental integration.

In October 1993, the presidents of Guatemala, El Salvador, Honduras, Nicaragua and Costa Rica signed a new **Central American Integration Treaty Protocol** to replace that of 1960 and set up new mechanisms for regional integration. The Treaty was the culmination of a series of annual presidential summits held since 1986 which, besides aiming for peace and economic integration, established a Central American Parliament and a Central American Court of Justice. Attempts at further economic and regional integration continue. Plans to create a **Free Trade Area of the Americas** (FTAA) appear to have failed, but the 2003 **Dominican Republic-Central American Free Trade Agreement** (DR-CAFTA) has now been signed by several nations including the Dominican Republic, Guatemala, El Salvador, Honduras, Nicaragua and Costa Rica.

The DR-CAFTA closely compliments the 2001 **Plan Puebla-Panama** (the PPP, also known as the Mesoamerican Integration and Development Project) an economic corridor stretching from Puebla, west of Mexico City, as far as Panama. Supporters of the plan see it as a means for economic development. Critics see it as a way of draining cheap labour and natural resources with little concern for the environment or long-term progress. Today, the PPP simmers on the back burner, but the desire for Central American nations to strengthen ties is regularly voiced. This is most apparent in the creation of Central America 4 (CA-4), a 2006 border control agreement between Guatemala, El Salvador, Honduras and Nicaragua, that opens up travel between the four nations. Regional meetings occur periodically to promote and encourage trust and cooperation, and while the final destination of such cooperation is far from clear, the Central America of today is far more productive and safer than it was in the 1980s and early 1990s.

Mexico

History

Spanish rule

The remarkable conquest of Mexico began when 34-year-old **Hernán Cortés** disembarked near the present Veracruz with about 500 men, some horses and cannon, on 21 April 1519. They marched into the interior and were admitted into the Aztec capital of Tenochtitlán in November. There they remained until 30 June of the following year, when they were expelled after a massacring a group of Aztec nobles. The next year Cortés came back with reinforcements and besieged the city. It fell on 30 August 1521, and was utterly razed. Cortés then turned to the conquest of the rest of the country.

By the end of the 16th century the Spaniards had founded most of the towns that are still important, tapped great wealth in mining, stock raising and sugar-growing, and firmly imposed their way of life and beliefs. Government was by a Spanish-born upper class, based on the subordination of the *indígena* and mestizo populations and there was a strict dependence on Spain for all things. As with the rest of Hispanic America, Spain built up resistance to itself by excluding from government both Spaniards born in Mexico and the small body of educated mestizos.

Independence

The flag of revolt was raised in 1810 by the curate of Dolores, **Miguel Hidalgo**, who collected 80,000 armed supporters. Had it not been for Hidalgo's loss of nerve, the capital might have been captured in the first month, but 11 years of fighting created bitter differences. A loyalist general, **Agustín de Iturbide**, joined the rebels and proclaimed an independent Mexico in 1821. A federal republic was created on 4 October 1824, with General Guadalupe Victoria as president. In 1836, Texas rebelled against the dictator, Santa Ana, and declared its Independence. It was annexed by the United States in 1845. War broke out and, under the terms of the peace treaty, the US acquired half Mexico's territory.

Benito Juárez

A period of liberal reform dominated by independent Mexico's great hero, the Zapoteco, **Benito Juárez**, began in 1857. The church, in alliance with the conservatives, hotly contested his programme and the constant civil strife wrecked the economy. Juárez was forced to suspend payment on the national debt, causing the French to invade and occupy Mexico City in 1863. They imposed the **Archduke Maximilian of Austria** as Mexican Emperor, but under US pressure, withdrew their troops in 1867. Maximilian was captured by the *Juaristas* at Querétaro, tried, and shot on 19 June. Juárez resumed control of the country and died in July 1872.

General Porfirio Díaz

Sebastián Lerdo de Tejada, the distinguished scholar who followed Juárez, was soon tricked out of office by **General Porfirio Díaz**, who ruled Mexico from 1876 to 1910. Díaz's paternal, though often ruthless, central authority introduced a period of 35 years of peace. A superficial prosperity followed, but the main mass of peasants had never been so wretched. It was this open contradiction between dazzling prosperity and hideous distress that led to the start of civil war (known as the Mexican Revolution) in November 1910, and to Porfirio Díaz's self-exile in Paris.

The Mexican revolution

A new leader, **Francisco Madero**, championed a programme of political and social reform, which included the restoration of stolen lands. Madero was initially supported by revolutionary leaders such as **Emiliano Zapata** in Morelos, **Pascual Orozco** in Chihuahua and **Pancho Villa**, also in the north. During his presidency (1911-1913), Madero neither satisfied his revolutionary supporters, nor pacified his reactionary enemies. After a coup in February 1913, led by General Victoriano Huerta, Madero was brutally murdered, but the great cry, '*Tierra y Libertad*' (Land and Freedom) was not to be quieted until the election of Alvaro Obregón to the Presidency in 1920. Before then, Mexico was in a state of civil war, leading first to the exile of Huerta in 1914, then the dominance of Venustiano Carranza's revolutionary faction over that of Zapata (assassinated in 1919) and Villa.

The PRI

In 1946, the official ruling party assumed the name **Partido Revolucionario Institucional (PRI)**, and held a virtual monopoly over all political activity. In the late 1980s, disaffected PRI members and others formed the breakaway **Partido de la Revolución Democrática (PRD)**, which rapidly gained support. On New Year's Day of the election year, 1994, at the moment when the North American Free Trade Agreement (NAFTA) came into force, a guerrilla group, The **Ejército Zapatista de Liberación Nacional** (EZLN) briefly took control of several towns in Chiapas. Despite ongoing unrest, PRI candidate **Ernesto Zedillo Ponce de León**, a US-trained economist and former education minister, won a comfortable majority in the August elections.

Ernesto Zedillo

On 20 December, just after his inauguration, Zedillo devalued the peso, claiming that political unrest was causing capital outflows. On 22 December a precipitate decision to allow the peso to float against the dollar caused an immediate crisis of confidence and investors in Mexico lost billions of dollars as the peso's value plummeted. Mexicans were hard hit by the recession and the ruling position of the PRI was damaged. In Chiapas, Zedillo suspended the controversial PRI governor, but the tension between the EZLN and the army continued as a 72-hour campaign to apprehend the EZLN leader, Subcomandante Marcos, failed. Talks recommenced in April, with the EZLN calling a ceasefire but the first peace accord was not signed until February 1996. Mid-term congressional elections held in July 1997 showed the PRI's grip on power was beginning to fade. They suffered a huge blow at the polls, and for the first time ever it lost control of Congress, winning only 239 seats. The PRD surged to become the second largest party in the lower house, with 125 deputies, while the right-wing PAN won 122.

Vicente Fox

During the 1999 presidential elections, Zedillo relinquished his traditional role in nominating his successor and the PRI had a US-style primary election to select a candidate. The **PAN**, meanwhile, chose former Coca-Cola executive **Vicente Fox** to lead their campaign. On 2 July 1999, Mexicans gave power to Fox, former governor of Guanajuato, and the PAN, prising it from the PRI for the first time in 71 years. An admirer of 'third way' politics and of ex-US President Bill Clinton and UK Prime Minister Tony Blair, Fox took office on 1 December 2000 announcing czar-led initiatives that would tackle government corruption, drug-trafficking, crime and poverty, and the economic conditions that drive migration to the US. One critic dismissively said Fox was "90% image and 10% ideas".

Felipe Calderón

Elections in July 2006 saw a new president leading Mexico. A close and ill-fought electoral result gave Felipe Calderón, the candidate of the ruling conservative National Action Party (PAN) a narrow win over Andrés Manuel López Obrador of the centre-left Party of the Democratic Revolution (PRD), pushing Roberto Madrazo of the Institutional Revolutionary Party (PRI) into third place. Calderón came to power looking to reduce poverty, violence, tax evasion, corruption and his own salary by 10%. Public infrastructure projects on roads, airports, bridges and dams would also intend to stem outward migration of Mexico's workforce. Ultimately, Calderón's term has been dominated by a war on drugs that has marred Mexico's northern states. Despite military-led crack-downs against the cartels and high-profile arrests of corrupt political stooges, tens of thousands lie dead. As violence seeps into other areas of the country, Calderón's approval remains at a low and many wonder if his strategy is working.

Culture

People

About 9% of Mexico's population are considered white, about 30% *indígena* (indigenous); with about 60% mestizos, a mixture in varying proportions of Spanish and *indígena*. Mexico also has infusions of other Europeans, as well as Arabs and Chinese. There is a national cultural prejudice in favour of the indigenous rather than the Spanish element, though this does not prevent *indígena* from being looked down on by the more Hispanic elements. There is hardly a single statue of Cortés in the whole of Mexico, although he does figure, pejoratively, in the frescoes of Diego Rivera and his contemporaries. On the other hand the two last Aztec emperors, Moctezuma and Cuauhtémoc, are national heroes.

The Mayans

The Yucatec Maya, occupying the Yucatán Peninsula, number some 2.45 million (with 892,723 Yucatec speakers) and are Mexico's biggest indigenous group after the Nahuas. The Yucatec Maya speak a single language with many distinct (but mutually intelligible) regional dialects. They lead lives with differing degrees of modernity. In eastern Chiapas, the Lacandón are a particularly fascinating, though sparsely numbered, lowland Maya group. Known as Hach Winik in their own language, which means 'real people', they are believed to be descended from refugees who fled Guatemala and Yucatán during the Spanish Conquest. In the highlands of Chiapas, the rugged topography provides niches for a network of 13 distinct ethnic groups, each with their own attire. Tzeltal, Tzotzil,

Tojolabal and Mam are their main languages. Community life is orientated around the family, a cargo system of civic duties, and religion – for which Alteños, as highlanders are called, are especially famous.

Land and environment

Geography

The structure of Mexico's land mass is extremely complicated, but may be simplified as a plateau flanked by ranges of mountains roughly paralleling the coasts. Geographically, North America is said to come to an end in the Isthmus of Tehuantepec, beyond which the land rises into the thinly populated highlands of Chiapas. Very different are the Gulf coast and Yucatán; half this area is classed as flat, and much of it gets enough rain the year round, leading to its having become one of the most important agricultural and cattle-raising areas in the country. The Gulf coast also provides most of Mexico's oil and sulphur.

Climate

The climate of the inland highlands is mostly mild, but with sharp changes of temperature between day and night, sunshine and shade. Generally, winter is the dry season and summer the wet season. Rain falls the year round in Tabasco state and along the Pacific coast of Chiapas. Extremes of weather do happen. In October 2005, the Yucatán Peninsula was savaged by Hurricane Wilma which stayed in the area for close to three days. In the summer of 2007, severe flooding affecting 700,000 people in the southeastern state of Tabasco, ruining crops, leaving 70% of the state under water and closing three of Mexico's main oil ports.

Guatemala

History

Under Pedro de Alvarado, the Spanish conquered Guatemala bit by bit from 1524 to 1697. The indigenous Maya died in their thousands from Western diseases and the survivors were forced to work and pay tribute under the *encomienda* system. In 1825 Guatemala became the capital of the Central American Federation until its dissolution in 1838. From 1839 to 1842, conservative governments restored Spanish institutions in a hark back to the colonial era. This trend was maintained by fiercely pro-church Rafael Carrera, who became president in 1844. He set about restoring church power and invited the Jesuits back into the country (they had been expelled in 1767). He went into exile in 1848 before returning to power in 1851 where he remained until 1865.

The 1871 Liberal Revolution

On Carrera's death, Conservative General Vicente Cerna ruled Guatemala until 1871, when General Justo Rufino Barrios successfully overthrew his regime and introduced a wave of Liberal leadership. **Miguel García Granados** (1871-1873) reigned briefly, expelling leading clerics and overturning Carrera's invitation to the Jesuits. Thereafter, **Justo Rufino Barrios** (1873-1885) himself was elected president. He too was vehemently anticlerical. He expropriated church property, using the proceeds to found a national bank, secularized education and marriage. New ports and railways were constructed and coffee production was reformed, transforming Guatemala into a major producer. This was largely accomplished through the confiscation of indigenous lands. Barrios also tried to restore the federation and when the idea foundered he resorted to dictatorial methods. He invaded El Salvador when they refused to cooperate and died in a battle at Chalachuapa. **Manuel Lisandro Barillas** (1885-1892) followed in his footsteps and again tried unsuccessfully to re-establish Central American union. The Liberal trend continued with **General José María Reina Barrios** (1892-1898), who confiscated his enemies' property and spent much time quashing internal rebellion. During his term the price of coffee crashed on the world market, but public works using public money continued to be built, causing widespread outrage and revolts. He was assassinated.

Dictatorship and the rise of the United Fruit Company

When **Manuel Estrada Cabrera** (1898-1920) came to power, his was the longest one-man rule in Central American history. Cabrera encouraged foreign investment, expansion of the railways and the United Fruit Company's foray into Guatemala, granting it some 800,000 ha for the planting of bananas. The company's privileges included a monopoly on transport and a free rein over their own affairs. American interests in Guatemala grew to the point where 40% of all exports were US controlled. Cabrera was eventually toppled amid widespread discontent. Carlos Herrera followed but the old style military did not like his approach. He was overthrown in a bloodless military coup, bringing José María Orellana to power. Orellana negotiated more concessions for United Fruit and the railway company. However, organized protests over plantation workers' rights grew and periodically met with government crackdowns. Orellana, unlike some of his predecessors, died a natural death in 1926.

Jorge Ubico

Jorge Ubico was an efficient but brutal dictator who came to power in 1931. He tightened political control, introduced a secret police, clamped down on workers' discontent and Communist movements, persecuted writers and intellectuals, promoted forced labour and fixed low wage rates. He also extended privileges to the United Fruit Company. These, and other issues, and the fact that he sought constant re-election, provoked widespread demonstrations calling for his resignation. In June 1944, following the death of a teacher in a protest demanding university autonomy, Ubico resigned and a triumvirate of generals assumed power.

October Revolution

On 20 October 1944 there was an armed uprising of La Guardia de Honor, backed by popular support. The military leaders drew up a democratic constitution, abolished forced labour, and upheld the autonomy of the university. Teacher **Juan José Arévalo** of the **Frente Popular Libertador** party was then elected president and drew up a plan of social reform. He separated the powers of state, introduced *comedores* for children of poor workers, set up the Department for Social Security, and accepted the existence of the Communist Party. He survived more than 20 military coups and finished his term of five years (1945-1950).

1954 US-backed military coup

Jacobo Arbenz Guzmán, a member of the 1944 military triumvirate, became the elected president in 1950. His 1952 Agrarian Reform Law saw the expropriation of large, underutilized estates without adequate compensation awarded to their owners – mainly the United Fruit Company, which for years had been under-declaring the value of its land for tax reasons. According to the company, of its 550,000 acres around the Caribbean, 85% of it was not farmed. It was offered a measly US$2.99 an acre for land (440,000 acres) which it said was worth US$75. The company's connections with high-powered players within the US Government and the CIA, and its constant allegation that Communism was percolating through the Guatemalan corridors of power, eventually persuaded the US to sponsor an overthrow of the Arbenz government. Military strikes were launched on the country in June 1954. At the end of the month Arbenz, under pressure from Guatemalan military and the US ambassador John Peurifoy, resigned.

Military rule

In June 1954 **Colonel Carlos Castillo Armas** took over the presidency. He persecuted and outlawed Communists. He was assassinated in 1957, which provoked a wave of violence and instability and for the next three decades the army and its right-wing supporters suppressed left-wing efforts, both constitutional and violent, to restore the gains made under Arévalo and Arbenz. Many thousands of people, mostly leftists but also many Maya without political orientation, were killed during this period.

The rise of the guerrilla movement

On 13 November 1960, a military group, inspired by revolution in Cuba, carried out an uprising against the government. It was suppressed but spawned the **Movimiento 13 de Noviembre**, which then joined forces with the **Guatemalan Workers' Party**. In 1962, student demonstrations ended in bloodshed, which resulted in the creation of the **Movimiento 12 de Abril**. These movements then merged to form **Fuerzas Armadas Rebeldes (FAR)** in 1962.

During this period, Arévalo made a move to re-enter the political fold. A coup d'état followed. Guerrilla and right-wing violence began to increase in the late 1960s. In the early 1970s the guerrillas re-focused. The FAR divided into FAR and the EGP (**Ejército Guerrillero de los Pobres**, Guerrilla Army of the Poor), which operated in the north of the country. In 1972 the **Organización Revolucionaria del Pueblo en Armas** (ORPA) was formed. The EGP was led by Rolando Morán, a supporter of the Cuban Revolution. The group's first action took place in the Ixil Triangle in 1975. The ORPA was led by Commandante Gaspar Ilom, also known as Rodrigo Asturias, son of Nobel Prize for Literature winner Miguel Angel Asturias.

The worst of the conflict

Throughout the 1970s and early 1980s the worst atrocities of the war were committed. **General Kjell Eugenio Laugerud García**'s presidency was characterized by escalating violence, which led the US to withdraw its support for the Guatemalan government in 1974. In 1976, a devastating earthquake struck Guatemala killing 23,000 people. This prompted widespread social movements in the country to improve the lives of the poor. At the same time, guerrilla activity surged. Meanwhile, the US, believing the human rights situation had improved, resumed military sales to Guatemala. But in 1981 the military unleashed a huge offensive against the guerrillas who united to confront it with the formation of the **Unidad Revolucionaria Nacional Guatemalteca** (URNG). The situation worsened when Ríos Montt came to power in 1982 following a coup d'état. He presided over the bloodiest period of violence with the introduction of the scorched-earth policy, massacring whole villages in an attempt to root out bands of guerrillas. Ríos Montt was ousted by his defence minister, General Oscar Mejías Victores, in a coup in August 1983.

Return of democracy

Mejía Victores permitted a Constituent Assembly to be elected in 1984, which drew up a new constitution and worked out a timetable for a return to democracy. He also created numerous 'model villages' to rehouse the displaced and persecuted Maya, who had fled in their thousands to the forests, the capital, Mexico and the US. Presidential elections in December 1985, were won by civilian Vinicio Cerezo Arévalo of the Christian Democrats (DC), who took office in January 1986. He was the first democratically elected President of Guatemala since 1966. In the 1990 elections **Jorge Serrano Elías** of the Solidarity Action Movement made Guatemalan history by being the first civilian to succeed a previous civilian president in a change of government.

Civil unrest

By 1993, however, the country was in disarray. The social policies pursued by the government had alienated nearly everybody and violence erupted on the streets. Amid growing civil unrest, President Serrano suspended the constitution, dissolved Congress and the Supreme Court, and imposed press censorship. International and domestic condemnation of his actions was immediate. After only a few days, Serrano was ousted by a combination of military, business and opposition leaders and a return to constitutional rule was promised. Congress approved a successor, Ramiro de León Carpio, previously the human rights ombudsman. He soon proved as capable as his predecessors, however, and the public's distaste of corrupt congressional deputies and ineffectual government did not diminish. The reform of election procedures and political parties had been called for by a referendum in 1994, which obliged Congressional elections to be called. The result gave a majority of seats to the **Guatemalan Republican Front** (FRG), led by ex-president Ríos Montt, who was elected to the presidency of Congress for 1994-1996. Ríos Montt's candidate in the 1995 presidential election, Alfonso Portillo, lost by a slim margin to Alvaro Arzú of the National Advancement Party. Arzú proposed to increase social spending, curtail tax evasion, combat crime and bring a speedy conclusion to peace negotiations with the URNG guerrillas.

Towards peace

One of the earliest moves made by President Serrano was to speed up the process of talks between the government and the URNG, which began in March 1990. The sides met in Mexico City in April 1991 to discuss such topics as democratization and human rights, a reduced role for the military, the rights of indigenous people, the resettlement of refugees and agrarian reform. Progress, however, was slow. In August 1995 an accord was drawn up with the aid of the UN's Guatemala mission (MINUGUA) and the Norwegian government. The timetable proved over-ambitious, but, on taking office in January 1996, President Arzú committed himself to signing a peace accord. In February 1996 he met the URNG leadership, who called a ceasefire in March. On 29 December 1996 a peace treaty was signed ending 36 years of armed conflict. An amnesty was agreed which would limit the scope of the Commission for Historical Clarification and prevent it naming names in its investigations of human rights abuses.

Peacetime elections and the Portillo Government

The 1999 elections went to a second round with self-confessed killer Alfonso Portillo of the FRG winning 62% of the vote against his rival Oscar Berger, the candidate of President Arzú's ruling PAN. Portillo subsequently promised to reform the armed forces, solve the killing of Bishop Gerardi and disband the elite presidential guard, so implicated in the human rights abuses. Common crime, as well as more sinister crimes such as lynchings, plagued Portillo's term and seemed to increase. Since the signing of the Peace Accords MINUGUA has verified 347 lynchings throughout the country.

The new millennium generally brought mixed results for justice. The former interior minister Byron Barrientos resigned in December 2001 and faced accusations of misappropriating US$6 million in state funds. He has now voluntarily brought himself before the courts. In June 2002, ex-president Jorge Serrano was ordered to be arrested on charges which included embezzlement of state funds. He remains exiled in Panama. In October 2002, a former colonel in the Guatemalan army, Colonel Juan Valencia Osorio, was found guilty of ordering the murder of anthropologist Myrna Mack and sentenced to 30 years' imprisonment. However, the appeal court overturned his conviction in 2003. Also in October 2002, the four men imprisoned for their role in the 1998 murder of Guatemalan Bishop Gerardi had their convictions overturned. A retrial was ordered. In 2003 Ríos Montt mounted a legal challenge to a rule which prohibits former coup leaders running for president. The constitutional court ruled he could stand in the autumn parliamentary elections. The UN High Commission for Human Rights announced it would open an office in Guatemala City. More details can be found at www.ghrc-usa.org.

Elections of 2003 and beyond

A new era in Guatemalan politics began with the election of **Oscar Berger** as president in December 2003. After coming second to Portillo in the 1999 elections as candidate for PAN, Berger led the newly formed **Gran Alianza Nacional** (GANA) to electoral victory with 54% of the vote over his centre-left rival Alvaro Colom. Berger assumed the presidency promising to improve access to clean water, education and health care for all citizens. He also persuaded indigenous leader and Nobel Prize winner Rigoberta Menchú to join his government to work towards a more just country.

Berger's presidency provided slight economic growth and attempts to strengthen the country's institutions, despite low tax revenues, organized crime, discrimination and poverty. Elections in November 2007 were also a close affair, with second round run-off providing Alvaro Colom with a narrow victory for the Unidad Nacional de la Esperanza (National Unity of Hope) and 53% of the vote. Colom took office vowing to fight poverty with a government that would have a Mayan face, while promising to reduce organized crime.

In recent years, Los Zetas drug gang, former wing of the Mexican Gulf Cartel, has moved into Guatemala, with smuggling concentrated in northern regions, particularly Petén. Dozens of murders have been linked with the ruthless gang, which is thought to include former members of the Kaibiles – the elite Guatemalan army squad, notorious for its brutalities during Guatemala's 1960-1996 civil war. By the end of 2010, Los Zetas' drug operations are thought to have spread to at least 75% of the country. Meanwhile, in 2011, President Alvaro Colom divorced his wife Sandra Torres, which will allow her to stand in this year's presidential elections. Under the Guatemalan constitution, a close relative of a president cannot stand for the presidency.

Culture

People

The word *ladino* applies to any person with a 'Latin' culture, speaking Spanish and wearing Western clothes, though they may be pure Amerindian by descent. The opposite of *ladino* is *indígena*; the definition is cultural, not racial. Guatemala's population in 2006 was estimated to be 13 million. The indigenous people of Guatemala are mainly of Maya descent. The largest of the 22 indigenous Maya groups are K'iche', Q'eqchi' and Mam. When the Spaniards arrived from Mexico in 1524 those who stayed settled in the southern highlands around Antigua and Guatemala City and intermarried with the groups of native subsistence farmers living there. This was the basis of the present mestizo population living in the cities and towns as well as in all parts of the southern highlands and in the flatlands along the Pacific coast; the indigenous population is still at its most dense in the western highlands and Alta Verapaz. They form two distinct cultures: the almost self-supporting indigenous system in the highlands, and the *ladino* commercial economy in the lowlands. About half the total population are classed as Amerindian (Maya) – estimates vary from 40-65%. The remaining populaton comprises: *ladino*, over 40%; white, 5%; black, 2%; and other mixed race or Chinese, 3.9%. A 2001 study revealed that there are 5,944,222 Maya; 3,800,405 *ladinos*; 6539 Garífuna; and 297 Xinca who are physically similar to the *ladinos*.

Costume and dress

Indigenous dress is particularly attractive, little changed from the time the Spaniards arrived: the colourful head-dresses, *huípiles* (tunics) and skirts of the women, the often richly patterned sashes and kerchiefs, the hatbands and tassels of the men vary greatly, often from village to village. Unfortunately a new outfit is costly, the indigenous people are poor, and denims are cheap. While men are adopting Western dress in many villages, women have been slower to change.

Religion

There is no official religion but about 70% consider themselves Roman Catholic. The other 30% are Protestant, mostly affiliated to evangelical churches, which have been very active in the country over the past 25 years.

Land and environment

A lowland ribbon, nowhere more than 50 km wide, runs the whole length of the Pacific shore. Cotton, sugar, bananas and maize are the chief crops of this strip. There is some stock raising as well. Summer rain is heavy and the lowland carries scrub forest. From this plain the highlands rise sharply to heights of between 2500 and 4000 m and stretch some 240 km to the north before sinking into the northern lowlands. A string of volcanoes juts boldly above the southern highlands along the Pacific. There are intermont basins at from 1500 to 2500 m in this volcanic area. Most of the people of Guatemala live in these basins, which are drained by short rivers into the Pacific and by longer ones into the Atlantic. One basin west of the capital, ringed by volcanoes and with no apparent outlet, is Lago de Atitlán. The southern highlands are covered with lush vegetation over a volcanic subsoil. This clears away in the central highlands, exposing the crystalline rock of the east-west running ranges. This area is lower but more rugged, with sharp-faced ridges and deep ravines modifying into gentle slopes and occasional valley lowlands as it loses height and approaches the Caribbean coastal levels and the flatlands of El Petén. The lower slopes of these highlands, from about 600 to 1500 m, are planted with coffee. Above 1500 m is given over to wheat and the main subsistence crops of maize and beans. Deforestation is becoming a serious problem. Where rainfall is low there are savannas; water for irrigation is now drawn from wells and these areas are being reclaimed for pasture and fruit growing. Two large rivers flow down to the Caribbean Gulf of Honduras from the highlands: one is the Río Motagua, 400 km long, rising among the southern volcanoes; the other, further north, is the Río Polochic, 298 km long, which drains into Lago de Izabal and the Bahía de Amatique. There are large areas of lowland in the lower reaches of both rivers, which are navigable for considerable distances; this was the great banana zone. To the northwest, bordering on Belize and Mexico's Yucatán Peninsula, lies the low, undulating tableland of El Petén almost one-third of the nation's territory. In some parts there is natural grassland, with woods and streams, suitable for cattle, but large areas are covered with dense hardwood forest. Since the 1970s large-scale tree-felling has reduced this tropical rainforest by some 40%, especially in the south and east. However, in the north, which now forms Guatemala's share of the Maya Biosphere Reserve, the forest is protected, but illegal logging still takes place.

Belize

History

Throughout the country, especially in the forests of the centre and south, there are many ruins of the Classic Maya period, which flourished here and in neighbouring Guatemala from the fourth to the ninth century and then, mysteriously (most probably because of drought), emigrated to Yucatán. It is estimated that the population was then 10 times what it is now.

The first settlers were English, with their black slaves from Jamaica, who came in about 1640 to cut logwood, then the source of textile dyes. The British Government made no claim to the territory but tried to secure the protection of the wood-cutters by treaties with Spain. Even after 1798, when a strong Spanish force was decisively beaten off at St George's Caye, the British Government still failed to claim the territory, though the settlers maintained that it had now become British by conquest.

When they achieved Independence from Spain in 1821, both Guatemala and Mexico laid claim to sovereignty over Belize, but these claims were rejected by Britain. Long before 1821, in defiance of Spain, the British settlers had established themselves as far south as the River Sarstoon, the present southern boundary. Independent Guatemala claimed that these settlers were trespassing and that Belize was a province of the new republic. By the middle of the 19th century Guatemalan fears of an attack by the United States led to a rapprochement with Britain. In 1859, a convention was signed by which Guatemala recognized the boundaries of Belize while, by Article 7, the United Kingdom undertook to contribute to the cost of a road from Guatemala City to the sea "near the settlement of Belize"; an undertaking that was never carried out.

Heartened by what it considered a final solution of the dispute, in 1862 Great Britain declared Belize, still officially a settlement, a colony, and a Crown Colony nine years later. Mexico, by treaty, renounced any claims it had on Belize in 1893, but Guatemala, which never ratified the 1859 agreement, renewed its claims periodically.

Independence and after

Belize became independent on 21 September 1981, following a United Nations declaration to that effect. Guatemala refused to recognize the independent state, but in 1986 President Cerezo of Guatemala announced an intention to drop his country's claim to Belize. A British military force was maintained in Belize from Independence until 1993, when the British government announced that the defence of Belize would be handed over to the government on 1 January 1994, and that it would reduce the 1200-strong garrison to about 100 soldiers who would organize jungle warfare training facilities. The last British troops were withdrawn in 1994 and finance was sought for the expansion of the Belize Defence Force. Belize was admitted into the OAS in 1991 following negotiations with Guatemala and Britain. As part of Guatemala's recognition of Belize as an independent nation (ratified by Congress in 1992), Britain will recompense Guatemala by providing financial and technical assistance to construct road, pipeline and port facilities that will guarantee Guatemala access to the Atlantic.

Border friction is an ongoing issue between Belize and Guatemala, and in early 2000 tensions overflowed when Guatemalans took some members of the Belizean Defence Force hostage for several days, eventually resulting in some Guatemalans being shot. Tensions were stretched to the limit, and periodically continue to rise and fall but now seem to have cooled and Guatemala has agreed to pursue its claim to half of Belizean territory through the international courts. Low-key negotiations continue between the two countries and in 2003 both countries agreed a draft settlement at Organization of American States (OAS) brokered talks. Progress was painfully slow, with Belize and Guatemala only signing up to a negotiation framework at the end of 2005.

Culture

The 2000 National Census put the population of Belize at 240,204, given an annual population growth of 2.7% from the 1991 census figure of 189,392. The urban/rural distribution continues to be roughly 50:50 as it was in 1991. The fastest-growing district over the 10-year period is Cayo which has gained at the expense of Orange Walk District and, to a far lesser extent, Belize District. The town of Orange Walk is now only a couple of hundred people more than San Ignacio/Santa Elena which has grown significantly – by Belizean standards – in the last 10 years.

People

About 30% of the population are predominantly black and of mixed ancestry, the so-called Creoles, a term widely used in the Caribbean. They predominate in Belize City, along the coast and on the navigable rivers. About 44% of the population are mestizo; 11% are Maya, who predominate in the north between the Hondo and New rivers and in the extreme south and west. About 7% of the population are Garífuna (black Caribs), descendants of those deported from St Vincent in 1797; they have a distinct language, and can be found in the villages and towns along the southern coast. They are good linguists, many speaking Mayan languages as well as Spanish and 'Creole' English. They also brought their culture and customs from the West Indies, including religious practices and ceremonies, for example Yankanu (John Canoe) dancing at Christmas time. The remainder are of unmixed European ancestry (the majority Mennonites, who speak a German dialect, and are particularly friendly and helpful) and a rapidly growing group of North Americans. The Mennonites fall into two groups, generally speaking: the most rigorous, in the Shipyard area on The New River, and the more 'integrated' in the west, Cayo district, who produce much of Belize's poultry, dairy goods and corn. The newest Mennonite settlements are east of Progresso Lagoon in the northeast. There are also East Indian and Chinese immigrants and their descendants.

Language and education

English is the official language, although for some 180,000 the lingua franca is 'Creole' English. Spanish is the lingua franca for about 130,000 people and is widely spoken in the northern and western areas. In addition, it is estimated that 22,000 people speak Mayan languages, 15,000 Garífuna and 3000 German. Free elementary education is available to everyone, and all the towns have secondary schools.

Land and environment

The coastlands are low and swampy with much mangrove, many salt and freshwater lagoons and some sandy beaches. In the north the land is low and flat, while in the southwest there is a heavily forested mountain massif with a general elevation of between 2000 and 3000 ft. In the east are the Maya Mountains, not yet wholly explored, and the Cockscomb Range which rises to a height of 3675 ft at Victoria Peak. Further west are some 250 square miles of the Mountain Pine Ridge, with large open spaces and some of the best scenery in the country.

From 10 to 40 miles off the coast an almost continuous, 184-mile line of reefs and cayes (or cays) provides shelter from the Caribbean, and forms the longest coral reef in the Western Hemisphere (the fifth-longest barrier reef in the world). Most of the cayes are quite tiny, but some have been developed into tourist resorts. Many have beautiful sandy beaches with clear, clean water, where swimming and diving are excellent. However, on the windward side of inhabited islands, domestic sewage is washed back on to the beaches, some of which are also affected by tar.

The most fertile areas of the country are in the foothills of the northern section of the Maya Mountains: citrus fruit is grown in the Stann Creek Valley, while in the valley of the Mopan, or upper Belize River, cattle raising and mixed farming are successful. The northern area of the country has long proved suitable for sugar cane production. In the south bananas and mangoes are cultivated. The lower valley of the Belize River is a rice-growing area as well as being used for mixed farming and citrus cultivation.

Global environmental change is also impacting Belize. Environmental groups included the Belizean Barrier Reef as one of four sites threatened by global climate change at a the 2007 World Heritage Convention. More locally, rain from two tropical storms caused flash flooding in the Stann Creek area and devastated papaya, shrimp and rice storage operations.

El Salvador

History

When Spanish expeditions arrived in El Salvador from Guatemala and Nicaragua, they found it quite densely populated by several indigenous groups, of whom the most populous were the **Pipiles**. By 1550, the Spaniards had occupied the country, many living in existing indigenous villages and towns. The settlers cultivated cocoa in the volcanic highlands and balsam along the coast, and introduced cattle to roam the grasslands freely. Towards the end of the 16th century, indigo became the big export crop: production was controlled by the Spaniards, and the indigenous population provided the workforce, many suffering illness as a result. A period of regional turmoil accompanied El Salvador's declaration of Independence from the newly autonomous political body of Central America in 1839: indigenous attempts to regain their traditional land rights were put down by force.

Coffee emerged as an important cash crop in the second half of the 19th century, bringing with it improvements in transport facilities and the final abolition of indigenous communal lands.

The land question was a fundamental cause of the peasant uprising of 1932, which was brutally crushed by the dictator **General Maximiliano Hernández Martínez**. Following his overthrow in 1944, the military did not relinquish power: a series of military coups kept them in control, while they protected the interests of the landowning oligarchy.

1980s Civil War

The most recent military coup, in October 1979, led to the formation of a civilian-military junta which promised far-reaching reforms. When these were not carried out, the opposition unified forming a broad coalition, the Frente Democrático Revolucionario, which adopted a military wing, the **Farabundo Martí National Liberation Front (FMLN)** in 1980. Later the same year, the Christian Democrat **Ingeniero José Napoleón Duarte** was named as President of the Junta. At about the same time, political tension reached the proportions of civil war.

Duarte was elected to the post of president in 1984, following a short administration headed by Dr Alvaro Magaña. Duarte's periods of power were characterized by a partly successful attempt at land reform, the nationalization of foreign trade and the banking system, and violence. In addition to deaths in combat, 40,000 civilians were killed between 1979 and 1984, mostly by right-wing death squads. Among the casualties was **Archbishop Oscar Romero**, who was shot while saying mass in March 1980. Nothing came of meetings between Duarte's government and the FMLN, which were aimed at seeking a peace agreement. The war continued in stalemate until 1989, by which time an estimated 70,000 had been killed. The Christian Democrats' inability to end the war, reverse the economic decline or rebuild after the 1986 earthquake, combined with their reputation for corruption, brought about a resurgence of support for the right-wing National Republican Alliance (ARENA). An FMLN offer to participate in presidential elections, dependent on certain conditions, was not accepted and the ARENA candidate, **Alfredo Cristiani**, won the presidency comfortably in March 1989, taking office in June. Peace talks again failed to produce results and in November 1989 the FMLN guerrillas staged their most ambitious offensive ever, which paralysed the capital and caused a violent backlash from government forces. FMLN-government negotiations resumed with UN mediation following the offensive, but the two sides could not reach agreement about the purging of the armed forces, which had become the most wealthy institution in the country following 10 years of US support.

Peace negotiations

Although El Salvador's most left-wing political party, the Unión Democrática Nacionalista, agreed to participate in municipal elections in 1991, the FMLN remained outside the electoral process, and the civil war continued unresolved. Talks were held in Venezuela and Mexico after initial agreement was reached in April on reforms to the electoral and judicial systems, but further progress was stalled over the restructuring of the armed forces and disarming the guerrillas. There were hopes that human rights would improve after the establishment in June 1991 of a UN Security Council human rights observer commission (ONUSAL), which was charged with verifying compliance with the human rights agreement signed by the Government and the FMLN in Geneva in April 1990. Finally, after considerable UN assistance, the FMLN and the Government signed a peace accord in New York in January 1992 and a formal ceasefire began the following month. A detailed schedule throughout 1992 was established to demobilize the FMLN, dismantle five armed forces elite battalions and to initiate land requests by ex-combatants from both sides. The demobilization process was reported as completed in December 1992, formally concluding the civil war. The US agreed at this point to 'forgive' a substantial portion of the US$2 billion international debt of El Salvador. In March 1993, the United Nations Truth Commission published its investigation of human rights abuses during the civil war. Five days later, the legislature approved a general amnesty for all those involved in criminal activities in the war. This included those named in the Truth Commission report. The Cristiani government was slow to implement not only the constitutional reforms proposed by the Truth Commission, but also the process of land reform and the establishment of the National Civilian Police (PNC). By 1995, when Cristiani's successor had taken office, the old national police force was demobilized, but the PNC suffered from a lack of resources for its proper establishment. In fact, the budget for the implementation of the final peace accords was inadequate and El Salvador had to ask the UN for financial assistance.

1994 elections and after

Presidential and congressional elections in 1994 failed to give an outright majority to any presidential candidate and **Calderón Sol** of ARENA won the run-off election. Besides his government's difficulties with the final stages of the peace accord, his first months in office were marked by rises in the cost of living, increases in crime, strikes and protests, and occupations of the Legislature by ex-combatants. Frustration at the slow rate of reform came in the form of criticism from the United Nations and in March 1997 through the ballot box. Only 41% of the electorate bothered to vote. In the National Assembly, Arena won 29 seats, narrowly beating the FMLN which increased its tally to 28 seats. The National Conciliation Party (PCN) won 11, the Christian Democrats (PDC) nine and minority parties seven seats. FMLN managed to run neck-and-neck with Arena until within a year of the March 1999 presidential elections. The party's inability to select a presidential candidate, however, caused it to lose ground rapidly. Arena's candidate, **Fransisco Flores**, won the election but still with a poor turn-out of less than 40% of the electorate. In the face of such a huge rejection of the political system Flores could not claim a clear mandate. Most interpreted the abstention as a lack of faith in any party's ability to solve the twin problems of poverty and crime. Elections in March 2004 won a five-year term for **Tony Saca**, the fourth successive victory for the right-wing Arena party. The former radio and TV presenter promised to crack down on criminal gangs and promote ties with the US.

Into the 21st century

If the devastating earthquakes of early 2001 were not enough for the country to deal with, droughts through the summer months led to a food crisis that required United Nations' intervention. Old rivalries flared briefly as Honduras expelled two Salvadorean diplomats on spying charges, displaying the fragility of the cordial relations with the northern neighbour. El Salvador also hosted the meeting of Mexican and Central America presidents to develop the controversial **Plan Puebla-Panama** regional integration project which would link the Mexican city of Puebla with Panama City along an economic investment corridor. In 2002, promising signs of progress and support for the future led US President Bush to call El Salvador one of the "really bright lights" in the region.

The country's lively landscape continued to shape events with the eruption of Ilamatepec volcano, also known as Santa Ana, in October 2005, quickly followed by the destructive floods and mudslides of Hurricane Stan which killed over 70 people, and forced over 36,000 to seek refuge in emergency shelters. In 2006 El Salvador continued to lead the way for regional integration as the first country to fully implement the Central American Free Trade Agreement with the US. The regional confidence continued and El Salvador and Honduras inaugurated their newly defined border in April 2006, bringing to an end the dispute that led to the outbreak of war between the two nations in 1969. In March 2011, the Inter-American Commission on Human Rights prepared to reopen the court case investigating the massacre of some 1000 civilians in village of El Mozote in December 1981, the bloodiest episode in the country's civil war. In the same month, US President Barack Obama offered US$200m to help El Salvador fight drug traffickers and gang violence. The money is part of the $1.5bn 'Mérida Initiative' announced in 2007 to combat the drugs cartels.

Culture

People

The population of 6.7 million people is far more homogeneous than that of Guatemala. The reason for this is that El Salvador lay comparatively isolated from the main stream of conquest, and had no precious metals to act as magnets for the Spaniards. The small number of Spanish settlers intermarried with those indigenous locals who survived the plagues brought from Europe to form a group of mestizos. There were only about half a million people as late as 1879. With the introduction of coffee, the population grew quickly and the new prosperity fertilized the whole economy, but the internal pressure of population has led to the occupation of all the available land. Several hundred thousand Salvadoreans have emigrated to neighbouring republics because of the shortage of land and the concentration of land ownership, and, more recently, because of the civil war.

Of the total population, some 10% are regarded as ethnic indigenous, although the traditional indigenous culture has almost completely vanished. Other estimates put the percentage of the pure indigenous population as low as 5%. The **Lenca** and the **Pipil**, the two surviving indigenous groups, are predominantly peasant farmers. Only 1% are of unmixed white ancestry, the rest are mestizos.

With a population of 322 to the square kilometre, El Salvador is the most densely populated country on the American mainland. Health and sanitation outside the capital and some of the main towns leave much to be desired.

Music and dance

The Mexican music industry seems to exert an overwhelming cultural influence, while the virtual absence of an indigenous population may also be partly responsible, since it is so often they who maintain traditions and connections with the past. Whatever the reason, the visitor who is seeking specifically Salvadorean native music will find little to satisfy him or her. El Salvador is an extension of 'marimba country', but songs and dances are often accompanied by the guitar and seem to lack a rhythm or style that can be pinpointed as specifically local. An exception is the music played on the *pito de caña* and *tambor* which accompanies the traditional dances called *Danza de los Historiantes*, *La Historia* or *Los Moros y Cristianos*. Over 30 types of dance have been identified, mostly in the west and centre of the country, although there are a few in the east. The main theme is the conflict between christianized and 'heretic' *indígenas* and the dances are performed as a ritual on the local saint's day.

Education and religion

State education is free and nominally obligatory. There are 43 universities, three national and the others private or church-affiliated. There is also a National School of Agriculture. The most famous are the government-financed Universidad Nacional and the Jesuit-run Universidad Centroamericana. Roman Catholicism is the prevailing religion.

Land and environment

El Salvador is the smallest, most densely populated and most integrated of the Central American republics. Its intermont basins are a good deal lower than those of Guatemala, rising to little more than 600 m at the capital, San Salvador. Across this upland and surmounting it run two more or less parallel rows of volcanoes, 14% of which are over 900 m high. The highest are Santa Ana (2365 m), San Vicente (2182 m), San Miguel (2130 m), and San Salvador (1893 m). One important result of this volcanic activity is that the highlands are covered with a deep layer of ash and lava which forms a porous soil ideal for coffee planting.

The total area of El Salvador is 21,000 sq km. Guatemala is to the west, Honduras to the north and east, and the Pacific coastline to the south is approximately 321 km long. Lowlands lie to the north and south of the high backbone. In the south, on the Pacific coast, the lowlands of Guatemala are confined to just east of Acajutla; beyond are lava promontories before another 30-km belt of lowlands where the 325-km long Río Lempa flows into the sea. The northern lowlands are in the wide depression along the course of the Río Lempa, buttressed to the south by the highlands of El Salvador and to the north by the basalt cliffs edging the highlands of Honduras. The highest point in El Salvador, Cerro El Pital (2730 m) is part of the mountain range bordering on Honduras. After 160 km the Lempa cuts through the southern uplands to reach the Pacific; the depression is prolonged southeast till it reaches the Gulf of Fonseca.

El Salvador is located on the southwest coast of the Central American Isthmus on the Pacific Ocean. As the only country in the region lacking access to the Caribbean Sea, it does not posses the flora associated with that particular coastal zone. El Salvador nevertheless has a wide variety of colourful, tropical vegetation; for example over 200 species of orchid grow all over the country. As a result of excessive forest cutting, and hence the destruction of their habitats, many of the animals (such as jaguars and crested eagles) once found in the highlands of the country, have diminished at an alarming rate. In response to this problem several nature reserves have been set up in areas where flora and fauna can be found in their most unspoilt state. Among these nature reserves are the Cerro Verde, Deininger Park, El Imposible Woods, El Jocatal Lagoon and the Montecristo Cloud Forest.

Honduras

History

Honduras was largely neglected by Spain and its colonists, who concentrated on their trading partners further north or south. The resulting disparity in levels of development between Honduras and its regional neighbours caused problems after Independence in 1821. Harsh partisan battles among provincial leaders resulted in the collapse of the Central American Federation in 1838. The national hero, **General Francisco Morazán** was a leader in unsuccessful attempts to maintain the Federation and the restoration of Central American unity was the main aim of foreign policy until 1922.

Banana Republic

Honduras has had a succession of military and civilian rulers and there have been 300 internal rebellions, civil wars and changes of government since Independence, most of them in the 20th century. Political instability in the past led to a lack of investment in economic infrastructure and socio-political integration, making Honduras one of the poorest countries in the Western Hemisphere. It earned its nickname of the 'Banana Republic' in the first part of the 20th century following the founding of a company in 1899, by the Vaccaro brothers of New Orleans, which eventually became the Standard Fruit Company and which was to make bananas the major export crop of Honduras. The United Fruit Company of Boston was also founded in 1899 and, 30 years later, was merged with the Cuyamel Fruit Company of Samuel Zemurray, who controlled the largest fruit interests in Honduras. United Fruit (UFCo), known as El Pulpo (the octopus), emerged as a major political influence in the region with strong links with several dictatorships.

The Great Depression

The 1929 Great Depression caused great hardship in the export-oriented economies of the region, and in Honduras it brought the rise of another authoritarian regime. **Tiburcio Cariás Andino** was elected in 1932 and, through his ties with foreign companies and other neighbouring dictators, he was able to hold on to power until renewed turbulence began in 1948, and he voluntarily withdrew from power a year later. The two political parties, the Liberals and the Nationals, came under the control of provincial military leaders and, after two more authoritarian Nationalist governments and a general strike in 1954 by radical labour unions on the north coast, young military reformists staged a palace coup in 1955. They installed a provisional junta and allowed elections for a constituent assembly in 1957. The assembly was led by the Liberal Party, which appointed **Dr Ramón Villeda Morales** as president, and transformed itself into a national legislature for six years. A newly created military academy graduated its first class in 1960, and the armed forces began to professionalize their leadership in conjunction with the civilian economic establishment. Conservative officers, nervous of a Cuban-style revolution, pre-empted elections in 1963 in a bloody coup which deposed Dr Villeda, exiled Liberal Party members and took control of the national police, which they organized into special security forces.

Football War
In 1969, Honduras and El Salvador were drawn into a bizarre episode known as the 'Football War', which took its name from its origin in a disputed decision in the third qualifying round of the World Cup. Its root cause, however, was the social tension aroused by migrating workers from overcrowded El Salvador to Honduras. In 13 days, 2000 people were killed before a ceasefire was arranged by the Organization of American States. A peace treaty was not signed until 1980, and the dispute provoked Honduras to withdraw from the Central American Common Market (CACM), which helped to hasten its demise.

Tensions between the two countries can still easily rise. Disputes over the border and fishing rights in the Gulf of Fonseca are a cause of friction, and in August 2001, Honduras expelled two Salvadoreans on spying charges. Honduras also has disputed land claims with Nicaragua to the east. However, regional cooperation is sufficiently well developed for regional conferences to tackle the problems with commitments to non-aggressive solutions.

Transition to democracy
The armed forces, led chiefly by **General López Arellano** and his protégés in the National Party, dominated government until 1982. López initiated land reform but, despite liberal policies, his regime was brought down in the mid-1970s by corruption scandals involving misuse of hurricane aid funds and bribes from the United Brands Company. His successors increased the size and power of the security forces and created the largest air force in Central America, while slowly preparing for a return to civilian rule. A constituent assembly was elected in 1980 and general elections held in 1981. A constitution was promulgated in 1982 and **President Roberto Suazo Córdoba** of the Liberal Party assumed power. During this period, Honduras cooperated closely with the USA on political and military issues, particularly in covert moves to destabilize Nicaragua's Sandinista government, and became host to some 12,000 right-wing Nicaraguan contra rebels. It was less willing to take a similar stand against the FMLN left-wing guerrillas in El Salvador for fear of renewing border tensions. In 1986 the first peaceful transfer of power between civilian presidents for 30 years took place when **José Azcona del Hoyo** (Liberal) won the elections. Close relations with the USA were maintained in the 1980s, Honduras had the largest Peace Corps Mission in the world, non-governmental and international voluntary agencies proliferated as the government became increasingly dependent upon US aid to finance its budget.

In 1989, the general elections were won by the right-wing **Rafael Leonardo Callejas Romero** of the National Party, which won a 14-seat majority in the National Assembly. Under the terms of the Central American Peace Plan, the contra forces were demobilized and disarmed by June 1990. The Honduran armed forces have come under greater pressure for reform as a result of US and domestic criticism of human rights abuses. A report published in April 1993 recommended a series of institutional reforms in the judiciary and security services, including the resolution by the Supreme Court of all cases of jurisdictional conflict between civilian and military courts. This and other measures led to some, but by no means all, improvements in respect of human rights.

Liberal government since 1993

In the campaign leading up to the 1993 general elections, the Liberal candidate, **Carlos Roberto Reina Idiáquez**, pledged to provide every citizen *"techo, trabajo, tierra y tortilla"* (roof, work, land and food), arguing for a more socially conscious face to the economic adjustment programme inaugurated by President Callejas. Although many of his economic policies were unpopular, and he was unable to alleviate widespread poverty in the short term, President Reina received approval for his handling of the military and investigations of human rights' abuses.

The 1997 presidential elections were again won by the Liberal candidate, **Carlos Flores Facusse**. He had the support of the business community, who believed he would control public spending and reduce the government deficit in line with IMF targets, but he also campaigned against economic austerity and in favour of bridging the gap between rich and poor. The passage of Hurricane Mitch over Honduras in October 1998 forced the Flores administration to refocus all its attention on rebuilding the country at all levels, social, economic and infrastructural.

Ricardo Maduro of the National Party was sworn in as president in January 2002. Elections in November 2005 were won by the Liberal Party's **Manuel Zelaya**, with a majority of just 75,000 votes. Zelaya had served in the government of Carlos Flores. On taking office he vowed to continue the fight against gang violence along with tackling corruption in government, creation of hundreds of thousands of badly needed jobs and support for CAFTA free trade agreement with the US.

But despite the determination, violence continues to dominate the political agenda, with prison riots and occasional ransoms of high-profile individuals undermining the rule of law. In 2007, Zelaya ordered national media outlets to carry government propaganda for two hours a day for 10 days to counteract a campaign of misinformation.

The Coup

In 2009, President Manuel Zelaya was ousted in a military coup. Troops seized the president early in the morning and sent him – still wearing his pyjamas – into exile in Costa Rica. The move followed the president's proposal to hold a referendum on changing the law to allow him to stand for a second term of office. When the head of the armed forces opposed the plan, Zelaya fired him, which triggered the coup. Zelaya now lives in the Dominican Republic. Meanwhile, recent presidential elections were won by **Porfirio 'Pepe' Lobo Sosa** of the right-wing National Party, with the largest number of votes ever recorded in Honduras' history. He took office in January, 2010. Honduras remains suspended from the Organization of American States (OAS).

Culture

People

2006 estimates put the population at just under seven million. The pure indigenous population is only an estimated 7% of the total population, and the percentage of pure Spanish or other European ancestry is even smaller. The two largest indigenous groups are the Chortis from Santa Rosa de Copán westwards to the border with Guatemala, and the Lencas in the departments of Lempira, Intibucá and, above all, in the highlands of La Paz.

There are also about 45,000 Miskito people who live on the Caribbean coast, alongside several communities of Garífunas (black Caribs). The population is 90% mestizo. Some 53% are peasant farmers or agricultural labourers, with a low standard of living.

Religion and education
Education is compulsory, but not all the rural children go to school – 33% of the population over the age of 10 have had no formal schooling. According to UNESCO 27.1% of people over 15 are illiterate. The Universidad Nacional, based in Tegucigalpa, has departments in Comayagua, San Pedro Sula and La Ceiba. Also in Tegucigalpa are the Universidad José Cecilio del Valle, Universidad Católica (with campuses in San Pedro Sula and Choluteca), Universidad Tecnológica Centro Americana and Universidad Pedagógica Nacional; there is also the Universidad de San Pedro Sula, Universidad Pedagógica Francisco Morazán and Universidad Tecnológica Centroamericana. The majority of the population is Catholic.

Music
The visitor seeking specifically Honduran native music will find little to satisfy him or her. Honduras shares with Belize and Guatemala the presence of Garífuna or black Caribs on the Caribbean coast. These descendants of indigenous Caribs and escaped black slaves were deported to the area from St Vincent in the late 18th century and continue to maintain a very separate identity, including their own religious observances, music and dances, profoundly African in spirit and style.

Land and environment
With a territory of 112,100 sq km, Honduras is larger than all the other Central American republics except Nicaragua. Bordered by Nicaragua, Guatemala and El Salvador, it has a narrow Pacific coastal strip, 124 km long on the Gulf of Fonseca, and a northern coast on the Caribbean of 640 km.

Inland, much of the country is mountainous: a rough plateau covered with volcanic ash and lava in the south, rising to peaks such as Cerro de las Minas in the Celaque range (2849 m), but with some intermont basins at between 900 and 1800 m. The volcanic detritus disappears to the north, revealing saw-toothed ranges which approach the coast at an angle; the one in the extreme northwest, along the border with Guatemala, disappears under the sea and shows itself again in the Bay Islands. At most places in the north there is only a narrow shelf of lowland between the sea and the sharp upthrust of the mountains, but along two rivers (the Aguán in the northeast, and the Ulúa in the northwest) long fingers of marshy lowland stretch inland between the ranges. The Ulúa lowland is particularly important; it is about 40 km wide and stretches southwards for 100 km where the city of San Pedro Sula is located. From its southern limit a deep gash continues across the highland to the Gulf of Fonseca on the Pacific. The distance between the Caribbean and the Pacific along this trough is 280 km; the altitude at the divide between the Río Comayagua, running into the Ulúa and the Caribbean, and the streams flowing into the Pacific, is only 950 m. In this trough lies Comayagua, the old colonial capital. The lowlands along the Gulf of Fonseca are narrower than they are along the Caribbean; there is no major thrust inland as there is along the Ulúa.

The prevailing winds are from the east, consequently the Caribbean coast has a high rainfall and is covered with deep tropical forest. The intermont basins, the valleys and the slopes sheltered from the prevailing winds bear oak and pine down to as low as 600 m.

Timber is almost the only fuel available. In the drier areas, north and south of Tegucigalpa, there are extensive treeless savannahs.

Today, land under some form of cultivation is only 18% of the total, while meadows and pastures make up 14% of total land use. Rugged terrain makes large areas unsuitable for any kind of agriculture. Nevertheless, there is undeveloped agricultural potential in the flat and almost unpopulated lands of the coastal plain east of Tela to Trujillo and Puerto Castilla, in the Aguán valley southward and in the region northeast of Juticalpa. The area to the northeast, known as the Mosquitia plain, is largely unexploited and little is known of its potential.

Climate

Rain is frequent on the Caribbean coast year-round; the heaviest occurs from September to February inclusive. In Tegucigalpa the dry season is normally from November to April inclusive. The coolest months are December and January, but this is when heavy rains fall on the north coast, which could impede travel. The driest months for this area are April and May, though they are very hot. However, weather predictions in this area have become more difficult in recent years, whether because of the *El Niño* phenomenon or for other reasons. Rain, when it comes, is usually heavy, but of short duration.

Nicaragua

History

Nicaragua was at the crossroads of northern and southern prehispanic cultures. The best understood are the Chorotegas, who came from Mexico around AD 800, and the Nicaraguas, who partially displaced the Chorotegas in the Pacific basin around AD 1200. The Nicaraguas set up a very successful society which traded with people from Mexico to Peru, but the most interesting pre-Columbian remains are the many petroglyphs and large basalt figures left by unnamed pre-Chorotega cultures, in particular on the islands of Zapatera and Ometepe. The Ramas and Mayagna, of South American lowland origin, populated the eastern seaboard regions, but are almost extinct today.

Conquest and colonization

In 1522, the Spanish explorer Gil González Dávila arrived overland from Panama, and searching for the wealthiest chief of all, arrived on the western shores of Lake Nicaragua to meet the famous Nicaraguas chief, Niqueragua. The chief and Dávila engaged in long philosophical conversations conducted through a translator and eventually the great chief agreed to accept Christianity. The Chorotega chieftain Diriangen, however, was less conducive to religious conversion and subsequently slaughtered Dávila's small force of troops. In 1524 the Spanish sent a stronger army and the local populace was overcome by Francisco Hernández de Córdoba. The colonies of Granada and León were subsequently founded and the local administrative centre was not wealthy Granada, with its profitable crops of sugar, cocoa, and indigo, but impoverished León, then barely able to subsist on its crops of maize, beans and rice. This reversal of the Spanish policy of choosing the most successful settlement as capital was due to the ease with which León could be reached from the Pacific. In 1852 Managua was chosen as a new capital as a compromise, following violent rivalry between Granada and León.

Walker's expedition

The infamous filibustering expedition of William Walker is an important event in Nicaraguan and Costa Rican history. William Walker (1824-1860) was born in Nashville, Tennessee, graduated and then studied medicine at Edinburgh and Heidelberg, being granted his MD in 1843. He then studied law and was called to the bar. In May 1855, he sailed for Nicaragua, where Liberal Party leaders had invited him to help them in their struggle against the Conservatives. In October he seized a steamer on Lake Nicaragua and was able to surprise and capture Granada. A new government was formed, and in June 1856 Walker was elected president. On 22 September, to gain support from the southern states in America, he suspended the Nicaraguan laws against slavery. Walker then attempted to take control of La Casona in the Guanacaste province of Costa Rica, only to be repelled by a coalition of Central American states. He surrendered to the US Navy to avoid capture in May 1857. In November 1857, he sailed from Mobile, Alabama with another expedition, but after landing near Greytown, Nicaragua, he was arrested and returned to the USA. In 1860 he sailed again from Mobile and landed in Honduras in his last attempt to conquer Central America. There he was taken prisoner by Captain Salmon, of the British Navy, and handed over to the Honduran authorities who tried and executed him on 12 September 1860. Walker's own book, *The War in Nicaragua*, is a fascinating document.

US involvement

US involvement in Nicaraguan affairs stretches back a long way. In 1909, US Marines assisted Nicaraguan Conservative leaders in an uprising to overthrow the Liberal president, José Santos Zelaya. In 1911 the USA pledged help in securing a loan to be guaranteed through the control of Nicaraguan customs by an American board. In 1912 the United States sent marines into Nicaragua to enforce control. Apart from short intervals, they stayed there until 1933. During the last five years of occupation, nationalists under **General Augusto César Sandino** waged a relentless guerrilla war against the US Marines. American forces were finally withdrawn in 1933, when President Franklin Roosevelt announced the 'Good Neighbour' policy, pledging non-intervention. An American-trained force, the Nicaraguan National Guard, was left behind, commanded by **Anastasio Somoza García**. Somoza's men assassinated General Sandino in February 1934 and Somoza himself took over the presidency in 1936. From 1932, with brief intervals, Nicaraguan affairs were dominated by this tyrant until he was assassinated in 1956. His two sons both served a presidential term and the younger, General **Anastasio Somoza Debayle**, dominated the country from 1963 until his deposition in 1979; he was later assassinated in Paraguay.

1978-1979 Revolution

The 1978 to 1979 Revolution against the Somoza Government by the Sandinista guerrilla organization (loosely allied to a broad opposition movement) resulted in extensive damage and many casualties (estimated at over 30,000) in certain parts of the country, especially in Managua, Estelí, León, Masaya, Chinandega and Corinto. After heavy fighting General Somoza resigned on 17 July 1979 and the government was taken over by a Junta representing the Sandinista guerrillas and their civilian allies. Real power was exercised by nine Sandinista *comandantes* whose chief short-term aim was reconstruction. A 47-member Council of State formally came into being in May 1980; supporters of the Frente Sandinista de Liberación Nacional (FSLN) had a majority.

Elections were held on 4 November 1984 for an augmented National Constituent Assembly with 96 seats; the Sandinista Liberation Front won 61 seats, and **Daniel Ortega Saavedra**, who had headed the Junta, was elected president. The failure of the Sandinista Government to meet the demands of a right-wing group, the Democratic Coordinating Board (CDN), led to this coalition boycotting the elections and to the US administration failing to recognize the democratically elected government.

The Sandinistas

Despite substantial official and private US support, anti-Sandinista guerrillas (the Contras) could boast no significant success in their war against the government. In 1988, the Sandinistas and the contras met for the first time to discuss the implementation of the Central American Peace Plan, drawn up by President Oscar Arias Sánchez of Costa Rica and signed in August 1987. By 1989, the contras, lacking funds and with diminished numbers, appeared to be a spent force. The Sandinista Government had brought major improvements in health and education, but the demands of the war and a complete US trade embargo did great damage to the economy as a whole. The electorate's desire for a higher standard of living was reflected in the outcome of the elections, when the US-supported candidate of the free market coalition group National Opposition Union (UNO), Señora **Violeta Chamorro**, won 55.2% of the vote, compared with 40.8% for President Ortega.

The USA was subsequently under considerable pressure to provide aid, but of the US$300 million promised for 1990 by the US Congress, only half had been distributed by May 1991. The lack of foreign financial assistance prevented any quick rebuilding of the economy. The Nicaraguan government's scant resources also did not permit it to give the disarmed contra forces the land that had been promised to them. Demilitarized Sandinistas and landless peasants also pressed for land in 1991, with a consequent rise in tension. Factions of the two groups rearmed, to be known as recontras and recompas; there were many bloody conflicts. Divisions within the UNO coalition, particularly between supporters of President Chamorro and those of Vice President Virgilio Godoy, added to the country's difficulties. Austerity measures introduced in early 1991, including a devaluation of the new córdoba. In January 1992, pacts signed between Government, recontras and recompas failed to stop occasional heavy fighting over the next two years. In 1994, however, a series of bilateral meetings, proposed by archbishop Miguel Obando y Bravo, significantly contributed to disarmament.

Movement towards a real and lasting peace

The achievement of a more peaceful state of affairs, if not reconciliation, did not remove other political tensions. After the UNO coalition realigned itself into new political groupings and returned to the National Assembly following a boycott in 1993, the FSLN began to fall apart in 1994. By early 1995, the Sandinistas had become irrevocably split between the orthodox wing, led by Daniel Ortega, and the Sandinista Renewal Movement (MRS), under Sergio Ramírez. The MRS accused the orthodox wing of betraying Sandinista principles by forming pacts with the technocrats and neo-liberals of the Government. The MRS was itself accused of opportunism. Linked to this was considerable manoeuvring over UNO-inspired constitutional reform.

The 1996 elections

In 1995 the National Assembly approved legislation governing the 20 October 1996 presidential elections. The front-runner was **Arnoldo Alemán**, former mayor of Managua, of the Liberal alliance. His main opponent was Daniel Ortega of the FSLN, who regarded Alemán's policies as a return to Somoza-style government. After reviewing the vote count because of allegations of fraud, the Supreme Electoral Council (CSE) declared Arnoldo Alemán had won 51% compared with 37.7% for Daniel Ortega. The FSLN called for new elections in Managua and Matagalpa as the OAS declared the elections fair but flawed. Ortega announced he would respect the legality but not the legitimacy of the Government of Alemán.

A new opportunity

In November of 2001, Daniel Ortega of the FSLN lost to **Enrique Bolaños** of the ruling Liberal Party (PLC). Voters chose Enrique Bolaños by more than 15 points in what many believed to be a vote against Ortega rather than approval of the Liberal Party. In Enrique Bolaños' first three months of office in 2002 he shocked many by taking a very aggressive stance against corruption and his administration exposed several cases of embezzlement under the Alemán adminstration. The desire to cleanse the past and clear the way for the future was apparent when in December 2003 former president Arnoldo Alemán was sentenced to 25 years in prison, later transferred to house arrest, for corruption including money laundering and embezzlement to a value of nearly US$100m.

President Bolaños' agreement to allow his predecessor to be investigated led to his alienation by some in the Liberal Party. The delicate balance of power in Congress has restricted the president's powers, and further changes were only avoided at the last minute when Bolaños made a pact with Sandinista leader Ortega. Elections for the new president took an interesting turn in April 2006 when the US urged Nicaragua to shun Ortega's left-wing Sandinista party. He was returned to power in November 2006.

Culture

People

With a population of 5.5 million, population density is low: 43 people per square kilometre, compared with El Salvador's 322. Nine out of 10 Nicaraguans live and work in the lowlands between the Pacific and the western shores of Lake Nicaragua, the southwestern shore of Lake Managua, and the southwestern sides of the row of volcanoes. In latter years settlers have taken to coffee-growing and cattle-rearing in the highlands at Matagalpa and Jinotega. Elsewhere, the highlands, save for an occasional mining camp, are very thinly settled.

The densely forested eastern lowlands fronting the Caribbean were neglected, because of the heavy rainfall and their consequent unhealthiness, until the British settled several colonies of Jamaicans in the 18th century at Bluefields and San Juan del Norte. But early this century the United Fruit Company of America (now United Brands) opened banana plantations inland from Puerto Cabezas, worked by blacks from Jamaica. Other companies followed suit along the coast, but the bananas were later attacked by Panama disease and exports today are small. Along the Mosquito coast there are still English-speaking communities of African, or mixed African and indigenous, descent. Besides the mestizo intermixtures of Spanish and indigenous (69%), there are pure blacks (9%), pure indigenous (5%) and mixtures of the two (mostly along the Atlantic coast).

A small proportion is of unmixed Spanish and other European descent. For a brief survey of the people of eastern Nicaragua, see page 697.

Music and dance

Nicaragua is 'marimba country' and the basic musical genre is the *son*, this time called the *Son Nica*. There are a number of popular dances for couples with the names of animals, like *La Vaca* (cow), *La Yeguita* (mare) and *El Toro* (bull). The folklore capital of Nicaragua is the city of Masaya and the musical heart of Masaya is the indigenous quarter of Monimbó. Here the marimba is king, but on increasingly rare occasions may be supported by the *chirimía* (oboe), *quijada de asno* (donkey's jaw) and *quijongo*, a single-string bow with gourd resonator. Some of the most traditional *sones* are *El Zañate*, *Los Novios* and *La Perra Renca*, while the more popular dances still to be found are *Las Inditas*, *Las Negras*, *Los Diablitos* and *El Torovenado*, all involving masked characters. Diriamba is another centre of tradition, notable for the folk play known as *El Güegüense*, accompanied by violin, flute and drum and the dance called *Toro Guaco*. The Caribbean coast is a totally different cultural region, home to the Miskito people and English-speaking black people of Jamaican origin concentrated around Bluefields. The latter have a maypole dance and their music is typically Afro-Caribbean, with banjos, accordions, guitars and of course drums as the preferred instruments.

Religion and education

Roman Catholicism is the prevailing religion, but there are Episcopal, Baptist, Methodist and other Protestant churches. Illiteracy was reduced by a determined campaign by the Sandinista government in the 1980s. Higher education at the Universidad Nacional Autónoma de Nicaragua at León, with three faculties at Managua, and the private Jesuit Universidad Centroamericana (UCA) at Managua is good. There are two separate Universidades Nacionales Autónomas de Nicaragua (UNAN).

Land and environment

Broadly speaking, there are three well-marked geographic regions in Nicaragua: **1)** A large triangular-shaped central mountain land beginning almost on the southern border with Costa Rica and broadening northwards; the prevailing moisture-laden northeast winds drench its eastern slopes, which are deeply forested with oak and pine on the drier, cooler heights. **2)** A belt of lowland plains which run from the Gulf of Fonseca, on the Pacific, to the Costa Rican border south of Lake Nicaragua. Out of it, to the east, rise the lava cliffs of the mountains to a height of 1500-2100 m. **3)** A wide belt of eastern lowland through which a number of rivers flow from the mountains into the Atlantic. In the plains are the two largest sheets of water in Central America and 10 crater lakes. The capital, Managua, is on the shores of Lake Managua (Xolotlán), 52 km long, 15-25 km wide, and 39 m above sea-level. Its maximum depth is only 30 m. The Río Tipitapa drains it into Lake Nicaragua, 148 km long, about 55 km at its widest, and 32 m above the sea; Granada is on its shores. The 190-km Río San Juan drains both lakes into the Caribbean and is one of 96 principal rivers in the country. The longest at 680 km is the Río Coco, on the border with Honduras. Lying at the intersection of three continental plates, Nicaragua has a very unstable, changing landscape. Through the Pacific basin runs a row of 28 major volcanoes, six of which were active during the 20th century.

Climate

The wet, warm winds of the Caribbean pour heavy rain on the Atlantic coastal zone, especially in the southern basin of the Río San Juan, with more than 6 m annually. While the dry season on the Atlantic coast is only short and not wholly dry, the Pacific dry season, or summer (November to April), becomes very dusty, especially when the winds begin to blow in February. There is a wide range of climates. Depending on altitude, average annual temperatures vary between 15° and 35°C. Midday temperatures in Managua range from 30° to 36°C, but readings of 38° are not uncommon between March and May, or of 40° in January and February in the west. It can get quite cold, especially after rain, in the Caribbean lowlands. Maximum daily humidity ranges from 90% to 100%.

Costa Rica

History

Spanish settlement

During his last voyage in September 1502, Columbus landed on the shores of what is now Costa Rica. Rumours of vast gold treasures (which never materialized) led to the name of Costa Rica (Rich Coast). The Spaniards settled in the Meseta Central, where the numbers of several thousand sedentary indigenous farmers were soon greatly diminished by the diseases brought by the settlers. Cártago was founded in 1563 by **Juan Vásquez de Coronado**, but there was almost no expansion for 145 years, when a small number left Cártago for the valleys of Aserrí and Escazú. They founded Heredia in 1717, and San José in 1737. Alajuela, not far from San José, was founded in 1782. The settlers were growing in numbers but were still poor and raising only subsistence crops.

Independence and coffee

Independence from Spain was declared in 1821 whereupon Costa Rica, with the rest of Central America, immediately became part of Mexico. This led to a civil war during which, two years later, the capital was moved from Cártago to San José. After Independence, the government sought anxiously for some product which could be exported and taxed for revenue. Coffee was successfully introduced from Cuba in 1808, making Costa Rica the first of the Central American countries to grow what was to become known as the golden bean. The Government offered free land to coffee growers, thus building up a peasant landowning class. In 1825 there was a trickle of exports, carried by mule to the ports. By 1846 there were ox-cart roads to Puntarenas. By 1850 there was a large flow of coffee to overseas markets which was greatly increased by the opening of a railway in 1890 from San José and Cártago to Puerto Limón along the valley of the River Reventazón. From 1850, coffee prosperity began to affect the country profoundly: the birth rate grew, land for coffee was free, and the peasant settlements started spreading, first down the Reventazón as far as Turrialba, then up the slopes of the volcanoes, then down the new railway from San José to the old Pacific port of Puntarenas.

Banana industry

Bananas were first introduced in 1878 making Costa Rica the first Central American republic to grow them. It is now the second largest exporter in the world. Labour was brought in from Jamaica to clear the forest and work the plantations. The industry grew and in 1913, the peak year, the Caribbean coastlands provided 11 million bunches for export. Since then the spread of disease has lowered exports and encouraged crop diversification. The United Fruit Company turned its attentions to the Pacific littoral, especially in the south around the port of Golfito. Although some of the Caribbean plantations were turned over to cacao, *abacá* (Manila hemp) and African palm, the region has regained its ascendancy over the Pacific littoral as a banana producer. By the end of the century over 50,000 ha were planted to bananas, mostly in the Atlantic lowlands.

In the 1990s Chiquita, Dole and Del Monte, the multinational fruit producers, came under international pressure over labour rights on their plantations. Two European campaign groups targeted working conditions in Costa Rica where, despite constitutional guarantees of union freedom, there was a poor record of labour rights abuse. Only 10% of Costa Rica's 50,000 banana workers were represented by unions. The rest preferred to join the less political *solidarista* associations, which provide cheap loans and promote savings, and thus avoid being blacklisted or harassed. Del Monte agreed in 1998 to talk to the unions after a decade of silence, while Chiquita declared its workers were free to choose trade union representation.

Democratic government

Costa Rica's long tradition of democracy began in 1889 and has continued to the present day, with only a few lapses. In 1917 the elected president **Alfredo González** was ousted by **Federico Tinoco**, who held power until 1919, when a counter-revolution and subsequent elections brought Julio Acosta to the presidency. Democratic and orderly government followed until the campaign of 1948 when violent protests and a general strike surrounded disputed results. A month of fighting broke out after the Legislative Assembly annulled the elections, leading to the abolition of the constitution and a junta being installed, led by **José Figueres Ferrer**. In 1949 a constituent assembly drew up a new constitution and abolished the army. The junta stepped down and **Otilio Ulate Blanco**, one of the candidates of the previous year, was inaugurated. In 1952, Figueres, a socialist, founded the Partido de Liberación Nacional, and was elected president in 1953. He dominated politics for the next two decades, serving as president in 1953-1958 and 1970-1974. The PLN introduced social welfare programmes and nationalization policies, while intervening conservative governments encouraged private enterprise. The PLN was again in power 1974-1978 (**Daniel Oduber Quirós**), 1982-1986 (**Luis Alberto Monge**), 19861-1990 (**Oscar Arias Sánchez**) and 1994-1998 (**José María Figueres**, son of José Figueres Ferrer).

President Arias drew up proposals for a peace pact in Central America and concentrated greatly on foreign policy initiatives. Efforts were made to expel Nicaraguan contras resident in Costa Rica and the country's official proclamation of neutrality, made in 1983, was reinforced. The Central American Peace Plan, signed by the five Central American presidents in Guatemala in 1987, earned Arias the Nobel Peace Prize, although progress in implementing its recommendations was slow. In the 1990 general elections, **Rafael Angel Calderón Fournier**, a conservative lawyer and candidate for the Social Christian Unity Party (PUSC), won a narrow victory, with 51% of the vote, over the candidate of the PLN. Calderón, the son of a former president who had been one of the candidates in the 1948 disputed elections, had previously stood for election in 1982 and 1986. The president's popularity slumped as the effects of his economic policies were felt on people's living standards, while his Government was brought into disrepute by allegations of corruption and links with 'narco' traffickers.

PLN government, 1994-1998

In the February 1994 elections another former president's son was elected by a narrow margin. **José María Figueres** of the PLN won 49.6% of the vote, 2.2% points ahead of his PUSC rival. In the Legislature, the PLN won 29 seats and the PUSC 25, while smaller parties won those that remained. The election was won on economic policies. Figueres argued against neo-liberal policies, claiming he would renegotiate agreements with the IMF and the World Bank, but in his first year of office a third Structural Adjustment Programme (backed by the international agencies and drawn up by the previous administration) was approved. A subsequent National Development Plan and a Plan to Fight Poverty contained a wide range of measures designed to promote economic stability and to improve the quality of life for many sectors of society. While the plans were partly responding to the protests that followed the approval of the Adjustment Programme, many of their proposals were at variance with the programme's policies.

1998 and 2002 elections

Elections were held in February 1998 and were won by the PUSC candidate, **Miguel Angel Rodríguez**, with 46.6% of the vote, 2% ahead of the PLN candidate. Thirty percent of voters abstained. The new president took office in May 1998, promising to make women, the young and the poor a priority for his government. Typically for Costa Rica, the elections of early 2002 ran on a frenzy of neutrality. **President Pacheco**, 68 years old, stimulated just enough support to win after the election went to a run-off when none of the three candidates won outright victory in the first round. The challenges to the candidates were to restimulate the economy, hit by the global downturn and the low coffee prices, and both claimed to be opposed to privatization of state-run industries.

Arias returns

Having successfully convinced Costa Rica's Congress to change the constitution and allow re-election, Oscar Arias was elected president in 2006, 16 years after serving his first term. The election was extremely close, and only decided after several recounts. President Arias, a strong supporter of the Central America Free Trade Agreement, has promised to stabilize the economy and to make Costa Rica one of the Latin America's most developed countries.

Culture

People

In all provinces over 98% of the population is white and mestizo except in Limón where 33.2% is black and 3.1% indigenous, of whom only 5000 survive in the whole country. There are three groups: the Bribri (3500), Boruca (1000) and Guatuso. Although officially protected, the living conditions of the indigenous population are very poor. In 1992 Costa Rica became the first Central American country to ratify the International Labour Organization treaty on indigenous populations and tribes. However, even in Limón, the percentage of blacks is falling: it was 57.1% in 1927. Many of them speak Jamaican English as their native tongue. Much of the Caribbean coastland, especially in the north, remains unoccupied. On the Pacific coastlands a white minority owns the land on the hacienda system which has been rejected in the uplands. About 46% of the people are mestizos. The population has risen sharply in the mountainous Peninsula of Nicoya, which is an important source of maize, rice and beans.

Music and dance

This is the southernmost in our string of 'marimba culture' countries. The guitar is also a popular instrument for accompanying folk dances, while the *chirimía* and *quijongo*, already encountered further north, have not yet totally died out in the Chorotega region of Guanacaste Province. This province is indeed the heartland of Costa Rican folklore and the Punto Guanacasteco, a heel-and-toe dance for couples, has been officially decreed to be the 'typical national dance', although it is not in fact traditional, but was composed at the turn of the last century by Leandro Cabalceta Brau during a brief sojourn in jail. There are other dances too, such as the *botijuela*, *tamborito* and *cambute*, but it must honestly be said that they will not be found in the countryside as a tradition, but are performed on stage when outsiders need to be shown some native culture. Among the country's most popular native performers are the duet **Los Talolingas**, authors of *La Guaria Morada*, regarded as the 'second national anthem', and **Lorenzo 'Lencho' Salazar**, whose humorous songs in the vernacular style are considered quintessentially Tico.

Some of the Republic's rapidly deculturizing indigenous groups have dances of their own, like the *Danza de los Diablitos* of the Borucas, the *Danza del Sol* and *Danza de la Luna* of the Chorotegas and the *Danza de los Huesos* of the Talamancas. A curious ocarina made of beeswax, the *dru mugata* is still played by the Guaymí people and is said to be the only truly pre-Columbian instrument still to be found. The drum and flute are traditional among various groups, but the guitar and accordion are moving in to replace them. As in the case of Nicaragua, the Caribbean coast of Costa Rica, centred on Puerto Limón, is inhabited by black people who came originally from the English-speaking islands and whose music reflects this origin. The sinkit seems to be a strictly local rhythm, but the calypso is popular and the cuadrille, square dance and maypole dance are also found. There is also a kind of popular hymn called the *saki*. Brass, percussion and string instruments are played, as well as the accordion.

Land and environment

Costa Rica lies between Nicaragua and Panama, with coastlines on the Caribbean (212 km) and the Pacific (1016 km). The distance between sea and sea ranges from 119-282 km. A low, thin line of hills between Lake Nicaragua and the Pacific is prolonged into northern Costa Rica with several volcanoes (including the active Volcán Arenal), broadening and rising into high and rugged mountains and volcanoes in the centre and south. The highest peak, Chirripó Grande, southeast of the capital, reaches 3820 m. Within these highlands are certain structural depressions; one of them, the Meseta Central, is of paramount importance. To the southwest this basin is rimmed by the comb of the Cordillera; at the foot of its slopes, inside the basin, are the present capital San José, and the old capital, Cártago. Northeast of these cities, about 30 km away, four volcano cones rise from a massive common pedestal. From northwest to southeast these are Poás (2704 m), Barva (2906 m), Irazú (3432 m) and Turrialba (3339 m). Irazú and Poás are intermittently active. Between the Cordillera and the volcanoes is the Meseta Central: an area of 5200 sq km at an altitude of between 900 and 1800 m, where two-thirds of the population live. The northeastern part of the basin is drained by the Reventazón through turbulent gorges into the Caribbean; the Río Grande de Tárcoles drains the western part of it into the Pacific.

There are lowlands on both coasts. On the Caribbean coast, the Nicaraguan lowland along the Río San Juan continues into Costa Rica, wide and sparsely inhabited as far as

Puerto Limón. A great deal of this land, particularly near the coast, is swampy; southeast of Puerto Limón the swamps continue as far as Panama in a narrow belt of lowland between sea and mountain.

The Gulf of Nicoya, on the Pacific side, thrusts some 65 km inland; its waters separate the mountains of the mainland from the 900-m-high mountains of the narrow Nicoya Peninsula. From a little to the south of the mouth of the Río Grande de Tercels, a lowland savannah stretches northwest past the port of Puntarenas and along the whole northeastern shore of the Gulf towards Nicaragua. Below the Río Grande de Tercels the savannah is pinched out by mountains, but there are other banana-growing lowlands to the south. Small quantities of African palm and cacao are now being grown in these lowlands. In the far south there are swampy lowlands again at the base of the Península de Osa and between the Golfo Dulce and the borders of Panama. Here there are 12,000 ha planted to bananas. The Río General, which flows into the Río Grande de Térraba, runs through a southern structural depression almost as large as the Meseta Central.

Panama

History

Camino Real

Panama City was founded in 1519 after a trail opened up between what is now the Pacific and the Caribbean. The Royal Road, or the *Camino Real*, ran from Panama City to Nombre de Dios until it was re-routed to Portobelo. An alternative route was used later for bulkier, less-valuable merchandise; it ran from Panama City to Las Cruces, on the Chagres River. Intruders were quickly attracted by the wealth passing over the Camino Real. **Sir Francis Drake** attacked Nombre de Dios, and in 1573 his men penetrated inland to Vera Cruz, further up the Chagres River on the Camino Real, plundering the town. Spain countered later attacks by building strongholds and forts to protect the route: among them San Felipe at the entrances to Portobelo and San Lorenzo at the mouth of the Chagres. Spanish galleons, loaded with treasure and escorted against attack, left Portobelo once a year. Perhaps the most famous pirate attack was by **Henry Morgan** in 1671. After capturing the fort of San Lorenzo, he pushed up the Chagres River to Las Cruces. From there he descended to Panama City, which he looted and burnt. The city was subsequently rebuilt on a new site, at the base of Ancón Hill, and fortified. With Britain and Spain at war, attacks reached their climax with Admiral Vernon's capture of Portobelo in 1739 and the fort of San Lorenzo the following year. Spain abandoned the route in 1746 and began trading round Cape Horn. Nonetheless, crossing between the Atlantic and Pacific became part of a Panamanian tradition and ultimately led to the construction of the Canal.

Panama Railroad

In 1821, Gran Colombia won Independence from Spain. Panama, in an event celebrated annually on 28 November, declared its own Independence and promptly joined Bolívar's Gran Colombia federation. Though known as the 'Sovereign State' of Panama it remained, even after the federation disintegrated, a province of Colombia. Some 30 years later, streams of men were once more moving up the Chagres and down to Panama City: the forty-niners on their way to the newly discovered gold fields of California, taking a quicker and safer route than the challenges of continental North America. Many perished on this 'road to hell', as it was called, and the gold rush brought into being a railway across the isthmus. The Panama Railroad from Colón (then only two streets) to Panama City took four years to build, with great loss of life. The first train ran on 26 November 1853. The railway was an enormous financial success until the re-routing of the Pacific Steam Navigation Company's ships round Cape Horn in 1867 and the opening of the first US transcontinental railroad in 1869 reduced its traffic.

Building of the Canal

Ferdinand de Lesseps, builder of the Suez Canal, arrived in Panama in 1881 to a hero's welcome, having decided to build a sea-level canal along the Chagres River and the Río Grande. Work started in 1882. About 30 km had been dug before the Company crashed in 1893, defeated by extravagance, corruption, tropical diseases (22,000 people died, mostly of yellow fever and malaria) and by engineering difficulties inherent in the construction of a canal without lift-locks. Eventually the Colombian government authorized the Company to sell all its rights and properties to the United States, but the Colombian Senate rejected the treaty, and the inhabitants of Panama, encouraged by the United States, declared their Independence on 3 November 1903. The United States intervened and, in spite of protests by Colombia, recognized the new republic. Colombia did not accept the severance until 1921.

Within two weeks of its Independence, Panama, represented in Washington by the controversial Frenchman **Philippe Bunau-Varilla**, signed a treaty granting to the USA 'in perpetuity' a 16-km-wide corridor across the isthmus over which the USA would exercise authority 'as if it were sovereign'. Bunau-Varilla, an official of the bankrupt French canal company, presented the revolutionary junta with the *fait accompli* of a signed treaty. The history of Panama then became that of two nations, with the Canal Zone governor, also a retired US general, responsible only to the President of the USA. Before beginning the task of building the Canal, the United States performed one of the greatest sanitary operations in history: the clearance from the area of the more malignant tropical diseases. The name of the physician **William Crawford Gorgas** will always be associated with this, as will that of the engineer **George Washington Goethals** with the actual building of the Canal. On 15 August 1914, the first official passage was made, by the ship *Ancón*.

1939 Treaty with USA

As a result of bitter resentment, the USA ended Panama's protectorate status in 1939 with a treaty which limited US rights of intervention. However, the disparity in living standards continued to provoke anti-US feeling, culminating in riots that began on 9 January 1964, resulting in the death of 23 Panamanians (the day is commemorated annually as Martyrs' Day), four US marines and the suspension of diplomatic relations for some months. In 1968 **Arnulfo Arias Madrid** was elected president for the third time and after only 10 days in office he was forcibly removed by the National Guard which installed a provisional junta. **Brigadier General Omar Torrijos Herrera** ultimately became Commander of the National Guard and principal power, dominating Panamanian politics for the next 13 years. Gradually, the theoretically civilian National Guard was converted into a full-scale army and renamed the Panama Defence Forces. Constitutional government was restored in 1972 after elections for a 505-member National Assembly of Community Representatives, which revised the 1946 constitution, elected **Demetrio Basilio Lakas Bahas** as president, and vested temporary extraordinary executive powers in General

Torrijos for six years. Torrijos' rule was characterized by his pragmatic nationalism; he carried out limited agrarian reform and nationalized major industries, yet satisfied business interests. Importantly, he reached agreement with the USA to restore Panamanian sovereignty over the Canal Zone and to close the US military bases by the year 2000. In 1978 elections for a new National Assembly were held and the new representatives elected **Arístedes Royo Sánchez** president of the country. General Torrijos resigned as Chief of Government but retained the powerful post of Commander of the National Guard until his death in a small plane air-crash in 1981. There followed several years of rapid governmental changes as tension rose between presidents and National Guard leaders.

General Noriega's Administration

Following an election in May 1984, **Nicolás Ardito Barletta** was inaugurated in October for a six-year term, though the fairness of the elections was widely questioned. He was removed from office by military pressure in September 1985 and replaced by **Eric Arturo Delvalle**, whose attempts to reduce the Guardia's influence, by then concentrated in the hands of **General Manuel Antonio Noriega Moreno**, led to his own removal in February 1988. **Manuel Solís Palma** was named president in his place. With the economy reeling and banks closed as a result of US economic sanctions, the campaign leading up to the election of May 1989 saw the growing influence of a movement called the *Civilista* Crusade, led by upper- and middle-class figures. When their coalition candidate, Guillermo Endara Galimany, triumphed over Noriega's candidate, Carlos Duque Jaén, the election was annulled by the military. General Noriega appointed Francisco Rodríguez as provisional president in September, but by December, General Noriega had formally assumed power as Head of State. These events provoked the US military invasion **Operation 'Just Cause'** on 20 December to overthrow him. He finally surrendered in mid-January, having first taken refuge in the Papal Nunciature on Christmas Eve. He was taken to the USA for trial on charges of drugs trafficking and other offences, and sentenced to 30 years in prison. **Guillermo Endara** was installed as president. The Panamanian Defence Forces were immediately remodelled into a new Public Force whose largest component is the civilian National Police. Panama has not had a regular army since. Noriega was released in September 2007 and extradited to France.

After 'Just Cause'

After the overthrow of General Noriega's administration, the US Senate approved a US$1 billion aid package including US$480 million in direct assistance to provide liquidity and get the economy moving again. The USA also put Panama under considerable pressure to sign a Treaty of Mutual Legal Assistance, which would limit bank secrecy and enable investigation into suspected drug traffickers' bank accounts. While structural, economic and legal changes impacted Panama in the early 1990s, Panama was still not without problems. Charges of corruption at the highest level were made by Panamanians and US officials. President Endara himself was weakened by allegations that his law firm had been involved with companies owned by drugs traffickers. Though the economy grew under Endara, street crime increased, social problems continued, there were isolated bombings and pro-military elements failed in a coup attempt.

1994 elections and after

The 1994 elections took place with 2000 local and international observers, and polling was largely incident-free and open. **Ernesto Pérez Balladares** of the Partido Revolucionario Democrático (PRD), won with less than a third of the popular vote. The PRD also won a narrow majority in the Legislative Assembly. Pérez Balladares, who appointed a cabinet containing members of opposition parties as well as from the PRD, gave priority to tackling the problems of social inequality, unemployment, deteriorating education standards and rising crime. In May 1999, **Mireya Moscoso** emerged victorious in presidential elections which saw a 78% voter turnout. Moscoso obtained 45% of the popular vote, ahead of her closest rival Martín Torrijos (son of General Omar Torrijos) with 38%. Moscoso took office on September 1, becoming the first female president of Panama, enjoying the honour of receiving control of the Panama Canal from the US on 31 December 1999, and the prospect of presiding over the nation's centennial celebrations in 2003. Elections in May 2004 saw **Martín Torrijos**, son of former dictator Omar Torrijos, win the presidential elections. His main legacy is the initiation of an ambitious expansion of the Canal, scheduled for completion in 2014. In 2009, supermarket magnate **Ricardo Martinelli** and his conservative Democratic Change party rode to power. It is too soon to judge the outcome of his term, but labour, environment and mineral code reforms have so far led to concerning clashes with protestors.

Culture

People

The population of 3.2 million is mostly of mixed descent but there are indigenous and black communities and a small Asian population. Most of the rural population live in the six provinces on the Pacific side, west of the Canal. There is only one rural population centre of any importance on the Caribbean: in Bocas del Toro, in the extreme northwest. Of the 60 indigenous tribes who inhabited the isthmus at the time of the Spanish conquest, only three have survived in any number: the Kunas (also spelt Cunas, particularly in Colombia) of the San Blas islands (50,000), the Guaymíes, who prefer to be called Ngöbe-Buglé, of the western provinces (80,000), and the Emberá-Wunan, formerly known as Chocóes of Darién (10,000). These, and a few others, such as the Naso, Bri-Bri and Bokotá, account for 6% of the total population. Indigenous opposition to the opening of copper mines at Cerro Colorado and demonstrations supporting greater autonomy for indigenous people in the area characterized 1996, but were inconclusive. However, an administrative enclave, the Comarca, providing for some Ngöbe-Buglé home rule, has been created. Numbers of African slaves escaped from their Spanish owners during the 16th century. They set up free communities in the Darién jungles and their Spanish-speaking descendants, known as *cimarrones*, still live there and in the Pearl Islands. The majority of Panama's blacks, often bilingual, are descended from English-speaking West Indians, brought in for the building of the railway in 1850, and later of the Canal. There are also a number of East Indians and Chinese, a few of whom, especially in the older generations, tend to cling to their own languages and customs.

Music and dance

Being at the crossroads of the Americas, where Central America meets South America and the Caribbean backs on to the Pacific, and being one of the smallest Latin American republics, Panama possesses an outstandingly rich and attractive musical culture. Albeit related to that of the Caribbean coast of Colombia and Venezuela, it is very different. The classic Panamanian folk dances are the *tambor* or *tamborito*, *cumbia*, *punto* and *mejorana*, largely centred on the central provinces of Coclé, and Veraguas and those of Herrera and Los Santos on the Península Azuero. Towns that are particularly noted for their musical traditions are Los Santos, Ocú, Las Tablas, Tonosí and Chorrera. The dances are for couples and groups of couples and the rhythms are lively and graceful, the man often dancing close to his partner without touching her, moving his hat in rhythmic imitation of fanning. The woman's *pollera* costume is arguably the most beautiful in Latin America and her handling of the voluminous skirt is an important element of the dance. The *tamborito* is considered to be Panama's national dance and is accompanied by three tall drums. The *cumbia*, which has a common origin with the better-known Colombian dance of the same name, has a fast variant called the *atravesado*, while the *punto* is slower and more stately. The name *mejorana* is shared by a small native guitar, a dance, a song form and a specific tune. The most common instruments to be found today are the tall drums that provide the basic beat, the violin, the guitar and the accordion. The *tuna* is a highly rhythmic musical procession with women's chorus and massed hand-clapping.

Turning to song, there are two traditional forms, both of Spanish origin: the *copla*, sung by women and accompanying the *tamborito*, and the *mejorana*, which is a male solo preserve, with the lyrics in the form of *décimas*, a verse form used by the great Spanish poets of the Golden Age. It is accompanied by the ukulele-like guitar of the same name. Quite unique to Panama are the *salomas* and *gritos*, the latter between two or more men. The yodelling and falsetto of the *salomas* are in fact carried over into the singing style and it is this element, more than any other, that gives Panamanian folk song its unique and instantly recognizable sound. There are other traditional masked street dances of a carnavalesque nature, such as the very African *congos*, the *diablicos sucios* (dirty little devils) and the *grandiablos* (big devils). In the area of the Canal there is a significant English-speaking black population, similar to those in Nicaragua and Costa Rica, who also sing calypso, while the Guaymí people (Ngöbe-Buglé) in the west and the Kuna and Chocó (Emberá-Wunan) of the San Blas islands and Darién isthmus possess their own song, rituals and very attractive flute music.

Land and environment

Panama is most easily visualized as a slightly stretched, horizontal 'S', with the 767-km Caribbean coastline on the north and the 1234-km Pacific coast on the south and lying between 7° and 10° north of the Equator. The Canal, which runs southeast-northwest, bisects the country; the mountains running along the isthmus divide the country from north to south. About one-third of the population lives in Panama City on the east side of the Canal at its southern terminus. Most of the rural population live in the quarter of the country south of the mountains and west of the Canal. At the border with Costa Rica there are several inactive volcanic cones, the boldest of which is the Volcán Barú, 3475 m high and the highest point in the country. The sharp-sided Cordillera de Talamanca continues southeast at a general altitude of about 900 m, but subsides suddenly southwest of Panama City. The next range, the San Blas, rises east of Colón (the city at the north end of the Canal) running parallel to the Caribbean coastline, into Colombia. Its highest peak Tacarcuna, at 1875 m, is in the heart of the Darién. A third range rises from the Pacific littoral in the southeast, running along the Pacific coast of Colombia as the Serranía de Baudó. Nature decreed a gap between the Talamanca and San Blas ranges in which the divide is no more than 87 m high. The ranges are so placed that the gap, through which the Canal runs, follows a line from northwest to southeast. To reach the Pacific from the Atlantic you must travel eastwards so when travelling through the Canal (as in much of the country) the sun rises over the Pacific and sets over the Atlantic. The rate of deforestation in Panama accelerated rapidly in the 1980s and early 1990s, but has fallen considerably. 70% of the country is classified as primary forest, more than any other Central American republic except Belize. The loss of forest in 1990 was estimated at 220,000 acres (89,000 ha), against felling of up to 154,000 acres (62,000 ha) per year between 1985 and 1989. The government reported a slowing of deforestation during 1993-1995, but in early 1996 estimated it was continuing at 2200 acres (900 ha) a year. Reports record a considerable decrease in deforestation between 2000 and 2005.

Wildlife

Mexico alone has over 430 mammal species, more than 960 different birds, around 720 reptiles and almost 300 amphibians; as for insects, there are definitely more than you want to know about, from beautiful butterflies to biting bugs. Even the smallest country in the area, El Salvador, which has little natural habitat remaining, can boast a total of 680 species of vertebrates (the UK has just 280 or so). This diversity is due to the fact that the area is the meeting place of two of the world's major biological regions – the Nearctic to the north and the Neotropical to the south. It has a remarkable geological and climatic complexity and consequently an enormous range of habitats, from desert in the north of Mexico to rainforests, dry forests, cloud forests, mangroves and stretches of wetlands further south in the tropical areas of the region.

When to go
In terms of wildlife, the best time to visit depends, obviously, on where you are and what you want to see, whether it's the sight of hundreds of thousands of migrating raptors passing over Central America between August and December, or that of nesting turtles along the coast from Mexico to Panama. The exact dates of the turtle season vary with the species, but June to October are peak times for many. In practise, planning will be required to get the timing right.

Spotting wildlife
Use local, **experienced guides** as these people will know what species are around and where to look for them and will often recognize bird calls and use these as an aid to spotting them. You should take **binoculars**; get a pair with a reasonable magnification and good light-gathering configurations (ie 10x40 or 8x40) for use in the dim light of the rainforests. They will also need to be reasonably waterproof. Another enormous aid to wildlife watching is a strong torch or, better still, a powerful **headlamp**. The latter not only leaves your hands free but it also helps when trying to spot eye shine of nocturnal mammals, the light reflected back from their eyes direct to yours. Some places, such as Monteverde Cloud Forest Reserve in Costa Rica and the Community Baboon Sanctuary in Belize, offer excellent night walks with guides, but with care you can equally well arrange your own. Another strategy to use is to select a likely looking spot – such as a fruiting fig or a watering hole (in dry country) – and wait for the animals to come to you.

Mammals

In Central America and Mexico mammals tend to be secretive, indeed the majority are nocturnal; hence the need for night walks if you are serious about finding them, though, even then, good views are comparatively rare. That said, you will certainly see some delightful creatures, with views of primates being more or less guaranteed. The rainforests throughout the region contain **spider monkeys**, **howler monkeys** and/or **capuchin monkeys**. The howlers are probably the most noticeable because, as their name suggests, they are inclined to make a huge row at times, especially early in the mornings and in the late afternoons. The Community Baboon Sanctuary in Belize was set up especially for the conservation of the **black howler monkey** and you've a good chance of seeing them in Tikal, Guatemala, in Parque Nacional Pico Bonito in Honduras, on the Omotepe Islands in Nicaragua and the rainforests of Costa Rica. The **spider monkey** is a much more agile, slender primate, swinging around high in the canopy, using its prehensile tail as a fifth limb and again found throughout the region. The smaller, **white-throated capuchins** are also commonly seen, moving around quite noisily in groups, searching for fruit and insects in the trees and even coming down to the ground to find food. Smaller again, and restricted to Panama and Costa Rica, is the **red-backed squirrel monkey**. The most likely places to see them are Corcovado and Manuel Antonio national parks in Costa Rica. Finally, for the daytime species, you may see a tamarin, both Geoffroy's and the cotton-top tamarin are present, but only in **Panama** (try Darién or Natural Metropolitano national parks). The New World, unlike Africa and Asia, has only one group (10 species) of nocturnal primates and this, appropriately enough, is the **night monkey**. Panama is the only country in the region to contain night monkeys.

Another mammal you are very likely to see in the southern countries of the region are sloths. Good places to look are Reserva Monteverde and the forests of Tortuguero and Manuel Antonio in Costa Rica. As they tend to stay in one area for days at a time, local guides are excellent at pointing them out. The most easily seen of the carnivores is not, sadly, the longed-for **jaguar**, but the ubiquitous **white-nosed coati**, a member of the racoon family. The females and their offspring go around in groups and are unmistakable with their long, ringed tails, frequently held in the air, and their long snouts sniffing around for insects and fruit in trees and on the ground. At many tourist sites, they hang around waiting to be fed by the visitors, in particular around Tikal and in the popular lowland national parks of Costa Rica. Members of the cat family are rarely seen; those in the area include the **bobcat** (in Mexico only), **jaguar**, **puma**, **ocelot** and **margay**. All are more likely to be seen at night, or, possibly, at dawn and dusk. In Belize, Cockscomb Basin Wildlife Sanctuary is also known as the Jaguar Reserve, so this area is as good a place as any to try your luck. Río Bravo and Chan Chich Lodge in Belize, Corcovado and Tortuguero national parks in Costa Rica and Reserva Biológica Indio Maíz in Nicaragua are also possibilities for the jaguar and the other small cats. The largest land mammal in Central America is **Baird's tapir**, weighing up to 300 kg. It is a forest species and very secretive, particularly so in areas where it is hunted. **Corcovado** and **Santa Rosa** national parks in Costa Rica are all places it might be seen, at least there is a reasonable chance of seeing its hoof prints. It might be seen at waterholes or be spotted swimming in rivers. More likely to be seen are **peccaries**, especially the collared peccary, medium sized pig-like animals that are active both day and night. The **collared peccary** can be found in both dry and rainforests throughout the region, while the **white-lipped peccary** is more common in wetter, evergreen forests. Both live in herds, of up to 100 individuals in the case of the white-lipped species. Found throughout the area, in drier, woodland patches, the white-tailed deer can easily be spotted, especially at dawn or dusk, or their bright eyeshine can be seen at night if you are out in a car or on foot with a torch. Also found from Mexico down into South America is the smaller red brocket; this, though, is a rainforest species and is more elusive. Rodent species you might come across include the agouti, which looks rather like a long-legged guinea pig and can be seen moving around on the forest floor. Considerably larger and stockier is the nocturnal paca (gibnut in Belize), another forest species found throughout the region, often near water where they hide when chased by predators. The world's largest rodent, the capybara, is also found near water, but in this region can be seen only in Panama, in Darién, for instance. Bats will usually be a quick fly past at night, impossible to identify but for the jagged flight path which is clearly not that of a bird. The nightly exodus of bats from caves near to El Zotz, in Petén, Guatemala is a spectacular sight. Others feed on fish, frogs, fruit and insects; probably the most notorious is the blood-sucking vampire bat, though it rarely attacks humans, instead feeding almost exclusively on domestic stock, such as cattle and goats.

Finally, marine mammals in the area include whales, dolphins and manatees. The last of these can be seen in Belize's Southern Lagoon, Lago Izabal in Guatemala or Cuero Y Salado Wildlife Reserve in Honduras. Whales and dolphins occur along both the Pacific and Atlantic coasts and can be watched at a number of sites as far south as Isla Iguana Wildlife Reserve in Panama.

Birds

It is true, the early bird gets the worm and the earlier you get up, the more species you'll see. All countries have very high numbers of birds on their lists but Panama is the haven for birdwatchers in this area; though relatively tiny, it boasts almost as many (922) bird species as Mexico. One of the best places to go in Panama is the Pipeline Road (Sendero Oleoducto) in Parque Nacional Soberanía. In this lowland rainforest area, brilliantly coloured species such as the violaceous and slaty-tailed trogans or the blue-crowned motmot can be seen, along with parrots, tanagers, hummingbirds, antbirds and many others during the day. It is also a good place to see the spectacular keel-billed toucan. At night, eight species of owl, including the crested, can be found, along with potoos and a variety of nightjars. Also, for serious birders, not to be missed in Panama is Parque Nacional Darién with mangroves, lowland and montane rainforest where numerous raptors can be seen, including king and black vultures, crested eagles and, if you're really lucky, the huge, monkey-eating harpy eagle with its 2-m wing span. Macaws, parrots and parakeets are common, along with toucans, hummingbirds, aracaris and tanagers. The golden-headed quetzal can be seen at higher altitudes in Parque Nacional Darién (Cerro Pirre) and nowhere else in Central America.

Many of these birds can be seen outside Panama. Toucans and the smaller toucanets are widespread throughout the tropical areas of the region with the ruins of Tikal offering good siting opportunities. Another popular sighting is the scarlet macaw easily spotted near Puerto Juárez, Costa Rica, and the region of El Perú and the Río San Juan in Guatemala. Hummingbirds too are a common sighting throughout the region, frequently drawn to sugar-feeders. The harpy eagle is extremely rare with sightings on the Osa Peninsula, Costa Rica a possibility and in the rainforest region of northern Guatemala, Belize and southern Mexico.

To find the resplendent quetzal, a brilliant emerald green bird, with males having a bright scarlet breast and belly and ostentatious long green streamers extending as much as 50 cm beyond the end of its tail, Monteverde Cloud Forest Reserve or the less atmospheric

Eddie Serrano Mirador in Costa Rica are a couple of the best places to go. You'll also have a good chance of spotting the quetzal in the Quetzal Biosphere Reserve in the Sierra de las Minas, Guatemala, where the bird is the national symbol and name of the currency.

In addition to the quetzal, Costa Rica, containing around 850 bird species, follows close on the heels of Panama as being a good country to visit for birdwatchers and **Monteverde** is a hotspot. Species there include black **guans, emerald toucanets, violet sabrewings, long-tailed manakins, three wattled bellbirds** and the threatened **bare-necked umbrellabird**. Mixed flocks of small birds such as **warblers, tanagers, woodcreepers** and **wood-wrens** can also be seen in the area. La Selva Biological Station, an area of rainforest in Costa Rica, is another area rich in rainforest species such as the **chestnut-billed toucan, mealy parrot** and **squirrel cuckoo**. A very different habitat, with, consequently, different birds, is found in the large wetland area of Parque Nacional Palo Verde in Costa Rica. Here one can see the **jabiru, black-necked stilt, spotted rail, bare-throated tiger heron, purple gallinule** and many other waterbirds. In the dry season, **ducks**, including the **black-bellied whistling duck, blue-billed teal, ring-necked duck** and **northern pintail**, congregate in this area in their thousands. More rarely seen here is the **white-faced whistling duck**. Many of these waterbirds can also be seen in Crooked Tree Wildlife Sanctuary in Belize.

Of course, all along the coasts are masses of different seabirds, including **pelicans, boobies** and the **magnificent frigate bird**. And in Mexico coastal, wetlands near Celestún and in Río Lagarto on the Yucután Peninsula provide good sightings of **pink flamingoes**.

If you are looking for real rarities, then try spotting the threatened **horned guam**, a highly distinctive and striking bird, that can be found only in high cloud forests of Mexico and Guatemala, for example, in El Triunfo Biosphere Reserve in Mexico.

Reptiles
This covers **snakes, lizards, crocodilians** and **turtles**. Mexico has more of these animals than any other country in the world. Throughout the whole region, though, you are not particularly likely to see snakes in the wild; for those wishing to do so, a snake farm or zoo is the best place to go. You might, though, be lucky on one of your walks and see a **boa constrictor**, or, again, a guide might know where one is resting. In contrast, **lizards** are everywhere, from small geckos walking up walls in your hotel room, catching insects attracted to the lights, to the large **iguanas** sunbathing in the tree tops. The **American crocodile** and **spectacled caiman** are both found throughout the area, with the latter being seen quite frequently. **Morlet's crocodile**, on the other hand, is found only in Mexico, Belize and Guatemala. Several species of both freshwater and sea **turtles** are present in the region. Parque Nacional Tortuguero in Costa Rica is a good place to see freshwater turtles and four species of marine turtle, while at Ostional Beach in Santa Rosa National Park you can watch masses of olive ridley turtles coming in to lay their eggs, particularly in September and October. You'll also be able to see nesting turtles along the Pacific coastal beaches of Nicaragua, in La Mosquitia, Honduras, Monterrico, Guatemala and Mexico.

Amphibians
You'll certainly hear frogs and toads, even if you do not see them. However, the brightly coloured **poison-dart frogs** and some of the tree frogs are well worth searching out. Look for them in damp places, under logs and moist leaf litter, in rock crevices and by ponds and streams, many will be more active at night. Monteverde and La Selva Reserves are both rich in amphibians, and a visit to Bocas del Toro will also reveal colourful amphibians on appropriately named Red Frog Beach.

Invertebrates

There are uncounted different species of invertebrates in the area. Probably, most desirable for ecotourists are the **butterflies**, though some of the **beetles**, such as the jewel **scarabs**, are also pretty spectacular. If you are fascinated by spiders, you can always go hunting for nocturnal **tarantulas**; **Lamanai** in **Belize** harbours four different species. There are **butterfly farms** in some of the countries, including Nicaragua (Los Guatusos Wildlife Reserve) and Costa Rica (eg el Jardín de Mariposas in Monteverde) that will give you a close up view of many different species. Watching **leaf-cutter ants** marching in long columns from a bush they are systematically destroying and taking the pieces of leaf to their nest, huge mounds on the forest floor, can be an absorbing sight, while marching columns of army ants, catching and killing all small beasts in their path, are best avoided.

Marine wildlife

Predicting the movement and location of marine animals is difficult, and often sightings of sharks and rays is chance. However, the **whale shark** makes a seasonal migration through the coastal waters of Belize and Honduras between March and May. Less natural shark encounters can be had off **Caye Caulker** (Belize) and **Isla Mujeres** (Yucatán, Mexico), where hand-feeding brings in **sting rays** and **nurse sharks** for close but safe encounters.

Index → *Entries in bold refer to maps*

Advertisers' index

Acknowledgements

First and foremost, a big thanks to Peter Hutchison, who is stepping down as the book's author after a decade of dedicated service. No less than eight editions have benefited from his expertise and insight – no small feat given the challenges of guidebook writing. Peter's departure as author marks the end of an era. His affable leadership will be sorely missed, but we also hope he will continue contributing in other ways. In this 19th edition, he deftly updated Costa Rica. Once again, many thanks to Peter, whose years of hard work have made the *Central America Handbook* the book it is today.

At the Footprint office, a big thank you to Felicity Laughton, Kevin Feeney, Pepi Bluck Emma Bryers and Alan Murphy.

A great many thanks to all the other authors who contributed to this fully revised 19th edition of the *Central America Handbook*. Starting with Southern Mexico, Geoff Groesbeck – author of *Footprint Mexico* – meticulously updated everything from Chiapas to the Yucatán. Neighbouring Belize benefitted from the expert input of Gardênia and Alex Robinson, authors of the forthcoming *Footprint Belize*. Huw Hennessey visited Guatemala, Honduras and El Salvador and did a very solid and commendable job of bringing those chapters up-to-date. Richard Arghiris covered Nicaragua and Panama, where he has been fortunate enough to spend the best part of two years travelling.

Thanks to the many colleagues and correspondents across Central America who provided updates, particularly Howard Rosenweig, who has been supplying excellent information on Copán Ruinas for years now. For specialist contributions from this or previous years we would like to thank: Caroline Harcourt for wildlife; Nigel Gallop for music and dance; John Alton for details on cargo ship cruises; Binka and Robin le Breton for motoring; Ashley Rawlings for motorcycling; Hallam Murray for cycling; Hilary Bradt for hiking and trekking; David Fishlow for language and Mark Eckstein for responsible tourism.

Special thanks Nigel Potter, Michèle Mühlemann, James Michie, Daniel Hoffer, Jim Goulder and Sebastian Moritz who were among the kind readers who took the time to write to us with their comments, criticisms and suggestions – these are always welcome and greatly appreciated.

Finally, many thanks to the hoteliers, restauranteurs, tour operators and others who kindly informed us when their contact details changed. Please note we are unlikely to include the details of a new establishment without specific recommendations, or ideally, a visit, but it is very useful to receive details about new telephone numbers, email and postal addresses, services provided, prices, and so on. Thanks.

Credits

Footprint credits
Project Editor: Felicity Laughton
Cover and colour section: Pepi Bluck,
Emma Bryers
Maps: Kevin Feeney

Managing Director: Andy Riddle
Commercial Director: Patrick Dawson
Publisher: Alan Murphy
Publishing Managers: Felicity Laughton
Nicola Gibbs
Digital Editors: Jo Williams, Tom Mellors
Marketing and PR: Liz Harper
Advertising: Renu Sibal
Finance and administration:
Elizabeth Taylor

Photograpy credits
Front cover: Red-eyed tree frog,
Costa Rica: Martin Van Lokven / FLPA
Back cover: Sololá, Guatemala: Bruno
Perousse / hemis.fr
Colour section: Page 1: Heinz Endler /
LOOK-foto / www.photolibrary.com;
Pages 2-3: Chichicastenango, Guatemala:
Sam Chadwick / Shutterstock.com;
Pages 6-7: Tikal, Guatemala: Gugli /
Dreamstime.com; **Page 8**: Volcán San
Cristóbal, Nicaragua: Terry Honeycutt /
Shutterstock.com

Printed in India by Nutech Print Services

Footprint feedback
We try as hard as we can to make each
Footprint guide as up to date as possible
but, of course, things always change. If you
want to let us know about your experiences –
good, bad or ugly – then don't delay, go to
www.footprintbooks.com and send in
your comments.

Publishing information
Footprint Central America
19th edition
© Footprint Handbooks Ltd
September 2011

ISBN: 978 1 907263 47 7
CIP DATA: A catalogue record for this book
is available from the British Library

® Footprint Handbooks and the Footprint
mark are a registered trademark of Footprint
Handbooks Ltd

Published by Footprint
6 Riverside Court
Lower Bristol Road
Bath BA2 3DZ, UK
T +44 (0)1225 469141
F +44 (0)1225 469461
www.footprinttravelguides.com

Distributed in the USA by Globe Pequot Press,
Guilford, Connecticut